"Edmund's®...

virtually every

safety informa

"Never pay retail. When buying a car, it is <u>imperative</u> that you know the dealer's cost. Refer to Edmund's® ... price guides for current information. Armed with this information, you can determine the price that provides the dealer with a <u>minimum</u> 'win' profit."

—Lisa Murr Chapman, **The Savvy Woman's Guide to Cars** (New York, NY: Bantam Books, 1995)

"First, whether you are buying or selling a used car, check its value in Edmund's® Used Car Prices.*"*

—Lesley Hazleton, **Everything Women Always Wanted to Know About Cars But Didn't Know Who to Ask** (New York, NY: Doubleday Books, 1995)

"Edmunds publishes a variety of useful guides ... buy the guide that deals specifically with the type of car you need. You can find out exactly what the car cost the dealership and what you should pay ... in Edmund's® auto books."

—Burke Leon, **The Insider's Guide to Buying a New or Used Car** (Cincinnati, OH: Betterway Books, 1993)

"If you really want the nitty-gritty, you're going to have to ... (get) ... Edmunds ... This little book is a gold mine for the curious car buyer.... It is an automobile fancier's delight, a straightforward, meaty compendium of raw facts ... and you will determine the exact cost of just about any car."

—Remar Sutton, **Don't Get Taken Every Time** (New York, NY: Penguin Books, 1997)

Most people have three things in common when they buy a car.

They pay too much.

They waste time.

They hate the experience.

Which is exactly why you should call the Consumers Car Club, a nationwide auto buying service. We offer the quickest and most convenient way to save time and money when you buy a new car or truck. Simple as that. Just tell us the vehicle and options you want (any make or model-foreign or domestic) and we'll get you a lower price than you can get on your own. Guaranteed in writing. We can factory order any domestic vehicle and usually save you even more. No haggling. No hassles. No games.

Don't forget to ask about our loans, leases and extended service contracts. It's a terrific way to save even more money on the purchase of your new car. For more information, call the Consumers Car Club at 1-800-CAR-CLUB (1-800-227-2582).

The Smart New Way to Buy Your Car™

All new cars arranged for sale are subject to price & availability from the selling franchised new car dealer.

FREE
COLOR CATALOGS

Ford®, Chevy®
GMC® or Toyota®
Truck & SUV

1000's of Great Accessories
Upgrade & Protect & Improve the Interior
Customize the Styling of Your Truck
Improve Horsepower and Mileage
Unique Bike, Sport & Cargo Racks
and Much More . . .

PERFORMANCE
PRODUCTS

Your Best Source of Performance Parts and Accessories

FREE Catalog Call 24 hours a day 800-297-5188
To Order Parts and Accessories CAll 800-853-6362
For a FREE catalog use this code: TX7C21

1999

Edmund's®

USED CARS

PRICES & RATINGS

"THE ORIGINAL CONSUMER PRICE AUTHORITY"

The Leading Resource For Do-It-Yourself Car Care

Chilton's® TOTAL CAR CARE

continues to be the Industry Leader in auto repair manuals, offering do-it-yourselfers of all levels TOTAL maintenance, service and repair information in an easy-to-use format, for virtually every vehicle on the road.

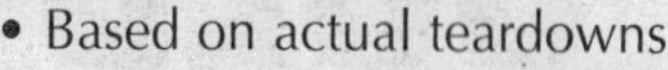

- Based on actual teardowns
- Hundreds of detailed photographs and exploded-view illustrations
- Trouble codes
- Electronic engine controls
- Vacuum and wiring diagrams
- Tune-up specifications and emission-controls data

Call Customer Service Toll Free 1-800-477-3996.
Mention Edmunds when you place your order.

An American tradition since 1925

1020 Andrew Drive, Suite 200 • West Chester, PA • 19380-4291
Phone: (610) 738-9280 • Fax: (610) 738-9370

Cover photo:
1998 GMC Jimmy

USED CARS

TABLE OF CONTENTS

ISBN: 0-87759-636-0
ISSN: 1086-8038

SPRING 1999 **VOL. U3301-9904**

1994 Lexus GS300

Edmund's® books are available at special quantity discounts when purchased in bulk by credit unions, corporations, organizations, and other special interest groups. Custom covers and/or customized copy on available pages may also be prepared to fit particular needs.

Some of the data used to compile Edmund's® Used Car ratings has been sourced from Intellichoice, Inc., 471 Division Street, Campbell, CA 95008.

Edmund's®

Edmund Publications Corp.
P.O. Box 18827 • Beverly Hills, CA 90209-4827

President: Peter Steinlauf *Vice President:* Lev R. Stark

EDITORIAL TEAM:

Editor-in-Chief:
Christian J. Wardlaw

Managing Editor:
B. Grant Whitmore

Senior Features Editor:
Greg Anderson

Features Editor:
Ingrid Loeffler Palmer

Technical Editor:
Karl A. Brauer

News Editor:
John Clor

Copy Editor:
Deborah Greenbaum

Photo Editor:
Robert E. Archbold

Director of Community:
Nancie Y. Meng

Editorial Communications Coordinator:
Michelle L. Good

Editorial Communications Assistant:
Debra Hunt

PRODUCTION TEAM:

Online Publications Production Manager:
Ali Spivak

Print Publications Production Manager:
Lynette R. Archbold

Print Publications Layout and Design:
Robert E. Archbold

New Vehicle Data Manager:
Scott Schapiro

Online Publications Production Assistant:
Andy Chase

Cover Design:
Karen Ross

BUSINESS TEAM:

Director of Business Development:
Daniel May

Director of Marketing:
Avi Steinlauf

Director of Organizational Development and Web Initiatives:
Jill S. Davidson

Controller:
Evvy Mankowitz

Administrative Assistant:
Sommer Marie Batchelor

TECHNICAL TEAM:

Director of Technology:
Robert Weiss

Director of Internet Development and Production:
Haim Hirsch

Senior Systems Administrator:
David Reid

System Administrator:
Jack Cate

Senior Programmer/Analyst:
Debby Katzir

Senior Media Specialist:
John Davis

Backup System Administrator:
Peter Brecht

© 1999 by Edmund Publications Corporation.
All rights reserved.
No reproduction in whole or in part may be made without explicit written permission from the publisher.

INTRODUCTION

Thanks for consulting *Edmund's® Used Cars Prices & Ratings*! You've made a wise purchase, because the values contained within this publication represent a current snapshot of the U.S. used car market as it exists for the consumer. Unlike other guides, we aren't publishing data sourced strictly from dealer-only auction houses or dealership sales records. Our values are based on advertised and actual transaction prices between private owners, between private owners and dealers, and between dealers. You won't find a dealer slant to our data, because one doesn't exist.

The Edmund's® Philosophy

For years Edmund's® followed tradition and published wholesale and retail values for vehicles. But we found that the commonly accepted method of providing a wholesale value and a retail value was based on a dealer's market, making such a system unreliable for and misleading to the average consumer. Dealers and private owners almost never sell a car for retail, and dealers almost never give wholesale value when assessing a trade-in. In years past we based our pricing on actual dealer advertised prices and auction data to generate retail and wholesale price. Our current pricing is gathered using a similar methodology, but we've modified the process to arrive at what we call Market Value and Trade-in Value.

Market Value

Market Value is a national average of prices asked by private sellers and dealers. Our source compiles hundreds of thousands of advertised prices nationwide, and interviews thousands of sellers by phone each week to find out their bottom-line price (the take price, as it is referred to in the industry), or the actual transaction price if the car has been sold. Data gleaned from telephone interviews, combined with national averages from the advertised price database, is used to create the Market Value. By including private sellers in the tabulation, we've effectively generated a more accurate, more reliable average value for any given make and model.

Trade-in Value

Trade-in Value is the amount that a consumer might expect to get from a dealer for a trade-in. Most dealers won't give a customer wholesale value (the average value a dealer could expect to receive at an auction) on a trade-in unless there is profit to be made from some other aspect of the deal. Why won't they? Because the dealer is assuming the customer's risk. If the car has a problem, the dealer must fix it. If

 © 1999 by Edmund Publications Corporation

the car is only in fair condition, the dealer must recondition it. If the car won't pass emissions inspection, the dealer must repair it. Then there is no guarantee that the car will sell on the dealer's used car lot, so the dealer must anticipate taking the car to the auction house, where a profit, no matter how meager, will be expected. So, when assessing a customer's trade-in, the dealer will value it lower than wholesale price. Our Trade-in Value, calculated as a percentage of Market Value, is designed to provide consumers with a more realistic guide to valuing a trade-in.

When buying or selling a car, a price close to Market Value is a fair price. When trading a car, a price close to Trade-in Value is a fair price. Keep in mind that dealers will use whatever regional price guide favors them the most to value your trade-in and price the used cars on their lot. Sometimes, they will consult two different guides; one that undervalues trades, and one that overvalues retail prices for used cars. Since Edmund's® does not cater to the dealer or sell dealer-specific value guides like many of our competitors, expect initial resistance by the dealer to the prices we publish, but don't give in to dealer claims that our numbers are wrong. Also, keep the following guideline in mind: *A car is only worth as much as someone is willing to pay for it.*

Recent Changes

We've added used vehicle values for 1998 models to this edition, and we've dropped values for 1988 vehicles. Space constraints in our book dictate that when a new model year is added, the oldest model year is dropped. This guide contains values for most vehicles built for model years 1989-1998.

Where's the Recall Data?

We've stopped publishing recall data, and here's the reason why. If you have Internet access, go to http://www.nhtsa.dot.gov, which is the address for the National Highway and Traffic Safety Administration's website. There you can search archives of recalls, technical service bulletins, and crash tests. The data found at this website is much more comprehensive and detailed than we could ever hope to provide, and you'll be better off arming yourself with this information before heading down to the local dealership for a chat with the service advisor.

How Do I Use Edmund's® Data?

Our editor-in-chief owns a 1997 Mazda Miata with a manual transmission. At this writing, the car has just 3,200 miles on the odometer. Options on his car include

 © 1999 by Edmund Publications Corporation

the leather package, air conditioning, alloy wheels, CD player, limited-slip differential, power mirrors, power windows and power steering. He would value his car like this:

	Trade-in Value	Market Value
1997 Mazda Miata	**$11215**	**$13515**
Air Conditioning	$565	$565
Alloy Wheels	$210	$210
CD Player	$355	$355
Leather Package	$785	$785
Limited Slip Differential	$255	$255
Power Mirrors	$80	$80
Power Steering	$245	$245
Power Windows	$150	$150
Rear Spoiler	$190	$190
Mileage Adjustment	+$1458	+$1458
TOTAL:	**$15508**	**$17808**

Since these figures are for a car in average shape, our editor could adjust the numbers slightly upward since his car is in showroom condition. However, he would then have to adjust the figure downward because winter has descended upon his home state and Miata sales in his region slow to a trickle when the weather turns cold.

This example illustrates a couple of important points. Vehicle condition can have an effect on vehicle value. Because our editor's car is in such good shape, and because he has all the maintenance receipts and original purchase paperwork, the car's value increases. Other variables can affect the price as well, such as demand for this particular model and the time of year that the car is sold.

However, just because our book claims a fair value for his car of about $17,810, that doesn't mean he can automatically sell it for that amount of money. *A used car is only worth as much as someone is willing to pay for it.*

Contact Us

We believe that this guide is much more accurate and easy-to-understand than ever before. If you have questions, comments, suggestions, or complaints, you can write to us at the following address:

 © 1999 by Edmund Publications Corporation

Automotive Editors
Edmund Publications Corporation
P.O. Box 18827
Beverly Hills, CA 90209-4827

Or, you can send us e-mail to editors@edmunds.com. We look forward to your feedback!

NOTE: All information and prices published herein are gathered from sources which, in the editors' opinion, are considered reliable, but under no circumstances is the reader to assume that this information is official or final. All prices are represented as average approximations only, in U.S. dollars. Unless otherwise noted, all prices are subject to change without notice. The publisher does not assume responsibility for errors of omission, commission, or interpretation. • All consumer information and pricing services advertised herein are not operated by nor are they the responsibility of the publisher. The publisher assumes no responsibility for claims made by advertisers regarding their products or services.

1997 Mazda Miata

 © 1999 by Edmund Publications Corporation

Understanding the Layout

Finding the Right Model

We've listed all makes and models in alphabetical order, from Acura to Volvo. To find the make and model you want to value, look at the title bar at the top of each page. The title bar defines each section of the book by listing the *Automobile Make* and *Model Year* covered on each page. When the proper section has been found, you can find the right model by looking at the gray shaded title bars that begin each model listing. In this gray bar, you will find the *Model Name* and *Model Year*. To distinguish cars from trucks, we've printed truck data over a gray background.

What's New and Ratings

Beneath the model title bar is a section of text, called a *Yearly Feature Update*, which explains what changed on the model for that particular model year. Next is a *Ratings Chart*, containing a synopsis of heavily researched data about the model you're valuing. Most of the vehicles covered in this book have a ratings chart, but some vehicles cannot be rated because there is not enough data to calculate accurate ratings. Below the ratings chart is a *Mileage Category Designation.*

Mileage Categories

Each vehicle in this guide has been assigned to a specific mileage category, which contains other vehicles with similar characteristics. For example, Category C contains mid-sized American cars like the Ford Contour. Category E contains economy cars like the Toyota Tercel. And, Category G contains compact pickups, compact SUVs, and minivans like the Chevrolet S-10, the Nissan Pathfinder, and the Dodge Caravan. The mileage adjustment table is keyed to each vehicle by category. Sometimes, different versions of the same model may fall into different categories. In this event, versions belonging to different categories will be listed separately within the individual model listing section.

Data Presentation

The first column of data contains a *Model Description* for each individual model that has pricing data. The number of doors, trim level, drive system (if something other than two-wheel drive), and body style are described here. The middle column is the baseline *Trade-in Value*, which is used to calculate the amount of money you might expect a dealership to offer you if you traded the car in. The third column is

 © 1999 by Edmund Publications Corporation

the baseline *Market Value*, which is used to calculate the amount of money you might expect to receive for your car on the open market, or the amount of money you might pay a dealership for a used car. Beneath the pricing data for each individual model you might find values for *Optional Equipment*. Conveniently located on the last page of this book is a *Mileage Adjustment Table*.

Pricing a Vehicle

Market or Trade-in Value?

To find an accurate value for a vehicle, you must make adjustments to the baseline values for equipment and mileage. Realistically, you should use Market Value if selling to a private party or buying from a private party or dealer, and use Trade-in Value if selling to a dealer.

Options and Packages

Below the baseline pricing data for most vehicles are lists of optional equipment that require price adjustments. If the vehicle you're valuing is equipped with any of these items, you must add the appropriate value to the baseline values. Also listed with the options are expensive option packages. For example, a BMW might be equipped with a Luxury Package that includes power leather seats, cruise control, an onboard computer, wood trim, special aluminum wheels, special interior trim, and special exterior trim. Some of these items might be found separately in the equipment list, and some might not. The published package price includes the intrinsic value for those items that are not otherwise listed as options. Most private sellers will be able to tell you if a vehicle is equipped with a certain package, but don't expect a dealer to know much about a used car except the price. Do your homework!

Transmissions

Our Market Value and Trade-in Value includes the standard transmission on that model, whether manual shift or automatic. Keep in mind that sometimes manufacturers would install a 3-speed automatic transmission as standard equipment, but would offer an upgraded 4-speed automatic transmission as an option. Newer Chevrolet Cavalier LS sedans provide an excellent example of this practice; the 3-speed automatic is standard, and the 4-speed automatic is optional. Don't assume that a listing for an optional automatic transmission means that the basic vehicle came with a stick shift.

 © 1999 by Edmund Publications Corporation

Engines

There are five basic engine types: gasoline; diesel; supercharged gasoline; turbocharged gasoline and turbocharged diesel. Some engines appear in the optional equipment listings. Each vehicle record is listed including the standard gasoline engine. Similarly, models with standard turbocharged or supercharged engines are listed individually. The only engines contained in the optional equipment lists are optional gasoline- or diesel-powered powerplants. Make sure you find out what engine is under the hood of the vehicle you're valuing. If the vehicle you're buying or selling has an optional engine, look for the value in the optional equipment list.

The Mileage Table

Once the proper adjusted value has been determined, you must further modify the price of the vehicle using the Mileage Table on the last page of this book. Edmund's links mileage adjustments directly to each vehicle category and presents the data in a single table. The table features an average mileage range for each category and model year, and provides an exact value to be added or subtracted **per mile** over or under the average mileage range. No other value guide provides such detailed, or realistic, mileage adjustments. Because the acceptable mileage range is based on an actual average mileage of all vehicles within a given category, an exotic car like the Acura NSX will be valued according to a substantially lower and tighter average mileage range than a mid-sized import like the Honda Accord. If the vehicle you're valuing has excessively high or low mileage, you should not add or subtract value in excess of half of the vehicle's adjusted trade-in value.

The Disclaimer

That's all there is to valuing a used car with Edmund's. Now you've got accurate ballpark values for trade-in value and market value. ***Keep the following in mind, however. Regional price differences, seasonal price differences, seasonal demand, vehicle condition, and the economic laws of supply and demand all help determine the actual worth of a used car. The values calculated using this guide are designed to represent average values nationwide for a used car in average condition, and should be used only as a guide to set an acceptable price range for selling or purchasing. None of the values published herein are intended to represent absolute values.***

 © 1999 by Edmund Publications Corporation

Pricing Examples

	Trade-in Value	Market Value
1. **1996 Ford Explorer XLT 4WD**	**$14,010**	**$17,515**
Automatic Transmission	515	515
Aluminum Alloy Wheels	190	190
AM/FM Stereo Tape	135	135
Dual Power Seats	350	350
JBL Sound System	425	425
Keyless Entry System	115	115
Leather Seats	425	425
Luggage Rack	85	85
Value before Mileage Adjustment	$16,250	$19,755
41,200 miles (Category G)	0	0
	--------	--------
TOTAL ADJUSTED VALUE:	**$16,250**	**$19,755**
2. **1993 Nissan Altima GXE**	**$4,720**	**$6,210**
Automatic Transmission	250	250
Air Conditioning	255	255
Cruise Control	75	75
Value before Mileage Adjustment	$5,300	$6,790
86,700 miles (Category D)	-392	-392
	--------	--------
TOTAL ADJUSTED VALUE:	**$4,908**	**$6,398**
3. **1991 BMW 325i**	**$6,260**	**$8,580**
Sport Package	380	380
Leather Seats	145	145
Power Sunroof	140	140
Value before Mileage Adjustment	$6,925	$9,245
76,550 miles (Category F)	+831	+831
	--------	--------
TOTAL ADJUSTED VALUE:	**$7,756**	**$10,076**

 © 1999 by Edmund Publications Corporation

HOW WE RATE THE CARS

Each spring, we update our ratings for used cars. Currently, we offer ratings for many vehicles built between 1989 and 1997. Edmund's ratings are presented in chart form, on a 1 to 10 numerical scale where 10 is best. Some ratings data is supplied by IntelliChoice, Inc., 471 Division Street, Campbell, CA 95008. IntelliChoice, a respected automotive data provider, has contributed information to our Safety and Reliability ratings for used cars and trucks.

Safety Rating

We examine nine factors that determine vehicle safety. First, we check frontal impact crash test data from the National Highway and Traffic Safety Administration (NHTSA). The NHTSA selects several models each year for crash testing, which is conducted at 35 mph into a fixed barrier. Federal standards require that all cars pass a 30 mph test to be sold in the United States. The higher speed used by the NHTSA allows for comparison outside of federal regulations. By crashing into a fixed barrier, the NHTSA simulates a head-on collision with another vehicle of similar size and weight traveling at the same rate of speed. The NHTSA assigns specific scores to the driver and front passenger. The higher the score, the more likely a person is to escape such a crash with minimal injuries. *If a vehicle has not been crash tested, we do not rate the vehicle in this category.* Crash test data is the most important ingredient of our safety score. Without it, a safety rating means little.

Other factors that are used to determine a safety rating include the number of times the model has been recalled for non-emissions-related issues and the presence of safety equipment like airbags and anti-lock brakes (ABS). On later model vehicles, offset crash test scores, which the Insurance Institute for Highway Safety (IIHS) began conducting in 1994, are rolled into the tabulation if available. In 1996, Volvo equipped their entire model lineup with side-impact airbags. Therefore, all 1996 and 1997 vehicles include side-impact airbags in the safety calculation. If a 1996 or 1997 model that is identical to a 1995 model but is not equipped with side-impact airbags has a slightly lower safety rating than the older vehicle, now you know why.

Important Note About Airbags and ABS: These days, it seems like everybody is talking about how unsafe these systems are. Edmund's® does not consider airbags or ABS to be unsafe. In defense of airbags, they have saved approximately 22 people for every one person they have killed. True, they shouldn't be killing anyone. Unfortunately, airbags were designed to protect a 165-lb. person not wearing a seatbelt. To accomplish this mandate, airbags must inflate rapidly, expanding at a rate of approximately 200 mph. Children and adults are getting

 © 1999 by Edmund Publications Corporation

hurt or killed every day because of these rapid inflation rates, but it is important to note that in almost all cases involving death, the person killed was not properly restrained by a seatbelt.

Problems with airbags seem particularly acute in low-speed collisions, such as tapping a car in a parking lot, which do not require the protection the airbag provides. The sensors that control the airbag may not be without fault or flaw, but neither are most other sophisticated systems in today's cars. The best way to avoid injury or loss with airbag-equipped cars is to sit as far away from the airbag as possible, wear your seat belt and strap youngsters into the back seat.

The lawmakers who forced automobile manufacturers to install airbags may have gone about doing so in a misguided and uneducated fashion, but the fact of the matter is that these supplemental restraints do save lives and are improved with each passing model year. In fact, many 1998 model year cars and trucks came equipped with airbags that deploy at lower speeds. This recently accepted lower deployment speed will save more properly belted vehicle occupants, but those who do not wear a seatbelt will be more at risk than if they rode in a vehicle with airbags that deployed at higher speeds.

Recent reports claim that vehicles equipped with anti-lock brakes are more likely to be involved in single vehicle crashes than cars that are not equipped with anti-lock brakes. Why is this? ABS is misunderstood, and is misused in general by the driving public.

Here are the facts. ABS will not shorten stopping distances. ABS will not prevent all skids. What ABS is designed to do, and it does this very well, is allow the driver to steer around danger while simultaneously using maximum braking ability. A car without ABS will skid when the wheels lock up, and when the car is skidding all steering ability is lost. So, in such a car, it is highly likely that the driver will lock up the brakes, skid the tires, and slide into whatever situation or object caused him to apply the brakes in the first place, thereby making the accident a two-vehicle crash.

With ABS, the driver can steer around the situation or object in the road because the front tires are not locked up. However, it is important that the driver steer carefully and not wildly. Once the car begins to change direction, it may begin to skid sideways if direction is changed too quickly. ABS cannot help control a lateral skid. One theory says that drivers of ABS-equipped cars are steering around immediate danger successfully, but then skidding laterally off the road and hitting a tree, a road sign, or a building. Also, some drivers of ABS-equipped cars may be pumping the brakes in moments of panic, because that's what has been taught for decades to stop a car without ABS.

 © 1999 by Edmund Publications Corporation

Owners of ABS-equipped cars should practice using the system in a vacant parking lot before the need to use ABS in a panic situation arises. For the record, Edmund's staff members prefer ABS on all surfaces except narrow dirt or gravel roads, where there is little room to steer and a locked tire can dig into the earth and drop speed more rapidly.

Finally, consider this. Bob Bondurant (famed racing legend and operator of the acclaimed Bob Bondurant School of High Performance Driving in Phoenix, AZ) told us that when ABS-equipped Mustangs were introduced to his fleet of student cars, the accident rate on his track dropped a whopping 40 percent. Bondurant believes in ABS, but conceeds that most drivers have no idea how to use them. Do all of us a favor – learn.

Reliability Rating

Our reliability rating is based on three factors that determine how trouble-free a vehicle is likely to be. Intellichoice, Inc. tracks complaints from vehicle owners. For any given make and model, we combine data regarding specific reported problem areas with the number of mechanically-related recalls issued by NHTSA. Finally, we consult our records regarding build quality inside and out when the car was new.

Performance Rating

We take into consideration a vehicle's ability to accelerate, stop, and turn, then compare to other models in the same vehicle class. So, the performance rating for the Toyota Tercel is to be compared to the Chevrolet Cavalier or Ford Escort rather than the Chevrolet Camaro or Ford Mustang. Additionally, we toss transmission performance and steering ability into the recipe. Since performance often means different things to different people, we'll define it this way. A fast car with good brakes, communicative steering, a smooth-shifting transmission, and the ability to get around a turn without keeling over and begging for mercy gets a higher rating than a car that, uh, doesn't.

Comfort Rating

Another subjective category, rated by our staffers, is overall comfort. We look for a comfortable position behind the steering wheel on a supportive seat with a clear view of gauges and an easy stretch to controls that operate with minimum amounts of concentration. A car or truck with a quiet ride that doesn't jar occupants, clear sightlines front and rear, and is easy to get in and out of will get a better score than

 © 1999 by Edmund Publications Corporation

one that rattles teeth and requires a stepladder to enter. So, if your idea of comfort is a rolling Barcalounger surrounded by look-alike chrome buttons and switches, you can ignore our rating.

Value Rating

To determine value, we examine nationally averaged theft rates, part costs if purchased at the dealership, the likelihood that a vehicle will break down or run reliably and average insurance rates based on claims losses from a nationally-known insurance company. The icing on the value cupcake is the vehicle's degree of versatility. A full-size 4WD Suburban is infinitely more useable than a Mazda Miata, and therefore, offers better overall versatility.

Overall Rating

Add 'em all together, and you come up with an overall rating. We do not weight the overall rating, allowing each factor to count equally toward the final tally. If any of the five factors is missing from the equation due to insufficient data, we do not provide an overall rating.

Important Note: If data was unavailable for more than two of the five factors, we did not rate the vehicle at all. For those cars without ratings, the reason a rating is not given in any category is because of scarce data for at least three of the rating factors listed above.

1993 Chevrolet Suburban

 © 1999 by Edmund Publications Corporation

Buying a Used Car:

- Visually inspect the car in daylight. If buying from a dealer, request that any items that are broken or damaged be repaired. If buying from a private seller, devalue the vehicle for broken or damaged items. Signs of paint overspray may indicate a history of bodywork.
- Have the car thoroughly inspected by a mechanic. If mechanical repair is necessary, devalue the vehicle accordingly.
- Have the car looked at by a body shop technician for signs of accident repair. Inspect the title, too. If the car has been wrecked and repaired, but has a clear title, chances are good that the vehicle is still in sound condition. If the vehicle is saddled with a salvage title, you should steer clear of it. This means it has been damaged so badly that the insurance company totaled it, and an enterprising person has repaired the vehicle for sale.
- Do a VIN search to help determine if the car has a clear title. Visit our website at http://www.edmunds.com to run a CarFax VIN report on any used car you're considering.
- Pay for the car with a cashier's check.
- Prepare a bill of sale. The bill of sale can be written in crayon on the back of a paper towel as long as a notary public witnesses the signatures of both parties. If the owner of the car has a lien against it, the bill of sale, when properly notarized, will serve as proof of purchase until the owner's loan is paid and you receive the title.

CAR FINANCE DOT COM ™
Instant
Lease & Loan Quotes
for New & Used Vehicles!
www.CarFinance.com/edmunds

 © 1999 by Edmund Publications Corporation

Selling a Used Car:

- Clean the vehicle thoroughly, and make sure it is in good operating condition.
- Make sure all paperwork related to the vehicle is in order, particularly the title and registration.
- Advertise, advertise, advertise in major newspapers and used car magazine classifieds. If possible, park the car in high-traffic areas with For Sale signs in the windows and flyers tucked under the wiper blade that explain why someone would want your car. However, beware of local ordinances prohibiting the display of vehicles for sale.
- Realize that Japanese cars are generally in more demand than most American and European cars on the used car market.

Trading a Used Car:

- Clean the vehicle thoroughly, and make sure it is in good operating condition.
- Make sure all paperwork related to the vehicle is in order, particularly the title and registration.
- Expect the dealer to offer far less than the car is worth. Negotiate as close to Trade-in Value as possible.
- Make sure the trade-in value doesn't get lost in the purchase or lease contract. Keep your eye on the ball.

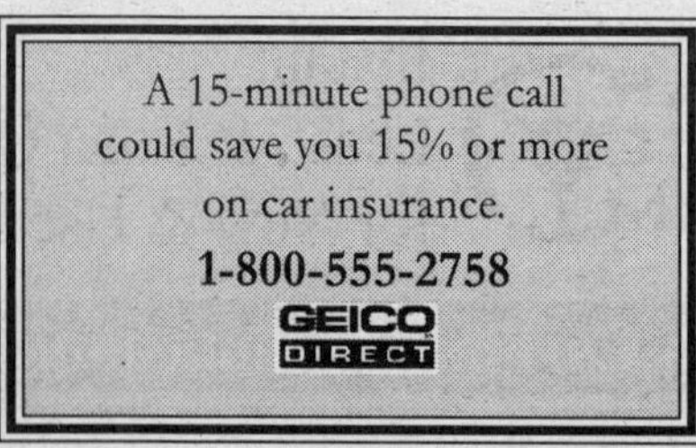

A 15-minute phone call
could save you 15% or more
on car insurance.
1-800-555-2758
GEICO
DIRECT

 © 1999 by Edmund Publications Corporation

Model Description	Trade-in Value	Market Value

ACURA Japan

1997 Acura TL

1998 ACURA

CL-SERIES 1998

A new 2.3L engine replaces last year's 2.2L unit. All CL models get a revised grille and new alloy wheels.

Category J

Model Description	Trade-in Value	Market Value
2 Dr 2.3 Cpe	16990	20230
2 Dr 2.3 Premium Cpe	17805	21195
2 Dr 3.0 Cpe	19875	23660
2 Dr 3.0 Premium Cpe	20645	24580

OPTIONS FOR CL-SERIES

Auto 4-Speed Transmission[Opt on 2.3, 2.3 Premium] +665
Rear Spoiler +310

INTEGRA 1998

A slight nose job, designed for a more aerodynamic approach, is added this year. LS, GS and GS-R models get a little more comfortable with a tilt- and height-adjustable driver's seat and new alloy wheels appear on the LS and GS-R. The performance edition Type R is available again this year.

Category E

Model Description	Trade-in Value	Market Value
2 Dr GS Hbk	14325	17260
4 Dr GS Sdn	14135	17030
2 Dr GS-R Hbk	15030	18110
4 Dr GS-R Sdn	15030	18110
2 Dr LS Hbk	13170	15865
4 Dr LS Sdn	13190	15890
2 Dr RS Hbk	11065	13335
2 Dr Type R Hbk	16650	20065

OPTIONS FOR INTEGRA

Auto 4-Speed Transmission +665
Air Conditioning[Opt on RS,Type R] +675
Aluminum/Alloy Wheels[Opt on RS] +265
Fog Lights +125
Keyless Entry System +125
Leather Seats[Std on GS] +740

RL-SERIES 1998

Slight suspension enhancements provide more sporty handling without sacrificing the ride.

Category A

Model Description	Trade-in Value	Market Value
4 Dr Premium Sdn	28685	34150
4 Dr Special Edition Sdn	27395	32610
4 Dr STD Sdn	26880	32000

OPTIONS FOR RL-SERIES

Navigation System +1710
Compact Disc Changer[Opt on STD] +725

SLX 1998

Acura's rebadged Isuzu Trooper gets more power and torque, a trick new 4WD system and revised styling for 1998.

Category G

Model Description	Trade-in Value	Market Value
4 Dr STD 4WD Wgn	20345	24220

TL-SERIES 1998

The premium level is gone, but the TL-Series gets more standard equipment.

Category A

Model Description	Trade-in Value	Market Value
4 Dr 2.5 Sdn	21015	25020
4 Dr 3.2 Sdn	22670	26990

1997 ACURA

CL-SERIES 1997

Introduced as a 1997 model, the 2.2CL is supposed to compete in the growing personal coupe segment. Like many Acura products, the 2.2CL is based on a Honda platform, in this case the Honda Accord. The 2.2CL's sights are aimed squarely at the personal coupe market segment that is currently dominated by cars like the Ford Thunderbird, BMW 3-Series and Chrysler Sebring.

RATINGS (SCALE OF 1-10)

Overall	Safety	Reliability	Performance	Comfort	Value
N/A	N/A	9.3	7.8	7.5	N/A

Category J

Model Description	Trade-in Value	Market Value
2 Dr 2.2 Cpe	14155	16855
2 Dr 2.2 Premium Cpe	14665	17455
2 Dr 3.0 Cpe	16660	19835
2 Dr 3.0 Premium Cpe	17165	20435

Don't forget to refer to the Mileage Adjustment Table at the back of this book!

© 1999 by Edmund Publications Corporation

Model Description	Trade-in Value	Market Value

OPTIONS FOR CL-SERIES

Auto 4-Speed Transmission[Opt on 2.2CL] +545

INTEGRA 1997

No major changes to what may be the last Acura Integra. The good news is that prices for Special Edition (now called GS), LS and RS models remain the same as last year.

RATINGS (SCALE OF 1-10)

Overall	Safety	Reliability	Performance	Comfort	Value
N/A	6.9	9.1	9.2	7.8	N/A

Category E		
2 Dr GS Hbk	13165	16055
4 Dr GS Sdn	13040	15900
2 Dr GS-R Hbk	13965	17030
4 Dr GS-R Sdn	14050	17135
2 Dr LS Hbk	12490	15235
4 Dr LS Sdn	12065	14715
2 Dr RS Hbk	10410	12695
2 Dr Type R Hbk	15560	18975

OPTIONS FOR INTEGRA

Auto 4-Speed Transmission +545
Air Conditioning[Opt on RS,Type R] +550
Aluminum/Alloy Wheels[Opt on LS] +215
AM/FM Stereo Tape[Std on LS] +210
Leather Seats[Std on GS] +605

RL-SERIES 1997

No changes for the 1997 3.5RL.

RATINGS (SCALE OF 1-10)

Overall	Safety	Reliability	Performance	Comfort	Value
N/A	N/A	9	8.2	8.9	4.2

Category A		
4 Dr Premium Sdn	25975	31295
4 Dr STD Sdn	25270	30445

OPTIONS FOR RL-SERIES

Elect. Navigation System +1360
Alarm System +185
Compact Disc Changer[Opt on STD] +590
Compact Disc W/fm/tape +475

SLX 1997

In typical Acura form, the SLX is one of the first luxury badged sport-utes to be released in this country. Based on the successful Isuzu Trooper, the SLX is very similar to its twin.

RATINGS (SCALE OF 1-10)

Overall	Safety	Reliability	Performance	Comfort	Value
6.8	6.5	8.7	6.8	7.6	4.6

Category G		
4 Dr Premium 4WD Wgn	20050	23870
4 Dr STD 4WD Wgn	18945	22555

TL-SERIES 1997

Vigor replacement designed to do battle with new Infiniti I30 and the Lexus ES300 in the near-luxury segment. Cleanly styled with room for four, the new TL-Series comes with either a 2.5- liter inline five-cylinder, or a smooth 3.2-liter V6.

RATINGS (SCALE OF 1-10)

Overall	Safety	Reliability	Performance	Comfort	Value
7.4	7.6	9.1	7.4	8	5.1

Category A		
4 Dr 2.5 Sdn	17495	21080
4 Dr 2.5 Premium Sdn	18880	22745
4 Dr 3.2 Sdn	20935	25220
4 Dr 3.2 Premium Sdn	22165	26705

1996 ACURA

INTEGRA 1996

All Integras get new wheel cover and alloy wheel designs this year, as well as green tinted glass. LS models receive body colored moldings. Three new colors can be applied to the 1996 Integra: pearls in red, green or black.

RATINGS (SCALE OF 1-10)

Overall	Safety	Reliability	Performance	Comfort	Value
7.3	6.9	9	9.2	7.8	3.5

Category E		
2 Dr GS-R Hbk	12730	16115
4 Dr GS-R Sdn	12510	15835
2 Dr LS Hbk	10980	13895
4 Dr LS Sdn	10785	13650
2 Dr RS Hbk	9435	11945
4 Dr RS Sdn	9435	11945
2 Dr Special Edition Hbk	11815	14955
4 Dr Special Edition Sdn	11625	14715

OPTIONS FOR INTEGRA

Auto 4-Speed Transmission +435
Air Conditioning[Opt on RS] +450
Aluminum/Alloy Wheels[Opt on LS] +175
Leather Seats[Opt on GS-R] +495

For a guaranteed low price on a new car in your area, call

1-800-CAR-CLUB

Don't forget to refer to the Mileage Adjustment Table at the back of this book!

 © 1999 by Edmund Publications Corporation

Model Description	Trade-in Value	Market Value

NSX 1996

The hardtop NSX is reintroduced to the Acura lineup.

Category K

2 Dr NSX-T Cpe	47440	55165

OPTIONS FOR NSX

Auto 4-Speed Transmission +1910

RL-SERIES 1996

The replacement for the Legend arrives wearing Acura's new alphanumeric naming system: the 3.5 RL. The 3.5 refers to the Acura's engine size. Detractors claim that the RL stands for little more than Revised Legend. While the 3.5 RL is definitely luxurious, we think that many will miss the Legend's sporty feel. The front wheels of the 3.5 RL are powered by a torquey V6 engine mated to an electronic four-speed automatic transmission. Other changes include 101 ways to isolate bumps, vibrations and road noise. Acura's new flagship promises to be about as noisy as a sensory deprivation chamber.

RATINGS (SCALE OF 1-10)

Overall	Safety	Reliability	Performance	Comfort	Value
N/A	N/A	9.3	8.2	8.9	3.2

Category A

4 Dr 3.5 Sdn	22240	27120
4 Dr 3.5 Premium Sdn	23485	28640

OPTIONS FOR RL-SERIES

Navigation System +1090
AM/FM Compact Disc Playr +290
Compact Disc Changer[Opt on 3.5] +485

SLX 1996

In typical Acura form, the SLX is one of the first luxury-badged sport-utes to be released in this country. Based on the successful Isuzu Trooper, the SLX is very similar to its twin.

RATINGS (SCALE OF 1-10)

Overall	Safety	Reliability	Performance	Comfort	Value
7	6.5	8.6	6.8	7.6	5.6

Category G

4 Dr STD 4WD Wgn	16915	20625

OPTIONS FOR SLX

Premium Pkg +1595
Dual Power Seats +350
Leather Seats +425
Limited Slip Diff +145
Power Moonroof +490

TL-SERIES 1996

Vigor replacement designed to do battle with new Infiniti I30 and the Lexus ES300 in the near-luxury segment. Cleanly styled with room for four, the new TL-Series comes with either a 2.5-liter inline five cylinder, or a smooth 3.2-liter V6.

RATINGS (SCALE OF 1-10)

Overall	Safety	Reliability	Performance	Comfort	Value
7.4	7.6	8.9	7.4	8	5

Category A

4 Dr 2.5 Sdn	15345	18715
4 Dr 2.5 Premium Sdn	16635	20285
4 Dr 3.2 Sdn	18535	22605
4 Dr 3.2 Premium Sdn	19765	24105

OPTIONS FOR TL-SERIES

Compact Disc Changer +485

1995 ACURA

INTEGRA 1995

A Special Edition model debuts, sporting leather interior, spoiler and larger tires. All LS models receive a sunroof.

RATINGS (SCALE OF 1-10)

Overall	Safety	Reliability	Performance	Comfort	Value
7.3	7.1	8.9	9.2	7.8	3.4

Category E

2 Dr GS-R Hbk	10865	14110
4 Dr GS-R Sdn	10880	14135
2 Dr LS Hbk	9260	12025
4 Dr LS Sdn	9280	12050
2 Dr RS Hbk	8020	10415
4 Dr RS Sdn	8155	10590
2 Dr Special Edition Hbk	10025	13015
4 Dr Special Edition Sdn	10090	13100

OPTIONS FOR INTEGRA

Auto 4-Speed Transmission +335
Air Conditioning[Opt on RS] +370
Alarm System +205
Aluminum/Alloy Wheels[Std on GS-R] +145
AM/FM Compact Disc Playr +215
Compact Disc W/fm/tape +315
Leather Seats[Opt on GS-R] +405
Rear Spoiler[Opt on LS,RS] +95

LEGEND 1995

Last year for the Acura flagship, the 1996 model will bear Acura's new alphanumeric nomenclature. No changes for this year's model.

RATINGS (SCALE OF 1-10)

Overall	Safety	Reliability	Performance	Comfort	Value
7.9	8	9.4	8.6	8	5.4

Don't forget to refer to the Mileage Adjustment Table at the back of this book!

© 1999 by Edmund Publications Corporation

Model Description	Trade-in Value	Market Value
Category A		
4 Dr GS Sdn	17320	21385
2 Dr L Cpe	17075	21080
4 Dr L Sdn	15215	18785
2 Dr LS Cpe	18020	22250
4 Dr LS Sdn	16720	20640
4 Dr SE Sdn	16940	20910

OPTIONS FOR LEGEND

Auto 4-Speed Transmission[Opt on GS,L,Cpe] +90
Compact Disc Changer[Opt on L] +395
Leather Seats[Opt on L Sdn] +310

NSX 1995

The NSX coupe is dropped in favor of the NSX-T. The "T" stands for targa; all 1995 models are so equipped. Designed to boost sales of this slow-selling sports car, the NSX-T is functionally very similar to its coupe sibling.

Model Description	Trade-in Value	Market Value
Category K		
2 Dr STD Cpe	42345	49815

OPTIONS FOR NSX

Auto 4-Speed Transmission +1560

1994 ACURA

INTEGRA 1994

Redesigned for 1994, the Integra sports a distinctive four headlight front-end. All models receive four-wheel disc brakes to aid stopping; LS and GS-R models get antilock brakes. GS-Rs get a ten-horsepower boost over last year to improve performance. Dual airbags finally replace the annoying motorized seat belts as the passive restraint system on the Integra.

RATINGS (SCALE OF 1-10)

Overall	Safety	Reliability	Performance	Comfort	Value
7.3	7.1	8.8	9.2	7.8	3.8

Model Description	Trade-in Value	Market Value
Category E		
2 Dr GS-R Hbk	9010	12015
4 Dr GS-R Sdn	9125	12165
2 Dr LS Hbk	7475	9965
4 Dr LS Sdn	7405	9875
2 Dr RS Hbk	6580	8770
4 Dr RS Sdn	6785	9045

OPTIONS FOR INTEGRA

Auto 4-Speed Transmission +280
Air Conditioning[Opt on RS] +300
Aluminum/Alloy Wheels[Opt on LS] +120
Compact Disc Changer +205
Keyless Entry System +55
Rear Spoiler[Opt on LS,Sdn] +75

LEGEND 1994

The base Legend is dropped from the line-up and a GS sedan is added. The new sedan offers the same 230-horsepower engine found in the coupe as well as traction control and a sport-tuned suspension. A new grille and bumpers find their way to all Legends and the LS coupe gets a new chin-spoiler. An automatically tilting steering wheel raises as soon as the key is removed from the ignition. Further improvements include a steering wheel position memory that is incorporated into the seat memory feature.

RATINGS (SCALE OF 1-10)

Overall	Safety	Reliability	Performance	Comfort	Value
7.8	8	9.3	8.6	8	5.4

Model Description	Trade-in Value	Market Value
Category A		
4 Dr GS Sdn	15035	18565
2 Dr L Cpe	14670	18110
4 Dr L Sdn	13140	16220
2 Dr LS Cpe	15420	19035
4 Dr LS Sdn	14375	17745

OPTIONS FOR LEGEND

Auto 4-Speed Transmission[Opt on GS,L,Cpe] +75
Leather Seats[Std on GS,LS,Cpe] +255

NSX 1994

Still no changes for the four-year-old NSX.

Model Description	Trade-in Value	Market Value
Category K		
2 Dr STD Cpe	35160	41855

OPTIONS FOR NSX

Auto 4-Speed Transmission +1485

VIGOR 1994

Dual airbags are now standard on all Vigors. Burled walnut trim replaces the Zebrano wood interior on all Vigors. GS models get a standard CD player. This is the final year for the Vigor.

Model Description	Trade-in Value	Market Value
Category D		
4 Dr GS Sdn	10285	13185
4 Dr LS Sdn	9330	11960

OPTIONS FOR VIGOR

Auto 4-Speed Transmission +280

1993 ACURA

INTEGRA 1993

An LS model is introduced to the Integra line-up. Standard leather upholstery, rear spoiler and bigger tires make this mid-level Integra attractive to luxury-oriented buyers. An improved warranty is offered this year that boosts coverage to four years/45,000 miles.

Don't forget to refer to the Mileage Adjustment Table at the back of this book!

© 1999 by Edmund Publications Corporation

Model Description	Trade-in Value	Market Value

RATINGS (SCALE OF 1-10)

Overall	Safety	Reliability	Performance	Comfort	Value
N/A	N/A	8.6	8.8	7.9	3.8

Category E		
2 Dr GS Hbk	6550	8970
4 Dr GS Sdn	6590	9030
2 Dr GS-R Hbk	7110	9740
2 Dr LS Hbk	6055	8295
4 Dr LS Sdn	5950	8155
2 Dr LS Special Hbk	6160	8440
2 Dr RS Hbk	5395	7390
4 Dr RS Sdn	5440	7450

OPTIONS FOR INTEGRA

Auto 4-Speed Transmission +225
Air Conditioning +245
Compact Disc W/fm/tape +210
Leather Seats[Opt on GS] +270
Theft Deterrent System +55

LEGEND 1993

Thirty more horsepower and a six-speed manual transmission make the Legend coupe a viable luxury-performance contender. A passenger airbag is now standard on the base Legend. Upgraded stereos are standard on the L and LS models. Warranty coverage is extended to four years/45,000 miles.

RATINGS (SCALE OF 1-10)

Overall	Safety	Reliability	Performance	Comfort	Value
7.8	8	9.2	8.6	8	5.3

Category A		
2 Dr L Cpe	11695	14805
4 Dr L Sdn	10675	13510
2 Dr LS Cpe	12550	15885
4 Dr LS Sdn	11540	14610
4 Dr STD Sdn	9905	12535

OPTIONS FOR LEGEND

Auto 4-Speed Transmission +245
AM/FM Compact Disc Playr +160
Compact Disc W/fm/tape +215
Leather Seats[Opt on L] +210

NSX 1993

A passenger airbag is introduced this year, as is a cupholder for the center console. Warranty coverage is improved from three years/36,000 miles to four years/45,000 miles.

Category K		
2 Dr STD Cpe	29930	36065

OPTIONS FOR NSX

Auto 4-Speed Transmission +1215

Model Description	Trade-in Value	Market Value

VIGOR 1993

A passenger airbag debuts on the up-level GS Vigor. Restyled front grille and sound insulation mark the other changes to this car. Warranty coverage increases to four years/45,000 miles.

Category D		
4 Dr GS Sdn	8120	10685
4 Dr LS Sdn	7340	9660

OPTIONS FOR VIGOR

Auto 4-Speed Transmission +225

1992 ACURA

INTEGRA 1992

A minor facelift and more horsepower are the only changes for the '92 Integra. A GS-R performance model is introduced for those who want to go a little bit faster. A VTEC engine, producing 160 horsepower, is standard on the GS-R.

RATINGS (SCALE OF 1-10)

Overall	Safety	Reliability	Performance	Comfort	Value
N/A	N/A	8.4	8.8	7.9	5.2

Category E		
2 Dr GS Hbk	5690	8125
4 Dr GS Sdn	5800	8290
2 Dr GS-R Hbk	6200	8860
2 Dr LS Hbk	4980	7115
4 Dr LS Sdn	5000	7140
2 Dr RS Hbk	4465	6375
4 Dr RS Sdn	4605	6575

OPTIONS FOR INTEGRA

Auto 4-Speed Transmission +185
Air Conditioning +200
Aluminum/Alloy Wheels[Opt on LS] +80
AM/FM Stereo Tape[Opt on RS] +75

LEGEND 1992

A passenger airbag joins the standard equipment list on LS models. Cupholders are finally available to front seat passengers. LS models are now available with heated front seats.

RATINGS (SCALE OF 1-10)

Overall	Safety	Reliability	Performance	Comfort	Value
7.8	7.5	8.8	8.6	8	6.2

Category A		
2 Dr L Cpe	9810	12905
4 Dr L Sdn	8935	11760
2 Dr LS Cpe	10575	13915
4 Dr LS Sdn	9745	12825
4 Dr STD Sdn	8315	10945

Don't forget to refer to the Mileage Adjustment Table at the back of this book!

 © 1999 by Edmund Publications Corporation

Model Description	Trade-in Value	Market Value

OPTIONS FOR LEGEND

Auto 4-Speed Transmission +195
Leather Seats[Opt on L] +170

NSX 1992

No changes for the sweetest looking car since the Porsche 911.

Category K

2 Dr STD Cpe	26000	31705

OPTIONS FOR NSX

Auto 4-Speed Transmission +975

VIGOR 1992

The Vigor is introduced to broaden Acura's market. It is a midsized near-luxury sedan based on the Honda Accord. Offered in two trim levels, the Vigor can be had with an automatic or manual transmission. Power comes via an inline five-cylinder engine. Antilock brakes, power everything and a security system are standard on the Vigor.

Category D

4 Dr GS Sdn	6785	9165
4 Dr LS Sdn	6420	8680

OPTIONS FOR VIGOR

Auto 4-Speed Transmission +185

1991 ACURA

INTEGRA 1991

No significant changes are made to the 1991 Integra.

RATINGS (SCALE OF 1-10)

Overall	Safety	Reliability	Performance	Comfort	Value
N/A	N/A	8.2	8.8	7.9	4.2

Category E

2 Dr GS Hbk	4685	6890
4 Dr GS Sdn	4640	6820
2 Dr LS Hbk	4210	6190
4 Dr LS Sdn	4130	6075
2 Dr LS Special Hbk	4250	6255
2 Dr RS Hbk	3780	5560
4 Dr RS Sdn	3745	5505

OPTIONS FOR INTEGRA

Auto 4-Speed Transmission +145
Air Conditioning +165
Aluminum/Alloy Wheels[Opt on LS] +65
AM/FM Stereo Tape[Opt on RS] +60

LEGEND 1991

Redesigned for 1991, the Legend gets longer and larger. A more powerful engine keeps this car competitive with domestic and import rivals.

RATINGS (SCALE OF 1-10)

Overall	Safety	Reliability	Performance	Comfort	Value
7.9	7.4	8.6	8.6	8	6.7

Category A

2 Dr L Cpe	8260	11010
4 Dr L Sdn	7190	9585
2 Dr LS Cpe	8830	11770
4 Dr LS Sdn	7890	10520
2 Dr STD Cpe	8150	10870
4 Dr STD Sdn	6715	8955

OPTIONS FOR LEGEND

Auto 4-Speed Transmission +160
Compact Disc Changer +175
Compact Disc W/fm/tape +140
Leather Seats[Opt on L] +140

1990 ACURA

INTEGRA 1990

The five-door hatchback is lost in the redesign of the Integra. The sedan and two-door hatchbacks continue. Horsepower and torque figures are up for this entry-level Acura, but so is weight. Suspension upgrades improve handling.

RATINGS (SCALE OF 1-10)

Overall	Safety	Reliability	Performance	Comfort	Value
N/A	N/A	7.9	8.8	7.9	4.6

Category E

2 Dr GS Hbk	3665	5640
4 Dr GS Sdn	3685	5670
2 Dr LS Hbk	3395	5225
4 Dr LS Sdn	3375	5195
2 Dr RS Hbk	3020	4650
4 Dr RS Sdn	2985	4595

OPTIONS FOR INTEGRA

Auto 4-Speed Transmission +120
Air Conditioning +135
Aluminum/Alloy Wheels[Std on GS,Sdn] +50
AM/FM Stereo Tape[Opt on RS] +50

LEGEND 1990

LS models get a spoiler. A new grille appears on all Legends. Interior changes include an authentic burled walnut center console and improved seats.

Category A

2 Dr L Cpe	5365	7250
4 Dr L Sdn	5070	6850
2 Dr LS Cpe	5850	7905
4 Dr LS Sdn	5520	7455
2 Dr STD Cpe	5030	6795
4 Dr STD Sdn	4560	6165

Don't forget to refer to the Mileage Adjustment Table at the back of this book!

© 1999 by Edmund Publications Corporation

Model Description	Trade-in Value	Market Value

OPTIONS FOR LEGEND

Auto 4-Speed Transmission +130
Leather Seats[Opt on L] +115
Power Sunroof[Std on L,LS,Cpe] +225

1989 ACURA

INTEGRA 1989

The Honda Civic-derived luxury sport coupes and sedans receive no changes in light of next year's redesign.

Category E

Model Description	Trade-in Value	Market Value
2 Dr LS Hbk	2185	3585
4 Dr LS Hbk	2230	3655
2 Dr RS Hbk	1890	3095
4 Dr RS Hbk	2065	3385

OPTIONS FOR INTEGRA

Auto 4-Speed Transmission +85
Air Conditioning +110
Aluminum/Alloy Wheels[Opt on RS] +45
AM/FM Stereo Tape +40

LEGEND 1989

The Acura flagship sedan gets a new rear suspension to improve handling. A driver airbag becomes standard in all models. Antilock brakes are available on the L and LS.

Category A

Model Description	Trade-in Value	Market Value
2 Dr L Cpe	4480	6220
4 Dr L Sdn	4250	5900
2 Dr LS Cpe	4570	6345
4 Dr LS Sdn	4420	6135
2 Dr STD Cpe	4230	5875
4 Dr STD Sdn	3990	5540

OPTIONS FOR LEGEND

Auto 4-Speed Transmission +110
Leather Seats[Std on LS,Cpe] +95
Power Sunroof[Std on L,LS,Cpe] +185

Instant
Lease & Loan Quotes
for New & Used Vehicles!
www.CarFinance.com/edmunds

Major Savings
On An
Extended Warranty
"YOU DESERVE THE BEST"
Call today for your free quote.
Pay up to 50% less than dealership prices!
http://www.edmunds.com/warranty 1-800-580-9889

Don't forget to refer to the Mileage Adjustment Table at the back of this book!

© 1999 by Edmund Publications Corporation

Model Description	Trade-in Value	Market Value

AUDI

Germany

1997 Audi A8

1998 AUDI

A4 1998

The 2.8 sedan gets a valve job resulting in 18 more horsepower and additional torque. Side-impact airbags are standard, as is traction control. Opt for the automatic and you'll get the same Tiptronic technology that allows Biff to manually shift Buffy's 911 Cabriolet. A new station wagon called Avant debuts, while the A4 1.8T gets new wheels, a sport package and an ambient temperature gauge. New colors and stereo improvements round out the changes for 1998.

Category J		
4 Dr Avant Wgn	23770	27640
4 Dr Quattro V6 4WD Sdn	23475	27295
4 Dr STD V6 Sdn	22355	25995

OPTIONS FOR A4

Auto 5-Speed Transmission[Std on Avant Wgn] +895
Bose Sound System +680
Compact Disc Changer +815
Heated Front Seats +345
Leather Seats +855
Power Moonroof +760
Special Factory Paint +1460

A6 1998

Stretch an A4 platform, add rounded styling with plenty of edges for character, toss in a sumptuously comfortable interior available in several "atmosphere" styles, blend it all with traditional Germanic handling, and what do you get? The excellent new Audi A6 sedan. Our only quibble is the with the dorky taillights, which appear to have been inspired by the Chevrolet S-10 pickup. The wagon is carried over from 1997.

Category J		
4 Dr Quattro 4WD Sdn	31950	37150
4 Dr STD Sdn	30425	35375

OPTIONS FOR A6

Enhanced Security Package +790
Warm Weather Package +1245
Bose Sound System +680
Compact Disc Changer +815
Dual Power Seats +610
Heated Front Seats +345
Leather Seats +855
Metallic Paint +675
Power Moonroof +760

1997 AUDI

A4 1997

A cheaper Audi A4 1.8T debuts, featuring a 150-horsepower 20-valve turbocharged inline four-cylinder engine and a base price in the low 20s. The 2.8 gains a revised decklid and expanded central locking features. All models have new cloth upholstery, and the console and armrests are trimmed with the same fabric as the seats. Three new colors debut for 1997.

RATINGS (SCALE OF 1-10)

Overall	Safety	Reliability	Performance	Comfort	Value
7.7	7.7	8.8	8.8	8.1	5

Category J		
4 Dr Quattro 4WD Sdn	20260	23560
4 Dr Quattro Turbo 4WD Sdn	18780	21840
4 Dr STD Sdn	18420	21420
4 Dr STD Turbo Sdn	17510	20360

OPTIONS FOR A4

Auto 5-Speed Transmission +660
Bose Sound System +555
Heated Front Seats +280
Leather Seats +700
Power Moonroof +620
Special Factory Paint +1195
Sport Seats +540

A6 1997

A new Quattro Value Package is available with a power glass sunroof, larger alloy wheels, bigger tires, and, of course, the quattro all-wheel drive system. Selective unlocking capability expands to the remote keyless entry fob, and the alarm system now features interior monitoring. Jacquard cloth upholstery is new, and three new colors debut: Tornado Red, Volcano Black metallic and Byzantine metallic.

Don't forget to refer to the Mileage Adjustment Table at the back of this book!

 © 1999 by Edmund Publications Corporation

Model Description	Trade-in Value	Market Value

RATINGS (SCALE OF 1-10)

Overall	Safety	Reliability	Performance	Comfort	Value
7.9	8.3	9.2	8	8	5.8

Category J

4 Dr Quattro 4WD Wgn	23805	27680
4 Dr Quattro 4WD Sdn	22575	26250

OPTIONS FOR A6

Bose Sound System +555
Dual Power Seats +500
Headlight Washers +170
Heated Front Seats +280
Leather Seats +700
Metallic Paint +550
Power Moonroof +620

A8 1997

Audi revolutionizes luxury sedan construction with the Audi Space Frame, which employs seven new aircraft-grade aluminum alloys to lighten weight and provide a tighter, more crashworthy structure. The new A8 is also the first passenger car equipped with six airbags. The usual accouterments associated with a premium German sedan are all in place.

Category L

4 Dr Quattro 4WD Sdn	39830	47420

OPTIONS FOR A8

Cold Weather Package +680
Polished Alloy Wheels +680
Warm Weather Package +1360
Bose Sound System[Opt on STD] +375
Heated Seats +240
Metallic Paint +410

CABRIOLET 1997

Category F

2 Dr STD Conv	24940	29340

OPTIONS FOR CABRIOLET

Premium Equipment Package +2015

1996 AUDI

A4 1996

All-new, the A4 replaces the compact 90. This car performs better than the lackluster 90, and features a full load of standard features. Plus, it's drop-dead gorgeous. For the first time, a five-speed automatic transmission is available with the optional Quattro all-wheel drive system.

RATINGS (SCALE OF 1-10)

Overall	Safety	Reliability	Performance	Comfort	Value
7.9	7.7	8.5	8.8	8.1	6.1

Category J

4 Dr Quattro 4WD Sdn	18125	21580
4 Dr STD Sdn	16055	19110

OPTIONS FOR A4

Auto 5-Speed Transmission +510
Bose Sound System +455
Heated Front Seats +230
Leather Seats +570
Leather Steering Wheel[Opt on STD] +55
Metallic Paint +450
Power Moonroof +510

A6 1996

Traction control systems have been improved this year. Fans of the manual transmission will mourn the loss of it; all 1996 A6 models are saddled with an automatic shifter.

RATINGS (SCALE OF 1-10)

Overall	Safety	Reliability	Performance	Comfort	Value
7.8	8.3	9.1	8	8	5.7

Category J

4 Dr Quattro 4WD Sdn	19590	23325
4 Dr Quattro 4WD Wgn	20690	24630
4 Dr STD Sdn	18140	21595
4 Dr STD Wgn	19695	23450

OPTIONS FOR A6

Bose Sound System +455
Dual Power Seats +410
Headlight Washers +140
Heated Front Seats +230
Leather Seats +570
Metallic Paint +450
Power Moonroof +510

CABRIOLET 1996

Better acceleration, a new radio, a new color and revised alloy wheels are the only changes.

Category F

2 Dr STD Conv	20105	24225

1995 AUDI

90 1995

Sport 90 model introduced, featuring lowered suspension.

Category D

4 Dr Quattro 4WD Sdn	13050	16520
4 Dr Sport Sdn	11520	14580
4 Dr STD Sdn	11320	14330

OPTIONS FOR 90

Auto 4-Speed Transmission +400
Climate Control for AC +135
Heated Front Seats +165

Don't forget to refer to the Mileage Adjustment Table at the back of this book!

 © 1999 by Edmund Publications Corporation

Model Description	Trade-in Value	Market Value

Keyless Entry System +135
Leather Seats +500
Power Sunroof +330
Tilt Steering Wheel +55

A6 1995

Subtle restyle brings new name. Sedan or wagon available in either front- or all-wheel drive. Wagon comes only with an automatic transmission.

RATINGS (SCALE OF 1-10)

Overall	Safety	Reliability	Performance	Comfort	Value
8.3	9.1	9.2	8	8	7

Category J

Model Description	Trade-in Value	Market Value
4 Dr Quattro 4WD Sdn	16375	19730
4 Dr Quattro 4WD Wgn	17065	20560
4 Dr STD Wgn	16345	19690
4 Dr STD Sdn	14365	17310

OPTIONS FOR A6

Auto 4-Speed Transmission[Std on Wgn] +400
AM/FM Compact Disc Playr +245
Bose Sound System +370
Dual Power Seats +335
Heated Front Seats +185
Leather Seats +465
Power Moonroof +415

CABRIOLET 1995

No changes.

Category F

Model Description	Trade-in Value	Market Value
2 Dr STD Conv	16735	20405

S6 1995

Category F

Model Description	Trade-in Value	Market Value
4 Dr STD Turbo 4WD Sdn	23560	28730

OPTIONS FOR S6

Compact Disc Changer +305

1994 AUDI

100 1994

Base sedan dropped. CS sedan gets standard automatic transmission. Rear ashtrays and cigarette lighters disappear from all models.

RATINGS (SCALE OF 1-10)

Overall	Safety	Reliability	Performance	Comfort	Value
N/A	N/A	9.1	8	8.1	7

Category D

Model Description	Trade-in Value	Market Value
4 Dr CS Sdn	12745	16550
4 Dr CS Quattro 4WD Sdn	13410	17420
4 Dr S Sdn	10965	14240
4 Dr S Wgn	11630	15105

OPTIONS FOR 100

Auto 4-Speed Transmission[Std on CS,Wgn] +295
Bose Sound System[Opt on S Sdn] +270
Compact Disc Changer +245
Headlight Washers +55
Heated Front Seats[Opt on S,Sdn] +135
Leather Seats[Opt on S Sdn] +410
Special Factory Paint +120

90 1994

Passenger airbag newly standard. S model can be equipped with leather and a power sunroof.

Category D

Model Description	Trade-in Value	Market Value
4 Dr CS Sdn	10900	14155
4 Dr CS Quattro 4WD Sdn	12770	16585
4 Dr S Sdn	9860	12800

OPTIONS FOR 90

Auto 4-Speed Transmission +295
Heated Front Seats +135
Power Sunroof[Opt on S] +270
Special Factory Paint +120

CABRIOLET 1994

Based on 90 platform. Features dual airbags, ABS, and 2.8-liter V6 engine. No manual transmission available. Rear window is plastic.

Category F

Model Description	Trade-in Value	Market Value
2 Dr STD Conv	15650	19560

OPTIONS FOR CABRIOLET

Heated Front Seats +125
Special Factory Paint +120

S4 1994

Category F

Model Description	Trade-in Value	Market Value
4 Dr STD Turbo 4WD Sdn	19290	24110

OPTIONS FOR S4

Compact Disc Changer +250
Special Factory Paint +120

V8 1994

Category F

Model Description	Trade-in Value	Market Value
4 Dr Quattro 4WD Sdn	15450	19315

OPTIONS FOR V8

Special Factory Paint +120

1993 AUDI

100 1993

Passenger airbag standard.

RATINGS (SCALE OF 1-10)

Overall	Safety	Reliability	Performance	Comfort	Value
N/A	N/A	8.7	8	8.1	6.9

Don't forget to refer to the Mileage Adjustment Table at the back of this book!

© 1999 by Edmund Publications Corporation

Model Description	Trade-in Value	Market Value
Category D		
4 Dr CS Sdn	9535	12880
4 Dr CS Quattro 4WD Sdn	11165	15085
4 Dr S Sdn	8310	11230
4 Dr STD Sdn	7650	10335

OPTIONS FOR 100

Auto 4-Speed Transmission[Std on CS,Wgn] +245
Heated Front Seats +110
Leather Seats[Opt on S] +335
Special Factory Paint +95

90 — 1993

All-new 90 model debuts, with 2.8-liter V6 under the hood. ABS and driver airbag standard. Quattro AWD system still available.

Model Description	Trade-in Value	Market Value
Category D		
4 Dr CS Sdn	7715	10430
4 Dr CS Quattro 4WD Sdn	9580	12945
4 Dr S Sdn	6985	9440

OPTIONS FOR 90

Auto 4-Speed Transmission +245
Heated Front Seats +110
Power Sunroof[Opt on S] +220
Special Factory Paint +95

S4 — 1993

Passenger airbag standard.

Model Description	Trade-in Value	Market Value
Category F		
4 Dr STD Turbo 4WD Sdn	16755	21760

V8 — 1993

Model Description	Trade-in Value	Market Value
Category F		
4 Dr Quattro 4WD Sdn	12740	16545

1992 AUDI

100 — 1992

Sheetmetal redesigned, and 2.8-liter V6 replaces five-cylinder motor. Quattro models available with automatic transmission. Driver airbag and ABS standard. All wagons are Quattro-equipped.

RATINGS (SCALE OF 1-10)

Overall	Safety	Reliability	Performance	Comfort	Value
N/A	N/A	8.6	8	8.1	6.9

Model Description	Trade-in Value	Market Value
Category D		
4 Dr CS Sdn	7435	10185
4 Dr CS Quattro 4WD Sdn	9980	13670
4 Dr CS Quattro 4WD Wgn	10055	13770
4 Dr S Sdn	7030	9630
4 Dr STD Sdn	6455	8840

OPTIONS FOR 100

Auto 4-Speed Transmission[Std on Wgn] +195
Pearlescent Met. Paint +230
AM/FM Stereo Tape[Opt on CS,S] +90
Headlight Washers[Std on Wgn] +35
Heated Front Seats[Std on Wgn] +90
Leather Seats[Std on Wgn] +275

S4 — 1992

200 designation dropped in favor of S4. Driver airbag and ABS standard.

Model Description	Trade-in Value	Market Value
Category F		
4 Dr STD Turbo Sdn	13720	18290

OPTIONS FOR S4

Aluminum/Alloy Wheels +75
Special Factory Paint +80

V8 — 1992

Model Description	Trade-in Value	Market Value
Category F		
4 Dr Quattro 4WD Sdn	10745	14330

OPTIONS FOR V8

Special Factory Paint +80

1991 AUDI

100 — 1991

100E dropped. New programmable four-speed automatic transmission for 100 models.

Model Description	Trade-in Value	Market Value
Category D		
4 Dr STD Sdn	5005	6855

OPTIONS FOR 100

Bose Sound System +145
Heated Front Seats +75
Leather Seats +225
Power Drivers Seat +70
Special Factory Paint +65

200 — 1991

New 20-valve turbo engine installed in 200 Quattro models.

Model Description	Trade-in Value	Market Value
Category F		
4 Dr Quattro Turbo 4WD Sdn	8060	10750
4 Dr STD Turbo Sdn	6975	9300

OPTIONS FOR 200

Heated Front Seats +70
Special Factory Paint +65

80 — 1991

Programmable four-speed automatic transmission introduced. 80 dumps weak 2.0-liter four-cylinder engine in favor of more powerful 2.3-liter five-cylinder engine.

Model Description	Trade-in Value	Market Value
Category D		
4 Dr STD Sdn	4335	5935

Don't forget to refer to the Mileage Adjustment Table at the back of this book!

 © 1999 by Edmund Publications Corporation

Model Description	Trade-in Value	Market Value

OPTIONS FOR 80

Auto 4-Speed Transmission +170
Anti-Lock Brakes[Opt on STD] +195
Heated Front Seats +75
Special Factory Paint +65
Sunroof +85

90 — 1991

Programmable four-speed automatic transmission introduced.

Category D

Model Description	Trade-in Value	Market Value
4 Dr Quattro 4WD Sdn	7255	9940
4 Dr STD Sdn	5050	6915

OPTIONS FOR 90

Heated Front Seats +75
Leather Seats +225
Power Drivers Seat +70
Special Factory Paint[Std on STD] +65
Trip Computer +50

V8 — 1991

Category F

Model Description	Trade-in Value	Market Value
4 Dr Quattro 4WD Sdn	7055	9405

OPTIONS FOR V8

Special Factory Paint +65

1990 AUDI

100 — 1990

No changes.

Category D

Model Description	Trade-in Value	Market Value
4 Dr Quattro 4WD Sdn	5015	6870
4 Dr STD Sdn	4125	5650

OPTIONS FOR 100

Bose Sound System +120
Leather Seats +185
Power Drivers Seat +55
Special Factory Paint +50

200 — 1990

No changes.

Category F

Model Description	Trade-in Value	Market Value
4 Dr STD Turbo Sdn	4935	6575

80 — 1990

No changes.

Category D

Model Description	Trade-in Value	Market Value
4 Dr Quattro 4WD Sdn	4200	5755
4 Dr STD Sdn	3280	4495

OPTIONS FOR 80

Auto 3-Speed Transmission +95
Anti-Lock Brakes +155
Power Sunroof +120
Special Factory Paint +50
Sport Seats +80
Sunroof +70

90 — 1990

No changes.

Category D

Model Description	Trade-in Value	Market Value
4 Dr Quattro 4WD Sdn	5535	7580
4 Dr STD Sdn	4605	6305

OPTIONS FOR 90

Auto 3-Speed Transmission +95
Heated Front Seats +60
Leather Seats +185
Power Drivers Seat +55
Special Factory Paint +50
Trip Computer +40

COUPE — 1990

New Coupe Quattro debuts, with 164-horsepower 20-valve engine.

Category F

Model Description	Trade-in Value	Market Value
2 Dr Quattro 4WD Cpe	6120	8160

OPTIONS FOR COUPE

Dual Power Seats +140
Heated Front Seats +55
Metallic Paint +70

V8 — 1990

Derived from 200 sedan, V8 Quattro features new sheetmetal, 3.6-liter V8 engine, all-wheel drive, ABS, driver airbag, and Bose audio system.

Category F

Model Description	Trade-in Value	Market Value
4 Dr Quattro 4WD Sdn	6945	9260

OPTIONS FOR V8

Special Factory Paint +55

1989 AUDI

100 — 1989

New name for 1989. Formerly Audi 5000. Non-turbo models designated 100; turbos called 200. All but base 100E have antilock brakes. Quattro AWD system is available on sedan, but only with manual transmission.

Category D

Model Description	Trade-in Value	Market Value
4 Dr E Sdn	2805	4065
4 Dr Quattro 4WD Sdn	3730	5405
4 Dr STD Sdn	3195	4635

OPTIONS FOR 100

Auto 3-Speed Transmission[Std on E] +75
Restraint System Pkg +215
Anti-Lock Brakes[Opt on E] +130
Leather Seats +150
Power Drivers Seat +45

Don't forget to refer to the Mileage Adjustment Table at the back of this book!

 © 1999 by Edmund Publications Corporation

Model Description	Trade-in Value	Market Value

200 — 1989

New name for 1989. Formerly Audi 5000. Non-turbo models designated 100; turbos called 200. 200 models get driver airbag. Quattro AWD system is available on sedan, but only with manual transmission.

Category F

Model Description	Trade-in Value	Market Value
4 Dr STD Turbo Sdn	3610	5015

OPTIONS FOR 200

Auto 3-Speed Transmission +75
Leather Seats[Opt on STD] +95

80 — 1989

Antilock brakes optional on 80 Quattro. New warranty covers all scheduled maintenance for three years or 50,000 miles.

Category D

Model Description	Trade-in Value	Market Value
4 Dr STD Sdn	2760	4000

OPTIONS FOR 80

Auto 3-Speed Transmission +70
AM/FM Stereo Tape +50
Heated Front Seats +50
Special Factory Paint +45

Major Savings On An Extended Warranty

"YOU DESERVE THE BEST"
Call today for your free quote.
Pay up to 50% less than dealership prices!

http://www.edmunds.com/warranty 1-800-580-9889

Get a great used car and apply for financing *online* at a price you must see to believe!

http://www.edmunds.com

Don't forget to refer to the Mileage Adjustment Table at the back of this book!

 © 1999 by Edmund Publications Corporation

Model Description	Trade-in Value	Market Value

BMW Germany

1990 BMW M3 Coupe

1998 BMW

3-SERIES 1998

BMW adds a 2.5-liter inline-six engine to their entry-level coupe and convertible, making them the cheapest six-cylinder BMWs in years. Also new are standard side-impact airbags for all front seat passengers in all models except the 318ti, which has side-impact airbags on its optional equipment list.

Model Description	Trade-in Value	Market Value
318i		
Category D		
4 Dr STD Sdn	18880	22210
318ti		
Category D		
2 Dr STD Hbk	17275	20325
323i		
Category D		
2 Dr STD Conv	27685	32570
323is		
Category D		
2 Dr STD Cpe	22830	26855
328i		
Category D		
2 Dr STD Conv	29855	35120
4 Dr STD Sdn	24990	29400
328is		
Category F		
2 Dr STD Cpe	26215	30840
M3		
Category J		
2 Dr STD Cpe	29425	34215
4 Dr STD Sdn	29050	33780

OPTIONS FOR 3-SERIES

Auto 4-Speed Transmission +810
Auto 5-Speed Transmission[Opt on M3] +995
California Roof +1330
Forged Alloy Wheels +1205
Rollover Protection System(Opt on Conv) +1205
Sport Handling Package +715
Aluminum/Alloy Wheels[Opt on 318i,318ti] +260
Compact Disc Changer +550
Cruise Control[Opt on 318ti,M3] +175
Dual Power Seats[Opt on M3] +610
Fog Lights[Opt on 318i,318ti] +55
Heated Front Seats +280
Keyless Entry System +250
Leather Seats[Std on M3] +590
Metallic Paint +255
Onboard Computer +330
Power Sunroof +565
Side Air Bag Restraint[Opt on 318ti] +240
Sport Suspension[Std on M3] +210

5-SERIES 1998

Side-impact airbags are now available for rear-seat passengers, as is break-resistant glass for the windows and moonroof.

Model Description	Trade-in Value	Market Value
528i		
Category F		
4 Dr STD Sdn	31090	36575
540i		
Category J		
4 Dr STD Sdn	38840	45160

OPTIONS FOR 5-SERIES

6-Speed Transmission[Opt on 540i] +2325
Auto 4-Speed Transmission +810
Comfort Seats +995
Navigation System +2155
Premium Package +2065
Sport Handling Package +1770
Heated Front Seats +280
Leather Seats[Opt on 528i] +590
Metallic Paint +350
Power Moonroof[Opt on 528i] +595
Premium Sound System +340
Sport Suspension +215

7-SERIES 1998

BMW introduces Dynamic Stability Control (DSC) to the big Bimmer. DSC is designed to automatically correct the yaw on all 7-Series cars, preventing plowing and fishtailing. Guess this means no more smoky burnouts in the Beverly Hilton's parking lot.

Don't forget to refer to the Mileage Adjustment Table at the back of this book!

 © 1999 by Edmund Publications Corporation

Model Description	Trade-in Value	Market Value

740i

Category L

4 Dr STD Sdn	44760	52660

740iL

Category L

4 Dr STD Sdn	49125	57795

750iL

Category L

4 Dr STD Sdn	59865	70430

OPTIONS FOR 7-SERIES

Comfort Seats +995
Elect Damping Control +1660
Navigation System +2080
Park Distance Control +750
Security Sun Roof +2160
Auto Load Leveling[Opt on 740iL] +895
Compact Disc W/fm/tape[Std on 750iL] +605
Heated Front Seats[Std on 750iL] +385
Metallic Paint +500
Power Sunroof +755

Z3 — 1998

The M Roadster, a 240-horsepower version of the Z3 convertible, arrives for 1998. An electric top also becomes available this year.

Category F

2 Dr 1.9 Conv	23290	27400
2 Dr 2.8 Conv	27300	32120
2 Dr M Conv	33945	39935

OPTIONS FOR Z3

Auto 4-Speed Transmission +810
Alloy Wheels W/17in.Tires +935
Extended Leather Trim +995
Heated Front Seats[Std on M] +280
Heated Power Mirrors[Std on M] +235
Leather Seats[Opt on 1.9] +590
Metallic Paint[Std on M] +350
Onboard Computer +330
Power Convertible Top[Std on M] +625
Premium Sound System[Opt on 1.9] +340
Side Air Bag Restraint +325

1997 BMW

3-SERIES — 1997

An M3 sedan has arrived at a store near you. Those of you claiming to want power and practicality no longer have an excuse for driving that old jalopy currently parked in your driveway. Buy one now. Also, All-Season Traction is now standard on all models.

RATINGS (SCALE OF 1-10)

Overall	Safety	Reliability	Performance	Comfort	Value
7.5	7.5	9.4	9.4	8	3

318i

Category D

2 Dr STD Conv	21115	25440
4 Dr STD Sdn	16970	20445

318is

Category F

2 Dr STD Cpe	19045	22405

318ti

Category D

2 Dr STD Hbk	14370	17315

328i

Category D

2 Dr Luxury Conv	28300	34095
2 Dr STD Conv	28150	33915
4 Dr STD Sdn	21960	26455

328is

Category F

2 Dr STD Cpe	24155	28420

M3

Category J

2 Dr STD Cpe	27570	32060
4 Dr STD Sdn	26850	31220

OPTIONS FOR 3-SERIES

Auto 4-Speed Transmission +680
Forged Alloy Wheels +985
Luxury Package +1495
Rollover Protection System(Opt on Conv) +985
Sports Package +615
Aluminum/Alloy Wheels[Opt on 318ti,318i] +210
AM/FM Compact Disc Playr +380
Compact Disc W/fm/tape +655
Heated Front Seats +230
Leather Seats[Std on M3,Luxury,328i STD Conv] +485
Onboard Computer +270
Power Sunroof +465
Premium Sound System +235
Sport Seats +325
Sport Suspension[Std on M3] +175

5-SERIES — 1997

The 5-Series is redesigned and introduced midway through 1996 as a 1997 model. Bearing a strong resemblance to its 3- and 7-Series siblings, the 5-Series offers a lot of car for a lot of money. The Touring wagons are no longer available, and the 3.0-liter V8 is history. New 5-Series models can be had as an entry level 528i or an exclusive 540i. Both models feature new engines, all-aluminum suspensions, improved brakes and available side impact airbag protection.

Don't forget to refer to the Mileage Adjustment Table at the back of this book!

© 1999 by Edmund Publications Corporation

Model Description	Trade-in Value	Market Value

RATINGS (SCALE OF 1-10)

Overall	Safety	Reliability	Performance	Comfort	Value
N/A	N/A	9.2	9.4	8.8	N/A

528i

Category F

4 Dr STD Sdn	27640	32520

540i

Category J

4 Dr STD Sdn	35725	41540

OPTIONS FOR 5-SERIES

6-Speed Transmission[Opt on 540i] +1455
Auto 4-Speed Transmission +580
Comfort Seats +715
Navigation System +1665
Premium Package +1010
Heated Front Seats +230
Leather Seats[Opt on 528i] +485
Power Moonroof[Opt on 528i] +485
Premium Sound System +280
Sport Suspension +305

7-SERIES 1997

BMW reintroduces the regular length 740i after the uproar caused over its cancellation for the 1996 model year. Like the rest of the 7-Series, the 740i has a standard equipment list that will leave the Sultan of Brunei drooling with desire.

740i

Category L

4 Dr STD Sdn	37620	44785

740iL

Category L

4 Dr STD Sdn	39505	47030

OPTIONS FOR 7-SERIES

Cold Weather Package +540
Comfort Seats +790
Elect Damping Control +1315
Navigation System +1840
Park Distance Control +590
Auto Load Leveling[Opt on 740iL] +730
Headlight Washers[Std on 750iL] +215
Heated Front Seats[Std on 750iL] +315

8-SERIES 1997

Engine displacement is bumped, making the 1997 840Ci and 850Ci a bit stronger than last year's models. BMW's five-speed Steptronic is now standard on both models.

840Ci

Category L

2 Dr STD Cpe	45575	54255

OPTIONS FOR 8-SERIES

Forged Alloy Wheels +820

Z3 1997

Hooray, the market for sports cars is alive and kicking. Despite the ever-increasing number of minivans and sport-utes on our clogged highways, there are still enough of us that like to drive to support this wonderful little car. As a reward for keeping the segment alive, BMW makes its 190-horsepower six-cylinder engine available in the Z3 2.8.

RATINGS (SCALE OF 1-10)

Overall	Safety	Reliability	Performance	Comfort	Value
N/A	N/A	8.6	8.6	7.5	N/A

Category F

2 Dr 1.9 Conv	21245	24995
2 Dr 2.8 Conv	26290	30925

OPTIONS FOR Z3

Auto 4-Speed Transmission +660
Extended Leather Trim +815
Compact Disc Changer +455
Heated Front Seats +230
Leather Seats[Opt on 1.9] +485
Onboard Computer +270
Traction Control System[Opt on 1.9] +480

1996 BMW

3-SERIES 1996

BMW's highly acclaimed 3-series receives new engines across the board. The 318 remains a 318 despite an increase in displacement to 1.9 liters. The six-cylinder model becomes the 328 with an improved engine that increases torque by a whopping 14 percent. Vented rear disc brakes aid the 328's stopping power by reducing brake fade. Automatic climate controls grace cabin occupants, except those in the 318ti, and improved sound systems are optional on all models.

RATINGS (SCALE OF 1-10)

Overall	Safety	Reliability	Performance	Comfort	Value
7.5	7.5	9.1	9.4	8	3.4

318i

Category D

2 Dr STD Conv	18785	23480
4 Dr STD Sdn	14820	18525

318is

Category F

2 Dr STD Cpe	16725	20155

318ti

Category D

2 Dr STD Hbk	11990	14985

Don't forget to refer to the Mileage Adjustment Table at the back of this book!

© 1999 by Edmund Publications Corporation

Model Description	Trade-in Value	Market Value

328i

Category D

2 Dr STD Conv	24385	30485
4 Dr STD Sdn	19445	24310

328is

Category F

2 Dr STD Cpe	20580	24795

M3

Category J

2 Dr STD Cpe	24245	28865

OPTIONS FOR 3-SERIES

Auto 4-Speed Transmission +530
Rollover Protection System(Opt on Conv) +790
Sports Package +510
Air Conditioning[Opt on 318ti] +460
Aluminum/Alloy Wheels[Opt on 318ti,318i Sdn] +170
AM/FM Compact Disc Playr +310
Cruise Control[Opt on 318ti,M3] +115
Heated Front Seats +185
Keyless Entry System +170
Leather Seats[Std on M3,328i STD Conv] +395
Onboard Computer +220
Power Sunroof[Opt on 318ti,M3] +380
Premium Sound System +195
Sport Seats +265
Sport Suspension +140
Tilt Steering Wheel[Opt on 318is] +70
Traction Control System +390

7-SERIES 1996

BMW's flagship gets stretched; the only 7-Series models available for 1996 are long wheelbase models. The 740iL receives a larger V8 that substantially increases torque. BMW's killer 440-watt sound system is now standard on the 750iL and optional on the 740iL. A sophisticated interior-motion theft-deterrent system is now available.

740iL

Category L

4 Dr STD Sdn	35195	41900

750iL

Category L

4 Dr STD Sdn	43830	52175

OPTIONS FOR 7-SERIES

Comfort Seats +655
Park Distance Control +490
Self Leveling Rear Suspen +600
Compact Disc Changer[Opt on 740i] +650
Headlight Washers[Std on 750iL] +175
Heated Front Seats[Opt on 740i] +255
Traction Control System[Opt on 740i] +890

Z3 1996

BMW follows Mazda's lead and introduces a roadster. This dreamy two-seater made its debut in the James Bond movie, *Golden Eye*, and has had enthusiasts across the country drooling over its smart styling and impressive refinement. Featured as the perfect Christmas gift in the 1995 Neiman Marcus Christmas catalog, BMW sold out of Z3s before the first one was released to the public.

RATINGS (SCALE OF 1-10)

Overall	Safety	Reliability	Performance	Comfort	Value
N/A	N/A	8.5	8.2	7.5	N/A

Category F

2 Dr 007 Conv	19445	23430
2 Dr STD Conv	19230	23170

OPTIONS FOR Z3

Auto 4-Speed Transmission +530
Heated Front Seats +185
Leather Seats +395
Onboard Computer +220
Traction Control System +390

1995 BMW

3-SERIES 1995

A new M3 coupe debuts with blistering performance and exceptional grace. Available only as a five-speed manual, the M3 has Z-rated tires, a limited-slip differential and 17-inch wheels. The 318 models gain a convertible. Two new packages debut that allow a driver to choose between a sports or luxury orientation.

RATINGS (SCALE OF 1-10)

Overall	Safety	Reliability	Performance	Comfort	Value
7.4	8.2	8.5	9.2	8	3.2

318i

Category D

2 Dr STD Conv	16205	20515
4 Dr STD Sdn	12040	15240

318is

Category F

2 Dr STD Cpe	13835	16870

318ti

Category D

2 Dr STD Hbk	11135	14095

325i

Category D

2 Dr STD Conv	20480	25925
4 Dr STD Sdn	16290	20620

Don't forget to refer to the Mileage Adjustment Table at the back of this book!

© 1999 by Edmund Publications Corporation

Model Description	Trade-in Value	Market Value

325is

Category F

2 Dr STD Cpe	17555	21410

M3

Category J

2 Dr STD Cpe	21395	25780

OPTIONS FOR 3-SERIES

Auto 4-Speed Transmission +405
Auto 5-Speed Transmission +535
Luxury Package +555
Rollover Protection Sys. +635
Sports Package +865
AM/FM Compact Disc Playr +225
Heated Front Seats +150
Keyless Entry System +135
Leather Seats[Opt on 318i,318is,318ti] +325
Onboard Computer +180
Power Sunroof[Opt on 318ti,M3] +310
Premium Sound System[Std on 325i] +155
Sport Seats +215
Sport Suspension +115
Traction Control System +320

5-SERIES 1995

BMW sports up its 540i by making a six-speed manual transmission available. That option includes 12-way power sport seats, a sport suspension and beefy anti-roll bars. Unfortunately, all models lose their V-rated tires in favor of wimpy H-rated tires in an attempt to improve fuel economy.

RATINGS (SCALE OF 1-10)

Overall	Safety	Reliability	Performance	Comfort	Value
N/A	N/A	8.4	8.8	8	N/A

525i

Category J

4 Dr STD Sdn	18865	22730
4 Dr Touring Wgn	19555	23560

530i

Category J

4 Dr STD Sdn	21245	25600

540i

Category J

4 Dr STD Sdn	23110	27845

OPTIONS FOR 5-SERIES

6-Speed Transmission[Opt on 540i] +400
Auto 4-Speed Transmission[Std on Touring] +445
Dual Power Sunroofs +590
Premium Package +700
AM/FM Compact Disc Playr +245
Heated Front Seats +185
Leather Seats[Opt on 525i] +465
Onboard Computer[Opt on 525i] +195
Power Sunroof[Std on 530i,540i] +555
Traction Control System +600

7-SERIES 1995

The big Bimmer is totally redesigned for 1995. The flagship sedan now features sleek styling and a lengthened wheelbase. Three models are available for 1995, including a new 740i regular-wheelbase model. The V-12 engine found in the 750iL gains 27 horsepower and 30 pounds/feet of torque. New interior refinements include a residual heat system which will continue to heat the car after the power has been turned off and 14-way power seats.

740i

Category L

4 Dr STD Sdn	28300	34515

740iL

Category L

4 Dr STD Sdn	29950	36525

750iL

Category L

4 Dr STD Sdn	35200	42930

OPTIONS FOR 7-SERIES

Comfort Seats +445
Park Distance Control +370
Compact Disc Changer[Std on 750iL] +530
Heated Front Seats[Std on 750iL] +210
Traction Control System[Std on 750iL] +725

8-SERIES 1995

No changes for the 8-Series.

840Ci

Category L

2 Dr STD Cpe	30100	36705

1994 BMW

3-SERIES 1994

Dual airbags appear on all 3-series models. A new six-cylinder convertible joins the stable and traction control becomes optional for all cars.

RATINGS (SCALE OF 1-10)

Overall	Safety	Reliability	Performance	Comfort	Value
7.1	7.9	7.5	9.2	8	2.7

318i

Category D

4 Dr STD Sdn	10980	14260

Category F

2 Dr STD Conv	14740	18425

Don't forget to refer to the Mileage Adjustment Table at the back of this book!

© 1999 by Edmund Publications Corporation

Model Description	Trade-in Value	Market Value

318is

Category F

2 Dr STD Cpe	11520	14400

325i

Category D		
4 Dr STD Sdn	13245	17205
Category F		
2 Dr STD Conv	18310	22890

325is

Category F

2 Dr STD Cpe	14930	18665

OPTIONS FOR 3-SERIES

Auto 4-Speed Transmission +335
Rollover Protection System(Opt on Conv) +515
AM/FM Compact Disc Playr +185
Heated Front Seats +125
Leather Seats[Opt on 318is,Sdn] +265
Onboard Computer +145
Premium Sound System +150
Sport Seats +180
Sport Suspension +95
Traction Control System +260

5-SERIES 1994

A passenger airbag debuts on all models and two new V8s join the lineup. The 535i and M5 are dropped. BMW's traction control system becomes standard on the 530i Touring and optional on other models. Both 525i models gain a premium sound system.

RATINGS (SCALE OF 1-10)

Overall	Safety	Reliability	Performance	Comfort	Value
N/A	N/A	8.1	8.8	8	N/A

525i

Category J

4 Dr STD Sdn	15330	18700
4 Dr Touring Wgn	16785	20470

530i

Category J

4 Dr STD Sdn	16850	20550
4 Dr Touring Wgn	18315	22335

540i

Category J

4 Dr STD Sdn	19135	23335

OPTIONS FOR 5-SERIES

Auto 4-Speed Transmission[Std on Touring] +370
Dual Power Sunroofs +490
AM/FM Compact Disc Playr +200
Heated Front Seats +155
Onboard Computer[Std on 540i] +160
Traction Control System[Opt on 525i,540i] +490

7-SERIES 1994

No changes for the 7-Series.

740i

Category L

4 Dr STD Sdn	18975	23720

740iL

Category L

4 Dr STD Sdn	20230	25285

OPTIONS FOR 7-SERIES

Elect Damping Control Susp. +555
Heated Front Seats[Std on 750iL] +170
Traction Control System[Std on 750iL] +595

8-SERIES 1994

Two new models are introduced to the 8-Series: the 840Ci and the 850CSi. The 840Ci has the same V8 power found in the 740 and 540. The 850CSi gets an increased displacement V12 that offers a whopping 372-horsepower. The CSi comes standard with a sports suspension and a six-speed manual transmission. Unfortunately, the introduction of the CSi takes away from the sportiness of the 850Ci, which is now saddled with a four-speed automatic as the only transmission choice.

840Ci

Category L

2 Dr STD Cpe	28140	35180

OPTIONS FOR 8-SERIES

Forged Alloy Wheels +410

1993 BMW

3-SERIES 1993

Four-bangers can now be equipped with an automatic transmission. Six-cylinder models get a variable valve timing system that improves low-end torque.

RATINGS (SCALE OF 1-10)

Overall	Safety	Reliability	Performance	Comfort	Value
6.5	6.2	6.8	9.2	8	2.5

318i

Category D

4 Dr STD Sdn	9145	12360

318is

Category F

2 Dr STD Cpe	10000	12985

Don't forget to refer to the Mileage Adjustment Table at the back of this book!

 © 1999 by Edmund Publications Corporation

Model Description	Trade-in Value	Market Value

325i

Category D

4 Dr STD Sdn	10860	14675

Category F

2 Dr STD Conv	13075	16980

325is

Category F

2 Dr STD Cpe	12200	15845

OPTIONS FOR 3-SERIES

Auto 4-Speed Transmission +260
Sports Package +255
Aluminum/Alloy Wheels[Opt on 318i] +95
Heated Front Seats +100
Leather Seats[Opt on Sdn] +215
Onboard Computer[Std on Conv] +120
Sport Seats +145
Sport Suspension +75

5-SERIES 1993

Bad news for trees and cows: wood trim and leather upholstery are now standard on the 525i. The 525i gets a variable valve timing system that improves low-end torque. The M5 gets new wheels for 1993.

RATINGS (SCALE OF 1-10)

Overall	Safety	Reliability	Performance	Comfort	Value
N/A	N/A	8.1	8.6	8	N/A

525i

Category J

4 Dr STD Sdn	13480	16640
4 Dr Touring Wgn	13725	16945

OPTIONS FOR 5-SERIES

Auto 4-Speed Transmission[Std on Touring] +260
Heated Front Seats[Opt on 525i] +125
Leather Seats[Opt on Touring] +310
Onboard Computer[Opt on 525i] +130

7-SERIES 1993

The 7-Series' cheapest model swaps V6 for V8 power. The entry-level 7-Series is now called the 740 to denote this change. The new engine has 282-horsepower that is mated to a five-speed automatic transmission. More wood for the interior, Z-rated tires, and an upgraded stereo round out the changes for the 1993 7-Series.

740i

Category L

4 Dr STD Sdn	16465	20845

740iL

Category L

4 Dr STD Sdn	17245	21825

OPTIONS FOR 7-SERIES

Elect Damp Cntrl Susp. +445
Heated Seats[Opt on 740i] +110
Traction Control System[Std on 750iL] +485

8-SERIES 1993

The 850i is now called the 850Ci. A passenger airbag is added to the standard equipment list, as is a split-fold rear seat. All interior materials have been upgraded over previous models.

850Ci

Category J

2 Dr STD Cpe	27825	34355

OPTIONS FOR 8-SERIES

Forged Alloy Wheels +305

1992 BMW

3-SERIES 1992

New sheetmetal for the 3-series; all the corners are rounded and the wheelbase is stretched. Interior space is marginally greater than previous models. A driver airbag is added to the equipment list. Buyers can choose between a sports or luxury package depending on their predilections.

RATINGS (SCALE OF 1-10)

Overall	Safety	Reliability	Performance	Comfort	Value
6.5	6	5.7	9.2	8	3.4

318i

Category D

2 Dr STD Conv	8750	11985
4 Dr STD Sdn	7820	10710

318is

Category F

2 Dr STD Cpe	8565	11425

325i

Category D

2 Dr STD Conv	10710	14675
4 Dr STD Sdn	9060	12410

325is

Category F

2 Dr STD Cpe	10000	13335

OPTIONS FOR 3-SERIES

Auto 4-Speed Transmission +195
Aluminum/Alloy Wheels[Opt on 318i] +75
Compact Disc W/fm/tape +240
Heated Front Seats[Std on 318i STD Conv] +85
Leather Seats[Opt on Sdn] +175
Onboard Computer[Std on Conv] +100

Don't forget to refer to the Mileage Adjustment Table at the back of this book!

© 1999 by Edmund Publications Corporation

Model Description	Trade-in Value	Market Value

5-SERIES 1992

The 525 loses some luxury items from its standard equipment list; the steering wheel is now wrapped in leatherette instead of leather and the spare tire is shod with a steel wheel instead of an alloy. The 535 gains options like a nifty on-board computer and a power-adjustable steering wheel with a position memory. A security system is now standard. The M5 gets better power steering and a higher final-drive ratio. A Touring model is introduced as a wagon body style.

RATINGS (SCALE OF 1-10)

Overall	Safety	Reliability	Performance	Comfort	Value
N/A	N/A	7.8	8.6	8	N/A

525i

Category J

4 Dr STD Sdn	10925	13830
4 Dr Touring Wgn	12005	15200

535i

Category J

4 Dr STD Sdn	13040	16510

OPTIONS FOR 5-SERIES

Auto 4-Speed Transmission[Std on 535i,Touring] +195
Auto Stability Control +315
Wood & Leather Pkg +275
Heated Front Seats +100
Leather Seats[Opt on 525i] +255
Onboard Computer[Opt on Touring] +105

7-SERIES 1992

7-Series cars equipped with an automatic transmission now have a shift interlock that prevents the car from being shifted out of park without simultaneously applying the brake. The one-touch-down power window feature now applies to all windows, not just the driver's. The 750iL model receives double-paned windows to improve noise reduction. All 1992 7-Series cars get a new Infinity stereo.

735i

Category L

4 Dr STD Sdn	12350	16035

735iL

Category L

4 Dr STD Sdn	13320	17300

750iL

Category L

4 Dr STD Sdn	15255	19810

OPTIONS FOR 7-SERIES

Auto Stability Control +315
Elect Damping Control +360
Heated Front Seats[Std on 750iL] +115

8-SERIES 1992

BMW's most expensive coupe gets a few tweaks for 1992. Models equipped with an automatic transmission now have a shift interlock to prevent the car from unintentionally being shifted out of park. BMW's Electronic Damping System is improved for 1992 as well, offering greater diversity between the sports and comfort settings.

850i

Category J

2 Dr STD Cpe	22520	28505

OPTIONS FOR 8-SERIES

Auto Stability Control +365
Elect Damping Control +360
Forged Alloy Wheels +245

1991 BMW

3-SERIES 1991

No changes for the 3-Series.

318i

Category D

2 Dr STD Conv	7095	9715
4 Dr STD Sdn	5295	7255

318is

Category F

2 Dr STD Sdn	5720	7630

325i

Category D

2 Dr STD Conv	9245	12665
2 Dr STD Sdn	6260	8580
4 Dr STD Sdn	6535	8955

325iX

Category F

2 Dr STD 4WD Sdn	9340	12450
4 Dr STD 4WD Sdn	8895	11855

M3

Category J

2 Dr STD Sdn	9825	12760

OPTIONS FOR 3-SERIES

Auto 3-Speed Transmission +130
Sport Handling Package +380
AM/FM Compact Disc Playr +100
Heated Front Seats +75
Leather Seats[Std on M3,Conv] +145
Power Drivers Seat +70
Power Sunroof[Std on M3] +140
Sport Seats +95
Sport Suspension +50
Sunroof[Std on 325iX] +80

Don't forget to refer to the Mileage Adjustment Table at the back of this book!

 © 1999 by Edmund Publications Corporation

Model Description	Trade-in Value	Market Value

5-SERIES 1991

No changes for the 1991 5-Series.

RATINGS (SCALE OF 1-10)

Overall	Safety	Reliability	Performance	Comfort	Value
N/A	N/A	7.7	8.6	8	N/A

525i

Category J

4 Dr STD Sdn	9230	11985

535i

Category J

4 Dr STD Sdn	10585	13745

M5

Category J

4 Dr STD Sdn	18380	23870

OPTIONS FOR 5-SERIES

Auto 4-Speed Transmission +70
Stability Control +255
Heated Front Seats +85
Leather Seats[Opt on 525i] +210

7-SERIES 1991

No changes for the 7-Series.

735i

Category L

4 Dr STD Sdn	10715	14095

735iL

Category L

4 Dr STD Sdn	11050	14535

750iL

Category L

4 Dr STD Sdn	11985	15770

OPTIONS FOR 7-SERIES

Electronic Susp. +295
Stability Control +255
Alarm System[Opt on 735i] +115
Heated Front Seats[Std on 750iL] +95

8-SERIES 1991

BMW's replacement for the 635CSi, the 850i offers V12 power, a six-speed manual transmission and rear-wheel drive. Standard traction control, a driver airbag, antilock brakes and power head restraints are a few of the safety features found on this expensive BMW coupe. A four-speed automatic transmission is an unfortunate option.

850i

Category J

2 Dr STD Cpe	19360	25145

OPTIONS FOR 8-SERIES

Electronic Susp. +295
Forged Alloy Wheels +200
Stability Control +300

1990 BMW

3-SERIES 1990

No changes for the 1990 3-Series.

325i

Category D

2 Dr STD Sdn	5630	7715
2 Dr STD Conv	7390	10120
4 Dr STD Sdn	5580	7645

325is

Category F

2 Dr STD Sdn	6765	9015

325iX

Category F

2 Dr STD 4WD Sdn	7730	10305
4 Dr STD 4WD Sdn	7505	10005

M3

Category J

2 Dr STD Sdn	9985	13315

OPTIONS FOR 3-SERIES

Auto 4-Speed Transmission +115
AM/FM Compact Disc Playr +80
Heated Front Seats +55
Leather Seats[Opt on 325i STD Sdn] +120
Power Sunroof[Std on 325is,M3] +115
Premium Sound System[Std on 325is,M3,Conv] +55

5-SERIES 1990

BMW Motorsports unleashes 5-Series M-car. Serious inquiries only; this car has a bone-jarring suspension and more performance than most drivers can handle.

RATINGS (SCALE OF 1-10)

Overall	Safety	Reliability	Performance	Comfort	Value
N/A	N/A	7.7	8.4	8	N/A

525i

Category J

4 Dr STD Sdn	7595	10125

535i

Category J

4 Dr STD Sdn	9130	12175

OPTIONS FOR 5-SERIES

Auto 4-Speed Transmission[Opt on 525i] +115
Heated Front Seats +70
Leather Seats[Opt on 525i] +170

Don't forget to refer to the Mileage Adjustment Table at the back of this book!

 © 1999 by Edmund Publications Corporation

Model Description	Trade-in Value	Market Value

7-SERIES 1990

No changes for the 7-Series.

735i

Category L

4 Dr STD Sdn	9080	12270

735iL

Category L

4 Dr STD Sdn	9750	13175

750iL

Category L

4 Dr STD Sdn	10470	14150

OPTIONS FOR 7-SERIES

Alarm System[Opt on 735i] +95
Heated Front Seats[Std on 750iL] +75

1989 BMW

3-SERIES 1989

New engines for the entire 325 family; horsepower is increased to 168. New tires are standard to accommodate this increase in speed. Body-color bumpers also debut.

325i

Category D

2 Dr STD Conv	6360	9220
2 Dr STD Sdn	4595	6660
4 Dr STD Sdn	4420	6405

325is

Category F

2 Dr STD Sdn	5280	7330

325iX

Category F

2 Dr STD 4WD Sdn	6135	8520
4 Dr STD 4WD Sdn	6080	8445

M3

Category J

2 Dr STD Sdn	8525	11675

OPTIONS FOR 3-SERIES

Auto 4-Speed Transmission +85
Heated Front Seats +45
Leather Seats[Std on 325is,M3,Conv] +95
Power Sunroof[Opt on 325i] +90
Premium Sound System[Opt on 325i STD Sdn] +45

5-SERIES 1989

An all-new 5-Series replaces the previous generation midsized offering from BMW. The wheelbase is extended but the overall length is shortened. Two models are offered, both are available as a five-speed manual or four-speed automatic.

RATINGS (SCALE OF 1-10)

Overall	Safety	Reliability	Performance	Comfort	Value
N/A	N/A	7.5	8.4	8	N/A

525i

Category J

4 Dr STD Sdn	6595	9035

535i

Category J

4 Dr STD Sdn	7350	10065

OPTIONS FOR 5-SERIES

Auto 4-Speed Transmission[Opt on 535i] +85
Heated Front Seats +55

6-SERIES 1989

635CSi

Category J

2 Dr STD Cpe	8015	10980

7-SERIES 1989

The big Bimmer is available as a 735i, 735iL, or 750iL. The L designation in the name indicates that the model has a long wheelbase. 1989 brings remote keyless entry for the 7-Series and Servotronic power steering. A trunk mounted six-disc CD changer is now standard equipment on the 750iL, optional on the 735.

735i

Category L

4 Dr STD Sdn	7190	9850

735iL

Category L

4 Dr STD Sdn	8075	11065

750iL

Category L

4 Dr STD Sdn	8950	12255

OPTIONS FOR 7-SERIES

Auto 4-Speed Transmission[Opt on 735i] +85
Heated Front Seats[Std on 750iL] +65

Get a great used car and apply for financing *online* at a price you must see to believe !

http://edmunds.com

Don't forget to refer to the Mileage Adjustment Table at the back of this book!

 © 1999 by Edmund Publications Corporation

BUICK USA

1995 Buick Riviera

1998 BUICK

CENTURY 1998

The addition of second-generation airbags, three new exterior colors, one new interior color and the availability of OnStar mobile communications are the modifications to the Century this year.

Category C

Model Description	Trade-in Value	Market Value
4 Dr Custom Sdn	13785	16610
4 Dr Limited Sdn	14775	17805

OPTIONS FOR CENTURY

Aluminum/Alloy Wheels +240
AM/FM Compact Disc Playr +320
Climate Control for AC +150
Cruise Control +170
Heated Power Mirrors[Opt on Custom] +115
Leather Seats +480
Power Drivers Seat +235
Power Moonroof +580

LE SABRE 1998

Cruise control is standard on base models, OnStar Mobile Communications is a dealer-installed option, Limited models get a couple of electrochromic mirrors, and new colors are on tap inside and out. Second-generation airbags are made standard.

Category B

Model Description	Trade-in Value	Market Value
4 Dr Custom Sdn	15620	18820
4 Dr Limited Sdn	18225	21955

OPTIONS FOR LE SABRE

Aluminum/Alloy Wheels[Opt on Custom] +275
AM/FM Compact Disc Playr +260
Auto Load Leveling +155
Dual Power Seats[Opt on Custom] +300
Keyless Entry System[Opt on Custom] +145
Leather Seats +550
Power Mirrors +80
Traction Control System +150

PARK AVENUE 1998

Exterior mirrors can be folded away, a new optional feature tilts the exterior mirrors down for curb viewing during reversing, dealers can install an OnStar Communications system and new colors are available inside and out. Second-generation airbags are made standard.

Category A

Model Description	Trade-in Value	Market Value
4 Dr STD Sdn	20075	23620
4 Dr Ultra Sprchgd Sdn	24220	28495

OPTIONS FOR PARK AVENUE

AM/FM Compact Disc Playr[Opt on STD] +435
Heads-up Display +230
Heated Front Seats[Opt on STD] +165
Heated Power Mirrors[Opt on STD] +85
Leather Seats[Opt on STD] +570
Power Moonroof +1190
Traction Control System[Opt on STD] +175

REGAL 1998

Regal LS gets a new standard four-speed automatic transmission, and three new exterior colors are available. Dealers will install an OnStar Mobile Communications system if the buyer desires, and second-generation airbags are added.

Category C

Model Description	Trade-in Value	Market Value
4 Dr 25TH Anniversary Sdn	15945	19215
4 Dr GS Sprchgd Sdn	17510	21095
4 Dr LS Sdn	14815	17850

OPTIONS FOR REGAL

Aluminum/Alloy Wheels[Opt on LS] +240
Chrome Wheels[Opt on GS,LS] +495
Climate Control for AC +150
Compact Disc W/fm/tape[Opt on GS,LS] +310
Dual Power Seats +480
Heated Front Seats +185
Leather Seats[Opt on LS] +480
Power Drivers Seat[Opt on LS] +235
Power Moonroof +580

RIVIERA 1998

Supercharged power is standard, OnStar satellite communications is a new option and de-powered airbags debut. Four exterior colors are new, suspension and steering have been massaged and a heated passenger seat with lumbar support has been added to the options list.

Category B

Model Description	Trade-in Value	Market Value
2 Dr STD Sprchgd Cpe	21460	25855

Don't forget to refer to the Mileage Adjustment Table at the back of this book!

 © 1999 by Edmund Publications Corporation

Model Description	Trade-in Value	Market Value

OPTIONS FOR RIVIERA

Chrome Wheels +610
Heated Front Seats +255
Power Moonroof +825
Special Factory Paint +185
Traction Control System +150

SKYLARK 1998

Skylark was sold strictly to fleets for 1998. If you're buying one used, chances are good that it was once a rental car.

Category C

4 Dr Custom Sdn	9455	11395

OPTIONS FOR SKYLARK

6 cyl 3.1 L Engine +370
Cruise Control +170
Power Windows +255

1997 BUICK

CENTURY 1997

After a decade and a half, Buick finally redesigns its bread-and-butter mid-size sedan, dropping the wagon variant in the process. A spunky 3.1-liter V6 engine, roomier interior, larger trunk and traditional Buick styling cues should convince Grandpa to trade the old warhorse in on a new one.

RATINGS (SCALE OF 1-10)

Overall	Safety	Reliability	Performance	Comfort	Value
N/A	N/A	8.8	8	7.9	6

Category C

4 Dr Custom Sdn	11845	14625
4 Dr Limited Sdn	12695	15675

OPTIONS FOR CENTURY

Prestige Package +585
Aluminum/Alloy Wheels +195
AM/FM Compact Disc Playr +260
Automatic Dimming Mirror +65
Climate Control for AC +120
Compact Disc W/fm/tape +250
Cruise Control +140
Dual Power Seats +395
Leather Seats +390
Power Drivers Seat +195
Power Moonroof +475

LE SABRE 1997

Buick freshens the somewhat stale LeSabre with new front and rear styling. Redesigned wheel selections, new seats on Custom models, and walnut instrument panel appliques round out the visual changes. Structurally, the LeSabre now meets side-impact standards. Oh, for your convenience, Buick engineers have made the coin holder larger.

RATINGS (SCALE OF 1-10)

Overall	Safety	Reliability	Performance	Comfort	Value
8.1	7.5	8.2	8.6	7.9	8.4

Category B

4 Dr Custom Sdn	12455	15190
4 Dr Limited Sdn	14585	17785

OPTIONS FOR LE SABRE

Prestige Package +500
Aluminum/Alloy Wheels[Opt on Custom] +225
AM/FM Compact Disc Playr +210
Automatic Dimming Mirror +60
Cruise Control[Opt on Custom] +145
Dual Power Seats[Opt on Custom] +245
Keyless Entry System[Opt on Custom] +120
Leather Seats +450
Power Drivers Seat +205
Power Mirrors[Opt on Custom] +65
Traction Control System +120

PARK AVENUE 1997

Buick engineers substantially improve the Park Avenue for 1997 by strengthening the body structure, improving interior ergonomics, and introducing a sleek new look. Powertrains are carried over, and two models are available: base and Ultra. Prices have risen, but the Park Avenue represents real value in comparison to other traditional luxury sedans.

RATINGS (SCALE OF 1-10)

Overall	Safety	Reliability	Performance	Comfort	Value
N/A	N/A	8.5	8.4	8.4	6.1

Category A

4 Dr STD Sdn	17470	20550
4 Dr Ultra Sprchgd Sdn	20135	23690

OPTIONS FOR PARK AVENUE

AM/FM Compact Disc Playr[Opt on STD] +355
Automatic Dimming Mirror +115
Chrome Wheels +760
Compact Disc Changer +590
Heated Front Seats[Opt on STD] +135
Heated Power Mirrors[Opt on STD] +70
Leather Seats[Opt on STD] +465
Power Moonroof +970
Traction Control System[Opt on STD] +145

REGAL 1997

Long overdue, Buick's complete redesign of the Regal means GM's premium division finally has a viable entry in the midsized sedan marketplace. The standard equipment list is a mile long, including ABS, traction control, dual-zone climate controls, heated exterior mirrors, retained accessory power and battery rundown protection.

Don't forget to refer to the Mileage Adjustment Table at the back of this book!

 © 1999 by Edmund Publications Corporation

Model Description	Trade-in Value	Market Value

RATINGS (SCALE OF 1-10)

Overall	Safety	Reliability	Performance	Comfort	Value
N/A	N/A	8.7	8.4	7.8	5.6

Category C

4 Dr GS Sprchgd Sdn	15375	18980
4 Dr LS Sdn	13805	17045

OPTIONS FOR REGAL

Aluminum/Alloy Wheels[Opt on LS] +195
Automatic Dimming Mirror +65
Chrome Wheels +405
Climate Control for AC +120
Compact Disc W/fm/tape +250
Heated Front Seats +155
Leather Seats[Opt on LS] +390
Power Drivers Seat +195
Power Moonroof +475

RIVIERA 1997

Upgraded transmissions, several new colors inside and out, additional standard equipment and new options summarize minimal changes to the Riviera in its third year.

RATINGS (SCALE OF 1-10)

Overall	Safety	Reliability	Performance	Comfort	Value
N/A	N/A	8.8	8.6	8	7.4

Category B

2 Dr STD Cpe	15710	19155
2 Dr STD Sprchgd Cpe	16455	20070

OPTIONS FOR RIVIERA

Automatic Dimming Mirror +60
Chrome Wheels +495
Heated Front Seats +210
Leather Seats +450
Power Moonroof +675
Traction Control System +120

SKYLARK 1997

Skylark gets minimal revisions this year. The standard equipment list is expanded and the car now meets 1997 side impact standards.

RATINGS (SCALE OF 1-10)

Overall	Safety	Reliability	Performance	Comfort	Value
7.8	7.7	8.5	7.2	7.3	8.1

Category C

2 Dr Custom Cpe	8065	9960
4 Dr Custom Sdn	8225	10155
2 Dr Gran Sport Cpe	10405	12845
4 Dr Gran Sport Sdn	10250	12655

OPTIONS FOR SKYLARK

6 cyl 3.1 L Engine[Opt on Custom] +295
Aluminum/Alloy Wheels[Opt on Custom] +195
AM/FM Stereo Tape[Opt on Custom] +110
Cruise Control[Opt on Custom] +140
Keyless Entry System +130
Leather Seats +390
Power Drivers Seat +195
Power Mirrors[Opt on Custom] +75
Power Moonroof +475
Power Windows[Opt on Custom] +205

1996 BUICK

CENTURY 1996

In many states, this design is just a decade away from antique car status. Wagons get the V6 as standard equipment. Power windows, cassette player, rear window defogger and a remote trunk release make the standard equipment list as this ancient A-body rolls into its final year of production.

RATINGS (SCALE OF 1-10)

Overall	Safety	Reliability	Performance	Comfort	Value
7.6	6.5	8.2	7.4	7.3	8.5

Category C

4 Dr STD Sdn	7295	9470
4 Dr STD Wgn	8000	10390

OPTIONS FOR CENTURY

6 cyl 3.1 L Engine[Opt on Sdn] +250
Auto 4-Speed Transmission[Opt on Sdn] +105
AM/FM Stereo Tape +90
Cruise Control +115
Keyless Entry System +105
Leather Seats +320
Luggage Rack +65
Power Drivers Seat +160
Power Mirrors +60
Wire Wheel Covers +125
Woodgrain Applique +175

LE SABRE 1996

Finally, the Series II engine is standard on LeSabre. Order the Gran Touring suspension, and get the same magnetic variable effort steering found on the Park Avenue Ultra. Now standard on the Custom is an electric rear window defogger and storage armrest. Limited trim levels get Twilight Sentinel, dual automatic ComforTemp climate controls, and a rear seat center armrest.

RATINGS (SCALE OF 1-10)

Overall	Safety	Reliability	Performance	Comfort	Value
8.1	7.5	8.2	8.6	7.9	8.3

Category B

4 Dr Custom Sdn	10095	12615
4 Dr Limited Sdn	12005	15005

OPTIONS FOR LE SABRE

Prestige Pkg +625
AM/FM Compact Disc Playr +175

Don't forget to refer to the Mileage Adjustment Table at the back of this book!

 © 1999 by Edmund Publications Corporation

Model Description	Trade-in Value	Market Value

Cruise Control[Opt on Custom] +120
Keyless Entry System[Opt on Custom] +100
Leather Seats +370
Power Drivers Seat +165
Power Mirrors[Opt on Custom] +55
Power Passenger Seat +170

PARK AVENUE 1996

Ultra gets new Series II supercharged engine as standard equipment, as well as magnetic variable effort steering gear. Colors and trim are revised, battery rundown protection is added, and long life engine components keep the Park going longer between maintenance stops.

RATINGS (SCALE OF 1-10)

Overall	Safety	Reliability	Performance	Comfort	Value
8.2	7.5	8.3	8.6	8.1	8.3

Category A

Model Description	Trade-in Value	Market Value
4 Dr STD Sdn	13885	17140
4 Dr Ultra Sprchgd Sdn	14855	18340

OPTIONS FOR PARK AVENUE

Luxury Package +870
Prestige Pkg +1030
AM/FM Compact Disc Playr +290
Automatic Dimming Mirror +90
Climate Control for AC[Opt on STD] +80
Dual Air Conditioning[Opt on STD] +30
Heated Front Seats +110
Heated Power Mirrors +55
Keyless Entry System[Opt on STD] +140
Leather Seats[Opt on STD] +380
Power Drivers Seat[Std on STD] +140
Power Moonroof +795
Traction Control System +120

REGAL 1996

The Series II 3.8-liter V6 is standard on Limited and Gran Sport, optional on base Custom models. Standard equipment now includes dual ComforTemp climate controls and a cassette player. Revised wheels, available in chrome, are standard on the Gran Sport. Base V6 is upgraded, and both engines feature long life engine components.

RATINGS (SCALE OF 1-10)

Overall	Safety	Reliability	Performance	Comfort	Value
N/A	N/A	8.5	7.4	7.6	7.7

Category C

Model Description	Trade-in Value	Market Value
2 Dr Custom Cpe	9615	12485
4 Dr Custom Sdn	9205	11955
2 Dr Gran Sport Cpe	10695	13890
4 Dr Gran Sport Sdn	10720	13920
4 Dr Limited Sdn	10215	13270
4 Dr Olympic Gold Sdn	9350	12145

OPTIONS FOR REGAL

6 cyl 3.8 L Engine[Opt on Custom] +205
AM/FM Compact Disc Playr +215
Keyless Entry System +105
Leather Seats +320
Power Drivers Seat[Std on Gran Sport] +160
Power Moonroof +390
Premium Sound System +220

RIVIERA 1996

Series II supercharged engine gives top-of-the-line Riv a 15 horsepower boost. There are new colors inside and out, real wood on the dash, and revised climate and radio controls. Chrome wheels are optional.

RATINGS (SCALE OF 1-10)

Overall	Safety	Reliability	Performance	Comfort	Value
N/A	N/A	8.3	8.6	8	7.7

Category B

Model Description	Trade-in Value	Market Value
2 Dr STD Cpe	13290	16610
2 Dr STD Sprchgd Cpe	13570	16965

OPTIONS FOR RIVIERA

Prestige Pkg +400
Chrome Wheels +405
Heated Front Seats +170
Leather Seats +370
Power Moonroof +550
Traction Control System +100

ROADMASTER 1996

Last year for Corvette-powered land yacht. All models are designated Collector's Editions.

RATINGS (SCALE OF 1-10)

Overall	Safety	Reliability	Performance	Comfort	Value
7.8	7.2	7.3	7.8	8.4	8.4

Category B

Model Description	Trade-in Value	Market Value
4 Dr Estate Wgn	15000	18750
4 Dr Limited Sdn	13925	17410
4 Dr STD Sdn	12635	15790

OPTIONS FOR ROADMASTER

Limited Pkg +610
Prestige Pkg +420
Auto Load Leveling +105
Camper/Towing Package +200
Compact Disc W/fm/tape +220
Heated Front Seats +170
Keyless Entry System[Std on Limited] +100
Leather Seats +370
Power Drivers Seat +165
Power Passenger Seat +170

SKYLARK 1996

Styling changes inside and out make the Skylark far more marketable, and credible. Dual airbags are new,

Don't forget to refer to the Mileage Adjustment Table at the back of this book!

 © 1999 by Edmund Publications Corporation

Model Description	Trade-in Value	Market Value	Model Description	Trade-in Value	Market Value

as are three-point seat belts mounted to the B-pillar where they should be. A new twin-cam engine replaces the 2.3-liter Quad 4, and automatic transmissions include traction control. Air conditioning, a rear window defroster, and a tilt wheel are now standard. Long life engine components round out the long list of improvements to Buick's lame duck.

RATINGS (SCALE OF 1-10)

Overall	Safety	Reliability	Performance	Comfort	Value
7.8	7.7	8.2	7.2	7.3	8.5

Category C

Model Description	Trade-in Value	Market Value
2 Dr Custom Cpe	7125	9250
4 Dr Custom Sdn	7270	9445
4 Dr Olympic Gold Sdn	7405	9620

OPTIONS FOR SKYLARK

6 cyl 3.1 L Engine +250
Gran Sport Pkg +730
AM/FM Stereo Tape +90
Cruise Control[Opt on Custom] +115
Keyless Entry System +105
Leather Seats +320
Power Drivers Seat +160
Power Moonroof +390
Power Windows +170

1995 BUICK

CENTURY 1995

Instruments newly backlit, and seats are revised.

RATINGS (SCALE OF 1-10)

Overall	Safety	Reliability	Performance	Comfort	Value
7.4	7.1	8	7.4	7.3	7.4

Category C

Model Description	Trade-in Value	Market Value
4 Dr Custom Sdn	6925	9110
4 Dr Limited Sdn	7305	9610
4 Dr Special Sdn	6345	8345
4 Dr Special Wgn	6485	8535

OPTIONS FOR CENTURY

6 cyl 3.1 L Engine[Opt on Special] +215
Auto 4-Speed Transmission[Opt on Special] +90
AM/FM Stereo Tape[Std on Limited] +75
Cruise Control[Std on Limited] +95
Keyless Entry System[Std on Limited] +85
Leather Seats[Std on Limited] +260
Luggage Rack +55
Power Drivers Seat[Std on Limited] +130
Power Mirrors[Std on Limited] +50
Power Windows[Opt on Special] +140
Premium Sound System +180
Wire Wheel Covers[Std on Limited] +100
Woodgrain Applique +140

LE SABRE 1995

New climate controls and radios are major changes.

RATINGS (SCALE OF 1-10)

Overall	Safety	Reliability	Performance	Comfort	Value
8.3	8.4	8.3	8.6	7.9	8.2

Category B

Model Description	Trade-in Value	Market Value
4 Dr Custom Sdn	8810	11295
4 Dr Limited Sdn	10535	13510

OPTIONS FOR LE SABRE

AM/FM Compact Disc Playr +140
Compact Disc W/fm/tape +180
Cruise Control[Opt on Custom] +95
Keyless Entry System[Opt on Custom] +80
Leather Seats +300
Power Drivers Seat[Opt on Custom] +135
Power Mirrors[Opt on Custom] +45
Power Passenger Seat +140
Premium Sound System +190
Traction Control System +80

PARK AVENUE 1995

Base engine upgraded to 3800 Series II status; makes 35 more horsepower than previous year. Base models get styling tweaks front and rear. New climate controls and radios are added.

RATINGS (SCALE OF 1-10)

Overall	Safety	Reliability	Performance	Comfort	Value
8.3	8.4	8.3	8.6	8.1	8.2

Category A

Model Description	Trade-in Value	Market Value
4 Dr STD Sdn	11540	14425
4 Dr Ultra Sprchgd Sdn	12405	15510

OPTIONS FOR PARK AVENUE

Luxury Package +440
Prestige Pkg +1105
AM/FM Compact Disc Playr +235
Climate Control for AC[Opt on STD] +65
Heated Front Seats +90
Keyless Entry System[Opt on STD] +115
Leather Seats[Opt on STD] +310
Power Moonroof +650
Power Passenger Seat[Opt on STD] +140
Premium Sound System +200
Traction Control System +95

REGAL 1995

New interior has dual airbags housed in revised instrument panel. Gauges are actually legible. Seats are new, too. Fake wood has been chopped from door panels. Exterior styling is updated.

Don't forget to refer to the Mileage Adjustment Table at the back of this book!

© 1999 by Edmund Publications Corporation

Model Description	Trade-in Value	Market Value

RATINGS (SCALE OF 1-10)

Overall	Safety	Reliability	Performance	Comfort	Value
N/A	N/A	7.7	7.4	7.6	8.1

Category C		
2 Dr Custom Cpe	7390	9720
4 Dr Custom Sdn	7425	9765
4 Dr Custom Select Sdn	7670	10090
2 Dr Gran Sport Cpe	8950	11780
4 Dr Gran Sport Sdn	8855	11650
4 Dr Limited Sdn	8650	11385

OPTIONS FOR REGAL

6 cyl 3.8 L Engine[Opt on Custom] +165
AM/FM Compact Disc Playr +175
AM/FM Stereo Tape[Opt on Custom] +75
Keyless Entry System[Std on Custom Select] +85
Leather Seats +260
Power Drivers Seat[Std on Custom Select] +130
Power Moonroof +320

RIVIERA 1995

All-new Riv debuts with controversial styling. Dual airbags and ABS are standard. Base engine is 3800 Series II V6; optional is a supercharged 3.8-liter. Traction control is optional.

RATINGS (SCALE OF 1-10)

Overall	Safety	Reliability	Performance	Comfort	Value
N/A	N/A	8.1	8.6	8	6.3

Category B		
2 Dr STD Cpe	11295	14480
2 Dr STD Sprchgd Cpe	11490	14730

OPTIONS FOR RIVIERA

AM/FM Compact Disc Playr +140
Heated Front Seats +140
Leather Seats +300
Power Moonroof +450
Traction Control System +80

ROADMASTER 1995

New radios and larger rearview mirrors are added. Cassette player is made standard. Wagon gets standard alloy wheels. New options are heated front seats and memory feature for power driver's seat.

RATINGS (SCALE OF 1-10)

Overall	Safety	Reliability	Performance	Comfort	Value
8	7.9	7.3	7.8	8.4	8.4

Category B		
4 Dr Estate Wgn	13385	17160
4 Dr Limited Sdn	11280	14465
4 Dr STD Sdn	9975	12785

OPTIONS FOR ROADMASTER

Limited Wagon Pkg +390
Auto Load Leveling +85
Camper/Towing Package +165
Climate Control for AC[Std on Limited] +80
Compact Disc W/fm/tape +180
Heated Front Seats +140
Keyless Entry System[Std on Limited] +80
Leather Seats +300
Power Drivers Seat[Std on Limited] +135
Power Passenger Seat[Std on Limited] +140

SKYLARK 1995

Rear suspension is revised. New base engine is 150-horsepower Quad 4, packing 35 more ponies than previous base engine. GS gets 3.1-liter V6 standard. Power sunroof is a new option.

RATINGS (SCALE OF 1-10)

Overall	Safety	Reliability	Performance	Comfort	Value
7.3	7.2	7.7	7.2	7	7.2

Category C		
2 Dr Custom Cpe	5305	6975
4 Dr Custom Sdn	5500	7235
2 Dr Gran Sport Cpe	7235	9520
4 Dr Gran Sport Sdn	7305	9615

OPTIONS FOR SKYLARK

6 cyl 3.1 L Engine[Opt on Custom] +215
Auto 4-Speed Transmission[Opt on Custom] +90
Air Conditioning[Opt on Custom] +360
AM/FM Stereo Tape[Opt on Custom] +75
Cruise Control[Opt on Custom] +95
Keyless Entry System +85
Leather Seats +260
Power Drivers Seat +130
Power Moonroof +320
Power Windows[Opt on Custom] +140

1994 BUICK

CENTURY 1994

A driver airbag and ABS are standard on all models. This marks the first time ABS is offered on the Century. Coupe trimmed from lineup. The 2.2-liter engine gains ten horsepower, and the optional 3.3-liter V6 is replaced by a 3.1-liter unit. When transmission is shifted into "Park," automatic door locks unlock themselves. Defeat this feature by removing a fuse. Tilt steering is standard on Special. New gauges debut.

RATINGS (SCALE OF 1-10)

Overall	Safety	Reliability	Performance	Comfort	Value
7.4	7	7.4	7.4	7.3	7.8

Don't forget to refer to the Mileage Adjustment Table at the back of this book!

 © 1999 by Edmund Publications Corporation

Model Description	Trade-in Value	Market Value
Category C		
4 Dr Custom Sdn	5265	7115
4 Dr Special Wgn	5430	7335
4 Dr Special Sdn	5040	6810

OPTIONS FOR CENTURY

6 cyl 3.1 L Engine +195
Auto 4-Speed Transmission +75
AM/FM Stereo Tape +60
Cruise Control +75
Keyless Entry System +70
Leather Seats +215
Power Drivers Seat +105
Power Mirrors +40
Power Windows +115

LE SABRE 1994

Passenger airbag installed. Solar-Ray tinted glass used for windshield. Traction control system able to cut engine power to slipping wheels in addition to applying brake. Front seat travel increased one inch.

RATINGS (SCALE OF 1-10)

Overall	Safety	Reliability	Performance	Comfort	Value
8.4	8.4	8.3	8.6	7.9	8.7

Model Description	Trade-in Value	Market Value
Category B		
4 Dr Custom Sdn	6695	8930
4 Dr Limited Sdn	8085	10780

OPTIONS FOR LE SABRE

AM/FM Stereo Tape[Opt on Custom] +65
Keyless Entry System[Opt on Custom] +65
Leather Seats +245
Power Drivers Seat[Opt on Custom] +110
Power Passenger Seat +115
Premium Sound System +155

PARK AVENUE 1994

Passenger airbag debuts, and Ultra model gets 20 more horsepower. Traction control system able to cut engine power to slipping wheels in addition to applying brake, and can be turned off via a dashboard-mounted switch. Remote keyless entry, power trunk pull-down and auto dimming rearview mirror added to Ultra standard equipment list. Front seat travel increased one inch. Heated front seats are newly optional.

RATINGS (SCALE OF 1-10)

Overall	Safety	Reliability	Performance	Comfort	Value
8.4	8.4	8.2	8.6	8.1	8.6

Model Description	Trade-in Value	Market Value
Category A		
4 Dr STD Sdn	8845	11340
4 Dr Ultra Sprchgd Sdn	9995	12810

OPTIONS FOR PARK AVENUE

Luxury Package +420
Prestige Package +610
AM/FM Compact Disc Playr +195
Astro Roof +510
Bose Sound System +255
Heated Front Seats +75
Keyless Entry System[Opt on STD] +90
Leather Seats[Opt on STD] +255
Power Passenger Seat[Opt on STD] +115
Traction Control System +80

REGAL 1994

Driver airbag and ABS standard on all Regals. 3.1-liter V6 gets 20 more horsepower. Power windows standard across the board, and automatic door locks automatically unlock when car is shifted into "Park." Defeat this feature by removing a fuse.

RATINGS (SCALE OF 1-10)

Overall	Safety	Reliability	Performance	Comfort	Value
7.5	6.7	6.8	8.2	7.3	8.5

Model Description	Trade-in Value	Market Value
Category C		
2 Dr Custom Cpe	6365	8600
4 Dr Custom Sdn	6250	8445
2 Dr Gran Sport Cpe	7250	9800
4 Dr Gran Sport Sdn	7260	9810
4 Dr Limited Sdn	6855	9265

OPTIONS FOR REGAL

6 cyl 3.8 L Engine[Opt on Custom] +145
AM/FM Stereo Tape +60
Cruise Control +75
Leather Seats +215
Power Drivers Seat +105
Power Moonroof +260
Premium Sound System +145

ROADMASTER 1994

Detuned Corvette engine transplanted into big Buick, giving Roadmaster 80 additional horsepower. Dual airbags housed in redesigned dashboard with new gauges.

RATINGS (SCALE OF 1-10)

Overall	Safety	Reliability	Performance	Comfort	Value
8.2	8	7.4	7.8	8.4	9.4

Model Description	Trade-in Value	Market Value
Category B		
4 Dr Estate Wgn	10090	13450
4 Dr Limited Sdn	9070	12095
4 Dr STD Sdn	7990	10655

OPTIONS FOR ROADMASTER

AM/FM Compact Disc Playr +115
Auto Load Leveling +70
Camper/Towing Package +135
Climate Control for AC[Opt on STD] +65
Keyless Entry System[Std on Limited] +65

Don't forget to refer to the Mileage Adjustment Table at the back of this book!

 © 1999 by Edmund Publications Corporation

Model Description	Trade-in Value	Market Value

Leather Seats +245
Power Drivers Seat[Opt on STD] +110
Power Passenger Seat[Std on Limited] +115

SKYLARK 1994

Driver airbag added to all models. New 3.1-liter V6 replaces 3.3-liter V6 from 1993. Automatic transmission gets overdrive gear. Gran Sport and Limited gain standard equipment including air conditioning, power windows, cruise control and tilt steering wheel. Automatic door locks automatically unlock when car is put in "Park." Defeat this feature by removing a fuse.

RATINGS (SCALE OF 1-10)

Overall	Safety	Reliability	Performance	Comfort	Value
7.3	7.2	7.7	7.2	7	7.2

Category C

Model Description	Trade-in Value	Market Value
2 Dr Custom Cpe	4720	6375
4 Dr Custom Sdn	4760	6435
2 Dr Gran Sport Cpe	6405	8655
4 Dr Gran Sport Sdn	6480	8760
4 Dr Limited Sdn	5565	7525

OPTIONS FOR SKYLARK

6 cyl 3.1 L Engine[Std on Gran Sport] +195
Auto 4-Speed Transmission[Std on Gran Sport] +75
Air Conditioning[Opt on Custom] +295
AM/FM Stereo Tape +60
Cruise Control[Opt on Custom] +75
Power Drivers Seat +105
Power Windows[Opt on Custom] +115

1993 BUICK

CENTURY 1993

Driver airbag standard on Custom and Limited; optional on Special. New 2.2-liter four-cylinder replaces old 2.5-liter unit with no loss of power. Fuel tank capacity increased.

RATINGS (SCALE OF 1-10)

Overall	Safety	Reliability	Performance	Comfort	Value
7.1	4.8	7.8	7.4	7.3	8.3

Category C

Model Description	Trade-in Value	Market Value
2 Dr Custom Cpe	4135	5820
4 Dr Custom Sdn	4135	5825
4 Dr Custom Wgn	4250	5985
4 Dr Limited Sdn	4445	6260
4 Dr Special Sdn	3860	5435
4 Dr Special Wgn	3800	5350

OPTIONS FOR CENTURY

6 cyl 3.3 L Engine +165
Auto 4-Speed Transmission +60
Prestige Package +300
Air Bag Restraint[Opt on Special] +155
AM/FM Stereo Tape +50
Cruise Control +65
Keyless Entry System +55
Leather Seats +175
Power Drivers Seat +85
Power Windows +90

LE SABRE 1993

Engine gets more torque, and ABS is standard on all models. Power door locks standard on all models, and Limited offers variable-assist steering.

RATINGS (SCALE OF 1-10)

Overall	Safety	Reliability	Performance	Comfort	Value
7.9	7.4	7.8	8.6	7.9	8

Category B

Model Description	Trade-in Value	Market Value
4 Dr 90th Anniversary Sdn	6060	8305
4 Dr Custom Sdn	5875	8045
4 Dr Limited Sdn	6715	9200

OPTIONS FOR LE SABRE

Luxury Package +390
Premium Package +285
Prestige Package +360
Aluminum/Alloy Wheels +100
AM/FM Stereo Tape[Opt on Custom,Limited] +55
Dual Power Seats +110
Keyless Entry System +55
Leather Seats +200
Power Drivers Seat[Opt on Custom,Limited] +90
Premium Sound System +125
Traction Control System +55
Wire Wheel Covers[Opt on Custom,Limited] +70

PARK AVENUE 1993

Base V6 gains power. Revisions made to grilles and taillights. An automatic ride control system adjusts the suspension between three different modes ranging from soft to firm.

RATINGS (SCALE OF 1-10)

Overall	Safety	Reliability	Performance	Comfort	Value
N/A	N/A	8.1	8.6	8.1	8.6

Category A

Model Description	Trade-in Value	Market Value
4 Dr STD Sdn	7245	9665
4 Dr Ultra Sprchgd Sdn	8050	10735

OPTIONS FOR PARK AVENUE

AM/FM Compact Disc Playr +160
Bose Sound System +210
Climate Control for AC[Opt on STD] +45
Keyless Entry System +75
Leather Seats[Opt on STD] +210
Power Passenger Seat[Opt on STD] +90
Power Sunroof +415
Traction Control System +65

Don't forget to refer to the Mileage Adjustment Table at the back of this book!

 © 1999 by Edmund Publications Corporation

Model Description	Trade-in Value	Market Value

REGAL 1993

A new transmission, grille and taillights debut. The 3.8-liter V6 gains torque. Fifteen-inch wheels replace 14-inch wheels. Optional on Limited and Gran Sport is a steering wheel with radio controls.

RATINGS (SCALE OF 1-10)

Overall	Safety	Reliability	Performance	Comfort	Value
7.1	4.9	6.7	8.2	7.3	8.4

Category C

Model Description	Trade-in Value	Market Value
2 Dr Custom Cpe	4945	6970
4 Dr Custom Sdn	5005	7050
2 Dr Gran Sport Cpe	6025	8485
4 Dr Gran Sport Sdn	5995	8445
2 Dr Limited Cpe	5425	7640
4 Dr Limited Sdn	5465	7695

OPTIONS FOR REGAL

6 cyl 3.8 L Engine[Std on Gran Sport] +110
Aluminum/Alloy Wheels[Std on Gran Sport] +85
AM/FM Stereo Tape +50
Anti-Lock Brakes[Opt on Custom] +190
Cruise Control +65
Leather Seats +175
Power Drivers Seat +85
Power Sunroof +210
Power Windows +90
Premium Sound System +120

RIVIERA 1993

Gran Touring model gets larger wheels and tires from defunct Reatta.

Category B

Model Description	Trade-in Value	Market Value
2 Dr STD Cpe	7645	10470

OPTIONS FOR RIVIERA

Aluminum/Alloy Wheels +100
AM/FM Compact Disc Playr +95
Keyless Entry System +55
Leather Seats +200
Power Sunroof +350
Premium Sound System +125

ROADMASTER 1993

Wagons get Solar-Ray tinted windshield. Both models receive power window lockout switch and more sound deadening.

RATINGS (SCALE OF 1-10)

Overall	Safety	Reliability	Performance	Comfort	Value
N/A	N/A	7.3	7.4	8.4	9.3

Category B

Model Description	Trade-in Value	Market Value
4 Dr Estate Wgn	7560	10355
4 Dr Limited Sdn	7325	10035
4 Dr STD Sdn	6590	9030

OPTIONS FOR ROADMASTER

Prestige Package +270
Aluminum/Alloy Wheels[Std on Estate] +100
AM/FM Compact Disc Playr +95
AM/FM Stereo Tape[Std on Limited] +55
Auto Load Leveling +55
Camper/Towing Package +110
Climate Control for AC +55
Leather Seats +200
Power Drivers Seat[Std on Limited] +90
Power Passenger Seat[Opt on Estate] +95

SKYLARK 1993

New entry-level Custom model debuts. Base engine loses five horsepower. Split-folding rear seat optional on Limited; not available on Custom. Adjustable Ride Control moves to GS options list from standard equipment roster.

RATINGS (SCALE OF 1-10)

Overall	Safety	Reliability	Performance	Comfort	Value
6.5	4.1	7	7.2	7	7

Category C

Model Description	Trade-in Value	Market Value
2 Dr Custom Cpe	3860	5440
4 Dr Custom Sdn	3730	5250
2 Dr Gran Sport Cpe	4760	6705
4 Dr Gran Sport Sdn	4925	6940
2 Dr Limited Cpe	4255	5995
4 Dr Limited Sdn	3895	5485

OPTIONS FOR SKYLARK

6 cyl 3.3 L Engine[Std on Gran Sport] +165
Air Conditioning +240
Aluminum/Alloy Wheels[Opt on Limited] +85
AM/FM Stereo Tape +50
Cruise Control +65
Power Drivers Seat +85
Power Windows +90

1992 BUICK

CENTURY 1992

Power door locks made standard. Custom models can be equipped with a trip odometer.

RATINGS (SCALE OF 1-10)

Overall	Safety	Reliability	Performance	Comfort	Value
6.9	4.3	7.3	7.4	7.3	8.2

Category C

Model Description	Trade-in Value	Market Value
2 Dr Custom Cpe	3280	4750
4 Dr Custom Wgn	4455	6460
4 Dr Custom Sdn	3420	4955
4 Dr Limited Wgn	4745	6880
4 Dr Limited Sdn	3605	5225
4 Dr Special Sdn	3260	4725

Don't forget to refer to the Mileage Adjustment Table at the back of this book!

© 1999 by Edmund Publications Corporation

Model Description	Trade-in Value	Market Value

OPTIONS FOR CENTURY

6 cyl 3.3 L Engine +125
Auto 4-Speed Transmission +50
AM/FM Stereo Tape +40
Cruise Control +50
Leather Seats +145
Power Drivers Seat +70
Power Windows +75

LE SABRE 1992

All-new car debuts based on 1991 Park Avenue redesign. ABS and driver airbag are standard. Coupe dropped; all LeSabres are sedans. 3.8-liter V6 gets more power. Theft-deterrent system and power windows made standard. Child-proof rear door locks are installed.

RATINGS (SCALE OF 1-10)

Overall	Safety	Reliability	Performance	Comfort	Value
7.8	6.9	7.7	8.6	7.9	7.9

Category B

Model Description	Trade-in Value	Market Value
4 Dr Custom Sdn	4630	6430
4 Dr Limited Sdn	5515	7665

OPTIONS FOR LE SABRE

Aluminum/Alloy Wheels +85
AM/FM Stereo Tape +45
Anti-Lock Brakes[Opt on Custom] +175
Leather Seats +165
Power Drivers Seat +75
Power Passenger Seat +75
Premium Sound System +105
Traction Control System +45
Wire Wheel Covers +55

PARK AVENUE 1992

Ultra gets 205-horsepower supercharged V6. Traction control is a new option. Variable-effort power steering and dual cupholders are new for all Park Avenues.

RATINGS (SCALE OF 1-10)

Overall	Safety	Reliability	Performance	Comfort	Value
N/A	N/A	7.8	8.6	8.1	8

Category A

Model Description	Trade-in Value	Market Value
4 Dr STD Sdn	5865	8150
4 Dr Ultra Sprchgd Sdn	6550	9095

OPTIONS FOR PARK AVENUE

Premium Pkg +185
Prestige Pkg +365
AM/FM Compact Disc Playr +130
Astro Roof +340
Bose Sound System +170
Climate Control for AC[Opt on STD] +35
Keyless Entry System +60
Leather Seats[Opt on STD] +170
Power Passenger Seat[Opt on STD] +75

REGAL 1992

Gran Sport no longer an option package; becomes a full-fledged model designation. ABS newly standard on Gran Sport and Limited. Power door locks made standard on all Regals. Power front passenger seat is new option.

RATINGS (SCALE OF 1-10)

Overall	Safety	Reliability	Performance	Comfort	Value
7	4.8	6.3	8.2	7.3	8.4

Category C

Model Description	Trade-in Value	Market Value
2 Dr Custom Cpe	3865	5600
4 Dr Custom Sdn	4080	5915
2 Dr Gran Sport Cpe	4860	7040
4 Dr Gran Sport Sdn	4915	7125
2 Dr Limited Cpe	4505	6530
4 Dr Limited Sdn	4435	6425

OPTIONS FOR REGAL

6 cyl 3.8 L Engine[Std on Gran Sport] +120
Aluminum/Alloy Wheels[Std on Gran Sport] +70
AM/FM Stereo Tape[Std on Gran Sport] +40
Anti-Lock Brakes[Opt on Custom] +155
Cruise Control +50
Leather Seats +145
Power Drivers Seat +70
Power Sunroof +170
Power Windows +75
Premium Sound System +100

RIVIERA 1992

Solar-control glass is standard. Brake system gets larger rotors and calipers.

Category B

Model Description	Trade-in Value	Market Value
2 Dr STD Cpe	6280	8720

OPTIONS FOR RIVIERA

Aluminum/Alloy Wheels +85
AM/FM Compact Disc Playr +75
Astro Roof +310
Bose Sound System +190
Leather Seats +165
Power Passenger Seat +75

ROADMASTER 1992

Wagon gets 5.7-liter engine. Sedan debuts.

RATINGS (SCALE OF 1-10)

Overall	Safety	Reliability	Performance	Comfort	Value
N/A	N/A	6.4	7.4	8.4	8.7

Category B

Model Description	Trade-in Value	Market Value
4 Dr Estate Wgn	6115	8495
4 Dr Limited Sdn	5925	8230
4 Dr STD Sdn	4925	6840

Don't forget to refer to the Mileage Adjustment Table at the back of this book!

© 1999 by Edmund Publications Corporation

OPTIONS FOR ROADMASTER
Aluminum/Alloy Wheels[Std on Estate] +85
AM/FM Stereo Tape[Std on Limited] +45
Camper/Towing Package +90
Climate Control for AC[Std on Limited] +45
Cruise Control[Opt on Estate] +55
Leather Seats +165
Power Drivers Seat[Std on Limited] +75
Power Passenger Seat[Std on Limited] +75

SKYLARK 1992

Redesign meant to bring younger buyers into showrooms backfires. Choice of four- or six-cylinder engines available. Automatic transmission is standard. ABS, power door locks and split-folding rear seat are standard. Still has door-mounted seatbelts. Adjustable Ride Control, standard on GS and optional on other Skylarks, allows driver to select one of three suspension settings.

RATINGS (SCALE OF 1-10)

Overall	Safety	Reliability	Performance	Comfort	Value
6.4	4.1	6.7	7.2	7	6.9

Category C

Model	Trade-in Value	Market Value
2 Dr Gran Sport Cpe	4010	5815
4 Dr Gran Sport Sdn	4055	5875
2 Dr STD Cpe	2930	4245
4 Dr STD Sdn	2790	4045

OPTIONS FOR SKYLARK
6 cyl 3.3 L Engine[Opt on STD] +125
Air Conditioning +200
AM/FM Stereo Tape +40
Cruise Control +50
Power Drivers Seat +70
Power Windows +75

1991 BUICK

CENTURY 1991

Remote keyless entry and steering wheel radio controls are newly available.

RATINGS (SCALE OF 1-10)

Overall	Safety	Reliability	Performance	Comfort	Value
6.7	3.8	7	7.4	7.3	8.1

Category C

Model	Trade-in Value	Market Value
2 Dr Custom Cpe	2730	4200
4 Dr Custom Wgn	2755	4240
4 Dr Custom Sdn	2655	4085
4 Dr Limited Wgn	3010	4630
4 Dr Limited Sdn	2915	4485

OPTIONS FOR CENTURY
6 cyl 3.3 L Engine +125
Auto 4-Speed Transmission +40
Prestige Pkg +170
AM/FM Stereo Tape +35
Cruise Control +40
Leather Seats +115
Power Door Locks +50
Power Drivers Seat +60
Power Windows +60

LE SABRE 1991

New 3.8-liter V6 engine replaces old one.

Category B

Model	Trade-in Value	Market Value
4 Dr Custom Sdn	3555	5010
2 Dr Limited Cpe	3920	5525
4 Dr Limited Sdn	4080	5745
2 Dr STD Cpe	3385	4770

OPTIONS FOR LE SABRE
AM/FM Stereo Tape +35
Anti-Lock Brakes +145
Leather Seats +135
Power Door Locks +50
Power Drivers Seat +60
Power Passenger Seat +65
Power Windows +60
Premium Sound System +85

PARK AVENUE 1991

All-new design debuts. New 3.8-liter V6 engine installed under the hood. Driver airbag and ABS are standard. Ultra gets standard dual-zone climate controls; this feature is optional on base car.

RATINGS (SCALE OF 1-10)

Overall	Safety	Reliability	Performance	Comfort	Value
N/A	N/A	7.7	8.6	8.1	7.9

Category A

Model	Trade-in Value	Market Value
4 Dr STD Sdn	4700	6715
4 Dr Ultra Sdn	5570	7955

OPTIONS FOR PARK AVENUE
AM/FM Compact Disc Playr +105
Astro Roof +275
Bose Sound System +140
Climate Control for AC +30
Keyless Entry System +50
Leather Seats[Opt on STD] +140
Power Passenger Seat[Opt on STD] +60

REATTA 1991

New transmission and alloy wheels debut. New 3.8-liter V6 installed under the hood. Final year for slow-selling sportster.

Category C

Model	Trade-in Value	Market Value
2 Dr STD Cpe	6755	10395

OPTIONS FOR REATTA
AM/FM Compact Disc Playr +80
Power Sunroof +140

Don't forget to refer to the Mileage Adjustment Table at the back of this book!

 © 1999 by Edmund Publications Corporation

Model Description	Trade-in Value	Market Value

REGAL 1991

Teensy analog gauges replace yucky digital readouts, except on Custom coupe. New 3.8-liter V6 is optional on Regal except Gran Sport, on which it is standard. ABS optional on all Regals.

RATINGS (SCALE OF 1-10)

Overall	Safety	Reliability	Performance	Comfort	Value
6.8	4.6	5.6	8.2	7.3	8.3

Category C

Model	Trade-in	Market
2 Dr Custom Cpe	3100	4770
4 Dr Custom Sdn	3200	4925
2 Dr Limited Cpe	3490	5365
4 Dr Limited Sdn	3455	5320

OPTIONS FOR REGAL

6 cyl 3.8 L Engine +85
Aluminum/Alloy Wheels +60
AM/FM Stereo Tape +35
Anti-Lock Brakes +125
Cruise Control +40
Leather Seats +115
Power Door Locks +50
Power Drivers Seat +60
Power Sunroof +140
Power Windows +60
Premium Sound System +80

RIVIERA 1991

Improved 3.8-liter V6 powers Riviera. Concert Sound II speaker system made standard. Retained accessory power means windows and sunroof can be shut after car is turned off.

Category B

Model	Trade-in	Market
2 Dr STD Cpe	4925	6940

OPTIONS FOR RIVIERA

Aluminum/Alloy Wheels +65
Astro Roof +255
Bose Sound System +155
Leather Seats +135
Power Passenger Seat +65

ROADMASTER 1991

Buick revives legendary moniker for huge new rear-drive wagon with glass Vista Roof over rear seat. ABS and driver airbag are standard. Powered by 5.0-liter V8.

RATINGS (SCALE OF 1-10)

Overall	Safety	Reliability	Performance	Comfort	Value
N/A	N/A	6.5	7.4	8.4	7.6

Category B

Model	Trade-in	Market
4 Dr Estate Wgn	4920	6930

OPTIONS FOR ROADMASTER

AM/FM Stereo Tape +35
Camper/Towing Package +75
Climate Control for AC +35
Leather Seats +135
Power Door Locks +50
Power Drivers Seat +60
Power Passenger Seat +65

SKYLARK 1991

No changes.

Category C

Model	Trade-in	Market
2 Dr Custom Cpe	2215	3410
4 Dr Custom Sdn	2315	3560
2 Dr Gran Sport Cpe	2560	3935
4 Dr Luxury Sdn	2685	4130
2 Dr STD Cpe	2050	3155
4 Dr STD Sdn	2125	3265

OPTIONS FOR SKYLARK

4 cyl 2.3 L Quad 4 Engine +130
6 cyl 3.3 L Engine +125
Air Conditioning +160
AM/FM Stereo Tape[Std on Gran Sport] +35
Anti-Lock Brakes +125
Power Door Locks +50
Power Drivers Seat +60
Power Windows +60

1990 BUICK

CENTURY 1990

New door trim, passive restraints and an improved suspension debut. Air conditioning moved to standard equipment list. 2.5-liter engine gets more power. Power seat switches relocated.

RATINGS (SCALE OF 1-10)

Overall	Safety	Reliability	Performance	Comfort	Value
6.6	3.8	6.9	7.4	7.3	7.6

Category C

Model	Trade-in	Market
2 Dr Custom Cpe	2345	3840
4 Dr Custom Wgn	2000	3280
4 Dr Custom Sdn	2085	3420
4 Dr Limited Sdn	2145	3520
4 Dr Limited Wgn	2100	3445

OPTIONS FOR CENTURY

6 cyl 3.3 L Engine +100
Auto 4-Speed Transmission +35
Cruise Control +35
Leather Seats +95
Power Door Locks +40
Power Drivers Seat +45
Power Windows +50

Don't forget to refer to the Mileage Adjustment Table at the back of this book!

 © 1999 by Edmund Publications Corporation

Model Description	Trade-in Value	Market Value

ELECTRA 1990

Cassette player and rear defogger made standard. Limited and Park Avenue get wire wheel covers; Limited and T-Type get cruise control. Steering feel is improved.

Category A

Model Description	Trade-in Value	Market Value
4 Dr Limited Sdn	3295	4915
4 Dr Park Ave Ultra Sdn	3755	5610
4 Dr Park Avenue Sdn	3395	5065
4 Dr T Type Sdn	3240	4840

OPTIONS FOR ELECTRA

Luxury Package +155
Prestige Pkg +170
Aluminum/Alloy Wheels[Opt on Limited,Park Avenue] +70
Anti-Lock Brakes[Opt on Limited,Park Avenue] +155
Astro Roof +225
Bose Sound System +115
Leather Seats[Std on Park Ave Ultra] +115
Power Door Locks[Opt on Limited,T Type] +35
Power Passenger Seat[Std on Park Ave Ultra] +50
Wire Wheel Covers[Std on Limited,T Type] +50

ESTATE WAGON 1990

LeSabre model dropped. Third seat can be deleted, and hood is garnished by new ornament.

Category B

Model Description	Trade-in Value	Market Value
4 Dr STD Wgn	2365	3640

OPTIONS FOR ESTATE WAGON

Camper/Towing Package +60
Leather Seats +110
Power Door Locks +40
Power Drivers Seat +50
Power Passenger Seat +50
Power Windows +50
Premium Sound System +70
Wire Wheel Covers +40
Woodgrain Applique +65

LE SABRE 1990

New front and rear styling debuts, including composite headlamps, new grille and body color fascia. T-Type model dropped. Steering feel is improved.

Category B

Model Description	Trade-in Value	Market Value
4 Dr Custom Sdn	2685	4130
2 Dr Limited Cpe	2840	4370
4 Dr Limited Sdn	3080	4735
2 Dr STD Cpe	2560	3940

OPTIONS FOR LE SABRE

Luxury Package +300
Popular Equipment Pkg +140
Prestige Pkg +130
AM/FM Stereo Tape +30
Anti-Lock Brakes +120
Leather Seats +110
Power Door Locks +40
Power Drivers Seat +50
Power Passenger Seat +50
Power Windows +50
Premium Sound System +70
Wire Wheel Covers +40

REATTA 1990

Convertible introduced. Coupe gets analog gauges. New stereo with cassette and CD player is available. Distracting Video Touch Screen replaced by conventional controls.

Category C

Model Description	Trade-in Value	Market Value
2 Dr STD Cpe	4985	8170
2 Dr STD Conv	8185	13415

OPTIONS FOR REATTA

AM/FM Compact Disc Playr +65
Power Sunroof +115

REGAL 1990

Sedan debuted midyear. New 3.8-liter engine is optional. ABS is part of SE package on Limited sedan. Leather is optional on Gran Sport coupe and Limited sedan.

RATINGS (SCALE OF 1-10)

Overall	Safety	Reliability	Performance	Comfort	Value
6.7	4.7	5.5	8.2	7.3	8.1

Category C

Model Description	Trade-in Value	Market Value
2 Dr Custom Cpe	2620	4290
2 Dr Limited Cpe	2790	4570

OPTIONS FOR REGAL

6 cyl 3.8 L Engine +65
Gran Sport Pkg +165
Anti-Lock Brakes +105
Cruise Control +35
Leather Seats +95
Power Door Locks +40
Power Drivers Seat +45
Power Sunroof +115
Power Windows +50

RIVIERA 1990

Video Touch Screen killed in favor of conventional radio and climate controls. Driver airbag added this year. Anti-theft ignition system made standard. Seats redesigned, and 14-way power adjustment is available. Taillights are revised. Ergonomics improved with relocated switches for various accessories.

Category B

Model Description	Trade-in Value	Market Value
2 Dr STD Cpe	3750	5770

OPTIONS FOR RIVIERA

Aluminum/Alloy Wheels +55
Anti-Lock Brakes +120
Astro Roof +205

Don't forget to refer to the Mileage Adjustment Table at the back of this book!

© 1999 by Edmund Publications Corporation

Model Description	Trade-in Value	Market Value

Bose Sound System +125
Leather Seats +110
Power Passenger Seat +50

SKYLARK 1990

Base 2.5-liter engine gets more horsepower. Turn signal chime reminds driver when signal has been on for more than half a mile.

Category C		
2 Dr Custom Cpe	1985	3255
4 Dr Custom Sdn	2035	3335
2 Dr Gran Sport Cpe	2235	3660
4 Dr Luxury Sdn	2390	3920
2 Dr STD Cpe	1865	3055
4 Dr STD Sdn	1610	2640

OPTIONS FOR SKYLARK

4 cyl 2.3 L Quad 4 Engine +100
6 cyl 3.3 L Engine +100
Air Conditioning +130
Aluminum/Alloy Wheels[Opt on Custom] +50
Power Door Locks +40
Power Drivers Seat +45
Power Windows +50

1989 BUICK

CENTURY 1989

Styling freshened, and a stronger V6 engine is dropped into the engine bay. Century gets Dynaride suspension. Dual outside mirrors made standard. Rear shoulder belts installed.

RATINGS (SCALE OF 1-10)

Overall	Safety	Reliability	Performance	Comfort	Value
6.8	3.7	7	7.4	7.3	8.5

Category C		
2 Dr Custom Cpe	1605	2815
4 Dr Custom Sdn	1410	2475
4 Dr Custom Wgn	1315	2305
4 Dr Estate Wgn	1605	2820
4 Dr Limited Sdn	1755	3080

OPTIONS FOR CENTURY

6 cyl 3.3 L Engine +95
Cruise Control +30
Leather Seats +80
Power Door Locks +30
Power Drivers Seat +40
Power Windows +40
Wire Wheel Covers +30

ELECTRA 1989

Park Avenue Ultra debuts with leather, ABS, alloys and 20-way power seats. Passive restraints new for 1989, as is remote keyless entry, a 100-mph speedometer, and optional blue leather in Park Avenue.

Category A		
4 Dr Limited Sdn	2375	3775
4 Dr Park Ave Ultra Sdn	3085	4900
4 Dr Park Avenue Sdn	2585	4105
4 Dr T Type Sdn	2475	3930
Category B		
4 Dr Estate Wgn	1895	3160

OPTIONS FOR ELECTRA

Prestige Group +215
Aluminum/Alloy Wheels[Opt on Limited,Park Avenue] +45
Anti-Lock Brakes[Opt on Limited,Park Avenue] +125
Astro Roof +185
Bose Sound System +95
Leather Seats[Std on Park Ave Ultra] +90
Power Passenger Seat[Std on Park Ave Ultra] +40
Wire Wheel Covers +30

LE SABRE 1989

Tilt steering wheel and trip odometer added to the standard equipment list. A 100-mph speedometer is added. More fake wood trim is slathered onto interior surfaces. Limited gets standard storage console with armrest; item is optional on Custom.

Category B		
4 Dr Custom Sdn	2105	3510
4 Dr Estate Wgn	1780	2965
2 Dr Limited Cpe	2135	3555
4 Dr Limited Sdn	2275	3795
2 Dr STD Cpe	1995	3325
2 Dr T Type Cpe	2290	3815

OPTIONS FOR LE SABRE

Anti-Lock Brakes +95
Leather Seats +90
Power Door Locks +35
Power Drivers Seat +40
Power Passenger Seat +40
Power Windows +40
Premium Sound System[Std on T Type] +55
Wire Wheel Covers +30

REATTA 1989

Remote keyless entry made standard. Cloth upholstery dropped. Trunk and fuel door releases moved from dashboard to glovebox.

Category C		
2 Dr STD Cpe	3905	6855

OPTIONS FOR REATTA

Power Sunroof +95

Don't forget to refer to the Mileage Adjustment Table at the back of this book!

 © 1999 by Edmund Publications Corporation

Model Description	Trade-in Value	Market Value

REGAL 1989

New options include ABS, power sunroof, CD player, and remote keyless entry. Midyear, a 3.1-liter V6 replaced 2.8-liter V6. Added to standard features list are air conditioning, rear shoulder belts, stereo, and tilt steering wheel. Power windows get automatic-down feature for driver's side.

RATINGS (SCALE OF 1-10)

Overall	Safety	Reliability	Performance	Comfort	Value
6.4	4.6	5.5	8.2	7.3	6.5

Category C

Model Description	Trade-in Value	Market Value
2 Dr Custom Cpe	1760	3085
2 Dr Limited Cpe	2120	3715

OPTIONS FOR REGAL

6 cyl 2.8 L Engine +85
Aluminum/Alloy Wheels +40
Anti-Lock Brakes +85
Cruise Control +30
Leather Seats +80
Power Door Locks +30
Power Drivers Seat +40
Power Sunroof +95
Power Windows +40
Premium Sound System +55

RIVIERA 1989

Length is up 11 inches, thanks to extra sheetmetal added aft of the passenger compartment. New grille and extra chrome trim added. Whitewalls and wire wheel covers replace blackwalls and alloy wheels. T-Type model dropped. Fake wood installed inside. Remote keyless entry is a new option.

Category B

Model Description	Trade-in Value	Market Value
2 Dr STD Cpe	2720	4535

OPTIONS FOR RIVIERA

Anti-Lock Brakes +95
Astro Roof +170
Leather Seats +90
Power Passenger Seat +40
Premium Sound System +55

SKYHAWK 1989

Rear shoulder belts, Dynaride suspension, and added sound insulation are standard. Final year for lame econocar.

Category E

Model Description	Trade-in Value	Market Value
2 Dr STD Cpe	800	1820
4 Dr STD Sdn	895	2030
4 Dr STD Wgn	785	1790

OPTIONS FOR SKYHAWK

Auto 3-Speed Transmission +55
Air Conditioning +110
AM/FM Stereo Tape +40
Cruise Control +30
Power Door Locks +30

SKYLARK 1989

More powerful V6 engine debuts. Four-cylinder engine gets more horsepower. Front styling updated with composite headlamps. Front bench seat replaces buckets.

Category C

Model Description	Trade-in Value	Market Value
2 Dr Custom Cpe	1485	2600
4 Dr Custom Sdn	1455	2550
2 Dr Limited Cpe	1510	2645
4 Dr Limited Sdn	1640	2880
4 Dr SE Sdn	1510	2645

OPTIONS FOR SKYLARK

4 cyl 2.3 L Quad 4 Engine +90
6 cyl 3.3 L Engine +95
Luxury Package +135
Air Conditioning +110
Flip-Up Sunroof +50
Leather Seats +80
Power Door Locks +30
Power Drivers Seat +40
Power Windows +40

Instant
Lease & Loan Quotes
for New & Used Vehicles!
www.CarFinance.com/edmunds

Don't forget to refer to the Mileage Adjustment Table at the back of this book!

 © 1999 by Edmund Publications Corporation

CADILLAC USA

1997 Cadillac DeVille

1998 CADILLAC

CATERA 1998

New radios are available across the board, and a new option is a power rear sunshade. Low-powered airbags arrived during the middle of the model year.

Category A

Model Description	Trade-in Value	Market Value
4 Dr STD Sdn	22825	26850

OPTIONS FOR CATERA

Leather Package +2120
Bose Sound System +570
Chrome Wheels +930
Dual Power Seats +315
Heated Seats +290
Leather Seats +570
Power Moonroof +1190

DE VILLE 1998

StabiliTrak, an integrated chassis control system that corrects four-wheel lateral skids, is available on base and d'Elegance. New radio systems debut, and door lock programmability is enhanced. An idiot light is added to warn about loose fuel caps, and new colors are available inside and out. Heated seats are added to the d'Elegance and Concours while the Concours also gets a much-needed alloy wheel redesign. Second-generation airbags debut as standard equipment.

Category A

Model Description	Trade-in Value	Market Value
4 Dr Concours Sdn	27145	31935
4 Dr D'elegance Sdn	26800	31530
4 Dr STD Sdn	24015	28250

OPTIONS FOR DE VILLE

Chrome Wheels[Std on D'elegance] +930
Compact Disc W/fm/tape[Opt on STD] +585
Heated Front Seats[Opt on STD] +165
Leather Seats[Opt on STD] +570
Power Moonroof +1190
Special Factory Paint +250

ELDORADO 1998

New radios, a revised interior electrochromic mirror, enhanced programmable features, second-generation airbags and the addition of StabiliTrak to the base model's option list are the major improvements for 1998.

Category A

Model Description	Trade-in Value	Market Value
2 Dr STD Cpe	26565	31250
2 Dr Touring Cpe	28940	34045

OPTIONS FOR ELDORADO

Bose Sound System[Opt on STD] +570
Chrome Wheels +930
Compact Disc Changer +725
Heated Front Seats[Opt on STD] +165
Leather Seats[Opt on STD] +570
Power Moonroof +1190

SEVILLE 1998

Cadillac redefines the American luxury car by debuting an athletic sedan that boasts the performance, style, refinement and technological innovation necessary to play ball on a global level.

Category A

Model Description	Trade-in Value	Market Value
4 Dr SLS Sdn	31110	36600
4 Dr STS Sdn	34340	40400

OPTIONS FOR SEVILLE

Adaptive Seat Package +1000
Personalization Package +1080
Bose Sound System[Opt on SLS] +570
Chrome Wheels +930
Compact Disc Changer +725
Heated Seats +290
Power Moonroof +1190

1997 CADILLAC

CATERA 1997

Cadillac leaps into the near luxury segment of the market with a stylish, German-engineered sedan that features a 200-horsepower V6, an impressive load of standard equipment, and proper rear-wheel drive.

RATINGS (SCALE OF 1-10)

Overall	Safety	Reliability	Performance	Comfort	Value
N/A	N/A	9.3	8.6	8.6	N/A

Category A

Model Description	Trade-in Value	Market Value
4 Dr STD Sdn	19590	23050

OPTIONS FOR CATERA

Leather Package +1360
Bose Sound System +465

Don't forget to refer to the Mileage Adjustment Table at the back of this book!

 © 1999 by Edmund Publications Corporation

Model Description	Trade-in Value	Market Value

Chrome Wheels +760
Dual Power Seats +255
Heated Seats +240
Leather Seats +465
Power Moonroof +970

DE VILLE 1997

DeVille undergoes a substantial revamp for 1997, including revised styling, the addition of standard side-impact airbags, and a fresh interior that is actually functional. Concours receives stability enhancement and road texture detection as part of its Integrated Chassis Control System (ICCS), while a new D'elegance model picks up where the defunct Fleetwood left off. Finally, the OnStar Services package provides DeVille owners with security and convenience features that will pinpoint the car's location at any given time or allow you to book a flight to Paris from the comfort of your driver's seat.

RATINGS (SCALE OF 1-10)

Overall	Safety	Reliability	Performance	Comfort	Value
7.8	7.7	8.1	8.2	8.3	6.8

Category A		
4 Dr Concours Sdn	22540	26515
4 Dr D'elegance Sdn	21860	25720
4 Dr STD Sdn	20170	23730

OPTIONS FOR DE VILLE
Chrome Wheels[Std on D'elegance] +760
Compact Disc Changer +590
Compact Disc W/fm/tape +475
Heated Front Seats +135
Leather Seats[Opt on STD] +465
Power Moonroof +970

ELDORADO 1997

Structural, suspension, and brake system enhancements are made across the board. Base models get MagnaSteer variable effort steering, while the Eldorado Touring Coupe (ETC) receives a new Integrated Chassis Control System (ICCS) that includes stability enhancement and road texture detection. All Eldos have slightly revised stereo and climate controls, and the OnStar services package is a slick new option that can notify emergency personnel where your disabled car is located or can allow you to book dinner reservations from the driver's seat.

RATINGS (SCALE OF 1-10)

Overall	Safety	Reliability	Performance	Comfort	Value
7.4	7.7	7.6	8.6	7.6	5.7

Category A		
2 Dr STD Cpe	24000	28235
2 Dr Touring Cpe	25440	29925

OPTIONS FOR ELDORADO
Automatic Dimming Mirror +115
Bose Sound System +465
Chrome Wheels +760
Compact Disc Changer +590
Heated Front Seats +135
Leather Seats[Opt on STD] +465
Power Moonroof +970

SEVILLE 1997

All Sevilles receive body structure, suspension, brake system, and interior enhancements. STS models get a new stability enhancement feature designed to correct lateral skids, and road texture detection, which helps modulate the ABS more effectively on rough roads. Enhanced personalization programmable packages are new to both models, as is a revised rear seatback and the availability of OnStar, a vehicle information and communications service. SLS models get MagnaSteer variable-effort steering.

RATINGS (SCALE OF 1-10)

Overall	Safety	Reliability	Performance	Comfort	Value
7.6	7.4	8	8.4	8.1	6.2

Category A		
4 Dr SLS Sdn	25365	29840
4 Dr STS Sdn	27365	32195

OPTIONS FOR SEVILLE
Automatic Dimming Mirror +115
Bose Sound System +465
Chrome Wheels +760
Compact Disc Changer +590
Heated Front Seats +135
Leather Seats[Opt on SLS] +465
Power Moonroof +970

1996 CADILLAC

DE VILLE 1996

Northstar V8 is installed in base DeVille, along with a new transmission, Integrated Chassis Control System, and Road-Sensing Suspension. Concours gets 25 horsepower boost to 300, along with a higher final-drive ratio for quicker pickup and an improved continuously-variable Road-Sensing Suspension. Automatic windshield wipers and new variable-effort steering are standard on the Concours. Daytime running lights debut on both of these monsters.

RATINGS (SCALE OF 1-10)

Overall	Safety	Reliability	Performance	Comfort	Value
7.9	7.8	8.3	8.2	8.3	6.8

Don't forget to refer to the Mileage Adjustment Table at the back of this book!

 © 1999 by Edmund Publications Corporation

Model Description	Trade-in Value	Market Value
Category A		
4 Dr Concours Sdn	18480	22815
4 Dr STD Sdn	16550	20430

OPTIONS FOR DE VILLE
Chrome Wheels +620
Compact Disc Changer +485
Heated Front Seats +110
Leather Seats[Opt on STD] +380
Power Moonroof +795

ELDORADO 1996

Sea Mist Green is a new interior and exterior color, and daytime running lights are standard. Eldorado gets new seats and revised audio systems. Touring Coupe interior is revised, with a center-stack console, bigger gauges, and seamless passenger airbag. Rainsense, an automatic windshield wiper system, is standard on the ETC, as is an updated continuously-variable Road-Sensing Suspension.

RATINGS (SCALE OF 1-10)

Overall	Safety	Reliability	Performance	Comfort	Value
7.5	7.8	7.8	8.6	7.6	5.6

Model Description	Trade-in Value	Market Value
Category A		
2 Dr STD Cpe	19220	23730
2 Dr Touring Cpe	20385	25170

OPTIONS FOR ELDORADO
Bose Sound System +380
Chrome Wheels +620
Compact Disc Changer +485
Heated Front Seats +110
Leather Seats[Opt on STD] +380
Power Moonroof +795

FLEETWOOD 1996

Final year for the longest production car sold in the U.S. Updates are limited to a new audio system, revised center storage armrest, and pre-wiring for Cadillac's Dual Mode cellular phone.

RATINGS (SCALE OF 1-10)

Overall	Safety	Reliability	Performance	Comfort	Value
N/A	N/A	7.3	7.6	8.1	6.7

Model Description	Trade-in Value	Market Value
Category A		
4 Dr STD Sdn	18495	22835

OPTIONS FOR FLEETWOOD
Camper/Towing Package +220
Chrome Wheels +620
Compact Disc W/fm/tape +390
Heated Seats +195
Leather Seats +380
Power Moonroof +795

SEVILLE 1996

All Sevilles get new seats and seat trim, redesigned sound systems, an integrated voice-activated cellular phone, daytime running lights, and programmable door lock functions and seating positions. The STS also receives an updated instrument panel with big gauges and a new center console, the Cadillac-exclusive Rainsense Wiper System (which detects rainfall and turns the wipers on automatically) and a newly improved continuously-variable Road-Sensing Suspension. Magnasteer variable-assist steering replaces the old speed-sensitive gear on last year's STS.

RATINGS (SCALE OF 1-10)

Overall	Safety	Reliability	Performance	Comfort	Value
7.7	7.5	8.1	8.4	8.1	6.1

Model Description	Trade-in Value	Market Value
Category A		
4 Dr SLS Sdn	19705	24325
4 Dr STS Sdn	21045	25985

OPTIONS FOR SEVILLE
Bose Sound System +380
Chrome Wheels +620
Compact Disc Changer +485
Heated Front Seats +110
Leather Seats[Opt on SLS] +380
Power Moonroof +795

1995 CADILLAC

DE VILLE 1995

Traction control is standard on base DeVille. Traction control can now be defeated via a dash-mounted switch. Headlights come on automatically when windshield wipers are activated. Chrome wheels can be ordered on Concours. Garage door opener is optional on DeVille; standard on Concours.

RATINGS (SCALE OF 1-10)

Overall	Safety	Reliability	Performance	Comfort	Value
8.1	8.6	8.2	8.2	8.3	7.2

Model Description	Trade-in Value	Market Value
Category A		
4 Dr Concours Sdn	15515	19395
4 Dr STD Sdn	13730	17165

OPTIONS FOR DE VILLE
Chrome Wheels +510
Compact Disc W/fm/tape +320
Heated Front Seats +90
Leather Seats[Opt on STD] +310
Power Moonroof +650

Don't forget to refer to the Mileage Adjustment Table at the back of this book!

 © 1999 by Edmund Publications Corporation

Model Description	Trade-in Value	Market Value

ELDORADO 1995

Northstar V8 power is increased. Electronic chassis controls now evaluate steering angle when deciding what to do with the Road Sensing Suspension, traction control, and ABS. Styling is slightly revised front and rear. Headlights come on automatically when windshield wipers are activated.

RATINGS (SCALE OF 1-10)

Overall	Safety	Reliability	Performance	Comfort	Value
7.7	8.6	7.9	8.6	7.6	5.7

Category A		
2 Dr STD Cpe	16105	20130
2 Dr Touring Cpe	17090	21360

OPTIONS FOR ELDORADO

Chrome Wheels +510
Compact Disc W/fm/tape +320
Heated Front Seats +90
Leather Seats[Opt on STD] +310
Power Moonroof +650

FLEETWOOD 1995

Traction control gets on/off switch. Platinum-tipped spark plugs are added, allowing tune-ups to occur every 100,000 miles. Antilockout feature added. Remote keyless entry, central unlocking, and fold-away outside mirrors are added. Garage door opener is new option.

RATINGS (SCALE OF 1-10)

Overall	Safety	Reliability	Performance	Comfort	Value
N/A	N/A	7.2	7.6	8.1	6.6

Category A		
4 Dr STD Sdn	14750	18440

OPTIONS FOR FLEETWOOD

Camper/Towing Package +180
Chrome Wheels +510
Compact Disc W/fm/tape +320
Heated Front Seats +90
Leather Seats +310
Power Moonroof +650

SEVILLE 1995

Northstar V8 power is increased. Electronic chassis controls now evaluate steering angle when deciding what to do with the Road Sensing Suspension, traction control, and ABS. Headlights come on automatically when windshield wipers are activated. Chrome wheels are new option.

RATINGS (SCALE OF 1-10)

Overall	Safety	Reliability	Performance	Comfort	Value
7.7	8.6	8	8.4	8.1	5.6

Category A		
4 Dr SLS Sdn	16250	20315
4 Dr STS Sdn	17540	21920

OPTIONS FOR SEVILLE

Chrome Wheels +510
Compact Disc W/fm/tape +320
Heated Front Seats +90
Leather Seats[Opt on SLS] +310
Power Moonroof +650

1994 CADILLAC

DE VILLE 1994

Redesigned with dual airbags, height-adjustable seat belts, and side-impact protection meeting 1997 standards. Base and Concours models available, with Concours replacing Touring Sedan. Concours comes with Northstar V8 and Road Sensing Suspension. Coupe DeVille and Sixty Special are retired. Base DeVille powered by 1993's 4.9-liter V8. Remote keyless entry is standard.

RATINGS (SCALE OF 1-10)

Overall	Safety	Reliability	Performance	Comfort	Value
N/A	N/A	8	8.2	8.3	8.1

Category A		
4 Dr Concours Sdn	12630	16190
4 Dr STD Sdn	11090	14215

OPTIONS FOR DE VILLE

AM/FM Compact Disc Playr +195
Astro Roof +510
Chrome Wheels +415
Heated Front Seats +75
Leather Seats[Opt on STD] +255
Traction Control System[Opt on STD] +80

ELDORADO 1994

Base model gets Northstar V8, Road Sensing Suspension, and traction control. Remote keyless entry and automatic door locks are made standard.

RATINGS (SCALE OF 1-10)

Overall	Safety	Reliability	Performance	Comfort	Value
7.7	8.6	7.9	8.6	7.6	5.6

Category A		
2 Dr STD Cpe	12785	16395
2 Dr Touring Cpe	13570	17395

OPTIONS FOR ELDORADO

Astro Roof +510
Chrome Wheels +415
Compact Disc W/fm/tape +260
Heated Front Seats +75
Leather Seats[Opt on STD] +255

Don't forget to refer to the Mileage Adjustment Table at the back of this book!

© 1999 by Edmund Publications Corporation

Model Description	Trade-in Value	Market Value

FLEETWOOD 1994

Detuned Corvette 5.7-liter engine makes its way under Fleetwood's gargantuan hood. Performance is much improved. New transmission comes with new engine. Brougham package includes padded vinyl roof and alloy wheels. Flash-to-pass is a new feature, and a battery saver is installed.

RATINGS (SCALE OF 1-10)

Overall	Safety	Reliability	Performance	Comfort	Value
N/A	N/A	7.4	7.6	8.1	7.1

Category A

Model Description	Trade-in Value	Market Value
4 Dr STD Sdn	11485	14725

OPTIONS FOR FLEETWOOD

Cloth Brougham Package +470
Leather Brougham Package +520
Astro Roof +510
Camper/Towing Package +145
Chrome Wheels +415
Compact Disc W/fm/tape +260
Heated Front Seats +75
Leather Seats +255

SEVILLE 1994

Base model now called SLS. SLS gets Northstar V8, traction control, and Road Sensing Suspension. Remote keyless entry is standard this year.

RATINGS (SCALE OF 1-10)

Overall	Safety	Reliability	Performance	Comfort	Value
7.8	8.6	7.8	8.4	8.1	6

Category A

Model Description	Trade-in Value	Market Value
4 Dr STD Sdn	13605	17440
4 Dr STS Sdn	13805	17695

OPTIONS FOR SEVILLE

Astro Roof +510
Chrome Wheels +415
Compact Disc W/fm/tape +260
Heated Front Seats +75
Leather Seats[Opt on STD] +255
Power Drivers Seat +90

1993 CADILLAC

60 SPECIAL 1993

Speed-sensitive steering debuts. Speed Sensitive Suspension is standard on all models. Grille is revised.

Category A

Model Description	Trade-in Value	Market Value
4 Dr STD Sdn	9020	12030

OPTIONS FOR 60 SPECIAL

Ultra Seating Pkg. +715
AM/FM Compact Disc Playr +160
Astro Roof +415
Chrome Wheels +340
Climate Control for AC +45
Heated Front Seats +60
Keyless Entry System +75
Leather Seats +210
Power Passenger Seat +90

ALLANTE 1993

Final year for ill-fated convertible, and this is the year to buy. Why? Only Allante with Northstar V8 engine. Along with the superb engine, Allante gets a new transmission, new traction control system, and a Road Sensing Suspension. Rear suspension is redesigned, and tires are rated to 155 mph. Audio system is revised, dual cupholders are added, alloy wheels are restyled, and seats are all-new. Buy one. Store it.

Category J

Model Description	Trade-in Value	Market Value
2 Dr STD Conv	22140	28025

OPTIONS FOR ALLANTE

Special Factory Paint +530

DE VILLE 1993

Fleetwood tag moved to big new rear drive sedan. Speed-sensitive steering debuts. Speed Sensitive Suspension is standard on all models. Grille is revised. Special Edition option packages include really cool stuff like gold trim and Phaeton roof.

RATINGS (SCALE OF 1-10)

Overall	Safety	Reliability	Performance	Comfort	Value
N/A	N/A	7.6	8	8	7.5

Category A

Model Description	Trade-in Value	Market Value
2 Dr STD Cpe	8730	11635
4 Dr STD Sdn	8295	11060
4 Dr Touring Sdn	9230	12305

OPTIONS FOR DE VILLE

AM/FM Compact Disc Playr +160
Astro Roof +415
Chrome Wheels +340
Leather Seats[Opt on STD] +210
Premium Sound System +135
Traction Control System +65

ELDORADO 1993

Touring Coupe gets stellar Northstar V8, Road Sensing Suspension, and traction control. Passenger airbag debuts. Rear suspension redesigned. Speed-sensitive steering made standard. Base Eldo gets Speed Sensitive Suspension standard. Sport Performance package is a blend of base model and TC with detuned Northstar. Sport Appearance package gives look of Sport Performance package with 4.9-liter V8 from base coupe. Got that?

Don't forget to refer to the Mileage Adjustment Table at the back of this book!

 © 1999 by Edmund Publications Corporation

Model Description	Trade-in Value	Market Value

RATINGS (SCALE OF 1-10)

Overall	Safety	Reliability	Performance	Comfort	Value
7.5	8.5	7.3	8.6	7.6	5.5

Category A

2 Dr STD Cpe	10390	13855
2 Dr Touring Cpe	10545	14065

OPTIONS FOR ELDORADO

8 cyl 4.6 L Engine +645
Sport Appear. Pkg. +265
Astro Roof +415
Automatic Dimming Mirror +50
Chrome Wheels +340
Compact Disc W/fm/tape +215
Heated Front Seats +60
Leather Seats +210
Traction Control System +65

FLEETWOOD 1993

Dual airbags and rounded styling characterize this Brougham replacement, which is based on stretched Chevy Caprice chassis. Length is up 4.1 inches. Yowza! Traction control and ABS are standard. Optional trailer tow group gives car a 7,000 lb. towing capacity. Goofy digital dashboard standard.

RATINGS (SCALE OF 1-10)

Overall	Safety	Reliability	Performance	Comfort	Value
N/A	N/A	6.8	7.2	8.1	7.9

Category A

4 Dr STD Sdn	9405	12540

OPTIONS FOR FLEETWOOD

AM/FM Compact Disc Playr +160
Astro Roof +415
Automatic Dimming Mirror +50
Heated Front Seats +60
Leather Seats +210

SEVILLE 1993

STS gets Northstar V8, Road Sensing Suspension, and traction control. Passenger airbag added to all Sevilles. Base Seville gets Speed Sensitive Suspension. Bigger fuel tank is added, rear suspension is redesigned, and a cupholder is added to center console. ABS and speed-sensitive steering standard on all Sevilles.

RATINGS (SCALE OF 1-10)

Overall	Safety	Reliability	Performance	Comfort	Value
7.6	8.5	7.2	8.4	8.1	5.8

Category A

4 Dr STD Sdn	9950	13270
4 Dr STS Sdn	10990	14650

OPTIONS FOR SEVILLE

AM/FM Compact Disc Playr +160
Astro Roof +415
Bose Sound System +210
Chrome Wheels +340
Heated Front Seats +60
Keyless Entry System[Opt on STD] +75
Leather Seats[Opt on STD] +210

1992 CADILLAC

ALLANTE 1992

No changes.

Category J

2 Dr STD Conv	14915	19120

OPTIONS FOR ALLANTE

Hardtop Roof +700
Special Factory Paint +435

BROUGHAM 1992

5.7-liter V8 escapes gas-guzzler tax. Towing capacity increased 2,000 lbs. Final edition.

Category A

4 Dr STD Sdn	7140	9915

OPTIONS FOR BROUGHAM

8 cyl 5.7 L Engine +60
D'elegance Package +380
Astro Roof +340
Automatic Dimming Mirror +40
Leather Seats +170
Wire Wheels +205

DE VILLE 1992

Traction control optional on base DeVille; standard on all others. Platinum-tipped spark plugs mean tune-ups happen every 100,000 miles. Power passenger seat made standard on DeVille. Electrochromic rearview mirror made standard on all models.

RATINGS (SCALE OF 1-10)

Overall	Safety	Reliability	Performance	Comfort	Value
N/A	N/A	7.5	8	8	7.4

Category A

2 Dr STD Cpe	6640	9220
4 Dr STD Sdn	6400	8890
4 Dr Touring Sdn	6885	9560

OPTIONS FOR DE VILLE

Phaeton Roof +265
AM/FM Compact Disc Playr +130
Astro Roof +340
Bose Sound System +170
Leather Seats[Opt on STD] +170

Don't forget to refer to the Mileage Adjustment Table at the back of this book!

 © 1999 by Edmund Publications Corporation

Model Description	Trade-in Value	Market Value

ELDORADO 1992

Complete makeover results in distinctly European-flavored coupe. Powertrains are carried over from 1991. ABS and driver airbag are standard. Sport interior option includes analog gauges rather than digital gauges.

RATINGS (SCALE OF 1-10)

Overall	Safety	Reliability	Performance	Comfort	Value
7.3	7.6	7.3	8.2	7.6	5.9

Category A

Model Description	Trade-in Value	Market Value
2 Dr STD Cpe	7920	11000

OPTIONS FOR ELDORADO

Stars & Stripes Package +215
Touring Pkg +690
Astro Roof +340
Automatic Dimming Mirror +40
Compact Disc W/fm/tape +175
Heated Front Seats +50
Leather Seats +170

FLEETWOOD 1992

Traction control standard. Platinum-tipped spark plugs mean tune-ups happen every 100,000 miles. Electrochromatic rearview mirror made standard on all models.

Category A

Model Description	Trade-in Value	Market Value
4 Dr Sixty Special Sdn	8185	11365
2 Dr STD Cpe	6985	9700
4 Dr STD Sdn	6970	9685

OPTIONS FOR FLEETWOOD

AM/FM Compact Disc Playr +130
Astro Roof +340
Bose Sound System +170
Leather Seats[Opt on STD] +170
Wire Wheel Covers +75

SEVILLE 1992

Complete makeover results in distinctly European-flavored sedan. Powertrains are carried over from 1991. ABS and driver airbag are standard. Sport interior option includes analog gauges rather than digital gauges. Leather upholstery and analog gauges are standard on STS.

RATINGS (SCALE OF 1-10)

Overall	Safety	Reliability	Performance	Comfort	Value
7.6	7.6	7.3	8.2	8.1	6.8

Category A

Model Description	Trade-in Value	Market Value
4 Dr STD Sdn	7520	10445
4 Dr STS Sdn	8340	11580

OPTIONS FOR SEVILLE

Phaeton Roof +265
AM/FM Compact Disc Playr +130
Astro Roof +340
Automatic Dimming Mirror +40
Heated Front Seats +50
Keyless Entry System[Opt on STD] +60
Leather Seats[Opt on STD] +170

1991 CADILLAC

ALLANTE 1991

Traction control debuts. Power latching mechanism added to manual top.

Category J

Model Description	Trade-in Value	Market Value
2 Dr STD Conv	12600	16360

OPTIONS FOR ALLANTE

Hardtop Roof +570
Special Factory Paint +355

BROUGHAM 1991

Standard and optional engines gain more power. Optional 5.7-liter motor slapped with gas-guzzler tax for city rating of 15 mpg.

Category A

Model Description	Trade-in Value	Market Value
4 Dr STD Sdn	5640	8055

OPTIONS FOR BROUGHAM

8 cyl 5.7 L Engine +50
D'elegance Package +360
Astro Roof +275
Leather Seats +140
Wire Wheels +165

DE VILLE 1991

Engine upgraded to 200-horsepower 4.9-liter V8 from 180-horsepower 4.5-liter V8. DeVille Touring Sedan debuted late in model year, with monotone exterior paint, performance tires, quicker-ratio steering, and thicker stabilizer bars.

RATINGS (SCALE OF 1-10)

Overall	Safety	Reliability	Performance	Comfort	Value
N/A	N/A	7.5	8	8	7.9

Category A

Model Description	Trade-in Value	Market Value
2 Dr STD Cpe	5595	7990
4 Dr STD Sdn	5485	7835
4 Dr Touring Sdn	6150	8790

OPTIONS FOR DE VILLE

Phaeton Roof +220
AM/FM Compact Disc Playr +105
Astro Roof +275
Bose Sound System +140
Leather Seats[Opt on STD] +140
Power Passenger Seat[Opt on STD] +60

Don't forget to refer to the Mileage Adjustment Table at the back of this book!

 © 1999 by Edmund Publications Corporation

Model Description	Trade-in Value	Market Value

ELDORADO 1991

Engine upgraded to 200-horsepower 4.9-liter V8 from 180-horsepower 4.5-liter V8. Transmission modified to generate better acceleration. Touring Coupe debuts, featuring Seville STS styling and suspension modifications.

Category A

2 Dr Biarritz Cpe	6295	8995
2 Dr STD Cpe	5955	8505

OPTIONS FOR ELDORADO

Touring Coupe Pkg +315
AM/FM Compact Disc Playr +105
Astro Roof +275
Bose Sound System +140
Leather Seats[Opt on STD] +140
Wire Wheel Covers[Opt on STD] +60

FLEETWOOD 1991

Engine upgraded to 200-horsepower 4.9-liter V8 from 180-horsepower 4.5-liter V8.

Category A

4 Dr Sixty Special Sdn	6365	9090
2 Dr STD Cpe	5695	8135
4 Dr STD Sdn	5920	8460

OPTIONS FOR FLEETWOOD

AM/FM Compact Disc Playr +105
Astro Roof +275
Bose Sound System +140
Leather Seats[Opt on STD] +140
Wire Wheel Covers +60

SEVILLE 1991

Engine upgraded to 200-horsepower 4.9-liter V8 from 180-horsepower 4.5-liter V8. Transmission modified to generate better acceleration.

Category A

4 Dr STD Sdn	5400	7715
4 Dr STS Sdn	6160	8805

OPTIONS FOR SEVILLE

Phaeton Roof +240
AM/FM Compact Disc Playr +105
Astro Roof +275
Bose Sound System +140
Leather Seats[Opt on STD] +140

1990 CADILLAC

ALLANTE 1990

CD player is standard, as is Natural Beige interior color.

Category J

2 Dr STD Conv	10635	13995

OPTIONS FOR ALLANTE

Hardtop Roof +465

BROUGHAM 1990

5.7-liter engine is optional, but only when ordered with trailer towing or Coachbuilder packages. ABS is standard. Composite headlights and new front bumper update Brougham's dated styling. Can't forget to mention the new standard padded vinyl roof, can we? Rear styling is updated as well.

Category A

4 Dr D'elegance Sdn	4430	6610
4 Dr STD Sdn	4255	6355

OPTIONS FOR BROUGHAM

8 cyl 5.7 L Engine +40
Astro Roof +225
Leather Seats +115
Power Passenger Seat[Opt on STD] +50
Premium Sound System +75
Wire Wheels +135

DE VILLE 1990

More powerful 4.5-liter V8 debuts. Driver airbag is made standard. Anti-theft ignition lock is standard.

RATINGS (SCALE OF 1-10)

Overall	Safety	Reliability	Performance	Comfort	Value
N/A	N/A	7.7	8	8	6.4

Category A

2 Dr STD Cpe	4415	6590
4 Dr STD Sdn	4165	6220

OPTIONS FOR DE VILLE

DeVille Spring Edition +340
Aluminum/Alloy Wheels +70
Anti-Lock Brakes +155
Astro Roof +225
Leather Seats +115
Power Passenger Seat +50
Premium Sound System +75

ELDORADO 1990

Stronger 4.5-liter V8 installed under the hood. Suspension is upgraded. Onboard computer added. Driver airbag is standard. Rear defogger, heated outside mirrors, and illuminated entry system made standard. Styling is tweaked.

Category A

2 Dr Biarritz Cpe	4650	6940
2 Dr STD Cpe	4395	6565

OPTIONS FOR ELDORADO

AM/FM Compact Disc Playr +85
Anti-Lock Brakes +155
Astro Roof +225

Don't forget to refer to the Mileage Adjustment Table at the back of this book!

 © 1999 by Edmund Publications Corporation

Model Description	Trade-in Value	Market Value

Leather Seats[Opt on STD] +115
Premium Sound System +75
Wire Wheel Covers[Opt on STD] +50

FLEETWOOD 1990

More powerful 4.5-liter V8 debuts. Driver airbag is made standard. Anti-theft ignition lock is standard.

Category A

4 Dr Sixty Special Sdn	4865	7260
2 Dr STD Cpe	5165	7710
4 Dr STD Sdn	4790	7145

OPTIONS FOR FLEETWOOD
AM/FM Compact Disc Playr +85
Astro Roof +225
Leather Seats[Opt on STD] +115
Premium Sound System +75
Wire Wheel Covers +50

SEVILLE 1990

Stronger 4.5-liter V8 installed under the hood. Suspension is upgraded. Onboard computer added. Driver airbag is standard. Rear defogger, heated outside mirrors, and illuminated entry system made standard. Styling is tweaked. STS gets dual exhaust system and firmer suspension.

Category A

4 Dr STD Sdn	4390	6555
4 Dr STS Sdn	4895	7310

OPTIONS FOR SEVILLE
Phaeton Roof +200
Anti-Lock Brakes[Opt on STD] +155
Astro Roof +225
Leather Seats[Opt on STD] +115
Premium Sound System +75

1989 CADILLAC

ALLANTE 1989

A 4.5-liter V8 replaces the original 4.1-liter unit. Variable-assist steering is added, along with automatically adjusting shock absorbers and bigger tires. The folding top has been redesigned; can be raised or lowered in 20 seconds. EPA gives Allante a 15 mpg rating in the city. Charcoal interior color is new, and a theft-deterrent system is standard.

Category J

2 Dr STD Conv	9135	12175

BROUGHAM 1989

Cruise control, intermittent wipers and remote trunk release are made standard. Grille is revised.

Category A

4 Dr D'elegance Sdn	3480	5520
4 Dr STD Sdn	3360	5330

OPTIONS FOR BROUGHAM
Formal Vinyl Roof +150
Astro Roof +185
Leather Seats +95
Power Passenger Seat[Opt on STD] +40
Wire Wheels +110

DE VILLE 1989

Restyled and made bigger to attract traditional Caddy buyers. Sedan grows 8.8 inches; coupe is 5.8 inches longer. Extra wheelbase gives sedan cavernous rear seat. Trunk capacity is up, too. ABS is optional on DeVille. Driver airbag is a new option.

RATINGS (SCALE OF 1-10)

Overall	Safety	Reliability	Performance	Comfort	Value
N/A	N/A	7.6	8	8	7.4

Category A

2 Dr STD Cpe	3125	4960
4 Dr STD Sdn	3220	5110

OPTIONS FOR DE VILLE
Aluminum/Alloy Wheels +55
Anti-Lock Brakes +125
Astro Roof +185
Leather Seats +95
Power Passenger Seat +40
Premium Sound System +60

ELDORADO 1989

Power front seats, express-down power driver's window, cassette player, and theft-deterrent system are all made standard. Maple interior trim comes with Biarritz package.

Category A

2 Dr Biarritz Cpe	3825	6075
2 Dr STD Cpe	3485	5530

OPTIONS FOR ELDORADO
AM/FM Compact Disc Playr +70
Anti-Lock Brakes +125
Astro Roof +185
Leather Seats +95
Power Passenger Seat[Opt on STD] +40
Premium Sound System +60
Wire Wheel Covers +40

FLEETWOOD 1989

Restyled and made bigger to attract traditional Caddy buyers. Sedan grows 8.8 inches; coupe is 5.8 inches longer. Extra wheelbase gives sedan cavernous rear seat. Trunk capacity is up, too. Fleetwood Coupe returns after two-year hiatus. Sixty Special gets Giugiaro-styled leather seats. ABS is standard. Driver airbag is a new option.

Don't forget to refer to the Mileage Adjustment Table at the back of this book!

 © 1999 by Edmund Publications Corporation

CADILLAC 89

Model Description	Trade-in Value	Market Value
Category A		
4 Dr Sixty Special Sdn	3715	5895
2 Dr STD Cpe	3750	5955
4 Dr STD Sdn	3505	5565

OPTIONS FOR FLEETWOOD

Astro Roof +185
Leather Seats[Opt on STD] +95
Power Passenger Seat[Opt on STD Sdn] +40
Premium Sound System +60

SEVILLE 1989

STS is made a regular production model after a brief run in 1988. 3,000 examples produced. Power front seats, express-down power driver's window, cassette player, theft-deterrent system, and maple interior trim all made standard.

Model Description	Trade-in Value	Market Value
Category A		
4 Dr STD Sdn	3315	5265
4 Dr STS Sdn	3765	5980

OPTIONS FOR SEVILLE

Phaeton Roof +150
AM/FM Compact Disc Playr +70
Anti-Lock Brakes[Opt on STD] +125
Astro Roof +185
Leather Seats[Opt on STD] +95
Premium Sound System +60

CAR FINANCE DOT COM
Instant
Lease & Loan Quotes
for New & Used Vehicles!
www.CarFinance.com/edmunds

A 15-minute phone call
could save you 15% or more
on car insurance.

1-800-555-2758

GEICO DIRECT

The Sensible Alternative

Don't forget to refer to the Mileage Adjustment Table at the back of this book!

© 1999 by Edmund Publications Corporation

CHEVROLET USA

1995 Chevrolet Suburban

1998 CHEVROLET

ASTRO 1998

New colors, improved clearcoating, a standard theft deterrent system (like anybody wants to steal one of these) and the addition of composite headlights and an uplevel grille to base models are all that's different on this year's Astro. Full-power airbags continue for 1998.

Category G		
2 Dr LS Pass. Van Ext	14645	17430
2 Dr LS 4WD Pass. Van Ext	16395	19515
2 Dr LT Pass. Van Ext	16135	19210
2 Dr LT 4WD Pass. Van Ext	17795	21180
2 Dr STD Cargo Van Ext	13675	16280
2 Dr STD Pass. Van Ext	13705	16320
2 Dr STD 4WD Pass. Van Ext	15350	18275
2 Dr STD 4WD Cargo Van Ext	15265	18170

OPTIONS FOR ASTRO

Aluminum/Alloy Wheels[Std on LT] +285
AM/FM Compact Disc Playr +320
Cruise Control[Opt on STD] +175
Dual Air Conditioning +840
Dual Power Seats +525
Keyless Entry System[Std on LT] +170
Leather Seats +640
Power Door Locks[Opt on STD] +190
Power Drivers Seat[Std on LT] +235
Power Mirrors[Opt on STD] +110
Power Windows[Opt on STD] +195
Rear Heater +170
Rear Window Defroster[Std on LT] +140
Tilt Steering Wheel[Opt on STD] +140

BLAZER 1998

Blazer gets a nose job and an interior redesign. New standard equipment includes a theft deterrent system, automatic headlight control, four-wheel disc brakes and dual airbags incorporating second-generation technology to reduce the bags' inflation force. New radios, colors, and a column-mounted automatic shift selector round out the major changes.

Category G		
2 Dr LS Utility	15645	18625
2 Dr LS 4WD Utility	16610	19775
4 Dr LS Wgn	17830	21230
4 Dr LS 4WD Wgn	18515	22040
4 Dr LT Wgn	19055	22685
4 Dr LT 4WD Wgn	19545	23265
2 Dr STD Utility	14105	16790
2 Dr STD 4WD Utility	14770	17585
4 Dr STD Wgn	16135	19210
4 Dr STD 4WD Wgn	16805	20005

OPTIONS FOR BLAZER

Auto 4-Speed Transmission[Opt on Utility] +740
Wide Stance Suspension +1420
Aluminum/Alloy Wheels[Opt on STD] +285
AM/FM Compact Disc Playr +320
Cruise Control[Opt on STD] +175
Fog Lights[Opt on LS] +120
Heated Front Seats +210
Keyless Entry System[Opt on LS] +170
Power Door Locks[Opt on STD] +190
Power Drivers Seat[Opt on LS] +235
Power Mirrors +110
Power Sunroof +670
Power Windows[Opt on STD] +195
Rear Window Defroster[Opt on STD] +140
Rear Window Wiper[Opt on STD] +125
Sport Suspension +400
Tilt Steering Wheel[Opt on STD] +140

C/K PICKUP 1998

This year's big news is a standard theft deterrent system, revised color choices, and fresh tailgate lettering. The Sport package has been dropped from the option list. Second generation airbags are standard on models under 8,600 GVWR.

C1500

Category H		
2 Dr Cheyenne Ext Cab SB	14130	16625
2 Dr Cheyenne Std Cab SB	13705	16125
2 Dr Cheyenne Std Cab Stepside SB	14245	16755
2 Dr Cheyenne Std Cab LB	13990	16460
2 Dr Cheyenne Ext Cab LB	14750	17355

Don't forget to refer to the Mileage Adjustment Table at the back of this book!

 © 1999 by Edmund Publications Corporation

CHEVROLET 98

Model Description	Trade-in Value	Market Value
2 Dr Silverado Ext Cab SB	16130	18975
2 Dr Silverado Std Cab SB	15590	18340
2 Dr Silverado Std Cab Stepside SB	16130	18975
2 Dr Silverado Ext Cab Stepside SB	16730	19685
2 Dr Silverado Ext Cab LB	15895	18700
2 Dr Silverado Std Cab LB	15875	18680
2 Dr WT Std Cab SB	12585	14805
2 Dr WT Std Cab LB	12900	15175

C2500

Category H

Model Description	Trade-in Value	Market Value
2 Dr Cheyenne Ext Cab SB	13930	16385
2 Dr Cheyenne Std Cab LB	13655	16065
2 Dr Silverado Ext Cab SB	18120	21320
2 Dr Silverado Std Cab LB	16835	19805

C3500

Category H

Model Description	Trade-in Value	Market Value
2 Dr Cheyenne Std Cab LB	16480	19385
2 Dr Cheyenne Ext Cab LB	17320	20375
4 Dr Cheyenne Crew Cab LB	18260	21485
2 Dr Silverado Ext Cab LB	19245	22640
2 Dr Silverado Std Cab LB	17610	20715
4 Dr Silverado Crew Cab LB	20605	24240

K1500

Category H

Model Description	Trade-in Value	Market Value
2 Dr Cheyenne 4WD Std Cab SB	15620	18375
2 Dr Cheyenne 4WD Ext Cab SB	16110	18950
2 Dr Cheyenne 4WD Std Cab Stepside SB	15990	18810
2 Dr Cheyenne 4WD Ext Cab LB	16220	19080
2 Dr Cheyenne 4WD Std Cab LB	15510	18245
2 Dr Silverado 4WD Std Cab SB	17685	20805
2 Dr Silverado 4WD Ext Cab SB	17745	20875
2 Dr Silverado 4WD Ext Cab Stepside SB	19190	22575
2 Dr Silverado 4WD Std Cab Stepside SB	18165	21370
2 Dr Silverado 4WD Std Cab LB	17925	21090
2 Dr Silverado 4WD Ext Cab LB	18360	21600
2 Dr WT 4WD Std Cab SB	15255	17945
2 Dr WT 4WD Std Cab LB	15510	18245

K2500 HD

Category H

Model Description	Trade-in Value	Market Value
2 Dr Cheyenne 4WD Ext Cab SB	16880	19860
2 Dr Cheyenne 4WD Std Cab LB	15275	17970
2 Dr Cheyenne 4WD Ext Cab LB	16975	19970
2 Dr Silverado 4WD Ext Cab SB	17935	21100
2 Dr Silverado 4WD Std Cab LB	17720	20850
2 Dr Silverado 4WD Ext Cab LB	18025	21205

K3500

Category H

Model Description	Trade-in Value	Market Value
2 Dr Cheyenne 4WD Std Cab LB	16855	19830
2 Dr Cheyenne 4WD Ext Cab LB	17550	20650
4 Dr Cheyenne 4WD Crew Cab LB	18140	21340
2 Dr Silverado 4WD Std Cab LB	18350	21590
2 Dr Silverado 4WD Ext Cab LB	19655	23125
4 Dr Silverado 4WD Crew Cab LB	20585	24220

OPTIONS FOR C/K PICKUP

8 cyl 5.0 L Engine[Std on C1500 Silverado Ext. Cab, C2500, K1500] +410
8 cyl 5.7 L Engine[Opt on C1500, C2500, K1500, K2500 LD] +830
8 cyl 7.4 L Engine +500
8 cyl 6.5 L Turbodsl Engine +2495
Auto 4-Speed Transmission +805
Air Conditioning[Std on Silverado] +670
Aluminum/Alloy Wheels +260
AM/FM Compact Disc Playr +245
Bed Liner +185
Camper/Towing Package +295
Cruise Control[Std on Silverado] +160
Dual Rear Wheels +700
Hinged Third Door (PU) +350
Keyless Entry System +125
Leather Seats +860
Power Door Locks[Opt on Cheyenne] +155
Power Drivers Seat +225
Rear Window Defroster +125
Skid Plates +90
Sliding Rear Window +95
Tilt Steering Wheel[Std on Silverado] +150

CAMARO 1998

Chevrolet dumps a 305-hp version of the Corvette's V8 engine under a new front end, adds standard four-wheel disc brakes on all models, adds a couple of new colors, makes second generation airbags standard, and revises trim levels. The mid-year SS package makes 320 horsepower. Uh, why were you considering that Mustang again?

Category F

Model Description	Trade-in Value	Market Value
2 Dr STD Cpe	12385	15105
2 Dr STD Conv	15985	19490
2 Dr Z28 Cpe	14050	17135
2 Dr Z28 Conv	18910	23060
2 Dr Z28 SS Cpe	16930	20645
2 Dr Z28 SS Conv	21860	26660

OPTIONS FOR CAMARO

Auto 4-Speed Transmission[Opt on STD] +675
Performance Package +975
Sport Appearance Package +1290
Aluminum/Alloy Wheels[Opt on STD] +260

Don't forget to refer to the Mileage Adjustment Table at the back of this book!

© 1999 by Edmund Publications Corporation

Model Description	Trade-in Value	Market Value

AM/FM Compact Disc Playr +410
Chrome Wheels +470
Cruise Control[Opt on STD, Cpe] +175
Fog Lights[Opt on STD, Cpe] +145
Glass Panel T-tops +860
Keyless Entry System[Opt on STD, Cpe] +145
Leather Seats +590
Limited Slip Diff[Opt on STD] +310
Power Door Locks[Opt on STD, Cpe] +165
Power Drivers Seat[Opt on STD, Cpe] +195
Power Mirrors[Opt on STD, Cpe] +100
Power Windows[Opt on STD, Z28, Cpe] +185
Rear Window Defroster[Opt on Cpe] +135

CAVALIER 1998

A Z24 convertible is introduced, cruise control is standard on all but base models, power windows and remote keyless entry are no longer available on base cars, and...hold on to your seats, buyers can no longer delete the AM/FM radio. Second-generation airbags debut on all models.

Category E

Model Description	Trade-in Value	Market Value
4 Dr LS Sdn	10185	12425
2 Dr RS Cpe	8755	10675
2 Dr STD Cpe	8215	10015
4 Dr STD Sdn	8080	9855
2 Dr Z24 Cpe	9785	11930
2 Dr Z24 Conv	11405	13910

OPTIONS FOR CAVALIER

4 cyl 2.4 L Engine[Opt on LS] +375
Auto 3-Speed Transmission +500
Auto 4-Speed Transmission[Std on LS] +650
Air Conditioning[Opt on RS, STD] +675
Aluminum/Alloy Wheels[Std on Z24] +265
AM/FM Compact Disc Playr +390
Cruise Control[Opt on STD] +185
Keyless Entry System[Std on Z24] +125
Power Door Locks[Std on Z24] +195
Power Mirrors[Std on Z24] +95
Power Sunroof +500
Power Windows[Std on Z24] +220
Rear Window Defroster[Std on Conv] +135
Tilt Steering Wheel[Opt on STD] +125
Traction Control System[Std on LS] +40

CHEVY VAN/EXPRESS 1998

All vans equipped with airbags switch to mini-module bag designs for the driver, but they still deploy with more force than second-generation types. A theft-deterrent system is standard, and three new colors debut.

G15

Category H

Model Description	Trade-in Value	Market Value
2 Dr LS Express Van	20455	24065
2 Dr STD Express Van	19110	22480
2 Dr STD Chevy Van	15705	18475

G25

Category H

Model Description	Trade-in Value	Market Value
2 Dr STD Chevy Van	15940	18755
2 Dr STD Chevy Van Ext	16590	19520

G35

Category H

Model Description	Trade-in Value	Market Value
2 Dr STD Chevy Van	15980	18800

OPTIONS FOR CHEVY VAN/EXPRESS

8 cyl 5.0 L Engine +410
8 cyl 5.7 L Engine[Opt on G15, G25 Chevy Van] +830
8 cyl 7.4 L Engine +500
8 cyl 6.5 L Turbodsl Engine +2495
8 Passenger Seating[Std on G15] +305
Air Conditioning[Opt on Chevy Van, Chevy Van Ext] +670
Aluminum/Alloy Wheels +260
AM/FM Compact Disc Playr +245
Cruise Control[Std on LS] +160
Dual Air Conditioning +1180
Heated Power Mirrors +100
Keyless Entry System +125
Power Door Locks[Std on LS] +155
Power Drivers Seat +225
Power Windows[Std on LS] +160
Rear Heater +185
Tilt Steering Wheel[Std on LS] +150

CORVETTE 1998

Two fresh colors are available, but the new convertible model steals the show. Equipped with a manual folding top, a hard tonneau that extends along the rear wall of the passenger compartment and a real live trunk that holds golf bags, this new drop top should prove quite popular. Lower-powered airbags are not available on the Corvette.

Category J

Model Description	Trade-in Value	Market Value
2 Dr STD Conv	37680	44325
2 Dr STD Cpe	32035	37685

OPTIONS FOR CORVETTE

6-Speed Transmission +675
Selective Damping System +1410
Sport Magnesium Wheels +2495
AM/FM Compact Disc Playr +450
Climate Control for AC +180
Dual Power Seats +610
Fog Lights +55
Glass Targa Top +530

LUMINA 1998

Last year's aborted LTZ sport sedan comes on strong for 1998, with a 200-horsepower 3800 V6 engine and machine-faced aluminum wheels. Four new exterior colors and one new interior color are also available on all Lumina models. To help give Lumina a more upscale

Don't forget to refer to the Mileage Adjustment Table at the back of this book!

 © 1999 by Edmund Publications Corporation

Model Description	Trade-in Value	Market Value

image than Malibu, an OnStar Mobile Communications system is a dealer-installed option. Second-generation airbags are standard equipment.

Category C

Model Description	Trade-in Value	Market Value
4 Dr LS Sdn	13020	15685
4 Dr LTZ Sdn	13285	16005
4 Dr STD Sdn	11340	13665

OPTIONS FOR LUMINA

6 cyl 3.8 L Engine[Opt on LTZ] +360
Aluminum/Alloy Wheels[Opt on STD] +240
AM/FM Compact Disc Playr +320
Anti-Lock Brakes[Opt on STD] +520
Cruise Control +170
Keyless Entry System +155
Leather Seats +480
Power Drivers Seat +235
Power Mirrors[Opt on STD] +90
Power Moonroof +580
Power Windows[Opt on STD] +255
Rear Window Defroster +135

MALIBU 1998

Leather trim is newly optional on LS models, aluminum wheels get an enhanced appearance, a sunroof can be ordered and Base models can be equipped with Medium Oak colored interior. Second-generation airbags debut.

Category C

Model Description	Trade-in Value	Market Value
4 Dr LS Sdn	13755	16575
4 Dr STD Sdn	10870	13095

OPTIONS FOR MALIBU

6 cyl 3.1 L Engine[Std on LS] +370
Aluminum/Alloy Wheels[Std on LS] +240
AM/FM Compact Disc Playr +320
Cruise Control[Std on LS] +170
Keyless Entry System[Std on LS] +155
Leather Seats +480
Power Door Locks[Std on LS] +200
Power Drivers Seat[Std on LS] +235
Power Mirrors[Std on LS] +90
Power Sunroof +580
Power Windows[Std on LS] +255
Rear Window Defroster[Std on LS] +135

METRO 1998

The Geo badge is replaced with a Chevy bowtie. Styling is updated front and rear. The LSi's four-cylinder engine gets four valves per cylinder for more power and better acceleration. Second-generation airbags are standard equipment. Wheel covers are revised, new radios, new interior fabrics, and the addition of California Gold Metallic to the paint palette round out the changes.

Category E

Model Description	Trade-in Value	Market Value
2 Dr LSi Hbk	6355	7750
4 Dr LSi Sdn	6515	7945
2 Dr STD Hbk	6120	7465

OPTIONS FOR METRO

Auto 3-Speed Transmission +480
Air Conditioning +675
AM/FM Compact Disc Playr +390
Anti-Lock Brakes +590
Power Door Locks +195
Power Steering +210
Rear Window Defroster +135
Rear Window Wiper +110

MONTE CARLO 1998

The Z34 model gets a different engine and fresh wheels. Second-generation airbags are added. New paint colors and one new interior hue round out the changes.

Category C

Model Description	Trade-in Value	Market Value
2 Dr LS Cpe	12585	15160
2 Dr Z34 Cpe	14060	16940

OPTIONS FOR MONTE CARLO

Aluminum/Alloy Wheels[Opt on LS] +240
AM/FM Compact Disc Playr +320
Cruise Control[Opt on LS] +170
Keyless Entry System[Opt on LS] +155
Leather Seats +480
Power Drivers Seat +235
Power Moonroof +580
Rear Window Defroster +135

PRIZM 1998

The Prizm is completely redesigned, though it might not look like it at first glance. Among the improvements are a larger standard engine, optional side airbags, an optional handling package for LSi models and new colors inside and out. Front airbags are of the de-powered variety.

Category E

Model Description	Trade-in Value	Market Value
4 Dr LSi Sdn	8225	10035
4 Dr STD Sdn	7820	9535

OPTIONS FOR PRIZM

Auto 3-Speed Transmission +410
Auto 4-Speed Transmission +665
Air Conditioning +675
Aluminum/Alloy Wheels +265
AM/FM Compact Disc Playr +390
Anti-Lock Brakes +590
Cruise Control +185
Power Door Locks[Opt on STD] +195
Power Sunroof +500
Power Windows +220
Rear Window Defroster +135
Side Air Bag Restraint +220
Tilt Steering Wheel +125

S10 PICKUP 1998

The S-10 gets a sheetmetal makeover and a new interior with dual airbags that incorporate second-generation technology for reduced force deployments. The basic

Don't forget to refer to the Mileage Adjustment Table at the back of this book!

 © 1999 by Edmund Publications Corporation

four-cylinder engine benefits from Vortec technology this year, while 4WD models now have four-wheel disc brakes and a more refined transfer case on trucks with an automatic transmission. New radios, automatic headlight control, and a standard theft-deterrent system sum up the changes.

Model Description	Trade-in Value	Market Value
Category G		
2 Dr LS Std Cab SB	9685	11530
2 Dr LS Ext Cab SB	9790	11655
2 Dr LS Std Cab Stepside SB	9840	11715
2 Dr LS Ext Cab Stepside SB	10165	12105
2 Dr LS Std Cab LB	9965	11860
2 Dr LS 4WD Ext Cab SB	13905	16555
2 Dr LS 4WD Std Cab SB	13850	16490
2 Dr LS 4WD Ext Cab Stepside SB	14250	16965
2 Dr LS 4WD Std Cab Stepside SB	13870	16515
2 Dr LS 4WD Std Cab LB	13760	16380
2 Dr STD Std Cab SB	9010	10725
2 Dr STD Std Cab LB	9525	11340
2 Dr STD 4WD Std Cab SB	13215	15735
2 Dr STD 4WD Std Cab LB	13400	15955
2 Dr ZR2 4WD Ext Cab SB	18775	22350
2 Dr ZR2 4WD Std Cab SB	18115	21565

OPTIONS FOR S10 PICKUP

6 cyl 4.3 L Engine[Opt on 2WD] +670
6 cyl 4.3 L Vortec Engine[Std on ZR2] +905
Auto 4-Speed Transmission[Std on ZR2] +890
Air Conditioning[Std on ZR2] +675
Aluminum/Alloy Wheels[Opt on LS] +285
AM/FM Compact Disc Playr +320
Cruise Control[Std on ZR2] +175
Fog Lights +120
Heavy Duty Suspension +115
Hinged Third Door (PU) +290
Keyless Entry System[Opt on LS] +170
Power Door Locks[Opt on LS] +190
Power Mirrors[Opt on LS] +110
Power Windows[Opt on LS] +195
Premium Sound System +300
Skid Plates[Std on ZR2] +115
Sliding Rear Window +100
Sport Suspension +400
Tilt Steering Wheel[Std on ZR2] +140

SUBURBAN 1998

New colors, a standard theft deterrent system, optional heated seats, second generation airbags, and an automatic 4WD system improve the 1998 Suburban.

Model Description	Trade-in Value	Market Value
Category H		
4 Dr C1500 Wgn	19015	22370
4 Dr C2500 Wgn	25040	29455
4 Dr K1500 4WD Wgn	22875	26910
4 Dr K2500 4WD Wgn	26410	31070

OPTIONS FOR SUBURBAN

8 cyl 7.4 L Engine[Opt on 2500] +500
8 cyl 6.5 L Turbodsl Engine[Opt on 2500] +2495
LS Package +2740
LT Package +3290
Air Conditioning +670
Aluminum/Alloy Wheels +260
AM/FM Compact Disc Playr +245
Camper/Towing Package +295
Cruise Control +160
Dual Air Conditioning +1180
Heated Front Seats +240
Keyless Entry System +125
Leather Seats +860
Power Drivers Seat +225
Power Mirrors +85
Power Windows +160
Privacy Glass +140
Rear Heater +185
Rear Window Defroster +125
Rear Window Wiper +115
Tilt Steering Wheel +150

TAHOE 1998

Autotrac is a new optional automatic four-wheel drive system that switches from 2WD to 4WD automatically as conditions warrant. A new option package includes heated seats and heated exterior mirrors. Second generation airbags deploy with less force than last year. A theft deterrent system is standard, and color selections are modified.

Model Description	Trade-in Value	Market Value
Category H		
2 Dr LS Utility	22180	26095
2 Dr LS 4WD Utility*	22960	27015
4 Dr LS Wgn	21510	25305
4 Dr LS 4WD Wgn	23120	27200
2 Dr LT Utility	23230	27325
2 Dr LT 4WD Utility	23945	28170
4 Dr LT Wgn	23500	27650
4 Dr LT 4WD Wgn	24160	28420
2 Dr STD 4WD Utility	19160	22545

OPTIONS FOR TAHOE

8 cyl 6.5 L Turbodsl Engine[Opt on 2 Dr] +2495
Air Conditioning[Opt on STD] +670
Aluminum/Alloy Wheels[Opt on STD] +260
AM/FM Compact Disc Playr +245
Camper/Towing Package +295
Cruise Control[Opt on STD] +160
Heated Front Seats +240
Rear Window Defroster[Opt on STD] +125
Rear Window Wiper[Opt on STD] +115
Running Boards +245
Tilt Steering Wheel[Opt on STD] +150

Don't forget to refer to the Mileage Adjustment Table at the back of this book!

 © 1999 by Edmund Publications Corporation

Model Description	Trade-in Value	Market Value

TRACKER 1998

Geo is gone, so all Trackers are now badged as Chevrolets. The LSi models are dropped, though an LSi equipment package is available on Base models. Two new colors are available. Second-generation airbags are standard.

Category G

Model Description	Trade-in Value	Market Value
2 Dr STD Conv	10545	12555
2 Dr STD 4WD Conv	11565	13770
4 Dr STD 4WD Wgn	11240	13380

OPTIONS FOR TRACKER

Auto 3-Speed Transmission +520
Auto 4-Speed Transmission +830
Air Conditioning +675
Aluminum/Alloy Wheels +285
AM/FM Compact Disc Playr +320
Anti-Lock Brakes +515
Auto Locking Hubs (4WD) +220
Cruise Control +175
Power Door Locks +190
Power Mirrors +110
Power Steering[Std on Wgn,4WD] +235
Power Windows +195
Rear Window Wiper +125

VENTURE 1998

Venture is the first minivan to get side-impact airbags. Other changes include the availability of a cargo van edition, a wider variety of dual door models, and an optional power sliding door on regular wheelbase vans. Power rear window vents are also added for 1998. Front airbags deploy with less force thanks to second-generation technology.

Category G

Model Description	Trade-in Value	Market Value
2 Dr LS Pass. Van Ext	16535	19685
2 Dr LS Pass. Van	16370	19490
2 Dr STD Pass. Van Ext	16100	19170
2 Dr STD Pass. Van	15085	17960
2 Dr STD Cargo Van Ext	15500	18455

OPTIONS FOR VENTURE

Aluminum/Alloy Wheels +285
AM/FM Compact Disc Playr +320
Cruise Control[Std on LS] +175
Keyless Entry System[Std on LS] +170
Power Drivers Seat +235
Power Windows[Std on LS] +195
Privacy Glass +225
Rear Window Defroster +140
Sliding Driver Side Door +445
Traction Control System +245

1997 CHEVROLET

ASTRO 1997

Daytime running lights debut, and LT models can be equipped with leather upholstery. Also optional this year is a HomeLink three-channel transmitter. Delayed entry/exit lighting is now standard on all Astro passenger vans. Transmission refinements mean smoother shifts, and electronic variable orifice steering eases steering effort at low speeds.

RATINGS (SCALE OF 1-10)

Overall	Safety	Reliability	Performance	Comfort	Value
7.4	7	8	6.8	6.5	8.6

Category G

Model Description	Trade-in Value	Market Value
2 Dr LS Pass. Van Ext	12710	15315
2 Dr LS 4WD Pass. Van Ext	14730	17745
2 Dr LT Pass. Van Ext	13955	16815
2 Dr LT 4WD Pass. Van Ext	15400	18555
2 Dr STD Cargo Van Ext	10910	13145
2 Dr STD Pass. Van Ext	11265	13570
2 Dr STD 4WD Pass. Van Ext	13030	15700
2 Dr STD 4WD Cargo Van Ext	13830	16660

OPTIONS FOR ASTRO

8 Passenger Seating[Opt on STD] +260
Aluminum/Alloy Wheels[Std on LT] +235
AM/FM Compact Disc Playr +260
Child Seats (2) +175
Cruise Control[Opt on STD] +145
Dual Air Conditioning +685
Keyless Entry System[Std on LT] +140
Leather Seats +520
Power Door Locks[Opt on STD] +155
Power Drivers Seat[Std on LT] +190
Power Mirrors[Std on LT] +90
Power Windows[Opt on STD] +160
Privacy Glass[Opt on STD] +185
Rear Heater +140
Tilt Steering Wheel[Opt on STD] +115

BLAZER 1997

Those who prefer a liftgate over a tailgate have that option on 1997 four-door Blazers. A power sunroof is a new option for all Blazers, and models equipped with LT decor are equipped with a HomeLink transmitter that will open your garage, among other things. All-wheel drive Blazers get four-wheel disc brakes, and automatic transmissions are revised for smoother shifting. Early production 4WD two-door Blazers could be ordered with a ZR2 suspension package, but by the time we got pricing, Chevrolet had cancelled the option. Base Blazers get a chrome grille, while LT four-door models have body-color grilles in six exterior colors. Two new paint colors round out the changes.

Don't forget to refer to the Mileage Adjustment Table at the back of this book!

 © 1999 by Edmund Publications Corporation

Model Description	Trade-in Value	Market Value

RATINGS (SCALE OF 1-10)

Overall	Safety	Reliability	Performance	Comfort	Value
7.2	5.3	8.3	8	7.9	6.5

Model Description	Trade-in Value	Market Value
Category G		
2 Dr LS Utility	14180	17085
2 Dr LS 4WD Utility	14735	17755
4 Dr LS Wgn	14895	17945
4 Dr LS 4WD Wgn	15885	19140
4 Dr LT Wgn	15950	19220
4 Dr LT 4WD Wgn	16805	20245
2 Dr STD Utility	12400	14940
2 Dr STD 4WD Utility	12650	15240
4 Dr STD Wgn	14005	16870
4 Dr STD 4WD Wgn	14270	17190

OPTIONS FOR BLAZER

Auto 4-Speed Transmission[Std on Wgn] +605
Wide Stance Suspension +1255
Aluminum/Alloy Wheels[Opt on STD] +235
AM/FM Compact Disc Playr +260
Cruise Control[Opt on STD] +145
Keyless Entry System[Opt on LS] +140
Power Door Locks[Opt on STD] +155
Power Drivers Seat[Opt on LS] +190
Power Mirrors[Opt on STD] +90
Power Sunroof +550
Power Windows[Opt on STD] +160
Running Boards +260
Skid Plates +95
Swing Out Tire Carrier[Opt on 4WD,Utility] +140
Tilt Steering Wheel[Opt on STD] +115

C/K PICKUP 1997

Order a truck under 8,600 lbs. GVWR, and you'll get a passenger airbag. The airbag can be deactivated when a rear-facing child safety seat is installed. Low-speed steering effort is reduced this year, and a refined transmission fluid pump results in smoother shifts. An alternative fuel version of the Vortec 5700 is available, but only on a specific model. K1500's get a tighter turning radius, and three new colors debut. The third door option will be more widely available, because it is now a required option on all C/K 1500 shortbed extended cab trucks.

RATINGS (SCALE OF 1-10)

Overall	Safety	Reliability	Performance	Comfort	Value
N/A	8.3	8.9	7.8	8.4	N/A

C1500

Model Description	Trade-in Value	Market Value
Category H		
2 Dr Cheyenne Std Cab SB	12260	14600
2 Dr Cheyenne Ext Cab SB	12495	14875
2 Dr Cheyenne Ext Cab Stepside SB	13110	15605
2 Dr Cheyenne Std Cab Stepside SB	12895	15355
2 Dr Cheyenne Ext Cab LB	12570	14965
2 Dr Cheyenne Std Cab LB	12400	14760
2 Dr Silverado Ext Cab SB	14015	16685
2 Dr Silverado Std Cab SB	13795	16420
2 Dr Silverado Std Cab Stepside SB	14405	17150
2 Dr Silverado Ext Cab Stepside SB	14635	17420
2 Dr Silverado Ext Cab LB	14150	16845
2 Dr Silverado Std Cab LB	13875	16515
2 Dr WT Std Cab SB	10155	12090
2 Dr WT Std Cab LB	10305	12265

C2500

Model Description	Trade-in Value	Market Value
Category H		
2 Dr Cheyenne Ext Cab SB	13270	15800
2 Dr Cheyenne Std Cab LB	12910	15370
2 Dr Silverado Ext Cab SB	15040	17900
2 Dr Silverado Std Cab LB	14405	17150

C2500 HD

Model Description	Trade-in Value	Market Value
Category H		
2 Dr Cheyenne Ext Cab LB	14470	17225
2 Dr Silverado Ext Cab LB	16360	19475

C3500

Model Description	Trade-in Value	Market Value
Category H		
2 Dr Cheyenne Ext Cab LB	15525	18480
2 Dr Cheyenne Std Cab LB	15120	18000
4 Dr Cheyenne Crew Cab LB	17095	20350
2 Dr Silverado Std Cab LB	16810	20010
2 Dr Silverado Ext Cab LB	17155	20420
4 Dr Silverado Crew Cab LB	17770	21150

K1500

Model Description	Trade-in Value	Market Value
Category H		
2 Dr Cheyenne 4WD Ext Cab SB	14610	17395
2 Dr Cheyenne 4WD Std Cab SB	14375	17115
2 Dr Cheyenne 4WD Std Cab Stepside SB	15000	17855
2 Dr Cheyenne 4WD Ext Cab Stepside SB	15260	18165
2 Dr Cheyenne 4WD Ext Cab LB	14695	17495
2 Dr Cheyenne 4WD Std Cab LB	14450	17205
2 Dr Silverado 4WD Std Cab SB	15715	18710
2 Dr Silverado 4WD Ext Cab SB	15960	19000
2 Dr Silverado 4WD Std Cab Stepside SB	16360	19480
2 Dr Silverado 4WD Ext Cab Stepside SB	16570	19725
2 Dr Silverado 4WD Ext Cab LB	16030	19085

Don't forget to refer to the Mileage Adjustment Table at the back of this book!

 © 1999 by Edmund Publications Corporation

Model Description	Trade-in Value	Market Value
2 Dr Silverado 4WD Std Cab LB	15785	18795
2 Dr WT 4WD Std Cab SB	12365	14720
2 Dr WT 4WD Std Cab LB	12470	14845

K2500 HD

Category H

Model Description	Trade-in Value	Market Value
2 Dr Cheyenne 4WD Ext Cab SB	16440	19570
2 Dr Cheyenne 4WD Std Cab LB	14860	17690
2 Dr Cheyenne 4WD Ext Cab LB	16440	19570
2 Dr Silverado 4WD Ext Cab SB	17270	20560
2 Dr Silverado 4WD Ext Cab LB	17345	20650
2 Dr Silverado 4WD Std Cab LB	16510	19650

K3500

Category H

Model Description	Trade-in Value	Market Value
2 Dr Cheyenne 4WD Std Cab LB	17325	20625
2 Dr Cheyenne 4WD Ext Cab LB	18460	21975
4 Dr Cheyenne 4WD Crew Cab LB	19085	22720
2 Dr Silverado 4WD Ext Cab LB	19385	23080
2 Dr Silverado 4WD Std Cab LB	18445	21960
4 Dr Silverado 4WD Crew Cab LB	19860	23645

OPTIONS FOR C/K PICKUP

8 cyl 5.0 L Engine +335
8 cyl 5.7 L Engine +705
8 cyl 7.4 L Engine +410
8 cyl 6.5 L Turbodsl Engine +2075
Auto 4-Speed Transmission +660
Air Conditioning[Std on Silverado] +550
Aluminum/Alloy Wheels +210
AM/FM Compact Disc Playr +200
Automatic Dimming Mirror[Std on Crew Cab] +95
Bed Liner +155
Camper/Towing Package +240
Cruise Control[Std on Silverado] +130
Dual Rear Wheels +570
Hinged Third Door (PU) +285
Keyless Entry System +110
Leather Seats +700
Power Door Locks[Opt on Cheyenne] +125
Power Drivers Seat +185
Tilt Steering Wheel[Std on Silverado] +120

CAMARO 1997

Chevrolet celebrates the Camaro's 30th Anniversary with a special-edition Z28 that emulates the appearance of the 1969 Z-28 Indy Pace Car with white paint, Hugger Orange stripes, and black-and-white houndstooth seat inserts. Interior revisions to seats, center console and dashboard freshen the look inside for 1997. Two new shades of gray are available for interiors, while exteriors get new green and purple hues. Tri-color taillamps debut, and new five-spoke alloy wheels are optional. On the safety front, daytime running lights are standard and side-impact regulations are met for the first time.

RATINGS (SCALE OF 1-10)

Overall	Safety	Reliability	Performance	Comfort	Value
7.3	8.3	7.8	9.2	6.6	4.7

Category F

Model Description	Trade-in Value	Market Value
2 Dr RS Conv	12645	15420
2 Dr RS Cpe	11400	13905
2 Dr STD Cpe	10605	12935
2 Dr STD Conv	11675	14240
2 Dr Z28 Conv	13590	16575
2 Dr Z28 Cpe	12755	15555
2 Dr Z28 SS Cpe	15840	19320
2 Dr Z28 SS Conv	18090	22060

OPTIONS FOR CAMARO

Auto 4-Speed Transmission[Std on Z28,SS] +535
Performance Package +770
Sport Suspension Package +800
Torsen Torque Sensing Axle +680
Aluminum/Alloy Wheels[Opt on STD] +210
AM/FM Compact Disc Playr +335
Cruise Control +140
Fog Lights +115
Glass Panel T-tops +700
Keyless Entry System +120
Leather Seats +485
Limited Slip Diff[Opt on RS,STD] +255
Power Door Locks +135
Power Drivers Seat +160
Power Mirrors +80
Power Windows +150
Special Factory Paint +225

CAVALIER 1997

The historically on-again off-again Rally Sport (RS) trim level is evidently on-again, attached for 1997 to the coupe and slotted between base and Z24 editions of the Cavalier. RS trim nets buyers the rear spoiler from the Z24, 15-inch tires, AM/FM stereo, tachometer, interior and exterior trim goodies, and a really cool (yeah, right) 3D rear quarter panel decal. Base coupes have new wheel covers and safety belt guide loops. All 1997 Cavaliers meet federal side-impact standards for the first time. One new interior color and three new exterior colors freshen the lineup.

RATINGS (SCALE OF 1-10)

Overall	Safety	Reliability	Performance	Comfort	Value
7.1	6.3	8.1	7.2	7.6	6.4

Category E

Model Description	Trade-in Value	Market Value
2 Dr LS Conv	9010	11260
4 Dr LS Sdn	8280	10350
2 Dr RS Cpe	7220	9025
2 Dr STD Cpe	6790	8485

Don't forget to refer to the Mileage Adjustment Table at the back of this book!

 © 1999 by Edmund Publications Corporation

Model Description	Trade-in Value	Market Value
4 Dr STD Sdn	6845	8555
2 Dr Z24 Cpe	7995	9995

OPTIONS FOR CAVALIER

4 cyl 2.4 L Engine[Opt on LS, Z24] +290
Auto 3-Speed Transmission[Std on LS] +360
Auto 4-Speed Transmission[Std on LS] +520
Air Conditioning[Opt on RS,STD] +550
Aluminum/Alloy Wheels[Std on Z24] +215
AM/FM Compact Disc Playr +320
Cruise Control +150
Keyless Entry System +100
Power Door Locks +160
Power Mirrors +75
Power Sunroof +410
Power Windows +180
Tilt Steering Wheel[Std on Z24] +100

CHEVY VAN/EXPRESS 1997

Dual airbags appear on the G3500 model, while daytime running lights and three fresh exterior colors make this van easier to see. (Editor's Note: If you can't see this monster van without DRL's, perhaps you should consider surrendering your driver's license.) Electronic variable orifice steering reduces effort at low speeds for easier parking, and automatic transmissions shift more smoothly.

G15

Category H

Model Description	Trade-in Value	Market Value
2 Dr LS Express Van	16620	19790
2 Dr STD Express Van	15890	18915
2 Dr STD Chevy Van	15325	18245

G25

Category H

Model Description	Trade-in Value	Market Value
2 Dr LS Express Van	15980	19025
2 Dr STD Chevy Van Ext	13605	16195
2 Dr STD Chevy Van	12885	15340
2 Dr STD Express Van	15315	18235

G35

Category H

Model Description	Trade-in Value	Market Value
2 Dr STD Chevy Van Ext	15730	18730
2 Dr STD Chevy Van	15010	17870

OPTIONS FOR CHEVY VAN/EXPRESS

8 cyl 5.0 L Engine +335
8 cyl 5.7 L Engine[Opt on G15] +705
8 cyl 7.4 L Engine +410
8 cyl 6.5 L Turbodsl Engine +2075
8 Passenger Seating[Std on G15] +250
Aluminum/Alloy Wheels +210
AM/FM Compact Disc Playr +200
Cruise Control[Std on LS] +130
Dual Air Conditioning +965
Keyless Entry System +110
Power Door Locks[Std on LS] +125
Power Drivers Seat +185
Power Windows[Std on LS] +130
Privacy Glass +115
Rear Heater +150
Tilt Steering Wheel[Std on LS] +120

CORVETTE 1997

Fifth-generation Corvette debuts 44 years after the original, and is better than ever with world-class build quality and performance at a bargain price.

Category J

Model Description	Trade-in Value	Market Value
2 Dr STD Cpe	28235	33615

OPTIONS FOR CORVETTE

6-Speed Transmission +600
Selective Damping System +1255
AM/FM Compact Disc Playr +370
Climate Control for AC +150
Dual Power Seats +500
Fog Lights +45
Glass Targa Top +435
Solid & Glass Targa Tops +635
Sport Seats +540

LUMINA 1997

Performance-oriented Lumina LTZ debuts, though a spoiler, special front and rear styling, graphics, and alloy wheels don't amount to performance in our book. Daytime running lamps are standard on all Luminas, and the power sunroof expected last year finally arrives. New colors and an oil life monitor round out changes to Lumina for 1997.

RATINGS (SCALE OF 1-10)

Overall	Safety	Reliability	Performance	Comfort	Value
7.8	7.6	8.5	7.6	7.3	7.8

Category C

Model Description	Trade-in Value	Market Value
4 Dr LS Sdn	10170	12555
4 Dr LTZ Sdn	10545	13020
4 Dr STD Sdn	8925	11015

OPTIONS FOR LUMINA

6 cyl 3.4 L Engine +745
Aluminum/Alloy Wheels[Opt on STD] +195
AM/FM Compact Disc Playr +260
Anti-Lock Brakes[Opt on STD] +425
Child Seat (1) +80
Cruise Control[Std on LS] +140
Keyless Entry System +130
Leather Seats +390
Power Drivers Seat +195
Power Moonroof +475
Power Windows[Opt on STD] +205

MALIBU 1997

Malibu returns after consumer clinics tell Chevrolet they want a tight, solid, roomy, fun-to-drive midsize sedan. Guess what? Chevrolet delivers.

Don't forget to refer to the Mileage Adjustment Table at the back of this book!

 © 1999 by Edmund Publications Corporation

Model Description	Trade-in Value	Market Value

RATINGS (SCALE OF 1-10)

Overall	Safety	Reliability	Performance	Comfort	Value
N/A	7.4	8.2	8.4	8.3	N/A

Category C		
4 Dr LS Sdn	11465	14155
4 Dr STD Sdn	9485	11710

OPTIONS FOR MALIBU

6 cyl 3.1 L Engine[Std on LS] +295
Aluminum/Alloy Wheels[Std on LS] +195
AM/FM Compact Disc Playr +260
Cruise Control[Std on LS] +140
Keyless Entry System[Std on LS] +130
Power Door Locks[Std on LS] +160
Power Drivers Seat[Std on LS] +195
Power Mirrors[Std on LS] +75
Power Windows[Std on LS] +205
Rear Window Defroster[Std on LS] +110

MONTE CARLO 1997

Hot-rod Z34 gets a new transmission, while all models have daytime running lights. Newly optional is a power sunroof. Two new colors freshen the rather dull sheetmetal.

RATINGS (SCALE OF 1-10)

Overall	Safety	Reliability	Performance	Comfort	Value
7.4	7.6	8.2	7.4	7.5	6.1

Category C		
2 Dr LS Cpe	10385	12825
2 Dr Z34 Cpe	11695	14440

OPTIONS FOR MONTE CARLO

Aluminum/Alloy Wheels[Opt on LS] +195
AM/FM Compact Disc Playr +260
Cruise Control[Opt on LS] +140
Keyless Entry System[Opt on LS] +130
Leather Seats +390
Power Drivers Seat +195
Power Sunroof +470

S10 PICKUP 1997

Chevy strengthens the 2WD S-10 frame by using tougher components. Refinements to the automatic transmission result in improved efficiency and smoother shifts. Four-wheel drive models have lighter-weight plug-in half shafts. Two new colors are available.

RATINGS (SCALE OF 1-10)

Overall	Safety	Reliability	Performance	Comfort	Value
N/A	5.1	7.7	6.6	8.1	N/A

Category G		
2 Dr LS Std Cab SB	8340	10045
2 Dr LS Ext Cab SB	8555	10305
2 Dr LS Std Cab Stepside SB	8885	10705
2 Dr LS Ext Cab Stepside SB	9075	10935
2 Dr LS Std Cab LB	8480	10220
2 Dr LS 4WD Std Cab SB	10745	12945
2 Dr LS 4WD Std Cab Stepside SB	11045	13305
2 Dr LS 4WD Ext Cab Stepside SB	11365	13695
2 Dr LS 4WD Std Cab LB	10950	13195
2 Dr STD Std Cab SB	7770	9365
2 Dr STD Std Cab LB	7915	9535
2 Dr STD 4WD Std Cab SB	10505	12660
2 Dr STD 4WD Std Cab LB	10635	12810

OPTIONS FOR S10 PICKUP

6 cyl 4.3 L Engine[Opt on 2WD] +510
6 cyl 4.3 L Vortec Engine +675
Auto 4-Speed Transmission +725
Wide Stance Suspension +1130
Air Conditioning +550
Aluminum/Alloy Wheels +235
AM/FM Compact Disc Playr +260
Cruise Control +145
Heavy Duty Suspension +95
Hinged Third Door (PU) +240
Keyless Entry System +140
Power Door Locks +155
Power Mirrors +90
Power Windows +160
Skid Plates +95
Tilt Steering Wheel +115

SUBURBAN 1997

Dual airbags debut, and a cargo area power lock switch makes locking up the vehicle after unloading cargo more convenient. Electronic Variable Orifice power steering lightens low-speed steering effort, and automatic transmissions are improved. Two new exterior colors are added to the paint roster.

RATINGS (SCALE OF 1-10)

Overall	Safety	Reliability	Performance	Comfort	Value
7.7	8.1	8	7.2	7.9	7.4

Category H		
4 Dr C1500 Wgn	19525	23245
4 Dr C2500 Wgn	20445	24340
4 Dr K1500 4WD Wgn	20755	24710
4 Dr K2500 4WD Wgn	21785	25935

OPTIONS FOR SUBURBAN

8 cyl 7.4 L Engine +410
8 cyl 6.5 L Turbodsl Engine +2075
LS Package +2120
LT Package +2385
Air Conditioning +550
Aluminum/Alloy Wheels +210
AM/FM Compact Disc Playr +200
Automatic Dimming Mirror[Std on K2500] +95

Don't forget to refer to the Mileage Adjustment Table at the back of this book!

 © 1999 by Edmund Publications Corporation

Model Description	Trade-in Value	Market Value

Camper/Towing Package +240
Cruise Control +130
Dual Air Conditioning +965
Keyless Entry System +110
Leather Seats +700
Power Drivers Seat +185
Power Mirrors +70
Power Windows +130
Privacy Glass +115
Rear Heater +150
Tilt Steering Wheel +120

TAHOE 1997

A passenger-side airbag is added, and the automatic transmission is improved. Electronic Variable Orifice steering debuts, and cargo areas have a power door lock switch. A new center console comes with high-back bucket seats, and two new paint colors are available.

RATINGS (SCALE OF 1-10)

Overall	Safety	Reliability	Performance	Comfort	Value
7.9	8.2	8.7	7.4	8	7.4

Category H

Model Description	Trade-in Value	Market Value
2 Dr LS Utility	19445	23150
2 Dr LS 4WD Utility	20205	24055
4 Dr LS Wgn	21235	25280
4 Dr LS 4WD Wgn	23020	27405
2 Dr LT Utility	20320	24195
2 Dr LT 4WD Utility	21365	25430
4 Dr LT Wgn	22130	26345
4 Dr LT 4WD Wgn	23890	28440
2 Dr STD 4WD Utility	18070	21510

OPTIONS FOR TAHOE

8 cyl 6.5 L Turbodsl Engine +2075
Air Conditioning[Opt on STD] +550
Aluminum/Alloy Wheels[Opt on STD] +210
AM/FM Compact Disc Playr +200
Camper/Towing Package +240
Cruise Control[Opt on STD] +130
Keyless Entry System[Std on LT,LS Utility] +110
Power Drivers Seat[Opt on LS] +185
Privacy Glass[Opt on STD] +115
Tilt Steering Wheel[Opt on STD] +120
Velour/Cloth Seats[Std on LS] +90

VENTURE 1997

Complete redesign of Chevy's minivan results in a new name, a left-side sliding door, optional traction control, a powerful standard engine, and a fun-to-drive demeanor. Nice van, except for the big chrome grille.

RATINGS (SCALE OF 1-10)

Overall	Safety	Reliability	Performance	Comfort	Value
7.6	7.5	8.2	7.8	7.9	6.8

Category G

Model Description	Trade-in Value	Market Value
2 Dr LS Pass. Van	12685	15280
2 Dr LS Pass. Van Ext	14010	16880
2 Dr STD Pass. Van	12590	15170
2 Dr STD Pass. Van Ext	13530	16300

OPTIONS FOR VENTURE

Aluminum/Alloy Wheels +235
AM/FM Compact Disc Playr +260
Child Seat (1) +120
Cruise Control +145
Dual Air Conditioning +685
Keyless Entry System +140
Power Drivers Seat +190
Power Windows +160
Privacy Glass +185
Sliding Driver Side Door +365
Traction Control System +200

1996 CHEVROLET

ASTRO 1996

A new interior with dual airbags, new radio systems, an improved V6, and three new paint colors make Astro an excellent minivan choice.

RATINGS (SCALE OF 1-10)

Overall	Safety	Reliability	Performance	Comfort	Value
7.3	7	7.7	6.8	6.5	8.5

Category G

Model Description	Trade-in Value	Market Value
2 Dr LS Pass. Van Ext	10695	13365
2 Dr LS 4WD Pass. Van Ext	11950	14940
2 Dr LT Pass. Van Ext	11510	14385
2 Dr LT 4WD Pass. Van Ext	12760	15950
2 Dr STD Pass. Van Ext	9505	11880
2 Dr STD Cargo Van Ext	8665	10830
2 Dr STD 4WD Pass. Van Ext	10740	13420
2 Dr STD 4WD Cargo Van Ext	10230	12790

OPTIONS FOR ASTRO

8 Passenger Seating[Opt on STD] +215
Aluminum/Alloy Wheels[Std on LT] +190
AM/FM Compact Disc Playr +215
Child Seats (2) +145
Cruise Control[Opt on STD] +115
Dual Air Conditioning +560
Keyless Entry System[Std on LT] +115
Power Door Locks[Opt on STD] +125
Power Drivers Seat[Std on LT] +155
Power Mirrors[Std on LT] +75
Power Windows[Opt on STD] +130
Privacy Glass[Opt on STD] +150
Rear Heater +115
Tilt Steering Wheel[Opt on STD] +95

Don't forget to refer to the Mileage Adjustment Table at the back of this book!

 © 1999 by Edmund Publications Corporation

BERETTA 1996

Final year for Beretta. Only change is the addition of long life coolant to the engine.

RATINGS (SCALE OF 1-10)

Overall	Safety	Reliability	Performance	Comfort	Value
6.8	6.3	8	7.8	7	5.1

Category E	Trade-in Value	Market Value
2 Dr STD Cpe	6155	8205
2 Dr Z26 Cpe	7865	10485

OPTIONS FOR BERETTA

6 cyl 3.1 L Engine[Opt on STD] +260
Auto 3-Speed Transmission +290
Auto 4-Speed Transmission[Opt on STD] +400
Aluminum/Alloy Wheels +175
AM/FM Compact Disc Playr +260
Cruise Control +120
Power Windows +145
Sunroof +195
Tilt Steering Wheel +85

BLAZER 1996

More power, available all-wheel drive, and five new colors improve the 1996 Blazer. A five-speed manual transmission is optional on two-door models.

RATINGS (SCALE OF 1-10)

Overall	Safety	Reliability	Performance	Comfort	Value
6.9	5.2	7.6	8	7.9	5.8

Category G	Trade-in Value	Market Value
2 Dr LS Utility	11915	14890
2 Dr LS 4WD Utility	13235	16545
4 Dr LS Wgn	12470	15590
4 Dr LS 4WD Wgn	13610	17015
4 Dr LT Wgn	13565	16955
4 Dr LT 4WD Wgn	14475	18090
2 Dr STD Utility	9910	12390
2 Dr STD 4WD Utility	11205	14010
4 Dr STD Wgn	11265	14080
4 Dr STD 4WD Wgn	11920	14895

OPTIONS FOR BLAZER

Auto 4-Speed Transmission[Std on Wgn] +475
AM/FM Compact Disc Playr +215
Cruise Control[Opt on STD] +115
Keyless Entry System[Std on LT] +115
Power Door Locks[Opt on STD] +125
Power Drivers Seat[Std on LT] +155
Power Mirrors[Opt on STD] +75
Power Windows[Opt on STD] +130
Running Boards +215
Skid Plates +75
Tilt Steering Wheel[Opt on STD] +95

C/K PICKUP 1996

Major engine improvements result in more horsepower and torque. Extended cab models can be equipped with an access panel that opens to the rear of the cab from the passenger side of the truck. Daytime running lights are added, and K1500 models offer an optional electronic shift transfer case.

RATINGS (SCALE OF 1-10)

Overall	Safety	Reliability	Performance	Comfort	Value
N/A	7.5	7.6	7.8	8.4	N/A

C1500

Category H	Trade-in Value	Market Value
2 Dr Cheyenne Std Cab SB	11180	13470
2 Dr Cheyenne Ext Cab SB	11485	13835
2 Dr Cheyenne Std Cab Stepside SB	11625	14005
2 Dr Cheyenne Ext Cab Stepside SB	11710	14105
2 Dr Cheyenne Ext Cab LB	11255	13560
2 Dr Cheyenne Std Cab LB	11130	13410
2 Dr Silverado Std Cab SB	12325	14850
2 Dr Silverado Ext Cab SB	12430	14975
2 Dr Silverado Std Cab Stepside SB	12920	15565
2 Dr Silverado Ext Cab Stepside SB	13040	15710
2 Dr Silverado Ext Cab LB	12600	15180
2 Dr Silverado Std Cab LB	12440	14990
2 Dr WT Std Cab SB	8935	10770
2 Dr WT Std Cab LB	9160	11035

C2500

Category H	Trade-in Value	Market Value
2 Dr Cheyenne Std Cab LB	11700	14095
2 Dr Silverado Std Cab LB	13435	16190

C3500

Category H	Trade-in Value	Market Value
2 Dr Cheyenne Ext Cab LB	15600	18795
2 Dr Cheyenne Std Cab LB	14685	17690
4 Dr Cheyenne Crew Cab LB	15745	18970
2 Dr Silverado Std Cab LB	16330	19675
2 Dr Silverado Ext Cab LB	18440	22220
4 Dr Silverado Crew Cab LB	17020	20505

K1500

Category H	Trade-in Value	Market Value
2 Dr Cheyenne 4WD Std Cab SB	12440	14990
2 Dr Cheyenne 4WD Ext Cab SB	12785	15405
2 Dr Cheyenne 4WD Ext Cab Stepside SB	13275	15995

Don't forget to refer to the Mileage Adjustment Table at the back of this book!

© 1999 by Edmund Publications Corporation

Model Description	Trade-in Value	Market Value
2 Dr Cheyenne 4WD Std Cab Stepside SB	13190	15890
2 Dr Cheyenne 4WD Std Cab LB	12700	15300
2 Dr Cheyenne 4WD Ext Cab LB	12810	15430
2 Dr Silverado 4WD Ext Cab SB	14070	16955
2 Dr Silverado 4WD Std Cab SB	13745	16565
2 Dr Silverado 4WD Ext Cab Stepside SB	14610	17600
2 Dr Silverado 4WD Std Cab Stepside SB	14305	17235
2 Dr Silverado 4WD Ext Cab LB	14130	17025
2 Dr Silverado 4WD Std Cab LB	13845	16680
2 Dr WT 4WD Std Cab SB	10460	12605
2 Dr WT 4WD Std Cab LB	10445	12585

K2500

Category H

Model Description	Trade-in Value	Market Value
2 Dr Cheyenne 4WD Ext Cab SB	13845	16680
2 Dr Cheyenne 4WD Std Cab LB	13425	16170
2 Dr Cheyenne 4WD Ext Cab LB	13790	16615
2 Dr Silverado 4WD Ext Cab SB	15345	18485
2 Dr Silverado 4WD Std Cab LB	14290	17215
2 Dr Silverado 4WD Ext Cab LB	15495	18670

K3500

Category H

Model Description	Trade-in Value	Market Value
2 Dr Cheyenne 4WD Std Cab LB	14980	18045
2 Dr Cheyenne 4WD Ext Cab LB	16645	20055
4 Dr Cheyenne 4WD Crew Cab LB	16905	20365
2 Dr Silverado 4WD Ext Cab LB	17470	21050
2 Dr Silverado 4WD Std Cab LB	15940	19205
4 Dr Silverado 4WD Crew Cab LB	17720	21350

OPTIONS FOR C/K PICKUP

8 cyl 5.0 L Engine +310
8 cyl 5.7 L Engine +560
8 cyl 7.4 L Engine +335
8 cyl 6.5 L Turbodsl Engine +1810
Auto 4-Speed Transmission +525
Air Conditioning[Std on Silverado] +450
AM/FM Compact Disc Playr +165
Automatic Dimming Mirror +80
Bed Liner +125
Camper/Towing Package +195
Cruise Control[Std on Silverado] +105
Dual Rear Wheels +470
Hinged Third Door (PU) +235
Keyless Entry System +90
Leather Seats +575
Power Door Locks[Std on Silverado] +105
Power Drivers Seat +150
Tilt Steering Wheel[Std on Silverado] +100

CAMARO 1996

Hot new base V6 whumps the Mustang. LT1 V8 whumps the Mustang GT, with ten additional horsepower. SLP Engineering provides a 300-horse Z28 SS, which gets whumped by the Mustang Cobra. An RS trim level debuts, and chrome aluminum wheels are optional.

RATINGS (SCALE OF 1-10)

Overall	Safety	Reliability	Performance	Comfort	Value
7.3	8.4	7.7	9.2	6.6	4.6

Category F

Model Description	Trade-in Value	Market Value
2 Dr RS Conv	10550	13190
2 Dr RS Cpe	9650	12060
2 Dr STD Conv	10280	12845
2 Dr STD Cpe	8245	10305
2 Dr Z28 Conv	11800	14750
2 Dr Z28 Cpe	11110	13885
2 Dr Z28 SS Conv	13545	16930
2 Dr Z28 SS Cpe	12870	16085

OPTIONS FOR CAMARO

Auto 4-Speed Transmission +420
Performance Package +640
R1 Wheels/tires Package +1035
Suspension Package +545
Torque-sensing Axle +545
Air Conditioning[Opt on STD Cpe] +460
Aluminum/Alloy Wheels[Opt on STD] +170
AM/FM Compact Disc Playr +275
Bose Sound System +280
Cruise Control +115
Fog Lights +95
Glass Panel T-tops +575
Keyless Entry System +95
Leather Seats +395
Limited Slip Diff[Opt on RS,STD] +205
Power Door Locks +110
Power Drivers Seat +130
Power Mirrors +65
Power Windows +125

CAPRICE 1996

Zero changes as Caprice enters final year of production.

RATINGS (SCALE OF 1-10)

Overall	Safety	Reliability	Performance	Comfort	Value
7.8	7.2	7.1	8.2	8.3	8.5

Category B

Model Description	Trade-in Value	Market Value
4 Dr STD Sdn	11900	14875

OPTIONS FOR CAPRICE

8 cyl 5.7 L Engine[Opt on Sdn] +285
Cruise Control +120
Dual Power Seats +200

Don't forget to refer to the Mileage Adjustment Table at the back of this book!

© 1999 by Edmund Publications Corporation

Model Description	Trade-in Value	Market Value

Keyless Entry System +100
Leather Seats +370
Power Windows +160

CAVALIER 1996

The 2.3-liter Quad 4 is replaced after just one year by a 2.4-liter Twin Cam engine. Four-speed automatic transmission includes traction control. Daytime running lights debut, remote keyless entry is optional on LS and Z24, and base models get new interior fabrics and an Appearance Package.

RATINGS (SCALE OF 1-10)

Overall	Safety	Reliability	Performance	Comfort	Value
7	6.2	7.4	7.2	7.6	6.7

Category E

Model	Trade-in	Market
2 Dr LS Conv	7500	10000
4 Dr LS Sdn	6810	9080
2 Dr STD Cpe	5710	7615
4 Dr STD Sdn	5985	7980
2 Dr Z24 Cpe	6940	9255

OPTIONS FOR CAVALIER

4 cyl 2.4 L Engine[Opt on LS] +185
Auto 3-Speed Transmission[Std on LS] +285
Auto 4-Speed Transmission +415
Air Conditioning[Opt on STD] +450
AM/FM Compact Disc Playr +260
Cruise Control +120
Keyless Entry System +80
Power Door Locks +130
Power Mirrors +60
Power Sunroof +335
Power Windows +145
Tilt Steering Wheel[Std on Z24] +85

CHEVY VAN/EXPRESS 1996

First all-new full-size cargo van for Chevrolet in 25 years sports dual airbags, standard four-wheel antilock brakes, up to 317 cubic feet of cargo room and 10,000 pounds of towing capacity. Full-frame construction replaces the less rugged unibody configuration of the previous model. Sportvan replacement, the Express, carries up to 15 passengers and offers full-frame rather than unibody construction. Dual airbags and four-wheel antilock brakes are standard. Long-wheelbase models can carry 317 cubic feet of cargo with the rear seats removed. 3500 models can tow up to 10,000 pounds.

G15

Category H

Model	Trade-in	Market
2 Dr STD Express Van	13925	16775
2 Dr STD Chevy Van	13100	15780

G25

Category H

Model	Trade-in	Market
2 Dr STD Chevy Van	11775	14185
2 Dr STD Chevy Van Ext	12485	15045

G35

Category H

Model	Trade-in	Market
2 Dr STD Chevy Van Ext	12195	14695
2 Dr STD Chevy Van	11400	13735

OPTIONS FOR CHEVY VAN/EXPRESS

8 cyl 5.0 L Engine +310
8 cyl 5.7 L Engine[Opt on G15] +560
8 cyl 7.4 L Engine +335
8 cyl 6.5 L Turbodsl Engine +1810
Aluminum/Alloy Wheels +175
AM/FM Compact Disc Playr +165
Cruise Control +105
Dual Air Conditioning +790
Power Door Locks +105
Power Drivers Seat +150
Power Windows +105
Rear Heater +125
Tilt Steering Wheel +100

CHEVY VAN/SPORTVAN CLASSIC 1996

Final year for ancient GM vans dating to 1971.

G30

Category H

Model	Trade-in	Market
2 Dr STD Chevy Van Ext	12195	14695
2 Dr STD Chevy Van	11315	13635
2 Dr STD Express Van Ext	13140	15830
2 Dr STD Express Van	12705	15310

OPTIONS FOR CHEVY VAN/SPORTVAN CLASSIC

8 cyl 6.5 L Dsl Engine +905
8 cyl 7.4 L Engine +335
15 Passenger Seating +400
Air Conditioning[Opt on STD] +450
AM/FM Stereo Tape[Opt on STD] +135
Cruise Control[Opt on STD] +105
Dual Air Conditioning +790
Power Door Locks[Opt on STD] +105
Power Windows[Opt on STD] +105
Privacy Glass +95
Rear Heater +125
Tilt Steering Wheel[Opt on STD] +100

CORSICA 1996

Chevy's fleet favorite rolls into the sunset with long life coolant.

RATINGS (SCALE OF 1-10)

Overall	Safety	Reliability	Performance	Comfort	Value
6.8	5.3	8	8	7.5	5.3

Category C

Model	Trade-in	Market
4 Dr STD Sdn	6320	8210

Don't forget to refer to the Mileage Adjustment Table at the back of this book!

 © 1999 by Edmund Publications Corporation

OPTIONS FOR CORSICA

6 cyl 3.1 L Engine +250
AM/FM Stereo Tape +90
Cruise Control +115
Power Windows +170
Tilt Steering Wheel +85

CORVETTE 1996

New 330-horsepower LT4 engine debuts on all manually-shifted Corvettes. Two special editions are available, the Collector Edition and the Grand Sport, to send the fourth-generation Vette off in style. Next year, an all-new Corvette debuts. Other additions for 1996 include a Selective Real Time Damping system for the shock absorbers, and a tooth jarring Z51 suspension setup.

Category J

Model	Trade-in	Market
2 Dr Grand Sport Cpe	21180	25825
2 Dr STD Conv	21945	26760
2 Dr STD Cpe	20365	24835

OPTIONS FOR CORVETTE

8 cyl 5.7 L LT4 Engine[Opt on STD,Conv] +755
Dual Roof Panels +495
Electronic Suspension +880
Bose Sound System +455
Climate Control for AC +120
Compact Disc W/fm/tape +395
Dual Power Seats +410
Power Drivers Seat +185
Solid & Glass Targa Tops +520
Sport Seats[Opt on STD] +440
Sport Suspension +250

IMPALA 1996

Big surprise. The car is finally correct with the addition of a tachometer and floor shifter, and General Motors kills it. Take note collectors; the 1996 Impala SS should be on your list.

RATINGS (SCALE OF 1-10)

Overall	Safety	Reliability	Performance	Comfort	Value
8	7.2	7.1	9	8.3	8.2

Category B

Model	Trade-in	Market
4 Dr SS Sdn	16450	20565

OPTIONS FOR IMPALA

AM/FM Compact Disc Playr +175
Keyless Entry System +100
Power Passenger Seat +170

LUMINA 1996

The ultimate family sedan is now available with an integrated child safety seat. Driver and passenger get their own climate controls. LS models offer available leather, and four-wheel disc brakes when equipped with the 3.4-liter V6.

RATINGS (SCALE OF 1-10)

Overall	Safety	Reliability	Performance	Comfort	Value
7.8	7.5	8.1	7.6	7.3	8.7

Category C

Model	Trade-in	Market
4 Dr LS Sdn	8350	10845
4 Dr STD Sdn	7455	9680

OPTIONS FOR LUMINA

6 cyl 3.4 L Engine +570
AM/FM Compact Disc Playr +215
Anti-Lock Brakes[Std on LS] +345
Child Seat (1) +65
Cruise Control +115
Keyless Entry System +105
Leather Seats +320
Power Drivers Seat +160
Power Windows[Std on LS] +170

LUMINA MINIVAN 1996

Last year for sloped-nose, plastic-bodied van. A 3.4-liter V6 good for 180 horsepower replaces standard and optional V6 engines from last year. Air conditioning, seven-passenger seating, and an electronically-controlled four-speed automatic transmission are standard.

RATINGS (SCALE OF 1-10)

Overall	Safety	Reliability	Performance	Comfort	Value
7.5	6.4	7.9	7.6	7.3	8.6

Category G

Model	Trade-in	Market
2 Dr STD Cargo Van	8150	10190
2 Dr STD Pass. Van	9625	12030

OPTIONS FOR LUMINA MINIVAN

Aluminum/Alloy Wheels +190
AM/FM Stereo Tape +135
Child Seat (1) +95
Cruise Control +115
Keyless Entry System +115
Power Door Locks +125
Power Drivers Seat +155
Power Mirrors +75
Power Sliding Door +195
Power Windows +130
Privacy Glass +150
Tilt Steering Wheel +95

MONTE CARLO 1996

Dual-zone climate controls reduce marital spats. The 3.4-liter V6 makes more power this year, and four-wheel disc brakes, standard on the Z34, are optional on the LS.

RATINGS (SCALE OF 1-10)

Overall	Safety	Reliability	Performance	Comfort	Value
7.4	7.5	7.5	7.4	7.5	6.9

Don't forget to refer to the Mileage Adjustment Table at the back of this book!

 © 1999 by Edmund Publications Corporation

Model Description	Trade-in Value	Market Value
Category C		
2 Dr LS Cpe	8775	11395
2 Dr Z34 Cpe	9900	12860

OPTIONS FOR MONTE CARLO

AM/FM Compact Disc Playr +215
Cruise Control[Opt on LS] +115
Keyless Entry System[Opt on LS] +105
Leather Seats +320
Power Drivers Seat +160
Power Sunroof +385

S10 PICKUP 1996

Improved V6 engines make more power and torque this year. A new five-speed manual gives four-cylinder models better acceleration, and four-bangers also get four-wheel antilock brakes. Extended cab models get third door access panel on the driver's side to make loading cargo and passengers easier. A new sport suspension turns the S-10 into a competent sports truck, and the new Sportside cargo box allows the S-Series to go head-to-head with the Ford Ranger Splash.

RATINGS (SCALE OF 1-10)

Overall	Safety	Reliability	Performance	Comfort	Value
N/A	5	7	6.6	8.1	N/A

Model Description	Trade-in Value	Market Value
Category G		
2 Dr LS Ext Cab SB	7590	9490
2 Dr LS Std Cab SB	7145	8930
2 Dr LS Ext Cab Stepside SB	7940	9930
2 Dr LS Std Cab Stepside SB	7720	9650
2 Dr LS Std Cab LB	7190	8990
2 Dr LS 4WD Std Cab SB	9510	11890
2 Dr LS 4WD Ext Cab SB	10345	12935
2 Dr LS 4WD Std Cab Stepside SB	9860	12325
2 Dr LS 4WD Std Cab LB	9410	11765
2 Dr STD Std Cab SB	6935	8670
2 Dr STD Std Cab LB	7040	8800
2 Dr STD 4WD Std Cab SB	9010	11260
2 Dr STD 4WD Std Cab LB	9085	11360

OPTIONS FOR S10 PICKUP

6 cyl 4.3 L Engine[Opt on 2WD] +420
6 cyl 4.3 L Vortec Engine +540
Auto 4-Speed Transmission +540
Wide Stance Suspension +845
Air Conditioning +450
Aluminum/Alloy Wheels +190
AM/FM Compact Disc Playr +215
Anti-Lock Brakes[Opt on 2WD] +345
Cruise Control +115
Heavy Duty Suspension +80
Hinged Third Door (PU) +195
Keyless Entry System +115
Power Door Locks +125
Power Mirrors +75
Power Windows +130
Tilt Steering Wheel +95

SUBURBAN 1996

Improved engines generate lots of horsepower and torque. Four-wheel drive models get an optional electronic shift transfer case. Daytime running lights, rear seat heating ducts, and two new paint colors summarize the changes to Chevy's Texas Cadillac.

RATINGS (SCALE OF 1-10)

Overall	Safety	Reliability	Performance	Comfort	Value
7.5	6.8	7.7	7.2	7.9	7.8

Model Description	Trade-in Value	Market Value
Category H		
4 Dr C1500 Wgn	17675	21295
4 Dr C2500 Wgn	18575	22380
4 Dr K1500 4WD Wgn	18890	22760
4 Dr K2500 4WD Wgn	19395	23370

OPTIONS FOR SUBURBAN

8 cyl 7.4 L Engine +335
8 cyl 6.5 L Turbodsl Engine +1810
LS Package +1440
LT Package +1640
Air Conditioning +450
AM/FM Compact Disc Playr +165
Automatic Dimming Mirror +80
Camper/Towing Package +195
Cruise Control +105
Dual Air Conditioning +790
Keyless Entry System +90
Leather Seats +575
Power Door Locks +105
Power Drivers Seat +150
Power Mirrors +55
Power Windows +105
Privacy Glass +95
Rear Heater +125
Tilt Steering Wheel +100

TAHOE 1996

For 1996, Tahoe gets 50 additional horsepower and more torque out of a new 5700 V8. Other improvements include rear seat heating ducts, quieter-riding P-metric tires, improved automatic transmissions, and extended interval service schedules. Daytime running lights are new for 1996, and for some reason, Chevy thinks a two-wheel drive two-door Tahoe will be a big seller.

RATINGS (SCALE OF 1-10)

Overall	Safety	Reliability	Performance	Comfort	Value
7.6	6.9	8.1	7.4	8	7.7

Model Description	Trade-in Value	Market Value
Category H		
2 Dr LS Utility	17595	21200
2 Dr LS 4WD Utility	17985	21670

Don't forget to refer to the Mileage Adjustment Table at the back of this book!

© 1999 by Edmund Publications Corporation

Model Description	Trade-in Value	Market Value
4 Dr LS Wgn	20825	25090
4 Dr LS 4WD Wgn	22520	27130
2 Dr LT Utility	18135	21850
2 Dr LT 4WD Utility	18640	22460
4 Dr LT Wgn	21095	25415
4 Dr LT 4WD Wgn	23020	27735
2 Dr STD Utility	16805	20245
2 Dr STD 4WD Utility	17470	21050

OPTIONS FOR TAHOE

8 cyl 6.5 L .Turbodsl Engine +1810
Auto 4-Speed Transmission[Std on STD Utility,Wgn] +510
Air Conditioning[Opt on STD] +450
Aluminum/Alloy Wheels[Opt on STD] +175
AM/FM Compact Disc Playr +165
Camper/Towing Package +195
Cruise Control[Opt on STD] +105
Keyless Entry System[Opt on LS] +90
Power Drivers Seat[Opt on LS] +150
Privacy Glass[Opt on STD] +95
Tilt Steering Wheel[Opt on STD,LS Utility] +100

1995 CHEVROLET

ASTRO 1995

Front sheetmetal is restyled. Regular-length versions are dropped from the lineup, leaving only the extended-length model. Multi-leaf steel springs replace single-leaf plastic springs. One engine is available, the 190-horsepower 4.3-liter V6. Air conditioning is newly standard, and remote keyless entry is a new option.

RATINGS (SCALE OF 1-10)

Overall	Safety	Reliability	Performance	Comfort	Value
7.3	6.1	7.4	7.2	6.6	9

Category G	Trade-in Value	Market Value
2 Dr CL Pass. Van Ext	8850	11200
2 Dr CL 4WD Pass. Van Ext	10685	13525
2 Dr CS Pass. Van Ext	8265	10460
2 Dr CS 4WD Pass. Van Ext	9645	12210
2 Dr LT Pass. Van Ext	9590	12140
2 Dr LT 4WD Pass. Van Ext	10945	13855
2 Dr STD Pass. Van Ext	8260	10455
2 Dr STD Cargo Van	7220	9140
2 Dr STD 4WD Pass. Van Ext	9495	12020
2 Dr STD 4WD Cargo Van	8995	11385

OPTIONS FOR ASTRO

8 Passenger Seating[Std on CL,LT] +175
AM/FM Compact Disc Playr +175
Cruise Control[Opt on STD] +95
Dual Air Conditioning +460
Keyless Entry System[Std on LT] +95
Power Door Locks[Std on CL,LT] +105
Power Drivers Seat +130
Power Mirrors[Std on LT] +60
Power Windows[Opt on CS,STD,CL Pass. Van Ext] +105
Privacy Glass[Opt on CS,STD,CL Pass. Van Ext] +125
Rear Heater +95
Tilt Steering Wheel[Opt on STD] +80

BERETTA 1995

Daytime running lights are newly standard. 170-horse Quad 4 engine is dropped, and 3.1-liter V6 loses five horsepower. Platinum-tipped spark plugs are standard on both engines.

RATINGS (SCALE OF 1-10)

Overall	Safety	Reliability	Performance	Comfort	Value
7	7	8.2	7.8	7	5.1

Category E	Trade-in Value	Market Value
2 Dr STD Cpe	4860	6655
2 Dr Z26 Cpe	6465	8855

OPTIONS FOR BERETTA

6 cyl 3.1 L Engine[Opt on STD] +570
Auto 3-Speed Transmission +245
Auto 4-Speed Transmission[Opt on STD] +445
AM/FM Compact Disc Playr +215
Cruise Control +100
Power Windows +120
Sunroof +155
Tilt Steering Wheel +70

BLAZER 1995

All-new SUV appears based on revamped S10. S10 nomenclature is dropped, and full-size Blazer becomes Tahoe. Four-wheel drive models have electronic transfer case as standard equipment. Spare tire on four-door model is mounted beneath cargo bay instead of in it. Five different suspension packages are available. One engine, a 195-horsepower 4.3-liter V6, is available. All-wheel drive is optional. Driver airbag and air conditioning are standard equipment.

RATINGS (SCALE OF 1-10)

Overall	Safety	Reliability	Performance	Comfort	Value
6.9	5.5	6.9	8	7.9	6.1

Category G	Trade-in Value	Market Value
2 Dr LS Utility	10810	13680
2 Dr LS 4WD Utility	11310	14315
4 Dr LS Wgn	11120	14075
4 Dr LS 4WD Wgn	11795	14930
4 Dr LT Wgn	11880	15040
4 Dr LT 4WD Wgn	12495	15815
2 Dr STD Utility	9340	11825
2 Dr STD 4WD Utility	9880	12505
4 Dr STD Wgn	9685	12255
4 Dr STD 4WD Wgn	10275	13005

Don't forget to refer to the Mileage Adjustment Table at the back of this book!

 © 1999 by Edmund Publications Corporation

Model Description	Trade-in Value	Market Value

OPTIONS FOR BLAZER

AM/FM Compact Disc Playr +175
Cruise Control[Opt on STD] +95
Keyless Entry System[Std on LT] +95
Power Door Locks[Opt on STD] +105
Power Drivers Seat[Std on LT] +130
Power Mirrors[Opt on STD] +60
Power Windows[Opt on STD] +105
Skid Plates +65
Swing Out Tire Carrier +95
Tilt Steering Wheel[Opt on STD] +80

C/K PICKUP 1995

New interior with driver airbag (models under 8,500 lb. GVWR) and standard four-wheel ABS debut. New dashboard features modular design with controls that are much easier to read and use. Power mirrors and remote keyless entry are new options. Uplevel radios come with automatic volume controls that raise or lower volume depending on vehicle speed.

RATINGS (SCALE OF 1-10)

Overall	Safety	Reliability	Performance	Comfort	Value
N/A	8.1	7.4	7.6	8.4	N/A

C1500

Category H

Model Description	Trade-in Value	Market Value
2 Dr Silverado Ext Cab SB	11095	13695
2 Dr Silverado Std Cab SB	10685	13190
2 Dr Silverado Ext Cab Stepside SB	11495	14190
2 Dr Silverado Std Cab Stepside SB	11075	13670
2 Dr Silverado Std Cab LB	10755	13280
2 Dr Silverado Ext Cab LB	11150	13765
2 Dr STD Std Cab SB	9540	11780
2 Dr STD Ext Cab SB	9635	11895
2 Dr STD Std Cab Stepside SB	10025	12375
2 Dr STD Ext Cab Stepside SB	10330	12755
2 Dr STD Std Cab LB	9710	11990
2 Dr STD Ext Cab LB	9980	12320
2 Dr WT Std Cab SB	8090	9990
2 Dr WT Std Cab LB	8215	10140

C2500

Category H

Model Description	Trade-in Value	Market Value
2 Dr Silverado Ext Cab SB	11925	14720
2 Dr Silverado Ext Cab LB	12195	15060
2 Dr Silverado Std Cab LB	11835	14610
2 Dr STD Ext Cab SB	11185	13805
2 Dr STD Ext Cab LB	11170	13790
2 Dr STD Std Cab LB	10795	13325

C3500

Category H

Model Description	Trade-in Value	Market Value
2 Dr Silverado Std Cab LB	13110	16185
2 Dr Silverado Ext Cab LB	13405	16545
4 Dr Silverado Crew Cab LB	14025	17315
2 Dr STD Std Cab LB	12335	15225
2 Dr STD Ext Cab LB	12570	15520
4 Dr STD Crew Cab LB	13250	16360

K1500

Category H

Model Description	Trade-in Value	Market Value
2 Dr Silverado 4WD Ext Cab SB	12285	15165
2 Dr Silverado 4WD Std Cab SB	11790	14555
2 Dr Silverado 4WD Std Cab Stepside SB	12320	15210
2 Dr Silverado 4WD Ext Cab Stepside SB	12670	15640
2 Dr Silverado 4WD Std Cab LB	11900	14695
2 Dr Silverado 4WD Ext Cab LB	12350	15245
2 Dr STD 4WD Ext Cab SB	11230	13865
2 Dr STD 4WD Std Cab SB	10595	13080
2 Dr STD 4WD Ext Cab Stepside SB	11625	14350
2 Dr STD 4WD Std Cab Stepside SB	11110	13715
2 Dr STD 4WD Std Cab LB	10705	13215
2 Dr STD 4WD Ext Cab LB	11305	13955
2 Dr WT 4WD Std Cab SB	9370	11565
2 Dr WT 4WD Std Cab LB	9150	11295

K2500

Category H

Model Description	Trade-in Value	Market Value
2 Dr Silverado 4WD Ext Cab SB	12770	15770
2 Dr Silverado 4WD Std Cab LB	12510	15445
2 Dr Silverado 4WD Ext Cab LB	13120	16195
2 Dr STD 4WD Ext Cab SB	11870	14655
2 Dr STD 4WD Std Cab LB	11575	14290
2 Dr STD 4WD Ext Cab LB	12145	14995

K3500

Category H

Model Description	Trade-in Value	Market Value
2 Dr Silverado 4WD Std Cab LB	13915	17175
2 Dr Silverado 4WD Ext Cab LB	15555	19205
4 Dr Silverado 4WD Crew Cab LB	16615	20515
2 Dr STD 4WD Std Cab LB	13345	16480
2 Dr STD 4WD Ext Cab LB	14485	17880
4 Dr STD 4WD Crew Cab LB	15785	19490

OPTIONS FOR C/K PICKUP

8 cyl 6.5 L Dsl Engine +955
8 cyl 5.0 L Engine +270
8 cyl 5.7 L Engine +335
8 cyl 7.4 L Engine +245
8 cyl 6.5 L Turbodsl Engine +1430
Auto 4-Speed Transmission +415

Don't forget to refer to the Mileage Adjustment Table at the back of this book!

 © 1999 by Edmund Publications Corporation

Model Description	Trade-in Value	Market Value

Air Conditioning[Opt on STD,WT,C3500 Silverado Std Cab LB,K3500 Silverado 4WD Std Cab LB] +365
AM/FM Compact Disc Playr +135
Bed Liner +100
Cruise Control[Opt on STD,WT] +90
Dual Rear Wheels +380
Keyless Entry System +70
Leather Seats +470
Power Door Locks[Opt on STD] +85
Power Drivers Seat +125
Power Mirrors +45
Tilt Steering Wheel[Opt on STD,WT] +80

CAMARO 1995

Z28 gets optional traction control. Z28 can now be ordered with body color roof and side mirrors (standard color is gloss black). Chrome-plated alloys are newly optional.

RATINGS (SCALE OF 1-10)

Overall	Safety	Reliability	Performance	Comfort	Value
7.4	9.1	7.1	9.2	6.6	4.9

Category F

Model	Trade-in	Market
2 Dr STD Cpe	7115	9120
2 Dr STD Conv	8885	11395
2 Dr Z28 Conv	10335	13250
2 Dr Z28 Cpe	9250	11855

OPTIONS FOR CAMARO

6 cyl 3.8 L Engine +155
Auto 4-Speed Transmission +340
Air Conditioning +380
AM/FM Compact Disc Playr +225
Bose Sound System +230
Cruise Control +95
Fog Lights +80
Glass Panel T-tops +470
Keyless Entry System +80
Leather Seats +325
Power Door Locks +90
Power Drivers Seat +110
Power Mirrors[Std on Cpe] +55
Power Windows +100

CAPRICE 1995

Impala SS styling treatment for C-pillar is carried over to more mainstream sedan. New seats and radios debut. Outside mirrors can be folded in, and a new option is a radio with speed-compensated volume control.

RATINGS (SCALE OF 1-10)

Overall	Safety	Reliability	Performance	Comfort	Value
7.9	7.9	6.9	8.2	8.3	8.4

Category B

Model	Trade-in	Market
4 Dr STD Wgn	9905	12700
4 Dr STD Sdn	9060	11615

OPTIONS FOR CAPRICE

8 cyl 5.7 L Engine[Std on Wgn] +245
AM/FM Stereo Tape[Std on Wgn] +80
Auto Load Leveling +85
Cruise Control +95
Keyless Entry System +80
Leather Seats +300
Power Drivers Seat +135
Power Mirrors +45
Power Windows +130

CAVALIER 1995

First redesign since 1982 debut. Sedan, coupe and convertible are available. Wagon is dropped. Sedan comes in base and LS trim. Coupe comes in base and Z24 trim. Convertible is available as LS only. Dual airbags and ABS are standard. Base engine is a 2.2-liter, 120-horsepower four-cylinder engine. Optional on LS sedan and convertible is the Z24's standard powerplant; a 2.3-liter DOHC four-cylinder making 150 horsepower.

RATINGS (SCALE OF 1-10)

Overall	Safety	Reliability	Performance	Comfort	Value
7.4	6.8	7.6	7.2	7.6	7.9

Category E

Model	Trade-in	Market
2 Dr LS Conv	6870	9410
4 Dr LS Sdn	5805	7955
2 Dr STD Cpe	4995	6845
4 Dr STD Sdn	5075	6955
2 Dr Z24 Cpe	6125	8390

OPTIONS FOR CAVALIER

4 cyl 2.3 L Quad 4 Engine[Opt on LS] +175
Auto 3-Speed Transmission[Std on LS] +200
Auto 4-Speed Transmission +220
Air Conditioning[Opt on STD] +370
AM/FM Compact Disc Playr +215
Cruise Control +100
Power Door Locks +105
Power Mirrors +50
Power Sunroof +275
Power Windows +120
Tilt Steering Wheel[Std on Z24] +70

CHEVY VAN/SPORTVAN 1995

No changes.

G10

Category H

Model	Trade-in	Market
2 Dr STD Chevy Van	9260	11430
2 Dr STD Chevy Van Ext	9450	11665

G20

Category H

Model	Trade-in	Market
2 Dr Beauville Sportvan	10405	12845
2 Dr STD Chevy Van Ext	7915	9770

Don't forget to refer to the Mileage Adjustment Table at the back of this book!

 © 1999 by Edmund Publications Corporation

CHEVROLET 95

Model Description	Trade-in Value	Market Value
2 Dr STD Chevy Van	7870	9715
2 Dr STD Sportvan	9470	11695

G30

Category H

Model Description	Trade-in Value	Market Value
2 Dr Beauville Sportvan Ext	11095	13700
2 Dr Beauville Sportvan	10580	13065
2 Dr STD Sportvan Ext	10130	12505
2 Dr STD Sportvan	9720	11995
2 Dr STD Chevy Van Ext	9100	11235
2 Dr STD Chevy Van	8575	10585

OPTIONS FOR CHEVY VAN/SPORTVAN

8 cyl 6.5 L Dsl Engine +955
8 cyl 5.0 L Engine +270
8 cyl 5.7 L Engine[Opt on G20,Chevy Van] +335
8 cyl 7.4 L Engine +245
16 Passenger Seating +170
Air Conditioning[Opt on G10,STD] +365
AM/FM Stereo Tape[Opt on G10,STD] +110
Cruise Control[Opt on G10,STD] +90
Dual Air Conditioning +645
Power Door Locks[Opt on G10,STD] +85
Power Windows[Opt on G10,STD] +85
Privacy Glass +75
Rear Heater +100
Tilt Steering Wheel[Opt on G10,STD] +80

CORSICA 1995

Daytime running lights debut. Rear suspension is revised, and larger tires are standard.

RATINGS (SCALE OF 1-10)

Overall	Safety	Reliability	Performance	Comfort	Value
6.9	5.8	7.9	8	7.5	5.2

Category C

Model Description	Trade-in Value	Market Value
4 Dr STD Sdn	5020	6605

OPTIONS FOR CORSICA

6 cyl 3.1 L Engine +215
AM/FM Stereo Tape +75
Cruise Control +95
Power Windows +140
Tilt Steering Wheel +70

CORVETTE 1995

ZR-1's brakes trickle down to base models. Front fenders get revised gills. Only 448 ZR-1s were produced in 1995.

Category J

Model Description	Trade-in Value	Market Value
2 Dr STD Cpe	16540	20415
2 Dr STD Conv	20355	25125
2 Dr ZR1 Cpe	25780	31830

OPTIONS FOR CORVETTE

Dual Roof Panels +425
Handling Package +915
Selective Ride Suspension +755
Bose Sound System +370
Climate Control for AC[Opt on STD] +100
Compact Disc W/fm/tape[Opt on STD] +325
Power Drivers Seat[Opt on STD] +150
Solid & Glass Targa Tops +425

IMPALA 1995

Dark Cherry and Green Gray paint colors join basic black. New seats and radios debut. Outside mirrors can be folded in, and a new option is a radio with speed-compensated volume control.

RATINGS (SCALE OF 1-10)

Overall	Safety	Reliability	Performance	Comfort	Value
8	7.9	6.9	9	8.3	8.1

Category B

Model Description	Trade-in Value	Market Value
4 Dr SS Sdn	13405	17185

OPTIONS FOR IMPALA

AM/FM Compact Disc Playr +140
Keyless Entry System +80
Power Passenger Seat +140

LUMINA 1995

Midsize sedan is redesigned; features dual airbags. Base and LS trim levels are available. ABS is optional on base model; standard on LS. Standard powerplant is a 160-horsepower 3.1-liter V6. Optional on LS is a 210-horsepower 3.4-liter V6. Air conditioning is standard.

RATINGS (SCALE OF 1-10)

Overall	Safety	Reliability	Performance	Comfort	Value
7.7	8.2	7.9	7.6	7.3	7.6

Category C

Model Description	Trade-in Value	Market Value
4 Dr LS Sdn	6980	9185
4 Dr STD Sdn	6490	8540

OPTIONS FOR LUMINA

6 cyl 3.4 L Engine +430
AM/FM Compact Disc Playr +175
Anti-Lock Brakes[Std on LS] +285
Cruise Control +95
Keyless Entry System +85
Power Drivers Seat +130
Power Windows[Std on LS] +140

LUMINA MINIVAN 1995

Transmission gets brake/shift interlock.

RATINGS (SCALE OF 1-10)

Overall	Safety	Reliability	Performance	Comfort	Value
7.2	6.9	7.2	7.6	7.3	6.8

Category G

Model Description	Trade-in Value	Market Value
2 Dr STD Cargo Van	6470	8185
2 Dr STD Pass. Van	7330	9280

Don't forget to refer to the Mileage Adjustment Table at the back of this book!

© 1999 by Edmund Publications Corporation

Model Description	Trade-in Value	Market Value

OPTIONS FOR LUMINA MINIVAN
6 cyl 3.8 L Engine +185
Auto 4-Speed Transmission +90
Air Conditioning +370
AM/FM Stereo Tape +110
Child Seat (1) +80
Cruise Control +95
Keyless Entry System +95
Power Door Locks +105
Power Drivers Seat +130
Power Mirrors +60
Power Windows +105
Privacy Glass +125
Tilt Steering Wheel +80

MONTE CARLO 1995

Chevy slaps revered moniker on coupe version of Lumina. Available in LS or Z34 trim levels. Dual airbags and ABS are standard. LS comes with 160-horsepower 3.1-liter V6, while Z34 is powered by 3.4-liter twin-cam V6 good for 210 horsepower. All Monte Carlos have automatic transmissions. Air conditioning is standard.

RATINGS (SCALE OF 1-10)

Overall	Safety	Reliability	Performance	Comfort	Value
7.4	8.2	7.1	7.4	7.5	7.1

Category C

Model Description	Trade-in Value	Market Value
2 Dr LS Cpe	7650	10065
2 Dr Z34 Cpe	8845	11640

OPTIONS FOR MONTE CARLO
Cruise Control[Opt on LS] +95
Keyless Entry System[Opt on LS] +85
Leather Seats +260
Power Drivers Seat +130
Power Mirrors[Opt on LS] +50

S10 PICKUP 1995

Driver airbag is added, and daytime running lights are standard. ZR2 off-road package can be ordered on the extended-cab. Power window and lock buttons are illuminated at night. Remote keyless entry is a new option. A single key operates both the door locks and the ignition. A manual transmission can now be ordered with the 191-horsepower 4.3-liter V6.

RATINGS (SCALE OF 1-10)

Overall	Safety	Reliability	Performance	Comfort	Value
N/A	5.1	7.1	6.6	8.1	N/A

Category G

Model Description	Trade-in Value	Market Value
2 Dr LS Std Cab SB	6290	7960
2 Dr LS Ext Cab SB	6810	8620
2 Dr LS Std Cab LB	6425	8135
2 Dr LS 4WD Std Cab SB	8335	10550
2 Dr LS 4WD Ext Cab SB	8820	11165
2 Dr LS 4WD Std Cab LB	8295	10500
2 Dr STD Std Cab SB	6270	7935
2 Dr STD Std Cab LB	6405	8110
2 Dr STD 4WD Std Cab SB	8150	10315
2 Dr STD 4WD Std Cab LB	8225	10410

OPTIONS FOR S10 PICKUP
6 cyl 4.3 L Engine[Opt on 2WD] +375
6 cyl 4.3 L CPI Engine +380
Auto 4-Speed Transmission +445
Wide Stance Suspension +770
Air Conditioning +370
AM/FM Compact Disc Playr +175
AM/FM Stereo Tape +110
Anti-Lock Brakes[Opt on 2WD] +280
Cruise Control +95
Heavy Duty Suspension +65
Keyless Entry System +95
Power Door Locks +105
Power Windows +105
Tilt Steering Wheel +80

SUBURBAN 1995

New interior with driver airbag debuts. New dashboard features modular design with controls that are much easier to read and use. 1500 models can now be ordered with turbodiesel engine. Brake/transmission shift interlock is added to automatic transmission. Seats and door panels are revised. New console on models with bucket seats features pivoting writing surface, along with rear cupholders and storage drawer. Uplevel radios come with automatic volume controls that raise or lower the volume depending on vehicle speed.

RATINGS (SCALE OF 1-10)

Overall	Safety	Reliability	Performance	Comfort	Value
7.5	7.5	7.5	7	7.9	7.7

Category H

Model Description	Trade-in Value	Market Value
4 Dr C1500 Wgn	15015	18540
4 Dr C2500 Wgn	15965	19705
4 Dr K1500 4WD Wgn	16360	20200
4 Dr K2500 4WD Wgn	17355	21430

OPTIONS FOR SUBURBAN
8 cyl 7.4 L Engine +245
8 cyl 6.5 L Turbodsl Engine +1430
LS Package +1505
LT Package +2025
Air Conditioning +365
AM/FM Compact Disc Playr +135
Automatic Dimming Mirror +65
Camper/Towing Package +160
Cruise Control +90
Dual Air Conditioning +645
Keyless Entry System +70
Leather Seats +470
Power Door Locks +85

Don't forget to refer to the Mileage Adjustment Table at the back of this book!

 © 1999 by Edmund Publications Corporation

Power Drivers Seat +125
Power Mirrors +45
Power Windows +85
Privacy Glass +75
Rear Heater +100
Tilt Steering Wheel +80

TAHOE 1995

Full-size SUV gets a new name as S10-based model takes Blazer moniker. New interior with driver airbag debuts. New dashboard features modular design with controls that are much easier to read and use. New five-door model is added midyear, nicely sized between Blazer and Suburban. New model is offered only in LS or LT trim with a 5.7-liter V8 and an automatic transmission in either 2WD or 4WD. Brake/transmission shift interlock is added to automatic transmission. New console on models with bucket seats features pivoting writing surface, along with rear cupholders and storage drawer.

RATINGS (SCALE OF 1-10)

Overall	Safety	Reliability	Performance	Comfort	Value
7.7	7.6	8.1	7.2	8	7.7

Category H

Model Description	Trade-in Value	Market Value
2 Dr LS 4WD Utility	15930	19665
4 Dr LS Wgn	15910	19640
4 Dr LS 4WD Wgn	19320	23850
2 Dr LT 4WD Utility	16475	20340
4 Dr LT Wgn	16505	20380
4 Dr LT 4WD Wgn	20000	24695
2 Dr STD 4WD Utility	14305	17660

OPTIONS FOR TAHOE

8 cyl 6.5 L Turbodsl Engine +1430
Auto 4-Speed Transmission[Std on Wgn] +415
Air Conditioning[Opt on STD] +365
AM/FM Compact Disc Playr +135
AM/FM Stereo Tape[Opt on STD] +110
Cruise Control[Opt on STD] +90
Keyless Entry System[Std on LT] +70
Power Door Locks[Opt on STD] +85
Power Drivers Seat[Opt on LS] +125
Privacy Glass[Opt on STD] +75
Tilt Steering Wheel[Opt on STD] +80

1994 CHEVROLET

ASTRO 1994

Driver airbag is made standard. Side door guard beams are stronger, and air conditioners use CFC-free refrigerant. A high-mount center brake light is added. Analog gauges get new graphics, and carpet is treated with Scotchgard.

RATINGS (SCALE OF 1-10)

Overall	Safety	Reliability	Performance	Comfort	Value
7.2	5.9	7	7.2	6.6	9.3

Category G

Model Description	Trade-in Value	Market Value
2 Dr CL Pass. Van Ext	6725	8735
2 Dr CL Pass. Van	6340	8230
2 Dr CL 4WD Pass. Van	9065	11775
2 Dr CL 4WD Pass. Van Ext	9920	12880
2 Dr LT Pass. Van	6550	8505
2 Dr LT Pass. Van Ext	7350	9545
2 Dr LT 4WD Pass. Van	10030	13030
2 Dr LT 4WD Pass. Van Ext	10410	13520
2 Dr STD Cargo Van Ext	5550	7205
2 Dr STD Pass. Van	5995	7785
2 Dr STD Pass. Van Ext	6360	8260
2 Dr STD Cargo Van	4990	6485
2 Dr STD 4WD Pass. Van Ext	8560	11115
2 Dr STD 4WD Cargo Van	7215	9370
2 Dr STD 4WD Cargo Van Ext	7380	9585
2 Dr STD 4WD Pass. Van	8345	10835

OPTIONS FOR ASTRO

6 cyl 4.3 L CPI Engine[Opt on 2WD] +205
8 Passenger Seating +140
Air Conditioning +300
AM/FM Stereo Tape +90
Cruise Control +80
Dual Air Conditioning +375
Power Door Locks +85
Power Drivers Seat +105
Power Windows +85
Privacy Glass[Std on LT] +100
Tilt Steering Wheel +65

BERETTA 1994

GT and GTZ are dropped in favor of Z26 model, which offers a standard 170-horsepower Quad 4 engine. Base models get ten more horsepower, and the 3.1-liter V6 makes an additional 20 horsepower, up to 160. Automatic transmission is unavailable with Quad 4; manual transmission is unavailable with V6. Door-mounted seatbelts are added. Automatic door locks lock doors once Beretta is underway, and unlock when car is stopped. Disable this feature by yanking a fuse. Interior lights shut off after ten minutes to save battery. Warning chime reminds driver that turn signal has been on for more than 3/4 mile.

RATINGS (SCALE OF 1-10)

Overall	Safety	Reliability	Performance	Comfort	Value
6.8	6.6	7.8	7.8	7	4.9

Category E

Model Description	Trade-in Value	Market Value
2 Dr STD Cpe	4180	5970
2 Dr Z26 Cpe	5080	7260

Don't forget to refer to the Mileage Adjustment Table at the back of this book!

 © 1999 by Edmund Publications Corporation

Model Description	Trade-in Value	Market Value

OPTIONS FOR BERETTA

6 cyl 3.1 L Engine +275
Auto 3-Speed Transmission +205
Auto 4-Speed Transmission +250
AM/FM Stereo Tape[Opt on STD] +115
Cruise Control +80
Power Windows +100
Sunroof +130
Tilt Steering Wheel +55

BLAZER 1994

Air conditioning receives CFC-free coolant. Side guard door beams are added. A new grille appears, and models equipped with a decor package get composite headlamps. A turbocharged diesel is newly optional. Third brake light is added.

Category H

Model Description	Trade-in Value	Market Value
2 Dr Silverado 4WD Utility	11910	14885
2 Dr Sport 4WD Utility	11515	14395
2 Dr STD 4WD Utility	10860	13575

OPTIONS FOR BLAZER

8 cyl 6.5 L Turbodsl Engine +1185
Auto 4-Speed Transmission +330
Air Conditioning[Opt on STD] +300
AM/FM Stereo Tape +90
Cruise Control[Opt on STD] +70
Power Door Locks[Std on Sport] +70
Power Drivers Seat +100
Power Windows[Std on Sport] +70
Tilt Steering Wheel[Opt on STD] +65

C/K PICKUP 1994

454 SS dropped. Grilles are restyled, side door guard beams are added, and a third brake light is installed. Leather seats are available. Front seatback on extended-cab models gets memory feature to improve entry and exit to rear seat. A 6.5-liter diesel replaces last year's 6.2-liter unit, and a turbocharged version is also available for 1500 and 2500 models.

RATINGS (SCALE OF 1-10)

Overall	Safety	Reliability	Performance	Comfort	Value
N/A	6	7.5	7.4	8.4	N/A

C1500

Category H

Model Description	Trade-in Value	Market Value
2 Dr Cheyenne Std Cab SB	8525	10655
2 Dr Cheyenne Ext Cab SB	8895	11115
2 Dr Cheyenne Std Cab Stepside SB	8855	11070
2 Dr Cheyenne Ext Cab Stepside SB	9255	11565
2 Dr Cheyenne Ext Cab LB	9360	11700
2 Dr Cheyenne Std Cab LB	8625	10780
2 Dr Silverado Std Cab SB	8795	10995
2 Dr Silverado Ext Cab SB	9190	11490
2 Dr Silverado Std Cab Stepside SB	9190	11490
2 Dr Silverado Ext Cab Stepside SB	9345	11680
2 Dr Silverado Ext Cab LB	9500	11875
2 Dr Silverado Std Cab LB	8960	11205
2 Dr STD Std Cab SB	8285	10355
2 Dr STD Ext Cab SB	8655	10820
2 Dr STD Ext Cab Stepside SB	8950	11185
2 Dr STD Std Cab Stepside SB	8615	10770
2 Dr STD Ext Cab LB	8735	10920
2 Dr STD Std Cab LB	8385	10480
2 Dr WT Std Cab SB	6765	8455
2 Dr WT Std Cab LB	6750	8440

C2500

Category H

Model Description	Trade-in Value	Market Value
2 Dr Cheyenne Ext Cab SB	9565	11955
2 Dr Cheyenne Std Cab LB	9090	11365
2 Dr Cheyenne Ext Cab LB	9705	12135
2 Dr Silverado Ext Cab SB	9675	12095
2 Dr Silverado Std Cab LB	9295	11620
2 Dr Silverado Ext Cab LB	9730	12165
2 Dr STD Ext Cab SB	9010	11260
2 Dr STD Ext Cab LB	9075	11345
2 Dr STD Std Cab LB	8815	11015

C3500

Category H

Model Description	Trade-in Value	Market Value
2 Dr Cheyenne Std Cab LB	10645	13305
2 Dr Cheyenne Ext Cab LB	10790	13490
4 Dr Cheyenne Crew Cab LB	11185	13980
2 Dr Silverado Ext Cab LB	11280	14100
2 Dr Silverado Std Cab LB	11165	13955
4 Dr Silverado Crew Cab LB	11460	14325
2 Dr STD Std Cab LB	10355	12940
2 Dr STD Ext Cab LB	10495	13120
4 Dr STD Crew Cab LB	10770	13465

K1500

Category H

Model Description	Trade-in Value	Market Value
2 Dr Cheyenne 4WD Ext Cab SB	10180	12730
2 Dr Cheyenne 4WD Std Cab SB	9610	12015
2 Dr Cheyenne 4WD Ext Cab Stepside SB	10235	12790
2 Dr Cheyenne 4WD Std Cab Stepside SB	9930	12410
2 Dr Cheyenne 4WD Ext Cab LB	10030	12540
2 Dr Cheyenne 4WD Std Cab LB	9645	12060
2 Dr Silverado 4WD Std Cab SB	9990	12490
2 Dr Silverado 4WD Ext Cab SB	10510	13135

Don't forget to refer to the Mileage Adjustment Table at the back of this book!

 © 1999 by Edmund Publications Corporation

Model Description	Trade-in Value	Market Value
2 Dr Silverado 4WD Ext Cab Stepside SB	10800	13500
2 Dr Silverado 4WD Std Cab Stepside SB	10300	12875
2 Dr Silverado 4WD Std Cab LB	10030	12535
2 Dr Silverado 4WD Ext Cab LB	10595	13245
2 Dr Sport 4WD Std Cab SB	9935	12420
2 Dr Sport 4WD Std Cab Stepside SB	10240	12800
2 Dr STD 4WD Ext Cab SB	9840	12305
2 Dr STD 4WD Std Cab SB	9330	11665
2 Dr STD 4WD Std Cab Stepside SB	9705	12130
2 Dr STD 4WD Ext Cab Stepside SB	9845	12310
2 Dr STD 4WD Std Cab LB	9220	11530
2 Dr STD 4WD Ext Cab LB	9920	12405
2 Dr WT 4WD Std Cab SB	7645	9555
2 Dr WT 4WD Std Cab LB	7730	9660

K2500

Category H

Model Description	Trade-in Value	Market Value
2 Dr Cheyenne 4WD Ext Cab SB	10605	13260
2 Dr Cheyenne 4WD Std Cab LB	9980	12475
2 Dr Cheyenne 4WD Ext Cab LB	10650	13310
2 Dr Silverado 4WD Ext Cab SB	10910	13635
2 Dr Silverado 4WD Ext Cab LB	11195	13995
2 Dr Silverado 4WD Std Cab LB	10555	13195
2 Dr STD 4WD Ext Cab SB	10125	12655
2 Dr STD 4WD Std Cab LB	9810	12265
2 Dr STD 4WD Ext Cab LB	10475	13090

K3500

Category H

Model Description	Trade-in Value	Market Value
2 Dr Cheyenne 4WD Std Cab LB	11620	14520
2 Dr Cheyenne 4WD Ext Cab LB	12390	15485
4 Dr Cheyenne 4WD Crew Cab LB	12465	15580
2 Dr Silverado 4WD Ext Cab LB	12535	15670
2 Dr Silverado 4WD Std Cab LB	11780	14725
4 Dr Silverado 4WD Crew Cab LB	12755	15945
2 Dr STD 4WD Ext Cab LB	12070	15085
2 Dr STD 4WD Std Cab LB	11380	14220
4 Dr STD 4WD Crew Cab LB	13095	16370

OPTIONS FOR C/K PICKUP

8 cyl 6.5 L Dsl Engine +975
8 cyl 5.0 L Engine +220
8 cyl 5.7 L Engine +265
8 cyl 7.4 L Engine +210
8 cyl 6.5 L Turbodsl Engine +1185
Auto 4-Speed Transmission +335
Sport Handling Package +360
Air Conditioning[Opt on STD,Work Truck] +300
AM/FM Stereo Tape[Std on Sport] +90
Bed Liner +85
Camper/Towing Package +130
Cruise Control[Std on Sport] +70
Dual Rear Wheels +310
Power Door Locks[Std on Sport] +70
Power Drivers Seat +100
Power Windows[Std on Sport] +70
Tilt Steering Wheel[Std on Sport] +65

CAMARO 1994

Convertible returns in base and Z28 trim. First-to-fourth shift pattern added to six-speed manual transmission to meet fuel economy regulations. Z28 with manual transmission gets revised gearing for better acceleration.

RATINGS (SCALE OF 1-10)

Overall	Safety	Reliability	Performance	Comfort	Value
7.4	9.2	7.4	9.2	6.6	4.4

Category F

Model Description	Trade-in Value	Market Value
2 Dr STD Cpe	6140	8080
2 Dr STD Conv	7770	10225
2 Dr Z28 Conv	9085	11955
2 Dr Z28 Cpe	7775	10230

OPTIONS FOR CAMARO

Auto 4-Speed Transmission +250
Air Conditioning +310
Bose Sound System +190
Fog Lights +65
Glass Panel T-tops +385
Keyless Entry System +65
Leather Seats +265
Power Door Locks +75
Power Drivers Seat +90
Power Windows +85

CAPRICE 1994

Passenger airbag added. New base engine for sedan is a 200-horsepower 4.3-liter V6. Optional on sedan and standard on wagon is a more powerful 260-horsepower 5.7-liter V8. Automatic transmissions get electronic controls. Pass-Key II is a standard theft-deterrent system, and CFC-free refrigerant is added to air conditioning systems.

RATINGS (SCALE OF 1-10)

Overall	Safety	Reliability	Performance	Comfort	Value
8	8	6.9	8.2	8.3	8.8

Category B

Model Description	Trade-in Value	Market Value
4 Dr LS Sdn	8120	10825
4 Dr STD Sdn	6690	8920
4 Dr STD Wgn	8480	11305

OPTIONS FOR CAPRICE

8 cyl 5.7 L Engine[Std on Wgn] +120
AM/FM Stereo Tape[Std on LS,Wgn] +65
Auto Load Leveling +70

Don't forget to refer to the Mileage Adjustment Table at the back of this book!

 © 1999 by Edmund Publications Corporation

Model Description	Trade-in Value	Market Value

Cruise Control[Std on LS] +80
Leather Seats +245
Power Door Locks[Std on LS] +90
Power Drivers Seat[Std on LS] +110
Power Windows[Std on LS] +110

CAVALIER 1994

Wagon is sold without trim designation. Base engine is up ten horsepower to 120. Automatic door locks unlock when ignition is turned off. Feature is defeated by yanking a fuse.

RATINGS (SCALE OF 1-10)

Overall	Safety	Reliability	Performance	Comfort	Value
N/A	N/A	7.5	6.6	6.8	8.4

Category E

Model Description	Trade-in Value	Market Value
2 Dr RS Cpe	3870	5530
2 Dr RS Conv	5085	7260
4 Dr RS Sdn	3845	5495
4 Dr STD Wgn	3775	5395
2 Dr VL Cpe	3185	4550
4 Dr VL Sdn	3125	4465
2 Dr Z24 Conv	6390	9130
2 Dr Z24 Cpe	5475	7820

OPTIONS FOR CAVALIER

6 cyl 3.1 L Engine[Std on Z24] +275
Auto 3-Speed Transmission[Opt on VL,Z24,RS Cpe] +185
Air Conditioning[Opt on VL] +300
AM/FM Stereo Tape[Std on Z24] +115
Cruise Control +80
Power Windows[Std on Conv] +100
Sunroof +130
Tilt Steering Wheel[Std on Z24] +55

CHEVY VAN/SPORTVAN 1994

Driver airbag is added to all models under 8,500 lb. GVWR. Side guard door beams are installed in front doors and a high-mount center brake light is added.

G10

Category H

Model Description	Trade-in Value	Market Value
2 Dr STD Chevy Van	8390	10485
2 Dr STD Chevy Van Ext	8890	11115

G20

Category H

Model Description	Trade-in Value	Market Value
2 Dr Beauville Sportvan	8580	10725
2 Dr STD Chevy Van	6795	8495
2 Dr STD Chevy Van Ext	6955	8695
2 Dr STD Sportvan	7565	9460

G30

Category H

Model Description	Trade-in Value	Market Value
2 Dr Beauville Sportvan Ext	8485	10605
2 Dr Beauville Sportvan	7995	9995
2 Dr STD Sportvan Ext	7845	9810
2 Dr STD Chevy Van Ext	7100	8875
2 Dr STD Chevy Van	6465	8080
2 Dr STD Sportvan	7295	9115

OPTIONS FOR CHEVY VAN/SPORTVAN

8 cyl 6.5 L Dsl Engine +975
8 cyl 5.0 L Engine +220
8 cyl 5.7 L Engine[Opt on G20] +265
8 cyl 7.4 L Engine +210
15 Passenger Seating +265
Air Conditioning[Opt on G10,STD] +300
AM/FM Stereo Tape +90
Cruise Control[Opt on G10,STD] +70
Dual Air Conditioning +525
Power Door Locks[Opt on G10,STD] +70
Power Windows[Opt on G10,STD] +70
Privacy Glass +65
Rear Heater +80
Tilt Steering Wheel[Opt on G10,STD] +65

CORSICA 1994

Door mounted seatbelts are added. Engines gain power; the 2.2-liter unit is up to 120 horsepower, and the optional 3.1-liter V6 now makes 160 horsepower. Sport Handling Package dropped from options list. Manual transmission dropped. Automatic door locks now unlock when car is shut off. This feature can be disabled by pulling a fuse. Interior lights will shut off automatically after ten minutes to save the battery. Warning chime sounds if turn signal is activated for more than 3/4 mile.

RATINGS (SCALE OF 1-10)

Overall	Safety	Reliability	Performance	Comfort	Value
7	5.8	7.5	8	7.5	6.1

Category C

Model Description	Trade-in Value	Market Value
4 Dr STD Sdn	3900	5270

OPTIONS FOR CORSICA

6 cyl 3.1 L Engine +195
AM/FM Stereo Tape +60
Cruise Control +75
Power Windows +115
Tilt Steering Wheel +55

CORVETTE 1994

Passenger airbag is added. Traction control is standard. A new steering wheel and redesigned seats are added inside. Leather upholstery is standard. Automatic transmission gets electronic shift controls and brake/transmission shift interlock. Convertible gets glass rear window with defogger. ZR-1 has new five-spoke alloys. Power windows gain express-down feature for driver's side. Selective Ride Control system has softer springs.

Don't forget to refer to the Mileage Adjustment Table at the back of this book!

© 1999 by Edmund Publications Corporation

Model Description	Trade-in Value	Market Value
Category J		
2 Dr STD Conv	16930	21160
2 Dr STD Cpe	15140	18925
2 Dr ZR1 Cpe	20030	25040

OPTIONS FOR CORVETTE

Adjustable Handling Pkg. +760
Selective Ride & Handling +630
Bose Sound System[Opt on STD] +305
Climate Control for AC[Opt on STD] +80
Compact Disc W/fm/tape +265
Power Drivers Seat[Opt on STD] +120
Solid & Glass Targa Tops +350

IMPALA 1994

Caprice-based sedan powered by 260-horsepower 5.7-liter V8 and sporting monochromatic black paint debuts to critical acclaim. Has four-wheel disc brakes, dual airbags, ABS, five-spoke alloys, and restyled C-pillars.

RATINGS (SCALE OF 1-10)

Overall	Safety	Reliability	Performance	Comfort	Value
8.1	8	6.9	9	8.3	8.5

Model Description	Trade-in Value	Market Value
Category B		
4 Dr SS Sdn	11165	14885

OPTIONS FOR IMPALA

AM/FM Compact Disc Playr +115
Keyless Entry System +65
Power Passenger Seat +115

LUMINA 1994

Base coupe is dropped from lineup. Manual transmission disappears.

RATINGS (SCALE OF 1-10)

Overall	Safety	Reliability	Performance	Comfort	Value
N/A	N/A	8	8.2	7.6	8.1

Model Description	Trade-in Value	Market Value
Category C		
2 Dr Euro Cpe	5875	7935
4 Dr Euro Sdn	5815	7855
4 Dr STD Sdn	4925	6655
2 Dr Z34 Cpe	6930	9360

OPTIONS FOR LUMINA

6 cyl 3.4 L Engine[Std on Z34] +415
AM/FM Stereo Tape[Opt on STD] +60
Anti-Lock Brakes[Opt on STD] +230
Cruise Control[Std on Z34] +75
Power Drivers Seat +105
Power Windows[Opt on STD] +115

LUMINA MINIVAN 1994

APV designation dropped in favor of more descriptive "Minivan" nomenclature. Front styling is revised; overall length drops three inches. Driver airbag is standard. Integrated child seats and remote keyless entry are newly optional. Midyear, traction control becomes available on LS model.

RATINGS (SCALE OF 1-10)

Overall	Safety	Reliability	Performance	Comfort	Value
7.6	6.9	7.4	7.6	7.5	8.5

Model Description	Trade-in Value	Market Value
Category G		
2 Dr STD Cargo Van	4710	6115
2 Dr STD Pass. Van	5895	7655

OPTIONS FOR LUMINA MINIVAN

6 cyl 3.8 L Engine +230
Auto 4-Speed Transmission +75
Air Conditioning +300
AM/FM Stereo Tape +90
Child Seat (1) +65
Cruise Control +80
Power Door Locks +85
Power Drivers Seat +105
Power Windows +85
Privacy Glass +100
Tilt Steering Wheel +65

S10 BLAZER 1994

Side-door guard beams and a high-mount center brake light are added. Front bench seat is now standard on four-door models.

RATINGS (SCALE OF 1-10)

Overall	Safety	Reliability	Performance	Comfort	Value
6	5.1	6.6	6.8	7.1	4.6

Model Description	Trade-in Value	Market Value
Category G		
2 Dr STD Utility	6215	8075
2 Dr STD 4WD Utility	7255	9420
4 Dr STD Wgn	7235	9395
4 Dr STD 4WD Wgn	8165	10605
2 Dr Tahoe Utility	6750	8765
2 Dr Tahoe 4WD Utility	7845	10185
4 Dr Tahoe Wgn	7460	9685
4 Dr Tahoe 4WD Wgn	8410	10920
2 Dr Tahoe LT Utility	7985	10370
2 Dr Tahoe LT 4WD Utility	9355	12145
4 Dr Tahoe LT Wgn	9200	11950
4 Dr Tahoe LT 4WD Wgn	10260	13325

OPTIONS FOR S10 BLAZER

6 cyl 4.3 L CPI Engine +205
Auto 4-Speed Transmission +335
Air Conditioning[Std on Tahoe LT] +300
AM/FM Stereo Tape[Std on Tahoe LT] +90
Cruise Control[Opt on STD] +80
Keyless Entry System[Std on Tahoe LT] +75
Power Door Locks[Std on Tahoe LT] +85
Power Drivers Seat[Std on Tahoe LT] +105
Power Windows[Std on Tahoe LT] +85
Tilt Steering Wheel[Opt on STD] +65

Don't forget to refer to the Mileage Adjustment Table at the back of this book!

 © 1999 by Edmund Publications Corporation

Model Description	Trade-in Value	Market Value

S10 PICKUP 1994

All-new truck debuts with more powerful engines and available four-wheel ABS. Side-door guard beams are standard. Rear ABS is standard on four cylinder models; V6 trucks get the new, four-wheel ABS system that works in both two- and four-wheel drive. ZR2 package is for serious off-roaders. Available only on regular-cab shortbed models, the ZR2 package includes four-inch wider track, three-inch height increase, off-road suspension and tires, wheel flares and thick skid plates. Base engine is 118-horse 2.2-liter four cylinder. Standard on 4WD models is a 165-horsepower 4.3-liter V6. Optional on all models is a 195-horsepower high output 4.3-liter V6. SS package available with high-output engine, sport suspension and alloy wheels.

RATINGS (SCALE OF 1-10)

Overall	Safety	Reliability	Performance	Comfort	Value
N/A	5.2	7.2	6.6	8.1	N/A

Category G	Trade-in Value	Market Value
2 Dr LS Ext Cab SB	6075	7890
2 Dr LS Std Cab SB	5785	7515
2 Dr LS Std Cab LB	5825	7565
2 Dr LS 4WD Std Cab SB	7095	9210
2 Dr LS 4WD Ext Cab SB	7560	9820
2 Dr LS 4WD Std Cab LB	7190	9340
2 Dr STD Std Cab SB	5635	7320
2 Dr STD Std Cab LB	5705	7410
2 Dr STD 4WD Std Cab SB	6855	8905
2 Dr STD 4WD Std Cab LB	6955	9030

OPTIONS FOR S10 PICKUP

6 cyl 4.3 L Engine[Opt on 2WD] +205
6 cyl 4.3 L CPI Engine +315
Auto 4-Speed Transmission +345
Wide Stance Package +625
Air Conditioning +300
AM/FM Stereo Tape +90
Anti-Lock Brakes[Opt on 2WD] +230
Cruise Control +80
Heavy Duty Suspension +50
Power Brakes[Std on LS,4WD,LB] +55
Power Door Locks +85
Power Windows +85
Tilt Steering Wheel +65

SUBURBAN 1994

Side-door guard beams are added, as well as a high-mounted center brake light. A turbocharged diesel is newly optional on 2500 models. A new grille appears.

RATINGS (SCALE OF 1-10)

Overall	Safety	Reliability	Performance	Comfort	Value
7	6.6	7.6	7	7.5	6.3

Category H	Trade-in Value	Market Value
4 Dr C1500 Wgn	12425	15530
4 Dr C2500 Wgn	13335	16670
4 Dr K1500 4WD Wgn	14180	17725
4 Dr K2500 4WD Wgn	14910	18640

OPTIONS FOR SUBURBAN

8 cyl 7.4 L Engine +210
8 cyl 6.5 L Turbodsl Engine +1185
Silverado Package +825
Air Conditioning +300
AM/FM Stereo Tape +90
Camper/Towing Package +130
Cruise Control +70
Dual Air Conditioning +525
Leather Seats +385
Power Door Locks +70
Power Drivers Seat +100
Power Windows +70
Rear Heater +80
Tilt Steering Wheel +65

1993 CHEVROLET

ASTRO 1993

Base 4.3-liter V6 gets 15 additional horsepower. Automatic transmission gets electronic shift controls and second-gear start feature. New speedometer reads to 100 mph. Driver airbag is offered as an option midyear.

RATINGS (SCALE OF 1-10)

Overall	Safety	Reliability	Performance	Comfort	Value
6.8	4.1	6.7	7.2	6.6	9.2

Category G	Trade-in Value	Market Value
2 Dr CL Pass. Van	5310	7085
2 Dr CL Pass. Van Ext	5585	7445
2 Dr CL 4WD Pass. Van Ext	6460	8610
2 Dr CL 4WD Pass. Van	6365	8485
2 Dr LT Pass. Van	5485	7310
2 Dr LT Pass. Van Ext	6175	8235
2 Dr LT 4WD Pass. Van Ext	7210	9610
2 Dr LT 4WD Pass. Van	6580	8770
2 Dr STD Cargo Van	4035	5385
2 Dr STD Cargo Van Ext	4090	5455
2 Dr STD Pass. Van	5025	6700
2 Dr STD Pass. Van Ext	5730	7640
2 Dr STD 4WD Cargo Van	5200	6935
2 Dr STD 4WD Cargo Van Ext	5330	7105
2 Dr STD 4WD Pass. Van	6225	8300

OPTIONS FOR ASTRO

6 cyl 4.3 L CPI Engine[Opt on CL,Pass. Van Ext,2WD] +140
8 Passenger Seating +115
Air Bag Restraint[Opt on CL,LT,Pass. Van Ext,2WD] +150

Don't forget to refer to the Mileage Adjustment Table at the back of this book!

 © 1999 by Edmund Publications Corporation

Model Description	Trade-in Value	Market Value

Air Conditioning +245
Aluminum/Alloy Wheels +105
AM/FM Stereo Tape +75
Cruise Control +65
Dual Air Conditioning +305
Power Door Locks +70
Power Drivers Seat +85
Power Windows +70
Privacy Glass[Std on LT] +80

BERETTA 1993

Standard engine on the GT is now a ridiculous 110-horsepower four-cylinder from the base car. The V6 is optional. GTZ's Quad 4 engine loses five horsepower to emissions regulations. A brake/shift interlock has been added to automatic transmissions. Manuals get an improved clutch.

RATINGS (SCALE OF 1-10)

Overall	Safety	Reliability	Performance	Comfort	Value
6.9	6.6	7.7	7.8	7	5.4

Category E

Model Description	Trade-in Value	Market Value
2 Dr GT Cpe	3545	5295
2 Dr GTZ Cpe	4640	6920
2 Dr STD Cpe	3245	4840

OPTIONS FOR BERETTA

6 cyl 3.1 L Engine +180
Auto 3-Speed Transmission +170
Air Conditioning[Std on GTZ] +245
AM/FM Stereo Tape +95
Cruise Control +65
Power Door Locks +70
Power Windows +80
Sunroof +105
Tilt Steering Wheel +45

BLAZER 1993

No changes.

Category H

Model Description	Trade-in Value	Market Value
2 Dr Silverado 4WD Utility	10140	12835
2 Dr Sport 4WD Utility	9900	12530
2 Dr STD 4WD Utility	9330	11810

OPTIONS FOR BLAZER

Auto 4-Speed Transmission +270
Air Conditioning[Opt on Sport,STD] +245
Aluminum/Alloy Wheels +95
AM/FM Stereo Tape +75
Cruise Control[Opt on Sport,STD] +60
Power Door Locks +55
Power Drivers Seat +85
Power Windows +60
Tilt Steering Wheel[Opt on Sport,STD] +55

C/K PICKUP 1993

Solar-Ray tinted glass is made standard. Cloth interior surfaces are now protected by Scotchgard fabric protection. Automatic transmissions get electronic shift controls. Base V6 gets five additional horsepower.

RATINGS (SCALE OF 1-10)

Overall	Safety	Reliability	Performance	Comfort	Value
N/A	5.6	8.3	7.4	8	N/A

C1500

Category H

Model Description	Trade-in Value	Market Value
2 Dr 454SS Std Cab SB	10775	13640
2 Dr Cheyenne Ext Cab SB	7185	9095
2 Dr Cheyenne Std Cab SB	6880	8710
2 Dr Cheyenne Ext Cab Stepside SB	7400	9365
2 Dr Cheyenne Std Cab Stepside SB	6840	8660
2 Dr Cheyenne Ext Cab LB	7270	9205
2 Dr Cheyenne Std Cab LB	6920	8760
2 Dr Silverado Ext Cab SB	7625	9650
2 Dr Silverado Std Cab SB	7110	9000
2 Dr Silverado Std Cab Stepside SB	7290	9230
2 Dr Silverado Ext Cab Stepside SB	7840	9925
2 Dr Silverado Ext Cab LB	7755	9815
2 Dr Silverado Std Cab LB	7110	9000
2 Dr Sport Std Cab Stepside SB	7165	9070
2 Dr STD Ext Cab SB	7160	9060
2 Dr STD Std Cab SB	6795	8600
2 Dr STD Std Cab Stepside SB	6660	8435
2 Dr STD Ext Cab Stepside SB	7365	9325
2 Dr STD Ext Cab LB	7235	9155
2 Dr STD Std Cab LB	6485	8210
2 Dr WT Std Cab LB	5595	7085

C2500

Category H

Model Description	Trade-in Value	Market Value
2 Dr Cheyenne Ext Cab SB	8185	10360
2 Dr Cheyenne Std Cab LB	7390	9355
2 Dr Cheyenne Ext Cab LB	8250	10440
2 Dr Silverado Ext Cab SB	8325	10535
2 Dr Silverado Std Cab LB	7925	10035
2 Dr Silverado Ext Cab LB	8355	10580
2 Dr STD Ext Cab SB	8130	10290
2 Dr STD Ext Cab LB	8195	10375
2 Dr STD Std Cab LB	7390	9355

Don't forget to refer to the Mileage Adjustment Table at the back of this book!

 © 1999 by Edmund Publications Corporation

Model Description	Trade-in Value	Market Value

C3500

Category H

Model Description	Trade-in Value	Market Value
2 Dr Cheyenne Std Cab LB	9010	11405
2 Dr Cheyenne Ext Cab LB	9700	12275
2 Dr Silverado Std Cab LB	9445	11955
2 Dr Silverado Ext Cab LB	10495	13285
4 Dr Silverado Crew Cab LB	11050	13985
4 Dr Silverado Turbodsl Crew Cab SB	10805	13680
2 Dr STD Std Cab LB	8640	10935
2 Dr STD Ext Cab LB	9585	12135
4 Dr STD Crew Cab LB	10475	13260

K1500

Category H

Model Description	Trade-in Value	Market Value
2 Dr Cheyenne 4WD Ext Cab SB	8705	11020
2 Dr Cheyenne 4WD Std Cab SB	7890	9990
2 Dr Cheyenne 4WD Ext Cab Stepside SB	8925	11300
2 Dr Cheyenne 4WD Std Cab Stepside SB	8175	10345
2 Dr Cheyenne 4WD Ext Cab LB	8785	11120
2 Dr Cheyenne 4WD Std Cab LB	7965	10080
2 Dr Silverado 4WD Ext Cab SB	9040	11440
2 Dr Silverado 4WD Std Cab SB	8360	10580
2 Dr Silverado 4WD Std Cab Stepside SB	8620	10915
2 Dr Silverado 4WD Ext Cab Stepside SB	9260	11720
2 Dr Silverado 4WD Std Cab LB	8355	10580
2 Dr Silverado 4WD Ext Cab LB	9115	11540
2 Dr STD 4WD Std Cab SB	7795	9865
2 Dr STD 4WD Ext Cab SB	8510	10775
2 Dr STD 4WD Ext Cab Stepside SB	8730	11055
2 Dr STD 4WD Std Cab Stepside SB	8075	10225
2 Dr STD 4WD Std Cab LB	7855	9945
2 Dr STD 4WD Ext Cab LB	8600	10885
2 Dr WT 4WD Std Cab LB	6700	8480

K2500

Category H

Model Description	Trade-in Value	Market Value
2 Dr Cheyenne 4WD Ext Cab SB	8820	11165
2 Dr Cheyenne 4WD Ext Cab LB	8880	11240
2 Dr Cheyenne 4WD Std Cab LB	8715	11030
2 Dr Silverado 4WD Ext Cab SB	9275	11745
2 Dr Silverado 4WD Ext Cab LB	9380	11870
2 Dr Silverado 4WD Std Cab LB	9125	11550
2 Dr STD 4WD Ext Cab SB	8715	11035
2 Dr STD 4WD Ext Cab LB	8730	11050
2 Dr STD 4WD Std Cab LB	8585	10870

K3500

Category H

Model Description	Trade-in Value	Market Value
2 Dr Cheyenne 4WD Ext Cab LB	10225	12945
2 Dr Cheyenne 4WD Std Cab LB	9790	12390
2 Dr Silverado 4WD Ext Cab LB	10435	13210
2 Dr Silverado 4WD Std Cab LB	9985	12635
4 Dr Silverado 4WD Crew Cab LB	12695	16065
2 Dr STD 4WD Std Cab LB	9790	12390
2 Dr STD 4WD Ext Cab LB	10140	12835
4 Dr STD 4WD Crew Cab LB	12055	15260

OPTIONS FOR C/K PICKUP

8 cyl 6.2 L Dsl Engine +655
8 cyl 5.0 L Engine +180
8 cyl 5.7 L Engine +255
8 cyl 7.4 L Engine +245
8 cyl 6.5 L Turbodsl Engine +855
Auto 4-Speed Transmission[Std on 454SS] +270
Sport Handling Package +325
Air Conditioning[Opt on Cheyenne,STD,Work Truck] +245
Aluminum/Alloy Wheels[Std on Sport] +95
AM/FM Stereo Tape[Std on Sport] +75
Bed Liner +70
Camper/Towing Package +110
Cruise Control[Std on 454SS,Sport,Silverado] +60
Dual Rear Wheels +255
Power Door Locks[Std on 454SS,Sport] +55
Power Drivers Seat +85
Power Windows[Std on 454SS,Sport] +60
Tilt Steering Wheel[Std on 454SS,Sport,Silverado] +55

CAMARO 1993

All-new sports coupe is redesigned for the first time in 12 years. Dual airbags and ABS are standard. Convertible disappears for one year. Available in base and Z28 trim. Base model powered by 3.4-liter V6; Z28 gets 5.7-liter V8 rated at 275 horsepower (115 more than base Camaro). Z28 has a six-speed manual transmission standard.

RATINGS (SCALE OF 1-10)

Overall	Safety	Reliability	Performance	Comfort	Value
7.5	9.1	7	9.2	6.6	5.4

Category F

Model Description	Trade-in Value	Market Value
2 Dr STD Cpe	5565	7420
2 Dr Z28 Cpe	6945	9255

OPTIONS FOR CAMARO

Auto 4-Speed Transmission +180
Air Conditioning +250
Aluminum/Alloy Wheels[Opt on STD] +95
Bose Sound System +155
Glass Panel T-tops +315
Power Door Locks +60
Power Drivers Seat +70
Power Windows +70

Don't forget to refer to the Mileage Adjustment Table at the back of this book!

 © 1999 by Edmund Publications Corporation

Model Description	Trade-in Value	Market Value

CAPRICE 1993

Rear styling is revised, and rear wheel wells are opened up. Rear track is increased 1.6 inches. LTZ gets a 180-horsepower 5.7-liter V8 standard. Acoustical package added to reduce noise. LS trim level gets gold accents on wheels and trim.

RATINGS (SCALE OF 1-10)

Overall	Safety	Reliability	Performance	Comfort	Value
7.9	7	7.2	7.6	8.3	9.4

Model Description	Trade-in Value	Market Value
Category B		
4 Dr LS Sdn	6175	8460
4 Dr LTZ Sdn	6325	8665
4 Dr STD Sdn	4915	6735
4 Dr STD Wgn	6470	8865

OPTIONS FOR CAPRICE

8 cyl 5.7 L Engine +75
AM/FM Stereo Tape +55
Auto Load Leveling +55
Cruise Control +65
Leather Seats +200
Power Door Locks[Std on LS,LTZ] +75
Power Drivers Seat +90
Power Windows[Std on LTZ] +90
Velour/Cloth Seats[Std on LS,LTZ] +70

CAVALIER 1993

Convertible gets glass rear window, and RS coupes and sedans can be equipped with the Z24's 3.1-liter V6. A CD player is a new option on VL models. RS gets Z24 interior trimmings.

RATINGS (SCALE OF 1-10)

Overall	Safety	Reliability	Performance	Comfort	Value
N/A	N/A	7.5	6.6	6.8	7.2

Model Description	Trade-in Value	Market Value
Category E		
2 Dr RS Conv	3870	5775
2 Dr RS Cpe	2910	4340
4 Dr RS Wgn	3060	4565
4 Dr RS Sdn	2880	4300
2 Dr VL Cpe	2510	3745
4 Dr VL Sdn	2545	3800
4 Dr VL Wgn	2435	3635
2 Dr Z24 Conv	5190	7745
2 Dr Z24 Cpe	4295	6415

OPTIONS FOR CAVALIER

6 cyl 3.1 L Engine[Opt on RS] +180
Auto 3-Speed Transmission[Std on Wgn] +150
Air Conditioning +245
AM/FM Stereo Tape +95
Cruise Control +65
Power Mirrors[Opt on VL] +35
Power Windows[Std on Conv] +80
Sunroof +105
Tilt Steering Wheel +45

CHEVY VAN/SPORTVAN 1993

Solar-Ray tinted glass and Scotchgard fabric protectant are both standard. Four-wheel ABS is a new standard feature. Remote keyless entry joins the options list.

Model Description	Trade-in Value	Market Value
G10		
Category H		
2 Dr Beauville Sportvan	7240	9165
2 Dr Beauville Sportvan Ext	7335	9285
2 Dr STD Sportvan Ext	7155	9060
2 Dr STD Chevy Van	5990	7585
2 Dr STD Chevy Van Ext	6440	8150
2 Dr STD Sportvan	7035	8905
G20		
Category H		
2 Dr Beauville Sportvan Ext	6295	7970
2 Dr STD Chevy Van	4910	6220
2 Dr STD Chevy Van Ext	5805	7350
2 Dr STD Sportvan Ext	5925	7495
G30		
Category H		
2 Dr Beauville Sportvan	6830	8645
2 Dr Beauville Sportvan Ext	6695	8470
2 Dr STD Chevy Van Ext	5665	7170
2 Dr STD Sportvan	6655	8425
2 Dr STD Sportvan Ext	6725	8515
2 Dr STD Chevy Van	5250	6645

OPTIONS FOR CHEVY VAN/SPORTVAN

8 cyl 6.2 L Dsl Engine +655
8 cyl 5.0 L Engine +180
8 cyl 5.7 L Engine[Opt on G10,G20,Chevy Van] +255
8 cyl 7.4 L Engine +245
12 Passenger Seating +190
8 Passenger Seating +110
Air Conditioning +245
AM/FM Stereo Tape +75
Cruise Control +60
Dual Air Conditioning +430
Power Door Locks +55
Power Windows +60
Privacy Glass +50
Rear Heater +65
Tilt Steering Wheel +55

CORSICA 1993

Wow. A brake/transmission shift interlock is added. Larger muffler is supposed to make Corsica quieter.

Don't forget to refer to the Mileage Adjustment Table at the back of this book!

 © 1999 by Edmund Publications Corporation

Model Description	Trade-in Value	Market Value

RATINGS (SCALE OF 1-10)

Overall	Safety	Reliability	Performance	Comfort	Value
6.8	5.8	7.5	6.8	7.3	6.5

Category C		
4 Dr LT Sdn	2790	3930

OPTIONS FOR CORSICA

6 cyl 3.1 L Engine +185
Auto 3-Speed Transmission +170
Air Conditioning +240
AM/FM Stereo Tape +50
Cruise Control +65
Power Door Locks +70
Power Drivers Seat +85
Power Windows +90
Tilt Steering Wheel +45

CORVETTE 1993

Base model gets narrower front tires and wider rear tires. LT1 V8 gets additional torque. ZR-1 horsepower is up to 405 this year. All models can be ordered in 40th Anniversary trim, consisting of Ruby Red paint and badging. Passive Keyless Entry is newly optional, and locks or unlocks the doors simply by having the key fob close to the car.

Category J		
2 Dr STD Conv	16295	20630
2 Dr STD Cpe	13865	17550
2 Dr ZR1 Cpe	19725	24970

OPTIONS FOR CORVETTE

Adjustable Handling Pkg. +410
Selective Ride Suspension +515
Bose Sound System +245
Climate Control for AC +65
Compact Disc W/fm/tape[Opt on STD] +215
Leather Seats[Opt on STD] +310
Power Drivers Seat[Opt on STD] +100
Solid & Glass Targa Tops +285

LUMINA 1993

Base sedans get five more horsepower this year, and base coupes now have standard V6 power. Doors lock automatically when vehicle reaches eight mph.

RATINGS (SCALE OF 1-10)

Overall	Safety	Reliability	Performance	Comfort	Value
N/A	N/A	7.5	8.2	7.6	8.5

Category C		
2 Dr Euro Cpe	4560	6425
4 Dr Euro Sdn	4545	6405
2 Dr STD Cpe	3840	5410
4 Dr STD Sdn	3570	5025
2 Dr Z34 Cpe	5865	8260

OPTIONS FOR LUMINA

6 cyl 3.1 L Engine[Std on Euro,Cpe] +185
6 cyl 3.4 L Engine[Std on Z34] +300
Auto 4-Speed Transmission +60
Air Conditioning[Opt on STD Sdn] +240
AM/FM Stereo Tape[Std on Z34] +50
Anti-Lock Brakes[Opt on STD] +190
Cruise Control[Std on Z34] +65
Power Drivers Seat +85
Power Windows +90
Tilt Steering Wheel[Std on Z34] +45

LUMINA MINIVAN 1993

Uplevel trim switches from CL to LS designation. Sunroof joins options list this year. Center console is redesigned to include dual cupholders.

RATINGS (SCALE OF 1-10)

Overall	Safety	Reliability	Performance	Comfort	Value
7.3	5.8	7.5	7.6	7.5	8.3

Category G		
2 Dr LS Pass. Van	5285	7050
2 Dr STD Pass. Van	4750	6335

OPTIONS FOR LUMINA MINIVAN

6 cyl 3.8 L Engine +190
Auto 4-Speed Transmission +60
Air Conditioning[Std on LS] +245
Aluminum/Alloy Wheels +105
AM/FM Stereo Tape +75
Cruise Control +65
Power Door Locks +70
Power Drivers Seat +85
Power Windows +70
Privacy Glass +80
Tilt Steering Wheel[Std on LS] +50

S10 BLAZER 1993

Two-door model available in LT trim. All models get two-tone paint scheme in LT trim. V6 engines get internal balance shaft designed to reduce vibration. Automatic transmission receives electronic shift controls and second-gear start feature. Manual lumbar adjusters are newly standard on front seats.

RATINGS (SCALE OF 1-10)

Overall	Safety	Reliability	Performance	Comfort	Value
6	5.1	6.5	6.8	7.1	4.4

Category G		
2 Dr STD Utility	4915	6555
2 Dr STD 4WD Utility	6100	8135
4 Dr STD Wgn	5775	7700
4 Dr STD 4WD Wgn	6690	8915
2 Dr Tahoe Utility	5215	6955
2 Dr Tahoe 4WD Utility	6240	8320
4 Dr Tahoe Wgn	5900	7865

Don't forget to refer to the Mileage Adjustment Table at the back of this book!

© 1999 by Edmund Publications Corporation

Model Description	Trade-in Value	Market Value
4 Dr Tahoe 4WD Wgn	6820	9095
2 Dr Tahoe LT Utility	6320	8425
2 Dr Tahoe LT 4WD Utility	7195	9595
4 Dr Tahoe LT Wgn	6905	9205
4 Dr Tahoe LT 4WD Wgn	8065	10755

OPTIONS FOR S10 BLAZER

6 cyl 4.3 L CPI Engine +140
Auto 4-Speed Transmission +275
Air Conditioning[Std on Tahoe LT] +245
Aluminum/Alloy Wheels +105
AM/FM Stereo Tape[Std on Tahoe LT] +75
Cruise Control[Std on Tahoe LT] +65
Leather Seats[Std on Tahoe LT] +235
Power Door Locks[Std on Tahoe LT] +70
Power Drivers Seat[Std on Tahoe LT] +85
Power Windows[Std on Tahoe LT] +70
Tilt Steering Wheel[Opt on STD] +50

S10 PICKUP 1993

V6 engines get internal balance shaft designed to reduce vibration. Automatic transmission gets electronic shift controls.

RATINGS (SCALE OF 1-10)

Overall	Safety	Reliability	Performance	Comfort	Value
N/A	3.4	7.7	7.2	7	N/A

Category G

Model Description	Trade-in Value	Market Value
2 Dr EL Std Cab SB	3525	4705
2 Dr EL 4WD Std Cab SB	5305	7075
2 Dr STD Ext Cab SB	4755	6335
2 Dr STD Std Cab SB	3925	5230
2 Dr STD Std Cab LB	3985	5315
2 Dr STD 4WD Ext Cab SB	5855	7805
2 Dr STD 4WD Std Cab SB	5700	7595
2 Dr STD 4WD Std Cab LB	5775	7700
2 Dr Tahoe Ext Cab SB	4810	6415
2 Dr Tahoe Std Cab SB	4280	5705
2 Dr Tahoe Std Cab LB	4325	5770
2 Dr Tahoe 4WD Std Cab SB	5950	7935
2 Dr Tahoe 4WD Ext Cab SB	6245	8325
2 Dr Tahoe 4WD Std Cab LB	6030	8035

OPTIONS FOR S10 PICKUP

6 cyl 2.8 L Engine +120
6 cyl 4.3 L Engine[Opt on 2WD] +190
Auto 4-Speed Transmission +270
Air Conditioning +245
Aluminum/Alloy Wheels[Std on Tahoe] +105
AM/FM Stereo Tape[Opt on EL,STD] +75
Cruise Control +65
Power Windows +70
Tilt Steering Wheel +50

SUBURBAN 1993

No changes.

RATINGS (SCALE OF 1-10)

Overall	Safety	Reliability	Performance	Comfort	Value
7	6.6	7.3	7	7.5	6.7

Category H

Model Description	Trade-in Value	Market Value
4 Dr C1500 Wgn	11400	14430
4 Dr C2500 Wgn	11980	15165
4 Dr K1500 4WD Wgn	11970	15155
4 Dr K2500 4WD Wgn	12710	16090

OPTIONS FOR SUBURBAN

8 cyl 7.4 L Engine +245
Silverado Package +645
Air Conditioning +245
Aluminum/Alloy Wheels +95
AM/FM Stereo Tape +75
Camper/Towing Package +110
Cruise Control +60
Dual Air Conditioning +430
Leather Seats +315
Power Door Locks +55
Power Drivers Seat +85
Power Windows +60
Rear Heater +65
Tilt Steering Wheel +55

1992 CHEVROLET

ASTRO 1992

Dutch rear door treatment is available. With Dutch doors, a rear washer/wiper and rear defogger can be ordered. All-wheel drive models get high-output 200-horsepower V6 standard. Engine is optional on 2WD models.

RATINGS (SCALE OF 1-10)

Overall	Safety	Reliability	Performance	Comfort	Value
6.7	4.2	7.2	7.2	6.6	8.3

Category G

Model Description	Trade-in Value	Market Value
2 Dr CL Pass. Van	4260	5835
2 Dr CL Pass. Van Ext	4665	6390
2 Dr CL 4WD Pass. Van Ext	6390	8755
2 Dr CL 4WD Pass. Van	5715	7830
2 Dr LT Pass. Van	4505	6170
2 Dr LT Pass. Van Ext	4760	6520
2 Dr LT 4WD Pass. Van	6180	8465
2 Dr LT 4WD Pass. Van Ext	6500	8905
2 Dr STD Pass. Van Ext	4450	6095
2 Dr STD Cargo Van	3080	4215
2 Dr STD Pass. Van	4070	5575
2 Dr STD Cargo Van Ext	3700	5070
2 Dr STD 4WD Pass. Van Ext	6335	8680
2 Dr STD 4WD Cargo Van	4620	6330

Don't forget to refer to the Mileage Adjustment Table at the back of this book!

 © 1999 by Edmund Publications Corporation

Model Description	Trade-in Value	Market Value
2 Dr STD 4WD Cargo Van Ext	5395	7395
2 Dr STD 4WD Pass. Van	5645	7730

OPTIONS FOR ASTRO
6 cyl 4.3 L CPI Engine +110
8 Passenger Seating +95
Air Conditioning +200
Aluminum/Alloy Wheels +85
AM/FM Stereo Tape +60
Dual Air Conditioning +250
Power Door Locks +55
Power Drivers Seat +70
Power Windows +60

BERETTA 1992

ABS is standard. Base engine gains 15 horsepower. GTZ gets revised gearing for better off-the-line acceleration. Base V6 models get gearing change designed to save fuel. Order a GTZ with the V6, and you'll get touring tires instead of high-performance rubber. Front brakes are slightly larger on all models.

RATINGS (SCALE OF 1-10)

Overall	Safety	Reliability	Performance	Comfort	Value
6.9	6.6	7.3	7.8	7	5.7

Category E

Model Description	Trade-in Value	Market Value
2 Dr GT Cpe	2990	4675
2 Dr GTZ Cpe	3565	5570
2 Dr STD Cpe	2445	3820

OPTIONS FOR BERETTA
6 cyl 3.1 L Engine +145
Auto 3-Speed Transmission +135
Air Conditioning[Std on GT] +200
AM/FM Stereo Tape +75
Cruise Control +55
Power Door Locks +55
Power Windows +65
Sunroof +85
Tilt Steering Wheel +35

BLAZER 1992

Totally redesigned and based on same platform and sheetmetal as C/K pickup. Six-passenger seating is standard. Cargo area gets fixed metal roof rather than fiberglass shell. Four-wheel ABS is standard and works in 4WD. New Sport appearance package includes two-tone paint and wheelwell flares. Diesel option is dropped. Five-speed manual is standard transmission. An automatic is optional. Shift-on-the-fly 4WD is standard.

Category H

Model Description	Trade-in Value	Market Value
2 Dr Silverado 4WD Utility	8570	11125
2 Dr Sport 4WD Utility	8395	10900
2 Dr STD 4WD Utility	8195	10640

OPTIONS FOR BLAZER
Auto 4-Speed Transmission +215
Air Conditioning +200
Aluminum/Alloy Wheels +75
AM/FM Stereo Tape +60
Cruise Control +50
Power Door Locks +45
Power Drivers Seat +70
Power Windows +45
Tilt Steering Wheel +45

C/K PICKUP 1992

Extended-cab models get Sportside box option. Crew Cab model is all-new, sporting same engineering and styling as rest of C/K line. Front buckets have been redesigned. Standard gauge cluster is restyled. Integral head restraints are added for outboard passengers. A new turbocharged 6.5-liter diesel V8 is optional in C/K 2500 and regular cab C/K 3500 models. Four-speed manual transmission is dropped.

RATINGS (SCALE OF 1-10)

Overall	Safety	Reliability	Performance	Comfort	Value
N/A	5.6	7.9	7.4	8	N/A

C1500

Category H

Model Description	Trade-in Value	Market Value
2 Dr 454SS Std Cab SB	8985	11670
2 Dr Scottsdale Ext Cab SB	6705	8710
2 Dr Scottsdale Std Cab SB	6150	7985
2 Dr Scottsdale Ext Cab Stepside SB	6595	8570
2 Dr Scottsdale Std Cab Stepside SB	6415	8330
2 Dr Scottsdale Ext Cab LB	6460	8390
2 Dr Scottsdale Std Cab LB	6265	8135
2 Dr Silverado Ext Cab SB	6505	8445
2 Dr Silverado Std Cab SB	6320	8205
2 Dr Silverado Std Cab Stepside SB	6660	8650
2 Dr Silverado Ext Cab Stepside SB	6840	8885
2 Dr Silverado Std Cab LB	6365	8265
2 Dr Silverado Ext Cab LB	6405	8320
2 Dr STD Ext Cab SB	6390	8300
2 Dr STD Std Cab SB	5910	7675
2 Dr STD Ext Cab Stepside SB	6185	8035
2 Dr STD Std Cab Stepside SB	6100	7920
2 Dr STD Ext Cab LB	6415	8330
2 Dr STD Std Cab LB	5960	7740
2 Dr WT Std Cab LB	4870	6320

Don't forget to refer to the Mileage Adjustment Table at the back of this book!

© 1999 by Edmund Publications Corporation

Model Description	Trade-in Value	Market Value
C2500		
Category H		
2 Dr Scottsdale Ext Cab SB	6980	9060
2 Dr Scottsdale Std Cab LB	6575	8535
2 Dr Scottsdale Ext Cab LB	7050	9155
2 Dr Silverado Ext Cab SB	7120	9245
2 Dr Silverado Std Cab LB	6685	8685
2 Dr Silverado Ext Cab LB	7195	9345
2 Dr STD Ext Cab SB	6820	8855
2 Dr STD Std Cab LB	6215	8070
2 Dr STD Ext Cab LB	6880	8935
C3500		
Category H		
2 Dr Scottsdale Ext Cab LB	8750	11365
2 Dr Scottsdale Std Cab LB	8545	11095
2 Dr Silverado Ext Cab LB	8930	11595
2 Dr Silverado Std Cab LB	8660	11245
2 Dr STD Ext Cab LB	8530	11075
2 Dr STD Std Cab LB	7775	10095
4 Dr STD Crew Cab LB	9380	12185
K1500		
Category H		
2 Dr Scottsdale 4WD Ext Cab SB	7990	10380
2 Dr Scottsdale 4WD Std Cab SB	7380	9580
2 Dr Scottsdale 4WD Std Cab Stepside SB	7585	9850
2 Dr Scottsdale 4WD Ext Cab Stepside SB	8190	10640
2 Dr Scottsdale 4WD Std Cab LB	7240	9400
2 Dr Scottsdale 4WD Ext Cab LB	8205	10655
2 Dr Silverado 4WD Ext Cab SB	8130	10560
2 Dr Silverado 4WD Std Cab SB	7530	9780
2 Dr Silverado 4WD Std Cab Stepside SB	7630	9910
2 Dr Silverado 4WD Ext Cab Stepside SB	8370	10870
2 Dr Silverado 4WD Std Cab LB	7385	9590
2 Dr Silverado 4WD Ext Cab LB	8260	10725
2 Dr STD 4WD Std Cab SB	7050	9155
2 Dr STD 4WD Ext Cab SB	7750	10060
2 Dr STD 4WD Std Cab Stepside SB	7280	9455
2 Dr STD 4WD Ext Cab Stepside SB	7820	10155
2 Dr STD 4WD Std Cab LB	7115	9240
2 Dr STD 4WD Ext Cab LB	7730	10040
2 Dr WT 4WD Std Cab LB	6125	7955
K2500		
Category H		
2 Dr Scottsdale 4WD Ext Cab SB	7895	10255
2 Dr Scottsdale 4WD Ext Cab LB	7970	10350
2 Dr Scottsdale 4WD Std Cab LB	7510	9755
2 Dr Silverado 4WD Ext Cab SB	8000	10390
2 Dr Silverado 4WD Std Cab LB	7625	9900
2 Dr Silverado 4WD Ext Cab LB	7915	10280
2 Dr STD 4WD Ext Cab SB	7570	9830
2 Dr STD 4WD Ext Cab LB	7690	9985
2 Dr STD 4WD Std Cab LB	7210	9360
K3500		
Category H		
2 Dr Scottsdale 4WD Ext Cab LB	9475	12305
2 Dr Silverado 4WD Ext Cab LB	9685	12580
2 Dr STD 4WD Ext Cab LB	9125	11850
2 Dr STD 4WD Std Cab LB	8375	10880
4 Dr STD 4WD Crew Cab LB	9700	12600

OPTIONS FOR C/K PICKUP

8 cyl 6.2 L Dsl Engine +510
8 cyl 5.0 L Engine +145
8 cyl 5.7 L Engine +205
8 cyl 7.4 L Engine[Opt on] +175
8 cyl 6.5 L Turbodsl Engine +650
Auto 4-Speed Transmission[Std on 454SS] +215
Heavy Duty Pkg +250
Sport Handling Package +220
Air Conditioning +200
Aluminum/Alloy Wheels +75
AM/FM Stereo Tape +60
Bed Liner +55
Camper/Towing Package +90
Cruise Control[Std on 454SS,Silverado] +50
Dual Rear Wheels +210
Power Door Locks[Std on 454SS] +45
Power Drivers Seat +70
Power Windows[Std on 454SS] +45
Tilt Steering Wheel[Std on 454SS,Silverado] +45

CAMARO 1992

Heritage Appearance option, essentially a couple of sport stripes and a dashboard plaque, commemorates Camaro's 25th anniversary. Z28 models get quicker steering and an improved suspension.

Model Description	Trade-in Value	Market Value
Category F		
2 Dr RS Conv	5965	8285
2 Dr RS Cpe	4155	5770
2 Dr Z28 Conv	7105	9865
2 Dr Z28 Cpe	5520	7670

OPTIONS FOR CAMARO

8 cyl 5.0 L Engine[Opt on RS] +90
8 cyl 5.7 L Engine +110
Auto 4-Speed Transmission +95
Air Conditioning +205

Don't forget to refer to the Mileage Adjustment Table at the back of this book!

 © 1999 by Edmund Publications Corporation

Model Description	Trade-in Value	Market Value

AM/FM Stereo Tape +50
Bose Sound System +125
Leather Seats +175
Power Door Locks +50
Power Drivers Seat +60
Power Windows +55
Special Factory Paint +80
T-Tops (solid/Colored) +230

CAPRICE 1992

Station wagon gets more powerful V8 option. Speedometer now reads to 100 mph, tilt steering is standard, and wagon's quarter vent windows are power operated.

RATINGS (SCALE OF 1-10)

Overall	Safety	Reliability	Performance	Comfort	Value
7.4	6.6	6.3	7.6	8.3	8.3

Category B

Model Description	Trade-in Value	Market Value
4 Dr Classic Sdn	4860	6750
4 Dr STD Sdn	3510	4875
4 Dr STD Wgn	5130	7125

OPTIONS FOR CAPRICE

8 cyl 5.7 L Engine +60
AM/FM Stereo Tape +45
Auto Load Leveling +45
Cruise Control +55
Leather Seats +165
Power Door Locks[Std on Classic] +60
Power Drivers Seat +75
Power Windows +70

CAVALIER 1992

ABS is standard, and base engines are bumped 15 horsepower to 110. RS and Z24 convertibles are back after two-year hiatus. Automatic door locks are added. VL and RS models get new wheelcovers. Z24 trades performance tires for touring.

RATINGS (SCALE OF 1-10)

Overall	Safety	Reliability	Performance	Comfort	Value
N/A	N/A	7.3	6.6	6.8	5.6

Category E

Model Description	Trade-in Value	Market Value
2 Dr RS Cpe	2250	3520
2 Dr RS Conv	3075	4805
4 Dr RS Wgn	2475	3865
4 Dr RS Sdn	2330	3645
2 Dr VL Cpe	1970	3080
4 Dr VL Wgn	2175	3400
4 Dr VL Sdn	2040	3190
2 Dr Z24 Conv	4165	6505
2 Dr Z24 Cpe	3310	5170

OPTIONS FOR CAVALIER

6 cyl 3.1 L Engine[Opt on RS] +145
Auto 3-Speed Transmission[Std on Wgn] +120
Air Conditioning +200
AM/FM Stereo Tape +75
Cruise Control +55
Power Windows[Std on Conv] +65
Sunroof +85
Tilt Steering Wheel +35

CHEVY VAN/SPORTVAN 1992

Minor suspension modifications improve the ride.

G10

Category H

Model Description	Trade-in Value	Market Value
2 Dr Beauville Sportvan	6095	7915
2 Dr Beauville Sportvan Ext	6170	8010
2 Dr STD Sportvan	5855	7605
2 Dr STD Sportvan Ext	5940	7715
2 Dr STD Chevy Van	4620	6005
2 Dr STD Chevy Van Ext	5090	6610

G20

Category H

Model Description	Trade-in Value	Market Value
2 Dr Beauville Sportvan Ext	4860	6310
2 Dr STD Chevy Van Ext	4460	5790
2 Dr STD Sportvan Ext	4555	5915
2 Dr STD Chevy Van	3905	5070

G30

Category H

Model Description	Trade-in Value	Market Value
2 Dr Beauville Sportvan Ext	6155	7995
2 Dr STD Sportvan Ext	5690	7390
2 Dr STD Chevy Van	4485	5825
2 Dr STD Sportvan	5450	7080
2 Dr STD Chevy Van Ext	4885	6345

OPTIONS FOR CHEVY VAN/SPORTVAN

8 cyl 6.2 L Dsl Engine +510
8 cyl 5.0 L Engine +145
8 cyl 5.7 L Engine[Opt on G10,G20,Chevy Van Ext] +205
8 cyl 7.4 L Engine +175
12 Passenger Seating +155
Air Conditioning +200
AM/FM Stereo Tape +60
Cruise Control +50
Dual Air Conditioning +350
Power Door Locks +45
Power Windows +45
Privacy Glass +40
Rear Heater +55
Tilt Steering Wheel +45

CORSICA 1992

Five-door hatchback is dropped. ABS is standard, and base engine makes more power. Manual transmission cannot be ordered with V6 this year. V6 models get

Don't forget to refer to the Mileage Adjustment Table at the back of this book!

 © 1999 by Edmund Publications Corporation

Model Description	Trade-in Value	Market Value

more fuel-efficient gearing. Front brakes are larger, and optional CD player gets theft-deterrent system. Outside mirrors are body-color.

RATINGS (SCALE OF 1-10)

Overall	Safety	Reliability	Performance	Comfort	Value
6.8	5.8	7.1	6.8	7.3	6.8

Category C

4 Dr LT Sdn	2205	3200

OPTIONS FOR CORSICA

6 cyl 3.1 L Engine +155
Auto 3-Speed Transmission +135
Air Conditioning +200
Aluminum/Alloy Wheels +70
AM/FM Stereo Tape +40
Cruise Control +50
Power Door Locks +60
Power Windows +75
Tilt Steering Wheel +35

CORVETTE 1992

New base V8 is the LT1 engine, making 300 horsepower. ZR-1 gets fender badging to distinguish itself from lesser Corvettes. All Corvettes get traction control standard. Speedometer swaps spots with the fuel gauge for better readability. A Quiet Car option adds weather-stripping and sound insulation.

Category J

2 Dr STD Conv	14020	17975
2 Dr STD Cpe	12015	15405
2 Dr ZR1 Cpe	17770	22780

OPTIONS FOR CORVETTE

Handling Package +500
Selective Suspension +415
Bose Sound System +200
Climate Control for AC[Opt on STD] +55
Compact Disc W/fm/tape[Opt on STD] +175
Leather Seats[Opt on STD] +255
Power Drivers Seat[Opt on STD] +80
Solid & Glass Targa Tops +230

LUMINA 1992

Euro sedan can be equipped with 3.4-liter twin-cam engine. Base engine loses five horsepower. ABS is standard on Z34 and Euro; optional on base models. A CD player joins the options sheet.

RATINGS (SCALE OF 1-10)

Overall	Safety	Reliability	Performance	Comfort	Value
N/A	N/A	7.2	8.2	7.6	8.3

Category C

2 Dr Euro Cpe	3495	5065
4 Dr Euro Sdn	3615	5240
2 Dr STD Cpe	2730	3960
4 Dr STD Sdn	2785	4035
2 Dr Z34 Cpe	4835	7005

OPTIONS FOR LUMINA

6 cyl 3.1 L Engine[Opt on STD] +155
6 cyl 3.4 L Engine[Std on Z34] +240
Auto 4-Speed Transmission +50
Euro 3.4 Pkg +410
Air Conditioning[Opt on STD] +200
AM/FM Stereo Tape[Std on Z34] +40
Anti-Lock Brakes[Opt on STD] +155
Cruise Control[Std on Z34] +50
Power Door Locks +60
Power Drivers Seat +70
Power Windows +75
Tilt Steering Wheel[Std on Z34] +35

LUMINA MINIVAN 1992

An optional 165-horsepower 3.8-liter V6 with a four-speed automatic is newly available. Wheels and tires are larger this year. Power mirrors and a four-way manual seat adjuster for the driver are new options.

RATINGS (SCALE OF 1-10)

Overall	Safety	Reliability	Performance	Comfort	Value
7.3	5.9	7.2	7.6	7.5	8.3

Category G

2 Dr CL Pass. Van	4045	5540
2 Dr STD Cargo Van	2710	3715
2 Dr STD Pass. Van	3845	5265

OPTIONS FOR LUMINA MINIVAN

6 cyl 3.8 L Engine +160
Auto 4-Speed Transmission +50
Air Conditioning[Std on CL] +200
Aluminum/Alloy Wheels +85
AM/FM Stereo Tape +60
Cruise Control +50
Power Door Locks +55
Power Drivers Seat +70
Power Windows +60
Tilt Steering Wheel[Std on CL] +40

S10 BLAZER 1992

Four-wheel ABS is standard on all models. Electronic-shift transfer case is added to options list of 4WD models. A high-performance 4.3-liter V6 debuts with 40 additional horsepower, bringing total output to 200 ponies. Bucket seats are redesigned, a new speedometer is installed, and a four-spoke steering wheel is added.

RATINGS (SCALE OF 1-10)

Overall	Safety	Reliability	Performance	Comfort	Value
5.9	3.9	6.8	6.8	7.1	4.9

Category G

2 Dr STD Utility	4400	6025
2 Dr STD 4WD Utility	5095	6975

Don't forget to refer to the Mileage Adjustment Table at the back of this book!

 © 1999 by Edmund Publications Corporation

Model Description	Trade-in Value	Market Value
4 Dr STD Wgn	4775	6540
2 Dr Tahoe Utility	4760	6520
2 Dr Tahoe 4WD Utility	5390	7385
4 Dr Tahoe Wgn	5050	6915
4 Dr Tahoe 4WD Wgn	5840	8000

OPTIONS FOR S10 BLAZER

6 cyl 4.3 L CPI Engine +110
Auto 4-Speed Transmission +215
LT Pkg +205
Air Conditioning +200
Aluminum/Alloy Wheels +85
AM/FM Stereo Tape +60
Cruise Control +50
Leather Seats +190
Power Door Locks +55
Power Windows +60
Tilt Steering Wheel +40

S10 PICKUP 1992

Base EL model can be equipped with four-wheel drive. Baja package dropped. Front bucket seats are redesigned, integral head restraints are added, and Extended Cabs can be equipped with leather seats. New speedometer and four-spoke steering wheel are installed. Premium sound system with CD player is added to options list. Four-wheel drive models can be equipped with an electronic-shift transfer case.

RATINGS (SCALE OF 1-10)

Overall	Safety	Reliability	Performance	Comfort	Value
N/A	3.5	7.5	7.2	7	N/A

Category G		
2 Dr EL Std Cab SB	3065	4195
2 Dr EL 4WD Std Cab SB	5190	7110
2 Dr STD Ext Cab SB	4035	5525
2 Dr STD Std Cab SB	3285	4500
2 Dr STD Std Cab LB	3400	4660
2 Dr STD 4WD Std Cab SB	5125	7020
2 Dr STD 4WD Ext Cab SB	5290	7245
2 Dr STD 4WD Std Cab LB	5225	7160
2 Dr Tahoe Std Cab SB	3530	4840
2 Dr Tahoe Ext Cab SB	4120	5645
2 Dr Tahoe Std Cab LB	3650	5000
2 Dr Tahoe 4WD Ext Cab SB	5365	7345
2 Dr Tahoe 4WD Std Cab SB	5235	7170
2 Dr Tahoe 4WD Std Cab LB	5340	7310

OPTIONS FOR S10 PICKUP

6 cyl 2.8 L Engine +95
6 cyl 4.3 L Engine[Opt on 2WD] +150
Auto 4-Speed Transmission +215
Air Conditioning +200
Aluminum/Alloy Wheels +85
AM/FM Stereo Tape +60
Cruise Control +50
Power Door Locks +55
Power Windows +60
Tilt Steering Wheel +40

SUBURBAN 1992

All-new design debuts based on platform and styling of C/K pickup. Cargo space and towing capacity are up. ABS works on all four wheels even in 4WD. Tailgate glass is lifted up instead of powered down. No diesel is offered. GM's Instatrac 4WD system is standard on K models.

RATINGS (SCALE OF 1-10)

Overall	Safety	Reliability	Performance	Comfort	Value
6.9	6.5	6.8	7	7.5	6.6

Category H		
4 Dr C1500 Wgn	8965	11640
4 Dr C2500 Wgn	9660	12545
4 Dr K1500 4WD Wgn	10115	13140
4 Dr K2500 4WD Wgn	10865	14115

OPTIONS FOR SUBURBAN

8 cyl 7.4 L Engine +175
Silverado Pkg +480
Air Conditioning +200
Aluminum/Alloy Wheels +75
AM/FM Stereo Tape +60
Camper/Towing Package +90
Cruise Control +50
Dual Air Conditioning +350
Power Door Locks +45
Power Drivers Seat +70
Power Windows +45
Rear Heater +55
Tilt Steering Wheel +45

1991 CHEVROLET

ASTRO 1991

Cargo models gain the 4.3-liter V6 as standard equipment. A revised Sport Package is available with sport suspension, rally wheels, front air dam with fog lights, and a sport steering wheel. Side and rear windows now have swing-out glass. Extended-length models can be ordered with the Sport Package.

RATINGS (SCALE OF 1-10)

Overall	Safety	Reliability	Performance	Comfort	Value
6.5	4.1	6.7	7.2	6.6	7.7

Category G		
2 Dr CL Pass. Van Ext	3660	5230
2 Dr CL Pass. Van	3120	4460
2 Dr CL 4WD Pass. Van	4555	6510
2 Dr CL 4WD Pass. Van Ext	5270	7525
2 Dr LT Pass. Van	3410	4870

Don't forget to refer to the Mileage Adjustment Table at the back of this book!

 © 1999 by Edmund Publications Corporation

Model Description	Trade-in Value	Market Value
2 Dr LT Pass. Van Ext	4025	5750
2 Dr LT 4WD Pass. Van	5005	7150
2 Dr LT 4WD Pass. Van Ext	5450	7785
2 Dr STD Pass. Van	2985	4260
2 Dr STD Cargo Van Ext	2760	3940
2 Dr STD Cargo Van	2335	3335
2 Dr STD Pass. Van Ext	3555	5075
2 Dr STD 4WD Pass. Van	4305	6150
2 Dr STD 4WD Pass. Van Ext	4985	7120
2 Dr STD 4WD Cargo Van Ext	4065	5810
2 Dr STD 4WD Cargo Van	3410	4870

OPTIONS FOR ASTRO

6 cyl 4.3 L HO Engine +85
Sport Handling Package +180
8 Passenger Seating +80
Air Conditioning +165
Aluminum/Alloy Wheels +70
AM/FM Stereo Tape +50
Dual Air Conditioning +205
Power Door Locks +45
Power Drivers Seat +55
Power Windows +50

BERETTA 1991

New dashboard debuts, and a driver airbag is added. Color-keyed lace-spoke alloys are available on GT, along with revised graphics. A CD player is newly optional. GTZ can be ordered with the more tame 3.1-liter V6 found in other Berettas so that folks who hate to shift their own gears can get a GTZ with an automatic transmission. All Quad 4 GTZs come with a five-speed only.

RATINGS (SCALE OF 1-10)

Overall	Safety	Reliability	Performance	Comfort	Value
6.5	5.5	6.9	7.8	7	5.2

Category E

Model Description	Trade-in Value	Market Value
2 Dr GT Cpe	2365	4010
2 Dr GTZ Cpe	2560	4340
2 Dr STD Cpe	1805	3055

OPTIONS FOR BERETTA

4 cyl 2.3 L Quad 4 Engine +30
6 cyl 3.1 L Engine[Opt on STD] +135
Auto 3-Speed Transmission +110
Air Conditioning[Opt on STD] +165
AM/FM Stereo Tape +60
Cruise Control +45
Power Door Locks +45
Power Windows +55
Sunroof +70
Tilt Steering Wheel +30

BLAZER 1991

Throttle-body fuel injection is improved, and more powerful alternator is standard.

Category H

Model Description	Trade-in Value	Market Value
2 Dr Silverado 4WD Utility	6140	8300
2 Dr STD 4WD Utility	6005	8115

OPTIONS FOR BLAZER

8 cyl 6.2 L Dsl Engine +465
Auto 4-Speed Transmission +175
Air Conditioning +165
Aluminum/Alloy Wheels +65
AM/FM Stereo Tape +50
Cruise Control +40
Power Door Locks +35
Power Windows +40
Tilt Steering Wheel +35

C/K PICKUP 1991

7.4-liter V8 is reworked, and can be mated to four-speed automatic transmission. 454 SS gets 25 more horsepower. New gauge cluster includes a tachometer. Bucket seats are a new option. Air conditioners get a new recirculation mode. Two-wheel drive models add tow hooks to the options list. W/T gets new steering wheel and revised outside mirrors.

RATINGS (SCALE OF 1-10)

Overall	Safety	Reliability	Performance	Comfort	Value
N/A	5.7	8.1	7.4	8	N/A

C1500

Category H

Model Description	Trade-in Value	Market Value
2 Dr Scottsdale Ext Cab SB	6040	8160
2 Dr Scottsdale Std Cab SB	5200	7030
2 Dr Scottsdale Std Cab Stepside SB	5415	7320
2 Dr Scottsdale Std Cab LB	5390	7285
2 Dr Scottsdale Ext Cab LB	5995	8100
2 Dr Silverado Std Cab SB	5315	7180
2 Dr Silverado Ext Cab SB	6080	8215
2 Dr Silverado Ext Cab Stepside SB	6080	8215
2 Dr Silverado Std Cab Stepside SB	5475	7400
2 Dr Silverado Std Cab LB	5445	7360
2 Dr Silverado Ext Cab LB	6085	8225
2 Dr STD Std Cab SB	5130	6935
2 Dr STD Ext Cab SB	5865	7930
2 Dr STD Std Cab Stepside SB	5360	7245
2 Dr STD Std Cab LB	5260	7110
2 Dr STD Ext Cab LB	5950	8040
2 Dr WT Std Cab LB	4435	5995

Don't forget to refer to the Mileage Adjustment Table at the back of this book!

 © 1999 by Edmund Publications Corporation

Model Description	Trade-in Value	Market Value
C2500		
Category H		
2 Dr Scottsdale Ext Cab SB	6085	8225
2 Dr Scottsdale Std Cab LB	5520	7460
2 Dr Scottsdale Ext Cab LB	6010	8120
2 Dr Silverado Ext Cab SB	6110	8255
2 Dr Silverado Std Cab LB	5625	7600
2 Dr Silverado Ext Cab LB	6080	8220
2 Dr STD Ext Cab SB	6030	8150
2 Dr STD Ext Cab LB	5975	8075
2 Dr STD Std Cab LB	5470	7395
C3500		
Category H		
2 Dr Scottsdale Std Cab LB	7325	9900
2 Dr Scottsdale Ext Cab LB	7725	10440
2 Dr Silverado Std Cab LB	7490	10120
2 Dr Silverado Ext Cab LB	7805	10550
2 Dr STD Std Cab LB	7230	9770
2 Dr STD Ext Cab LB	7695	10395
K1500		
Category H		
2 Dr Scottsdale 4WD Ext Cab SB	6705	9060
2 Dr Scottsdale 4WD Std Cab SB	6370	8605
2 Dr Scottsdale 4WD Std Cab Stepside SB	6610	8930
2 Dr Scottsdale 4WD Std Cab LB	6455	8720
2 Dr Scottsdale 4WD Ext Cab LB	6805	9200
2 Dr Silverado 4WD Ext Cab SB	6765	9145
2 Dr Silverado 4WD Std Cab SB	6525	8820
2 Dr Silverado 4WD Std Cab Stepside SB	6655	8995
2 Dr Silverado 4WD Ext Cab Stepside SB	6865	9280
2 Dr Silverado 4WD Ext Cab LB	6895	9320
2 Dr Silverado 4WD Std Cab LB	6530	8825
2 Dr STD 4WD Std Cab SB	6425	8685
2 Dr STD 4WD Ext Cab SB	6625	8950
2 Dr STD 4WD Std Cab Stepside SB	6580	8895
2 Dr STD 4WD Std Cab LB	6265	8465
2 Dr STD 4WD Ext Cab LB	6675	9020
2 Dr WT 4WD Std Cab LB	5755	7775
K2500		
Category H		
2 Dr Scottsdale 4WD Ext Cab SB	7350	9935
2 Dr Scottsdale 4WD Std Cab LB	6570	8875
2 Dr Scottsdale 4WD Ext Cab LB	7440	10050
2 Dr Silverado 4WD Ext Cab SB	7380	9975
2 Dr Silverado 4WD Ext Cab LB	7585	10250
2 Dr Silverado 4WD Std Cab LB	6630	8960
2 Dr STD 4WD Ext Cab SB	7315	9885
2 Dr STD 4WD Std Cab LB	6505	8790
2 Dr STD 4WD Ext Cab LB	7375	9965
K3500		
Category H		
2 Dr Scottsdale 4WD Ext Cab LB	8665	11710
2 Dr Scottsdale 4WD Std Cab LB	7730	10445
2 Dr Silverado 4WD Ext Cab LB	8750	11825
2 Dr Silverado 4WD Std Cab LB	7820	10570
2 Dr STD 4WD Ext Cab LB	8550	11555
2 Dr STD 4WD Std Cab LB	7615	10290

OPTIONS FOR C/K PICKUP

8 cyl 6.2 L Dsl Engine +465
8 cyl 5.0 L Engine +120
8 cyl 5.7 L Engine +165
8 cyl 7.4 L Engine +160
Auto 4-Speed Transmission[Std on 454SS] +175
Heavy Duty Pkg +195
Sport Handling Package +250
Air Conditioning[Std on 454SS] +165
Aluminum/Alloy Wheels +65
AM/FM Stereo Tape +50
Anti-Lock Brakes +105
Camper/Towing Package +70
Cruise Control[Std on 454SS] +40
Power Door Locks[Std on 454SS] +35
Power Windows[Std on 454SS] +40
Tilt Steering Wheel[Std on 454SS] +35

CAMARO 1991

Chevy loses IROC sponsorship to Dodge, and right to use IROC name. Z28 nomenclature returns on top-level Camaro. Order your RS with the 5.0-liter V8 engine, and you can opt for a 16-inch wheel and tire combination. Z28 models have a revised hood, scooped rocker panels, and a more aggressive rear spoiler. Color-keyed alloys are available.

Model Description	Trade-in Value	Market Value
Category F		
2 Dr RS Conv	5065	7130
2 Dr RS Cpe	3425	4825
2 Dr Z28 Conv	6080	8565
2 Dr Z28 Cpe	4660	6560

OPTIONS FOR CAMARO

8 cyl 5.0 L Engine[Opt on RS] +70
8 cyl 5.7 L Engine +95
Auto 4-Speed Transmission +105
Air Conditioning +170
AM/FM Stereo Tape +40
Leather Seats +145
Power Door Locks +40
Power Drivers Seat +50
Power Windows +45
T-Tops (solid/Colored) +190

Don't forget to refer to the Mileage Adjustment Table at the back of this book!

 © 1999 by Edmund Publications Corporation

Model Description	Trade-in Value	Market Value

CAPRICE 1991

Shamu arrives! Sedan and wagon are totally re ...ahem, designed. Retain rear-wheel drive. Standard engine is a 5.0-liter V8. Driver airbag and ABS are standard. Wagon provides over 92 cubic feet of cargo volume. LTZ model added midyear sporting wider tires, sport suspension, and heavy-duty cooling and braking systems.

RATINGS (SCALE OF 1-10)

Overall	Safety	Reliability	Performance	Comfort	Value
7.3	6.7	6.2	7.6	8.3	7.6

Category B

Model Description	Trade-in Value	Market Value
4 Dr Classic Sdn	3945	5555
4 Dr STD Sdn	2775	3905
4 Dr STD Wgn	4400	6200

OPTIONS FOR CAPRICE

AM/FM Stereo Tape +35
Cruise Control +45
Leather Seats +135
Power Door Locks[Std on Classic] +50
Power Drivers Seat +60
Power Windows[Std on Classic] +60
Tilt Steering Wheel +35

CAVALIER 1991

Styling is revised front and rear for a more aerodynamic look. Cupholders and storage cubbies are added to a restyled dashboard. RS trim level reappears for coupe and sedan after two-year hiatus. Z51 Performance Handling Package is available on Cavalier RS coupe, and includes sport suspension, performance tires and gauge package. Scotchgard protectant covers cloth seats and door trim. Z24 gets new alloy wheels.

RATINGS (SCALE OF 1-10)

Overall	Safety	Reliability	Performance	Comfort	Value
N/A	N/A	6.8	6.6	6.8	5.6

Category E

Model Description	Trade-in Value	Market Value
2 Dr RS Conv	2745	4650
2 Dr RS Cpe	1735	2940
4 Dr RS Sdn	1775	3010
4 Dr RS Wgn	1880	3185
2 Dr VL Cpe	1435	2435
4 Dr VL Sdn	1445	2450
4 Dr VL Wgn	1545	2620
2 Dr Z24 Cpe	2400	4070

OPTIONS FOR CAVALIER

6 cyl 3.1 L Engine[Opt on Wgn] +135
Auto 3-Speed Transmission[Std on Wgn] +95
Air Conditioning +165
AM/FM Stereo Tape +60
Cruise Control +45
Power Door Locks[Std on Conv] +45
Power Windows[Std on Conv] +55
Sunroof +70
Tilt Steering Wheel +30

CHEVY VAN/SPORTVAN 1991

7.4-liter engine can be equipped with a four-speed automatic transmission.

G10

Category H

Model Description	Trade-in Value	Market Value
2 Dr STD Chevy Van Ext	4455	6015
2 Dr STD Chevy Van	4200	5675
2 Dr STD Sportvan	5145	6955

G20

Category H

Model Description	Trade-in Value	Market Value
2 Dr Beauville Sportvan	4765	6440
2 Dr STD Chevy Van	3240	4375
2 Dr STD Sportvan	4325	5845

G30

Category H

Model Description	Trade-in Value	Market Value
2 Dr Beauville Sportvan Ext	4260	5755
2 Dr Beauville Sportvan	4195	5670
2 Dr STD Chevy Van	3090	4180
2 Dr STD Sportvan Ext	4030	5445
2 Dr STD Sportvan	3845	5200
2 Dr STD Chevy Van Ext	3335	4510

OPTIONS FOR CHEVY VAN/SPORTVAN

8 cyl 6.2 L Dsl Engine +465
8 cyl 5.0 L Engine +120
8 cyl 5.7 L Engine[Std on G30,Chevy Van Ext] +165
8 cyl 7.4 L Engine +160
Heavy Duty Pkg +185
12 Passenger Seating +125
Air Conditioning +165
AM/FM Stereo Tape +50
Cruise Control +40
Dual Air Conditioning +290
Power Door Locks +35
Power Windows +40
Privacy Glass +35
Rear Heater +45
Tilt Steering Wheel +35

CORSICA 1991

New dashboard debuts, and a driver airbag is added. LTZ model is dropped, leaving one trim level available. Sport Handling Package includes LTZ suspension, trim, and wheels. A CD player joins the options sheet.

RATINGS (SCALE OF 1-10)

Overall	Safety	Reliability	Performance	Comfort	Value
6.4	4.7	6.8	6.8	7.3	6.3

Don't forget to refer to the Mileage Adjustment Table at the back of this book!

 © 1999 by Edmund Publications Corporation

Model Description	Trade-in Value	Market Value
Category C		
4 Dr LT Sdn	1815	2790
4 Dr LT Hbk	1905	2930

OPTIONS FOR CORSICA

6 cyl 3.1 L Engine +105
Auto 3-Speed Transmission +110
Air Conditioning +160
Aluminum/Alloy Wheels +60
AM/FM Stereo Tape +35
Cruise Control +40
Power Door Locks +50
Power Windows +60
Tilt Steering Wheel +30

CORVETTE 1991

Styling is tweaked front and rear for a more aerodynamic appearance. All Corvettes get the ZR-1's rear styling treatment. New alloy wheels are standard across the line.

Model Description	Trade-in Value	Market Value
Category J		
2 Dr STD Cpe	10530	13675
2 Dr STD Conv	12465	16190
2 Dr ZR1 Cpe	17020	22105

OPTIONS FOR CORVETTE

Adj. Leather Seats +220
Electronic Ride Select. +340
AM/FM Compact Disc Playr +110
Bose Sound System +165
Leather Seats[Opt on STD] +210
Power Drivers Seat[Opt on STD] +65
Solid & Glass Targa Tops +190

LUMINA 1991

Euro models get standard alloy wheels. Newly optional is a Delco/Bose sound system. Coupes can be ordered in new Z34 trim, which comes standard with a 3.4-liter twin-cam V6, sport suspension, and louvered hood.

RATINGS (SCALE OF 1-10)

Overall	Safety	Reliability	Performance	Comfort	Value
N/A	N/A	6.7	8.2	7.6	8.3

Model Description	Trade-in Value	Market Value
Category C		
2 Dr Euro Cpe	2715	4180
4 Dr Euro Sdn	2730	4195
2 Dr STD Cpe	2070	3180
4 Dr STD Sdn	2150	3310
2 Dr Z34 Cpe	3855	5930

OPTIONS FOR LUMINA

6 cyl 3.1 L Engine[Opt on STD] +105
Auto 4-Speed Transmission +40
Air Conditioning[Opt on STD] +160
AM/FM Stereo Tape[Std on Z34] +35
Cruise Control[Std on Z34] +40
Power Door Locks +50
Power Drivers Seat +60
Power Windows +60
Tilt Steering Wheel[Std on Z34] +30

LUMINA MINIVAN 1991

A CD player is newly optional. Non-reflective carpet is added to the top of the dashboard.

RATINGS (SCALE OF 1-10)

Overall	Safety	Reliability	Performance	Comfort	Value
6.9	4.9	7.6	7	7.5	7.7

Model Description	Trade-in Value	Market Value
Category G		
2 Dr CL Pass. Van	3125	4460
2 Dr STD Cargo Van	2195	3135
2 Dr STD Pass. Van	2930	4190

OPTIONS FOR LUMINA MINIVAN

Air Conditioning +165
Aluminum/Alloy Wheels +70
AM/FM Stereo Tape +50
Cruise Control +45
Power Door Locks +45
Power Drivers Seat +55
Power Windows +50
Tilt Steering Wheel +35

R3500 PICKUP 1991

Model Description	Trade-in Value	Market Value
Category H		
4 Dr Silverado Crew Cab LB	6165	8330
4 Dr STD Crew Cab LB	5575	7535

OPTIONS FOR R3500 PICKUP

8 cyl 6.2 L Dsl Engine +465
8 cyl 7.4 L Engine +160
Auto 4-Speed Transmission +195
Air Conditioning +165
AM/FM Stereo Tape +50
Cruise Control +40
Dual Rear Wheels +170
Power Door Locks +35
Power Windows +40
Tilt Steering Wheel +35

S10 BLAZER 1991

Four-door models get new Sport Package on the options list. It includes two-tone paint, alloy wheels, and chrome trim. A heavy-duty battery is standard on all models, and 2WD Blazers can be equipped with 15-inch alloy wheels. Front bench seat option will give four-door models six-passenger capacity. Softer suspension available midyear with Tahoe LT trim.

RATINGS (SCALE OF 1-10)

Overall	Safety	Reliability	Performance	Comfort	Value
5.6	3.7	5.8	6.8	7.1	4.4

Don't forget to refer to the Mileage Adjustment Table at the back of this book!

 © 1999 by Edmund Publications Corporation

Model Description	Trade-in Value	Market Value
Category G		
2 Dr Sport Utility	3745	5355
2 Dr Sport 4WD Utility	4285	6120
4 Dr Sport Wgn	4240	6055
4 Dr Sport 4WD Wgn	4765	6810
2 Dr STD Utility	3560	5085
2 Dr STD 4WD Utility	4065	5810
4 Dr STD Wgn	3995	5705
4 Dr STD 4WD Wgn	4640	6625
2 Dr Tahoe Utility	3695	5280
2 Dr Tahoe 4WD Utility	4245	6065
4 Dr Tahoe Wgn	4110	5870
4 Dr Tahoe 4WD Wgn	4685	6690

OPTIONS FOR S10 BLAZER

Auto 4-Speed Transmission +175
LT Pkg +195
Air Conditioning +165
Aluminum/Alloy Wheels +70
AM/FM Stereo Tape +50
Cruise Control +45
Leather Seats +155
Power Door Locks +45
Power Windows +50
Tilt Steering Wheel +35

S10 PICKUP 1991

Exterior facelift that includes a new grille, fresh trim, and restyled wheels debuted early in 1990. Four-wheel drive models get the 4.3-liter V6 as standard equipment. Durango trim is dropped. Midyear, the base four-cylinder powerplant gets more horsepower.

RATINGS (SCALE OF 1-10)

Overall	Safety	Reliability	Performance	Comfort	Value
N/A	3.4	7.2	7.2	7	N/A

Model Description	Trade-in Value	Market Value
Category G		
2 Dr Baja 4WD Ext Cab SB	5010	7155
2 Dr Baja 4WD Std Cab SB	4170	5955
2 Dr Baja 4WD Std Cab LB	4445	6350
2 Dr EL Std Cab SB	2365	3380
2 Dr STD Std Cab SB	2665	3805
2 Dr STD Ext Cab SB	3030	4330
2 Dr STD Std Cab LB	2725	3895
2 Dr STD 4WD Std Cab SB	4030	5760
2 Dr STD 4WD Ext Cab SB	4785	6835
2 Dr STD 4WD Std Cab LB	4220	6030
2 Dr Tahoe Std Cab SB	2890	4125
2 Dr Tahoe Ext Cab SB	3140	4485
2 Dr Tahoe Std Cab LB	2970	4245
2 Dr Tahoe 4WD Std Cab SB	4065	5810
2 Dr Tahoe 4WD Ext Cab SB	4830	6900
2 Dr Tahoe 4WD Std Cab LB	4285	6120

OPTIONS FOR S10 PICKUP

6 cyl 2.8 L Engine +80
6 cyl 4.3 L Engine[Opt on 2WD] +125
Auto 4-Speed Transmission +175
Air Conditioning +165
Aluminum/Alloy Wheels +70
AM/FM Stereo Tape +50
Cruise Control +45
Power Door Locks +45
Power Windows +50
Tilt Steering Wheel +35

SUBURBAN 1991

Manual transmission is dropped.

Model Description	Trade-in Value	Market Value
Category H		
4 Dr R1500 Wgn	5760	7785
4 Dr R2500 Wgn	6055	8180
4 Dr V1500 4WD Wgn	7410	10010
4 Dr V2500 4WD Wgn	7880	10645

OPTIONS FOR SUBURBAN

8 cyl 6.2 L Dsl Engine +465
8 cyl 7.4 L Engine +160
Silverado Pkg +305
Air Conditioning +165
Aluminum/Alloy Wheels +65
AM/FM Stereo Tape +50
Camper/Towing Package +70
Cruise Control +40
Dual Air Conditioning +290
Power Door Locks +35
Power Windows +40
Rear Heater +45
Tilt Steering Wheel +35

V3500 PICKUP 1991

Model Description	Trade-in Value	Market Value
Category H		
4 Dr Silverado 4WD Crew Cab LB	7295	9855
4 Dr STD 4WD Crew Cab LB	6790	9175

OPTIONS FOR V3500 PICKUP

8 cyl 6.2 L Dsl Engine +465
8 cyl 7.4 L Engine +160
Auto 4-Speed Transmission +175
Air Conditioning +165
AM/FM Stereo Tape +50
Cruise Control +40
Dual Rear Wheels +170
Power Door Locks +35
Power Windows +40
Tilt Steering Wheel +35

For a guaranteed low price on a new car in your area, call
1-800-CAR-CLUB

Don't forget to refer to the Mileage Adjustment Table at the back of this book!

 © 1999 by Edmund Publications Corporation

1990 CHEVROLET

ASTRO 1990

All-wheel drive is newly optional, and an extended body style is introduced. Standard engine on passenger models is a 150-horsepower 4.3-liter V6. The optional sport suspension will not be available on AWD vans. Four-wheel ABS is standard on all but commercially-purchased cargo vans.

RATINGS (SCALE OF 1-10)

Overall	Safety	Reliability	Performance	Comfort	Value
6.5	4	6.3	7.2	6.6	8.1

Category G

Model	Trade-in	Market
2 Dr CL Pass. Van	2775	4205
2 Dr CL Pass. Van Ext	3165	4795
2 Dr CL 4WD Pass. Van Ext	4765	7220
2 Dr CL 4WD Pass. Van	4190	6350
2 Dr LT Pass. Van	3130	4745
2 Dr LT Pass. Van Ext	3390	5135
2 Dr LT 4WD Pass. Van	4330	6560
2 Dr LT 4WD Pass. Van Ext	5155	7810
2 Dr STD Pass. Van	2720	4125
2 Dr STD Cargo Van Ext	2350	3565
2 Dr STD Cargo Van	2150	3260
2 Dr STD Pass. Van Ext	2880	4360
2 Dr STD 4WD Cargo Van Ext	3725	5645
2 Dr STD 4WD Pass. Van Ext	4490	6800
2 Dr STD 4WD Pass. Van	3995	6055
2 Dr STD 4WD Cargo Van	3350	5070

OPTIONS FOR ASTRO

6 cyl 4.3 L Engine +100
Sport Handling Package +215
8 Passenger Seating +65
Air Conditioning +135
Aluminum/Alloy Wheels +55
AM/FM Stereo Tape +40
Dual Air Conditioning +165
Power Door Locks +40
Power Drivers Seat +45
Power Windows +40

BERETTA 1990

GTZ model debuts, with high-output version of Quad 4 engine. GTZ has 180-horsepower, and is available only with five-speed transmission. Short-lived GTU is dropped. An aggressively hyped convertible model never made it to production. Base 2.0-liter engine is swapped for peppier 2.2-liter unit. Optional V6 goes from 2.8 liters to 3.1, and now makes 140 horsepower. Air conditioning is made standard on all but the base model. All Berettas get new cloth seat covers and cushions.

RATINGS (SCALE OF 1-10)

Overall	Safety	Reliability	Performance	Comfort	Value
6.2	5.2	6.3	7.8	6.8	5

Category E

Model	Trade-in	Market
2 Dr GT Cpe	1655	3180
2 Dr GTZ Cpe	1740	3345
2 Dr STD Cpe	1230	2365

OPTIONS FOR BERETTA

6 cyl 3.1 L Engine[Opt on STD] +115
Auto 3-Speed Transmission +90
Air Conditioning[Opt on STD] +135
Aluminum/Alloy Wheels[Std on GTZ] +50
Power Door Locks +40
Power Windows +45
Sunroof +55

BLAZER 1990

Rear-wheel ABS that works only in 2WD is added.

Category H

Model	Trade-in	Market
2 Dr Silverado 4WD Utility	5315	7385
2 Dr STD 4WD Utility	5120	7110

OPTIONS FOR BLAZER

8 cyl 6.2 L Dsl Engine +390
Auto 4-Speed Transmission +140
Air Conditioning +135
Aluminum/Alloy Wheels +50
AM/FM Stereo Tape +40
Cruise Control +30
Power Door Locks +30
Power Windows +30
Tilt Steering Wheel +30

C/K PICKUP 1990

Stripped W/T (Work Truck) model is added to serve as a serious, and affordable, work truck. C/K 2500 Crew Cab model dropped. 454 SS model introduced, with powerful 7.4-liter V8 and sport suspension installed in regular-cab shortbox.

RATINGS (SCALE OF 1-10)

Overall	Safety	Reliability	Performance	Comfort	Value
N/A	5.5	7.4	7.4	8	N/A

C1500

Category H

Model	Trade-in	Market
2 Dr 454SS Std Cab SB	7140	9920
2 Dr Scottsdale Std Cab SB	4570	6345
2 Dr Scottsdale Ext Cab SB	5150	7150
2 Dr Scottsdale Std Cab Stepside SB	4675	6495
2 Dr Scottsdale Ext Cab LB	5225	7255
2 Dr Scottsdale Std Cab LB	4940	6860
2 Dr Silverado Std Cab SB	4815	6690
2 Dr Silverado Ext Cab SB	5265	7315

Don't forget to refer to the Mileage Adjustment Table at the back of this book!

 © 1999 by Edmund Publications Corporation

Model Description	Trade-in Value	Market Value
2 Dr Silverado Std Cab Stepside SB	4890	6790
2 Dr Silverado Ext Cab LB	5340	7420
2 Dr Silverado Std Cab LB	4995	6940
2 Dr STD Ext Cab SB	5060	7025
2 Dr STD Std Cab SB	4465	6200
2 Dr STD Ext Cab Stepside SB	5090	7070
2 Dr STD Std Cab Stepside SB	4530	6290
2 Dr STD Ext Cab LB	5105	7090
2 Dr STD Std Cab LB	4675	6490
2 Dr WT Std Cab LB	4075	5660

C2500

Category H

Model Description	Trade-in Value	Market Value
2 Dr Scottsdale Ext Cab SB	5050	7015
2 Dr Scottsdale Std Cab LB	4910	6820
2 Dr Scottsdale Ext Cab LB	5190	7205
2 Dr Silverado Ext Cab SB	5140	7140
2 Dr Silverado Std Cab LB	5150	7150
2 Dr Silverado Ext Cab LB	5315	7385
2 Dr STD Ext Cab SB	5020	6970
2 Dr STD Std Cab LB	4815	6685
2 Dr STD Ext Cab LB	5095	7075

C3500

Category H

Model Description	Trade-in Value	Market Value
2 Dr Scottsdale Ext Cab LB	6680	9280
2 Dr Scottsdale Std Cab LB	6465	8975
2 Dr Silverado Ext Cab LB	6930	9620
2 Dr Silverado Std Cab LB	6495	9020
2 Dr STD Std Cab LB	6330	8790
2 Dr STD Ext Cab LB	6620	9195

K1500

Category H

Model Description	Trade-in Value	Market Value
2 Dr Scottsdale 4WD Std Cab SB	5665	7870
2 Dr Scottsdale 4WD Ext Cab SB	6195	8605
2 Dr Scottsdale 4WD Std Cab Stepside SB	5610	7790
2 Dr Scottsdale 4WD Std Cab LB	5655	7850
2 Dr Scottsdale 4WD Ext Cab LB	6155	8550
2 Dr Silverado 4WD Ext Cab SB	6255	8685
2 Dr Silverado 4WD Std Cab SB	5880	8165
2 Dr Silverado 4WD Std Cab Stepside SB	5755	7995
2 Dr Silverado 4WD Ext Cab LB	6320	8780
2 Dr Silverado 4WD Std Cab LB	5660	7860
2 Dr STD 4WD Ext Cab SB	6010	8350
2 Dr STD 4WD Std Cab SB	5620	7805
2 Dr STD 4WD Std Cab Stepside SB	5600	7780
2 Dr STD 4WD Std Cab LB	5615	7795
2 Dr STD 4WD Ext Cab LB	6090	8460
2 Dr WT 4WD Std Cab LB	4575	6355

K2500

Category H

Model Description	Trade-in Value	Market Value
2 Dr Scottsdale 4WD Ext Cab SB	6170	8570
2 Dr Scottsdale 4WD Std Cab LB	5475	7600
2 Dr Scottsdale 4WD Ext Cab LB	6235	8660
2 Dr Silverado 4WD Ext Cab SB	6205	8620
2 Dr Silverado 4WD Std Cab LB	5605	7785
2 Dr Silverado 4WD Ext Cab LB	6320	8780
2 Dr STD 4WD Ext Cab SB	6140	8525
2 Dr STD 4WD Std Cab LB	5470	7595
2 Dr STD 4WD Ext Cab LB	6155	8550

K3500

Category H

Model Description	Trade-in Value	Market Value
2 Dr Scottsdale 4WD Ext Cab LB	6915	9600
2 Dr Scottsdale 4WD Std Cab LB	6350	8820
2 Dr Silverado 4WD Std Cab LB	6405	8895
2 Dr Silverado 4WD Ext Cab LB	7150	9930
2 Dr STD 4WD Std Cab LB	6270	8705
2 Dr STD 4WD Ext Cab LB	6850	9515

OPTIONS FOR C/K PICKUP

8 cyl 6.2 L Dsl Engine +390
8 cyl 5.0 L Engine +95
8 cyl 5.7 L Engine +125
Auto 3-Speed Transmission[Std on 454SS] +105
Auto 4-Speed Transmission +140
Sport Handling Pkg +145
Air Conditioning[Std on 454SS] +135
Aluminum/Alloy Wheels +50
AM/FM Stereo Tape +40
Camper/Towing Package +60
Cruise Control[Std on 454SS] +30
Dual Rear Wheels +140
Power Door Locks[Std on 454SS] +30
Power Windows[Std on 454SS] +30
Tilt Steering Wheel[Std on 454SS] +30

CAMARO 1990

Driver airbag is standard. The 2.8-liter V6 is replaced by a 3.1-liter motor making 140 horsepower. The 5.7-liter V8 is redesigned with lighter-weight pistons. IROC models get a limited-slip differential, and IROC convertibles have new 16-inch alloy wheels. Delco/Bose sound system is upgraded. Buyers can order a Flame Red interior, though we don't know why they would.

Category F

Model Description	Trade-in Value	Market Value
2 Dr IROC Z Conv	5915	8575
2 Dr IROC Z Cpe	4180	6060
2 Dr RS Conv	4875	7060
2 Dr RS Cpe	2740	3970

OPTIONS FOR CAMARO

8 cyl 5.0 L Engine[Opt on RS Cpe] +80
8 cyl 5.7 L Engine +90
Auto 4-Speed Transmission +85

Don't forget to refer to the Mileage Adjustment Table at the back of this book!

 © 1999 by Edmund Publications Corporation

Model Description	Trade-in Value	Market Value

Air Conditioning +140
AM/FM Stereo Tape +35
Leather Seats +120
Power Door Locks +35
Power Drivers Seat +40
Power Windows +35
T-Tops (solid/Colored) +155

CAPRICE 1990

No changes.

Category B		
4 Dr Classic Sdn	2935	4515
4 Dr Classic Wgn	2380	3660
4 Dr Classic Brougham Sdn	3100	4775
4 Dr LS Brougham Sdn	3410	5250
4 Dr STD Sdn	2185	3360

OPTIONS FOR CAPRICE

Leather Seats +110
Power Door Locks +40
Power Drivers Seat +50
Power Windows +50
Wire Wheel Covers +40

CAVALIER 1990

Convertible model disappears. New engines have more power; base 2.2-liter motor pumps out 95 horsepower, while the 3.1-liter V6 makes 140 horsepower. Door-mounted passive seatbelts have been added. Seats and fabrics are new this year. RS trim level reappears on wagon models.

RATINGS (SCALE OF 1-10)

Overall	Safety	Reliability	Performance	Comfort	Value
N/A	N/A	6.8	6.6	6.8	5.4

Category E		
2 Dr RS Cpe	1455	2795
2 Dr STD Cpe	1280	2460
4 Dr STD Wgn	1190	2285
4 Dr STD Sdn	1205	2315
2 Dr VL Cpe	1050	2025
4 Dr VL Wgn	1120	2155
4 Dr VL Sdn	1105	2125
2 Dr Z24 Cpe	1825	3505

OPTIONS FOR CAVALIER

6 cyl 3.1 L Engine[Opt on STD] +115
Auto 3-Speed Transmission +75
Air Conditioning +135
Aluminum/Alloy Wheels +50
Power Door Locks +40
Power Windows +45
Sunroof +55

CELEBRITY 1990

Sedan model dropped, leaving only a wagon. Base engine makes more power, and optional 2.8-liter V6 is replaced by a 3.1-liter motor that makes 135 horsepower. All models get a heavy-duty suspension. The rear seat is now of the split-folding variety. Door-mounted passive restraints have been added.

Category C		
4 Dr Eurosport Wgn	1915	3145
4 Dr STD Wgn	1900	3115

OPTIONS FOR CELEBRITY

6 cyl 3.1 L Engine +100
Auto 4-Speed Transmission[Opt on STD] +35
Air Conditioning[Opt on STD] +130
Aluminum/Alloy Wheels +50
Power Door Locks +40
Power Drivers Seat +45
Power Windows +50

CHEVY VAN/SPORTVAN 1990

No changes.

G10

Category H		
2 Dr Beauville Sportvan	3995	5550
2 Dr Beauville Sportvan Ext	4130	5735
2 Dr STD Sportvan	3055	4240
2 Dr STD Chevy Van Ext	2695	3740
2 Dr STD Sportvan Ext	3065	4260
2 Dr STD Chevy Van	2610	3625

G20

Category H		
2 Dr Beauville Sportvan	4370	6070
2 Dr STD Chevy Van	3150	4375
2 Dr STD Sportvan	3515	4880
2 Dr STD Chevy Van Ext	3620	5030

G30

Category H		
2 Dr Beauville Sportvan	4175	5795
2 Dr STD Chevy Van	3380	4695
2 Dr STD Sportvan	3985	5535
2 Dr STD Chevy Van Ext	3535	4910

OPTIONS FOR CHEVY VAN/SPORTVAN

8 cyl 6.2 L Dsl Engine +390
8 cyl 5.0 L Engine +95
8 cyl 5.7 L Engine[Opt on G10,G20,Chevy Van Ext] +125
8 cyl 7.4 L Engine +75
Auto 4-Speed Transmission[Std on G30,Beauville, Sportvan] +40
12 Passenger Seating +100
Air Conditioning +135

Don't forget to refer to the Mileage Adjustment Table at the back of this book!

 © 1999 by Edmund Publications Corporation

Model Description	Trade-in Value	Market Value

Dual Air Conditioning +235
Power Door Locks +30
Power Windows +30

CORSICA 1990

Base model replaced by LT trim level. A 2.2-liter engine replaces the base 2.0-liter motor. A 3.1-liter V6 replaces the 2.8-liter V6. Seats get new cloth covers and cushions. All models except the LT comes with air conditioning standard.

RATINGS (SCALE OF 1-10)

Overall	Safety	Reliability	Performance	Comfort	Value
6.2	4	6.2	6.8	6.9	7.4

Category C		
4 Dr LT Sdn	1590	2605
4 Dr LT Hbk	1585	2600
4 Dr LTZ Sdn	2005	3285

OPTIONS FOR CORSICA

6 cyl 3.1 L Engine[Opt on LT] +100
Auto 3-Speed Transmission +90
Air Conditioning[Opt on LT] +130
Aluminum/Alloy Wheels +50
Power Door Locks +40
Power Windows +50

CORVETTE 1990

King-of-the-hill ZR-1 appears with aluminum DOHC 32-valve 5.7-liter V8 built by Mercury Marine. ZF six-speed transmission is standard on ZR-1, as is blistering performance and ultra-wide rear wheels. ZR-1 is distinguished by unique rear-body work. All Corvettes get a driver airbag and ABS. New dashboard debuts with several analog gauges and a real glovebox. Base Corvettes get five additional horsepower. The radiator is sloped for better cooling. 17-inch alloys are lighter-weight. A 200-watt sound system with cassette or CD player is available.

Category J		
2 Dr STD Conv	11510	15140
2 Dr STD Cpe	9835	12940
2 Dr ZR1 Cpe	16365	21530

OPTIONS FOR CORVETTE

Electronic Ride Selection +280
Handling Suspension (FX3) +280
Roof Option +150
AM/FM Compact Disc Playr +90
Bose Sound System +135
Leather Seats[Opt on STD] +170
Power Drivers Seat[Opt on STD] +55
Solid & Glass Targa Tops +155

LUMINA 1990

Sedan bowed in March, 1989. Coupe is added this year. Base engine is a 110-horsepower 2.5-liter four cylinder. Optional is a 135-horsepower 3.1-liter V6. Euro models include V6 engine, sport suspension, air conditioning, bigger wheels, and decklid spoiler.

RATINGS (SCALE OF 1-10)

Overall	Safety	Reliability	Performance	Comfort	Value
N/A	N/A	6.4	8.2	7.6	8.1

Category C		
2 Dr Euro Cpe	2135	3495
4 Dr Euro Sdn	2165	3545
2 Dr STD Cpe	1685	2760
4 Dr STD Sdn	1705	2790

OPTIONS FOR LUMINA

6 cyl 3.1 L Engine[Opt on STD] +100
Auto 4-Speed Transmission +35
Air Conditioning[Opt on STD] +130
Aluminum/Alloy Wheels +50
Power Door Locks +40
Power Drivers Seat +45
Power Windows +50

LUMINA MINIVAN 1990

New minivan suffering from inadequate powerplant debuts. Body panels are composite plastic mounted to a steel-space frame. Modular seating accommodates up to seven passengers. Standard and only engine is a 3.1-liter V6 offering 120 measly horsepower.

RATINGS (SCALE OF 1-10)

Overall	Safety	Reliability	Performance	Comfort	Value
6.7	4.9	7	7	7.5	7.2

Category G		
2 Dr CL Pass. Van	3200	4850
2 Dr STD Pass. Van	2910	4410

OPTIONS FOR LUMINA MINIVAN

Air Conditioning[Std on CL] +135
Aluminum/Alloy Wheels +55
Power Door Locks +40
Power Drivers Seat +45
Power Windows +40

R3500 PICKUP 1990

Category H		
4 Dr Silverado Crew Cab LB	5505	7650
4 Dr STD Crew Cab LB	5280	7330

OPTIONS FOR R3500 PICKUP

8 cyl 6.2 L Dsl Engine +390
8 cyl 7.4 L Engine +75
Auto 3-Speed Transmission +110
Air Conditioning +135

Don't forget to refer to the Mileage Adjustment Table at the back of this book!

 © 1999 by Edmund Publications Corporation

Model Description	Trade-in Value	Market Value

Dual Rear Wheels +140
Power Door Locks +30
Power Windows +30

S10 BLAZER 1990

A four-door model with standard four-wheel ABS is added to the lineup, and the 2.8-liter engine is dropped in favor of a more powerful 160-horsepower 4.3-liter V6.

RATINGS (SCALE OF 1-10)

Overall	Safety	Reliability	Performance	Comfort	Value
6.3	3.7	7.4	6.8	7.1	6.3

Category G

Model Description	Trade-in Value	Market Value
2 Dr Sport Utility	3115	4715
2 Dr Sport 4WD Utility	3370	5110
2 Dr STD 4WD Utility	3275	4960
2 Dr Tahoe Utility	3175	4810
2 Dr Tahoe 4WD Utility	3415	5180

OPTIONS FOR S10 BLAZER
Auto 4-Speed Transmission +140
Air Conditioning +135
Aluminum/Alloy Wheels[Opt on STD,Tahoe] +55
Leather Seats +125
Power Door Locks +40
Power Windows +40
Tilt Steering Wheel +30

S10 PICKUP 1990

No changes.

RATINGS (SCALE OF 1-10)

Overall	Safety	Reliability	Performance	Comfort	Value
N/A	3.4	6.8	7.2	7	N/A

Category G

Model Description	Trade-in Value	Market Value
2 Dr Baja 4WD Std Cab SB	3640	5515
2 Dr Durango Std Cab SB	2250	3405
2 Dr Durango Std Cab LB	2355	3565
2 Dr Durango 4WD Std Cab SB	3570	5410
2 Dr Durango 4WD Ext Cab SB	3720	5635
2 Dr Durango 4WD Std Cab LB	3465	5250
2 Dr EL Std Cab SB	2095	3170
2 Dr STD Std Cab SB	2200	3330
2 Dr STD Ext Cab SB	2905	4405
2 Dr STD Std Cab LB	2245	3405
2 Dr STD 4WD Ext Cab SB	3640	5515
2 Dr STD 4WD Std Cab SB	3390	5140
2 Dr STD 4WD Std Cab LB	3410	5165
2 Dr Tahoe Std Cab SB	2285	3465
2 Dr Tahoe Ext Cab SB	3080	4665
2 Dr Tahoe Std Cab LB	2410	3650
2 Dr Tahoe 4WD Std Cab SB	3540	5360
2 Dr Tahoe 4WD Ext Cab SB	3665	5555
2 Dr Tahoe 4WD Std Cab LB	3505	5315

OPTIONS FOR S10 PICKUP
6 cyl 2.8 L Engine +60
6 cyl 4.3 L Engine[Opt on 2WD] +100
Auto 4-Speed Transmission +145
Air Conditioning +135
Aluminum/Alloy Wheels +55
Auto Locking Hubs (4WD) +45
Power Door Locks +40
Power Windows +40

SUBURBAN 1990

Rear-wheel ABS that works only in 2WD is added.

Category H.

Model Description	Trade-in Value	Market Value
4 Dr R1500 Wgn	5035	6990
4 Dr R2500 Wgn	5185	7200
4 Dr V1500 4WD Wgn	6070	8430
4 Dr V2500 4WD Wgn	6290	8740

OPTIONS FOR SUBURBAN
8 cyl 6.2 L Dsl Engine +390
8 cyl 7.4 L Engine +75
Auto 3-Speed Transmission +105
Auto 4-Speed Transmission[Opt on V15] +140
Silverado Package +240
Suburban Silverado Package +225
Air Conditioning +135
Aluminum/Alloy Wheels +50
Camper/Towing Package +60
Dual Air Conditioning +235
Power Door Locks +30
Power Windows +30

V3500 PICKUP 1990

Category H

Model Description	Trade-in Value	Market Value
4 Dr STD 4WD Crew Cab LB	7645	10620

OPTIONS FOR V3500 PICKUP
8 cyl 6.2 L Dsl Engine +390
8 cyl 7.4 L Engine +75
Auto 3-Speed Transmission +110
Air Conditioning +135
Dual Rear Wheels +140
Power Door Locks +30
Power Windows +30

1989 CHEVROLET

ASTRO 1989

Rear-wheel ABS is added. Standard gauges have been upgraded. Power steering, front stabilizer bar and 27-gallon fuel tank move from options sheet to standard equipment list. Outboard seating positions get shoulder belts. Optional four-seat seating package is dropped. Midyear, a sport suspension package is introduced.

Don't forget to refer to the Mileage Adjustment Table at the back of this book!

 © 1999 by Edmund Publications Corporation

Model Description	Trade-in Value	Market Value

RATINGS (SCALE OF 1-10)

Overall	Safety	Reliability	Performance	Comfort	Value
6.3	3.2	6.4	7.2	6.6	7.9

Category G

Model Description	Trade-in Value	Market Value
2 Dr CL Pass. Van	2220	3640
2 Dr LT Pass. Van	2490	4085
2 Dr STD Cargo Van	1930	3160
2 Dr STD Pass. Van	2105	3455

OPTIONS FOR ASTRO

6 cyl 4.3 L Engine[Opt on Cargo Van] +50
Auto 4-Speed Transmission +85
8 Passenger Seating +50
Air Conditioning +110
Aluminum/Alloy Wheels +45
AM/FM Stereo Tape +35
Power Door Locks +30
Power Drivers Seat +40
Power Windows +30

BERETTA 1989

Base models get GT trim, and GT gets alloy wheels, new seat fabric and a split-folding rear seatback. Base model has larger tires. Midyear, the GTU debuts, featuring unique trim, aero body panels and alloy wheels.

RATINGS (SCALE OF 1-10)

Overall	Safety	Reliability	Performance	Comfort	Value
6.3	5.2	6.1	7.8	6.8	5.9

Category E

Model Description	Trade-in Value	Market Value
2 Dr GT Cpe	1170	2655
2 Dr STD Cpe	935	2125

OPTIONS FOR BERETTA

6 cyl 2.8 L Engine[Std on GT] +90
Auto 3-Speed Transmission +65
GTU Package +300
Air Conditioning[Std on GT] +110
Aluminum/Alloy Wheels +45
Power Door Locks +30
Power Windows +35
Sunroof +45

BLAZER 1989

Suspension refinements net a smoother, quieter ride. Front styling is revised to resemble C/K pickup.

Category H

Model Description	Trade-in Value	Market Value
2 Dr Silverado 4WD Utility	4100	5940
2 Dr STD 4WD Utility	3545	5140

OPTIONS FOR BLAZER

8 cyl 6.2 L Dsl Engine +290
Auto 4-Speed Transmission +110
Air Conditioning +110
Aluminum/Alloy Wheels +40

C/K PICKUP 1989

A new extended-cab model with a shortbox is introduced. Also new, C/K 2500 models with 8,600 lb. GVWR and a K3500 Heavy Hauler Duallie with 10,000 lb. GVWR.

RATINGS (SCALE OF 1-10)

Overall	Safety	Reliability	Performance	Comfort	Value
N/A	5.5	7.2	7.4	8	N/A

C1500

Category H

Model Description	Trade-in Value	Market Value
2 Dr Scottsdale Ext Cab SB	4615	6690
2 Dr Scottsdale Std Cab SB	4295	6225
2 Dr Scottsdale Std Cab Stepside SB	4260	6175
2 Dr Scottsdale Std Cab LB	4330	6275
2 Dr Scottsdale Ext Cab LB	4555	6605
2 Dr Silverado Std Cab SB	4325	6265
2 Dr Silverado Ext Cab SB	4660	6750
2 Dr Silverado Std Cab Stepside SB	4470	6480
2 Dr Silverado Ext Cab LB	4620	6695
2 Dr Silverado Std Cab LB	4355	6315
2 Dr STD Std Cab SB	4265	6185
2 Dr STD Ext Cab SB	4490	6505
2 Dr STD Std Cab Stepside SB	4255	6170
2 Dr STD Std Cab LB	4275	6200
2 Dr STD Ext Cab LB	4420	6410

C2500

Category H

Model Description	Trade-in Value	Market Value
2 Dr Scottsdale Ext Cab LB	4800	6960
2 Dr Scottsdale Std Cab LB	3890	5635
2 Dr Silverado Ext Cab LB	5190	7520
2 Dr Silverado Std Cab LB	3945	5720
2 Dr STD Ext Cab SB	4645	6730
2 Dr STD Ext Cab LB	4585	6650
2 Dr STD Std Cab LB	3695	5360

C3500

Category H

Model Description	Trade-in Value	Market Value
2 Dr Scottsdale Std Cab LB	5120	7420
2 Dr Silverado Std Cab LB	5430	7870
2 Dr Silverado Ext Cab LB	6065	8790
2 Dr STD Std Cab LB	4970	7205
2 Dr STD Ext Cab LB	5875	8515

K1500

Category H

Model Description	Trade-in Value	Market Value
2 Dr Scottsdale 4WD Ext Cab SB	5455	7905
2 Dr Scottsdale 4WD Std Cab SB	4980	7220
2 Dr Scottsdale 4WD Std Cab Stepside SB	5160	7480
2 Dr Scottsdale 4WD Ext Cab LB	5560	8060

Don't forget to refer to the Mileage Adjustment Table at the back of this book!

 © 1999 by Edmund Publications Corporation

Model Description	Trade-in Value	Market Value
2 Dr Scottsdale 4WD Std Cab LB	4870	7055
2 Dr Silverado 4WD Ext Cab SB	5590	8100
2 Dr Silverado 4WD Std Cab SB	5035	7300
2 Dr Silverado 4WD Std Cab Stepside SB	5205	7540
2 Dr Silverado 4WD Ext Cab LB	5630	8160
2 Dr Silverado 4WD Std Cab LB	4925	7140
2 Dr STD 4WD Std Cab SB	4560	6610
2 Dr STD 4WD Ext Cab SB	5330	7725
2 Dr STD 4WD Std Cab LB	4735	6865
2 Dr STD 4WD Ext Cab LB	5060	7330

K2500

Category H

Model Description	Trade-in Value	Market Value
2 Dr Scottsdale 4WD Ext Cab LB	5450	7900
2 Dr Scottsdale 4WD Std Cab LB	4915	7120
2 Dr Silverado 4WD Ext Cab LB	5515	7990
2 Dr Silverado 4WD Std Cab LB	5010	7260
2 Dr STD 4WD Ext Cab LB	5430	7865
2 Dr STD 4WD Std Cab LB	4875	7065

K3500

Category H

Model Description	Trade-in Value	Market Value
2 Dr Scottsdale 4WD Std Cab LB	5750	8330
2 Dr Scottsdale 4WD Ext Cab LB	6880	9970
2 Dr Silverado 4WD Ext Cab LB	6715	9730
2 Dr Silverado 4WD Std Cab LB	5895	8540
2 Dr STD 4WD Std Cab LB	5640	8170
2 Dr STD 4WD Ext Cab LB	6455	9355

OPTIONS FOR C/K PICKUP

8 cyl 6.2 L Dsl Engine +290
8 cyl 5.0 L Engine +80
8 cyl 5.7 L Engine +100
Auto 3-Speed Transmission +85
Auto 4-Speed Transmission +110
Heavy Duty Pkg +130
Sport Handling Package +120
Air Conditioning +110
Aluminum/Alloy Wheels +40
AM/FM Stereo Tape +35
Camper/Towing Package +50
Dual Rear Wheels +115

CAMARO 1989

RS coupe replaces Sport Coupe in lineup; has 2.8-liter V6 standard. RS convertible gets 170-horsepower 5.0-liter V8, which is optional on RS coupe. Pass-key theft deterrent is added to all Camaros.

Category F

Model Description	Trade-in Value	Market Value
2 Dr IROC Z Conv	4835	7215
2 Dr IROC Z Cpe	3770	5630
2 Dr RS Conv	4090	6100
2 Dr RS Cpe	2330	3475

OPTIONS FOR CAMARO

8 cyl 5.0 L Engine[Opt on RS Cpe] +55
8 cyl 5.0 L TPI Engine +100
8 cyl 5.7 L Engine +140
Auto 4-Speed Transmission +65
Air Conditioning +115
Leather Seats +95
Power Drivers Seat +30
Power Windows +30
T-Tops (solid/Colored) +125

CAPRICE 1989

Air conditioning and V8 power come standard this year. Sedans get fuel injection. Three-point rear seatbelts are added, and a cargo net is newly optional on sedans.

Category B

Model Description	Trade-in Value	Market Value
4 Dr Classic Wgn	1745	2910
4 Dr Classic Sdn	2050	3415
4 Dr Classic Brougham Sdn	2505	4175
4 Dr LS Brougham Sdn	2785	4645
4 Dr STD Sdn	1845	3075

OPTIONS FOR CAPRICE

Leather Seats +90
Power Door Locks +35
Power Drivers Seat +40
Power Windows +40
Wire Wheel Covers +30

CAVALIER 1989

Steering wheels are self-aligning this year, and are supposed to reduce chest injury in an accident. RS trim level becomes an option package. V6 is standard on Z24 and optional on wagons. Z24 coupe gets split-folding seatback; item is optional on base coupe and sedan. Z24 gets gas-pressurized shocks. All models receive rear shoulder belts.

RATINGS (SCALE OF 1-10)

Overall	Safety	Reliability	Performance	Comfort	Value
N/A	N/A	6.3	6.6	6.8	6.3

Category E

Model Description	Trade-in Value	Market Value
2 Dr STD Cpe	800	1820
4 Dr STD Wgn	800	1815
4 Dr STD Sdn	910	2070
2 Dr VL Cpe	795	1800
2 Dr Z24 Cpe	1295	2945
2 Dr Z24 Conv	1780	4045

OPTIONS FOR CAVALIER

6 cyl 2.8 L Engine[Opt on STD] +90
Auto 3-Speed Transmission +55
Air Conditioning +110
Aluminum/Alloy Wheels[Std on Z24] +45
Power Door Locks[Std on Conv] +30
Power Windows[Std on Conv] +35

Don't forget to refer to the Mileage Adjustment Table at the back of this book!

© 1999 by Edmund Publications Corporation

Model Description	Trade-in Value	Market Value

CELEBRITY 1989

Coupe is dropped from lineup. Base 2.5-liter engine receives more horsepower midyear. Manual transmission is canceled (only a few hundred were sold during 1987/1988).

Category C		
4 Dr STD Wgn	1315	2305
4 Dr STD Sdn	1355	2380

OPTIONS FOR CELEBRITY

6 cyl 2.8 L Engine +85
Air Conditioning +110
Aluminum/Alloy Wheels +40
Power Door Locks +30
Power Drivers Seat +40
Power Windows +40

CHEVY VAN/SPORTVAN 1989

A 7.4-liter V8 is new to the options list.

G10

Category H		
2 Dr STD Sportvan Ext	3275	4750
2 Dr STD Sportvan	3150	4565
2 Dr STD Chevy Van	2635	3820
2 Dr STD Chevy Van Ext	2965	4295

G20

Category H		
2 Dr Beauville Sportvan	3465	5025
2 Dr STD Chevy Van	2675	3880
2 Dr STD Sportvan	3030	4395
2 Dr STD Chevy Van Ext	2730	3955

G30

Category H		
2 Dr Beauville Sportvan	3320	4815
2 Dr STD Chevy Van	2260	3275
2 Dr STD Sportvan	3300	4780

OPTIONS FOR CHEVY VAN/SPORTVAN

8 cyl 6.2 L Dsl Engine +290
8 cyl 5.0 L Engine +80
8 cyl 5.7 L Engine[Opt on G10,G20,Chevy Van] +100
Auto 4-Speed Transmission[Std on G30] +65
12 Passenger Seating +85
Air Conditioning +110
Dual Air Conditioning +190

CORSICA 1989

Four-door hatchback model is added. Sporty LTZ trim is newly available, and includes a split-folding rear seat, V6 engine, sport suspension, alloy wheels, and performance tires.

RATINGS (SCALE OF 1-10)

Overall	Safety	Reliability	Performance	Comfort	Value
5.9	4	5.9	6.8	6.9	6

Category C		
4 Dr LTZ Sdn	1535	2695
4 Dr STD Hbk	1240	2180
4 Dr STD Sdn	1295	2270

OPTIONS FOR CORSICA

6 cyl 2.8 L Engine[Opt on STD] +85
Auto 3-Speed Transmission +65
Air Conditioning[Opt on STD] +110
Aluminum/Alloy Wheels[Opt on STD] +40
Power Door Locks +30
Power Windows +40

CORVETTE 1989

A six-speed manual transmission is available. Coupes with six-speed and optional Z51 Performance Handling Package will be eligible for new Selective Ride Control, which allows driver to select between touring, sport, and competition suspension settings. Midyear, convertibles get optional hard top with heated rear window.

Category J		
2 Dr STD Conv	10290	13715
2 Dr STD Cpe	9295	12395

OPTIONS FOR CORVETTE

Seat Package +140
Suspension Pkg +230
Bose Sound System +110
Climate Control for AC +30
Leather Seats +140
Power Drivers Seat +45
Solid & Glass Targa Tops +125

R2500 1989

Category H		
4 Dr Silverado Crew Cab LB	5345	7745

OPTIONS FOR R2500

8 cyl 6.2 L Dsl Engine +290
8 cyl 7.4 L Engine +65
Auto 3-Speed Transmission +85
Air Conditioning +110

R30 1989

Category H		
4 Dr Silverado Crew Cab LB	5775	8370

OPTIONS FOR R30

8 cyl 5.7 L Engine +100
8 cyl 7.4 L Engine +65
Auto 3-Speed Transmission +75
Air Conditioning +110
Dual Rear Wheels +115

Don't forget to refer to the Mileage Adjustment Table at the back of this book!

 © 1999 by Edmund Publications Corporation

Model Description	Trade-in Value	Market Value

R3500 PICKUP 1989

Category H

Model Description	Trade-in Value	Market Value
4 Dr Silverado Crew Cab LB	5295	7675
4 Dr STD Crew Cab LB	5140	7445

OPTIONS FOR R3500 PICKUP

8 cyl 6.2 L Dsl Engine +290
8 cyl 7.4 L Engine +65
Auto 3-Speed Transmission +85
Air Conditioning +110
Dual Rear Wheels +115

S10 BLAZER 1989

Rear-wheel ABS that operates in 2WD mode only is new, and rear shoulder belts are added. Instatrac 4WD system is revised when equipped with standard 2.8-liter V6. Power steering is made standard. Rear wiper/ washer and digital gauges are new to options list.

RATINGS (SCALE OF 1-10)

Overall	Safety	Reliability	Performance	Comfort	Value
6.1	3.2	6.9	6.8	7.1	6.2

Category G

Model Description	Trade-in Value	Market Value
2 Dr Sport Utility	2540	4165
2 Dr Sport 4WD Utility	2635	4315
2 Dr STD Utility	2360	3865
2 Dr STD 4WD Utility	2470	4050
2 Dr Tahoe Utility	2525	4140
2 Dr Tahoe 4WD Utility	2580	4225

OPTIONS FOR S10 BLAZER

6 cyl 4.3 L Engine +50
Auto 4-Speed Transmission +110
High Country Pkg +140
Air Conditioning +110
Aluminum/Alloy Wheels +45
Leather Seats +105
Power Door Locks +30
Power Windows +30

S10 PICKUP 1989

Four-wheel drive models get the 2.8-liter V6 and power steering standard. Rear-wheel ABS that operates in 2WD mode only is added.

RATINGS (SCALE OF 1-10)

Overall	Safety	Reliability	Performance	Comfort	Value
N/A	4.3	6.9	7.2	7	N/A

Category G

Model Description	Trade-in Value	Market Value
2 Dr Baja 4WD Std Cab SB	2855	4680
2 Dr Durango Std Cab SB	1835	3005
2 Dr Durango Std Cab LB	2255	3265
2 Dr Durango 4WD Std Cab SB	2830	4640
2 Dr Durango 4WD Ext Cab SB	3025	4960
2 Dr Durango 4WD Std Cab LB	2835	4645
2 Dr EL Std Cab SB	1870	3065
2 Dr STD Ext Cab SB	2285	3745
2 Dr STD Std Cab SB	1995	3270
2 Dr STD Std Cab LB	1990	3260
2 Dr STD 4WD Ext Cab SB	2845	4665
2 Dr STD 4WD Std Cab LB	2750	4510
2 Dr Tahoe Ext Cab SB	2375	3890
2 Dr Tahoe Std Cab SB	2040	3345
2 Dr Tahoe Std Cab LB	2020	3310
2 Dr Tahoe 4WD Std Cab SB	2675	4390
2 Dr Tahoe 4WD Ext Cab SB	3085	5060
2 Dr Tahoe 4WD Std Cab LB	2795	4585

OPTIONS FOR S10 PICKUP

6 cyl 2.8 L Engine[Opt on 2WD] +55
6 cyl 4.3 L Engine +50
Auto 4-Speed Transmission +110
Air Conditioning +110
Aluminum/Alloy Wheels +45
Power Door Locks[Opt on Baja,STD,Tahoe] +30
Power Drivers Seat +40
Power Windows +30

SUBURBAN 1989

Trim treatments are revised. Front styling updated to resemble C/K pickup.

Category H

Model Description	Trade-in Value	Market Value
4 Dr R1500 Wgn	4595	6655
4 Dr R2500 Wgn	4680	6785
4 Dr V1500 4WD Wgn	5000	7245
4 Dr V2500 4WD Wgn	5235	7585

OPTIONS FOR SUBURBAN

8 cyl 6.2 L Dsl Engine +290
8 cyl 7.4 L Engine +65
Auto 3-Speed Transmission +85
Auto 4-Speed Transmission[Std on R15] +100
Silverado Package +190
Air Conditioning +110
Aluminum/Alloy Wheels +40
Camper/Towing Package +50
Dual Air Conditioning +190

V3500 PICKUP 1989

Category H

Model Description	Trade-in Value	Market Value
4 Dr Scottsdale 4WD Crew Cab LB	6490	9410
4 Dr Silverado 4WD Crew Cab LB	6515	9440
4 Dr STD 4WD Crew Cab LB	6425	9315

OPTIONS FOR V3500 PICKUP

8 cyl 6.2 L Dsl Engine +290
8 cyl 7.4 L Engine +65
Auto 3-Speed Transmission +85
Air Conditioning +110
Dual Rear Wheels +115

Don't forget to refer to the Mileage Adjustment Table at the back of this book!

 © 1999 by Edmund Publications Corporation

CHRYSLER USA

1995 Chrysler Sebring

1998 CHRYSLER

CIRRUS 1998

There's just one model to choose from this year, as Chrysler says "goodbye" to the base LX, and "hello" to a higher price. That means that leather seats, a powered driver's seat, a 2.5-liter V6 engine, a tilt wheel, and power windows, locks, and mirrors are now standard equipment. The LXi also comes in five new colors and as with all other Chrysler products, depowered airbags are standard.

Category C

Model Description	Trade-in Value	Market Value
4 Dr LXi Sdn	12755	15370

OPTIONS FOR CIRRUS

Chrome Wheels +495
Leather Seats +480
Power Drivers Seat +235
Power Moonroof +580

CONCORDE 1998

The Concorde is all-new for 1998. The only thing they didn't change is the name.

Category B

Model Description	Trade-in Value	Market Value
4 Dr LX Sdn	15500	18675
4 Dr LXi Sdn	18240	21975

OPTIONS FOR CONCORDE

Aluminum/Alloy Wheels[Opt on LX] +275
Anti-Lock Brakes[Opt on LX] +595
Compact Disc W/fm/tape +325
Dual Power Seats[Opt on LX] +300
Power Moonroof +825
Traction Control System[Opt on LX] +150

SEBRING 1998

Evolutionary, mostly aesthetic changes enhance the Sebrings this year. The Sebring Coupe LX and LXi now offer a black and gray interior, and the exterior color of the day is "Caffe Latte" (not to be confused with Macchiato or Cappuccino).

Category C

Model Description	Trade-in Value	Market Value
2 Dr JX Conv	13360	16095
2 Dr JXi Conv	17325	20875
2 Dr LX Cpe	10545	12705
2 Dr LXi Cpe	14645	17645

OPTIONS FOR SEBRING

6 cyl 2.5 L Engine[Std on LXi] +585
Auto 4-Speed Transmission[Opt on LX] +580
Aluminum/Alloy Wheels[Opt on JX, LX] +240
Anti-Lock Brakes[Opt on JX, LX] +520
Chrome Wheels +495
Compact Disc W/fm/tape[Std on LXi] +310
Cruise Control[Opt on JX, LX] +170
Heated Power Mirrors[Opt on JX] +115
Keyless Entry System[Opt on JX, LX] +155
Leather Seats[Opt on LXi] +480
Power Door Locks[Opt on JX, LX] +200
Power Drivers Seat[Std on JXi] +235
Power Mirrors +90
Power Sunroof +580
Power Windows[Opt on LX] +255
Remote Trunk Release[Opt on JX] +70
Traction Control System +235

TOWN & COUNTRY 1998

Chrysler's luxury minivans get a few improvements this year, with the addition of a new Chrysler-signature grille, more powerful 3.8-liter V-6, high-performance headlights, and three fancy new colors.

Category G

Model Description	Trade-in Value	Market Value
2 Dr LX Pass. Van Ext	18115	21565
2 Dr LX 4WD Pass. Van Ext	19685	23435
2 Dr LXi Pass. Van Ext	21550	25655
2 Dr LXi 4WD Pass. Van Ext	22465	26745
2 Dr SX Pass. Van	17080	20335

OPTIONS FOR TOWN & COUNTRY

6 cyl 3.8 L Engine[Std on LXi, 4WD] +360
Auto Load Leveling[Std on LXi, 4WD] +190
Camper/Towing Package +240
Compact Disc W/fm/tape[Std on LXi] +565
Dual Air Conditioning[Opt on LX] +840
Garage Door Opener[Std on LXi] +100
Heated Front Seats +210
Leather Seats[Std on LXi] +640
Power Drivers Seat +235
Rear Heater[Opt on LX] +170
Special Factory Paint +120

Don't forget to refer to the Mileage Adjustment Table at the back of this book!

 © 1999 by Edmund Publications Corporation

1997 CHRYSLER

CIRRUS 1997

New wheels for everyone; the LXi trim level gets chrome wheels and the LX gets optional aluminum wheels. The Gold Package is also available on the LX, for any driver who wants to be mistaken for Slick Jimmy, your friendly, neighborhood pimp. On a more positive note, an in-dash CD changer is now available on LX and LXi models, as is a trip computer.

RATINGS (SCALE OF 1-10)

Overall	Safety	Reliability	Performance	Comfort	Value
N/A	N/A	7.5	7.6	7.6	7.1

Category C

Model	Trade-in Value	Market Value
4 Dr LX Sdn	9235	11400
4 Dr LXi Sdn	10605	13090

OPTIONS FOR CIRRUS

6 cyl 2.5 L Engine +615
Aluminum/Alloy Wheels +195
AM/FM Compact Disc Playr +260
Child Seat (1) +80
Gold Package +255
Keyless Entry System[Opt on LX] +130
Power Drivers Seat[Opt on LX] +195
Trip Computer +125

CONCORDE 1997

The 3.5-liter engine is now standard on the LX trim level. An upgraded stereo debuts along with hood-mounted windshield-washer nozzles. The automatic transmission receives refinements.

RATINGS (SCALE OF 1-10)

Overall	Safety	Reliability	Performance	Comfort	Value
N/A	N/A	8.4	8.2	8.4	8.9

Category B

Model	Trade-in Value	Market Value
4 Dr LX Sdn	10980	13390
4 Dr LXi Sdn	13315	16240

OPTIONS FOR CONCORDE

Aluminum/Alloy Wheels[Std on LXi] +225
Anti-Lock Brakes[Std on LXi] +485
Compact Disc W/fm/tape +265
Dual Power Seats +245
Leather Seats[Opt on LX] +450
Power Moonroof +675
Premium Sound System[Opt on LX] +285
Traction Control System[Opt on LX] +120

LHS 1997

What's new for 1997? Deep Amethyst Pearl Paint. Oh yeah, the automatic transmission receives some fine-tuning.

RATINGS (SCALE OF 1-10)

Overall	Safety	Reliability	Performance	Comfort	Value
8.2	7.6	8.6	8.4	8.1	8.4

Category A

Model	Trade-in Value	Market Value
4 Dr STD Sdn	14615	17190

OPTIONS FOR LHS

Compact Disc W/fm/tape +475
Power Moonroof +970

SEBRING 1997

Chrysler redesigns the Sebring for 1997, adding a new grille, bodyside cladding, headlights, taillights, wheel covers, and front and rear fascias. Models equipped with the 2.5-liter V6 also get a handling package. After just one year in production, the Sebring Convertible receives a rash of changes. The most significant are a quieter intake manifold for the 2.4-liter engine, and the availability of Chrysler's AutoStick transmission. Other changes include the addition of new colors, auto-dimming mirror, trip computer, enhanced vehicle theft system, and damage-resistant power antenna to the options list.

RATINGS (SCALE OF 1-10)

Overall	Safety	Reliability	Performance	Comfort	Value
7.4	7.9	8.1	7.6	7.5	6.2

Category C

Model	Trade-in Value	Market Value
2 Dr JX Conv	12270	15150
2 Dr JXi Conv	14390	17765
2 Dr LX Cpe	9585	11830
2 Dr LXi Cpe	12305	15190

OPTIONS FOR SEBRING

6 cyl 2.5 L Engine[Std on LXi] +615
Auto 4-Speed Transmission[Opt on LX] +470
Aluminum/Alloy Wheels[Opt on JX,LX] +195
Anti-Lock Brakes[Opt on JX,LX] +425
Compact Disc Changer +355
Compact Disc W/fm/tape[Std on LXi] +250
Cruise Control[Opt on JX,LX] +140
Heated Power Mirrors[Opt on JX] +95
Keyless Entry System[Opt on JX,LX] +130
Leather Seats[Opt on LXi] +390
Power Door Locks[Opt on JX,LX] +160
Power Drivers Seat[Std on JXi] +195
Power Sunroof +470
Power Windows[Opt on LX] +205

TOWN & COUNTRY 1997

Chrysler's luxury minivans get a few improvements this year, as AWD extended length models are added to the lineup. Also new this year is a sporty SX model, which replaces last year's LX as the regular length Town & Country. Families with kids will love the standard left side sliding door on this vehicle.

Don't forget to refer to the Mileage Adjustment Table at the back of this book!

 © 1999 by Edmund Publications Corporation

Model Description	Trade-in Value	Market Value

RATINGS (SCALE OF 1-10)

Overall	Safety	Reliability	Performance	Comfort	Value
7.8	7.3	8.1	7.4	7.8	8.2

Model Description	Trade-in Value	Market Value
Category G		
2 Dr LX Pass. Van Ext	17130	20640
2 Dr LX 4WD Pass. Van Ext	17915	21585
2 Dr LXi Pass. Van Ext	19030	22925
2 Dr LXi 4WD Pass. Van Ext	20345	24510
2 Dr SX Pass. Van	17130	20640

OPTIONS FOR TOWN & COUNTRY

6 cyl 3.8 L Engine[Std on LXi,LX 4WD] +280
Auto Load Leveling[Std on LXi,LX 4WD] +155
Child Seats (2) +175
Compact Disc W/fm/tape[Std on LXi] +465
Dual Air Conditioning[Std on LXi] +685
Leather Seats[Std on LXi] +520
Luggage Rack[Std on LXi] +105
Power Drivers Seat +190

1996 CHRYSLER

CIRRUS 1996

Base LX model gets a four-cylinder engine in a cost-cutting move. Uplevel LXi gets revised torque converter for better V6 response. A power sunroof, chrome-plated aluminum wheels, and new colors are available for 1996.

RATINGS (SCALE OF 1-10)

Overall	Safety	Reliability	Performance	Comfort	Value
N/A	N/A	6.7	7.6	7.6	6.3

Model Description	Trade-in Value	Market Value
Category C		
4 Dr LX Sdn	8100	10520
4 Dr LXi Sdn	9460	12290

OPTIONS FOR CIRRUS

6 cyl 2.5 L Engine[Opt on LX] +550
Aluminum/Alloy Wheels +160
AM/FM Compact Disc Playr +215
Child Seat (1) +65
Chrome Wheels +330
Power Drivers Seat[Opt on LX] +160
Power Sunroof +385

CONCORDE 1996

Improved headlight illumination, a revised exterior appearance, a quieter interior and new colors bow on all Concorde models. Base cars get standard 16-inch wheels. LXi models get gold accented wheels and trim.

RATINGS (SCALE OF 1-10)

Overall	Safety	Reliability	Performance	Comfort	Value
8.3	7.6	8.3	8.2	8.4	8.9

Model Description	Trade-in Value	Market Value
Category B		
4 Dr LX Sdn	9930	12415
4 Dr LXi Sdn	10910	13640

OPTIONS FOR CONCORDE

6 cyl 3.5 L Engine +355
Child Seat (1) +55
Climate Control for AC[Opt on LX] +100
Compact Disc W/fm/tape +220
Dual Power Seats +200
Keyless Entry System +100
Power Moonroof +550
Premium Sound System[Opt on LX] +235
Traction Control System[Opt on LX] +100
Trip Computer[Opt on LX] +120

LHS 1996

A quieter interior and new colors entice buyers for 1996. Revised sound systems and a HomeLink Universal transmitter that opens your garage door for you when you pull in the driveway debut.

RATINGS (SCALE OF 1-10)

Overall	Safety	Reliability	Performance	Comfort	Value
8	7.6	8.3	8.4	8.1	7.8

Model Description	Trade-in Value	Market Value
Category A		
4 Dr STD Sdn	12550	15490

OPTIONS FOR LHS

AM/FM Compact Disc Playr +290
Infinity Sound System +165
Power Moonroof +795

NEW YORKER 1996

Gets same changes as LHS, plus added standard equipment over last year's New Yorker. After a short 1996 production run, the New Yorker is axed from the lineup in favor of the more popular LHS.

RATINGS (SCALE OF 1-10)

Overall	Safety	Reliability	Performance	Comfort	Value
8	7.6	8.3	8.4	8.1	7.8

Model Description	Trade-in Value	Market Value
Category B		
4 Dr STD Sdn	10520	13150

OPTIONS FOR NEW YORKER

Compact Disc Changer +275
Leather Seats +370
Power Moonroof +550
Power Passenger Seat +170
Traction Control System +100

SEBRING 1996

Remote keyless entry system gets a panic feature, and a HomeLink Universal Transmitter debuts on this suave sport coupe. Three new paint colors are also available.

Don't forget to refer to the Mileage Adjustment Table at the back of this book!

 © 1999 by Edmund Publications Corporation

Model Description	Trade-in Value	Market Value

Chrysler dumps its final K-Car variant this year in favor of the fine looking Sebring Convertible. Based on the Cirrus platform and drivetrains, this drop top shares only the name of the Sebring coupe.

RATINGS (SCALE OF 1-10)

Overall	Safety	Reliability	Performance	Comfort	Value
7	7.8	7.3	7.6	7.5	4.9

Category C		
2 Dr JX Conv	10265	13335
2 Dr JXi Conv	13050	16950
2 Dr LX Cpe	8315	10795
2 Dr LXi Cpe	10350	13440

OPTIONS FOR SEBRING

6 cyl 2.5 L Engine[Opt on JX,LX] +550
Auto 4-Speed Transmission[Opt on LX] +355
Anti-Lock Brakes[Opt on JX] +345
Compact Disc Changer +290
Compact Disc W/fm/tape +205
Cruise Control[Opt on JX,LX] +115
Keyless Entry System[Opt on JX,LX] +105
Leather Seats[Opt on LXi] +320
Power Door Locks[Opt on JX,LX] +135
Power Drivers Seat[Std on JXi] +160
Power Sunroof +385
Power Windows[Opt on LX] +170
Premium Sound System[Opt on LX] +220

TOWN & COUNTRY 1996

Totally redesigned for 1996, the T&C raises the bar for luxury minivans. In a departure from last year, the T&C is offered in a short wheelbase version, and is available in two trim levels: LX and LXi. New innovations include a driver's side passenger door, dual-zone temperature controls, and a one-hand latch system on the integrated child safety seats.

RATINGS (SCALE OF 1-10)

Overall	Safety	Reliability	Performance	Comfort	Value
7.6	7.3	7.7	7.4	7.8	8

Category G		
2 Dr LX Pass. Van	12875	16095
2 Dr LXi Pass. Van Ext	16375	20470
2 Dr STD Pass. Van Ext	13760	17200

OPTIONS FOR TOWN & COUNTRY

6 cyl 3.8 L Engine[Std on LXi] +235
Captain Chairs (4)[Std on LXi] +350
Child Seats (2) +145
Compact Disc W/fm/tape[Std on LXi] +380
Dual Air Conditioning[Opt on STD] +560
Infinity Sound System +330
Keyless Entry System[Std on LXi] +115
Leather Seats[Std on LXi] +425
Luggage Rack[Std on LXi] +85
Power Drivers Seat +155
Sliding Driver Side Door[Std on LXi] +295
Sunscreen Glass[Std on LXi] +195

1995 CHRYSLER

CIRRUS 1995

The Cirrus is replacing the LeBaron sedan. A cab-forward design, a 164-horsepower V6 coupled with an automatic transmission, dual airbags, antilock brakes, air conditioning, power door locks, and power windows are just a few of the improvements this car has over the LeBaron.

RATINGS (SCALE OF 1-10)

Overall	Safety	Reliability	Performance	Comfort	Value
N/A	N/A	6.3	7.6	7.6	7.1

Category C		
4 Dr LX Sdn	7350	9675
4 Dr LXi Sdn	8005	10535

OPTIONS FOR CIRRUS

4 cyl 2.4 L Engine +195
AM/FM Compact Disc Playr +175
Child Seat (1) +55
Power Drivers Seat[Opt on LX] +130
Premium Sound System[Opt on LX] +180

CONCORDE 1995

No significant changes for the 1995 Concorde.

RATINGS (SCALE OF 1-10)

Overall	Safety	Reliability	Performance	Comfort	Value
8.3	8.4	7.8	8.2	8.4	8.7

Category B		
4 Dr STD Sdn	8350	10705

OPTIONS FOR CONCORDE

6 cyl 3.5 L Engine +325
Aluminum/Alloy Wheels +150
Child Seat (1) +45
Infinity Sound System +295
Keyless Entry System +80
Leather Seats +300
Power Drivers Seat +135
Power Moonroof +450
Power Passenger Seat +140
Traction Control System +80

LE BARON 1995

The last of the K-cars, the LeBaron convertible rides into the sunset in GTC trim.

RATINGS (SCALE OF 1-10)

Overall	Safety	Reliability	Performance	Comfort	Value
7.8	8.5	7.7	7.8	6.6	8.5

Don't forget to refer to the Mileage Adjustment Table at the back of this book!

 © 1999 by Edmund Publications Corporation

Model Description	Trade-in Value	Market Value
Category C		
2 Dr GTC Conv	6905	9085

OPTIONS FOR LE BARON

AM/FM Compact Disc Playr +175
Anti-Lock Brakes +285
Cruise Control +95
Keyless Entry System +85
Leather Seats +260
Power Door Locks +110
Power Drivers Seat +130
Premium Sound System +180
Trip Computer +85

LHS 1995

No changes to the highly acclaimed LHS.

RATINGS (SCALE OF 1-10)

Overall	Safety	Reliability	Performance	Comfort	Value
8.1	8.4	7.9	8.4	8.1	7.6

Model Description	Trade-in Value	Market Value
Category A		
4 Dr STD Sdn	10385	12980

OPTIONS FOR LHS

AM/FM Compact Disc Playr +235
Power Moonroof +650

NEW YORKER 1995

No changes to the highly acclaimed New Yorker.

RATINGS (SCALE OF 1-10)

Overall	Safety	Reliability	Performance	Comfort	Value
8.1	8.4	7.9	8.4	8.1	7.6

Model Description	Trade-in Value	Market Value
Category B		
4 Dr STD Sdn	8645	11085

OPTIONS FOR NEW YORKER

Climate Control for AC +80
Infinity Sound System +295
Keyless Entry System +80
Leather Seats +300
Power Moonroof +450
Power Passenger Seat +140
Traction Control System +80

SEBRING 1995

Chrysler's sporty replacement for the LeBaron coupe is the Sebring. Based on the Dodge Avenger, the Sebring offers more luxury and less performance than its corporate cousin. The Sebring is available as a four-cylinder LX or an upscale 2.5-liter V6 LXi; both come standard with an automatic transmission.

RATINGS (SCALE OF 1-10)

Overall	Safety	Reliability	Performance	Comfort	Value
7.4	8.3	7.1	7.6	7.5	6.3

Model Description	Trade-in Value	Market Value
Category C		
2 Dr LX Cpe	7215	9490
2 Dr LXi Cpe	8970	11800

OPTIONS FOR SEBRING

6 cyl 2.5 L Engine[Opt on LX] +430
Auto 4-Speed Transmission[Opt on LX] +305
AM/FM Compact Disc Playr +175
Cruise Control[Opt on LX] +95
Keyless Entry System[Opt on LX] +85
Leather Seats +260
Power Door Locks[Opt on LX] +110
Power Drivers Seat +130
Power Sunroof +315
Power Windows[Opt on LX] +140
Premium Sound System +180

TOWN & COUNTRY 1995

There are no changes for the 1995 Town & Country.

RATINGS (SCALE OF 1-10)

Overall	Safety	Reliability	Performance	Comfort	Value
8	8.6	7.5	7.8	8	8

Model Description	Trade-in Value	Market Value
Category G		
2 Dr STD Pass. Van	11055	13995
2 Dr STD 4WD Pass. Van	11310	14315

OPTIONS FOR TOWN & COUNTRY

AM/FM Compact Disc Playr +175
Child Seats (2) +115

1994 CHRYSLER

CONCORDE 1994

The base 3.3-liter engine is upped to 161 horsepower. A flexible-fuel version of the Concorde is available that will allow the car to run on alternative fuels such as methanol. Variable-assist power steering and a touring suspension are also added to the standard equipment list.

RATINGS (SCALE OF 1-10)

Overall	Safety	Reliability	Performance	Comfort	Value
8.2	8.4	7.5	8.2	8.4	8.5

Model Description	Trade-in Value	Market Value
Category B		
4 Dr STD Sdn	6455	8605

OPTIONS FOR CONCORDE

6 cyl 3.5 L Engine +270
Aluminum/Alloy Wheels +125
AM/FM Compact Disc Playr +115
Child Seat (1) +35
Infinity Sound System +240
Keyless Entry System +65
Leather Seats +245
Power Door Locks +90

Don't forget to refer to the Mileage Adjustment Table at the back of this book!

 © 1999 by Edmund Publications Corporation

Model Description	Trade-in Value	Market Value

Power Drivers Seat +110
Power Moonroof +370
Power Windows +110
Traction Control System +65

LE BARON 1994

The two-door coupe is cancelled, leaving the convertible and sedan in place. The 100-horsepower four-cylinder engine is dropped, leaving the 141-horsepower V6 as the sole powerplant.

RATINGS (SCALE OF 1-10)

Overall	Safety	Reliability	Performance	Comfort	Value
7.6	8.5	7.5	7.8	6.6	7.7

Category C

Model	Trade-in	Market
2 Dr GTC Conv	5780	7815
4 Dr Landau Sdn	5615	7585
4 Dr LE Sdn	5235	7075

OPTIONS FOR LE BARON

6 cyl 3.0 L Engine[Opt on LE] +255
Auto 4-Speed Transmission[Opt on LE] +65
Air Conditioning[Opt on LE] +295
Aluminum/Alloy Wheels +105
AM/FM Compact Disc Playr +140
Anti-Lock Brakes +230
Cruise Control[Opt on GTC] +75
Infinity Sound System +270
Leather Seats +215
Power Door Locks[Opt on GTC,LE] +90
Power Drivers Seat +105
Premium Sound System +145
Trip Computer +70

LHS 1994

The de-chromed LHS model is the sporty edition of the New Yorker.

RATINGS (SCALE OF 1-10)

Overall	Safety	Reliability	Performance	Comfort	Value
8	8.4	7.5	8.4	8.1	7.5

Category A

Model	Trade-in	Market
4 Dr STD Sdn	8440	10820

OPTIONS FOR LHS

AM/FM Compact Disc Playr +195

NEW YORKER 1994

An all-new New Yorker replaces the stodgy car of yesterday. Improved handling, styling and luxury mark a significant change in direction for the once-ailing Chrysler corporation.

RATINGS (SCALE OF 1-10)

Overall	Safety	Reliability	Performance	Comfort	Value
8	8.4	7.5	8.4	8.1	7.5

Category B

Model	Trade-in	Market
4 Dr STD Sdn	6765	9020

OPTIONS FOR NEW YORKER

Aluminum/Alloy Wheels +125
AM/FM Compact Disc Playr +115
Climate Control for AC +65
Keyless Entry System +65
Leather Seats +245
Power Moonroof +370
Power Passenger Seat +115
Premium Sound System +155
Traction Control System +65

TOWN & COUNTRY 1994

A passenger airbag joins the standard equipment list of the Chrysler Town & Country, once again pushing the envelope of the growing minivan segment. A larger engine is also available in the 1994 Town & Country.

RATINGS (SCALE OF 1-10)

Overall	Safety	Reliability	Performance	Comfort	Value
7.7	8.6	7.2	7.8	8	6.9

Category G

Model	Trade-in	Market
2 Dr STD Pass. Van	9015	11705
2 Dr STD 4WD Pass. Van	10390	13490

OPTIONS FOR TOWN & COUNTRY

AM/FM Compact Disc Playr +145
Child Seats (2) +95

1993 CHRYSLER

CONCORDE 1993

Chrysler's new near-luxury sedan is designed to compete with cars like the Acura Vigor and the Lexus ES 300. Standard antilock brakes, dual airbags, an optional integrated child-seat, and optional traction control are some of the Concorde's available safety features. Cab-forward design and a long wheelbase insure good passenger space and a comfortable ride for all occupants. A 3.5-liter V6 engine that produces 214 horsepower is available instead of the standard 3.3-liter V6 that produces 153 horsepower.

RATINGS (SCALE OF 1-10)

Overall	Safety	Reliability	Performance	Comfort	Value
8	8.4	7.3	8.2	8.4	7.9

Category B

Model	Trade-in	Market
4 Dr STD Sdn	5525	7565

OPTIONS FOR CONCORDE

6 cyl 3.5 L Engine +190
Aluminum/Alloy Wheels +100
AM/FM Compact Disc Playr +95
Child Seat (1) +30
Cruise Control +65

Don't forget to refer to the Mileage Adjustment Table at the back of this book!

 © 1999 by Edmund Publications Corporation

Model Description	Trade-in Value	Market Value

Keyless Entry System +55
Leather Seats +200
Power Door Locks +75
Power Drivers Seat +90
Power Passenger Seat +95
Power Windows +90
Premium Sound System +125
Traction Control System +55

FIFTH AVENUE 1993

A new stereo is available on the Fifth Avenue; buyers can now choose between a CD player or a cassette player for their listening pleasure. A tamper-resistant odometer is also added; this means that the miles displayed should be true.

Category C

4 Dr STD Sdn	5445	7670

OPTIONS FOR FIFTH AVENUE

6 cyl 3.8 L Engine +110
Aluminum/Alloy Wheels +85
AM/FM Compact Disc Playr +115
AM/FM Stereo Tape +50
Anti-Lock Brakes +190
Infinity Sound System +220
Keyless Entry System +55
Leather Seats +175
Power Passenger Seat +80
Premium Sound System +120

IMPERIAL 1993

A new stereo is available on the Imperial. Buyers can choose between a CD player or a cassette player. A tamper-resistant odometer is also added; this means that the miles displayed should be true.

Category A

4 Dr STD Sdn	6205	8270

OPTIONS FOR IMPERIAL

Aluminum/Alloy Wheels +125
AM/FM Compact Disc Playr +160
Dual Power Seats +115
Keyless Entry System +75
Leather Seats +210

LE BARON 1993

The turbocharged engine is dropped and a new grille is added.

RATINGS (SCALE OF 1-10)

Overall	Safety	Reliability	Performance	Comfort	Value
6.9	5.9	7.3	7.8	6.6	6.8

Category C

2 Dr GTC Conv	4950	6975
2 Dr GTC Cpe	4705	6630
4 Dr Landau Sdn	4930	6940
4 Dr LE Sdn	4120	5805
2 Dr LX Conv	5330	7505
2 Dr LX Cpe	5055	7120
2 Dr STD Conv	4380	6170
2 Dr STD Cpe	4030	5680

OPTIONS FOR LE BARON

6 cyl 3.0 L Engine[Opt on LE,STD] +210
Auto 4-Speed Transmission[Std on Landau,LX] +120
Air Conditioning[Opt on LE,STD] +240
Aluminum/Alloy Wheels[Std on GTC Conv] +85
AM/FM Compact Disc Playr +115
Anti-Lock Brakes +190
Cruise Control[Opt on STD] +65
Leather Seats[Std on LX Conv] +175
Power Door Locks[Std on GTC,LX] +70
Power Drivers Seat[Std on LX Conv] +85
Power Windows[Opt on Landau,LE] +90
Premium Sound System +120
Sport Suspension[Opt on LX] +50
Trip Computer +55

NEW YORKER 1993

This is the last model year for the New Yorker in its current form. Interior changes include a six-way power seat and an upgraded stereo.

Category B

4 Dr Salon Sdn	5135	7030

OPTIONS FOR NEW YORKER

Aluminum/Alloy Wheels +100
AM/FM Stereo Tape +55
Anti-Lock Brakes +215
Cruise Control +65
Infinity Sound System +200
Keyless Entry System +55
Leather Seats +200
Power Door Locks +75
Power Passenger Seat +95

TOWN & COUNTRY 1993

A stainless-steel exhaust system, new wheels and adjustable front shoulder belts are the main changes for the 1993 Town & Country.

RATINGS (SCALE OF 1-10)

Overall	Safety	Reliability	Performance	Comfort	Value
7.2	6.8	6.9	7.8	8	6.8

Category G

2 Dr STD Pass. Van	7015	9355
2 Dr STD 4WD Pass. Van	8065	10755

OPTIONS FOR TOWN & COUNTRY

Air Conditioning +245
AM/FM Compact Disc Playr +115
Leather Seats +235

Don't forget to refer to the Mileage Adjustment Table at the back of this book!

© 1999 by Edmund Publications Corporation

Model Description	Trade-in Value	Market Value

1992 CHRYSLER

FIFTH AVENUE 1992

The Fifth Avenue gets revised front-end styling that includes a new hood, grille and headlights.

Category C

4 Dr STD Sdn	4515	6545

OPTIONS FOR FIFTH AVENUE

6 cyl 3.8 L Engine +120
Aluminum/Alloy Wheels +70
AM/FM Stereo Tape +40
Anti-Lock Brakes +155
Climate Control for AC +45
Infinity Sound System +180
Keyless Entry System +45
Leather Seats +145
Power Passenger Seat +65
Power Sunroof +170
Premium Sound System +100

IMPERIAL 1992

No changes for 1992.

Category A

4 Dr STD Sdn	5000	6945

OPTIONS FOR IMPERIAL

Electronic Features Pkg +440
Infinity Sound System +75
Keyless Entry System +60
Leather Seats +170

LE BARON 1992

Antilock brakes become an available option on the 1992 LeBaron. A transmission interlock also joins the list of safety equipment. Designed to keep the car from being started while in gear, the interlock requires that the clutch be fully depressed before the car will start. LeBarons equipped with an automatic transmission require that the brake pedal be fully depressed before the vehicle can be shifted out of park. This year there are three trim levels available for the LeBaron, including a Landau and base model that have a 100-horsepower four-cylinder engine.

RATINGS (SCALE OF 1-10)

Overall	Safety	Reliability	Performance	Comfort	Value
6.7	5.8	6.8	7.8	6.6	6.7

Category C

2 Dr GTC Cpe	3365	4880
2 Dr GTC Conv	3945	5715
4 Dr Landau Sdn	3760	5450
2 Dr LX Cpe	3920	5680
2 Dr LX Conv	4465	6470
4 Dr LX Sdn	3615	5240
2 Dr STD Cpe	3110	4505
2 Dr STD Conv	3680	5330
4 Dr STD Sdn	2855	4140

OPTIONS FOR LE BARON

6 cyl 3.0 L Engine[Std on GTC,LX] +170
Auto 3-Speed Transmission[Opt on GTC,STD Conv] +75
Auto 4-Speed Transmission[Std on LX] +95
Air Conditioning[Opt on STD,LX Sdn] +200
Aluminum/Alloy Wheels[Std on GTC,LX Sdn] +70
AM/FM Stereo Tape[Std on Landau] +40
Anti-Lock Brakes +155
Cruise Control[Std on GTC,Landau,LX,Sdn] +50
Leather Seats[Std on LX Conv] +145
Power Door Locks[Opt on Landau,STD,Sdn] +60
Power Drivers Seat[Std on LX Conv] +70
Power Windows[Opt on Landau,Sdn] +75
Premium Sound System +100

NEW YORKER 1992

Revised styling results in rounded front and rear corners on Chrysler's midsized luxury cars. The landau top is reintroduced and an electromagnetic mirror is added to the options list.

Category B

4 Dr Salon Sdn	4310	5985

OPTIONS FOR NEW YORKER

AM/FM Stereo Tape +45
Anti-Lock Brakes +175
Cruise Control +55
Dual Power Seats +90
Infinity Sound System +160
Keyless Entry System +45
Leather Seats +165
Power Door Locks +60
Power Sunroof +285

TOWN & COUNTRY 1992

The Town & Country can finally be ordered without the awful wood paneling that looks more at home in a midwestern basement than on the side of a passenger vehicle.

RATINGS (SCALE OF 1-10)

Overall	Safety	Reliability	Performance	Comfort	Value
7.1	6.1	6.1	7.8	8	7.7

Category G

2 Dr STD Pass. Van	6080	8330
2 Dr STD 4WD Pass. Van	6655	9115

OPTIONS FOR TOWN & COUNTRY

Dual Air Conditioning +250
Leather Seats +190

Don't forget to refer to the Mileage Adjustment Table at the back of this book!

© 1999 by Edmund Publications Corporation

Model Description	Trade-in Value	Market Value

1991 CHRYSLER

IMPERIAL 1991

No changes for 1991.

Category A

4 Dr STD Sdn	4255	6080

OPTIONS FOR IMPERIAL

6 cyl 3.8 L Engine +50
Electronic Features Pkg +275
Infinity Sound System +60
Keyless Entry System +50
Leather Seats +140

LE BARON 1991

No major changes for the 1991 Chrysler LeBaron.

RATINGS (SCALE OF 1-10)

Overall	Safety	Reliability	Performance	Comfort	Value
6.7	5.8	6.6	7.8	6.6	6.6

Category C

2 Dr GTC Conv	3270	5030
2 Dr GTC Cpe	3030	4660
2 Dr GTC Turbo Conv	3350	5155
2 Dr Highline Conv	2925	4500
2 Dr Highline Cpe	2635	4055
2 Dr Highline Turbo Conv	3050	4695
2 Dr Premium LX Cpe	3235	4975
2 Dr Premium LX Conv	3470	5335
4 Dr STD Sdn	2585	3975

OPTIONS FOR LE BARON

6 cyl 3.0 L Engine[Opt on Highline,STD] +135
Auto 3-Speed Transmission[Opt on GTC,Highline] +40
Auto 4-Speed Transmission[Opt on GTC,Highline] +85
Air Conditioning[Opt on Highline] +160
Aluminum/Alloy Wheels[Std on GTC] +60
AM/FM Stereo Tape[Std on STD] +35
Anti-Lock Brakes +125
Cruise Control[Opt on Highline] +40
Infinity Sound System +150
Leather Seats[Opt on GTC,STD] +115
Power Door Locks[Opt on Highline,STD] +50
Power Drivers Seat +60
Power Windows[Opt on STD] +60
Sunroof +75
Trip Computer +40

NEW YORKER 1991

No changes for the 1991 New Yorker.

Category B

4 Dr Fifth Avenue Sdn	3840	5410
4 Dr Salon Sdn	3720	5235

OPTIONS FOR NEW YORKER

6 cyl 3.8 L Engine +50
Electronic Features Pkg +245
Luxury Package +255
Aluminum/Alloy Wheels +65
AM/FM Stereo Tape +35
Anti-Lock Brakes +145
Climate Control for AC +35
Cruise Control[Opt on Salon] +45
Dual Power Seats +75
Infinity Sound System +130
Keyless Entry System +35
Leather Seats +135
Power Door Locks[Opt on Salon] +50
Power Sunroof +235

TOWN & COUNTRY 1991

Antilock brakes and a driver airbag are added to the all-new Town & Country option lists.

RATINGS (SCALE OF 1-10)

Overall	Safety	Reliability	Performance	Comfort	Value
7.2	5.6	6	7.8	8	8.6

Category G

2 Dr STD Pass. Van	5240	7485

OPTIONS FOR TOWN & COUNTRY

Captain Chairs (4) +130
Dual Air Conditioning +205
Premium Sound System +75

1990 CHRYSLER

FIFTH AVENUE 1990

Wow, this car gets big changes in 1990. Chrysler swaps the V8 for V6 power, which actually improves this beast's performance. This totally redesigned sedan now rides on a front-wheel drive platform borrowed from the Dodge Dynasty. Luxury content is up and rear seat passengers will appreciate the commodious leg room.

Category C

4 Dr Mark Cross Sdn	3005	4925

OPTIONS FOR FIFTH AVENUE

Electronic Features Pkg +150
Aluminum/Alloy Wheels +50
Anti-Lock Brakes +105
Power Passenger Seat[Opt on STD] +45
Premium Sound System +65

IMPERIAL 1990

Yet another Chrysler Imperial is unleashed on the unsuspecting public. This one has front-wheel drive and is larger than the New Yorker Fifth Avenue. It is loaded with standard equipment and is equipped with Chrysler's new 3.3 V6 engine and a four-speed transmission.

Don't forget to refer to the Mileage Adjustment Table at the back of this book!

 © 1999 by Edmund Publications Corporation

Model Description	Trade-in Value	Market Value
Category A		
4 Dr STD Sdn	3605	5380

OPTIONS FOR IMPERIAL

Premium Sound System +75

LE BARON 1990

The LeBaron hatchback is dropped, moving the Chrysler coupe and convertible closer to enthusiast respectability. A new V6 engine is introduced offering smoother operation than the raspy turbo. Speaking of turbos, the next generation turbo is released for the LeBaron; horsepower figures are the same but turbo lag is reduced. A LeBaron Sedan is reintroduced this year with a 3.0-liter engine and room for six.

RATINGS (SCALE OF 1-10)

Overall	Safety	Reliability	Performance	Comfort	Value
6.5	5.2	6.3	7.8	6.6	6.6

Model Description	Trade-in Value	Market Value
Category C		
2 Dr GT Cpe	2270	3725
2 Dr GT Conv	2640	4325
2 Dr GT Turbo Conv	2705	4430
2 Dr GT Turbo Cpe	2485	4075
2 Dr GTC Turbo Conv	2760	4525
2 Dr GTC Turbo Cpe	2340	3840
2 Dr Highline Conv	2455	4025
2 Dr Highline Cpe	1980	3250
2 Dr Highline Turbo Conv	2470	4050
2 Dr Highline Turbo Cpe	2050	3360
2 Dr Premium Conv	2895	4745
2 Dr Premium Cpe	2570	4215
4 Dr STD Sdn	2285	3750

OPTIONS FOR LE BARON

6 cyl 3.0 L Engine[Opt on Highline] +110
Auto 3-Speed Transmission[Opt on GT,GTC] +60
Auto 4-Speed Transmission[Opt on GT,Highline] +60
Air Conditioning[Opt on Highline] +130
Aluminum/Alloy Wheels[Std on GT,GTC] +50
Cruise Control[Opt on Highline,Premium Cpe] +35
Leather Seats[Std on GTC Turbo Conv] +95
Power Door Locks[Opt on Highline,STD] +40
Power Drivers Seat[Std on GTC] +45
Power Windows[Opt on STD] +50
Premium Sound System +65
Sunroof +60

NEW YORKER 1990

The New Yorker Landau and Salon models are introduced to the New Yorker lineup, as is a Chrysler-built 3.3-liter V6 engine. A new four-speed automatic is mated to the new powerplant.

Model Description	Trade-in Value	Market Value
Category B		
4 Dr Mark Cross Sdn	3155	4855
4 Dr Salon Sdn	2505	3855
Category C		
4 Dr Landau Sdn	2415	3960

OPTIONS FOR NEW YORKER

Air Conditioning[Opt on Salon] +130
Aluminum/Alloy Wheels +50
Anti-Lock Brakes +105
Cruise Control[Std on Mark Cross] +35
Leather Seats[Opt on Landau] +95
Power Door Locks[Std on Mark Cross] +40
Power Drivers Seat[Std on Mark Cross] +45
Power Passenger Seat[Std on Mark Cross] +45
Power Sunroof +115
Power Windows[Opt on Salon] +50
Premium Sound System +65

TC 1990

Model Description	Trade-in Value	Market Value
Category J		
2 Dr STD Turbo Conv	8520	11210

OPTIONS FOR TC

Hardtop Roof +465

TOWN & COUNTRY 1990

Chrysler releases an upscale version of its popular minivan. Luxury appointments and fake wood-grain body-side paneling hearken back to the days of the full-size luxury station wagon. Power comes via 3.3-liter V6 engine that is good for 150 horsepower.

Model Description	Trade-in Value	Market Value
Category G		
2 Dr STD Pass. Van	4405	6675

OPTIONS FOR TOWN & COUNTRY

Dual Air Conditioning +165

1989 CHRYSLER

CONQUEST 1989

Model Description	Trade-in Value	Market Value
Category F		
2 Dr TSi Turbo Hbk	2590	3870

OPTIONS FOR CONQUEST

Auto 4-Speed Transmission +95
Air Conditioning +115
Leather Seats +95
Sunroof +55

FIFTH AVENUE 1989

A driver airbag is now standard on all Fifth Avenues. A few luxury options are added to the this luxo-cruiser, but the Fifth Avenue is basically unchanged.

Model Description	Trade-in Value	Market Value
Category C		
4 Dr STD Sdn	1675	2940

OPTIONS FOR FIFTH AVENUE

Luxury Package +190
Cruise Control +30
Leather Seats +80

Don't forget to refer to the Mileage Adjustment Table at the back of this book!

 © 1999 by Edmund Publications Corporation

Model Description	Trade-in Value	Market Value

Power Door Locks +30
Power Drivers Seat +40
Power Passenger Seat +35
Power Sunroof +95

LE BARON 1989

The sedan and wagon body styles are dropped in favor of the better-selling coupe and hatchback. The remaining models are available with a 2.5-liter turbocharged engine. The coupe and convertible are now equipped with a driver airbag. Performance models, denoted by a GTC or GTS suffix, are distinguished by their special exterior graphics, low-profile tires, and alloy wheels. The high-performance engine is a 2.2-liter turbocharged four-cylinder that produces 174-horsepower.

RATINGS (SCALE OF 1-10)

Overall	Safety	Reliability	Performance	Comfort	Value
6.5	5.3	6.4	7.8	6.4	6.5

Model Description	Trade-in Value	Market Value
Category C		
2 Dr GT Turbo Cpe	1575	2765
2 Dr GT Turbo Conv	1965	3445
2 Dr GTC Turbo Conv	2060	3615
2 Dr GTC Turbo Cpe	1650	2895
4 Dr GTS Turbo Hbk	1685	2960
2 Dr Highline Conv	1810	3175
2 Dr Highline Cpe	1380	2425
2 Dr Highline Turbo Conv	1865	3275
2 Dr Highline Turbo Cpe	1430	2505
4 Dr Highline Hbk	1545	2710
4 Dr Highline Turbo Hbk	1630	2860
2 Dr Premium Cpe	1580	2775
2 Dr Premium Conv	1920	3365
2 Dr Premium Turbo Conv	2040	3580
2 Dr Premium Turbo Cpe	1625	2855
4 Dr Premium Turbo Hbk	1730	3035

OPTIONS FOR LE BARON

4 cyl 2.5 L Engine[Std on Premium,Conv,Cpe] +40
Auto 3-Speed Transmission +60
Luxury Package +190
Air Conditioning[Opt on Highline] +110
Aluminum/Alloy Wheels[Std on GT,GTC,GTS] +40
Cruise Control[Std on GT,GTC,GTS,Premium Turbo Conv] +30
Leather Seats[Std on GTC] +80
Power Door Locks[Opt on Highline] +30
Power Drivers Seat[Std on GTC] +40
Power Sunroof +95
Power Windows[Std on GTC,GTS,GT Turbo Conv, Premium Turbo Conv] +40
Premium Sound System[Std on GTS] +55

NEW YORKER 1989

This year the Chrysler flagship gets a new four-speed automatic transmission and added luxury features. Horsepower is also increased from last year's 136 to this year's 141. A "turn signal on" warning system is standard, and notifies inattentive drivers that their turn signal has been on for more than half-a-mile. Hmmm... Do we really want these people on the road?

Model Description	Trade-in Value	Market Value
Category B		
4 Dr Mark Cross Sdn	2250	3755
4 Dr STD Sdn	1825	3045
Category C		
4 Dr Landau Sdn	1810	3175

OPTIONS FOR NEW YORKER

Aluminum/Alloy Wheels +40
Anti-Lock Brakes +85
Cruise Control[Opt on STD] +30
Dual Power Seats +50
Leather Seats[Opt on Landau] +80
Power Door Locks[Opt on STD] +30
Power Sunroof +95
Premium Sound System +55
Wire Wheel Covers +30

TC 1989

Model Description	Trade-in Value	Market Value
Category J		
2 Dr STD Turbo Conv	6900	9200

Instant
Lease & Loan Quotes
for New & Used Vehicles!

www.CarFinance.com/edmunds

Don't forget to refer to the Mileage Adjustment Table at the back of this book!

© 1999 by Edmund Publications Corporation

Model Description	Trade-in Value	Market Value

DODGE USA

1994 Dodge Ram 1500 2WD

1998 DODGE

AVENGER 1998

Interior fabrics are new, as is a black and gray color scheme. The ES model gets a new Sport package that affects appearance, not performance. Also available for the ES are new 16-inch aluminum wheels and a rear sway bar that improves handling.

Model Description	Trade-in Value	Market Value
Category F		
2 Dr ES Cpe	11000	13415
2 Dr STD Cpe	10375	12655

OPTIONS FOR AVENGER

6 cyl 2.5 L Engine +535
Auto 4-Speed Transmission +580
Air Conditioning[Std on ES] +690
Aluminum/Alloy Wheels[Std on ES] +260
Anti-Lock Brakes +600
Compact Disc W/fm/tape +435
Cruise Control[Std on ES] +175
Keyless Entry System +145
Leather Seats +590
Leather Steering Wheel[Std on ES] +100
Power Door Locks +165
Power Drivers Seat +195
Power Mirrors +100
Power Sunroof +565
Power Windows +185

CARAVAN 1998

Available this year is a 3.8-liter V6 that puts out 180 horsepower and 240 foot-pounds of torque. And for convenience, Caravans come with rear-seat mounted grocery bag hooks, and driver's-side easy-entry Quad seating. All Chrysler products are equipped with "Next Generation" depowered airbags.

Model Description	Trade-in Value	Market Value
Category G		
2 Dr Grand Pass. Van	14390	17130
2 Dr Grand ES Pass. Van	19475	23185
2 Dr Grand ES 4WD Pass. Van	21830	25990
2 Dr Grand LE Pass. Van	18095	21540
2 Dr Grand LE 4WD Pass. Van	18690	22250
2 Dr Grand SE Pass. Van	15930	18960
2 Dr Grand SE 4WD Pass. Van	16520	19665
2 Dr LE Pass. Van	17020	20260
2 Dr SE Pass. Van	14195	16900
2 Dr STD Pass. Van	13240	15765

OPTIONS FOR CARAVAN

6 cyl 3.0 L Engine[Std on Grand, SE] +360
6 cyl 3.3 L Engine[Std on Grand ES, Grand LE, LE] +430
6 cyl 3.8 L Engine[Std on 4WD] +360
Auto 4-Speed Transmission[Opt on Grand, STD] +210
Air Conditioning[Std on Grand ES,Grand LE, LE,4WD] +675
Aluminum/Alloy Wheels[Std on Grand ES] +285
AM/FM Compact Disc Playr +320
Anti-Lock Brakes[Opt on Grand, STD] +515
Auto Load Leveling[Std on 4WD] +190
Captain Chairs (4) +525
Cruise Control[Opt on Grand, STD] +175
Dual Air Conditioning +840
Keyless Entry System[Opt on Grand SE, SE] +170
Leather Seats +640
Power Door Locks[Std on Grand ES, Grand LE, LE] +190
Power Drivers Seat +235
Power Mirrors[Opt on Grand, STD] +110
Power Windows[Opt on Grand SE, SE] +195
Rear Window Defroster[Std on Grand ES, Grand LE, LE] +140
Sliding Driver Side Door[Opt on STD] +445
Special Factory Paint +120
Sunscreen Glass[Std on Grand ES,Grand LE,LE] +295
Tilt Steering Wheel[Opt on Grand, STD] +140
Traction Control System +245

DAKOTA 1998

The Dakota R/T, featuring a 250-horsepower V8, is available for those seeking a performance pickup. The passenger airbag can now be deactivated in all Dakotas, so a rear-facing child seat is perfectly safe. The Dakota is also available in three new colors.

Model Description	Trade-in Value	Market Value
Category G		
2 Dr R/T Sport Ext Cab SB	15175	18065
2 Dr R/T Sport Std Cab SB	13775	16395
2 Dr SLT Ext Cab SB	12215	14540
2 Dr SLT Std Cab SB	11510	13700
2 Dr SLT Std Cab LB	11505	13695
2 Dr SLT 4WD Std Cab SB	15125	18005
2 Dr SLT 4WD Ext Cab SB	15490	18440
2 Dr Sport Ext Cab SB	11915	14185

Don't forget to refer to the Mileage Adjustment Table at the back of this book!

 © 1999 by Edmund Publications Corporation

Model Description	Trade-in Value	Market Value
2 Dr Sport Std Cab SB	11055	13160
2 Dr Sport Std Cab LB	11065	13170
2 Dr Sport 4WD Ext Cab SB	15230	18130
2 Dr Sport 4WD Std Cab SB	15010	17870
2 Dr STD Ext Cab SB	11250	13390
2 Dr STD Std Cab SB	10245	12195
2 Dr STD Std Cab LB	10285	12245
2 Dr STD 4WD Ext Cab SB	14205	16910
2 Dr STD 4WD Std Cab SB	13505	16075

OPTIONS FOR DAKOTA

6 cyl 3.9 L Engine[Std on 4WD, SLT 2WD Ext Cab SB] +415
8 cyl 5.2 L Engine +725
8 cyl 5.9 L Engine[Std on R/T Sport] +1315
Auto 4-Speed Transmission[Std on R/T Sport] +790
Air Conditioning[Std on SLT] +675
AM/FM Compact Disc Playr +320
Anti-Lock Brakes +515
Bed Liner +230
Cruise Control[Std on R/T Sport] +175
Fog Lights +120
Keyless Entry System +170
Limited Slip Diff[Std on R/T Sport] +220
Power Door Locks +190
Power Drivers Seat +235
Power Mirrors +110
Power Windows +195
Sliding Rear Window +100
Tilt Steering Wheel[Std on R/T Sport] +140

DURANGO 1998

As the most recent addition to the Dodge truck lineup, the Durango makes quite an entry. Offering the most cargo space in its class, along with eight-passenger seating and three-and-a-half tons of towing capacity, the Durango is the most versatile sport-utility on the market.

Category H

Model Description	Trade-in Value	Market Value
4 Dr SLT 4WD Wgn	21020	24730
4 Dr STD 4WD Wgn	20310	23895

OPTIONS FOR DURANGO

8 cyl 5.2 L Engine +485
8 cyl 5.9 L Engine +490
Anti-Lock Brakes +420
Camper/Towing Package +295
Compact Disc W/fm/tape +265
Fog Lights +95
Leather Seats +860
Limited Slip Diff +210
Power Drivers Seat +225
Third Seat +525

INTREPID 1998

Completely redesigned for 1998, the Intrepid is a sedan that has the graceful styling of a coupe, thanks to a continuation of Chrysler's cab-forward design. Dodge's trademark cross hair grille dominates the front end along with two large, sparkling headlights. And the new Intrepid is powered by your choice of two new V6 engines.

Category B

Model Description	Trade-in Value	Market Value
4 Dr ES Sdn	16635	20040
4 Dr STD Sdn	14810	17845

OPTIONS FOR INTREPID

AM/FM Compact Disc Playr +260
Anti-Lock Brakes[Std on ES] +595
Climate Control for AC +145
Dual Power Seats +300
Keyless Entry System[Std on ES] +145
Leather Seats +550
Power Drivers Seat[Std on ES] +250
Power Moonroof +825
Traction Control System +150

NEON 1998

An R/T appearance package makes people think you're driving a Viper! Improved option packages, LEV emissions and next-generation airbags round out the changes. More work has been done to quiet the Neon's boisterous demeanor.

Category E

Model Description	Trade-in Value	Market Value
2 Dr Competition Cpe	8235	10040
4 Dr Competition Sdn	8460	10320
2 Dr Highline Cpe	7680	9365
4 Dr Highline Sdn	7635	9310
2 Dr R/T Cpe	10760	13120
4 Dr R/T Sdn	11315	13795
2 Dr Sport Cpe	8485	10345
4 Dr Sport Sdn	8535	10410

OPTIONS FOR NEON

Auto 3-Speed Transmission +500
Competition Package +1255
Air Conditioning[Std on R/T, Sport] +675
Aluminum/Alloy Wheels[Std on R/T] +265
AM/FM Compact Disc Playr +390
Anti-Lock Brakes +590
Cruise Control +185
Keyless Entry System +125
Power Door Locks +195
Power Mirrors +95
Power Windows +220
Rear Window Defroster[Opt on Competition] +135
Tilt Steering Wheel +125

RAM PICKUP 1998

All Rams get a totally redesigned interior, standard passenger-side airbag with cutoff switch, and all airbags are "depowered" for safety.

Don't forget to refer to the Mileage Adjustment Table at the back of this book!

 © 1999 by Edmund Publications Corporation

RAM 1500

Category H

Model Description	Trade-in Value	Market Value
2 Dr Laramie SLT Ext Cab SB	16525	19445
2 Dr Laramie SLT Std Cab SB	13920	16380
2 Dr Laramie SLT Ext Cab LB	16745	19700
2 Dr Laramie SLT Std Cab LB	14115	16605
2 Dr Laramie SLT 4WD Std Cab SB	18805	22125
2 Dr Laramie SLT 4WD Ext Cab SB	19190	22575
2 Dr Laramie SLT 4WD Ext Cab LB	19080	22450
2 Dr Laramie SLT 4WD Std Cab LB	19060	22425
4 Dr Laramie SLT Ext Cab SB	18110	21310
4 Dr Laramie SLT Ext Cab LB	18760	22070
4 Dr Laramie SLT 4WD Ext Cab SB	19395	22815
4 Dr Laramie SLT 4WD Ext Cab LB	19665	23140
2 Dr SS/T Std Cab SB	15945	18760
2 Dr ST Std Cab SB	11900	14000
2 Dr ST Ext Cab SB	14220	16730
2 Dr ST Ext Cab LB	14495	17055
2 Dr ST Std Cab LB	12770	15025
2 Dr ST 4WD Ext Cab SB	16445	19350
2 Dr ST 4WD Std Cab SB	15985	18805
2 Dr ST 4WD Std Cab LB	15920	18730
2 Dr ST 4WD Ext Cab LB	16975	19970
4 Dr ST Ext Cab SB	14400	16940
4 Dr ST Ext Cab LB	14690	17285
4 Dr ST 4WD Ext Cab SB	17070	20080
4 Dr ST 4WD Ext Cab LB	17505	20590
2 Dr WS Std Cab SB	11025	12970
2 Dr WS Std Cab LB	10485	12335

RAM 2500

Category H

Model Description	Trade-in Value	Market Value
2 Dr Laramie SLT Ext Cab SB	21890	25755
2 Dr Laramie SLT Std Cab LB	20500	24115
2 Dr Laramie SLT Ext Cab LB	21395	25170
2 Dr Laramie SLT 4WD Ext Cab SB	25135	29570
2 Dr Laramie SLT 4WD Std Cab LB	23815	28020
2 Dr Laramie SLT 4WD Ext Cab LB	25290	29750
4 Dr Laramie SLT Ext Cab SB	20745	24405
4 Dr Laramie SLT Ext Cab LB	20980	24685
4 Dr Laramie SLT 4WD Ext Cab SB	26675	31385
4 Dr Laramie SLT 4WD Ext Cab LB	26845	31580
2 Dr ST Ext Cab SB	19605	23065
2 Dr ST Ext Cab LB	20435	24040
2 Dr ST Std Cab LB	18715	22020
2 Dr ST 4WD Ext Cab SB	22860	26895
2 Dr ST 4WD Ext Cab LB	23760	27955
2 Dr ST 4WD Std Cab LB	22085	25985
4 Dr ST Ext Cab SB	20030	23565
4 Dr ST Ext Cab LB	20020	23555
4 Dr ST 4WD Ext Cab SB	24715	29075
4 Dr ST 4WD Ext Cab LB	23775	27970

RAM 3500

Category H

Model Description	Trade-in Value	Market Value
2 Dr Laramie SLT Std Cab LB	20590	24220
2 Dr Laramie SLT 4WD Std Cab LB	23495	27645
4 Dr Laramie SLT Ext Cab LB	21870	25730
4 Dr Laramie SLT 4WD Ext Cab LB	25915	30490
2 Dr ST Std Cab LB	18430	21685
2 Dr ST 4WD Std Cab LB	21325	25085
4 Dr ST Ext Cab LB	19810	23305
4 Dr ST 4WD Ext Cab LB	23735	27925

OPTIONS FOR RAM PICKUP

10 cyl 8.0 L Engine +810
6 cyl 5.9 L Turbodsl Engine +3695
8 cyl 5.2 L Engine[Std on Ext Cab, 4WD] +485
8 cyl 5.9 L Engine[Std on Ram 2500, Ram 3500, SS/T] +490
Auto 4-Speed Transmission +790
Air Conditioning[Opt on ST, WS] +670
Aluminum/Alloy Wheels[Opt on Ram 2500, ST] +260
AM/FM Compact Disc Playr +245
Anti-Lock Brakes +420
Bed Liner +185
Camper/Towing Package +295
Cruise Control[Opt on ST, WS] +160
Fog Lights[Std on SS/T] +95
Heated Power Mirrors[Std on Ram 3500, Laramie SLT, SS/T] +100
Keyless Entry System +125
Leather Seats +860
Limited Slip Diff +210
Power Drivers Seat +225
Skid Plates[Std on Ram 3500] +90
Sliding Rear Window +95
Tilt Steering Wheel[Opt on ST, WS] +150
Tutone Paint +220

RAM VAN/WAGON 1998

A minor redesign this year includes better build quality, so we're told. Of note are the appearance of dual airbags in the revised dash and upgrades to the brakes, front

Don't forget to refer to the Mileage Adjustment Table at the back of this book!

© 1999 by Edmund Publications Corporation

doors and sound system. The V8 engines have also been relocated forward to reduce the size of that annoying "doghouse."

B150

Category H

2 Dr Maxi Ram Van Ext	15150	17825
2 Dr SLT Ram Wagon	16470	19380
2 Dr STD Ram Van	13475	15855
2 Dr STD Ram Van Ext	13610	16010
2 Dr STD Ram Wagon	15555	18300

B250

Category H

2 Dr Maxi Ram Van Ext	13610	16010
2 Dr SLT Ram Wagon Ext	16085	18920
2 Dr STD Ram Wagon Ext	15870	18670
2 Dr STD Ram Van Ext	13430	15800

B350

Category H

2 Dr Maxi Ram Van Ext	14465	17020
2 Dr Maxi Ram Wagon Ext	16375	19265
2 Dr SLT Maxi Ram Wagon Ext	17605	20710
2 Dr STD Ram Van Ext	13865	16310

OPTIONS FOR RAM VAN/WAGON

8 cyl 5.2 L Engine[Opt on B150] +485
8 cyl 5.9 L Engine +490
Auto 4-Speed Transmission[Opt on B150] +250
Air Conditioning[Opt on Ram Van, Ram Van Ext] +670
Aluminum/Alloy Wheels +260
AM/FM Compact Disc Playr +245
Anti-Lock Brakes +420
Cruise Control +160
Keyless Entry System +125
Power Door Locks +155
Power Drivers Seat +225
Power Mirrors +85
Power Windows +160
Premium Sound System +335
Rear Heater +185
Rear Window Defroster +125
Sunscreen Glass +210

STRATUS 1998

The 2.4-liter engine with automatic transmission is now standard on the ES. New colors are available this year and numerous refinements were made to reduce NVH.

Category C

4 Dr ES Sdn	11215	13510
4 Dr STD Sdn	9115	10980

OPTIONS FOR STRATUS

4 cyl 2.4 L Engine[Std on ES] +375
6 cyl 2.5 L Engine +585
Auto 4-Speed Transmission[Std on ES] +875
AM/FM Compact Disc Playr +320
Anti-Lock Brakes +520
Cruise Control[Std on ES] +170
Heated Power Mirrors[Std on ES] +115
Keyless Entry System +155
Leather Seats +480
Power Door Locks[Std on ES] +200
Power Drivers Seat +235
Power Sunroof +580
Power Windows[Std on ES] +255

1997 DODGE

AVENGER 1997

Front and rear styling is updated, while ES models lose the standard V6 engine. The V6 is available on base and ES models, and includes 17-inch wheels and tires on the ES. New colors inside and out and two additional speakers with cassette stereos further broaden the appeal of this roomy coupe.

RATINGS (SCALE OF 1-10)

Overall	Safety	Reliability	Performance	Comfort	Value
7.5	7.7	8.4	7.6	7.6	6.2

Category F

2 Dr ES Cpe	11065	13495
2 Dr STD Cpe	9190	11205

OPTIONS FOR AVENGER

6 cyl 2.5 L Engine +525
Auto 4-Speed Transmission +470
Air Conditioning[Std on ES] +565
Aluminum/Alloy Wheels[Std on ES] +210
Anti-Lock Brakes[Std on ES] +490
Compact Disc W/fm/tape +355
Cruise Control[Std on ES] +140
Keyless Entry System +120
Leather Seats +485
Power Door Locks +135
Power Drivers Seat +160
Power Sunroof +465
Power Windows +150

CARAVAN 1997

Traction control is a new option, so long as you get LE or ES trim, and an enhanced accident response system will automatically unlock the doors and illuminate the interior when an airbag deploys. Appearance and equipment refinements complete the modest changes to this best-in-class minivan.

RATINGS (SCALE OF 1-10)

Overall	Safety	Reliability	Performance	Comfort	Value
7.5	7.3	7.7	6.6	7.4	8.3

Category G

2 Dr ES Pass. Van	14725	17740
2 Dr Grand Pass. Van	12195	14690
2 Dr Grand ES Pass. Van	16505	19885

Don't forget to refer to the Mileage Adjustment Table at the back of this book!

 © 1999 by Edmund Publications Corporation

Model Description	Trade-in Value	Market Value
2 Dr Grand ES 4WD Pass. Van	17030	20520
2 Dr Grand LE Pass. Van	15935	19200
2 Dr Grand LE 4WD Pass. Van	16785	20225
2 Dr Grand SE Pass. Van	13460	16215
2 Dr Grand SE 4WD Pass. Van	14330	17270
2 Dr LE Pass. Van	13705	16510
2 Dr SE Pass. Van	11550	13915
2 Dr STD Pass. Van	10475	12620

OPTIONS FOR CARAVAN

6 cyl 3.0 L Engine +470
6 cyl 3.3 L Engine[Opt on Grand,Grand SE,SE, STD] +620
6 cyl 3.8 L Engine[Opt on ES,LE] +280
Auto 4-Speed Transmission[Opt on Grand,STD] +170
Sport Handling Package +650
7 Passenger Seating[Opt on STD] +370
Air Conditioning[Opt on Grand,Grand SE,SE,STD] +550
Aluminum/Alloy Wheels[Std on ES,Grand ES] +235
Anti-Lock Brakes[Opt on Grand,STD] +420
Auto Load Leveling +155
Captain Chairs (4) +430
Child Seats (2) +175
Compact Disc W/fm/tape +465
Cruise Control[Opt on Grand,STD] +145
Dual Air Conditioning +685
Keyless Entry System[Opt on Grand SE,SE] +140
Leather Seats +520
Luggage Rack +105
Power Door Locks[Opt on Grand,Grand SE,SE, STD] +155
Power Drivers Seat +190
Power Windows[Opt on Grand SE,SE] +160
Premium Sound System +245
Sliding Driver Side Door[Opt on Grand,Grand SE, SE,STD] +365
Traction Control System +200

DAKOTA 1997

What's new? The entire truck, that's what. Powertrains are carried over, but everything else is new. Distinctions? Tightest turning circle in class, roomiest cabs and dual airbags are standard. Faux pas? No third door option, and the passenger airbag cannot be deactivated, so a rear-facing child seat is out of the question unless you cram it into the rear of the Club Cab.

RATINGS (SCALE OF 1-10)

Overall	Safety	Reliability	Performance	Comfort	Value
N/A	7.2	8.6	7	7.1	N/A

Category G

Model Description	Trade-in Value	Market Value
2 Dr SLT Ext Cab SB	11920	14360
2 Dr SLT Std Cab SB	10580	12745
2 Dr SLT Std Cab LB	10650	12830
2 Dr SLT 4WD Ext Cab SB	13785	16610
2 Dr SLT 4WD Std Cab SB	13545	16320
2 Dr Sport Ext Cab SB	11450	13795
2 Dr Sport Std Cab SB	10300	12410
2 Dr Sport Std Cab LB	10385	12510
2 Dr Sport 4WD Ext Cab SB	13010	15675
2 Dr Sport 4WD Std Cab SB	12655	15245
2 Dr STD Std Cab SB	9700	11690
2 Dr STD Ext Cab SB	10990	13240
2 Dr STD Std Cab LB	9600	11570
2 Dr STD 4WD Ext Cab SB	12705	15310
2 Dr STD 4WD Std Cab SB	12240	14750

OPTIONS FOR DAKOTA

6 cyl 3.9 L Engine +340
8 cyl 5.2 L Engine +570
Auto 4-Speed Transmission +645
Air Conditioning[Std on SLT] +550
Anti-Lock Brakes +420
Camper/Towing Package +195
Compact Disc W/fm/tape +465
Cruise Control +145
Keyless Entry System +140
Limited Slip Diff +180
Power Door Locks +155
Power Windows +160
Skid Plates +95
Velour/Cloth Seats[Opt on STD,Std Cab LB] +120

INTREPID 1997

Few changes as first-generation Intrepid enters final year of production. A Sport Group including the 3.5-liter V6 engine is optional on base models, which also get an upgraded cassette stereo standard. Bolt-on wheel covers debut, and a new exterior color is introduced. Automatic transmissions get new software.

RATINGS (SCALE OF 1-10)

Overall	Safety	Reliability	Performance	Comfort	Value
8.3	7.2	8.3	8.4	8.6	8.9

Category B

Model Description	Trade-in Value	Market Value
4 Dr ES Sdn	12615	15385
4 Dr STD Sdn	10920	13315

OPTIONS FOR INTREPID

6 cyl 3.5 L Engine[Std on ES] +130
Anti-Lock Brakes[Std on ES] +485
Climate Control for AC +120
Compact Disc W/fm/tape +265
Dual Power Seats +245
Keyless Entry System[Std on ES] +120
Power Moonroof +675
Premium Sound System +285
Traction Control System +120

NEON 1997

Sport trim level disappears in favor of Sport Package for Highline models. Twin-cam engine is now optional

Don't forget to refer to the Mileage Adjustment Table at the back of this book!

 © 1999 by Edmund Publications Corporation

Model Description	Trade-in Value	Market Value

on Highline models. Federal side-impact standards are met for the first time. More work has been done to quiet the Neon's boisterous demeanor.

RATINGS (SCALE OF 1-10)

Overall	Safety	Reliability	Performance	Comfort	Value
7.4	6.4	8.2	7.4	7.6	7.4

Category E

Model Description	Trade-in Value	Market Value
2 Dr Highline Cpe	6755	8445
4 Dr Highline Sdn	7170	8960
2 Dr Sport Cpe	7990	9985
4 Dr Sport Sdn	7990	9985
2 Dr STD Cpe	5940	7425
4 Dr STD Sdn	5955	7440

OPTIONS FOR NEON

4 cyl 2.0 L DOHC Engine +100
Auto 3-Speed Transmission +395
Competition Package +920
Air Conditioning[Opt on STD] +550
Aluminum/Alloy Wheels +215
AM/FM Compact Disc Playr +320
Anti-Lock Brakes +480
Child Seat (1) +80
Cruise Control +150
Keyless Entry System +100
Power Door Locks +160
Power Moonroof +395
Power Windows +180
Tilt Steering Wheel +100

RAM PICKUP 1997

No major changes to this popular truck for 1997. Refinements include available leather seating and woodgrain trim on SLT models, optional remote keyless entry, and standard deep-tinted quarter glass on Club Cab models. Newly available is a combination CD/cassette stereo. Items from the 1996 Indy 500 Special Edition are available in a new Sport Package upgrade. Fresh interior and exterior colors sum up the changes this year.

RATINGS (SCALE OF 1-10)

Overall	Safety	Reliability	Performance	Comfort	Value
N/A	5.8	8.5	7	8	N/A

RAM 1500

Category H

Model Description	Trade-in Value	Market Value
2 Dr Laramie SLT Ext Cab SB	14525	17290
2 Dr Laramie SLT Std Cab SB	13265	15790
2 Dr Laramie SLT Ext Cab LB	14585	17365
2 Dr Laramie SLT Std Cab LB	13330	15870
2 Dr Laramie SLT 4WD Ext Cab SB	16515	19660
2 Dr Laramie SLT 4WD Std Cab SB	15575	18540
2 Dr Laramie SLT 4WD Std Cab LB	15665	18645
2 Dr Laramie SLT 4WD Ext Cab LB	16760	19955
2 Dr LT Std Cab SB	11710	13940
2 Dr LT Std Cab LB	11765	14005
2 Dr LT 4WD Std Cab SB	14005	16670
2 Dr LT 4WD Std Cab LB	14095	16780
2 Dr SS/T Std Cab SB	12920	15380
2 Dr ST Ext Cab SB	13175	15685
2 Dr ST Ext Cab LB	13250	15775
2 Dr ST 4WD Ext Cab SB	15145	18030
2 Dr ST 4WD Ext Cab LB	15215	18115
2 Dr WS Std Cab SB	9300	11070
2 Dr WS Std Cab LB	9370	11155

RAM 2500

Category H

Model Description	Trade-in Value	Market Value
2 Dr Laramie SLT Ext Cab SB	17190	20465
2 Dr Laramie SLT Ext Cab LB	17270	20560
2 Dr Laramie SLT Std Cab LB	16230	19320
2 Dr Laramie SLT 4WD Ext Cab SB	18050	21490
2 Dr Laramie SLT 4WD Ext Cab LB	18125	21580
2 Dr Laramie SLT 4WD Std Cab LB	16700	19880
2 Dr LT Std Cab LB	14925	17765
2 Dr LT 4WD Std Cab LB	15345	18265
2 Dr ST Ext Cab SB	16220	19310
2 Dr ST Ext Cab LB	16295	19400
2 Dr ST Std Cab LB	15165	18055
2 Dr ST 4WD Ext Cab SB	17055	20305
2 Dr ST 4WD Std Cab LB	15645	18625
2 Dr ST 4WD Ext Cab LB	17130	20395

RAM 3500

Category H

Model Description	Trade-in Value	Market Value
2 Dr Laramie SLT Ext Cab LB	19780	23550
2 Dr Laramie SLT Std Cab LB	18700	22265
2 Dr Laramie SLT 4WD Std Cab LB	19165	22815
2 Dr Laramie SLT 4WD Ext Cab LB	20180	24025
2 Dr LT Std Cab LB	17240	20525
2 Dr LT 4WD Std Cab LB	18830	22415
2 Dr ST Ext Cab LB	18360	21860
2 Dr ST Std Cab LB	17490	20825
2 Dr ST 4WD Ext Cab LB	18995	22615
2 Dr ST 4WD Std Cab LB	18885	22480

Don't forget to refer to the Mileage Adjustment Table at the back of this book!

 © 1999 by Edmund Publications Corporation

Model Description	Trade-in Value	Market Value

OPTIONS FOR RAM PICKUP

10 cyl 8.0 L Engine +660
6 cyl 5.9 L Turbodsl Engine +2955
8 cyl 5.2 L Engine +300
8 cyl 5.9 L Engine +380
Auto 4-Speed Transmission +645
Sport Appearance Group +535
Air Conditioning[Opt on LT,ST,WS] +550
Aluminum/Alloy Wheels[Std on SS/T] +210
Anti-Lock Brakes +345
Camper/Towing Package +240
Chrome Wheels[Std on Laramie SLT] +200
Compact Disc W/fm/tape +215
Cruise Control[Opt on LT,ST,WS] +130
Keyless Entry System +110
Leather Seats +700
Limited Slip Diff +175
Power Drivers Seat +185
Premium Sound System +275
Rear Step Bumper[Std on Laramie SLT,SS/T] +105
Skid Plates[Std on Ram 3500 ST 4WD Ext Cab LB] +75

RAM VAN/WAGON 1997

New this year are wider cargo doors, upgraded stereo systems, and an improved ignition switch with anti-theft protection. Front quarter vent windows disappear for 1997, and underhood service points feature colored identification.

RATINGS (SCALE OF 1-10)

Overall	Safety	Reliability	Performance	Comfort	Value
N/A	6.5	8.4	6.2	6.9	N/A

B150

Category H

Model	Trade-in	Market
2 Dr SLT Ram Wagon	13650	16250
2 Dr STD Ram Van Ext	11650	13870
2 Dr STD Ram Van	10830	12890
2 Dr STD Ram Wagon	12130	14440

B250

Category H

Model	Trade-in	Market
2 Dr Maxi Ram Van Ext	14240	16955
2 Dr SLT Ram Wagon Ext	15495	18445
2 Dr STD Ram Van Ext	13040	15525
2 Dr STD Ram Van	12405	14765
2 Dr STD Ram Wagon Ext	13800	16430

B350

Category H

Model	Trade-in	Market
2 Dr Maxi Ram Van Ext	12650	15060
2 Dr Maxi Ram Wagon Ext	13655	16255
2 Dr SLT Ram Wagon Ext	14580	17355
2 Dr SLT Maxi Ram Wagon Ext	15345	18265
2 Dr STD Ram Wagon Ext	13345	15885
2 Dr STD Ram Van Ext	11585	13795

OPTIONS FOR RAM VAN/WAGON

8 cyl 5.2 L Engine[Std on B350,B250 Ram Wagon Ext] +300
8 cyl 5.9 L Engine +380
Auto 4-Speed Transmission[Std on B350,Ram Wagon Ext] +205
Tradesman Upfitter Pkg. +675
Air Conditioning[Opt on Ram Van,Ram Van Ext] +550
Aluminum/Alloy Wheels +210
AM/FM Compact Disc Playr +200
Anti-Lock Brakes +345
Camper/Towing Package +240
Chrome Bumpers[Std on SLT] +115
Chrome Wheels[Opt on STD] +200
Cruise Control[Opt on Maxi,STD] +130
Dual Air Conditioning[Opt on B150,B250,Maxi,STD] +965
Keyless Entry System[Opt on Maxi,STD] +110
Limited Slip Diff +175
Power Door Locks[Opt on Maxi,STD] +125
Power Drivers Seat +185
Power Windows[Opt on Maxi,STD] +130
Premium Sound System +275

STRATUS 1997

Subtle styling revisions are the most obvious change to the Stratus for 1997. Sound systems have been improved, rear seat heat ducts benefit from improved flow, and the optional 2.4-liter engine runs quieter. New colors and a revised console round out changes.

RATINGS (SCALE OF 1-10)

Overall	Safety	Reliability	Performance	Comfort	Value
N/A	N/A	7.5	7	7.8	7.1

Category C

Model	Trade-in	Market
4 Dr ES Sdn	9135	11280
4 Dr STD Sdn	7590	9370

OPTIONS FOR STRATUS

4 cyl 2.4 L Engine +295
6 cyl 2.5 L Engine +615
Auto 4-Speed Transmission +615
Anti-Lock Brakes[Std on ES] +425
Child Seat (1) +80
Compact Disc W/fm/tape +250
Cruise Control[Std on ES] +140
Keyless Entry System +130
Leather Seats +390
Lighted Entry System +110
Power Door Locks[Std on ES] +160
Power Windows[Std on ES] +205

VIPER 1997

One new color, flame red, with or without white stripes, is available for 1997. Silver, sparkle gold or yellow gold wheels come with red Vipers. The original blue with white stripes paint scheme is available as an option, as are last year's standard polished aluminum wheels. The

Don't forget to refer to the Mileage Adjustment Table at the back of this book!

 © 1999 by Edmund Publications Corporation

Model Description	Trade-in Value	Market Value

RT/10 roadster is set to return later this year, with dual airbags, power windows and door locks, and the 450-horsepower V10 from the GTS. Also set to debut on the revamped drop top are the four-wheel independent suspension and adjustable pedals from the GTS.

Category K

Model Description	Trade-in Value	Market Value
2 Dr GTS Cpe	48585	57840

OPTIONS FOR VIPER

Blue Pearlcoat Paint +815
Air Conditioning[Std on GTS] +815

1996 DODGE

AVENGER 1996

Dodge's sporty coupe gets a panic mode for the remote keyless entry system and a HomeLink transmitter that will open your garage door. ES models get new seat fabric, and three new colors are on the roster.

RATINGS (SCALE OF 1-10)

Overall	Safety	Reliability	Performance	Comfort	Value
7.1	7.7	7.7	7.6	7.6	4.9

Category F

Model Description	Trade-in Value	Market Value
2 Dr ES Cpe	9785	12230
2 Dr STD Cpe	7640	9550

OPTIONS FOR AVENGER

Auto 4-Speed Transmission[Std on ES] +355
Air Conditioning[Std on ES] +460
Anti-Lock Brakes[Std on ES] +400
Compact Disc W/fm/tape +290
Cruise Control[Std on ES] +115
Keyless Entry System +95
Leather Seats +395
Power Door Locks +110
Power Drivers Seat +130
Power Sunroof +380
Power Windows +125
Premium Sound System +225

CARAVAN 1996

Completely redesigned with cavernous interiors, best-in-class driveability, and new innovations such as the optional driver's side passenger door. Caravan, and the extended-length Grand Caravan, have dethroned the Ford Windstar, once again reigning as king of the minivans.

RATINGS (SCALE OF 1-10)

Overall	Safety	Reliability	Performance	Comfort	Value
7.3	7.3	7.3	6.6	7.4	8.1

Category G

Model Description	Trade-in Value	Market Value
2 Dr ES Pass. Van	12195	15245
2 Dr Grand Pass. Van	9960	12450
2 Dr Grand ES Pass. Van	13635	17045
2 Dr Grand LE Pass. Van	13400	16750
2 Dr Grand SE Pass. Van	11115	13895
2 Dr LE Pass. Van	11760	14695
2 Dr SE Pass. Van	9510	11890
2 Dr STD Pass. Van	8580	10720

OPTIONS FOR CARAVAN

6 cyl 3.0 L Engine +390
6 cyl 3.3 L Engine[Opt on Grand SE,SE] +470
6 cyl 3.3 L CNG Engine +480
6 cyl 3.8 L Engine[Opt on LE, ES] +235
Auto 4-Speed Transmission[Opt on SE,STD] +110
7 Passenger Seating[Opt on STD] +300
Air Conditioning[Opt on Grand,Grand SE,SE,STD] +450
Anti-Lock Brakes[Opt on SE,STD] +345
Captain Chairs (4) +350
Child Seats (2) +145
Compact Disc W/fm/tape +380
Cruise Control[Opt on Grand,STD] +115
Dual Air Conditioning +560
Infinity Sound System +330
Keyless Entry System[Std on LE] +115
Leather Seats +425
Luggage Rack +85
Power Door Locks[Opt on Grand,Grand SE,SE, STD] +125
Power Drivers Seat +155
Power Windows[Opt on Grand SE,SE] +130
Sliding Driver Side Door +295

DAKOTA 1996

America's first midsized pickup gets a more powerful standard four-cylinder engine, revised sound system, and three new colors.

RATINGS (SCALE OF 1-10)

Overall	Safety	Reliability	Performance	Comfort	Value
N/A	6.4	7.5	7	7.1	N/A

Category G

Model Description	Trade-in Value	Market Value
2 Dr SLT Std Cab SB	9000	11250
2 Dr SLT Ext Cab SB	9770	12215
2 Dr SLT Std Cab LB	9230	11540
2 Dr SLT 4WD Std Cab SB	11355	14195
2 Dr SLT 4WD Ext Cab SB	11420	14270
2 Dr SLT 4WD Std Cab LB	10870	13590
2 Dr Sport Ext Cab SB	8535	10665
2 Dr Sport Std Cab SB	8305	10380
2 Dr Sport 4WD Std Cab SB	10815	13520
2 Dr Sport 4WD Ext Cab SB	10930	13660
2 Dr STD Std Cab SB	7970	9960
2 Dr STD Ext Cab SB	8570	10715
2 Dr STD Std Cab LB	8050	10060
2 Dr STD 4WD Std Cab SB	9910	12385
2 Dr STD 4WD Ext Cab SB	10110	12640
2 Dr STD 4WD Std Cab LB	9730	12165

Don't forget to refer to the Mileage Adjustment Table at the back of this book!

 © 1999 by Edmund Publications Corporation

Model Description	Trade-in Value	Market Value
2 Dr WS Std Cab SB	6720	8400
2 Dr WS Std Cab LB	6560	8200
2 Dr WS 4WD Std Cab SB	9450	11815
2 Dr WS 4WD Std Cab LB	9575	11965

OPTIONS FOR DAKOTA

6 cyl 3.9 L Engine +375
8 cyl 5.2 L Engine +400
Auto 4-Speed Transmission +500
Air Conditioning[Std on SLT] +450
Aluminum/Alloy Wheels[Opt on SLT] +190
AM/FM Compact Disc Playr +215
Anti-Lock Brakes +345
Camper/Towing Package +160
Chrome Bumpers[Std on SLT] +90
Chrome Wheels[Std on SLT] +135
Cruise Control[Opt on Sport,STD] +115
Limited Slip Diff +145
Power Door Locks +125
Power Windows +130
Premium Sound System +200
Velour/Cloth Seats[Std on SLT,Sport,Ext Cab] +95

INTREPID 1996

ES carries over, but the base model gets several improvements to remain competitive with the new Ford Taurus. ES styling cues and 16-inch wheels come standard on the base Intrepid. New colors and seat fabrics update this full-size sedan, and all Intrepids get noise, vibration and harshness improvements.

RATINGS (SCALE OF 1-10)

Overall	Safety	Reliability	Performance	Comfort	Value
8.2	7.2	8	8.4	8.6	8.8

Category B

Model Description	Trade-in Value	Market Value
4 Dr ES Sdn	9505	11880
4 Dr STD Sdn	8660	10820

OPTIONS FOR INTREPID

6 cyl 3.5 L Engine +355
Aluminum/Alloy Wheels +185
AM/FM Compact Disc Playr +175
Anti-Lock Brakes[Std on ES] +395
Child Seat (1) +55
Climate Control for AC +100
Keyless Entry System +100
Leather Seats +370
Power Drivers Seat +165
Power Moonroof +550
Power Passenger Seat +170
Traction Control System +100

NEON 1996

A raft of improvements make the sprightly Neon even more attractive to compact buyers. Base models get more equipment, and the ugly gray bumpers are history. A base coupe is newly available. Interior noise levels are supposedly subdued this year. ABS is available across the board this year. An optional power sunroof debuts midyear.

RATINGS (SCALE OF 1-10)

Overall	Safety	Reliability	Performance	Comfort	Value
7.2	6.3	7.3	7.4	7.6	7.2

Category E

Model Description	Trade-in Value	Market Value
2 Dr Highline Cpe	5585	7450
4 Dr Highline Sdn	5520	7360
2 Dr Sport Cpe	6140	8190
4 Dr Sport Sdn	6025	8035
2 Dr STD Cpe	4960	6610
4 Dr STD Sdn	4975	6635

OPTIONS FOR NEON

4 cyl 2.0 L DOHC Engine[Std on Sport] +80
Auto 3-Speed Transmission +295
Air Conditioning +450
AM/FM Compact Disc Playr +260
Anti-Lock Brakes[Std on Sport] +395
Child Seat (1) +65
Cruise Control +120
Power Door Locks[Std on Sport] +130
Power Steering[Opt on STD] +140
Power Windows +145
Rear Spoiler[Std on Sport] +115
Tilt Steering Wheel[Std on Sport] +85

RAM PICKUP 1996

Best-selling Ram has a more powerful diesel engine for 1996, an available "Camper Special" suspension package, and new wheels on the 1500 SLT and Sport. Two new colors, a revised sound system, and easy-to-find yellow under-hood service point identification all debut for 1996.

RATINGS (SCALE OF 1-10)

Overall	Safety	Reliability	Performance	Comfort	Value
N/A	N/A	8	7	8	N/A

RAM 1500

Category H

Model Description	Trade-in Value	Market Value
2 Dr Laramie SLT Std Cab SB	12030	14495
2 Dr Laramie SLT Ext Cab SB	12525	15090
2 Dr Laramie SLT Ext Cab LB	12765	15380
2 Dr Laramie SLT Std Cab LB	12065	14535
2 Dr Laramie SLT 4WD Ext Cab SB	14045	16925
2 Dr Laramie SLT 4WD Std Cab SB	13790	16615
2 Dr Laramie SLT 4WD Std Cab LB	13885	16730
2 Dr Laramie SLT 4WD Ext Cab LB	14145	17040

Don't forget to refer to the Mileage Adjustment Table at the back of this book!

 © 1999 by Edmund Publications Corporation

Model Description	Trade-in Value	Market Value
2 Dr LT Std Cab SB	10445	12585
2 Dr LT Std Cab LB	10535	12690
2 Dr LT 4WD Std Cab SB	12415	14960
2 Dr LT 4WD Std Cab LB	12590	15170
2 Dr ST Ext Cab SB	11445	13790
2 Dr ST Ext Cab LB	11445	13790
2 Dr ST 4WD Ext Cab SB	12860	15490
2 Dr ST 4WD Ext Cab LB	13065	15740
2 Dr WS Std Cab SB	8515	10260
2 Dr WS Std Cab LB	8600	10365

RAM 2500

Category H

Model Description	Trade-in Value	Market Value
2 Dr Laramie SLT Ext Cab SB	13880	16720
2 Dr Laramie SLT Std Cab LB	13620	16410
2 Dr Laramie SLT Ext Cab LB	13905	16755
2 Dr Laramie SLT 4WD Ext Cab SB	15385	18535
2 Dr Laramie SLT 4WD Std Cab LB	14265	17190
2 Dr Laramie SLT 4WD Ext Cab LB	15510	18685
2 Dr LT Std Cab LB	12145	14630
2 Dr LT 4WD Std Cab LB	12430	14975
2 Dr ST Ext Cab SB	13175	15875
2 Dr ST Std Cab LB	12725	15335
2 Dr ST Ext Cab LB	13245	15955
2 Dr ST 4WD Ext Cab SB	13905	16755
2 Dr ST 4WD Ext Cab LB	13970	16835
2 Dr ST 4WD Std Cab LB	13005	15670

RAM 3500

Category H

Model Description	Trade-in Value	Market Value
2 Dr Laramie SLT Std Cab LB	15950	19220
2 Dr Laramie SLT Ext Cab LB	16175	19490
2 Dr Laramie SLT 4WD Std Cab LB	17045	20535
2 Dr Laramie SLT 4WD Ext Cab LB	17380	20940
2 Dr LT Std Cab LB	14930	17985
2 Dr LT 4WD Std Cab LB	15725	18950
2 Dr ST Std Cab LB	15165	18270
2 Dr ST Ext Cab LB	15685	18895
2 Dr ST 4WD Std Cab LB	15940	19205
2 Dr ST 4WD Ext Cab LB	16325	19670

OPTIONS FOR RAM PICKUP

10 cyl 8.0 L Engine +255
6 cyl 5.9 L Turbodsl Engine +2245
8 cyl 5.2 L Engine +230
8 cyl 5.9 L Engine +330
Auto 4-Speed Transmission +505
Air Conditioning[Opt on LT,ST,WS] +450
Aluminum/Alloy Wheels[Std on Laramie SLT] +175
AM/FM Compact Disc Playr +165
Anti-Lock Brakes +280
Bed Liner +125
Camper/Towing Package +195
Chrome Bumpers[Opt on ST] +95
Chrome Wheels[Opt on LT,ST] +165
Cruise Control[Opt on LT,ST,WS] +105
Limited Slip Diff +140
Power Door Locks[Opt on LT,ST] +105
Power Drivers Seat +150
Premium Sound System +225
Rear Step Bumper[Std on Laramie SLT] +85
Skid Plates +60
Split Front Bench Seat +190

RAM VAN/WAGON 1996

New interior and exterior colors, a revised stereo system, and improved ventilation freshen this ancient design. Also new: a higher GVWR and new cruise control switches.

RATINGS (SCALE OF 1-10)

Overall	Safety	Reliability	Performance	Comfort	Value
N/A	6.5	7.8	6.2	6.9	N/A

B150

Category H

Model Description	Trade-in Value	Market Value
2 Dr SLT Ram Wagon	10840	13060
2 Dr STD Ram Van	8305	10005
2 Dr STD Ram Van Ext	8400	10120
2 Dr STD Ram Wagon	9275	11175

B250

Category H

Model Description	Trade-in Value	Market Value
2 Dr Maxi Ram Van Ext	12195	14690
2 Dr SLT Ram Wagon Ext	14880	17930
2 Dr STD Ram Van Ext	12005	14465
2 Dr STD Ram Van	10955	13200
2 Dr STD Ram Wagon Ext	12990	15650

B350

Category H

Model Description	Trade-in Value	Market Value
2 Dr Maxi Ram Van Ext	10350	12465
2 Dr Maxi Ram Wagon Ext	11295	13610
2 Dr SLT Ram Wagon Ext	12960	15615
2 Dr SLT Maxi Ram Wagon Ext	13270	15990
2 Dr STD Ram Van Ext	9575	11535
2 Dr STD Ram Wagon Ext	11095	13365

OPTIONS FOR RAM VAN/WAGON

8 cyl 5.2 L Engine[Std on B350] +230
8 cyl 5.9 L Engine +330
Auto 4-Speed Transmission[Std on B350] +135
Air Conditioning[Std on B350 Ram Wagon] +450
AM/FM Compact Disc Playr +165
Anti-Lock Brakes[Opt on B350,Maxi,Ram Van, Ram Van Ext] +280

Don't forget to refer to the Mileage Adjustment Table at the back of this book!

 © 1999 by Edmund Publications Corporation

Model Description	Trade-in Value	Market Value

Camper/Towing Package +195
Chrome Bumpers[Std on SLT] +95
Chrome Wheels[Opt on STD] +165
Cruise Control[Opt on Maxi,STD] +105
Dual Air Conditioning[Opt on B150,B250,Maxi,STD] +790
Keyless Entry System[Std on SLT,SLT Maxi] +90
Limited Slip Diff +140
Power Door Locks[Opt on Maxi,STD] +105
Power Drivers Seat +150
Power Windows[Opt on Maxi,STD] +105
Premium Sound System +225
Velour/Cloth Seats[Opt on B150,STD] +75

STEALTH 1996

Final year for slow-selling Japanese-built sports car. A new rear spoiler and body-color roof mark the 1996 model. A chrome 18"-wheel package is available with Pirelli P-Zero tires and base models get an optional Infinity sound system.

Category F

2 Dr R/T Hbk	13140	16430
2 Dr STD Hbk	11605	14510

OPTIONS FOR STEALTH

Auto 4-Speed Transmission +480
Anti-Lock Brakes +400
Cruise Control[Std on 4WD] +115
Keyless Entry System[Std on 4WD] +95
Leather Seats +395
Power Door Locks[Std on 4WD] +110
Power Sunroof +380
Power Windows[Std on 4WD] +125

STRATUS 1996

Excellent midsized sedan gets a more responsive torque converter when equipped with the 2.5-liter V6. New colors and a power sunroof are also new for 1996.

RATINGS (SCALE OF 1-10)

Overall	Safety	Reliability	Performance	Comfort	Value
N/A	N/A	6.7	7	7.8	6.3

Category C

4 Dr ES Sdn	7730	10040
4 Dr STD Sdn	6885	8940

OPTIONS FOR STRATUS

4 cyl 2.4 L Engine +245
6 cyl 2.5 L Engine +550
Auto 4-Speed Transmission +450
AM/FM Compact Disc Playr +215
Anti-Lock Brakes[Std on ES] +345
Child Seat (1) +65
Keyless Entry System +105
Leather Seats +320
Lighted Entry System +90
Power Door Locks[Std on ES] +135
Power Drivers Seat +160
Power Sunroof +385
Power Windows[Std on ES] +170
Premium Sound System +220

VIPER 1996

Final year for Viper in current form. More power is eked from the V10 engine via a low-restriction rear outlet exhaust system, and an optional hardtop with sliding side curtains is available. Five-spoke aluminum wheels and three exterior styling themes replace the trim on the 1995 Viper. GTS coupe begins production when convertibles have completed their run. Scheduled to pace the 1996 Indianapolis 500, the GTS will arrive in showrooms with dual airbags and air conditioning.

Category K

2 Dr GTS Cpe	43870	52225
2 Dr RT/10 Conv	40310	47990

OPTIONS FOR VIPER

Air Conditioning[Std on GTS] +665
Hardtop Roof +1390

1995 DODGE

AVENGER 1995

New coupe is late replacement for Daytona. Based on a Mitsubishi Galant platform, the Avenger is about the size of a Camry coupe. Base and ES models are available. Base cars have a 2.0-liter 140-horsepower four-cylinder engine underhood. ES gets a Mitsubishi-built 2.5-liter V6 making 155 horsepower. An automatic is the only transmission available on the ES. ABS is optional on base models; standard on ES. All Avengers have dual airbags, height-adjustable driver's seat, split-folding rear seat, rear defroster, and tilt steering wheel.

RATINGS (SCALE OF 1-10)

Overall	Safety	Reliability	Performance	Comfort	Value
7.5	8.5	7.4	7.6	7.6	6.3

Category F

2 Dr ES Cpe	8525	10930
2 Dr Highline Cpe	6735	8630

OPTIONS FOR AVENGER

Auto 4-Speed Transmission[Std on ES] +305
Air Conditioning[Std on ES] +380
AM/FM Compact Disc Playr +225
Anti-Lock Brakes[Std on ES] +330
Cruise Control[Std on ES] +95
Infinity Sound System +315
Keyless Entry System +80
Leather Seats +325
Power Door Locks +90
Power Drivers Seat +110
Power Sunroof +310
Power Windows +100
Premium Sound System +185

Don't forget to refer to the Mileage Adjustment Table at the back of this book!

 © 1999 by Edmund Publications Corporation

Model Description	Trade-in Value	Market Value

CARAVAN 1995

Newly optional is a 3.3-liter V6 engine designed to operate on compressed natural gas. Sport and SE decor packages are available this year. The five-speed manual transmission, available only with the four-cylinder engine, has been canceled.

RATINGS (SCALE OF 1-10)

Overall	Safety	Reliability	Performance	Comfort	Value
7.9	8.3	7.1	7.4	8.3	8.5

Model Description	Trade-in Value	Market Value
Category G		
2 Dr ES Pass. Van	8915	11285
2 Dr Grand Pass. Van	7515	9510
2 Dr Grand ES Pass. Van	10670	13505
2 Dr Grand ES 4WD Pass. Van	10820	13695
2 Dr Grand LE Pass. Van	10040	12705
2 Dr Grand LE 4WD Pass. Van	10180	12885
2 Dr Grand SE Pass. Van	8490	10750
2 Dr Grand SE 4WD Pass. Van	8555	10830
2 Dr LE Pass. Van	8720	11040
2 Dr SE Pass. Van	7050	8920
2 Dr STD Pass. Van	6315	7995
2 Dr STD Cargo Van	5485	6940
2 Dr STD Cargo Van Ext	6245	7910

OPTIONS FOR CARAVAN

6 cyl 3.0 L Engine[Opt on STD] +105
6 cyl 3.3 L Engine[Opt on ES,LE,SE] +325
6 cyl 3.3 L CNG Engine +390
6 cyl 3.8 L Engine +185
Auto 4-Speed Transmission[Opt on SE,Cargo Van, STD] +90
7 Passenger Seating[Opt on STD] +245
Air Conditioning[Opt on Grand,Grand SE,SE,STD] +370
Anti-Lock Brakes[Std on ES,Grand ES,Grand LE, LE,4WD] +280
Captain Chairs (4) +285
Child Seats (2) +115
Cruise Control[Opt on Grand,STD] +95
Dual Air Conditioning +460
Keyless Entry System[Opt on Grand SE,SE] +95
Leather Seats +350
Luggage Rack +70
Power Door Locks[Opt on Grand,Grand SE,SE, STD] +105
Power Drivers Seat +130
Power Windows +105
Premium Sound System +165

DAKOTA 1995

A 2WD Club Cab Sport is added to the model mix.

RATINGS (SCALE OF 1-10)

Overall	Safety	Reliability	Performance	Comfort	Value
N/A	7.1	7.8	7	7.1	N/A

Model Description	Trade-in Value	Market Value
Category G		
2 Dr SLT Ext Cab SB	8280	10480
2 Dr SLT Std Cab SB	7380	9340
2 Dr SLT Std Cab LB	7825	9905
2 Dr SLT 4WD Ext Cab SB	10185	12895
2 Dr SLT 4WD Std Cab SB	9985	12640
2 Dr SLT 4WD Std Cab LB	10110	12800
2 Dr Sport Std Cab SB	6700	8480
2 Dr Sport Ext Cab SB	7300	9240
2 Dr Sport 4WD Std Cab SB	9075	11485
2 Dr Sport 4WD Ext Cab SB	9110	11530
2 Dr STD Ext Cab SB	7440	9420
2 Dr STD Std Cab SB	6540	8280
2 Dr STD Std Cab LB	6940	8785
2 Dr STD 4WD Std Cab SB	8750	11075
2 Dr STD 4WD Ext Cab SB	8990	11380
2 Dr STD 4WD Std Cab LB	8870	11230
2 Dr WS Std Cab SB	5710	7230
2 Dr WS Std Cab LB	6105	7730
2 Dr WS 4WD Std Cab SB	8110	10265
2 Dr WS 4WD Std Cab LB	8225	10410

OPTIONS FOR DAKOTA

6 cyl 3.9 L Engine +305
8 cyl 5.2 L Engine +335
Auto 4-Speed Transmission +410
Air Conditioning[Std on SLT] +370
AM/FM Compact Disc Playr +175
Anti-Lock Brakes +280
Camper/Towing Package +130
Chrome Bumpers +70
Chrome Wheels[Std on SLT] +110
Cruise Control[Std on SLT Ext Cab SB] +95
Limited Slip Diff +120
Power Door Locks +105
Power Windows +105
Premium Sound System +165
Rear Step Bumper[Opt on WS] +65
Sliding Rear Window[Std on SLT] +55
Velour/Cloth Seats[Std on SLT,Sport,Ext Cab] +80

INTREPID 1995

ABS is standard on ES, rather than optional. Traction control is a new ES option.

RATINGS (SCALE OF 1-10)

Overall	Safety	Reliability	Performance	Comfort	Value
8.2	7.9	7.5	8.4	8.6	8.5

Model Description	Trade-in Value	Market Value
Category B		
4 Dr ES Sdn	8180	10485
4 Dr STD Sdn	6825	8750

OPTIONS FOR INTREPID

6 cyl 3.3 L FLEX Engine +65
6 cyl 3.5 L Engine +325
AM/FM Compact Disc Playr +140

Don't forget to refer to the Mileage Adjustment Table at the back of this book!

 © 1999 by Edmund Publications Corporation

Anti-Lock Brakes[Std on ES] +325
Child Seat (1) +45
Climate Control for AC +80
Cruise Control[Std on ES] +95
Dual Power Seats +160
Keyless Entry System +80
Power Door Locks[Std on ES] +115
Power Drivers Seat +135
Power Moonroof +450
Power Windows[Std on ES] +130
Traction Control System +80

NEON 1995

This spunky Shadow replacement is cleverly designed, adequately powered, and cute to boot. Base, Highline and Sport models are available. Coupe and sedan body styles are offered. All except Sport Coupe have a 132-horsepower, 2.0-liter four-cylinder engine. Sport Coupe gets a 150-horsepower twin-cam edition of the base motor. Dual airbags are standard on all models; ABS is standard on Sport and optional on others. Integrated child seats are optional.

RATINGS (SCALE OF 1-10)

Overall	Safety	Reliability	Performance	Comfort	Value
7	6.1	6.7	7.4	7.6	7.1

Category E

Model	Trade-in Value	Market Value
2 Dr Highline Cpe	4540	6215
4 Dr Highline Sdn	4455	6105
2 Dr Sport Cpe	4970	6805
4 Dr Sport Sdn	4925	6745
4 Dr STD Sdn	4035	5525

OPTIONS FOR NEON

4 cyl 2.0 L DOHC Engine[Std on Sport] +65
Auto 3-Speed Transmission +225
Air Conditioning +370
AM/FM Compact Disc Playr +215
Anti-Lock Brakes[Std on Sport] +320
Child Seat (1) +50
Cruise Control +100
Power Door Locks[Std on Sport] +105
Power Steering[Opt on STD] +115
Power Windows +120
Premium Sound System +155
Rear Spoiler[Opt on Sdn] +95
Tilt Steering Wheel[Std on Sport] +70
Tinted Glass[Opt on STD] +45

RAM PICKUP 1995

A Club Cab model is added in 1500-, 2500-, and 3500-series levels with either two- or four-wheel drive. The Club Cab is available only in ST or Laramie SLT trim. Regular-cab models can be equipped with Sport trim midyear. Sport models have a sport suspension, chrome wheels, and a body-color grille with fog lights. Four-wheel ABS moves to the 3500 options list midyear.

RATINGS (SCALE OF 1-10)

Overall	Safety	Reliability	Performance	Comfort	Value
N/A	N/A	7.7	7	8	N/A

RAM 1500

Category H

Model	Trade-in Value	Market Value
2 Dr Laramie SLT Std Cab SB	10035	12385
2 Dr Laramie SLT Ext Cab SB	10870	13420
2 Dr Laramie SLT Ext Cab LB	10950	13520
2 Dr Laramie SLT Std Cab LB	10095	12465
2 Dr Laramie SLT 4WD Std Cab SB	11685	14425
2 Dr Laramie SLT 4WD Ext Cab SB	12255	15125
2 Dr Laramie SLT 4WD Std Cab LB	11810	14580
2 Dr Laramie SLT 4WD Ext Cab LB	12330	15225
2 Dr LT Std Cab SB	8720	10765
2 Dr LT Std Cab LB	8725	10770
2 Dr LT 4WD Std Cab SB	10475	12930
2 Dr LT 4WD Std Cab LB	10630	13125
2 Dr ST Ext Cab SB	9635	11895
2 Dr ST Ext Cab LB	9705	11980
2 Dr ST 4WD Ext Cab SB	10840	13385
2 Dr ST 4WD Ext Cab LB	11110	13715
2 Dr WS Std Cab SB	6985	8620
2 Dr WS Std Cab LB	7075	8735

RAM 2500

Category H

Model	Trade-in Value	Market Value
2 Dr Laramie SLT Ext Cab LB	12450	15370
2 Dr Laramie SLT Std Cab LB	11580	14295
2 Dr Laramie SLT 4WD Ext Cab SB	13315	16440
2 Dr Laramie SLT 4WD Std Cab LB	12515	15450
2 Dr Laramie SLT 4WD Ext Cab LB	13280	16395
2 Dr LT Std Cab LB	10620	13110
2 Dr LT 4WD Std Cab LB	11385	14055
2 Dr Sport Ext Cab SB	11890	14680
2 Dr Sport 4WD Ext Cab SB	12520	15460
2 Dr ST Ext Cab SB	11190	13815
2 Dr ST Std Cab LB	10645	13145
2 Dr ST Ext Cab LB	11290	13935
2 Dr ST 4WD Ext Cab SB	11820	14590
2 Dr ST 4WD Std Cab LB	11580	14295
2 Dr ST 4WD Ext Cab LB	12005	14820

Don't forget to refer to the Mileage Adjustment Table at the back of this book!

 © 1999 by Edmund Publications Corporation

RAM 3500

Category H

Model Description	Trade-in Value	Market Value
2 Dr Laramie SLT Std Cab LB	13095	16170
2 Dr Laramie SLT Ext Cab LB	13125	16205
2 Dr Laramie SLT 4WD Std Cab LB	14600	18025
2 Dr Laramie SLT 4WD Ext Cab LB	15815	19525
2 Dr LT Std Cab LB	11985	14800
2 Dr LT 4WD Std Cab LB	13065	16125
2 Dr ST Std Cab LB	12160	15015
2 Dr ST Ext Cab LB	12235	15105
2 Dr ST 4WD Ext Cab LB	14650	18085

OPTIONS FOR RAM PICKUP

10 cyl 8.0 L Engine +210
6 cyl 5.9 L Turbodsl Engine +1820
8 cyl 5.2 L Engine +200
8 cyl 5.9 L Engine +270
Auto 4-Speed Transmission +415
Sport Appearance Grp +380
Air Conditioning[Std on Laramie SLT] +365
Aluminum/Alloy Wheels +140
AM/FM Compact Disc Playr +135
Anti-Lock Brakes +230
Camper/Towing Package +160
Chrome Wheels[Opt on LT,ST] +135
Cruise Control[Std on Laramie SLT] +90
Limited Slip Diff +115
Power Door Locks[Opt on LT,ST] +85
Power Drivers Seat +125
Power Windows[Opt on ST] +85
Premium Sound System +185
Rear Step Bumper[Opt on Ram 3500,WS] +70
Skid Plates +50

RAM VAN/WAGON 1995

A driver airbag is added, and four-wheel ABS is now standard on Wagons and Vans sent to conversion outfitters. LE trim changes to SLT. Chrome wheels and a CD player are new options.

RATINGS (SCALE OF 1-10)

Overall	Safety	Reliability	Performance	Comfort	Value
N/A	7.2	7.7	6.2	6.9	N/A

B150

Category H

Model Description	Trade-in Value	Market Value
2 Dr SLT Ram Wagon	9465	11685
2 Dr STD Ram Van Ext	7215	8905
2 Dr STD Ram Wagon	8145	10055
2 Dr STD Ram Van	6925	8550

B250

Category H

Model Description	Trade-in Value	Market Value
2 Dr Maxi Ram Van Ext	7485	9245
2 Dr Maxi Ram Wagon Ext	8310	10260
2 Dr SLT Ram Wagon Ext	10760	13285
2 Dr SLT Ram Wagon	9755	12045
2 Dr STD Ram Wagon	8165	10080
2 Dr STD Ram Van	7245	8945
2 Dr STD Ram Van Ext	7385	9115

B350

Category H

Model Description	Trade-in Value	Market Value
2 Dr SLT Ram Wagon	10130	12505
2 Dr SLT Ram Wagon Ext	10165	12550
2 Dr STD Ram Van Ext	7690	9495
2 Dr STD Ram Van	7595	9375
2 Dr STD Ram Wagon	8425	10400
2 Dr STD Ram Wagon Ext	9040	11160

OPTIONS FOR RAM VAN/WAGON

8 cyl 5.2 L Engine[Std on B350,Ram Wagon Ext] +200
8 cyl 5.9 L Engine +270
Auto 4-Speed Transmission[Std on B350] +110
Rear A/C W/Rear Heater +365
Air Conditioning[Std on B250 SLT] +365
AM/FM Compact Disc Playr +135
Anti-Lock Brakes[Opt on Ram Van,Ram Van Ext] +230
Chrome Bumpers[Std on SLT] +75
Chrome Wheels[Std on SLT] +135
Cruise Control[Std on SLT] +90
Dual Air Conditioning[Opt on B250,STD] +645
Keyless Entry System[Std on SLT] +70
Limited Slip Diff[Opt on B250,B350] +115
Power Door Locks[Opt on Maxi,STD] +85
Power Drivers Seat +125
Power Windows[Opt on Maxi,STD] +85
Premium Sound System +185
Velour/Cloth Seats[Opt on B150,Maxi,STD] +60

SPIRIT 1995

Flexible fuel model, and optional four-speed automatic transmission, are dropped. A three-speed automatic continues as standard equipment.

RATINGS (SCALE OF 1-10)

Overall	Safety	Reliability	Performance	Comfort	Value
7.1	6.7	8	6.8	7.4	6.8

Category C

Model Description	Trade-in Value	Market Value
4 Dr STD Sdn	5430	7150

OPTIONS FOR SPIRIT

6 cyl 3.0 L Engine +355
Power Door Locks +110
Power Drivers Seat +130
Power Windows +140

Don't forget to refer to the Mileage Adjustment Table at the back of this book!

© 1999 by Edmund Publications Corporation

Model Description	Trade-in Value	Market Value

STEALTH 1995

Chromed 18-inch aluminum wheels are available on R/T Turbo.

RATINGS (SCALE OF 1-10)

Overall	Safety	Reliability	Performance	Comfort	Value
N/A	N/A	8	9.4	6.8	N/A

Category F

Model Description	Trade-in Value	Market Value
2 Dr R/T Hbk	11865	15210
2 Dr R/T Turbo 4WD Hbk	14545	18645
2 Dr STD Hbk	10370	13295

OPTIONS FOR STEALTH

Auto 4-Speed Transmission +395
Anti-Lock Brakes[Std on 4WD] +330
Chrome Wheels +255
Compact Disc Changer +305
Cruise Control[Opt on STD] +95
Keyless Entry System +80
Leather Seats +325
Power Door Locks[Std on 4WD] +90
Power Sunroof +310
Power Windows[Std on 4WD] +100

STRATUS 1995

Spirit replacement features cutting-edge styling and class-leading accommodations. Dual airbags and ABS are standard. Base and ES models are available. Base model has 2.4-liter four-cylinder engine making 140 horsepower and a four-speed automatic transmission. ES is powered by 155-horsepower Mitsubishi 2.5-liter V6. A credit option on the ES is the Neon's 2.0-liter four hooked to a five-speed manual transmission.

RATINGS (SCALE OF 1-10)

Overall	Safety	Reliability	Performance	Comfort	Value
N/A	N/A	6.6	7	7.8	7.1

Category C

Model Description	Trade-in Value	Market Value
4 Dr ES Sdn	7525	9905
4 Dr STD Sdn	6525	8590

OPTIONS FOR STRATUS

4 cyl 2.4 L Engine +195
Auto 4-Speed Transmission[Std on ES] +325
AM/FM Compact Disc Playr +175
Anti-Lock Brakes[Std on ES] +285
Child Seat (1) +55
Keyless Entry System +85
Leather Seats +260
Lighted Entry System +75
Power Door Locks[Std on ES] +110
Power Drivers Seat +130
Power Windows[Std on ES] +140
Premium Sound System +180

VIPER 1995

No changes.

Category K

Model Description	Trade-in Value	Market Value
2 Dr RT/10 Conv	33750	41155

OPTIONS FOR VIPER

Air Conditioning +545

1994 DODGE

CARAVAN 1994

A passenger airbag is added to a redesigned dashboard, and new side door guard beams meet 1997 passenger car safety standards. All-wheel drive is no longer available on regular-length models. Bumpers are restyled, and seats with integrated child seats can be reclined for the first time.

RATINGS (SCALE OF 1-10)

Overall	Safety	Reliability	Performance	Comfort	Value
7.7	8.3	6.5	7.4	8.3	7.9

Category G

Model Description	Trade-in Value	Market Value
2 Dr ES Pass. Van	7565	9825
2 Dr Grand Pass. Van	6405	8320
2 Dr Grand ES Pass. Van	8410	10920
2 Dr Grand ES 4WD Pass. Van	8635	11215
2 Dr Grand LE Pass. Van	8315	10800
2 Dr Grand LE 4WD Pass. Van	8490	11025
2 Dr Grand SE Pass. Van	6815	8850
2 Dr Grand SE 4WD Pass. Van	7225	9385
2 Dr LE Pass. Van	7390	9595
2 Dr SE Pass. Van	6220	8080
2 Dr STD Pass. Van	5170	6715
2 Dr STD Cargo Van	3710	4815
2 Dr STD Cargo Van Ext	4965	6450

OPTIONS FOR CARAVAN

6 cyl 3.0 L Engine[Opt on STD] +40
6 cyl 3.3 L Engine[Opt on Grand,SE] +225
6 cyl 3.8 L Engine +160
Auto 3-Speed Transmission[Opt on STD] +145
Auto 4-Speed Transmission[Opt on Grand,SE, STD] +225
7 Passenger Seating[Opt on SE,STD] +200
Air Conditioning[Std on Grand LE,LE] +300
AM/FM Compact Disc Playr +145
Anti-Lock Brakes +230
Captain Chairs (4) +235
Child Seats (2) +95
Cruise Control[Opt on Grand,STD] +80
Dual Air Conditioning +375
Heavy Duty Suspension[Opt on LE] +50
Infinity Sound System +220
Keyless Entry System[Std on Grand LE,LE] +75
Leather Seats +285

Don't forget to refer to the Mileage Adjustment Table at the back of this book!

 © 1999 by Edmund Publications Corporation

Model Description	Trade-in Value	Market Value

Lighted Entry System[Opt on Grand SE] +55
Power Door Locks[Std on Grand LE,LE] +85
Power Drivers Seat +105
Power Windows[Std on LE] +85
Sport Suspension +180

COLT 1994

A driver airbag debuts. ES trim replaces GL nomenclature. Order ABS on an ES sedan and you'll get rear discs instead of drums. The optional 1.8-liter engine is available on the coupe this year, but only with ES trim. Sedans gain standard power steering. Air conditioners use CFC-free refrigerant.

RATINGS (SCALE OF 1-10)

Overall	Safety	Reliability	Performance	Comfort	Value
6.5	5.5	7.1	8	7.4	4.6

Category E		
2 Dr ES Sdn	3400	4860
4 Dr ES Sdn	3845	5490
2 Dr STD Sdn	3285	4695
4 Dr STD Sdn	3730	5325

OPTIONS FOR COLT

4 cyl 1.8 L Engine[Opt on ES Sdn] +165
Auto 3-Speed Transmission +190
Auto 4-Speed Transmission +250
Air Conditioning +300
Aluminum/Alloy Wheels +120
AM/FM Stereo Tape +115
Anti-Lock Brakes +265
Cruise Control +80
Power Door Locks +85
Power Windows +100

DAKOTA 1994

Driver airbag is added, along with side guard door beams. LE trim level now called SLT. A strengthened roof now meets passenger car crush standards. The 5.2-liter V8 loses horsepower but gains torque.

RATINGS (SCALE OF 1-10)

Overall	Safety	Reliability	Performance	Comfort	Value
N/A	7	7.3	7	7.1	N/A

Category G		
2 Dr SLT Std Cab SB	6570	8535
2 Dr SLT Ext Cab SB	6925	8995
2 Dr SLT Std Cab LB	7065	9175
2 Dr SLT 4WD Std Cab SB	8255	10720
2 Dr SLT 4WD Ext Cab SB	8695	11290
2 Dr SLT 4WD Std Cab LB	8615	11190
2 Dr Sport Std Cab SB	5725	7440
2 Dr Sport Ext Cab SB	6625	8600
2 Dr Sport 4WD Std Cab SB	8150	10585
2 Dr Sport 4WD Ext Cab SB	8335	10825
2 Dr STD Std Cab SB	5620	7300
2 Dr STD Ext Cab SB	6500	8440
2 Dr STD Std Cab LB	6520	8465
2 Dr STD 4WD Std Cab SB	8020	10415
2 Dr STD 4WD Ext Cab SB	8125	10555
2 Dr STD 4WD Std Cab LB	8375	10880
2 Dr WS Std Cab SB	5455	7085
2 Dr WS Std Cab LB	6320	8210
2 Dr WS 4WD Std Cab SB	7665	9955
2 Dr WS 4WD Std Cab LB	7980	10365

OPTIONS FOR DAKOTA

6 cyl 3.9 L Engine +195
8 cyl 5.2 L Engine +255
Auto 4-Speed Transmission +335
Air Conditioning[Opt on Sport,STD,WS] +300
AM/FM Stereo Tape[Opt on STD,WS] +90
Anti-Lock Brakes +230
Camper/Towing Package +105
Chrome Bumpers[Std on SLT] +60
Chrome Wheels[Std on SLT] +90
Cruise Control[Opt on Sport,STD] +80
Intermittent Wipers[Opt on STD,WS] +30
Limited Slip Diff +100
Power Door Locks +85
Power Windows +85
Premium Sound System +135
Rear Step Bumper[Opt on STD,WS] +55

INTREPID 1994

Base engine is upgraded with eight more horsepower. A flexible-fuel model is introduced to all states except California. Standard equipment now includes air conditioning and a touring suspension. ES models gain variable-assist power steering, which is optional on base models with the Wheel and Handling Group. New options include a power sunroof, security alarm and power cloth passenger seat.

RATINGS (SCALE OF 1-10)

Overall	Safety	Reliability	Performance	Comfort	Value
8.1	7.9	7.3	8.4	8.6	8.4

Category B		
4 Dr ES Sdn	6795	9055
4 Dr STD Sdn	5700	7600

OPTIONS FOR INTREPID

6 cyl 3.5 L Engine +270
Anti-Lock Brakes +265
Child Seat (1) +35
Climate Control for AC +65
Compact Disc W/fm/tape +145
Cruise Control[Std on ES] +80
Dual Power Seats +135
Keyless Entry System +65
Leather Seats +245
Power Door Locks +90

Don't forget to refer to the Mileage Adjustment Table at the back of this book!

 © 1999 by Edmund Publications Corporation

Model Description	Trade-in Value	Market Value

Power Moonroof +370
Power Windows +110
Traction Control System +65

RAM PICKUP 1994

Brand-new truck replaces 22-year-old D-Series model. New truck sports big-rig styling, driver airbag, available V10 engine, and a commodious cabin. All 1994 Rams are regular-cab models in shortbed or longbed configuration with 2WD or 4WD. Optional on 1500 and 2500 models is four-wheel ABS that works in both 2WD and 4WD.

RATINGS (SCALE OF 1-10)

Overall	Safety	Reliability	Performance	Comfort	Value
N/A	N/A	7.6	7	8	N/A

RAM 1500

Category H

Model Description	Trade-in Value	Market Value
2 Dr Laramie SLT Std Cab SB	8315	10395
2 Dr Laramie SLT Std Cab LB	8420	10525
2 Dr Laramie SLT 4WD Std Cab SB	10140	12675
2 Dr Laramie SLT 4WD Std Cab LB	10235	12790
2 Dr LT Std Cab SB	7280	9100
2 Dr LT Std Cab LB	7360	9200
2 Dr LT 4WD Std Cab SB	9095	11370
2 Dr LT 4WD Std Cab LB	9190	11490
2 Dr ST Std Cab SB	7350	9185
2 Dr ST Std Cab LB	7380	9230
2 Dr ST 4WD Std Cab SB	9305	11630
2 Dr ST 4WD Std Cab LB	9315	11645
2 Dr WS Std Cab SB	7115	8895
2 Dr WS Std Cab LB	7255	9070

RAM 2500

Category H

Model Description	Trade-in Value	Market Value
2 Dr Laramie SLT Std Cab LB	9915	12395
2 Dr Laramie SLT 4WD Std Cab LB	10910	13640
2 Dr LT Std Cab LB	8855	11070
2 Dr LT 4WD Std Cab LB	10070	12585
2 Dr ST Std Cab LB	8945	11180
2 Dr ST 4WD Std Cab LB	10120	12650

RAM 3500

Category H

Model Description	Trade-in Value	Market Value
2 Dr Laramie SLT Std Cab LB	12550	15685
2 Dr Laramie SLT 4WD Std Cab LB	12880	16105
2 Dr LT Std Cab LB	11535	14415
2 Dr LT 4WD Std Cab LB	11915	14895
2 Dr ST Std Cab LB	11675	14595
2 Dr ST 4WD Std Cab LB	12050	15065

OPTIONS FOR RAM PICKUP
10 cyl 8.0 L Engine +175
6 cyl 5.9 L Turbodsl Engine +1630
8 cyl 5.2 L Engine +180
8 cyl 5.9 L Engine +190
Auto 4-Speed Transmission +335
Air Conditioning[Opt on LT,ST,WS] +300
Anti-Lock Brakes +190
Bed Liner +85
Camper/Towing Package +130
Chrome Bumpers[Opt on LT] +60
Chrome Wheels[Opt on LT,ST] +110
Compact Disc W/fm/tape +120
Cruise Control[Opt on LT,ST,WS] +70
Limited Slip Diff +95
Power Drivers Seat +100
Premium Sound System +150
Rear Step Bumper +60

RAM VAN/WAGON 1994

A reskinned full-size van debuted in mid-1993, featuring new front and rear styling. Early-build vans did not include side door guard beams for the front doors or improved roof crush protection. Air conditioning now uses CFC-free refrigerant.

RATINGS (SCALE OF 1-10)

Overall	Safety	Reliability	Performance	Comfort	Value
N/A	6.3	7.8	6.2	6.9	N/A

B150

Category H

Model Description	Trade-in Value	Market Value
2 Dr LE Ram Wagon	7335	9170
2 Dr STD Ram Van Ext	6635	8295
2 Dr STD Ram Van	5525	6905
2 Dr STD Ram Wagon	6360	7950

B250

Category H

Model Description	Trade-in Value	Market Value
2 Dr LE Ram Wagon	8620	10780
2 Dr Maxi Ram Wagon	7915	9890
2 Dr Maxi Ram Van Ext	7170	8965
2 Dr STD Ram Wagon	7390	9235
2 Dr STD Ram Van	6925	8655
2 Dr STD Ram Van Ext	6955	8695

B350

Category H

Model Description	Trade-in Value	Market Value
2 Dr LE Ram Wagon Ext	9775	12220
2 Dr LE Ram Wagon	9190	11485
2 Dr Maxi Ram Van Ext	7370	9210
2 Dr Maxi LE Ram Wagon	9990	12490
2 Dr STD Ram Wagon Ext	8080	10100
2 Dr STD Ram Van Ext	7170	8960
2 Dr STD Ram Wagon	8015	10020

Don't forget to refer to the Mileage Adjustment Table at the back of this book!

© 1999 by Edmund Publications Corporation

Model Description	Trade-in Value	Market Value

OPTIONS FOR RAM VAN/WAGON

8 cyl 5.2 L Engine[Std on B350,B250 LE Ram Wagon] +180
8 cyl 5.9 L Engine +190
Auto 4-Speed Transmission[Std on B350] +95
Air Conditioning[Std on LE] +300
Aluminum/Alloy Wheels +115
AM/FM Stereo Tape +90
Anti-Lock Brakes +190
Auxiliary Fuel Tank +75
Cruise Control[Opt on Maxi,STD] +70
Dual Air Conditioning[Opt on B250] +525
Infinity Sound System +65
Keyless Entry System[Opt on Maxi,STD] +60
Limited Slip Diff +95
Power Door Locks[Opt on Maxi,STD] +70
Power Windows[Opt on Maxi,STD] +70
Premium Sound System +150
Velour/Cloth Seats[Std on LE,Maxi LE] +50

SHADOW 1994

Four-door hatchback production stops midyear. Front passengers are now restrained by the dreaded motorized seatbelt to comply with federal regulations. Air conditioning runs on CFC-free coolant this year.

RATINGS (SCALE OF 1-10)

Overall	Safety	Reliability	Performance	Comfort	Value
6.5	6.5	7.1	7.2	6.8	5.2

Category E

Model Description	Trade-in Value	Market Value
2 Dr ES Hbk	3705	5290
4 Dr ES Hbk	3865	5520
2 Dr STD Hbk	3250	4640
4 Dr STD Hbk	3425	4895

OPTIONS FOR SHADOW

4 cyl 2.5 L Engine[Std on ES] +105
6 cyl 3.0 L Engine +295
Auto 3-Speed Transmission +205
Auto 4-Speed Transmission +270
Air Conditioning +300
Aluminum/Alloy Wheels +120
AM/FM Compact Disc Playr +175
Anti-Lock Brakes +265
Cruise Control +80
Power Door Locks +85
Power Drivers Seat +110
Power Windows +100
Premium Sound System +125
Sunroof +130

SPIRIT 1994

Motorized seatbelt is introduced for front passengers. Highline and ES trim designations are retired in favor of ... well, nothing. All 1994 Spirits come equipped one way, with various option packages available.

RATINGS (SCALE OF 1-10)

Overall	Safety	Reliability	Performance	Comfort	Value
7.2	6.6	7.7	6.8	7.4	7.5

Category C

Model Description	Trade-in Value	Market Value
4 Dr D Sdn	4550	6145
4 Dr STD Sdn	4330	5855

OPTIONS FOR SPIRIT

6 cyl 3.0 L Engine +255
Auto 4-Speed Transmission +65
AM/FM Stereo Tape +60
Anti-Lock Brakes +230
Power Door Locks +90
Power Drivers Seat +105
Power Windows +115

STEALTH 1994

Passenger airbag is added. R/T Turbo gains 20 horsepower and a six-speed transmission. ES trim level is dropped. Styling is slightly revised front and rear, revealing the addition of projector-beam headlamps in place of the hidden lights used previously. CFC-free refrigerant is used in the air conditioning system, and R/T models can be painted a really bright shade of yellow.

RATINGS (SCALE OF 1-10)

Overall	Safety	Reliability	Performance	Comfort	Value
N/A	N/A	7.9	9.4	6.8	N/A

Category F

Model Description	Trade-in Value	Market Value
2 Dr R/T Hbk	9255	12180
2 Dr R/T Turbo 4WD Hbk	12720	16735
2 Dr R/T Luxury Hbk	10290	13540
2 Dr STD Hbk	9185	12085

OPTIONS FOR STEALTH

Auto 4-Speed Transmission +360
Air Conditioning[Std on R/T Luxury,4WD] +310
AM/FM Stereo Tape +75
Anti-Lock Brakes[Std on 4WD] +270
Chrome Wheels +210
Compact Disc Changer[Opt on R/T,STD] +250
Cruise Control[Std on R/T Luxury,4WD] +80
Keyless Entry System[Opt on R/T,STD] +65
Leather Seats +265
Power Door Locks[Std on R/T Luxury,4WD] +75
Power Sunroof +255
Power Windows[Std on R/T Luxury,4WD] +85
Premium Sound System[Std on R/T Luxury,4WD] +150
Rear Spoiler[Std on R/T Luxury,4WD] +105

Don't forget to refer to the Mileage Adjustment Table at the back of this book!

 © 1999 by Edmund Publications Corporation

1993 DODGE

CARAVAN 1993

No changes.

RATINGS (SCALE OF 1-10)

Overall	Safety	Reliability	Performance	Comfort	Value
7.3	6.4	6	7.4	8.3	8.3

Category G		
2 Dr ES Pass. Van	6020	8030
2 Dr ES 4WD Pass. Van	6665	8890
2 Dr Grand Pass. Van	4985	6645
2 Dr Grand ES Pass. Van	6725	8965
2 Dr Grand LE Pass. Van	6475	8635
2 Dr Grand LE 4WD Pass. Van	6845	9125
2 Dr Grand SE Pass. Van	5440	7250
2 Dr Grand SE 4WD Pass. Van	5580	7440
2 Dr LE Pass. Van	5535	7380
2 Dr LE 4WD Pass. Van	6290	8390
2 Dr SE Pass. Van	4455	5940
2 Dr SE 4WD Pass. Van	5085	6780
2 Dr STD Cargo Van Ext	3225	4300
2 Dr STD Cargo Van	2590	3450
2 Dr STD Pass. Van	3825	5105

OPTIONS FOR CARAVAN

6 cyl 3.0 L Engine[Opt on SE,STD] +115
6 cyl 3.3 L Engine[Std on Grand ES,Grand LE,Grand SE,4WD] +200
Auto 3-Speed Transmission[Opt on STD] +70
Auto 4-Speed Transmission[Opt on SE Pass. Van, LE Pass. Van] +180
7 Passenger Seating[Std on Grand ES] +165
Air Conditioning[Std on ES,Grand ES, Grand LE, LE] +245
Aluminum/Alloy Wheels +105
AM/FM Compact Disc Playr +115
Anti-Lock Brakes +185
Captain Chairs (4) +190
Child Seats (2) +80
Cruise Control[Opt on Grand,Grand SE,SE,STD] +65
Dual Air Conditioning +305
Leather Seats +235
Luggage Rack +45
Power Door Locks[Opt on Grand,Grand SE,SE,STD] +70
Power Drivers Seat +85
Power Windows +70
Premium Sound System +110

COLT 1993

Complete redesign results in two- and four-door notchback models; the hatchback is dropped. Coupes and sedans come in base or GL trim. Coupe and base sedan are powered by same 1.5-liter engine from last year. GL sedan has a stronger 113-horsepower 1.8-liter engine; this powerplant is optional on base sedan. GL sedan is only Colt that can be equipped with optional ABS.

RATINGS (SCALE OF 1-10)

Overall	Safety	Reliability	Performance	Comfort	Value
N/A	N/A	6.9	8	7.4	6.6

Category E		
2 Dr GL Sdn	2765	4130
4 Dr GL Sdn	2775	4140
2 Dr STD Sdn	2370	3535
4 Dr STD Sdn	2600	3885

OPTIONS FOR COLT

4 cyl 1.8 L Engine[Std on GL] +115
Auto 3-Speed Transmission +155
Auto 4-Speed Transmission +205
Air Conditioning +245
Aluminum/Alloy Wheels +95
AM/FM Stereo Tape +95
Anti-Lock Brakes +215
Cruise Control +65
Power Door Locks +70
Power Steering +75
Power Windows +80

DAKOTA 1993

Sport model gets new graphics.

RATINGS (SCALE OF 1-10)

Overall	Safety	Reliability	Performance	Comfort	Value
N/A	4.8	7.1	7	7.1	N/A

Category G		
2 Dr LE Std Cab SB	5265	7020
2 Dr LE Ext Cab SB	6030	8040
2 Dr LE Std Cab LB	5355	7140
2 Dr LE 4WD Std Cab SB	6595	8790
2 Dr LE 4WD Ext Cab SB	7195	9595
2 Dr LE 4WD Std Cab LB	6680	8910
2 Dr S Std Cab SB	4405	5875
2 Dr Sport Std Cab SB	4740	6320
2 Dr Sport 4WD Std Cab SB	6165	8225
2 Dr STD Std Cab SB	4600	6135
2 Dr STD Ext Cab SB	5265	7020
2 Dr STD Std Cab LB	4695	6260
2 Dr STD 4WD Std Cab SB	6150	8200
2 Dr STD 4WD Ext Cab SB	6595	8795
2 Dr STD 4WD Std Cab LB	6155	8205

OPTIONS FOR DAKOTA

6 cyl 3.9 L Engine +160
8 cyl 5.2 L Engine +260
Auto 4-Speed Transmission +270
Dakota Snowplow Prep Grp. +230
Air Conditioning[Std on LE] +245
Aluminum/Alloy Wheels[Opt on STD] +105

Don't forget to refer to the Mileage Adjustment Table at the back of this book!

 © 1999 by Edmund Publications Corporation

AM/FM Stereo Tape[Opt on S,STD] +75
Anti-Lock Brakes +185
Camper/Towing Package +85
Chrome Bumpers +50
Chrome Wheels +75
Cruise Control[Std on LE] +65
Limited Slip Diff +80
Power Door Locks +70
Power Steering[Std on LE,Sport,4WD] +85
Power Windows +70
Premium Sound System +110
Rear Step Bumper[Opt on S,STD] +45

DAYTONA 1993

ABS is now available on base model. IROC loses turbocharged engine, though the limited-edition IROC R/T continues with turbo power.

Model Description	Trade-in Value	Market Value
Category C		
2 Dr ES Hbk	3435	4840
2 Dr STD Hbk	3100	4370
Category F		
2 Dr IROC Hbk	4650	6200

OPTIONS FOR DAYTONA

6 cyl 3.0 L Engine[Std on IROC] +210
Auto 3-Speed Transmission +170
Auto 4-Speed Transmission +215
Cloth Pwr Enthusiast Seats +230
Air Conditioning[Std on IROC R/T] +240
Aluminum/Alloy Wheels[Opt on STD] +85
AM/FM Compact Disc Playr +115
Anti-Lock Brakes[Opt on ES] +190
Cruise Control +65
Leather Seats +175
Power Door Locks +60
Power Drivers Seat +70
Power Windows +70
Premium Sound System +120
Tilt Steering Wheel +45

DYNASTY 1993

Audio system is upgraded, a tamper-resistant odometer is added, and a stainless steel exhaust system is installed.

Model Description	Trade-in Value	Market Value
Category C		
4 Dr LE Sdn	3825	5385
4 Dr STD Sdn	3135	4420

OPTIONS FOR DYNASTY

6 cyl 3.0 L Engine[Std on LE] +165
6 cyl 3.3 L Engine +210
Auto 4-Speed Transmission[Std on LE] +40
Air Conditioning +240
AM/FM Stereo Tape +50
Anti-Lock Brakes +190
Cruise Control +65
Keyless Entry System +55
Leather Seats +175
Power Door Locks +70
Power Drivers Seat +85
Power Passenger Seat +80
Power Windows +90
Premium Sound System +120
Wire Wheel Covers +65

INTREPID 1993

This midsized car represents the beginning of a revolution at Chrysler. Introducing cab-forward styling, Intrepid is powered by one of two V6 engines and comes in base or ES trim. ES model has four-wheel disc brakes. ABS is optional on base and ES. All Intrepids are equipped with dual airbags and height-adjustable seatbelts, while integrated child seats are optional.

RATINGS (SCALE OF 1-10)

Overall	Safety	Reliability	Performance	Comfort	Value
7.9	7.8	6.7	8.4	8.6	7.8

Model Description	Trade-in Value	Market Value
Category B		
4 Dr ES Sdn	5135	7035
4 Dr STD Sdn	4480	6135

OPTIONS FOR INTREPID

6 cyl 3.5 L Engine +190
Air Conditioning +245
Aluminum/Alloy Wheels +100
Anti-Lock Brakes +215
Child Seat (1) +30
Climate Control for AC +55
Compact Disc W/fm/tape +120
Cruise Control +65
Leather Seats +200
Power Door Locks +75
Power Drivers Seat +90
Power Passenger Seat +95
Power Windows +90
Premium Sound System +125
Traction Control System +55

RAM 50 PICKUP 1993

Rear-wheel ABS reappears as standard equipment on all models.

Model Description	Trade-in Value	Market Value
Category G		
2 Dr SE Std Cab SB	2885	3850
2 Dr STD Std Cab SB	2665	3550
2 Dr STD Std Cab LB	2780	3705

OPTIONS FOR RAM 50 PICKUP

Auto 4-Speed Transmission +215
Air Conditioning +245
AM/FM Stereo Tape +75
Cruise Control +65
Power Door Locks +70
Power Steering[Opt on 2WD] +85
Power Windows +70
Rear Step Bumper +45

Don't forget to refer to the Mileage Adjustment Table at the back of this book!

 © 1999 by Edmund Publications Corporation

Model Description	Trade-in Value	Market Value

RAM PICKUP 1993

The optional 5.9-liter V8 is upgraded. New steel and alloy wheel designs debut.

RAM 150

Category H

Model Description	Trade-in Value	Market Value
2 Dr LE Ext Cab SB	7205	9120
2 Dr LE Std Cab SB	5915	7490
2 Dr LE Ext Cab LB	7290	9225
2 Dr LE Std Cab LB	5995	7590
2 Dr LE 4WD Std Cab SB	7015	8880
2 Dr LE 4WD Std Cab LB	7225	9145
2 Dr LE 4WD Ext Cab LB	10130	12820
2 Dr STD Ext Cab SB	6785	8590
2 Dr STD Std Cab SB	5110	6470
2 Dr STD Ext Cab LB	6865	8690
2 Dr STD Std Cab LB	5190	6565
2 Dr STD 4WD Std Cab SB	6560	8300
2 Dr STD 4WD Ext Cab LB	9350	11835
2 Dr STD 4WD Std Cab LB	6625	8390

RAM 250

Category H

Model Description	Trade-in Value	Market Value
2 Dr LE Std Cab LB	6855	8680
2 Dr LE Turbodsl Ext Cab LB	8910	11275
2 Dr LE 4WD Ext Cab LB	10020	12680
2 Dr STD Std Cab LB	6460	8180
2 Dr STD 4WD Ext Cab LB	9595	12145

RAM 350

Category H

Model Description	Trade-in Value	Market Value
2 Dr LE Turbodsl Ext Cab LB	9430	11935
2 Dr LE Turbodsl 4WD Ext Cab LB	11355	14375
2 Dr STD Std Cab LB	8265	10465
2 Dr STD Turbodsl Ext Cab LB	8475	10730
2 Dr STD Turbodsl 4WD Ext Cab LB	10505	13300

OPTIONS FOR RAM PICKUP

6 cyl 5.9 L Turbodsl Engine +1175
8 cyl 5.2 L Engine +165
8 cyl 5.9 L Engine +180
Auto 3-Speed Transmission +200
Auto 4-Speed Transmission +270
Snow Plow Prep Pkg +250
Air Conditioning[Opt on STD] +245
Aluminum/Alloy Wheels +95
AM/FM Stereo Tape[Opt on STD] +75
Camper/Towing Package +110
Chrome Step Bumper +65
Cruise Control[Opt on STD] +60
Dual Rear Wheels +255
Limited Slip Diff +75
Power Door Locks[Opt on STD] +55
Power Windows[Opt on STD] +60
Premium Sound System +125
Rear Step Bumper[Opt on STD] +45
Skid Plates +35

RAM VAN/WAGON 1993

The optional 5.9-liter V8 is upgraded.

B150

Category H

Model Description	Trade-in Value	Market Value
2 Dr LE Ram Wagon	5970	7555
2 Dr LE Ram Wagon Ext	6005	7600
2 Dr STD Ram Wagon	5500	6960
2 Dr STD Ram Wagon Ext	5550	7025
2 Dr STD Ram Van Ext	4675	5920
2 Dr STD Ram Van	4640	5875
2 Dr Value Ram Wagon	5820	7365
2 Dr Value Ram Wagon Ext	5880	7440

B250

Category H

Model Description	Trade-in Value	Market Value
2 Dr LE Ram Wagon Ext	7330	9280
2 Dr LE Maxi Ram Wagon Ext	7730	9785
2 Dr Maxi Ram Van Ext	6190	7840
2 Dr Maxi Ram Wagon Ext	7250	9175
2 Dr STD Ram Van	5640	7140
2 Dr STD Ram Van Ext	5835	7385
2 Dr STD Ram Wagon Ext	6720	8505
2 Dr Value Ram Wagon Ext	7030	8900
2 Dr Value Maxi Ram Wagon Ext	7565	9575

B350

Category H

Model Description	Trade-in Value	Market Value
2 Dr LE Ram Wagon Ext	7220	9140
2 Dr LE Ram Wagon	7040	8915
2 Dr Maxi Ram Van Ext	5880	7445
2 Dr STD Ram Wagon	6640	8405
2 Dr STD Ram Wagon Ext	6920	8760
2 Dr STD Ram Van Ext	5535	7005
2 Dr Value Ram Wagon Ext	7130	9025
2 Dr Value Ram Wagon	6895	8725

OPTIONS FOR RAM VAN/WAGON

8 cyl 5.2 L Engine[Std on B350,LE Maxi,Value Maxi, B250 Maxi Ram Wagon Ext] +165
8 cyl 5.9 L Engine +180
Auto 3-Speed Transmission[Opt on B150,Ram Van, Ram Van Ext] +100
Auto 4-Speed Transmission[Std on B350] +140
8 Pass W/Travel Seat Pkg +275
Air Conditioning[Opt on Maxi,STD,B150, LE Ram Wagon Ext] +245
Aluminum/Alloy Wheels +95
AM/FM Stereo Tape +75
Cruise Control[Std on LE,LE Maxi] +60
Dual Air Conditioning +430
Limited Slip Diff +75

Don't forget to refer to the Mileage Adjustment Table at the back of this book!

© 1999 by Edmund Publications Corporation

Model Description	Trade-in Value	Market Value

Power Door Locks[Opt on Value] +55
Power Windows[Opt on Value] +60
Premium Sound System[Opt on Value] +125

RAMCHARGER 1993

The optional 5.9-liter V8 is upgraded.

Category H

Model Description	Trade-in Value	Market Value
2 Dr Canyon Sport 4WD Utility	7855	9945
2 Dr LE 4WD Utility	7470	9455
2 Dr S 4WD Utility	6875	8700
2 Dr STD 4WD Utility	7330	9280

OPTIONS FOR RAMCHARGER

8 cyl 5.9 L Engine +165
Ramcharger Snow Plow Pkg.+320
Air Conditioning[Std on LE] +245
Aluminum/Alloy Wheels +95
AM/FM Stereo Tape +75
Camper/Towing Package +110
Cruise Control[Std on LE] +60
Limited Slip Diff +75
Power Door Locks[Std on LE] +55
Power Windows[Std on LE] +60
Premium Sound System +125
Velour/Cloth Seats[Opt on Canyon Sport,S,4WD] +40

SHADOW 1993

America model is dropped. Convertible disappears midyear. ABS is newly optional.

RATINGS (SCALE OF 1-10)

Overall	Safety	Reliability	Performance	Comfort	Value
6.7	6.5	7.9	7.2	6.8	5.1

Category E

Model Description	Trade-in Value	Market Value
2 Dr ES Hbk	2990	4460
2 Dr ES Conv	3985	5945
4 Dr ES Hbk	3080	4595
2 Dr Highline Conv	3665	5475
2 Dr STD Hbk	2625	3920
4 Dr STD Hbk	2720	4060

OPTIONS FOR SHADOW

4 cyl 2.5 L Engine[Opt on STD] +85
6 cyl 3.0 L Engine +210
Auto 3-Speed Transmission +170
Auto 4-Speed Transmission +210
Air Conditioning +245
Aluminum/Alloy Wheels +95
AM/FM Compact Disc Playr +145
Anti-Lock Brakes +215
Cruise Control +65
Power Door Locks +70
Power Drivers Seat +90
Power Windows[Opt on STD] +80
Premium Sound System +105
Sunroof +105

SPIRIT 1993

LE and R/T models are dropped from lineup. Turbocharged engines are banished. Four thousand flexible-fuel models are produced. Grille is now color keyed. CD player is added to options list. Rear styling is revised..

RATINGS (SCALE OF 1-10)

Overall	Safety	Reliability	Performance	Comfort	Value
7.1	6.1	7.8	6.8	7.4	7.4

Category C

Model Description	Trade-in Value	Market Value
4 Dr ES Sdn	4195	5910
4 Dr Highline Sdn	3285	4630

OPTIONS FOR SPIRIT

6 cyl 3.0 L Engine +210
Auto 3-Speed Transmission[Std on ES] +125
Auto 4-Speed Transmission +170
Air Conditioning +240
Aluminum/Alloy Wheels[Std on ES] +85
AM/FM Stereo Tape +50
Anti-Lock Brakes +190
Cruise Control[Std on ES] +65
Power Door Locks +70
Power Drivers Seat +85
Power Windows +90
Premium Sound System +120

STEALTH 1993

Base model gets ES sill moldings, while R/T's spoiler is optional across the line. R/T Turbo can be ordered with chrome wheels. Remote keyless entry and a CD changer are new options.

RATINGS (SCALE OF 1-10)

Overall	Safety	Reliability	Performance	Comfort	Value
N/A	6.3	7.5	9.4	6.8	N/A

Category F

Model Description	Trade-in Value	Market Value
2 Dr ES Hbk	6840	9120
2 Dr R/T Hbk	9105	12135
2 Dr R/T Turbo 4WD Hbk	10510	14015
2 Dr STD Hbk	6450	8600

OPTIONS FOR STEALTH

Auto 4-Speed Transmission +260
Air Conditioning[Std on R/T] +250
AM/FM Stereo Tape +60
Anti-Lock Brakes[Std on R/T] +220
Chrome Wheels +170
Compact Disc Changer +205
Cruise Control[Std on R/T] +65
Keyless Entry System +50
Leather Seats +215
Power Door Locks[Std on R/T] +60
Power Sunroof +205

Don't forget to refer to the Mileage Adjustment Table at the back of this book!

 © 1999 by Edmund Publications Corporation

Model Description	Trade-in Value	Market Value

Power Windows[Std on R/T] +70
Premium Sound System[Std on R/T] +125
Rear Spoiler[Std on R/T] +85

1992 DODGE

CARAVAN 1992

Integrated child seats are a new option. Exterior door handles are flush-mounted, and new wheels debut.

RATINGS (SCALE OF 1-10)

Overall	Safety	Reliability	Performance	Comfort	Value
7	5.8	5.5	7.4	8.3	8.2

Category G	Trade-in Value	Market Value
2 Dr ES Pass. Van	4815	6595
2 Dr ES 4WD Pass. Van	5480	7510
2 Dr Grand Pass. Van	4020	5505
2 Dr Grand ES Pass. Van	5680	7780
2 Dr Grand ES 4WD Pass. Van	5980	8195
2 Dr Grand LE Pass. Van	5520	7565
2 Dr Grand LE 4WD Pass. Van	5815	7965
2 Dr Grand SE Pass. Van	4440	6080
2 Dr Grand SE 4WD Pass. Van	4825	6610
2 Dr LE Pass. Van	4715	6460
2 Dr LE 4WD Pass. Van	5475	7495
2 Dr SE Pass. Van	3615	4955
2 Dr SE 4WD Pass. Van	4410	6045
2 Dr STD Cargo Van Ext	2860	3920
2 Dr STD Cargo Van	2295	3140
2 Dr STD Pass. Van	3110	4265
2 Dr STD 4WD Cargo Van Ext	3700	5070
2 Dr STD 4WD Cargo Van	3020	4140

OPTIONS FOR CARAVAN

6 cyl 3.0 L Engine[Opt on SE,STD] +95
6 cyl 3.3 L Engine[Std on Grand ES,Grand LE,Grand SE,Cargo Van,4WD] +185
Auto 3-Speed Transmission[Opt on STD] +105
Auto 4-Speed Transmission[Std on ES,Grand ES,Grand LE,Grand SE,LE,4WD] +140
7 Passenger Seating[Opt on STD] +135
Air Conditioning[Opt on Grand,Grand SE,SE,STD] +200
Aluminum/Alloy Wheels[Std on ES,Grand ES] +85
AM/FM Compact Disc Playr +95
Anti-Lock Brakes +155
Captain Chairs (4) +155
Child Seats (2) +65
Cruise Control[Opt on Grand,Grand SE,SE,STD] +50
Dual Air Conditioning +250
Infinity Sound System +145
Leather Seats +190
Luggage Rack +40
Power Door Locks[Opt on Grand,Grand SE,SE,STD] +55
Power Drivers Seat +70
Power Windows[Opt on Grand SE,SE] +60

COLT 1992

GL models can be equipped with a digital clock, but all Colts lose options such as factory floor mats, intermittent wipers, wheel trim rings, and alloy wheels.

Category E	Trade-in Value	Market Value
2 Dr GL Hbk	2290	3575
2 Dr STD Hbk	1905	2975

OPTIONS FOR COLT

Auto 3-Speed Transmission +135
Air Conditioning +200
AM/FM Stereo Tape +75
Power Steering +60

DAKOTA 1992

V6 and V8 engines get more power. The V6 is up considerably, from 125 to 180 horsepower. V8 models add a whopping 65 horsepower and 30 lb./ft. of torque. Four-wheel drive models can be equipped with an optional Off-Road Appearance package.

RATINGS (SCALE OF 1-10)

Overall	Safety	Reliability	Performance	Comfort	Value
N/A	4.7	7.2	7	7.1	N/A

Category G	Trade-in Value	Market Value
2 Dr LE Std Cab SB	3895	5335
2 Dr LE Ext Cab SB	4855	6650
2 Dr LE Std Cab LB	4055	5560
2 Dr LE 4WD Ext Cab SB	5685	7785
2 Dr LE 4WD Std Cab SB	5215	7145
2 Dr LE 4WD Std Cab LB	5280	7235
2 Dr S Std Cab SB	3235	4430
2 Dr Sport Std Cab SB	3805	5210
2 Dr Sport Ext Cab SB	4705	6450
2 Dr Sport 4WD Ext Cab SB	5520	7565
2 Dr Sport 4WD Std Cab SB	4960	6795
2 Dr STD Std Cab SB	3525	4825
2 Dr STD Ext Cab SB	4450	6095
2 Dr STD Std Cab LB	3680	5040
2 Dr STD 4WD Ext Cab SB	5370	7355
2 Dr STD 4WD Std Cab SB	4870	6670
2 Dr STD 4WD Std Cab LB	4955	6785

OPTIONS FOR DAKOTA

6 cyl 3.9 L Engine +130
8 cyl 5.2 L Engine +205
Auto 4-Speed Transmission +215
Snow Plow Prep Pkg +185
Air Conditioning +200
Aluminum/Alloy Wheels[Std on Sport] +85
AM/FM Stereo Tape[Std on Sport] +60
Camper/Towing Package +70
Chrome Bumpers +40
Cruise Control +50
Limited Slip Diff +65

Don't forget to refer to the Mileage Adjustment Table at the back of this book!

 © 1999 by Edmund Publications Corporation

Model Description	Trade-in Value	Market Value

Power Door Locks +55
Power Steering[Std on Sport,4WD] +70
Power Windows +60
Premium Sound System +90
Rear Step Bumper[Std on Sport] +35

DAYTONA 1992

Front and rear styling is revised, unsuccessfully. ABS is a new option. Shelby model is replaced midyear by IROC R/T model, powered by a 224-horsepower 2.2-liter turbocharged engine and limited to a production run of 800 units.

Model Description	Trade-in Value	Market Value
Category C		
2 Dr ES Hbk	2870	4160
2 Dr STD Hbk	2510	3635
Category F		
2 Dr IROC Hbk	3950	5490
2 Dr IROC R/T Turbo Hbk	5260	7305

OPTIONS FOR DAYTONA

6 cyl 3.0 L Engine[Std on IROC] +170
Auto 3-Speed Transmission +135
Auto 4-Speed Transmission +155
Air Conditioning +200
Aluminum/Alloy Wheels[Opt on STD] +70
AM/FM Compact Disc Playr +95
Anti-Lock Brakes +155
Cruise Control +50
Power Door Locks +50
Power Drivers Seat[Std on IROC R/T] +60
Power Windows +55
Premium Sound System +100
Rear Spoiler[Opt on STD] +40
Sunroof +90
Tilt Steering Wheel +35

DYNASTY 1992

Child-proof door locks are added, and options include an overhead console with storage bin and console with cassette storage.

Model Description	Trade-in Value	Market Value
Category C		
4 Dr LE Sdn	3240	4695
4 Dr STD Sdn	2730	3955

OPTIONS FOR DYNASTY

6 cyl 3.0 L Engine[Std on LE] +125
6 cyl 3.3 L Engine +170
Air Conditioning +200
Aluminum/Alloy Wheels +70
AM/FM Stereo Tape +40
Cruise Control +50
Power Door Locks +60
Power Windows +75
Split Front Bench Seat[Std on LE] +50
Tilt Steering Wheel +35

MONACO 1992

No changes.

Model Description	Trade-in Value	Market Value
Category C		
4 Dr LE Sdn	1745	2525

OPTIONS FOR MONACO

Air Conditioning[Opt on LE] +200
Aluminum/Alloy Wheels +70
AM/FM Stereo Tape[Opt on LE] +40
Anti-Lock Brakes +155
Cruise Control +50
Power Door Locks +60
Power Drivers Seat +70
Power Windows +75
Premium Sound System +100

RAM 50 PICKUP 1992

The V6 engine, rear ABS, and extended-cab models are dropped from the lineup. Left are regular-cab trucks in 2WD or 4WD equipped with base or SE trim.

Model Description	Trade-in Value	Market Value
Category G		
2 Dr SE Std Cab SB	3015	4130
2 Dr SE Std Cab LB	2980	4080
2 Dr STD Std Cab SB	2745	3760
2 Dr STD Std Cab LB	2790	3820
2 Dr STD 4WD Std Cab SB	3800	5205

OPTIONS FOR RAM 50 PICKUP

Auto 4-Speed Transmission +170
Air Conditioning +200
AM/FM Stereo Tape +60
Chrome Wheels[Std on SE] +60
Limited Slip Diff +65
Power Steering[Std on SE,4WD] +70
Rear Step Bumper +35

RAM PICKUP 1992

Gasoline engines make more horsepower, and the Cummins Turbo Diesel engine is newly optional on Club Cab models. A one-ton duallie is introduced. Club Cabs have larger fuel tanks.

RAM 150

Model Description	Trade-in Value	Market Value
Category H		
2 Dr LE Ext Cab SB	6415	8330
2 Dr LE Std Cab SB	4465	5800
2 Dr LE Ext Cab LB	6510	8455
2 Dr LE Std Cab LB	4535	5885
2 Dr LE 4WD Std Cab SB	5690	7390
2 Dr LE 4WD Std Cab LB	5830	7570
2 Dr STD Std Cab SB	4360	5660
2 Dr STD Ext Cab SB	6360	8260
2 Dr STD Std Cab LB	4385	5695
2 Dr STD Ext Cab LB	6440	8365

Don't forget to refer to the Mileage Adjustment Table at the back of this book!

 © 1999 by Edmund Publications Corporation

Model Description	Trade-in Value	Market Value
2 Dr STD 4WD Std Cab SB	5490	7130
2 Dr STD 4WD Std Cab LB	5675	7365

RAM 250

Category H

Model Description	Trade-in Value	Market Value
2 Dr LE Std Cab LB	6495	8430
2 Dr LE 4WD Std Cab LB	6845	8890
2 Dr STD Std Cab LB	6030	7830
2 Dr STD 4WD Std Cab LB	6675	8670

RAM 350

Category H

Model Description	Trade-in Value	Market Value
2 Dr LE Turbodsl Ext Cab LB	7780	10105
2 Dr LE Turbodsl 4WD Ext Cab LB	9830	12765
2 Dr STD Turbodsl Ext Cab LB	7445	9670
2 Dr STD Turbodsl 4WD Ext Cab LB	9780	12705

OPTIONS FOR RAM PICKUP

6 cyl 5.9 L Turbodsl Engine +950
8 cyl 5.2 L Engine +110
8 cyl 5.9 L Engine +145
Auto 3-Speed Transmission +160
Auto 4-Speed Transmission +215
Snow Plow Prep Pkg +200
Air Conditioning +200
Aluminum/Alloy Wheels +75
AM/FM Stereo Tape +60
Camper/Towing Package +90
Cruise Control +50
Dual Rear Wheels[Opt on 4WD] +210
Limited Slip Diff +65
Power Door Locks +45
Power Windows +45
Premium Sound System +100
Rear Step Bumper +40

RAM VAN/WAGON 1992

Alloy wheels and moldings are revised, and two engines get an infusion of horsepower.

B150

Category H

Model Description	Trade-in Value	Market Value
2 Dr LE Ram Wagon	5495	7140
2 Dr STD Ram Van Ext	4980	6470
2 Dr STD Ram Van	4225	5485
2 Dr STD Ram Wagon	5060	6575

B250

Category H

Model Description	Trade-in Value	Market Value
2 Dr LE Ram Wagon Ext	6640	8625
2 Dr LE Maxi Ram Wagon Ext	6710	8715
2 Dr Maxi Ram Wagon Ext	6505	8445
2 Dr Maxi Ram Van Ext	5430	7050
2 Dr STD Ram Van	4930	6400
2 Dr STD Ram Van Ext	4995	6485
2 Dr STD Ram Wagon Ext	5810	7545

B350

Category H

Model Description	Trade-in Value	Market Value
2 Dr LE Ram Wagon Ext	5850	7595
2 Dr Maxi Ram Wagon Ext	6180	8030
2 Dr Maxi Ram Van Ext	5375	6980
2 Dr STD Ram Van Ext	4885	6345
2 Dr STD Ram Wagon Ext	5650	7335

OPTIONS FOR RAM VAN/WAGON

8 cyl 5.2 L Engine[Std on B350] +110
8 cyl 5.9 L Engine[Opt on B150,B250,B350] +145
Auto 3-Speed Transmission[Opt on B150,Ram Van, Ram Van Ext] +80
Auto 4-Speed Transmission +110
Travel Seating Pkg +225
Air Conditioning[Opt on B150,B250,Maxi,STD] +200
AM/FM Stereo Tape +60
Cruise Control[Opt on B150,B250,Maxi,STD] +50
Dual Air Conditioning +350
Limited Slip Diff +65
Power Door Locks[Opt on B150,B250,Maxi,STD] +45
Power Windows[Opt on B150,B250,Maxi,STD] +45

RAMCHARGER 1992

The 5.2-liter engine gains 50 horsepower, and manual transmissions have five speeds rather than four. A Canyon Sport trim level is available this year.

Category H

Model Description	Trade-in Value	Market Value
2 Dr Canyon Sport 4WD Utility	5975	7755
2 Dr LE 4WD Utility	5720	7430
2 Dr S 4WD Utility	5000	6495
2 Dr STD 4WD Utility	5380	6985

OPTIONS FOR RAMCHARGER

8 cyl 5.9 L Engine +110
Auto 4-Speed Transmission[Opt on 4WD] +215
Air Conditioning +200
Aluminum/Alloy Wheels +75
AM/FM Stereo Tape +60
Cruise Control +50
Limited Slip Diff +65
Power Door Locks +45
Power Windows +45
Velour/Cloth Seats +35

SHADOW 1992

ES model gets body-color bumpers. Midyear, the turbo engine found in the ES is swapped for a 3.0-liter V6.

RATINGS (SCALE OF 1-10)

Overall	Safety	Reliability	Performance	Comfort	Value
6.5	5.9	7.1	7.2	6.8	5.4

Category E

Model Description	Trade-in Value	Market Value
2 Dr America Hbk	1940	3030
4 Dr America Hbk	1970	3080
2 Dr ES Hbk	2495	3900
2 Dr ES Conv	2595	4055

Don't forget to refer to the Mileage Adjustment Table at the back of this book!

© 1999 by Edmund Publications Corporation

Model Description	Trade-in Value	Market Value
4 Dr ES Hbk	2510	3925
2 Dr Highline Conv	2425	3785
2 Dr Highline Hbk	2115	3305
4 Dr Highline Hbk	2210	3450

OPTIONS FOR SHADOW

4 cyl 2.5 L Engine[Std on ES,Conv] +70
6 cyl 3.0 L Engine +180
Auto 3-Speed Transmission +135
Auto 4-Speed Transmission +170
Air Conditioning +200
Aluminum/Alloy Wheels[Std on ES] +80
AM/FM Stereo Tape +75
Cruise Control +55
Power Door Locks +55
Power Drivers Seat +75
Power Windows +65
Premium Sound System +85
Sunroof +85

SPIRIT 1992

R/T gets revised gear ratios to make it accelerate faster, and revised suspension tuning to make it handle better. V6 models can be equipped with a three-speed automatic instead of a four-speed unit. Alloy wheels are restyled.

RATINGS (SCALE OF 1-10)

Overall	Safety	Reliability	Performance	Comfort	Value
7.1	6.1	7.5	6.8	7.4	7.8

Model Description	Trade-in Value	Market Value
Category C		
4 Dr ES Sdn	3085	4470
4 Dr LE Sdn	2830	4100
4 Dr STD Sdn	2360	3415

OPTIONS FOR SPIRIT

6 cyl 3.0 L Engine[Std on ES] +170
Auto 3-Speed Transmission[Std on LE] +135
Auto 4-Speed Transmission +115
Air Conditioning +200
Aluminum/Alloy Wheels[Opt on LE,STD] +70
AM/FM Stereo Tape[Opt on LE,STD] +40
Anti-Lock Brakes +155
Cruise Control[Opt on STD] +50
Power Door Locks +60
Power Drivers Seat +70
Power Windows +75
Premium Sound System +100

STEALTH 1992

A tilt/removable glass sunroof becomes available midyear.

RATINGS (SCALE OF 1-10)

Overall	Safety	Reliability	Performance	Comfort	Value
N/A	6.3	7.5	9.4	6.8	N/A

Model Description	Trade-in Value	Market Value
Category F		
2 Dr ES Hbk	5770	8010
2 Dr R/T Hbk	7165	9950
2 Dr R/T Turbo 4WD Hbk	8810	12235
2 Dr STD Hbk	5060	7025

OPTIONS FOR STEALTH

Auto 4-Speed Transmission +205
Air Conditioning[Std on R/T] +205
Aluminum/Alloy Wheels[Opt on STD] +75
Anti-Lock Brakes[Std on R/T] +180
Compact Disc W/fm/tape +130
Cruise Control[Std on R/T] +50
Leather Seats +175
Power Door Locks[Std on R/T] +50
Power Windows[Std on R/T] +55
Premium Sound System[Opt on ES] +100
Sunroof +95

1991 DODGE

CARAVAN 1991

Van is substantially reworked,-with new styling, new interior, available all-wheel drive, and optional ABS. A driver airbag is standard on models built after February 1, 1991. All models have an automatic transmission, and the turbocharged model has been dropped.

RATINGS (SCALE OF 1-10)

Overall	Safety	Reliability	Performance	Comfort	Value
7	5.3	5.3	7.4	8.3	8.6

Model Description	Trade-in Value	Market Value
Category G		
2 Dr ES Pass. Van	4090	5845
2 Dr ES 4WD Pass. Van	4235	6050
2 Dr Grand LE Pass. Van	4025	5750
2 Dr Grand LE 4WD Pass. Van	4830	6900
2 Dr Grand SE Pass. Van	3200	4570
2 Dr Grand SE 4WD Pass. Van	4060	5800
2 Dr LE Pass. Van	3930	5615
2 Dr LE 4WD Pass. Van	4280	6115
2 Dr SE Pass. Van	3045	4350
2 Dr SE 4WD Pass. Van	3450	4930
2 Dr STD Cargo Van Ext	2435	3480
2 Dr STD Pass. Van	2565	3665
2 Dr STD Cargo Van	2105	3010
2 Dr STD 4WD Cargo Van Ext	2865	4090
2 Dr STD 4WD Cargo Van	2280	3260

OPTIONS FOR CARAVAN

6 cyl 3.0 L Engine[Std on ES,Cargo Van Ext] +145
6 cyl 3.3 L Engine[Opt on ES,SE,LE,STD,Cargo Van Ext] +115
Auto 4-Speed Transmission[Std on ES,Grand LE,Grand SE,Cargo Van,Cargo Van Ext,4WD] +35
Luxury Package +190
Premium Decor Pkg +160

Don't forget to refer to the Mileage Adjustment Table at the back of this book!

© 1999 by Edmund Publications Corporation

Model Description	Trade-in Value	Market Value

7 Passenger Seating[Opt on STD] +110
Air Bag Restraint +100
Air Conditioning[Std on ES,Grand LE,LE] +165
Aluminum/Alloy Wheels[Std on ES] +70
AM/FM Stereo Tape +50
Anti-Lock Brakes +125
Captain Chairs (4) +130
Child Seats (2) +50
Cruise Control[Std on ES,Grand LE,LE] +45
Dual Air Conditioning +205
Leather Seats +155
Luggage Rack +30
Power Door Locks[Std on ES,Grand LE,LE] +45
Power Drivers Seat +55
Power Windows +50
Premium Sound System +75

COLT 1991

GT model dropped from lineup due to lack of interest.

Category E

Model Description	Trade-in Value	Market Value
2 Dr GL Hbk	1480	2510
2 Dr STD Hbk	1445	2450
4 Dr STD Wgn	2210	3745
4 Dr STD 4WD Wgn	2300	3900

OPTIONS FOR COLT

Auto 3-Speed Transmission +105
Air Conditioning +165
Aluminum/Alloy Wheels +65
AM/FM Stereo Tape +60
Cruise Control +45
Power Door Locks +45
Power Steering[Std on 4WD] +50
Power Windows +55

DAKOTA 1991

Base four-cylinder engine gets more horsepower. Club Cab can be ordered with four-wheel drive. Slow-selling convertible model is dropped from lineup. Front styling is freshened with composite headlamps (LE and Sport), new bumper, new grille, and extended sheetmetal to better accommodate the optional V8 engine. Exterior door handles are now metal instead of plastic. Front disc brake calipers are larger. Ignition and lock keys are double-sided.

RATINGS (SCALE OF 1-10)

Overall	Safety	Reliability	Performance	Comfort	Value
N/A	4.6	6.7	6.6	7.1	N/A

Category G

Model Description	Trade-in Value	Market Value
2 Dr LE Std Cab SB	3575	5110
2 Dr LE Ext Cab SB	3755	5365
2 Dr LE Std Cab LB	3655	5220
2 Dr LE 4WD Ext Cab SB	5150	7360
2 Dr LE 4WD Std Cab SB	4630	6615
2 Dr LE 4WD Std Cab LB	4685	6695
2 Dr S Std Cab SB	2805	4005
2 Dr SE Std Cab SB	3350	4785
2 Dr SE Ext Cab SB	3530	5045
2 Dr SE Std Cab LB	3400	4860
2 Dr SE 4WD Ext Cab SB	4830	6900
2 Dr SE 4WD Std Cab SB	4450	6355
2 Dr SE 4WD Std Cab LB	4510	6440
2 Dr Sport Std Cab SB	3795	5420
2 Dr Sport Ext Cab SB	3515	5020
2 Dr Sport Std Cab LB	3830	5470
2 Dr Sport 4WD Ext Cab SB	5490	7840
2 Dr Sport 4WD Std Cab SB	4600	6570
2 Dr Sport 4WD Std Cab LB	4905	7005
2 Dr STD Ext Cab SB	3420	4885
2 Dr STD Std Cab SB	3205	4580
2 Dr STD Std Cab LB	3280	4685
2 Dr STD 4WD Ext Cab SB	4785	6835
2 Dr STD 4WD Std Cab SB	4290	6130
2 Dr STD 4WD Std Cab LB	4475	6395

OPTIONS FOR DAKOTA

6 cyl 3.9 L Engine +105
8 cyl 5.2 L Engine +195
Auto 4-Speed Transmission +175
Snow Plow Prep Pkg +150
Air Conditioning +165
Aluminum/Alloy Wheels +70
AM/FM Stereo Tape +50
Camper/Towing Package +60
Cruise Control +45
Limited Slip Diff +55
Power Door Locks +45
Power Steering[Std on 4WD] +55
Power Windows +50
Premium Sound System +75
Rear Step Bumper +30

DAYTONA 1991

No changes.

Category C

Model Description	Trade-in Value	Market Value
2 Dr ES Hbk	2080	3195
2 Dr STD Hbk	1790	2750

OPTIONS FOR DAYTONA

6 cyl 3.0 L Engine[Std on IROC] +135
Auto 3-Speed Transmission +110
Auto 4-Speed Transmission +125
CS Competition Pkg +430
Air Conditioning +160
AM/FM Compact Disc Playr +80
Cruise Control +40
Leather Seats +115
Power Door Locks +50
Power Drivers Seat +60
Power Windows +60
Premium Sound System +80
Rear Spoiler[Opt on STD] +35

Don't forget to refer to the Mileage Adjustment Table at the back of this book!

 © 1999 by Edmund Publications Corporation

DYNASTY 1991

Remote keyless entry is a new option, available with a security system and illuminated entry in an option package. Door glass is thicker, and front suspensions are improved.

Category C

Model Description	Trade-in Value	Market Value
4 Dr LE Sdn	2420	3720
4 Dr STD Sdn	2005	3085

OPTIONS FOR DYNASTY

6 cyl 3.0 L Engine[Std on LE] +135
6 cyl 3.3 L Engine +125
Luxury Package +175
Air Conditioning +160
AM/FM Stereo Tape +35
Anti-Lock Brakes +125
Cruise Control +40
Dual Power Seats +115
Keyless Entry System +40
Leather Seats +115
Power Door Locks +50
Power Sunroof +140
Power Windows +60
Premium Sound System +80

MONACO 1991

No changes.

Category C

Model Description	Trade-in Value	Market Value
4 Dr ES Sdn	2250	3460
4 Dr LE Sdn	1750	2695

OPTIONS FOR MONACO

Air Conditioning[Opt on LE] +160
AM/FM Stereo Tape[Opt on LE] +35
Anti-Lock Brakes +125
Cruise Control +40
Keyless Entry System +40
Leather Seats +115
Power Door Locks +50
Power Drivers Seat +60
Power Windows +60
Premium Sound System +80

RAM 50 PICKUP 1991

Rear-wheel ABS is standard on top models. V6 engine is infused with additional power. Upholstery is revised.

Category G

Model Description	Trade-in Value	Market Value
2 Dr SE Std Cab SB	2820	4025
2 Dr STD Std Cab SB	2690	3840
2 Dr STD Std Cab LB	2770	3955

OPTIONS FOR RAM 50 PICKUP

Auto 4-Speed Transmission +135
Air Conditioning +165
AM/FM Stereo Tape +50
Bucket Seats[Opt on SE] +60
Chrome Wheels +50
Power Steering[Std on LE,4WD] +55
Rear Step Bumper[Std on LE] +30

RAM PICKUP 1991

New rear step bumper increases towing capacity from 3,000 to 5,000 pounds. An intercooler for turbodiesel models debuts midyear. Grille is revised, and Ram's-head hood ornament has been axed.

RAM 150

Category H

Model Description	Trade-in Value	Market Value
2 Dr LE Std Cab SB	3660	4945
2 Dr LE Ext Cab SB	4620	6245
2 Dr LE Std Cab LB	3770	5095
2 Dr LE Ext Cab LB	4550	6150
2 Dr LE 4WD Std Cab SB	5080	6865
2 Dr LE 4WD Std Cab LB	5170	6985
2 Dr S Std Cab SB	3365	4550
2 Dr S Std Cab LB	3475	4695
2 Dr S 4WD Std Cab SB	4735	6400
2 Dr S 4WD Std Cab LB	4830	6525
2 Dr SE Std Cab SB	3550	4795
2 Dr SE Std Cab LB	3655	4940
2 Dr SE 4WD Std Cab SB	4915	6645
2 Dr SE 4WD Std Cab LB	4975	6720
2 Dr STD Std Cab SB	3510	4745
2 Dr STD Ext Cab SB	4220	5700
2 Dr STD Ext Cab LB	4155	5620
2 Dr STD Std Cab LB	3620	4890
2 Dr STD 4WD Std Cab SB	4885	6600
2 Dr STD 4WD Std Cab LB	4970	6715

RAM 250

Category H

Model Description	Trade-in Value	Market Value
2 Dr LE Std Cab LB	5500	7435
2 Dr LE 4WD Std Cab LB	6415	8670
2 Dr SE Std Cab LB	5265	7115
2 Dr SE 4WD Std Cab LB	6305	8520
2 Dr STD Std Cab LB	5045	6815
2 Dr STD 4WD Std Cab LB	6265	8465

RAM 350

Category H

Model Description	Trade-in Value	Market Value
2 Dr LE Std Cab LB	6490	8770
2 Dr SE Std Cab LB	6045	8170
2 Dr STD Std Cab LB	5990	8095

OPTIONS FOR RAM PICKUP

6 cyl 5.9 L Turbodsl Engine +675
8 cyl 5.2 L Engine +105
8 cyl 5.9 L Engine +115
4-Speed Transmission +45
Auto 3-Speed Transmission +130
Auto 4-Speed Transmission +175
Snow Plow Pkg +210
Air Conditioning +165

Don't forget to refer to the Mileage Adjustment Table at the back of this book!

 © 1999 by Edmund Publications Corporation

Model Description	Trade-in Value	Market Value

Aluminum/Alloy Wheels +65
AM/FM Stereo Tape +50
Cruise Control +40
Dual Rear Wheels +170
Limited Slip Diff +50
Power Door Locks +35
Power Windows +40
Rear Step Bumper +30

RAM VAN/WAGON 1991

Cruise control buttons now located on steering wheel. A new air conditioning outlet next to the second rear seat of Wagons improves cooling.

B150

Category H

Model Description	Trade-in Value	Market Value
2 Dr LE Ram Wagon	3670	4960
2 Dr LE Ram Wagon Ext	4135	5590
2 Dr STD Ram Wagon	3415	4615
2 Dr STD Ram Van	2870	3875
2 Dr STD Ram Van Ext	2915	3940

B250

Category H

Model Description	Trade-in Value	Market Value
2 Dr LE Ram Wagon Ext	4160	5625
2 Dr LE Ram Wagon	4080	5515
2 Dr STD Ram Van	3185	4300
2 Dr STD Ram Van Ext	3255	4400
2 Dr STD Ram Wagon	3775	5100
2 Dr STD Ram Wagon Ext	3840	5190

B350

Category H

Model Description	Trade-in Value	Market Value
2 Dr LE Ram Wagon Ext	4445	6010
2 Dr LE Ram Wagon	4370	5905
2 Dr Maxi Ram Wagon Ext	4285	5790
2 Dr STD Ram Wagon Ext	4280	5780
2 Dr STD Ram Van	3610	4875
2 Dr STD Ram Wagon	4230	5715
2 Dr STD Ram Van Ext	3650	4930

OPTIONS FOR RAM VAN/WAGON

8 cyl 5.2 L Engine[Std on B350] +115
8 cyl 5.9 L Engine[Std on Maxi] +105
Auto 3-Speed Transmission[Opt on B150,Ram Van,Ram Van Ext] +65
Auto 4-Speed Transmission[Std on B350,B150 STD Ram Van Ext] +90
Travel Seating Pkg +250
Air Conditioning +165
AM/FM Stereo Tape +50
Captain Chairs (2) +110
Cruise Control +40
Dual Air Conditioning +290
Limited Slip Diff +50
Power Door Locks +35
Power Windows +40
Premium Sound System +80

RAMCHARGER 1991

Front styling is revised with a new grille and the exclusion of the Ram's head hood ornament. A stronger rear bumper provides more towing capacity. Models equipped with a manual transmission can be ordered with tilt steering.

Category H

Model Description	Trade-in Value	Market Value
2 Dr LE 4WD Utility	5170	6985
2 Dr S 4WD Utility	4410	5960
2 Dr STD 4WD Utility	5000	6755

OPTIONS FOR RAMCHARGER

8 cyl 5.9 L Engine +105
Auto 4-Speed Transmission[Opt on 4WD] +175
Snow Plow Pkg +195
Air Conditioning +165
Aluminum/Alloy Wheels +65
AM/FM Stereo Tape +50
Camper/Towing Package +70
Cruise Control +40
Limited Slip Diff +50
Power Door Locks +35
Power Windows +40
Premium Sound System +80

SHADOW 1991

A bargain-basement America model is introduced, and convertible body style is added to the lineup.

RATINGS (SCALE OF 1-10)

Overall	Safety	Reliability	Performance	Comfort	Value
6.4	5.8	6.3	7.4	6.8	5.8

Category E

Model Description	Trade-in Value	Market Value
2 Dr America Hbk	1525	2580
4 Dr America Hbk	1660	2815
2 Dr ES Hbk	1875	3180
2 Dr ES Conv	2465	4175
2 Dr ES Turbo Conv	2405	4080
4 Dr ES Hbk	2045	3470
2 Dr Highline Conv	2285	3875
2 Dr Highline Hbk	1655	2805
2 Dr Highline Turbo Conv	2210	3750
4 Dr Highline Hbk	1800	3055

OPTIONS FOR SHADOW

4 cyl 2.5 L Engine[Std on ES,Conv] +55
Auto 3-Speed Transmission +110
Air Conditioning +165
AM/FM Stereo Tape +60
Cruise Control +45
Power Door Locks +45
Power Drivers Seat +60
Power Windows[Std on Conv] +55
Sunroof +70

Don't forget to refer to the Mileage Adjustment Table at the back of this book!

 © 1999 by Edmund Publications Corporation

Model Description	Trade-in Value	Market Value

SPIRIT 1991

R/T trim level debuts with monochromatic paint scheme, sport-tuned suspension, 2.2-liter twin-cam turbocharged engine good for 224 horsepower, and 6.5 second zero-to-60 times. Four-wheel ABS is newly optional on all Spirit models.

RATINGS (SCALE OF 1-10)

Overall	Safety	Reliability	Performance	Comfort	Value
7.1	6	7.2	6.8	7.4	8.3

Category C

Model Description	Trade-in Value	Market Value
4 Dr ES Sdn	2445	3760
4 Dr ES Turbo Sdn	2680	4125
4 Dr LE Sdn	2260	3480
4 Dr LE Turbo Sdn	2630	4045
4 Dr R/T Turbo Sdn	3155	4855
4 Dr STD Sdn	1915	2945

OPTIONS FOR SPIRIT

6 cyl 3.0 L Engine[Std on ES] +135
Auto 3-Speed Transmission[Std on LE] +85
Auto 4-Speed Transmission +110
Air Conditioning[Std on R/T] +160
AM/FM Stereo Tape[Opt on LE,STD] +35
Anti-Lock Brakes +125
Cruise Control[Opt on STD] +40
Flip-Up Sunroof +75
Power Door Locks +50
Power Drivers Seat +60
Power Windows +60
Premium Sound System +80
Special Seats[Std on ES,LE,R/T] +60

STEALTH 1991

Brand-new sports car based on Mitsubishi 3000GT is available with front- or all-wheel drive. Four-wheel steering is standard with the all-wheel drive R/T Turbo model, powered by a twin-turbocharged 300-horsepower V6. Basic models have either a 164-horse SOHC V6 engine or a DOHC V6 making 222 horsepower.

RATINGS (SCALE OF 1-10)

Overall	Safety	Reliability	Performance	Comfort	Value
N/A	6.2	7.1	9.4	6.8	N/A

Category F

Model Description	Trade-in Value	Market Value
2 Dr ES Hbk	5135	7230
2 Dr R/T Hbk	6520	9180
2 Dr R/T Turbo 4WD Hbk	7240	10200
2 Dr STD Hbk	4455	6275

OPTIONS FOR STEALTH

Auto 4-Speed Transmission +160
Air Conditioning[Std on R/T] +170
Anti-Lock Brakes[Std on R/T] +145
Compact Disc W/fm/tape +105
Cruise Control[Std on R/T] +40
Leather Seats +145
Power Door Locks[Std on R/T] +40
Power Windows[Std on R/T] +45
Premium Sound System[Std on R/T] +85

1990 DODGE

CARAVAN 1990

All models get a 20-gallon fuel tank. New 3.3-liter V6 option is added to Grand Caravan engine lineup.

Category G

Model Description	Trade-in Value	Market Value
2 Dr ES Pass. Van	2695	4080
2 Dr ES Turbo Pass. Van	2625	3975
2 Dr Grand LE Pass. Van	2915	4415
2 Dr Grand SE Pass. Van	2545	3855
2 Dr LE Pass. Van	2580	3910
2 Dr LE Turbo Pass. Van	2560	3880
2 Dr SE Pass. Van	2170	3285
2 Dr SE Turbo Pass. Van	2045	3100
2 Dr STD Cargo Van Ext	1880	2850
2 Dr STD Cargo Van	1710	2590
2 Dr STD Pass. Van	1950	2960
2 Dr STD Turbo Pass. Van	1925	2915

OPTIONS FOR CARAVAN

6 cyl 3.0 L Engine[Std on ES] +145
6 cyl 3.3 L Engine[Opt on STD] +195
Auto 3-Speed Transmission +95
Auto 4-Speed Transmission[Opt on ES,LE,SE,STD] +120
Royal Pkg +195
Sun Roof Pkg +135
7 Passenger Seating[Opt on SE,STD] +90
Air Conditioning[Std on ES,Grand LE,LE] +135
Aluminum/Alloy Wheels[Std on ES] +55
AM/FM Stereo Tape +40
Cruise Control[Std on ES,Grand LE,LE] +35
Dual Air Conditioning +165
Leather Seats +125
Power Door Locks[Std on ES,Grand LE,LE] +40
Power Drivers Seat[Std on LE] +45
Power Sunroof +135
Power Windows[Std on ES,Grand LE,LE] +40
Premium Sound System +60

COLT 1990

Outstanding GT model loses turbocharged engine. To compensate, a 1.6-liter twin-cam has been installed in the GT, making 113 horsepower. That's 22 fewer ponies than in 1989. Other changes include a switch from E to GL trim for the midrange hatchback. Vista 4WD system is now full-time rather than part-time. Vista body-side moldings and the grille have fresh appearance.

Don't forget to refer to the Mileage Adjustment Table at the back of this book!

 © 1999 by Edmund Publications Corporation

Model Description	Trade-in Value	Market Value
Category E		
4 Dr DL Wgn	1735	3335
4 Dr DL 4WD Wgn	1835	3530
2 Dr GL Hbk	1020	1960
2 Dr GT Hbk	1355	2605
2 Dr STD Hbk	900	1735
4 Dr STD Wgn	1480	2845
4 Dr STD 4WD Wgn	1770	3400

OPTIONS FOR COLT

Auto 3-Speed Transmission +85
Auto 4-Speed Transmission +110
Performance Pkg +250
Sport Appearance Package +135
Air Conditioning +135
Aluminum/Alloy Wheels +50
AM/FM Stereo Tape +50
Cruise Control +35
Power Door Locks +40
Power Steering[Std on 4WD] +40
Power Windows +45

DAKOTA 1990

Big news is the addition of an extended-cab model. Base, SE, LE, and Sport versions of new Club Cab are available. Shelby model dropped from lineup, while convertible availability expands to base trim.

RATINGS (SCALE OF 1-10)

Overall	Safety	Reliability	Performance	Comfort	Value
N/A	4.7	6.9	6.6	7.1	N/A

Model Description	Trade-in Value	Market Value
Category G		
2 Dr LE Ext Cab SB	3000	4545
2 Dr LE Std Cab SB	2530	3835
2 Dr LE Std Cab LB	2635	3990
2 Dr LE 4WD Std Cab SB	3160	4790
2 Dr LE 4WD Std Cab LB	3210	4865
2 Dr S Std Cab SB	2365	3585
2 Dr SE Ext Cab SB	2905	4405
2 Dr SE Std Cab SB	2510	3800
2 Dr SE Std Cab LB	2575	3905
2 Dr SE 4WD Std Cab SB	3035	4600
2 Dr SE 4WD Std Cab LB	3110	4710
2 Dr Sport Ext Cab SB	3075	4655
2 Dr Sport Std Cab SB	2800	4240
2 Dr Sport 4WD Std Cab SB	3425	5185
2 Dr Sport Convertible 4WD Std Cab SB	3825	5795
2 Dr STD Std Cab SB	2400	3635
2 Dr STD Ext Cab SB	2810	4260
2 Dr STD Std Cab LB	2405	3645
2 Dr STD 4WD Std Cab SB	2990	4530
2 Dr STD 4WD Std Cab LB	3060	4640

OPTIONS FOR DAKOTA

6 cyl 3.9 L Engine +85
Auto 4-Speed Transmission +140
Air Conditioning +135
Aluminum/Alloy Wheels +55
AM/FM Stereo Tape[Opt on LE,S,SE,STD] +40
Camper/Towing Package +50
Cruise Control +35
Limited Slip Diff +45
Power Door Locks +40
Power Steering[Std on Convertible,4WD] +45
Power Windows +40
Premium Sound System +60

DAYTONA 1990

Top-shelf Turbo II engine replaced by Turbo IV, which utilizes a variable-nozzle turbine to reduce turbo lag. Manual transmission has been reworked to provide less shift lever travel and easier use. Optional on base and ES models is a Mitsubishi-built V6 engine. Instrument panel is completely revised.

Model Description	Trade-in Value	Market Value
Category C		
2 Dr ES Hbk	1595	2615
2 Dr ES Turbo Hbk	1770	2900
2 Dr STD Hbk	1530	2510
2 Dr STD Turbo Hbk	1600	2625
Category F		
2 Dr Shelby Turbo Hbk	2280	3305

OPTIONS FOR DAYTONA

6 cyl 3.0 L Engine +110
Auto 3-Speed Transmission +70
Auto 4-Speed Transmission +105
CS Performance Pkg +195
Air Conditioning +130
Aluminum/Alloy Wheels[Opt on STD] +50
Cruise Control +35
Leather Seats +95
Power Door Locks +35
Power Drivers Seat +40
Power Windows +35
Premium Sound System +65
Sunroof +60
T-Tops (solid/Colored) +155

DYNASTY 1990

Driver airbag debuts. A new 3.3-liter V6 engine is available. New options include an automatic day/night mirror, and leather seating for LE models. Power windows can have a one-touch down feature for the driver's side, and bumpers are upgraded to withstand five-mph impacts. Outboard rear seat passengers are treated to three-point seatbelts.

Model Description	Trade-in Value	Market Value
Category C		
4 Dr LE Sdn	1940	3185
4 Dr STD Sdn	1735	2840

Don't forget to refer to the Mileage Adjustment Table at the back of this book!

 © 1999 by Edmund Publications Corporation

Model Description	Trade-in Value	Market Value

OPTIONS FOR DYNASTY

6 cyl 3.0 L Engine[Std on LE] +100
6 cyl 3.3 L Engine +110
Air Conditioning +130
Aluminum/Alloy Wheels +50
Anti-Lock Brakes +105
Cruise Control +35
Leather Seats +95
Power Door Locks +40
Power Drivers Seat +45
Power Passenger Seat +45
Power Sunroof +115
Power Windows +50

MONACO 1990

New model is virtually identical to Eagle Premier. LS and ES trim levels are available, with ES including four-wheel disc brakes, touring suspension and alloy wheels. An automatic is the only transmission choice.

Category C

Model Description	Trade-in Value	Market Value
4 Dr ES Sdn	1700	2785
4 Dr LE Sdn	1425	2335

OPTIONS FOR MONACO

Air Conditioning[Opt on LE] +130
Aluminum/Alloy Wheels +50
Cruise Control +35
Keyless Entry System +30
Leather Seats +95
Power Door Locks +40
Power Drivers Seat +45
Power Passenger Seat +45
Power Sunroof +115
Power Windows +50
Premium Sound System +65

OMNI 1990

A driver airbag is added to this ancient econocar. Production finally ceased midyear.

Category E

Model Description	Trade-in Value	Market Value
4 Dr America Hbk	770	1480

OPTIONS FOR OMNI

Air Conditioning +135
AM/FM Stereo Tape +50
Power Steering +40
Rally Wheels +45

RAM 50 PICKUP 1990

Sport trim becomes SE, while extended-cabs are now known as Sport Cabs. A V6 engine is newly standard on 4WD models.

Category G

Model Description	Trade-in Value	Market Value
2 Dr SE Std Cab SB	2145	3245
2 Dr STD Std Cab SB	1980	3000

OPTIONS FOR RAM 50 PICKUP

Auto 4-Speed Transmission +115
Air Conditioning +135
AM/FM Stereo Tape +40
Chrome Wheels +40
Cruise Control +35
Power Door Locks +40
Power Steering[Std on LE,4WD] +45
Power Windows +40

RAM PICKUP 1990

Finally, an extended-cab model is available in D150 and D250 series. D100 trucks dropped from the lineup.

RAM 150

Category H

Model Description	Trade-in Value	Market Value
2 Dr LE Ext Cab SB	3750	5210
2 Dr LE Std Cab SB	3170	4400
2 Dr LE Std Cab LB	3170	4400
2 Dr LE Ext Cab LB	3815	5300
2 Dr LE 4WD Std Cab SB	4120	5720
2 Dr LE 4WD Std Cab LB	4200	5835
2 Dr LE 4WD Ext Cab LB	4330	6010
2 Dr S Std Cab SB	2570	3570
2 Dr S Std Cab LB	2840	3945
2 Dr S 4WD Std Cab SB	3925	5455
2 Dr S 4WD Std Cab LB	3990	5540
2 Dr SE Std Cab SB	3060	4245
2 Dr SE Std Cab LB	3125	4340
2 Dr SE 4WD Std Cab SB	4100	5695
2 Dr SE 4WD Std Cab LB	4145	5755
2 Dr STD Ext Cab SB	3490	4850
2 Dr STD Std Cab SB	3030	4210
2 Dr STD Ext Cab LB	3510	4875
2 Dr STD Std Cab LB	2890	4015
2 Dr STD 4WD Std Cab SB	4005	5565
2 Dr STD 4WD Std Cab LB	4070	5650
2 Dr STD 4WD Ext Cab LB	4225	5870

RAM 250

Category H

Model Description	Trade-in Value	Market Value
2 Dr LE Std Cab LB	3810	5295
2 Dr LE 4WD Ext Cab LB	5510	7650
2 Dr LE 4WD Std Cab LB	4690	6515
2 Dr SE Std Cab LB	3740	5190
2 Dr SE 4WD Std Cab LB	4620	6420
2 Dr STD Std Cab LB	3605	5010
2 Dr STD 4WD Ext Cab LB	5185	7200
2 Dr STD 4WD Std Cab LB	4570	6350

RAM 350

Category H

Model Description	Trade-in Value	Market Value
2 Dr LE Std Cab LB	4920	6830
2 Dr SE Std Cab LB	4850	6740
2 Dr STD Std Cab LB	4790	6650

Don't forget to refer to the Mileage Adjustment Table at the back of this book!

 © 1999 by Edmund Publications Corporation

Model Description	Trade-in Value	Market Value

OPTIONS FOR RAM PICKUP

6 cyl 5.9 L Turbodsl Engine +535
8 cyl 5.2 L Engine +90
8 cyl 5.9 L Engine +90
4-Speed Transmission[Opt on] +35
Auto 3-Speed Transmission +105
Auto 4-Speed Transmission +140
Snow Plow Prep Pkg +165
Air Conditioning +135
Aluminum/Alloy Wheels +50
AM/FM Stereo Tape +40
Cruise Control +30
Dual Rear Wheels +140
Limited Slip Diff +40
Power Door Locks +30
Power Windows +30
Premium Sound System +65

RAM VAN/WAGON 1990

Prospector trim dropped, as well as Value Wagon and Long Range Ram Van models.

B150

Category H

Model Description	Trade-in Value	Market Value
2 Dr LE Ram Wagon	2870	3990
2 Dr STD Ram Van	2170	3015
2 Dr STD Ram Wagon	2265	3145
2 Dr STD Ram Van Ext	2280	3170

B250

Category H

Model Description	Trade-in Value	Market Value
2 Dr LE Ram Wagon Ext	3550	4930
2 Dr LE Ram Wagon	3180	4415
2 Dr STD Ram Wagon Ext	2985	4150
2 Dr STD Ram Wagon	2920	4055
2 Dr STD Ram Van	2830	3930
2 Dr STD Ram Van Ext	3120	4335

B350

Category H

Model Description	Trade-in Value	Market Value
2 Dr LE Ram Wagon Ext	4020	5585
2 Dr STD Ram Wagon Ext	3860	5360
2 Dr STD Ram Van	3135	4355
2 Dr STD Ram Van Ext	3260	4530
2 Dr STD Ram Wagon	3620	5030

OPTIONS FOR RAM VAN/WAGON

8 cyl 5.2 L Engine[Std on B350] +90
8 cyl 5.9 L Engine +90
Auto 3-Speed Transmission[Opt on B150 ,B250] +55
Auto 4-Speed Transmission[Std on B350] +65
Travel Seating Pkg +205
Air Conditioning +135
Aluminum/Alloy Wheels +50
AM/FM Stereo Tape +40
Cruise Control +30
Dual Air Conditioning +235
Limited Slip Diff +40
Power Door Locks +30
Power Windows +30
Premium Sound System +65

RAMCHARGER 1990

Base 100-series model is replaced by a 150-series S trim level. Prospector trim package dropped.

Category H

Model Description	Trade-in Value	Market Value
2 Dr LE 4WD Utility	3775	5245
2 Dr S 4WD Utility	2945	4090
2 Dr STD 4WD Utility	3690	5125

OPTIONS FOR RAMCHARGER

8 cyl 5.9 L Engine +90
Auto 4-Speed Transmission[Opt on 4WD] +140
Snow Plow Pkg-Ramcharger +160
Air Conditioning +135
Aluminum/Alloy Wheels +50
AM/FM Stereo Tape +40
Camper/Towing Package +60
Cruise Control +30
Limited Slip Diff +40
Power Door Locks +30
Power Windows +30
Premium Sound System +65

SHADOW 1990

A driver airbag is installed. An optional Turbo IV engine with variable-nozzle turbine pumps 174 horsepower to Shadow ES's front axle. Manual transmissions have been redesigned.

RATINGS (SCALE OF 1-10)

Overall	Safety	Reliability	Performance	Comfort	Value
6.6	5.5	6.6	7.4	6.8	6.8

Category E

Model Description	Trade-in Value	Market Value
2 Dr ES Hbk	1280	2455
2 Dr ES Turbo Hbk	1420	2730
4 Dr ES Hbk	1375	2645
4 Dr ES Turbo Hbk	1570	3025
2 Dr STD Hbk	1200	2305
2 Dr STD Turbo Hbk	1225	2350
4 Dr STD Hbk	1335	2570
4 Dr STD Turbo Hbk	1545	2975

OPTIONS FOR SHADOW

4 cyl 2.5 L Engine +45
4 cyl 2.5 L Turbo Engine +130
Auto 3-Speed Transmission +90
Competition Pkg +165
Air Conditioning +135
Aluminum/Alloy Wheels[Std on ES] +50
AM/FM Stereo Tape[Std on ES] +50
Cruise Control +35
Power Door Locks +40
Power Drivers Seat +50

Don't forget to refer to the Mileage Adjustment Table at the back of this book!

 © 1999 by Edmund Publications Corporation

Power Windows +45
Premium Sound System +55
Sunroof +55

SPIRIT 1990

Base models can be equipped with V6 power. A driver airbag is newly standard. ES model gets four-wheel disc brakes and more sound insulation.

RATINGS (SCALE OF 1-10)

Overall	Safety	Reliability	Performance	Comfort	Value
7	5.5	6.9	6.8	7.4	8.2

Category C

Model Description	Trade-in Value	Market Value
4 Dr ES Sdn	1945	3190
4 Dr ES Turbo Sdn	2010	3295
4 Dr LE Sdn	1615	2645
4 Dr LE Turbo Sdn	1755	2875
4 Dr STD Sdn	1565	2565
4 Dr STD Turbo Sdn	1595	2615

OPTIONS FOR SPIRIT

6 cyl 3.0 L Engine[Std on ES] +110
Auto 3-Speed Transmission +95
Auto 4-Speed Transmission +105
Air Conditioning +130
Aluminum/Alloy Wheels[Std on ES] +50
Cruise Control[Opt on STD] +35
Power Door Locks +40
Power Drivers Seat +45
Power Windows +50
Premium Sound System +65
Sunroof +60

1989 DODGE

ARIES 1989

Wagon dropped from lineup. 2.5-liter engine picks up four additional horsepower. Underhood service points are brightly marked this year to make them easy to find, probably because you'll need to find them often. Stereo system now has four speakers.

Category C

Model Description	Trade-in Value	Market Value
2 Dr America Sdn	835	1470
4 Dr America Sdn	885	1550

OPTIONS FOR ARIES

4 cyl 2.5 L Engine +40
Auto 3-Speed Transmission +75
Air Conditioning +110
Cruise Control +30
Power Door Locks +30
Power Steering +35

CARAVAN 1989

A turbocharged engine is an option on SE and LE models, teamed with either a five-speed manual or a three-speed automatic transmission. A four-speed automatic transmission debuts, only available with the 3.0-liter V6 Grand Caravan. Also new is a four-speed automatic, only available with the optional 3.0-liter V6. Dodge Dynasty suspension components supposedly reduce ride harshness. LE's can now be equipped with leather seating, and higher-line models also get an optional power motor to close the rear vent windows. Air conditioning is made standard on LE. SE and LE get a power liftgate release standard. The optional gauge package now includes a tachometer.

Category G

Model Description	Trade-in Value	Market Value
2 Dr ES Turbo Pass. Van	1805	2955
2 Dr Grand LE Pass. Van	2110	3460
2 Dr Grand SE Pass. Van	1900	3115
2 Dr Grand SE Turbo Pass. Van	1825	2990
2 Dr LE Pass. Van	1820	2980
2 Dr LE Turbo Pass. Van	1765	2890
2 Dr SE Pass. Van	1760	2885
2 Dr SE Turbo Pass. Van	1630	2675
2 Dr STD Cargo Van Ext	1555	2550
2 Dr STD Pass. Van	1495	2450
2 Dr STD Cargo Van	1230	2020
2 Dr STD Turbo Pass. Van	1290	2120

OPTIONS FOR CARAVAN

6 cyl 3.0 L Engine[Std on ES,Grand LE] +135
Auto 3-Speed Transmission +75
Auto 4-Speed Transmission[Std on Grand LE] +100
Luxury Package +250
Royal Decor Pkg +115
Turbo Sport Pkg +140
7 Passenger Seating[Opt on ES,LE,SE,STD] +75
Air Conditioning[Std on ES,Grand LE,LE] +110
AM/FM Stereo Tape +35
Cruise Control +30
Dual Air Conditioning +135
Electric Sunroof +95
Power Door Locks +30
Power Drivers Seat +40
Power Sunroof +110
Power Windows +30
Premium Sound System +50
Woodgrain Applique[Opt on Grand LE,Non-Turbo Models] +45

COLT 1989

Hatchback is completely redesigned, and wagon is carried over with a new full-time 4WD version available. Sedan model is dropped. Hatchback comes in base, E, and turbocharged GT trim. GT uses a twin-cam turbo

 © 1999 by Edmund Publications Corporation

Model Description	Trade-in Value	Market Value

engine making 135 horsepower. Base and E have an 81-horsepower 1.5-liter engine. Four-wheel drive Wagon has an 87-horsepower 1.8-liter motor. On the Vista, rear outboard passengers get shoulder safety belts, and the optional power windows have a new express-down feature.

Category E

Model Description	Trade-in Value	Market Value
4 Dr DL Wgn	965	2195
4 Dr DL 4WD Wgn	1300	2955
2 Dr E Hbk	660	1500
2 Dr GT Hbk	800	1815
2 Dr GT Turbo Hbk	815	1855
2 Dr STD Hbk	600	1365
4 Dr STD Wgn	800	1820
4 Dr STD 4WD Wgn	1080	2455
4 Dr Vista Wgn	940	2140
4 Dr Vista 4WD Wgn	1110	2520

OPTIONS FOR COLT

Auto 3-Speed Transmission +65
Air Conditioning +110
Aluminum/Alloy Wheels +45
AM/FM Stereo Tape +40
Cruise Control +30
Power Door Locks +30
Power Steering[Std on 4WD] +35
Power Windows +35
Premium Sound System +45

DAKOTA 1989

A convertible edition of the Sport model is introduced, and is available in two- or four-wheel drive. The gauge package has been made standard. New SE decor package includes wheel covers, bright trim, cloth interior, and dual mirrors. Shelby performance model introduced midyear with V8 power.

RATINGS (SCALE OF 1-10)

Overall	Safety	Reliability	Performance	Comfort	Value
N/A	4.7	6.7	6.6	7.1	N/A

Category G

Model Description	Trade-in Value	Market Value
2 Dr LE Std Cab SB	2040	3345
2 Dr LE Std Cab LB	2170	3560
2 Dr LE 4WD Std Cab SB	2960	4850
2 Dr LE 4WD Std Cab LB	3010	4935
2 Dr S Std Cab SB	2105	3450
2 Dr SE Std Cab SB	2010	3295
2 Dr SE Std Cab LB	2125	3480
2 Dr SE 4WD Std Cab SB	2850	4675
2 Dr SE 4WD Std Cab LB	2955	4845
2 Dr Shelby Std Cab SB	4015	6585
2 Dr Sport Std Cab SB	2515	4120
2 Dr Sport 4WD Std Cab SB	3130	5130
2 Dr Sport Convertible Std Cab SB	3075	5040
2 Dr Sport Convertible 4WD Std Cab SB	3475	5695
2 Dr STD Std Cab SB	1990	3265
2 Dr STD Std Cab LB	1995	3270
2 Dr STD 4WD Std Cab SB	2685	4400
2 Dr STD 4WD Std Cab LB	2910	4770

OPTIONS FOR DAKOTA

6 cyl 3.9 L Engine +65
Auto 4-Speed Transmission[Std on Shelby] +110
Air Conditioning[Std on Shelby] +110
Aluminum/Alloy Wheels[Opt on LE,SE,STD] +45
AM/FM Stereo Tape[Opt on LE,S,SE,STD] +35
Camper/Towing Package +40
Cruise Control +30
Limited Slip Diff[Std on Shelby] +35
Power Door Locks[Std on Sport Convertble] +30
Power Steering[Std on Shelby,Sport Convertble, 4WD] +40
Power Windows[Std on Sport Convertble] +30

DAYTONA 1989

New front and rear styling freshens the exterior, and all models get four-wheel disc brakes standard. Pacifica model becomes ES. Driver airbag added as standard equipment late in 1988. ES Turbo has new 150-horsepower 2.5-liter engine. Shelby model loses the Z suffix and gets a trick new paint scheme. Shelby also gets new alloy wheels. Order T-tops and you'll be treated to a new interior sunshade. Want to go fast on the cheap? Order a base model with the C/S Competition Package, which includes lots of Shelby performance bits but sheds 200 pounds off Shelby's weight.

Model Description	Trade-in Value	Market Value
Category C		
2 Dr ES Hbk	1215	2135
2 Dr STD Hbk	960	1680
2 Dr STD Turbo Hbk	1010	1770
Category F		
2 Dr ES Turbo Hbk	1480	2210
2 Dr Shelby Turbo Hbk	1900	2835

OPTIONS FOR DAYTONA

Auto 3-Speed Transmission +60
CS Competition Pkg +250
Air Conditioning +110
Aluminum/Alloy Wheels[Opt on STD] +40
Cruise Control +30
Leather Seats +95
Power Drivers Seat +30
Power Windows +30
Premium Sound System +55
Sunroof +50
T-Tops (solid/Colored) +125

Don't forget to refer to the Mileage Adjustment Table at the back of this book!

 © 1999 by Edmund Publications Corporation

Model Description	Trade-in Value	Market Value

DIPLOMAT 1989

No changes for final year.

Category C

4 Dr Salon Sdn	895	1575

OPTIONS FOR DIPLOMAT

Air Conditioning[Std on SE] +110
Cruise Control[Std on SE] +30
Power Door Locks +30
Power Drivers Seat +40
Power Windows +40
Wire Wheel Covers +30

DYNASTY 1989

Take "Dy" from the name and what do you have? Exactly. For 1989, Dynasty has more power and a new four-speed automatic transmission. ABS is optional. New options this year include six-way power driver's seat with memory and an anti-theft system ... like you'll need it.

Category C

4 Dr LE Sdn	1675	2940
4 Dr STD Sdn	1630	2860

OPTIONS FOR DYNASTY

6 cyl 3.0 L Engine[Std on LE] +95
Air Conditioning +110
Aluminum/Alloy Wheels +40
Anti-Lock Brakes +85
Cruise Control +30
Power Door Locks +30
Power Drivers Seat +40
Power Passenger Seat +35
Power Sunroof +95
Power Windows +40
Premium Sound System +55

LANCER 1989

Shelby package becomes production trim level.

Category C

4 Dr ES Turbo Hbk	1150	2020

OPTIONS FOR LANCER

Auto 3-Speed Transmission +75
Sport Appearance Package +130
Air Conditioning[Opt on STD] +110
Aluminum/Alloy Wheels[Opt on STD] +40
Cruise Control[Opt on ES,STD] +30
Leather Seats[Opt on ES] +80
Power Door Locks[Opt on STD] +30
Power Drivers Seat[Opt on ES,STD] +40
Power Sunroof +95
Power Windows[Opt on ES,STD] +40

OMNI 1989

2.2-liter engine gets modifications designed to make it run quieter. Underhood service points are brightly marked for easy visibility.

Category E

4 Dr America Hbk	545	1235

OPTIONS FOR OMNI

Auto 3-Speed Transmission +65
Air Conditioning +110
AM/FM Stereo Tape +40
Power Steering +35

RAIDER 1989

A 141-horsepower V6 is a new option. Black front trim is added around the grille and headlights, and the optional rear seat now folds down or tips up for added flexibility. Get the rear seat and you'll get new shoulder belts for outboard passengers. Interior door panels and front seats are new, and front passengers can view themselves in the new visor vanity mirror. Ordering the V6 qualifies you for optional power windows, power locks and cruise control.

Category G

2 Dr STD 4WD Utility	2865	4695

OPTIONS FOR RAIDER

6 cyl 3.0 L Engine +135
Auto 4-Speed Transmission +100
Air Conditioning +110
Aluminum/Alloy Wheels +45
AM/FM Stereo Tape +35
Power Door Locks +30
Power Windows +30

RAM 100 PICKUP 1989

Rear-wheel ABS is added. 5.2-liter V8 gets 17 percent boost in horsepower this year, and other engines are also improved with the addition of electronic fuel injection.

Category H

2 Dr STD Std Cab SB	2475	3585
2 Dr STD Std Cab LB	2495	3615

OPTIONS FOR RAM 100 PICKUP

8 cyl 5.2 L Engine +75
4-Speed Transmission[Std on 4WD] +30
Auto 3-Speed Transmission +85
Auto 4-Speed Transmission +110
Air Conditioning +110
AM/FM Stereo Tape +35
Camper/Towing Package +50
Limited Slip Diff +35

RAM 50 PICKUP 1989

Sport model has new monochromatic paint treatment.

Category G

2 Dr Custom Std Cab LB	2005	3290
2 Dr Sport Std Cab SB	1595	2615
2 Dr STD Std Cab SB	1485	2440
2 Dr STD Ext Cab SB	2395	3925

Don't forget to refer to the Mileage Adjustment Table at the back of this book!

 © 1999 by Edmund Publications Corporation

Model Description	Trade-in Value	Market Value
2 Dr STD Std Cab LB	1940	3175
2 Dr STD 4WD Std Cab SB	2165	3555
2 Dr STD 4WD Std Cab LB	2200	3610

OPTIONS FOR RAM 50 PICKUP

Auto 4-Speed Transmission +95
Air Conditioning +110
Aluminum/Alloy Wheels +45
AM/FM Stereo Tape +35
Chrome Wheels[Std on Sport] +30
Limited Slip Diff +35
Power Steering[Std on Sport,4WD] +40
Premium Sound System +50

RAM PICKUP 1989

Rear-wheel ABS is added. A duallie model is introduced midyear. Those who want to tow heavy loads will want to consider the new 5.9-liter Cummins Turbo Diesel engine. It makes 160 horsepower at 2,500 rpm and 400 lb./ft. of torque at 1,700 rpm. 5.2-liter V8 gets 17 percent boost in horsepower this year, and other engines are also improved with the addition of electronic fuel injection.

RAM 150

Category H

Model Description	Trade-in Value	Market Value
2 Dr LE Std Cab SB	2670	3870
2 Dr LE Std Cab LB	2695	3910
2 Dr LE 4WD Std Cab SB	3400	4930
2 Dr LE 4WD Std Cab LB	3440	4985
2 Dr STD Std Cab SB	2430	3525
2 Dr STD Std Cab LB	2465	3570
2 Dr STD 4WD Std Cab SB	3335	4835
2 Dr STD 4WD Std Cab LB	3385	4905

RAM 250

Category H

Model Description	Trade-in Value	Market Value
2 Dr LE Std Cab LB	3080	4465
2 Dr LE 4WD Std Cab LB	3915	5675
2 Dr STD Std Cab LB	3025	4385
2 Dr STD 4WD Std Cab LB	3930	5700

RAM 350

Category H

Model Description	Trade-in Value	Market Value
2 Dr LE Std Cab LB	4140	6000

OPTIONS FOR RAM PICKUP

6 cyl 5.9 L Turbodsl Engine +310
8 cyl 5.2 L Engine +70
8 cyl 5.9 L Engine +75
4-Speed Transmission[Std on RAM 250,RAM 350, 4WD] +30
Auto 3-Speed Transmission +85
Auto 4-Speed Transmission +110
Prospector Package +235
Air Conditioning +110
AM/FM Stereo Tape +35
Dual Rear Wheels +115
Limited Slip Diff +35
Premium Sound System +55

RAM VAN/WAGON 1989

New B150 Value and Long Range vans are added to lineup.

B150

Category H

Model Description	Trade-in Value	Market Value
2 Dr STD Ram Van	1650	2395
2 Dr STD Ram Wagon	1965	2845
2 Dr STD Ram Wagon Ext	2020	2925

B250

Category H

Model Description	Trade-in Value	Market Value
2 Dr LE Ram Wagon Ext	3165	4590
2 Dr LE Ram Wagon	2985	4325
2 Dr STD Ram Van Ext	2520	3655
2 Dr STD Ram Van	1990	2885
2 Dr STD Ram Wagon Ext	2615	3790
2 Dr STD Ram Wagon	2405	3485

B350

Category H

Model Description	Trade-in Value	Market Value
2 Dr LE Ram Wagon Ext	3055	4425
2 Dr STD Ram Van	2605	3775
2 Dr STD Ram Van Ext	2655	3845
2 Dr STD Ram Wagon Ext	2950	4275
2 Dr STD Ram Wagon	2820	4090

OPTIONS FOR RAM VAN/WAGON

8 cyl 5.2 L Engine[Std on B350,B150, Ram Van Ext] +70
8 cyl 5.9 L Engine +75
Auto 3-Speed Transmission +40
Prospector Package +230
Seat/Bed Combination +165
Aluminum/Alloy Wheels +40
AM/FM Stereo Tape +35
Camper/Towing Package +50
Dual Air Conditioning +190
Limited Slip Diff +35
Premium Sound System +55

RAMCHARGER 1989

Engines get electronic fuel injection. Gas-charged shock absorbers are added. A new stereo system bows.

Category H

Model Description	Trade-in Value	Market Value
2 Dr D150 LE Utility	2370	3435
2 Dr W100 4WD Utility	3080	4460
2 Dr W150 4WD Utility	3250	4715
2 Dr W150 LE 4WD Utility	3335	4835

OPTIONS FOR RAMCHARGER

8 cyl 5.9 L Engine +70
Auto 3-Speed Transmission[Opt on W100,W150] +85
Prospector Package +225
Air Conditioning +110
Aluminum/Alloy Wheels +40

Don't forget to refer to the Mileage Adjustment Table at the back of this book!

 © 1999 by Edmund Publications Corporation

Model Description	Trade-in Value	Market Value

AM/FM Stereo Tape +35
Camper/Towing Package +50
Limited Slip Diff +35

SHADOW 1989

New body-color grille is added to all Shadows, and flush headlamps replace the former recessed lights. Rear outboard passengers get shoulder belts, and redesigned front seats result in more rear leg room. Shadow ES gets new 150-horsepower turbo engine and revised alloys. A six-way power driver's seat is a new option. Five new colors debut. ES suspension altered to provide better handling. Want ES performance but not ES price? Get a base Shadow equipped with the new Competition Package.

RATINGS (SCALE OF 1-10)

Overall	Safety	Reliability	Performance	Comfort	Value
6.3	4.4	6.1	7.4	6.8	6.7

Category E		
2 Dr STD Hbk	780	1770
2 Dr STD Turbo Hbk	820	1860
4 Dr STD Hbk	835	1900
4 Dr STD Turbo Hbk	885	2015

OPTIONS FOR SHADOW

4 cyl 2.5 L Engine +40
Auto 3-Speed Transmission +75
Air Conditioning +110
Aluminum/Alloy Wheels +45
AM/FM Stereo Tape +40
Cruise Control +30
Power Door Locks +30
Power Drivers Seat +40
Power Windows +35
Premium Sound System +45
Rear Spoiler +30
Sunroof +45

SPIRIT 1989

All-new sedan replaces Dodge 600. Base engine is 100-horsepower 2.5-liter four; optional is a 150-horsepower turbocharged version of the same engine. Base, LE, and ES trim are available, with ES carrying the turbo motor standard. Optional on ES only is a 141-horsepower V6. LE and ES have a standard split-folding rear seat.

RATINGS (SCALE OF 1-10)

Overall	Safety	Reliability	Performance	Comfort	Value
N/A	N/A	6.8	6.8	7.4	8.1

Category C		
4 Dr ES Sdn	1715	3015
4 Dr ES Turbo Sdn	1575	2765
4 Dr LE Sdn	1240	2180
4 Dr LE Turbo Sdn	1315	2310
4 Dr STD Sdn	1180	2070
4 Dr STD Turbo Sdn	1280	2250

OPTIONS FOR SPIRIT

Auto 3-Speed Transmission +75
Auto 4-Speed Transmission +85
Air Conditioning +110
Aluminum/Alloy Wheels[Std on ES] +40
Cruise Control[Opt on STD] +30
Power Door Locks +30
Power Drivers Seat +40
Power Windows +40
Premium Sound System +55
Sunroof +50

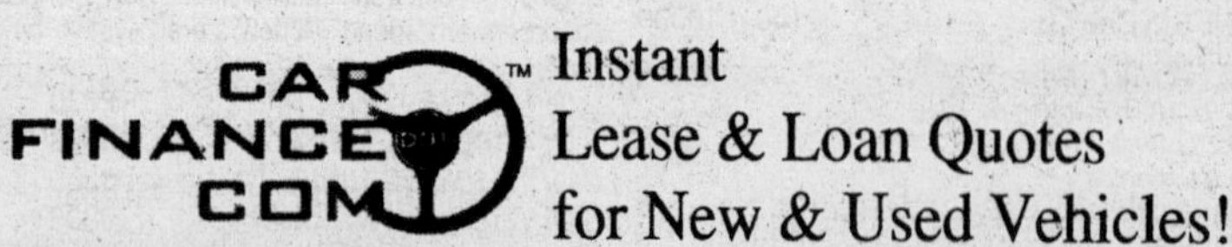

CAR
FINANCE
COM
Instant
Lease & Loan Quotes
for New & Used Vehicles!
www.CarFinance.com/edmunds

Don't forget to refer to the Mileage Adjustment Table at the back of this book!

© 1999 by Edmund Publications Corporation

EAGLE USA

1993 Eagle Talon

1998 EAGLE

TALON 1998

Eagle is in its final year of production. New silver exterior badging is an appearance aid, as is the new black and gray interior. A new four-speaker CD/cassette player is now optional on the ESi, and all Talons benefit from Chrysler's next generation depowered airbags.

Category F

Model	Trade-in	Market
2 Dr ESi Hbk	10755	13115
2 Dr STD Hbk	10620	12950

OPTIONS FOR TALON

Auto 4-Speed Transmission +620
Air Conditioning +690
Aluminum/Alloy Wheels[Opt on ESi] +260
AM/FM Compact Disc Playr +410
Anti-Lock Brakes +600
Cruise Control[Std on 4WD] +175
Keyless Entry System +145
Power Door Locks[Std on 4WD] +165
Power Mirrors[Opt on ESi] +100
Power Sunroof +565
Power Windows[Std on 4WD] +185
Rear Window Defroster[Std on TSi] +135

1997 EAGLE

TALON 1997

Eagle's sporty Talon sees a host of changes as Chrysler Corp. seeks to rescue this endangered species. New front and rear fascias, bodyside cladding, bright new paint colors and "sparkle" wheels and wheel covers are guaranteed to attract attention to this overshadowed model. A bargain-basement Talon is introduced with minimal standard equipment to serve as a value leader for the model.

RATINGS (SCALE OF 1-10)

Overall	Safety	Reliability	Performance	Comfort	Value
6.9	6.8	7.9	8.4	6.6	5

Category F

Model	Trade-in	Market
2 Dr ESi Hbk	9325	11370
2 Dr STD Hbk	9050	11035
2 Dr TSi Turbo Hbk	10220	12465
2 Dr TSi Turbo 4WD Hbk	12290	14990

OPTIONS FOR TALON

Auto 4-Speed Transmission +535
Air Conditioning +565
Aluminum/Alloy Wheels[Opt on ESi] +210
Anti-Lock Brakes +490
Compact Disc W/fm/tape +355
Cruise Control[Std on 4WD] +140
Keyless Entry System +120
Leather Seats +485
Limited Slip Diff +255
Power Door Locks[Std on 4WD] +135
Power Drivers Seat +160
Power Sunroof +465
Power Windows[Std on 4WD] +150
Premium Sound System +280

VISION 1997

The 3.5-liter engine currently exclusive to the TSi is now available on the ESi. Automatic transmission refinements are intended to improve shifting. Eagle Vision ESis gets an improved stereo. A new color, Deep Amethyst Pearl, is now available.

RATINGS (SCALE OF 1-10)

Overall	Safety	Reliability	Performance	Comfort	Value
8.3	7.2	8.3	8.4	8.5	8.9

Category B

Model	Trade-in	Market
4 Dr ESi Sdn	10185	12425
4 Dr TSi Sdn	12270	14965

OPTIONS FOR VISION

Anti-Lock Brakes[Opt on ESi] +485
Compact Disc W/fm/tape +265
Keyless Entry System[Opt on ESi] +120
Leather Seats +450
Lighted Entry System[Opt on ESi] +70
Power Drivers Seat +205
Power Moonroof +675
Trip Computer[Opt on ESi] +145

Don't forget to refer to the Mileage Adjustment Table at the back of this book!

 © 1999 by Edmund Publications Corporation

1996 EAGLE

TALON 1996

Based on Mitsubishi mechanicals, Talon receives minor upgrades for 1996, including revised sound systems, a panic alarm, a HomeLink transmitter, and two new colors. ESi trim level gets standard 16-inch wheels.

RATINGS (SCALE OF 1-10)

Overall	Safety	Reliability	Performance	Comfort	Value
6.8	6.8	7.8	8.4	6.6	4.5

Category F	Trade-in Value	Market Value
2 Dr ESi Hbk	8030	10035
2 Dr STD Hbk	7690	9615
2 Dr TSi Turbo Hbk	9345	11680
2 Dr TSi Turbo 4WD Hbk	10180	12725

OPTIONS FOR TALON

Auto 4-Speed Transmission +425
Air Conditioning +460
Aluminum/Alloy Wheels +170
Anti-Lock Brakes +400
Compact Disc W/fm/tape +290
Cruise Control[Std on 4WD] +115
Leather Seats +395
Power Door Locks[Std on 4WD] +110
Power Drivers Seat +130
Power Sunroof +380
Power Windows[Std on 4WD] +125

VISION 1996

An automanual transmission called AutoStick gives the 1996 Vision a feature to distinguish it as Chrysler's premier sport sedan. Interiors have been quieted down, and the ESi gets standard 16-inch wheels. Headlight illumination has been improved, new colors and seat fabrics are on board, and improved sound systems debut; all in the hope that some interest can be sparked in this slow-selling Eagle.

RATINGS (SCALE OF 1-10)

Overall	Safety	Reliability	Performance	Comfort	Value
8.2	7.2	8.2	8.4	8.5	8.8

Category B	Trade-in Value	Market Value
4 Dr ESi Sdn	9180	11475
4 Dr TSi Sdn	10555	13190

OPTIONS FOR VISION

Anti-Lock Brakes[Opt on ESi] +395
Child Seat (1) +55
Compact Disc W/fm/tape +220
Keyless Entry System[Opt on ESi] +100
Leather Seats +370
Power Drivers Seat[Opt on ESi] +165
Power Moonroof +550
Premium Sound System +235

1995 EAGLE

SUMMIT 1995

Dual airbags for the slow-selling Eagle Summit are the only changes for 1995.

RATINGS (SCALE OF 1-10)

Overall	Safety	Reliability	Performance	Comfort	Value
6.6	6.5	7.2	8.2	7	4.2

Category E	Trade-in Value	Market Value
2 Dr DL Cpe	4445	6085
4 Dr DL Wgn	5940	8135
2 Dr ESi Cpe	4590	6290
4 Dr ESi Sdn	5730	7850
4 Dr LX Sdn	5615	7690
4 Dr LX Wgn	6060	8300

OPTIONS FOR SUMMIT

4 cyl 1.8 L Engine[Opt on Cpe] +290
4 cyl 2.4 L Engine[Opt on DL Wgn] +80
Auto 3-Speed Transmission +235
Auto 4-Speed Transmission +315
Air Conditioning +370
AM/FM Stereo Tape +140
Anti-Lock Brakes +320
Cruise Control +100
Keyless Entry System +65
Luggage Rack +60
Power Door Locks[Std on LX] +105
Power Steering[Opt on Cpe] +115
Power Windows +120
Tilt Steering Wheel[Opt on ESi] +70
Tutone Paint[Std on LX] +65

TALON 1995

The Talon is redesigned for 1995. The new model features gorgeous curves and more power. Base engine creeps up to 140 horsepower, the turbo to 210 horsepower. Dual airbags replace the antiquated motorized seat belts on the previous edition, and the Talon now meets 1997 federal side-impact standards.

RATINGS (SCALE OF 1-10)

Overall	Safety	Reliability	Performance	Comfort	Value
6.8	7.5	7.7	8.4	6.6	3.9

Category F	Trade-in Value	Market Value
2 Dr ESi Hbk	6590	8450
2 Dr TSi Turbo Hbk	8000	10255
2 Dr TSi Turbo 4WD Hbk	8870	11370

OPTIONS FOR TALON

Auto 4-Speed Transmission +365
Air Conditioning +380
Anti-Lock Brakes +330
Compact Disc W/fm/tape +240

Don't forget to refer to the Mileage Adjustment Table at the back of this book!

 © 1999 by Edmund Publications Corporation

Model Description	Trade-in Value	Market Value

Cruise Control[Std on 4WD] +95
Keyless Entry System +80
Leather Seats +325
Power Door Locks[Std on 4WD] +90
Power Drivers Seat +110
Power Sunroof +310
Power Windows[Std on 4WD] +100

VISION 1995

No changes to the Vision.

RATINGS (SCALE OF 1-10)

Overall	Safety	Reliability	Performance	Comfort	Value
8.2	7.9	7.7	8.4	8.5	8.6

Category B		
4 Dr ESi Sdn	7475	9585
4 Dr TSi Sdn	8805	11285

OPTIONS FOR VISION

6 cyl 3.5 L Engine[Opt on ESi] +325
AM/FM Compact Disc Playr +140
Anti-Lock Brakes[Opt on ESi] +325
Child Seat (1)[Opt on TSi] +45
Climate Control for AC[Opt on ESi] +80
Keyless Entry System[Opt on ESi] +80
Leather Seats +300
Power Drivers Seat[Opt on ESi] +135
Power Moonroof +450
Power Passenger Seat +140
Traction Control System +80

1994 EAGLE

SUMMIT 1994

A driver airbag is added to the standard equipment list of the Eagle Summit. CFC-free air conditioning is now standard on all models equipped with air conditioning. Power steering is standard on all sedan models.

RATINGS (SCALE OF 1-10)

Overall	Safety	Reliability	Performance	Comfort	Value
N/A	N/A	7.1	8.2	7	4.6

Category E		
2 Dr DL Cpe	2825	4035
4 Dr DL Wgn	4560	6515
2 Dr ES Cpe	3205	4580
4 Dr ES Sdn	3875	5540
2 Dr ESi Cpe	3260	4660
4 Dr ESi Sdn	4045	5780
4 Dr LX Sdn	3505	5005
4 Dr LX Wgn	4925	7035

OPTIONS FOR SUMMIT

4 cyl 2.4 L Engine[Opt on DL] +65
Auto 3-Speed Transmission +190
Auto 4-Speed Transmission +250
Air Conditioning +300
AM/FM Stereo Tape +115
Anti-Lock Brakes +265
Cruise Control +80
Keyless Entry System +55
Luggage Rack +50
Power Door Locks[Std on LX] +85
Power Steering[Opt on ES Cpe] +95
Power Windows +100
Tilt Steering Wheel[Opt on ES,ESi] +55

TALON 1994

No changes for the Talon.

RATINGS (SCALE OF 1-10)

Overall	Safety	Reliability	Performance	Comfort	Value
N/A	N/A	7.8	8.4	6.8	3.9

Category F		
2 Dr DL Hbk	4685	6165
2 Dr ES Hbk	5530	7275
2 Dr TSi Turbo Hbk	6330	8330
2 Dr TSi Turbo 4WD Hbk	6805	8955

OPTIONS FOR TALON

Auto 4-Speed Transmission +290
Air Conditioning +310
Aluminum/Alloy Wheels[Std on 4WD] +115
Anti-Lock Brakes +270
Compact Disc W/fm/tape +195
Cruise Control +80
Leather Seats +265
Power Door Locks +75
Power Steering[Opt on DL] +135
Power Windows +85
Premium Sound System +150
Sunroof +145

VISION 1994

ESi models restyled to resemble their TSi stablemates by adding body cladding and a similar front fascia. The ESi's engine gains an increase in horsepower for 1994 as well. A flexible fuel version of the Vision is released in all states but California.

RATINGS (SCALE OF 1-10)

Overall	Safety	Reliability	Performance	Comfort	Value
8.1	7.9	7.4	8.4	8.5	8.5

Category B		
4 Dr ESi Sdn	6135	8180
4 Dr TSi Sdn	6865	9150

OPTIONS FOR VISION

AM/FM Compact Disc Playr +115
Child Seat (1) +35
Climate Control for AC[Opt on ESi] +65
Infinity Sound System +240
Leather Seats +245
Lighted Entry System +35
Overhead Console[Opt on ESi] +145

Don't forget to refer to the Mileage Adjustment Table at the back of this book!

 © 1999 by Edmund Publications Corporation

Model Description	Trade-in Value	Market Value

Power Drivers Seat[Opt on ESi] +110
Power Passenger Seat +115
Traction Control System +65

1993 EAGLE

SUMMIT 1993

The Eagle Summit is redesigned and in the process loses its hatchback. Offered as a coupe or sedan, the new Summit is longer than the one it replaces which translates into more interior room for passengers. The Summit is now available as a base DL or upscale ES. Fortunately, the 113-horsepower engine can be had on both models. Antilock brakes are a thoughtful option on the ES models and wagons. The minivan/station wagon hybrid is positioned to take advantage of those consumers who want the convenience of a minivan and the driveability of a car. There is seating for five in the Summit Wagon which is available as a DL, LX, or all-wheel drive model.

RATINGS (SCALE OF 1-10)

Overall	Safety	Reliability	Performance	Comfort	Value
N/A	N/A	7	8.2	7	6.6

Category E	Trade-in Value	Market Value
2 Dr DL Cpe	2375	3545
4 Dr DL Sdn	3025	4515
4 Dr DL Wgn	3555	5305
2 Dr ES Cpe	2710	4045
4 Dr ES Sdn	3305	4935
4 Dr LX Wgn	3745	5590

OPTIONS FOR SUMMIT

4 cyl 1.8 L Engine[Std on ES,Wgn] +115
4 cyl 2.4 L Engine[Opt on DL Wgn] +55
Auto 3-Speed Transmission +155
Auto 4-Speed Transmission +210
Air Conditioning +245
Aluminum/Alloy Wheels +95
AM/FM Stereo Tape +95
Anti-Lock Brakes +215
Cruise Control +65
Luggage Rack +40
Power Door Locks +70
Power Steering[Opt on ES,Sdn] +75
Power Windows +80
Tilt Steering Wheel[Opt on ES] +45

TALON 1993

The Talon gets a new base model to attract bargain shoppers. The new Talon DL comes standard with a disappointing 92-horsepower engine. Geez, that's just a little more than the base Summit. The former base model is renamed the ES.

RATINGS (SCALE OF 1-10)

Overall	Safety	Reliability	Performance	Comfort	Value
N/A	N/A	7.7	8.4	6.8	4.4

Category F	Trade-in Value	Market Value
2 Dr DL Hbk	3885	5180
2 Dr ES Hbk	4560	6080
2 Dr TSi Turbo Hbk	5500	7330
2 Dr TSi Turbo 4WD Hbk	6020	8030

OPTIONS FOR TALON

Auto 4-Speed Transmission +240
Air Conditioning +250
Aluminum/Alloy Wheels[Std on 4WD] +95
Anti-Lock Brakes +220
Compact Disc W/fm/tape +160
Cruise Control +65
Leather Seats +215
Power Door Locks +60
Power Steering[Opt on DL] +110
Power Windows +70
Premium Sound System +125
Sunroof +120

VISION 1993

Eagle receives its version of the Chrysler LH sedan in the form of the Vision. Available as an ESi or TSi, the Vision features cab-forward styling, dual airbags, V6 power, and available antilock brakes. TSi models are the sportier of the two, it comes equipped with a touring suspension, standard antilock brakes, a 214-horsepower engine, and sixteen-inch wheels.

RATINGS (SCALE OF 1-10)

Overall	Safety	Reliability	Performance	Comfort	Value
7.9	7.8	6.8	8.4	8.5	7.9

Category B	Trade-in Value	Market Value
4 Dr ESi Sdn	4815	6595
4 Dr TSi Sdn	5710	7820

OPTIONS FOR VISION

AM/FM Compact Disc Playr +95
Anti-Lock Brakes[Opt on ESi] +215
Child Seat (1) +30
Climate Control for AC[Opt on ESi] +55
Cruise Control[Opt on ESi] +65
Dual Power Seats +110
Keyless Entry System +55
Leather Seats +200
Power Door Locks[Opt on ESi] +75
Power Windows +90
Premium Sound System +125
Traction Control System +55

Don't forget to refer to the Mileage Adjustment Table at the back of this book!

 © 1999 by Edmund Publications Corporation

1992 EAGLE

PREMIER 1992

Exterior tweaks to the Premier include a new grille, tail lights and new paint.

Category C

Model	Trade-in Value	Market Value
4 Dr ES Sdn	2475	3585
4 Dr ES Limited Sdn	3200	4640
4 Dr LX Sdn	2055	2980

OPTIONS FOR PREMIER

Aluminum/Alloy Wheels[Opt on ES,LX] +70
Anti-Lock Brakes[Opt on ES,LX] +155
Compact Disc W/fm/tape +90
Cruise Control[Opt on LX] +50
Keyless Entry System +45
Leather Seats[Opt on ES] +145
Lighted Entry System +40
Power Door Locks[Opt on LX] +60
Power Drivers Seat[Opt on ES,LX] +70
Power Windows[Opt on ES,LX] +75
Premium Sound System[Opt on ES,LX] +100

SUMMIT 1992

Cloth seats are now optional on base models for those who don't like the adhesive quality imparted by vinyl seats in the summer.

Category E

Model	Trade-in Value	Market Value
4 Dr DL Wgn	2970	4640
2 Dr ES Hbk	2350	3675
4 Dr ES Sdn	2565	4010
4 Dr LX Wgn	3095	4840
2 Dr STD Hbk	2095	3270
4 Dr STD Sdn	2325	3635
4 Dr STD 4WD Wgn	3245	5070

OPTIONS FOR SUMMIT

4 cyl 2.4 L Engine +45
Auto 3-Speed Transmission +135
Auto 4-Speed Transmission +170
Air Conditioning +200
Aluminum/Alloy Wheels +80
AM/FM Stereo Tape +75
Anti-Lock Brakes +175
Cruise Control +55
Luggage Rack +30
Power Door Locks +55
Power Steering[Opt on STD Sdn] +60
Power Windows +65

TALON 1992

The Talon is redesigned for 1992, getting a new grille, headlights, taillights and sheetmetal.

RATINGS (SCALE OF 1-10)

Overall	Safety	Reliability	Performance	Comfort	Value
N/A	N/A	7.5	8.4	6.8	3.3

Category F

Model	Trade-in Value	Market Value
2 Dr STD Hbk	3565	4950
2 Dr TSi Turbo Hbk	4100	5695
2 Dr TSi Turbo 4WD Hbk	4640	6440

OPTIONS FOR TALON

Auto 4-Speed Transmission +195
Air Conditioning +205
Aluminum/Alloy Wheels[Std on 4WD] +75
Anti-Lock Brakes +180
Compact Disc W/fm/tape +130
Cruise Control +50
Leather Seats +175
Power Door Locks +50
Power Windows +55
Premium Sound System +100
Sunroof +95

1991 EAGLE

PREMIER 1991

No changes for the Premier.

Category C

Model	Trade-in Value	Market Value
4 Dr ES Sdn	2335	3595
4 Dr ES Limited Sdn	2945	4530
4 Dr LX Sdn	1890	2910

OPTIONS FOR PREMIER

Aluminum/Alloy Wheels[Opt on ES,LX] +60
AM/FM Compact Disc Playr +80
Anti-Lock Brakes[Opt on ES,LX] +125
Cruise Control[Opt on LX] +40
Keyless Entry System[Opt on ES,LX] +40
Leather Seats[Opt on ES] +115
Lighted Entry System +35
Power Door Locks[Opt on LX] +50
Power Drivers Seat[Opt on ES,LX] +60
Power Windows[Opt on ES,LX] +60
Premium Sound System[Opt on ES,LX] +80
Trip Computer +40

SUMMIT 1991

No changes to the Summit.

Category E

Model	Trade-in Value	Market Value
2 Dr ES Hbk	1380	2340
4 Dr ES Sdn	1705	2885
2 Dr STD Hbk	1340	2270
4 Dr STD Sdn	1515	2570

OPTIONS FOR SUMMIT

Auto 3-Speed Transmission +110
Auto 4-Speed Transmission +135
Air Conditioning +165
Aluminum/Alloy Wheels +65

Don't forget to refer to the Mileage Adjustment Table at the back of this book!

 © 1999 by Edmund Publications Corporation

Model Description	Trade-in Value	Market Value

AM/FM Stereo Tape +60
Cruise Control +45
Power Door Locks +45
Power Steering[Opt on STD,Hbk] +50
Power Windows +55
Rear Spoiler +40

TALON 1991

Antilock brakes are now available on the Talon.

RATINGS (SCALE OF 1-10)

Overall	Safety	Reliability	Performance	Comfort	Value
N/A	N/A	7.3	8.4	6.8	4.3

Category F

Model Description	Trade-in Value	Market Value
2 Dr STD Hbk	2985	4205
2 Dr TSi Turbo Hbk	3375	4750
2 Dr TSi Turbo 4WD Hbk	3720	5235

OPTIONS FOR TALON

Auto 4-Speed Transmission +155
Air Conditioning +170
Aluminum/Alloy Wheels[Std on 4WD] +65
Anti-Lock Brakes +145
Cruise Control +40
Leather Seats +145
Power Door Locks +40
Power Windows +45
Premium Sound System +85
Sunroof +80

1990 EAGLE

PREMIER 1990

The Premier's enthusiast-oriented ES model is introduced in 1990. Noticeably missing on this alleged sports sedan is a manual transmission. A power sunroof and CD player are added to the Premier's option list.

Category C

Model Description	Trade-in Value	Market Value
4 Dr ES Sdn	1525	2505
4 Dr ES Limited Sdn	1895	3105
4 Dr LX Sdn	1250	2055

OPTIONS FOR PREMIER

Air Conditioning[Opt on LX] +130
Aluminum/Alloy Wheels[Opt on ES,LX] +50
AM/FM Compact Disc Playr +65
Cruise Control[Opt on ES,LX] +35
Leather Seats[Opt on ES] +95
Power Door Locks[Opt on ES,LX] +40
Power Drivers Seat[Opt on ES,LX] +45
Power Passenger Seat[Opt on ES,LX] +45
Power Windows[Opt on ES,LX] +50
Premium Sound System[Opt on ES,LX] +65
Trip Computer[Opt on LX] +30

SUMMIT 1990

An ES sport model is added to the Summit line-up, as is a truly inexpensive base model. The LX model's three-speed automatic is replaced by a four-speed this year. All automatics get a shift-lock feature that prevents the car from being shifted out of "Park" unless the brake pedal is fully depressed.

Category E

Model Description	Trade-in Value	Market Value
4 Dr DL Sdn	1125	2160
4 Dr ES Sdn	1190	2285
4 Dr STD Sdn	945	1815

OPTIONS FOR SUMMIT

Auto 3-Speed Transmission +85
Auto 4-Speed Transmission +115
Air Conditioning +135
Aluminum/Alloy Wheels +50
AM/FM Stereo Tape +50
Cruise Control +35
Power Door Locks +40
Power Steering[Opt on DL,STD] +40
Power Windows +45
Premium Sound System +55

TALON 1990

A cool new sports coupe is offered through Eagle: it's called the Talon. Available with a turbo or normally aspirated engine, this little rocket redefines the inexpensive sports coupe. Available all-wheel drive and 190-horsepower distinguish the Talon from nearly everything else in this segment.

RATINGS (SCALE OF 1-10)

Overall	Safety	Reliability	Performance	Comfort	Value
N/A	N/A	7.3	8.4	6.8	5.8

Category F

Model Description	Trade-in Value	Market Value
2 Dr STD Hbk	2580	3740
2 Dr TSi Turbo Hbk	2960	4290
2 Dr TSi Turbo 4WD Hbk	3175	4600

OPTIONS FOR TALON

Auto 4-Speed Transmission +115
Air Conditioning +140
Aluminum/Alloy Wheels +50
AM/FM Compact Disc Playr +80
Cruise Control +35
Leather Seats +120
Power Door Locks +35
Power Windows +35
Premium Sound System +70

Don't forget to refer to the Mileage Adjustment Table at the back of this book!

 © 1999 by Edmund Publications Corporation

1989 EAGLE

MEDALLION 1989

The French-built Medallion gets a redesigned dashboard.

Category C

4 Dr DL Sdn	980	1715
4 Dr LX Sdn	1015	1785

OPTIONS FOR MEDALLION

Auto 3-Speed Transmission[Opt on Sdn] +65
Air Conditioning +110
Aluminum/Alloy Wheels +40
Cruise Control +30
Power Door Locks +30
Power Sunroof +95
Power Windows +40
Premium Sound System +55

PREMIER 1989

Premiers with five-passenger seating get a floor-mounted shift lever.

Category C

4 Dr ES Sdn	1230	2160
4 Dr ES Limited Sdn	1490	2615
4 Dr LX Sdn	1215	2135

OPTIONS FOR PREMIER

6 cyl 3.0 L Engine[Opt on LX] +95
Air Conditioning[Opt on ES,LX] +110
Aluminum/Alloy Wheels[Opt on ES,LX] +40
Cruise Control[Opt on ES,LX] +30
Leather Seats[Opt on ES] +80
Power Door Locks[Opt on ES,LX] +30
Power Drivers Seat[Opt on ES,LX] +40
Power Passenger Seat[Opt on ES,LX] +35
Power Windows[Opt on ES,LX] +40
Premium Sound System[Opt on ES,LX] +55

SUMMIT 1989

This Diamond Star subcompact bows as Eagle's bargain-basement entry. Available as a base DL or uplevel LX, the Summit comes standard with an 81-horsepower four-cylinder engine. A performance package is available for the LX model that features a 113-horsepower DOHC inline-four, a sport suspension and four-wheel disc brakes.

Category E

4 Dr DL Sdn	825	1875
4 Dr LX Sdn	1050	2385

OPTIONS FOR SUMMIT

Auto 3-Speed Transmission +70
Auto 4-Speed Transmission +90
DOHC Package +110
Air Conditioning +110
Aluminum/Alloy Wheels +45
AM/FM Stereo Tape +40
Cruise Control +30
Power Door Locks +30
Power Steering[Opt on DL] +35
Power Windows +35
Premium Sound System +45

Edmund's Town Hall

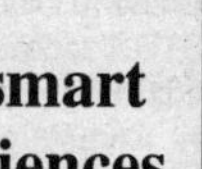

Get answers from our editors, scope out smart shopping strategies and share your experiences in our new talk area. Just enter the following address in your web browser:

http://townhall.edmunds.com

Don't forget to refer to the Mileage Adjustment Table at the back of this book!

 © 1999 by Edmund Publications Corporation

Model Description	Trade-in Value	Market Value

FORD USA

1997 Ford F-150

1998 FORD

CLUB WAGON/ECONOLINE 1998

New interior and exterior packages appear on the Club Wagon and Econoline vans.

E-150

Category H

Model Description	Trade-in Value	Market Value
2 Dr Chateau Club Wagon	20040	23575
2 Dr STD Econoline	14285	16805
2 Dr XL Club Wagon	17445	20525
2 Dr XLT Club Wagon	17695	20815

E-250

Category H

Model Description	Trade-in Value	Market Value
2 Dr STD Econoline	15210	17895
2 Dr STD Econoline Ext	17050	20060

E-350

Category H

Model Description	Trade-in Value	Market Value
2 Dr Chateau Club Wagon	21710	25540
2 Dr STD Econoline	17810	20950
2 Dr STD Econoline Ext	18785	22100
2 Dr XL Club Wagon	19615	23075
2 Dr XL Club Wagon Ext	20725	24385
2 Dr XLT Club Wagon Ext	21460	25250
2 Dr XLT Club Wagon	21075	24795

OPTIONS FOR CLUB WAGON/ECONOLINE

10 cyl 6.8 L Engine +500
8 cyl 4.6 L Engine +540
8 cyl 5.4 L Engine[Std on E-350] +760
8 cyl 7.3 L Turbodsl Engine +4025
12 Passenger Seating[Std on XL,Club Wagon] +515
Air Conditioning[Std on Chateau, XL, XLT] +670
Aluminum/Alloy Wheels[Opt on XLT] +260
Anti-Lock Brakes[Std on Chateau, XL, XLT] +420
Cruise Control +160
Dual Air Conditioning +1180
Keyless Entry System +125
Power Door Locks[Std on Chateau, XLT] +155
Power Drivers Seat +225
Power Mirrors +85
Power Windows[Std on Chateau, XLT] +160
Privacy Glass +140
Tilt Steering Wheel +150

CONTOUR 1998

A redesigned face gives this Ford more character, but the new taillight treatment is almost identical to the Contour's sibling, the Mercury Mystique. New alloy wheels and a slightly more commodious rear seat debut. The outstanding SVT model provides the performance of a BMW 328i at the price of a Buick Century. Mid-year changes included a model consolidation, the addition of de-powered airbags, as well as improved handling and new wheels for the SVT.

Category C

Model Description	Trade-in Value	Market Value
4 Dr GL Sdn	8150	9820
4 Dr LX Sdn	8370	10085
4 Dr SE Sdn	8675	10450
4 Dr STD Sdn	7315	8815
4 Dr SVT Sdn	13415	16165

OPTIONS FOR CONTOUR

6 cyl 2.5 L Engine[Std on SE, SVT] +585
Auto 4-Speed Transmission +675
Air Conditioning[Std on SVT] +665
Aluminum/Alloy Wheels[Opt on GL, LX] +240
AM/FM Compact Disc Playr +320
Anti-Lock Brakes[Std on SVT] +520
Cruise Control[Std on SVT] +170
Keyless Entry System[Std on SVT] +155
Leather Seats[Std on SVT] +480
Power Door Locks[Opt on GL, LX] +200
Power Drivers Seat[Std on SVT] +235
Power Mirrors[Opt on GL] +90
Power Moonroof +580
Power Windows[Std on SVT] +255
Rear Window Defroster[Std on SE, SVT] +135
Traction Control System[Opt on SE] +235

CROWN VICTORIA 1998

A formal roofline graces this favorite of police officers and taxi drivers. To further add to the Crown Victoria's driving excitement, the power steering and suspension have been improved.

Category B

Model Description	Trade-in Value	Market Value
4 Dr LX Sdn	18345	22100
4 Dr STD Sdn	16730	20155

OPTIONS FOR CROWN VICTORIA

Aluminum/Alloy Wheels +275
Anti-Lock Brakes +595

Don't forget to refer to the Mileage Adjustment Table at the back of this book!

 © 1999 by Edmund Publications Corporation

Model Description	Trade-in Value	Market Value

Climate Control for AC +145
Dual Power Seats +300
Keyless Entry System[Std on LX] +145
Leather Seats +550
Power Drivers Seat[Std on LX] +250
Traction Control System +150

ESCORT 1998

Packages are reshuffled on Ford's entry-level cars. Available this year as sedans, wagons or stylish coupes, the Ford Escort now qualifies as a low emissions vehicle, thanks to the car's split-port induction 2.0-liter four-cylinder engine.

Category E

Model Description	Trade-in Value	Market Value
4 Dr LX Sdn	7655	9340
4 Dr SE Sdn	8195	9995
4 Dr SE Wgn	8170	9965
2 Dr ZX2 Cool Cpe	8335	10165
2 Dr ZX2 Hot Cpe	8700	10610

OPTIONS FOR ESCORT

Auto 4-Speed Transmission +645
Air Conditioning[Std on SE] +675
Aluminum/Alloy Wheels +265
Anti-Lock Brakes +590
Cruise Control +185
Keyless Entry System[Std on SE] +125
Luggage Rack +105
Power Door Locks +195
Power Mirrors[Std on SE] +95
Power Moonroof +485
Power Windows +220
Premium Sound System +285
Rear Window Defroster[Std on SE] +135
Rear Window Wiper +110
Tilt Steering Wheel +125

EXPEDITION 1998

After an insanely successful first year, the Ford Expedition pounds its way into 1998 without changes.

Category H

Model Description	Trade-in Value	Market Value
4 Dr Eddie Bauer Wgn	22970	27025
4 Dr Eddie Bauer 4WD Wgn	23750	27940
4 Dr XLT Wgn	22165	26075
4 Dr XLT 4WD Wgn	22960	27015

OPTIONS FOR EXPEDITION

8 cyl 5.4 L Engine +760
Load Leveling Suspension +675
Aluminum/Alloy Wheels[Opt on XLT] +260
Camper/Towing Package +295
Compact Disc Changer +360
Compact Disc W/fm/tape +265
Cruise Control[Opt on XLT] +160
Dual Air Conditioning +1180
Fog Lights[Opt on XLT] +95
Heated Front Seats +240
Heated Power Mirrors +100
Leather Seats[Opt on XLT] +860
Power Drivers Seat[Opt on XLT] +225
Privacy Glass[Opt on XLT] +140
Running Boards +245
Third Seat +525

EXPLORER 1998

The Ford Explorer gets a restyled tailgate for 1998.

Category G

Model Description	Trade-in Value	Market Value
4 Dr Eddie Bauer Wgn	17660	21025
4 Dr Eddie Bauer 4WD Wgn	17955	21375
4 Dr Limited Wgn	18855	22450
4 Dr Limited 4WD Wgn	19360	23045
2 Dr Sport Utility	15785	18795
2 Dr Sport 4WD Utility	16305	19410
4 Dr XL Wgn	16780	19975
4 Dr XL 4WD Wgn	16995	20235
4 Dr XLT Wgn	17465	20790
4 Dr XLT 4WD Wgn	17465	20790

OPTIONS FOR EXPLORER

6 cyl 4.0 L Engine[Opt on Sport, XLT] +450
8 cyl 5.0 L Engine +735
Auto 4-Speed Transmission +415
Auto 5-Speed Transmission[Std on Eddie Bauer, Limited] +885
Aluminum/Alloy Wheels[Opt on XL] +285
Climate Control for AC[Std on Limited] +165
Compact Disc Changer +430
Compact Disc W/fm/tape[Std on Limited] +565
Cruise Control[Opt on Sport, XL] +175
Dual Power Seats[Std on Limited] +525
Fog Lights[Std on Limited] +120
Keyless Entry System[Std on Limited] +170
Leather Seats[Std on Limited] +640
Power Drivers Seat[Opt on Sport, XLT] +235
Power Moonroof +735
Rear Heater[Std on Limited] +170
Rear Window Defroster[Opt on Sport, XL] +140
Rear Window Wiper[Opt on Sport, XL] +125
Running Boards[Std on Limited] +320
Tilt Steering Wheel[Opt on XL] +140
Tutone Paint[Opt on XLT] +220

F-SERIES PICKUP 1998

The 1998 F-150 gets a 50th Anniversary decal affixed to the lower left corner of the windshield. Other changes include making the locking tailgate standard on XLT and Lariat trims, optional on XL and Standard models. Fog lights become optional this year on all four-wheel drive models except for the Lariat, which gets them standard. An STX package featuring 17-inch tires, aluminum wheels, and color-keyed grille debuts as an option for the XLT 2WD. The Lariat receives a color-keyed steering

Don't forget to refer to the Mileage Adjustment Table at the back of this book!

 © 1999 by Edmund Publications Corporation

column, leather-wrapped steering wheel, and outside power signal mirrors. Silver Metallic paint replaces Silver Frost paint, and Light Denim Blue replaces Portofino Blue.

F-150

Category H

Model Description	Trade-in Value	Market Value
2 Dr Lariat Ext Cab SB	15680	18445
2 Dr Lariat Std Cab SB	15600	18350
2 Dr Lariat Std Cab Stepside SB	16375	19265
2 Dr Lariat Ext Cab Stepside SB	16490	19400
2 Dr Lariat Std Cab LB	15855	18655
2 Dr Lariat Ext Cab LB	15895	18700
2 Dr Lariat 4WD Ext Cab SB	17740	20870
2 Dr Lariat 4WD Std Cab SB	17335	20395
2 Dr Lariat 4WD Std Cab Stepside SB	17935	21100
2 Dr Lariat 4WD Ext Cab Stepside SB	18235	21455
2 Dr Lariat 4WD Std Cab LB	17560	20660
2 Dr Lariat 4WD Ext Cab LB	17955	21125
2 Dr STD Std Cab SB	10950	12885
2 Dr STD Ext Cab SB	11235	13215
2 Dr STD Std Cab LB	11150	13115
2 Dr STD Ext Cab LB	11485	13510
2 Dr STD 4WD Std Cab SB	13300	15650
2 Dr STD 4WD Ext Cab SB	13870	16315
2 Dr STD 4WD Std Cab LB	13650	16060
2 Dr STD 4WD Ext Cab LB	14230	16740
2 Dr XL Ext Cab SB	12310	14480
2 Dr XL Std Cab SB	11900	14000
2 Dr XL Std Cab Stepside SB	12535	14745
2 Dr XL Ext Cab Stepside SB	12885	15160
2 Dr XL Std Cab LB	12150	14295
2 Dr XL Ext Cab LB	12535	14745
2 Dr XL 4WD Std Cab SB	13965	16430
2 Dr XL 4WD Ext Cab SB	14650	17235
2 Dr XL 4WD Std Cab Stepside SB	14420	16965
2 Dr XL 4WD Ext Cab Stepside SB	15120	17790
2 Dr XL 4WD Std Cab LB	14045	16525
2 Dr XL 4WD Ext Cab LB	14875	17500
2 Dr XLT Std Cab SB	13125	15440
2 Dr XLT Ext Cab SB	13485	15865
2 Dr XLT Ext Cab Stepside SB	14045	16525
2 Dr XLT Std Cab Stepside SB	13370	15730
2 Dr XLT Std Cab LB	13200	15530
2 Dr XLT Ext Cab LB	13715	16135
2 Dr XLT 4WD Std Cab SB	15655	18420
2 Dr XLT 4WD Ext Cab SB	16230	19095
2 Dr XLT 4WD Ext Cab Stepside SB	16740	19695
2 Dr XLT 4WD Std Cab Stepside SB	16415	19310
2 Dr XLT 4WD Ext Cab LB	16460	19360
2 Dr XLT 4WD Std Cab LB	15895	18700

F-250

Category H

Model Description	Trade-in Value	Market Value
2 Dr Lariat Ext Cab SB	20275	23855
2 Dr Lariat Std Cab LB	18970	22320
2 Dr Lariat 4WD Ext Cab SB	22135	26040
2 Dr Lariat 4WD Std Cab LB	21440	25225
2 Dr STD Ext Cab SB	15435	18160
2 Dr STD Std Cab LB	14500	17060
2 Dr STD 4WD Ext Cab SB	17400	20470
2 Dr STD 4WD Std Cab LB	16930	19920
2 Dr XL Ext Cab SB	15480	18210
2 Dr XL Std Cab LB	14960	17600
2 Dr XL 4WD Ext Cab SB	17720	20850
2 Dr XL 4WD Std Cab LB	17515	20605
2 Dr XLT Ext Cab SB	17300	20350
2 Dr XLT Std Cab LB	16990	19990
2 Dr XLT 4WD Ext Cab SB	20200	23765
2 Dr XLT 4WD Std Cab LB	17880	21035

OPTIONS FOR F-SERIES PICKUP

8 cyl 4.6 L Engine[Std on F-150 4WD, F-250, Lariat] +540
8 cyl 5.4 L Engine +760
Auto 4-Speed Transmission +825
Air Conditioning +670
Aluminum/Alloy Wheels[Std on Lariat] +260
AM/FM Compact Disc Playr +245
Anti-Lock Brakes[Std on Lariat] +420
Camper/Towing Package +295
Chrome Wheels[Std on Lariat] +245
Cruise Control +160
Fog Lights[Std on Lariat] +95
Keyless Entry System +125
Leather Steering Wheel[Opt on XLT] +55
Power Drivers Seat +225
Power Mirrors[Std on Lariat, XLT Stepside] +85
Skid Plates +90
Sliding Rear Window +95
Tilt Steering Wheel +150

MUSTANG 1998

The Mustang gains standard equipment, such as power windows and door locks, air conditioning, and premium sound. Options are shuffled as well, making it easier to choose the car you want. GT models get a slight boost in power.

Don't forget to refer to the Mileage Adjustment Table at the back of this book!

 © 1999 by Edmund Publications Corporation

Model Description	Trade-in Value	Market Value
Category F		
2 Dr Cobra Conv	21310	25990
2 Dr Cobra Cpe	17800	21710
2 Dr GT Conv	16500	20120
2 Dr GT Cpe	13920	16975
2 Dr STD Cpe	11840	14440
2 Dr STD Conv	13230	16135

OPTIONS FOR MUSTANG

Auto 4-Speed Transmission +675
Air Conditioning +690
Aluminum/Alloy Wheels +260
Anti-Lock Brakes[Std on Cobra] +600
Compact Disc W/fm/tape +435
Cruise Control[Std on Cobra] +175
Leather Seats +590
Power Drivers Seat[Opt on STD] +195
Rear Window Defroster[Std on Cobra] +135

RANGER 1998

The Ranger gets new sheetmetal, a new grille and revised headlamps. The wheelbase on regular cab models has been stretched to provide more cabin room and the displacement of the base engine has been increased. A short- and long-arm (SLA) suspension replaces the Twin-I-Beam suspension found on last year's models. A four-door Ranger join the lineup mid-year.

Model Description	Trade-in Value	Market Value
Category G		
2 Dr Splash Std Cab Stepside SB	11330	13490
2 Dr Splash Ext Cab Stepside SB	11750	13990
2 Dr Splash 4WD Ext Cab Stepside SB	13920	16570
2 Dr Splash 4WD Std Cab Stepside SB	13290	15820
2 Dr XL Std Cab SB	8825	10505
2 Dr XL Ext Cab SB	9625	11460
2 Dr XL Ext Cab Stepside SB	10730	12775
2 Dr XL Std Cab Stepside SB	9165	10910
2 Dr XL Std Cab LB	9205	10960
2 Dr XL 4WD Ext Cab SB	12645	15050
2 Dr XL 4WD Std Cab SB	11685	13915
2 Dr XL 4WD Ext Cab Stepside SB	12980	15450
2 Dr XL 4WD Std Cab Stepside SB	11975	14255
2 Dr XL 4WD Std Cab LB	12015	14305
2 Dr XLT Std Cab SB	9945	11840
2 Dr XLT Ext Cab SB	10335	12305
2 Dr XLT Std Cab Stepside SB	10285	12245
2 Dr XLT Ext Cab Stepside SB	10675	12710
2 Dr XLT Std Cab LB	10395	12375
2 Dr XLT 4WD Std Cab SB	12030	14325
2 Dr XLT 4WD Ext Cab SB	12560	14955
2 Dr XLT 4WD Std Cab Stepside SB	12320	14665
2 Dr XLT 4WD Ext Cab Stepside SB	12900	15355
2 Dr XLT 4WD Std Cab LB	12450	14825

OPTIONS FOR RANGER

6 cyl 3.0 L Engine[Std on 4WD, Splash 2WD Ext Cab] +430
6 cyl 4.0 L Engine +745
Auto 4-Speed Transmission +910
Auto 5-Speed Transmission +940
Air Conditioning +675
Aluminum/Alloy Wheels[Opt on XL, XLT, Ext Cab] +285
AM/FM Compact Disc Playr +320
Anti-Lock Brakes +515
Bed Liner +230
Chrome Wheels[Opt on XLT] +200
Cruise Control +175
Fog Lights +120
Keyless Entry System +170
Power Door Locks +190
Power Mirrors[Opt on XLT] +110
Power Windows +195
Sliding Rear Window[Opt on XL, XLT, Std Cab, 2WD] +100
Tilt Steering Wheel +140

TAURUS 1998

A mild facelift, revised trim levels and fewer options are the only changes to Ford's mid-size sedan.

Model Description	Trade-in Value	Market Value
Category C		
4 Dr LX Sdn	12620	15205
4 Dr SE Sdn	13495	16260
4 Dr SE Wgn	16115	19415
Category F		
4 Dr SHO Sdn	17035	20775

OPTIONS FOR TAURUS

6 cyl 3.0 L DOHC Engine[Opt on LX, SE] +410
Aluminum/Alloy Wheels +240
Anti-Lock Brakes[Std on SHO] +520
Chrome Wheels[Opt on SE] +470
Climate Control for AC[Opt on SE] +140
Compact Disc Changer[Opt on SE] +430
Dual Power Seats[Opt on SE] +480
Heated Power Mirrors[Opt on SE] +115
Keyless Entry System[Opt on LX, Wgn] +145
Leather Seats +480
Power Door Locks[Opt on LX] +165
Power Drivers Seat +235
Power Moonroof[Opt on SE] +580

Don't forget to refer to the Mileage Adjustment Table at the back of this book!

 © 1999 by Edmund Publications Corporation

Model Description	Trade-in Value	Market Value

WINDSTAR 1998

Ford widens the driver's door as a stop-gap measure until the 1999 Windstar arrives with a fourth door. Subtle styling revisions and a new Limited model round out the changes for 1998.

Category G

2 Dr GL Pass. Van	12635	15040
2 Dr LX Pass. Van	17015	20255
2 Dr STD Pass. Van	12115	14420

OPTIONS FOR WINDSTAR

6 cyl 3.8 L Engine[Std on Limited, LX] +360
Air Conditioning[Std on LX] +675
Aluminum/Alloy Wheels[Opt on GL] +285
AM/FM Compact Disc Playr +320
Captain Chairs (4)[Opt on GL, LX] +525
Cruise Control[Opt on GL, STD] +175
Dual Air Conditioning[Opt on GL, LX] +840
JBL Sound System +635
Keyless Entry System +170
Leather Seats[Opt on LX] +640
Power Door Locks[Opt on GL, STD] +190
Power Drivers Seat[Opt on GL] +235
Power Mirrors[Opt on GL, STD] +110
Power Windows[Opt on GL, STD] +195
Privacy Glass +225
Rear Window Defroster[Std on Limited] +140
Tilt Steering Wheel[Opt on GL, STD] +140
Traction Control System +245

1997 FORD

AEROSTAR 1997

Ford's aging minivan gets a five-speed "swap-shift" automatic transmission this year. The sound system is upgraded and the seats are restyled as well.

RATINGS (SCALE OF 1-10)

Overall	Safety	Reliability	Performance	Comfort	Value
7.3	5.8	7.9	6.8	7.5	8.7

Category G

2 Dr STD Cargo Van	8240	9930
2 Dr XLT Pass. Van Ext	11560	13930
2 Dr XLT Pass. Van	9875	11900
2 Dr XLT 4WD Pass. Van Ext	12430	14975

OPTIONS FOR AEROSTAR

6 cyl 4.0 L Engine[Opt on 2WD] +560
Air Conditioning[Opt on STD] +550
Aluminum/Alloy Wheels +235
AM/FM Compact Disc Playr +260
AM/FM Stereo Tape +165
Captain Chairs (4) +430
Child Seat (1) +120
Cruise Control +145
Dual Air Conditioning +685
Luggage Rack +105
Power Door Locks +155
Power Windows +160
Running Boards +260

ASPIRE 1997

This Kia-built entry-level Ford gets a higher final drive ratio on models equipped with an automatic transmission. New wheel covers, paint choices and interior trim are the only other changes.

RATINGS (SCALE OF 1-10)

Overall	Safety	Reliability	Performance	Comfort	Value
7	6.6	8.7	7.2	7.3	5

Category E

2 Dr STD Hbk	4780	5975
4 Dr STD Hbk	5275	6595

OPTIONS FOR ASPIRE

Auto 3-Speed Transmission +450
Air Conditioning +550
AM/FM Stereo Tape +210
Anti-Lock Brakes +480
Power Steering +170
Rear Window Defroster +110

CLUB WAGON/ECONOLINE 1997

More power? Ford's full-size minivans are now the only ones in the segment to offer V10 power. Multiple overhead-cam engines also debut in models across the board. Econoline vans get standard four-wheel ABS this year.

RATINGS (SCALE OF 1-10)

Overall	Safety	Reliability	Performance	Comfort	Value
N/A	8	9	7	7.5	N/A

E-150

Category H

2 Dr Chateau Club Wagon	17165	20435
2 Dr STD Econoline	12955	15425
2 Dr XL Club Wagon	13850	16490
2 Dr XLT Club Wagon	14525	17290

E-250

Category H

2 Dr STD Econoline Ext	13075	15565
2 Dr STD Econoline	12515	14900

E-350

Category H

2 Dr Chateau Club Wagon	17285	20575
2 Dr STD Econoline Ext	13750	16370
2 Dr STD Econoline	13215	15730
2 Dr XL Club Wagon Ext	15580	18545

Don't forget to refer to the Mileage Adjustment Table at the back of this book!

 © 1999 by Edmund Publications Corporation

Model Description	Trade-in Value	Market Value
2 Dr XL Club Wagon	14895	17735
2 Dr XLT Club Wagon Ext	16065	19125
2 Dr XLT Club Wagon	15605	18575

OPTIONS FOR CLUB WAGON/ECONOLINE

10 cyl 6.8 L Engine +280
8 cyl 4.6 L Engine +400
8 cyl 5.4 L Engine[Std on E-350] +555
8 cyl 7.3 L Turbodsl Engine +2835
Air Conditioning[Std on Chateau,XLT] +550
Aluminum/Alloy Wheels[Opt on XL,XLT] +210
AM/FM Stereo Tape[Std on Chateau] +165
Anti-Lock Brakes[Opt on STD] +345
Camper/Towing Package +240
Chrome Bumpers[Std on Chateau,XLT] +115
Cruise Control[Std on Chateau] +130
Dual Air Conditioning +965
Keyless Entry System +110
Limited Slip Diff +175
Power Door Locks[Std on Chateau,XLT] +125
Power Drivers Seat +185
Power Windows[Std on Chateau,XLT] +130
Velour/Cloth Seats[Std on Chateau,XLT] +90

CONTOUR 1997

The addition of a Sport Package for the GL and LX models and the inclusion of a standard trunk light are the only changes for the 1997 Contour.

RATINGS (SCALE OF 1-10)

Overall	Safety	Reliability	Performance	Comfort	Value
7.6	7	7.7	8.4	7.9	6.8

Category C

Model Description	Trade-in Value	Market Value
4 Dr GL Sdn	7115	8785
4 Dr LX Sdn	7685	9485
4 Dr SE Sdn	8930	11025

OPTIONS FOR CONTOUR

6 cyl 2.5 L Engine[Std on SE] +615
Auto 4-Speed Transmission +555
Air Conditioning +540
Aluminum/Alloy Wheels[Std on SE] +195
AM/FM Compact Disc Playr +260
Anti-Lock Brakes +425
Cruise Control +140
Keyless Entry System +130
Leather Seats +390
Power Door Locks +160
Power Drivers Seat +195
Power Moonroof +475
Power Windows +205
Rear Spoiler[Opt on GL] +110
Traction Control System +190

CROWN VICTORIA 1997

After a mild facelift last year, the Crown Vic soldiers on with a few color changes, improved power steering, and the addition of rear air suspension to the handling package.

RATINGS (SCALE OF 1-10)

Overall	Safety	Reliability	Performance	Comfort	Value
8.2	8.1	8.5	7.7	8.3	8.4

Category B

Model Description	Trade-in Value	Market Value
4 Dr LX Sdn	12630	15400
4 Dr STD Sdn	12440	15170

OPTIONS FOR CROWN VICTORIA

Handling/Performance Package +745
Aluminum/Alloy Wheels +225
AM/FM Stereo Tape +120
Anti-Lock Brakes +485
Climate Control for AC +120
Cruise Control +145
Dual Power Seats +245
Keyless Entry System +120
Leather Seats +450
Power Door Locks +170
Premium Sound System +285
Traction Control System +120
Trip Computer +145

ESCORT 1997

The Ford Escort is totally redesigned this year with improvements across the board. The most noticeable improvements are in the powertrain and ride quality. New sheetmetal gives the Escort a rounder, more aerodynamic appearance as well. To the chagrin of bargain-basement enthusiasts, the GT hatchback version is dropped.

RATINGS (SCALE OF 1-10)

Overall	Safety	Reliability	Performance	Comfort	Value
7.1	6.6	8.6	7.2	7.3	5.7

Category E

Model Description	Trade-in Value	Market Value
4 Dr LX Sdn	6450	8060
4 Dr LX Wgn	6350	7940
4 Dr STD Sdn	6290	7865

OPTIONS FOR ESCORT

Auto 4-Speed Transmission +500
Air Conditioning +550
Aluminum/Alloy Wheels +215
AM/FM Stereo Tape +210
Anti-Lock Brakes +480
Child Seat (1) +80
Compact Disc Changer +380
Cruise Control +150
Keyless Entry System +100
Luggage Rack +90

Don't forget to refer to the Mileage Adjustment Table at the back of this book!

© 1999 by Edmund Publications Corporation

Model Description	Trade-in Value	Market Value

Power Door Locks +160
Power Windows +180
Tilt Steering Wheel +100

EXPEDITION 1997

Ford's replacement for the aging Bronco is the all-new Expedition. Based on the hugely successful 1997 F-150 platform, this full-size sport-utility vehicle is poised to do battle with the wildly popular Chevrolet Tahoe and GMC Yukon. Ford has priced the Expedition aggressively and stands to steal some sales from GM customers who have been told that they'll have to wait four months for their full-size SUV.

RATINGS (SCALE OF 1-10)

Overall	Safety	Reliability	Performance	Comfort	Value
7.6	8.5	8.4	6.8	7.9	6.7

Category H

Model Description	Trade-in Value	Market Value
4 Dr Eddie Bauer Wgn	20560	24475
4 Dr Eddie Bauer 4WD Wgn	21470	25555
4 Dr XLT Wgn	20200	24050
4 Dr XLT 4WD Wgn	21270	25320

OPTIONS FOR EXPEDITION

8 cyl 5.4 L Engine +555
Load Leveling Suspension +555
Aluminum/Alloy Wheels[Opt on XLT] +210
Camper/Towing Package +240
Chrome Wheels +200
Compact Disc W/fm/tape +215
Cruise Control[Opt on XLT] +130
Dual Air Conditioning +965
Leather Seats[Opt on XLT] +700
Limited Slip Diff +175
Luggage Rack[Opt on XLT] +90
Power Drivers Seat[Opt on XLT] +185
Power Moonroof +660
Running Boards +200
Skid Plates +75
Third Seat +430

EXPLORER 1997

Ford's best-selling Explorer receives a few appreciated improvements this year. A new SOHC V6 engine is now available, providing nearly as much power as the 5.0-liter V8. Also new is a five-speed automatic transmission, the first ever offered by an American auto manufacturer, which is standard on V6 models equipped with automatic.

RATINGS (SCALE OF 1-10)

Overall	Safety	Reliability	Performance	Comfort	Value
7.8	7.5	7.7	7.8	7.1	8.8

Category G

Model Description	Trade-in Value	Market Value
4 Dr Eddie Bauer Wgn	15690	18900
4 Dr Eddie Bauer 4WD Wgn	16665	20075
4 Dr Limited Wgn	17650	21265
4 Dr Limited 4WD Wgn	18560	22365
2 Dr Sport Utility	13705	16510
2 Dr Sport 4WD Utility	14280	17205
2 Dr XL Utility	12225	14730
2 Dr XL 4WD Utility	13280	16000
4 Dr XL Wgn	13345	16075
4 Dr XL 4WD Wgn	14320	17255
4 Dr XLT Wgn	14870	17915
4 Dr XLT 4WD Wgn	15675	18885

OPTIONS FOR EXPLORER

6 cyl 4.0 L Engine[Opt on Sport,XL,XLT] +290
8 cyl 5.0 L Engine +825
Auto 4-Speed Transmission +540
Auto 5-Speed Transmission[Opt on Sport,XL,XLT] +725
AM/FM Stereo Tape[Std on Eddie Bauer] +165
Camper/Towing Package +195
Child Seat (1) +120
Chrome Wheels[Opt on Sport] +165
Climate Control for AC[Std on Limited] +135
Compact Disc Changer +350
Cruise Control[Opt on XL] +145
Dual Power Seats[Opt on Sport,XLT] +430
JBL Sound System[Std on Limited] +520
Keyless Entry System[Std on Limited] +140
Leather Seats[Std on Limited] +520
Limited Slip Diff +180
Luggage Rack[Opt on Sport,XL,XLT] +105
Power Door Locks[Opt on XL] +155
Power Moonroof +600
Power Windows[Opt on XL] +160
Running Boards[Std on Limited] +260

F-SERIES PICKUP 1997

Everything is new. New engines, new sheetmetal, and a new suspension compliment dual airbags and class-leading side impact protection in this user-friendly heavy hauler. All SuperCab models get a third door for easy access to the rear compartment. Styling is slightly different depending on what drive system is selected.

RATINGS (SCALE OF 1-10)

Overall	Safety	Reliability	Performance	Comfort	Value
N/A	7.7	8.1	6.6	7.8	N/A

F-150

Category H

Model Description	Trade-in Value	Market Value
2 Dr Lariat Ext Cab SB	13680	16285
2 Dr Lariat Std Cab SB	13485	16055
2 Dr Lariat Ext Cab Stepside SB	14175	16875
2 Dr Lariat Std Cab Stepside SB	13795	16425
2 Dr Lariat Ext Cab LB	13775	16400
2 Dr Lariat Std Cab LB	13540	16120

Don't forget to refer to the Mileage Adjustment Table at the back of this book!

© 1999 by Edmund Publications Corporation

Model Description	Trade-in Value	Market Value
2 Dr Lariat 4WD Ext Cab SB	15265	18170
2 Dr Lariat 4WD Std Cab SB	14870	17705
2 Dr Lariat 4WD Ext Cab Stepside SB	15760	18760
2 Dr Lariat 4WD Std Cab Stepside SB	15160	18050
2 Dr Lariat 4WD Std Cab LB	15140	18020
2 Dr Lariat 4WD Ext Cab LB	15355	18280
2 Dr STD Std Cab SB	11135	13255
2 Dr STD Ext Cab SB	11155	13280
2 Dr STD Std Cab LB	11215	13350
2 Dr STD Ext Cab LB	11220	13355
2 Dr STD 4WD Std Cab SB	12395	14755
2 Dr STD 4WD Ext Cab SB	13240	15760
2 Dr STD 4WD Ext Cab LB	13330	15870
2 Dr STD 4WD Std Cab LB	12480	14855
2 Dr XL Std Cab SB	11220	13360
2 Dr XL Ext Cab SB	11385	13555
2 Dr XL Std Cab Stepside SB	11720	13955
2 Dr XL Ext Cab Stepside SB	11795	14040
2 Dr XL Ext Cab LB	11220	13355
2 Dr XL Std Cab LB	11215	13350
2 Dr XL 4WD Ext Cab SB	13585	16170
2 Dr XL 4WD Std Cab SB	12510	14890
2 Dr XL 4WD Std Cab Stepside SB	12880	15335
2 Dr XL 4WD Ext Cab Stepside SB	14130	16825
2 Dr XL 4WD Ext Cab LB	13730	16345
2 Dr XL 4WD Std Cab LB	12575	14970
2 Dr XLT Std Cab SB	12160	14475
2 Dr XLT Ext Cab SB	12195	14515
2 Dr XLT Std Cab Stepside SB	12510	14895
2 Dr XLT Ext Cab Stepside SB	12730	15155
2 Dr XLT Std Cab LB	12225	14555
2 Dr XLT Ext Cab LB	12285	14625
2 Dr XLT 4WD Ext Cab SB	14205	16910
2 Dr XLT 4WD Std Cab SB	13320	15860
2 Dr XLT 4WD Ext Cab Stepside SB	14685	17485
2 Dr XLT 4WD Std Cab Stepside SB	13005	15480
2 Dr XLT 4WD Std Cab LB	13390	15940
2 Dr XLT 4WD Ext Cab LB	14285	17010

F-250

Category H

Model Description	Trade-in Value	Market Value
2 Dr Lariat Ext Cab SB	16815	20015
2 Dr Lariat Std Cab LB	16410	19535
2 Dr Lariat 4WD Ext Cab SB	18345	21840
2 Dr Lariat 4WD Std Cab LB	17595	20945
2 Dr STD Ext Cab SB	14195	16895
2 Dr STD Std Cab LB	13975	16635
2 Dr STD 4WD Ext Cab SB	15890	18915
2 Dr STD 4WD Std Cab LB	15150	18035
2 Dr XL Ext Cab SB	14195	16895
2 Dr XL Std Cab LB	14050	16725
2 Dr XL 4WD Ext Cab SB	15400	18335
2 Dr XL 4WD Std Cab LB	15215	18115
2 Dr XLT Ext Cab SB	15020	17885
2 Dr XLT Std Cab LB	14855	17685
2 Dr XLT 4WD Ext Cab SB	16580	19740
2 Dr XLT 4WD Std Cab LB	15940	18975

F-250 HEAVY DUTY

Category H

Model Description	Trade-in Value	Market Value
2 Dr XL Ext Cab SB	15215	18115
2 Dr XL Std Cab LB	13155	15660
2 Dr XL Ext Cab LB	14995	17850
2 Dr XL 4WD Ext Cab SB	15820	18830
2 Dr XL 4WD Ext Cab LB	15600	18570
2 Dr XL 4WD Std Cab LB	14415	17160
4 Dr XL Crew Cab SB	18385	21885
4 Dr XL 4WD Crew Cab SB	20180	24025
2 Dr XLT Ext Cab SB	17385	20695
2 Dr XLT Ext Cab LB	17290	20585
2 Dr XLT Std Cab LB	15020	17880
2 Dr XLT 4WD Ext Cab SB	17860	21260
2 Dr XLT 4WD Ext Cab LB	17770	21155
2 Dr XLT 4WD Std Cab LB	16290	19395
4 Dr XLT Crew Cab SB	19780	23550
4 Dr XLT 4WD Crew Cab SB	22520	26810

F-350

Category H

Model Description	Trade-in Value	Market Value
2 Dr XL Ext Cab LB	17090	20345
2 Dr XL Std Cab LB	16375	19495
2 Dr XL 4WD Std Cab LB	17655	21020
4 Dr XL Crew Cab LB	17975	21400
4 Dr XL 4WD Crew Cab LB	18495	22020
2 Dr XLT Std Cab LB	18465	21985
2 Dr XLT Ext Cab LB	19200	22855
2 Dr XLT 4WD Std Cab LB	18615	22165
4 Dr XLT Crew Cab LB	19905	23695
4 Dr XLT 4WD Crew Cab LB	20325	24195

OPTIONS FOR F-SERIES PICKUP

8 cyl 4.6 L Engine +400
8 cyl 5.4 L Engine +555
8 cyl 7.5 L Engine +260
8 cyl 7.3 L Turbodsl Engine +2835
Auto 4-Speed Transmission +615
Off-Road Equipment Group +485
Air Conditioning[Opt on F-150,F-250] +550
Aluminum/Alloy Wheels[Std on Lariat] +210
Anti-Lock Brakes[Std on Lariat] +345
Camper/Towing Package +240

Don't forget to refer to the Mileage Adjustment Table at the back of this book!

 © 1999 by Edmund Publications Corporation

Model Description	Trade-in Value	Market Value

Chrome Wheels[Opt on XL,XLT] +200
Compact Disc W/fm/tape +215
Cruise Control[Opt on F-150,F-250] +130
Dual Rear Wheels +570
Keyless Entry System +110
Limited Slip Diff +175
Power Drivers Seat +185
Rear Step Bumper +105
Skid Plates +75
Tutone Paint +180

MUSTANG 1997

While messing around with the rest of their models, Ford decided to take it easy with changes to the Mustang. GT models and base convertibles get new interior color options, and 'Stangs equipped with an automatic transmission (what fun) get a thicker shift lever. New 17-inch aluminum wheels are optional on the GT. Lastly, the Passive Anti-Theft System has been introduced to all Mustangs in an attempt decrease this vehicle's extremely high theft rating.

RATINGS (SCALE OF 1-10)

Overall	Safety	Reliability	Performance	Comfort	Value
N/A	7	8.7	8.8	7.3	N/A

Category F

Model Description	Trade-in Value	Market Value
2 Dr Cobra Conv	18105	22080
2 Dr Cobra Cpe	15985	19495
2 Dr GT Cpe	11545	14080
2 Dr GT Conv	13975	17045
2 Dr STD Conv	11790	14380
2 Dr STD Cpe	9580	11680

OPTIONS FOR MUSTANG

Auto 4-Speed Transmission +555
Air Conditioning[Std on Cobra] +565
Aluminum/Alloy Wheels[Opt on STD] +210
Anti-Lock Brakes[Std on Cobra] +490
Compact Disc W/fm/tape +355
Cruise Control[Std on Cobra] +140
Keyless Entry System[Std on Cobra] +120
Leather Seats +485
Limited Slip Diff[Std on Cobra] +255
Power Door Locks[Std on Cobra,Conv] +135
Power Drivers Seat[Std on Cobra] +160
Power Windows[Std on Cobra,Conv] +150
Premium Sound System +280
Rear Spoiler[Opt on STD,Cpe] +190

PROBE 1997

Ford adds a GTS Sport Appearance Package to the GT's option sheet. The package includes a rear spoiler, racing stripes and 16-inch chrome wheels.

RATINGS (SCALE OF 1-10)

Overall	Safety	Reliability	Performance	Comfort	Value
N/A	7.2	8.2	9	7.4	N/A

Category E

Model Description	Trade-in Value	Market Value
2 Dr GT Hbk	9260	11575
2 Dr STD Hbk	7870	9835

OPTIONS FOR PROBE

Auto 4-Speed Transmission +610
Air Conditioning +550
Aluminum/Alloy Wheels[Std on GT] +215
AM/FM Compact Disc Playr +320
Anti-Lock Brakes +480
Chrome Wheels +265
Cruise Control +150
Keyless Entry System +100
Leather Seats +605
Power Door Locks +160
Power Drivers Seat +200
Power Sunroof +410
Power Windows +180

RANGER 1997

Ford introduces its brand-new five-speed automatic transmission to the Ranger lineup. Available with the V6 engines, the five-speed automatic is designed to improve the Ranger's acceleration, towing, and hill climbing ability.

RATINGS (SCALE OF 1-10)

Overall	Safety	Reliability	Performance	Comfort	Value
N/A	6.5	9	7.2	7.3	N/A

Category G

Model Description	Trade-in Value	Market Value
2 Dr Splash Ext Cab Stepside SB	11745	14150
2 Dr Splash Std Cab Stepside SB	9585	11550
2 Dr Splash 4WD Ext Cab Stepside SB	13210	15915
2 Dr Splash 4WD Std Cab Stepside SB	12710	15315
2 Dr STX 4WD Ext Cab SB	11685	14080
2 Dr STX 4WD Std Cab SB	11150	13435
2 Dr STX 4WD Std Cab LB	11340	13660
2 Dr XL Ext Cab SB	8575	10335
2 Dr XL Std Cab SB	7145	8610
2 Dr XL Ext Cab Stepside SB	8555	10310
2 Dr XL Std Cab Stepside SB	7135	8595
2 Dr XL Std Cab LB	7240	8720
2 Dr XL 4WD Ext Cab SB	10830	13050
2 Dr XL 4WD Std Cab SB	10485	12630
2 Dr XL 4WD Std Cab Stepside SB	10445	12585
2 Dr XL 4WD Ext Cab Stepside SB	10815	13030
2 Dr XL 4WD Std Cab LB	10570	12735
2 Dr XLT Std Cab SB	7775	9370

Don't forget to refer to the Mileage Adjustment Table at the back of this book!

 © 1999 by Edmund Publications Corporation

Model Description	Trade-in Value	Market Value
2 Dr XLT Ext Cab SB	9025	10870
2 Dr XLT Std Cab Stepside SB	7760	9350
2 Dr XLT Ext Cab Stepside SB	9025	10870
2 Dr XLT Std Cab LB	7860	9470
2 Dr XLT 4WD Ext Cab SB	11180	13470
2 Dr XLT 4WD Std Cab SB	11005	13260
2 Dr XLT 4WD Std Cab Stepside SB	10965	13210
2 Dr XLT 4WD Ext Cab Stepside SB	11180	13470
2 Dr XLT 4WD Std Cab LB	11115	13390

OPTIONS FOR RANGER

6 cyl 3.0 L Engine +470
6 cyl 4.0 L Engine +560
Auto 4-Speed Transmission +710
Auto 5-Speed Transmission +735
Air Conditioning +550
Aluminum/Alloy Wheels[Std on Splash] +235
AM/FM Compact Disc Playr +260
Anti-Lock Brakes +420
Bed Liner +190
Chrome Wheels[Opt on XLT] +165
Cruise Control +145
Keyless Entry System +140
Limited Slip Diff +180
Power Door Locks +155
Power Drivers Seat +190
Power Steering[Std on Splash,STX,Ext Cab,4WD] +190
Power Windows +160

TAURUS 1997

After totally redesigning the Taurus for 1996, Ford is taking it slow with changes for '97. A few new exterior color choices are added and there are minor changes to a couple of optional equipment packages.

RATINGS (SCALE OF 1-10)

Overall	Safety	Reliability	Performance	Comfort	Value
7.8	7.1	8.2	8	8	7.7

Model Description	Trade-in Value	Market Value
Category C		
4 Dr G Sdn	9300	11480
4 Dr GL Wgn	9955	12290
4 Dr GL Sdn	9620	11880
4 Dr LX Sdn	11490	14185
4 Dr LX Wgn	11635	14365
Category F		
4 Dr SHO Sdn	14485	17665

OPTIONS FOR TAURUS

Aluminum/Alloy Wheels[Opt on G,GL] +195
AM/FM Compact Disc Playr +260
Anti-Lock Brakes[Std on SHO] +425
Child Seat (1) +80
Chrome Wheels +385
Climate Control for AC +115
Cruise Control[Std on SHO] +140
Keyless Entry System +120
Leather Seats +390
Power Door Locks[Opt on G,GL] +135
Power Drivers Seat[Opt on GL] +160
Power Moonroof +475
Third Seat +115

THUNDERBIRD 1997

The Thunderbird receives few updates this year. A revised center console, a few new colors, and standard four-wheel disc brakes are the big news for 1997.

RATINGS (SCALE OF 1-10)

Overall	Safety	Reliability	Performance	Comfort	Value
7.7	7.9	8.1	8	7.9	6.4

Model Description	Trade-in Value	Market Value
Category C		
2 Dr LX Cpe	10395	12835

OPTIONS FOR THUNDERBIRD

8 cyl 4.6 L Engine +505
Aluminum/Alloy Wheels +195
Anti-Lock Brakes +425
Chrome Wheels +405
Compact Disc W/fm/tape +250
Keyless Entry System +130
Leather Seats +390
Power Drivers Seat +195
Power Moonroof +475
Premium Sound System +270
Traction Control System +190

WINDSTAR 1997

Nothing is new for the 1997 Ford Windsar.

RATINGS (SCALE OF 1-10)

Overall	Safety	Reliability	Performance	Comfort	Value
7.6	8.4	8.3	6.8	7.3	7

Model Description	Trade-in Value	Market Value
Category G		
2 Dr GL Pass. Van	12335	14860
2 Dr LX Pass. Van	14465	17430
2 Dr STD Cargo Van	10835	13055

OPTIONS FOR WINDSTAR

6 cyl 3.8 L Engine[Std on LX] +280
Air Conditioning[Std on LX] +550
Aluminum/Alloy Wheels[Opt on GL] +235
AM/FM Compact Disc Playr +260
Child Seats (2) +175
Cruise Control[Std on LX] +145
Dual Air Conditioning +685
Keyless Entry System +140
Leather Seats +520
Luggage Rack +105
Power Door Locks[Std on LX] +155
Power Windows[Std on LX] +160
Traction Control System +200

Don't forget to refer to the Mileage Adjustment Table at the back of this book!

 © 1999 by Edmund Publications Corporation

1996 FORD

AEROSTAR 1996

Smoother shifting transmission debuts, along with revised A/C controls and a new radio with visible controls. Solar tinted glass is standard.

RATINGS (SCALE OF 1-10)

Overall	Safety	Reliability	Performance	Comfort	Value
7.4	5.8	7.7	6.8	7.5	9.1

Model Description	Trade-in Value	Market Value
Category G		
2 Dr STD Cargo Van	6925	8660
2 Dr XLT Pass. Van Ext	8855	11070
2 Dr XLT Pass. Van	8540	10670
2 Dr XLT 4WD Pass. Van Ext	10525	13155

OPTIONS FOR AEROSTAR

6 cyl 4.0 L Engine[Opt on 2WD] +420
Air Conditioning[Opt on STD] +450
Aluminum/Alloy Wheels +190
AM/FM Compact Disc Playr +215
Captain Chairs (4) +350
Child Seat (1) +95
Cruise Control[Opt on STD,Pass. Van] +115
Dual Air Conditioning +560
Luggage Rack +85
Power Door Locks +125
Power Windows +130

ASPIRE 1996

Korean-built minicompact loses the SE trim level and several items of standard and optional equipment. Four new colors debut.

RATINGS (SCALE OF 1-10)

Overall	Safety	Reliability	Performance	Comfort	Value
7.1	6.6	8.4	7.2	7.3	5.9

Model Description	Trade-in Value	Market Value
Category E		
2 Dr STD Hbk	3915	5220
4 Dr STD Hbk	4100	5465

OPTIONS FOR ASPIRE

Auto 3-Speed Transmission +345
Air Conditioning +450
AM/FM Stereo Tape +170
Anti-Lock Brakes +395
Power Steering +140

BRONCO 1996

Trick new turn signal system is embedded in side view mirrors. Otherwise, minor trim changes mark the passing of the last Bronco.

RATINGS (SCALE OF 1-10)

Overall	Safety	Reliability	Performance	Comfort	Value
7.1	8	7.8	6.4	6.6	6.6

Model Description	Trade-in Value	Market Value
Category H		
2 Dr Eddie Bauer 4WD Utility	14275	17195
2 Dr XL 4WD Utility	12845	15475
2 Dr XLT 4WD Utility	13560	16340

OPTIONS FOR BRONCO

8 cyl 5.8 L Engine +520
Auto 4-Speed Transmission[Opt on XL,XLT] +555
Air Conditioning[Opt on XL,XLT] +450
AM/FM Compact Disc Playr +165
Camper/Towing Package +195
Chrome Wheels +165
Keyless Entry System +90
Leather Seats +575
Limited Slip Diff +140
Power Door Locks +105
Power Windows +105
Rear Window Defroster[Opt on XL,XLT] +85
Velour/Cloth Seats[Std on XLT] +75

CLUB WAGON/ECONOLINE 1996

For Club Wagon, the flip-out rear door glass is replaced by that of the fixed variety, four new colors are available, and E-150 models get plastic hubcaps. For Econoline, monster 14,050 GVWR E-350 van and van cutaway are introduced.

RATINGS (SCALE OF 1-10)

Overall	Safety	Reliability	Performance	Comfort	Value
N/A	7	8.5	6.8	7.9	N/A

E-150

Model Description	Trade-in Value	Market Value
Category H		
2 Dr Chateau Club Wagon	15050	18130
2 Dr STD Econoline	12070	14545
2 Dr XL Econoline	12615	15200
2 Dr XL Club Wagon	11850	14275
2 Dr XLT Club Wagon	13245	15955

E-250

Model Description	Trade-in Value	Market Value
Category H		
2 Dr STD Econoline Ext	10435	12575
2 Dr STD Econoline	9740	11730
2 Dr XL Econoline Ext	11030	13290
2 Dr XL Econoline	10420	12555

E-350

Model Description	Trade-in Value	Market Value
Category H		
2 Dr Chateau Club Wagon	14490	17460
2 Dr STD Econoline	10735	12935
2 Dr STD Econoline Ext	10910	13145
2 Dr XL Econoline	10955	13200
2 Dr XL Club Wagon	11115	13395
2 Dr XL Club Wagon Ext	11565	13935
2 Dr XL Econoline Ext	11165	13450
2 Dr XLT Club Wagon Ext	12075	14550
2 Dr XLT Club Wagon	11865	14295

Don't forget to refer to the Mileage Adjustment Table at the back of this book!

 © 1999 by Edmund Publications Corporation

Model Description	Trade-in Value	Market Value

OPTIONS FOR CLUB WAGON/ECONOLINE

8 cyl 5.0 L Engine +310
8 cyl 5.8 L Engine +520
8 cyl 7.5 L Engine +470
8 cyl 7.3 L Turbodsl Engine +2475
Auto 4-Speed Transmission[Opt on E-250,E-350, STD] +165
Air Conditioning[Std on XLT] +450
Aluminum/Alloy Wheels[Std on Chateau] +175
AM/FM Stereo Tape[Std on Chateau] +135
Anti-Lock Brakes[Opt on Econoline,Econoline Ext] +280
Camper/Towing Package +195
Chrome Bumpers[Std on Chateau,XLT,E-150] +95
Cruise Control[Std on Chateau] +105
Dual Air Conditioning[Std on Chateau] +790
Keyless Entry System +90
Limited Slip Diff +140
Power Door Locks[Opt on STD, XL Club Wagon] +105
Power Drivers Seat +150
Power Windows[Opt on STD, XL Club Wagon] +105

CONTOUR 1996

Designers sculpt and adjust interior seating to make more leg and head room in the back seat. Five new colors are available, improvements to shift effort on manual transmission models, and the deletion of the bright trim insert in the bumpers make the 1996 Contour more competitive.

RATINGS (SCALE OF 1-10)

Overall	Safety	Reliability	Performance	Comfort	Value
7.5	6.9	7.4	8.4	7.9	6.8

Category C		
4 Dr GL Sdn	6300	8180
4 Dr LX Sdn	6730	8745
4 Dr SE Sdn	7475	9705

OPTIONS FOR CONTOUR

6 cyl 2.5 L Engine[Std on SE] +550
Auto 4-Speed Transmission +425
Air Conditioning +445
AM/FM Compact Disc Playr +215
Anti-Lock Brakes +345
Keyless Entry System +105
Leather Seats +320
Power Door Locks +135
Power Drivers Seat +160
Power Moonroof +390
Power Windows +170

CROWN VICTORIA 1996

A new steering wheel and gas cap are standard, and some equipment has been dropped from the roster, including the JBL sound system and trailer towing package.

RATINGS (SCALE OF 1-10)

Overall	Safety	Reliability	Performance	Comfort	Value
8.1	8	7.9	7.7	8.3	8.8

Category B		
4 Dr LX Sdn	10675	13345
4 Dr STD Sdn	9990	12485

OPTIONS FOR CROWN VICTORIA

Handling/Performance Package +570
Anti-Lock Brakes +395
Climate Control for AC +100
Cruise Control +120
Dual Power Seats +200
Keyless Entry System +100
Leather Seats +370
Power Door Locks +140
Premium Sound System +235
Traction Control System +100
Trip Computer +120

ESCORT 1996

Last year for the second-generation Escort. The 1.9-liter engine gets 100,000 mile tune-up interval. Automatic transmissions have lower final drive ratio when coupled with 1.9-liter engine to improve acceleration. Sport/Appearance Group available on four-door models. Ultra Violet decor no longer offered on GT. Integrated child safety seat, added during 1995 model year, continues for 1996 on sedan and wagon.

RATINGS (SCALE OF 1-10)

Overall	Safety	Reliability	Performance	Comfort	Value
7	6.6	8.1	6.8	7.3	6.1

Category E		
2 Dr GT Hbk	6380	8505
2 Dr LX Hbk	4815	6420
4 Dr LX Hbk	4840	6450
4 Dr LX Sdn	5090	6790
4 Dr LX Wgn	5080	6770
2 Dr STD Hbk	4495	5995

OPTIONS FOR ESCORT

Auto 4-Speed Transmission +425
Air Conditioning +450
AM/FM Compact Disc Playr +260
Anti-Lock Brakes +395
Child Seat (1) +65
Cruise Control +120
Luggage Rack +70
Power Door Locks +130
Power Moonroof +325
Power Steering[Std on GT] +140
Power Windows +145
Rear Spoiler[Opt on LX] +115
Tilt Steering Wheel +85

Don't forget to refer to the Mileage Adjustment Table at the back of this book!

 © 1999 by Edmund Publications Corporation

Model Description	Trade-in Value	Market Value

EXPLORER 1996

The long-awaited V8 AWD Explorers are available in XLT, Eddie Bauer or Limited Edition flavors. An integrated child safety seat is optional, and the Expedition model has been replaced by a Premium trim package for the Sport. Limited models get an exclusive color choice.

RATINGS (SCALE OF 1-10)

Overall	Safety	Reliability	Performance	Comfort	Value
7.8	7.5	7.5	7.6	7.1	9.2

Category G

Model Description	Trade-in Value	Market Value
4 Dr Eddie Bauer Wgn	14230	17790
4 Dr Eddie Bauer 4WD Wgn	14790	18490
4 Dr Limited Wgn	15550	19435
4 Dr Limited 4WD Wgn	15885	19855
2 Dr Sport Utility	11665	14585
2 Dr Sport 4WD Utility	12720	15895
2 Dr XL Utility	10355	12945
2 Dr XL 4WD Utility	12060	15075
4 Dr XL Wgn	11820	14775
4 Dr XL 4WD Wgn	12380	15475
4 Dr XLT Wgn	13350	16690
4 Dr XLT 4WD Wgn	14010	17515

OPTIONS FOR EXPLORER

8 cyl 5.0 L Engine +525
Auto 4-Speed Transmission[Opt on Sport,XL,XLT] +515
Premium Sport Package +1315
Aluminum/Alloy Wheels +190
AM/FM Stereo Tape[Std on Eddie Bauer] +135
Camper/Towing Package +160
Child Seat (1) +95
Chrome Wheels[Opt on Sport] +135
Climate Control for AC[Std on Limited] +110
Compact Disc Changer +290
Cruise Control[Opt on XL] +115
Dual Power Seats[Opt on XLT] +350
JBL Sound System[Std on Limited] +425
Keyless Entry System[Opt on Sport,XLT, Eddie Bauer] +115
Leather Seats[Std on Limited] +425
Limited Slip Diff +145
Luggage Rack[Opt on Sport,XL,XLT] +85
Power Door Locks[Opt on XL] +125
Power Moonroof +490
Power Windows[Opt on XL] +130
Running Boards[Std on Limited] +215

F-SERIES PICKUP 1996

Until an all-new truck goes into production for release in the spring, we're stuck with the same old truck that's been on the road since 1980. The Lightning has been axed from the 1996 lineup. Two new F-250 models debut, and both F-250 and F-350 models receive improvements.

RATINGS (SCALE OF 1-10)

Overall	Safety	Reliability	Performance	Comfort	Value
N/A	6.6	7.9	6.8	7.4	N/A

F-150

Category H

Model Description	Trade-in Value	Market Value
2 Dr Eddie Bauer Ext Cab SB	11165	13450
2 Dr Eddie Bauer Std Cab SB	10655	12840
2 Dr Eddie Bauer Ext Cab Stepside SB	11165	13450
2 Dr Eddie Bauer Std Cab Stepside SB	10670	12855
2 Dr Eddie Bauer Std Cab LB	10735	12935
2 Dr Eddie Bauer Ext Cab LB	11230	13535
2 Dr Eddie Bauer 4WD Std Cab SB	12175	14670
2 Dr Eddie Bauer 4WD Ext Cab SB	12995	15655
2 Dr Eddie Bauer 4WD Ext Cab Stepside SB	12925	15570
2 Dr Eddie Bauer 4WD Std Cab Stepside SB	12175	14670
2 Dr Eddie Bauer 4WD Std Cab LB	12270	14780
2 Dr Eddie Bauer 4WD Ext Cab LB	12995	15655
2 Dr Special Std Cab SB	6950	8370
2 Dr Special Ext Cab SB	7725	9305
2 Dr Special Std Cab LB	7120	8575
2 Dr Special Ext Cab LB	8140	9805
2 Dr Special 4WD Std Cab SB	10380	12505
2 Dr Special 4WD Std Cab LB	10910	13145
2 Dr XL Std Cab SB	8955	10790
2 Dr XL Ext Cab SB	9375	11295
2 Dr XL Std Cab Stepside SB	8965	10805
2 Dr XL Ext Cab Stepside SB	9455	11395
2 Dr XL Ext Cab LB	9525	11480
2 Dr XL Std Cab LB	8950	10785
2 Dr XL 4WD Std Cab SB	10510	12665
2 Dr XL 4WD Ext Cab SB	10965	13210
2 Dr XL 4WD Ext Cab Stepside SB	10965	13210
2 Dr XL 4WD Std Cab Stepside SB	10510	12665
2 Dr XL 4WD Std Cab LB	10500	12655
2 Dr XL 4WD Ext Cab LB	11030	13290
2 Dr XLT Std Cab SB	10530	12685
2 Dr XLT Ext Cab SB	10905	13140

Don't forget to refer to the Mileage Adjustment Table at the back of this book!

 © 1999 by Edmund Publications Corporation

Model Description	Trade-in Value	Market Value
2 Dr XLT Std Cab Stepside SB	10420	12555
2 Dr XLT Ext Cab Stepside SB	10905	13140
2 Dr XLT Std Cab LB	10605	12775
2 Dr XLT Ext Cab LB	10975	13220
2 Dr XLT 4WD Ext Cab SB	12295	14815
2 Dr XLT 4WD Std Cab SB	11915	14355
2 Dr XLT 4WD Std Cab Stepside SB	11915	14355
2 Dr XLT 4WD Ext Cab Stepside SB	12340	14870
2 Dr XLT 4WD Std Cab LB	12010	14465
2 Dr XLT 4WD Ext Cab LB	12360	14895

F-250

Category H

Model Description	Trade-in Value	Market Value
2 Dr XL Ext Cab SB	13255	15970
2 Dr XL Ext Cab LB	12860	15495
2 Dr XL Std Cab LB	10340	12455
2 Dr XL 4WD Ext Cab SB	14475	17440
2 Dr XL 4WD Ext Cab LB	14130	17025
2 Dr XL 4WD Std Cab LB	12185	14680
4 Dr XL Crew Cab LB	15670	18880
4 Dr XL 4WD Crew Cab LB	16260	19590
2 Dr XLT Ext Cab SB	14925	17985
2 Dr XLT Std Cab LB	11590	13960
2 Dr XLT Ext Cab LB	14535	17510
2 Dr XLT 4WD Ext Cab SB	16185	19500
2 Dr XLT 4WD Std Cab LB	13550	16325
2 Dr XLT 4WD Ext Cab LB	15795	19030
4 Dr XLT Crew Cab LB	17335	20885
4 Dr XLT 4WD Crew Cab LB	17805	21450

F-350

Category H

Model Description	Trade-in Value	Market Value
2 Dr XL Ext Cab LB	15585	18775
2 Dr XL Std Cab LB	13940	16795
2 Dr XL 4WD Std Cab LB	15690	18905
4 Dr XL Crew Cab LB	16375	19725
4 Dr XL 4WD Crew Cab LB	17480	21060
2 Dr XLT Std Cab LB	15565	18755
2 Dr XLT Ext Cab LB	17130	20640
2 Dr XLT 4WD Std Cab LB	16585	19980
4 Dr XLT Crew Cab LB	17570	21170
4 Dr XLT 4WD Crew Cab LB	18665	22490

OPTIONS FOR F-SERIES PICKUP

8 cyl 5.0 L Engine +310
8 cyl 5.8 L Engine +520
8 cyl 7.5 L Engine +470
8 cyl 7.3 L Turbodsl Engine +2475
Auto 3-Speed Transmission +405
Auto 4-Speed Transmission +530
Air Conditioning[Opt on Special,XL] +450
Anti-Lock Brakes +280
Camper/Towing Package +195
Chrome Wheels[Opt on XL] +165
Compact Disc W/fm/tape +175
Cruise Control[Opt on Special,XL] +105
Dual Rear Wheels +470
Keyless Entry System +90
Limited Slip Diff +140
Power Door Locks[Opt on XL] +105
Power Drivers Seat +150
Power Windows[Opt on XL] +105
Rear Bench Seat +185
Skid Plates +60
Tilt Steering Wheel[Opt on Special,XL] +100

MUSTANG 1996

After much anticipation among enthusiasts, Ford plugs a 4.6-liter modular V8 into its pony car. Too bad it doesn't make any more power than the old 5.0-liter motor it replaces. Suspension and steering upgrades compliment the new engine, which does live up to its promise in the limited-edition 305-horsepower Cobra. Base cars also get engine improvements, and all Mustangs get minor styling revisions. Collectors hint: The GTS model, a midyear 1995 V8 base Mustang, has been dropped. Buy one if you can find one.

RATINGS (SCALE OF 1-10)

Overall	Safety	Reliability	Performance	Comfort	Value
6.9	6.9	8	8.8	7.3	3.5

Category F

Model Description	Trade-in Value	Market Value
2 Dr Cobra Cpe	14375	17970
2 Dr Cobra Conv	15385	19230
2 Dr GT Conv	12525	15655
2 Dr GT Cpe	10520	13150
2 Dr STD Cpe	8070	10090
2 Dr STD Conv	10155	12695

OPTIONS FOR MUSTANG

Auto 4-Speed Transmission +425
Mystic Metallic Paint +425
Air Conditioning[Std on Cobra] +460
Anti-Lock Brakes[Std on Cobra] +400
Compact Disc W/fm/tape +290
Cruise Control[Std on Cobra] +115
Keyless Entry System[Std on Cobra] +95
Leather Seats +395
Power Door Locks[Std on Cobra,Conv] +110
Power Drivers Seat[Std on Cobra] +130
Power Windows[Std on Cobra,Conv] +125
Premium Sound System +225
Rear Spoiler[Std on Cobra,Conv] +155

PROBE 1996

Ford concentrates on the SE and GT trim levels this year, revising and simplifying options lists and making minor cosmetic and trim revisions.

Don't forget to refer to the Mileage Adjustment Table at the back of this book!

 © 1999 by Edmund Publications Corporation

Model Description	Trade-in Value	Market Value

RATINGS (SCALE OF 1-10)

Overall	Safety	Reliability	Performance	Comfort	Value
7	7.2	8	9	7.4	3.7

Model Description	Trade-in Value	Market Value
Category E		
2 Dr GT Hbk	7280	9705
2 Dr SE Hbk	6460	8615
2 Dr STD Hbk	6330	8445

OPTIONS FOR PROBE

Auto 4-Speed Transmission +425
Air Conditioning +450
AM/FM Compact Disc Playr +260
Anti-Lock Brakes +395
Chrome Wheels +215
Cruise Control +120
Keyless Entry System +80
Leather Seats +495
Power Door Locks +130
Power Drivers Seat +165
Power Sunroof +335
Power Windows +145
Tilt Steering Wheel +85

RANGER 1996

An optional passenger-side airbag is available, and it comes with a switch that will disable the system if a child seat is installed in the truck. Cool, huh? Super Cab models get standard privacy glass, Splash models lose that putrid green tape stripe, and the Flareside box from the Splash is now available on two-wheel drive, four-cylinder XL and XLT models.

RATINGS (SCALE OF 1-10)

Overall	Safety	Reliability	Performance	Comfort	Value
N/A	6.5	8.8	7.2	7.3	N/A

Model Description	Trade-in Value	Market Value
Category G		
2 Dr Splash Std Cab Stepside SB	8485	10605
2 Dr Splash Ext Cab Stepside SB	9515	11895
2 Dr Splash 4WD Std Cab Stepside SB	10535	13170
2 Dr Splash 4WD Ext Cab Stepside SB	10960	13700
2 Dr STX 4WD Std Cab SB	10030	12535
2 Dr STX 4WD Ext Cab SB	10340	12925
2 Dr STX 4WD Std Cab LB	10135	12670
2 Dr XL Std Cab SB	6600	8250
2 Dr XL Ext Cab SB	7340	9175
2 Dr XL Ext Cab Stepside SB	7340	9175
2 Dr XL Std Cab Stepside SB	6570	8210
2 Dr XL Std Cab LB	6715	8390
2 Dr XL 4WD Std Cab SB	8620	10780
2 Dr XL 4WD Ext Cab SB	9600	12005
2 Dr XL 4WD Ext Cab Stepside SB	9610	12010
2 Dr XL 4WD Std Cab Stepside SB	8685	10855
2 Dr XL 4WD Std Cab LB	8850	11065
2 Dr XLT Ext Cab SB	7840	9805
2 Dr XLT Std Cab SB	6845	8555
2 Dr XLT Std Cab Stepside SB	6835	8540
2 Dr XLT Ext Cab Stepside SB	7840	9805
2 Dr XLT Std Cab LB	6975	8720
2 Dr XLT 4WD Ext Cab SB	9420	11775
2 Dr XLT 4WD Std Cab SB	9270	11590
2 Dr XLT 4WD Ext Cab Stepside SB	9420	11775
2 Dr XLT 4WD Std Cab Stepside SB	9315	11640
2 Dr XLT 4WD Std Cab LB	9330	11665

OPTIONS FOR RANGER

6 cyl 3.0 L Engine +390
6 cyl 4.0 L Engine +420
Auto 4-Speed Transmission +570
Air Conditioning +450
AM/FM Compact Disc Playr +215
Anti-Lock Brakes[Opt on 2WD] +345
Bed Liner +155
Chrome Wheels[Opt on XL,XLT] +135
Cruise Control +115
Dual Air Bag Restraints +235
Keyless Entry System +115
Limited Slip Diff +145
Power Door Locks +125
Power Drivers Seat +155
Power Steering[Std on Splash,STX,Ext Cab,4WD] +155
Power Windows +130

TAURUS 1996

All-new Taurus debuts in sedan and wagon format, available in GL, LX, and SHO trim levels. New or substantially revised engines and suspensions improve the performance of the Taurus, while several functional innovations make the car easier and more enjoyable to drive.

RATINGS (SCALE OF 1-10)

Overall	Safety	Reliability	Performance	Comfort	Value
7.8	7.1	7.8	8	8	8

Model Description	Trade-in Value	Market Value
Category C		
4 Dr G Sdn	7840	10185
4 Dr GL Sdn	7945	10315
4 Dr GL Wgn	8270	10740
4 Dr LX Wgn	9785	12705
4 Dr LX Sdn	9550	12405
Category F		
4 Dr SHO Sdn	13490	16860

Don't forget to refer to the Mileage Adjustment Table at the back of this book!

 © 1999 by Edmund Publications Corporation

Model Description	Trade-in Value	Market Value

OPTIONS FOR TAURUS

AM/FM Compact Disc Playr +215
Anti-Lock Brakes[Std on SHO] +345
Child Seat (1) +65
Chrome Wheels[Opt on LX] +315
Climate Control for AC +95
Cruise Control[Std on SHO] +115
Keyless Entry System +95
Leather Seats[Opt on LX] +320
Power Door Locks[Opt on GL] +110
Power Drivers Seat[Opt on GL] +130
Power Moonroof +390
Premium Sound System +220
Third Seat +95

THUNDERBIRD 1996

Revised styling greatly improves the look of the Thunderbird for 1996. The Super Coupe is deleted, replaced by a Sport Package for the V8 model. Base V6 engines have been upgraded, and go 100,000 miles between tune-ups. Equipment rosters have been shuffled.

RATINGS (SCALE OF 1-10)

Overall	Safety	Reliability	Performance	Comfort	Value
7.6	7.9	7.5	8	7.9	6.6

Category C		
2 Dr LX Cpe	8590	11155

OPTIONS FOR THUNDERBIRD

AM/FM Compact Disc Playr +215
Anti-Lock Brakes +345
Chrome Wheels +330
Climate Control for AC +100
Keyless Entry System +105
Leather Seats +320
Power Drivers Seat +160
Power Moonroof +390
Premium Sound System +220
Traction Control System +155

WINDSTAR 1996

Holy Smokes! That's just what the front tires will be doing, unless you find one with the optional traction control system. Ford boosted output on the 3.8-liter V6 from 155 to 200 horsepower. Trim and equipment have been revised, and four-wheel disc brakes come with traction control or the tow package. A new integrated child safety seat has been added to the options list. Tune-ups happen every 100,000 miles.

RATINGS (SCALE OF 1-10)

Overall	Safety	Reliability	Performance	Comfort	Value
7.5	8.3	7.7	6.8	7.3	7.4

Category G		
2 Dr GL Pass. Van	10040	12545
2 Dr LX Pass. Van	13340	16675
2 Dr STD Cargo Van	7125	8905

OPTIONS FOR WINDSTAR

6 cyl 3.8 L Engine[Std on LX] +235
Air Conditioning[Std on LX] +450
AM/FM Compact Disc Playr +215
Child Seats (2) +145
Cruise Control +115
Dual Air Conditioning +560
Keyless Entry System +115
Luggage Rack +85
Power Door Locks[Std on LX] +125
Power Windows[Std on LX] +130
Traction Control System +165

1995 FORD

AEROSTAR 1995

The XL and Eddie Bauer trim levels are dropped; only the XLT remains. The AWD system is only available in extended-length versions. Antilock brakes become standard for the Aerostar.

RATINGS (SCALE OF 1-10)

Overall	Safety	Reliability	Performance	Comfort	Value
7.2	6.1	7.2	6.6	7.5	8.5

Category G		
2 Dr STD Cargo Van	5360	6785
2 Dr XLT Pass. Van Ext	7790	9860
2 Dr XLT Pass. Van	6820	8635
2 Dr XLT 4WD Pass. Van Ext	9515	12045

OPTIONS FOR AEROSTAR

6 cyl 4.0 L Engine[Opt on 2WD] +340
Air Conditioning[Opt on STD] +370
AM/FM Stereo Tape[Std on 4WD] +110
Camper/Towing Package +130
Captain Chairs (4) +285
Child Seat (1) +80
Cruise Control[Opt on STD] +95
Dual Air Conditioning +460
Luggage Rack +70
Power Door Locks[Std on 4WD] +105
Power Windows[Std on 4WD] +105

ASPIRE 1995

Commonly referred to as the Expire, the latest runabout from Ford has little to offer but economy. Available as a two- or four door hatchback, the Aspire comes with dual airbags and available antilock brakes.

RATINGS (SCALE OF 1-10)

Overall	Safety	Reliability	Performance	Comfort	Value
7.5	7.3	8.2	7.2	7.3	7.3

Don't forget to refer to the Mileage Adjustment Table at the back of this book!

 © 1999 by Edmund Publications Corporation

Model Description	Trade-in Value	Market Value
Category E		
2 Dr SE Hbk	3640	4990
2 Dr STD Hbk	3195	4375
4 Dr STD Hbk	3110	4260

OPTIONS FOR ASPIRE

Auto 3-Speed Transmission +260
Air Conditioning +370
AM/FM Compact Disc Playr +215
Anti-Lock Brakes +320
Power Steering +115
Premium Sound System +155
Rear Window Defroster +75

BRONCO 1995

An available Sport Package and new exterior styling for the Eddie Bauer model are the sole changes for 1995.

RATINGS (SCALE OF 1-10)

Overall	Safety	Reliability	Performance	Comfort	Value
7.3	8.8	7.6	6.4	6.6	6.9

Model Description	Trade-in Value	Market Value
Category H		
2 Dr Eddie Bauer 4WD Utility	12265	15140
2 Dr XL 4WD Utility	10775	13305
2 Dr XLT 4WD Utility	11390	14065

OPTIONS FOR BRONCO

8 cyl 5.8 L Engine +410
Auto 4-Speed Transmission[Opt on XL,XLT] +465
Air Conditioning[Opt on XL,XLT] +365
AM/FM Compact Disc Playr +135
Camper/Towing Package +160
Chrome Wheels +135
Keyless Entry System +70
Leather Seats +470
Limited Slip Diff +115
Power Door Locks +85
Power Windows +85
Velour/Cloth Seats +60

CLUB WAGON/ECONOLINE 1995

The optional diesel engine gets a turbocharger. Heavy-duty versions of the van receive the driver airbag that became standard on light-duty models in 1992.

RATINGS (SCALE OF 1-10)

Overall	Safety	Reliability	Performance	Comfort	Value
N/A	7.7	8.6	6.8	7.9	N/A

E-150

Model Description	Trade-in Value	Market Value
Category H		
2 Dr Chateau Club Wagon	11695	14435
2 Dr STD Econoline	9865	12180
2 Dr XL Econoline	10640	13135
2 Dr XL Club Wagon	9305	11490
2 Dr XLT Club Wagon	10550	13025

E-250

Model Description	Trade-in Value	Market Value
Category H		
2 Dr STD Econoline	8330	10285
2 Dr STD Econoline Ext	8850	10925
2 Dr XL Econoline	8630	10655
2 Dr XL Econoline Ext	9385	11585

E-350

Model Description	Trade-in Value	Market Value
Category H		
2 Dr Chateau Club Wagon	10970	13545
2 Dr STD Econoline	9895	12215
2 Dr STD Econoline Ext	10530	13005
2 Dr XL Club Wagon	8865	10945
2 Dr XL Econoline Ext	10975	13550
2 Dr XL Club Wagon Ext	9620	11875
2 Dr XL Econoline	10305	12725
2 Dr XLT Club Wagon Ext	10495	12960
2 Dr XLT Club Wagon	9885	12205

OPTIONS FOR CLUB WAGON/ECONOLINE

8 cyl 5.0 L Engine +270
8 cyl 5.8 L Engine +410
8 cyl 7.5 L Engine +390
8 cyl 7.3 L Turbodsl Engine +1985
Auto 4-Speed Transmission[Opt on E-250,E-350] +135
Air Conditioning[Opt on STD,XL] +365
AM/FM Stereo Tape[Std on Chateau] +110
Anti-Lock Brakes[Std on Club Wagon,Club Wagon Ext] +230
Camper/Towing Package[Opt on E-150,E-250,Club Wagon] +160
Chrome Bumpers[Opt on] +75
Cruise Control[Std on Chateau] +90
Dual Air Conditioning +645
Keyless Entry System +70
Limited Slip Diff +115
Power Door Locks[Opt on STD, XL] +85
Power Drivers Seat +125
Power Windows[Opt on STD, XL] +85
Velour/Cloth Seats[Std on XL] +60

CONTOUR 1995

The Contour replaces the much maligned Tempo in an attempt to compete with European and Japanese compacts. Based on the European Mondeo, the Contour has front-wheel drive and dual airbags. Traction control and antilock brakes are available on all models, as is a V6 engine that produces an impressive 170 horsepower.

RATINGS (SCALE OF 1-10)

Overall	Safety	Reliability	Performance	Comfort	Value
7.6	7.5	7	8.4	7.9	7.1

Don't forget to refer to the Mileage Adjustment Table at the back of this book!

 © 1999 by Edmund Publications Corporation

Model Description	Trade-in Value	Market Value
Category C		
4 Dr GL Sdn	5450	7175
4 Dr LX Sdn	5925	7795
4 Dr SE Sdn	6515	8570

OPTIONS FOR CONTOUR

6 cyl 2.5 L Engine[Std on SE] +430
Auto 4-Speed Transmission +365
Air Conditioning +360
Anti-Lock Brakes +285
Compact Disc W/fm/tape +170
Cruise Control +95
Keyless Entry System +85
Leather Seats +260
Power Door Locks +110
Power Drivers Seat +130
Power Moonroof +320
Power Windows +140
Premium Sound System +180

CROWN VICTORIA 1995

New grille, trunk lid, wheels, and bumpers freshen the Crown Victoria's styling. Rear window defroster and heated outside mirrors move from the options list to the standard equipment roster. A new interior includes a revised stereo, backlit door switches, restyled instrument panel, and a fresh climate control system.

RATINGS (SCALE OF 1-10)

Overall	Safety	Reliability	Performance	Comfort	Value
7.9	8.7	7.5	7.7	8.3	7.4

Model Description	Trade-in Value	Market Value
Category B		
4 Dr LX Sdn	8465	10850
4 Dr STD Sdn	8130	10425

OPTIONS FOR CROWN VICTORIA

Handling/Performance Package +345
Aluminum/Alloy Wheels +150
AM/FM Stereo Tape +80
Anti-Lock Brakes +325
Camper/Towing Package +165
Climate Control for AC +80
Cruise Control +95
Dual Power Seats +160
Keyless Entry System +80
Leather Seats +300
Power Door Locks +115
Premium Sound System +190
Traction Control System +80

ESCORT 1995

A passenger airbag is now available but the motorized seat belts mysteriously remain. A more powerful, optional air conditioner appears in the revised instrument panel. An integrated child seat is available on sedans and wagons.

RATINGS (SCALE OF 1-10)

Overall	Safety	Reliability	Performance	Comfort	Value
6.8	7.2	7.9	6.8	7.3	5.1

Model Description	Trade-in Value	Market Value
Category E		
2 Dr GT Hbk	5160	7065
2 Dr LX Hbk	4070	5575
4 Dr LX Hbk	4145	5680
4 Dr LX Wgn	4010	5495
4 Dr LX Sdn	4325	5925
2 Dr STD Hbk	3700	5065

OPTIONS FOR ESCORT

Auto 4-Speed Transmission +365
Air Conditioning +370
AM/FM Compact Disc Playr +215
Anti-Lock Brakes +320
Child Seat (1) +50
Cruise Control +100
Luggage Rack +60
Power Door Locks +105
Power Moonroof +265
Power Steering[Std on GT] +115
Power Windows +120
Premium Sound System +155
Rear Spoiler[Opt on LX] +95
Tilt Steering Wheel +70

EXPLORER 1995

Dual airbags top the changes for the redesigned Explorer. Integrated child safety seats are optional on four-door models. Exterior changes include new sheetmetal, headlights, grille, taillights, and side moldings. The Control-Trac four-wheel drive system automatically sends power to front wheels if it senses rear wheel slippage. This feature can be locked in for full-time four-wheeling.

RATINGS (SCALE OF 1-10)

Overall	Safety	Reliability	Performance	Comfort	Value
7.6	8.1	7	7.6	7.1	8.4

Model Description	Trade-in Value	Market Value
Category G		
4 Dr Eddie Bauer Wgn	12400	15695
4 Dr Eddie Bauer 4WD Wgn	13085	16560
2 Dr Expedition 4WD Utility	11920	15085
4 Dr Limited Wgn	13515	17110
4 Dr Limited 4WD Wgn	13870	17555
2 Dr Sport Utility	9585	12130
2 Dr Sport 4WD Utility	10930	13835
2 Dr XL Utility	8600	10890
2 Dr XL 4WD Utility	9955	12605
4 Dr XL Wgn	10360	13110
4 Dr XL 4WD Wgn	10880	13775
4 Dr XLT Wgn	11720	14840
4 Dr XLT 4WD Wgn	12230	15480

Don't forget to refer to the Mileage Adjustment Table at the back of this book!

 © 1999 by Edmund Publications Corporation

Model Description	Trade-in Value	Market Value

OPTIONS FOR EXPLORER

Auto 4-Speed Transmission[Opt on Sport,XL,XLT] +420
Aluminum/Alloy Wheels +155
AM/FM Stereo Tape[Opt on Sport,XL,XLT] +110
Camper/Towing Package +130
Climate Control for AC[Std on Limited] +90
Compact Disc Changer +235
Cruise Control[Opt on XL] +95
Dual Power Seats[Opt on Sport,XLT] +285
JBL Sound System[Std on Limited] +350
Keyless Entry System[Opt on Sport,XLT, Eddie Bauer] +95
Leather Seats[Std on Limited] +350
Limited Slip Diff +120
Luggage Rack[Opt on Sport,XL,XLT] +70
Power Door Locks[Opt on XL] +105
Power Moonroof +400
Power Windows[Opt on XL] +105
Running Boards[Std on Limited] +175

F-SERIES PICKUP 1995

The Lightning model returns after a one-year hiatus and a new turbo-diesel engine is made available.

RATINGS (SCALE OF 1-10)

Overall	Safety	Reliability	Performance	Comfort	Value
N/A	7.3	7.5	6.8	7.4	N/A

F-150

Category H

Model Description	Trade-in Value	Market Value
2 Dr Eddie Bauer Ext Cab SB	9875	12190
2 Dr Eddie Bauer Std Cab SB	9100	11230
2 Dr Eddie Bauer Std Cab Stepside SB	9535	11770
2 Dr Eddie Bauer Ext Cab Stepside SB	10260	12670
2 Dr Eddie Bauer Ext Cab LB	9945	12275
2 Dr Eddie Bauer Std Cab LB	9150	11300
2 Dr Eddie Bauer 4WD Ext Cab SB	11480	14170
2 Dr Eddie Bauer 4WD Std Cab SB	10585	13070
2 Dr Eddie Bauer 4WD Std Cab Stepside SB	11030	13615
2 Dr Eddie Bauer 4WD Ext Cab Stepside SB	11865	14650
2 Dr Eddie Bauer 4WD Ext Cab LB	11540	14250
2 Dr Eddie Bauer 4WD Std Cab LB	10685	13190
2 Dr Lightning Std Cab SB	11580	14295
2 Dr Special Ext Cab SB	8195	10120
2 Dr Special Std Cab SB	6345	7835
2 Dr Special Ext Cab LB	8195	10120
2 Dr Special Std Cab LB	6425	7935
2 Dr Special 4WD Std Cab SB	7480	9235
2 Dr Special 4WD Std Cab LB	7585	9360
2 Dr XL Ext Cab SB	8155	10065
2 Dr XL Std Cab SB	7650	9445
2 Dr XL Ext Cab Stepside SB	8610	10630
2 Dr XL Std Cab Stepside SB	8085	9985
2 Dr XL Ext Cab LB	8290	10235
2 Dr XL Std Cab LB	7710	9515
2 Dr XL 4WD Ext Cab SB	9785	12080
2 Dr XL 4WD Std Cab SB	9070	11195
2 Dr XL 4WD Ext Cab Stepside SB	10185	12575
2 Dr XL 4WD Std Cab Stepside SB	9510	11740
2 Dr XL 4WD Std Cab LB	9165	11315
2 Dr XL 4WD Ext Cab LB	9855	12165
2 Dr XLT Std Cab SB	8985	11090
2 Dr XLT Ext Cab SB	9315	11500
2 Dr XLT Ext Cab Stepside SB	9855	12165
2 Dr XLT Std Cab Stepside SB	9415	11625
2 Dr XLT Std Cab LB	9030	11150
2 Dr XLT Ext Cab LB	9315	11500
2 Dr XLT 4WD Ext Cab SB	10840	13380
2 Dr XLT 4WD Std Cab SB	10195	12585
2 Dr XLT 4WD Ext Cab Stepside SB	11225	13860
2 Dr XLT 4WD Std Cab Stepside SB	10630	13125
2 Dr XLT 4WD Ext Cab LB	10910	13470
2 Dr XLT 4WD Std Cab LB	10460	12915

F-250

Category H

Model Description	Trade-in Value	Market Value
2 Dr Special Ext Cab LB	10190	12580
2 Dr XL Std Cab LB	9255	11425
2 Dr XL Ext Cab LB	10525	12995
2 Dr XL 4WD Std Cab LB	11110	13715
2 Dr XL 4WD Ext Cab LB	11765	14520
2 Dr XLT Std Cab LB	10445	12895
2 Dr XLT Ext Cab LB	11690	14435
2 Dr XLT 4WD Std Cab LB	12135	14985
2 Dr XLT 4WD Ext Cab LB	13040	16100

F-350

Category H

Model Description	Trade-in Value	Market Value
2 Dr XL Ext Cab LB	12165	15015
2 Dr XL Std Cab LB	11860	14640
2 Dr XL 4WD Std Cab LB	12095	14935
4 Dr XL Crew Cab LB	12355	15255
4 Dr XL 4WD Crew Cab LB	13565	16745
2 Dr XLT Ext Cab LB	13140	16220

Don't forget to refer to the Mileage Adjustment Table at the back of this book!

© 1999 by Edmund Publications Corporation

Model Description	Trade-in Value	Market Value
2 Dr XLT Std Cab LB	13105	16180
2 Dr XLT 4WD Std Cab LB	13310	16430
4 Dr XLT Crew Cab LB	13145	16230
4 Dr XLT 4WD Crew Cab LB	14835	18315

OPTIONS FOR F-SERIES PICKUP

8 cyl 5.0 L Engine +270
8 cyl 5.8 L Engine +410
8 cyl 7.5 L Engine +390
8 cyl 7.3 L Turbodsl Engine +1985
Auto 3-Speed Transmission +330
Auto 4-Speed Transmission[Std on Lightning] +435
Air Conditioning[Opt on Special,XL] +365
AM/FM Compact Disc Playr +135
Camper/Towing Package +160
Chrome Wheels[Opt on XL] +135
Cruise Control[Opt on Special,XL] +90
Dual Rear Wheels +380
Keyless Entry System +70
Limited Slip Diff +115
Power Drivers Seat +125
Premium Sound System +185
Skid Plates +50

MUSTANG 1995

A power driver's seat moves from the standard equipment list to the options list. A powerful new stereo with a CD changer also debuts on the options list.

RATINGS (SCALE OF 1-10)

Overall	Safety	Reliability	Performance	Comfort	Value
7.1	7.5	7.6	8.8	7.3	4.4

Model Description	Trade-in Value	Market Value
Category F		
2 Dr Cobra Conv	12605	16160
2 Dr Cobra Cpe	11510	14760
2 Dr GT Conv	10415	13355
2 Dr GT Cpe	9125	11700
2 Dr GTS Cpe	8120	10410
2 Dr STD Conv	8775	11245
2 Dr STD Cpe	6745	8645

OPTIONS FOR MUSTANG

Auto 4-Speed Transmission +355
Air Conditioning +380
Anti-Lock Brakes[Std on Cobra] +330
Compact Disc W/fm/tape +240
Cruise Control +95
Keyless Entry System +80
Leather Seats[Opt on GT] +325
Power Door Locks[Std on Cobra,GT,Conv] +90
Power Drivers Seat +110
Power Windows[Std on Cobra,GT,Conv] +100
Rear Spoiler[Opt on STD] +130
Remote Trunk Release +35

PROBE 1995

The SE Package becomes a trim level. Base and GT models receive new taillights. GTs receive 16-inch directional wheels. The rear-window wiper washer, four-way seat height adjuster and graphic equalizer have been deleted from the option list.

RATINGS (SCALE OF 1-10)

Overall	Safety	Reliability	Performance	Comfort	Value
7	7.8	7.5	9	7.4	3.6

Model Description	Trade-in Value	Market Value
Category E		
2 Dr SE Hbk	6090	8340
2 Dr STD Hbk	5630	7710
Category F		
2 Dr GT Hbk	6850	8780

OPTIONS FOR PROBE

Auto 4-Speed Transmission +355
Air Conditioning[Std on SE] +370
AM/FM Compact Disc Playr +215
Anti-Lock Brakes +320
Chrome Wheels +255
Cruise Control[Std on SE] +95
Keyless Entry System +65
Leather Seats +325
Power Door Locks[Std on SE] +90
Power Drivers Seat +110
Power Sunroof +275
Power Windows[Std on SE] +100

RANGER 1995

A driver airbag and optional four-wheel antilock brakes are two of the features added to the safety equipment roster of the capable Ford Ranger. SuperCab models can now be had with a power driver's seat.

RATINGS (SCALE OF 1-10)

Overall	Safety	Reliability	Performance	Comfort	Value
N/A	6.7	8.4	7.2	7.3	N/A

Model Description	Trade-in Value	Market Value
Category G		
2 Dr Splash Ext Cab Stepside SB	8210	10390
2 Dr Splash Std Cab Stepside SB	6935	8775
2 Dr Splash 4WD Ext Cab Stepside SB	9715	12300
2 Dr Splash 4WD Std Cab Stepside SB	9555	12095
2 Dr STX 4WD Ext Cab SB	8865	11220
2 Dr STX 4WD Std Cab SB	8475	10725
2 Dr STX 4WD Std Cab LB	8100	10250
2 Dr XL Std Cab SB	5545	7020
2 Dr XL Ext Cab SB	6620	8380

Don't forget to refer to the Mileage Adjustment Table at the back of this book!

 © 1999 by Edmund Publications Corporation

Model Description	Trade-in Value	Market Value
2 Dr XL Std Cab LB	5645	7145
2 Dr XL 4WD Ext Cab SB	8525	10790
2 Dr XL 4WD Std Cab SB	7270	9200
2 Dr XL 4WD Std Cab LB	7500	9490
2 Dr XLT Ext Cab SB	6690	8465
2 Dr XLT Std Cab SB	6020	7620
2 Dr XLT Std Cab LB	6015	7615
2 Dr XLT 4WD Std Cab SB	7995	10120
2 Dr XLT 4WD Ext Cab SB	8660	10960
2 Dr XLT 4WD Std Cab LB	8085	10235

OPTIONS FOR RANGER

6 cyl 3.0 L Engine +325
6 cyl 4.0 L Engine +340
Auto 4-Speed Transmission +465
Air Conditioning +370
AM/FM Compact Disc Playr +175
Anti-Lock Brakes[Opt on 2WD] +280
Chrome Wheels[Std on Splash] +110
Cruise Control +95
Limited Slip Diff[Std on Splash 4WD Ext Cab Stepside SB,STX 4WD Ext Cab SB,XLT 4WD Ext Cab SB] +120
Power Door Locks +105
Power Drivers Seat +130
Power Steering[Std on Splash,STX,Ext Cab,4WD] +130
Power Windows +105
Velour/Cloth Seats +80

TAURUS 1995

Sport edition model is introduced as an SE. The SE includes aluminum wheels, sport bucket seats, air conditioning, and a rear defroster. The base engine has been revised to decrease engine noise.

RATINGS (SCALE OF 1-10)

Overall	Safety	Reliability	Performance	Comfort	Value
7.9	7.6	7.8	8	7.8	8.4

Model Description	Trade-in Value	Market Value
Category C		
4 Dr GL Sdn	6030	7935
4 Dr GL Wgn	6320	8315
4 Dr LX Wgn	7390	9725
4 Dr LX Sdn	6990	9200
4 Dr SE Sdn	6470	8510
Category F		
4 Dr SHO Sdn	8330	10680

OPTIONS FOR TAURUS

6 cyl 3.0 L FLEX Engine +210
6 cyl 3.8 L Engine[Opt on GL,SE] +280
Auto 4-Speed Transmission[Opt on SHO] +355
Anti-Lock Brakes[Std on SHO] +285
Center Console[Opt on GL] +35
Climate Control for AC[Opt on LX] +75
Compact Disc W/fm/tape +170
Cruise Control[Std on SHO] +95
Keyless Entry System[Std on SHO] +80
Leather Seats +260
Power Door Locks[Opt on GL] +90
Power Drivers Seat[Opt on GL] +110
Power Moonroof +320
Power Passenger Seat +120
Power Windows[Opt on GL] +100
Premium Sound System[Opt on LX] +180
Third Seat +75

THUNDERBIRD 1995

The trunk mounted CD changer is deleted in favor of an in-dash CD-player. Variable-assist power steering is lost from the standard equipment list.

RATINGS (SCALE OF 1-10)

Overall	Safety	Reliability	Performance	Comfort	Value
7.9	8.7	7.7	8	7.9	7.2

Model Description	Trade-in Value	Market Value
Category C		
2 Dr LX Cpe	6975	9175
Category F		
2 Dr SC Sprchgd Cpe	10030	12860

OPTIONS FOR THUNDERBIRD

8 cyl 4.6 L Engine +275
Auto 4-Speed Transmission[Opt on SC] +355
AM/FM Compact Disc Playr +175
Anti-Lock Brakes[Opt on LX] +285
Climate Control for AC[Opt on LX] +75
Keyless Entry System +80
Leather Seats[Opt on LX] +260
Power Door Locks[Opt on LX] +90
Power Moonroof +320
Power Passenger Seat +120
Premium Sound System +180

WINDSTAR 1995

This year, Ford introduces its version of the front-wheel drive minivan. Designed to replace the archaic Aerostar, the Windstar offers an extensive standard equipment list. Dual airbags, antilock brakes, a four-speed automatic transmission, and V6 power are just a few of the things Windstar owners will find included on their vehicle. The Windstar has seating for seven that includes a unique integrated child seat: an attractive feature for a family with toddlers.

RATINGS (SCALE OF 1-10)

Overall	Safety	Reliability	Performance	Comfort	Value
7.5	9.1	7.3	6.6	7.3	7.2

Model Description	Trade-in Value	Market Value
Category G		
2 Dr 1995.5 Cargo Van	7130	9030
2 Dr GL Pass. Van	7785	9855
2 Dr GL 1995.5 Pass. Van	7805	9880
2 Dr LX Pass. Van	10250	12975
2 Dr LX 1995.5 Pass. Van	10425	13195
2 Dr STD Cargo Van	6635	8395

Don't forget to refer to the Mileage Adjustment Table at the back of this book!

 © 1999 by Edmund Publications Corporation

Model Description	Trade-in Value	Market Value

OPTIONS FOR WINDSTAR

6 cyl 3.8 L Engine[Opt on 1995.5] +185
Air Conditioning[Std on LX] +370
AM/FM Compact Disc Playr +175
Child Seat (1) +80
Cruise Control[Std on LX] +95
Dual Air Conditioning +460
Keyless Entry System +95
Leather Seats +350
Luggage Rack +70
Power Door Locks[Std on LX] +105
Power Windows[Std on LX] +105

1994 FORD

AEROSTAR 1994

A high-mounted rear brake light is standard. No other changes to Ford's venerable minivan.

RATINGS (SCALE OF 1-10)

Overall	Safety	Reliability	Performance	Comfort	Value
7	6.2	7.4	6.6	7.5	7.5

Category G

Model Description	Trade-in Value	Market Value
2 Dr Eddie Bauer Pass. Van Ext	7975	10360
2 Dr Eddie Bauer Pass. Van	7145	9280
2 Dr Eddie Bauer 4WD Pass. Van	7920	10285
2 Dr Eddie Bauer 4WD Pass. Van Ext	8285	10760
2 Dr STD Cargo Van	4110	5340
2 Dr STD Cargo Van Ext	4880	6340
2 Dr STD 4WD Cargo Van	5215	6770
2 Dr STD 4WD Cargo Van Ext	6005	7800
2 Dr Window Cargo Van	4155	5395
2 Dr Window Cargo Van Ext	4970	6455
2 Dr Window 4WD Cargo Van	5295	6875
2 Dr Window 4WD Cargo Van Ext	6005	7800
2 Dr XL Pass. Van	5065	6575
2 Dr XL Pass. Van Ext	5785	7515
2 Dr XL 4WD Pass. Van	6000	7790
2 Dr XL 4WD Pass. Van Ext	6530	8480
2 Dr XL Plus Pass. Van	5490	7130
2 Dr XL Plus Pass. Van Ext	5945	7725
2 Dr XL Plus 4WD Pass. Van	6660	8645
2 Dr XL Plus 4WD Pass. Van Ext	7140	9275
2 Dr XLT Pass. Van	6345	8240
2 Dr XLT Pass. Van Ext	6860	8910
2 Dr XLT 4WD Pass. Van	6665	8660
2 Dr XLT 4WD Pass. Van Ext	7430	9650

OPTIONS FOR AEROSTAR

6 cyl 4.0 L Engine[Std on Cargo Van,4WD, Eddie Bauer Pass. Van Ext] +170
Auto 4-Speed Transmission[Std on Eddie Bauer,XLT, 4WD] +280
Air Conditioning[Std on XLT] +300
AM/FM Stereo Tape +90
Captain Chairs (4) +235
Child Seat (1) +65
Cruise Control[Std on Eddie Bauer,XLT] +80
Dual Air Conditioning[Std on Eddie Bauer] +375
Leather Seats +285
Luggage Rack[Std on Eddie Bauer] +60
Power Door Locks[Std on Eddie Bauer] +85
Power Windows[Std on Eddie Bauer] +85
Premium Sound System[Opt on XLT] +135

ASPIRE 1994

Ford introduces the Aspire as a replacement for the aging Festiva. This little econobox has a 1.3-liter inline-four that produces a measly 63 horsepower. The Aspire is available with a five-speed manual or a three-speed automatic transmission. If you are seriously looking at the Aspire, you may want to consider a bike. It will undoubtedly get you where you want to go faster than this car.

RATINGS (SCALE OF 1-10)

Overall	Safety	Reliability	Performance	Comfort	Value
7.2	7.3	8	7.2	7.3	6.2

Category E

Model Description	Trade-in Value	Market Value
2 Dr SE Hbk	2990	4275
2 Dr STD Hbk	2640	3775
4 Dr STD Hbk	2600	3715

OPTIONS FOR ASPIRE

Auto 3-Speed Transmission +215
Air Conditioning +300
AM/FM Compact Disc Playr +175
Anti-Lock Brakes +265
Power Steering +95
Premium Sound System +125
Rear Window Defroster +60

BRONCO 1994

The 1994 Bronco receives a driver airbag and door guard beams. ABS now works in two-wheel drive and four-wheel drive.

RATINGS (SCALE OF 1-10)

Overall	Safety	Reliability	Performance	Comfort	Value
7.2	8.8	7.4	6.4	6.6	6.9

Category H

Model Description	Trade-in Value	Market Value
2 Dr Eddie Bauer 4WD Utility	10970	13715
2 Dr XL 4WD Utility	9555	11940
2 Dr XLT 4WD Utility	10020	12520

OPTIONS FOR BRONCO

8 cyl 5.8 L Engine +315
Auto 4-Speed Transmission[Opt on XL,XLT] +345
Air Conditioning[Opt on XL,XLT] +300
AM/FM Compact Disc Playr +110

Don't forget to refer to the Mileage Adjustment Table at the back of this book!

 © 1999 by Edmund Publications Corporation

Model Description	Trade-in Value	Market Value

Camper/Towing Package +130
Chrome Wheels +110
Keyless Entry System +60
Leather Seats +385
Limited Slip Diff +95
Power Door Locks +70
Power Windows +70
Swing Out Tire Carrier +60
Velour/Cloth Seats +50

CLUB WAGON/ECONOLINE 1994

Four-wheel antilock brakes replace previous rear-wheel antilock brakes.

RATINGS (SCALE OF 1-10)

Overall	Safety	Reliability	Performance	Comfort	Value
N/A	7.8	8.3	6.8	7.9	N/A

E-150

Category H

Model Description	Trade-in Value	Market Value
2 Dr Chateau Club Wagon	9485	11855
2 Dr STD Econoline	8505	10630
2 Dr XL Club Wagon	7625	9530
2 Dr XL Econoline	8520	10655
2 Dr XLT Club Wagon	8640	10800

E-250

Category H

Model Description	Trade-in Value	Market Value
2 Dr STD Econoline Ext	6865	8580
2 Dr STD Econoline	6770	8465
2 Dr XL Econoline	7115	8890

E-350

Category H

Model Description	Trade-in Value	Market Value
2 Dr Chateau Club Wagon	10845	13555
2 Dr STD Econoline	8865	11080
2 Dr STD Econoline Ext	10015	12515
2 Dr XL Club Wagon	9050	11310
2 Dr XL Club Wagon Ext	9660	12080
2 Dr XL Econoline	9500	11875
2 Dr XLT Club Wagon	9520	11900
2 Dr XLT Club Wagon Ext	10030	12535

OPTIONS FOR CLUB WAGON/ECONOLINE

8 cyl 7.3 L Dsl Engine +940
8 cyl 5.0 L Engine +220
8 cyl 5.8 L Engine +315
8 cyl 7.5 L Engine +330
Auto 4-Speed Transmission[Std on Chateau,Club Wagon Ext,E-150 XL Club Wagon,E-150 XLT Club Wagon] +110
High Capacity A/C +380
High Capacity A/C w/Aux Heater +690
Air Conditioning[Std on Chateau,E-150 XLT Club Wagon] +300
AM/FM Stereo Tape[Std on Chateau] +90
Anti-Lock Brakes[Opt on STD,Econoline] +190
Camper/Towing Package[Std on E-350 STD Econoline, E-350 Club Wagon,E-350 Club Wagon Ext] +130
Chrome Bumpers[Opt on STD] +60
Cruise Control +70
Dual Air Conditioning +525
Limited Slip Diff +95
Power Door Locks[Opt on STD] +70
Power Drivers Seat[Std on Chateau] +100
Power Passenger Seat +90
Power Windows[Opt on STD, XL] +70
Premium Sound System +150
Velour/Cloth Seats[Opt on STD, XL Club Wagon] +50

CROWN VICTORIA 1994

A passenger airbag is now standard. Air conditioning gets CFC-free refrigerant.

RATINGS (SCALE OF 1-10)

Overall	Safety	Reliability	Performance	Comfort	Value
8.1	8	7.7	7.7	8.3	8.7

Category B

Model Description	Trade-in Value	Market Value
4 Dr LX Sdn	6760	9015
4 Dr S Sdn	6730	8970
4 Dr STD Sdn	6540	8720

OPTIONS FOR CROWN VICTORIA

Aluminum/Alloy Wheels +125
AM/FM Stereo Tape +65
Anti-Lock Brakes +265
Climate Control for AC +65
Cruise Control[Std on S] +80
Keyless Entry System +65
Leather Seats +245
Power Door Locks +90
Premium Sound System +155
Traction Control System +65

ESCORT 1994

A driver airbag debuts on all models. Antilock brakes are now available on the GT. The LX-E sedan is dropped from the lineup.

RATINGS (SCALE OF 1-10)

Overall	Safety	Reliability	Performance	Comfort	Value
6.9	6.2	7.8	6.8	7.6	6

Category E

Model Description	Trade-in Value	Market Value
2 Dr GT Hbk	3995	5705
2 Dr LX Hbk	3260	4655
4 Dr LX Sdn	3500	5000
4 Dr LX Hbk	3360	4800
4 Dr LX Wgn	3240	4630
2 Dr STD Hbk	2840	4060

OPTIONS FOR ESCORT

Auto 4-Speed Transmission +295
Air Conditioning +300
AM/FM Compact Disc Playr +175

Don't forget to refer to the Mileage Adjustment Table at the back of this book!

 © 1999 by Edmund Publications Corporation

Model Description	Trade-in Value	Market Value

Anti-Lock Brakes +265
Cruise Control +80
Luggage Rack +50
Power Door Locks +85
Power Moonroof +215
Power Steering[Std on GT] +95
Power Windows +100
Premium Sound System +125
Rear Spoiler[Opt on LX] +75

EXPLORER 1994

New wheels and a power equipment group for the Eddie Bauer model are the only changes to this year's Explorer.

RATINGS (SCALE OF 1-10)

Overall	Safety	Reliability	Performance	Comfort	Value
7.3	5.5	6.9	7.4	8.3	8.5

Category G

Model Description	Trade-in Value	Market Value
2 Dr Eddie Bauer Utility	8820	11455
2 Dr Eddie Bauer 4WD Utility	9105	11825
4 Dr Eddie Bauer Wgn	8700	11300
4 Dr Eddie Bauer 4WD Wgn	9610	12480
4 Dr Limited Wgn	10125	13150
4 Dr Limited 4WD Wgn	10645	13825
2 Dr Sport Utility	7360	9560
2 Dr Sport 4WD Utility	7630	9905
2 Dr XL Utility	7010	9105
2 Dr XL 4WD Utility	7510	9750
4 Dr XL Wgn	7260	9430
4 Dr XL 4WD Wgn	7905	10270
4 Dr XLT Wgn	8510	11055
4 Dr XLT 4WD Wgn	9460	12285

OPTIONS FOR EXPLORER

Auto 4-Speed Transmission[Std on Limited] +330
Air Conditioning[Std on Limited] +300
Camper/Towing Package +105
Compact Disc W/fm/tape +255
Cruise Control[Opt on Sport,XL] +80
JBL Sound System +285
Keyless Entry System[Std on Limited] +75
Leather Seats[Std on Limited] +285
Limited Slip Diff +100
Luggage Rack[Opt on Sport,XL, XLT Wgn] +60
Power Door Locks[Opt on Sport,XL] +85
Power Windows[Opt on Sport,XL] +85
Running Boards +140

F-SERIES PICKUP 1994

A driver airbag becomes part of the standard equipment list on the light-duty trucks. Side-door beams and a high-mounted third taillight round out the safety changes for this year. New options include a CD player and a unique tri-fold seat that turns into a center armrest.

RATINGS (SCALE OF 1-10)

Overall	Safety	Reliability	Performance	Comfort	Value
N/A	7.1	6.9	6.8	7.4	N/A

F-150

Category H

Model Description	Trade-in Value	Market Value
2 Dr Eddie Bauer Ext Cab LB	8580	10725
2 Dr Lightning Std Cab SB	10130	12660
2 Dr S Std Cab SB	5145	6430
2 Dr S Ext Cab SB	7020	8775
2 Dr S Std Cab LB	5210	6515
2 Dr S Ext Cab LB	7140	8925
2 Dr S 4WD Std Cab SB	7975	9965
2 Dr S 4WD Std Cab LB	8010	10010
2 Dr XL Ext Cab SB	7090	8865
2 Dr XL Std Cab SB	6575	8215
2 Dr XL Ext Cab Stepside SB	7305	9130
2 Dr XL Std Cab Stepside SB	6610	8260
2 Dr XL Ext Cab LB	7105	8880
2 Dr XL Std Cab LB	6635	8295
2 Dr XL 4WD Ext Cab SB	8460	10575
2 Dr XL 4WD Std Cab SB	8005	10005
2 Dr XL 4WD Std Cab Stepside SB	8270	10340
2 Dr XL 4WD Ext Cab Stepside SB	8740	10925
2 Dr XL 4WD Std Cab LB	8095	10120
2 Dr XL 4WD Ext Cab LB	8530	10665
2 Dr XLT Std Cab SB	7290	9110
2 Dr XLT Ext Cab SB	7815	9770
2 Dr XLT Std Cab Stepside SB	7540	9425
2 Dr XLT Ext Cab Stepside SB	8040	10050
2 Dr XLT Std Cab LB	7350	9185
2 Dr XLT Ext Cab LB	8005	10010
2 Dr XLT 4WD Ext Cab SB	9260	11575
2 Dr XLT 4WD Std Cab SB	8935	11165
2 Dr XLT 4WD Ext Cab Stepside SB	9460	11825
2 Dr XLT 4WD Std Cab Stepside SB	9280	11600
2 Dr XLT 4WD Ext Cab LB	9275	11595
2 Dr XLT 4WD Std Cab LB	8980	11225

F-250

Category H

Model Description	Trade-in Value	Market Value
2 Dr S Ext Cab LB	9010	11260
2 Dr XL Ext Cab LB	9135	11420
2 Dr XL Std Cab LB	7675	9595
2 Dr XL 4WD Ext Cab LB	10325	12905
2 Dr XL 4WD Std Cab LB	9555	11945
2 Dr XLT Ext Cab LB	10095	12620
2 Dr XLT Std Cab LB	8520	10650

Don't forget to refer to the Mileage Adjustment Table at the back of this book!

 © 1999 by Edmund Publications Corporation

Model Description	Trade-in Value	Market Value
2 Dr XLT 4WD Std Cab LB	10505	13130
2 Dr XLT 4WD Ext Cab LB	11275	14090

F-350

Category H

Model Description	Trade-in Value	Market Value
2 Dr XL Std Cab LB	10345	12930
2 Dr XL Ext Cab LB	11095	13870
2 Dr XL 4WD Std Cab LB	10600	13250
4 Dr XL Crew Cab LB	11720	14650
4 Dr XL 4WD Crew Cab LB	12855	16070
2 Dr XLT Std Cab LB	11990	14985
2 Dr XLT Ext Cab LB	12190	15235
2 Dr XLT 4WD Std Cab LB	12550	15685
4 Dr XLT Crew Cab LB	12375	15470
4 Dr XLT 4WD Crew Cab LB	12975	16220

OPTIONS FOR F-SERIES PICKUP

8 cyl 7.3 L Dsl Engine +940
8 cyl 5.0 L Engine +220
8 cyl 5.8 L Engine +315
8 cyl 7.5 L Engine +330
8 cyl 7.3 L Turbodsl Engine +1405
Auto 3-Speed Transmission +260
Auto 4-Speed Transmission[Std on Lightning] +345
Air Conditioning[Opt on S,XL] +300
AM/FM Compact Disc Playr +110
Camper/Towing Package +130
Cruise Control[Opt on S,XL] +70
Dual Rear Wheels +310
Keyless Entry System +60
Power Door Locks[Std on F-250,F-350,Eddie Bauer, Lightning] +70
Power Drivers Seat +100
Power Windows[Std on F-250,F-350,Eddie Bauer, Lightning] +70
Premium Sound System +150
Rear Step Bumper +60

MUSTANG 1994

New sheetmetal for the venerable pony. The LX model and hatchback are dropped. The base Mustang gets a 3.8-liter V6, and GT models receive a boost in horsepower. Four-wheel disc brakes are standard on both Mustangs and ABS finally becomes an available option. A passenger airbag, power driver's seat, and tilt steering wheel become standard in 1994. Convertibles are available with a removable hardtop.

RATINGS (SCALE OF 1-10)

Overall	Safety	Reliability	Performance	Comfort	Value
7.2	7.6	7.7	8.8	7.3	4.8

Category F

Model Description	Trade-in Value	Market Value
2 Dr Cobra Cpe	10450	13750
2 Dr Cobra Conv	12895	16965
2 Dr GT Cpe	8065	10615
2 Dr GT Conv	9710	12775
2 Dr STD Cpe	5920	8000
2 Dr STD Conv	7590	9985

OPTIONS FOR MUSTANG

Auto 4-Speed Transmission +295
Air Conditioning +295
Anti-Lock Brakes[Std on Cobra] +230
Compact Disc W/fm/tape +135
Cruise Control +75
Keyless Entry System +65
Leather Seats[Opt on GT,STD,Cpe] +265
Power Door Locks[Opt on STD Cpe] +75
Power Windows[Opt on STD Cpe] +85
Premium Sound System +145
Rear Spoiler[Opt on STD] +60

PROBE 1994

Dual airbags are now standard on all Probes. A Sport Appearance Package is available for base models.

RATINGS (SCALE OF 1-10)

Overall	Safety	Reliability	Performance	Comfort	Value
7.1	7.9	7.6	9	7.4	3.5

Category E

Model Description	Trade-in Value	Market Value
2 Dr SE Hbk	4440	6340
2 Dr STD Hbk	4320	6175

Category F

Model Description	Trade-in Value	Market Value
2 Dr GT Hbk	5925	7795

OPTIONS FOR PROBE

Auto 4-Speed Transmission +295
Air Conditioning +300
AM/FM Compact Disc Playr +175
Anti-Lock Brakes +265
Cruise Control +80
Keyless Entry System +55
Leather Seats +265
Power Door Locks +75
Power Drivers Seat +90
Power Sunroof +225
Power Windows +85

RANGER 1994

Side-impact door beams are installed on the Ranger to protect occupants. The Splash model is now available as a SuperCab. Look out, the Splash 2WD holds the road better than most sport coupes.

RATINGS (SCALE OF 1-10)

Overall	Safety	Reliability	Performance	Comfort	Value
N/A	4.9	7.9	7.2	7.3	N/A

Category G

Model Description	Trade-in Value	Market Value
2 Dr Splash Ext Cab Stepside SB	6650	8635
2 Dr Splash Std Cab Stepside SB	5920	7685
2 Dr Splash 4WD Ext Cab Stepside SB	8130	10560

Don't forget to refer to the Mileage Adjustment Table at the back of this book!

 © 1999 by Edmund Publications Corporation

Model Description	Trade-in Value	Market Value
2 Dr Splash 4WD Std Cab Stepside SB	7885	10240
2 Dr STX Ext Cab SB	6480	8415
2 Dr STX Std Cab SB	5800	7535
2 Dr STX Std Cab LB	5875	7630
2 Dr STX 4WD Std Cab SB	7325	9510
2 Dr STX 4WD Ext Cab SB	7600	9870
2 Dr STX 4WD Std Cab LB	7540	9790
2 Dr XL Std Cab SB	4625	6010
2 Dr XL Ext Cab SB	5600	7270
2 Dr XL Std Cab LB	4650	6035
2 Dr XL 4WD Std Cab SB	6745	8760
2 Dr XL 4WD Ext Cab SB	7320	9505
2 Dr XL 4WD Std Cab LB	6850	8895
2 Dr XLT Std Cab SB	4930	6405
2 Dr XLT Ext Cab SB	5950	7730
2 Dr XLT Std Cab LB	5035	6535
2 Dr XLT 4WD Ext Cab SB	7470	9700
2 Dr XLT 4WD Std Cab SB	7125	9255
2 Dr XLT 4WD Std Cab LB	7250	9420

OPTIONS FOR RANGER

6 cyl 3.0 L Engine +170
6 cyl 4.0 L Engine +225
Auto 4-Speed Transmission +365
Air Conditioning +300
AM/FM Compact Disc Playr +145
Cruise Control +80
Limited Slip Diff +100
Power Door Locks +85
Power Steering[Std on Splash,STX,Ext Cab,4WD] +105
Power Windows +85
Premium Sound System +135

TAURUS 1994

The passenger airbag is finally a standard equipment item. GL models receive 15-inch wheels and all Tauruses get a new steering wheel. Cellular phones are a new option.

RATINGS (SCALE OF 1-10)

Overall	Safety	Reliability	Performance	Comfort	Value
8	7.6	7.6	8	7.8	8.8

Model Description	Trade-in Value	Market Value
Category C		
4 Dr GL Wgn	5020	6785
4 Dr GL Sdn	4670	6315
4 Dr LX Wgn	6290	8495
4 Dr LX Sdn	6040	8165
Category F		
4 Dr SHO Sdn	7230	9515

OPTIONS FOR TAURUS

6 cyl 3.8 L Engine[Opt on GL,LX] +205
Auto 4-Speed Transmission[Opt on SHO] +295
Air Conditioning[Std on LX,SHO] +295
Anti-Lock Brakes[Std on SHO] +230
Climate Control for AC[Opt on LX] +65
Compact Disc W/fm/tape +135
Cruise Control[Std on SHO] +75
Keyless Entry System +65
Leather Seats[Std on SHO] +215
Power Door Locks[Std on LX,SHO] +75
Power Drivers Seat[Opt on GL,Wgn] +90
Power Moonroof +260
Power Passenger Seat +100
Power Windows[Std on LX,SHO] +85
Premium Sound System +145
Third Seat +60

TEMPO 1994

CFC-free air conditioning refrigerant and redesigned seat belts are the only changes this year. The Tempo is mercifully retired after this model year in favor of the new Contour.

RATINGS (SCALE OF 1-10)

Overall	Safety	Reliability	Performance	Comfort	Value
6.8	5.2	7.3	7.6	7.1	6.9

Model Description	Trade-in Value	Market Value
Category C		
2 Dr GL Sdn	3450	4660
4 Dr GL Sdn	3450	4660
4 Dr LX Sdn	3700	5000

OPTIONS FOR TEMPO

6 cyl 3.0 L Engine +255
Auto 3-Speed Transmission +200
Air Bag Restraint +190
Air Conditioning +295
AM/FM Stereo Tape +60
Cruise Control +75
Power Door Locks[Opt on GL] +90
Power Drivers Seat +105
Power Windows +115

THUNDERBIRD 1994

Dual airbags make their first appearance on the Thunderbird. An optional 4.6-liter V8 replaces last year's 5.0-liter V8. Electronic shift controls with an overdrive lockout switch improve traction from a standstill. Dual cupholders complement the center console and the airbags are housed in a restyled dashboard.

RATINGS (SCALE OF 1-10)

Overall	Safety	Reliability	Performance	Comfort	Value
7.6	8.7	7.5	8	7.9	5.8

Model Description	Trade-in Value	Market Value
Category C		
2 Dr LX Cpe	6165	8330
Category F		
2 Dr SC Sprchgd Cpe	8990	11825

Don't forget to refer to the Mileage Adjustment Table at the back of this book!

© 1999 by Edmund Publications Corporation

OPTIONS FOR THUNDERBIRD

8 cyl 4.6 L Engine +210
Auto 4-Speed Transmission[Opt on SC] +295
Anti-Lock Brakes[Opt on LX] +230
Climate Control for AC[Opt on LX] +65
Compact Disc Changer +195
Cruise Control[Opt on SC] +75
Keyless Entry System +65
Leather Seats +215
Power Door Locks[Opt on SC] +75
Power Drivers Seat[Opt on SC] +90
Power Moonroof +260
Power Passenger Seat +100
Premium Sound System +145
Traction Control System +105

1993 FORD

AEROSTAR 1993

An integrated child seat is introduced as an option.

RATINGS (SCALE OF 1-10)

Overall	Safety	Reliability	Performance	Comfort	Value
7.2	6.2	7.1	6.6	7.5	8.4

Category G

Model Description	Trade-in Value	Market Value
2 Dr Eddie Bauer Pass. Van Ext	6835	9110
2 Dr Eddie Bauer Pass. Van	6220	8290
2 Dr Eddie Bauer 4WD Pass. Van	6670	8895
2 Dr Eddie Bauer 4WD Pass. Van Ext	7260	9680
2 Dr STD Cargo Van Ext	3835	5115
2 Dr STD Cargo Van	3015	4020
2 Dr STD 4WD Cargo Van	3805	5075
2 Dr Window Cargo Van	3180	4240
2 Dr Window 4WD Cargo Van	4080	5435
2 Dr XL Pass. Van Ext	4625	6170
2 Dr XL Pass. Van	3895	5195
2 Dr XL 4WD Pass. Van Ext	5665	7555
2 Dr XL 4WD Pass. Van	5225	6965
2 Dr XL Plus Pass. Van Ext	4655	6210
2 Dr XL Plus Pass. Van	4050	5400
2 Dr XL Plus 4WD Pass. Van	5400	7200
2 Dr XLT Pass. Van	5080	6770
2 Dr XLT Pass. Van Ext	5510	7345
2 Dr XLT 4WD Pass. Van Ext	6480	8640
2 Dr XLT Plus Pass. Van	5350	7130
2 Dr XLT Plus 4WD Pass. Van	5620	7490

OPTIONS FOR AEROSTAR

6 cyl 4.0 L Engine[Std on 4WD, Eddie Bauer] +145
Auto 4-Speed Transmission[Std on Eddie Bauer,XLT, XLT Plus,4WD] +225
Air Conditioning[Std on XLT,XLT Plus,Eddie Bauer] +245
Aluminum/Alloy Wheels[Std on Eddie Bauer] +105
AM/FM Stereo Tape +75
Captain Chairs (4)[Opt on XL,XL Plus,XLT,XLT Plus, Pass. Van Ext] +190
Child Seat (1) +55
Chrome Wheels +75
Cruise Control[Opt on STD,XL,XL Plus] +65
Dual Air Conditioning[Std on Eddie Bauer] +305
Leather Seats +235
Luggage Rack[Std on Eddie Bauer] +45
Power Door Locks[Std on Eddie Bauer] +70
Power Windows[Std on Eddie Bauer] +70
Premium Sound System[Std on Eddie Bauer] +110

BRONCO 1993

Four-wheel antilock brakes introduced on the 1993 Bronco.

RATINGS (SCALE OF 1-10)

Overall	Safety	Reliability	Performance	Comfort	Value
6.6	6.4	6.9	6.4	6.6	6.9

Category H

Model Description	Trade-in Value	Market Value
2 Dr Eddie Bauer 4WD Utility	9360	11850
2 Dr STD 4WD Utility	8180	10355
2 Dr XLT 4WD Utility	8620	10910

OPTIONS FOR BRONCO

8 cyl 5.8 L Engine +260
Auto 4-Speed Transmission[Opt on STD,XLT] +280
Air Conditioning[Opt on STD,XLT] +245
Aluminum/Alloy Wheels[Opt on XLT] +95
AM/FM Stereo Tape +75
Camper/Towing Package +110
Leather Seats +315
Limited Slip Diff +75
Power Door Locks +55
Power Drivers Seat +85
Power Windows +60
Swing Out Tire Carrier[Std on XLT] +50
Velour/Cloth Seats[Std on Eddie Bauer] +40

CLUB WAGON/ECONOLINE 1993

No changes to the newly redesigned Ford Club Wagon.

RATINGS (SCALE OF 1-10)

Overall	Safety	Reliability	Performance	Comfort	Value
N/A	7.8	8.2	6.8	7.9	N/A

E-150

Category H

Model Description	Trade-in Value	Market Value
2 Dr Chateau Club Wagon	7890	9985
2 Dr Custom Club Wagon	6725	8510
2 Dr Custom Super Dsl Club Wagon	8170	10340
2 Dr STD Econoline	7095	8980
2 Dr XL Econoline	7295	9235
2 Dr XLT Club Wagon	7050	8925
2 Dr XLT Super Club Wagon Ext	7125	9020
2 Dr XLT Super Dsl Club Wagon	8245	10435

Don't forget to refer to the Mileage Adjustment Table at the back of this book!

© 1999 by Edmund Publications Corporation

Model Description	Trade-in Value	Market Value

E-250

Category H

Model Description	Trade-in Value	Market Value
2 Dr STD Econoline Ext	6160	7795
2 Dr STD Econoline	5685	7200
2 Dr XL Econoline Ext	6345	8035
2 Dr XL Econoline	5845	7395

E-350

Category H

Model Description	Trade-in Value	Market Value
2 Dr Custom Super Club Wagon Ext	6560	8305
2 Dr STD Econoline	5455	6905
2 Dr STD Econoline Ext	6130	7760
2 Dr XL Econoline Ext	6220	7870
2 Dr XL Econoline	5735	7260
2 Dr XLT Super Club Wagon Ext	6970	8825

OPTIONS FOR CLUB WAGON/ECONOLINE

8 cyl 7.3 L Dsl Engine +805
8 cyl 5.0 L Engine +180
8 cyl 5.8 L Engine +260
8 cyl 7.5 L Engine +290
Auto 4-Speed Transmission[Std on Chateau,Custom, XLT] +90
Club Wagon Seat/Bed Package +305
Air Conditioning[Std on Chateau] +245
Aluminum/Alloy Wheels[Std on Chateau] +95
AM/FM Stereo Tape[Std on Chateau] +75
Camper/Towing Package[Opt on Custom,STD,XL] +110
Chrome Bumpers[Std on Chateau,XLT,XLT Super] +50
Cruise Control[Std on Chateau] +60
Limited Slip Diff +75
Power Door Locks[Std on Chateau,XLT,XLT Super] +55
Power Drivers Seat[Std on Chateau] +85
Power Windows[Std on Chateau,XLT,XLT Super] +60
Velour/Cloth Seats[Opt on E-250,Custom,Custom Super,STD,XL] +40

CROWN VICTORIA 1993

The touring sedan is no longer available. Front-end styling changes include the addition of a grille. Cupholders finally appear in the dashboard. An express-down feature shows up for the driver's side window. An electronic overdrive lock-out debuts on the automatic transmission and a traction control system is available with the antilock brakes option. A 10-disc CD changer and an auto-dimming mirror are new options.

RATINGS (SCALE OF 1-10)

Overall	Safety	Reliability	Performance	Comfort	Value
7.7	7.1	7.3	7.5	8.3	8.5

Category B

Model Description	Trade-in Value	Market Value
4 Dr LX Sdn	5530	7575
4 Dr STD Sdn	5130	7025

OPTIONS FOR CROWN VICTORIA

Luxury Group +285
Air Bag Restraint[Opt on LX] +195
Aluminum/Alloy Wheels +100
AM/FM Stereo Tape +55
Anti-Lock Brakes +215
Climate Control for AC +55
Compact Disc Changer +150
Cruise Control +65
Dual Power Seats +110
Keyless Entry System +55
Leather Seats +200
Power Door Locks +75
Premium Sound System +125
Traction Control System +55
Trip Computer +65

ESCORT 1993

Minor styling changes to all trim-levels include new taillights and grille. GT models receive a new spoiler and wheels. The LX models receive body color spoilers.

RATINGS (SCALE OF 1-10)

Overall	Safety	Reliability	Performance	Comfort	Value
6.6	4.7	7.5	6.8	7.6	6.4

Category E

Model Description	Trade-in Value	Market Value
2 Dr GT Hbk	3065	4575
2 Dr LX Hbk	2670	3985
4 Dr LX Hbk	2725	4065
4 Dr LX Wgn	2490	3715
4 Dr LX Sdn	2810	4190
4 Dr LX-E Sdn	3365	5020
2 Dr STD Hbk	2430	3625

OPTIONS FOR ESCORT

Auto 4-Speed Transmission +220
Air Conditioning +245
AM/FM Stereo Tape[Opt on LX,STD] +95
Cruise Control +65
Luggage Rack +40
Power Door Locks +70
Power Moonroof +175
Power Steering[Opt on LX,STD] +75
Power Windows +80
Premium Sound System +105
Rear Spoiler[Opt on LX] +60

EXPLORER 1993

A new steering wheel and instrument panel freshen the Explorer's interior. New wheels are the only exterior changes. Explorers gain four-wheel antilock brakes that work in both two- and four-wheel drive modes.

RATINGS (SCALE OF 1-10)

Overall	Safety	Reliability	Performance	Comfort	Value
7.3	4.7	6.5	7.4	8.3	9.5

Don't forget to refer to the Mileage Adjustment Table at the back of this book!

 © 1999 by Edmund Publications Corporation

FORD 93

Model Description	Trade-in Value	Market Value
Category G		
2 Dr Eddie Bauer Utility	6640	8850
2 Dr Eddie Bauer 4WD Utility	7490	9990
4 Dr Eddie Bauer Wgn	7180	9575
4 Dr Eddie Bauer 4WD Wgn	7870	10495
4 Dr Limited Wgn	8015	10685
4 Dr Limited 4WD Wgn	8580	11440
2 Dr Sport Utility	5510	7345
2 Dr Sport 4WD Utility	6320	8425
2 Dr XL Utility	5385	7180
2 Dr XL 4WD Utility	6200	8270
4 Dr XL Wgn	6100	8130
4 Dr XL 4WD Wgn	6490	8650
4 Dr XLT Wgn	6785	9045
4 Dr XLT 4WD Wgn	7510	10010

OPTIONS FOR EXPLORER

Auto 4-Speed Transmission[Std on Limited] +270
Air Conditioning[Std on Limited] +245
Aluminum/Alloy Wheels[Opt on XL] +105
AM/FM Compact Disc Playr +115
Camper/Towing Package +85
Cruise Control[Opt on Sport,XL] +65
Dual Power Seats[Opt on XLT] +190
Keyless Entry System +60
Leather Seats[Std on Limited] +235
Limited Slip Diff +80
Luggage Rack[Opt on Sport,XL,XLT] +45
Power Door Locks[Opt on Sport,XL] +70
Power Windows[Opt on Sport,XL] +70
Premium Sound System +110
Running Boards +115
Sunroof +90

F-SERIES PICKUP 1993

No changes for the 1993 F-Series.

RATINGS (SCALE OF 1-10)

Overall	Safety	Reliability	Performance	Comfort	Value
N/A	5.4	6.8	6.8	7.4	N/A

F-150

Model Description	Trade-in Value	Market Value
Category H		
2 Dr Lightning Std Cab SB	8900	11265
2 Dr S Std Cab SB	4400	5565
2 Dr S Std Cab LB	4560	5775
2 Dr S 4WD Std Cab SB	5865	7425
2 Dr S 4WD Std Cab LB	6000	7595
2 Dr XL Ext Cab SB	6205	7855
2 Dr XL Std Cab SB	5745	7270
2 Dr XL Std Cab Stepside SB	6015	7615
2 Dr XL Ext Cab Stepside SB	6425	8130
2 Dr XL Std Cab LB	5845	7395
2 Dr XL Ext Cab LB	6290	7965
2 Dr XL 4WD Ext Cab SB	7410	9380
2 Dr XL 4WD Std Cab SB	6860	8680
2 Dr XL 4WD Ext Cab Stepside SB	7615	9640
2 Dr XL 4WD Std Cab Stepside SB	7095	8980
2 Dr XL 4WD Ext Cab LB	7445	9425
2 Dr XL 4WD Std Cab LB	6930	8775
2 Dr XLT Std Cab SB	6510	8240
2 Dr XLT Ext Cab SB	6545	8285
2 Dr XLT Std Cab Stepside SB	6485	8210
2 Dr XLT Ext Cab Stepside SB	6805	8615
2 Dr XLT Ext Cab LB	6685	8460
2 Dr XLT Std Cab LB	6495	8220
2 Dr XLT 4WD Ext Cab SB	7955	10070
2 Dr XLT 4WD Std Cab SB	7535	9540
2 Dr XLT 4WD Std Cab Stepside SB	7820	9900
2 Dr XLT 4WD Ext Cab Stepside SB	8205	10390
2 Dr XLT 4WD Ext Cab LB	8105	10260
2 Dr XLT 4WD Std Cab LB	7605	9630

F-250

Model Description	Trade-in Value	Market Value
Category H		
2 Dr XL Std Cab LB	6765	8560
2 Dr XL Ext Cab LB	8045	10185
2 Dr XL 4WD Std Cab LB	8200	10380
2 Dr XL 4WD Ext Cab LB	8665	10970
2 Dr XLT Ext Cab LB	8650	10950
2 Dr XLT Std Cab LB	7565	9575
2 Dr XLT 4WD Std Cab LB	8685	10990
2 Dr XLT 4WD Ext Cab LB	9405	11905

F-350

Model Description	Trade-in Value	Market Value
Category H		
2 Dr XL Ext Cab LB	8975	11360
2 Dr XL Std Cab LB	8880	11240
2 Dr XL 4WD Std Cab SB	9980	12630
2 Dr XL 4WD Std Cab LB	9990	12650
4 Dr XL Crew Cab LB	9205	11650
4 Dr XL 4WD Crew Cab LB	11050	13985
2 Dr XLT Ext Cab LB	10035	12700
2 Dr XLT Std Cab LB	9805	12410
2 Dr XLT 4WD Std Cab LB	10840	13720
4 Dr XLT Crew Cab LB	10245	12965
4 Dr XLT 4WD Crew Cab LB	11725	14840

OPTIONS FOR F-SERIES PICKUP

8 cyl 7.3 L Dsl Engine +805
8 cyl 5.0 L Engine +180
8 cyl 5.8 L Engine +260
8 cyl 7.5 L Engine +290
8 cyl 7.3 L Turbodsl Engine +1125
4-Speed Transmission +35

Don't forget to refer to the Mileage Adjustment Table at the back of this book!

© 1999 by Edmund Publications Corporation

Model Description	Trade-in Value	Market Value

Auto 3-Speed Transmission +210
Auto 4-Speed Transmission[Std on Lightning] +280
Air Conditioning[Opt on Lightning,S,XL, XLT] +245
Aluminum/Alloy Wheels[Std on Lightning] +95
AM/FM Stereo Tape[Std on XLT] +75
Camper/Towing Package +110
Cruise Control[Opt on XL, XLT] +60
Dual Rear Wheels +255
Limited Slip Diff[Std on Lightning] +75
Power Door Locks[Opt on XL, XLT] +55
Power Windows[Opt on XL, XLT] +60
Rear Step Bumper +45
Skid Plates +35
Sliding Rear Window +35

FESTIVA 1993

No changes to the 1993 Festiva.

RATINGS (SCALE OF 1-10)

Overall	Safety	Reliability	Performance	Comfort	Value
6.1	4.6	7.9	6.2	6.9	5

Model Description	Trade-in Value	Market Value
Category E		
2 Dr GL Hbk	2475	3695
2 Dr L Hbk	2045	3055

OPTIONS FOR FESTIVA

Auto 3-Speed Transmission +155
Air Conditioning +245
AM/FM Stereo Tape +95
Rear Spoiler +60
Rear Window Defroster +50
Sunroof +105

MUSTANG 1993

The Cobra is introduced to the lineup. Two hundred forty-five horsepower, a beefy suspension, and four-wheel disc brakes distinguish it from other Mustangs. Improved stereos grace all Mustangs this year.

RATINGS (SCALE OF 1-10)

Overall	Safety	Reliability	Performance	Comfort	Value
N/A	N/A	7.3	7.8	6.3	3.8

Model Description	Trade-in Value	Market Value
Category C		
2 Dr LX Cpe	3550	5000
2 Dr LX Conv	4570	6435
2 Dr LX Hbk	3620	5095
Category F		
2 Dr Cobra Hbk	9080	12110
2 Dr GT Conv	7120	9490
2 Dr GT Hbk	6485	8645
2 Dr LX 5.0 Cpe	5660	7550
2 Dr LX 5.0 Hbk	5835	7775
2 Dr LX 5.0 Conv	7090	9450

OPTIONS FOR MUSTANG

Auto 4-Speed Transmission +180
Air Conditioning +240
Aluminum/Alloy Wheels[Opt on LX] +85
AM/FM Compact Disc Playr +115
Chrome Wheels +170
Cruise Control +65
Leather Seats +215
Power Door Locks[Std on Conv] +60
Power Drivers Seat +70
Power Windows[Std on Conv] +70
Rear Spoiler[Opt on Conv] +50
Sunroof +110

PROBE 1993

A driver airbag becomes standard on the restyled Probe. The Probe's wheelbase stretches four inches and its curb weight jumps 100 pounds. The slow-selling LX model is dropped. Four-cylinder engines in the base model are good for 115 horsepower; GT models get a twin-cam 2.5-liter V6 engine that makes 164. Antilock brakes become optional for all Probes.

RATINGS (SCALE OF 1-10)

Overall	Safety	Reliability	Performance	Comfort	Value
6.8	6.1	7.3	9	7.4	4.4

Model Description	Trade-in Value	Market Value
Category C		
2 Dr STD Hbk	3730	5255
Category F		
2 Dr GT Hbk	4755	6335

OPTIONS FOR PROBE

Auto 4-Speed Transmission +220
Air Conditioning +240
Aluminum/Alloy Wheels[Std on GT] +85
AM/FM Compact Disc Playr +115
Anti-Lock Brakes +190
Cruise Control +65
Keyless Entry System +50
Leather Seats +175
Power Door Locks +60
Power Drivers Seat[Std on GT] +70
Power Sunroof +205
Power Windows +70

RANGER 1993

The classy looking Ranger Splash is introduced in 1993, offering the first flareside cargo box in the small pickup class. The rest of the Ranger lineup gets new sheetmetal.

RATINGS (SCALE OF 1-10)

Overall	Safety	Reliability	Performance	Comfort	Value
N/A	5	8.1	7.2	7.3	N/A

Model Description	Trade-in Value	Market Value
Category G		
2 Dr Splash Std Cab Stepside SB	4950	6600
2 Dr Splash 4WD Std Cab Stepside SB	6675	8900
2 Dr Sport Std Cab SB	3915	5220

Don't forget to refer to the Mileage Adjustment Table at the back of this book!

 © 1999 by Edmund Publications Corporation

Model Description	Trade-in Value	Market Value
2 Dr Sport Std Cab LB	4000	5330
2 Dr Sport 4WD Std Cab SB	5735	7645
2 Dr Sport 4WD Std Cab LB	5840	7790
2 Dr STX Ext Cab SB	5155	6875
2 Dr STX Std Cab SB	4795	6395
2 Dr STX Std Cab LB	4895	6525
2 Dr STX 4WD Ext Cab SB	6450	8600
2 Dr STX 4WD Std Cab SB	6225	8300
2 Dr STX 4WD Std Cab LB	6325	8435
2 Dr XL Ext Cab SB	4530	6040
2 Dr XL Std Cab SB	3805	5075
2 Dr XL Std Cab LB	3905	5205
2 Dr XL 4WD Ext Cab SB	6415	8555
2 Dr XL 4WD Std Cab SB	5670	7560
2 Dr XL 4WD Std Cab LB	5770	7695
2 Dr XLT Std Cab SB	4140	5520
2 Dr XLT Ext Cab SB	4900	6530
2 Dr XLT Std Cab LB	4240	5655
2 Dr XLT 4WD Ext Cab SB	6320	8425
2 Dr XLT 4WD Std Cab SB	6015	8020
2 Dr XLT 4WD Std Cab LB	6120	8160

OPTIONS FOR RANGER

6 cyl 3.0 L Engine +145
6 cyl 4.0 L Engine +200
Auto 4-Speed Transmission +300
Air Conditioning +245
Aluminum/Alloy Wheels[Std on Splash] +105
AM/FM Compact Disc Playr +115
Cruise Control +65
Limited Slip Diff +80
Power Door Locks +70
Power Steering[Opt on XL 2WD Std Cab] +85
Power Windows +70
Premium Sound System +110

TAURUS 1993

SHOs finally receive an optional automatic transmission. The base L model is dropped in favor of the new entry-level Taurus GL. Body-color bumpers and side moldings are now standard.

RATINGS (SCALE OF 1-10)

Overall	Safety	Reliability	Performance	Comfort	Value
7.6	7	7	8	7.8	8.2

Model Description	Trade-in Value	Market Value
Category C		
4 Dr GL Wgn	3965	5580
4 Dr GL Sdn	3585	5050
4 Dr LX Sdn	4925	6940
4 Dr LX Wgn	5350	7535
Category F		
4 Dr SHO Sdn	5605	7470

OPTIONS FOR TAURUS

6 cyl 3.0 L FLEX Engine +220
6 cyl 3.8 L Engine +170
Auto 4-Speed Transmission[Opt on SHO] +195
Air Conditioning[Opt on GL] +240
Aluminum/Alloy Wheels[Opt on GL] +85
AM/FM Compact Disc Playr +115
Anti-Lock Brakes[Std on SHO] +190
Climate Control for AC[Opt on LX] +50
Cruise Control[Std on SHO] +65
Dual Air Bag Restraints +150
Dual Power Seats +175
Leather Seats +175
Power Door Locks[Opt on GL] +60
Power Moonroof +210
Power Windows[Opt on GL] +70
Premium Sound System +120
Third Seat +50

TEMPO 1993

Say goodbye to the GLS. GL and LX Tempos have removable cupholders and a leather-wrapped shift knob. A driver airbag is optional on both models.

RATINGS (SCALE OF 1-10)

Overall	Safety	Reliability	Performance	Comfort	Value
6.7	4.4	7.7	7.6	7.1	6.9

Model Description	Trade-in Value	Market Value
Category C		
2 Dr GL Sdn	2715	3825
4 Dr GL Sdn	2720	3830
4 Dr LX Sdn	3020	4255

OPTIONS FOR TEMPO

6 cyl 3.0 L Engine +210
Auto 3-Speed Transmission +170
Air Bag Restraint +155
Air Conditioning +240
Aluminum/Alloy Wheels +85
AM/FM Stereo Tape +50
Cruise Control +65
Power Door Locks[Opt on GL] +70
Power Drivers Seat +85
Power Windows +90

THUNDERBIRD 1993

Base and Sport models are discontinued. Restyled alloy wheels and a new steering wheel complete the changes to the 1993 Thunderbird.

RATINGS (SCALE OF 1-10)

Overall	Safety	Reliability	Performance	Comfort	Value
6.9	5.8	7.1	6.8	8	7

Model Description	Trade-in Value	Market Value
Category C		
2 Dr LX Cpe	4670	6580
Category F		
2 Dr SC Sprchgd Cpe	6595	8795

Don't forget to refer to the Mileage Adjustment Table at the back of this book!

© 1999 by Edmund Publications Corporation

OPTIONS FOR THUNDERBIRD

8 cyl 5.0 L Engine +345
Auto 4-Speed Transmission[Opt on SC] +180
Aluminum/Alloy Wheels[Opt on LX] +85
AM/FM Compact Disc Playr +115
Anti-Lock Brakes +190
Climate Control for AC +50
Cruise Control[Opt on SC] +65
Keyless Entry System +50
Leather Seats +175
Power Door Locks[Opt on SC] +60
Power Drivers Seat +70
Power Moonroof +210
Power Passenger Seat +80
Premium Sound System +120

1992 FORD

AEROSTAR 1992

A driver airbag becomes standard on passenger and cargo models. A new dashboard includes redesigned climate controls. On automatics, the shift lever moves from the floor to the column. High-back front bucket seats are now standard for all trim levels. Leather seats are available for the Eddie Bauer model. Outboard rear-seat passengers get a shoulder belt. A new grille and headlights appear on the exterior.

RATINGS (SCALE OF 1-10)

Overall	Safety	Reliability	Performance	Comfort	Value
7.1	6.2	6.8	6.6	7.5	8.2

Category G	Trade-in Value	Market Value
2 Dr Eddie Bauer Pass. Van Ext	5175	7085
2 Dr Eddie Bauer Pass. Van	4515	6185
2 Dr Eddie Bauer 4WD Pass. Van	5025	6880
2 Dr Eddie Bauer 4WD Pass. Van Ext	5585	7655
2 Dr STD Cargo Van Ext	2925	4010
2 Dr STD Cargo Van	2450	3360
2 Dr STD 4WD Cargo Van	2705	3705
2 Dr STD 4WD Cargo Van Ext	3260	4465
2 Dr XL Pass. Van Ext	3850	5275
2 Dr XL Pass. Van	3245	4450
2 Dr XL 4WD Pass. Van	3540	4850
2 Dr XL 4WD Pass. Van Ext	4115	5635
2 Dr XLT Pass. Van	3865	5295
2 Dr XLT Pass. Van Ext	4550	6235
2 Dr XLT 4WD Pass. Van	4215	5775
2 Dr XLT 4WD Pass. Van Ext	4895	6705

OPTIONS FOR AEROSTAR

6 cyl 4.0 L Engine[Std on 4WD] +140
Auto 4-Speed Transmission[Opt on 2WD] +185
Plus Pkg +280
Seat/Bed Combination +230
Air Conditioning[Std on XLT] +200
Aluminum/Alloy Wheels[Opt on STD,XL,XLT] +85
AM/FM Stereo Tape +60
Captain Chairs (4) +155
Cruise Control[Opt on STD,XL] +50
Dual Air Conditioning[Opt on XL,XLT] +250
Leather Seats +190
Luggage Rack[Opt on XL,XLT] +40
Power Door Locks[Opt on STD,XL] +55
Power Windows[Opt on STD,XL] +60
Premium Sound System[Opt on STD,XL,XLT] +90
Running Boards +95

BRONCO 1992

Freshened front-end styling and the addition of the XLT and Eddie Bauer models are the main changes for 1992.

RATINGS (SCALE OF 1-10)

Overall	Safety	Reliability	Performance	Comfort	Value
6.3	5.6	6.1	6.4	6.6	6.7

Category H	Trade-in Value	Market Value
2 Dr Custom 4WD Utility	6810	8845
2 Dr Eddie Bauer 4WD Utility	7495	9735
2 Dr XLT 4WD Utility	7180	9325

OPTIONS FOR BRONCO

8 cyl 5.0 L Engine[Opt on Custom,XLT] +145
8 cyl 5.8 L Engine +210
Auto 4-Speed Transmission +225
Air Conditioning[Opt on Custom,XLT] +200
Aluminum/Alloy Wheels[Opt on Custom,XLT] +75
AM/FM Stereo Tape +60
Camper/Towing Package +90
Cruise Control[Opt on Custom,XLT] +50
Leather Seats +255
Limited Slip Diff +65
Power Door Locks +45
Power Windows +45
Velour/Cloth Seats[Std on Eddie Bauer] +35

CLUB WAGON/ECONOLINE 1992

Fully redesigned, Ford's full-size van receives a new body, lights, suspension and fuel tank. New safety features include a driver's side airbag and a high-mounted third brake light.

RATINGS (SCALE OF 1-10)

Overall	Safety	Reliability	Performance	Comfort	Value
N/A	7	7.7	6.8	7.9	N/A

E-150

Category H	Trade-in Value	Market Value
2 Dr Chateau Club Wagon	6495	8435
2 Dr STD Econoline Ext	5715	7420
2 Dr STD Club Wagon	6155	7995
2 Dr STD Econoline	5495	7135

Don't forget to refer to the Mileage Adjustment Table at the back of this book!

© 1999 by Edmund Publications Corporation

Model Description	Trade-in Value	Market Value
2 Dr XL Econoline Ext	5790	7520
2 Dr XL Econoline	5550	7205
2 Dr XLT Club Wagon	6470	8405

E-250

Category H

Model Description	Trade-in Value	Market Value
2 Dr STD Econoline	4620	6000
2 Dr STD Econoline Ext	5085	6605
2 Dr XL Econoline Ext	5170	6715
2 Dr XL Econoline	4690	6090

E-350

Category H

Model Description	Trade-in Value	Market Value
2 Dr Chateau Club Wagon Ext	6300	8185
2 Dr Chateau Dsl Club Wagon	6405	8315
2 Dr STD Econoline Ext	5485	7125
2 Dr STD Econoline	5000	6495
2 Dr Super Club Wagon Ext	5895	7660
2 Dr Super Dsl Club Wagon	6010	7810
2 Dr XL Econoline Ext	5670	7365
2 Dr XL Dsl Econoline	5665	7355
2 Dr XLT Club Wagon	5915	7685
2 Dr XLT Club Wagon Ext	6070	7885

OPTIONS FOR CLUB WAGON/ECONOLINE

8 cyl 7.3 L Dsl Engine +690
8 cyl 5.0 L Engine +145
8 cyl 5.8 L Engine +210
8 cyl 7.5 L Engine +230
Auto 4-Speed Transmission[Std on E-150 Club Wagon] +75
Seat/Bed Pkg +245
Air Conditioning +200
Aluminum/Alloy Wheels +75
AM/FM Stereo Tape +60
Camper/Towing Package[Std on E-150 Econoline Ext, E-350 Econoline,E-350 Econoline Ext] +90
Chrome Bumpers +40
Cruise Control +50
Dual Air Conditioning +350
Limited Slip Diff +65
Power Door Locks +45
Power Drivers Seat +70
Power Windows +45

CROWN VICTORIA 1992

After a total redesign, the corny LTD moniker is dropped from name and the station wagon body style is deleted from the Crown Vic's lineup. Suspension improvements include gas-charged shock absorbers and rear stabilizer bars. Antilock brakes are optional but four-wheel disc brakes are standard.

RATINGS (SCALE OF 1-10)

Overall	Safety	Reliability	Performance	Comfort	Value
7.6	7.2	7.3	7.5	8.3	7.9

Category B

Model Description	Trade-in Value	Market Value
4 Dr LX Sdn	4325	6010
4 Dr STD Sdn	4070	5650
4 Dr Touring Sdn	5065	7030

OPTIONS FOR CROWN VICTORIA

Aluminum/Alloy Wheels[Std on Touring] +85
AM/FM Stereo Tape +45
Anti-Lock Brakes[Std on Touring] +175
Climate Control for AC +45
Cruise Control[Std on Touring] +55
Keyless Entry System +45
Leather Seats +165
Power Door Locks +60
Power Drivers Seat[Std on Touring] +75
Power Passenger Seat[Opt on LX] +75
Premium Sound System +105
Traction Control System[Opt on LX] +45
Trip Computer +55

ESCORT 1992

A notchback sedan is introduced as an LX-E trim-level; it offers four-wheel disc brakes, the GT engine, and GT interior touches. The Pony Comfort Group option makes air conditioning and power steering available on the base model.

RATINGS (SCALE OF 1-10)

Overall	Safety	Reliability	Performance	Comfort	Value
6.4	4.7	7.1	6.8	7.6	5.8

Category E

Model Description	Trade-in Value	Market Value
2 Dr GT Hbk	2195	3425
2 Dr LX Hbk	1890	2955
4 Dr LX Wgn	1905	2980
4 Dr LX Hbk	2025	3165
4 Dr LX Sdn	2070	3240
4 Dr LX-E Sdn	2440	3810
2 Dr Pony Hbk	1700	2660

OPTIONS FOR ESCORT

Auto 4-Speed Transmission +180
Air Conditioning +200
AM/FM Stereo Tape[Opt on LX,Pony] +75
Cruise Control +55
Luggage Rack +30
Power Door Locks +55
Power Moonroof +145
Power Steering[Opt on LX,Pony] +60
Power Windows +65
Premium Sound System +85

EXPLORER 1992

A 3.55 axle replaces last years 3.27 on four-wheel drive models. A one-touch-down driver's window becomes standard on all Explorers equipped with power windows.

Don't forget to refer to the Mileage Adjustment Table at the back of this book!

© 1999 by Edmund Publications Corporation

Model Description	Trade-in Value	Market Value

Eddie Bauer models receive color-keyed alloy wheels. A tilt-open sunroof is now available without an option package.

RATINGS (SCALE OF 1-10)

Overall	Safety	Reliability	Performance	Comfort	Value
6.6	4.8	6.3	7.4	8.3	6.5

Category G

Model Description	Trade-in Value	Market Value
2 Dr Eddie Bauer Utility	5315	7280
2 Dr Eddie Bauer 4WD Utility	6225	8530
4 Dr Eddie Bauer Wgn	6270	8585
4 Dr Eddie Bauer 4WD Wgn	6775	9280
2 Dr Sport Utility	4925	6750
2 Dr Sport 4WD Utility	6050	8290
2 Dr XL Utility	4790	6565
2 Dr XL 4WD Utility	5850	8015
4 Dr XL Wgn	5205	7130
4 Dr XL 4WD Wgn	6010	8230
4 Dr XLT Wgn	6060	8300
4 Dr XLT 4WD Wgn	6395	8760

OPTIONS FOR EXPLORER

Auto 4-Speed Transmission +215
Sport Bucket Seats +215
Air Conditioning +200
Aluminum/Alloy Wheels[Opt on XL, XLT 4WD] +85
AM/FM Compact Disc Playr +95
Auto Locking Hubs (4WD)[Opt on XL,XLT] +65
Camper/Towing Package +70
Cruise Control[Std on Eddie Bauer, XLT] +50
Flip-Up Sunroof +85
Leather Seats +190
Limited Slip Diff +65
Luggage Rack[Std on Eddie Bauer] +40
Power Door Locks[Std on Eddie Bauer, XLT] +55
Power Drivers Seat[Opt on XLT] +70
Power Passenger Seat[Opt on XLT] +65
Power Windows[Std on Eddie Bauer, XLT] +60
Premium Sound System +90
Sunroof +75

F-SERIES PICKUP 1992

New front sheetmetal, a redesigned dashboard, and the return of the Flareside mark the changes for the 1992 F-Series. Climate controls are simplified and stereo controls are moved closer to the driver.

RATINGS (SCALE OF 1-10)

Overall	Safety	Reliability	Performance	Comfort	Value
N/A	5.6	7.1	6.8	7.4	N/A

F-150

Category H

Model Description	Trade-in Value	Market Value
2 Dr S Ext Cab SB	4485	5820
2 Dr S Std Cab SB	3870	5025
2 Dr S Ext Cab LB	4660	6050
2 Dr S Std Cab LB	3965	5150
2 Dr S 4WD Std Cab SB	5395	7010
2 Dr S 4WD Std Cab LB	5515	7160
2 Dr STD Std Cab SB	4965	6450
2 Dr STD Ext Cab SB	5230	6790
2 Dr STD Std Cab Stepside SB	5220	6780
2 Dr STD Ext Cab Stepside SB	5500	7140
2 Dr STD Ext Cab LB	5380	6985
2 Dr STD Std Cab LB	4980	6470
2 Dr STD 4WD Std Cab SB	6530	8480
2 Dr STD 4WD Ext Cab SB	6530	8480
2 Dr STD 4WD Ext Cab Stepside SB	6775	8800
2 Dr STD 4WD Std Cab Stepside SB	6720	8730
2 Dr STD 4WD Std Cab LB	6515	8460
2 Dr STD 4WD Ext Cab LB	6535	8490
2 Dr XL Std Cab SB	5015	6515
2 Dr XL Ext Cab SB	5345	6940
2 Dr XL Ext Cab Stepside SB	5565	7230
2 Dr XL Std Cab Stepside SB	5270	6845
2 Dr XL Ext Cab LB	5450	7075
2 Dr XL Std Cab LB	5100	6625
2 Dr XL 4WD Std Cab SB	6635	8615
2 Dr XL 4WD Ext Cab SB	6665	8655
2 Dr XL 4WD Ext Cab Stepside SB	6900	8960
2 Dr XL 4WD Std Cab Stepside SB	6780	8805
2 Dr XL 4WD Ext Cab LB	6605	8580
2 Dr XL 4WD Std Cab LB	6595	8565

F-250

Category H

Model Description	Trade-in Value	Market Value
2 Dr STD Ext Cab LB	6940	9010
2 Dr STD Std Cab LB	6415	8335
2 Dr STD 4WD Ext Cab LB	8095	10515
2 Dr STD 4WD Std Cab LB	6955	9030

F-350

Category H

Model Description	Trade-in Value	Market Value
2 Dr STD Ext Cab LB	7875	10225
2 Dr STD Std Cab LB	7655	9940
2 Dr STD 4WD Std Cab LB	8770	11390
4 Dr STD Crew Cab LB	8020	10415
4 Dr STD 4WD Crew Cab LB	8920	11585

OPTIONS FOR F-SERIES PICKUP

8 cyl 7.3 L Dsl Engine +690
8 cyl 5.0 L Engine +145
8 cyl 5.8 L Engine +210
8 cyl 7.5 L Engine +230
Auto 3-Speed Transmission +200
Auto 4-Speed Transmission +225

Don't forget to refer to the Mileage Adjustment Table at the back of this book!

 © 1999 by Edmund Publications Corporation

Model Description	Trade-in Value	Market Value

Nite Trim Pkg +640
Air Conditioning +200
Aluminum/Alloy Wheels +75
AM/FM Stereo Tape +60
Camper/Towing Package +90
Chrome Wheels +75
Cruise Control +50
Dual Rear Wheels +210
Limited Slip Diff +65
Power Door Locks +45
Power Windows +45
Rear Step Bumper +40

FESTIVA 1992

The GL gets alloy wheels. Sport trim and a spoiler are part of the GL's optional Sport Package.

RATINGS (SCALE OF 1-10)

Overall	Safety	Reliability	Performance	Comfort	Value
6.2	4.6	8.2	6.2	6.9	5

Model Description	Trade-in Value	Market Value
Category E		
2 Dr GL Hbk	1770	2765
2 Dr L Hbk	1495	2340

OPTIONS FOR FESTIVA

Auto 3-Speed Transmission +125
Air Conditioning +200
AM/FM Stereo Tape +75
Rear Spoiler +50
Rear Window Defroster +40
Sunroof +85

MUSTANG 1992

LX models receive color-keyed body side moldings and bumper rub strips. All models get a new dome lamp.

RATINGS (SCALE OF 1-10)

Overall	Safety	Reliability	Performance	Comfort	Value
N/A	N/A	7.4	7.8	6.3	4.8

Model Description	Trade-in Value	Market Value
Category C		
2 Dr LX Hbk	3285	4760
2 Dr LX Cpe	3140	4550
2 Dr LX Conv	4150	6010
Category F		
2 Dr GT Hbk	5385	7480
2 Dr GT Conv	6260	8690
2 Dr LX 5.0 Conv	6035	8380
2 Dr LX 5.0 Cpe	4745	6590
2 Dr LX 5.0 Hbk	4885	6785

OPTIONS FOR MUSTANG

Auto 4-Speed Transmission +145
Air Conditioning +200
Aluminum/Alloy Wheels[Opt on LX] +70
AM/FM Stereo Tape +40
Cruise Control +50
Leather Seats +175
Power Door Locks[Std on Conv] +50
Power Drivers Seat +60
Power Windows[Std on Conv] +55
Premium Sound System +100
Sunroof +90

PROBE 1992

The Sport Option Package becomes available for the LX model. A rear window defroster, interval wipers, power mirrors, tinted glass, and a tilt steering wheel are no longer standard on the GT or LX.

Model Description	Trade-in Value	Market Value
Category E		
2 Dr GL Hbk	2535	3960
2 Dr LX Hbk	2820	4405
Category F		
2 Dr GT Turbo Hbk	3470	4815

OPTIONS FOR PROBE

Auto 4-Speed Transmission +180
Air Conditioning +200
Aluminum/Alloy Wheels[Std on GT] +75
AM/FM Compact Disc Playr +115
Anti-Lock Brakes +175
Climate Control for AC +40
Cruise Control +50
Leather Seats +175
Power Door Locks +50
Power Drivers Seat +60
Power Windows +55
Sunroof +85

RANGER 1992

No changes to the 1992 Ford Ranger.

Model Description	Trade-in Value	Market Value
Category G		
2 Dr Custom Std Cab SB	2945	4035
2 Dr Custom Std Cab LB	3020	4140
2 Dr Custom 4WD Std Cab SB	4505	6175
2 Dr Custom 4WD Std Cab LB	4460	6110
2 Dr S Std Cab SB	2815	3855
2 Dr Sport Std Cab SB	3035	4160
2 Dr Sport Std Cab LB	3110	4260
2 Dr Sport 4WD Std Cab SB	4585	6280
2 Dr Sport 4WD Std Cab LB	4665	6390
2 Dr STD Ext Cab SB	3675	5035
2 Dr STD 4WD Ext Cab SB	5010	6865
2 Dr STX Std Cab SB	3865	5295
2 Dr STX Ext Cab SB	3995	5475
2 Dr STX Std Cab LB	3875	5305
2 Dr STX 4WD Ext Cab SB	5270	7220
2 Dr STX 4WD Std Cab LB	5170	7080
2 Dr XLT Std Cab SB	3275	4485
2 Dr XLT Ext Cab SB	3760	5150
2 Dr XLT Std Cab LB	3305	4525
2 Dr XLT 4WD Std Cab SB	4855	6655

Don't forget to refer to the Mileage Adjustment Table at the back of this book!

© 1999 by Edmund Publications Corporation

Model Description	Trade-in Value	Market Value
2 Dr XLT 4WD Ext Cab SB	5135	7030
2 Dr XLT 4WD Std Cab LB	4895	6705

OPTIONS FOR RANGER

6 cyl 2.9 L Engine +135
6 cyl 3.0 L Engine[Std on STX] +140
6 cyl 4.0 L Engine +185
Auto 4-Speed Transmission +230
Chrome Rally Bar Pkg +230
Chrome Sport Appear Pkg +205
Air Conditioning +200
Aluminum/Alloy Wheels +85
AM/FM Stereo Tape[Std on STX , XLT] +60
Auto Locking Hubs (4WD) +65
Cruise Control[Opt on Custom,Sport,STD,XLT,4WD] +50
Limited Slip Diff +65
Power Door Locks +55
Power Drivers Seat +70
Power Steering[Std on STD,STX,Ext Cab,4WD, XLT] +70
Power Windows +60
Rear Step Bumper[Opt on S,Sport] +35
Velour/Cloth Seats[Std on STX,XLT] +45

TAURUS 1992

A passenger airbag is now optional. Interior changes include a new dash. Restyled sheetmetal replaces everything but the doors. Antilock brakes are standard on the SHO and optional on other models. The SHO receives distinctive front-end styling. Wagons get an optional remote lift gate release.

RATINGS (SCALE OF 1-10)

Overall	Safety	Reliability	Performance	Comfort	Value
7.6	7	6.9	8	7.8	8.1

Model Description	Trade-in Value	Market Value
Category C		
4 Dr GL Wgn	3100	4495
4 Dr GL Sdn	2855	4140
4 Dr L Wgn	3005	4355
4 Dr L Sdn	2615	3785
4 Dr LX Sdn	4000	5795
4 Dr LX Wgn	4370	6330
Category F		
4 Dr SHO Sdn	4575	6355

OPTIONS FOR TAURUS

6 cyl 3.8 L Engine[Opt on GL] +120
Air Conditioning[Std on LX,SHO] +200
Aluminum/Alloy Wheels[Opt on GL] +70
AM/FM Compact Disc Playr +95
Anti-Lock Brakes[Std on SHO] +155
Climate Control for AC +40
Cruise Control[Std on SHO] +50
Dual Air Bag Restraints +120
Keyless Entry System +45
Leather Seats +145
Power Door Locks[Std on LX,SHO] +50
Power Moonroof +175
Power Windows[Std on LX,SHO] +55
Premium Sound System[Std on SHO] +100
Third Seat +40

TEMPO 1992

V6 power becomes available but the four-wheel drive option departs. Rear stabilizer bars are added to V6 models and sequential-port fuel injection appears on all Tempos. The GLS model receives fog lamps, alloy wheels and 15-inch tires.

RATINGS (SCALE OF 1-10)

Overall	Safety	Reliability	Performance	Comfort	Value
6.6	4.4	7.3	7.6	7.1	6.3

Model Description	Trade-in Value	Market Value
Category C		
2 Dr GL Sdn	2160	3135
4 Dr GL Sdn	2100	3045
2 Dr GLS Sdn	2640	3830
4 Dr GLS Sdn	2650	3845
4 Dr LX Sdn	2385	3455

OPTIONS FOR TEMPO

6 cyl 3.0 L Engine[Std on GLS] +170
Auto 3-Speed Transmission +135
Air Bag Restraint +125
Air Conditioning[Std on GLS] +200
AM/FM Stereo Tape[Std on GLS] +40
Cruise Control +50
Power Door Locks[Std on LX] +60
Power Drivers Seat +70
Power Windows +75
Premium Sound System +100

THUNDERBIRD 1992

A V8 engine is available on the Base and LX Thunderbird; standard on the new Sport. The Sport has alloy wheels and V8 fender badges.

RATINGS (SCALE OF 1-10)

Overall	Safety	Reliability	Performance	Comfort	Value
6.9	5.8	6.9	6.8	8	6.9

Model Description	Trade-in Value	Market Value
Category C		
2 Dr LX Cpe	4165	6040
2 Dr Sport Cpe	4420	6405
2 Dr STD Cpe	3635	5265
Category F		
2 Dr SC Sprchgd Cpe	5230	7265

OPTIONS FOR THUNDERBIRD

8 cyl 5.0 L Engine[Std on Sport] +270
Auto 4-Speed Transmission[Opt on SC] +145
Aluminum/Alloy Wheels[Opt on LX,STD] +70
AM/FM Compact Disc Playr +95
Anti-Lock Brakes[Std on SC] +155
Climate Control for AC +40
Cruise Control[Opt on STD] +50

Don't forget to refer to the Mileage Adjustment Table at the back of this book!

 © 1999 by Edmund Publications Corporation

Model Description	Trade-in Value	Market Value

Keyless Entry System +45
Leather Seats +145
Power Door Locks[Std on LX] +50
Power Drivers Seat[Std on LX] +60
Power Moonroof +175
Power Passenger Seat +65
Premium Sound System +100

1991 FORD

AEROSTAR 1991

A new sport appearance package debuts on XL and XLT models; it includes running boards and a front air dam. The towing harness is upgraded and a door ajar dummy-light appears for rear doors. The Eddie Bauer trim-level is added this year.

RATINGS (SCALE OF 1-10)

Overall	Safety	Reliability	Performance	Comfort	Value
6.6	4.4	6.5	6.6	7.3	8.1

Category G

Model Description	Trade-in Value	Market Value
2 Dr Eddie Bauer Pass. Van	3535	5050
2 Dr Eddie Bauer Pass. Van Ext	3845	5490
2 Dr Eddie Bauer 4WD Pass. Van	4160	5945
2 Dr Eddie Bauer 4WD Pass. Van Ext	4805	6865
2 Dr STD Cargo Van	1870	2670
2 Dr STD Pass. Van	2680	3825
2 Dr STD Cargo Van Ext	2425	3460
2 Dr STD 4WD Cargo Van Ext	3125	4465
2 Dr STD 4WD Cargo Van	2560	3660
2 Dr XL Pass. Van Ext	3045	4350
2 Dr XL Pass. Van	2770	3960
2 Dr XL 4WD Pass. Van Ext	3740	5345
2 Dr XL 4WD Pass. Van	3300	4715
2 Dr XLT Pass. Van	3100	4430
2 Dr XLT Pass. Van Ext	3525	5035
2 Dr XLT 4WD Pass. Van Ext	3940	5630
2 Dr XLT 4WD Pass. Van	3455	4940

OPTIONS FOR AEROSTAR

6 cyl 4.0 L Engine[Opt on 2WD] +120
Auto 4-Speed Transmission[Opt on XL,XLT] +135
Seat/Bed Combination +175
Air Conditioning[Std on Eddie Bauer, XLT] +165
Aluminum/Alloy Wheels +70
AM/FM Stereo Tape[Opt on STD,XL,XLT] +50
Camper/Towing Package +60
Captain Chairs (4) +130
Cruise Control[Std on Eddie Bauer, XLT] +45
Dual Air Conditioning[Opt on STD,XL,XLT] +205
Luggage Rack[Opt on STD,XL,XLT] +30
Power Door Locks +45
Power Windows +50
Premium Sound System[Opt on STD,XL,XLT] +75

BRONCO 1991

A four-speed automatic transmission replaces the three-speed unit. A silver-anniversary edition is available.

Category H

Model Description	Trade-in Value	Market Value
2 Dr Custom 4WD Utility	5330	7200
2 Dr Eddie Bauer 4WD Utility	6020	8135
2 Dr Slvr Anniversary 4WD Utility	5740	7755
2 Dr XLT 4WD Utility	5915	7995
2 Dr XLT Nite 4WD Utility	5915	7995

OPTIONS FOR BRONCO

8 cyl 5.0 L Engine[Opt on Custom,XLT] +120
8 cyl 5.8 L Engine +165
Auto 4-Speed Transmission[Std on Slvr Anniversary] +185
Air Conditioning[Opt on Custom] +165
Aluminum/Alloy Wheels[Opt on Custom,XLT] +65
AM/FM Stereo Tape[Opt on Custom] +50
Camper/Towing Package +70
Cruise Control[Opt on Custom] +40
Leather Seats[Opt on Custom, XLT] +210
Limited Slip Diff +50
Power Door Locks[Opt on Custom] +35
Power Windows[Opt on Custom] +40
Swing Out Tire Carrier[Opt on Custom,XLT] +35

CLUB WAGON/ECONOLINE 1991

The short wheelbase model is dropped but a Heavy Duty workhorse becomes available. Optional 15-inch deep-dish wheels are available for those who want that "sporty" full-size van look.

E-150

Category H

Model Description	Trade-in Value	Market Value
2 Dr STD Econoline Ext	3955	5345
2 Dr STD Econoline	3695	4995
2 Dr XL Econoline	3765	5090
2 Dr XL Econoline Ext	4475	6050
2 Dr XLT Club Wagon	4800	6490

E-250

Category H

Model Description	Trade-in Value	Market Value
2 Dr STD Econoline	3585	4840
2 Dr STD Club Wagon	4430	5985
2 Dr STD Econoline Ext	3965	5360
2 Dr XLT Club Wagon	4900	6625

E-350

Category H

Model Description	Trade-in Value	Market Value
2 Dr STD Econoline Ext	3880	5240
2 Dr STD Econoline	3745	5065
2 Dr Super Club Wagon Ext	4730	6395
2 Dr Super Club Wagon	4360	5890
2 Dr XLT Club Wagon Ext	4865	6575

Don't forget to refer to the Mileage Adjustment Table at the back of this book!

 © 1999 by Edmund Publications Corporation

OPTIONS FOR CLUB WAGON/ECONOLINE

8 cyl 7.3 L Dsl Engine +460
8 cyl 5.0 L Engine +120
8 cyl 5.8 L Engine +165
8 cyl 7.5 L Engine +175
Auto 4-Speed Transmission[Std on E-150 XLT Club Wagon] +60
Air Conditioning +165
Aluminum/Alloy Wheels +65
AM/FM Stereo Tape[Std on XLT Club Wagon] +50
Camper/Towing Package[Std on E-250 XLT Club Wagon] +70
Chrome Bumpers +35
Cruise Control[Std on E-250 XLT Club Wagon] +40
Dual Air Conditioning[Std on E-250 XLT Club Wagon] +290
Limited Slip Diff +50
Power Door Locks[Std on E-250 XLT Club Wagon] +35
Power Drivers Seat +55
Power Windows[Std on E-250 XLT Club Wagon] +40
Swing Out Tire Carrier +35

CROWN VICTORIA 1991

No changes to the 1991 Crown Victoria.

Category B		
4 Dr Cntry Squire LX Wgn	2985	4205
4 Dr Cntry Squire Wgn	2570	3615
4 Dr LX Wgn	2760	3885
4 Dr LX Sdn	3235	4555
4 Dr S Sdn	2420	3405
4 Dr STD Sdn	2935	4135
4 Dr STD Wgn	2310	3250

OPTIONS FOR CROWN VICTORIA

AM/FM Stereo Tape +35
Cruise Control +45
Leather Seats +135
Power Door Locks +50
Premium Sound System +85
Third Seat[Opt on Country Squire] +35

ESCORT 1991

A totally redesigned Escort bows in 1991. New engines, sheetmetal and interiors round out the changes for this car that is based on the Mazda Protege.

RATINGS (SCALE OF 1-10)

Overall	Safety	Reliability	Performance	Comfort	Value
6.2	4.6	6.6	6.8	7.6	5.6

Category E		
2 Dr GT Hbk	1770	3000
2 Dr LX Hbk	1430	2425
4 Dr LX Hbk	1465	2485
4 Dr LX Wgn	1515	2565
2 Dr Pony Hbk	1285	2180

OPTIONS FOR ESCORT

Auto 4-Speed Transmission +145
Air Conditioning +165
AM/FM Stereo Tape[Std on GT] +60
Cruise Control +45
Power Door Locks +45
Power Steering[Std on GT] +50
Premium Sound System +70
Tilt Steering Wheel +30

EXPLORER 1991

New model introduced to replace aging Bronco II. The Explorer is one of the bigger compact sport utilities and comes in two- or four-door models. A 4.0-liter V6 engine powers two- and four-wheel drive models. Part-time four-wheel drive can be engaged with the push of a button.

RATINGS (SCALE OF 1-10)

Overall	Safety	Reliability	Performance	Comfort	Value
6.6	4.8	6	7.4	8.3	6.4

Category G		
2 Dr Eddie Bauer Utility	4825	6890
2 Dr Eddie Bauer 4WD Utility	5440	7775
4 Dr Eddie Bauer Wgn	5110	7300
4 Dr Eddie Bauer 4WD Wgn	5690	8130
2 Dr Sport Utility	3860	5515
2 Dr Sport 4WD Utility	4465	6380
2 Dr XL Utility	3765	5380
2 Dr XL 4WD Utility	4460	6375
4 Dr XL Wgn	4320	6175
4 Dr XL 4WD Wgn	4795	6850
4 Dr XLT Wgn	4755	6795
4 Dr XLT 4WD Wgn	5340	7630

OPTIONS FOR EXPLORER

Auto 4-Speed Transmission +175
Air Conditioning +165
Aluminum/Alloy Wheels[Opt on XL Sport] +70
AM/FM Compact Disc Playr +80
Auto Locking Hubs (4WD)[Opt on Sport,XL,XLT] +55
Camper/Towing Package +60
Cruise Control[Opt on Sport,XL] +45
Leather Seats +155
Limited Slip Diff +55
Luggage Rack[Std on Eddie Bauer] +30
Power Door Locks[Opt on Sport,XL] +45
Power Drivers Seat +55
Power Windows[Opt on Sport,XL] +50
Premium Sound System +75
Rear Window Wiper[Opt on XL,XLT, Sport] +30
Sunroof +60

F-SERIES PICKUP 1991

A Nite Appearance Package is offered and the 5.0-liter engine is now available with the four-speed automatic

Don't forget to refer to the Mileage Adjustment Table at the back of this book!

 © 1999 by Edmund Publications Corporation

Model Description	Trade-in Value	Market Value

transmission. F-250 and 350s receive auto-locking hubs. Ford's touch-drive transfer case replaces the older, floor-mounted system.

F-150

Category H

Model Description	Trade-in Value	Market Value
2 Dr S Std Cab SB	3245	4385
2 Dr S Std Cab LB	3305	4465
2 Dr STD Ext Cab SB	4445	6010
2 Dr STD Std Cab SB	4200	5675
2 Dr STD Ext Cab LB	4505	6090
2 Dr STD Std Cab LB	4255	5750
2 Dr STD 4WD Ext Cab SB	5775	7805
2 Dr STD 4WD Std Cab SB	5380	7270
2 Dr STD 4WD Std Cab LB	5480	7405
2 Dr STD 4WD Ext Cab LB	5785	7820
2 Dr XL Std Cab SB	4345	5870
2 Dr XL Ext Cab SB	4520	6110
2 Dr XL Std Cab LB	4400	5945
2 Dr XL Ext Cab LB	4580	6185
2 Dr XL 4WD Ext Cab SB	5925	8005
2 Dr XL 4WD Std Cab SB	5380	7270
2 Dr XL 4WD Std Cab LB	5590	7555
2 Dr XL 4WD Ext Cab LB	5860	7920

F-250

Category H

Model Description	Trade-in Value	Market Value
2 Dr STD Ext Cab LB	6140	8295
2 Dr STD Std Cab LB	5315	7180
2 Dr STD 4WD Std Cab LB	5935	8020
2 Dr STD 4WD Ext Cab LB	6675	9020
2 Dr XL Std Cab LB	5375	7265
2 Dr XL Ext Cab LB	6230	8420
2 Dr XL 4WD Std Cab LB	6005	8115
2 Dr XL 4WD Ext Cab LB	6765	9140

F-350

Category H

Model Description	Trade-in Value	Market Value
2 Dr STD Ext Cab LB	6685	9030
2 Dr STD Std Cab LB	6205	8390
2 Dr STD 4WD Std Cab LB	6945	9385
4 Dr STD Crew Cab LB	6945	9385
4 Dr STD 4WD Crew Cab LB	7830	10580
2 Dr XL 4WD Std Cab LB	6975	9430

OPTIONS FOR F-SERIES PICKUP

8 cyl 7.3 L Dsl Engine +460
8 cyl 5.0 L Engine +120
8 cyl 5.8 L Engine +165
8 cyl 7.5 L Engine +175
Auto 3-Speed Transmission +160
Auto 4-Speed Transmission +185
Heavy Duty Pkg +295
Air Conditioning +165
Aluminum/Alloy Wheels +65
AM/FM Stereo Tape +50
Camper/Towing Package +70
Cruise Control +40
Dual Rear Wheels +170
Limited Slip Diff +50
Power Door Locks +35
Power Windows +40
Rear Step Bumper +30

FESTIVA 1991

The L Plus model is dropped. The LX is renamed GL and gets body-color bumpers and color-keyed wheels in the process.

RATINGS (SCALE OF 1-10)

Overall	Safety	Reliability	Performance	Comfort	Value
6.1	4.6	7.9	6.2	6.9	5

Category E

Model Description	Trade-in Value	Market Value
2 Dr GL Hbk	1035	1750
2 Dr L Hbk	1015	1720

OPTIONS FOR FESTIVA

Auto 3-Speed Transmission +105
Air Conditioning +165
AM/FM Stereo Tape +60
Flip-Up Sunroof +70
Power Steering +50
Rear Window Defroster +30

MUSTANG 1991

New wheels appear on the GT and LX 5.0 Mustangs.

RATINGS (SCALE OF 1-10)

Overall	Safety	Reliability	Performance	Comfort	Value
N/A	N/A	7.3	7.8	6.3	4.2

Model Description	Trade-in Value	Market Value
Category C		
2 Dr LX Hbk	2495	3840
2 Dr LX Conv	3440	5290
2 Dr LX Cpe	2375	3655
Category F		
2 Dr GT Hbk	4640	6535
2 Dr GT Conv	5090	7170
2 Dr LX 5.0 Hbk	3930	5540
2 Dr LX 5.0 Cpe	3785	5330
2 Dr LX 5.0 Conv	4600	6480

OPTIONS FOR MUSTANG

Auto 4-Speed Transmission +120
Air Conditioning +160
AM/FM Stereo Tape +35
Cruise Control +40
Leather Seats +115
Power Door Locks[Std on Conv] +40
Power Windows[Std on Conv] +45
Premium Sound System +80

Don't forget to refer to the Mileage Adjustment Table at the back of this book!

 © 1999 by Edmund Publications Corporation

Model Description	Trade-in Value	Market Value

PROBE 1991

All Probes get revised front and rear styling. GT models lose their body-side cladding resulting in a cleaner look.

Model Description	Trade-in Value	Market Value
Category E		
2 Dr GL Hbk	1905	3225
2 Dr LX Hbk	2165	3665
Category F		
2 Dr GT Turbo Hbk	2960	4170

OPTIONS FOR PROBE

Auto 4-Speed Transmission +145
Air Conditioning +165
AM/FM Compact Disc Playr +100
Anti-Lock Brakes +145
Climate Control for AC +35
Cruise Control +40
Flip-Up Sunroof +70
Leather Seats +180
Power Door Locks +40
Power Drivers Seat +50
Power Windows +45
Premium Sound System +70

RANGER 1991

Ford introduces a Sport model to the Ranger stable. Equipped with an optional V6 engine, alloy wheels, and snazzy graphics, the Ranger Sport promises to be one of the hottest vehicles in the high-school parking lot.

Model Description	Trade-in Value	Market Value
Category G		
2 Dr Custom Ext Cab SB	3320	4740
2 Dr Custom Std Cab SB	2690	3840
2 Dr Custom Std Cab LB	2780	3975
2 Dr Custom 4WD Std Cab SB	3710	5300
2 Dr Custom 4WD Ext Cab SB	4345	6205
2 Dr Custom 4WD Std Cab LB	3785	5410
2 Dr S Std Cab SB	2230	3190
2 Dr Sport Std Cab SB	2830	4040
2 Dr Sport Std Cab LB	2915	4160
2 Dr Sport 4WD Std Cab SB	4030	5755
2 Dr Sport 4WD Std Cab LB	4160	5940
2 Dr STX Std Cab SB	3050	4355
2 Dr STX Ext Cab SB	3515	5025
2 Dr STX Std Cab LB	3085	4410
2 Dr STX 4WD Std Cab SB	4165	5950
2 Dr STX 4WD Ext Cab SB	4625	6605
2 Dr STX 4WD Std Cab LB	4270	6095
2 Dr XLT Ext Cab SB	3420	4885
2 Dr XLT Std Cab SB	2965	4235
2 Dr XLT Std Cab LB	3050	4355
2 Dr XLT 4WD Std Cab SB	4125	5890
2 Dr XLT 4WD Ext Cab SB	4405	6295
2 Dr XLT 4WD Std Cab LB	4205	6010

OPTIONS FOR RANGER

6 cyl 2.9 L Engine +100
6 cyl 3.0 L Engine +120
6 cyl 4.0 L Engine +145
Auto 4-Speed Transmission +170
Sport Appearance Package +160
Air Conditioning +165
Aluminum/Alloy Wheels +70
AM/FM Stereo Tape[Opt on Custom,Sport,STX,Std Cab,2WD] +50
Auto Locking Hubs (4WD)[Opt on Custom,Sport,STX, Std Cab] +55
Cruise Control +45
Limited Slip Diff +55
Power Door Locks +45
Power Steering[Std on Ext Cab,4WD] +55
Rear Step Bumper[Std on Ext Cab] +30

TAURUS 1991

Sequential multi-port fuel injection systems are added to the Taurus.

Model Description	Trade-in Value	Market Value
Category C		
4 Dr GL Sdn	2095	3225
4 Dr GL Wgn	2370	3650
4 Dr L Wgn	2275	3500
4 Dr L Sdn	1965	3025
4 Dr LX Wgn	3290	5060
4 Dr LX Sdn	3085	4745
Category F		
4 Dr SHO Sdn	3855	5430

OPTIONS FOR TAURUS

6 cyl 3.0 L Engine[Std on LX,SHO,Wgn] +135
6 cyl 3.8 L Engine +110
Air Conditioning[Opt on GL,L] +160
AM/FM Compact Disc Playr +80
Anti-Lock Brakes[Opt on GL,L] +125
Climate Control for AC +35
Cruise Control[Std on SHO] +40
Keyless Entry System +35
Leather Seats +115
Power Door Locks[Opt on GL,L] +40
Power Drivers Seat[Opt on GL,L] +50
Power Passenger Seat +55
Power Sunroof +140
Power Windows[Opt on GL,L] +45
Premium Sound System +80

TEMPO 1991

No significant changes for the 1991 Tempo.

RATINGS (SCALE OF 1-10)

Overall	Safety	Reliability	Performance	Comfort	Value
6.7	4.5	7.3	7.2	7.1	7.4

Model Description	Trade-in Value	Market Value
Category C		
2 Dr GL Sdn	1675	2580
4 Dr GL Sdn	1720	2650

Don't forget to refer to the Mileage Adjustment Table at the back of this book!

 © 1999 by Edmund Publications Corporation

Model Description	Trade-in Value	Market Value
2 Dr GLS Sdn	1880	2890
4 Dr GLS Sdn	1935	2975
2 Dr L Sdn	1620	2495
4 Dr L Sdn	1660	2555
4 Dr LX Sdn	1910	2940
4 Dr STD 4WD Sdn	2070	3185

OPTIONS FOR TEMPO

Auto 3-Speed Transmission[Std on STD] +110
Air Conditioning +160
AM/FM Stereo Tape[Std on GLS,LX] +35
Cruise Control +40
Power Door Locks[Std on LX] +50
Power Drivers Seat +60
Power Windows[Std on LX] +60
Premium Sound System +80

THUNDERBIRD 1991

No changes for the 1991 Thunderbird.

RATINGS (SCALE OF 1-10)

Overall	Safety	Reliability	Performance	Comfort	Value
6.7	5.7	6.4	6.8	8	6.8

Model Description	Trade-in Value	Market Value
Category C		
2 Dr LX Cpe	3290	5060
2 Dr STD Cpe	2865	4405
Category F		
2 Dr SC Sprchgd Cpe	4695	6615

OPTIONS FOR THUNDERBIRD

8 cyl 5.0 L Engine +220
Auto 4-Speed Transmission[Opt on SC] +120
AM/FM Compact Disc Playr +80
Anti-Lock Brakes[Std on SC] +125
Climate Control for AC +35
Cruise Control[Opt on STD] +40
Dual Power Seats +115
Keyless Entry System +35
Leather Seats +115
Power Door Locks[Opt on STD] +40
Power Moonroof +145
Premium Sound System +80

1990 FORD

AEROSTAR 1990

Rear-wheel antilock brakes and full-time all-wheel drive become available. A 4.0-liter V6 is also available. An under-seat locking storage compartment is now standard on the Aerostar and will store small valuables.

RATINGS (SCALE OF 1-10)

Overall	Safety	Reliability	Performance	Comfort	Value
6.2	4	5.7	6.6	7.3	7.5

Model Description	Trade-in Value	Market Value
Category G		
2 Dr Eddie Bauer Pass. Van Ext	3110	4710
2 Dr Eddie Bauer Pass. Van	2860	4335
2 Dr Eddie Bauer 4WD Pass. Van	3735	5660
2 Dr Eddie Bauer 4WD Pass. Van Ext	4145	6280
2 Dr STD Cargo Van	1750	2650
2 Dr STD Cargo Van Ext	2160	3275
2 Dr STD Pass. Van Ext	2580	3910
2 Dr STD Pass. Van	2425	3675
2 Dr STD 4WD Cargo Van Ext	2565	3890
2 Dr STD 4WD Pass. Van Ext	3060	4640
2 Dr STD 4WD Pass. Van	2760	4185
2 Dr STD 4WD Cargo Van	2170	3290
2 Dr XL Pass. Van Ext	2725	4130
2 Dr XL Pass. Van	2475	3755
2 Dr XL Cargo Van	1950	2955
2 Dr XL 4WD Pass. Van Ext	3200	4850
2 Dr XL 4WD Pass. Van	2990	4530
2 Dr XLT Pass. Van	2595	3935
2 Dr XLT Pass. Van Ext	3045	4615
2 Dr XLT 4WD Pass. Van Ext	3255	4935
2 Dr XLT 4WD Pass. Van	3065	4645

OPTIONS FOR AEROSTAR

6 cyl 4.0 L Engine[Opt on 2WD] +105
Auto 4-Speed Transmission[Opt on 2WD] +110
Electronics Pkg +170
Exterior Appearance Pkg +130
Air Conditioning[Opt on STD,Cargo Van,XL,XLT] +135
Aluminum/Alloy Wheels[Opt on STD,XL,XLT] +55
AM/FM Stereo Tape[Opt on STD,XL] +40
Captain Chairs (4) +105
Cruise Control[Std on Eddie Bauer] +35
Dual Air Conditioning[Opt on STD,XL,XLT] +165
Power Door Locks[Std on Eddie Bauer] +40
Power Windows[Std on Eddie Bauer] +40
Premium Sound System[Opt on STD,XL,XLT] +60
Rear Window Defroster[Opt on STD,XL,XLT] +30

BRONCO 1990

No changes for 1990.

Model Description	Trade-in Value	Market Value
Category H		
2 Dr Custom 4WD Utility	4625	6425
2 Dr Eddie Bauer 4WD Utility	5345	7425
2 Dr XLT 4WD Utility	4745	6590

OPTIONS FOR BRONCO

8 cyl 5.0 L Engine[Opt on Custom,XLT] +95
8 cyl 5.8 L Engine +135
Auto 4-Speed Transmission +150
Air Conditioning[Opt on Custom,XLT] +135
Aluminum/Alloy Wheels +50
AM/FM Stereo Tape[Opt on Custom,XLT] +40
Camper/Towing Package +60

Don't forget to refer to the Mileage Adjustment Table at the back of this book!

 © 1999 by Edmund Publications Corporation

Model Description	Trade-in Value	Market Value

Cruise Control[Opt on Custom,XLT] +30
Limited Slip Diff +40
Power Door Locks[Opt on Custom,XLT] +30
Power Windows[Opt on Custom,XLT] +30

BRONCO II 1990

New floor mats appear on the Eddie Bauer trim level. Louder horn debuts.

Category G

Model Description	Trade-in Value	Market Value
2 Dr Eddie Bauer Utility	2600	3935
2 Dr Eddie Bauer 4WD Utility	3185	4825
2 Dr Sport Utility	2430	3685
2 Dr Sport 4WD Utility	2900	4395
2 Dr XL Utility	2350	3555
2 Dr XL 4WD Utility	2740	4150
2 Dr XLT Utility	2525	3830
2 Dr XLT 4WD Utility	2940	4455

OPTIONS FOR BRONCO II

Auto 4-Speed Transmission +160
Air Conditioning[Std on Eddie Bauer] +135
Aluminum/Alloy Wheels[Std on Eddie Bauer] +55
AM/FM Stereo Tape +40
Auto Locking Hubs (4WD)[Std on Eddie Bauer] +45
Cruise Control[Std on Eddie Bauer] +35
Limited Slip Diff +45
Power Door Locks[Std on Eddie Bauer] +40
Power Windows[Std on Eddie Bauer] +40
Premium Sound System +60
Swing Out Tire Carrier +35

CLUB WAGON/ECONOLINE 1990

No changes for 1990.

E-150

Category H

Model Description	Trade-in Value	Market Value
2 Dr STD Club Wagon	3990	5540
2 Dr STD Econoline Ext	3560	4945
2 Dr STD Econoline	3030	4210
2 Dr XL Econoline	3450	4790
2 Dr XL Econoline Ext	3685	5115
2 Dr XLT Club Wagon	4280	5945

E-250

Category H

Model Description	Trade-in Value	Market Value
2 Dr STD Econoline Ext	3110	4320
2 Dr STD Econoline	2775	3850
2 Dr STD Club Wagon	3425	4755
2 Dr XL Econoline Ext	3220	4470
2 Dr XL Econoline	2920	4055
2 Dr XLT Club Wagon	3925	5450

E-350

Category H

Model Description	Trade-in Value	Market Value
2 Dr STD Econoline Ext	3295	4575
2 Dr STD Club Wagon	3715	5160
2 Dr STD Club Wagon Ext	3875	5385
2 Dr STD Econoline	3205	4450
2 Dr XL Econoline Ext	3415	4745
2 Dr XL Dsl Econoline	4540	6305
2 Dr XLT Club Wagon Ext	4220	5865
2 Dr XLT Club Wagon	3935	5460

OPTIONS FOR CLUB WAGON/ECONOLINE

8 cyl 7.3 L Dsl Engine +390
8 cyl 5.0 L Engine +95
8 cyl 5.8 L Engine +135
8 cyl 7.5 L Engine +140
Auto 4-Speed Transmission[Std on E-150 STD Club Wagon,E-150 XLT Club Wagon] +45
Air Conditioning +135
AM/FM Stereo Tape +40
Camper/Towing Package +60
Cruise Control +30
Dual Air Conditioning +235
Limited Slip Diff +40
Power Door Locks +30
Power Windows +30

CROWN VICTORIA 1990

A driver airbag becomes standard and the instrument panel is redesigned.

Category B

Model Description	Trade-in Value	Market Value
4 Dr Cntry Squire LX Wgn	2560	3940
4 Dr Cntry Squire Wgn	2320	3565
4 Dr LX Wgn	2515	3870
4 Dr LX Sdn	2860	4400
4 Dr STD Sdn	2570	3950
4 Dr STD Wgn	2205	3395

OPTIONS FOR CROWN VICTORIA

Aluminum/Alloy Wheels +55
AM/FM Stereo Tape +30
Cruise Control +35
Leather Seats +110
Power Door Locks +40
Power Drivers Seat +50
Power Passenger Seat +50
Premium Sound System +70
Third Seat[Opt on Country Squire] +30

ESCORT 1990

No changes.

Category E

Model Description	Trade-in Value	Market Value
2 Dr GT Hbk	1240	2385
2 Dr LX Hbk	1080	2080
4 Dr LX Hbk	970	1860
4 Dr LX Wgn	1140	2190
2 Dr Pony Hbk	925	1780

OPTIONS FOR ESCORT

Auto 3-Speed Transmission +85
Air Conditioning +135

Don't forget to refer to the Mileage Adjustment Table at the back of this book!

 © 1999 by Edmund Publications Corporation

Model Description	Trade-in Value	Market Value

AM/FM Stereo Tape +50
Cruise Control +35
Power Steering[Opt on LX] +40

F-SERIES PICKUP 1990

No major changes for the 1990 F-series.

F-150

Category H

Model Description	Trade-in Value	Market Value
2 Dr S Std Cab SB	3035	4215
2 Dr S Std Cab LB	3235	4490
2 Dr STD Ext Cab SB	4065	5645
2 Dr STD Std Cab SB	3940	5470
2 Dr STD Std Cab LB	3995	5550
2 Dr STD Ext Cab LB	4110	5705
2 Dr STD 4WD Std Cab SB	4380	6080
2 Dr STD 4WD Ext Cab SB	4990	6930
2 Dr STD 4WD Ext Cab LB	5105	7085
2 Dr STD 4WD Std Cab LB	4565	6340
2 Dr XL Ext Cab SB	4350	6040
2 Dr XL Std Cab SB	4005	5560
2 Dr XL Ext Cab LB	4415	6130
2 Dr XL Std Cab LB	4020	5580
2 Dr XL 4WD Std Cab SB	4850	6735
2 Dr XL 4WD Ext Cab SB	5105	7090
2 Dr XL 4WD Ext Cab LB	5135	7135
2 Dr XL 4WD Std Cab LB	5030	6985

F-250

Category H

Model Description	Trade-in Value	Market Value
2 Dr STD Std Cab LB	4545	6310
2 Dr STD Ext Cab LB	5200	7225
2 Dr STD 4WD Std Cab LB	5295	7355
2 Dr STD 4WD Ext Cab LB	5960	8280
2 Dr XL Ext Cab LB	5355	7435
2 Dr XL Std Cab LB	4705	6535
2 Dr XL 4WD Ext Cab LB	6070	8430
2 Dr XL 4WD Std Cab LB	5365	7450

F-350

Category H

Model Description	Trade-in Value	Market Value
2 Dr STD Ext Cab LB	6115	8490
2 Dr STD Std Cab LB	5900	8195
2 Dr STD 4WD Std Cab LB	6335	8800
4 Dr STD Crew Cab LB	6265	8700
4 Dr STD 4WD Crew Cab LB	7660	10640
2 Dr XL Std Cab LB	6050	8400
2 Dr XL Ext Cab LB	6265	8700
2 Dr XL 4WD Std Cab LB	6600	9170
4 Dr XL Crew Cab LB	6370	8845
4 Dr XL 4WD Crew Cab LB	7755	10770

OPTIONS FOR F-SERIES PICKUP

8 cyl 7.3 L Dsl Engine +390
8 cyl 5.0 L Engine +95
8 cyl 5.8 L Engine +135
8 cyl 7.5 L Engine +140
Auto 3-Speed Transmission +115
Auto 4-Speed Transmission +150
Sport Appearance Package +165
Suspension Pkg +130
Air Conditioning +135
AM/FM Stereo Tape +40
Camper/Towing Package +60
Cruise Control +30
Dual Rear Wheels +140
Limited Slip Diff +40
Power Door Locks +30
Power Windows +30

FESTIVA 1990

A five-speed manual transmission and fuel injection becomes standard. New seat cushions and a restyled grille are the only other changes.

RATINGS (SCALE OF 1-10)

Overall	Safety	Reliability	Performance	Comfort	Value
6.2	4.6	7.9	6.2	6.9	5.4

Category E

Model Description	Trade-in Value	Market Value
2 Dr L Hbk	810	1560
2 Dr L Plus Hbk	820	1575
2 Dr LX Hbk	945	1815

OPTIONS FOR FESTIVA

Auto 3-Speed Transmission +85
Air Conditioning +135
Aluminum/Alloy Wheels +50
AM/FM Stereo[Opt on L] +50
AM/FM Stereo Tape +50
Power Steering +40
Sunroof +55

MUSTANG 1990

A driver airbag becomes standard. Knee bolsters and a leather-wrapped steering wheel complete interior changes. The exterior receives clear coat paint.

RATINGS (SCALE OF 1-10)

Overall	Safety	Reliability	Performance	Comfort	Value
N/A	N/A	7.2	7.8	6.3	3.7

Model Description	Trade-in Value	Market Value
Category C		
2 Dr LX Hbk	2275	3735
2 Dr LX Conv	3140	5150
2 Dr LX Cpe	2185	3580
Category F		
2 Dr GT Hbk	4035	5850
2 Dr GT Conv	4630	6710
2 Dr LX Limited Conv	3760	5445
2 Dr LX 5.0 Cpe	3645	5285
2 Dr LX 5.0 Hbk	3385	4910

Don't forget to refer to the Mileage Adjustment Table at the back of this book!

 © 1999 by Edmund Publications Corporation

Model Description	Trade-in Value	Market Value

OPTIONS FOR MUSTANG
Auto 4-Speed Transmission +100
Air Conditioning +130
Cruise Control +35
Leather Seats +120
Power Door Locks[Opt on Cpe,Hbk] +35
Power Windows[Opt on Cpe,Hbk] +35
Premium Sound System +70
Sunroof +60

PROBE 1990

A multitude of engine choices are available with the addition of the 3.0-liter V6 to the LX models. Antilock brakes become standard on the GT and optional on the LX. An automatic transmission becomes available on the GT.

Model Description	Trade-in Value	Market Value
Category E		
2 Dr GL Hbk	1470	2830
2 Dr LX Hbk	1695	3265
Category F		
2 Dr GT Turbo Hbk	2345	3400

OPTIONS FOR PROBE
Auto 4-Speed Transmission +120
Air Conditioning +135
Aluminum/Alloy Wheels[Std on GT] +50
AM/FM Compact Disc Playr +80
Anti-Lock Brakes +120
Climate Control for AC +30
Cruise Control +35
Flip-Up Sunroof +60
Leather Seats +120
Power Door Locks +35
Power Drivers Seat +40
Power Windows +35
Premium Sound System +70

RANGER 1990

No changes for the Ford Ranger.

Model Description	Trade-in Value	Market Value
Category G		
2 Dr S Std Cab SB	1980	3000
2 Dr S Std Cab LB	2125	3220
2 Dr S 4WD Std Cab SB	2780	4210
2 Dr S 4WD Std Cab LB	2835	4295
2 Dr Sport Std Cab SB	2330	3535
2 Dr Sport Ext Cab SB	2810	4260
2 Dr Sport Std Cab LB	2375	3595
2 Dr Sport 4WD Ext Cab SB	3555	5390
2 Dr Sport 4WD Std Cab SB	3045	4610
2 Dr Sport 4WD Std Cab LB	3080	4670
2 Dr STD Std Cab SB	2160	3275
2 Dr STD Ext Cab SB	2490	3775
2 Dr STD Std Cab LB	2200	3335
2 Dr STD 4WD Ext Cab SB	3420	5185
2 Dr STD 4WD Std Cab SB	2935	4445
2 Dr STD 4WD Std Cab LB	3035	4595
2 Dr STX 4WD Ext Cab SB	3795	5750
2 Dr STX 4WD Std Cab SB	3295	4995
2 Dr STX 4WD Std Cab LB	3240	4910
2 Dr XLT Ext Cab SB	2770	4195
2 Dr XLT Std Cab SB	2345	3555
2 Dr XLT Std Cab LB	2385	3615
2 Dr XLT 4WD Ext Cab SB	3725	5645
2 Dr XLT 4WD Std Cab SB	3150	4775
2 Dr XLT 4WD Std Cab LB	3190	4835

OPTIONS FOR RANGER
6 cyl 2.9 L Engine +105
6 cyl 4.0 L Engine +105
Auto 4-Speed Transmission +150
Ranger Sport Appear Pkg +130
Air Conditioning +135
Aluminum/Alloy Wheels +55
AM/FM Stereo Tape[Std on XLT] +40
Auto Locking Hubs (4WD) +45
Cruise Control +35
Limited Slip Diff +45
Power Door Locks +40
Power Steering[Std on STX,Ext Cab,4WD] +45
Power Windows +40

TAURUS 1990

Antilock brakes are available for all Tauruses. A driver airbag becomes available on the Taurus as well.

Model Description	Trade-in Value	Market Value
Category C		
4 Dr GL Sdn	1695	2775
4 Dr GL Wgn	1845	3025
4 Dr L Sdn	1585	2595
4 Dr L Wgn	1765	2895
4 Dr LX Wgn	2290	3760
4 Dr LX Sdn	2180	3570
Category F		
4 Dr SHO Sdn	2990	4335

OPTIONS FOR TAURUS
6 cyl 3.0 L Engine[Std on LX,SHO,Wgn] +110
6 cyl 3.8 L Engine +110
Air Conditioning[Std on LX,SHO] +130
Aluminum/Alloy Wheels[Std on SHO] +50
Anti-Lock Brakes[Std on SHO] +105
Climate Control for AC +30
Cruise Control[Std on SHO] +35
Keyless Entry System +30
Leather Seats +95
Power Door Locks[Std on LX,SHO] +35
Power Drivers Seat[Std on LX,SHO] +40
Power Passenger Seat +45
Power Sunroof +115
Power Windows[Std on LX,SHO] +35
Premium Sound System +65

Don't forget to refer to the Mileage Adjustment Table at the back of this book!

 © 1999 by Edmund Publications Corporation

Model Description	Trade-in Value	Market Value

TEMPO 1990

Rear shoulder belts become standard on the 1990 Tempo.

RATINGS (SCALE OF 1-10)

Overall	Safety	Reliability	Performance	Comfort	Value
6.7	4.5	7.1	7.2	7.1	7.4

Model Description	Trade-in Value	Market Value
Category C		
2 Dr GL Sdn	1370	2245
4 Dr GL Sdn	1365	2235
2 Dr GLS Sdn	1480	2430
4 Dr GLS Sdn	1555	2555
4 Dr LX Sdn	1595	2615
4 Dr STD 4WD Sdn	1595	2615

OPTIONS FOR TEMPO

Auto 3-Speed Transmission[Std on STD] +95
Sport Appearance Package +195
Air Bag Restraint +85
Air Conditioning +130
Cruise Control +35
Power Door Locks[Std on LX] +40
Power Drivers Seat +45
Power Windows +50
Premium Sound System +65

THUNDERBIRD 1990

Thirty-fifth anniversary model. No changes.

RATINGS (SCALE OF 1-10)

Overall	Safety	Reliability	Performance	Comfort	Value
6.3	5.6	6	6.8	8	5

Model Description	Trade-in Value	Market Value
Category C		
2 Dr LX Cpe	2600	4260
2 Dr STD Cpe	2285	3750
Category F		
2 Dr SC Sprchgd Cpe	3555	5150

OPTIONS FOR THUNDERBIRD

Auto 4-Speed Transmission[Opt on SC] +95
Aluminum/Alloy Wheels[Std on SC] +50
Anti-Lock Brakes[Std on SC] +105
Cruise Control[Std on LX] +35
Keyless Entry System +30
Leather Seats +95
Power Door Locks[Std on LX] +35
Power Drivers Seat[Std on LX] +40
Power Passenger Seat +45
Power Sunroof +115
Premium Sound System +65

1989 FORD

AEROSTAR 1989

An extended-length Aerostar joins the line-up and an XL Sport package is added to the option list. A new grille debuts with a matching front bumper. Flat-fold rear seatbacks improve cargo space and cabin storage bins appear on the extended-length models. Fuel capacity increases to 21 gallons.

RATINGS (SCALE OF 1-10)

Overall	Safety	Reliability	Performance	Comfort	Value
6.2	3.8	5.7	6.6	7.3	7.8

Model Description	Trade-in Value	Market Value
Category G		
2 Dr Eddie Bauer Pass. Van Ext	2220	3640
2 Dr Eddie Bauer Pass. Van	2135	3500
2 Dr STD Cargo Van Ext	1755	2880
2 Dr STD Cargo Van	1295	2120
2 Dr XL Pass. Van Ext	2090	3430
2 Dr XL Pass. Van	1835	3010
2 Dr XLT Pass. Van	1975	3235
2 Dr XLT Pass. Van Ext	2160	3545

OPTIONS FOR AEROSTAR

Auto 4-Speed Transmission +85
Air Conditioning[Std on XLT] +110
Aluminum/Alloy Wheels[Opt on STD,XL,XLT] +45
AM/FM Stereo Tape[Std on XLT] +35
Camper/Towing Package +40
Captain Chairs (4) +85
Cruise Control[Opt on STD,XL] +30
Dual Air Conditioning[Opt on STD,XL,XLT] +135
Limited Slip Diff +35
Power Door Locks[Opt on XL,XLT] +30
Power Windows[Opt on XL,XLT] +30
Premium Sound System[Opt on STD,XL,XLT] +50

BRONCO 1989

No changes.

Model Description	Trade-in Value	Market Value
Category H		
2 Dr Custom 4WD Utility	3980	5770
2 Dr Eddie Bauer 4WD Utility	4515	6540
2 Dr XLT 4WD Utility	4075	5905

OPTIONS FOR BRONCO

8 cyl 5.0 L Engine[Opt on Custom,XLT] +80
8 cyl 5.8 L Engine +100
Auto 3-Speed Transmission +95
Auto 4-Speed Transmission +115
Air Conditioning[Opt on Custom,XLT] +110
AM/FM Stereo Tape[Opt on Custom,XLT] +35
Camper/Towing Package +50
Limited Slip Diff +35

BRONCO II 1989

A new front end appears with a new hood, front fenders, aerodynamic headlights, and a redesigned bumper. Standard AM/FM stereos appear in the F-Series styled dashboard. The automatic transmission shifter is relocated to the column. A new front axle and power-steering valve is introduced to help improve handling.

Don't forget to refer to the Mileage Adjustment Table at the back of this book!

 © 1999 by Edmund Publications Corporation

Model Description	Trade-in Value	Market Value
Category G		
2 Dr Eddie Bauer Utility	2300	3770
2 Dr Eddie Bauer 4WD Utility	2605	4265
2 Dr Sport Utility	2170	3555
2 Dr Sport 4WD Utility	2495	4090
2 Dr XL Utility	2130	3490
2 Dr XL 4WD Utility	2460	4035
2 Dr XLT Utility	2145	3515
2 Dr XLT 4WD Utility	2480	4065

OPTIONS FOR BRONCO II

Auto 4-Speed Transmission +130
Air Conditioning[Opt on Sport,XL] +110
Aluminum/Alloy Wheels[Opt on XL,XLT] +45
AM/FM Stereo Tape[Opt on Sport,XL] +35
Auto Locking Hubs (4WD)[Std on XLT] +35
Cruise Control[Std on Eddie Bauer] +30
Limited Slip Diff +35
Power Door Locks[Std on Eddie Bauer] +30
Power Windows[Std on Eddie Bauer] +30
Swing Out Tire Carrier[Opt on 2WD] +30

CLUB WAGON/ECONOLINE 1989

No changes.

E-150

Model Description	Trade-in Value	Market Value
Category H		
2 Dr STD Club Wagon	3490	5055
2 Dr STD Econoline	2175	3150
2 Dr STD Econoline Ext	2685	3895
2 Dr XL Econoline	2700	3910
2 Dr XLT Club Wagon	3545	5140

E-250

Model Description	Trade-in Value	Market Value
Category H		
2 Dr STD Club Wagon	2845	4125
2 Dr STD Econoline Ext	2580	3735
2 Dr STD Econoline	2275	3300
2 Dr XL Econoline	2370	3435
2 Dr XLT Club Wagon	2925	4235

E-350

Model Description	Trade-in Value	Market Value
Category H		
2 Dr STD Econoline Ext	2725	3950
2 Dr STD Econoline	2555	3700
2 Dr STD Club Wagon	3230	4680
2 Dr XLT Club Wagon Ext	3370	4880
2 Dr XLT Club Wagon	3280	4755

OPTIONS FOR CLUB WAGON/ECONOLINE

8 cyl 7.3 L Dsl Engine +270
8 cyl 5.0 L Engine +80
8 cyl 5.8 L Engine +100
8 cyl 7.5 L Engine +120
Auto 3-Speed Transmission[Opt on E-150 Econoline] +55
Auto 4-Speed Transmission +95
7-Passenger Seat/Bed Pkg +135
Air Conditioning +110
AM/FM Stereo Tape +35
Camper/Towing Package +50
Dual Air Conditioning +190
Limited Slip Diff +35

CROWN VICTORIA 1989

An engine system warning light replaces the oil light.

Model Description	Trade-in Value	Market Value
Category B		
4 Dr Cntry Squire LX Wgn	1890	3155
4 Dr Cntry Squire Wgn	1775	2955
4 Dr LX Wgn	1815	3020
4 Dr LX Sdn	2280	3795
4 Dr S Sdn	1910	3180
4 Dr STD Sdn	1990	3320
4 Dr STD Wgn	1730	2880

OPTIONS FOR CROWN VICTORIA

8 cyl 5.8 L Engine +60
Aluminum/Alloy Wheels +45
Cruise Control +30
Dual Power Seats +50
Leather Seats +90
Power Door Locks +35
Power Windows[Std on Cntry Squire LX,LX] +40
Premium Sound System +55
Trip Computer +30

ESCORT 1989

EXP model is discontinued.

Model Description	Trade-in Value	Market Value
Category E		
2 Dr GT Hbk	800	1815
2 Dr LX Hbk	760	1720
4 Dr LX Hbk	745	1695
4 Dr LX Wgn	735	1670
2 Dr Pony Hbk	675	1540

OPTIONS FOR ESCORT

Auto 3-Speed Transmission +60
Air Conditioning +110
AM/FM Stereo Tape +40
Cruise Control +30
Power Steering[Opt on LX] +35
Premium Sound System +45

F-SERIES PICKUP 1989

Automatic locking hubs introduced midyear for F-150 four-wheel drives.

F-150

Model Description	Trade-in Value	Market Value
Category H		
2 Dr S Std Cab SB	3135	4540
2 Dr S Std Cab LB	3250	4710
2 Dr STD Std Cab SB	3310	4795
2 Dr STD Ext Cab SB	3655	5300
2 Dr STD Ext Cab LB	3745	5425
2 Dr STD Std Cab LB	3375	4890

Don't forget to refer to the Mileage Adjustment Table at the back of this book!

 © 1999 by Edmund Publications Corporation

Model Description	Trade-in Value	Market Value
2 Dr STD 4WD Ext Cab SB	4540	6575
2 Dr STD 4WD Std Cab SB	4120	5970
2 Dr STD 4WD Std Cab LB	4170	6045
2 Dr XL Std Cab SB	3395	4920
2 Dr XL Ext Cab SB	3685	5345
2 Dr XL Ext Cab LB	3810	5520
2 Dr XL Std Cab LB	3560	5160
2 Dr XL 4WD Std Cab SB	3775	5475
2 Dr XL 4WD Std Cab LB	4280	6200
2 Dr XL 4WD Ext Cab LB	4530	6565

F-250

Category H

Model Description	Trade-in Value	Market Value
2 Dr STD Ext Cab LB	4325	6270
2 Dr STD Std Cab LB	4190	6075
2 Dr STD 4WD Std Cab LB	5025	7280
2 Dr STD 4WD Ext Cab LB	5620	8145
2 Dr XL Std Cab LB	4335	6280
2 Dr XL 4WD Std Cab LB	5195	7525
2 Dr XL 4WD Ext Cab LB	5690	8250

F-350

Category H

Model Description	Trade-in Value	Market Value
2 Dr STD Std Cab LB	5360	7765
2 Dr STD 4WD Std Cab LB	5940	8610
4 Dr STD Crew Cab LB	5485	7950
4 Dr STD 4WD Crew Cab LB	6115	8865
2 Dr XL 4WD Std Cab LB	6085	8820

OPTIONS FOR F-SERIES PICKUP

8 cyl 7.3 L Dsl Engine +270
8 cyl 5.0 L Engine +80
8 cyl 5.8 L Engine +100
8 cyl 7.5 L Engine +120
Auto 3-Speed Transmission +95
Auto 4-Speed Transmission +120
Suspension Pkg +105
XLT Lariat Trim Pkg +275
Air Conditioning +110
Aluminum/Alloy Wheels +40
AM/FM Stereo Tape +35
Camper/Towing Package +50
Dual Rear Wheels +115
Limited Slip Diff +35

FESTIVA 1989

An automatic transmission is introduced to this budget hatchback.

RATINGS (SCALE OF 1-10)

Overall	Safety	Reliability	Performance	Comfort	Value
6	4.6	7.6	6.2	6.9	4.9

Category E

Model Description	Trade-in Value	Market Value
2 Dr L Hbk	650	1480
2 Dr L Plus Hbk	675	1535
2 Dr LX Hbk	690	1565

OPTIONS FOR FESTIVA

Auto 3-Speed Transmission +70
Air Conditioning +110
Aluminum/Alloy Wheels +45
AM/FM Stereo Tape +40

MUSTANG 1989

Power windows and door locks are now standard on the LX and GT convertibles.

RATINGS (SCALE OF 1-10)

Overall	Safety	Reliability	Performance	Comfort	Value
N/A	N/A	7	7.8	6.3	4.6

Model Description	Trade-in Value	Market Value
Category C		
2 Dr LX Hbk	1625	2850
2 Dr LX Conv	2295	4030
2 Dr LX Cpe	1560	2735
Category F		
2 Dr GT Hbk	2865	4280
2 Dr GT Conv	3915	5845
2 Dr LX 5.0 Hbk	3065	4570
2 Dr LX 5.0 Conv	3610	5390
2 Dr LX 5.0 Cpe	2940	4390

OPTIONS FOR MUSTANG

Auto 4-Speed Transmission +70
Air Conditioning +110
Aluminum/Alloy Wheels[Opt on LX] +40
Cruise Control +30
Leather Seats +80
Power Windows[Std on Conv] +30
Premium Sound System +55
Sunroof +55

PROBE 1989

Ford's new front-wheel drive sport coupe comes in three trim levels: GL, LX and GT. GL and LX models are equipped with a 2.2-liter four-cylinder engine and the GT has a turbocharged version of the same, rated at 145 horsepower. GT models also have four-wheel disc brakes and are available with antilock.

Model Description	Trade-in Value	Market Value
Category E		
2 Dr GL Hbk	975	2210
2 Dr LX Hbk	1055	2395
Category F		
2 Dr GT Turbo Hbk	1960	2925

OPTIONS FOR PROBE

Auto 4-Speed Transmission +85
Air Conditioning +110
Aluminum/Alloy Wheels[Std on GT] +40
Anti-Lock Brakes +95
Cruise Control +30
Flip-Up Sunroof +50
Power Drivers Seat +30
Power Windows +30
Premium Sound System +45

Don't forget to refer to the Mileage Adjustment Table at the back of this book!

 © 1999 by Edmund Publications Corporation

Model Description	Trade-in Value	Market Value

RANGER 1989

Ford's excellent compact pickup is offered in short and long bed models with a SuperCab available for those who need more interior space. A multitude of engine choices are available to suit nearly anyone's needs.

Category G

Model Description	Trade-in Value	Market Value
2 Dr S Std Cab SB	1700	2785
2 Dr S Std Cab LB	1720	2820
2 Dr STD Ext Cab SB	2105	3445
2 Dr STD Std Cab SB	1940	3180
2 Dr STD Std Cab LB	1990	3260
2 Dr STD 4WD Std Cab SB	2630	4310
2 Dr STD 4WD Ext Cab SB	2810	4610
2 Dr STD 4WD Std Cab LB	2755	4520
2 Dr STX Std Cab SB	2020	3315
2 Dr STX Ext Cab SB	2145	3515
2 Dr STX Std Cab LB	2060	3380
2 Dr STX 4WD Ext Cab SB	3155	5175
2 Dr STX 4WD Std Cab SB	2790	4575
2 Dr STX 4WD Std Cab LB	2900	4755
2 Dr STX GT Std Cab SB	2130	3490
2 Dr XLT Std Cab SB	1990	3260
2 Dr XLT Ext Cab SB	2150	3525
2 Dr XLT Std Cab LB	2020	3315
2 Dr XLT 4WD Ext Cab SB	3005	4925
2 Dr XLT 4WD Std Cab SB	2700	4430
2 Dr XLT 4WD Std Cab LB	2845	4665

OPTIONS FOR RANGER

6 cyl 2.9 L Engine +95
Auto 4-Speed Transmission +120
Black Sport Appear Pkg +115
Chrome Sport Appear Pkg +150
Air Conditioning +110
Aluminum/Alloy Wheels[Std on STX GT] +45
AM/FM Stereo Tape[Std on XLT] +35
Auto Locking Hubs (4WD) +35
Bed Liner +40
Cruise Control +30
Limited Slip Diff[Std on STX GT] +35
Power Door Locks +30
Power Steering[Std on Ext Cab,4WD, XLT] +40
Power Windows +30

TAURUS 1989

The high-performance Taurus SHO is added to the Taurus lineup. The Taurus SHO has a 220-horsepower V6 engine and four-wheel disc brakes. Ground effects, fog lights and aluminum wheels distinguish this vehicle from other Tauruses.

Category C

Model Description	Trade-in Value	Market Value
4 Dr GL Wgn	1515	2660
4 Dr GL Sdn	1340	2345
4 Dr L Sdn	1220	2140
4 Dr L Wgn	1355	2380
4 Dr LX Wgn	1805	3165
4 Dr LX Sdn	1710	2995
Category F		
4 Dr SHO Sdn	2410	3600

OPTIONS FOR TAURUS

6 cyl 3.0 L Engine[Std on LX,SHO,Wgn] +95
6 cyl 3.8 L Engine +55
Air Conditioning[Opt on GL,L] +110
Aluminum/Alloy Wheels[Std on SHO] +40
Cruise Control[Std on SHO] +30
Leather Seats +80
Power Drivers Seat[Opt on GL,L] +30
Power Moonroof +95
Power Passenger Seat +35
Power Windows[Opt on GL,L] +30
Premium Sound System +55

TEMPO 1989

Gas-pressure struts are added to the GL. All models get an emission system warning light. A center armrest becomes standard on the GLS.

RATINGS (SCALE OF 1-10)

Overall	Safety	Reliability	Performance	Comfort	Value
6.3	4.5	6.6	7.2	7.1	6

Category C

Model Description	Trade-in Value	Market Value
2 Dr GL Sdn	1100	1930
4 Dr GL Sdn	1150	2015
2 Dr GLS Sdn	1115	1960
4 Dr GLS Sdn	1205	2115
4 Dr LX Sdn	1245	2185
4 Dr STD 4WD Sdn	1420	2490

OPTIONS FOR TEMPO

Auto 3-Speed Transmission[Std on STD] +70
Sport Appearance Package +160
Air Bag Restraint +70
Air Conditioning +110
Cruise Control +30
Power Door Locks[Std on LX] +30
Power Drivers Seat +40
Power Windows +40
Premium Sound System +55

THUNDERBIRD 1989

The redesigned Thunderbird gets an increased wheelbase and improved interior measurements in every direction. An independent suspension debuts in the T-Bird. GL and LX Thunderbirds are powered by 3.8-liter V6s. The Super Coupe is powered by a supercharged V6. Four-wheel antilock brakes are standard on the Super Coupe and optional on the other models. Speed sensitive steering is standard on the

Don't forget to refer to the Mileage Adjustment Table at the back of this book!

 © 1999 by Edmund Publications Corporation

Model Description	Trade-in Value	Market Value

LX and Super Coupe. All models get air conditioning and power windows. Super Coupes have an Automatic Adjustable Suspension. Base and SC models have analog gauges; LX models have digital.

RATINGS (SCALE OF 1-10)

Overall	Safety	Reliability	Performance	Comfort	Value
6.4	5.7	6.1	6.8	8	5.4

Model Description	Trade-in Value	Market Value
Category C		
2 Dr LX Cpe	1955	3430
2 Dr STD Cpe	1755	3075
Category F		
2 Dr SC Sprchgd Cpe	3660	5465

OPTIONS FOR THUNDERBIRD

Auto 4-Speed Transmission[Opt on SC] +70
Aluminum/Alloy Wheels[Std on SC] +40
Anti-Lock Brakes[Std on SC] +85
Cruise Control[Opt on STD] +30
Leather Seats +80
Power Drivers Seat[Opt on STD] +30
Power Moonroof +95
Power Passenger Seat[Std on SC] +35
Premium Sound System +55

A 15-minute phone call could save you 15% or more on car insurance.

1-800-555-2758

The Sensible Alternative

Get a great used car and apply for financing *online* at a price you must see to believe!

http://www.edmunds.com

Don't forget to refer to the Mileage Adjustment Table at the back of this book!

 © 1999 by Edmund Publications Corporation

1994 Geo Prizm

1997 GEO

METRO 1997

Geo drops the base sedan variant of the Metro for 1997. A new convenience package is available on LSi models, and the LSi hatchback comes with the larger 1.3-liter engine standard. Two new colors debut.

RATINGS (SCALE OF 1-10)

Overall	Safety	Reliability	Performance	Comfort	Value
6.4	6.5	8.3	6.6	6.4	4.4

Category E	Trade-in Value	Market Value
2 Dr LSi Hbk	5260	6415
4 Dr LSi Sdn	5515	6725
2 Dr STD Hbk	4555	5555

OPTIONS FOR METRO

Auto 3-Speed Transmission +390
Air Conditioning +550
Anti-Lock Brakes +480
Compact Disc W/fm/tape +470
Power Door Locks +160
Power Steering +170
Rear Window Defroster +110

PRIZM 1997

The Prizm is essentially carried over for 1997, sporting new door trim panels, standard power steering, new exterior colors, and strengthened side-impact protection.

RATINGS (SCALE OF 1-10)

Overall	Safety	Reliability	Performance	Comfort	Value
7.1	6.5	8.9	8	7.8	4.4

Category E	Trade-in Value	Market Value
4 Dr LSi Sdn	7535	9185
4 Dr STD Sdn	7120	8685

OPTIONS FOR PRIZM

4 cyl 1.8 L Engine +230
Auto 3-Speed Transmission +325
Auto 4-Speed Transmission +525
Air Conditioning +550
Aluminum/Alloy Wheels +215
Anti-Lock Brakes +480
Child Seat (1) +80
Compact Disc W/fm/tape +470
Cruise Control +150
Leather Seats +605
Power Door Locks +160
Power Sunroof +410
Power Windows +180
Rear Window Defroster +110

TRACKER 1997

After a heavy makeover for 1996, changes for 1997 are limited. Convertibles get a standard fold-and-stow rear bench seat along with an enhanced evaporative emissions system. All Trackers can be painted Sunset Red Metallic or Azurite Blue Metallic for the first time. Prices have been at or near 1996 levels in an effort to make the Tracker more attractive to folks shopping Kia Sportage, Toyota RAV4 and Honda CR-V.

RATINGS (SCALE OF 1-10)

Overall	Safety	Reliability	Performance	Comfort	Value
6.2	5.5	8.7	6.4	6.8	3.4

Category G	Trade-in Value	Market Value
4 Dr LSi 4WD Wgn	8155	9710
2 Dr STD Conv	6980	8310
2 Dr STD 4WD Conv	7805	9290
4 Dr STD 4WD Wgn	7840	9330

OPTIONS FOR TRACKER

Auto 3-Speed Transmission +425
Auto 4-Speed Transmission +645
Air Conditioning +550
Aluminum/Alloy Wheels +235
Anti-Lock Brakes +420
Auto Locking Hubs (4WD) +180
Compact Disc W/fm/tape +465
Cruise Control +145
Power Door Locks +155
Power Steering[Std on LSi,Wgn,4WD] +190
Power Windows +160
Skid Plates +95

Don't forget to refer to the Mileage Adjustment Table at the back of this book!

 © 1999 by Edmund Publications Corporation

Model Description	Trade-in Value	Market Value

1996 GEO

METRO 1996

A zoned rear window defroster clears the center of the Metro's tiny rear backlight first, base coupes get dual exterior mirrors, and LSi coupes get cool hubcaps and body-color bumpers that keep it from looking like a refugee from some third-world country.

RATINGS (SCALE OF 1-10)

Overall	Safety	Reliability	Performance	Comfort	Value
6.4	6.5	8.2	6.6	6.4	4.3

Category E

Model	Trade-in Value	Market Value
2 Dr LSi Hbk	4220	5340
4 Dr LSi Sdn	4400	5570
2 Dr STD Hbk	3440	4355
4 Dr STD Sdn	4065	5145

OPTIONS FOR METRO

4 cyl 1.3 L Engine[Opt on Hbk] +185
Auto 3-Speed Transmission +260
Air Conditioning +450
Anti-Lock Brakes +395
Compact Disc W/fm/tape +385
Power Door Locks +130
Power Steering +140

PRIZM 1996

An integrated child safety seat is optional on the LSi, and daytime running lights debut, making the Prizm more visible to other motorists, and radar-toting police officers. Three new exterior colors and added equipment to the base model round out the changes to this excellent compact.

RATINGS (SCALE OF 1-10)

Overall	Safety	Reliability	Performance	Comfort	Value
7.3	6.6	9.2	8	7.8	4.9

Category E

Model	Trade-in Value	Market Value
4 Dr LSi Sdn	6245	7905
4 Dr STD Sdn	6235	7895

OPTIONS FOR PRIZM

4 cyl 1.8 L Engine +185
Auto 3-Speed Transmission +255
Auto 4-Speed Transmission +415
Air Conditioning +450
Anti-Lock Brakes +395
Child Seat (1) +65
Compact Disc W/fm/tape +385
Cruise Control +120
Leather Seats +495
Power Door Locks +130
Power Steering +140
Power Sunroof +335
Power Windows +145

TRACKER 1996

A new four-door model joins the lineup, and dual airbags are standard on all Trackers. Four-wheel antilock brakes are optional. Revised styling freshens the new exterior, and daytime running lights make the Tracker more conspicuous to motorists. In a switch from tradition, tasteful exterior colors are newly available. Cruise control is a new convenience option.

RATINGS (SCALE OF 1-10)

Overall	Safety	Reliability	Performance	Comfort	Value
6.1	5.5	8.3	6.4	6.8	3.8

Category G

Model	Trade-in Value	Market Value
2 Dr LSi Conv	6530	7960
2 Dr LSi 4WD Conv	7225	8810
4 Dr LSi Wgn	6750	8235
4 Dr LSi 4WD Wgn	7605	9275
2 Dr STD Conv	5930	7230
2 Dr STD 4WD Conv	7060	8610
4 Dr STD Wgn	6225	7590
4 Dr STD 4WD Wgn	7410	9035

OPTIONS FOR TRACKER

Auto 3-Speed Transmission +320
Auto 4-Speed Transmission +415
Air Conditioning +450
Aluminum/Alloy Wheels +190
Anti-Lock Brakes +345
Auto Locking Hubs (4WD) +145
Compact Disc W/fm/tape +380
Cruise Control +115
Power Door Locks +125
Power Steering[Std on Wgn,LSi 4WD Conv] +155
Power Windows +130
Skid Plates +75

1995 GEO

METRO 1995

All-new car is larger than previous model, and comes as a two-door hatchback or four-door sedan in base or LSi trim. Dual airbags are standard. ABS is optional on all models. Hatchbacks get the carryover 1.0-liter three-cylinder motor. Optional on LSi hatchback and standard on sedans is a 70-horsepower 1.3-liter four-cylinder engine. Daytime running lights are standard.

RATINGS (SCALE OF 1-10)

Overall	Safety	Reliability	Performance	Comfort	Value
6.5	7	7.6	6.6	6.4	4.7

Category E

Model	Trade-in Value	Market Value
2 Dr LSi Hbk	3340	4335
4 Dr LSi Sdn	3800	4935

Don't forget to refer to the Mileage Adjustment Table at the back of this book!

© 1999 by Edmund Publications Corporation

Model Description	Trade-in Value	Market Value
2 Dr STD Hbk	3090	4010
4 Dr STD Sdn	3615	4700

OPTIONS FOR METRO

4 cyl 1.3 L Engine[Opt on Hbk] +160
Auto 3-Speed Transmission +225
Air Conditioning +370
Anti-Lock Brakes +320
Compact Disc W/fm/tape +315
Power Door Locks +105
Power Steering +115
Rear Window Defroster +75

PRIZM 1995

Base 1.6-liter engine loses horsepower. All models get new wheelcovers, and leather is newly optional on LSi.

RATINGS (SCALE OF 1-10)

Overall	Safety	Reliability	Performance	Comfort	Value
7.4	7.2	8.7	8	7.8	5.4

Category E

Model Description	Trade-in Value	Market Value
4 Dr LSi Sdn	5730	7440
4 Dr STD Sdn	5565	7225

OPTIONS FOR PRIZM

4 cyl 1.8 L Engine +290
Auto 3-Speed Transmission +220
Auto 4-Speed Transmission +355
Air Conditioning +370
Aluminum/Alloy Wheels +145
Anti-Lock Brakes +320
Compact Disc W/fm/tape +315
Cruise Control +100
Leather Seats +405
Power Door Locks +105
Power Steering +115
Power Sunroof +275
Power Windows +120

TRACKER 1995

All 4WD models and Massachusetts-bound Trackers get 95-horsepower engine. Convertible top has been redesigned for easier operation. Expressions Packages offer color-coordinated tops and wheels.

RATINGS (SCALE OF 1-10)

Overall	Safety	Reliability	Performance	Comfort	Value
5.6	2.7	8.3	6.2	7	3.6

Category G

Model Description	Trade-in Value	Market Value
2 Dr LSi 4WD Conv	5965	7365
2 Dr LSi 4WD Utility	6420	7925
2 Dr STD Conv	5390	6650
2 Dr STD 4WD Conv	5755	7105
2 Dr STD 4WD Utility	5835	7205

OPTIONS FOR TRACKER

Auto 3-Speed Transmission +265
Air Conditioning +370
Aluminum/Alloy Wheels +155
Compact Disc W/fm/tape +310
Skid Plates +65

1994 GEO

METRO 1994

Convertible is dropped. LSi trim level is discarded. CFC-free refrigerant is added to air conditioning systems.

RATINGS (SCALE OF 1-10)

Overall	Safety	Reliability	Performance	Comfort	Value
N/A	N/A	8	6.6	7.1	4.4

Category E

Model Description	Trade-in Value	Market Value
2 Dr STD Hbk	2710	3615
4 Dr STD Hbk	2590	3450
2 Dr XFi Hbk	2445	3260

OPTIONS FOR METRO

Auto 3-Speed Transmission +185
Air Conditioning +300
AM/FM Stereo Tape +115
Rear Window Defroster +60

PRIZM 1994

Passenger airbag is added. Air conditioners get CFC-free coolant.

RATINGS (SCALE OF 1-10)

Overall	Safety	Reliability	Performance	Comfort	Value
7.5	7.3	8.9	8	7.8	5.3

Category E

Model Description	Trade-in Value	Market Value
4 Dr LSi Sdn	4305	5740
4 Dr STD Sdn	4240	5655

OPTIONS FOR PRIZM

4 cyl 1.8 L Engine +165
Auto 3-Speed Transmission +185
Auto 4-Speed Transmission +295
Air Conditioning +300
Aluminum/Alloy Wheels +120
Anti-Lock Brakes +265
Compact Disc W/fm/tape +255
Cruise Control +80
Leather Seats +330
Power Door Locks +85
Power Steering +95
Power Sunroof +225
Power Windows +100
Premium Sound System +125

Don't forget to refer to the Mileage Adjustment Table at the back of this book!

 © 1999 by Edmund Publications Corporation

Model Description	Trade-in Value	Market Value

TRACKER 1994

Trackers sold in California and New York get 95-horsepower version of 1.6-liter engine to clear emissions hurdles. Four-wheel drive models trade on-/off-road tires for better riding all-season type rubber. Alloy wheels have been restyled. Center console gets cupholders. Interior fabrics are new. Optional is a CD/cassette player.

RATINGS (SCALE OF 1-10)

Overall	Safety	Reliability	Performance	Comfort	Value
5.5	2.7	8.2	6.2	7	3.6

Category G	Trade-in Value	Market Value
2 Dr LSi 4WD Utility	5280	6595
2 Dr LSi 4WD Conv	5100	6375
2 Dr STD Conv	4165	5205
2 Dr STD 4WD Conv	4795	5990
2 Dr STD 4WD Utility	5005	6260

OPTIONS FOR TRACKER

Auto 3-Speed Transmission +220
Air Conditioning +300
Aluminum/Alloy Wheels +130
Compact Disc W/fm/tape +255
Luggage Rack +60
Power Steering[Opt on STD] +105
Skid Plates +50

1993 GEO

METRO 1993

Automatic door locks are added. Convertibles can have an optional CD player.

RATINGS (SCALE OF 1-10)

Overall	Safety	Reliability	Performance	Comfort	Value
N/A	N/A	7.7	6.6	7.1	4.7

Category E	Trade-in Value	Market Value
2 Dr LSi Hbk	2855	3910
2 Dr LSi Conv	3285	4500
4 Dr LSi Hbk	3280	4495
2 Dr STD Hbk	2530	3470
4 Dr STD Hbk	2760	3785
2 Dr XFi Hbk	2260	3095

OPTIONS FOR METRO

Auto 3-Speed Transmission +120
Air Conditioning +245
AM/FM Stereo Tape +95
Rear Window Defroster[Std on LSi] +50

PRIZM 1993

Totally redesigned and available in base or LSi trim in sedan configuration. A driver airbag is standard. ABS is available. Still based on Toyota Corolla design. Standard engine is a 108-horsepower DOHC 1.6-liter engine. Available on LSi models is a twin-cam 1.8-liter engine making 115 horsepower.

RATINGS (SCALE OF 1-10)

Overall	Safety	Reliability	Performance	Comfort	Value
7.2	5.9	8.7	8	7.8	5.8

Category E	Trade-in Value	Market Value
4 Dr LSi Sdn	3705	5070
4 Dr STD Sdn	3500	4795

OPTIONS FOR PRIZM

4 cyl 1.8 L Engine +115
Auto 3-Speed Transmission +150
Auto 4-Speed Transmission +235
Air Conditioning +245
Aluminum/Alloy Wheels +95
AM/FM Compact Disc Playr +145
Anti-Lock Brakes +215
Cruise Control +65
Power Door Locks +70
Power Steering +75
Power Sunroof +185
Power Windows +80
Rear Window Defroster +50

STORM 1993

Hatchback model is dropped. Base engine loses five horsepower, but peak torque is made at lower rpm. Base models can be equipped with alloys. A CD player is optional.

RATINGS (SCALE OF 1-10)

Overall	Safety	Reliability	Performance	Comfort	Value
5.8	5	7	7.8	5.9	3.3

Category E	Trade-in Value	Market Value
2 Dr GSi Cpe	3990	5465
2 Dr STD Cpe	3320	4550

OPTIONS FOR STORM

Auto 3-Speed Transmission +165
Auto 4-Speed Transmission +225
Air Conditioning +245
Aluminum/Alloy Wheels[Opt on STD] +95
AM/FM Compact Disc Playr +145

TRACKER 1993

Radios get revised controls.

RATINGS (SCALE OF 1-10)

Overall	Safety	Reliability	Performance	Comfort	Value
5.5	2.7	8	6.2	7	3.5

Category G	Trade-in Value	Market Value
2 Dr LSi 4WD Utility	4315	5530
2 Dr LSi 4WD Conv	4110	5270
2 Dr STD Conv	3510	4500

Don't forget to refer to the Mileage Adjustment Table at the back of this book!

 © 1999 by Edmund Publications Corporation

Model Description	Trade-in Value	Market Value
2 Dr STD 4WD Utility	4135	5300
2 Dr STD 4WD Conv	3965	5085

OPTIONS FOR TRACKER

Auto 3-Speed Transmission +180
Air Conditioning +245
Aluminum/Alloy Wheels +105
AM/FM Stereo Tape +75
Power Steering +85

1992 GEO

METRO 1992

Styling is revised front and rear. A new instrument panel is installed. New wheelcovers are installed on base and LSi models. Four-door hatchbacks get child safety rear-door locks.

RATINGS (SCALE OF 1-10)

Overall	Safety	Reliability	Performance	Comfort	Value
N/A	N/A	7.4	6.6	7.1	4.6

Category E

Model Description	Trade-in Value	Market Value
2 Dr LSi Conv	2455	3510
2 Dr LSi Hbk	2345	3350
4 Dr LSi Hbk	2400	3430
2 Dr STD Hbk	2085	2980
4 Dr STD Hbk	2175	3110
2 Dr XFi Hbk	1820	2600

OPTIONS FOR METRO

Auto 3-Speed Transmission +120
Air Conditioning +200
AM/FM Stereo Tape +75
Rear Window Defroster[Std on LSi] +40

PRIZM 1992

Four-door hatchback is dropped.

Category E

Model Description	Trade-in Value	Market Value
4 Dr GSi Sdn	3360	4800
4 Dr LSi Sdn	2910	4160
4 Dr STD Sdn	2750	3925

OPTIONS FOR PRIZM

Auto 3-Speed Transmission +120
Auto 4-Speed Transmission +190
Air Conditioning[Opt on STD] +200
AM/FM Stereo Tape +75
Cruise Control +55
Power Door Locks[Std on LSi] +55
Power Steering[Opt on STD] +60
Power Sunroof +150
Power Windows +65

STORM 1992

Styling is revised front and rear. GSi models get new 1.8-liter engine making 140 horsepower.

RATINGS (SCALE OF 1-10)

Overall	Safety	Reliability	Performance	Comfort	Value
6.2	5	7.3	7.8	5.9	4.8

Category E

Model Description	Trade-in Value	Market Value
2 Dr 2+2 Cpe	2500	3570
2 Dr GSi Cpe	2990	4270
2 Dr STD Hbk	2330	3325

OPTIONS FOR STORM

Auto 3-Speed Transmission +135
Auto 4-Speed Transmission +180
Air Conditioning +200
Aluminum/Alloy Wheels[Opt on 2+2,STD] +80
AM/FM Stereo Tape +75

TRACKER 1992

Dashboard is slightly revised and a tilt steering column is a new option. Center console includes cupholders. New seat fabrics and cloth bolsters are added.

RATINGS (SCALE OF 1-10)

Overall	Safety	Reliability	Performance	Comfort	Value
5.4	2.4	7.7	6.2	7	3.8

Category G

Model Description	Trade-in Value	Market Value
2 Dr LSi 4WD Utility	3730	4975
2 Dr LSi 4WD Conv	3225	4295
2 Dr STD Conv	2210	2950
2 Dr STD 4WD Conv	2990	3990
2 Dr STD 4WD Utility	3520	4695

OPTIONS FOR TRACKER

Auto 3-Speed Transmission +145
Air Conditioning +200
Aluminum/Alloy Wheels +85
AM/FM Stereo Tape +60
Power Steering +70
Rear Window Defroster[Opt on STD] +40
Rear Window Wiper[Opt on STD] +40

1991 GEO

METRO 1991

LSi Convertible debuts, and includes driver airbag and larger tires. Convertible seats only two.

RATINGS (SCALE OF 1-10)

Overall	Safety	Reliability	Performance	Comfort	Value
N/A	N/A	7.2	6.6	7.1	4.5

Category E

Model Description	Trade-in Value	Market Value
2 Dr LSi Conv	1855	2725
2 Dr LSi Hbk	1720	2530
4 Dr LSi Hbk	1635	2400
2 Dr STD Hbk	1665	2445
4 Dr STD Hbk	1610	2365
2 Dr XFi Hbk	1490	2190

Don't forget to refer to the Mileage Adjustment Table at the back of this book!

 © 1999 by Edmund Publications Corporation

Model Description	Trade-in Value	Market Value

OPTIONS FOR METRO

Auto 3-Speed Transmission +95
Air Conditioning +165
AM/FM Stereo Tape +60
Power Steering +50
Rear Window Defroster[Std on LSi] +30

PRIZM 1991

Horsepower is up to 102 on base models and 130 on GSi models.

Category E

Model Description	Trade-in Value	Market Value
4 Dr GSi Sdn	2700	3975
4 Dr GSi Hbk	2860	4205
4 Dr STD Hbk	2310	3400
4 Dr STD Sdn	2305	3385

OPTIONS FOR PRIZM

Auto 3-Speed Transmission +95
Auto 4-Speed Transmission +155
LSi Pkg +265
Air Conditioning +165
AM/FM Stereo Tape +60
Cruise Control +45
Power Door Locks +45
Power Steering[Opt on STD] +50
Power Sunroof +120
Power Windows +55

STORM 1991

A funky looking three-door hatchback joins the lineup with squared-off rear styling like that found on Honda Civic. New hatchback is available only in base trim. Base engine is up 25 horsepower to 95. GSi gets horsepower boost to 130.

RATINGS (SCALE OF 1-10)

Overall	Safety	Reliability	Performance	Comfort	Value
5.8	5	6.8	7.8	5.9	3.8

Category E

Model Description	Trade-in Value	Market Value
2 Dr 2+2 Cpe	2060	3030
2 Dr GSi Cpe	2460	3615
2 Dr STD Hbk	1975	2905

OPTIONS FOR STORM

Auto 3-Speed Transmission +110
Auto 4-Speed Transmission +150
Air Conditioning +165
AM/FM Stereo Tape +60
Rear Spoiler +40

TRACKER 1991

Rear antilock brakes are standard, and work only in 2WD. Four-wheel drive LSi models get auto-locking front hubs.

RATINGS (SCALE OF 1-10)

Overall	Safety	Reliability	Performance	Comfort	Value
5.5	2.4	7.7	6.2	7	4.4

Category G

Model Description	Trade-in Value	Market Value
2 Dr LSi 4WD Utility	3660	4945
2 Dr LSi 4WD Conv	3045	4115
2 Dr STD Conv	2550	3445
2 Dr STD 4WD Utility	3530	4770
2 Dr STD 4WD Conv	2950	3985

OPTIONS FOR TRACKER

Auto 3-Speed Transmission +115
Air Conditioning +165
Aluminum/Alloy Wheels +70
AM/FM Stereo Tape +50
Power Steering +55

1990 GEO

METRO 1990

Passive front seatbelts are added, and automatics get a new brake/transmission shift interlock. Fuel sipper strippo model is now called XFi and gets 53 mpg in the city. XFi engine makes only 49 horsepower. Four-door hatch is now available in base trim.

RATINGS (SCALE OF 1-10)

Overall	Safety	Reliability	Performance	Comfort	Value
N/A	N/A	7.1	6.6	7.1	4.5

Category E

Model Description	Trade-in Value	Market Value
2 Dr LSi Conv	1610	2475
2 Dr LSi Hbk	1290	1985
4 Dr LSi Hbk	1190	1830
2 Dr STD Hbk	1210	1865
4 Dr STD Hbk	1060	1630
2 Dr XFi Hbk	1025	1580

OPTIONS FOR METRO

Auto 3-Speed Transmission +75
Air Conditioning +135
AM/FM Stereo Tape +50

PRIZM 1990

Sporty GSi models added to lineup, powered by a 115-horsepower version of standard DOHC 1.6-liter engine. GSi trim adds body-color bumpers, power steering, four-wheel disc brakes and a tachometer.

Category E

Model Description	Trade-in Value	Market Value
4 Dr GSi Sdn	2090	3210
4 Dr GSi Hbk	2230	3425
4 Dr STD Sdn	1880	2890
4 Dr STD Hbk	1945	2990

Don't forget to refer to the Mileage Adjustment Table at the back of this book!

 © 1999 by Edmund Publications Corporation

Model Description	Trade-in Value	Market Value

OPTIONS FOR PRIZM

Auto 3-Speed Transmission +70
Auto 4-Speed Transmission +130
Air Conditioning +135
AM/FM Stereo Tape +50
Cruise Control +35
Power Door Locks +40
Power Steering[Opt on STD] +40
Power Sunroof +100
Power Windows +45

STORM 1990

Small sport coupe based on Isuzu Impulse. Sold in base or GSi trim. Driver airbag is standard. Base models have 70 horsepower; GSi models are boosted to 125 horsepower.

RATINGS (SCALE OF 1-10)

Overall	Safety	Reliability	Performance	Comfort	Value
5.7	5	6.6	7.8	5.9	3.4

Category E

Model Description	Trade-in Value	Market Value
2 Dr 2+2 Cpe	1490	2295
2 Dr GSi Cpe	1855	2855

OPTIONS FOR STORM

Auto 3-Speed Transmission +90
Auto 4-Speed Transmission +125
Air Conditioning +135
Aluminum/Alloy Wheels +50
AM/FM Stereo Tape +50

TRACKER 1990

Production moved to Canada, and Trackers are sold nationwide. Convertible gets LSi trim level. Air conditioning and automatic transmission are now optional on all Trackers.

RATINGS (SCALE OF 1-10)

Overall	Safety	Reliability	Performance	Comfort	Value
5.6	2.4	7.3	6.2	7	5.2

Category G

Model Description	Trade-in Value	Market Value
2 Dr LSi 4WD Conv	2585	3590
2 Dr LSi 4WD Utility	2830	3930
2 Dr STD 4WD Utility	2540	3525
2 Dr STD 4WD Conv	2430	3375

OPTIONS FOR TRACKER

Auto 3-Speed Transmission +95
Air Conditioning +135
AM/FM Stereo Tape +40
Power Steering +45

1989 GEO

METRO 1989

All-new subcompact sold as a two- or four-door hatchback in base or LSi trim. Power comes from a three-cylinder 1.0-liter engine that makes 55 horsepower.

RATINGS (SCALE OF 1-10)

Overall	Safety	Reliability	Performance	Comfort	Value
N/A	N/A	6.9	6.6	7.1	4.4

Category E

Model Description	Trade-in Value	Market Value
2 Dr LSi Hbk	1075	1765
4 Dr LSi Hbk	955	1560
2 Dr STD Hbk	820	1345

OPTIONS FOR METRO

Auto 3-Speed Transmission +55
Air Conditioning +110
AM/FM Stereo Tape +40
Sunroof +45

PRIZM 1989

Nova replacement is based on Toyota Corolla design. Sold as a four-door sedan and a four-door hatchback in base or LSi trim. A twin-cam 1.6-liter engine good for 95 horsepower powers Prizm.

Category E

Model Description	Trade-in Value	Market Value
4 Dr STD Hbk	1670	2735
4 Dr STD Sdn	1630	2670

OPTIONS FOR PRIZM

Auto 3-Speed Transmission +55
Air Conditioning +110
AM/FM Stereo Tape +40
Cruise Control +30
Power Door Locks +30
Power Steering +35
Power Sunroof +80
Power Windows +35

SPECTRUM 1989

Turbo model dropped from this Isuzu-built hatchback and sedan.

Category E

Model Description	Trade-in Value	Market Value
2 Dr STD Hbk	865	1415
4 Dr STD Sdn	965	1580

OPTIONS FOR SPECTRUM

Auto 3-Speed Transmission +55
Air Conditioning +110
AM/FM Stereo Tape +40
Cruise Control +30
Power Steering +35

Don't forget to refer to the Mileage Adjustment Table at the back of this book!

 © 1999 by Edmund Publications Corporation

Model Description	Trade-in Value	Market Value

TRACKER 1989

First year for spunky sport-utility vehicle. Convertible and hardtop models are sold in base trim; LSi trim is reserved for hardtops only. Initially available in just 12 coastal states, the first 10,000 Trackers are imported from Japan. An 80-horsepower 1.6-liter engine powers Tracker. Four-wheel drive models come with manual locking front hubs.

RATINGS (SCALE OF 1-10)

Overall	Safety	Reliability	Performance	Comfort	Value
5.8	2.4	7.2	6.2	7	6.1

Model Description	Trade-in Value	Market Value
Category G		
2 Dr LSi 4WD Utility	2105	3050
2 Dr STD 4WD Utility	1885	2730
2 Dr STD 4WD Conv	1865	2705

OPTIONS FOR TRACKER

Air Conditioning[Opt on STD] +110
AM/FM Stereo Tape +35

Major Savings On An Extended Warranty

"YOU DESERVE THE BEST"

Call today for your free quote.

Pay up to 50% less than dealership prices!

http://www.edmunds.com/warranty 1-800-580-9889

A 15-minute phone call could save you 15% or more on car insurance.

1-800-555-2758

GEICO DIRECT

The Sensible Alternative

Don't forget to refer to the Mileage Adjustment Table at the back of this book!

 © 1999 by Edmund Publications Corporation

Model Description	Trade-in Value	Market Value

GMC USA

1995 GMC Suburban

1998 GMC

C/K PICKUP 1998

With an all-new Sierra just one year away, changes are minimal. Diesel engines make more power and torque, extended cab models get rear heater ducts, a PassLock theft deterrent system is standard, 1500-series trucks get reduced rolling resistance tires and three new colors debut. Second generation airbags are standard.

C1500

Category H

Model Description	Trade-in Value	Market Value
2 Dr SL Ext Cab SB	14040	16515
2 Dr SL Std Cab SB	13555	15945
2 Dr SL Std Cab Stepside SB	13710	16130
2 Dr SL Std Cab LB	13830	16270
2 Dr SL Ext Cab LB	14315	16840
2 Dr SLE Std Cab SB	15730	18505
2 Dr SLE Ext Cab SB	15815	18605
2 Dr SLE Std Cab Stepside SB	16335	19215
2 Dr SLE Ext Cab Stepside SB	16515	19430
2 Dr SLE Std Cab LB	15845	18640
2 Dr SLE Ext Cab LB	16080	18920
2 Dr SLT Ext Cab SB	17155	20185
2 Dr SLT Std Cab SB	16705	19650
2 Dr SLT Ext Cab Stepside SB	17605	20710
2 Dr SLT Std Cab Stepside SB	17345	20405
2 Dr SLT Std Cab LB	16925	19910
2 Dr SLT Ext Cab LB	17325	20385
2 Dr Special Std Cab SB	12930	15210
2 Dr Special Std Cab LB	13155	15475

C2500

Category H

Model Description	Trade-in Value	Market Value
2 Dr SL Std Cab LB	16475	19385
2 Dr SLE Std Cab LB	18290	21515
2 Dr SLT Std Cab LB	19585	23040

C3500

Category H

Model Description	Trade-in Value	Market Value
4 Dr SL Crew Cab LB	19970	23495
4 Dr SLE Crew Cab LB	23825	28030
4 Dr SLT Crew Cab LB	25335	29805

K1500

Category H

Model Description	Trade-in Value	Market Value
2 Dr SL 4WD Std Cab SB	15045	17700
2 Dr SL 4WD Ext Cab SB	15785	18570
2 Dr SL 4WD Std Cab Stepside SB	15925	18735
2 Dr SL 4WD Std Cab LB	15115	17785
2 Dr SL 4WD Ext Cab LB	15680	18445
2 Dr SLE 4WD Ext Cab SB	17485	20570
2 Dr SLE 4WD Std Cab SB	16590	19520
2 Dr SLE 4WD Std Cab Stepside SB	17320	20375
2 Dr SLE 4WD Ext Cab Stepside SB	18090	21285
2 Dr SLE 4WD Ext Cab LB	17260	20310
2 Dr SLE 4WD Std Cab LB	16825	19795
2 Dr SLT 4WD Std Cab SB	18010	21190
2 Dr SLT 4WD Ext Cab SB	18430	21685
2 Dr SLT 4WD Ext Cab Stepside SB	19495	22935
2 Dr SLT 4WD Std Cab Stepside SB	18500	21765
2 Dr SLT 4WD Ext Cab LB	19055	22415
2 Dr SLT 4WD Std Cab LB	18260	21480
2 Dr Special 4WD Std Cab SB	14910	17540
2 Dr Special 4WD Std Cab LB	15165	17840

K2500 HD

Category H

Model Description	Trade-in Value	Market Value
2 Dr SL 4WD Ext Cab SB	16385	19280
2 Dr SL 4WD Ext Cab LB	16470	19375
2 Dr SL 4WD Std Cab LB	16110	18955
2 Dr SLE 4WD Ext Cab SB	18840	22165
2 Dr SLE 4WD Std Cab LB	18310	21540
2 Dr SLE 4WD Ext Cab LB	18905	22240
2 Dr SLT 4WD Ext Cab SB	21105	24830
2 Dr SLT 4WD Std Cab LB	20560	24190
2 Dr SLT 4WD Ext Cab LB	20905	24595

Don't forget to refer to the Mileage Adjustment Table at the back of this book!

 © 1999 by Edmund Publications Corporation

Model Description	Trade-in Value	Market Value

K3500

Category H

Model Description	Trade-in Value	Market Value
4 Dr SL 4WD Crew Cab LB	20695	24345
4 Dr SLE 4WD Crew Cab LB	24255	28535
4 Dr SLT 4WD Crew Cab LB	25615	30135

OPTIONS FOR C/K PICKUP

8 cyl 5.0 L Engine[Std on C1500 Ext Cab, C2500, K1500 4WD Ext Cab] +410
8 cyl 5.7 L Engine[Opt on C1500, C2500, K1500] +830
8 cyl 7.4 L Engine +500
8 cyl 6.5 L Turbodsl Engine +2495
Auto 4-Speed Transmission[Std on C1500 Ext Cab Stepside] +805
Air Conditioning[Std on SLE, SLT] +670
Aluminum/Alloy Wheels[Std on SLT] +260
AM/FM Compact Disc Playr +245
Bed Liner +185
Camper/Towing Package +295
Cruise Control[Std on SLE, SLT] +160
Dual Rear Wheels[Std on Ext Cab] +700
Hinged Third Door (PU) +350
Keyless Entry System[Opt on SLE] +125
Power Door Locks[Std on SLE, SLT] +155
Power Drivers Seat[Opt on SLE] +225
Privacy Glass +140
Rear Window Defroster +125
Sliding Rear Window +95
Tilt Steering Wheel[Std on SLE, SLT] +150

JIMMY 1998

A revised interior contains dual second-generation airbags, improved climate controls and available premium sound systems. Outside, the front bumper, grille and headlights are new. Side cladding is restyled and SLT models have new alloy wheels. Fresh colors inside and out sum up the changes.

Category G

Model Description	Trade-in Value	Market Value
2 Dr SL 4WD Utility	14770	17585
4 Dr SL Wgn	15880	18905
4 Dr SL 4WD Wgn	16875	20090
4 Dr SLE Wgn	18095	21540
4 Dr SLE 4WD Wgn	19080	22715
2 Dr SLS Sport 4WD Utility	17340	20640
4 Dr SLS Sport Wgn	17980	21405
4 Dr SLS Sport 4WD Wgn	18975	22590
4 Dr SLT Wgn	18965	22575
4 Dr SLT 4WD Wgn	19900	23690

OPTIONS FOR JIMMY

Aluminum/Alloy Wheels[Opt on SL] +285
AM/FM Compact Disc Playr +320
Cruise Control[Opt on SL] +175
Heated Front Seats +210
Keyless Entry System[Std on SLE, SLT] +170
Luggage Rack[Opt on SL] +130
Power Door Locks[Opt on SL] +190
Power Drivers Seat[Std on SLE, SLT] +235
Power Mirrors[Opt on SL] +110
Power Moonroof +735
Power Windows[Opt on SL] +195
Rear Window Defroster[Opt on SL] +140
Rear Window Wiper[Opt on SL] +125
Tilt Steering Wheel[Opt on SL] +140

SAFARI 1998

New colors, a theft deterrent system and automatic transmission refinements are the changes to the Safari. This van is one of the few GM models that retains full-power airbags for 1998.

Category G

Model Description	Trade-in Value	Market Value
2 Dr SL Cargo Van Ext	13350	15895
2 Dr SLE Pass. Van Ext	15320	18240
2 Dr SLE 4WD Pass. Van Ext	17795	21185
2 Dr SLT Pass. Van Ext	16685	19865
2 Dr SLT 4WD Pass. Van Ext	18975	22590
2 Dr SLX Pass. Van Ext	13435	15990
2 Dr SLX 4WD Pass. Van Ext	16460	19595

OPTIONS FOR SAFARI

8 Passenger Seating[Opt on SLX] +320
Aluminum/Alloy Wheels[Std on SLT] +285
AM/FM Compact Disc Playr[Std on SLT] +320
Cruise Control[Opt on SL, SLX] +175
Dual Air Conditioning +840
Dual Power Seats +525
Keyless Entry System[Std on SLT] +170
Leather Seats +640
Power Door Locks[Opt on SL, SLX] +190
Power Drivers Seat[Std on SLT] +235
Power Mirrors[Std on SLT] +110
Power Windows[Opt on SL, SLX] +195
Premium Sound System +300
Privacy Glass[Opt on SL, SLX] +225
Rear Heater +170
Rear Window Defroster +140
Rear Window Wiper +125
Tilt Steering Wheel[Opt on SL, SLX] +140

SAVANA 1998

New colors, transmission enhancements, more power for the diesel engine, revised uplevel stereos and the addition of a PassLock theft deterrent system mark the changes for 1998. A mini-module driver's airbag is new, but it and the passenger airbag still deploy at full-force levels.

G15

Category H

Model Description	Trade-in Value	Market Value
2 Dr SLE Pass. Van	20350	23940
2 Dr STD Cargo Van	18370	21610
2 Dr STD Pass. Van	19575	23030

Don't forget to refer to the Mileage Adjustment Table at the back of this book!

 © 1999 by Edmund Publications Corporation

Model Description	Trade-in Value	Market Value

OPTIONS FOR SAVANA

8 cyl 5.0 L Engine +410
8 cyl 5.7 L Engine[Std on G25 Pass. Van, G25 Pass. Van Ext., G35] +830
Air Conditioning[Opt on Cargo Van, Cargo Van Ext] +670
Aluminum/Alloy Wheels +260
AM/FM Compact Disc Playr +245
Cruise Control[Opt on STD] +160
Dual Air Conditioning +1180
Keyless Entry System +125
Power Door Locks[Opt on STD] +155
Power Drivers Seat +225
Power Windows[Opt on STD] +160
Privacy Glass +140
Rear Heater +185
Tilt Steering Wheel[Opt on STD] +150

SONOMA 1998

Styling is re-tuned inside and out, resulting in a sleeker look and better interior ergonomics. Dual second-generation airbags are standard, and seats are upgraded for improved comfort and appearance. Four-wheel disc brakes are standard on 4WD models and uplevel stereos are new for 1998. New colors inside and out round out the changes.

Category G		
2 Dr SL Std Cab SB	10225	12170
2 Dr SL Std Cab LB	10045	11960
2 Dr SLE Ext Cab SB	11920	14190
2 Dr SLE Std Cab SB	11265	13410
2 Dr SLE 4WD Ext Cab SB	15425	18365
2 Dr SLS Sport Ext Cab SB	11170	13300
2 Dr SLS Sport Std Cab SB	10850	12915
2 Dr SLS Sport Std Cab Stepside SB	11070	13180
2 Dr SLS Sport Ext Cab Stepside SB	11540	13740
2 Dr SLS Sport Std Cab LB	11120	13240
2 Dr SLS Sport 4WD Ext Cab SB	15095	17970
2 Dr SLS Sport 4WD Ext Cab Stepside SB	15275	18185

OPTIONS FOR SONOMA

6 cyl 4.3 L Engine[Opt on 2WD] +670
6 cyl 4.3 L Vortec Engine +905
Auto 4-Speed Transmission +890
Highrider Suspension Package +1135
Air Conditioning +675
Aluminum/Alloy Wheels[Std on SLE] +285
AM/FM Compact Disc Playr +320
Cruise Control +175
Heavy Duty Suspension[Opt on SL, Std Cab, 4WD] +115
Hinged Third Door (PU) +290
Keyless Entry System +170
Power Door Locks +190
Power Mirrors +110
Power Windows +195
Sliding Rear Window +100
Sport Suspension +400
Tilt Steering Wheel +140

SUBURBAN 1998

De-powered second-generation airbags protect front seat occupants for 1998. A new innovation called carpeted floor mats finally appears inside the big 'Burban. Standard equipment now includes PassLock theft deterrent system, power driver's seat, electrochromic rearview mirror, and automatic four-wheel drive on K-series models.

Category H		
4 Dr C1500 Wgn	22795	26815
4 Dr C2500 Wgn	23295	27405
4 Dr K1500 4WD Wgn	24200	28470
4 Dr K2500 4WD Wgn	25080	29505

OPTIONS FOR SUBURBAN

8 cyl 7.4 L Engine[Opt on 2500] +500
8 cyl 6.5 L Turbodsl Engine[Opt on 2500] +2495
SLE Package +3050
SLT Package +3565
Air Conditioning +670
Aluminum/Alloy Wheels +260
Camper/Towing Package +295
Compact Disc W/fm/tape +265
Cruise Control +160
Dual Air Conditioning +1180
Heated Front Seats +240
Keyless Entry System +125
Leather Seats +860
Power Drivers Seat +225
Power Mirrors +85
Power Windows +160
Privacy Glass +140
Rear Heater +185
Rear Window Defroster +125
Rear Window Wiper +115
Running Boards +245
Tilt Steering Wheel +150

YUKON 1998

The two-door model gets the ax this year. Rear seat passengers are cooled by a newly optional rear air conditioning system. A host of new standard features has been added, including carpeted floor mats. Three new colors spruce up the outside a bit, and second-generation airbags are standard inside.

Category H		
4 Dr SLE Wgn	22820	26850
4 Dr SLE 4WD Wgn	23160	27245
4 Dr SLT Wgn	23590	27750
4 Dr SLT 4WD Wgn	24700	29060

Don't forget to refer to the Mileage Adjustment Table at the back of this book!

 © 1999 by Edmund Publications Corporation

Model Description	Trade-in Value	Market Value

OPTIONS FOR YUKON

Luxury Convenience Group +685
Compact Disc W/fm/tape[Opt on SLE] +265
Dual Air Conditioning[Opt on SLE] +1180
Heated Front Seats +240
Running Boards +245

1997 GMC

C/K PICKUP 1997

A passenger airbag is added, along with speed sensitive steering that reduces low-speed effort. K1500 models have a tighter turning radius for better maneuverability. Automatic transmissions are refined to provide smoother shifts and improved efficiency. Three new paint colors debut.

RATINGS (SCALE OF 1-10)

Overall	Safety	Reliability	Performance	Comfort	Value
N/A	8.6	9.2	7.8	8.4	N/A

C1500

Category H

Model Description	Trade-in Value	Market Value
2 Dr GT Std Cab SB	13730	16345
2 Dr SL Ext Cab SB	12670	15085
2 Dr SL Std Cab SB	12385	14740
2 Dr SL Std Cab Stepside SB	12675	15090
2 Dr SL Ext Cab Stepside SB	13280	15810
2 Dr SL Std Cab LB	12115	14420
2 Dr SL Ext Cab LB	13030	15510
2 Dr SLE Ext Cab SB	13760	16380
2 Dr SLE Std Cab SB	13485	16055
2 Dr SLE Std Cab Stepside SB	14135	16825
2 Dr SLE Ext Cab Stepside SB	14370	17110
2 Dr SLE Std Cab LB	13570	16155
2 Dr SLE Ext Cab LB	13835	16470
2 Dr SLT Std Cab SB	14580	17360
2 Dr SLT Ext Cab SB	14820	17645
2 Dr SLT Ext Cab Stepside SB	15515	18470
2 Dr SLT Std Cab Stepside SB	15230	18130
2 Dr SLT Std Cab LB	14670	17460
2 Dr SLT Ext Cab LB	14895	17735
2 Dr Special Std Cab SB	11000	13095
2 Dr Special Std Cab LB	11385	13555

C2500

Category H

Model Description	Trade-in Value	Market Value
2 Dr SL Ext Cab SB	15895	18920
2 Dr SL Std Cab LB	15330	18250
2 Dr SLE Ext Cab SB	17125	20385
2 Dr SLE Std Cab LB	16425	19555
2 Dr SLT Ext Cab SB	17905	21315
2 Dr SLT Std Cab LB	17245	20530

C3500

Category H

Model Description	Trade-in Value	Market Value
2 Dr SL Std Cab LB	17275	20565
2 Dr SL Ext Cab LB	18485	22005
4 Dr SL Crew Cab LB	19660	23405
2 Dr SLE Ext Cab LB	19640	23380
2 Dr SLE Std Cab LB	18475	21990
4 Dr SLE Crew Cab LB	20970	24965
2 Dr SLT Std Cab LB	19235	22895
2 Dr SLT Ext Cab LB	20530	24440
4 Dr SLT Crew Cab LB	21735	25875

K1500

Category H

Model Description	Trade-in Value	Market Value
2 Dr SL 4WD Std Cab SB	14185	16885
2 Dr SL 4WD Ext Cab SB	14250	16960
2 Dr SL 4WD Ext Cab Stepside SB	14860	17690
2 Dr SL 4WD Std Cab Stepside SB	14830	17655
2 Dr SL 4WD Ext Cab LB	14320	17050
2 Dr SL 4WD Std Cab LB	14275	16995
2 Dr SLE 4WD Ext Cab SB	15885	18910
2 Dr SLE 4WD Std Cab SB	15760	18760
2 Dr SLE 4WD Ext Cab Stepside SB	16515	19660
2 Dr SLE 4WD Std Cab Stepside SB	16365	19485
2 Dr SLE 4WD Ext Cab LB	15975	19020
2 Dr SLE 4WD Std Cab LB	15830	18845
2 Dr SLT 4WD Std Cab SB	16590	19750
2 Dr SLT 4WD Ext Cab SB	16695	19875
2 Dr SLT 4WD Ext Cab Stepside SB	17480	20810
2 Dr SLT 4WD Std Cab Stepside SB	17315	20615
2 Dr SLT 4WD Std Cab LB	16680	19860
2 Dr SLT 4WD Ext Cab LB	16775	19970
2 Dr Special 4WD Std Cab SB	14020	16690
2 Dr Special 4WD Std Cab LB	14110	16795

K2500 HD

Category H

Model Description	Trade-in Value	Market Value
2 Dr SL 4WD Ext Cab SB	15865	18885
2 Dr SL 4WD Std Cab LB	15030	17890
2 Dr SL 4WD Ext Cab LB	15930	18965
2 Dr SLE 4WD Ext Cab SB	17210	20490
2 Dr SLE 4WD Std Cab LB	16225	19315
2 Dr SLE 4WD Ext Cab LB	17260	20545
2 Dr SLT 4WD Ext Cab SB	18190	21655
2 Dr SLT 4WD Std Cab LB	17730	21110
2 Dr SLT 4WD Ext Cab LB	18245	21720

Don't forget to refer to the Mileage Adjustment Table at the back of this book!

 © 1999 by Edmund Publications Corporation

Model Description	Trade-in Value	Market Value

K3500

Category H

Model Description	Trade-in Value	Market Value
2 Dr SL 4WD Ext Cab LB	19220	22880
2 Dr SL 4WD Std Cab LB	17785	21175
4 Dr SL 4WD Crew Cab LB	20045	23860
2 Dr SLE 4WD Std Cab LB	18925	22530
2 Dr SLE 4WD Ext Cab LB	20305	24170
4 Dr SLE 4WD Crew Cab LB	21180	25210
2 Dr SLT 4WD Std Cab LB	19625	23365
2 Dr SLT 4WD Ext Cab LB	21100	25115
4 Dr SLT 4WD Crew Cab LB	22045	26245

OPTIONS FOR C/K PICKUP

8 cyl 5.0 L Engine +335
8 cyl 5.7 L Engine +705
8 cyl 7.4 L Engine +410
8 cyl 6.5 L Turbodsl Engine +2075
Auto 4-Speed Transmission +660
Air Conditioning[Opt on SL,Special] +550
Aluminum/Alloy Wheels[Std on SLT] +210
AM/FM Compact Disc Playr +200
Bed Liner +155
Camper/Towing Package +240
Chrome Wheels[Std on GT] +200
Compact Disc W/fm/tape +215
Cruise Control[Opt on SL,Special] +130
Dual Rear Wheels +570
Hinged Third Door (PU) +285
Keyless Entry System[Opt on SLE] +110
Locking Differential +170
Power Door Locks[Opt on GT,SL] +125
Power Drivers Seat[Opt on SLE] +185
Rear Step Bumper +105
Skid Plates +75

JIMMY 1997

Highrider off-road package deleted as GMC realigns Jimmy as luxury sport-ute. Instead, buyers can opt for a Gold Edition in one of four colors. New options include a power sunroof and HomeLink universal transmitter. In a fit of good taste, Radar Purple and Bright Teal paint colors are replaced by Fairway Green and Smoky Caramel.

RATINGS (SCALE OF 1-10)

Overall	Safety	Reliability	Performance	Comfort	Value
6.9	5.3	8	8	7.9	5.5

Category G

Model Description	Trade-in Value	Market Value
2 Dr SL 4WD Utility	13545	16320
4 Dr SL Wgn	13310	16035
4 Dr SL 4WD Wgn	13575	16360
4 Dr SLE Wgn	15260	18385
4 Dr SLE 4WD Wgn	15705	18920
2 Dr SLS Sport 4WD Utility	14585	17570
4 Dr SLS Sport Wgn	15180	18290
4 Dr SLS Sport 4WD Wgn	15600	18795
4 Dr SLT Wgn	16155	19460
4 Dr SLT 4WD Wgn	16405	19765

OPTIONS FOR JIMMY

Aluminum/Alloy Wheels[Opt on SL] +235
AM/FM Compact Disc Playr +260
Camper/Towing Package +195
Cruise Control[Std on SLE,SLS Sport,SLT] +145
Keyless Entry System[Std on SLT] +140
Luggage Rack[Std on SLE,SLS Sport,SLT] +105
Power Door Locks[Std on SLE,SLS Sport,SLT] +155
Power Drivers Seat[Std on SLT] +190
Power Moonroof +600
Power Windows[Std on SLE,SLS Sport,SLT] +160
Premium Sound System[Std on SLT] +245
Skid Plates +95
Swing Out Tire Carrier +140

SAFARI 1997

Illuminated entry and daytime running lights debut this year, along with a couple of new colors and automatic transmission improvements. SLT models can be equipped with leather seating, and a HomeLink three-channel transmitter is optional. Speed-sensitive power steering makes parking easier.

RATINGS (SCALE OF 1-10)

Overall	Safety	Reliability	Performance	Comfort	Value
7.3	6.9	7.7	6.8	6.5	8.6

Category G

Model Description	Trade-in Value	Market Value
2 Dr SL Cargo Van Ext	10590	12760
2 Dr SL 4WD Cargo Van Ext	13805	16635
2 Dr SLE Pass. Van Ext	12445	14990
2 Dr SLE 4WD Pass. Van Ext	15275	18405
2 Dr SLT Pass. Van Ext	13620	16410
2 Dr SLT 4WD Pass. Van Ext	16085	19375
2 Dr SLX Pass. Van Ext	11170	13455
2 Dr SLX 4WD Pass. Van Ext	14135	17030

OPTIONS FOR SAFARI

Aluminum/Alloy Wheels[Std on SLT] +235
Camper/Towing Package +195
Chrome Wheels +165
Compact Disc W/fm/tape +465
Cruise Control[Opt on SL, SLX] +145
Dual Air Conditioning +685
Dual Power Seats +430
Keyless Entry System[Std on SLT] +140
Leather Seats +520
Luggage Rack[Std on SLT] +105
Power Door Locks[Opt on SL,SLX] +155
Power Drivers Seat[Std on SLT] +190
Power Windows[Opt on SL,SLX] +160

SAVANA 1997

G3500 models get dual airbags, while daytime running lights are a new standard feature. Speed-sensitive steering reduces effort at low speeds. Chrome-plated wheels are a new option.

Don't forget to refer to the Mileage Adjustment Table at the back of this book!

 © 1999 by Edmund Publications Corporation

Model Description	Trade-in Value	Market Value

Remote keyless entry key fobs are redesigned, and automatic transmissions provide better fuel economy and smoother shifts.

G15

Category H

2 Dr SLE Pass. Van	17070	20320
2 Dr STD Pass. Van	16325	19435
2 Dr STD Cargo Van	15305	18225

G35

Category H

2 Dr SLE Pass. Van Ext	16020	19075
2 Dr SLE Pass. Van	15345	18265
2 Dr STD Pass. Van	14175	16875
2 Dr STD Pass. Van Ext	14850	17680
2 Dr STD Cargo Van Ext	14350	17085
2 Dr STD Cargo Van	13720	16335

OPTIONS FOR SAVANA

8 cyl 5.0 L Engine +335
8 cyl 5.7 L Engine[Std on G35] +705
8 cyl 7.4 L Engine +410
8 cyl 6.5 L Turbodsl Engine +2075
Air Conditioning[Opt on Cargo Van,Cargo Van Ext] +550
Aluminum/Alloy Wheels +210
Camper/Towing Package +240
Chrome Bumpers[Std on SLE] +115
Chrome Wheels +200
Compact Disc W/fm/tape +215
Cruise Control[Std on SLE] +130
Dual Air Conditioning[Opt on G15 Savana] +965
Dual Power Seats +315
Keyless Entry System +110
Locking Differential +170
Power Door Locks[Std on SLE] +125
Power Windows[Std on SLE] +130

SONOMA 1997

Nothing much. Changes are limited to availability of the Sport Suspension on extended cab models, engine and transmission improvements, lighter-weight plug-in half shafts for 4WD Sonomas, and console-mounted shifter for trucks equipped with a center console and bucket seats. New colors arrive, and the remote keyless entry key fob is redesigned.

RATINGS (SCALE OF 1-10)

Overall	Safety	Reliability	Performance	Comfort	Value
N/A	4.9	7.7	6.6	8.1	N/A

Category G

2 Dr SL Std Cab SB	8305	10005
2 Dr SL Std Cab LB	8220	9900
2 Dr SL 4WD Std Cab SB	11585	13955
2 Dr SL 4WD Std Cab LB	11690	14080
2 Dr SLE Ext Cab SB	9320	11230
2 Dr SLE Std Cab SB	9150	11025
2 Dr SLE Std Cab Stepside SB	9480	11425
2 Dr SLE Ext Cab Stepside SB	9915	11945
2 Dr SLE 4WD Std Cab SB	12410	14950
2 Dr SLE 4WD Ext Cab Stepside SB	13940	16795
2 Dr SLE 4WD Std Cab Stepside SB	12620	15205
2 Dr SLS Sport Ext Cab SB	9045	10895
2 Dr SLS Sport Std Cab SB	8490	10230
2 Dr SLS Sport Ext Cab Stepside SB	9115	10980
2 Dr SLS Sport Std Cab Stepside SB	8845	10655
2 Dr SLS Sport Std Cab LB	8825	10630
2 Dr SLS Sport 4WD Std Cab SB	12115	14595
2 Dr SLS Sport 4WD Ext Cab Stepside SB	12660	15250
2 Dr SLS Sport 4WD Std Cab Stepside SB	12585	15160
2 Dr SLS Sport 4WD Std Cab LB	12220	14720

OPTIONS FOR SONOMA

6 cyl 4.3 L Engine +510
6 cyl 4.3 L Vortec Engine +675
Auto 4-Speed Transmission +725
Highrider Suspension Package +1185
Air Conditioning +550
Aluminum/Alloy Wheels[Std on SLE] +235
AM/FM Compact Disc Playr +260
AM/FM Stereo Tape +165
Cruise Control +145
Power Door Locks +155
Power Windows +160
Tilt Steering Wheel +115
Tutone Paint[Opt on SLS Sport] +180

SUBURBAN 1997

GMC has added a passenger side airbag and a power lock switch in the cargo compartment. SLE and SLT trim now includes rear heat and air conditioning, as well as remote keyless entry. Uplevel SLT trim also includes a combination CD and cassette player stereo system. All Suburbans receive speed-sensitive power steering, and 4WD models have a tighter turning circle. Two new colors freshen the dated exterior design this year.

RATINGS (SCALE OF 1-10)

Overall	Safety	Reliability	Performance	Comfort	Value
7.7	8.1	8	7.2	7.9	7.4

Don't forget to refer to the Mileage Adjustment Table at the back of this book!

© 1999 by Edmund Publications Corporation

Model Description	Trade-in Value	Market Value
Category H		
4 Dr C1500 Wgn	18870	22465
4 Dr C2500 Wgn	20795	24755
4 Dr K1500 4WD Wgn	20590	24510
4 Dr K2500 4WD Wgn	21300	25355

OPTIONS FOR SUBURBAN

8 cyl 7.4 L Engine +410
8 cyl 6.5 L Turbodsl Engine +2075
Folding Center/Rear Seats +805
SLE Package +2260
SLT Package +2460
Air Conditioning +550
Aluminum/Alloy Wheels +210
Camper/Towing Package +240
Compact Disc W/fm/tape +215
Cruise Control +130
Dual Air Conditioning +965
Keyless Entry System +110
Leather Seats +700
Luggage Rack +90
Power Drivers Seat +185
Power Windows +130
Running Boards +200
Skid Plates +75

YUKON 1997

Dual airbags, speed-sensitive steering and a tighter turning circle for 4WD models. A power lock switch is added to the cargo compartment, and SLT models have a standard CD/cassette combo stereo. Remote keyless entry is standard on four-door models, and on SLE and SLT two-door models. Newly optional on four-door models is a rear air conditioning unit.

RATINGS (SCALE OF 1-10)

Overall	Safety	Reliability	Performance	Comfort	Value
7.8	7.8	8.4	7.4	8	7.4

Model Description	Trade-in Value	Market Value
Category H		
2 Dr SL Utility	17210	20485
2 Dr SL 4WD Utility	18680	22240
2 Dr SLE Utility	19460	23165
2 Dr SLE 4WD Utility	20940	24930
4 Dr SLE Wgn	21015	25015
4 Dr SLE 4WD Wgn	22560	26855
2 Dr SLT Utility	20575	24495
2 Dr SLT 4WD Utility	21975	26160
4 Dr SLT Wgn	22160	26380
4 Dr SLT 4WD Wgn	23930	28490

OPTIONS FOR YUKON

8 cyl 6.5 L Turbodsl Engine +2075
Air Conditioning[Opt on SL] +550
Aluminum/Alloy Wheels[Opt on SL] +210
Camper/Towing Package +240
Compact Disc W/fm/tape[Std on SLT] +215
Cruise Control[Opt on SL] +130
Dual Air Conditioning +965
Keyless Entry System[Opt on SL,SLE] +110
Power Drivers Seat[Std on SLT] +185
Running Boards +200
Skid Plates +75

1996 GMC

C/K PICKUP 1996

Extended cab models get a trick new side-access panel on the passenger side of the truck. Engines are dramatically improved across the board, daytime running lights debut, and long-life engine coolant gets changed about the same time you make your last payment. Spark plugs last 100,000 miles. Passenger car tires on 1500 models improve the ride and make the Sierra quieter. Heat ducts keep rear passengers' tootsies warm on extended cab models. Four-wheel drive models get optional electronic shift-on-the-fly, and illuminated entry is a nice new touch.

RATINGS (SCALE OF 1-10)

Overall	Safety	Reliability	Performance	Comfort	Value
N/A	7.7	8.5	7.8	8.4	N/A

C1500

Model Description	Trade-in Value	Market Value
Category H		
2 Dr SL Ext Cab SB	11270	13580
2 Dr SL Std Cab SB	11000	13255
2 Dr SL Ext Cab Stepside SB	11580	13950
2 Dr SL Std Cab Stepside SB	11410	13750
2 Dr SL Std Cab LB	11100	13370
2 Dr SL Ext Cab LB	11485	13840
2 Dr SLE Std Cab SB	11985	14440
2 Dr SLE Ext Cab SB	12180	14675
2 Dr SLE Ext Cab Stepside SB	12710	15310
2 Dr SLE Std Cab Stepside SB	12480	15035
2 Dr SLE Ext Cab LB	12260	14770
2 Dr SLE Std Cab LB	12080	14555
2 Dr SLT Std Cab SB	13000	15660
2 Dr SLT Ext Cab SB	13195	15900
2 Dr SLT Std Cab Stepside SB	13515	16285
2 Dr SLT Ext Cab Stepside SB	13775	16595
2 Dr SLT Ext Cab LB	13300	16025
2 Dr SLT Std Cab LB	13070	15745
2 Dr Special Std Cab SB	10475	12620
2 Dr Special Std Cab LB	10445	12585

C2500

Model Description	Trade-in Value	Market Value
Category H		
2 Dr SL Ext Cab SB	13155	15850
2 Dr SL Std Cab LB	12550	15120
2 Dr SL Ext Cab LB	13100	15785
2 Dr SLE Ext Cab SB	13525	16295

Don't forget to refer to the Mileage Adjustment Table at the back of this book!

 © 1999 by Edmund Publications Corporation

Model Description	Trade-in Value	Market Value
2 Dr SLE Std Cab LB	13195	15900
2 Dr SLE Ext Cab LB	13525	16295
2 Dr SLT Ext Cab SB	15070	18155
2 Dr SLT Std Cab LB	14860	17905

C3500

Category H

Model Description	Trade-in Value	Market Value
2 Dr SL Ext Cab LB	15620	18820
4 Dr SL Crew Cab LB	17055	20550
2 Dr SLE Ext Cab LB	16785	20225
4 Dr SLE Crew Cab LB	18095	21800
2 Dr SLT Ext Cab LB	17295	20840
4 Dr SLT Crew Cab LB	18905	22775

K1500

Category H

Model Description	Trade-in Value	Market Value
2 Dr SL 4WD Ext Cab SB	12760	15375
2 Dr SL 4WD Std Cab SB	12025	14485
2 Dr SL 4WD Ext Cab Stepside SB	13285	16005
2 Dr SL 4WD Std Cab Stepside SB	12540	15110
2 Dr SL 4WD Ext Cab LB	13080	15760
2 Dr SL 4WD Std Cab LB	12050	14520
2 Dr SLE 4WD Ext Cab SB	13990	16855
2 Dr SLE 4WD Std Cab SB	13625	16415
2 Dr SLE 4WD Std Cab Stepside SB	14140	17035
2 Dr SLE 4WD Ext Cab Stepside SB	14620	17615
2 Dr SLE 4WD Ext Cab LB	14170	17070
2 Dr SLE 4WD Std Cab LB	13650	16445
2 Dr SLT 4WD Std Cab SB	14315	17245
2 Dr SLT 4WD Ext Cab SB	14910	17965
2 Dr SLT 4WD Std Cab Stepside SB	14830	17865
2 Dr SLT 4WD Ext Cab Stepside SB	15440	18600
2 Dr SLT 4WD Std Cab LB	14345	17285
2 Dr SLT 4WD Ext Cab LB	15090	18180
2 Dr Special 4WD Std Cab SB	11740	14145
2 Dr Special 4WD Std Cab LB	11780	14190

K2500

Category H

Model Description	Trade-in Value	Market Value
2 Dr SL 4WD Ext Cab SB	15015	18090
2 Dr SL 4WD Std Cab LB	14530	17505
2 Dr SL 4WD Ext Cab LB	15065	18155
2 Dr SLE 4WD Ext Cab SB	15365	18515
2 Dr SLE 4WD Std Cab LB	15540	18720
2 Dr SLE 4WD Ext Cab LB	15915	19175
2 Dr SLT 4WD Std Cab LB	16170	19480
2 Dr SLT 4WD Ext Cab LB	16345	19695

K3500

Category H

Model Description	Trade-in Value	Market Value
2 Dr SL 4WD Ext Cab LB	17940	21615
2 Dr SL 4WD Std Cab LB	16795	20235
4 Dr SL 4WD Crew Cab LB	18425	22200
2 Dr SLE 4WD Ext Cab LB	18935	22815
2 Dr SLE 4WD Std Cab LB	17830	21480
4 Dr SLE 4WD Crew Cab LB	19420	23395
2 Dr SLT 4WD Ext Cab LB	19710	23745
2 Dr SLT 4WD Std Cab LB	18490	22275
4 Dr SLT 4WD Crew Cab LB	20175	24305

OPTIONS FOR C/K PICKUP

8 cyl 5.0 L Engine +310
8 cyl 5.7 L Engine +560
8 cyl 7.4 L Engine +335
8 cyl 6.5 L Turbodsl Engine +1810
Auto 4-Speed Transmission +530
Air Conditioning[Std on SLE,SLT] +450
Aluminum/Alloy Wheels[Std on SLT] +175
Bed Liner +125
Camper/Towing Package +195
Chrome Bumpers[Opt on SL] +95
Chrome Wheels +165
Compact Disc W/fm/tape +175
Cruise Control[Std on SLE,SLT] +105
Dual Rear Wheels +470
Hinged Third Door (PU) +235
Keyless Entry System[Opt on SLE] +90
Locking Differential +140
Power Door Locks[Opt on SL] +105
Power Drivers Seat[Opt on SLE] +150
Rear Step Bumper +85
Skid Plates +60

JIMMY 1996

GMC's popular compact sport utility gets a super-duper optional off-road package called Highrider, as well as an available five-speed transmission. Either of these are available on two-door models only. All Jimmys receive glow-in-the-day headlights and long-life engine coolant. Spark plugs last 100,000 miles. All-wheel drive, which became optional in mid-1995, continues. Conspicuously absent is a passenger airbag.

RATINGS (SCALE OF 1-10)

Overall	Safety	Reliability	Performance	Comfort	Value
6.9	5.3	7.3	8	7.9	5.8

Category G

Model Description	Trade-in Value	Market Value
2 Dr SL Utility	10855	13570
4 Dr SL Wgn	11625	14530
4 Dr SL 4WD Wgn	12770	15960
4 Dr SLE Wgn	12740	15925

Don't forget to refer to the Mileage Adjustment Table at the back of this book!

 © 1999 by Edmund Publications Corporation

Model Description	Trade-in Value	Market Value
4 Dr SLE 4WD Wgn	13700	17120
2 Dr SLS Utility	11660	14575
2 Dr SLS 4WD Utility	12365	15455
4 Dr SLS Wgn	12605	15755
4 Dr SLS 4WD Wgn	13615	17020
4 Dr SLT Wgn	13230	16535
4 Dr SLT 4WD Wgn	14190	17735
2 Dr STD Utility	10710	13390
2 Dr STD 4WD Utility	10795	13495
4 Dr STD Wgn	11300	14125
4 Dr STD 4WD Wgn	12075	15095

OPTIONS FOR JIMMY

Aluminum/Alloy Wheels[Opt on SL,STD] +190
AM/FM Compact Disc Playr +215
Camper/Towing Package +160
Cruise Control[Opt on STD] +115
Keyless Entry System[Std on SLT] +115
Limited Slip Diff +145
Luggage Rack[Opt on STD] +85
Power Door Locks[Opt on STD] +125
Power Drivers Seat[Std on SLT] +155
Power Windows[Opt on STD] +130
Premium Sound System[Std on SLT] +200
Skid Plates +75
Swing Out Tire Carrier +115

SAFARI 1996

An all-new interior debuts with dual airbags, more leg and foot room, and a host of other features. Important among them are the availability of dual integrated child seats and a child-proof lock on the right side sliding door. Under seat heat ducts help warm the rear passengers, and new audio systems include a radio that can be tuned independently by rear seat passengers without disturbing the listening pleasure, or program, that the front occupants are enjoying.

RATINGS (SCALE OF 1-10)

Overall	Safety	Reliability	Performance	Comfort	Value
7.2	6.9	7.5	6.8	6.5	8.5

Category G

Model Description	Trade-in Value	Market Value
2 Dr SL Cargo Van Ext	10095	12620
2 Dr SL 4WD Cargo Van Ext	12450	15560
2 Dr SLE Pass. Van Ext	10850	13560
2 Dr SLE 4WD Pass. Van Ext	13380	16725
2 Dr SLT Pass. Van Ext	12345	15430
2 Dr SLT 4WD Pass. Van Ext	14090	17610
2 Dr SLX Pass. Van Ext	10635	13290
2 Dr SLX 4WD Pass. Van Ext	12530	15665
2 Dr STD Pass. Van Ext	10560	13195
2 Dr STD 4WD Pass. Van Ext	12405	15510

OPTIONS FOR SAFARI

Aluminum/Alloy Wheels[Std on SLT] +190
Camper/Towing Package +160
Chrome Wheels +135
Compact Disc W/fm/tape +380
Cruise Control[Opt on SL] +115
Dual Air Conditioning +560
Keyless Entry System[Opt on SLE] +115
Luggage Rack[Std on SLT] +85
Power Door Locks[Opt on SL,STD] +125
Power Drivers Seat[Std on SLT] +155
Power Passenger Seat +150
Power Windows[Opt on SL] +130

SAVANA 1996

G15

Category H

Model Description	Trade-in Value	Market Value
2 Dr STD Pass. Van	15560	18750
2 Dr STD Cargo Van	15095	18190

OPTIONS FOR SAVANA

8 cyl 5.0 L Engine +310
8 cyl 5.7 L Engine[Std on G35 Savana,G25 Savana] +560
Air Conditioning[Opt on Cargo Van,Cargo Van Ext] +450
Aluminum/Alloy Wheels +175
Camper/Towing Package +195
Chrome Bumpers +95
Compact Disc W/fm/tape +175
Cruise Control +105
Dual Air Conditioning +790
Power Door Locks +105
Power Drivers Seat +150
Power Passenger Seat +140
Power Windows +105

SONOMA 1996

Extended cab models get an optional driver's side rear access panel. All Sonomas are now equipped with four-wheel ABS. A new sport suspension turns the Sonoma into a Miata with a big trunk (so long as you provide an aftermarket sunroof), and a snazzy Sportside box ends Ford's reign as lord of compact stepsides. A new five-speed transmission improves shifter location and operation when equipped with the base four-cylinder. Still missing is the availability of a passenger airbag.

RATINGS (SCALE OF 1-10)

Overall	Safety	Reliability	Performance	Comfort	Value
N/A	4.8	7	6.6	8.1	N/A

Category G

Model Description	Trade-in Value	Market Value
2 Dr SL Std Cab SB	7095	8870
2 Dr SL Std Cab LB	7180	8975
2 Dr SL 4WD Std Cab SB	10060	12575
2 Dr SL 4WD Std Cab LB	10145	12680
2 Dr SLE Ext Cab SB	8080	10095
2 Dr SLE Std Cab SB	7430	9285
2 Dr SLE Ext Cab Stepside SB	8080	10095

Don't forget to refer to the Mileage Adjustment Table at the back of this book!

 © 1999 by Edmund Publications Corporation

Model Description	Trade-in Value	Market Value
2 Dr SLE 4WD Std Cab SB	10575	13220
2 Dr SLE 4WD Ext Cab SB	11090	13860
2 Dr SLE 4WD Ext Cab Stepside SB	11080	13855
2 Dr SLS Sport Std Cab SB	7115	8895
2 Dr SLS Sport Ext Cab SB	7710	9635
2 Dr SLS Sport Ext Cab Stepside SB	7525	9405
2 Dr SLS Sport Std Cab Stepside SB	7115	8895
2 Dr SLS Sport Std Cab LB	7205	9005
2 Dr SLS Sport 4WD Std Cab SB	10075	12590
2 Dr SLS Sport 4WD Ext Cab SB	10545	13185
2 Dr SLS Sport 4WD Std Cab Stepside SB	10105	12630
2 Dr SLS Sport 4WD Ext Cab Stepside SB	10540	13175
2 Dr SLS Sport 4WD Std Cab LB	10160	12705

OPTIONS FOR SONOMA

6 cyl 4.3 L Engine +420
6 cyl 4.3 L Vortec Engine +540
Auto 4-Speed Transmission +585
Highrider Suspension Package +940
Air Conditioning +450
Aluminum/Alloy Wheels[Std on SLE] +190
AM/FM Compact Disc Playr +215
Camper/Towing Package +160
Cruise Control +115
Hinged Third Door (PU) +195
Keyless Entry System +115
Limited Slip Diff +145
Power Door Locks +125
Power Windows +130
Premium Sound System +200
Skid Plates +75
Tutone Paint[Opt on SLS Sport] +145

SUBURBAN 1996

Giant SUV gets daytime running lights to make it more visible to other drivers. This is akin to installing field lighting on the bow of the Queen Mary. New V8s, quieter tires, and long-life spark plugs and coolant make the Suburban more satisfying to skipper. Rear passengers get warmer faster, thanks to new rear-seat heat ducting. Illuminated entry is newly standard, and electronic 4WD controls are a new option.

RATINGS (SCALE OF 1-10)

Overall	Safety	Reliability	Performance	Comfort	Value
7.5	6.8	7.7	7.2	7.9	7.8

Model Description	Trade-in Value	Market Value
Category H		
4 Dr C1500 Wgn	17190	20715
4 Dr C2500 Wgn	18360	22120
4 Dr K1500 4WD Wgn	18770	22610
4 Dr K2500 4WD Wgn	19915	23990

OPTIONS FOR SUBURBAN

8 cyl 7.4 L Engine +335
8 cyl 6.5 L Turbodsl Engine +1810
Folding Center/Rear Seats +645
SLE Package +1360
SLT Package +1850
Air Conditioning +450
Camper/Towing Package[Std on C2500] +195
Compact Disc W/fm/tape +175
Cruise Control +105
Dual Air Conditioning +790
Keyless Entry System +90
Leather Seats +575
Luggage Rack +75
Power Door Locks +105
Power Drivers Seat +150
Power Windows +105
Skid Plates +60

VANDURA/RALLY WAGON 1996

G35

Model Description	Trade-in Value	Market Value
Category H		
2 Dr STD Vandura	10810	13020
2 Dr STD Vandura Ext	11430	13770
2 Dr STD Rally Wagon Ext	12675	15270
2 Dr STD Rally Wagon	12090	14570
2 Dr STX Rally Wagon Ext	13730	16540
2 Dr STX Rally Wagon	13145	15840

OPTIONS FOR VANDURA/RALLY WAGON

8 cyl 6.5 L Dsl Engine +905
8 cyl 7.4 L Engine +335
Air Conditioning[Opt on STD] +450
AM/FM Compact Disc Playr +165
Camper/Towing Package +195
Chrome Bumpers[Opt on Vandura, Vandura Ext] +95
Cruise Control[Opt on STD] +105
Dual Air Conditioning +790
Keyless Entry System +90
Power Door Locks[Opt on STD] +105
Power Windows[Opt on STD] +105
Premium Sound System +225

YUKON 1996

Just what we need: a two-wheel drive two-door Yukon. A new 5700 Vortec V8 gets long-life coolant and spark plugs, as well as a hefty bump in power and torque. Passenger car tires on less stout Yukons result in a softer, quieter ride. Rear heat ducts, illuminated entry, and height-adjustable seat belts debut. Four-wheel drive models get a newly optional electronic shift mechanism.

Don't forget to refer to the Mileage Adjustment Table at the back of this book!

 © 1999 by Edmund Publications Corporation

Model Description	Trade-in Value	Market Value

RATINGS (SCALE OF 1-10)

Overall	Safety	Reliability	Performance	Comfort	Value
7.6	6.9	8	7.4	8	7.8

Category H

Model Description	Trade-in Value	Market Value
2 Dr SL Utility	16455	19825
2 Dr SL 4WD Utility	17725	21355
2 Dr SLE Utility	16785	20220
2 Dr SLE 4WD Utility	17925	21595
4 Dr SLE Wgn	21080	25400
4 Dr SLE 4WD Wgn	22495	27105
2 Dr SLT Utility	17630	21240
2 Dr SLT 4WD Utility	18980	22870
4 Dr SLT Wgn	21550	25965
4 Dr SLT 4WD Wgn	23020	27735

OPTIONS FOR YUKON

8 cyl 6.5 L Turbodsl Engine +1810
Air Conditioning[Opt on SL] +450
Aluminum/Alloy Wheels[Opt on SL] +175
Camper/Towing Package +195
Compact Disc W/fm/tape +175
Cruise Control[Opt on SL] +105
Keyless Entry System[Opt on SL,SLE] +90
Power Drivers Seat[Opt on SLE, SLT] +150
Rear Window Defroster[Opt on SL] +85
Running Boards +165
Skid Plates +60

1995 GMC

C/K PICKUP 1995

New interior with driver airbag (models under 8,500 lb. GVWR) and standard four-wheel ABS debut. Sport package is dropped. New dashboard features modular design with controls that are much easier to read and use. Power mirrors and remote keyless entry are new options. Uplevel radios come with automatic volume controls that raise or lower volume depending on vehicle speed.

RATINGS (SCALE OF 1-10)

Overall	Safety	Reliability	Performance	Comfort	Value
N/A	8.5	8.5	7.6	8.4	N/A

C1500

Category H

Model Description	Trade-in Value	Market Value
2 Dr SL Std Cab SB	9550	11790
2 Dr SL Ext Cab SB	9780	12075
2 Dr SL Std Cab Stepside SB	10120	12490
2 Dr SL Ext Cab Stepside SB	10240	12640
2 Dr SL Std Cab LB	10070	12430
2 Dr SL Ext Cab LB	10155	12535
2 Dr SLE Ext Cab SB	10900	13460
2 Dr SLE Std Cab SB	10710	13225
2 Dr SLE Std Cab Stepside SB	11135	13745
2 Dr SLE Ext Cab Stepside SB	11270	13915
2 Dr SLE Ext Cab LB	10965	13535
2 Dr SLE Std Cab LB	10920	13485
2 Dr SLT Ext Cab SB	11550	14260
2 Dr SLT Ext Cab Stepside SB	11925	14725
2 Dr SLT Ext Cab LB	11620	14350
2 Dr Special Std Cab SB	7740	9560
2 Dr Special Std Cab LB	7815	9650

C2500

Category H

Model Description	Trade-in Value	Market Value
2 Dr SL Ext Cab SB	10895	13450
2 Dr SL Ext Cab LB	10820	13355
2 Dr SL Std Cab LB	10475	12930
2 Dr SLE Ext Cab SB	11910	14705
2 Dr SLE Ext Cab LB	12260	15135
2 Dr SLE Std Cab LB	11545	14255
2 Dr SLT Ext Cab SB	12770	15765
2 Dr SLT Ext Cab LB	12845	15855

C3500

Category H

Model Description	Trade-in Value	Market Value
2 Dr SL Std Cab LB	13530	16705
2 Dr SL Ext Cab LB	13755	16980
4 Dr SL Crew Cab LB	15575	19230
2 Dr SLE Std Cab LB	14190	17520
2 Dr SLE Ext Cab LB	14410	17790
4 Dr SLE Crew Cab LB	17035	21030
2 Dr SLT Ext Cab LB	15095	18635

K1500

Category H

Model Description	Trade-in Value	Market Value
2 Dr SL 4WD Std Cab SB	11195	13820
2 Dr SL 4WD Ext Cab SB	11900	14695
2 Dr SL 4WD Std Cab Stepside SB	11720	14470
2 Dr SL 4WD Ext Cab Stepside SB	12300	15185
2 Dr SL 4WD Ext Cab LB	11980	14790
2 Dr SL 4WD Std Cab LB	11185	13810
2 Dr SLE 4WD Ext Cab SB	12470	15390
2 Dr SLE 4WD Std Cab SB	12120	14960
2 Dr SLE 4WD Ext Cab Stepside SB	12855	15875
2 Dr SLE 4WD Std Cab Stepside SB	12750	15740
2 Dr SLE 4WD Std Cab LB	12210	15070
2 Dr SLE 4WD Ext Cab LB	12535	15475
2 Dr SLS 4WD Ext Cab SB	11980	14790
2 Dr SLS 4WD Ext Cab Stepside SB	12435	15350
2 Dr SLT 4WD Ext Cab SB	13115	16195

Don't forget to refer to the Mileage Adjustment Table at the back of this book!

 © 1999 by Edmund Publications Corporation

Model Description	Trade-in Value	Market Value
2 Dr SLT 4WD Ext Cab Stepside SB	13515	16685
2 Dr SLT 4WD Ext Cab LB	13195	16295
2 Dr Special 4WD Std Cab SB	9125	11265
2 Dr Special 4WD Std Cab LB	9220	11380

K2500

Category H

Model Description	Trade-in Value	Market Value
2 Dr SL 4WD Ext Cab SB	11975	14780
2 Dr SL 4WD Ext Cab LB	12035	14860
2 Dr SL 4WD Std Cab LB	11400	14075
2 Dr SLE 4WD Ext Cab SB	12675	15650
2 Dr SLE 4WD Ext Cab LB	13020	16075
2 Dr SLE 4WD Std Cab LB	12430	15345
2 Dr SLT 4WD Ext Cab SB	13305	16430
2 Dr SLT 4WD Ext Cab LB	13650	16850

K3500

Category H

Model Description	Trade-in Value	Market Value
2 Dr SL 4WD Ext Cab LB	14490	17890
2 Dr SL 4WD Std Cab LB	12370	15275
4 Dr SL 4WD Crew Cab LB	14730	18185
2 Dr SLE 4WD Std Cab LB	13135	16220
2 Dr SLE 4WD Ext Cab LB	15210	18780
4 Dr SLE 4WD Crew Cab LB	15515	19155
2 Dr SLT 4WD Ext Cab LB	15690	19370

OPTIONS FOR C/K PICKUP

8 cyl 5.0 L Engine +270
8 cyl 5.7 L Engine +335
8 cyl 7.4 L Engine +245
8 cyl 6.5 L Turbodsl Engine +1430
Auto 4-Speed Transmission +415
Air Conditioning[Std on SLE , SLT] +365
Bed Liner +100
Camper/Towing Package +160
Chrome Bumpers[Opt on C1500,K1500] +75
Chrome Wheels +135
Compact Disc W/fm/tape +145
Cruise Control[Std on SLE,SLT] +90
Dual Rear Wheels +380
Keyless Entry System[Opt on SL,SLE] +70
Limited Slip Diff +115
Locking Differential +115
Power Door Locks[Std on SLE,SLT] +85
Power Drivers Seat[Opt on SLE] +125
Premium Sound System +185
Rear Step Bumper +70
Skid Plates +50

JIMMY 1995

All-new SUV appears based on revamped Sonoma. Four-wheel drive models have electronic transfer case as standard equipment. Spare tire on four-door model is mounted beneath cargo bay instead of in it. Five different suspension packages are available. One engine, a 195-horsepower 4.3-liter V6, is available. All-wheel drive is optional. Driver airbag and air conditioning are standard equipment.

RATINGS (SCALE OF 1-10)

Overall	Safety	Reliability	Performance	Comfort	Value
6.9	5.6	6.9	8	7.9	6.1

Category G

Model Description	Trade-in Value	Market Value
2 Dr SL Utility	9900	12530
2 Dr SL 4WD Utility	10465	13250
4 Dr SLE Wgn	11210	14190
4 Dr SLE 4WD Wgn	11535	14600
2 Dr SLS Utility	10640	13465
2 Dr SLS 4WD Utility	11345	14365
4 Dr SLS Wgn	10925	13830
4 Dr SLS 4WD Wgn	11445	14485
4 Dr SLT Wgn	12085	15295
4 Dr SLT 4WD Wgn	12210	15455
2 Dr STD Utility	9350	11835
2 Dr STD 4WD Utility	9865	12485
4 Dr STD Wgn	9925	12565
4 Dr STD 4WD Wgn	10295	13030

OPTIONS FOR JIMMY

AM/FM Compact Disc Playr +175
Camper/Towing Package +130
Cruise Control[Opt on STD] +95
Keyless Entry System[Std on SLT] +95
Limited Slip Diff +120
Luggage Rack[Opt on STD] +70
Power Door Locks[Opt on STD] +105
Power Drivers Seat[Std on SLT] +130
Power Windows[Opt on STD] +105
Premium Sound System[Std on SLT Wgn] +165
Skid Plates +65
Swing Out Tire Carrier +95

SAFARI 1995

Front sheetmetal is restyled. Regular-length versions are dropped from the lineup, leaving only the extended model. Multileaf steel springs replace single-leaf plastic springs. One engine is available, the 190-horsepower 4.3-liter V6. Air conditioning is newly standard, and remote keyless entry is a new option.

RATINGS (SCALE OF 1-10)

Overall	Safety	Reliability	Performance	Comfort	Value
7.3	6.1	7.4	7.2	6.6	9

Category G

Model Description	Trade-in Value	Market Value
2 Dr SL Cargo Van Ext	8115	10270
2 Dr SL 4WD Cargo Van Ext	8600	10885
2 Dr SLE Pass. Van Ext	9015	11410
2 Dr SLE 4WD Pass. Van Ext	9850	12470
2 Dr SLT Pass. Van Ext	9720	12300

Don't forget to refer to the Mileage Adjustment Table at the back of this book!

 © 1999 by Edmund Publications Corporation

Model Description	Trade-in Value	Market Value
2 Dr SLT 4WD Pass. Van Ext	10520	13315
2 Dr SLX Pass. Van Ext	8475	10730
2 Dr SLX 4WD Pass. Van Ext	9380	11875
2 Dr STD Pass. Van Ext	8345	10565
2 Dr STD 4WD Pass. Van Ext	9220	11670

OPTIONS FOR SAFARI

AM/FM Compact Disc Playr +175
Camper/Towing Package +130
Cruise Control[Opt on SL] +95
Dual Air Conditioning +460
Keyless Entry System[Std on SLT] +95
Limited Slip Diff +120
Luggage Rack +70
Power Door Locks[Std on SLE,SLT] +105
Power Drivers Seat +130
Power Windows[Std on SLT] +105
Premium Sound System +165

SONOMA 1995

Driver airbag is added, and daytime running lights are standard. Highrider off-road package can be ordered on the Club Coupe. Power window and lock buttons are illuminated at night. Remote keyless entry is a new option. A single key operates both the door locks and the ignition. A manual transmission can now be ordered with the 191-horsepower 4.3-liter V6.

RATINGS (SCALE OF 1-10)

Overall	Safety	Reliability	Performance	Comfort	Value
N/A	4.9	7.1	6.6	8.1	N/A

Category G

Model Description	Trade-in Value	Market Value
2 Dr SL Std Cab SB	6235	7895
2 Dr SL Std Cab LB	6190	7835
2 Dr SL 4WD Std Cab SB	8525	10790
2 Dr SL 4WD Std Cab LB	8300	10510
2 Dr SLE Std Cab SB	6960	8810
2 Dr SLE Ext Cab SB	7230	9150
2 Dr SLE 4WD Ext Cab SB	9450	11960
2 Dr SLE 4WD Std Cab SB	9230	11685
2 Dr SLS Ext Cab SB	6740	8535
2 Dr SLS Std Cab SB	6695	8470
2 Dr SLS Std Cab LB	6635	8395
2 Dr SLS 4WD Ext Cab SB	9025	11425
2 Dr SLS 4WD Std Cab SB	8940	11315
2 Dr SLS 4WD Std Cab LB	8795	11135

OPTIONS FOR SONOMA

6 cyl 4.3 L Engine +375
6 cyl 4.3 L CPI Engine +380
Auto 4-Speed Transmission +450
Highrider Suspension +770
Air Conditioning +370
AM/FM Compact Disc Playr +175
Anti-Lock Brakes[Opt on 2WD] +280
Camper/Towing Package +130
Cruise Control +95
Keyless Entry System +95
Limited Slip Diff +120
Power Door Locks +105
Power Windows +105
Premium Sound System +165
Rear Step Bumper[Opt on SL] +65
Skid Plates +65
Velour/Cloth Seats +80

SUBURBAN 1995

New interior with driver airbag debuts. New dashboard features modular design with controls that are much easier to read and use. 1500 models can now be ordered with turbodiesel engine. Brake/transmission shift interlock is added to automatic transmission. Seats and door panels are revised. New console on models with bucket seats features pivoting writing surface, along with rear cupholders and storage drawer. Uplevel radios come with automatic volume controls that raise or lower the volume depending on vehicle speed.

RATINGS (SCALE OF 1-10)

Overall	Safety	Reliability	Performance	Comfort	Value
7.5	7.5	7.5	7	7.9	7.7

Category H

Model Description	Trade-in Value	Market Value
4 Dr C1500 Wgn	15010	18530
4 Dr C2500 Wgn	15885	19610
4 Dr K1500 4WD Wgn	16635	20535
4 Dr K2500 4WD Wgn	17420	21510

OPTIONS FOR SUBURBAN

8 cyl 7.4 L Engine +245
8 cyl 6.5 L Turbodsl Engine +1430
Folding Center/Rear Seats +530
SLE Package +1485
SLT Package +1850
Air Conditioning +365
Camper/Towing Package[Std on C2500] +160
Compact Disc W/fm/tape +145
Cruise Control +90
Dual Air Conditioning +645
Keyless Entry System +70
Leather Seats +470
Luggage Rack +60
Power Door Locks +85
Power Drivers Seat +125
Power Windows +85
Skid Plates +50

VANDURA/RALLY WAGON 1995

No changes.

G15

Category H

Model Description	Trade-in Value	Market Value
2 Dr STD Vandura	11410	14085
2 Dr STD Vandura Ext	11435	14115

Don't forget to refer to the Mileage Adjustment Table at the back of this book!

 © 1999 by Edmund Publications Corporation

Model Description	Trade-in Value	Market Value
G25		
Category H		
2 Dr STD Vandura Ext	9705	11980
2 Dr STD Rally Wagon	10955	13525
2 Dr STD Vandura	9530	11765
2 Dr STX Rally Wagon	12060	14885
G35		
Category H		
2 Dr STD Rally Wagon Ext	10625	13115
2 Dr STD Vandura	8970	11075
2 Dr STD Vandura Ext	9410	11620
2 Dr STD Rally Wagon	10190	12580
2 Dr STX Rally Wagon	11075	13675
2 Dr STX Rally Wagon Ext	11750	14510

OPTIONS FOR VANDURA/RALLY WAGON

8 cyl 6.5 L Dsl Engine +955
8 cyl 5.0 L Engine +270
8 cyl 5.7 L Engine[Opt on G25] +335
8 cyl 7.4 L Engine +245
Air Conditioning[Std on STX] +365
AM/FM Compact Disc Playr +135
Camper/Towing Package +160
Chrome Bumpers[Opt on G15,Vandura,Vandura Ext] +75
Cruise Control[Std on STX] +90
Dual Air Conditioning +645
Keyless Entry System +70
Limited Slip Diff +115
Power Door Locks[Std on STX] +85
Power Windows[Std on STX] +85
Premium Sound System +185

YUKON 1995

New interior with driver airbag debuts. New dashboard features modular design with controls that are much easier to read and use. New four-door model is added midyear, nicely sized between Jimmy and Suburban. New model is offered only in SLE or SLT trim with a 5.7-liter V8 and an automatic transmission in either 2WD or 4WD. Brake/transmission shift interlock is added to automatic transmission. New console on models with bucket seats features pivoting writing surface, along with rear cupholders and storage drawer.

RATINGS (SCALE OF 1-10)

Overall	Safety	Reliability	Performance	Comfort	Value
7.7	7.6	7.8	7.2	8	7.7

For a guaranteed low price on a new car in your area, call
1-800-CAR-CLUB

Model Description	Trade-in Value	Market Value
Category H		
2 Dr SLE 4WD Utility	16060	19830
4 Dr SLE Wgn	16150	19940
4 Dr SLE 4WD Wgn	19570	24160
2 Dr SLT 4WD Utility	16515	20390
4 Dr SLT Wgn	16720	20645
4 Dr SLT 4WD Wgn	20115	24835
2 Dr STD 4WD Utility	14190	17520

OPTIONS FOR YUKON

8 cyl 6.5 L Turbodsl Engine +1430
Auto 4-Speed Transmission[Std on Wgn] +415
Air Conditioning[Opt on STD] +365
Camper/Towing Package +160
Compact Disc W/fm/tape +145
Cruise Control[Opt on STD] +90
Keyless Entry System[Opt on SLE] +70
Power Door Locks[Opt on STD] +85
Power Drivers Seat[Opt on SLE] +125
Running Boards +135
Skid Plates +50

1994 GMC

C/K PICKUP 1994

Grilles are restyled, side door guard beams are added, and a third brake light is installed. Leather seats are included in new SLT package. Front seatback on Club Coupe models gets memory feature to improve entry and exit to rear seat. A 6.5-liter diesel replaces last year's 6.2-liter unit.

RATINGS (SCALE OF 1-10)

Overall	Safety	Reliability	Performance	Comfort	Value
N/A	6.2	8.1	7.4	8.4	N/A

Model Description	Trade-in Value	Market Value
C1500		
Category H		
2 Dr SL Std Cab SB	8250	10310
2 Dr SL Ext Cab SB	8665	10835
2 Dr SL Std Cab Stepside SB	8590	10740
2 Dr SL Ext Cab Stepside SB	8965	11205
2 Dr SL Std Cab LB	8350	10435
2 Dr SL Ext Cab LB	8980	11225
2 Dr SLE Std Cab SB	8390	10490
2 Dr SLE Ext Cab SB	9100	11375
2 Dr SLE Std Cab Stepside SB	8720	10895
2 Dr SLE Ext Cab Stepside SB	9400	11750
2 Dr SLE Ext Cab LB	9170	11465
2 Dr SLE Std Cab LB	8470	10585
2 Dr SLT Ext Cab SB	9730	12160
2 Dr SLT Ext Cab Stepside SB	9920	12405
2 Dr Special Std Cab SB	6640	8300
2 Dr Special Std Cab LB	6675	8340
2 Dr STD Std Cab SB	7900	9875

Don't forget to refer to the Mileage Adjustment Table at the back of this book!

 © 1999 by Edmund Publications Corporation

Model Description	Trade-in Value	Market Value
2 Dr STD Std Cab Stepside SB	8130	10160
2 Dr STD Ext Cab LB	8715	10890
2 Dr STD Std Cab LB	7875	9845

C2500

Category H

Model Description	Trade-in Value	Market Value
2 Dr SL Ext Cab SB	11220	14025
2 Dr SL Std Cab LB	9265	11580
2 Dr SL Ext Cab LB	11300	14125
2 Dr SLE Ext Cab SB	11755	14695
2 Dr SLE Std Cab LB	9930	12410
2 Dr SLE Ext Cab LB	11835	14795
2 Dr STD Ext Cab SB	10980	13725
2 Dr STD Ext Cab LB	11060	13825
2 Dr STD Std Cab LB	9065	11330

C3500

Category H

Model Description	Trade-in Value	Market Value
2 Dr SL Ext Cab LB	12305	15380
2 Dr SL Std Cab LB	11240	14050
2 Dr SLE Std Cab LB	11725	14655
2 Dr SLE Ext Cab LB	12440	15550
2 Dr STD Std Cab LB	11000	13750
2 Dr STD Ext Cab LB	12065	15080

K1500

Category H

Model Description	Trade-in Value	Market Value
2 Dr SL 4WD Std Cab SB	9930	12415
2 Dr SL 4WD Std Cab Stepside SB	10000	12500
2 Dr SL 4WD Std Cab LB	9500	11880
2 Dr SLE 4WD Ext Cab SB	10580	13225
2 Dr SLE 4WD Std Cab SB	10080	12605
2 Dr SLE 4WD Std Cab Stepside SB	10130	12665
2 Dr SLE 4WD Ext Cab Stepside SB	10880	13595
2 Dr SLE 4WD Ext Cab LB	10650	13315
2 Dr SLE 4WD Std Cab LB	9940	12430
2 Dr SLT 4WD Ext Cab SB	11500	14375
2 Dr SLT 4WD Ext Cab Stepside SB	11905	14880
2 Dr SLT 4WD Ext Cab LB	11605	14510
2 Dr Special 4WD Std Cab SB	7770	9710
2 Dr Special 4WD Std Cab LB	7860	9825
2 Dr STD 4WD Ext Cab SB	10105	12630
2 Dr STD 4WD Std Cab SB	9505	11880
2 Dr STD 4WD Ext Cab Stepside SB	10405	13005
2 Dr STD 4WD Std Cab Stepside SB	9450	11810
2 Dr STD 4WD Ext Cab LB	10225	12785
2 Dr STD 4WD Std Cab LB	9400	11750

K2500

Category H

Model Description	Trade-in Value	Market Value
2 Dr SL 4WD Ext Cab SB	11230	14040
2 Dr SL 4WD Std Cab LB	10575	13220
2 Dr SL 4WD Ext Cab LB	11405	14255
2 Dr SLE 4WD Ext Cab SB	11335	14170
2 Dr SLE 4WD Ext Cab LB	11520	14400
2 Dr SLE 4WD Std Cab LB	10710	13385
2 Dr STD 4WD Ext Cab SB	11095	13870
2 Dr STD 4WD Std Cab LB	10310	12885
2 Dr STD 4WD Ext Cab LB	11165	13955

OPTIONS FOR C/K PICKUP

8 cyl 6.5 L Dsl Engine +975
8 cyl 5.0 L Engine +220
8 cyl 5.7 L Engine +265
8 cyl 7.4 L Engine +210
8 cyl 6.5 L Turbodsl Engine +1185
Auto 4-Speed Transmission +335
Deluxe Two Tone +460
Sport Handling Package +385
Air Conditioning[Std on SLE ,SLT] +300
Aluminum/Alloy Wheels +115
Bed Liner +85
Camper/Towing Package +130
Chrome Bumpers +60
Chrome Wheels +110
Cruise Control[Std on SLT] +70
Dual Rear Wheels[Opt on Crew Cab,Std Cab] +310
Limited Slip Diff +95
Locking Differential +95
Power Door Locks[Std on SLT] +70
Power Drivers Seat[Std on SLT] +100
Power Windows[Std on SLT] +70
Premium Sound System[Std on SLT] +150
Rear Step Bumper +60
Skid Plates +40

S15 JIMMY 1994

Side-door guard beams and a high-mounted center brake light are added. Front bench seat is now standard on four-door models.

RATINGS (SCALE OF 1-10)

Overall	Safety	Reliability	Performance	Comfort	Value
6	5.1	6.6	6.8	7.1	4.6

Category G

Model Description	Trade-in Value	Market Value
2 Dr SLE Utility	7105	9225
2 Dr SLE 4WD Utility	8520	11065
4 Dr SLE Wgn	8115	10540
4 Dr SLE 4WD Wgn	9960	12935
2 Dr SLS Utility	6435	8355
2 Dr SLS 4WD Utility	7695	9995
4 Dr SLS Wgn	7740	10055
4 Dr SLS 4WD Wgn	9650	12530

Don't forget to refer to the Mileage Adjustment Table at the back of this book!

© 1999 by Edmund Publications Corporation

Model Description	Trade-in Value	Market Value
2 Dr SLT Utility	7790	10115
2 Dr SLT 4WD Utility	9070	11780
4 Dr SLT Wgn	8685	11280
4 Dr SLT 4WD Wgn	10510	13650
2 Dr STD Utility	6310	8190
2 Dr STD 4WD Utility	7435	9655
4 Dr STD Wgn	7225	9380
4 Dr STD 4WD Wgn	8340	10830

OPTIONS FOR S15 JIMMY

6 cyl 4.3 L CPI Engine +205
Auto 4-Speed Transmission +335
Air Conditioning[Opt on SLS,STD] +300
AM/FM Compact Disc Playr +145
Camper/Towing Package +105
Cruise Control[Std on SLE ,SLT] +80
Keyless Entry System[Std on SLT] +75
Limited Slip Diff +100
Luggage Rack[Std on SLE,SLT] +60
Power Door Locks[Std on SLT, SLE] +85
Power Drivers Seat[Opt on SLE,SLS,STD] +105
Power Windows[Std on SLT,SLE Wgn] +85
Premium Sound System +135
Skid Plates +50

SAFARI 1994

Driver airbag is made standard. Side-door guard beams are stronger, and air conditioners use CFC-free refrigerant. A high-mount center brake light is added. Analog gauges get new graphics, and carpet is treated with Scotchgard.

RATINGS (SCALE OF 1-10)

Overall	Safety	Reliability	Performance	Comfort	Value
7.3	6	7.3	7.2	6.6	9.3

Category G

Model Description	Trade-in Value	Market Value
2 Dr SLE Pass. Van	6785	8810
2 Dr SLE Pass. Van Ext	7775	10095
2 Dr SLE 4WD Pass. Van Ext	8185	10630
2 Dr SLT Pass. Van	7260	9430
2 Dr SLT 4WD Pass. Van Ext	8695	11290
2 Dr SLX Pass. Van	6580	8545
2 Dr SLX Pass. Van Ext	7260	9430
2 Dr STD Pass. Van Ext	7015	9110
2 Dr STD Cargo Van Ext	6065	7875
2 Dr STD Cargo Van	5500	7145
2 Dr STD Pass. Van	6400	8310
2 Dr STD 4WD Pass. Van	7090	9205
2 Dr STD 4WD Cargo Van	6570	8530
2 Dr STD 4WD Cargo Van Ext	7165	9305
2 Dr STD 4WD Pass. Van Ext	7800	10130

OPTIONS FOR SAFARI

6 cyl 4.3 L CPI Engine[Std on 4WD] +205
Air Conditioning +300
AM/FM Compact Disc Playr +145
Camper/Towing Package +105
Chrome Bumpers +60
Cruise Control[Std on SLT] +80
Dual Air Conditioning +375
Keyless Entry System +75
Limited Slip Diff +100
Luggage Rack[Std on SLT Pass. Van] +60
Power Drivers Seat +105
Power Windows[Std on SLT] +85
Premium Sound System +135

SONOMA 1994

All-new truck debuts with more powerful engines and available four-wheel ABS. Side-door guard beams are standard. Rear ABS is standard on four-cylinder models; V6 trucks get the new four-wheel ABS system that works in both two- and four-wheel drive. Highrider package is for serious off-roaders. Available only on regular-cab shortbed models, the Highrider includes four-inch wider track, three-inch height increase, off-road suspension and tires, wheel flares, and thick skid plates. Base engine is 118-horse 2.2-liter four cylinder. Standard on 4WD models is a 165-horsepower 4.3-liter V6. Optional on all models is a 195-horsepower high output 4.3-liter V6.

RATINGS (SCALE OF 1-10)

Overall	Safety	Reliability	Performance	Comfort	Value
N/A	4.9	6.9	6.6	8.1	N/A

Category G

Model Description	Trade-in Value	Market Value
2 Dr SL Std Cab SB	5315	6905
2 Dr SL Std Cab LB	5225	6785
2 Dr SL 4WD Std Cab SB	7340	9530
2 Dr SL 4WD Std Cab LB	7165	9305
2 Dr SLE Std Cab SB	5660	7350
2 Dr SLE Ext Cab SB	6000	7795
2 Dr SLE Std Cab LB	5535	7190
2 Dr SLE 4WD Std Cab LB	7730	10040
2 Dr SLS Ext Cab SB	5960	7740
2 Dr SLS Std Cab SB	5645	7335
2 Dr SLS 4WD Std Cab SB	7440	9660
2 Dr SLS 4WD Ext Cab SB	7805	10135

OPTIONS FOR SONOMA

6 cyl 4.3 L Engine +205
6 cyl 4.3 L CPI Engine +315
Auto 4-Speed Transmission +345
Air Conditioning +300
Aluminum/Alloy Wheels +130
AM/FM Compact Disc Playr +145
Anti-Lock Brakes[Opt on 2WD] +230
Camper/Towing Package +105
Cruise Control +80
Limited Slip Diff +100
Power Door Locks +85

Don't forget to refer to the Mileage Adjustment Table at the back of this book!

 © 1999 by Edmund Publications Corporation

Model Description	Trade-in Value	Market Value

Power Windows +85
Premium Sound System +135
Skid Plates +50

SUBURBAN 1994

Side-door guard beams are added, as well as a high-mounted center brake light. A turbocharged diesel is newly optional on 2500 models. A new grille appears.

RATINGS (SCALE OF 1-10)

Overall	Safety	Reliability	Performance	Comfort	Value
6.9	6.5	7.3	7	7.5	6.3

Category H

Model Description	Trade-in Value	Market Value
4 Dr C1500 Wgn	12595	15745
4 Dr C2500 Wgn	13295	16615
4 Dr K1500 4WD Wgn	14335	17915
4 Dr K2500 4WD Wgn	15220	19025

OPTIONS FOR SUBURBAN

8 cyl 7.4 L Engine +210
8 cyl 6.5 L Turbodsl Engine +1185
SLE Decor Group +670
Air Conditioning +300
AM/FM Stereo Tape +90
Camper/Towing Package +130
Cruise Control +70
Dual Air Conditioning +525
Leather Seats +385
Limited Slip Diff +95
Luggage Rack +50
Power Door Locks +70
Power Drivers Seat +100
Power Mirrors +35
Power Windows +70
Premium Sound System +150
Skid Plates +40

VANDURA/RALLY WAGON 1994

Driver airbag is added to all models under 8,500 lb. GVWR. Side-door guard beams are installed in front doors and a high-mounted center brake light is added.

G15

Category H

Model Description	Trade-in Value	Market Value
2 Dr STD Vandura Ext	9505	11880
2 Dr STD Vandura	9230	11540

G25

Category H

Model Description	Trade-in Value	Market Value
2 Dr STD Vandura Ext	8760	10950
2 Dr STD Rally Wagon	8405	10505
2 Dr STD Vandura	8685	10855
2 Dr STX Rally Wagon	9190	11490

G35

Category H

Model Description	Trade-in Value	Market Value
2 Dr STD Vandura Ext	7830	9785
2 Dr STD Rally Wagon	8650	10810
2 Dr STD Vandura	7220	9025
2 Dr STD Rally Wagon Ext	9355	11695

OPTIONS FOR VANDURA/RALLY WAGON

8 cyl 6.5 L Dsl Engine +975
8 cyl 5.0 L Engine +220
8 cyl 5.7 L Engine[Opt on G25,Vandura] +265
8 cyl 7.4 L Engine +210
8 cyl 6.2 L Turbodsl Engine +615
Air Conditioning[Std on STX] +300
AM/FM Compact Disc Playr +110
Camper/Towing Package +130
Captain Chairs (2)[Std on STX] +200
Chrome Bumpers[Opt on G15,Vandura,Vandura Ext] +60
Cruise Control +70
Dual Air Conditioning +525
Keyless Entry System +60
Leather Seats +385
Limited Slip Diff +95
Power Door Locks +70
Power Windows +70
Premium Sound System +150

YUKON 1994

Air conditioning receives CFC-free coolant. Side-door guard beams are added. A new grille appears, and models equipped with a decor package get composite headlamps. A turbocharged diesel is newly optional. Third brake light is added.

Category H

Model Description	Trade-in Value	Market Value
2 Dr SLE 4WD Utility	11880	14850
2 Dr Sport 4WD Utility	11875	14845
2 Dr STD 4WD Utility	11160	13950

OPTIONS FOR YUKON

8 cyl 6.5 L Turbodsl Engine +1185
Auto 4-Speed Transmission +330
Air Conditioning[Std on Sport] +300
AM/FM Stereo Tape[Std on Sport] +90
Camper/Towing Package +130
Cruise Control[Std on Sport] +70
Luggage Rack +50
Power Door Locks[Std on Sport] +70
Power Drivers Seat +100
Power Windows[Std on Sport] +70
Premium Sound System +150
Skid Plates +40
Tilt Steering Wheel[Std on Sport] +65

1993 GMC

C/K PICKUP 1993

Solar-Ray tinted glass is made standard. Cloth interior surfaces are now protected by Scotchgard fabric protection. Automatic transmissions get electronic shift controls. Base V6 gets five additional horsepower.

Don't forget to refer to the Mileage Adjustment Table at the back of this book!

 © 1999 by Edmund Publications Corporation

RATINGS (SCALE OF 1-10)

Overall	Safety	Reliability	Performance	Comfort	Value
N/A	5.6	8.5	7.4	8	N/A

Model Description	Trade-in Value	Market Value
C1500		
Category H		
2 Dr SLE Ext Cab SB	7515	9510
2 Dr SLE Std Cab SB	7465	9445
2 Dr SLE Ext Cab Stepside SB	7720	9770
2 Dr SLE Std Cab Stepside SB	7540	9545
2 Dr SLE Ext Cab LB	7585	9600
2 Dr SLE Std Cab LB	7440	9415
2 Dr SLX Ext Cab SB	7630	9660
2 Dr SLX Std Cab SB	7520	9520
2 Dr SLX Ext Cab Stepside SB	7565	9580
2 Dr SLX Ext Cab LB	7430	9405
2 Dr Special Std Cab LB	6645	8410
2 Dr STD Ext Cab SB	7190	9100
2 Dr STD Std Cab SB	7000	8860
2 Dr STD Std Cab Stepside SB	7225	9145
2 Dr STD Ext Cab Stepside SB	7385	9350
2 Dr STD Std Cab LB	7045	8920
2 Dr STD Ext Cab LB	7255	9185
C2500		
Category H		
2 Dr SLE Ext Cab SB	10345	13095
2 Dr SLE Std Cab LB	9665	12235
2 Dr SLE Ext Cab LB	10375	13135
2 Dr SLX Ext Cab SB	10210	12925
2 Dr SLX Ext Cab LB	10110	12800
2 Dr SLX Std Cab LB	9430	11935
2 Dr STD Ext Cab SB	9460	11975
2 Dr STD Std Cab LB	9285	11755
2 Dr STD Ext Cab LB	9525	12060
C3500		
Category H		
2 Dr SLE Ext Cab LB	10910	13815
2 Dr SLE Std Cab LB	10395	13160
4 Dr SLE Crew Cab LB	11535	14600
2 Dr SLX Std Cab LB	10270	13000
2 Dr SLX Ext Cab LB	10785	13655
2 Dr STD Std Cab LB	10155	12855
2 Dr STD Ext Cab LB	10505	13300
4 Dr STD Crew Cab LB	11190	14165
K1500		
Category H		
2 Dr SLE 4WD Ext Cab SB	8680	10990
2 Dr SLE 4WD Std Cab SB	8590	10875
2 Dr SLE 4WD Ext Cab Stepside SB	8825	11170
2 Dr SLE 4WD Std Cab Stepside SB	8660	10965
2 Dr SLE 4WD Ext Cab LB	8905	11275
2 Dr SLE 4WD Std Cab LB	8700	11010
2 Dr SLX 4WD Ext Cab SB	8580	10865
2 Dr SLX 4WD Ext Cab LB	8645	10940
2 Dr Special 4WD Std Cab LB	7415	9385
2 Dr Sport 4WD Std Cab SB	8725	11045
2 Dr STD 4WD Std Cab SB	8515	10780
2 Dr STD 4WD Ext Cab SB	8570	10845
2 Dr STD 4WD Ext Cab LB	8630	10925
2 Dr STD 4WD Std Cab LB	8615	10905
K2500		
Category H		
2 Dr SLE 4WD Ext Cab SB	9795	12400
2 Dr SLE 4WD Ext Cab LB	9900	12535
2 Dr SLE 4WD Std Cab LB	9340	11825
2 Dr SLX 4WD Ext Cab SB	9790	12395
2 Dr SLX 4WD Std Cab LB	9160	11595
2 Dr SLX 4WD Ext Cab LB	9865	12490
2 Dr STD 4WD Ext Cab SB	9690	12265
2 Dr STD 4WD Std Cab LB	9130	11555
2 Dr STD 4WD Ext Cab LB	9685	12260
K3500		
Category H		
2 Dr SL Turbodsl 4WD Ext Cab LB	8840	11190

OPTIONS FOR C/K PICKUP

8 cyl 6.2 L Dsl Engine +655
8 cyl 5.0 L Engine +180
8 cyl 5.7 L Engine +255
8 cyl 7.4 L Engine +245
8 cyl 6.5 L Turbodsl Engine +855
Auto 4-Speed Transmission +270
Sport Handling Pkg +260
Air Conditioning[Std on SL] +245
Aluminum/Alloy Wheels +95
AM/FM Stereo Tape +75
Bed Liner +70
Camper/Towing Package +110
Chrome Wheels +90
Cruise Control +60
Dual Rear Wheels +255
Limited Slip Diff +75
Locking Differential +75
Power Door Locks +55
Power Drivers Seat +85
Power Windows +60
Premium Sound System +125
Rear Step Bumper +45
Skid Plates +35

Don't forget to refer to the Mileage Adjustment Table at the back of this book!

 © 1999 by Edmund Publications Corporation

Model Description	Trade-in Value	Market Value

S15 JIMMY 1993

Two-door model available in SLT trim. Four-door models get monochromatic paint scheme in SLS trim. V6 engines get internal balance shaft designed to reduce vibration. Automatic transmission receives electronic shift controls and second-gear start feature. Manual lumbar adjusters are newly standard on front seats. Typhoon can be ordered in white as well as black.

RATINGS (SCALE OF 1-10)

Overall	Safety	Reliability	Performance	Comfort	Value
5.9	5.1	6.2	6.8	7.1	4.4

Category G

Model	Trade-in	Market
2 Dr SLE Utility	5810	7750
2 Dr SLE 4WD Utility	6590	8790
4 Dr SLE Wgn	5690	7590
4 Dr SLE 4WD Wgn	6645	8860
2 Dr SLS Utility	5665	7555
2 Dr SLS 4WD Utility	6490	8650
4 Dr SLS 4WD Wgn	6465	8620
2 Dr SLT Utility	6270	8365
2 Dr SLT 4WD Utility	6890	9190
4 Dr SLT Wgn	7080	9440
4 Dr SLT 4WD Wgn	7505	10005
2 Dr STD Utility	5365	7155
2 Dr STD 4WD Utility	6345	8460

OPTIONS FOR S15 JIMMY

6 cyl 4.3 L CPI Engine +140
Auto 4-Speed Transmission +255
Air Conditioning[Std on SLT Wgn] +245
Aluminum/Alloy Wheels[Opt on SLE,STD] +105
AM/FM Compact Disc Playr +115
Camper/Towing Package +85
Cruise Control[Std on SLT Wgn] +65
Keyless Entry System[Std on SLT Wgn] +60
Leather Seats[Std on SLT] +235
Limited Slip Diff +80
Luggage Rack[Std on SLT Wgn] +45
Power Door Locks[Std on SLT Wgn] +70
Power Drivers Seat[Std on SLT] +85
Power Rear Window +30
Power Windows[Std on SLT Wgn] +70
Premium Sound System +110

SAFARI 1993

Base 4.3-liter V6 gets 15 additional horsepower. Automatic transmission gets electronic shift controls and second-gear start feature. New speedometer reads to 100 mph. Driver airbag is offered as an option midyear.

RATINGS (SCALE OF 1-10)

Overall	Safety	Reliability	Performance	Comfort	Value
6.8	4.1	6.7	7.2	6.6	9.2

Category G

Model	Trade-in	Market
2 Dr GT Sport Pass. Van Ext	6045	8060
2 Dr SLE Pass. Van	5535	7375
2 Dr SLE Pass. Van Ext	6130	8175
2 Dr SLE 4WD Pass. Van	5910	7885
2 Dr SLT Pass. Van	5720	7625
2 Dr SLT 4WD Pass. Van	6330	8440
2 Dr SLT 4WD Pass. Van Ext	6900	9200
2 Dr STD Pass. Van	5135	6850
2 Dr STD Cargo Van Ext	4575	6095
2 Dr STD Pass. Van Ext	5795	7730
2 Dr STD Cargo Van	4065	5425
2 Dr STD 4WD Pass. Van	5750	7670
2 Dr STD 4WD Cargo Van Ext	6015	8020
2 Dr STD 4WD Pass. Van Ext	6410	8550

OPTIONS FOR SAFARI

6 cyl 4.3 L CPI Engine[Std on 4WD] +140
Air Bag Restraint[Std on Cargo Van Ext] +150
Air Conditioning +245
Aluminum/Alloy Wheels +105
AM/FM Compact Disc Playr +115
Camper/Towing Package +85
Chrome Bumpers +50
Cruise Control +65
Dual Air Conditioning +305
Limited Slip Diff +80
Luggage Rack +45
Power Door Locks +70
Power Drivers Seat +85
Power Windows +70
Premium Sound System +110

SONOMA 1993

V6 engines get internal balance shaft designed to reduce vibration. Automatic transmission gets electronic shift controls. Syclone dropped.

RATINGS (SCALE OF 1-10)

Overall	Safety	Reliability	Performance	Comfort	Value
N/A	3.2	7.7	7.2	7	N/A

Category G

Model	Trade-in	Market
2 Dr SLE Ext Cab SB	5050	6735
2 Dr SLE Std Cab SB	4365	5820
2 Dr SLE 4WD Ext Cab SB	6575	8765
2 Dr SLE 4WD Std Cab SB	5340	7120
2 Dr SLE 4WD Std Cab LB	5395	7195
2 Dr SLS Std Cab SB	4075	5430
2 Dr SLS Ext Cab SB	5015	6685
2 Dr SLS 4WD Ext Cab SB	6470	8625
2 Dr SLS 4WD Std Cab SB	5400	7200
2 Dr SLS 4WD Std Cab LB	5315	7085
2 Dr Special Std Cab SB	3730	4975
2 Dr Special 4WD Std Cab SB	4985	6645

Don't forget to refer to the Mileage Adjustment Table at the back of this book!

 © 1999 by Edmund Publications Corporation

Model Description	Trade-in Value	Market Value
2 Dr STD Ext Cab SB	4790	6385
2 Dr STD Std Cab SB	3760	5010
2 Dr STD 4WD Std Cab SB	5165	6890
2 Dr STD 4WD Ext Cab SB	6390	8520
2 Dr STD 4WD Std Cab LB	5080	6770

OPTIONS FOR SONOMA

6 cyl 2.8 L Engine +120
6 cyl 4.3 L Engine +140
6 cyl 4.3 L CPI Engine +190
Auto 4-Speed Transmission +270
Air Conditioning +245
Aluminum/Alloy Wheels +105
AM/FM Stereo[Opt on Special] +60
AM/FM Stereo Tape +75
Cruise Control +65
Power Mirrors[Std on SLE] +40
Power Steering[Opt on 2WD] +85
Tilt Steering Wheel +50

SUBURBAN 1993

No changes.

RATINGS (SCALE OF 1-10)

Overall	Safety	Reliability	Performance	Comfort	Value
7	6.6	7.3	7	7.5	6.7

Category H

Model Description	Trade-in Value	Market Value
4 Dr C1500 Wgn	10750	13605
4 Dr C2500 Wgn	11435	14475
4 Dr K1500 4WD Wgn	12505	15830
4 Dr K2500 4WD Wgn	13100	16580

OPTIONS FOR SUBURBAN

8 cyl 7.4 L Engine +245
SLE Decor Group +700
Air Conditioning +245
Aluminum/Alloy Wheels +95
AM/FM Stereo Tape +75
Camper/Towing Package +110
Cruise Control +60
Dual Air Conditioning +430
Leather Seats +315
Luggage Rack +40
Power Door Locks +55
Power Drivers Seat +85
Power Passenger Seat +75
Power Windows +60
Premium Sound System +125
Skid Plates +35

TYPHOON 1993

Typhoon can be ordered in white as well as black.

Category I

Model Description	Trade-in Value	Market Value
2 Dr STD Turbo 4WD Utility	13560	17845

OPTIONS FOR TYPHOON

AM/FM Compact Disc Playr +40
Luggage Rack +40

VANDURA/RALLY WAGON 1993

Solar-Ray tinted glass and Scotchgard fabric protectant are both standard. Four-wheel ABS is a new standard feature. Remote keyless entry joins the options list.

G15

Category H

Model Description	Trade-in Value	Market Value
2 Dr STD Rally Wagon	8040	10180
2 Dr STD Rally Wagon Ext	8060	10205
2 Dr STD Vandura	6785	8590
2 Dr STD Vandura Ext	6800	8605
2 Dr STX Rally Wagon	8590	10870

G25

Category H

Model Description	Trade-in Value	Market Value
2 Dr STD Vandura	5780	7315
2 Dr STD Rally Wagon Ext	6865	8690
2 Dr STD Vandura Ext	5910	7480
2 Dr STX Rally Wagon Ext	7015	8880

OPTIONS FOR VANDURA/RALLY WAGON

8 cyl 6.2 L Dsl Engine +655
8 cyl 5.0 L Engine +180
8 cyl 5.7 L Engine[Std on G35] +255
Air Conditioning +245
Aluminum/Alloy Wheels +95
AM/FM Compact Disc Playr +90
Camper/Towing Package +110
Chrome Bumpers[Opt on Vandura,Vandura Ext] +50
Cruise Control +60
Dual Air Conditioning +430
Keyless Entry System +45
Power Door Locks +55
Power Windows +60
Premium Sound System +125

YUKON 1993

No changes.

Category H

Model Description	Trade-in Value	Market Value
2 Dr SLE 4WD Utility	10540	13340
2 Dr Sport GT 4WD Utility	10665	13505
2 Dr STD 4WD Utility	9990	12645

OPTIONS FOR YUKON

Auto 4-Speed Transmission +270
Air Conditioning[Opt on STD] +245
Aluminum/Alloy Wheels[Opt on STD] +95
AM/FM Stereo Tape[Opt on STD] +75
Camper/Towing Package +110
Cruise Control[Opt on STD] +60
Luggage Rack +40
Power Door Locks +55
Power Drivers Seat +85
Power Windows +60
Premium Sound System +125
Skid Plates +35

Don't forget to refer to the Mileage Adjustment Table at the back of this book!

 © 1999 by Edmund Publications Corporation

Model Description	Trade-in Value	Market Value

1992 GMC

C/K PICKUP 1992

Extended-cab models get Sportside box option. Crew Cab model is all-new, sporting same engineering and styling as rest of Sierra line. Front buckets have been redesigned. Standard gauge cluster is restyled. Integral head restraints are added for outboard passengers. A new turbocharged 6.5-liter diesel V8 is optional in C/K 2500 and regular-cab C/K 3500 models. Four-speed manual transmission is dropped.

RATINGS (SCALE OF 1-10)

Overall	Safety	Reliability	Performance	Comfort	Value
N/A	5.6	8	7.4	8	N/A

C1500

Category H

Model Description	Trade-in Value	Market Value
2 Dr SLE Ext Cab SB	6740	8755
2 Dr SLE Std Cab SB	6455	8385
2 Dr SLE Std Cab Stepside SB	6495	8440
2 Dr SLE Ext Cab Stepside SB	6740	8750
2 Dr SLE Std Cab LB	6420	8335
2 Dr SLE Ext Cab LB	6735	8745
2 Dr SLX Std Cab SB	6370	8270
2 Dr SLX Ext Cab SB	6595	8565
2 Dr SLX Ext Cab Stepside SB	6705	8710
2 Dr SLX Std Cab Stepside SB	6320	8210
2 Dr SLX Std Cab LB	6240	8105
2 Dr SLX Ext Cab LB	6625	8605
2 Dr Special Std Cab LB	5085	6605
2 Dr STD Ext Cab SB	6370	8275
2 Dr STD Std Cab SB	6215	8070
2 Dr STD Ext Cab Stepside SB	6580	8545
2 Dr STD Ext Cab LB	6390	8300
2 Dr STD Std Cab LB	6210	8065

C2500

Category H

Model Description	Trade-in Value	Market Value
2 Dr SLE Ext Cab SB	7095	9215
2 Dr SLE Ext Cab LB	7075	9190
2 Dr SLE Std Cab LB	6495	8440
2 Dr SLX Ext Cab SB	6845	8890
2 Dr SLX Ext Cab LB	6850	8900
2 Dr SLX Std Cab LB	6485	8425
2 Dr STD Ext Cab SB	6755	8770
2 Dr STD Ext Cab LB	6755	8775
2 Dr STD Std Cab LB	6455	8380

C3500

Category H

Model Description	Trade-in Value	Market Value
2 Dr SLE Ext Cab LB	8345	10835
2 Dr SLX Ext Cab LB	8045	10445
2 Dr STD Ext Cab LB	7975	10355
4 Dr STD Crew Cab LB	9510	12350

K1500

Category H

Model Description	Trade-in Value	Market Value
2 Dr SLE 4WD Std Cab SB	7165	9305
2 Dr SLE 4WD Ext Cab SB	8365	10865
2 Dr SLE 4WD Std Cab Stepside SB	7330	9520
2 Dr SLE 4WD Ext Cab Stepside SB	8605	11175
2 Dr SLE 4WD Std Cab LB	7165	9300
2 Dr SLE 4WD Ext Cab LB	8445	10970
2 Dr SLX 4WD Ext Cab SB	8225	10685
2 Dr SLX 4WD Std Cab SB	7050	9160
2 Dr SLX 4WD Std Cab Stepside SB	7170	9310
2 Dr SLX 4WD Ext Cab Stepside SB	8375	10875
2 Dr SLX 4WD Std Cab LB	7005	9095
2 Dr SLX 4WD Ext Cab LB	8220	10675
2 Dr Special 4WD Std Cab LB	6130	7960
2 Dr STD 4WD Std Cab SB	6850	8895
2 Dr STD 4WD Ext Cab SB	8135	10565
2 Dr STD 4WD Std Cab Stepside SB	7100	9220
2 Dr STD 4WD Ext Cab Stepside SB	8305	10785
2 Dr STD 4WD Ext Cab LB	8150	10585
2 Dr STD 4WD Std Cab LB	6900	8960

K2500

Category H

Model Description	Trade-in Value	Market Value
2 Dr SLE 4WD Ext Cab SB	8485	11020
2 Dr SLE 4WD Std Cab LB	7450	9675
2 Dr SLE 4WD Ext Cab LB	8540	11095
2 Dr SLX 4WD Ext Cab SB	8465	10995
2 Dr SLX 4WD Std Cab LB	7170	9315
2 Dr SLX 4WD Ext Cab LB	8510	11055
2 Dr STD 4WD Ext Cab SB	8370	10870
2 Dr STD 4WD Ext Cab LB	8415	10925
2 Dr STD 4WD Std Cab LB	7145	9280

K3500

Category H

Model Description	Trade-in Value	Market Value
2 Dr STD 4WD Ext Cab LB	8865	11510

OPTIONS FOR C/K PICKUP

8 cyl 6.2 L Dsl Engine +510
8 cyl 5.0 L Engine +145
8 cyl 5.7 L Engine +205
8 cyl 7.4 L Engine +175
8 cyl 6.5 L Turbodsl Engine +650
Auto 4-Speed Transmission +215
Heavy Duty Pkg +260

Don't forget to refer to the Mileage Adjustment Table at the back of this book!

© 1999 by Edmund Publications Corporation

Model Description	Trade-in Value	Market Value

Sport Handling Package +205
Air Conditioning +200
Aluminum/Alloy Wheels +75
AM/FM Stereo Tape +60
Bed Liner +55
Camper/Towing Package +90
Cruise Control +50
Dual Rear Wheels +210
Limited Slip Diff +65
Locking Differential +60
Power Brakes[Opt on C3500 SLX Std Cab LB] +45
Power Door Locks +45
Power Windows +45
Premium Sound System +100
Rear Step Bumper +40
Skid Plates +30

S15 JIMMY 1992

Four-wheel ABS is standard on all models. Electronic-shift transfer case is added to options list; comes standard with SLT trim. A high-performance 4.3-liter V6 debuts with 40 additional horsepower, bringing total output to 200 ponies. Bucket seats are redesigned, a new speedometer is installed, and a four-spoke steering wheel is added.

RATINGS (SCALE OF 1-10)

Overall	Safety	Reliability	Performance	Comfort	Value
5.9	3.9	6.5	6.8	7.1	4.9

Category G

Model Description	Trade-in Value	Market Value
2 Dr SLE Utility	4315	5915
2 Dr SLE 4WD Utility	5505	7540
4 Dr SLT Wgn	5300	7260
4 Dr SLT 4WD Wgn	5760	7890
2 Dr STD Utility	4225	5785
2 Dr STD 4WD Utility	5230	7165
4 Dr STD Wgn	4775	6540
4 Dr STD 4WD Wgn	5235	7170

OPTIONS FOR S15 JIMMY

Auto 4-Speed Transmission +215
Air Conditioning +200
Aluminum/Alloy Wheels +85
AM/FM Compact Disc Playr +95
Camper/Towing Package +70
Cruise Control +50
Leather Seats +190
Limited Slip Diff +65
Luggage Rack +40
Power Door Locks +55
Power Windows +60
Premium Sound System +90

SAFARI 1992

Dutch rear door treatment is available. With Dutch doors, a rear washer/wiper and rear defogger can be ordered. All-wheel drive models get high-output, 200-horsepower V6 standard. Engine is optional on 2WD models.

RATINGS (SCALE OF 1-10)

Overall	Safety	Reliability	Performance	Comfort	Value
6.6	4.1	6.9	7.2	6.6	8.3

Category G

Model Description	Trade-in Value	Market Value
2 Dr SLE Pass. Van Ext	5140	7040
2 Dr SLE Pass. Van	4970	6810
2 Dr SLE 4WD Pass. Van	5185	7105
2 Dr SLT Pass. Van Ext	5740	7865
2 Dr SLT Pass. Van	5215	7140
2 Dr SLT 4WD Pass. Van	5310	7275
2 Dr SLT 4WD Pass. Van Ext	5920	8110
2 Dr STD Cargo Van	3750	5135
2 Dr STD Pass. Van Ext	5090	6970
2 Dr STD Pass. Van	4580	6275
2 Dr STD Cargo Van Ext	4225	5790
2 Dr STD 4WD Pass. Van	4795	6570
2 Dr STD 4WD Pass. Van Ext	5360	7340
2 Dr STD 4WD Cargo Van Ext	4925	6750

OPTIONS FOR SAFARI

6 cyl 4.3 L CPI Engine[Std on 4WD] +110
Air Conditioning +200
Aluminum/Alloy Wheels +85
AM/FM Compact Disc Playr +95
Camper/Towing Package +70
Chrome Bumpers +40
Cruise Control +50
Dual Air Conditioning +250
Limited Slip Diff +65
Luggage Rack +40
Power Door Locks +55
Power Drivers Seat +70
Power Windows +60
Premium Sound System +90
Rear Step Bumper +35

SONOMA 1992

New GT model debuts, available on regular-cab shortbed 2WD models and including many Syclone styling cues along with high-output 4.3-liter V6. Front bucket seats are redesigned, integral head restraints are added, and Club Coupes can be equipped with leather seats. New speedometer and four-spoke steering wheel are installed. Premium sound system with CD player is added to options list. Four-wheel drive models can be equipped with an electronic-shift transfer case.

RATINGS (SCALE OF 1-10)

Overall	Safety	Reliability	Performance	Comfort	Value
N/A	3	7.5	7.2	7	N/A

Category G

Model Description	Trade-in Value	Market Value
2 Dr GT Std Cab SB	6290	8615
2 Dr SLE Ext Cab SB	4205	5760
2 Dr SLE Std Cab SB	3465	4750
2 Dr SLE Std Cab LB	3515	4815

Don't forget to refer to the Mileage Adjustment Table at the back of this book!

 © 1999 by Edmund Publications Corporation

Model Description	Trade-in Value	Market Value
2 Dr SLE 4WD Ext Cab SB	5540	7590
2 Dr SLE 4WD Std Cab SB	4595	6295
2 Dr SLE 4WD Std Cab LB	4670	6395
2 Dr Special Std Cab SB	3230	4430
2 Dr Special 4WD Std Cab SB	4400	6030
2 Dr STD Std Cab SB	3285	4505
2 Dr STD Ext Cab SB	4125	5650
2 Dr STD Std Cab LB	3380	4625
2 Dr STD 4WD Std Cab SB	4445	6090
2 Dr STD 4WD Ext Cab SB	5320	7285
2 Dr STD 4WD Std Cab LB	4550	6230

OPTIONS FOR SONOMA

6 cyl 2.8 L Engine +95
6 cyl 4.3 L Engine +110
6 cyl 4.3 L CPI Engine +150
Auto 4-Speed Transmission[Std on GT,Syclone] +215
Air Conditioning[Std on GT] +200
Aluminum/Alloy Wheels[Opt on SLE,STD] +85
AM/FM Compact Disc Playr +95
Bucket Seats +70
Camper/Towing Package +70
Cruise Control[Opt on SLE,STD] +50
Leather Seats +190
Limited Slip Diff[Opt on SLE,STD] +65
Power Door Locks[Opt on SLE,STD] +55
Power Steering[Std on GT,Ext Cab,4WD] +70
Power Windows[Opt on SLE,STD] +60
Premium Sound System[Std on GT] +90
Rear Step Bumper +35
Skid Plates +35

SUBURBAN 1992

All-new design debuts based on platform and styling of Sierra. Cargo space and towing capacity are up. ABS works on all four wheels even in 4WD. Tailgate glass is lifted up instead of powered down. No diesel is offered. GM's Instatrac 4WD system is standard on K models.

RATINGS (SCALE OF 1-10)

Overall	Safety	Reliability	Performance	Comfort	Value
6.9	6.6	7.1	7	7.5	6.6

Category H

Model Description	Trade-in Value	Market Value
4 Dr C1500 Wgn	9805	12730
4 Dr C2500 Wgn	10020	13015
4 Dr K1500 4WD Wgn	10095	13110
4 Dr K2500 4WD Wgn	10650	13830

OPTIONS FOR SUBURBAN

8 cyl 7.4 L Engine +175
SLE Package +480
Air Conditioning +200
Aluminum/Alloy Wheels +75
AM/FM Stereo Tape +60
Camper/Towing Package +90
Cruise Control +50
Dual Air Conditioning +350
Limited Slip Diff +65
Luggage Rack +35
Power Door Locks +45
Power Drivers Seat +70
Power Windows +45
Premium Sound System +100
Skid Plates +30

TYPHOON 1992

Typhoon blows into town, featuring Syclone powertrain wrapped in two-door Jimmy body.

Category I

Model Description	Trade-in Value	Market Value
2 Dr STD Turbo 4WD Utility	12455	16390

OPTIONS FOR TYPHOON

AM/FM Compact Disc Playr +35
Ground Effects Package +45
Luggage Rack +30

VANDURA/RALLY WAGON 1992

Minor suspension modifications improve the ride.

G15

Category H

Model Description	Trade-in Value	Market Value
2 Dr STD Rally Wagon	6520	8465
2 Dr STD Rally Wagon Ext	6675	8670
2 Dr STD Vandura Ext	5675	7370
2 Dr STD Vandura	5610	7285
2 Dr STX Rally Wagon	6625	8605

G25

Category H

Model Description	Trade-in Value	Market Value
2 Dr STD Vandura	4960	6440
2 Dr STD Rally Wagon Ext	6140	7975
2 Dr STX Rally Wagon Ext	6575	8540

OPTIONS FOR VANDURA/RALLY WAGON

8 cyl 6.2 L Dsl Engine +510
8 cyl 5.0 L Engine +145
8 cyl 5.7 L Engine[Opt on G15,G25,Vandura] +205
127In. Wheelbase +230
Air Conditioning +200
Aluminum/Alloy Wheels +75
AM/FM Stereo Tape +60
Camper/Towing Package +90
Cruise Control +50
Dual Air Conditioning +350
Keyless Entry System +40
Limited Slip Diff +65
Power Door Locks +45
Power Windows +45
Premium Sound System +100

YUKON 1992

Totally redesigned and based on same platform and sheetmetal as Sierra pickup, the old Jimmy becomes the Yukon to differentiate it from the Sonoma-based Jimmy. Six-

Don't forget to refer to the Mileage Adjustment Table at the back of this book!

 © 1999 by Edmund Publications Corporation

Model Description	Trade-in Value	Market Value

passenger seating is standard. Cargo area gets fixed metal roof rather than fiberglass shell. Four-wheel ABS is standard and works in 4WD. New Sport appearance package includes two-tone paint and wheelwell flares. Diesel option is dropped. Five-speed manual is standard transmission. An automatic is optional. Shift-on-the-fly 4WD is standard.

Category H

Model Description	Trade-in Value	Market Value
2 Dr SLE 4WD Utility	9110	11830
2 Dr Sport 4WD Utility	8975	11655
2 Dr STD 4WD Utility	8720	11325

OPTIONS FOR YUKON

Auto 4-Speed Transmission +215
Sport Handling Package +390
Air Conditioning +200
Aluminum/Alloy Wheels +75
AM/FM Stereo Tape +60
Camper/Towing Package +90
Cruise Control +50
Limited Slip Diff +65
Luggage Rack +35
Power Door Locks +45
Power Drivers Seat +70
Power Windows +45
Premium Sound System +100

1991 GMC

C/K PICKUP 1991

7.4-liter V8 is reworked, and can be mated to four-speed automatic transmission. New gauge cluster includes a tachometer. Bucket seats are a new option. Air conditioners get a new recirculation mode. Two-wheel drive models add tow hooks to the options list. Special gets new steering wheel and revised outside mirrors.

RATINGS (SCALE OF 1-10)

Overall	Safety	Reliability	Performance	Comfort	Value
N/A	5.7	8.1	7.4	8	N/A

C1500

Category H

Model Description	Trade-in Value	Market Value
2 Dr SLE Ext Cab SB	5965	8060
2 Dr SLE Std Cab SB	5390	7285
2 Dr SLE Std Cab Stepside SB	5295	7155
2 Dr SLE Std Cab LB	5400	7295
2 Dr SLE Ext Cab LB	6040	8165
2 Dr SLX Ext Cab SB	5910	7990
2 Dr SLX Std Cab SB	5265	7115
2 Dr SLX Std Cab Stepside SB	5260	7105
2 Dr SLX Std Cab LB	5345	7225
2 Dr SLX Ext Cab LB	5975	8075
2 Dr STD Ext Cab SB	5780	7810
2 Dr STD Std Cab SB	5105	6900
2 Dr STD Std Cab Stepside SB	5235	7070
2 Dr STD Ext Cab Stepside SB	5830	7880
2 Dr STD Ext Cab LB	5865	7925
2 Dr STD Std Cab LB	5185	7010

C2500

Category H

Model Description	Trade-in Value	Market Value
2 Dr SLE Ext Cab SB	6440	8700
2 Dr SLE Std Cab LB	5640	7620
2 Dr SLE Ext Cab LB	6435	8695
2 Dr SLX Ext Cab SB	6380	8620
2 Dr SLX Std Cab LB	5585	7545
2 Dr SLX Ext Cab LB	6450	8715
2 Dr STD Ext Cab SB	6255	8455
2 Dr STD Ext Cab LB	6325	8545
2 Dr STD Std Cab LB	5330	7205

K1500

Category H

Model Description	Trade-in Value	Market Value
2 Dr SLE 4WD Ext Cab SB	6895	9315
2 Dr SLE 4WD Std Cab SB	6300	8515
2 Dr SLE 4WD Std Cab Stepside SB	6575	8885
2 Dr SLE 4WD Std Cab LB	6280	8490
2 Dr SLE 4WD Ext Cab LB	6960	9405
2 Dr SLX 4WD Std Cab SB	6280	8490
2 Dr SLX 4WD Ext Cab SB	6805	9195
2 Dr SLX 4WD Std Cab Stepside SB	6460	8735
2 Dr SLX 4WD Ext Cab LB	6870	9285
2 Dr SLX 4WD Std Cab LB	6240	8435
2 Dr STD 4WD Std Cab SB	6180	8350
2 Dr STD 4WD Ext Cab SB	6770	9150
2 Dr STD 4WD Std Cab Stepside SB	6225	8415
2 Dr STD 4WD Ext Cab LB	6780	9160
2 Dr STD 4WD Std Cab LB	6135	8290

K2500

Category H

Model Description	Trade-in Value	Market Value
2 Dr SLE 4WD Ext Cab SB	7055	9535
2 Dr SLE 4WD Std Cab LB	6580	8890
2 Dr SLE 4WD Ext Cab LB	7155	9670
2 Dr SLX 4WD Ext Cab SB	6995	9455
2 Dr SLX 4WD Ext Cab LB	7060	9540
2 Dr SLX 4WD Std Cab LB	6485	8765
2 Dr STD 4WD Ext Cab SB	6945	9390
2 Dr STD 4WD Ext Cab LB	7020	9485
2 Dr STD 4WD Std Cab LB	6395	8640

OPTIONS FOR C/K PICKUP

8 cyl 6.2 L Dsl Engine +465
8 cyl 5.0 L Engine +120
8 cyl 5.7 L Engine +165

Don't forget to refer to the Mileage Adjustment Table at the back of this book!

 © 1999 by Edmund Publications Corporation

Model Description	Trade-in Value	Market Value

8 cyl 7.4 L Engine +160
Auto 4-Speed Transmission +175
Heavy Duty Pkg +195
Sport Handling Pkg +170
Air Conditioning +165
Aluminum/Alloy Wheels +65
AM/FM Stereo Tape +50
Bed Liner +45
Camper/Towing Package +70
Cruise Control +40
Limited Slip Diff +50
Locking Differential +50
Power Door Locks +35
Power Windows +40
Premium Sound System +80

JIMMY 1991

Throttle-body fuel injection is improved, and more powerful alternator is standard.

Category H		
2 Dr STD 4WD Utility	4785	6465

OPTIONS FOR JIMMY

8 cyl 6.2 L Dsl Engine +465
Auto 4-Speed Transmission +175
SLE Package +220
Air Conditioning +165
Aluminum/Alloy Wheels +65
AM/FM Stereo Tape +50
Camper/Towing Package +70
Cruise Control +40
Limited Slip Diff +50
Power Door Locks +35
Power Windows +40
Premium Sound System +80

S15 JIMMY 1991

Four-door models get new Gypsy package on the options list. It includes two-tone paint, alloy wheels and chrome trim. A heavy-duty battery is standard on all models, and 2WD Jimmys can be equipped with 15-inch alloy wheels. Front bench seat option will give four-door six passenger capacity. SLT Touring Package with softer suspension added midyear.

RATINGS (SCALE OF 1-10)

Overall	Safety	Reliability	Performance	Comfort	Value
5.6	3.7	5.8	6.8	7.1	4.4

Category G		
2 Dr SLE Utility	4150	5925
2 Dr SLE 4WD Utility	4665	6665
4 Dr SLE 4WD Wgn	5245	7490
2 Dr SLS Utility	4110	5875
2 Dr SLS 4WD Utility	4550	6500
4 Dr SLS Wgn	4665	6660
4 Dr SLS 4WD Wgn	5115	7305
4 Dr SLT 4WD Wgn	5440	7770
2 Dr STD Utility	3720	5315
2 Dr STD 4WD Utility	4460	6370
4 Dr STD Wgn	4315	6160
4 Dr STD 4WD Wgn	4795	6850

OPTIONS FOR S15 JIMMY

Auto 4-Speed Transmission +175
Air Conditioning[Std on SLT] +165
Aluminum/Alloy Wheels[Opt on SLE,STD] +70
AM/FM Stereo Tape +50
Camper/Towing Package +60
Cruise Control[Std on SLT] +45
Leather Seats[Std on SLT] +155
Limited Slip Diff +55
Luggage Rack[Std on SLT] +30
Power Door Locks[Std on SLT] +45
Power Windows[Std on SLT] +50
Premium Sound System[Std on SLT] +75
Swing Out Tire Carrier +40

SAFARI 1991

Cargo models gain the 4.3-liter V6 as standard equipment. A new GT model is available with sport suspension, rally wheels, front air dam, fog lights, and a sport steering wheel. Side and rear windows now have swing-out glass. Extended-length models can now be ordered with the Sport Appearance Package. A high-output, 4.3-liter V6 option is expected midyear.

RATINGS (SCALE OF 1-10)

Overall	Safety	Reliability	Performance	Comfort	Value
6.5	4.1	6.7	7.2	6.6	7.7

Category G		
2 Dr SLE Pass. Van	3665	5235
2 Dr SLE Pass. Van Ext	4145	5925
2 Dr SLE 4WD Pass. Van	4300	6145
2 Dr SLE 4WD Pass. Van Ext	4740	6775
2 Dr SLT Pass. Van	3985	5695
2 Dr SLT Pass. Van Ext	4495	6420
2 Dr SLT 4WD Pass. Van	4660	6655
2 Dr SLT 4WD Pass. Van Ext	5105	7295
2 Dr STD Cargo Van Ext	3105	4435
2 Dr STD Pass. Van Ext	3885	5545
2 Dr STD Pass. Van	3460	4940
2 Dr STD Cargo Van	2630	3760
2 Dr STD 4WD Cargo Van	3230	4615
2 Dr STD 4WD Pass. Van	4150	5930
2 Dr STD 4WD Cargo Van Ext	3885	5550
2 Dr STD 4WD Pass. Van Ext	4465	6380

OPTIONS FOR SAFARI

6 cyl 4.3 L HO Engine +85
Sport Handling Package +180
Air Conditioning +165
Aluminum/Alloy Wheels +70

Don't forget to refer to the Mileage Adjustment Table at the back of this book!

 © 1999 by Edmund Publications Corporation

Model Description	Trade-in Value	Market Value

AM/FM Stereo Tape +50
Camper/Towing Package +60
Chrome Bumpers +30
Cruise Control +45
Dual Air Conditioning +205
Limited Slip Diff +55
Luggage Rack +30
Power Door Locks +45
Power Drivers Seat +55
Power Windows +50
Premium Sound System +75

SONOMA 1991

Introduced in January, 1990, Sonoma is a S15 Pickup with a new name and an exterior facelift that includes a new grille, fresh trim and restyled wheels. Four-wheel drive models get the 4.3-liter V6 as standard equipment. High Sierra trim is dropped, and Sierra Classic trim is changed to SLE. Midyear, the base four-cylinder powerplant gets more horsepower. Also available is Syclone, an all-wheel drive turbocharged V6 terror with a Corvette automatic transmission, four-wheel ABS, and 280 horsepower. GMC says acceleration from zero-to-60 is accomplished in 4.6 seconds.

RATINGS (SCALE OF 1-10)

Overall	Safety	Reliability	Performance	Comfort	Value
N/A	2.9	7.1	7.2	7	N/A

Category G

Model Description	Trade-in Value	Market Value
2 Dr SLE Ext Cab SB	3390	4840
2 Dr SLE Std Cab SB	3165	4525
2 Dr SLE Std Cab LB	3125	4465
2 Dr SLE 4WD Std Cab SB	4140	5915
2 Dr SLE 4WD Ext Cab SB	4360	6225
2 Dr SLE 4WD Std Cab LB	4300	6140
2 Dr Special Std Cab SB	2540	3625
2 Dr STD Ext Cab SB	3355	4790
2 Dr STD Std Cab SB	3005	4295
2 Dr STD Std Cab LB	3070	4385
2 Dr STD 4WD Std Cab SB	4090	5840
2 Dr STD 4WD Ext Cab SB	4255	6080
2 Dr STD 4WD Std Cab LB	4185	5980

OPTIONS FOR SONOMA

6 cyl 2.8 L Engine +80
6 cyl 4.3 L Engine +125
Auto 4-Speed Transmission[Opt on SLE,STD] +175
Air Conditioning[Opt on SLE,Special,STD] +165
Aluminum/Alloy Wheels +70
AM/FM Stereo Tape[Opt on SLE,Special,STD] +50
Camper/Towing Package +60
Cruise Control[Opt on SLE,STD] +45
Leather Seats +155
Limited Slip Diff[Opt on SLE,STD] +55
Power Door Locks[Opt on SLE,STD] +45
Power Steering[Std on Ext Cab,4WD] +55
Power Windows[Opt on SLE,STD] +50

Premium Sound System +75
Rear Step Bumper +30

SUBURBAN 1991

Manual transmission is dropped.

Category H

Model Description	Trade-in Value	Market Value
4 Dr R1500 Wgn	6390	8640
4 Dr R2500 Wgn	6515	8805
4 Dr V1500 4WD Wgn	6980	9430
4 Dr V2500 4WD Wgn	7410	10015

OPTIONS FOR SUBURBAN

8 cyl 6.2 L Dsl Engine +465
8 cyl 7.4 L Engine +160
SLE Package +330
Air Conditioning +165
Aluminum/Alloy Wheels +65
AM/FM Stereo Tape +50
Camper/Towing Package +70
Cruise Control +40
Dual Air Conditioning +290
Limited Slip Diff +50
Luggage Rack +30
Power Door Locks +35
Power Windows +40
Premium Sound System +80
Rear Bench Seat +65

SYCLONE 1991

This Sonoma pickup is an all-wheel drive turbocharged V6 terror with a Corvette automatic transmission, four-wheel ABS and 280 horsepower. GMC says acceleration from zero-to-60 is accomplished in 4.6 seconds.

Category I

Model Description	Trade-in Value	Market Value
2 Dr STD Turbo 4WD Std Cab SB	10670	14225

OPTIONS FOR SYCLONE

Premium Sound System +30

VANDURA/RALLY WAGON 1991

7.4-liter engine can be equipped with a four-speed automatic transmission.

G15

Category H

Model Description	Trade-in Value	Market Value
2 Dr STD Rally Wagon	5730	7740
2 Dr STD Vandura	4530	6120
2 Dr STD Rally Wagon Ext	5745	7765
2 Dr STD Vandura Ext	4560	6160

G25

Category H

Model Description	Trade-in Value	Market Value
2 Dr STD Vandura Ext	5415	7315
2 Dr STD Vandura	5400	7295
2 Dr STD Rally Wagon	6525	8815
2 Dr STX Rally Wagon	6965	9415

Don't forget to refer to the Mileage Adjustment Table at the back of this book!

 © 1999 by Edmund Publications Corporation

Model Description	Trade-in Value	Market Value

OPTIONS FOR VANDURA/RALLY WAGON

8 cyl 6.2 L Dsl Engine +465
8 cyl 5.0 L Engine +120
8 cyl 5.7 L Engine[Opt on G25,G15] +165
Heavy Duty Pkg +185
Air Conditioning +165
Aluminum/Alloy Wheels +65
AM/FM Stereo Tape +50
Camper/Towing Package +70
Cruise Control +40
Dual Air Conditioning +290
Limited Slip Diff +50
Power Door Locks +35
Power Windows +40
Premium Sound System +80

1990 GMC

C/K PICKUP 1990

Stripped Special model is added to serve as a serious work truck. C/K 2500 Bonus Cab model dropped.

RATINGS (SCALE OF 1-10)

Overall	Safety	Reliability	Performance	Comfort	Value
N/A	5.5	7.4	7.4	8	N/A

C1500

Category H

Model Description	Trade-in Value	Market Value
2 Dr SLE Ext Cab SB	5440	7560
2 Dr SLE Std Cab SB	4600	6385
2 Dr SLE Std Cab Stepside SB	4890	6795
2 Dr SLE Std Cab LB	4855	6745
2 Dr SLE Ext Cab LB	5340	7420
2 Dr SLX Std Cab SB	4385	6090
2 Dr SLX Ext Cab SB	5200	7220
2 Dr SLX Std Cab Stepside SB	4330	6015
2 Dr SLX Ext Cab LB	5245	7285
2 Dr SLX Std Cab LB	4440	6170
2 Dr STD Ext Cab SB	5070	7040
2 Dr STD Std Cab SB	4250	5905
2 Dr STD Std Cab Stepside SB	4195	5825
2 Dr STD Ext Cab LB	5115	7105
2 Dr STD Std Cab LB	4315	5995

C2500

Category H

Model Description	Trade-in Value	Market Value
2 Dr SLE Ext Cab LB	5275	7325
2 Dr SLE Std Cab LB	5150	7155
2 Dr SLX Std Cab LB	5035	6990
2 Dr STD Std Cab LB	4755	6605
2 Dr STD Ext Cab LB	5220	7245

C3500

Category H

Model Description	Trade-in Value	Market Value
2 Dr SLE Std Cab LB	6350	8820
2 Dr SLE Ext Cab LB	7000	9725
2 Dr SLX Std Cab LB	6280	8720
2 Dr SLX Ext Cab LB	6930	9625
2 Dr STD Ext Cab LB	6820	9475
2 Dr STD Std Cab LB	6270	8710

K1500

Category H

Model Description	Trade-in Value	Market Value
2 Dr SLE 4WD Ext Cab SB	6355	8825
2 Dr SLE 4WD Std Cab SB	5880	8165
2 Dr SLE 4WD Ext Cab Stepside SB	6455	8965
2 Dr SLE 4WD Std Cab Stepside SB	5755	7995
2 Dr SLE 4WD Std Cab LB	5660	7860
2 Dr SLE 4WD Ext Cab LB	6450	8960
2 Dr SLX 4WD Std Cab SB	5525	7675
2 Dr SLX 4WD Ext Cab SB	6260	8695
2 Dr SLX 4WD Std Cab LB	5550	7705
2 Dr SLX 4WD Ext Cab LB	6355	8830
2 Dr Special 4WD Std Cab LB	5155	7165
2 Dr STD 4WD Ext Cab SB	6160	8560
2 Dr STD 4WD Std Cab SB	5575	7740
2 Dr STD 4WD Ext Cab LB	6140	8530
2 Dr STD 4WD Std Cab LB	5595	7770

K2500

Category H

Model Description	Trade-in Value	Market Value
2 Dr SLE 4WD Ext Cab SB	6230	8650
2 Dr SLE 4WD Ext Cab LB	6230	8655
2 Dr SLE 4WD Std Cab LB	5560	7725
2 Dr SLX 4WD Ext Cab SB	6175	8575
2 Dr SLX 4WD Std Cab LB	5490	7620
2 Dr STD 4WD Ext Cab SB	6055	8410
2 Dr STD 4WD Std Cab LB	5380	7475

K3500

Category H

Model Description	Trade-in Value	Market Value
2 Dr SLE 4WD Ext Cab LB	7350	10205
2 Dr STD 4WD Std Cab LB	6325	8785
2 Dr STD 4WD Ext Cab LB	7260	10080

OPTIONS FOR C/K PICKUP

8 cyl 6.2 L Dsl Engine +390
8 cyl 5.0 L Engine +95
8 cyl 5.7 L Engine +125
Auto 3-Speed Transmission +105
Auto 4-Speed Transmission +140
Heavy Duty Pkg +185
Sport Handling Pkg +150
Air Conditioning +135
Aluminum/Alloy Wheels +50
AM/FM Stereo Tape +40
Camper/Towing Package +60
Cruise Control +30
Dual Rear Wheels +140
Limited Slip Diff +40

Don't forget to refer to the Mileage Adjustment Table at the back of this book!

 © 1999 by Edmund Publications Corporation

Model Description	Trade-in Value	Market Value

Locking Differential +40
Power Door Locks +30
Power Windows +30
Premium Sound System +65

JIMMY 1990

Rear-wheel ABS that works only in 2WD is added.

Category H

Model Description	Trade-in Value	Market Value
2 Dr Sierra Classic 4WD Utility	5355	7435
2 Dr STD 4WD Utility	5085	7060

OPTIONS FOR JIMMY

8 cyl 6.2 L Dsl Engine +390
Auto 4-Speed Transmission +140
Air Conditioning +135
Aluminum/Alloy Wheels +50
AM/FM Stereo Tape +40
Cruise Control +30
Limited Slip Diff +40
Power Door Locks +30
Power Windows +30
Premium Sound System +65

R35 PICKUP 1990

Category H

Model Description	Trade-in Value	Market Value
4 Dr SLE Crew Cab LB	6280	8725
4 Dr STD Crew Cab LB	6250	8680

OPTIONS FOR R35 PICKUP

8 cyl 6.2 L Dsl Engine +390
8 cyl 7.4 L Engine +75
Auto 3-Speed Transmission +110
Air Conditioning +135
AM/FM Stereo Tape +40
Cruise Control +30
Limited Slip Diff +40
Power Door Locks +30
Power Windows +30
Premium Sound System +65

S15 1990

No changes.

RATINGS (SCALE OF 1-10)

Overall	Safety	Reliability	Performance	Comfort	Value
N/A	3.5	7	7.2	7	N/A

Category G

Model Description	Trade-in Value	Market Value
2 Dr EL Std Cab SB	2285	3460
2 Dr High Sierra Ext Cab SB	3060	4635
2 Dr High Sierra Std Cab SB	2550	3865
2 Dr High Sierra Std Cab LB	2625	3975
2 Dr High Sierra 4WD Ext Cab SB	3680	5575
2 Dr High Sierra 4WD Std Cab SB	3530	5345
2 Dr High Sierra 4WD Std Cab LB	3525	5340
2 Dr Sierra Classic Ext Cab SB	2990	4530
2 Dr Sierra Classic Std Cab SB	2400	3635
2 Dr Sierra Classic Std Cab LB	2410	3655
2 Dr Sierra Classic 4WD Ext Cab SB	3645	5520
2 Dr Sierra Classic 4WD Std Cab SB	3500	5300
2 Dr Sierra Classic 4WD Std Cab LB	3490	5290
2 Dr STD Ext Cab SB	2925	4435
2 Dr STD Std Cab SB	2305	3495
2 Dr STD Std Cab LB	2355	3570
2 Dr STD 4WD Std Cab SB	3460	5245
2 Dr STD 4WD Ext Cab SB	3590	5440
2 Dr STD 4WD Std Cab LB	3400	5155

OPTIONS FOR S15

6 cyl 2.8 L Engine +60
6 cyl 4.3 L Engine +100
Auto 4-Speed Transmission +140
Air Conditioning +135
Aluminum/Alloy Wheels +55
AM/FM Stereo Tape +40
Camper/Towing Package +50
Cruise Control +35
Limited Slip Diff +45
Power Door Locks +40
Power Steering[Opt on 2WD] +45
Power Windows +40
Premium Sound System +60

S15 JIMMY 1990

A four-door model with standard four-wheel ABS is added to the lineup, and the 2.8-liter engine is dropped in favor of the more powerful 160-horsepower 4.3-liter V6.

RATINGS (SCALE OF 1-10)

Overall	Safety	Reliability	Performance	Comfort	Value
6.1	3.9	6.3	6.8	7.1	6.3

Category G

Model Description	Trade-in Value	Market Value
2 Dr Gypsy Utility	3305	5005
2 Dr Gypsy 4WD Utility	3385	5130
2 Dr Sierra Classic Utility	3150	4770
2 Dr Sierra Classic 4WD Utility	3375	5115
2 Dr STD Utility	2905	4405
2 Dr STD 4WD Utility	3295	4995

OPTIONS FOR S15 JIMMY

Auto 4-Speed Transmission +140
Air Conditioning +135
Aluminum/Alloy Wheels[Std on Gypsy] +55
AM/FM Stereo Tape +40
Camper/Towing Package +50
Cruise Control +35
Leather Seats +125
Limited Slip Diff +45

Don't forget to refer to the Mileage Adjustment Table at the back of this book!

 © 1999 by Edmund Publications Corporation

Model Description	Trade-in Value	Market Value

Power Door Locks +40
Power Windows +40
Premium Sound System +60
Sunroof +50
Swing Out Tire Carrier +35

SAFARI 1990

All-wheel drive is newly optional, and an extended body style is introduced. Standard engine on passenger models is a 150-horsepower 4.3-liter V6. The optional sport suspension, and the Sport Appearance Package, will not be available on AWD vans. Four-wheel ABS is standard on all but commercially purchased cargo vans.

RATINGS (SCALE OF 1-10)

Overall	Safety	Reliability	Performance	Comfort	Value
6.5	4	6.3	7.2	6.6	8.1

Category G

Model Description	Trade-in Value	Market Value
2 Dr SLE Pass. Van Ext	3385	5125
2 Dr SLE Pass. Van	2930	4440
2 Dr SLE 4WD Pass. Van Ext	4770	7230
2 Dr SLE 4WD Pass. Van	4220	6395
2 Dr SLT Pass. Van	3155	4785
2 Dr SLT Pass. Van Ext	3430	5195
2 Dr SLT 4WD Pass. Van Ext	4865	7370
2 Dr SLT 4WD Pass. Van	4310	6530
2 Dr SLX Pass. Van	2720	4125
2 Dr SLX Pass. Van Ext	2970	4505
2 Dr SLX 4WD Pass. Van	3975	6025
2 Dr SLX 4WD Pass. Van Ext	4575	6935
2 Dr STD Cargo Van Ext	2385	3610
2 Dr STD Cargo Van	2160	3270
2 Dr STD 4WD Cargo Van	3360	5090

OPTIONS FOR SAFARI

6 cyl 4.3 L Engine[Std on SLE,SLT,SLX,4WD] +100
GT Pkg +185
Air Conditioning +135
Aluminum/Alloy Wheels +55
AM/FM Stereo Tape +40
Camper/Towing Package +50
Cruise Control +35
Dual Air Conditioning +165
Limited Slip Diff +45
Power Door Locks +40
Power Drivers Seat +45
Power Windows +40
Premium Sound System +60

SUBURBAN 1990

Rear-wheel ABS that works in 2WD only is added.

Category H

Model Description	Trade-in Value	Market Value
4 Dr R1500 Wgn	5015	6965
4 Dr R2500 Wgn	5260	7305
4 Dr V1500 4WD Wgn	6035	8380
4 Dr V2500 4WD Wgn	6165	8560

OPTIONS FOR SUBURBAN

8 cyl 6.2 L Dsl Engine +390
8 cyl 7.4 L Engine +75
Auto 3-Speed Transmission +105
Auto 4-Speed Transmission[Std on R15] +140
SLE Package +265
Air Conditioning +135
Aluminum/Alloy Wheels +50
AM/FM Stereo Tape +40
Camper/Towing Package +60
Cruise Control +30
Dual Air Conditioning +235
Limited Slip Diff +40
Power Door Locks +30
Power Windows +30
Premium Sound System +65

V3500 PICKUP 1990

Category H

Model Description	Trade-in Value	Market Value
4 Dr STD 4WD Crew Cab LB	7495	10410

OPTIONS FOR V3500 PICKUP

8 cyl 6.2 L Dsl Engine +390
8 cyl 7.4 L Engine +75
Auto 3-Speed Transmission +110
Air Conditioning +135
AM/FM Stereo Tape +40
Cruise Control +30
Limited Slip Diff +40
Power Door Locks +30
Power Windows +30
Premium Sound System +65

VANDURA/RALLY WAGON 1990

No changes.

G15

Category H

Model Description	Trade-in Value	Market Value
2 Dr STD Vandura	3190	4430
2 Dr STD Vandura Ext	3320	4610
2 Dr STD Rally Wagon	4450	6180
2 Dr STD Rally Wagon Ext	4505	6255

G25

Category H

Model Description	Trade-in Value	Market Value
2 Dr STD Vandura Ext	3595	4990
2 Dr STD Vandura	3230	4485
2 Dr STD Rally Wagon	3990	5540
2 Dr STX Rally Wagon	4440	6165

G35

Category H

Model Description	Trade-in Value	Market Value
2 Dr STD Rally Wagon	3835	5325
2 Dr STD Vandura	3260	4530

Don't forget to refer to the Mileage Adjustment Table at the back of this book!

 © 1999 by Edmund Publications Corporation

Model Description	Trade-in Value	Market Value

OPTIONS FOR VANDURA/RALLY WAGON

8 cyl 6.2 L Dsl Engine +390
8 cyl 5.0 L Engine +95
8 cyl 5.7 L Engine[Opt on G15,G25,Vandura] +125
8 cyl 7.4 L Engine +75
Auto 4-Speed Transmission[Std on STX,Rally Wagon, Rally Wagon Ext] +40
Air Conditioning +135
Aluminum/Alloy Wheels +50
AM/FM Stereo Tape +40
Camper/Towing Package +60
Cruise Control +30
Dual Air Conditioning +235
Leather Seats +170
Limited Slip Diff +40
Power Door Locks +30
Power Windows +30
Premium Sound System +65

1989 GMC

C/K PICKUP 1989

A new Club Coupe model with a shortbox is introduced. Also new, C/K 2500 models with 8,600 lb. GVWR and a K3500 Heavy Hauler Duallie with 10,000 lb. GVWR.

RATINGS (SCALE OF 1-10)

Overall	Safety	Reliability	Performance	Comfort	Value
N/A	5.5	7.3	7.4	8	N/A

C1500

Category H

Model Description	Trade-in Value	Market Value
2 Dr SLE Ext Cab SB	4560	6610
2 Dr SLE Std Cab SB	4255	6165
2 Dr SLE Std Cab Stepside SB	4335	6280
2 Dr SLE Ext Cab LB	4610	6680
2 Dr SLE Std Cab LB	4355	6315
2 Dr SLX Std Cab Stepside SB	4230	6130
2 Dr SLX Std Cab LB	4230	6130
2 Dr SLX Ext Cab LB	4530	6565
2 Dr STD Std Cab SB	3900	5650
2 Dr STD Ext Cab LB	4415	6400
2 Dr STD Std Cab LB	4190	6075

C2500

Category H

Model Description	Trade-in Value	Market Value
2 Dr SLE Ext Cab LB	4835	7005
2 Dr SLE Std Cab LB	3895	5650
2 Dr SLX Ext Cab LB	4725	6850
2 Dr SLX Std Cab LB	3870	5610
2 Dr STD Ext Cab SB	4560	6610
2 Dr STD Std Cab LB	3695	5360
2 Dr STD Ext Cab LB	4550	6595

C3500

Category H

Model Description	Trade-in Value	Market Value
2 Dr SLE Std Cab LB	5350	7755
2 Dr SLE Ext Cab LB	6065	8790
2 Dr SLX Std Cab LB	5050	7320
2 Dr STD Std Cab LB	5000	7250
2 Dr STD Ext Cab LB	5820	8435

K1500

Category H

Model Description	Trade-in Value	Market Value
2 Dr SLE 4WD Ext Cab SB	5375	7790
2 Dr SLE 4WD Std Cab SB	4955	7185
2 Dr SLE 4WD Std Cab Stepside SB	5080	7360
2 Dr SLE 4WD Std Cab LB	5130	7435
2 Dr SLX 4WD Std Cab Stepside SB	4800	6955
2 Dr SLX 4WD Ext Cab LB	5190	7525
2 Dr SLX 4WD Std Cab LB	4720	6840
2 Dr STD 4WD Std Cab SB	4600	6665
2 Dr STD 4WD Std Cab Stepside SB	4760	6900
2 Dr STD 4WD Ext Cab LB	4990	7230
2 Dr STD 4WD Std Cab LB	4690	6795

K2500

Category H

Model Description	Trade-in Value	Market Value
2 Dr SLE 4WD Std Cab LB	5035	7295
2 Dr SLE 4WD Ext Cab LB	5540	8030
2 Dr SLX 4WD Ext Cab SB	5330	7730
2 Dr SLX 4WD Std Cab LB	4910	7115
2 Dr SLX 4WD Ext Cab LB	5385	7800
2 Dr STD 4WD Ext Cab LB	5360	7765
2 Dr STD 4WD Std Cab LB	4870	7055

K3500

Category H

Model Description	Trade-in Value	Market Value
2 Dr SLE 4WD Ext Cab LB	6525	9455
2 Dr SLE 4WD Std Cab LB	5860	8490
2 Dr SLX 4WD Std Cab LB	5820	8440
2 Dr STD 4WD Ext Cab LB	6420	9305

OPTIONS FOR C/K PICKUP

8 cyl 6.2 L Dsl Engine +290
8 cyl 5.0 L Engine +80
8 cyl 5.7 L Engine +100
Auto 3-Speed Transmission +85
Auto 4-Speed Transmission +110
Heavy Duty Pkg +130
Air Conditioning +110
Aluminum/Alloy Wheels +40
AM/FM Stereo Tape +35
Camper/Towing Package +50
Dual Rear Wheels +115

Don't forget to refer to the Mileage Adjustment Table at the back of this book!

© 1999 by Edmund Publications Corporation

Model Description	Trade-in Value	Market Value

Limited Slip Diff +35
Locking Differential +35
Premium Sound System +55

JIMMY 1989

Suspension refinements net a smoother, quieter ride. Front styling is revised to resemble Sierra pickup.

Category H

Model	Trade-in	Market
2 Dr Sierra Classic 4WD Utility	4370	6335
2 Dr SLE 4WD Utility	4270	6190
2 Dr STD 4WD Utility	3985	5775

OPTIONS FOR JIMMY

8 cyl 6.2 L Dsl Engine +290
Auto 4-Speed Transmission +110
Air Conditioning +110
Aluminum/Alloy Wheels +40
AM/FM Stereo Tape +35
Camper/Towing Package +50
Limited Slip Diff +35
Premium Sound System +55

R35 PICKUP 1989

Category H

Model	Trade-in	Market
4 Dr SLE Crew Cab LB	5180	7505
4 Dr STD Crew Cab LB	4985	7225

OPTIONS FOR R35 PICKUP

8 cyl 6.2 L Dsl Engine +290
8 cyl 7.4 L Engine +65
Auto 3-Speed Transmission +85
Air Conditioning +110
AM/FM Stereo Tape +35
Chrome Step Bumper +30
Limited Slip Diff +35
Premium Sound System +55

S15 1989

Four-wheel drive models get the 2.8-liter V6 and power steering standard. Rear-wheel ABS that operates in 2WD mode only is added.

RATINGS (SCALE OF 1-10)

Overall	Safety	Reliability	Performance	Comfort	Value
N/A	4.3	6.8	7.2	7	N/A

Category G

Model	Trade-in	Market
2 Dr EL Std Cab SB	1840	3015
2 Dr High Sierra Ext Cab SB	2265	3715
2 Dr High Sierra Std Cab SB	1930	3170
2 Dr High Sierra Std Cab LB	1990	3265
2 Dr High Sierra 4WD Ext Cab SB	2990	4900
2 Dr Sierra Classic Std Cab SB	1980	3245
2 Dr Sierra Classic Ext Cab SB	2450	4015
2 Dr Sierra Classic Std Cab LB	2020	3310
2 Dr Sierra Classic 4WD Ext Cab SB	3115	5105
2 Dr Sierra Classic 4WD Std Cab SB	2845	4660
2 Dr Sierra Classic 4WD Std Cab LB	2780	4560
2 Dr STD Ext Cab SB	2190	3590
2 Dr STD Std Cab SB	1930	3160
2 Dr STD Std Cab LB	1990	3260
2 Dr STD 4WD Ext Cab SB	2770	4535
2 Dr STD 4WD Std Cab LB	2660	4360

OPTIONS FOR S15

6 cyl 2.8 L Engine +50
6 cyl 4.3 L Engine +55
Auto 4-Speed Transmission +110
Air Conditioning +110
Aluminum/Alloy Wheels +45
AM/FM Stereo Tape +35
Camper/Towing Package +40
Cruise Control +30
Limited Slip Diff +35
Power Door Locks +30
Power Steering[Opt on 2WD] +40
Power Windows +30
Premium Sound System +50

S15 JIMMY 1989

Rear-wheel ABS that operates in 2WD mode only, and rear shoulder belts are added. Instatrac 4WD system is revised when equipped with standard 2.8-liter V6. Power steering is made standard. Rear wiper/washer and digital gauges are new to options list.

RATINGS (SCALE OF 1-10)

Overall	Safety	Reliability	Performance	Comfort	Value
5.9	3.4	6.1	6.8	7.1	6.2

Category G

Model	Trade-in	Market
2 Dr Gypsy Utility	2475	4060
2 Dr Gypsy 4WD Utility	2610	4280
2 Dr Sierra Classic Utility	2420	3970
2 Dr Sierra Classic 4WD Utility	2580	4225
2 Dr STD Utility	2360	3865
2 Dr STD 4WD Utility	2450	4015

OPTIONS FOR S15 JIMMY

6 cyl 4.3 L Engine +50
Auto 4-Speed Transmission +110
Timberline Pkg +140
Air Conditioning +110
Aluminum/Alloy Wheels +45
AM/FM Stereo Tape +35
Camper/Towing Package +40
Cruise Control +30
Leather Seats +105

Don't forget to refer to the Mileage Adjustment Table at the back of this book!

 © 1999 by Edmund Publications Corporation

Model Description	Trade-in Value	Market Value

Limited Slip Diff +35
Power Door Locks +30
Power Windows +30
Premium Sound System +50
Sunroof +40
Swing Out Tire Carrier +30

SAFARI 1989

Rear-wheel ABS is added. Standard gauges have been upgraded. Power steering, front stabilizer bar and 27-gallon fuel tank move from options sheet to standard equipment list. Outboard seating positions get shoulder belts. Optional four-seat seating package is dropped. Midyear, a sport suspension package is introduced.

RATINGS (SCALE OF 1-10)

Overall	Safety	Reliability	Performance	Comfort	Value
6.3	3.4	6.4	7.2	6.6	8.1

Category G

Model	Trade-in	Market
2 Dr SLE Pass. Van	2560	4195
2 Dr SLT Pass. Van	2625	4300
2 Dr SLX Pass. Van	2240	3670
2 Dr STD Cargo Van	1935	3170

OPTIONS FOR SAFARI

6 cyl 4.3 L Engine[Opt on STD] +50
Auto 4-Speed Transmission +85
Air Conditioning +110
Aluminum/Alloy Wheels +45
AM/FM Stereo Tape +35
Camper/Towing Package +40
Cruise Control +30
Dual Air Conditioning +135
Limited Slip Diff +35
Power Door Locks +30
Power Drivers Seat +40
Power Windows +30
Premium Sound System +50

SUBURBAN 1989

Trim treatments are revised. Front styling updated to resemble Sierra.

Category H

Model	Trade-in	Market
4 Dr R1500 Wgn	4410	6390
4 Dr R2500 Wgn	4565	6620
4 Dr V1500 4WD Wgn	4945	7165
4 Dr V2500 4WD Wgn	5180	7505

OPTIONS FOR SUBURBAN

8 cyl 6.2 L Dsl Engine +290
8 cyl 7.4 L Engine +65
Auto 3-Speed Transmission +85
Auto 4-Speed Transmission[Std on R15] +110
Seat Package +130
Sierra SLE Pkg +210
Air Conditioning +110
Aluminum/Alloy Wheels +40

AM/FM Stereo Tape +35
Camper/Towing Package +50
Dual Air Conditioning +190
Limited Slip Diff +35
Premium Sound System +55

V3500 PICKUP 1989

Category H

Model	Trade-in	Market
4 Dr SLE 4WD Crew Cab LB	6710	9725

OPTIONS FOR V3500 PICKUP

8 cyl 6.2 L Dsl Engine +290
8 cyl 7.4 L Engine +65
Auto 3-Speed Transmission +85
Air Conditioning +110
AM/FM Stereo Tape +35
Limited Slip Diff +35

VANDURA/RALLY WAGON 1989

A 7.4-liter V8 is new to the options list.

G15

Category H

Model	Trade-in	Market
2 Dr STD Vandura Ext	2835	4110
2 Dr STD Rally Wagon Ext	3240	4695
2 Dr STD Rally Wagon	3105	4500
2 Dr STD Vandura	2580	3740

G25

Category H

Model	Trade-in	Market
2 Dr STD Rally Wagon	3085	4470
2 Dr STD Vandura	2710	3925
2 Dr STX Rally Wagon	3465	5025

G35

Category H

Model	Trade-in	Market
2 Dr STD Vandura	2310	3350
2 Dr STD Rally Wagon	3245	4705
2 Dr STX Rally Wagon	3285	4765

OPTIONS FOR VANDURA/RALLY WAGON

8 cyl 6.2 L Dsl Engine +290
8 cyl 5.0 L Engine +80
8 cyl 5.7 L Engine[Opt on G15,G25,Vandura] +100
Auto 4-Speed Transmission[Std on G35] +65
Air Conditioning +110
Aluminum/Alloy Wheels +40
AM/FM Stereo Tape +35
Camper/Towing Package +50
Dual Air Conditioning +190
Limited Slip Diff +35
Premium Sound System +55

For a guaranteed low price on a new car in your area, call
1-800-CAR-CLUB

Don't forget to refer to the Mileage Adjustment Table at the back of this book!

 © 1999 by Edmund Publications Corporation

Model Description	Trade-in Value	Market Value

HONDA
Japan

1993 Honda Civic

1998 HONDA

ACCORD 1998

Honda redesigns its best-seller for 1998. A 3.0-liter V6 engine makes its debut in LX and EX models, marking the first six-cylinder VTEC in the Honda lineup. The standard 2.3-liter four-banger is also re-engineered, as is the chassis. And the new interior design creates more room inside than any of Accord's competitors.

Category E

Model Description	Trade-in Value	Market Value
4 Dr DX Sdn	10960	13205
2 Dr EX Cpe	14205	17115
4 Dr EX Sdn	15300	18430
2 Dr EX V6 Cpe	17825	21475
4 Dr EX V6 Sdn	17445	21020
2 Dr LX Cpe	13015	15685
4 Dr LX Sdn	12850	15485
2 Dr LX V6 Cpe	15935	19200
4 Dr LX V6 Sdn	15195	18305

OPTIONS FOR ACCORD

Auto 4-Speed Transmission[Std on EX V6, LX V6] +665
Air Conditioning[Opt on DX] +675
Aluminum/Alloy Wheels[Std on EX, EX V6] +265
Anti-Lock Brakes[Std on EX, EX V6, LX V6] +590
Leather Seats[Std on EX V6] +740
Power Drivers Seat[Std on EX V6, LX V6] +245

CIVIC 1998

Last year's best-selling small car gets minor revisions: select models get new wheelcovers, a rear hatch handle, and map lights.

Category E

Model Description	Trade-in Value	Market Value
2 Dr CX Hbk	7620	9185
2 Dr DX Hbk	8400	10120
2 Dr DX Cpe	8570	10325
4 Dr DX Sdn	8795	10595
2 Dr EX Cpe	11555	13925
4 Dr EX Sdn	11670	14065
2 Dr HX Cpe	10020	12070
4 Dr LX Sdn	10600	12770

OPTIONS FOR CIVIC

Auto 4-Speed Transmission +705
Air Conditioning[Std on EX, LX] +675
AM/FM Compact Disc Playr +390
Power Steering[Opt on CX] +210

CR-V 1998

A manual transmission lowers the ante, making the CR-V a more attractive value than before. Also available is a front-wheel drive LX model, and the EX trim level now includes a CD player, anti-lock brakes, and remote keyless entry.

Category G

Model Description	Trade-in Value	Market Value
4 Dr EX 4WD Wgn	14610	17395
4 Dr LX 4WD Wgn	13510	16080

OPTIONS FOR CR-V

Auto 4-Speed Transmission[Std on 2WD] +665

ODYSSEY 1998

The engine is upgraded to a more sophisticated 2.3-liter, good for an extra 10 horsepower and seven foot-pounds of torque. New looks up front come from a revised bumper and grille, and the interior gets dressed in new fabric.

Category G

Model Description	Trade-in Value	Market Value
4 Dr EX Pass. Van	17540	20880
4 Dr LX Pass. Van	16210	19295

OPTIONS FOR ODYSSEY

6 Passenger Seating[Opt on LX] +400
Captain Chairs (4)[Opt on LX] +525

PASSPORT 1998

Like its Isuzu Rodeo counterpart, the Passport has been completely revised from top to bottom. The Passport gets modernized styling, a user-friendly interior, more V6 power and added room for passengers and cargo.

Category G

Model Description	Trade-in Value	Market Value
4 Dr EX 4WD Wgn	19180	22835
4 Dr LX 4WD Wgn	16240	19330

OPTIONS FOR PASSPORT

Auto 4-Speed Transmission[Opt on LX] +955
Leather Seats +640
Limited Slip Diff[Opt on LX] +220
Swing Out Tire Carrier +170

Don't forget to refer to the Mileage Adjustment Table at the back of this book!

© 1999 by Edmund Publications Corporation

Model Description	Trade-in Value	Market Value

PRELUDE 1998

The Prelude doesn't change for 1998, because you don't mess with success. (Pssst, buy this car!)

Category F

2 Dr STD Cpe	15765	18550
2 Dr Type SH Cpe	18150	21350

OPTIONS FOR PRELUDE

Auto 4-Speed Transmission +830

1997 HONDA

ACCORD 1997

Changes to the ever-popular Accord include the deletion of antilock brakes on the LX five-speed models and the discontinuation of the EX coupes with leather. No other changes for the 1997 Accord.

RATINGS (SCALE OF 1-10)

Overall	Safety	Reliability	Performance	Comfort	Value
7.6	6.9	9.1	7.8	8	6.3

Category E

4 Dr DX Sdn	9440	11510
2 Dr EX Cpe	13055	15925
4 Dr EX Wgn	13805	16835
4 Dr EX Sdn	13345	16275
4 Dr EX V6 Sdn	15525	18930
2 Dr LX Cpe	11220	13685
4 Dr LX Sdn	11480	14000
4 Dr LX Wgn	11570	14110
4 Dr LX V6 Sdn	13420	16370
2 Dr Special Edition Cpe	12810	15620
4 Dr Special Edition Sdn	13055	15920
4 Dr Value Sdn	10510	12815

OPTIONS FOR ACCORD

Auto 4-Speed Transmission[Opt on DX,LX,EX Sdn,EX Cpe] +545
Air Conditioning[Opt on DX] +550
Aluminum/Alloy Wheels[Opt on LX] +215
Anti-Lock Brakes[Opt on LX] +480
Compact Disc W/fm/tape[Opt on EX,EX V6] +470
Leather Seats[Opt on EX] +605
Power Drivers Seat[Opt on EX] +200

CIVIC 1997

For some reason, Honda deletes the Civic EX Coupe five-speed with ABS model. Maybe they think that people who like to row their own gears don't worry about whether they can stop or not. DX models receive new wheel covers, all Civics get 14-inch wheels, and the LX sedan gets air conditioning.

RATINGS (SCALE OF 1-10)

Overall	Safety	Reliability	Performance	Comfort	Value
7.3	6.6	8.9	8.2	7.8	5

Category E

2 Dr CX Hbk	7030	8570
2 Dr DX Hbk	7625	9300
2 Dr DX Cpe	8125	9910
4 Dr DX Sdn	8250	10060
2 Dr EX Cpe	10670	13010
4 Dr EX Sdn	10655	12995
2 Dr HX Cpe	9235	11265
4 Dr LX Sdn	9605	11715

OPTIONS FOR CIVIC

Auto 4-Speed Transmission +610
Air Conditioning[Std on EX,LX] +550
AM/FM Compact Disc Playr +320
Anti-Lock Brakes[Opt on Cpe] +480
Leather Seats +605
Power Steering[Std on EX,HX,LX,DX,Sdn] +170
Rear Spoiler +140

CIVIC DEL SOL 1997

No changes to Honda's two-seater.

RATINGS (SCALE OF 1-10)

Overall	Safety	Reliability	Performance	Comfort	Value
N/A	N/A	8.8	8.4	7.6	4.1

Category F

2 Dr S Cpe	9505	11450
2 Dr Si Cpe	10930	13165
2 Dr VTEC Cpe	12100	14580

OPTIONS FOR CIVIC DEL SOL

Auto 4-Speed Transmission +605
Air Conditioning +565
Power Steering[Opt on S] +245

CR-V 1997

Priced competitively with mini-utes, the CR-V offers cargo capacity that is in line with what compact sport-utility buyers are accustomed to. The CR-V comes in one trim level and is available with antilock brakes.

RATINGS (SCALE OF 1-10)

Overall	Safety	Reliability	Performance	Comfort	Value
N/A	7.4	N/A	7.8	8.5	N/A

Category G

4 Dr STD 4WD Wgn	14265	16985

OPTIONS FOR CR-V

Aluminum/Alloy Wheels +235
AM/FM Compact Disc Playr +260
Anti-Lock Brakes +420
Luggage Rack +105

Don't forget to refer to the Mileage Adjustment Table at the back of this book!

 © 1999 by Edmund Publications Corporation

Model Description	Trade-in Value	Market Value

ODYSSEY 1997

No changes for the 1997 Honda Odyssey.

RATINGS (SCALE OF 1-10)

Overall	Safety	Reliability	Performance	Comfort	Value
7.4	7.5	9.4	7.2	7.1	5.6

Category G		
4 Dr EX Pass. Van	15825	18840
4 Dr LX Pass. Van	13880	16525

OPTIONS FOR ODYSSEY

AM/FM Compact Disc Playr +260
Captain Chairs (4)[Opt on LX] +430
Luggage Rack +105

PASSPORT 1997

Honda drops the slow-selling DX four-cylinder Passport.

RATINGS (SCALE OF 1-10)

Overall	Safety	Reliability	Performance	Comfort	Value
6.7	6.8	8	7	7.1	4.8

Category G		
4 Dr EX Wgn	14845	17675
4 Dr EX 4WD Wgn	16345	19455
4 Dr LX Wgn	12445	14820
4 Dr LX 4WD Wgn	13705	16315

OPTIONS FOR PASSPORT

Auto 4-Speed Transmission[Opt on LX,4WD] +740
Air Conditioning[Std on EX,4WD] +550
Limited Slip Diff[Opt on LX] +180

PRELUDE 1997

The Prelude is totally redesigned for 1997. A base model is available with a five-speed manual or four-speed automatic gearbox, but the top-of-the-line Type SH model, featuring Honda's new Active Torque Transfer System, can only be had as a manual. Both the base and Type SH Preludes feature last year's VTEC engine which produces 195-horsepower for 1997.

RATINGS (SCALE OF 1-10)

Overall	Safety	Reliability	Performance	Comfort	Value
N/A	N/A	9.1	8.6	6.9	4.7

Category F		
2 Dr STD Cpe	14535	17515
2 Dr Type SH Cpe	16640	20050

1996 HONDA

ACCORD 1996

All Accords get revised styling, featuring new taillights and bumper covers. Wagons have a new roof rack, while sedans boast a new pass-through ski sack.

RATINGS (SCALE OF 1-10)

Overall	Safety	Reliability	Performance	Comfort	Value
7.4	6.9	9	7.8	8	5.4

Category E		
4 Dr 25th Anniversary Sdn	9835	12445
4 Dr DX Sdn	8565	10840
2 Dr EX Cpe	11680	14785
4 Dr EX Wgn	12155	15385
4 Dr EX Sdn	11860	15010
4 Dr EX V6 Sdn	13410	16975
2 Dr LX Cpe	10050	12725
4 Dr LX Sdn	10240	12965
4 Dr LX Wgn	10340	13085
4 Dr LX V6 Sdn	11720	14835

OPTIONS FOR ACCORD

Auto 4-Speed Transmission[Opt on DX,LX,EX Cpe,EX Sdn] +435
Air Conditioning[Opt on DX] +450
Aluminum/Alloy Wheels[Opt on LX,LX V6] +175
Anti-Lock Brakes[Opt on LX] +395
Compact Disc W/fm/tape +385
Leather Seats[Opt on EX] +495
Power Drivers Seat[Opt on EX Sdn] +165

CIVIC 1996

Keeping to their legendary four-year redesign schedule, Honda engineers have created a larger, more powerful, and more contemporary Civic for 1996. This is a great car for those concerned about reliability and value, but who don't want to sacrifice style.

RATINGS (SCALE OF 1-10)

Overall	Safety	Reliability	Performance	Comfort	Value
7.4	6.6	8.7	8.2	7.8	5.9

Category E		
2 Dr CX Hbk	6235	7895
2 Dr DX Cpe	7325	9275
2 Dr DX Hbk	6790	8595
4 Dr DX Sdn	7725	9780
2 Dr EX Cpe	9500	12025
4 Dr EX Sdn	9675	12250
2 Dr HX Cpe	8110	10265
4 Dr LX Sdn	8065	10210

OPTIONS FOR CIVIC

Auto 4-Speed Transmission +490
Air Conditioning[Std on EX] +450
Aluminum/Alloy Wheels[Opt on DX] +175
AM/FM Stereo Tape +170
Anti-Lock Brakes[Opt on LX,Cpe] +395
Compact Disc Changer +310
Power Steering[Std on EX,HX,LX,DX Sdn] +140
Rear Spoiler +115

Don't forget to refer to the Mileage Adjustment Table at the back of this book!

 © 1999 by Edmund Publications Corporation

Model Description	Trade-in Value	Market Value

CIVIC DEL SOL 1996

No changes to the 1996 del Sol.

RATINGS (SCALE OF 1-10)

Overall	Safety	Reliability	Performance	Comfort	Value
N/A	N/A	8.5	8.4	7.6	4

Category F		
2 Dr S Cpe	8650	10680
2 Dr Si Cpe	9845	12155
2 Dr VTEC Cpe	10920	13480

OPTIONS FOR CIVIC DEL SOL

Auto 4-Speed Transmission +470
Air Conditioning +460
Power Steering[Opt on S] +200

ODYSSEY 1996

Minivan-wagon hybrid carries into 1996 sans changes.

RATINGS (SCALE OF 1-10)

Overall	Safety	Reliability	Performance	Comfort	Value
7.6	7.5	9.4	7.2	7.1	6.6

Category G		
4 Dr EX Pass. Van	13590	16570
4 Dr LX Pass. Van	13325	16250

OPTIONS FOR ODYSSEY

Captain Chairs (4)[Opt on LX] +350

PASSPORT 1996

New wheels, dual airbags, available ABS, and a stronger V6 engine are the changes for the 1996 Isuzu Rodeo, er, we mean Passport.

RATINGS (SCALE OF 1-10)

Overall	Safety	Reliability	Performance	Comfort	Value
7	6.6	7.8	7	7.1	6.7

Category G		
4 Dr DX Wgn	9815	11965
4 Dr EX Wgn	13915	16970
4 Dr EX 4WD Wgn	14905	18180
4 Dr LX Wgn	11210	13670
4 Dr LX 4WD Wgn	12485	15225

OPTIONS FOR PASSPORT

Auto 4-Speed Transmission[Opt on LX,4WD] +595
Air Conditioning[Std on EX,4WD] +450

PRELUDE 1996

This is the last year for the current-generation Prelude. All of the really exciting stuff happens in 1997.

RATINGS (SCALE OF 1-10)

Overall	Safety	Reliability	Performance	Comfort	Value
7	7.4	8.9	9	6.8	3.1

Category F		
2 Dr S Cpe	11365	14030
2 Dr Si Cpe	12855	15870
2 Dr VTEC Cpe	14525	17935

OPTIONS FOR PRELUDE

Auto 4-Speed Transmission +435

1995 HONDA

ACCORD 1995

Finally, a V6 is offered in the midsized Honda! Unfortunately, it fails to improve performance figures because of the mandatory automatic transmission. V6 Accords gain different front styling as a result of the increased size of the engine bay. All V6 Accords come with standard antilock brakes.

RATINGS (SCALE OF 1-10)

Overall	Safety	Reliability	Performance	Comfort	Value
7.4	7.5	8.6	7.8	8	5.4

Category E		
4 Dr DX Sdn	7295	9475
2 Dr EX Cpe	9880	12830
4 Dr EX Sdn	10040	13035
4 Dr EX Wgn	10390	13490
4 Dr EX V6 Sdn	11430	14845
2 Dr LX Cpe	8470	11000
4 Dr LX Wgn	8810	11440
4 Dr LX Sdn	8655	11240
4 Dr LX V6 Sdn	9835	12775

OPTIONS FOR ACCORD

Auto 4-Speed Transmission[Opt on DX,LX,EX Cpe,EX Sdn] +335
Air Conditioning[Opt on DX] +370
Anti-Lock Brakes[Opt on LX] +320
Compact Disc W/fm/tape +315
Leather Seats[Std on EX V6] +405
Power Drivers Seat[Opt on EX] +135

CIVIC 1995

No changes for the last year of the current Civic.

RATINGS (SCALE OF 1-10)

Overall	Safety	Reliability	Performance	Comfort	Value
7.1	6.5	8.6	8	8	4.4

Category E		
2 Dr CX Hbk	5325	6915
2 Dr DX Cpe	6360	8260
2 Dr DX Hbk	6035	7840
4 Dr DX Sdn	6495	8435
2 Dr EX Cpe	7900	10260
4 Dr EX Sdn	8400	10905

Don't forget to refer to the Mileage Adjustment Table at the back of this book!

 © 1999 by Edmund Publications Corporation

Model Description	Trade-in Value	Market Value
4 Dr LX Sdn	7010	9105
2 Dr Si Hbk	7070	9185
2 Dr VX Hbk	6225	8085

OPTIONS FOR CIVIC

Auto 4-Speed Transmission +370
Air Conditioning[Std on EX Sdn] +370
Aluminum/Alloy Wheels[Opt on EX] +145
AM/FM Stereo Tape[Opt on DX] +140
Anti-Lock Brakes[Opt on LX,Cpe] +320
Power Steering[Opt on DX Hbk] +115
Premium Sound System +155
Rear Spoiler +95

CIVIC DEL SOL 1995

Antilock brakes are now standard on VTEC models. Power door locks are also new to the standard equipment lists of Si and VTEC models. All del Sols get a remote trunk release.

RATINGS (SCALE OF 1-10)

Overall	Safety	Reliability	Performance	Comfort	Value
N/A	N/A	8.5	8.4	7.6	4.5

Category F

Model Description	Trade-in Value	Market Value
2 Dr S Cpe	7680	9600
2 Dr Si Cpe	8695	10870
2 Dr VTEC Cpe	9710	12140

OPTIONS FOR CIVIC DEL SOL

Auto 4-Speed Transmission +385
Air Conditioning +380
Power Steering[Opt on S] +165

ODYSSEY 1995

Honda finally gets its minivan in the form of the Odyssey. Unique to the Odyssey is five-door design that includes four passenger car-like swing-out doors. LX and EX models come standard with antilock brakes and dual airbags.

RATINGS (SCALE OF 1-10)

Overall	Safety	Reliability	Performance	Comfort	Value
7.5	8.2	8.9	7.2	7.1	6

Category G

Model Description	Trade-in Value	Market Value
4 Dr EX Pass. Van	12785	15785
4 Dr LX Pass. Van	11500	14195

OPTIONS FOR ODYSSEY

Captain Chairs (4) +285
Luggage Rack[Opt on LX] +70

PASSPORT 1995

Midyear change gives the Passport a driver airbag.

RATINGS (SCALE OF 1-10)

Overall	Safety	Reliability	Performance	Comfort	Value
7.2	7	7.9	7	7.1	6.8

Category G

Model Description	Trade-in Value	Market Value
4 Dr DX Wgn	8545	10545
4 Dr DX 1995.5 Wgn	8710	10750
4 Dr EX 4WD Wgn	12840	15850
4 Dr EX 1995.5 Wgn	12265	15145
4 Dr EX 1995.5 4WD Wgn	13110	16185
4 Dr LX Wgn	10355	12785
4 Dr LX 4WD Wgn	10575	13055
4 Dr LX 1995.5 Wgn	10475	12935
4 Dr LX 1995.5 4WD Wgn	10745	13265

OPTIONS FOR PASSPORT

Auto 4-Speed Transmission +515
Air Conditioning[Opt on DX,2WD] +370
Aluminum/Alloy Wheels[Opt on LX] +155
AM/FM Stereo Tape[Opt on DX] +110
Leather Seats +350
Limited Slip Diff[Opt on LX] +120
Luggage Rack +70
Running Boards +175

PRELUDE 1995

The ill-conceived Si 4WS is mercifully dropped from the Prelude lineup. The fourth-generation Prelude is nearing the end of its life. Few changes for 1995 except the addition of air conditioning to the standard equipment list of S models.

RATINGS (SCALE OF 1-10)

Overall	Safety	Reliability	Performance	Comfort	Value
7.1	8.1	8.9	9	6.8	2.6

Category F

Model Description	Trade-in Value	Market Value
2 Dr S Cpe	9460	11825
2 Dr SE Cpe	11450	14315
2 Dr Si Cpe	10650	13310
2 Dr VTEC Cpe	12080	15105

OPTIONS FOR PRELUDE

Auto 4-Speed Transmission +335

1994 HONDA

ACCORD 1994

Once again, Honda's best-selling model is redesigned. Changes for 1994 make the vehicle more competitive with its midsize rival, the Ford Taurus. Shorter and wider than the previous generation Accord, the 1994 model is available in three trim levels. Antilock brakes are standard on the EX and are finally available on the LX and DX. New engines across the board improve horsepower figures for all Accords.

RATINGS (SCALE OF 1-10)

Overall	Safety	Reliability	Performance	Comfort	Value
7.5	7.5	8.8	7.8	8	5.3

Don't forget to refer to the Mileage Adjustment Table at the back of this book!

 © 1999 by Edmund Publications Corporation

Accord (continued)

Category E

Model Description	Trade-in Value	Market Value
2 Dr DX Cpe	6070	8090
4 Dr DX Sdn	6225	8305
2 Dr EX Cpe	8235	10980
4 Dr EX Wgn	8505	11335
4 Dr EX Sdn	8365	11155
2 Dr LX Cpe	7065	9425
4 Dr LX Sdn	7200	9600
4 Dr LX Wgn	7400	9865

OPTIONS FOR ACCORD

Auto 4-Speed Transmission +280
Air Conditioning[Opt on DX] +300
AM/FM Compact Disc Playr +175
Anti-Lock Brakes[Std on EX] +265
Leather Seats +330

CIVIC 1994

The passenger airbag is now standard on all Civics. Antilock brakes are optional on the LX sedan, EX coupe and Si hatchback.

RATINGS (SCALE OF 1-10)

Overall	Safety	Reliability	Performance	Comfort	Value
7.5	6.5	8.6	8	8	6.4

Category E

Model Description	Trade-in Value	Market Value
2 Dr CX Hbk	4245	5660
2 Dr DX Hbk	4775	6370
2 Dr DX Cpe	5175	6905
4 Dr DX Sdn	5250	7000
2 Dr EX Cpe	6680	8910
4 Dr EX Sdn	6830	9110
4 Dr LX Sdn	5850	7800
2 Dr Si Hbk	5985	7980
2 Dr VX Hbk	4940	6590

OPTIONS FOR CIVIC

Auto 4-Speed Transmission +305
Air Conditioning[Std on EX Sdn] +300
Aluminum/Alloy Wheels[Std on VX] +120
AM/FM Compact Disc Playr +175
Anti-Lock Brakes[Opt on LX,Si,Cpe] +265
Cruise Control[Opt on DX] +80
Leather Seats +330
Power Door Locks[Opt on VX] +85
Power Steering[Std on EX,LX,Si,Sdn] +95
Rear Spoiler +75

CIVIC DEL SOL 1994

VTEC technology makes its way to the del Sol giving buyers a choice of three models. VTEC del Sols offer 35 more horsepower than the Si. A passenger airbag joins the standard equipment list for all models. VTEC del Sols gain performance-oriented upgrades that include a beefier suspension, larger tires and bigger brakes.

RATINGS (SCALE OF 1-10)

Overall	Safety	Reliability	Performance	Comfort	Value
N/A	N/A	7.9	8.4	7.6	4.3

Category F

Model Description	Trade-in Value	Market Value
2 Dr S Cpe	6460	8180
2 Dr Si Cpe	7105	8990
2 Dr VTEC Cpe	7820	9900

OPTIONS FOR CIVIC DEL SOL

Auto 4-Speed Transmission +320
Air Conditioning +310
AM/FM Stereo Tape[Opt on S] +75
Power Steering[Opt on S] +135

PASSPORT 1994

Honda loyalists waiting for the launch of a Honda sport utility should be thrilled with the Passport, until they discover that it's an Isuzu. Based on the highly successful Rodeo, the Honda Passport has very little to distinguish it from its less expensive twin. Two- and four-wheel drive models are available in three trim levels ranging from the budget-minded DX to the top-end EX.

RATINGS (SCALE OF 1-10)

Overall	Safety	Reliability	Performance	Comfort	Value
6.5	4.1	7.8	7	7.4	6.2

Category G

Model Description	Trade-in Value	Market Value
4 Dr DX Wgn	6735	8415
4 Dr EX 4WD Wgn	10185	12730
4 Dr LX Wgn	8490	10610
4 Dr LX 4WD Wgn	8750	10935

OPTIONS FOR PASSPORT

Auto 4-Speed Transmission +385
Air Conditioning[Opt on DX,2WD] +300
AM/FM Stereo Tape[Std on EX] +90
Luggage Rack +60

PRELUDE 1994

Dual airbags are standard on all Preludes this year. Improved interior ergonomics, freshened front-end styling, and environmentally conscious CFC-free air conditioning are also welcome changes to this car.

RATINGS (SCALE OF 1-10)

Overall	Safety	Reliability	Performance	Comfort	Value
7.2	8.1	8.9	9	6.8	3.1

Category F

Model Description	Trade-in Value	Market Value
2 Dr S Cpe	7545	9550
2 Dr Si Cpe	9140	11570
2 Dr Si 4WS Cpe	9840	12455
2 Dr VTEC Cpe	10175	12880

Don't forget to refer to the Mileage Adjustment Table at the back of this book!

 © 1999 by Edmund Publications Corporation

OPTIONS FOR PRELUDE

Auto 4-Speed Transmission +280
Air Conditioning[Opt on S] +310
Aluminum/Alloy Wheels[Opt on S] +115
Rear Spoiler[Opt on Si] +105

1993 HONDA

ACCORD 1993

The SE model is re-introduced as the top of the line Accord. A passenger airbag is added.

RATINGS (SCALE OF 1-10)

Overall	Safety	Reliability	Performance	Comfort	Value
N/A	N/A	8.1	8	8.4	5.4

Category E

Model	Trade-in	Market
4 Dr 10th Anniversary Sdn	6835	9360
2 Dr DX Cpe	4915	6735
4 Dr DX Sdn	5105	6990
2 Dr EX Cpe	6685	9160
4 Dr EX Sdn	6610	9055
4 Dr EX Wgn	7115	9745
2 Dr LX Cpe	5915	8105
4 Dr LX Sdn	6120	8385
4 Dr LX Wgn	6630	9085
2 Dr SE Cpe	7315	10025
4 Dr SE Sdn	7490	10260

OPTIONS FOR ACCORD

Auto 4-Speed Transmission[Opt on DX,EX,LX] +225
Air Conditioning[Opt on DX] +245
Aluminum/Alloy Wheels[Opt on LX] +95
AM/FM Stereo Tape[Opt on DX] +95
Anti-Lock Brakes[Opt on LX] +215
Leather Seats[Std on SE] +270

CIVIC 1993

A coupe body style is added to the Civic stable. EX models get standard power steering and a sunroof. A passenger airbag is available on the EX coupe.

RATINGS (SCALE OF 1-10)

Overall	Safety	Reliability	Performance	Comfort	Value
6.9	5.1	8.6	8	8	4.9

Category E

Model	Trade-in	Market
2 Dr CX Hbk	3575	4895
2 Dr DX Hbk	4080	5590
2 Dr DX Cpe	4465	6115
4 Dr DX Sdn	4510	6180
2 Dr EX Cpe	5600	7675
4 Dr EX Sdn	5540	7585
4 Dr LX Sdn	4905	6720
2 Dr Si Hbk	4985	6830
2 Dr VX Hbk	4260	5835

OPTIONS FOR CIVIC

Auto 4-Speed Transmission +250
Air Conditioning +245
Aluminum/Alloy Wheels[Opt on EX] +95
AM/FM Compact Disc Playr +145
Cruise Control[Opt on VX] +65
Dual Air Bag Restraints +190
Power Steering[Opt on DX Cpe] +75
Rear Spoiler +60

CIVIC DEL SOL 1993

The sun, that's what Honda wants you to think of when you picture this open-air replacement for the CRX. Poised to recapture some of the two-seater market from the Mazda Miata, the del Sol offers solid performance and value. Usable trunk space and improved body rigidity are the benefits the del Sol has over its rivals. We think, however, that the Miata's superior horsepower and rear-wheel drive will prove to be more fun in the long run.

RATINGS (SCALE OF 1-10)

Overall	Safety	Reliability	Performance	Comfort	Value
N/A	N/A	8.4	8.4	7.6	4.4

Category F

Model	Trade-in	Market
2 Dr S Cpe	5555	7215
2 Dr Si Cpe	6140	7970

OPTIONS FOR CIVIC DEL SOL

Auto 4-Speed Transmission +260
Air Conditioning +250
AM/FM Stereo Tape +60
Power Door Locks +60

PRELUDE 1993

More power, in the form of Honda's exclusive VTEC system, is available to the Prelude. A boost of 30 horsepower for top-end Preludes means that that this car won't be the laughingstock of stoplight drags anymore.

RATINGS (SCALE OF 1-10)

Overall	Safety	Reliability	Performance	Comfort	Value
6.9	7	8.9	9	6.8	3.1

Category F

Model	Trade-in	Market
2 Dr S Cpe	6805	8840
2 Dr Si Cpe	7760	10075
2 Dr Si 4WS Cpe	8315	10800
2 Dr VTEC Cpe	8800	11425

OPTIONS FOR PRELUDE

Auto 4-Speed Transmission +225
Air Conditioning[Opt on S] +250
AM/FM Compact Disc Playr +150

Don't forget to refer to the Mileage Adjustment Table at the back of this book!

 © 1999 by Edmund Publications Corporation

1992 HONDA

ACCORD 1992

The SE model is dropped. The EX model gains antilock brakes with rear discs instead of drums. Horsepower is up in the EX sedans, ten more than last year's 130. A driver airbag is added to the standard equipment list.

RATINGS (SCALE OF 1-10)

Overall	Safety	Reliability	Performance	Comfort	Value
N/A	N/A	7.8	8	8.4	6.2

Category E		
2 Dr DX Cpe	4050	5790
4 Dr DX Sdn	4245	6065
2 Dr EX Cpe	5510	7875
4 Dr EX Wgn	6165	8805
4 Dr EX Sdn	5675	8110
2 Dr LX Cpe	4850	6930
4 Dr LX Sdn	5015	7165
4 Dr LX Wgn	5500	7855

OPTIONS FOR ACCORD

Auto 4-Speed Transmission +185
Air Conditioning[Opt on DX] +200
Aluminum/Alloy Wheels[Opt on LX] +80
AM/FM Stereo Tape[Opt on DX,EX Wgn] +75
Leather Seats +220
Luggage Rack +30

CIVIC 1992

A driver airbag is standard on all new Civics. Unfortunately, the wagon body style is dropped from the lineup. VTEC power is available by way of the top-end EX model. All sedans now have power steering added to their standard equipment list.

RATINGS (SCALE OF 1-10)

Overall	Safety	Reliability	Performance	Comfort	Value
7	5.1	8.2	8	8	5.7

Category E		
2 Dr CX Hbk	3040	4345
2 Dr DX Hbk	3585	5120
4 Dr DX Sdn	3685	5260
4 Dr EX Sdn	4615	6595
4 Dr LX Sdn	4035	5765
2 Dr Si Hbk	4110	5870
2 Dr VX Hbk	3655	5225

OPTIONS FOR CIVIC

Auto 4-Speed Transmission +185
Air Conditioning +200
Aluminum/Alloy Wheels[Std on VX] +80
AM/FM Stereo Tape +75
Power Steering[Opt on DX Hbk] +60
Rear Spoiler[Opt on Si] +50

PRELUDE 1992

Totally redesigned for 1992, the fourth generation Prelude sports a driver airbag in all models and a standard passenger airbag on the Si 4WS. Antilock brakes are still available only on Si models.

RATINGS (SCALE OF 1-10)

Overall	Safety	Reliability	Performance	Comfort	Value
7.2	7	8.7	9	6.8	4.5

Category F		
2 Dr S Cpe	5930	7905
2 Dr Si Cpe	6850	9135

OPTIONS FOR PRELUDE

Auto 4-Speed Transmission +185
Air Conditioning[Opt on S] +205
Compact Disc W/fm/tape +130
Leather Seats +175
Rear Spoiler +70

1991 HONDA

ACCORD 1991

Honda introduces a leather-trimmed SE model to the lineup to compete in the upscale market.

RATINGS (SCALE OF 1-10)

Overall	Safety	Reliability	Performance	Comfort	Value
N/A	N/A	7	8	8.4	6.9

Category E		
2 Dr DX Cpe	3420	5030
4 Dr DX Sdn	3570	5255
2 Dr EX Cpe	4590	6745
4 Dr EX Wgn	5120	7530
4 Dr EX Sdn	4715	6930
2 Dr LX Cpe	4000	5885
4 Dr LX Wgn	4540	6675
4 Dr LX Sdn	4150	6100
4 Dr SE Sdn	5395	7935

OPTIONS FOR ACCORD

Auto 4-Speed Transmission[Std on SE] +150
Air Conditioning[Opt on DX] +165
AM/FM Stereo Tape[Opt on DX] +60
Cruise Control[Opt on DX] +45
Leather Seats[Opt on EX] +180

CIVIC 1991

Few changes for Honda's popular subcompact. A complete redesign is expected for 1992.

Category E		
2 Dr DX Hbk	2905	4270
4 Dr DX Sdn	2950	4335
4 Dr EX Sdn	3455	5080

Don't forget to refer to the Mileage Adjustment Table at the back of this book!

 © 1999 by Edmund Publications Corporation

Model Description	Trade-in Value	Market Value
4 Dr LX Sdn	3205	4715
2 Dr Si Hbk	3215	4730
2 Dr STD Hbk	2610	3835
4 Dr STD Wgn	3050	4485
4 Dr STD 4WD Wgn	3460	5090

OPTIONS FOR CIVIC

Auto 4-Speed Transmission +165
Air Conditioning +165
AM/FM Stereo Tape +60
Cruise Control[Std on EX,LX] +45
Power Steering[Std on EX,LX,Si,4WD] +50
Rear Spoiler +40

CIVIC CRX 1991

This is the last year for the Honda CRX. Stiff competition from Toyota and Mazda are forcing this superb two-seater into obscurity. The CRX's large luggage storage and peppy performance will be missed.

Category E

Model Description	Trade-in Value	Market Value
2 Dr HF Cpe	2870	4225
2 Dr Si Cpe	3545	5215
2 Dr STD Cpe	3190	4695

OPTIONS FOR CIVIC CRX

Auto 4-Speed Transmission +120
Air Conditioning +165
AM/FM Stereo Tape +60
Cruise Control +45

PRELUDE 1991

1991 is the last year for the third-generation Prelude, so no major changes in face of next year's redesign.

Category F

Model Description	Trade-in Value	Market Value
2 Dr 2.0 Si Cpe	4690	6250
2 Dr Si Cpe	5105	6805

OPTIONS FOR PRELUDE

Auto 4-Speed Transmission +150
Air Conditioning +170
Aluminum/Alloy Wheels +65
AM/FM Compact Disc Playr +100
Anti-Lock Brakes +145
Power Door Locks +40
Rear Spoiler +55

1990 HONDA

ACCORD 1990

The Accord is entirely redesigned for 1990. Nearly five inches longer than the previous model, the 1990 Accord has considerably more interior space than last year's model.

RATINGS (SCALE OF 1-10)

Overall	Safety	Reliability	Performance	Comfort	Value
N/A	N/A	7.5	8	8.4	6.9

Category E

Model Description	Trade-in Value	Market Value
2 Dr DX Cpe	2935	4520
4 Dr DX Sdn	3095	4760
2 Dr EX Cpe	3740	5750
4 Dr EX Sdn	3855	5930
2 Dr LX Cpe	3395	5225
4 Dr LX Sdn	3450	5310

OPTIONS FOR ACCORD

Auto 4-Speed Transmission +125
Air Conditioning[Opt on DX] +135
Aluminum/Alloy Wheels[Opt on LX] +50
AM/FM Stereo Tape[Std on EX,LX,Cpe] +50
Cruise Control[Opt on DX] +35
Leather Seats +145

CIVIC 1990

New bumpers are given to the hatchbacks and sedans. New front and rear light combinations also appear on the 1990 Civic. A top-of-the-line EX version is added.

Category E

Model Description	Trade-in Value	Market Value
2 Dr DX Hbk	2370	3650
4 Dr DX Sdn	2350	3615
4 Dr EX Sdn	2705	4165
4 Dr LX Sdn	2555	3930
2 Dr Si Hbk	2535	3900
2 Dr STD Hbk	2140	3290
4 Dr STD Wgn	2315	3565
4 Dr STD 4WD Wgn	2735	4210

OPTIONS FOR CIVIC

Auto 4-Speed Transmission +140
Air Conditioning +135
Aluminum/Alloy Wheels +50
AM/FM Stereo Tape +50
Cruise Control[Std on EX,LX] +35
Power Steering[Opt on DX,STD] +40
Rear Spoiler +35

CIVIC CRX 1990

All CRXs are equipped with passive restraint seatbelts. New wheel covers are among the only other changes to this peppy little car.

Category E

Model Description	Trade-in Value	Market Value
2 Dr HF Cpe	2345	3610
2 Dr Si Cpe	2805	4315
2 Dr STD Cpe	2565	3945

OPTIONS FOR CIVIC CRX

Auto 4-Speed Transmission +100
Air Conditioning +135
AM/FM Stereo Tape +50
Cruise Control +35

Don't forget to refer to the Mileage Adjustment Table at the back of this book!

© 1999 by Edmund Publications Corporation

Model Description	Trade-in Value	Market Value

PRELUDE 1990

Antilock brakes are finally available on Honda's pricey pocket rocket. Minor styling updates are the only other changes.

Category F

Model Description	Trade-in Value	Market Value
2 Dr S Cpe	3735	4980
2 Dr Si Cpe	4305	5745

OPTIONS FOR PRELUDE

4 cyl 2.1 L Engine +335
Auto 4-Speed Transmission +125
4 Wheel Steering +175
Air Conditioning[Opt on S] +140
Aluminum/Alloy Wheels[Opt on S] +50
Anti-Lock Brakes +120
Power Door Locks +35
Rear Spoiler +45

1989 HONDA

ACCORD 1989

Honda's mainstay continues into 1989 with few revisions. Available as a coupe, hatchback, or sedan, the Accord is due for a makeover next year. The sole change for 1989 is the addition of the SEi sedan.

Category E

Model Description	Trade-in Value	Market Value
2 Dr DX Cpe	2165	3545
2 Dr DX Hbk	2085	3420
4 Dr DX Sdn	2310	3785
4 Dr LX Sdn	2320	3800
2 Dr LXi Cpe	2530	4145
2 Dr LXi Hbk	2355	3855
4 Dr LXi Sdn	2470	4050
2 Dr SEi Cpe	2710	4440
4 Dr SEi Sdn	2620	4290

OPTIONS FOR ACCORD

Auto 4-Speed Transmission +85
Air Conditioning[Opt on DX] +110
Aluminum/Alloy Wheels[Opt on LX] +45
AM/FM Stereo Tape[Opt on DX] +40
Cruise Control[Std on LX,LXi,SEi,Sdn] +30
Premium Sound System[Opt on LXi] +45

CIVIC 1989

Fun-to-drive Si hatchback is resurrected. Automatic transmission becomes available on the four-wheel drive wagon.

Category E

Model Description	Trade-in Value	Market Value
2 Dr DX Hbk	1760	2885
4 Dr DX Sdn	1845	3025
4 Dr LX Sdn	2010	3300
2 Dr Si Hbk	1995	3270
2 Dr STD Hbk	1545	2535
4 Dr STD Wgn	2005	3285
4 Dr STD 4WD Wgn	2305	3775
4 Dr Wagovan Wgn	2010	3300

OPTIONS FOR CIVIC

Auto 4-Speed Transmission +100
Air Conditioning +110
AM/FM Stereo Tape +40
Cruise Control +30
Power Steering[Std on LX,Si,4WD] +35

CIVIC CRX 1989

The Civic-related CRX returns virtually unchanged after last year's redesign. This attractive two-seater is available in three models that range from the environmentally friendly HF to the enthusiast oriented Si. Performance is uniformly good in this front-wheel drive car.

Category E

Model Description	Trade-in Value	Market Value
2 Dr HF Cpe	1710	2805
2 Dr Si Cpe	2300	3770
2 Dr STD Cpe	1855	3040

OPTIONS FOR CIVIC CRX

Auto 4-Speed Transmission +75
Air Conditioning +110
AM/FM Stereo Tape +40
Cruise Control +30

PRELUDE 1989

Honda's sport coupe entry is unchanged from the 1988 redesign that brought us the first example of four-wheel steering in a production car.

Category F

Model Description	Trade-in Value	Market Value
2 Dr S Cpe	2880	4000
2 Dr Si Cpe	3355	4665
2 Dr Si 4WS Cpe	3740	5195

OPTIONS FOR PRELUDE

Auto 4-Speed Transmission +100
Air Conditioning[Opt on S] +115
Aluminum/Alloy Wheels[Opt on S] +40
Leather Seats +95

A 15-minute phone call could save you 15% or more on car insurance.

1-800-555-2758

GEICO DIRECT

Don't forget to refer to the Mileage Adjustment Table at the back of this book!

 © 1999 by Edmund Publications Corporation

Model Description	Trade-in Value	Market Value

HYUNDAI S. Korea

1995 Hyundai Sonata

1998 HYUNDAI

ACCENT 1998

The Accent GSi replaces the Accent GT this year. New front and rear fascias, and new engine mounts, which reduce engine vibration and harshness, are the only other changes to Hyundai's smallest car.

Category E

Model Description	Trade-in Value	Market Value
4 Dr GL Sdn	6605	8050
2 Dr GS Hbk	6160	7515
2 Dr GSi Hbk	6950	8475
2 Dr L Hbk	5775	7040

OPTIONS FOR ACCENT

Auto 4-Speed Transmission +630
Air Conditioning +675
AM/FM Compact Disc Playr +390
Anti-Lock Brakes +590
Flip-Up Sunroof +295
Keyless Entry System +125

ELANTRA 1998

No changes to the Elantra for 1998.

Category E

Model Description	Trade-in Value	Market Value
4 Dr GLS Sdn	8045	9810
4 Dr GLS Wgn	7965	9715
4 Dr STD Sdn	7235	8825
4 Dr STD Wgn	7435	9070

OPTIONS FOR ELANTRA

Auto 4-Speed Transmission[Std on GLS Wgn] +665
Air Conditioning +675
Aluminum/Alloy Wheels +265
AM/FM Compact Disc Playr +390
Anti-Lock Brakes +590
Cruise Control +185
Keyless Entry System +125
Power Moonroof +485

SONATA 1998

No changes to the Sonata for 1998.

Category D

Model Description	Trade-in Value	Market Value
4 Dr GL Sdn	9740	11880
4 Dr GL V6 Sdn	9810	11965
4 Dr GLS Sdn	10900	13295
4 Dr STD Sdn	8370	10205

OPTIONS FOR SONATA

Auto 4-Speed Transmission[Opt on STD] +665
Anti-Lock Brakes +790
Cruise Control[Std on GLS] +200
Keyless Entry System +250
Leather Seats +915
Power Moonroof +695

TIBURON 1998

Base Tiburons get the 2.0-liter 140-horsepower engine as standard equipment.

Category E

Model Description	Trade-in Value	Market Value
2 Dr FX Hbk	10650	12985
2 Dr STD Hbk	10100	12315

OPTIONS FOR TIBURON

Auto 4-Speed Transmission +665
Air Conditioning +675
Aluminum/Alloy Wheels[Std on FX] +265
Anti-Lock Brakes +590
Cruise Control +185
Fog Lights[Std on FX] +125
Keyless Entry System +125
Leather Seats +740
Power Sunroof +500

1997 HYUNDAI

ACCENT 1997

In the absence of truly ground-breaking improvement, Hyundai revises trim levels, adding GS hatchback and GL sedan mid-range models.

Category E

Model Description	Trade-in Value	Market Value
4 Dr GL Sdn	5330	6835
2 Dr GS Hbk	5225	6700
2 Dr GT Hbk	6070	7780
2 Dr L Hbk	5110	6550

OPTIONS FOR ACCENT

Auto 4-Speed Transmission +515
Air Conditioning +550
AM/FM Compact Disc Playr +320
AM/FM Stereo Tape +210
Anti-Lock Brakes +480
Flip-Up Sunroof +240

Don't forget to refer to the Mileage Adjustment Table at the back of this book!

 © 1999 by Edmund Publications Corporation

Model Description	Trade-in Value	Market Value

Keyless Entry System +100
Power Steering[Std on GT] +170
Rear Spoiler[Std on GT] +140

ELANTRA 1997

Elantra rolls into 1997 with zero changes, save for a slight price increase.

Category E

Model Description	Trade-in Value	Market Value
4 Dr GLS Wgn	7245	9290
4 Dr GLS Sdn	6615	8480
4 Dr STD Wgn	6085	7805
4 Dr STD Sdn	6050	7755

OPTIONS FOR ELANTRA

Auto 4-Speed Transmission[Opt on STD] +545
Air Conditioning +550
Aluminum/Alloy Wheels +215
AM/FM Compact Disc Playr +320
Anti-Lock Brakes +480
Cruise Control +150
Keyless Entry System +100
Luggage Rack[Opt on GLS] +90
Power Moonroof +395
Rear Spoiler +140

SONATA 1997

Sheetmetal is all-new, and gives Sonata a more substantial look despite somewhat controversial retro-style front fascia and grille. Flush-fitting doors and restyled exterior mirrors help quiet the ride, while horn activation switches from spoke button to center steering wheel pad.

Category D

Model Description	Trade-in Value	Market Value
4 Dr GL Sdn	8360	10320
4 Dr GLS Sdn	9205	11365
4 Dr STD Sdn	7180	8860

OPTIONS FOR SONATA

6 cyl 3.0 L Engine[Opt on GL] +680
Auto 4-Speed Transmission[Opt on STD] +545
Anti-Lock Brakes +645
Compact Disc W/fm/tape +655
Cruise Control[Opt on GL] +165
Keyless Entry System +205
Leather Seats +750
Power Moonroof +565

TIBURON 1997

Loosely based on the 1993 HCD-II concept car, the Tiburon (Spanish for shark) debuts as a budget sport coupe that promises to gobble competitors such as the Toyota Paseo like so much chum.

Category E

Model Description	Trade-in Value	Market Value
2 Dr FX Hbk	8460	10845
2 Dr STD Hbk	7360	9440

OPTIONS FOR TIBURON

Auto 4-Speed Transmission +545
Air Conditioning +550
Aluminum/Alloy Wheels[Std on FX] +215
Anti-Lock Brakes +480
Center Console[Std on FX] +65
Compact Disc W/fm/tape +470
Cruise Control +150
Fog Lights[Std on FX] +105
Keyless Entry System +100
Leather Seats +605
Power Sunroof +410
Rear Spoiler[Std on FX] +140

1996 HYUNDAI

ACCENT 1996

Hyundai is painting the Accent in some new colors this year, and height-adjustable seat belt anchors are standard. Front and rear center consoles with cupholders debut, and optional air conditioning is now CFC-free. A new 105-horsepower GT hatch debuted midyear.

Category E

Model Description	Trade-in Value	Market Value
2 Dr GT Hbk	5075	6855
2 Dr L Hbk	4010	5420
2 Dr STD Hbk	4210	5690
4 Dr STD Sdn	4140	5590

OPTIONS FOR ACCENT

Auto 4-Speed Transmission +410
Air Conditioning +450
AM/FM Compact Disc Playr +260
Anti-Lock Brakes +395
Power Steering[Std on GT] +140
Rear Spoiler[Std on GT] +115
Sunroof +195

ELANTRA 1996

All-new Elantra is a slickly styled sedan or wagon featuring dual airbags, side-impact protection, and a more powerful engine. Pricing is up as well, pushing this Hyundai squarely into Dodge Neon and Honda Civic territory.

Category E

Model Description	Trade-in Value	Market Value
4 Dr GLS Wgn	6265	8465
4 Dr GLS Sdn	5570	7525
4 Dr STD Wgn	5255	7100
4 Dr STD Sdn	4920	6650

OPTIONS FOR ELANTRA

Auto 4-Speed Transmission[Opt on STD,Sdn] +475
Air Conditioning +450
Aluminum/Alloy Wheels +175
AM/FM Compact Disc Playr +260
Anti-Lock Brakes +395

Don't forget to refer to the Mileage Adjustment Table at the back of this book!

 © 1999 by Edmund Publications Corporation

Model Description	Trade-in Value	Market Value

Cruise Control +120
Rear Spoiler +115
Sunroof +195

SONATA 1996

Noise, vibration, and harshness are quelled with the addition of insulation to the floor and cowl, and liquid-filled V6 engine mounts. ABS is available as a stand-alone option on the GLS, and Steel Gray joins the color chart. Upgraded seat fabric comes in the base and GL models, while all Sonatas get CFC-free A/C.

Category D

Model Description	Trade-in Value	Market Value
4 Dr GL Sdn	6950	8910
4 Dr GL V6 Sdn	7340	9410
4 Dr GLS Sdn	7745	9930
4 Dr STD Sdn	6335	8120

OPTIONS FOR SONATA

Auto 4-Speed Transmission[Opt on STD] +435
Anti-Lock Brakes +530
Compact Disc W/fm/tape +535
Cruise Control[Std on GLS] +135
Leather Seats +610
Power Moonroof +465

1995 HYUNDAI

ACCENT 1995

Dramatically improved car replaces Excel in lineup. Dual airbags are standard, and ABS is optional. Power comes from the 1.5-liter Alpha engine which debuted in 1993 Scoupe.

Category E

Model Description	Trade-in Value	Market Value
2 Dr L Hbk	3025	4260
2 Dr STD Hbk	3430	4830
4 Dr STD Sdn	3460	4870

OPTIONS FOR ACCENT

Auto 4-Speed Transmission +385
Air Conditioning +370
AM/FM Stereo Tape +140
Anti-Lock Brakes +320
Power Steering +115
Sunroof +155

ELANTRA 1995

No changes.

Category E

Model Description	Trade-in Value	Market Value
4 Dr GLS Sdn	3870	5455
4 Dr SE Sdn	3620	5100
4 Dr STD Sdn	3410	4800

OPTIONS FOR ELANTRA

4 cyl 1.8 L Engine[Std on GLS] +290
Auto 4-Speed Transmission +325
Air Conditioning +370
Aluminum/Alloy Wheels +145
AM/FM Stereo Tape[Std on GLS] +140
Anti-Lock Brakes +320
Cruise Control +100
Power Moonroof +265
Premium Sound System +155
Rear Spoiler[Std on SE] +95

SCOUPE 1995

No changes.

Category E

Model Description	Trade-in Value	Market Value
2 Dr LS Cpe	4565	6430
2 Dr STD Cpe	3775	5320

OPTIONS FOR SCOUPE

Auto 4-Speed Transmission +300
Air Conditioning +370
Aluminum/Alloy Wheels[Opt on LS] +145
AM/FM Compact Disc Playr +215
Flip-Up Sunroof +160
Power Steering[Std on LS] +115
Premium Sound System +155

SONATA 1995

Brand new Sonata debuted in mid-1994. Dual airbags are standard. A 137-horsepower engine powers base and GL models while a 142-horsepower V6 is optional on midlevel GL and standard on GLS. Both engines are Mitsubishi-based designs. New car meets 1997 side-impact standards. Air conditioning and cassette stereo are standard on all models.

Category D

Model Description	Trade-in Value	Market Value
4 Dr GL Sdn	5435	7060
4 Dr GL V6 Sdn	5725	7430
4 Dr GLS Sdn	5980	7765
4 Dr STD Sdn	4740	6155

OPTIONS FOR SONATA

Auto 4-Speed Transmission[Opt on STD] +360
Anti-Lock Brakes +430
Compact Disc W/fm/tape +440
Cruise Control[Std on GLS] +110
Leather Seats +500
Power Moonroof +380
Power Sunroof +330

1994 HYUNDAI

ELANTRA 1994

Styling is updated, and a driver airbag is standard. ABS is optional on GLS models. CFC-free refrigerant replaces freon in Elantra's air conditioning system.

Category E

Model Description	Trade-in Value	Market Value
4 Dr GLS Sdn	3030	4525
4 Dr STD Sdn	2645	3950

Don't forget to refer to the Mileage Adjustment Table at the back of this book!

© 1999 by Edmund Publications Corporation

Model Description	Trade-in Value	Market Value

OPTIONS FOR ELANTRA

4 cyl 1.8 L Engine[Opt on STD] +165
Auto 4-Speed Transmission +270
Air Conditioning +300
Aluminum/Alloy Wheels +120
AM/FM Compact Disc Playr +175
Anti-Lock Brakes +265
Cruise Control +80
Power Sunroof +225

EXCEL 1994

Four-speed manual dropped from base car in favor of five-speed unit. Base sedan is discontinued. New interior fabrics and wheel covers spruce up the Excel. Air conditioners get CFC-free coolant.

Category E

Model Description	Trade-in Value	Market Value
4 Dr GL Sdn	2225	3320
2 Dr GS Hbk	2390	3565
2 Dr STD Hbk	1980	2955

OPTIONS FOR EXCEL

Auto 4-Speed Transmission +210
Air Conditioning +300
AM/FM Stereo Tape[Opt on STD] +115
Power Steering +95
Power Sunroof +225

SCOUPE 1994

Base and LS models receive new interior fabrics, wheel covers and revised trim molding. CFC-free refrigerant is added to the air conditioner.

Category E

Model Description	Trade-in Value	Market Value
2 Dr LS Cpe	3300	4930
2 Dr STD Cpe	2850	4250

OPTIONS FOR SCOUPE

Auto 4-Speed Transmission +250
Air Conditioning +300
Aluminum/Alloy Wheels +120
AM/FM Compact Disc Playr +175
Flip-Up Sunroof +130
Power Steering[Std on LS] +95

SONATA 1994

No changes.

Category D

Model Description	Trade-in Value	Market Value
4 Dr GLS Sdn	3730	4975
4 Dr GLS V6 Sdn	4125	5500
4 Dr STD Sdn	3290	4385
4 Dr V6 Sdn	3690	4920

OPTIONS FOR SONATA

Auto 4-Speed Transmission[Opt on GLS,STD] +290
Aluminum/Alloy Wheels[Opt on GLS] +165
Anti-Lock Brakes +355
Compact Disc W/fm/tape +360
Cruise Control[Opt on STD,V6] +90
Leather Seats +410
Power Door Locks[Opt on STD,V6] +100
Power Sunroof +270
Power Windows[Opt on STD,V6] +100

1993 HYUNDAI

ELANTRA 1993

Base model gets a black grille, while GLS features a body-color piece. GLS also gets new wheelcovers and steering wheel. All automatic models and the five-speed GLS get a new 1.8-liter engine good for 124 horsepower.

Category E

Model Description	Trade-in Value	Market Value
4 Dr GLS Sdn	2360	3810
4 Dr STD Sdn	2145	3460

OPTIONS FOR ELANTRA

4 cyl 1.8 L Engine[Opt on STD] +115
Auto 4-Speed Transmission +215
Air Conditioning +245
Aluminum/Alloy Wheels +95
AM/FM Stereo Tape[Opt on STD] +95
Cruise Control +65
Power Sunroof +185

EXCEL 1993

Slight styling revisions update Excel.

Category E

Model Description	Trade-in Value	Market Value
4 Dr GL Sdn	1950	3145
2 Dr GS Hbk	2070	3340
2 Dr STD Hbk	1925	3105
4 Dr STD Sdn	1820	2935

OPTIONS FOR EXCEL

Auto 4-Speed Transmission +180
Air Conditioning +245
Aluminum/Alloy Wheels +95
AM/FM Stereo Tape[Opt on STD] +95
Power Steering +75
Sunroof +105

SCOUPE 1993

Styling updates, a new engine, and a new Turbo model summarize the big news for 1993. The new motor is a 1.5-liter SOHC four-cylinder designed and built by Hyundai. Called Alpha, the new engine makes 92 horsepower in base and LS Scoupes; 115 horsepower in Turbo format. Turbos are available only with a manual transmission. Dashboard is slightly revised and features rotary climate controls.

Category E

Model Description	Trade-in Value	Market Value
2 Dr LS Cpe	2400	3870
2 Dr STD Cpe	2345	3785
2 Dr STD Turbo Cpe	2665	4295

Don't forget to refer to the Mileage Adjustment Table at the back of this book!

© 1999 by Edmund Publications Corporation

Model Description	Trade-in Value	Market Value

OPTIONS FOR SCOUPE
Auto 4-Speed Transmission +175
Air Conditioning +245
Aluminum/Alloy Wheels[Std on Turbo] +95
AM/FM Stereo Tape[Std on LS,Turbo] +95
Power Steering[Std on LS,Turbo] +75
Sunroof +105

SONATA 1993

Front air intake is now body-color, and new wheelcovers debut.

Category D

4 Dr GLS Sdn	2970	4180
4 Dr STD Sdn	2885	4060

OPTIONS FOR SONATA
6 cyl 3.0 L Engine +240
Auto 4-Speed Transmission +225
Aluminum/Alloy Wheels +135
AM/FM Compact Disc Playr +170
Anti-Lock Brakes +290
Cruise Control[Opt on STD] +75
Leather Seats +335
Power Door Locks[Opt on STD] +80
Power Sunroof +220
Power Windows[Opt on STD] +80

1992 HYUNDAI

ELANTRA 1992

Brand-new compact is slotted between Excel and Sonata. All models come standard with a 113-horsepower 1.6-liter twin-cam four-cylinder engine. Horsepower drops to 105 with the automatic transmission.

Category E

4 Dr GLS Sdn	1710	2950
4 Dr STD Sdn	1515	2610

OPTIONS FOR ELANTRA
Auto 4-Speed Transmission +160
Air Conditioning +200
Aluminum/Alloy Wheels +80
AM/FM Stereo Tape[Opt on STD] +75
Cruise Control +55
Power Sunroof +150
Premium Sound System +85

EXCEL 1992

GLS sedan dropped from lineup.

Category E

4 Dr GL Sdn	1650	2845
2 Dr GS Hbk	1605	2770
2 Dr STD Hbk	1375	2370
4 Dr STD Sdn	1415	2440

Model Description	Trade-in Value	Market Value

OPTIONS FOR EXCEL
Auto 4-Speed Transmission +145
Air Conditioning +200
Aluminum/Alloy Wheels +80
AM/FM Stereo Tape[Opt on STD] +75
Power Steering +60
Sunroof +85

SCOUPE 1992

No changes.

Category E

2 Dr LS Cpe	1660	2860
2 Dr STD Cpe	1475	2545

OPTIONS FOR SCOUPE
Auto 4-Speed Transmission +140
Air Conditioning +200
Aluminum/Alloy Wheels +80
AM/FM Stereo Tape[Std on LS] +75
Cruise Control +55
Power Drivers Seat +75
Power Steering[Std on LS] +60
Premium Sound System +85
Sunroof +85

SONATA 1992

Styling is tweaked, ABS is optional on GLS V6 models, and a new 2.0-liter twin-cam engine replaces the less-powerful 2.4-liter base unit.

Category D

4 Dr GLS Sdn	2450	3655
4 Dr STD Sdn	2320	3460

OPTIONS FOR SONATA
6 cyl 3.0 L Engine +335
Auto 4-Speed Transmission +185
Air Conditioning[Opt on STD] +210
Aluminum/Alloy Wheels[Opt on STD] +110
AM/FM Compact Disc Playr +140
Anti-Lock Brakes +235
Cruise Control[Opt on STD] +60
Leather Seats +275
Power Door Locks[Opt on STD] +65
Power Moonroof +205
Power Windows[Opt on STD] +65
Premium Sound System +85

1991 HYUNDAI

EXCEL 1991

No changes.

Category E

4 Dr GL Sdn	900	1765
4 Dr GL SE Sdn	935	1830
4 Dr GLS Sdn	1050	2055
2 Dr GS Hbk	1105	2165
2 Dr GS SE Hbk	1125	2205

Don't forget to refer to the Mileage Adjustment Table at the back of this book!

 © 1999 by Edmund Publications Corporation

Model Description	Trade-in Value	Market Value
2 Dr STD Hbk	1005	1965
4 Dr STD Sdn	795	1560

OPTIONS FOR EXCEL

Auto 4-Speed Transmission +135
Air Conditioning +165
Aluminum/Alloy Wheels[Opt on GLS,GS] +65
AM/FM Stereo Tape[Opt on GL,GS,STD] +60
Power Steering[Std on GLS] +50
Premium Sound System +70
Rear Spoiler[Opt on GS] +40
Sunroof +70

SCOUPE 1991

"Sports" coupe debuts based on Excel underpinnings. Car gets its own coupe styling, interior and Lotus-tuned suspension. Scoupe has a whopping 81 horsepower; a shorter final-drive ratio makes Scoupe slightly speedier than the slooooooow Excel.

Category E

Model Description	Trade-in Value	Market Value
2 Dr LS Cpe	1140	2230
2 Dr SE Cpe	1175	2300
2 Dr STD Cpe	1010	1980

OPTIONS FOR SCOUPE

Auto 4-Speed Transmission +105
Air Conditioning +165
Aluminum/Alloy Wheels +65
AM/FM Stereo Tape[Opt on STD] +60
Cruise Control +45
Power Steering[Opt on STD] +50
Premium Sound System +70
Sunroof +70

SONATA 1991

Child-proof rear door locks are added.

Category D

Model Description	Trade-in Value	Market Value
4 Dr GLS Sdn	1815	2705
4 Dr GLS SE Sdn	2010	3000
4 Dr STD Sdn	1650	2465

OPTIONS FOR SONATA

6 cyl 3.0 L Engine[Std on GLS SE] +150
Auto 4-Speed Transmission[Std on GLS SE] +145
Radio Option +260
Air Conditioning[Opt on STD] +170
Aluminum/Alloy Wheels[Std on GLS SE] +90
AM/FM Compact Disc Playr +115
Cruise Control[Opt on STD] +50
Leather Seats[Opt on GLS] +225
Power Door Locks[Opt on STD] +55
Power Windows[Opt on STD] +55
Premium Sound System +70

1990 HYUNDAI

EXCEL 1990

All-new Excel debuts. Engine is improved, with more horsepower and torque. Automatic transmission is redesigned, and manual transmission shifts more smoothly. For the first time, a tilt wheel is optional.

Category E

Model Description	Trade-in Value	Market Value
4 Dr GL Hbk	620	1405
4 Dr GL Sdn	760	1725
4 Dr GLS Sdn	865	1965
2 Dr GS Hbk	775	1765
2 Dr STD Hbk	600	1365
4 Dr STD Sdn	750	1700

OPTIONS FOR EXCEL

Auto 4-Speed Transmission +85
Air Conditioning +135
Aluminum/Alloy Wheels +50
AM/FM Stereo Tape[Std on GLS] +50
Power Steering +40
Power Sunroof +100
Premium Sound System +55

SONATA 1990

GLS gets new grille, upholstery and tinted glass. A V6 was added early in the model year. Premium sound and leather interior are offered for the first time. Automatic transmission gets an available power/normal shift selector.

Category D

Model Description	Trade-in Value	Market Value
4 Dr GLS Sdn	1380	2120
4 Dr GLS V6 Sdn	1670	2570
4 Dr STD Sdn	1175	1810
4 Dr V6 Sdn	1395	2145

OPTIONS FOR SONATA

Auto 4-Speed Transmission[Opt on GLS,STD] +115
Air Conditioning +140
Aluminum/Alloy Wheels +75
AM/FM Stereo Tape[Opt on STD,V6] +60
Cruise Control[Opt on STD,V6] +40
Keyless Entry System +50
Leather Seats +185
Power Door Locks[Opt on STD,V6] +45
Power Sunroof +120
Power Windows[Opt on STD,V6] +45
Premium Sound System +55

For a guaranteed low price on a new car in your area, call
1-800-CAR-CLUB

Don't forget to refer to the Mileage Adjustment Table at the back of this book!

 © 1999 by Edmund Publications Corporation

Model Description	Trade-in Value	Market Value

1989 HYUNDAI

EXCEL 1989

Bumper-to-bumper warranty increased to 3 years/ 36,000 miles.

Category E

Model Description	Trade-in Value	Market Value
2 Dr GL Hbk	415	1545
4 Dr GL Hbk	350	1290
4 Dr GL Sdn	335	1240
4 Dr GLS Sdn	415	1540
4 Dr GLS Hbk	380	1415
2 Dr GS Hbk	450	1660
2 Dr STD Hbk	295	1090
4 Dr STD Sdn	330	1220

OPTIONS FOR EXCEL

Auto 3-Speed Transmission +65
Auto 4-Speed Transmission +65
Air Conditioning +110
Aluminum/Alloy Wheels[Std on GS] +45
AM/FM Stereo Tape[Opt on GL,STD] +40
Power Steering +35
Power Sunroof +80
Premium Sound System +45

SONATA 1989

New front-wheel drive sedan intended to compete with Honda Accord, Toyota Camry and Ford Taurus. Sonata is styled by Giorgio Giugiaro, and features mostly Hyundai engineering. The engine, however, is a Mitsubishi unit.

Category D

Model Description	Trade-in Value	Market Value
4 Dr GLS Sdn	885	1455
4 Dr GLS V6 Sdn	935	1530
4 Dr STD Sdn	725	1190

OPTIONS FOR SONATA

Auto 4-Speed Transmission[Opt on GLS,STD] +85
Air Conditioning +115
Aluminum/Alloy Wheels +60
AM/FM Stereo Tape[Opt on STD,V6] +50
Cruise Control[Opt on STD] +35
Power Door Locks[Opt on STD] +35
Power Sunroof +100
Power Windows[Opt on STD] +35
Premium Sound System +45

www.CarFinance.com/edmunds

A 15-minute phone call could save you 15% or more on car insurance.

1-800-555-2758

The Sensible Alternative

Don't forget to refer to the Mileage Adjustment Table at the back of this book!

© 1999 by Edmund Publications Corporation

INFINITI

Japan

1993 Infiniti J30

1998 INFINITI

I30 — 1998

Side-impact airbags make their way into the Infiniti I30, as do new headlamps, taillamps, center console and wheels.

Category D

Model Description	Trade-in Value	Market Value
4 Dr STD Sdn	18670	22225
4 Dr Touring Sdn	21085	25105

OPTIONS FOR I30

Auto 4-Speed Transmission[Opt on Touring] +830
Infiniti Communicator +745
Heated Front Seats[Opt on STD] +305
Heated Power Mirrors[Opt on STD] +75
Leather Seats[Opt on STD] +915
Power Moonroof[Opt on STD] +695

Q45 — 1998

The Q45 gets front seatbelt pretensioners. No other changes for Infiniti's flagship.

Category J

Model Description	Trade-in Value	Market Value
4 Dr STD Sdn	28430	33845
4 Dr Touring Sdn	29500	35120

OPTIONS FOR Q45

Infiniti Communicator +745
Compact Disc Changer[Opt on STD] +815
Heated Front Seats[Opt on STD] +345

QX4 — 1998

No changes to the QX4.

Category G

Model Description	Trade-in Value	Market Value
4 Dr STD 4WD Wgn	23690	28200

OPTIONS FOR QX4

Compact Disc Changer +430
Heated Front Seats +210
Power Moonroof +735

1997 INFINITI

I30 — 1997

A few new paint colors are the only changes to the 1997 I30.

RATINGS (SCALE OF 1-10)

Overall	Safety	Reliability	Performance	Comfort	Value
7.4	6.8	9.4	8.4	8	4.1

Category D

Model Description	Trade-in Value	Market Value
4 Dr STD Sdn	16835	20285
4 Dr Touring Sdn	18215	21945

OPTIONS FOR I30

Auto 4-Speed Transmission +330
Heated Front Seats[Opt on STD] +250
Leather Seats[Opt on STD] +750
Limited Slip Diff[Opt on STD] +335
Power Moonroof[Opt on STD] +565

J30 — 1997

There are no changes to the 1997 Infiniti J30.

RATINGS (SCALE OF 1-10)

Overall	Safety	Reliability	Performance	Comfort	Value
7.8	7.6	9.7	8.4	8.5	4.5

Category J

Model Description	Trade-in Value	Market Value
4 Dr 1997.5 Sdn	18070	21510
4 Dr 1997.5 Touring Sdn	18685	22245
4 Dr STD Sdn	18070	21510
4 Dr Touring Sdn	18685	22245

Q45 — 1997

This totally redesigned car has almost nothing in common with its predecessor. Power now comes via a 4.1-liter V8 engine and is still delivered through the rear wheels. The Q45 no longer has aspirations to be a sports sedan, its prime duties now are interstate cruising.

RATINGS (SCALE OF 1-10)

Overall	Safety	Reliability	Performance	Comfort	Value
N/A	N/A	9.1	8.4	9	5.1

Category J

Model Description	Trade-in Value	Market Value
4 Dr 1997.5 Sdn	27375	32590
4 Dr 1997.5 Touring Sdn	27975	33305
4 Dr STD Sdn	27375	32590
4 Dr Touring Sdn	27375	32590

Don't forget to refer to the Mileage Adjustment Table at the back of this book!

© 1999 by Edmund Publications Corporation

Model Description	Trade-in Value	Market Value

OPTIONS FOR Q45

Heated Front Seats[Opt on STD] +280

QX4 1997

A version of Nissan's wonderful four-wheeler is introduced by Infiniti, aiming to compete with the Mercury Mountaineer, Acura SLX and Land Rover Discovery. Differences between the QX4 and the Pathfinder include the Q's full-time four-wheel drive system, a more luxurious interior, and substantially different sheetmetal.

RATINGS (SCALE OF 1-10)

Overall	Safety	Reliability	Performance	Comfort	Value
6.9	7	8.7	7	7.3	4.6

Category G

Model Description	Trade-in Value	Market Value
4 Dr STD 4WD Wgn	21930	26105

OPTIONS FOR QX4

Heated Front Seats +175
Limited Slip Diff +180
Power Moonroof +600

1996 INFINITI

G20 1996

Emergency locking front and rear seat belts have been installed, and fake wood is applied on models equipped with the Leather Appointment Package. This is the last year for the entry-level Infinti.

RATINGS (SCALE OF 1-10)

Overall	Safety	Reliability	Performance	Comfort	Value
N/A	N/A	9	8.6	7.8	5.9

Category D

Model Description	Trade-in Value	Market Value
4 Dr STD Sdn	9725	12155
4 Dr Touring Sdn	11080	13850

OPTIONS FOR G20

Auto 4-Speed Transmission +545
Dual Power Seats[Opt on STD] +465
Keyless Entry System[Opt on STD] +170
Leather Seats[Opt on STD] +610
Power Moonroof[Opt on STD] +465

I30 1996

New luxo-sport sedan based on the Nissan Maxima arrived during 1995. Slotted between the G20 and the J30, the I30 competes with the Lexus ES 300, BMW 3-Series, and the new Acura TL-Series. If you like big chrome grilles, this is the car to buy.

RATINGS (SCALE OF 1-10)

Overall	Safety	Reliability	Performance	Comfort	Value
7.5	6.8	9.3	8.4	8	5.1

Category D

Model Description	Trade-in Value	Market Value
4 Dr STD Sdn	13680	17100
4 Dr Touring Sdn	15050	18815

OPTIONS FOR I30

Auto 4-Speed Transmission +500
Heated Front Seats[Opt on STD] +205
Leather Seats[Opt on STD] +610
Limited Slip Diff[Opt on STD] +270
Power Moonroof[Opt on STD] +465

J30 1996

Three new colors join the paint palette.

RATINGS (SCALE OF 1-10)

Overall	Safety	Reliability	Performance	Comfort	Value
7.7	7.6	9.6	8.4	8.5	4.4

Category J

Model Description	Trade-in Value	Market Value
4 Dr STD Sdn	14730	17965
4 Dr Touring Sdn	15235	18580

Q45 1996

Active suspension model is canceled, but two new exterior colors are available.

RATINGS (SCALE OF 1-10)

Overall	Safety	Reliability	Performance	Comfort	Value
N/A	N/A	9.3	8.6	9.1	5.8

Category J

Model Description	Trade-in Value	Market Value
4 Dr STD Sdn	20580	25100
4 Dr Touring Sdn	20760	25320

OPTIONS FOR Q45

Compact Disc W/fm/tape +395
Heated Front Seats +230
Traction Control System +730

1995 INFINITI

G20 1995

All-season tires are added to the G20. No other changes are made to the entry-level Infiniti.

RATINGS (SCALE OF 1-10)

Overall	Safety	Reliability	Performance	Comfort	Value
N/A	N/A	8.7	8.6	7.8	5.4

Category D

Model Description	Trade-in Value	Market Value
4 Dr STD Sdn	9040	11440
4 Dr Touring Sdn	9755	12350

OPTIONS FOR G20

Auto 4-Speed Transmission +445
Dual Power Seats +380
Keyless Entry System[Opt on STD] +135
Leather Seats[Opt on STD] +500
Power Moonroof[Opt on STD] +380

Don't forget to refer to the Mileage Adjustment Table at the back of this book!

 © 1999 by Edmund Publications Corporation

J30 1995

Redesigned taillights, power lumbar support for the driver's seat, and an anti-glare mirror mark the changes for the 1995 J30.

RATINGS (SCALE OF 1-10)

Overall	Safety	Reliability	Performance	Comfort	Value
7.9	8.3	9.2	8.4	8.5	4.9

Category J

Model Description	Trade-in Value	Market Value
4 Dr STD Sdn	13680	16890

OPTIONS FOR J30

Touring Package +705
Rear Spoiler +170

Q45 1995

Alloy wheels for the base model are about the only changes for the Q45.

RATINGS (SCALE OF 1-10)

Overall	Safety	Reliability	Performance	Comfort	Value
N/A	N/A	9.3	8.6	9.1	5.8

Category J

Model Description	Trade-in Value	Market Value
4 Dr A Sdn	18995	23455
4 Dr STD Sdn	18115	22365

OPTIONS FOR Q45

Touring Pkg +650
Compact Disc Changer[Std on A] +445
Heated Front Seats[Std on A] +185
Traction Control System[Std on A] +600

1994 INFINITI

G20 1994

No changes to the G20.

RATINGS (SCALE OF 1-10)

Overall	Safety	Reliability	Performance	Comfort	Value
N/A	N/A	8.5	8.6	7.8	6.4

Category D

Model Description	Trade-in Value	Market Value
4 Dr STD Sdn	7685	9855

OPTIONS FOR G20

Auto 4-Speed Transmission +370
Dual Power Seats +310
Keyless Entry System +110
Leather Seats +410
Limited Slip Diff +180
Power Moonroof +310
Rear Spoiler +155

J30 1994

Heated front seats and the addition of two speakers further pamper passengers in the J30.

RATINGS (SCALE OF 1-10)

Overall	Safety	Reliability	Performance	Comfort	Value
7.7	8.3	8.9	8.4	8.5	4.3

Category J

Model Description	Trade-in Value	Market Value
4 Dr STD Sdn	12015	15020

OPTIONS FOR J30

Touring Package +760
Rear Spoiler +140

Q45 1994

A passenger airbag appears on the restyled 1994 Infiniti. Changes to the grille, bumpers and fog lights will distinguish this car from previous models.

RATINGS (SCALE OF 1-10)

Overall	Safety	Reliability	Performance	Comfort	Value
N/A	N/A	8.9	8.6	9.1	5.6

Category J

Model Description	Trade-in Value	Market Value
4 Dr A Sdn	15585	19485
4 Dr STD Sdn	14760	18450

OPTIONS FOR Q45

Touring Package +945
Heated Front Seats[Std on A] +155
Traction Control System[Std on A] +490

1993 INFINITI

G20 1993

Driver and passenger airbags are introduced as a midyear change to the G20.

RATINGS (SCALE OF 1-10)

Overall	Safety	Reliability	Performance	Comfort	Value
N/A	N/A	8.4	8.6	7.8	6.3

Category D

Model Description	Trade-in Value	Market Value
4 Dr STD Sdn	6435	8465

OPTIONS FOR G20

Auto 4-Speed Transmission +275
Dual Power Seats +255
Keyless Entry System +90
Leather Seats +335
Power Sunroof +220

J30 1993

A new introduction to the Infiniti lineup, the J30 really shakes things up. Love it or hate it, this car certainly turns heads. Powered by a 210-horsepower V6 gleaned from the Nissan 300ZX, the J30 is shifted by a four-speed automatic transmission. Dual airbags are standard on the J30, as are antilock brakes.

Don't forget to refer to the Mileage Adjustment Table at the back of this book!

 © 1999 by Edmund Publications Corporation

Model Description	Trade-in Value	Market Value

RATINGS (SCALE OF 1-10)

Overall	Safety	Reliability	Performance	Comfort	Value
7.6	8.3	8.9	8.4	8.5	3.8

Category J

4 Dr STD Sdn	9345	12135

OPTIONS FOR J30

Touring Package +515
Rear Spoiler +115

Q45 1993

Interior designers get a hold of the Q, sprucing, coloring and covering everything in beautiful new materials; even the clock on this car masquerades as a hand-crafted timepiece. Additional touches include map pockets to the front seat backs.

RATINGS (SCALE OF 1-10)

Overall	Safety	Reliability	Performance	Comfort	Value
N/A	N/A	8.7	9	8.4	5.7

Category J

4 Dr A Sdn	11365	14755
4 Dr STD Sdn	10975	14255

OPTIONS FOR Q45

Touring Package +820
Traction Control System +400

1992 INFINITI

G20 1992

New tires and an automatic transmission are introduced on Infiniti junior.

RATINGS (SCALE OF 1-10)

Overall	Safety	Reliability	Performance	Comfort	Value
N/A	N/A	8.2	8.6	7.8	6.2

Category D

4 Dr STD Sdn	5100	6895

OPTIONS FOR G20

Auto 4-Speed Transmission +220
Leather Seats +275
Power Sunroof +180

M30 1992

Unique, door opening system is introduced to the M30; this system enables both doors to be locked/unlocked from either door. This car is replaced by the more exotic looking J30 in 1993.

Category J

2 Dr STD Conv	8785	11710
2 Dr STD Cpe	6935	9245

OPTIONS FOR M30

AM/FM Stereo Tape[Std on Cpe] +245

Q45 1992

High-performance tires and new exterior colors are available on the 1992 Q45.

RATINGS (SCALE OF 1-10)

Overall	Safety	Reliability	Performance	Comfort	Value
N/A	N/A	8.2	9	8.4	5.9

Category J

4 Dr A Sdn	9170	12225
4 Dr STD Sdn	8865	11820

OPTIONS FOR Q45

Touring Package +610
Rear Spoiler +95
Traction Control System +325

1991 INFINITI

G20 1991

Infiniti's entry-level sedan is the new G20. Based on the Japanese market Nissan Primera, but suitably well-dressed to call itself an Infiniti, the G20 is designed to lure not-yet-affluent car buyers into the Infiniti family.

RATINGS (SCALE OF 1-10)

Overall	Safety	Reliability	Performance	Comfort	Value
N/A	N/A	7.9	8.6	7.8	5.6

Category D

4 Dr STD Sdn	4280	5865

OPTIONS FOR G20

Auto 4-Speed Transmission +160
AM/FM Compact Disc Playr +115
Leather Seats +225
Power Sunroof +150

M30 1991

No significant changes for the midsized offering from Infiniti.

Category J

2 Dr STD Conv	8095	10795
2 Dr STD Cpe	5945	7930

Q45 1991

Four-wheel steering is introduced to the Infiniti flagship. Full Active Suspension is available on the Q45, enabling the car to react much more quickly to changes in car position than a vehicle with conventional shock absorbers.

RATINGS (SCALE OF 1-10)

Overall	Safety	Reliability	Performance	Comfort	Value
N/A	N/A	8	9	8.4	5.9

Don't forget to refer to the Mileage Adjustment Table at the back of this book!

 © 1999 by Edmund Publications Corporation

Model Description	Trade-in Value	Market Value
Category J		
4 Dr A Sdn	7985	10645
4 Dr STD Sdn	7760	10345

OPTIONS FOR Q45

Touring Pkg +500
AM/FM Compact Disc Playr +110
Cellular Telephone +330
Traction Control System +265

1990 INFINITI

M30 1990

Based on a popular Japanese sedan, the M30 is introduced to the American market. Fans of the Maxima will appreciate the engine in the M30, which is lifted straight out of the Nissan parts bin. The rear-wheel drive, however, gives this car a distinct advantage over other Japanese luxury imports. Antilock brakes and an automatic transmission are standard on the M30.

Model Description	Trade-in Value	Market Value
Category J		
2 Dr STD Cpe	4835	6535

Q45 1990

The new flagship for Infiniti, the Q45 is the third entry into the growing Japanese luxury segment. Distinctive styling and a powerful 270-horsepower V8 engine make this car desirable, as does the extensive standard equipment list and luxurious interior appointments.

RATINGS (SCALE OF 1-10)

Overall	Safety	Reliability	Performance	Comfort	Value
N/A	N/A	7.9	9	8.4	5.1

Model Description	Trade-in Value	Market Value
Category J		
4 Dr STD Sdn	6900	9320

OPTIONS FOR Q45

Touring Pkg +415
Compact Disc W/fm/tape +120

Instant
Lease & Loan Quotes
for New & Used Vehicles!

www.CarFinance.com/edmunds

Edmund's

Get answers from our editors, scope out smart shopping strategies and share your experiences in our new talk area. Just enter the following address in your web browser:

http://townhall.edmunds.com

Don't forget to refer to the Mileage Adjustment Table at the back of this book!

© 1999 by Edmund Publications Corporation

Model Description	Trade-in Value	Market Value

ISUZU Japan

1996 Isuzu Oasis

1998 ISUZU

AMIGO 1998

Isuzu reintroduces its convertible sport utility after a three-year hiatus. This model comes with a modest four-cylinder engine, but the powerful V6 from the Rodeo is available and turns this 4WD droptop into a screamer.

Category G		
2 Dr S 4WD Utility	13045	15530
2 Dr S V6 4WD Utility	14390	17130

OPTIONS FOR AMIGO

Air Conditioning +675
Aluminum/Alloy Wheels +285
AM/FM Compact Disc Playr +320
Cruise Control +175
Fog Lights +120
Keyless Entry System +170
Power Door Locks +190
Power Mirrors +110
Power Windows +195
Tilt Steering Wheel +140

HOMBRE 1998

Four-wheel drive arrives, finally. Also new are a theft deterrent system and dual airbags housed in a revised instrument panel, with a passenger-side airbag cutoff switch so the kiddies can ride up front.

Category G		
2 Dr S Std Cab SB	8940	10640
2 Dr XS Std Cab SB	9545	11360
2 Dr XS Ext Cab SB	10855	12925
2 Dr XS V6 Ext Cab SB	12550	14940

OPTIONS FOR HOMBRE

Auto 4-Speed Transmission[Std on XS V6] +890
Air Conditioning +675
Aluminum/Alloy Wheels[Std on S,4WD] +285
AM/FM Compact Disc Playr +320
Cruise Control +175
Power Door Locks +190
Power Mirrors +110
Power Windows +195
Sliding Rear Window +100
Tilt Steering Wheel +140

RODEO 1998

Though it may not look like it, Isuzu has completely revised the Rodeo from top to bottom, giving it more modern styling, a user-friendly interior, more V6 power, and added room for passengers and cargo.

Category G		
4 Dr LS Wgn	17240	20525
4 Dr LS 4WD Wgn	18830	22415
4 Dr S Wgn	14060	16735
4 Dr S V6 Wgn	14585	17365
4 Dr S V6 4WD Wgn	15595	18565

OPTIONS FOR RODEO

Auto 4-Speed Transmission[Std on LS] +830
Air Conditioning[Std on LS] +675
AM/FM Compact Disc Playr +320
Cruise Control[Std on LS] +175
Fog Lights[Std on LS] +120
Heated Power Mirrors[Std on LS] +50
Keyless Entry System[Std on LS] +170
Power Door Locks[Std on LS] +190
Power Windows[Std on LS] +195
Swing Out Tire Carrier[Opt on S, S V6, 2WD] +170
Tilt Steering Wheel[Std on LS] +140

TROOPER 1998

A bigger and lighter engine provides huge improvements in horsepower and torque (up 13 and 22 percent, respectively). And the new Torque On Demand (TOD) drive system replaces conventional four-high mode for better performance on paved or slippery roads.

Category G		
4 Dr Luxury 4WD Wgn	19125	22765
4 Dr S 4WD Wgn	16885	20100

OPTIONS FOR TROOPER

Auto 4-Speed Transmission[Opt on S] +1040
Leather Seating Package +695
Performance Package +1385
AM/FM Compact Disc Playr +320
Compact Disc Changer[Opt on S] +430
Dual Power Seats[Opt on S] +525
Heated Front Seats[Opt on S] +210

Don't forget to refer to the Mileage Adjustment Table at the back of this book!

 © 1999 by Edmund Publications Corporation

Leather Seats[Opt on S] +640
Limited Slip Diff +220
Privacy Glass +225
Running Boards +320

1997 ISUZU

HOMBRE 1997

A Spacecab model debuts, with seating for five passengers and your choice of four-cylinder or V6 power. Other news includes two fresh paint colors and revised graphics.

RATINGS (SCALE OF 1-10)

Overall	Safety	Reliability	Performance	Comfort	Value
N/A	5.6	8.6	6.6	7.9	N/A

Category G		
2 Dr S Std Cab SB	7150	8510
2 Dr XS Ext Cab SB	8525	10150
2 Dr XS Std Cab SB	7295	8685
2 Dr XS V6 Ext Cab SB	9575	11400

OPTIONS FOR HOMBRE

Auto 4-Speed Transmission[Opt on S,XS] +675
Air Conditioning +550
AM/FM Compact Disc Playr +260
Cruise Control +145
Power Door Locks +155
Power Windows +160
Rear Step Bumper +100

OASIS 1997

Cruise control is added to the S model's standard equipment list, and four new colors are available.

RATINGS (SCALE OF 1-10)

Overall	Safety	Reliability	Performance	Comfort	Value
7.4	7.5	9.4	7.2	7.1	5.6

Category G		
4 Dr LS Pass. Van	15170	18060
4 Dr S Pass. Van	13475	16040

OPTIONS FOR OASIS

AM/FM Compact Disc Playr +260
Luggage Rack[Opt on S] +105

RODEO 1997

All 4WD models get a standard shift-on-the-fly transfer case, and improvements have been made to reduce noise, vibration and harshness.

RATINGS (SCALE OF 1-10)

Overall	Safety	Reliability	Performance	Comfort	Value
6.9	6.6	8	7	7.1	5.8

Category G		
4 Dr LS Wgn	13750	16370
4 Dr LS 4WD Wgn	15135	18020
4 Dr S Wgn	11370	13535
4 Dr S V6 Wgn	11565	13770
4 Dr S V6 4WD Wgn	12610	15010

OPTIONS FOR RODEO

Auto 4-Speed Transmission[Opt on S V6,4WD] +740
Air Conditioning[Std on LS] +550
Aluminum/Alloy Wheels[Std on LS] +235
Anti-Lock Brakes +420
Compact Disc W/fm/tape +465
Cruise Control[Std on LS] +145
Keyless Entry System +140
Leather Seats +520
Limited Slip Diff +180
Luggage Rack[Std on LS] +105
Moonroof +240
Power Door Locks[Std on LS] +155
Power Windows[Std on LS] +160
Running Boards +260
Swing Out Tire Carrier[Opt on S] +140

TROOPER 1997

Antilock brakes are now standard on all models, and dealers get a wider profit margin to help increase sales. Despite delirious requests by a certain consumer group, Isuzu will not equip the Trooper with training wheels for 1997.

RATINGS (SCALE OF 1-10)

Overall	Safety	Reliability	Performance	Comfort	Value
7.3	7.1	8.1	6.8	7.7	7

Category G		
4 Dr Limited 4WD Wgn	21815	25970
4 Dr LS 4WD Wgn	18455	21970
4 Dr S 4WD Wgn	14100	16785

OPTIONS FOR TROOPER

Auto 4-Speed Transmission[Opt on S] +850
Air Conditioning[Opt on S] +550
Alarm System[Opt on S] +240
Aluminum/Alloy Wheels[Opt on S] +235
AM/FM Compact Disc Playr +260
Cruise Control[Opt on S] +145
Dual Power Seats[Opt on LS] +430
Heated Front Seats[Opt on LS] +175
Keyless Entry System[Opt on LS,S] +140
Leather Seats[Opt on LS] +520
Limited Slip Diff[Opt on LS,S] +180
Power Door Locks[Opt on S] +155
Power Moonroof[Opt on LS] +600
Power Windows[Opt on S] +160
Running Boards +260

Don't forget to refer to the Mileage Adjustment Table at the back of this book!

© 1999 by Edmund Publications Corporation

1996 ISUZU

HOMBRE 1996

In a switch from history, Isuzu clones a Chevy S-10 and dumps its Japanese-built compact truck. Sheetmetal is unique to Isuzu, but everything else is pure General Motors.

RATINGS (SCALE OF 1-10)

Overall	Safety	Reliability	Performance	Comfort	Value
N/A	5.5	8.1	6.6	7.9	N/A

Category G

Model Description	Trade-in Value	Market Value
2 Dr S Std Cab SB	6620	8075
2 Dr XS Std Cab SB	7065	8615

OPTIONS FOR HOMBRE

Air Conditioning +450
AM/FM Stereo Tape +135
Rear Step Bumper[Opt on S] +80

OASIS 1996

New Isuzu minivan is a clone of the Honda Odyssey, except for the grille, badging and wheels. The Isuzu offers a better warranty, too.

RATINGS (SCALE OF 1-10)

Overall	Safety	Reliability	Performance	Comfort	Value
7.6	7.5	9.4	7.2	7.1	6.6

Category G

Model Description	Trade-in Value	Market Value
4 Dr LS Pass. Van	14165	17275
4 Dr S Pass. Van	12450	15180

OPTIONS FOR OASIS

AM/FM Compact Disc Playr +215
Cruise Control[Opt on S] +115
Luggage Rack[Opt on S] +85

RODEO 1996

Finally, Isuzu's Rodeo can be equipped with four-wheel antilock brakes, and 4WD models get a standard shift-on-the-fly system. New style wheels debut, and the engine now makes 190 horsepower. Increased wheel track improves ride quality, and spare tire covers are redesigned.

RATINGS (SCALE OF 1-10)

Overall	Safety	Reliability	Performance	Comfort	Value
7	6.6	7.8	7	7.1	6.7

Category G

Model Description	Trade-in Value	Market Value
4 Dr LS Wgn	11855	14460
4 Dr LS 4WD Wgn	13105	15980
4 Dr S Wgn	9505	11590
4 Dr S V6 Wgn	9565	11665
4 Dr S V6 4WD Wgn	10905	13300

OPTIONS FOR RODEO

Auto 4-Speed Transmission[Opt on S V6,4WD] +595
Air Conditioning[Std on LS] +450
Aluminum/Alloy Wheels[Std on LS] +190
AM/FM Compact Disc Playr +215
Anti-Lock Brakes +345
Cruise Control[Std on LS] +115
Keyless Entry System +115
Leather Seats +425
Limited Slip Diff +145
Luggage Rack[Std on LS] +85
Moonroof +195
Power Door Locks[Std on LS] +125
Power Windows[Std on LS] +130
Running Boards +215
Swing Out Tire Carrier[Opt on S] +115

TROOPER 1996

More standard equipment, a horsepower boost for the SOHC V6 engine, and standard shift-on-the-fly debut for 1996.

RATINGS (SCALE OF 1-10)

Overall	Safety	Reliability	Performance	Comfort	Value
7.4	6.6	8	6.8	7.7	7.9

Category G

Model Description	Trade-in Value	Market Value
4 Dr Limited 4WD Wgn	19890	24260
4 Dr LS 4WD Wgn	15535	18945
4 Dr S 4WD Wgn	11290	13770
4 Dr SE 4WD Wgn	19635	23945

OPTIONS FOR TROOPER

Auto 4-Speed Transmission[Opt on S] +685
Air Conditioning[Opt on S] +450
Aluminum/Alloy Wheels[Opt on S] +190
AM/FM Compact Disc Playr +215
Anti-Lock Brakes[Opt on LS,S] +345
Cruise Control[Opt on S] +115
Dual Power Seats[Opt on LS] +350
Keyless Entry System[Std on SE] +115
Leather Seats[Opt on LS] +425
Limited Slip Diff[Std on SE] +145
Power Door Locks[Opt on S] +125
Power Moonroof[Opt on LS] +490
Power Windows[Opt on S] +130
Running Boards +215

1995 ISUZU

HALF TON PICKUP 1995

Spacecab, V6 power and automatic transmission are canceled for 1995. All that's left are four-cylinder regular-cab trucks in 2WD or 4WD. California didn't get any 1995 Pickups, thanks to strict emissions regulations.

Don't forget to refer to the Mileage Adjustment Table at the back of this book!

 © 1999 by Edmund Publications Corporation

Model Description	Trade-in Value	Market Value
Category G		
2 Dr S Std Cab SB	4805	5935
2 Dr S Std Cab LB	4805	5935
2 Dr S 4WD Std Cab SB	6850	8455

OPTIONS FOR HALF TON PICKUP

Wheel Pkg +360
Air Conditioning +370
AM/FM Stereo Tape +110
Power Steering[Opt on 2WD] +130
Rear Step Bumper +65

RODEO 1995

S V6 models can be equipped with a Bright Package in conjunction with the Preferred Equipment Package. It includes lots of chrome trim and aluminum wheels.

RATINGS (SCALE OF 1-10)

Overall	Safety	Reliability	Performance	Comfort	Value
6.9	6.9	7.7	7	7.1	5.8

Model Description	Trade-in Value	Market Value
Category G		
4 Dr LS Wgn	11505	14205
4 Dr LS 4WD Wgn	12340	15235
4 Dr S Wgn	7955	9825
4 Dr S 4WD Wgn	8870	10950
4 Dr S V6 Wgn	8235	10165

OPTIONS FOR RODEO

Auto 4-Speed Transmission[Opt on S,S V6,4WD] +480
Bright Pkg +475
Air Conditioning[Std on LS] +370
Aluminum/Alloy Wheels[Std on LS] +155
Anti-Lock Brakes +280
Compact Disc W/fm/tape +310
Cruise Control[Std on LS] +95
Dual Air Bag Restraints[Opt on S,S V6,2WD] +195
Keyless Entry System +95
Limited Slip Diff +120
Luggage Rack[Std on LS] +70
Power Door Locks[Std on LS] +105
Power Windows[Std on LS] +105
Running Boards +175
Sunroof +135
Swing Out Tire Carrier[Opt on S] +95

TROOPER 1995

Dual airbags are standard. Styling is revised. A new top-of-the-line trim level debuts. The Limited has a power sunroof, leather upholstery, heated seats, and wood grain trim. Suspensions have been reworked to provide a better ride.

RATINGS (SCALE OF 1-10)

Overall	Safety	Reliability	Performance	Comfort	Value
7.5	7.5	8.3	6.8	7.7	7.1

Model Description	Trade-in Value	Market Value
Category G		
4 Dr Limited 4WD Wgn	15470	19095
4 Dr LS 4WD Wgn	13010	16060
2 Dr RS 4WD Utility	12420	15335
4 Dr S 4WD Wgn	9835	12140
4 Dr SE 4WD Wgn	15240	18815

OPTIONS FOR TROOPER

Auto 4-Speed Transmission[Opt on LS,RS,S] +515
Air Conditioning[Opt on S] +370
Aluminum/Alloy Wheels[Opt on S] +155
AM/FM Compact Disc Playr +175
Anti-Lock Brakes[Opt on S] +280
Cruise Control[Opt on S] +95
Keyless Entry System[Opt on S] +95
Limited Slip Diff[Opt on S] +120
Power Door Locks[Opt on S] +105
Power Windows[Opt on S] +105
Premium Sound System[Opt on S] +165

1994 ISUZU

AMIGO 1994

Automatic transmission disappears from options list, and base 2.3-liter four-cylinder engine is no longer available. Power steering, power outside mirrors, a center floor console, and 16-inch tires are all newly standard.

Model Description	Trade-in Value	Market Value
Category G		
2 Dr S Utility	6065	7580
2 Dr S 4WD Utility	6460	8075
2 Dr XS Utility	6750	8435
2 Dr XS 4WD Utility	7040	8800

OPTIONS FOR AMIGO

Air Conditioning +300
AM/FM Stereo Tape +90
Sunroof[Opt on S,2WD] +110

HALF TON PICKUP 1994

Vent windows are dropped. Models with 2.6-liter engine get standard power steering. Outside mirrors are revised.

Model Description	Trade-in Value	Market Value
Category G		
2 Dr S Ext Cab SB	4950	6190
2 Dr S Std Cab LB	4250	5310
2 Dr S 4WD Std Cab SB	6195	7745
2 Dr S 2.6 Ext Cab SB	5025	6280
2 Dr S 2.6 Std Cab SB	4345	5430
2 Dr STD Std Cab SB	4180	5220

OPTIONS FOR HALF TON PICKUP

6 cyl 3.1 L Engine +320
Tire/Wheel Package +310
Air Conditioning +300
AM/FM Stereo Tape +90

Don't forget to refer to the Mileage Adjustment Table at the back of this book!

© 1999 by Edmund Publications Corporation

Model Description	Trade-in Value	Market Value

Chrome Bumpers +60
Power Steering[Std on Ext Cab,4WD] +105
Rear Step Bumper +55

RODEO 1994

S model gets standard power steering. LS models are equipped with standard air conditioning. Front vent windows are dropped. All V6 models come with standard rear wiper/washer and tailgate spare tire carrier.

RATINGS (SCALE OF 1-10)

Overall	Safety	Reliability	Performance	Comfort	Value
6.5	4	7.5	7	7.4	6.5

Category G		
4 Dr LS Wgn	9490	11860
4 Dr LS 4WD Wgn	9880	12350
4 Dr S Wgn	6810	8510
4 Dr S 4WD Wgn	7630	9535
4 Dr S V6 Wgn	6905	8630

OPTIONS FOR RODEO

Auto 4-Speed Transmission[Opt on S,S V6,4WD] +385
Air Conditioning[Std on LS] +300
Compact Disc W/fm/tape +255
Cruise Control[Std on LS] +80
Keyless Entry System +75
Limited Slip Diff +100
Luggage Rack[Std on LS] +60
Power Door Locks[Std on LS] +85
Power Windows[Std on LS] +85
Sunroof +110
Swing Out Tire Carrier[Opt on 2WD] +75

TROOPER 1994

Four-wheel ABS filters down to the Trooper S options sheet. Gray leather upholstery is a new options for the LS model, and it includes heated front seats with power adjustments. RS gets new alloys.

RATINGS (SCALE OF 1-10)

Overall	Safety	Reliability	Performance	Comfort	Value
7.2	4.3	8	7.8	7.8	8.2

Category G		
4 Dr LS 4WD Wgn	11100	13875
2 Dr RS 4WD Utility	9800	12250
4 Dr S 4WD Wgn	8125	10155
4 Dr SE 4WD Wgn	11870	14835

OPTIONS FOR TROOPER

Auto 4-Speed Transmission[Std on SE] +425
Heated Leather Pwr Seats +280
Air Conditioning[Opt on S] +300
AM/FM Compact Disc Playr +145
Anti-Lock Brakes[Opt on S] +230
Cruise Control[Opt on S] +80
Dual Power Seats[Opt on LS] +235
Heated Front Seats[Opt on LS] +95
Leather Seats[Opt on LS] +285
Limited Slip Diff[Opt on S] +100
Power Door Locks[Opt on S] +85
Power Sunroof[Opt on LS] +300
Power Windows[Opt on S] +85

1993 ISUZU

AMIGO 1993

Amigo gets a new grille.

Category G		
2 Dr S Utility	4925	6315
2 Dr S 4WD Utility	5255	6735
2 Dr XS Utility	5515	7070
2 Dr XS 4WD Utility	5850	7500

OPTIONS FOR AMIGO

4 cyl 2.6 L Engine[Std on XS,4WD] +255
Auto 4-Speed Transmission +270
Amigo Tire/Wheel Pkg +245
Air Conditioning +245
Aluminum/Alloy Wheels[Opt on S,2WD] +105
AM/FM Stereo Tape +75
Sunroof +90

HALF TON PICKUP 1993

LS trim level dropped. Two models discontinued: one-ton Longbed and 4WD Spacecab. A new grille graces the front of the Pickup.

Category G		
2 Dr S Ext Cab SB	4150	5320
2 Dr S Std Cab SB	4030	5165
2 Dr S Std Cab LB	4045	5185
2 Dr S 4WD Std Cab SB	5565	7130
2 Dr S 2.6 Std Cab SB	4190	5375

OPTIONS FOR HALF TON PICKUP

6 cyl 3.1 L Engine +255
Pick Up 4WD Bright Package +505
Air Conditioning +245
Aluminum/Alloy Wheels +105
AM/FM Stereo Tape +75
Power Steering[Std on S 2.6,Ext Cab,4WD] +85
Rear Step Bumper +45

RODEO 1993

More potent V6 engine filters into Rodeo from big brother Trooper. Horsepower boost equals 55 ponies. A new grille is installed up front.

RATINGS (SCALE OF 1-10)

Overall	Safety	Reliability	Performance	Comfort	Value
6.5	4.1	7.5	7	7.4	6.3

Don't forget to refer to the Mileage Adjustment Table at the back of this book!

 © 1999 by Edmund Publications Corporation

Model Description	Trade-in Value	Market Value
Category G		
4 Dr LS Wgn	7550	9680
4 Dr LS 4WD Wgn	7730	9910
4 Dr S Wgn	5970	7655
4 Dr S 4WD Wgn	6625	8495
4 Dr S V6 Wgn	6220	7975

OPTIONS FOR RODEO
Auto 4-Speed Transmission +295
Rodeo Tire/Wheel Pkg +290
Air Conditioning +245
Aluminum/Alloy Wheels +105
AM/FM Compact Disc Playr +115
Cruise Control[Std on LS] +65
Limited Slip Diff +80
Luggage Rack[Std on LS] +45
Sunroof +90

TROOPER 1993

A short-wheelbase two-door model joins the lineup in RS trim. Four-wheel ABS is optional on this stubby new model.

RATINGS (SCALE OF 1-10)

Overall	Safety	Reliability	Performance	Comfort	Value
6.9	4.1	8.2	7.8	7.8	6.5

Model Description	Trade-in Value	Market Value
Category G		
4 Dr LS 4WD Wgn	9360	12000
2 Dr RS 4WD Utility	7920	10155
4 Dr S 4WD Wgn	6835	8765

OPTIONS FOR TROOPER
Auto 4-Speed Transmission +350
4-Sensor Anti Lock Brakes +335
Air Conditioning[Opt on S] +245
Aluminum/Alloy Wheels[Opt on S] +105
AM/FM Compact Disc Playr +115
Cruise Control[Opt on S] +65
Limited Slip Diff[Opt on S] +80
Power Door Locks[Opt on S] +70
Power Sunroof +245
Power Windows[Opt on S] +70
Premium Sound System[Opt on S] +110

1992 ISUZU

AMIGO 1992

Those who hate shifting their own gears are in luck; an automatic is newly optional.

Model Description	Trade-in Value	Market Value
Category G		
2 Dr S Utility	4480	5970
2 Dr S 4WD Utility	4810	6410
2 Dr XS Utility	4900	6535
2 Dr XS 4WD Utility	5655	7545

OPTIONS FOR AMIGO
4 cyl 2.6 L Engine[Std on XS,4WD] +180
Auto 4-Speed Transmission +220
Air Conditioning +200
Aluminum/Alloy Wheels[Opt on S,2WD] +85
AM/FM Stereo Tape +60
Power Steering[Std on XS,4WD] +70
Sunroof +75

HALF TON PICKUP 1992

No changes.

Model Description	Trade-in Value	Market Value
Category G		
2 Dr LS Ext Cab SB	3670	4895
2 Dr S Ext Cab SB	3100	4130
2 Dr S Std Cab SB	2670	3560
2 Dr S Std Cab LB	2725	3635
2 Dr S 4WD Std Cab SB	4420	5895

OPTIONS FOR HALF TON PICKUP
4 cyl 2.6 L Engine[Std on LS,Ext Cab,4WD] +100
6 cyl 3.1 L Engine +180
Auto 4-Speed Transmission +215
Air Conditioning +200
Aluminum/Alloy Wheels[Opt on S] +85
AM/FM Stereo Tape[Opt on S] +60
Cruise Control +50
Power Door Locks +55
Power Steering[Std on LS,4WD] +70
Power Windows +60
Rear Step Bumper +35

RODEO 1992

No changes.

RATINGS (SCALE OF 1-10)

Overall	Safety	Reliability	Performance	Comfort	Value
6.4	4.1	7.5	6.6	7.4	6.3

Model Description	Trade-in Value	Market Value
Category G		
4 Dr LS Wgn	6130	8175
4 Dr LS 4WD Wgn	6365	8485
4 Dr LX 4WD Wgn	6570	8755
4 Dr S Wgn	4595	6125
4 Dr S 4WD Wgn	5605	7475
4 Dr S V6 Wgn	5395	7190
4 Dr XS Wgn	5430	7240
4 Dr XS 4WD Wgn	5975	7965

OPTIONS FOR RODEO
Auto 3-Speed Transmission +215
Auto 4-Speed Transmission +240
Air Conditioning +200
Aluminum/Alloy Wheels[Opt on S] +85
AM/FM Stereo Tape[Std on LS,LX] +60
Cruise Control +50
Limited Slip Diff[Opt on LS] +65
Luggage Rack +40

Don't forget to refer to the Mileage Adjustment Table at the back of this book!

 © 1999 by Edmund Publications Corporation

Model Description	Trade-in Value	Market Value

Power Door Locks +55
Power Steering[Opt on S Wgn] +70
Power Windows +60
Sunroof +75
Swing Out Tire Carrier +50

STYLUS 1992

RS gets ten more horsepower, thanks to a larger 1.8-liter twin-cam engine.

Category E		
4 Dr RS Sdn	2505	3575
4 Dr S Sdn	2025	2890

OPTIONS FOR STYLUS

Auto 3-Speed Transmission +135
Air Conditioning +200
Aluminum/Alloy Wheels[Opt on S] +80
AM/FM Stereo Tape +75
Cruise Control +55
Power Door Locks +55
Power Steering[Opt on S] +60
Power Windows +65

TROOPER 1992

Beefy SUV moves upscale with total redesign that renders it longer, wider, taller, and heavier. Four-wheel ABS is optional on LS models. A new Isuzu-designed 3.2-liter V6 powers Trooper; base models have an SOHC unit, while LS models get a DOHC engine good for 190 horsepower.

RATINGS (SCALE OF 1-10)

Overall	Safety	Reliability	Performance	Comfort	Value
6.8	4.1	7.9	7.8	7.8	6.4

Category G		
4 Dr LS 4WD Wgn	7700	10265
4 Dr S 4WD Wgn	5925	7900

OPTIONS FOR TROOPER

Auto 4-Speed Transmission +280
Air Conditioning[Opt on S] +200
AM/FM Compact Disc Playr +95
Anti-Lock Brakes[Std on S] +155
Limited Slip Diff[Opt on S] +65
Power Sunroof +200
Premium Sound System[Opt on S] +90

1991 ISUZU

AMIGO 1991

Warranty changes from 3 years/36,000 miles to 3 years/50,000 miles. Rust coverage is extended to 6 years/100,000 miles from 3 years/unlimited mileage. New powertrain warranty is good for 5 years/60,000 miles. XS gets locking center console standard; item is optional on S. New paint colors, graphics and alloy wheels debut.

Category G		
2 Dr S Utility	3350	4525
2 Dr S 4WD Utility	3920	5300
2 Dr XS Utility	3635	4915
2 Dr XS 4WD Utility	4285	5790

OPTIONS FOR AMIGO

4 cyl 2.6 L Engine[Std on XS,4WD] +115
Air Conditioning +165
Aluminum/Alloy Wheels[Opt on S,2WD] +70
AM/FM Stereo Tape +50
Power Steering[Std on XS,4WD] +55
Sunroof +60

HALF TON PICKUP 1991

Warranty changes from 3 years/36,000 miles to 3 years/50,000 miles. Rust coverage extended to 6 years/100,000 miles. New powertrain warranty is good for 5 years/60,000 miles. A 3.1-liter GM V-6 is newly optional. Grille and tailgate graphics are revised with new lettering. LS models get standard sliding rear window. On 2WD with 2.6-liter engine, drums replace the rear discs.

Category G		
2 Dr LS Ext Cab SB	3215	4345
2 Dr LS 4WD Std Cab SB	4565	6170
2 Dr S Ext Cab SB	2880	3895
2 Dr S Std Cab SB	2395	3240
2 Dr S Std Cab LB	2470	3335
2 Dr S 4WD Std Cab SB	3735	5045

OPTIONS FOR HALF TON PICKUP

4 cyl 2.6 L Engine[Std on LS,Ext Cab,4WD] +70
6 cyl 3.1 L Engine[Opt on S] +115
Auto 4-Speed Transmission +165
Power Pkg +155
Air Conditioning +165
Aluminum/Alloy Wheels[Opt on S] +70
AM/FM Stereo Tape[Opt on S] +50
Cruise Control +45
Power Door Locks +45
Power Steering[Std on LS,Ext Cab,4WD] +55
Power Windows +50

IMPULSE 1991

New RS model debuts equipped with turbocharged engine and all-wheel drive, two items twin Geo Storm never received. RS turbo makes 160 horsepower and can be equipped with optional ABS. Also new is an aberration called Impulse XS hatchback. Warranty changes from 3 years/36,000 miles to 3 years/50,000 miles. Rust coverage is extended to 6 years/100,000 miles from 3 years/unlimited mileage. New powertrain warranty is good for 5 years/60,000 miles.

Don't forget to refer to the Mileage Adjustment Table at the back of this book!

 © 1999 by Edmund Publications Corporation

Model Description	Trade-in Value	Market Value
Category E		
2 Dr RS Turbo 4WD Cpe	2935	4315
2 Dr XS Cpe	2220	3265
2 Dr XS Hbk	2255	3320

OPTIONS FOR IMPULSE

Auto 4-Speed Transmission +150
Air Conditioning +165
Aluminum/Alloy Wheels[Opt on XS] +65
AM/FM Stereo Tape[Opt on XS] +60
Cruise Control +45
Power Door Locks +45
Power Sunroof +120
Power Windows +55
Premium Sound System +70

RODEO 1991

New Pickup-based sport utility debuts. Built in Indiana. Available with two- or four-wheel drive with either Isuzu-built four cylinder or GM-sourced V6. Rodeo features a long wheelbase for ride comfort and excellent rear seat leg room. Four-wheel disc brakes accompany V6 engines.

RATINGS (SCALE OF 1-10)

Overall	Safety	Reliability	Performance	Comfort	Value
6.2	4	7.1	6.6	7.4	5.8

Model Description	Trade-in Value	Market Value
Category G		
4 Dr LS Wgn	5350	7235
4 Dr LS 4WD Wgn	5615	7590
4 Dr S Wgn	3900	5270
4 Dr S 4WD Wgn	5020	6785
4 Dr S V6 Wgn	4200	5675
4 Dr XS Wgn	4510	6095
4 Dr XS 4WD Wgn	5210	7040

OPTIONS FOR RODEO

Auto 4-Speed Transmission +190
Air Conditioning +165
Aluminum/Alloy Wheels[Std on XS] +70
AM/FM Stereo Tape[Std on LS Wgn] +50
Cruise Control +45
Luggage Rack +30
Power Door Locks +45
Power Steering[Opt on S Wgn] +55
Power Windows +50
Premium Sound System +75
Sunroof +60
Swing Out Tire Carrier[Opt on LS,S,S V6,2WD] +40

STYLUS 1991

New sedan based on Impulse running gear includes standard driver airbag. XS is quite a spry sport sedan with 130-horsepower twin-cam 1.6-liter engine.

Model Description	Trade-in Value	Market Value
Category E		
4 Dr S Sdn	1800	2645
4 Dr XS Sdn	2035	2990

OPTIONS FOR STYLUS

Auto 3-Speed Transmission +95
Air Conditioning +165
AM/FM Stereo Tape +60
Cruise Control +45
Power Door Locks +45
Power Steering[Opt on S] +50
Power Sunroof +120
Power Windows +55
Premium Sound System +70
Rear Spoiler +40

TROOPER 1991

Warranty changes from 3 years/36,000 miles to 3 years/50,000 miles. Rust coverage is extended to 6 years/100,000 miles from 3 years/unlimited mileage. New powertrain warranty is good for 5 years/60,000 miles.

Model Description	Trade-in Value	Market Value
Category G		
4 Dr LS 4WD Wgn	4915	6645
4 Dr S 4WD Wgn	4220	5700
4 Dr SE 4WD Wgn	5015	6775
4 Dr XS 4WD Wgn	4665	6305

OPTIONS FOR TROOPER

6 cyl 2.8 L Engine[Opt on S] +80
Auto 4-Speed Transmission +220
Air Conditioning +165
Aluminum/Alloy Wheels[Opt on S] +70
AM/FM Stereo Tape[Opt on S] +50
Auto Locking Hubs (4WD) +55
Camper/Towing Package[Opt on S] +60
Luggage Rack[Opt on S,XS] +30

1990 ISUZU

AMIGO 1990

A removable stereo is a new option.

Model Description	Trade-in Value	Market Value
Category G		
2 Dr S Utility	2545	3535
2 Dr S 4WD Utility	3450	4790
2 Dr XS Utility	2700	3750
2 Dr XS 4WD Utility	3585	4975

OPTIONS FOR AMIGO

4 cyl 2.6 L Engine[Std on XS,4WD] +105
Air Conditioning +135
Aluminum/Alloy Wheels[Opt on S] +55
AM/FM Stereo Tape +40
Power Steering[Std on XS,4WD] +45
Sunroof +50

Don't forget to refer to the Mileage Adjustment Table at the back of this book!

 © 1999 by Edmund Publications Corporation

Model Description	Trade-in Value	Market Value

HALF TON PICKUP 1990

Rear-wheel ABS debuts. System works only in 2WD.

Category G		
2 Dr LS Std Cab SB	2335	3240
2 Dr LS Ext Cab SB	3195	4435
2 Dr LS 4WD Std Cab SB	3415	4740
2 Dr S Std Cab SB	1910	2650
2 Dr S Ext Cab SB	2695	3740
2 Dr S Std Cab LB	2075	2880
2 Dr S 4WD Std Cab SB	3170	4400
2 Dr XS Std Cab SB	2020	2805
2 Dr XS Ext Cab SB	2820	3915
2 Dr XS 4WD Std Cab SB	3350	4655

OPTIONS FOR HALF TON PICKUP

4 cyl 2.6 L Engine[Std on LS,XS,Ext Cab,4WD] +105
Auto 4-Speed Transmission +135
Power Pkg +130
Air Conditioning +135
Aluminum/Alloy Wheels[Std on XS] +55
AM/FM Stereo Tape[Std on LS] +40
Cruise Control +35
Power Door Locks +40
Power Steering[Std on LS,Ext Cab,4WD] +45
Power Windows +40

IMPULSE 1990

Totally redesigned car carrying traditional Impulse styling cues. Identical in structure and engineering to Geo Storm. XS model has 130 horsepower normally-aspirated motor and front-wheel drive. Driver airbag is standard.

Category E		
2 Dr XS Hbk	1950	3000

OPTIONS FOR IMPULSE

Auto 4-Speed Transmission +125
Air Conditioning +135
Aluminum/Alloy Wheels +50
AM/FM Stereo Tape +50
Cruise Control +35
Flip-Up Sunroof +60
Power Door Locks +40
Power Windows +45
Premium Sound System +55

TROOPER 1990

S model gets full carpeting, dual outside mirrors and improved instrumentation. XS model is available only with V6 engine. After one season, the short-wheelbase two-door model is dropped.

Category G		
4 Dr LS 4WD Wgn	3985	5535
4 Dr S 4WD Wgn	3730	5180
4 Dr XS 4WD Wgn	3820	5305

OPTIONS FOR TROOPER

6 cyl 2.8 L Engine[Opt on S] +60
Auto 4-Speed Transmission +180
Air Conditioning +135
Aluminum/Alloy Wheels +55
AM/FM Stereo Tape[Opt on S] +40
Camper/Towing Package +50

1989 ISUZU

AMIGO 1989

New convertible SUV based on Pickup design. Available in two- or four-wheel drive with choice of two four-cylinder engines.

Category G		
2 Dr S Utility	2305	3340
2 Dr S 4WD Utility	2965	4295
2 Dr XS Utility	2515	3650
2 Dr XS 4WD Utility	3160	4580

OPTIONS FOR AMIGO

4 cyl 2.6 L Engine[Std on XS,4WD] +60
Air Conditioning +110
Aluminum/Alloy Wheels[Opt on S] +45
AM/FM Stereo Tape +35
Power Steering[Std on XS,4WD] +40
Sunroof +40

HALF TON PICKUP 1989

No changes.

Category G		
2 Dr LS Std Cab SB	2140	3100
2 Dr LS Ext Cab SB	2330	3375
2 Dr LS 4WD Ext Cab SB	2855	4140
2 Dr LS 4WD Std Cab SB	2645	3830
2 Dr S Ext Cab SB	2200	3190
2 Dr S Std Cab LB	1865	2700
2 Dr S 4WD Std Cab SB	2490	3610
2 Dr XS Ext Cab SB	2295	3325
2 Dr XS 4WD Std Cab SB	2815	4080

OPTIONS FOR HALF TON PICKUP

4 cyl 2.6 L Engine[Std on LS,XS,Ext Cab,4WD] +60
Auto 4-Speed Transmission +70
Air Conditioning +110
Aluminum/Alloy Wheels[Std on LS] +45
AM/FM Stereo Tape[Std on LS] +35
Cruise Control +30
Power Door Locks +30
Power Steering[Std on LS,Ext Cab,4WD] +40
Power Windows +30

Don't forget to refer to the Mileage Adjustment Table at the back of this book!

 © 1999 by Edmund Publications Corporation

Model Description	Trade-in Value	Market Value

I-MARK 1989

New DOHC engine debuts with 125 horsepower. To get this motor, you must get an RS with a five-speed manual transmission. RS model has Lotus-tuned suspension and comes in red, black or gray. Optional is a Recaro package that includes sport seats and glass sunroof. LS models also have Lotus-tuned suspension, but are powered by a 110-horsepower turbocharged 1.5-liter engine. New Sunsport model is based on S hatchback and includes a power canvas roof, body-color trim, and sport seats.

Category E

Model Description	Trade-in Value	Market Value
2 Dr RS Hbk	1250	2050
2 Dr RS Turbo Hbk	1320	2160
4 Dr RS Sdn	1195	1960
4 Dr RS Turbo Sdn	1355	2220
2 Dr S Hbk	980	1605
4 Dr S Sdn	860	1410
2 Dr XS Hbk	1215	1995
4 Dr XS Sdn	1150	1885

OPTIONS FOR I-MARK

Auto 3-Speed Transmission +60
Recaro Pkg +120
Sunsports Pkg +150
Air Conditioning +110
AM/FM Stereo Tape[Opt on S,XS,RS Turbo Sdn] +40
Cruise Control +30
Power Door Locks +30
Power Steering[Opt on S] +35
Sunroof[Std on LS] +45

IMPULSE 1989

Body-color bumpers are standard.

Category E

Model Description	Trade-in Value	Market Value
2 Dr STD Hbk	1630	2670
2 Dr STD Turbo Hbk	1940	3175

OPTIONS FOR IMPULSE

Auto 4-Speed Transmission +75

TROOPER II 1989

New short-wheelbase two-door debuts. Four-door model gets an optional GM-sourced 2.8-liter 125-horsepower V6 engine. Base four-cylinder Isuzu engine produces 120 horsepower.

Category G

Model Description	Trade-in Value	Market Value
4 Dr LS 4WD Wgn	3190	4625
2 Dr RS 4WD Utility	3370	4885
4 Dr S 4WD Wgn	3075	4455
4 Dr XS 4WD Wgn	3125	4530

OPTIONS FOR TROOPER II

6 cyl 2.8 L Engine +55
Auto 4-Speed Transmission +120
Air Conditioning +110
Aluminum/Alloy Wheels[Std on LS] +45
AM/FM Stereo Tape[Opt on S] +35
Auto Locking Hubs (4WD)[Std on LS] +35
Power Door Locks +30
Power Windows +30

Get a great used car and apply for financing *online* at a price you must see to believe!

http://www.edmunds.com

Don't forget to refer to the Mileage Adjustment Table at the back of this book!

 © 1999 by Edmund Publications Corporation

JAGUAR Britain

1995 Jaguar XJ12

1998 JAGUAR

VANDEN PLAS 1998

A new V8 engine, taken from the XK coupe and convertible, makes its way into the engine bay. A revised instrument panel greatly improves interior ergonomics. Cruise and satellite stereo controls are located on the steering wheel.

Category J

	Trade-in Value	Market Value
4 Dr STD Sdn	46580	54165

OPTIONS FOR VANDEN PLAS

All Weather Package +1050
Compact Disc Changer +815
Harman Kardon Sound Sys +1495
Heated Seats +300

XJ-SERIES 1998

A new V8 engine, taken from the XK coupe and convertible, makes its way into the engine bay. A revised instrument panel greatly improves interior ergonomics. Cruise and satellite stereo controls are located on the steering wheel.

XJ8

Category J

	Trade-in Value	Market Value
4 Dr STD Sdn	39390	45805

XJ8L

Category J

	Trade-in Value	Market Value
4 Dr STD Sdn	41650	48430

OPTIONS FOR XJ-SERIES

All Weather Package +1050

1997 JAGUAR

XJ-SERIES 1997

XJ6

Category J

	Trade-in Value	Market Value
4 Dr STD Sdn	32700	38025

XJ6L

Category J

	Trade-in Value	Market Value
4 Dr STD Sdn	33930	39455

XJR

Category L

	Trade-in Value	Market Value
4 Dr STD Sprchgd Sdn	37555	44710

OPTIONS FOR XJ-SERIES

All Weather Package +1360

XK8 1997

Category J

	Trade-in Value	Market Value
2 Dr STD Conv	47125	54795
2 Dr STD Cpe	44590	51850

OPTIONS FOR XK8

All-Weather Package +1360
Chrome Wheels +975
Compact Disc Changer +665
Traction Control System +895

1996 JAGUAR

VANDEN PLAS 1996

Category J

	Trade-in Value	Market Value
4 Dr STD Sdn	30605	36435

OPTIONS FOR VANDEN PLAS

All Weather Package +540
Chrome Wheels +795
Compact Disc Changer +545
Traction Control System +730

XJ-SERIES 1996

XJ12

Category J

	Trade-in Value	Market Value
4 Dr STD Sdn	36125	43005

XJ6

Category J

	Trade-in Value	Market Value
4 Dr STD Sdn	28440	33860

XJR

Category L

	Trade-in Value	Market Value
4 Dr STD Sprchgd Sdn	34030	40510

Don't forget to refer to the Mileage Adjustment Table at the back of this book!

 © 1999 by Edmund Publications Corporation

Model Description	Trade-in Value	Market Value

XJS 1996

After a mighty 20-year reign, the XJS is put out to pasture. The only model offered for 1996 is the six-cylinder convertible; the most popular XJS in its remarkable history. The changes for 1996 include new wheels, new bucket seats, additional chrome exterior trim, and an adjustable, wood-trimmed steering wheel.

Category J

Model Description	Trade-in Value	Market Value
2 Dr 2+2 Conv	30940	36835

OPTIONS FOR XJS

Chrome Wheels +795
Compact Disc Changer +545
Sport Suspension +250

1995 JAGUAR

XJ-SERIES 1995

XJ12

Category J

Model Description	Trade-in Value	Market Value
4 Dr STD Sdn	29640	35710

XJ6

Category J

Model Description	Trade-in Value	Market Value
4 Dr STD Sdn	22280	26840
4 Dr Vanden Plas Sdn	24795	29875

XJR

Category L

Model Description	Trade-in Value	Market Value
4 Dr STD Sprchgd Sdn	27635	33705

XJS

Category J

Model Description	Trade-in Value	Market Value
2 Dr STD Cpe	24500	29520
2 Dr STD Conv	26670	32135
2 Dr V12 Conv	30700	36985
2 Dr V12 Cpe	28130	33890

OPTIONS FOR XJ-SERIES

Luxury Package +565

1994 JAGUAR

XJ-SERIES 1994

XJ12

Category J

Model Description	Trade-in Value	Market Value
4 Dr STD Sdn	16795	20485

XJ6

Category J

Model Description	Trade-in Value	Market Value
4 Dr STD Sdn	14585	17785
4 Dr Vanden Plas Sdn	16785	20470

XJS

Category J

Model Description	Trade-in Value	Market Value
2 Dr 4.0L Cpe	20260	24705
2 Dr 4.0L Conv	20290	24745
2 Dr 6.0L Conv	24375	29725
2 Dr 6.0L Cpe	23375	28505

OPTIONS FOR XJ-SERIES

Paint (non Standard) +555
Sport Handling Package +370

1993 JAGUAR

XJ-SERIES 1993

XJ6

Category J

Model Description	Trade-in Value	Market Value
4 Dr STD Sdn	11355	14020
4 Dr Vanden Plas Sdn	13065	16130

XJS

Category J

Model Description	Trade-in Value	Market Value
2 Dr STD Cpe	14550	17960
2 Dr STD Conv	17475	21575

1992 JAGUAR

XJ-SERIES 1992

XJ6

Category J

Model Description	Trade-in Value	Market Value
4 Dr Majestic Sdn	12035	15235
4 Dr Sovereign Sdn	9745	12340
4 Dr STD Sdn	8735	11060
4 Dr Vanden Plas Sdn	11165	14130

XJS

Category J

Model Description	Trade-in Value	Market Value
2 Dr STD Conv	15985	20230
2 Dr STD Cpe	12365	15655

1991 JAGUAR

XJ-SERIES 1991

XJ6

Category J

Model Description	Trade-in Value	Market Value
4 Dr Sovereign Sdn	7945	10315
4 Dr STD Sdn	7085	9200
4 Dr Vanden Plas Sdn	9080	11790

XJS

Category J

Model Description	Trade-in Value	Market Value
2 Dr STD Conv	14355	18645
2 Dr STD Cpe	9875	12825

Don't forget to refer to the Mileage Adjustment Table at the back of this book!

 © 1999 by Edmund Publications Corporation

1990 JAGUAR

XJ-SERIES 1990

Model Description	Trade-in Value	Market Value
XJ6		
Category J		
4 Dr Sovereign Sdn	6780	9045
4 Dr STD Sdn	6145	8190
4 Dr Vanden Majestic Sdn	8290	11050
4 Dr Vanden Plas Sdn	7565	10085
XJS		
Category J		
2 Dr STD Conv	11925	15900
2 Dr STD Cpe	8655	11540

1989 JAGUAR

XJ-SERIES 1989

Model Description	Trade-in Value	Market Value
XJ6		
Category J		
4 Dr STD Sdn	5460	7480
4 Dr Vanden Plas Sdn	5880	8055
XJS		
Category J		
2 Dr Rouge Cpe	8675	11885
2 Dr STD Conv	9965	13655
2 Dr STD Cpe	7185	9845

Major Savings On An Extended Warranty

"YOU DESERVE THE BEST"

Call today for your free quote.

Pay up to 50% less than dealership prices!

http://www.edmunds.com/warranty 1-800-580-9889

A 15-minute phone call could save you 15% or more on car insurance.

1-800-555-2758

GEICO DIRECT

The Sensible Alternative

Don't forget to refer to the Mileage Adjustment Table at the back of this book!

 © 1999 by Edmund Publications Corporation

JEEP USA

1997 Jeep Wrangler

1998 JEEP

CHEROKEE 1998

Cherokee Classic and Limited replace the Cherokee Country. A new 2.5-liter four-cylinder engine is now the base engine for the SE, available with an optional three-speed automatic. New colors include Chili Pepper Red, Emerald Green and Deep Amethyst.

Category G		
4 Dr Classic Wgn	16215	19300
4 Dr Classic 4WD Wgn	16945	20175
4 Dr Limited Wgn	18435	21950
4 Dr Limited 4WD Wgn	18530	22060
2 Dr SE 4WD Utility	13895	16545
4 Dr SE Wgn	12740	15170
4 Dr SE 4WD Wgn	13620	16215
2 Dr Sport 4WD Utility	14145	16835
4 Dr Sport Wgn	13940	16600
4 Dr Sport 4WD Wgn	14550	17320

OPTIONS FOR CHEROKEE

6 cyl 4.0 L Engine[Opt on SE] +745
Auto 4-Speed Transmission[Opt on SE, Sport] +785
Air Conditioning[Std on Limited] +675
Aluminum/Alloy Wheels[Opt on SE, Sport] +285
Anti-Lock Brakes +515
Auto Locking Hubs (4WD)[Opt on Utility] +220
Compact Disc W/fm/tape +565
Cruise Control[Std on Limited] +175
Fog Lights +120
Keyless Entry System[Std on Limited] +170
Leather Seats[Opt on Classic] +640
Power Door Locks[Std on Limited] +190
Power Drivers Seat[Std on Limited] +235
Power Mirrors[Opt on SE, Sport] +110
Power Windows[Std on Limited] +195
Rear Window Defroster[Std on Limited] +140
Rear Window Wiper[Opt on SE, Sport] +125
Sunscreen Glass[Opt on Sport] +295
Tilt Steering Wheel[Std on Limited] +140

GRAND CHEROKEE 1998

A 5.9-liter V8 making 245 horsepower and 345 foot-pounds torque powers the Grand Cherokee 5.9 Limited, making it the mightiest of all Jeeps. With the addition of the 5.9, the putrid Orvis model dies. Two new colors and "next-generation" airbags round out the changes.

Category G		
4 Dr 5.9 Limited 4WD Wgn	24365	29005
4 Dr Laredo Wgn	17920	21330
4 Dr Laredo 4WD Wgn	18865	22460
4 Dr Limited Wgn	21040	25045
4 Dr Limited 4WD Wgn	22200	26430
4 Dr TSi Wgn	18665	22220
4 Dr TSi 4WD Wgn	20160	24000

OPTIONS FOR GRAND CHEROKEE

8 cyl 5.2 L Engine +725
Camper/Towing Package +240
Compact Disc W/fm/tape[Opt on Laredo, TSi] +565
Dual Power Seats[Opt on Laredo,TSi] +525
Fog Lights[Opt on Laredo,TSi] +120
Heated Front Seats[Std on 5.9 Limited] +210
Heated Power Mirrors[Opt on Laredo, TSi] +50
Leather Seats[Opt on Laredo, TSi] +640
Locking Differential[Std on 5.9 Limited] +250
Power Sunroof[Std on 5.9 Limited] +670
Sunscreen Glass[Opt on Laredo, TSi] +295

WRANGLER 1998

Jeep has improved off-road capability by increasing the axle ratio offered with the 4.0-liter engine and revising the torsion bar for better steering. Optional this year are a tilting driver's seat, automatic speed control, a combination CD/cassette stereo, a new Smart Key Immobilizer theft deterrent system and two new colors.

Category G		
2 Dr Sahara 4WD Utility	15970	19010
2 Dr SE 4WD Utility	11935	14210
2 Dr Sport 4WD Utility	13810	16445

OPTIONS FOR WRANGLER

Auto 3-Speed Transmission +520
Color Match Dual Roofs +1495
Air Conditioning +675
Aluminum/Alloy Wheels[Opt on Sport] +285
AM/FM Stereo Tape[Std on Sahara] +205
Anti-Lock Brakes +515
Compact Disc W/fm/tape +565
Cruise Control +175
Fog Lights[Opt on Sport] +120
Hardtop Roof +640

Don't forget to refer to the Mileage Adjustment Table at the back of this book!

 © 1999 by Edmund Publications Corporation

Model Description	Trade-in Value	Market Value

Rear Window Defroster +140
Rear Window Wiper +125
Tilt Steering Wheel[Std on Sahara] +140
Velour/Cloth Seats[Std on Sahara] +145

1997 JEEP

CHEROKEE 1997

A new interior sporting modern instrumentation debuts. Front and rear styling is refined, and the rear liftgate is now stamped from steel. Multi-plex wiring is designed to improve reliability of the electrical system, while a new paint process aims to polish the finish of all Cherokees.

RATINGS (SCALE OF 1-10)

Overall	Safety	Reliability	Performance	Comfort	Value
7.1	6.3	8.1	7.4	7	6.4

Category G	Trade-in Value	Market Value
4 Dr Country Wgn	14315	17245
4 Dr Country 4WD Wgn	15440	18600
2 Dr SE Utility	10535	12690
2 Dr SE 4WD Utility	11650	14035
4 Dr SE Wgn	10325	12440
4 Dr SE 4WD Wgn	11370	13700
2 Dr Sport Utility	12115	14595
2 Dr Sport 4WD Utility	12780	15395
4 Dr Sport Wgn	11825	14245
4 Dr Sport 4WD Wgn	12785	15405

OPTIONS FOR CHEROKEE

6 cyl 4.0 L Engine[Opt on SE] +560
Auto 4-Speed Transmission[Std on Country] +640
Air Conditioning +550
Aluminum/Alloy Wheels[Std on Country] +235
Anti-Lock Brakes +420
Camper/Towing Package +195
Compact Disc W/fm/tape +465
Cruise Control +145
Keyless Entry System[Opt on Sport] +140
Leather Seats +520
Locking Differential +205
Luggage Rack[Std on Country] +105
Power Door Locks[Opt on Sport] +155
Power Drivers Seat +190
Power Windows[Opt on Sport] +160
Skid Plates +95

GRAND CHEROKEE 1997

Last year's integrated child safety seat has mysteriously disappeared from press kit and dealer order sheet radar. Other big news is the availability of the optional 5.2-liter V8 engine in 2WD models, and a six-cylinder that qualifies the JGC as a Transitional Low Emissions Vehicle (TLEV) in California. Refinements have been made to the ABS system, entry-level cassette stereo, and floor carpet fit. In January, a sporty TSi model debuted with monotone paint, special aluminum wheels, and other goodies.

RATINGS (SCALE OF 1-10)

Overall	Safety	Reliability	Performance	Comfort	Value
7.3	7.2	8.1	7.6	7.6	6.1

Category G	Trade-in Value	Market Value
4 Dr Laredo Wgn	15705	18920
4 Dr Laredo 4WD Wgn	16130	19435
4 Dr Limited Wgn	18920	22800
4 Dr Limited 4WD Wgn	18970	22855
4 Dr TSi Wgn	16535	19920
4 Dr TSi 4WD Wgn	17610	21215

OPTIONS FOR GRAND CHEROKEE

8 cyl 5.2 L Engine +570
Luxury Group +530
Camper/Towing Package +195
Compact Disc W/fm/tape +465
Dual Power Seats[Std on Limited] +430
Infinity Sound System[Std on Limited] +400
Leather Seats[Std on Limited] +520
Limited Slip Diff +180
Locking Differential +205
Power Sunroof +550
Skid Plates +95

WRANGLER 1997

Jeep has totally redesigned the original sport-ute. A Quadra-coil suspension improves on and off-road manners; while dual airbags and optional antilock brakes increase the Wrangler's ability to keep occupants safe. Round, retro-style headlights add a nostalgic touch to this venerable ground-pounder. Fortunately, none of these refinements soften the Wrangler's tough exterior. A restyled interior includes integrated air vents, a glovebox, and car-like stereo controls and accessory switches.

RATINGS (SCALE OF 1-10)

Overall	Safety	Reliability	Performance	Comfort	Value
7	7.4	8.1	7	5.6	6.9

Category G	Trade-in Value	Market Value
2 Dr Sahara 4WD Utility	13585	16370
2 Dr SE 4WD Utility	10625	12800
2 Dr Sport 4WD Utility	12295	14815

OPTIONS FOR WRANGLER

Auto 3-Speed Transmission +370
Air Conditioning +550
Aluminum/Alloy Wheels[Opt on Sport] +235
AM/FM Stereo Tape[Std on Sahara] +165
Anti-Lock Brakes +420
Bucket Seats[Opt on SE] +195
Hardtop Roof +520

Don't forget to refer to the Mileage Adjustment Table at the back of this book!

 © 1999 by Edmund Publications Corporation

Model Description	Trade-in Value	Market Value

Locking Differential +205
Power Steering[Opt on SE] +190
Velour/Cloth Seats[Std on Sahara] +120

1996 JEEP

CHEROKEE 1996

Perennial favorite rolls into 1996 with improved engines, new colors, upgraded Selec-Trac four-wheel drive system, more standard equipment, and the same sheetmetal that it wore on introduction day in 1983.

RATINGS (SCALE OF 1-10)

Overall	Safety	Reliability	Performance	Comfort	Value
6.7	5.8	6.8	7.4	6.6	6.7

Category G

Model Description	Trade-in Value	Market Value
4 Dr Country Wgn	10845	13555
4 Dr Country 4WD Wgn	11790	14735
2 Dr SE Utility	8225	10280
2 Dr SE 4WD Utility	9405	11760
4 Dr SE Wgn	8630	10790
4 Dr SE 4WD Wgn	9610	12010
2 Dr Sport Utility	9400	11750
2 Dr Sport 4WD Utility	10275	12840
4 Dr Sport Wgn	9360	11700
4 Dr Sport 4WD Wgn	10340	12925

OPTIONS FOR CHEROKEE

6 cyl 4.0 L Engine[Opt on SE] +420
Auto 4-Speed Transmission +485
Off-Road Suspension Pkg +415
Air Conditioning +450
Aluminum/Alloy Wheels +190
Anti-Lock Brakes +345
Camper/Towing Package +160
Compact Disc W/fm/tape +380
Cruise Control +115
Keyless Entry System +115
Leather Seats +425
Limited Slip Diff +145
Locking Differential +165
Luggage Rack[Std on Country] +85
Power Door Locks +125
Power Drivers Seat +155
Power Windows +130
Skid Plates +75

GRAND CHEROKEE 1996

Jeep turns its flagship into an Explorer killer with dual airbags, revised styling, a better V6 engine, improved front suspension, and an upgraded Selec-Trac four-wheel drive system. Interiors have been restyled, featuring new luxury doodads and an optional integrated child safety seat. Trim levels are two: Laredo and Limited. The gaudy Orvis continues as an option on the Limited. It's almost perfect; if they could just get rid of that pesky spare tire in the cargo hold.

RATINGS (SCALE OF 1-10)

Overall	Safety	Reliability	Performance	Comfort	Value
7.2	7.1	7.4	7.6	7.6	6.4

Category G

Model Description	Trade-in Value	Market Value
4 Dr Laredo Wgn	13155	16445
4 Dr Laredo 4WD Wgn	13990	17490
4 Dr Limited Wgn	15800	19745
4 Dr Limited 4WD Wgn	16930	21165

OPTIONS FOR GRAND CHEROKEE

8 cyl 5.2 L Engine +400
Camper/Towing Package +160
Child Seat (1) +95
Compact Disc W/fm/tape +380
Infinity Sound System[Opt on Laredo] +330
Leather Seats[Opt on Laredo] +425
Limited Slip Diff +145
Locking Differential +165
Power Sunroof +450
Skid Plates +75

1995 JEEP

CHEROKEE 1995

Driver airbag is added on all models. SE model gets reclining bucket seats.

RATINGS (SCALE OF 1-10)

Overall	Safety	Reliability	Performance	Comfort	Value
6.8	6.4	6.7	7.4	6.6	6.7

Category G

Model Description	Trade-in Value	Market Value
4 Dr Country Wgn	8805	11145
4 Dr Country 4WD Wgn	10155	12850
2 Dr SE Utility	6775	8575
2 Dr SE 4WD Utility	8180	10355
4 Dr SE Wgn	6945	8795
4 Dr SE 4WD Wgn	8255	10450
2 Dr Sport Utility	7235	9160
2 Dr Sport 4WD Utility	8690	11000
4 Dr Sport Wgn	7475	9460
4 Dr Sport 4WD Wgn	8820	11165

OPTIONS FOR CHEROKEE

6 cyl 4.0 L Engine[Opt on SE] +340
Auto 4-Speed Transmission +400
Off-Road Suspension Pkg +340
Air Conditioning +370
AM/FM Stereo Tape +110
Anti-Lock Brakes +280
Camper/Towing Package +130
Center Console[Std on Country] +70
Keyless Entry System +95
Leather Seats +350

Don't forget to refer to the Mileage Adjustment Table at the back of this book!

 © 1999 by Edmund Publications Corporation

Model Description	Trade-in Value	Market Value

Limited Slip Diff +120
Locking Differential +135
Luggage Rack[Std on Country] +70
Power Door Locks +105
Power Drivers Seat +130
Power Windows +105
Skid Plates +65

GRAND CHEROKEE 1995

Rear disc brakes are added to all models. An Orvis trim package is added to the Limited 4WD. New options are an integrated child safety seat and a flip-up liftgate window. Optional V8 engine gets a torque increase. A 2WD Limited model is newly available. A power sunroof is added to the options list.

RATINGS (SCALE OF 1-10)

Overall	Safety	Reliability	Performance	Comfort	Value
7.2	6.9	7.6	7.6	7.8	6.3

Category G

Model Description	Trade-in Value	Market Value
4 Dr Laredo Wgn	11225	14210
4 Dr Laredo 4WD Wgn	11935	15110
4 Dr Limited Wgn	13720	17365
4 Dr Limited 4WD Wgn	14715	18630
4 Dr SE Wgn	10220	12940
4 Dr SE 4WD Wgn	10990	13915

OPTIONS FOR GRAND CHEROKEE

8 cyl 5.2 L Engine +335
Up Country Suspension Grp +355
AM/FM Compact Disc Playr +175
Camper/Towing Package +130
Child Seat (1) +80
Dual Power Seats +285
Infinity Sound System[Std on Limited] +270
Leather Seats[Std on Limited] +350
Limited Slip Diff +120
Locking Differential +135
Power Sunroof +365
Skid Plates +65

WRANGLER 1995

S model can be equipped with new Rio Grande package. Renegade is dropped from lineup. An optional dome light can be attached to the optional sound bar.

RATINGS (SCALE OF 1-10)

Overall	Safety	Reliability	Performance	Comfort	Value
6	4.1	7.3	6.6	5.9	6.1

Category G

Model Description	Trade-in Value	Market Value
2 Dr Rio Grande 4WD Utility	8375	10605
2 Dr S 4WD Utility	7920	10025
2 Dr Sahara 4WD Utility	11355	14375
2 Dr SE 4WD Utility	10320	13065

OPTIONS FOR WRANGLER

Auto 3-Speed Transmission +280
Air Conditioning +370
Aluminum/Alloy Wheels +155
AM/FM Stereo Tape[Opt on S] +110
Anti-Lock Brakes +280
Hardtop Roof +350
Locking Differential +135
Power Steering[Opt on S] +130
Velour/Cloth Seats[Opt on S] +80

1994 JEEP

CHEROKEE 1994

Side-door guard beams have been added, and center high-mounted brake light is new. Base model gets SE nomenclature.

RATINGS (SCALE OF 1-10)

Overall	Safety	Reliability	Performance	Comfort	Value
6.4	4.7	6.9	7.4	6.6	6.2

Category G

Model Description	Trade-in Value	Market Value
2 Dr Country Utility	7000	9090
2 Dr Country 4WD Utility	7635	9915
4 Dr Country Wgn	7400	9610
4 Dr Country 4WD Wgn	8270	10740
2 Dr SE Utility	5360	6965
2 Dr SE 4WD Utility	6670	8660
4 Dr SE Wgn	6150	7985
4 Dr SE 4WD Wgn	6810	8845
2 Dr Sport Utility	6285	8160
2 Dr Sport 4WD Utility	6775	8800
4 Dr Sport Wgn	6380	8285
4 Dr Sport 4WD Wgn	7295	9475

OPTIONS FOR CHEROKEE

6 cyl 4.0 L Engine[Opt on SE] +170
Auto 4-Speed Transmission +335
Off-Road Suspension Pkg +280
Air Conditioning +300
AM/FM Stereo Tape +90
Anti-Lock Brakes +230
Camper/Towing Package +105
Cruise Control +80
Keyless Entry System +75
Leather Seats +285
Limited Slip Diff +100
Locking Differential +110
Luggage Rack[Std on Country] +60
Power Door Locks +85
Power Drivers Seat +105
Power Windows +85
Skid Plates +50

Don't forget to refer to the Mileage Adjustment Table at the back of this book!

 © 1999 by Edmund Publications Corporation

GRAND CHEROKEE 1994

Side-door guard beams are added for 1994. Grand Wagoneer trim level is dropped. Base model is now called SE. Limited gets rear disc brakes.

RATINGS (SCALE OF 1-10)

Overall	Safety	Reliability	Performance	Comfort	Value
7	7	7.6	7.6	7.8	5.2

Category G

Model Description	Trade-in Value	Market Value
4 Dr Laredo Wgn	9140	11870
4 Dr Laredo 4WD Wgn	9400	12210
4 Dr Limited 4WD Wgn	12300	15970
4 Dr SE Wgn	8230	10690
4 Dr SE 4WD Wgn	8610	11185

OPTIONS FOR GRAND CHEROKEE

8 cyl 5.2 L Engine +255
Auto 4-Speed Transmission[Std on Limited,2WD] +335
Camper/Towing Package[Std on Limited] +105
Compact Disc W/fm/tape +255
Dual Power Seats +235
Infinity Sound System[Std on Limited] +220
Keyless Entry System[Opt on SE] +75
Leather Seats[Std on Limited] +285
Limited Slip Diff +100
Power Door Locks[Opt on SE] +85
Power Windows[Opt on SE] +85
Skid Plates +50

WRANGLER 1994

The four-cylinder engine can be saddled with an automatic transmission this year. Base trim is now termed SE. Center high-mounted brake light is added.

RATINGS (SCALE OF 1-10)

Overall	Safety	Reliability	Performance	Comfort	Value
5.9	4	6.9	6.6	5.9	6

Category G

Model Description	Trade-in Value	Market Value
2 Dr Renegade 4WD Utility	10295	13370
2 Dr S 4WD Utility	6950	9030
2 Dr Sahara 4WD Utility	9950	12920
2 Dr SE 4WD Utility	8965	11640
2 Dr Sport 4WD Utility	9125	11850

OPTIONS FOR WRANGLER

Auto 3-Speed Transmission +230
Air Conditioning +300
AM/FM Stereo Tape[Opt on S,SE,Sport] +90
Anti-Lock Brakes +230
Chrome Bumpers +60
Hardtop Roof +285
Limited Slip Diff +100
Locking Differential +110
Power Steering[Opt on S,SE] +105
Velour/Cloth Seats[Opt on SE,Sport] +65

1993 JEEP

CHEROKEE 1993

Lineup is shuffled to make room for Grand Cherokee. Country trim replaces Limited. Base prices fall substantially, but models are decontented to achieve lower price.

RATINGS (SCALE OF 1-10)

Overall	Safety	Reliability	Performance	Comfort	Value
6.3	4.6	6.6	7.4	6.6	6.1

Category G

Model Description	Trade-in Value	Market Value
2 Dr Country Utility	6090	8115
2 Dr Country 4WD Utility	6475	8635
4 Dr Country Wgn	6065	8090
4 Dr Country 4WD Wgn	6890	9190
2 Dr Sport Utility	5235	6980
2 Dr Sport 4WD Utility	5985	7980
4 Dr Sport Wgn	5520	7360
4 Dr Sport 4WD Wgn	6135	8180
2 Dr STD Utility	4465	5955
2 Dr STD 4WD Utility	5580	7445
4 Dr STD Wgn	5020	6690
4 Dr STD 4WD Wgn	5865	7820

OPTIONS FOR CHEROKEE

6 cyl 4.0 L Engine[Opt on STD] +145
Auto 4-Speed Transmission +270
Off-road Suspension Pkg +230
Air Conditioning +245
Aluminum/Alloy Wheels[Std on Country] +105
AM/FM Stereo Tape +75
Anti-Lock Brakes +185
Camper/Towing Package +85
Cruise Control +65
Keyless Entry System +60
Luggage Rack[Std on Country] +45
Power Door Locks +70
Power Drivers Seat +85
Power Windows +70
Premium Sound System +110
Skid Plates +40
Swing Out Tire Carrier[Std on Sport 4WD Wgn] +60

GRAND CHEROKEE 1993

Introduced in April, 1992, Grand Cherokee gets a V8 engine option and a Grand Wagoneer model that includes the V8 and fake-wood siding. Late in the year, 2WD models in Base and Laredo trim are introduced. A driver airbag and ABS that works in 2WD or 4WD are standard.

RATINGS (SCALE OF 1-10)

Overall	Safety	Reliability	Performance	Comfort	Value
7	6.9	7	7.6	7.8	5.6

Don't forget to refer to the Mileage Adjustment Table at the back of this book!

 © 1999 by Edmund Publications Corporation

Model Description	Trade-in Value	Market Value
Category G		
4 Dr Laredo Wgn	7540	10050
4 Dr Laredo 4WD Wgn	7775	10365
4 Dr Limited 4WD Wgn	9960	13280
4 Dr STD Wgn	6495	8660
4 Dr STD 4WD Wgn	6975	9300

OPTIONS FOR GRAND CHEROKEE

8 cyl 5.2 L Engine +260
Auto 4-Speed Transmission[Std on Limited,2WD] +265
Up Country Suspension Grp +235
Air Conditioning[Std on Limited] +245
Aluminum/Alloy Wheels[Std on Limited] +105
AM/FM Compact Disc Playr +115
Camper/Towing Package +85
Cruise Control[Opt on STD] +65
Keyless Entry System[Std on Limited] +60
Leather Seats[Opt on Laredo] +235
Locking Differential +90
Luggage Rack[Opt on STD] +45
Power Door Locks[Std on Limited] +70
Power Drivers Seat[Opt on Laredo] +85
Power Passenger Seat[Opt on Laredo] +80
Power Windows[Std on Limited] +70
Premium Sound System[Std on Limited] +110
Skid Plates +40

GRAND WAGONEER 1993

Model Description	Trade-in Value	Market Value
Category G		
4 Dr STD 4WD Wgn	9725	12965

OPTIONS FOR GRAND WAGONEER

AM/FM Compact Disc Playr +115

WRANGLER 1993

ABS that works in both two- and four-wheel drive is newly optional with six-cylinder engines. Islander model disappears. Other changes include a stainless steel exhaust system, tamper-resistant odometer, and tinted plastic windows for the convertible. Sport package includes new graphics and five-spoke steel wheels.

RATINGS (SCALE OF 1-10)

Overall	Safety	Reliability	Performance	Comfort	Value
5.7	4.3	6.5	6.6	5.9	5.4

Model Description	Trade-in Value	Market Value
Category G		
2 Dr Renegade 4WD Utility	8125	10835
2 Dr S 4WD Utility	5930	7910
2 Dr Sahara 4WD Utility	8065	10750
2 Dr STD 4WD Utility	6915	9220

OPTIONS FOR WRANGLER

6 cyl 4.0 L Engine[Opt on S,STD] +145
Auto 3-Speed Transmission +175
Sport Handling Package +355
Air Conditioning +245
Aluminum/Alloy Wheels[Std on Renegade] +105
AM/FM Stereo Tape +75
Anti-Lock Brakes +185
Hardtop Roof +235
Locking Differential +90
Power Steering[Opt on S,STD] +85

1992 JEEP

CHEROKEE 1992

Sport models gain a glass sunroof option, while Laredos get vent windows. All radios now have an integral digital clock. Leather upholstery is available on Laredo for the first time. Detachable cupholders are added to the center console.

RATINGS (SCALE OF 1-10)

Overall	Safety	Reliability	Performance	Comfort	Value
6.6	4.7	6.5	7.4	6.6	7.7

Model Description	Trade-in Value	Market Value
Category G		
4 Dr Briarwood 4WD Wgn	7120	9755
2 Dr Laredo 4WD Utility	5485	7510
4 Dr Laredo Wgn	5285	7235
4 Dr Laredo 4WD Wgn	5795	7940
4 Dr Limited 4WD Wgn	7370	10095
2 Dr Sport 4WD Utility	4815	6595
4 Dr Sport Wgn	4360	5975
4 Dr Sport 4WD Wgn	5135	7035
2 Dr STD Utility	4485	6145
2 Dr STD 4WD Utility	4670	6400
4 Dr STD Wgn	4300	5890
4 Dr STD 4WD Wgn	5060	6930

OPTIONS FOR CHEROKEE

6 cyl 4.0 L Engine[Opt on Laredo,Sport,STD] +140
Auto 4-Speed Transmission[Opt on Laredo,Sport, STD] +215
Off Road Package +240
Sport Handling Package +190
Air Conditioning[Opt on Laredo,Sport,STD] +200
Aluminum/Alloy Wheels[Std on Briarwood,Limited, Laredo Wgn] +85
AM/FM Compact Disc Playr +95
Anti-Lock Brakes +155
Camper/Towing Package +70
Cruise Control[Opt on Laredo,Sport,STD] +50
Keyless Entry System[Opt on Laredo,Sport,STD] +50
Leather Seats[Opt on Laredo,Sport,STD] +190
Locking Differential +75
Luggage Rack[Opt on Laredo,Sport,STD] +40
Power Door Locks[Opt on Laredo,Sport,STD] +55
Power Drivers Seat[Opt on Laredo,Sport,STD] +70
Power Passenger Seat[Opt on Laredo,Sport,STD] +65
Power Windows[Opt on Laredo,Sport,STD] +60
Premium Sound System +90
Sunroof +75

Don't forget to refer to the Mileage Adjustment Table at the back of this book!

 © 1999 by Edmund Publications Corporation

COMANCHE 1992

Sport option group debuts. Radios have digital clocks. Detachable cupholders are added to center console.

Category G	Trade-in Value	Market Value
2 Dr Eliminator 4WD Std Cab SB	4345	5950
2 Dr Eliminator 4WD Std Cab LB	4360	5975
2 Dr Pioneer 4WD Std Cab SB	4230	5795
2 Dr Pioneer 4WD Std Cab LB	4245	5820
2 Dr Sport 4WD Std Cab SB	4155	5695
2 Dr Sport 4WD Std Cab LB	4175	5715
2 Dr STD 4WD Std Cab SB	4005	5485
2 Dr STD 4WD Std Cab LB	4025	5515

OPTIONS FOR COMANCHE

6 cyl 4.0 L Engine +140
5-Speed Transmission +50
Auto 4-Speed Transmission +245
Big Ton Pkg +185
Off Road Package +235
Air Conditioning +200
Aluminum/Alloy Wheels +85
AM/FM Stereo Tape +60
Cruise Control +50
Locking Differential +75
Power Steering +70
Rear Step Bumper +35
Skid Plates +35
Sliding Rear Window +30

WRANGLER 1992

Three-point seatbelts anchored to the roll bar are added. New colors round out the changes.

RATINGS (SCALE OF 1-10)

Overall	Safety	Reliability	Performance	Comfort	Value
5.6	4.2	6	6.6	5.9	5.4

Category G	Trade-in Value	Market Value
2 Dr Islander 4WD Utility	6385	8745
2 Dr Renegade 4WD Utility	6640	9100
2 Dr S 4WD Utility	5225	7160
2 Dr Sahara 4WD Utility	6500	8905
2 Dr STD 4WD Utility	6065	8305

OPTIONS FOR WRANGLER

6 cyl 4.0 L Engine +140
Auto 3-Speed Transmission +140
Air Conditioning +200
Aluminum/Alloy Wheels +85
AM/FM Stereo Tape +60
Chrome Bumpers +40
Fog Lights +35
Hardtop Roof +190
Locking Differential +75
Rear Bench Seat[Opt on S] +100
Velour/Cloth Seats +45

1991 JEEP

CHEROKEE 1991

Two new models, the Sport four-door and top-of-the-line Briarwood, join the lineup. Child-proof rear door locks are added to four-door models. A security alarm system is a new option. Power is increased for both engines. An automatic transmission is no longer available with the base four-cylinder engine.

RATINGS (SCALE OF 1-10)

Overall	Safety	Reliability	Performance	Comfort	Value
6.3	4.4	6	7.4	6.6	7.1

Category G	Trade-in Value	Market Value
4 Dr Briarwood 4WD Wgn	6035	8625
2 Dr Laredo 4WD Utility	4645	6640
4 Dr Laredo Wgn	4210	6015
4 Dr Laredo 4WD Wgn	4930	7040
4 Dr Limited 4WD Wgn	6160	8805
2 Dr Sport Utility	3755	5360
2 Dr Sport 4WD Utility	4235	6050
4 Dr Sport Wgn	3625	5180
4 Dr Sport 4WD Wgn	4415	6310
2 Dr STD Utility	3605	5150
2 Dr STD 4WD Utility	4190	5985
4 Dr STD Wgn	3555	5080
4 Dr STD 4WD Wgn	4345	6210

OPTIONS FOR CHEROKEE

6 cyl 4.0 L Engine[Opt on Laredo,Sport,STD] +120
Auto 4-Speed Transmission[Opt on Laredo,Sport, STD] +175
Cherokee Off Road Package +195
Air Conditioning[Opt on Laredo,Sport,STD] +165
Aluminum/Alloy Wheels[Opt on Sport,STD] +70
AM/FM Stereo Tape[Opt on Laredo,Sport,STD] +50
Anti-Lock Brakes +125
Camper/Towing Package +60
Cruise Control[Opt on Laredo,Sport,STD] +45
Dual Power Seats[Opt on Laredo] +130
Keyless Entry System[Opt on Laredo] +40
Leather Seats[Opt on Laredo,STD] +155
Limited Slip Diff +55
Luggage Rack[Opt on Sport,STD] +30
Power Door Locks[Opt on Laredo,Sport,STD] +45
Power Windows[Opt on Laredo,Sport,STD] +50
Sunroof +60

COMANCHE 1991

Power is increased for both engines, and five new colors are available.

Category G	Trade-in Value	Market Value
2 Dr Eliminator 4WD Std Cab SB	3450	4925
2 Dr Eliminator 4WD Std Cab LB	3550	5070

Don't forget to refer to the Mileage Adjustment Table at the back of this book!

 © 1999 by Edmund Publications Corporation

Model Description	Trade-in Value	Market Value
2 Dr Pioneer 4WD Std Cab SB	3320	4745
2 Dr Pioneer 4WD Std Cab LB	3430	4905
2 Dr STD 4WD Std Cab SB	3285	4695
2 Dr STD 4WD Std Cab LB	3350	4785

OPTIONS FOR COMANCHE

6 cyl 4.0 L Engine[Opt on Eliminator,STD] +120
5-Speed Transmission +40
Automatic-Column Shift +200
Automatic-Floor Shift +160
Big Ton Pkg +150
Suspension Pkg +195
Air Conditioning +165
Aluminum/Alloy Wheels +70
AM/FM Stereo Tape +50
Cruise Control +45
Limited Slip Diff +55
Power Steering +55
Rear Step Bumper +30

GRAND WAGONEER 1991

Five new exterior colors and one new interior color debut.

Category H

Model Description	Trade-in Value	Market Value
4 Dr STD 4WD Wgn	6635	8970

OPTIONS FOR GRAND WAGONEER

Camper/Towing Package +70
Limited Slip Diff +50
Power Sunroof +280

WRANGLER 1991

New Renegade option replaces Laredo and adds fender flares, fog lights and alloy wheels. A new six-cylinder engine boosts horsepower substantially, from 112 with the old 4.2-liter unit to 180 with the new 4.0-liter motor. Four-cylinder models also get a slight bump in power. New seats with reclining backrests are new to all models except S. A sound bar is also available on all models except S.

RATINGS (SCALE OF 1-10)

Overall	Safety	Reliability	Performance	Comfort	Value
5.4	4	5.9	6.6	5.9	4.8

Category G

Model Description	Trade-in Value	Market Value
2 Dr Islander 4WD Utility	5500	7855
2 Dr Renegade 4WD Utility	6030	8610
2 Dr S 4WD Utility	4440	6345
2 Dr Sahara 4WD Utility	5810	8300
2 Dr STD 4WD Utility	5450	7785

OPTIONS FOR WRANGLER

6 cyl 4.0 L Engine +120
Auto 3-Speed Transmission +115
Air Conditioning +165
Aluminum/Alloy Wheels +70
AM/FM Stereo Tape +50
Hardtop Roof +155
Limited Slip Diff +55
Power Steering +55
Rear Bench Seat[Opt on S] +85
Velour/Cloth Seats +35

1990 JEEP

CHEROKEE 1990

AM/FM stereo is newly standard. Rear seats get three-point seatbelts, and an overhead console is a new option.

RATINGS (SCALE OF 1-10)

Overall	Safety	Reliability	Performance	Comfort	Value
6.2	4.1	5.5	7.4	6.6	7.4

Category G

Model Description	Trade-in Value	Market Value
2 Dr Laredo 4WD Utility	4020	6090
4 Dr Laredo Wgn	3540	5365
4 Dr Laredo 4WD Wgn	4225	6405
2 Dr Limited 4WD Utility	4715	7145
4 Dr Limited 4WD Wgn	5030	7620
2 Dr Pioneer 4WD Utility	3610	5470
4 Dr Pioneer Wgn	3175	4815
4 Dr Pioneer 4WD Wgn	3830	5805
2 Dr Sport Utility	3070	4650
2 Dr Sport 4WD Utility	3605	5465
2 Dr STD Utility	2735	4145
2 Dr STD 4WD Utility	3525	5340
4 Dr STD Wgn	2965	4490
4 Dr STD 4WD Wgn	3665	5555

OPTIONS FOR CHEROKEE

6 cyl 4.0 L Engine[Opt on Sport,STD] +105
Auto 4-Speed Transmission[Std on Limited] +140
Off Road Package +150
Air Conditioning[Std on Limited] +135
Aluminum/Alloy Wheels[Std on Laredo,Limited] +55
AM/FM Compact Disc Playr +65
Anti-Lock Brakes +100
Camper/Towing Package +50
Cruise Control[Std on Limited] +35
Dual Power Seats[Opt on Laredo] +105
Keyless Entry System[Std on Limited] +35
Limited Slip Diff +45
Power Door Locks[Std on Limited] +40
Power Windows[Std on Limited] +40
Premium Sound System[Std on Limited] +60
Sunroof +50
Swing Out Tire Carrier +35
Velour/Cloth Seats[Opt on Sport,STD] +30

Don't forget to refer to the Mileage Adjustment Table at the back of this book!

© 1999 by Edmund Publications Corporation

Model Description	Trade-in Value	Market Value

COMANCHE 1990

No changes.

Category G

Model Description	Trade-in Value	Market Value
2 Dr Eliminator 4WD Std Cab SB	2725	4125
2 Dr Pioneer 4WD Std Cab SB	2565	3890
2 Dr Pioneer 4WD Std Cab LB	2615	3965
2 Dr STD 4WD Std Cab SB	2480	3755
2 Dr STD 4WD Std Cab LB	2530	3835

OPTIONS FOR COMANCHE

6 cyl 4.0 L Engine[Std on Eliminator] +105
5-Speed Transmission[Std on Eliminator] +35
Auto 3-Speed Transmission +155
Off Road Package +155
Air Conditioning +135
Aluminum/Alloy Wheels[Std on Eliminator] +55
AM/FM Stereo Tape +40
Cruise Control +35
Limited Slip Diff +45
Power Steering[Std on Eliminator] +45

GRAND WAGONEER 1990

Rear seats get three-point seatbelts.

Category H

Model Description	Trade-in Value	Market Value
4 Dr STD 4WD Wgn	5220	7250

OPTIONS FOR GRAND WAGONEER

Camper/Towing Package +60
Limited Slip Diff +40
Power Sunroof +230

WAGONEER 1990

Rear seats get three-point seatbelts.

Category G

Model Description	Trade-in Value	Market Value
4 Dr Limited 4WD Wgn	4960	7515

OPTIONS FOR WAGONEER

AM/FM Stereo Tape +40
Anti-Lock Brakes +100
Camper/Towing Package +50
Limited Slip Diff +45
Premium Sound System +60
Sunroof +50

WRANGLER 1990

Locking half doors are available for the first time. Order a hardtop and you'll get a new rear window wiper/washer. Front seats gain improved lateral support, and Sahara and Laredo models get a larger 20-gallon fuel tank. S models have a wider variety of options.

RATINGS (SCALE OF 1-10)

Overall	Safety	Reliability	Performance	Comfort	Value
5.3	3.8	6.1	6.2	5.9	4.8

Category G

Model Description	Trade-in Value	Market Value
2 Dr Islander 4WD Utility	4665	7065
2 Dr Laredo 4WD Utility	5035	7630
2 Dr S 4WD Utility	3910	5920
2 Dr Sahara 4WD Utility	4815	7295
2 Dr STD 4WD Utility	4540	6875

OPTIONS FOR WRANGLER

6 cyl 4.2 L Engine[Std on Laredo] +75
Auto 3-Speed Transmission +95
Air Conditioning +135
Aluminum/Alloy Wheels[Std on Laredo] +55
AM/FM Stereo Tape +40
Cruise Control +35
Hardtop Roof[Std on Laredo] +125
Limited Slip Diff +45
Power Steering[Std on Laredo,Sahara] +45
Rear Bench Seat +70
Velour/Cloth Seats[Opt on Islander,STD] +30

1989 JEEP

CHEROKEE 1989

Six-cylinder models with automatic transmissions and Selec-Trac can be equipped with ABS that works in both 2WD and 4WD. Old 13.5-gallon fuel tank is replaced by a 20-gallon unit. Power steering is newly standard on base models. Remote keyless entry is a new standard feature on Limited. Chief model dropped. Pioneer trim is new.

RATINGS (SCALE OF 1-10)

Overall	Safety	Reliability	Performance	Comfort	Value
6.2	4.2	5.6	7.4	6.6	7.3

Category G

Model Description	Trade-in Value	Market Value
2 Dr Laredo 4WD Utility	3160	5180
4 Dr Laredo Wgn	2845	4670
4 Dr Laredo 4WD Wgn	3280	5380
2 Dr Limited 4WD Utility	3770	6180
4 Dr Limited 4WD Wgn	3935	6445
2 Dr Pioneer 4WD Utility	3085	5060
4 Dr Pioneer Wgn	2520	4135
4 Dr Pioneer 4WD Wgn	2870	4705
2 Dr Sport 4WD Utility	3030	4970
2 Dr STD Utility	2525	4140
2 Dr STD 4WD Utility	2810	4610
4 Dr STD Wgn	2480	4065
4 Dr STD 4WD Wgn	2850	4675

OPTIONS FOR CHEROKEE

6 cyl 4.0 L Engine[Std on Limited] +80
Auto 4-Speed Transmission[Std on Limited] +110
Off Road Package +125
Air Conditioning[Std on Limited] +110
Aluminum/Alloy Wheels[Opt on Pioneer,STD] +45

Don't forget to refer to the Mileage Adjustment Table at the back of this book!

 © 1999 by Edmund Publications Corporation

Model Description	Trade-in Value	Market Value

AM/FM Stereo Tape[Std on Limited] +35
Anti-Lock Brakes +85
Auto Locking Hubs (4WD)[Std on Limited] +35
Camper/Towing Package +40
Cruise Control[Std on Limited] +30
Keyless Entry System[Std on Limited] +30
Limited Slip Diff +35
Power Door Locks[Std on Limited] +30
Power Drivers Seat[Opt on Laredo] +40
Power Passenger Seat[Opt on Laredo] +35
Power Windows[Std on Limited] +30
Sunroof +40
Swing Out Tire Carrier +30

COMANCHE 1989

Longbed models get new 23.5-gallon fuel tank, and tinted glass is standard. Chief package replaced by Pioneer trim. Laredo trim disappears in favor of SporTruck.

Category G

Model Description	Trade-in Value	Market Value
2 Dr Eliminator Std Cab SB	2250	3690
2 Dr Pioneer Std Cab SB	2065	3385
2 Dr Pioneer Std Cab LB	2205	3615
2 Dr Pioneer 4WD Std Cab SB	2335	3830
2 Dr Pioneer 4WD Std Cab LB	2450	4020
2 Dr STD Std Cab SB	2000	3280
2 Dr STD Std Cab LB	2115	3470
2 Dr STD 4WD Std Cab SB	2295	3760
2 Dr STD 4WD Std Cab LB	2380	3905

OPTIONS FOR COMANCHE

6 cyl 4.0 L Engine[Std on Eliminator] +80
Auto 3-Speed Transmission +125
Air Conditioning +110
Aluminum/Alloy Wheels[Std on Eliminator] +45
AM/FM Stereo Tape +35
Camper/Towing Package +40
Cruise Control +30
Limited Slip Diff +35
Power Steering[Std on Eliminator,Pioneer,4WD] +40

GRAND WAGONEER 1989

A new overhead console is standard, except with sunroof, and it features remote keyless entry, front and rear lighting, temperature gauge, and compass. Sunvisors get illuminated vanity mirrors.

Category G

Model Description	Trade-in Value	Market Value
4 Dr STD 4WD Wgn	3765	6170

OPTIONS FOR GRAND WAGONEER

Camper/Towing Package +40
Electric Sunroof +95
Limited Slip Diff +35

WAGONEER 1989

Six-cylinder models with automatic transmissions and Selec-Trac can be equipped with ABS that works in both 2WD and 4WD. Old 13.5-gallon fuel tank is replaced by a 20-gallon unit. Remote keyless entry is a new standard feature. Dual power mirrors, fog lamps and a tachometer are made standard.

Category G

Model Description	Trade-in Value	Market Value
4 Dr Limited 4WD Wgn	3725	6110

OPTIONS FOR WAGONEER

AM/FM Stereo Tape +35
Anti-Lock Brakes +85
Camper/Towing Package +40
Limited Slip Diff +35
Sunroof +40

WRANGLER 1989

New Islander model joins lineup.

RATINGS (SCALE OF 1-10)

Overall	Safety	Reliability	Performance	Comfort	Value
5.5	3.7	5.6	6.2	5.9	6.2

Category G

Model Description	Trade-in Value	Market Value
2 Dr Islander 4WD Utility	3785	6200
2 Dr Laredo 4WD Utility	3995	6550
2 Dr S 4WD Utility	3630	5950
2 Dr Sahara 4WD Utility	3955	6480
2 Dr STD 4WD Utility	3775	6190

OPTIONS FOR WRANGLER

6 cyl 4.2 L Engine[Std on Laredo] +55
Auto 3-Speed Transmission +65
Air Conditioning +110
Aluminum/Alloy Wheels[Std on Laredo] +45
AM/FM Stereo Tape +35
Cruise Control +30
Hardtop Roof[Std on Laredo] +105
Limited Slip Diff +35
Power Steering[Std on Laredo,Sahara] +40

A 15-minute phone call
could save you 15% or more
on car insurance.
1-800-555-2758
GEICO
DIRECT

Don't forget to refer to the Mileage Adjustment Table at the back of this book!

 © 1999 by Edmund Publications Corporation

KIA

S. Korea

1997 Kia Sephia

1998 KIA

SEPHIA 1998

The Sephia is totally redesigned for 1998.

Category E

Model	Trade-in	Market
4 Dr LS Sdn	7430	9060
4 Dr STD Sdn	6485	7910

OPTIONS FOR SEPHIA

Auto 4-Speed Transmission +810
Air Conditioning +675
Aluminum/Alloy Wheels +265
AM/FM Compact Disc Playr +390
Anti-Lock Brakes +590
Cruise Control +185
Power Door Locks +195
Power Mirrors +95
Power Steering[Std on LS] +210
Power Windows +220

SPORTAGE 1998

There are lots of improvements this year for the Sportage, including a new grille, new alloy wheels, tilt steering wheel, passenger-side airbag, better brakes, improved air conditioning and four-wheel ABS that replaces last year's rear-wheel ABS.

Category G

Model	Trade-in	Market
4 Dr EX Wgn	12515	15080
4 Dr EX 4WD Wgn	13595	16380
4 Dr STD Wgn	9505	11450
4 Dr STD 4WD Wgn	10010	12060

OPTIONS FOR SPORTAGE

Auto 4-Speed Transmission +830
Air Conditioning[Std on EX] +675
Aluminum/Alloy Wheels[Std on EX, 4WD] +285
AM/FM Compact Disc Playr[Std on EX] +320
Anti-Lock Brakes +515
Leather Seats +640

1997 KIA

SEPHIA 1997

RS models get body-color bumpers this year, and a tan interior is newly available with black exterior paint.

Category E

Model	Trade-in	Market
4 Dr GS Sdn	6435	8250
4 Dr LS Sdn	5755	7380
4 Dr RS Sdn	4835	6195

OPTIONS FOR SEPHIA

Auto 4-Speed Transmission +615
Air Conditioning +550
Aluminum/Alloy Wheels +215
AM/FM Compact Disc Playr +320
AM/FM Stereo Tape[Std on GS] +210
Anti-Lock Brakes +480
Power Steering[Opt on RS] +170
Premium Sound System +230

SPORTAGE 1997

An automatic transmission is offered on 2WD models, and the EX trim level is available in 2WD for the first time. Power door locks, a theft deterrent system, and a spare tire carrier are all standard on all Sportages for 1997. A new option is a CD player. Sportage gets a new grille. A tan interior can be combined with black paint for the first time. Base 2WD models lose their standard alloy wheels.

Category G

Model	Trade-in	Market
4 Dr EX Wgn	9545	11640
4 Dr EX 4WD Wgn	10355	12630
4 Dr STD Wgn	8900	10855
4 Dr STD 4WD Wgn	9340	11390

OPTIONS FOR SPORTAGE

Auto 4-Speed Transmission +680
Air Conditioning +550
Aluminum/Alloy Wheels[Std on EX,4WD] +235
AM/FM Compact Disc Playr +260
Leather Seats +520
Luggage Rack[Std on EX] +105
Swing Out Tire Carrier[Std on EX,4WD] +140

1996 KIA

SEPHIA 1996

Styling and suspension tweaks, dual airbags, and new twin-cam motors appeared with the introduction of the 1995.5 Sephia. These improvements, along with interior revisions and improved equipment levels, make the Kia

Don't forget to refer to the Mileage Adjustment Table at the back of this book!

 © 1999 by Edmund Publications Corporation

more competitive in the compact sedan marketplace. Sephia now meets 1997 side-impact standards, and GS models can be equipped with antilock brakes. Sephia comes with 5 year/60,000 mile powertrain coverage.

Category E

Model	Trade-in	Market
4 Dr GS Sdn	5430	7335
4 Dr LS Sdn	4690	6335
4 Dr RS Sdn	3960	5350

OPTIONS FOR SEPHIA

Auto 4-Speed Transmission +480
Air Conditioning +450
AM/FM Stereo Tape[Std on GS] +170
Anti-Lock Brakes +395
Power Steering[Opt on RS] +140
Premium Sound System +190

SPORTAGE 1996

The world's first knee airbag arrives in conjunction with a driver airbag, and a two-wheel drive edition is available this year. A spirited twin-cam engine arrived late in 1995, and cured Sportage's power ills.

Category G

Model	Trade-in	Market
4 Dr EX Wgn	7635	9545
4 Dr EX 4WD Wgn	8770	10960
4 Dr STD Wgn	7330	9160
4 Dr STD 4WD Wgn	8300	10375

OPTIONS FOR SPORTAGE

4 cyl 2.0 L DOHC Engine +410
Auto 4-Speed Transmission +560
Air Conditioning +450
AM/FM Stereo Tape +135
Leather Seats +425
Luggage Rack +85
Swing Out Tire Carrier +115

1995 KIA

SEPHIA 1995

Oh no, another Korean manufacturer trying to break into the American market. But wait, this one is actually worth considering; a lot of help from Mazda and Ford mean that this little upstart is actually making fairly reliable little cars. The Sephia has plenty of Mazda parts and Kia has a long history of building durable, cheap cars.

Category E

Model	Trade-in	Market
4 Dr GS Sdn	4035	5680
4 Dr GS 1995.5 Sdn	4405	6205
4 Dr LS Sdn	3665	5160
4 Dr LS 1995.5 Sdn	3775	5320
4 Dr RS Sdn	3225	4540
4 Dr RS 1995.5 Sdn	3300	4650

OPTIONS FOR SEPHIA

4 cyl 1.6 L DOHC Engine +50
4 cyl 1.8 L Engine +290
Auto 4-Speed Transmission +375
Air Conditioning +370
AM/FM Stereo Tape[Std on GS] +140
Cruise Control[Opt on GS] +100
Dual Air Bag Restraints +285
Power Steering[Opt on RS,RS 1995.5] +115
Premium Sound System +155

SPORTAGE 1995

Another mini-SUV is introduced, competing with everything from the Jeep Cherokee to the Geo Tracker. The Sportage offers comfortable seating for four, ample storage space, and available four-wheel drive. Designed with Ford and Mazda, with suspension tuning by Lotus, the Sportage should provide a good deal of fun and durability.

Category G

Model	Trade-in	Market
4 Dr EX 4WD Wgn	7355	9550
4 Dr STD 4WD Wgn	7070	9185

OPTIONS FOR SPORTAGE

4 cyl 2.0 L Engine +335
Auto 4-Speed Transmission +445
Air Conditioning +370
AM/FM Stereo Tape +110
Leather Seats +350
Luggage Rack +70
Swing Out Tire Carrier +95

1994 KIA

SEPHIA 1994

New subcompact sedan from South Korea based on 1990-1994 Mazda Protege platform and powered by a 1.6-liter 88-horsepower four-cylinder engine. Sold only in the western and southwestern regions of the U.S.

Category E

Model	Trade-in	Market
4 Dr GS Sdn	3705	5535
4 Dr LS Sdn	3150	4700
4 Dr RS Sdn	2745	4095

OPTIONS FOR SEPHIA

Auto 4-Speed Transmission +280
Air Conditioning +300
AM/FM Stereo Tape[Std on GS] +115
Cruise Control +80
Power Steering[Opt on RS] +95
Premium Sound System +125

Don't forget to refer to the Mileage Adjustment Table at the back of this book!

© 1999 by Edmund Publications Corporation

LAND ROVER Britain

1996 Land Rover Discovery

1998 LAND ROVER

DISCOVERY 1998

Changes to the Discovery include interior trim enhancements for the LE and LSE. The rearview mirror also features map lights for the first time.

Model Description	Trade-in Value	Market Value
Category H		
4 Dr 50TH Anniversary 4WD Wgn	29315	33700
4 Dr LE 4WD Wgn	27090	31140
4 Dr LSE 4WD Wgn	29395	33785

OPTIONS FOR DISCOVERY

Compact Disc Changer[Opt on LE] +360
Dual Air Conditioning +1180
Rear Jump Seats +210
Special Factory Paint +115

RANGE ROVER 1998

Range Rover models get a new Harmon Kardon audio system this year. Other changes include a new upholstery stitch pattern and a leather-wrapped gearshift knob.

Model Description	Trade-in Value	Market Value
Category H		
4 Dr 4.0 SE 4WD Wgn	42715	49095
4 Dr 4.6 HSE 4WD Wgn	48870	56170
4 Dr 50TH Anniversary 4WD Wgn	44965	51685

OPTIONS FOR RANGE ROVER

Special Factory Paint +115

1997 LAND ROVER

DISCOVERY 1997

A diversity antenna is added, and all interiors are trimmed with polished burled walnut. The sunroof has darker tinting, the airbag system benefits from simplified operation, and engine management is improved. Three new exterior colors debut: Oxford Blue, Rioja Red and Charleston Green.

Model Description	Trade-in Value	Market Value
Category H		
4 Dr LSE 4WD Wgn	24060	27975
4 Dr SD 4WD Wgn	22010	25595
4 Dr SE 4WD Wgn	23200	26975
4 Dr SE7 4WD Wgn	23715	27575
4 Dr XD 4WD Wgn	23280	27070

OPTIONS FOR DISCOVERY

Auto 4-Speed Transmission[Std on SE,XD] +340
Leather Rear Jump Seats +660
Compact Disc Changer +295
Dual Power Seats[Opt on SD] +315
Leather Seats[Opt on SD] +700
Luggage Rack[Std on XD] +90
Rear Jump Seats[Std on SE7] +175

RANGE ROVER 1997

4.0 SE gets three new exterior colors (Oxford Blue, Rioja Red and White Gold, all matched to Saddle leather interior), a HomeLink transmitter, and jeweled wheel center caps. The 4.6 HSE gets three new exterior colors (British Racing Green, Monza Red, AA Yellow), one new interior color (Lightstone with contrasting piping), and a leather shift handle.

Model Description	Trade-in Value	Market Value
Category H		
4 Dr 4.0 SE 4WD Wgn	36015	41880
4 Dr 4.6 HSE 4WD Wgn	41780	48580

OPTIONS FOR RANGE ROVER

Kensington Interior Pkg. +2040
Vitesse Package +2040

1996 LAND ROVER

DISCOVERY 1996

Three new trim levels, a revised engine that gets better around-town fuel economy, new colors, increased seat travel, and new power seats sum up the changes for 1996.

Model Description	Trade-in Value	Market Value
Category H		
4 Dr SD 4WD Wgn	18740	22045
4 Dr SE 4WD Wgn	19760	23250
4 Dr SE7 4WD Wgn	20095	23640

OPTIONS FOR DISCOVERY

Auto 4-Speed Transmission[Std on SE] +630
Compact Disc Changer +240
Compact Disc W/fm/tape +175
Leather Seats[Opt on SD] +575
Third Seat[Std on SE7] +350

Don't forget to refer to the Mileage Adjustment Table at the back of this book!

 © 1999 by Edmund Publications Corporation

Model Description	Trade-in Value	Market Value

RANGE ROVER 1996

Base 4.0 SE model is unchanged for 1996. A new, more powerful 4.6 HSE model debuts, giving buyers extra horsepower, fat wheels and tires, mud flaps, and chrome exhaust for a $7,000 premium over the 4.0 SE.

Category H

Model	Trade-in	Market
4 Dr 4.0 SE 4WD Wgn	30005	35300
4 Dr 4.6 HSE 4WD Wgn	35500	41765

OPTIONS FOR RANGE ROVER

AM/FM Compact Disc Playr +165

1995 LAND ROVER

DEFENDER 1995

Category G

Model	Trade-in	Market
2 Dr STD 4WD Utility	21075	28480

OPTIONS FOR DEFENDER

Full Top & Safari Cage +625
Air Conditioning +370

DISCOVERY 1995

Category H

Model	Trade-in	Market
4 Dr STD 4WD Wgn	16145	19220

OPTIONS FOR DISCOVERY

Auto 4-Speed Transmission +515
Dual Power Moonroofs +735
Jump Seat +390
Leather Jump Seat +435
Dual Air Conditioning +645
Leather Seats +470

RANGE ROVER 1995

Category H

Model	Trade-in	Market
4 Dr 4.0 SE 4WD Wgn	24450	29105
4 Dr County Classic 4WD Wgn	23175	27590
4 Dr County LWB 4WD Wgn	23415	27875

OPTIONS FOR RANGE ROVER

Body Kit +890
Interior Trim/Light Stone +390

1994 LAND ROVER

DISCOVERY 1994

Category H

Model	Trade-in	Market
4 Dr STD 4WD Wgn	13850	16685

OPTIONS FOR DISCOVERY

Auto 4-Speed Transmission +410
Dual Air Conditioning +525
Leather Seats +385
Power Moonroof +360
Rear Jump Seats +95

RANGE ROVER 1994

Category H

Model	Trade-in	Market
4 Dr County LWB 4WD Wgn	18280	22025
4 Dr County SWB 4WD Wgn	16010	19290

OPTIONS FOR RANGE ROVER

Black Sable Edition +390

1993 LAND ROVER

RANGE ROVER 1993

Category H

Model	Trade-in	Market
4 Dr County 4WD Wgn	14410	17360
4 Dr LWB 4WD Wgn	16210	19530

OPTIONS FOR RANGE ROVER

Chrome Wheels +90
Compact Disc Changer +130
Running Boards +90

1992 LAND ROVER

RANGE ROVER 1992

Category H

Model	Trade-in	Market
4 Dr County 4WD Wgn	12320	15400
4 Dr LSE 4WD Wgn	12605	15755
4 Dr STD 4WD Wgn	11805	14755

OPTIONS FOR RANGE ROVER

Third Seat +155

1991 LAND ROVER

RANGE ROVER 1991

Category H

Model	Trade-in	Market
4 Dr County SE 4WD Wgn	10920	13820
4 Dr Great Divide 4WD Wgn	10625	13450
4 Dr STD 4WD Wgn	10465	13245

OPTIONS FOR RANGE ROVER

Power Sunroof[Opt on STD] +280
Premium Sound System +80

1990 LAND ROVER

RANGE ROVER 1990

Category H

Model	Trade-in	Market
4 Dr County 4WD Wgn	8635	11215
4 Dr STD 4WD Wgn	8355	10850

OPTIONS FOR RANGE ROVER

AM/FM Compact Disc Playr +50
Power Sunroof +230
Premium Sound System +65

Don't forget to refer to the Mileage Adjustment Table at the back of this book!

© 1999 by Edmund Publications Corporation

Model Description	Trade-in Value	Market Value
1989 LAND ROVER		
RANGE ROVER 1989		
Category H		
4 Dr County 4WD Wgn	7570	10095
4 Dr STD 4WD Wgn	6980	9305

OPTIONS FOR RANGE ROVER
Compact Disc Changer +60
Power Sunroof[Opt on STD] +190

Get a great used car and apply for financing *online* at a price you must see to believe !

http://edmunds.com

Major Savings On An Extended Warranty

"YOU DESERVE THE BEST"
Call today for your free quote.
Pay up to 50% less than dealership prices!

http://www.edmunds.com/warranty 1-800-580-9889

A 15-minute phone call could save you 15% or more on car insurance.

1-800-555-2758

GEICO DIRECT

The Sensible Alternative

Don't forget to refer to the Mileage Adjustment Table at the back of this book!

 © 1999 by Edmund Publications Corporation

LEXUS

Japan

1994 Lexus GS 300

1998 LEXUS

ES300 — 1998

Side-impact airbags debut on Lexus's entry-level car, as does an engine immobilizer anti-theft system and an optional Nakamichi audio system. Reduced force front airbags are also new on all 1998 Lexus models.

Category J

4 Dr STD Sdn	23155	27565

OPTIONS FOR ES300

Chrome Wheels +1190
Compact Disc Changer +815
Heated Front Seats +345
Leather Seats +855
Nakamichi Sound System +970
Power Moonroof +760
Traction Control System +1095

GS — 1998

A totally redesigned GS appears for 1998. Featuring the familiar inline-six engine of the previous model in the GS300 or an overhead cam V8 with continuously variable valve timing in the GS400, the new cars live up to the promise of providing serious fun in an elegant package.

GS300

Category J

4 Dr STD Sdn	27880	33190

GS400

Category J

4 Dr STD Sdn	33675	40090

OPTIONS FOR GS

Navigation System +1870

LS400 — 1998

Lexus further refines its flagship by introducing a new four-cam V8 engine that features continuously variable valve timing. Also new this year is a five-speed automatic transmission, Vehicle Skid Control (VSC) and a host of interior improvements.

Category L

4 Dr STD Sdn	36910	41945

OPTIONS FOR LS400

Navigation System +1870
Auto Load Leveling +895
Chrome Wheels +1215
Compact Disc Changer +975
Heated Front Seats +385
Nakamichi Sound System +900
Power Moonroof +745

1997 LEXUS

ES300 — 1997

The entry-level Lexus has been totally redesigned this year, growing in nearly every dimension. Lexus manages to eke out more power from the ES300's 3.0-liter V6 engine. No longer just a dressed-up Camry, the ES300 has finally come into its own.

RATINGS (SCALE OF 1-10)

Overall	Safety	Reliability	Performance	Comfort	Value
7.9	7.7	9.7	8.2	8.8	5.1

Category J

4 Dr STD Sdn	21500	25595

OPTIONS FOR ES300

Chrome Wheels +975
Compact Disc Changer +665
Leather Seats +700
Power Moonroof +620
Traction Control System +895

LS400 — 1997

Side-impact airbags are standard, yet, the price doesn't go up! Magic? You be the judge.

RATINGS (SCALE OF 1-10)

Overall	Safety	Reliability	Performance	Comfort	Value
N/A	N/A	9.9	8	9.4	6.4

Category L

4 Dr Coach Sdn	35885	41250
4 Dr STD Sdn	34665	39845

OPTIONS FOR LS400

Drivers Memory System +545
Cellular Telephone +650
Chrome Wheels +995
Compact Disc Changer[Opt on STD] +795

Don't forget to refer to the Mileage Adjustment Table at the back of this book!

© 1999 by Edmund Publications Corporation

Model Description	Trade-in Value	Market Value

Nakamichi Sound System +735
Power Moonroof[Opt on STD] +610
Traction Control System +1085

LX450 — 1997

There are no changes to the 1997 LX450.

RATINGS (SCALE OF 1-10)

Overall	Safety	Reliability	Performance	Comfort	Value
N/A	N/A	9.1	7.6	8	N/A

Category G

Model	Trade-in	Market
4 Dr STD 4WD Wgn	33145	39460

OPTIONS FOR LX450
F&R Locking Diff. Axles +610
Compact Disc Changer +350
Luggage Rack +105
Power Moonroof +600
Running Boards +260
Trailer Hitch +195

SC — 1997

SC300

Category J

Model	Trade-in	Market
2 Dr STD Cpe	26130	31110

SC400

Category J

Model	Trade-in	Market
2 Dr STD Cpe	31590	37605

OPTIONS FOR SC
Leather Trim Package +510

1996 LEXUS

ES300 — 1996

Two new colors are available.

RATINGS (SCALE OF 1-10)

Overall	Safety	Reliability	Performance	Comfort	Value
7.9	7.7	9.2	8.4	8.1	6.3

Category J

Model	Trade-in	Market
4 Dr STD Sdn	17720	21610

OPTIONS FOR ES300
Chrome Wheels +795
Compact Disc Changer +545
Leather Seats +570
Power Moonroof +510

GS300 — 1996

A five-speed automatic transmission makes the GS 300 feel more sporty, while rear styling revisions and five new exterior colors update the suave exterior. 1997 side-impact standards are met this year, and the power moonroof features one-touch operation.

RATINGS (SCALE OF 1-10)

Overall	Safety	Reliability	Performance	Comfort	Value
8	7.1	9.9	8.6	9.1	5.6

Category J

Model	Trade-in	Market
4 Dr STD Sdn	21865	26660

OPTIONS FOR GS300
Chrome Wheels +795
Compact Disc Changer +545
Leather Seats +570
Nakamichi Sound System +650
Power Moonroof +510
Traction Control System +730

LS400 — 1996

Deep Jewel Green Pearl is newly available on the paint palette.

RATINGS (SCALE OF 1-10)

Overall	Safety	Reliability	Performance	Comfort	Value
N/A	N/A	9.8	8	9.4	6.4

Category L

Model	Trade-in	Market
4 Dr STD Sdn	30315	35665

OPTIONS FOR LS400
Chrome Wheels +810
Compact Disc Changer +650
Nakamichi Sound System +600
Power Moonroof +500
Traction Control System +890

LX450 — 1996

Lexus clones a Toyota Land Cruiser, puts some fancy wheels on it, and slathers leather and wood all over the interior to capitalize on the booming sport-ute market.

RATINGS (SCALE OF 1-10)

Overall	Safety	Reliability	Performance	Comfort	Value
N/A	N/A	8.9	7.6	8	N/A

Category G

Model	Trade-in	Market
4 Dr STD 4WD Wgn	29375	35820

OPTIONS FOR LX450
F&R Locking Differential +490
Compact Disc Changer +290
Luggage Rack +85
Power Moonroof +490
Running Boards +215

SC — 1996

SC300

Category J

Model	Trade-in	Market
2 Dr STD Cpe	23495	28650

SC400

Category J

Model	Trade-in	Market
2 Dr STD Cpe	28235	34435

Don't forget to refer to the Mileage Adjustment Table at the back of this book!

 © 1999 by Edmund Publications Corporation

Model Description	Trade-in Value	Market Value

1995 LEXUS

ES300 1995

Styling is freshened, and chrome wheels are available. Trunk-mounted CD changer is a new option.

RATINGS (SCALE OF 1-10)

Overall	Safety	Reliability	Performance	Comfort	Value
8	8.4	9.1	8.4	8.1	5.8

Category J

4 Dr STD Sdn	15700	19385

OPTIONS FOR ES300

Chrome Wheels +650
Compact Disc Changer +445
Leather Seats +465
Power Moonroof +415

GS300 1995

No changes.

RATINGS (SCALE OF 1-10)

Overall	Safety	Reliability	Performance	Comfort	Value
8.2	7.8	9.7	8.6	9.1	6

Category J

4 Dr STD Sdn	19235	23745

OPTIONS FOR GS300

Compact Disc Changer +445
Leather Seats +465
Nakamichi Sound System +530
Power Moonroof +415
Traction Control System +600

LS400 1995

All-new car looks pretty much the same as it has for half a decade. The interior and trunk are larger, the engine more powerful, and the car is quicker than before. Six-disc CD changer is dash-mounted.

RATINGS (SCALE OF 1-10)

Overall	Safety	Reliability	Performance	Comfort	Value
N/A	N/A	9.5	8	9.4	6.3

Category L

4 Dr STD Sdn	25525	30390

OPTIONS FOR LS400

AM/FM Compact Disc Playr +355
Chrome Wheels +665
Compact Disc Changer +530
Nakamichi Sound System +490
Power Moonroof +405
Traction Control System +725

SC 1995

SC300

Category J

2 Dr STD Cpe	19990	24680

SC400

Category J

2 Dr STD Cpe	22920	28300

1994 LEXUS

ES300 1994

Passenger airbag added. New 3.0-liter engine has twin cams, aluminum block, and a few more horsepower. Several convenience features are now standard, including an outside temperature gauge.

RATINGS (SCALE OF 1-10)

Overall	Safety	Reliability	Performance	Comfort	Value
8	8.4	9.1	8.4	8.1	5.8

Category J

4 Dr STD Sdn	13330	16660

OPTIONS FOR ES300

Cellular Telephone +600
Compact Disc Changer +365
Leather Seats +380
Power Moonroof +340

GS300 1994

No changes.

RATINGS (SCALE OF 1-10)

Overall	Safety	Reliability	Performance	Comfort	Value
8.3	7.8	9.8	8.6	9.1	6

Category J

4 Dr STD Sdn	16350	20440

OPTIONS FOR GS300

Compact Disc Changer +365
Leather Seats +380
Nakamichi Sound System +435
Power Moonroof +340
Traction Control System +490

LS400 1994

Minor trim revisions.

RATINGS (SCALE OF 1-10)

Overall	Safety	Reliability	Performance	Comfort	Value
N/A	N/A	9.7	9	9.3	6.3

Category L

4 Dr STD Sdn	20225	24660

Don't forget to refer to the Mileage Adjustment Table at the back of this book!

 © 1999 by Edmund Publications Corporation

Model Description	Trade-in Value	Market Value

OPTIONS FOR LS400

Electric Air Suspension +630
Compact Disc Changer +435
Nakamichi Sound System +400
Power Moonroof +335
Traction Control System +595

SC 1994

SC300

Category J

2 Dr STD Cpe	16875	21090

SC400

Category J

2 Dr STD Cpe	18660	23330

OPTIONS FOR SC

Leather Trim Package +325

1993 LEXUS

ES300 1993

A fuel cap tether and automatic-locking safety belt retractors are added.

RATINGS (SCALE OF 1-10)

Overall	Safety	Reliability	Performance	Comfort	Value
8.1	8.4	8.9	8.4	8.1	6.7

Category J

4 Dr STD Sdn	10530	13675

OPTIONS FOR ES300

Compact Disc Changer +295
Leather Seats +310
Power Moonroof +280

GS300 1993

New sports sedan looks great, but fails to deliver much performance. Arrived late in 1993 with dual airbags, ABS and CFC-free air conditioning.

RATINGS (SCALE OF 1-10)

Overall	Safety	Reliability	Performance	Comfort	Value
8.3	7.8	9.5	8.6	9.1	6.4

Category J

4 Dr STD Sdn	13815	17940

OPTIONS FOR GS300

Portable Plus Telephone +510
Cellular Telephone +490
Chrome Wheels +435
Compact Disc Changer +295
Leather Seats +310
Nakamichi Sound System +355
Power Moonroof +280
Traction Control System +400

Model Description	Trade-in Value	Market Value

LS400 1993

Passenger airbag added. New alloy wheels debut. Brakes and tires are bigger. Styling is touched up, and interiors receive a host of upgrades. CFC-free air conditioning replaces Freon-based unit.

RATINGS (SCALE OF 1-10)

Overall	Safety	Reliability	Performance	Comfort	Value
N/A	N/A	9.8	9	9.3	4.5

Category L

4 Dr STD Sdn	16290	20365

OPTIONS FOR LS400

Cellular Telephone +290
Compact Disc Changer +355
Nakamichi Sound System +330
Power Moonroof +270
Traction Control System +485

SC 1993

SC300

Category J

2 Dr STD Cpe	14035	18225

SC400

Category J

2 Dr STD Cpe	15570	20225

1992 LEXUS

ES300 1992

Camry-based replacement for ES250. ABS and driver airbag are standard.

RATINGS (SCALE OF 1-10)

Overall	Safety	Reliability	Performance	Comfort	Value
7.8	7.4	8.7	8.4	8.1	6.1

Category J

4 Dr STD Sdn	8885	11845

OPTIONS FOR ES300

Auto 4-Speed Transmission +220
AM/FM Compact Disc Playr +135
Leather Seats +255
Power Moonroof +225

LS400 1992

No changes.

RATINGS (SCALE OF 1-10)

Overall	Safety	Reliability	Performance	Comfort	Value
N/A	N/A	9.7	9	9.3	6.2

Category L

4 Dr STD Sdn	13390	16735

Don't forget to refer to the Mileage Adjustment Table at the back of this book!

 © 1999 by Edmund Publications Corporation

OPTIONS FOR LS400

Memory System +195
AM/FM Compact Disc Playr +195
Compact Disc Changer +290
Power Moonroof +220
Premium Sound System +195
Traction Control System +395

SC 1992

SC300

Category J

2 Dr STD Cpe	11750	15665

SC400

Category J

2 Dr STD Cpe	13340	17785

1991 LEXUS

ES250 1991

No changes.

Category D

4 Dr STD Sdn	5620	7700

OPTIONS FOR ES250

Auto 4-Speed Transmission +150
Compact Disc W/fm/tape +195
Leather Seats +225
Power Drivers Seat +70
Power Sunroof +150
Premium Sound System +70

LS400 1991

No changes.

RATINGS (SCALE OF 1-10)

Overall	Safety	Reliability	Performance	Comfort	Value
N/A	N/A	9.5	9	9.3	5.6

Category L

4 Dr STD Sdn	11075	14195

OPTIONS FOR LS400

Air Suspension System +300
Memory System +160
AM/FM Compact Disc Playr +155
Leather Seats +250
Nakamichi Sound System +220
Power Moonroof +180
Premium Sound System +160
Traction Control System +325

1990 LEXUS

ES250 1990

Camry-based luxury compact meant to serve as entry-level car for new Lexus division.. ABS and driver airbag are standard.

Category D

4 Dr STD Sdn	4960	6890

OPTIONS FOR ES250

Auto 4-Speed Transmission +125
Compact Disc W/fm/tape +160
Leather Seats +185
Power Drivers Seat +55
Power Sunroof +120

LS400 1990

Brand new flagship for brand new Toyota luxury division. ABS and driver airbag are standard. Traction control is optional.

RATINGS (SCALE OF 1-10)

Overall	Safety	Reliability	Performance	Comfort	Value
N/A	N/A	9.1	9	9.3	4.4

Category L

4 Dr STD Sdn	9620	12660

OPTIONS FOR LS400

Air Suspension System +250
Memory System +130
AM/FM Compact Disc Playr +130
Cellular Telephone +160
Compact Disc Changer +195
Keyless Entry System +40
Leather Seats +200
Nakamichi Sound System +180
Power Sunroof +150
Traction Control System +265

A 15-minute phone call
could save you 15% or more
on car insurance.
1-800-555-2758
GEICO DIRECT

Don't forget to refer to the Mileage Adjustment Table at the back of this book!

© 1999 by Edmund Publications Corporation

LINCOLN USA

1997 Lincoln Mark VIII

1998 LINCOLN

CONTINENTAL 1998

Lincoln's front-wheel drive luxo-barge gets a bigger grille (just what it needs) and rounded corners. It also gets an interior freshening that replaces the digital clock with an analog timepiece.

Category A		
4 Dr STD Sdn	25685	30220

OPTIONS FOR CONTINENTAL

RESCU Package +890
Chrome Wheels +930
Compact Disc Changer +725
Heated Front Seats +165
JBL Sound System +465
Power Moonroof +1190

MARK VIII 1998

No changes to Lincoln's muscle car.

Category A		
2 Dr LSC Cpe	27120	31905
2 Dr STD Cpe	26715	31430

OPTIONS FOR MARK VIII

AM/FM Compact Disc Playr +435
Chrome Wheels[Opt on STD] +930
Compact Disc Changer +725
Heated Front Seats +165
Power Moonroof +1190

NAVIGATOR 1998

This all-new entrant into the luxury SUV market is the first truck ever sold by Lincoln. Based on the highly-acclaimed Ford Expedition, the Navigator is powered by a 5.4-liter SOHC V8 engine and has standard goodies that include illuminated running boards, a load-leveling air suspension and standard anti-lock brakes. This truck also features one of the largest grilles this side of a Kenworth.

Category H		
4 Dr STD Wgn	28765	33840
4 Dr STD 4WD Wgn	31430	36980

OPTIONS FOR NAVIGATOR

Chrome Wheels +245
Compact Disc Changer +360
Dual Air Conditioning +1180
Limited Slip Diff[Opt on 2WD] +210
Power Moonroof +805

TOWN CAR 1998

Lincoln redesigns its Town Car this year, making it lower, stiffer and faster. The interior is nicely improved as well, with softer seats and better positioned controls.

Category A		
4 Dr Cartier Sdn	30040	35340
4 Dr Executive Sdn	27905	32825
4 Dr Signature Sdn	29115	34255

OPTIONS FOR TOWN CAR

Chrome Wheels +930
Compact Disc Changer +725
Heated Front Seats[Std on Cartier] +165
JBL Sound System[Std on Cartier] +465
Leather Seats[Std on Cartier] +570
Power Moonroof +1190
Traction Control System[Std on Cartier] +175

1997 LINCOLN

CONTINENTAL 1997

The changes to the 1997 Continental are minor this year. The first is the addition of a single-key locking system that locks the doors, glove box, and trunk with a turn of the wrist. The second is the addition of all-speed traction control. Lastly, the Continental receives a minor interior and exterior facelift.

RATINGS (SCALE OF 1-10)

Overall	Safety	Reliability	Performance	Comfort	Value
N/A	N/A	8.4	7.6	8.1	6.7

Category A		
4 Dr STD Sdn	19640	23105

OPTIONS FOR CONTINENTAL

RESCU Package +870
Cellular Telephone +490
Chrome Wheels +760
Compact Disc Changer +590
Power Moonroof +970

Don't forget to refer to the Mileage Adjustment Table at the back of this book!

 © 1999 by Edmund Publications Corporation

Model Description	Trade-in Value	Market Value

MARK VIII 1997

Lincoln thoroughly updates this personal coupe, lighting the darn thing up like a Christmas tree in the process. The Mark now has high-intensity discharge front headlamps, cornering lamps, a neon rear applique, and puddle lamps. Wow, you'll see this thing from miles away. The hood, grille and interior have also been slightly redesigned.

RATINGS (SCALE OF 1-10)

Overall	Safety	Reliability	Performance	Comfort	Value
N/A	N/A	9	8.4	7.9	5.9

Category A

Model	Trade-in	Market
2 Dr LSC Cpe	20365	23955
2 Dr STD Cpe	20045	23585

OPTIONS FOR MARK VIII

AM/FM Compact Disc Playr +355
Cellular Telephone +490
Chrome Wheels[Opt on STD] +760
Compact Disc Changer +590
Power Moonroof +970

TOWN CAR 1997

The Town Car's power steering has been improved. Watch out, Mario!

RATINGS (SCALE OF 1-10)

Overall	Safety	Reliability	Performance	Comfort	Value
7.6	8.3	8.5	7.4	8.4	5.6

Category A

Model	Trade-in	Market
4 Dr Cartier Sdn	22410	26365
4 Dr Executive Sdn	19645	23110
4 Dr Signature Sdn	20810	24480

OPTIONS FOR TOWN CAR

Cellular Telephone +490
Chrome Wheels +760
Compact Disc Changer +590
JBL Sound System[Std on Cartier] +380
Leather Seats[Std on Cartier] +465
Power Moonroof +970
Traction Control System[Std on Cartier] +145

1996 LINCOLN

CONTINENTAL 1996

The big news for Continental is an optional gee-whiz rescue unit that uses a Global Positioning Satellite to pinpoint your location for roadside assistance, medical, and law enforcement personnel in the event of an emergency. Likely the greatest safety advance since airbags and antilock brakes. Also new are run-flat Michelin tires, a 75th Diamond Anniversary Edition, and a standard anti-theft system. It's getting there.

RATINGS (SCALE OF 1-10)

Overall	Safety	Reliability	Performance	Comfort	Value
N/A	N/A	8.1	7.6	8.1	7.1

Category A

Model	Trade-in	Market
4 Dr STD Sdn	15890	19615

OPTIONS FOR CONTINENTAL

RESCU Package +795
Cellular Telephone +400
Chrome Wheels +620
Compact Disc Changer +485
JBL Sound System +310
Power Moonroof +795
Traction Control System +120

MARK VIII 1996

Last year's limited-edition LSC model goes full-time for 1996. Eight new colors are available, and borderless floor mats debut. A Touring Package and 75th Diamond Anniversary model are offered.

RATINGS (SCALE OF 1-10)

Overall	Safety	Reliability	Performance	Comfort	Value
N/A	N/A	8.7	8.4	7.9	6.3

Category A

Model	Trade-in	Market
2 Dr LSC Cpe	16725	20650
2 Dr STD Cpe	16400	20250

OPTIONS FOR MARK VIII

Cellular Telephone +400
Chrome Wheels[Opt on STD] +620
Compact Disc Changer +485
Power Moonroof +795
Traction Control System +120

TOWN CAR 1996

Engine upgrades, new automatic climate controls, and real wood on the dashboard in Cartier models sum up the changes to the Town Car.

RATINGS (SCALE OF 1-10)

Overall	Safety	Reliability	Performance	Comfort	Value
7.9	8.3	8.2	7.4	8.4	7.3

Category A

Model	Trade-in	Market
4 Dr Cartier Sdn	18465	22795
4 Dr Executive Sdn	16150	19940
4 Dr Signature Sdn	17090	21100

OPTIONS FOR TOWN CAR

Cellular Telephone +400
Compact Disc Changer +485
JBL Sound System[Std on Cartier] +310
Leather Seats[Std on Cartier] +380
Power Moonroof +795
Traction Control System[Std on Cartier] +120

Don't forget to refer to the Mileage Adjustment Table at the back of this book!

 © 1999 by Edmund Publications Corporation

1995 LINCOLN

CONTINENTAL 1995

An all-new Continental is released with a V8 DOHC engine. A new suspension system that adjusts the shock absorbers to the prevailing driving conditions debuts, as does a memory seat system that will retain the seating preferences for two people. The new Continental has swoopier styling which is geared towards attracting a more youthful audience.

RATINGS (SCALE OF 1-10)

Overall	Safety	Reliability	Performance	Comfort	Value
N/A	N/A	7.8	7.6	8.1	5.7

Category A

Model	Trade-in Value	Market Value
4 Dr STD Sdn	13365	16710

OPTIONS FOR CONTINENTAL

Cellular Telephone +330
Chrome Wheels +510
Compact Disc Changer +395
Power Moonroof +650
Traction Control System +95

MARK VIII 1995

Lincoln's premium touring coupe receives significant changes across the board. A new instrument panel houses a new stereo with larger buttons. A feature called retained accessory power makes an appearance on the Mark VIII, allowing passengers ten seconds to close the window after the car is turned off.

RATINGS (SCALE OF 1-10)

Overall	Safety	Reliability	Performance	Comfort	Value
N/A	N/A	8.7	8.4	7.9	6.3

Category A

Model	Trade-in Value	Market Value
2 Dr LSC Cpe	13725	17155
2 Dr STD Cpe	13725	17155

OPTIONS FOR MARK VIII

Cellular Telephone +330
Chrome Wheels +510
Compact Disc Changer +395
Power Moonroof +650
Traction Control System +95

TOWN CAR 1995

Exterior changes on the Town Car include new headlights, grille, taillights, bumpers, and bodyside molding. The outside mirrors have been moved forward slightly to increase visibility. An electronic steering switch selector allows the driver to select the type of steering effort they want. The instrument panel includes a redesigned two-spoke steering wheel, illuminated switches, and improved stereos with larger controls. Signature and Cartier models get steering wheel-mounted stereo and climate controls. A gate access unit integrated into the driver's side visor allows up to three frequencies to be programmed into its memory.

RATINGS (SCALE OF 1-10)

Overall	Safety	Reliability	Performance	Comfort	Value
8	9	7.9	7.4	8.4	7.3

Category A

Model	Trade-in Value	Market Value
4 Dr Cartier Sdn	15020	18775
4 Dr Executive Sdn	13015	16265
4 Dr Signature Sdn	13855	17320

OPTIONS FOR TOWN CAR

Cellular Telephone +330
Compact Disc Changer +395
JBL Sound System[Std on Cartier] +255
Leather Seats[Std on Cartier] +310
Power Moonroof +650
Traction Control System[Std on Cartier] +95

1994 LINCOLN

CONTINENTAL 1994

Suspension changes improve the Continental's ride. A memory feature on the remote keyless entry automatically adjusts the driver's seat to a pre-set position each time it's activated. Exterior changes include revised taillamps, grille and rocker moldings. A retractable trunk cord is standard on all Continentals; it is designed to keep the trunk from bouncing around when it has to be left open for large loads.

RATINGS (SCALE OF 1-10)

Overall	Safety	Reliability	Performance	Comfort	Value
N/A	N/A	7.3	7.6	7.6	6.5

Category A

Model	Trade-in Value	Market Value
4 Dr Executive Sdn	8745	11210
4 Dr Signature Sdn	9430	12090

OPTIONS FOR CONTINENTAL

AM/FM Compact Disc Playr +195
Cellular Telephone +270
Keyless Entry System[Opt on Executive] +90
Power Moonroof +530
Power Passenger Seat[Opt on Executive] +115

MARK VIII 1994

Chrome wheels are now an available option on the Mark VIII. There is a memory feature for the seats and outside mirrors.

RATINGS (SCALE OF 1-10)

Overall	Safety	Reliability	Performance	Comfort	Value
N/A	N/A	8.7	8.4	7.9	6.2

Don't forget to refer to the Mileage Adjustment Table at the back of this book!

 © 1999 by Edmund Publications Corporation

Model Description	Trade-in Value	Market Value
Category A		
2 Dr STD Cpe	10655	13660

OPTIONS FOR MARK VIII

AM/FM Compact Disc Playr +195
Cellular Telephone +270
Chrome Wheels +415
Compact Disc Changer +325
Power Moonroof +530
Traction Control System +80

TOWN CAR 1994

A dual exhaust system on the Town Car is made standard this year, upping horsepower to 210. All models receive solar tinted glass. The Jack Nicklaus Special Edition has been dropped.

RATINGS (SCALE OF 1-10)

Overall	Safety	Reliability	Performance	Comfort	Value
N/A	N/A	8.5	7	8	7.2

Model Description	Trade-in Value	Market Value
Category A		
4 Dr Cartier Sdn	11445	14675
4 Dr Executive Sdn	9680	12410
4 Dr Signature Sdn	10490	13450

OPTIONS FOR TOWN CAR

Cellular Telephone +270
Compact Disc Changer +325
JBL Sound System[Std on Cartier] +205
Keyless Entry System[Opt on Executive] +90
Leather Seats[Std on Cartier] +255
Power Moonroof +530
Traction Control System +80

1993 LINCOLN

CONTINENTAL 1993

Bucket seats are available this year with a handy center console. The Signature series gets remote keyless entry, aluminum wheels, and the Comfort and Convenience Group added to its standard features list. Both models receive adjustable seatbelt anchor points.

RATINGS (SCALE OF 1-10)

Overall	Safety	Reliability	Performance	Comfort	Value
N/A	N/A	7	7.6	7.6	5.8

Model Description	Trade-in Value	Market Value
Category A		
4 Dr Executive Sdn	6580	8775
4 Dr Signature Sdn	6830	9110

OPTIONS FOR CONTINENTAL

AM/FM Compact Disc Playr +160
Cellular Telephone +220
Dual Power Seats[Opt on Executive] +115
Keyless Entry System[Opt on Executive] +75
Power Sunroof +415
Premium Sound System[Opt on Executive] +135

MARK VIII 1993

The Mark VIII debuts replacing the dated Mark VII. Based on the Thunderbird platform, the new Mark has a sportier feel than previous models. A twin-cam 4.6-liter V8 produces 280 horsepower in the Mark VIII, and the transmission is an electronically controlled four-speed automatic.

RATINGS (SCALE OF 1-10)

Overall	Safety	Reliability	Performance	Comfort	Value
N/A	N/A	8.1	8.4	7.9	4.3

Model Description	Trade-in Value	Market Value
Category A		
2 Dr STD Cpe	8690	11590

OPTIONS FOR MARK VIII

Cellular Telephone +220
Compact Disc Changer +265
Compact Disc W/fm/tape +215
Power Sunroof +415

TOWN CAR 1993

Styling changes and an optional Handling Package mark the differences in this year's Town Car. The formerly optional geometric aluminum wheels are made standard and the grille and headlights are slightly altered. The Handling Package consists of a firmer suspension and larger tires. The Executive series gains some features that were standard on the other models.

RATINGS (SCALE OF 1-10)

Overall	Safety	Reliability	Performance	Comfort	Value
N/A	N/A	8.1	7	8	6.6

Model Description	Trade-in Value	Market Value
Category A		
4 Dr Cartier Sdn	9120	12160
4 Dr Executive Sdn	7670	10230
4 Dr Signature Sdn	8345	11125

OPTIONS FOR TOWN CAR

Cellular Telephone +220
Compact Disc Changer +265
Leather Seats[Std on Cartier] +210
Power Sunroof +415
Premium Sound System[Std on Cartier] +135

1992 LINCOLN

CONTINENTAL 1992

The passenger airbag is revived this year and two trim-levels are available, the Signature and the Executive. Several optional safety features debut this year, such as an electrochromatic rearview mirror and a remote keyless entry system with a panic button.

Don't forget to refer to the Mileage Adjustment Table at the back of this book!

 © 1999 by Edmund Publications Corporation

RATINGS (SCALE OF 1-10)

Overall	Safety	Reliability	Performance	Comfort	Value
N/A	N/A	6.9	7.6	7.6	5.8

Category A

Model Description	Trade-in Value	Market Value
4 Dr Executive Sdn	5065	7035
4 Dr Signature Sdn	5615	7795

OPTIONS FOR CONTINENTAL

Aluminum/Alloy Wheels[Opt on Executive] +105
Cellular Telephone +180
Compact Disc W/fm/tape +175
Keyless Entry System[Opt on Executive] +60
Power Moonroof +355
Premium Sound System +110

MARK VII 1992

The final year for the Mark VII, changes are limited to minor alterations of the interior.

Category A

Model Description	Trade-in Value	Market Value
2 Dr Bill Blass Cpe	6595	9160
2 Dr LSC Cpe	6790	9430

OPTIONS FOR MARK VII

AM/FM Compact Disc Playr +130
Cellular Telephone +180
Power Moonroof +355
Premium Sound System +110

TOWN CAR 1992

Transmission adaptations include electronic shift controls, overdrive lockout, and a feature that won't allow the car to be shifted out of park unless the brake is on.

RATINGS (SCALE OF 1-10)

Overall	Safety	Reliability	Performance	Comfort	Value
N/A	N/A	8	7	8	7

Category A

Model Description	Trade-in Value	Market Value
4 Dr Cartier Sdn	7045	9780
4 Dr Executive Sdn	6130	8515
4 Dr Signature Sdn	6530	9070

OPTIONS FOR TOWN CAR

Aluminum/Alloy Wheels[Opt on Executive] +105
AM/FM Compact Disc Playr +130
Cellular Telephone +180
JBL Sound System[Std on Cartier] +140
Keyless Entry System[Opt on Executive] +60
Leather Seats +170
Power Moonroof +355
Power Passenger Seat[Opt on Executive] +75
Premium Sound System +110

1991 LINCOLN

CONTINENTAL 1991

A passenger airbag is available only in a portion of these cars since they ran out of propellant halfway through the production run.

RATINGS (SCALE OF 1-10)

Overall	Safety	Reliability	Performance	Comfort	Value
N/A	N/A	6.6	7.6	7.6	7.1

Category A

Model Description	Trade-in Value	Market Value
4 Dr Signature Sdn	4280	6115
4 Dr STD Sdn	3815	5455

OPTIONS FOR CONTINENTAL

Aluminum/Alloy Wheels[Opt on STD] +85
AM/FM Compact Disc Playr +105
Cellular Telephone +145
Keyless Entry System[Opt on STD] +50
Power Passenger Seat[Opt on STD] +60
Power Sunroof +275

MARK VII 1991

No significant changes to the Mark VII.

Category A

Model Description	Trade-in Value	Market Value
2 Dr Bill Blass Cpe	5435	7760
2 Dr LSC Cpe	5465	7810

OPTIONS FOR MARK VII

AM/FM Compact Disc Playr +105
Cellular Telephone +145
Power Sunroof +275

TOWN CAR 1991

An impressive 4.6-liter overhead cam V8 engine debuts in the Town Car. Offering 40 to 60 more horsepower, depending on the exhaust system, than the previous 5.0-liter V8. The new Town Car has quite a bit more pizzazz than many luxo-barges.

RATINGS (SCALE OF 1-10)

Overall	Safety	Reliability	Performance	Comfort	Value
N/A	N/A	7.3	7	8	6.9

Category A

Model Description	Trade-in Value	Market Value
4 Dr Cartier Sdn	6010	8590
4 Dr Signature Sdn	5430	7755
4 Dr STD Sdn	4865	6950

OPTIONS FOR TOWN CAR

Aluminum/Alloy Wheels[Opt on STD] +85
AM/FM Compact Disc Playr +105
Cellular Telephone +145
JBL Sound System[Std on Cartier] +115
Keyless Entry System[Opt on STD] +50
Leather Seats[Std on Cartier] +140
Power Passenger Seat[Opt on STD] +60

Don't forget to refer to the Mileage Adjustment Table at the back of this book!

 © 1999 by Edmund Publications Corporation

Model Description	Trade-in Value	Market Value

Power Sunroof +275
Traction Control System +45

1990 LINCOLN

CONTINENTAL 1990

A serious-looking aerodynamic grille appears on the nose of the Continental and new taillamps illuminate the rear.

RATINGS (SCALE OF 1-10)

Overall	Safety	Reliability	Performance	Comfort	Value
N/A	N/A	6.3	7.6	7.6	7.1

Category A

4 Dr Signature Sdn	3495	5215
4 Dr STD Sdn	3125	4660

OPTIONS FOR CONTINENTAL

Aluminum/Alloy Wheels[Opt on STD] +70
AM/FM Compact Disc Playr +85
Cellular Telephone +120
JBL Sound System +95
Keyless Entry System[Opt on STD] +40
Power Passenger Seat[Opt on STD] +50
Power Sunroof +225

MARK VII 1990

The Mark VII receives a standard driver airbag. The LSC receives new wheels.

Category A

2 Dr Bill Blass Cpe	3925	5860
2 Dr LSC Cpe	3945	5890

OPTIONS FOR MARK VII

AM/FM Compact Disc Playr +85
Cellular Telephone +120
Leather Seats +115
Power Sunroof +225

TOWN CAR 1990

The Town Car gets new sheetmetal. Rounded edges and aerodynamic shapes produce a car that looks much more modern than its predecessor.

RATINGS (SCALE OF 1-10)

Overall	Safety	Reliability	Performance	Comfort	Value
N/A	N/A	6.7	6.8	8	6.3

Category A

4 Dr Cartier Sdn	4680	6985
4 Dr Signature Sdn	4405	6575
4 Dr STD Sdn	4025	6005

OPTIONS FOR TOWN CAR

Aluminum/Alloy Wheels[Opt on STD] +70
AM/FM Compact Disc Playr +85
Anti-Lock Brakes +155
Cellular Telephone +120
JBL Sound System +95
Keyless Entry System[Opt on STD] +40
Leather Seats[Std on Cartier] +115
Power Passenger Seat +50
Power Sunroof +225

1989 LINCOLN

CONTINENTAL 1989

Dual airbags are available on the 1989 Lincoln Continental. The addition of the passenger airbag necessitated a dashboard change. Little else is different on this four-door, six-passenger front-wheel drive behemoth.

RATINGS (SCALE OF 1-10)

Overall	Safety	Reliability	Performance	Comfort	Value
N/A	N/A	5.8	7.6	7.6	6.5

Category A

4 Dr Signature Sdn	2715	4310
4 Dr STD Sdn	2495	3960

OPTIONS FOR CONTINENTAL

Aluminum/Alloy Wheels[Opt on STD] +55
AM/FM Compact Disc Playr +70
Compact Disc W/fm/tape +95
Keyless Entry System[Opt on STD] +35
Power Moonroof +195
Power Passenger Seat +40
Premium Sound System +60

MARK VII 1989

The only significant change for the 1989 Mark VII is the addition of a dummy light for the computer controlled engine-management system. This warning light was previously available on California models.

Category A

2 Dr Bill Blass Cpe	2995	4755
2 Dr LSC Cpe	3070	4870

OPTIONS FOR MARK VII

Premium Sound System +60

TOWN CAR 1989

No significant changes for the 1989 Town Car.

Category A

4 Dr Cartier Sdn	3025	4800
4 Dr Signature Sdn	2875	4565
4 Dr STD Sdn	2650	4210

OPTIONS FOR TOWN CAR

Aluminum/Alloy Wheels[Opt on STD] +55
AM/FM Compact Disc Playr +70
Dual Power Seats[Opt on STD] +50
Keyless Entry System[Opt on STD] +35
Leather Seats[Std on Cartier] +95
Premium Sound System +60

Don't forget to refer to the Mileage Adjustment Table at the back of this book!

 © 1999 by Edmund Publications Corporation

Model Description	Trade-in Value	Market Value

MAZDA

Japan

1995 Mazda Millenia

1998 MAZDA

626 1998

Mazda redesigns the 626, giving it more upscale styling, more powerful engines, a tighter body and increased cargo and people space while retaining the sedan's distinctive sporting nature.

Category D

Model Description	Trade-in Value	Market Value
4 Dr DX Sdn	9415	11210
4 Dr ES Sdn	15465	18410
4 Dr LX Sdn	11680	13905
4 Dr LX V6 Sdn	13725	16340

OPTIONS FOR 626

Auto 4-Speed Transmission +665
Air Conditioning[Opt on DX] +700
Aluminum/Alloy Wheels[Std on ES] +375
AM/FM Compact Disc Playr[Opt on DX] +465
Anti-Lock Brakes[Opt on LX] +790
Bose Sound System[Std on ES] +605
Keyless Entry System[Opt on LX] +250
Leather Seats[Opt on LX] +915
Power Drivers Seat[Std on ES] +285
Power Moonroof[Std on ES] +695

B-SERIES PICKUP 1998

Fresh styling, a revised front suspension, a larger regular cab, a more powerful 2.5-liter four-cylinder engine, a stiffer frame and a new 4WD system ensure that Mazda's compact truck will remain competitive through the end of the century.

Category G

Model Description	Trade-in Value	Market Value
2 Dr B2500 SE Std Cab SB	8145	9700
2 Dr B2500 SE Ext Cab SB	9460	11265
2 Dr B2500 SX Std Cab SB	7800	9285
2 Dr B3000 SE Ext Cab SB	11630	13845
2 Dr B3000 SE 4WD Ext Cab SB	12745	15175
2 Dr B3000 SE 4WD Std Cab SB	11820	14075
2 Dr B3000 SX 4WD Std Cab SB	11360	13525
2 Dr B4000 SE Ext Cab SB	12115	14420
2 Dr B4000 SE 4WD Ext Cab SB	12870	15320

OPTIONS FOR B-SERIES PICKUP

Auto 4-Speed Transmission +890
Auto 5-Speed Transmission[Opt on B4000] +920
Air Conditioning +675
Aluminum/Alloy Wheels +285
AM/FM Compact Disc Playr +320
Anti-Lock Brakes +515
Bed Liner +230
Cruise Control +175
Fog Lights +120
Keyless Entry System +170
Power Door Locks +190
Power Mirrors +110
Power Windows +195
Sliding Rear Window +100
Tilt Steering Wheel +140

MILLENIA 1998

Millenia carries over into 1998 with no changes.

Category D

Model Description	Trade-in Value	Market Value
4 Dr S Sdn	24345	28985
4 Dr STD Sdn	15980	19020

OPTIONS FOR MILLENIA

Premium Package +715
Bose Sound System[Std on S] +605
Dual Power Seats[Std on S] +695
Heated Front Seats +305
Heated Power Mirrors +75
Keyless Entry System[Std on S] +250
Leather Seats[Std on S] +915
Power Moonroof[Std on S] +695
Traction Control System[Std on S] +675

MPV 1998

A CD player is now standard.

Category G

Model Description	Trade-in Value	Market Value
2 Dr ES Pass. Van	17710	21085
2 Dr ES 4WD Pass. Van	20550	24465
2 Dr LX Pass. Van	14550	17320
2 Dr LX 4WD Pass. Van	18005	21435

OPTIONS FOR MPV

Air Conditioning +675
Aluminum/Alloy Wheels[Std on ES,4WD] +285
Auto Load Leveling[Opt on LX] +190
Dual Air Conditioning +840
Keyless Entry System +170
Leather Seats[Opt on LX] +640
Power Moonroof +735
Privacy Glass +225

Don't forget to refer to the Mileage Adjustment Table at the back of this book!

 © 1999 by Edmund Publications Corporation

Model Description	Trade-in Value	Market Value

PROTEGE 1998

A CD player is standard on ES and LX. It also comes on DX models equipped with an option package.

Category E

Model Description	Trade-in Value	Market Value
4 Dr DX Sdn	7895	9510
4 Dr ES Sdn	10655	12840
4 Dr LX Sdn	9175	11050

OPTIONS FOR PROTEGE

Auto 4-Speed Transmission +665
Air Conditioning[Std on ES] +675
Aluminum/Alloy Wheels +265
AM/FM Compact Disc Playr[Opt on DX] +390
Anti-Lock Brakes +590
Keyless Entry System +125
Power Moonroof +485

1997 MAZDA

626 1997

LX V6 and ES models gain power and torque, while the four-cylinder LX gets a Lexus-like trim package that includes two-tone paint, chrome wheel covers, leather interior, and other creature comforts. Audio systems are revised and two new colors debut.

RATINGS (SCALE OF 1-10)

Overall	Safety	Reliability	Performance	Comfort	Value
7.8	7.2	8.9	9	8.1	5.6

Category D

Model Description	Trade-in Value	Market Value
4 Dr DX Sdn	8750	10545
4 Dr ES Sdn	13310	16040
4 Dr LX Sdn	10130	12205
4 Dr LX V6 Sdn	11585	13955

OPTIONS FOR 626

Auto 4-Speed Transmission +525
Air Conditioning[Opt on DX] +575
Aluminum/Alloy Wheels[Opt on LX] +305
AM/FM Stereo Tape[Opt on DX] +245
Anti-Lock Brakes[Std on ES] +645
Keyless Entry System[Std on ES] +205
Leather Seats[Std on ES] +750
Power Antenna[Std on ES] +80
Power Drivers Seat[Std on ES] +230
Power Moonroof[Std on ES] +565

B-SERIES PICKUP 1997

The lineup is trimmed, leaving just B2300 and B4000 models available. SE-5 designation returns to bolster marketing efforts. B4000 pickups can be equipped with a new five-speed automatic transmission.

RATINGS (SCALE OF 1-10)

Overall	Safety	Reliability	Performance	Comfort	Value
N/A	6.5	8.7	7.2	7.3	N/A

Category G

Model Description	Trade-in Value	Market Value
2 Dr B2300 Std Cab SB	7520	8955
2 Dr B2300 SE Ext Cab SB	9060	10785
2 Dr B2300 SE Std Cab SB	8605	10245
2 Dr B4000 4WD Std Cab SB	10930	13010
2 Dr B4000 4WD Ext Cab SB	11705	13935
2 Dr B4000 SE Ext Cab SB	9205	10960
2 Dr B4000 SE 4WD Ext Cab SB	12130	14440

OPTIONS FOR B-SERIES PICKUP

Auto 4-Speed Transmission +725
Auto 5-Speed Transmission +750
Air Conditioning +550
Aluminum/Alloy Wheels +235
AM/FM Compact Disc Playr +260
Anti-Lock Brakes +420
Bed Liner +190
Compact Disc Changer +350
Cruise Control +145
Keyless Entry System +140
Limited Slip Diff +180
Power Door Locks +155
Power Steering[Std on B4000,B4000 SE,Ext Cab] +190
Power Windows +160
Premium Sound System +245
Rear Step Bumper[Opt on Ext Cab] +100

MIATA 1997

Mazda adds a Touring Package to the options list, consisting of alloy wheels, power steering, leather-wrapped steering wheel, power mirrors, power windows, and door map pockets. Midyear a new M-Edition debuts, sporting Marina Green paint and chromed alloy wheels. Summertime brings the limited-production STO-Edition, of which 1,500 were produced.

RATINGS (SCALE OF 1-10)

Overall	Safety	Reliability	Performance	Comfort	Value
7.3	6.3	8.8	9.2	7.1	5.1

Category F

Model Description	Trade-in Value	Market Value
2 Dr MX-5 Conv	11215	13515
2 Dr MX-5 M-Edition Conv	13260	15975

OPTIONS FOR MIATA

Auto 4-Speed Transmission +600
Leather Package +785
Air Conditioning[Opt on MX-5] +565
Aluminum/Alloy Wheels[Opt on MX-5] +210
Anti-Lock Brakes +490
Compact Disc W/fm/tape[Opt on MX-5] +355
Cruise Control[Opt on MX-5] +140
Hardtop Roof +935
Leather Seats[Opt on MX-5] +485
Limited Slip Diff[Opt on MX-5] +255
Power Steering[Opt on MX-5] +245
Power Windows[Opt on MX-5] +150
Rear Spoiler +190
Sport Suspension +175

Don't forget to refer to the Mileage Adjustment Table at the back of this book!

 © 1999 by Edmund Publications Corporation

Model Description	Trade-in Value	Market Value

MILLENIA 1997

Models equipped with leather are upgraded this year with an eight-way power passenger seat, 16-inch alloy wheels, and revised final drive ratio for better low-end response. S models also get the power passenger seat. All Millenias have a new rear-window-mounted diversity antenna, a new sound system with in-dash CD player, revised center console design, and Michelin tires.

RATINGS (SCALE OF 1-10)

Overall	Safety	Reliability	Performance	Comfort	Value
7.5	7.7	9	8.4	7.9	4.6

Category D

Model	Trade-in	Market
4 Dr L Sdn	15930	19190
4 Dr S Sdn	18285	22030
4 Dr STD Sdn	15640	18840

OPTIONS FOR MILLENIA

Bose Sound System +495
Traction Control System[Std on S] +550

MPV 1997

Four-wheel ABS is standard across the board, and all but the LX 2WD model are dressed in dorky All-Sport exterior trim.

RATINGS (SCALE OF 1-10)

Overall	Safety	Reliability	Performance	Comfort	Value
7.5	7.7	8.4	7.6	7.6	6.1

Category G

Model	Trade-in	Market
2 Dr ES Pass. Van	15955	18995
2 Dr ES 4WD Pass. Van	16495	19640
2 Dr LX Pass. Van	14100	16785
2 Dr LX 4WD Pass. Van	14560	17335

OPTIONS FOR MPV

Air Conditioning +550
Aluminum/Alloy Wheels[Std on ES,4WD] +235
Compact Disc W/fm/tape +465
Dual Air Conditioning +685
Keyless Entry System +140
Luggage Rack[Std on ES,4WD] +105
Power Moonroof +600

MX6 1997

All LS models get a rear spoiler.

RATINGS (SCALE OF 1-10)

Overall	Safety	Reliability	Performance	Comfort	Value
7.5	7.2	8.7	9	7.9	4.7

Category F

Model	Trade-in	Market
2 Dr LS Cpe	13760	16580
2 Dr STD Cpe	10995	13245

OPTIONS FOR MX6

Auto 4-Speed Transmission +545
Air Conditioning[Std on LS] +565
Aluminum/Alloy Wheels[Std on LS] +210
Anti-Lock Brakes +490
Keyless Entry System[Std on LS] +120
Leather Seats +485
Power Drivers Seat +160
Power Sunroof[Std on LS] +465
Rear Spoiler[Std on LS] +190

PROTEGE 1997

Styling revisions inside and out update this roomy compact nicely.

RATINGS (SCALE OF 1-10)

Overall	Safety	Reliability	Performance	Comfort	Value
N/A	N/A	8.9	7.8	7.4	5.4

Category E

Model	Trade-in	Market
4 Dr DX Sdn	6780	8265
4 Dr ES Sdn	8830	10765
4 Dr LX Sdn	7745	9445

OPTIONS FOR PROTEGE

Auto 4-Speed Transmission +545
Air Conditioning[Std on ES] +550
Aluminum/Alloy Wheels +215
AM/FM Stereo Tape[Opt on DX] +210
Anti-Lock Brakes +480
Power Moonroof +395

1996 MAZDA

626 1996

Chrome is tacked on front and rear, and the hood is raised a bit to give the 626 a more substantial look. ABS is available as a stand alone option on LX and LX V6 models for the first time (formerly, you had to buy an option package), and side-impact protection meets 1997 standards.

RATINGS (SCALE OF 1-10)

Overall	Safety	Reliability	Performance	Comfort	Value
7.6	7.2	8.7	9	8.1	5

Category D

Model	Trade-in	Market
4 Dr DX Sdn	7335	9170
4 Dr ES Sdn	11165	13955
4 Dr LX Sdn	8475	10590
4 Dr LX V6 Sdn	9745	12180

OPTIONS FOR 626

Auto 4-Speed Transmission +435
Air Conditioning[Opt on DX] +470
AM/FM Stereo Tape[Opt on DX] +200
Anti-Lock Brakes[Std on ES] +530

Don't forget to refer to the Mileage Adjustment Table at the back of this book!

 © 1999 by Edmund Publications Corporation

Model Description	Trade-in Value	Market Value

Keyless Entry System[Std on ES] +170
Power Drivers Seat[Std on ES] +190
Power Moonroof[Std on ES] +465

B-SERIES PICKUP 1996

A passenger side airbag comes with SE Plus and LE trim levels, and it can be deactivated in the event that a rear facing child safety seat is installed. SE models also get new chrome bumpers.

RATINGS (SCALE OF 1-10)

Overall	Safety	Reliability	Performance	Comfort	Value
N/A	6.5	8.5	7.2	7.3	N/A

Category G	Trade-in Value	Market Value
2 Dr B2300 Std Cab SB	6780	8270
2 Dr B2300 Ext Cab SB	7505	9155
2 Dr B2300 Std Cab LB	6900	8410
2 Dr B2300 4WD Std Cab SB	9675	11800
2 Dr B2300 SE Std Cab SB	8100	9875
2 Dr B2300 SE Ext Cab SB	8420	10265
2 Dr B3000 4WD Ext Cab SB	10080	12290
2 Dr B3000 SE Ext Cab SB	9030	11015
2 Dr B4000 LE Ext Cab SB	9940	12125
2 Dr B4000 LE 4WD Ext Cab SB	11900	14510
2 Dr B4000 SE 4WD Ext Cab SB	11350	13840
2 Dr B4000 SE 4WD Std Cab SB	11180	13635

OPTIONS FOR B-SERIES PICKUP

Auto 4-Speed Transmission +570
Air Conditioning[Std on B4000 LE] +450
Aluminum/Alloy Wheels[Std on B4000 LE] +190
Anti-Lock Brakes +345
Bed Liner +155
Compact Disc Changer +290
Cruise Control +115
Lighted Entry System +80
Power Door Locks +125
Power Windows +130
Premium Sound System +200
Rear Jump Seats[Std on B4000 LE] +125

MIATA 1996

Side-impact standards for 1997 are met a year early, and to offset the added weight, Mazda boosts power and torque.

RATINGS (SCALE OF 1-10)

Overall	Safety	Reliability	Performance	Comfort	Value
7.3	6.3	8.9	9.2	7.1	5.1

Category F	Trade-in Value	Market Value
2 Dr MX-5 Conv	10310	12725
2 Dr MX-5 M-Edition Conv	11300	13950

OPTIONS FOR MIATA

Auto 4-Speed Transmission +500
Sensory Sound System +480
Air Conditioning[Opt on MX-5] +460
Aluminum/Alloy Wheels[Opt on MX-5] +170
Anti-Lock Brakes[Opt on MX-5] +400
Cruise Control[Opt on MX-5] +115
Hardtop Roof +765
Leather Seats[Opt on MX-5] +395
Limited Slip Diff[Opt on MX-5] +205
Power Steering[Opt on MX-5] +200
Power Windows[Opt on MX-5] +125
Rear Spoiler +155
Sport Suspension +145

MILLENIA 1996

The Millenia S gets revised bright-finish alloy wheels.

RATINGS (SCALE OF 1-10)

Overall	Safety	Reliability	Performance	Comfort	Value
7.5	7.7	9	8.4	7.9	4.6

Category D	Trade-in Value	Market Value
4 Dr L Sdn	13590	16990
4 Dr S Sdn	15120	18905
4 Dr STD Sdn	13295	16620

OPTIONS FOR MILLENIA

Bose Sound System +405
Traction Control System[Std on S] +450

MPV 1996

New styling up front, a fourth door on the driver's side, and a revised instrument panel with dual airbags sum up the changes to Mazda's attempt at a minivan.

RATINGS (SCALE OF 1-10)

Overall	Safety	Reliability	Performance	Comfort	Value
7.4	7.7	8.3	7.6	7.6	6

Category G	Trade-in Value	Market Value
2 Dr DX Pass. Van	9600	11705
2 Dr ES Pass. Van	11780	14365
2 Dr ES 4WD Pass. Van	13790	16820
2 Dr LX Pass. Van	10845	13225
2 Dr LX 4WD Pass. Van	12395	15115

OPTIONS FOR MPV

Air Conditioning +450
Aluminum/Alloy Wheels[Opt on 2WD] +190
AM/FM Compact Disc Playr +215
Dual Air Conditioning +560
Keyless Entry System +115
Power Moonroof +490

MX6 1996

No changes for 1995.

RATINGS (SCALE OF 1-10)

Overall	Safety	Reliability	Performance	Comfort	Value
7.4	7.2	8.6	9	7.9	4.1

Don't forget to refer to the Mileage Adjustment Table at the back of this book!

 © 1999 by Edmund Publications Corporation

Model Description	Trade-in Value	Market Value
Category F		
2 Dr LS Cpe	11220	13850
2 Dr M-Edition Cpe	12035	14855
2 Dr STD Cpe	9670	11940

OPTIONS FOR MX6

Auto 4-Speed Transmission +435
Air Conditioning[Opt on STD] +460
Aluminum/Alloy Wheels[Opt on STD] +170
Anti-Lock Brakes[Opt on LS,STD] +400
Keyless Entry System[Opt on STD] +95
Leather Seats[Opt on LS] +395
Power Drivers Seat[Opt on LS] +130
Power Sunroof[Opt on STD] +380
Rear Spoiler[Opt on LS,STD] +155

PROTEGE 1996

No changes for 1996.

RATINGS (SCALE OF 1-10)

Overall	Safety	Reliability	Performance	Comfort	Value
N/A	N/A	8.9	7.8	7.4	5.9

Model Description	Trade-in Value	Market Value
Category E		
4 Dr DX Sdn	6410	8115
4 Dr ES Sdn	7940	10050
4 Dr LX Sdn	6950	8800

OPTIONS FOR PROTEGE

Auto 4-Speed Transmission +435
Air Conditioning[Std on ES] +450
AM/FM Stereo Tape[Opt on DX] +170
Anti-Lock Brakes +395
Keyless Entry System +80
Power Moonroof +325

1995 MAZDA

626 1995

ES gets remote keyless entry, which is available on LX and LX-V6 models. New wheels and wheelcovers are added across the board.

RATINGS (SCALE OF 1-10)

Overall	Safety	Reliability	Performance	Comfort	Value
7.9	7.8	8.2	9	8.1	6.4

Model Description	Trade-in Value	Market Value
Category D		
4 Dr DX Sdn	6475	8200
4 Dr ES Sdn	9820	12435
4 Dr LX Sdn	7460	9445
4 Dr LX V6 Sdn	8545	10820

OPTIONS FOR 626

Auto 4-Speed Transmission +355
Air Conditioning[Opt on DX] +385
Aluminum/Alloy Wheels[Opt on LX] +205
AM/FM Stereo Tape[Opt on DX] +165
Anti-Lock Brakes[Std on ES] +430
Keyless Entry System[Std on ES] +135
Power Drivers Seat[Std on ES] +155
Power Moonroof[Std on ES] +380

929 1995

Leather seats, wood trim and remote keyless entry are standard. Final year for sleek executive sedan.

RATINGS (SCALE OF 1-10)

Overall	Safety	Reliability	Performance	Comfort	Value
N/A	N/A	8.3	8.2	8.4	3.9

Model Description	Trade-in Value	Market Value
Category D		
4 Dr STD Sdn	12080	15295

OPTIONS FOR 929

Limited Slip Diff +220

B-SERIES PICKUP 1995

Redesigned dashboard with driver airbag debuts. Four-wheel ABS is standard on 4WD and 2WD B4000 models.

RATINGS (SCALE OF 1-10)

Overall	Safety	Reliability	Performance	Comfort	Value
N/A	6.7	8.1	7.2	7.3	N/A

Model Description	Trade-in Value	Market Value
Category G		
2 Dr B2300 Std Cab SB	6565	8105
2 Dr B2300 Ext Cab SB	7145	8820
2 Dr B2300 Std Cab LB	6530	8060
2 Dr B2300 4WD Std Cab SB	7830	9670
2 Dr B2300 SE Ext Cab SB	7605	9390
2 Dr B2300 SE Std Cab SB	7185	8870
2 Dr B3000 SE Ext Cab SB	7860	9705
2 Dr B3000 SE Std Cab SB	7680	9480
2 Dr B3000 SE 4WD Ext Cab SB	9180	11330
2 Dr B4000 LE Ext Cab SB	8750	10805
2 Dr B4000 LE 4WD Ext Cab SB	10705	13220
2 Dr B4000 SE Ext Cab SB	8300	10250
2 Dr B4000 SE 4WD Std Cab SB	9465	11685
2 Dr B4000 SE 4WD Ext Cab SB	10000	12345

OPTIONS FOR B-SERIES PICKUP

Auto 4-Speed Transmission +465
Air Conditioning[Std on B4000 LE] +370
Aluminum/Alloy Wheels +155
AM/FM Stereo Tape[Opt on B2300] +110
Auto Locking Hubs (4WD)[Std on B4000 SE] +120
Bed Liner +125
Compact Disc Changer +235
Cruise Control +95
Keyless Entry System +95
Limited Slip Diff +120
Power Door Locks +105
Power Drivers Seat +130

Don't forget to refer to the Mileage Adjustment Table at the back of this book!

 © 1999 by Edmund Publications Corporation

Model Description	Trade-in Value	Market Value

Power Steering[Std on SE,LE,Ext Cab,4WD] +130
Power Windows +105
Premium Sound System +165

MIATA 1995

Option packages are revised, and a gorgeous M-Edition with Merlot Mica paint, tan top, tan leather interior, and 15-inch BBS rims is available.

RATINGS (SCALE OF 1-10)

Overall	Safety	Reliability	Performance	Comfort	Value
7.5	6.9	8.7	9.2	7.1	5.5

Category F	Trade-in Value	Market Value
2 Dr MX-5 Conv	8375	10470
2 Dr MX-5 M-Edition Conv	10055	12565

OPTIONS FOR MIATA

Auto 4-Speed Transmission +380
Leather Pkg +990
Sensory Sound System +390
Air Conditioning[Opt on MX-5] +380
Aluminum/Alloy Wheels[Opt on MX-5] +140
Anti-Lock Brakes[Opt on MX-5] +330
Compact Disc W/fm/tape +240
Cruise Control[Opt on MX-5] +95
Hardtop Roof +625
Limited Slip Diff +170
Power Steering[Opt on MX-5] +165
Power Windows[Opt on MX-5] +100
Rear Spoiler +130
Sport Seats +240
Sport Suspension +120

MILLENIA 1995

Luxury-oriented refugee from aborted Amati luxury channel. Positioned to do battle with entry-level Lexus, Infiniti and BMW models. S models have 2.3-liter V6 with Miller-cycle technology and 210 horsepower. Dual airbags and ABS are standard on all models. The Millenia S adds traction control.

RATINGS (SCALE OF 1-10)

Overall	Safety	Reliability	Performance	Comfort	Value
7.5	8.4	8.4	8.4	7.9	4.4

Category D	Trade-in Value	Market Value
4 Dr S Sdn	12345	15625
4 Dr STD Sdn	10985	13905

OPTIONS FOR MILLENIA

Bose Sound System +330
Compact Disc Changer +300
Keyless Entry System[Std on S] +135
Leather Seats[Std on S] +500
Power Moonroof[Std on S] +380
Power Passenger Seat[Std on S] +175
Traction Control System[Std on S] +370

MPV 1995

New lineup includes L, LX and LXE trim levels. All come with seven-passenger seating. Four-cylinder engine has been dropped.

RATINGS (SCALE OF 1-10)

Overall	Safety	Reliability	Performance	Comfort	Value
7.3	6.5	8.2	7.8	7.6	6.4

Category G	Trade-in Value	Market Value
2 Dr L Pass. Van	8620	10640
2 Dr LX Pass. Van	9480	11705
2 Dr LX 4WD Pass. Van	10370	12805
2 Dr LXE Pass. Van	11010	13595
2 Dr LXE 4WD Pass. Van	11965	14770

OPTIONS FOR MPV

Air Conditioning +370
Aluminum/Alloy Wheels +155
Camper/Towing Package[Opt on LX] +130
Dual Air Conditioning +460
Keyless Entry System +95
Power Moonroof +400

MX3 1995

GS model, and its cool 1.8-liter V6 engine, vanishes. ABS is available only with manual transmission.

Category E	Trade-in Value	Market Value
2 Dr STD Hbk	6020	7820

OPTIONS FOR MX3

Auto 4-Speed Transmission +355
Air Conditioning +370
Aluminum/Alloy Wheels +145
Anti-Lock Brakes +320
Cruise Control +100
Power Door Locks +105
Power Sunroof +275
Power Windows +120

MX6 1995

No changes for 1995.

RATINGS (SCALE OF 1-10)

Overall	Safety	Reliability	Performance	Comfort	Value
7.4	7.9	8.3	9	7.9	4

Category F	Trade-in Value	Market Value
2 Dr LS Cpe	9490	11865
2 Dr STD Cpe	7340	9175

OPTIONS FOR MX6

Auto 4-Speed Transmission +355
Air Conditioning[Std on LS] +380
Aluminum/Alloy Wheels +140
Anti-Lock Brakes +330
Keyless Entry System +80

Don't forget to refer to the Mileage Adjustment Table at the back of this book!

 © 1999 by Edmund Publications Corporation

Model Description	Trade-in Value	Market Value

Leather Seats +325
Power Sunroof[Std on LS] +310
Rear Spoiler +130

PROTEGE 1995

Totally redesigned, the Protege grows substantially in interior volume. Has ten more cubic feet of volume than Honda Civic. Dual airbags are finally added. ABS is standard on ES trim level; optional on LX.

RATINGS (SCALE OF 1-10)

Overall	Safety	Reliability	Performance	Comfort	Value
N/A	N/A	8.4	7.8	7.4	5.8

Category E

Model	Trade-in Value	Market Value
4 Dr DX Sdn	5005	6500
4 Dr ES Sdn	6475	8405
4 Dr LX Sdn	5660	7350

OPTIONS FOR PROTEGE

Auto 4-Speed Transmission +355
Air Conditioning[Std on ES] +370
Aluminum/Alloy Wheels +145
AM/FM Stereo Tape[Opt on DX] +140
Anti-Lock Brakes[Opt on LX] +320
Power Moonroof +265

RX-7 1995

CFC-free refrigerant is added to air conditioner. Touring package ousted. Red leather option dumped. Last year for RX-7.

Category F

Model	Trade-in Value	Market Value
2 Dr STD Turbo Rotary Cpe	18025	22530

OPTIONS FOR RX-7

Auto 4-Speed Transmission +400
Leather Seats +325
Power Sunroof +310
Rear Spoiler +130
Sport Suspension +120

1994 MAZDA

323 1994

No changes. Final year for homely, slow-selling hatchback.

RATINGS (SCALE OF 1-10)

Overall	Safety	Reliability	Performance	Comfort	Value
6.3	4.3	7.4	6.8	7	5.8

Category E

Model	Trade-in Value	Market Value
2 Dr STD Hbk	2940	3920

OPTIONS FOR 323

Auto 4-Speed Transmission +280
Air Conditioning +300
AM/FM Stereo Tape +115
Power Steering +95
Velour/Cloth Seats +30

626 1994

Passenger airbag added. LX-V6 debuts. Four-cylinder models get new Ford transmission for smoother shifting than previous Mazda unit. ABS becomes standard on ES trim level, as well as leather seats and power sunroof.

RATINGS (SCALE OF 1-10)

Overall	Safety	Reliability	Performance	Comfort	Value
7.6	7.9	8	9	8.1	5.2

Category D

Model	Trade-in Value	Market Value
4 Dr DX Sdn	6045	7750
4 Dr ES Sdn	8135	10425
4 Dr LX Sdn	6085	7800
4 Dr LX V6 Sdn	7245	9290

OPTIONS FOR 626

Auto 4-Speed Transmission +295
Air Conditioning[Opt on DX] +315
Aluminum/Alloy Wheels +165
Anti-Lock Brakes[Std on ES] +355
Cruise Control[Opt on DX] +90
Heated Power Mirrors[Std on ES] +35
Power Door Locks[Opt on DX] +100
Power Drivers Seat[Std on ES] +125
Power Moonroof[Std on ES] +310
Power Windows[Opt on DX] +100

929 1994

Trimmed to one model. Console cupholder added, height-adjustable seatbelts debut, and a limited-slip differential is included with the Cold Package. Premium Package adds remote keyless entry. New alloy wheels are standard.

RATINGS (SCALE OF 1-10)

Overall	Safety	Reliability	Performance	Comfort	Value
N/A	N/A	8.1	8.2	8.4	5.6

Category D

Model	Trade-in Value	Market Value
4 Dr STD Sdn	9645	12365

OPTIONS FOR 929

Premium Package +790
Cellular Telephone +360
Compact Disc Changer +245
Leather Seats +410
Power Drivers Seat +125
Power Passenger Seat +140

B-SERIES PICKUP 1994

Mazda revises the styling of Ford's Ranger, slaps its name on the tailgate, and has a new compact pickup to sell. Base, SE and LE trim levels are offered in two- or four-wheel drive and two bodystyles.

Don't forget to refer to the Mileage Adjustment Table at the back of this book!

 © 1999 by Edmund Publications Corporation

Model Description	Trade-in Value	Market Value

RATINGS (SCALE OF 1-10)

Overall	Safety	Reliability	Performance	Comfort	Value
N/A	4.9	7.7	7.2	7.3	N/A

Category G		
2 Dr B2300 Std Cab SB	5055	6320
2 Dr B2300 Ext Cab SB	5900	7375
2 Dr B2300 SE Std Cab SB	5860	7325
2 Dr B3000 4WD Std Cab SB	6885	8610
2 Dr B3000 4WD Ext Cab SB	7150	8940
2 Dr B3000 SE Std Cab SB	5960	7450
2 Dr B3000 SE Ext Cab SB	6645	8305
2 Dr B3000 SE Std Cab LB	5830	7285
2 Dr B4000 LE Ext Cab SB	7185	8980
2 Dr B4000 LE 4WD Ext Cab SB	8080	10105
2 Dr B4000 SE Std Cab LB	5865	7330
2 Dr B4000 SE 4WD Std Cab SB	6955	8695
2 Dr B4000 SE 4WD Ext Cab SB	7455	9315

OPTIONS FOR B-SERIES PICKUP

Auto 4-Speed Transmission[Std on B4000 LE] +535
Air Conditioning +300
Aluminum/Alloy Wheels +130
AM/FM Compact Disc Playr +145
Bed Liner +105
Power Door Locks[Std on B4000 LE] +85
Power Steering[Opt on B2300 Std Cab SB] +105
Power Windows[Std on B4000 LE] +85

MIATA 1994

Dual airbags arrive, and a 1.8-liter four cylinder making 128 horsepower replaces the original 1.6-liter engine. Sharp new alloy wheels debut. Optional automatic gets electronic shift controls. Larger diameter disc brakes are standard. Bigger gas tank added. New R package debuts with sportier suspension. Superman Blue replaced by Montego Blue. M-Edition is painted Montego Blue with chromed alloys.

RATINGS (SCALE OF 1-10)

Overall	Safety	Reliability	Performance	Comfort	Value
7.5	6.9	8.5	9.2	7.1	5.9

Category F		
2 Dr MX-5 Conv	7840	9925
2 Dr MX-5 M-Edition Conv	8550	10820

OPTIONS FOR MIATA

Auto 4-Speed Transmission +245
Air Conditioning[Opt on MX-5] +310
Aluminum/Alloy Wheels[Opt on MX-5] +115
Anti-Lock Brakes +270
Compact Disc W/fm/tape +195
Cruise Control[Opt on MX-5] +80
Hardtop Roof +510
Leather Seats[Opt on MX-5] +265
Limited Slip Diff[Opt on MX-5] +140
Power Antenna[Opt on MX-5] +30
Power Steering[Opt on MX-5] +135
Power Windows[Opt on MX-5] +85
Rear Spoiler +105
Sport Suspension +95

MPV 1994

Side-door impact beams are added. Four-wheel disc brakes are new. Standard tire size increases.

RATINGS (SCALE OF 1-10)

Overall	Safety	Reliability	Performance	Comfort	Value
7.2	6.3	8	7.8	7.6	6.3

Category G		
2 Dr STD Pass. Van	7105	8880
2 Dr STD 4WD Pass. Van	8525	10660

OPTIONS FOR MPV

6 cyl 3.0 L Engine[Opt on 2WD] +225
Luxury Package +490
7 Passenger Seating[Opt on 2WD] +200
Air Conditioning +300
Aluminum/Alloy Wheels +130
AM/FM Compact Disc Playr +145
Camper/Towing Package +105
Cruise Control +80
Dual Air Conditioning +375
Keyless Entry System +75
Leather Seats +285
Power Door Locks +85
Power Moonroof +325
Power Windows +85

MX3 1994

Base model gets more power, and a passenger airbag is added. ABS can be ordered on base models for the first time. Can't get ABS on GS with automatic transmission. Base cars can be equipped with power sunroof. Both models get new wheels.

Category E		
2 Dr GS Hbk	6365	8490
2 Dr STD Hbk	5445	7260

OPTIONS FOR MX3

Auto 4-Speed Transmission +325
Air Conditioning +300
Aluminum/Alloy Wheels +120
Anti-Lock Brakes +265
Cruise Control +80
Power Door Locks +85
Power Sunroof +225
Power Windows +100

MX6 1994

Passenger airbag debuts. Air conditioning and power sunroof become standard on LS.

Don't forget to refer to the Mileage Adjustment Table at the back of this book!

 © 1999 by Edmund Publications Corporation

Model Description	Trade-in Value	Market Value

RATINGS (SCALE OF 1-10)

Overall	Safety	Reliability	Performance	Comfort	Value
7.2	7.9	7.9	9	7.9	3.3

Category F

Model Description	Trade-in Value	Market Value
2 Dr LS Cpe	7780	9850
2 Dr STD Cpe	6435	8145

OPTIONS FOR MX6

Auto 4-Speed Transmission +295
Air Conditioning[Std on LS] +310
Aluminum/Alloy Wheels +115
Anti-Lock Brakes +270
Leather Seats +265
Power Drivers Seat +90
Power Sunroof[Std on LS] +255
Rear Spoiler +105

NAVAJO 1994

Restyled alloy wheels are new. Since Ford won't give Mazda a four-door version of Explorer to sell, this is final year for Navajo as Mazda picks up its toys and goes home to pout.

RATINGS (SCALE OF 1-10)

Overall	Safety	Reliability	Performance	Comfort	Value
7.5	5.7	7.4	7.6	8.3	8.4

Category G

Model Description	Trade-in Value	Market Value
2 Dr DX 4WD Utility	7545	9430
2 Dr LX 4WD Utility	8695	10870

OPTIONS FOR NAVAJO

Auto 4-Speed Transmission +330
Air Conditioning +300
AM/FM Compact Disc Playr +145
Camper/Towing Package +105
Cruise Control +80
Leather Seats +285
Limited Slip Diff +100
Luggage Rack +60
Moonroof +130
Power Drivers Seat +105

PROTEGE 1994

Minor styling revisions include new grille, headlamps, hood and front fascia.

RATINGS (SCALE OF 1-10)

Overall	Safety	Reliability	Performance	Comfort	Value
N/A	N/A	8.4	8.2	7.4	5.3

Category E

Model Description	Trade-in Value	Market Value
4 Dr DX Sdn	3895	5190
4 Dr LX Sdn	4485	5980
4 Dr Special Sdn	3570	4755

OPTIONS FOR PROTEGE

Auto 4-Speed Transmission +285
Air Conditioning +300
Aluminum/Alloy Wheels +120
AM/FM Stereo Tape[Opt on DX] +115
Power Door Locks[Opt on DX] +85
Power Sunroof +225
Power Windows[Opt on DX] +100
Tilt Steering Wheel[Opt on DX] +55

RX-7 1994

Dual airbags appear, and softer suspension settings are available. Seatbacks get map pockets, and power windows have a driver express-down feature.

Category F

Model Description	Trade-in Value	Market Value
2 Dr STD Turbo Rotary Cpe	14205	17980

OPTIONS FOR RX-7

Auto 4-Speed Transmission +335
R-2 Package +555
Touring Package +410
AM/FM Compact Disc Playr +185
Bose Sound System +190
Leather Seats +265
Power Moonroof +265
Rear Spoiler +105
Sport Suspension +95

1993 MAZDA

323 1993

No changes.

RATINGS (SCALE OF 1-10)

Overall	Safety	Reliability	Performance	Comfort	Value
6.2	4.3	7.2	6.8	7	5.7

Category E

Model Description	Trade-in Value	Market Value
2 Dr SE Hbk	3020	4140
2 Dr STD Hbk	2715	3720

OPTIONS FOR 323

Auto 4-Speed Transmission +220
Air Conditioning +245
AM/FM Stereo Tape +95
Power Steering +75

626 1993

Completely redesigned for 1993. First import-badged car to be classified domestic by EPA. Driver airbag is standard, and ABS is optional. Top-end ES model gets 2.5-liter V6 engine. DX and LX powered by four-cylinder motor.

RATINGS (SCALE OF 1-10)

Overall	Safety	Reliability	Performance	Comfort	Value
7.2	6.1	7.9	9	8.1	5.1

Category D

Model Description	Trade-in Value	Market Value
4 Dr DX Sdn	4605	6060
4 Dr ES Sdn	6220	8180
4 Dr LX Sdn	4740	6240

Don't forget to refer to the Mileage Adjustment Table at the back of this book!

© 1999 by Edmund Publications Corporation

OPTIONS FOR 626

Auto 4-Speed Transmission +240
Air Conditioning[Opt on DX] +255
Alarm System[Opt on LX] +170
Aluminum/Alloy Wheels[Opt on LX] +135
AM/FM Compact Disc Playr +170
Anti-Lock Brakes +290
Compact Disc W/fm/tape +290
Cruise Control[Opt on DX] +75
Leather Seats +335
Power Door Locks[Opt on DX] +80
Power Drivers Seat +105
Power Moonroof +255
Power Windows[Opt on DX] +80

929 — 1993

Glass moonroof replaces steel offering. Revised alloy wheels, optional wood trim and optional power passenger's seat are new for 1993.

RATINGS (SCALE OF 1-10)

Overall	Safety	Reliability	Performance	Comfort	Value
N/A	N/A	7.8	8.2	8.4	5.4

Category D	Trade-in Value	Market Value
4 Dr STD Sdn	7920	10420

OPTIONS FOR 929

Premium Package +420
Compact Disc Changer +200
Leather Seats +335
Power Passenger Seat +115
Premium Sound System +105

B-SERIES PICKUP — 1993

No changes.

Category G	Trade-in Value	Market Value
2 Dr B2200 Ext Cab SB	4880	6255
2 Dr B2200 Std Cab SB	3905	5005
2 Dr B2200 Std Cab LB	3935	5040
2 Dr B2600i Ext Cab SB	4970	6375
2 Dr B2600i 4WD Ext Cab SB	6080	7795
2 Dr B2600i 4WD Std Cab SB	5785	7415

OPTIONS FOR B-SERIES PICKUP

Auto 4-Speed Transmission +240
Air Conditioning +245
Aluminum/Alloy Wheels +105
AM/FM Stereo Tape +75
Bed Liner +85
Chrome Wheels +75
Power Steering[Std on B2600i,Ext Cab] +85
Rear Step Bumper +45

MIATA — 1993

Limited Edition available with black paint and red leather interior; just 1,500 were produced. Yellow dropped from paint roster. Tan roof and leather interior optional on red and white cars. A 130-watt Sensory Sound System is newly optional.

RATINGS (SCALE OF 1-10)

Overall	Safety	Reliability	Performance	Comfort	Value
7.3	6.2	8.5	8.8	7.1	6

Category F	Trade-in Value	Market Value
2 Dr MX-5 Conv	6435	8355
2 Dr MX-5 Limited Conv	7195	9345

OPTIONS FOR MIATA

Auto 4-Speed Transmission +225
Air Conditioning[Opt on MX-5] +250
Aluminum/Alloy Wheels[Opt on MX-5] +95
AM/FM Compact Disc Playr +150
Anti-Lock Brakes[Opt on MX-5] +220
Cruise Control[Opt on MX-5] +65
Hardtop Roof +415
Leather Seats[Opt on MX-5] +215
Limited Slip Diff[Opt on MX-5] +115
Power Steering[Opt on MX-5] +110
Power Windows[Opt on MX-5] +70

MPV — 1993

Keyless entry system added to options list. Driver airbag added midyear.

RATINGS (SCALE OF 1-10)

Overall	Safety	Reliability	Performance	Comfort	Value
7	5.3	8.1	7.8	7.6	6.3

Category G	Trade-in Value	Market Value
2 Dr STD Pass. Van	6315	8100
2 Dr STD Cargo Van	5130	6580
2 Dr STD 4WD Pass. Van	6835	8765

OPTIONS FOR MPV

6 cyl 3.0 L Engine[Opt on 2WD] +200
Air Conditioning +245
Aluminum/Alloy Wheels[Opt on 2WD] +105
Camper/Towing Package +85
Compact Disc W/fm/tape +205
Cruise Control +65
Dual Air Conditioning +305
Keyless Entry System +60
Leather Seats +235
Power Door Locks +70
Power Moonroof +265
Power Windows +70

MX3 — 1993

A cassette stereo is made standard, and Laguna Blue Metallic is a new color.

Category E	Trade-in Value	Market Value
2 Dr GS Hbk	5170	7080
2 Dr Special Hbk	5460	7480
2 Dr STD Hbk	4140	5670

Don't forget to refer to the Mileage Adjustment Table at the back of this book!

 © 1999 by Edmund Publications Corporation

Model Description	Trade-in Value	Market Value

OPTIONS FOR MX3

Auto 4-Speed Transmission +220
Air Conditioning +245
Aluminum/Alloy Wheels[Opt on STD] +95
AM/FM Compact Disc Playr +145
Anti-Lock Brakes +215
Cruise Control[Opt on GS] +65
Power Door Locks[Opt on GS,STD] +70
Power Sunroof[Opt on GS] +185
Power Windows[Opt on GS,STD] +80

MX6 — 1993

All-new this year, sporting dramatically swept bodywork and a speedy LS model with 2.5-liter V6 engine. EPA says MX-6 is a domestic car. Driver airbag standard, while ABS is optional.

RATINGS (SCALE OF 1-10)

Overall	Safety	Reliability	Performance	Comfort	Value
N/A	N/A	7.5	9	7.9	4.8

Category F

Model Description	Trade-in Value	Market Value
2 Dr LS Cpe	6130	7960
2 Dr STD Cpe	5025	6530

OPTIONS FOR MX6

Auto 4-Speed Transmission +245
Air Conditioning +250
Aluminum/Alloy Wheels[Std on LS] +95
AM/FM Compact Disc Playr +150
Anti-Lock Brakes +220
Leather Seats +215
Power Drivers Seat +70
Power Sunroof +205
Rear Spoiler +85

NAVAJO — 1993

Four-wheel ABS is newly standard.

RATINGS (SCALE OF 1-10)

Overall	Safety	Reliability	Performance	Comfort	Value
7.5	5	7.4	7.6	8.3	9.4

Category G

Model Description	Trade-in Value	Market Value
2 Dr DX 4WD Utility	6350	8145
2 Dr LX 4WD Utility	6805	8725

OPTIONS FOR NAVAJO

Auto 4-Speed Transmission +270
Navajo LX Leather Pkg +490
Air Conditioning +245
AM/FM Compact Disc Playr +115
Camper/Towing Package +85
Cruise Control +65
Leather Seats +235
Luggage Rack +45
Power Drivers Seat +85
Sunroof +90

PROTEGE — 1993

Trim and equipment revisions.

RATINGS (SCALE OF 1-10)

Overall	Safety	Reliability	Performance	Comfort	Value
N/A	N/A	8.2	8.2	7.4	5.7

Category E

Model Description	Trade-in Value	Market Value
4 Dr DX Sdn	3335	4570
4 Dr LX Sdn	3785	5185

OPTIONS FOR PROTEGE

Auto 4-Speed Transmission +220
Air Conditioning +245
Aluminum/Alloy Wheels +95
AM/FM Stereo Tape[Opt on LX] +95
Power Sunroof +185
Tilt Steering Wheel[Opt on DX] +45

RX-7 — 1993

All-new supercar designed with a singular purpose: speed. Convertible dropped. 2+2 version canceled. Twin-turbo rotary engine is standard. Driver airbag and ABS are standard.

Category F

Model Description	Trade-in Value	Market Value
2 Dr STD Turbo Rotary Cpe	11560	15010

OPTIONS FOR RX-7

Auto 4-Speed Transmission +260
R-1 Package +370
Touring Pkg +350
AM/FM Compact Disc Playr +150
Bose Sound System +155
Leather Seats +215
Power Sunroof +205
Premium Sound System +125
Rear Spoiler +85

1992 MAZDA

323 — 1992

New taillights debut.

RATINGS (SCALE OF 1-10)

Overall	Safety	Reliability	Performance	Comfort	Value
6.1	4.3	6.9	6.8	7	5.5

Category E

Model Description	Trade-in Value	Market Value
2 Dr SE Hbk	2265	3235
2 Dr STD Hbk	2095	2995

OPTIONS FOR 323

Auto 4-Speed Transmission +170
Air Conditioning +200
AM/FM Stereo Tape +75
Power Steering +60
Rear Window Wiper +30

Don't forget to refer to the Mileage Adjustment Table at the back of this book!

© 1999 by Edmund Publications Corporation

Model Description	Trade-in Value	Market Value

626 1992

Touring Sedan is dropped.

Category D

Model Description	Trade-in Value	Market Value
4 Dr DX Sdn	3575	4830
4 Dr LX Sdn	3925	5305

OPTIONS FOR 626

Auto 4-Speed Transmission +195
Air Conditioning +210
Aluminum/Alloy Wheels +110
AM/FM Stereo Tape[Opt on DX] +90
Anti-Lock Brakes +235
Cruise Control[Opt on DX] +60
Power Moonroof +205

929 1992

Completely redesigned. Dual airbags and antilock brakes are standard.

RATINGS (SCALE OF 1-10)

Overall	Safety	Reliability	Performance	Comfort	Value
N/A	N/A	7.7	8.2	8.4	5.9

Category D

Model Description	Trade-in Value	Market Value
4 Dr STD Sdn	6745	9115

OPTIONS FOR 929

Compact Disc Changer +165
Leather Seats +275
Power Moonroof +205
Power Passenger Seat +95
Premium Sound System +85

B-SERIES PICKUP 1992

New steering wheel and minor trim changes. Extended-cab models get new rear lap/shoulder seatbelts.

Category G

Model Description	Trade-in Value	Market Value
2 Dr B2200 Std Cab SB	3345	4460
2 Dr B2200 Ext Cab SB	4160	5545
2 Dr B2200 Std Cab LB	3335	4450
2 Dr B2600i Ext Cab SB	4180	5570
2 Dr B2600i Std Cab SB	3395	4525
2 Dr B2600i 4WD Std Cab SB	5045	6725
2 Dr B2600i 4WD Ext Cab SB	5445	7260

OPTIONS FOR B-SERIES PICKUP

Auto 4-Speed Transmission +195
Air Conditioning +200
Aluminum/Alloy Wheels +85
AM/FM Stereo Tape +60
Bed Liner +70
Chrome Wheels +60
Power Steering[Std on B2600i,Ext Cab] +70
Rear Step Bumper +35

MIATA 1992

Silver paint dropped in favor of yellow and black. Remote trunk release added. Optional hardtop gets rear window defogger. Brilliant Black special edition available.

RATINGS (SCALE OF 1-10)

Overall	Safety	Reliability	Performance	Comfort	Value
6.9	6.2	8.3	8.8	7.1	4.4

Category F

Model Description	Trade-in Value	Market Value
2 Dr MX-5 Conv	5560	7410

OPTIONS FOR MIATA

Auto 4-Speed Transmission +185
Package C +185
Air Conditioning +205
Aluminum/Alloy Wheels +75
AM/FM Compact Disc Playr +120
Anti-Lock Brakes +180
Cruise Control +50
Hardtop Roof +340
Leather Seats +175
Limited Slip Diff +90
Power Steering +90
Power Windows +55
Premium Sound System +100

MPV 1992

Eight-passenger seating and power moonroof added to options list. Five-speed manual transmission dropped. V6 engine gets five additional horsepower. New alloy wheels debut.

RATINGS (SCALE OF 1-10)

Overall	Safety	Reliability	Performance	Comfort	Value
7.3	4.9	7.6	7.8	7.6	8.4

Category G

Model Description	Trade-in Value	Market Value
2 Dr STD Pass. Van	4950	6600
2 Dr STD Cargo Van	3365	4490
2 Dr STD 4WD Pass. Van	6100	8135

OPTIONS FOR MPV

6 cyl 3.0 L Engine[Opt on 2WD] +185
Luxury Package +425
Air Conditioning +200
Aluminum/Alloy Wheels[Opt on 2WD] +85
AM/FM Compact Disc Playr +95
Camper/Towing Package +70
Cruise Control +50
Dual Air Conditioning +250
Leather Seats +190
Power Door Locks +55
Power Moonroof +220
Power Windows +60

Don't forget to refer to the Mileage Adjustment Table at the back of this book!

 © 1999 by Edmund Publications Corporation

Model Description	Trade-in Value	Market Value

MX3 1992

All-new sport coupe takes over where Honda CRX left off. A 1.8-liter V6 engine, the industry's smallest, is standard on GS models. ABS optional on GS.

Category E

Model	Trade-in	Market
2 Dr GS Hbk	3990	5700
2 Dr STD Hbk	3150	4500

OPTIONS FOR MX3

Auto 4-Speed Transmission +170
Air Conditioning +200
Aluminum/Alloy Wheels[Std on GS] +80
AM/FM Compact Disc Playr +115
Anti-Lock Brakes +175
Cruise Control +55
Power Door Locks +55
Power Sunroof +150
Power Windows +65

MX6 1992

No changes.

Category F

Model	Trade-in	Market
2 Dr DX Cpe	3350	4465
2 Dr LX Cpe	3710	4950

OPTIONS FOR MX6

Auto 4-Speed Transmission +195
Air Conditioning +205
Aluminum/Alloy Wheels[Opt on LX] +75
Cruise Control[Opt on DX] +50
Power Sunroof +170
Rear Spoiler[Std on GT] +70

NAVAJO 1992

A base model joins the lineup, called DX. Upper trim level becomes LX. Two-wheel drive is now available in either trim level.

RATINGS (SCALE OF 1-10)

Overall	Safety	Reliability	Performance	Comfort	Value
6.9	5.1	7.1	7.6	8.3	6.4

Category G

Model	Trade-in	Market
2 Dr DX Utility	4270	5695
2 Dr DX 4WD Utility	4910	6545
2 Dr LX Utility	5115	6815
2 Dr LX 4WD Utility	5450	7265

OPTIONS FOR NAVAJO

Auto 4-Speed Transmission +210
Air Conditioning +200
AM/FM Stereo Tape +60
Camper/Towing Package +70
Cruise Control +50
Leather Seats +190
Luggage Rack +40
Moonroof +90
Power Drivers Seat +70

PROTEGE 1992

New taillights are added, and the all-wheel drive model is dropped.

RATINGS (SCALE OF 1-10)

Overall	Safety	Reliability	Performance	Comfort	Value
N/A	N/A	8	8.2	7.4	5.6

Category E

Model	Trade-in	Market
4 Dr DX Sdn	2535	3620
4 Dr LX Sdn	3015	4310

OPTIONS FOR PROTEGE

Auto 4-Speed Transmission +170
Air Conditioning +200
Aluminum/Alloy Wheels +80
AM/FM Stereo Tape[Opt on DX] +75
Power Steering[Opt on DX] +60
Power Sunroof +150
Tilt Steering Wheel[Opt on DX] +35

1991 MAZDA

323 1991

No changes.

RATINGS (SCALE OF 1-10)

Overall	Safety	Reliability	Performance	Comfort	Value
6	4.3	6.8	6.8	7	5

Category E

Model	Trade-in	Market
2 Dr SE Hbk	1965	2885
2 Dr STD Hbk	1745	2565

OPTIONS FOR 323

Auto 4-Speed Transmission +140
Air Conditioning +165
AM/FM Stereo Tape +60
Power Steering +50

626 1991

New option packages added.

Category D

Model	Trade-in	Market
4 Dr DX Sdn	2795	3830
4 Dr GT Turbo Hbk	3225	4420
4 Dr LE Sdn	3445	4720
4 Dr LX Sdn	3130	4290
4 Dr LX Hbk	3205	4390

OPTIONS FOR 626

Auto 4-Speed Transmission +145
Air Conditioning[Std on LE] +170
Aluminum/Alloy Wheels[Opt on LX] +90
AM/FM Stereo Tape[Opt on DX] +75
Anti-Lock Brakes +195
Cruise Control[Opt on DX] +50
Power Sunroof[Std on LE] +150
Premium Sound System +70

Don't forget to refer to the Mileage Adjustment Table at the back of this book!

 © 1999 by Edmund Publications Corporation

Model Description	Trade-in Value	Market Value

929 1991

Lace alloys standard on all models. Two new option packages are available.

Category D		
4 Dr S Sdn	4525	6200
4 Dr STD Sdn	4175	5720

OPTIONS FOR 929

Compact Disc W/fm/tape +195
Leather Seats +225
Power Passenger Seat +75

B-SERIES PICKUP 1991

Four-wheel drive models get new grille and fender flares. Regular cab models get headrests.

Category G		
2 Dr B2200 Std Cab SB	2810	3795
2 Dr B2200 Ext Cab SB	3510	4745
2 Dr B2200 Std Cab LB	2620	3545
2 Dr B2600i Std Cab SB	2850	3855
2 Dr B2600i Ext Cab SB	3530	4770
2 Dr B2600i 4WD Ext Cab SB	4705	6355
2 Dr B2600i 4WD Std Cab SB	4070	5500

OPTIONS FOR B-SERIES PICKUP

Auto 4-Speed Transmission +160
Air Conditioning +165
Aluminum/Alloy Wheels +70
AM/FM Stereo Tape +50
Bed Liner +55
Chrome Wheels +50
Power Steering[Std on B2600i,Ext Cab] +55
Rear Step Bumper +30

MIATA 1991

Special edition painted British Racing Green; 4,000 units produced. ABS is a new option.

RATINGS (SCALE OF 1-10)

Overall	Safety	Reliability	Performance	Comfort	Value
6.9	6	7.6	8.8	7.1	4.8

Category F		
2 Dr MX-5 Conv	5255	7005
2 Dr MX-5 Special Conv	5515	7350

OPTIONS FOR MIATA

Auto 4-Speed Transmission +115
Air Conditioning[Opt on MX-5] +170
Aluminum/Alloy Wheels +65
Anti-Lock Brakes +145
Cruise Control[Opt on MX-5] +40
Hardtop Roof +280
Limited Slip Diff[Opt on MX-5] +75
Power Steering[Opt on MX-5] +75
Power Windows[Opt on MX-5] +45

MPV 1991

Luxury package with lace alloy wheels, leather seats and two-tone paint debuts.

RATINGS (SCALE OF 1-10)

Overall	Safety	Reliability	Performance	Comfort	Value
7.2	4.9	7.4	7.8	7.6	8.3

Category G		
2 Dr STD Pass. Van	4010	5420
2 Dr STD Cargo Van	2855	3855
2 Dr STD 4WD Pass. Van	5040	6815

OPTIONS FOR MPV

6 cyl 3.0 L Engine[Opt on 2WD] +145
Auto 4-Speed Transmission[Std on Cargo Van, 4WD] +145
Value Pkg +545
Air Conditioning +165
Aluminum/Alloy Wheels[Opt on 2WD] +70
AM/FM Compact Disc Playr +80
Camper/Towing Package[Opt on 2WD] +60
Cruise Control +45
Dual Air Conditioning +205
Leather Seats +155
Luggage Rack +30
Power Door Locks +45
Power Windows +50
Premium Sound System +75

MX6 1991

GT 4WS dropped.

Category F		
2 Dr DX Cpe	3070	4095
2 Dr GT Turbo Cpe	3650	4870
2 Dr LE Cpe	3555	4740
2 Dr LX Cpe	3330	4440

OPTIONS FOR MX6

Auto 4-Speed Transmission +145
Air Conditioning[Std on LE] +170
Aluminum/Alloy Wheels[Opt on LX] +65
AM/FM Compact Disc Playr +100
Anti-Lock Brakes +145
Cruise Control[Opt on DX] +40
Power Sunroof[Std on LE] +140
Rear Spoiler[Opt on DX,LX] +55

NAVAJO 1991

Reskinned two-door Ford Explorer gives Mazda its first sport-utility vehicle. Single trim level with 4WD and rear antilock brakes available.

RATINGS (SCALE OF 1-10)

Overall	Safety	Reliability	Performance	Comfort	Value
6.7	5	6.5	7.6	8.3	6.3

Don't forget to refer to the Mileage Adjustment Table at the back of this book!

 © 1999 by Edmund Publications Corporation

Model Description	Trade-in Value	Market Value
Category G		
2 Dr STD 4WD Utility	4955	6700

OPTIONS FOR NAVAJO

Auto 4-Speed Transmission +175
Air Conditioning +165
Aluminum/Alloy Wheels +70
AM/FM Stereo Tape +50
Camper/Towing Package +60
Cruise Control +45
Leather Seats +155
Luggage Rack +30
Sunroof +60
Tilt Steering Wheel +35

PROTEGE 1991

No changes.

RATINGS (SCALE OF 1-10)

Overall	Safety	Reliability	Performance	Comfort	Value
N/A	N/A	7.9	8.2	7.4	5

Model Description	Trade-in Value	Market Value
Category E		
4 Dr DX Sdn	2160	3175
4 Dr LX Sdn	2530	3720

OPTIONS FOR PROTEGE

Auto 4-Speed Transmission +140
Air Conditioning +165
Aluminum/Alloy Wheels +65
AM/FM Stereo Tape[Std on LX] +60
Power Steering[Opt on DX] +50
Power Sunroof +120
Tilt Steering Wheel[Opt on DX] +30

RX-7 1991

Lineup trimmed to three models: base, Turbo and convertible. ABS is standard on Turbo. A driver airbag is standard on the convertible.

Model Description	Trade-in Value	Market Value
Category F		
2 Dr STD Rotary Conv	6825	9105
2 Dr STD Rotary Cpe	4950	6600
2 Dr Turbo Rotary Cpe	6575	8765

OPTIONS FOR RX-7

Auto 4-Speed Transmission +150
Cruise Control[Std on Turbo,Conv] +40
Leather Seats[Std on Conv] +145
Power Sunroof[Opt on STD] +140
Premium Sound System[Opt on STD] +85
Tilt Steering Wheel[Opt on STD] +35

1990 MAZDA

323 1990

Completely redesigned, 323 is available as hatchback only.

RATINGS (SCALE OF 1-10)

Overall	Safety	Reliability	Performance	Comfort	Value
6	4.3	6.7	6.8	7	5.4

Model Description	Trade-in Value	Market Value
Category E		
2 Dr SE Hbk	1765	2715
2 Dr STD Hbk	1620	2495

OPTIONS FOR 323

Auto 4-Speed Transmission +115
Air Conditioning +135
AM/FM Stereo Tape +50
Power Steering +40

626 1990

Some production moved to Michigan plant that produces MX-6 and Ford Probe. A new grille, alloy wheels, taillights, upholstery, and steering wheel debut.

Model Description	Trade-in Value	Market Value
Category D		
4 Dr DX Sdn	2480	3445
4 Dr GT Turbo Hbk	2900	4025
4 Dr LX Hbk	2630	3655
4 Dr LX Sdn	2630	3650

OPTIONS FOR 626

Auto 4-Speed Transmission +120
Air Conditioning +140
Aluminum/Alloy Wheels[Std on GT] +75
AM/FM Compact Disc Playr +95
Anti-Lock Brakes +155
Cruise Control[Opt on DX] +40
Power Sunroof +120

929 1990

A new sport version called 929 S arrives with more power, upgraded suspension and standard ABS. A new grille, new bumpers and lower bodyside molding are added. All 929s get two-tone paint.

Model Description	Trade-in Value	Market Value
Category D		
4 Dr S Sdn	3710	5155
4 Dr STD Sdn	3500	4860

OPTIONS FOR 929

AM/FM Compact Disc Playr +95
Anti-Lock Brakes[Std on S] +155
Leather Seats +185

B-SERIES PICKUP 1990

New five-spoke alloys debut on options list. 2.6-liter engine is optional on 2WD models. Rear wheel ABS now standard. LE-5 replaces LX model.

Model Description	Trade-in Value	Market Value
Category G		
2 Dr B2200 Std Cab SB	2505	3480
2 Dr B2200 Ext Cab SB	2900	4030
2 Dr B2200 Std Cab LB	2460	3420
2 Dr B2600i Ext Cab SB	3130	4350
2 Dr B2600i Std Cab SB	2655	3690

Don't forget to refer to the Mileage Adjustment Table at the back of this book!

 © 1999 by Edmund Publications Corporation

Model Description	Trade-in Value	Market Value
2 Dr B2600i 4WD Std Cab SB	3670	5100
2 Dr B2600i 4WD Ext Cab SB	4055	5630

OPTIONS FOR B-SERIES PICKUP

Auto 4-Speed Transmission +115
LE5 Luxury Package +135
Air Conditioning +135
Aluminum/Alloy Wheels +55
AM/FM Stereo Tape +40
Power Steering[Opt on B2200] +45

MIATA 1990

The love affair begins. 116 horsepower from 1.6-liter inline four. Driver airbag is standard. Available in red, white, blue and silver.

RATINGS (SCALE OF 1-10)

Overall	Safety	Reliability	Performance	Comfort	Value
7.3	5.6	8	8.8	7.1	6.9

Category F

Model Description	Trade-in Value	Market Value
2 Dr MX-5 Conv	4650	6205

OPTIONS FOR MIATA

Auto 4-Speed Transmission +120
Air Conditioning +140
Aluminum/Alloy Wheels +50
AM/FM Compact Disc Playr +80
Cruise Control +35
Hardtop Roof +230
Limited Slip Diff +60
Power Steering +60
Power Windows +35
Rear Spoiler +45

MPV 1990

A dual-range five-speed manual transmission is new.

RATINGS (SCALE OF 1-10)

Overall	Safety	Reliability	Performance	Comfort	Value
6.9	4.9	7.3	7.8	7.6	7

Category G

Model Description	Trade-in Value	Market Value
2 Dr LX Pass. Van	4245	5900
2 Dr STD Cargo Van	2510	3485
2 Dr STD Pass. Van	3900	5420
2 Dr STD 4WD Pass. Van	4410	6125

OPTIONS FOR MPV

6 cyl 3.0 L Engine[Std on 4WD] +145
Auto 4-Speed Transmission[Std on LX] +105
Air Conditioning +135
Aluminum/Alloy Wheels[Std on LX,4WD] +55
AM/FM Compact Disc Playr +65
Camper/Towing Package[Opt on 2WD] +50
Cruise Control[Std on LX] +35
Dual Air Conditioning +165
Power Door Locks[Std on LX] +40
Power Windows[Std on LX] +40

MX6 1990

No changes.

Category F

Model Description	Trade-in Value	Market Value
2 Dr 4WS Turbo Cpe	3500	4670
2 Dr DX Cpe	2700	3595
2 Dr GT Turbo Cpe	3215	4285
2 Dr LX Cpe	2860	3810

OPTIONS FOR MX6

Auto 4-Speed Transmission +120
Air Conditioning +140
Aluminum/Alloy Wheels[Opt on DX,LX] +50
AM/FM Compact Disc Playr +80
Anti-Lock Brakes +120
Cruise Control[Opt on DX] +35
Power Sunroof[Std on 4WS] +115
Rear Spoiler[Opt on LX] +45

PROTEGE 1990

Formerly the 323 sedan, this redesigned model is available in two trim levels.

RATINGS (SCALE OF 1-10)

Overall	Safety	Reliability	Performance	Comfort	Value
N/A	N/A	7.7	8.2	7.4	5.9

Category E

Model Description	Trade-in Value	Market Value
4 Dr LX Sdn	1920	2955
4 Dr SE Sdn	1730	2660

OPTIONS FOR PROTEGE

Auto 4-Speed Transmission +115
Air Conditioning +135
Aluminum/Alloy Wheels +50
AM/FM Stereo Tape +50
Cruise Control +35
Power Steering[Opt on SE] +40
Power Sunroof +100

RX-7 1990

No changes.

Category F

Model Description	Trade-in Value	Market Value
2 Dr GTU Rotary Cpe	3640	4855
2 Dr GTUs Rotary Cpe	3735	4975
2 Dr GXL Rotary Cpe	4080	5440
2 Dr 2+2 GXL Rotary Cpe	4080	5440
2 Dr STD Rotary Conv	5790	7715
2 Dr Turbo Rotary Cpe	4960	6615

OPTIONS FOR RX-7

Auto 3-Speed Transmission +100
Auto 4-Speed Transmission +125
Air Conditioning[Opt on GTU,GTUs,STD] +140
AM/FM Compact Disc Playr +80
Leather Seats[Std on STD] +120
Power Sunroof[Opt on GTU] +115

Don't forget to refer to the Mileage Adjustment Table at the back of this book!

 © 1999 by Edmund Publications Corporation

Model Description	Trade-in Value	Market Value

1989 MAZDA

323 — 1989

Station wagon and GT sedan are axed from the lineup.

Category E

4 Dr LX Sdn	1270	2080
2 Dr SE Hbk	1210	1985
4 Dr SE Sdn	1270	2080
2 Dr STD Hbk	1195	1960
4 Dr STD Sdn	1260	2065

OPTIONS FOR 323

Auto 4-Speed Transmission +95
Air Conditioning +110
Aluminum/Alloy Wheels +45
AM/FM Stereo Tape +40
Cruise Control +30
Power Door Locks +30
Power Steering[Std on LX] +35
Power Windows +35
Sunroof +45

626 — 1989

Four-wheel steering is dropped from lineup. ABS is optional on turbocharged Touring Sedan.

Category D

4 Dr DX Sdn	1980	2870
4 Dr LX Sdn	2095	3040
4 Dr Touring Hbk	2130	3090
4 Dr Touring Turbo Hbk	2690	3895

OPTIONS FOR 626

Auto 4-Speed Transmission +95
Air Conditioning +115
Aluminum/Alloy Wheels[Std on Turbo] +60
AM/FM Compact Disc Playr +75
Anti-Lock Brakes +130
Cruise Control[Opt on DX] +35
Power Sunroof[Std on Turbo] +100
Premium Sound System +45

929 — 1989

Power moonroof and power driver's seat are made standard. Five-speed manual transmission dropped. ABS is optional.

Category D

4 Dr STD Sdn	2665	3860

OPTIONS FOR 929

AM/FM Compact Disc Playr +75
Anti-Lock Brakes +130
Leather Seats +150

B-SERIES PICKUP — 1989

Four-wheel drive models get more powerful 2.6-liter engine.

Category G

2 Dr B2200 Ext Cab SB	2360	3420
2 Dr B2200 Std Cab SB	1935	2805
2 Dr B2200 Std Cab LB	2095	3040
2 Dr B2200 LX Ext Cab SB	2565	3720
2 Dr B2200 SE5 Ext Cab SB	2415	3500
2 Dr B2200 SE5 Std Cab SB	1975	2860
2 Dr B2200 SE5 Std Cab LB	2140	3105
2 Dr B2600i 4WD Std Cab SB	2950	4275
2 Dr B2600i LX 4WD Ext Cab SB	3710	5375
2 Dr B2600i SE5 4WD Std Cab SB	2990	4330
2 Dr B2600i SE5 4WD Ext Cab SB	3510	5085

OPTIONS FOR B-SERIES PICKUP

Auto 4-Speed Transmission +85
Air Conditioning +110
AM/FM Stereo Tape +35
Cruise Control[Std on B2200 LX,B2600i LX] +30
Power Steering[Opt on B2200,B2200 SE5] +40

MPV — 1989

Mazda's first minivan debuts with rear-wheel drive and a 4WD option.

RATINGS (SCALE OF 1-10)

Overall	Safety	Reliability	Performance	Comfort	Value
6.7	4.6	7.2	7.8	7.6	6.4

Category G

2 Dr STD Pass. Van	2840	4120
2 Dr STD 4WD Pass. Van	4060	5880

OPTIONS FOR MPV

6 cyl 3.0 L Engine[Opt on 2WD] +135
Auto 4-Speed Transmission[Std on 4WD] +95
Luxury Package +110
Air Conditioning +110
Aluminum/Alloy Wheels[Opt on 2WD] +45
AM/FM Compact Disc Playr +50
Camper/Towing Package[Opt on 2WD] +40
Cruise Control +30
Dual Air Conditioning +135
Power Door Locks +30
Power Windows +30
Premium Sound System +50

MX6 — 1989

GT 4WS is added to the lineup; includes four-wheel steering. ABS is optional on GT models.

Category F

2 Dr DX Cpe	1960	2720
2 Dr GT Turbo Cpe	2300	3190
2 Dr LX Cpe	2225	3090

OPTIONS FOR MX6

Auto 4-Speed Transmission +95
Air Conditioning +115
Aluminum/Alloy Wheels[Opt on DX,LX] +40

Don't forget to refer to the Mileage Adjustment Table at the back of this book!

 © 1999 by Edmund Publications Corporation

Model Description	Trade-in Value	Market Value

Anti-Lock Brakes +100
Cruise Control[Opt on DX] +30
Power Sunroof[Std on 4WS] +90
Premium Sound System[Opt on DX,LX] +55
Rear Spoiler[Opt on LX] +40

RX-7 1989

1988 model carried over during first part of model year. Mild restyle, along with engine and transmission upgrades, accompany delayed 1989 version. ABS optional on GXL and Turbo.

Model Description	Trade-in Value	Market Value
Category F		
2 Dr 1989.5 Rotary Conv	4930	6850
2 Dr 1989.5 GTU-S Rotary Cpe	3140	4360
2 Dr 1989.5 Turbo Rotary Cpe	3635	5050

OPTIONS FOR RX-7
Auto 4-Speed Transmission +100
Air Conditioning[Opt on 1989.5 GTU] +115
AM/FM Compact Disc Playr +65
Cruise Control[Opt on 1989.5 GTU] +30
Leather Seats +95
Power Sunroof[Opt on 1989.5 GTU] +90

Edmund's Town Hall

Get answers from our editors, scope out smart shopping strategies and share your experiences in our new talk area. Just enter the following address in your web browser:

http://townhall.edmunds.com

Get a great used car and apply for financing *online* at a price you must see to believe!

http://www.edmunds.com

Don't forget to refer to the Mileage Adjustment Table at the back of this book!

 © 1999 by Edmund Publications Corporation

MERCEDES Germany

1997 Mercedes-Benz C230

1998 MERCEDES-BENZ

C-CLASS 1998

The C280 is the lucky recipient of Mercedes' new V-type engine technology, receiving a 2.8-liter unit for the engine bay. BabySmart car seats, Brake Assist and side airbags also debut on the C-Class this year.

C230

Category L

Model Description	Trade-in Value	Market Value
4 Dr STD Sdn	21625	25440

C280

Category L

Model Description	Trade-in Value	Market Value
4 Dr STD Sdn	24695	29050

OPTIONS FOR C-CLASS

Xenon Headlamps +800
Bose Sound System[Opt on C230] +460
Compact Disc Changer +975
Dual Power Seats[Opt on C230] +725
Heated Front Seats +385
Leather Seats +1015
Power Moonroof +745
Sport Suspension +135
Telescopic Steering Whl +155
Traction Control System +1330

CLK320 1998

Mercedes rolls out an all-new sport coupe that is an amalgamation of C- and SLK-Class technologies, with E-Class style up front. The CLK is infused with the same 3.2-liter V6 that has made its way into the ML320 and E320. Those who have spent an obscene amount of money on the BMW 840Ci must be scratching their heads at this one; the CLK cost half when new.

Category L

Model Description	Trade-in Value	Market Value
2 Dr STD Cpe	35815	42140

OPTIONS FOR CLK320

K2 Option Package +700
K4 Option Package +1340
Compact Disc Changer +975
Heated Front Seats +385
Power Moonroof +745

E-CLASS 1998

All-wheel drive comes to the Mercedes' E-Class lineup via the E320 sedan and all-new E320 wagon. Like the rest of Mercedes' model lineup, E-Class cars formerly powered by an inline-six engine now receive a more fuel efficient V6 unit that is also supposed to improve the cars' low-end torque. The 1998 E-Class cars receive the benefit of BabySmart airbags which are able to detect the presence of a Mercedes' car seat in the front passenger seat and disable the front passenger airbag. Brake Assist is also a new feature, which aids drivers' stopping distance in a panic stop situation.

E320

Category L

Model Description	Trade-in Value	Market Value
4 Dr STD Sdn	35105	41300
4 Dr STD Wgn	35685	41985

OPTIONS FOR E-CLASS

Elect. Stability Program +825
Option Package E1 +1000
Parktronic System +810
Xenon Headlamps +795
Bose Sound System +460
Compact Disc Changer +975
Heated Front Seats +385
Leather Seats[Opt on Wgn] +1015
Power Moonroof +745

ML320 1998

Mercedes enters the sport-ute fray with the introduction of the ML320. Designed from a clean sheet of paper, the ML320 offers the best of the car and truck worlds.

Category G

Model Description	Trade-in Value	Market Value
4 Dr STD 4WD Wgn	28110	34280

OPTIONS FOR ML320

M1 Option Package +1300
M4 Option Package +675
Compact Disc Changer +430
Dual Power Seats +525
Heated Front Seats +210
Leather Seats +640
Power Moonroof +735
Privacy Glass +225

Don't forget to refer to the Mileage Adjustment Table at the back of this book!

 © 1999 by Edmund Publications Corporation

SL-CLASS 1998

The bargain basement, ha ha, SL320 has been discontinued this year, leaving only the wallet busting SL500 and SL600. The big news is the $10,000 price reduction of the SL500; this car cost only $79,900 when new.

SL500

Category J

Model Description	Trade-in Value	Market Value
2 Dr STD Conv	61135	71085

OPTIONS FOR SL-CLASS

Adapt Damping System +3650
Removable Panorama Roof +2990
Xenon Headlamps +800
Heated Front Seats[Opt on SL500] +345
Traction Control System +1095

SLK 1998

Mercedes-Benz releases an all-new retractable-hardtop roadster. Powered by a supercharged 2.3-liter engine, which is hooked to a five-speed automatic transmission, the SLK races to 60 mph in just over seven seconds.

Category J

Model Description	Trade-in Value	Market Value
2 Dr STD Sprchgd Conv	33590	39060

OPTIONS FOR SLK

Compact Disc Changer +815
Heated Front Seats +345

1997 MERCEDES-BENZ

C-CLASS 1997

The C220 is replaced by a more powerful C230. The C36 gains more horsepower. All C-Class models have redesigned headlamps.

RATINGS (SCALE OF 1-10)

Overall	Safety	Reliability	Performance	Comfort	Value
7.9	7.5	9.4	8.6	8.1	5.8

C230

Category L

Model Description	Trade-in Value	Market Value
4 Dr STD Sdn	20235	24090

C280

Category L

Model Description	Trade-in Value	Market Value
4 Dr STD Sdn	24170	28770

C36

Category L

Model Description	Trade-in Value	Market Value
4 Dr STD Sdn	34795	41425

OPTIONS FOR C-CLASS

Bose Sound System[Opt on C230] +375
Cellular Telephone +650
Compact Disc Changer +795
Dual Power Seats[Opt on C230] +590
Leather Seats[Std on C36] +830
Limited Slip Diff +885
Power Moonroof[Std on C36] +610
Sport Suspension +110
Telescopic Steering Whl +125
Traction Control System +1085

E-CLASS 1997

The Mercedes-Benz E300D and E320 receive the driver-adaptable five-speed automatic transmission. The E-Class also has a smart sensor to determine if anyone is sitting in the passenger seat and to determine whether or not to deploy the air bag. The E420 can be had with a Sport Package.

RATINGS (SCALE OF 1-10)

Overall	Safety	Reliability	Performance	Comfort	Value
N/A	N/A	9.2	9.4	8.6	6.3

E300D

Category L

Model Description	Trade-in Value	Market Value
4 Dr STD Dsl Sdn	28925	34430

E320

Category L

Model Description	Trade-in Value	Market Value
4 Dr STD Sdn	32430	38610

E420

Category L

Model Description	Trade-in Value	Market Value
4 Dr STD Sdn	36010	42870

OPTIONS FOR E-CLASS

Option Package E4 +995
Sport Package E6 +1895
Xenon Headlamps +640
Bose Sound System[Std on E420] +375
Cellular Telephone +650
Chrome Wheels +995
Compact Disc Changer +795
Compact Disc W/fm/tape +495
Leather Seats[Opt on E300D] +830
Limited Slip Diff[Opt on E320] +885
Power Moonroof +610

S-CLASS 1997

It's a big year for the big Benz. After a few years of relatively minor changes, the S-Class gets its share of the fun that has been flying around the Stuttgart design studios. Side impact air bags debut in all S-Class cars this year. S-Class coupes get new front bumpers. All cars get new alloy wheels. A Parktronic system is available for those who aren't comfortable parking their $100,000 car in a narrow space. Mercedes' outstanding Automatic Slip Reduction (ASR) traction control system is finally available on the S320s. Lastly, a rain sensor system is now standard on all models. (It adjusts the speed of the wipers to the intensity of the rain.)

Don't forget to refer to the Mileage Adjustment Table at the back of this book!

 © 1999 by Edmund Publications Corporation

Model Description	Trade-in Value	Market Value
S320		
Category L		
4 Dr LWB Sdn	40630	48370
4 Dr SWB Sdn	40630	48370
S420		
Category L		
4 Dr STD Sdn	46115	54895
S500		
Category L		
2 Dr STD Cpe	61760	73525
4 Dr STD Sdn	54785	65220

OPTIONS FOR S-CLASS

Adapt Damping System +1520
Four Place Power Seating +3710
Parktronic System +650
Power Rear Seat Adjusters +1170
Xenon Headlamps +645
Auto Load Leveling[Opt on S320,S420] +730
Traction Control System[Opt on S420,S500] +1085

SL-CLASS 1997

A Panorama hardtop is now available, and it helps improve top-up visibility. ASR traction control is now standard on the SL320. A rain sensor is now standard on all models as well.

Model Description	Trade-in Value	Market Value
SL320		
Category J		
2 Dr STD Conv	51360	59720
SL500		
Category J		
2 Dr STD Conv	58170	67640

OPTIONS FOR SL-CLASS

Adapt Damping System +2940
Removable Panorama Roof +2380
Xenon Headlamps +645
Traction Control System[Opt on SL500] +895

1996 MERCEDES-BENZ

C-CLASS 1996

An infrared remote security system, dual cupholders in the console, a delayed headlamp dousing system, and reconfigured option packages mark the changes to the baby Benz.

RATINGS (SCALE OF 1-10)

Overall	Safety	Reliability	Performance	Comfort	Value
7.9	7.5	9.3	8.6	8.1	5.8

Model Description	Trade-in Value	Market Value
C220		
Category L		
4 Dr STD Sdn	18650	22205
C280		
Category L		
4 Dr STD Sdn	22270	26515
C36		
Category L		
4 Dr STD Sdn	31460	37455

OPTIONS FOR C-CLASS

Bose Sound System[Opt on C220] +305
Cellular Telephone +530
Compact Disc Changer +650
Leather Seats[Std on C36] +680
Limited Slip Diff +720
Power Moonroof[Std on C36] +500
Power Passenger Seat +220
Telescopic Steering Whl[Std on C36] +100
Traction Control System +890

E-CLASS 1996

All-new and sporting a face anybody's mother could love, the E-Class comes in three flavors: E300 Diesel, E320 and E420. A new front suspension and larger wheels and tires provide better handling response, while optional gas-discharge headlamps mark new technology. Side-impact airbags are included in the doors of all E-Class models. E420's can be had with ESP, which is a new safety system that makes sure the E420 is under control at all times. The E420 also gets a new five-speed transmission.

RATINGS (SCALE OF 1-10)

Overall	Safety	Reliability	Performance	Comfort	Value
N/A	N/A	8.8	9.4	8.6	5

Model Description	Trade-in Value	Market Value
E300D		
Category L		
4 Dr STD Dsl Sdn	26190	31180
E320		
Category L		
4 Dr STD Sdn	29400	35000

OPTIONS FOR E-CLASS

Xenon Headlamps +520
Bose Sound System +305
Cellular Telephone +530
Compact Disc Changer +650
Leather Seats[Std on E320] +680
Limited Slip Diff +720
Power Moonroof +500

S-CLASS 1996

No cosmetic improvements to the S-Class this year; everything new is under the skin. ESP is standard on the S600 and optional on all other models. ESP is a safety system designed to help the driver keep the S-Class under control at all times. V8 and V12 versions

Don't forget to refer to the Mileage Adjustment Table at the back of this book!

 © 1999 by Edmund Publications Corporation

get a new five-speed automatic, and all models get a standard power glass sunroof and smog sensing climate control system. The S350 Turbodiesel is history.

S320

Category L

4 Dr LWB Sdn	38070	45320
4 Dr SWB Sdn	38070	45320

S420

Category L

4 Dr STD Sdn	42770	50920

S500

Category L

2 Dr STD Cpe	55465	66030
4 Dr STD Sdn	49025	58360

OPTIONS FOR S-CLASS

Adapt Damping System +1390
Four Place Power Seating +2935
Rear Axle Level Control +485
Power Moonroof +500

SL-CLASS 1996

Tweaked styling and new alloys freshen the exterior of the SL roadster. Underneath, ESP keeps drivers on track in lousy driving conditions. It comes standard on the SL600; can be ordered for the SL320 and SL500. Side airbags are standard across the board. A five-speed automatic is included with SL500 and SL600. Cool gas-discharge headlamps are not available on the SL320.

SL320

Category J

2 Dr STD Conv	44120	52520

SL500

Category J

2 Dr STD Conv	52180	62120

OPTIONS FOR SL-CLASS

Adapt Damping System +2260
Slip Control +900

1995 MERCEDES-BENZ

C-CLASS 1995

The AMG-prepared C36 is introduced to the C-Class family. This little mighty mouse runs circles around its lesser siblings and gives BMW M3 owners something to think about. Only 300 copies of the C36 are available in 1995; get one if you can.

RATINGS (SCALE OF 1-10)

Overall	Safety	Reliability	Performance	Comfort	Value
7.6	8.1	8.6	8.6	8.1	4.3

C220

Category L

4 Dr STD Sdn	16475	20095

C280

Category L

4 Dr STD Sdn	18690	22790

C36

Category L

4 Dr STD Sdn	29220	35635

OPTIONS FOR C-CLASS

Option Package C1 +1100
Bose Sound System[Opt on C220] +250
Leather Seats[Std on C36] +555
Limited Slip Diff +590
Power Moonroof +405
Power Passenger Seat[Opt on C220] +180
Telescopic Steering Whl +85
Traction Control System +725

E-CLASS 1995

No changes for the last year of this rendition of the E-Class.

RATINGS (SCALE OF 1-10)

Overall	Safety	Reliability	Performance	Comfort	Value
N/A	N/A	8.9	8.8	8.4	5.2

E300D

Category L

4 Dr STD Dsl Sdn	20625	25150

E320

Category L

2 Dr STD Cpe	30095	36700
2 Dr STD Conv	39825	48565
4 Dr STD Sdn	23980	29240
4 Dr STD Wgn	24990	30475

E420

Category L

4 Dr STD Sdn	26220	31975

OPTIONS FOR E-CLASS

Option Package E1 +1040
Option Package E2 +480
Sportline Pkg +485
Cellular Telephone +435
Compact Disc Changer +530
Leather Seats[Opt on E300D,Wgn] +555
Limited Slip Diff +590
Premium Sound System[Std on E420,Cpe] +355
Telescopic Steering Whl[Opt on E300D,Wgn] +85

S-CLASS 1995

Minuscule exterior changes and a drop in price are about the only changes to the S-Class.

Don't forget to refer to the Mileage Adjustment Table at the back of this book!

 © 1999 by Edmund Publications Corporation

Model Description	Trade-in Value	Market Value

S320
Category L

4 Dr LWB Sdn	32790	39985
4 Dr SWB Sdn	32095	39140

S420
Category L

4 Dr STD Sdn	34845	42490

S500
Category L

2 Dr STD Cpe	47495	57920
4 Dr STD Sdn	40995	49990

S600
Category L

2 Dr STD Cpe	59975	73140

OPTIONS FOR S-CLASS

Adapt Damping System +1135
Four Place Power Seating +2400
Rear Axle Level Control +395
Cellular Telephone +435
Power Moonroof +405

SL-CLASS 1995

Traction control is now standard on the SL320. Price cuts are the only other change for the Mercedes roadster.

SL320
Category J

2 Dr STD Conv	39410	47480

SL500
Category J

2 Dr STD Conv	44990	54205

SL600
Category J

2 Dr STD Conv	47560	57300

OPTIONS FOR SL-CLASS

Adapt Damping System +1845
Slip Control +735
Cellular Telephone +735

1994 MERCEDES-BENZ

C-CLASS 1994

This peppy replacement for the 190 is long-awaited. Longer and wider than the 190, the C-Class gives rear seat passengers more room. Standard on the C-Class are dual airbags, a wood-trimmed interior, four-wheel antilock brakes and a power sunroof. The C-Class cars are available in four- or six-cylinder flavors with a standard automatic transmission.

RATINGS (SCALE OF 1-10)

Overall	Safety	Reliability	Performance	Comfort	Value
7.9	8.1	8.5	8.6	8.1	6.1

C220
Category L

4 Dr STD Sdn	14760	18450

C280
Category L

4 Dr STD Sdn	16655	20820

OPTIONS FOR C-CLASS

Leather Seats +455
Limited Slip Diff +480
Power Moonroof +335
Power Passenger Seat[Opt on C220] +150
Premium Sound System +290
Traction Control System +595

E-CLASS 1994

In an effort at simplification, Mercedes renames its 300-Class, now calling it the E-Class. Like the new C-Class, the numeral after the E indicates the engine's size. Pretty cool, huh? Coupe, convertible, sedan and wagon body styles are still offered.

RATINGS (SCALE OF 1-10)

Overall	Safety	Reliability	Performance	Comfort	Value
N/A	N/A	8.8	8.8	8.4	5.2

E320
Category L

2 Dr STD Cpe	24790	30985
2 Dr STD Conv	37075	46345
4 Dr STD Wgn	20370	25465
4 Dr STD Sdn	19605	24510

E420
Category L

4 Dr STD Sdn	21370	26715

E500
Category L

4 Dr STD Sdn	36035	45045

OPTIONS FOR E-CLASS

Sportline Package +540
Leather Seats[Opt on Wgn] +455
Premium Sound System[Opt on E320 STD Sdn] +290
Sport Suspension +60
Tilt Steering Wheel[Opt on Wgn] +125
Traction Control System[Std on E500] +595

S-CLASS 1994

The big Benz gains Mercedes's new alphanumeric nomenclature that makes it easier to identify the vehicle family and engine size. Fuel economy is improved for

Don't forget to refer to the Mileage Adjustment Table at the back of this book!

 © 1999 by Edmund Publications Corporation

the S-Class, and all but the S600 switch to H-rated tires for increased traction in inclement weather.

S320

Category L

Model Description	Trade-in Value	Market Value
4 Dr STD Sdn	27475	34340

S350D

Category L

Model Description	Trade-in Value	Market Value
4 Dr STD Turbodsl Sdn	25610	32010

S420

Category L

Model Description	Trade-in Value	Market Value
4 Dr STD Sdn	29685	37105

S500

Category L

Model Description	Trade-in Value	Market Value
2 Dr STD Cpe	38895	48620
4 Dr STD Sdn	33180	41480

S600

Category L

Model Description	Trade-in Value	Market Value
2 Dr STD Cpe	50860	63575

OPTIONS FOR S-CLASS

Adapt Damping System +915
Four Place Seating +1815
Level Control Suspension +320
Rear Power Seatback +385
Cellular Telephone[Opt on S500] +355
Power Sunroof +340
Traction Control System[Opt on S320,S420] +595

SL-CLASS 1994

The SL300 becomes the SL320 as a new powerplant slips into the engine bay. Offering the same horsepower as the previous engine, the SL320 throws out considerably more torque than last year's model. A Bose stereo is added to the standard equipment lists of the entire SL-Class.

SL320

Category J

Model Description	Trade-in Value	Market Value
2 Dr STD Conv	34280	41805

SL500

Category J

Model Description	Trade-in Value	Market Value
2 Dr STD Conv	40590	49500

SL600

Category J

Model Description	Trade-in Value	Market Value
2 Dr STD Conv	47985	58520

OPTIONS FOR SL-CLASS

Adapt Damping System +1490
Removable Hard Top +2410
Traction Control System[Opt on SL320] +490

1993 MERCEDES-BENZ

190 1993

No changes for the little Mercedes that could; still a good car at a relatively good price. A new model replaces the 190 for 1994.

190E

Category L

Model Description	Trade-in Value	Market Value
4 Dr 2.6 Sdn	10815	13695
4 Dr STD Sdn	9680	12250

OPTIONS FOR 190

Auto 4-Speed Transmission +275
190E 2.6 Sportline Pkg +475
Auto Locking Differential +335
Cellular Telephone +290
Compact Disc W/fm/tape +220
Dual Power Seats[Opt on STD] +265
Leather Seats +370
Limited Slip Diff +395
Power Sunroof +275
Sport Suspension +50
Traction Control System +485

300 1993

All but the turbo models receive a larger engine. A driver airbag is finally standard on the 300-Class Mercedes. A 300 CE cabriolet model is brought into the fold; it has a power top and a pop-up roll bar similar to the one found on the SL-roadsters.

300CE

Category L

Model Description	Trade-in Value	Market Value
2 Dr STD Conv	34660	43870
2 Dr STD Cpe	23245	29420

300D

Category L

Model Description	Trade-in Value	Market Value
4 Dr STD Turbodsl Sdn	16590	21000

300E

Category L

Model Description	Trade-in Value	Market Value
4 Dr 2.8 Sdn	14210	17990
4 Dr 4matic 4WD Sdn	18110	22925
4 Dr STD Sdn	15920	20150

300SD

Category L

Model Description	Trade-in Value	Market Value
4 Dr STD Turbodsl Sdn	24515	31030

300SE

Category L

Model Description	Trade-in Value	Market Value
4 Dr STD Sdn	23810	30135

300SL

Category L

Model Description	Trade-in Value	Market Value
2 Dr STD Conv	30410	38495

Don't forget to refer to the Mileage Adjustment Table at the back of this book!

 © 1999 by Edmund Publications Corporation

Model Description	Trade-in Value	Market Value

300TE

Category L

4 Dr STD Wgn	18245	23095

OPTIONS FOR 300

Auto 5-Speed Transmission[Opt on 300SL] +335
300E Sportline Pkg +515
Adapt Damping System +950
Auto Locking Differential +335
CE Sportline Pkg +320
Four Place Seating +1355
Power Rear Seat Back +310
Rear Axle Level Cntrl Sus +260
AM/FM Compact Disc Playr +235
Cellular Telephone +290
Leather Seats[Opt on 300D,300TE,2.8] +370
Power Moonroof +270
Premium Sound System[Opt on 300D,2.8] +240
Sport Suspension +50
Third Seat +340
Traction Control System +485

400 — 1993

The 400SE becomes the 400SEL in order to compete with the longer wheelbase sedans from BMW.

400E

Category L

4 Dr STD Sdn	18180	23015

400SEL

Category L

4 Dr STD Sdn	25870	32745

OPTIONS FOR 400

Adapt Damping System +825
Four Place Seating +1570
Power Rear Seat Back +310
Rear Axle Level Cntrl Sus +260
Cellular Telephone +290
Compact Disc Changer +355
Power Moonroof +270
Traction Control System +485

500 — 1993

No changes to 500-Series models.

500E

Category L

4 Dr STD Sdn	29950	37910

500SEL

Category L

4 Dr STD Sdn	28340	35875

500SL

Category L

2 Dr STD Conv	34710	43940

OPTIONS FOR 500

Adapt Damping System +910
Four Place Seating +1355
Cellular Telephone +290
Power Moonroof +270

1992 MERCEDES-BENZ

190 — 1992

A sportline package is now available on the six-cylinder 190E 2.6. The package consists of go-fast goodies like V-rated tires, a sport-tuned suspension and quicker steering.

190E

Category L

4 Dr 2.6 Sdn	9410	12220
4 Dr STD Sdn	8340	10835

OPTIONS FOR 190

Auto 4-Speed Transmission +220
Sportline Pack +305
Auto Load Leveling +265
Dual Power Seats +215
Leather Seats +305
Power Sunroof +225

300 — 1992

No changes for 1992.

300CE

Category L

2 Dr STD Cpe	17505	22735

300D

Category L

4 Dr STD Turbodsl Sdn	13340	17325

300E

Category L

4 Dr 3.0 Sdn	14000	18180
4 Dr 4matic 4WD Sdn	15550	20195
4 Dr STD Sdn	12240	15895

300SD

Category L

4 Dr STD Turbodsl Sdn	20120	26125

300SE

Category L

4 Dr STD Sdn	20465	26580

300SL

Category L

2 Dr STD Conv	27565	35795

300TE

Category L

4 Dr 4matic 4WD Wgn	16865	21900
4 Dr STD Wgn	15175	19710

Don't forget to refer to the Mileage Adjustment Table at the back of this book!

 © 1999 by Edmund Publications Corporation

Model Description	Trade-in Value	Market Value

OPTIONS FOR 300

Auto 4-Speed Transmission[Opt on 300SL] +245
Adapt Damping System +760
Four Place Seating Pkg +1250
Rear Power Seats +250
Sportline Pkg +430
Alarm System[Opt on 300D,300E STD Sdn] +145
Auto Load Leveling[Std on 300TE] +265
Dual Air Bag Restraints[Std on 300SD,300SL] +165
Leather Seats[Opt on 300D,300TE,300E STD Sdn] +305
Power Sunroof +225
Premium Sound System[Opt on 300D,300E STD Sdn] +195
Third Seat +275

400 — 1992

A new model is introduced to the lineup of midsize Mercedes: the 400E. It offers V8 power, a first in this line of cars, and comes standard with an automatic transmission. Dual airbags are now standard on these pricey sedans, as are neat features like traction control, a five-speed automatic transmission, heated front seats, double paned side-windows, and a self-leveling system.

400E

Category L

4 Dr STD Sdn	15180	19715

400SE

Category L

4 Dr STD Sdn	22050	28635

OPTIONS FOR 400

Adapt Damping System +660
Four Place Seating Pkg +1250
Power Seatback Recliner +250
Auto Load Leveling +265
Power Passenger Seat +100
Power Sunroof +225
Traction Control System +395

500 — 1992

A new 500E model is introduced to the Mercedes top-drawer lineup.

500E

Category L

4 Dr STD Sdn	27030	35100

500SEL

Category L

4 Dr STD Sdn	24050	31230

500SL

Category L

2 Dr STD Conv	31225	40555

OPTIONS FOR 500

Adapt Damping System +725
Four Place Seating +1260
Air Bag Restraint[Std on 500E] +160
Cellular Telephone +235
Power Moonroof +220

1991 MERCEDES-BENZ

190 — 1991

A four-cylinder gas powered model is reintroduced to the 190 line-up.

190E

Category L

4 Dr 2.6 Sdn	8015	10550
4 Dr STD Sdn	6865	9035

OPTIONS FOR 190

Auto 4-Speed Transmission +90
Dual Power Seats[Opt on STD] +175
Leather Seats +250
Limited Slip Diff +265
Power Drivers Seat +85
Power Sunroof +185
Traction Control System +325

300 — 1991

No major changes for this recently overhauled Mercedes.

300CE

Category L

2 Dr STD Cpe	14940	19655

300D

Category L

4 Dr STD Turbodsl Sdn	10440	13740

300E

Category L

4 Dr 2.6 Sdn	10005	13165
4 Dr 4matic 4WD Sdn	13700	18025
4 Dr STD Sdn	11590	15250

300SE

Category L

4 Dr STD Sdn	12975	17070

300SEL

Category L

4 Dr STD Sdn	12925	17005

300SL

Category L

2 Dr STD Conv	25385	33405

300TE

Category L

4 Dr 4matic 4WD Wgn	14405	18955
4 Dr STD Wgn	13830	18195

Don't forget to refer to the Mileage Adjustment Table at the back of this book!

© 1999 by Edmund Publications Corporation

Model Description	Trade-in Value	Market Value

OPTIONS FOR 300

Auto 4-Speed Transmission[Opt on 300SL] +200
Adapt Damping System +755
Four Place Seating Pkg +615
Dual Air Bag Restraints[Std on 300SL] +135
Leather Seats[Opt on 300D,2.6,300E STD Sdn] +250
Power Sunroof +185
Premium Sound System[Opt on 300D,2.6,300E STD Sdn] +160
Special Factory Paint[Opt on 300D,2.6,300E STD Sdn] +90
Third Seat +225
Tilt Steering Wheel[Opt on 300D,2.6] +70

350 — 1991

No changes.

350SD

Category L

Model	Trade-in	Market
4 Dr STD Turbodsl Sdn	14860	19555

350SDL

Category L

Model	Trade-in	Market
4 Dr STD Turbodsl Sdn	14665	19295

OPTIONS FOR 350

Four Place Seating Pkg +615
Leather Seats +250
Power Sunroof +185

420 — 1991

No changes.

420SEL

Category L

Model	Trade-in	Market
4 Dr STD Sdn	14215	18705

OPTIONS FOR 420

Four Place Seating Pkg +615
Power Sunroof +185

500 — 1991

We wait in anticipation as Mercedes readies its new flagship. Unfortunately, there are no major changes in the interim.

500SL

Category L

Model	Trade-in	Market
2 Dr STD Conv	27990	36830

OPTIONS FOR 500

Adapt Damping System +755

560 — 1991

We wait in anticipation as Mercedes readies its new flagship. Unfortunately, there are no major changes in the interim.

560SEC

Category L

Model	Trade-in	Market
2 Dr STD Cpe	19840	26105

560SEL

Category L

Model	Trade-in	Market
4 Dr STD Sdn	15600	20525

OPTIONS FOR 560

Four Place Seating Pkg +475

1990 MERCEDES-BENZ

190 — 1990

No changes for the baby Benz.

190E

Category L

Model	Trade-in	Market
4 Dr STD Sdn	6685	9035

OPTIONS FOR 190

Auto 4-Speed Transmission +150
Dual Power Seats +145
Leather Seats +200
Power Sunroof +150

300 — 1990

Big changes for the midsized offering from Mercedes. The 260 is now called the Mercedes 300E 2.6 to indicate that it is indeed a 300 and not a 190. The 300CE gains a boost in horsepower by adding two more valves per cylinder. The central locking system will now handily close the windows and sunroof as well as lock the doors. The interior has been made more luxurious by adding more leather and wood to everything. SL Roadster is completely redesigned.

300CE

Category L

Model	Trade-in	Market
2 Dr STD Cpe	12955	17510

300E

Category L

Model	Trade-in	Market
4 Dr 2.6 Sdn	8265	11170
4 Dr STD Sdn	10060	13595

300SE

Category L

Model	Trade-in	Market
4 Dr STD Sdn	11285	15255

300SEL

Category L

Model	Trade-in	Market
4 Dr STD Sdn	11065	14955

300SL

Category L

Model	Trade-in	Market
2 Dr STD Conv	22465	30355

Don't forget to refer to the Mileage Adjustment Table at the back of this book!

 © 1999 by Edmund Publications Corporation

Model Description	Trade-in Value	Market Value

300TE

Category L

4 Dr STD Wgn	11595	15670

OPTIONS FOR 300

Auto 4-Speed Transmission[Opt on 300SL,300TE STD Wgn] +85
Four Place Seating Pkg +500
Air Bag Restraint[Std on 300SEL,300SL,2.6] +110
Alarm System[Opt on 2.6] +95
Leather Seats[Opt on 300D,300TE,2.6] +200
Power Drivers Seat[Opt on 300D,2.6] +70
Power Passenger Seat[Opt on 2.6] +65
Power Sunroof[Opt on 300TE] +150
Premium Sound System[Opt on 300E STD Sdn] +130
Special Factory Paint +75
Third Seat +185

420 — 1990

No major changes for 1990.

420SEL

Category L

4 Dr STD Sdn	11720	15835

OPTIONS FOR 420

Four Place Seating Pkg +500

500 — 1990

Goodness gracious, the roadsters sure look different than last year. Appealing to a more youthful audience, Mercedes ditched the long, sedate look in favor of an aerodynamic, almost racy sports car. Available with a 320-horsepower V8, this car is the most powerful in its class. The convertible top is entirely automatic and a pop-up roll bar will protect occupants in the event of a roll-over accident.

500SL

Category L

2 Dr STD Conv	26250	35475

OPTIONS FOR 500

Special Factory Paint +75

560 — 1990

The 560 coupe and sedan receive no changes.

560SEC

Category L

2 Dr STD Cpe	16755	22640

560SEL

Category L

4 Dr STD Sdn	13145	17760

OPTIONS FOR 560

Four Place Seating Pkg +385

1989 MERCEDES-BENZ

190 — 1989

The four-cylinder model has been dropped from the 190E line-up, leaving the 158-horsepower V6 as the only gas-powered engine available for this car. All 190s get new body-side moldings and restyled bumpers.

190E

Category L

4 Dr STD Sdn	6260	8575

OPTIONS FOR 190

Auto 4-Speed Transmission +125
Leather Seats +165
Power Drivers Seat +60
Power Passenger Seat +55
Power Sunroof +125

190D — 1989

Category L

4 Dr STD Dsl Sdn	6070	8310

OPTIONS FOR 190D

Leather Seats +165
Power Drivers Seat +60
Power Passenger Seat +55
Power Sunroof +125

260 — 1989

The availability of a passenger airbag is the biggest change for the 1989 260 Mercedes. Unfortunately, the manual transmission is no longer available; all models are now saddled with the four-speed automatic. Cold weather residents will appreciate the heated windshield wiper nozzles that aid the melting of snow and ice on freezing days.

260E

Category L

4 Dr STD Sdn	7035	9635

OPTIONS FOR 260

Dual Air Bag Restraints +90
Leather Seats +165
Power Drivers Seat +60
Power Passenger Seat +55
Power Sunroof +125

300 — 1989

The availability of a passenger airbag is the biggest change for the 1989 300 Mercedes. Unfortunately, the manual transmission is no longer available; all models are now saddled with the four-speed automatic. Cold weather residents will appreciate the heated windshield wiper nozzles that aid the melting of snow and ice on freezing days.

Don't forget to refer to the Mileage Adjustment Table at the back of this book!

 © 1999 by Edmund Publications Corporation

Model Description	Trade-in Value	Market Value
300CE		
Category L		
2 Dr STD Cpe	11025	15105
300E		
Category L		
4 Dr STD Sdn	8095	11090
300SE		
Category L		
4 Dr STD Sdn	9345	12800
300SEL		
Category L		
4 Dr STD Sdn	9650	13220
300TE		
Category L		
4 Dr STD Wgn	9305	12745

OPTIONS FOR 300

Four Place Seat Pkg +385
Leather Seats[Opt on 300E,300TE] +165
Power Sunroof +125
Premium Sound System +105
Third Seat +150

For a guaranteed low price on a new car in your area, call
1-800-CAR-CLUB

420 — 1989

A passenger airbag is a new option on the Mercedes 420; models with this feature gain a lockable center console as compensation for the loss of their glovebox. New exterior colors and the addition of an extra-supple leather interior round out the changes for Mercedes' luxury line.

Model Description	Trade-in Value	Market Value
420SEL		
Category L		
4 Dr STD Sdn	9785	13405

OPTIONS FOR 420

Four Place Seat Pkg +385
Compact Disc W/fm/tape +100
Power Sunroof +125

560 — 1989

A revised final-drive ratio is the only change to Mercedes aging SL roadster.

Model Description	Trade-in Value	Market Value
560SEC		
Category L		
2 Dr STD Cpe	13820	18930
560SEL		
Category L		
4 Dr STD Sdn	11325	15510
560SL		
Category L		
2 Dr STD Conv	18235	24980

Get a great used car and apply for financing *online* at a price you must see to believe!

http://www.edmunds.com

Don't forget to refer to the Mileage Adjustment Table at the back of this book!

 © 1999 by Edmund Publications Corporation

Model Description	Trade-in Value	Market Value

MERCURY USA

1995 Mercury Sable

1998 MERCURY

GRAND MARQUIS 1998

Vive le Grand Marquis! The last of the American rear-drive sedans gets substantial improvements this year, including a new instrument panel, new steering gear and an improved ride, thanks to a Watt's linkage suspension. All-speed traction control debuts this year as well.

Category B		
4 Dr GS Sdn	16910	20375
4 Dr LS Sdn	17970	21650

OPTIONS FOR GRAND MARQUIS

Aluminum/Alloy Wheels +275
AM/FM Compact Disc Playr +260
Anti-Lock Brakes +595
Climate Control for AC +145
Dual Power Seats +300
Keyless Entry System[Opt on GS] +145
Leather Seats +550
Traction Control System +150

MOUNTAINEER 1998

The Mountaineer gets minor front and rear styling tweaks as it enters its second year of production. In addition, a new model, with full-time four-wheel drive, receives the SOHC V6 and five-speed automatic transmission that became available on the Explorer last year.

Category H		
4 Dr STD Wgn	19630	23095
4 Dr STD 4WD Wgn	19945	23465

OPTIONS FOR MOUNTAINEER

8 cyl 5.0 L Engine +410
Chrome Wheels +245
Climate Control for AC +490
Compact Disc Changer +360
Compact Disc W/fm/tape +265
Dual Power Seats +380
Keyless Entry System +125
Leather Seats +860
Power Drivers Seat +225
Power Moonroof +805
Running Boards +245

MYSTIQUE 1998

The 1998 Mystique receives a freshened interior and exterior that includes new wheels and a new front end. Mechanical enhancements include 100,000-mile maintenance intervals for the 2.0-liter Zetec engine, improved manual transmission shifter feel, improved NVH and improved air conditioning performance. New interior pieces are intended to distinguish the Mystique from its otherwise-identical twin, the Ford Contour.

Category C		
4 Dr GS Sdn	9930	11965
4 Dr LS Sdn	10945	13185

OPTIONS FOR MYSTIQUE

Auto 4-Speed Transmission +675
Aluminum/Alloy Wheels[Opt on GS] +240
AM/FM Compact Disc Playr +320
Anti-Lock Brakes +520
Fog Lights[Opt on GS] +80
Keyless Entry System[Opt on GS] +155
Leather Seats +480
Power Drivers Seat[Opt on GS] +235
Power Moonroof +580

SABLE 1998

A mild facelift and fewer options are the only change to Mercury's mid-size sedan.

Category C		
4 Dr GS Sdn	12350	14880
4 Dr LS Sdn	13030	15700
4 Dr LS Wgn	13155	15850

OPTIONS FOR SABLE

6 cyl 3.0 L DOHC Engine +410
Aluminum/Alloy Wheels[Opt on GS] +240
Anti-Lock Brakes +520
Chrome Wheels +495
Climate Control for AC +150
Compact Disc Changer +430
Dual Power Seats +480
Heated Power Mirrors +115
Keyless Entry System[Opt on GS] +155
Leather Seats +480
Power Drivers Seat[Opt on GS] +235
Power Moonroof +580

Don't forget to refer to the Mileage Adjustment Table at the back of this book!

 © 1999 by Edmund Publications Corporation

Model Description	Trade-in Value	Market Value

TRACER 1998

No changes to Mercury's recently redesigned entry-level car.

Category E

4 Dr GS Sdn	7740	9440
4 Dr LS Sdn	9150	11160

OPTIONS FOR TRACER

Auto 4-Speed Transmission +675
Air Conditioning[Opt on GS] +675
Aluminum/Alloy Wheels +265
Anti-Lock Brakes +590
Cruise Control +185
Keyless Entry System[Opt on GS] +125
Power Door Locks +195
Power Mirrors[Opt on GS] +95
Power Windows +220
Rear Window Defroster[Opt on GS] +135
Tilt Steering Wheel +125

VILLAGER 1998

No changes to the 1998 Villager as Mercury readies a replacement.

Category G

2 Dr GS Cargo Van	15320	18235
2 Dr GS Pass. Van	15945	18985
2 Dr LS Pass. Van	19300	22975
2 Dr Nautica Pass. Van	20680	24615

OPTIONS FOR VILLAGER

7 Passenger Seating[Opt on GS] +450
Air Conditioning[Opt on GS] +675
Aluminum/Alloy Wheels[Opt on GS, LS] +285
Anti-Lock Brakes[Opt on GS] +515
Climate Control for AC +165
Compact Disc W/fm/tape +565
Cruise Control +175
Dual Air Conditioning +840
Dual Power Seats +525
Keyless Entry System +170
Leather Seats[Opt on LS] +640
Power Door Locks[Opt on GS] +190
Power Drivers Seat +235
Power Mirrors[Opt on GS] +110
Power Moonroof +735
Power Windows[Opt on GS] +195
Premium Sound System +300
Privacy Glass[Opt on GS] +225
Rear Window Defroster[Opt on GS] +140

1997 MERCURY

COUGAR 1997

Mercury gives you the chance to buy a special anniversary edition replete with plenty of badges, a special interior and a few luxury doo-dads.

RATINGS (SCALE OF 1-10)

Overall	Safety	Reliability	Performance	Comfort	Value
7.7	7.9	8.4	8	7.8	6.4

Category C

2 Dr XR7 Cpe	10395	12835

OPTIONS FOR COUGAR

8 cyl 4.6 L Engine +505
Aluminum/Alloy Wheels +195
AM/FM Compact Disc Playr +260
Anti-Lock Brakes +425
Cruise Control +140
Dual Power Seats +395
Keyless Entry System +130
Power Door Locks +160
Power Drivers Seat +195
Power Moonroof +475
Premium Sound System +270
Sport Suspension +115
Traction Control System +190

GRAND MARQUIS 1997

After a mild facelift last year, the Grand Marquis soldiers on with a few color changes, improved power steering and the addition of rear air suspension to the handling package.

RATINGS (SCALE OF 1-10)

Overall	Safety	Reliability	Performance	Comfort	Value
8.2	8.1	8.5	7.7	8.3	8.4

Category B

4 Dr GS Sdn	13240	16145
4 Dr LS Sdn	13425	16370

OPTIONS FOR GRAND MARQUIS

Handling Package +695
Aluminum/Alloy Wheels +225
Anti-Lock Brakes +485
Cruise Control +145
Keyless Entry System +120
Leather Seats +450
Power Door Locks +170
Premium Sound System +285
Traction Control System +120
Trip Computer +145

MOUNTAINEER 1997

The all-new Mercury Mountaineer is yet another entrant into the booming luxury sport-utility market. Based on the wildly successful Ford Explorer, the Mountaineer is intended to appeal to outdoor sophisticates rather than true roughnecks. Distinguishing characteristics of the Mountaineer include four-wheel antilock brakes, a pushrod V8 engine and optional all-wheel drive.

Don't forget to refer to the Mileage Adjustment Table at the back of this book!

 © 1999 by Edmund Publications Corporation

Model Description	Trade-in Value	Market Value

RATINGS (SCALE OF 1-10)

Overall	Safety	Reliability	Performance	Comfort	Value
8	7.8	8.5	7.8	7.3	8.8

Category H

Model Description	Trade-in Value	Market Value
4 Dr STD Wgn	16670	19845
4 Dr STD 4WD Wgn	17405	20720

OPTIONS FOR MOUNTAINEER

Camper/Towing Package +240
Child Seat (1) +135
Compact Disc Changer +295
Compact Disc W/fm/tape +215
Keyless Entry System +110
Leather Seats +700
Luggage Rack +90
Power Drivers Seat +185
Power Moonroof +660
Running Boards +200

MYSTIQUE 1997

The addition of a Spree Package for the GS model and the inclusion of a tilt steering wheel and standard trunk light are the only changes for the 1997 Mystique.

RATINGS (SCALE OF 1-10)

Overall	Safety	Reliability	Performance	Comfort	Value
7.7	7.1	8	8.4	7.9	6.9

Category C

Model Description	Trade-in Value	Market Value
4 Dr GS Sdn	7345	9065
4 Dr LS Sdn	8185	10105
4 Dr STD Sdn	7230	8925

OPTIONS FOR MYSTIQUE

6 cyl 2.5 L Engine +615
Auto 4-Speed Transmission +555
Air Conditioning +540
Aluminum/Alloy Wheels[Opt on GS] +195
AM/FM Compact Disc Playr +260
AM/FM Stereo Tape[Std on LS] +110
Anti-Lock Brakes +425
Cruise Control +140
Keyless Entry System +130
Leather Seats +390
Power Door Locks +160
Power Drivers Seat[Opt on GS] +195
Power Moonroof +475
Power Windows +205
Premium Sound System +270

SABLE 1997

The 1997 Sable LS can now be had with Ford's outstanding Mach audio system. Other changes, occurring at the end of the 1996 model year, include the addition of a mass airflow sensor to the Vulcan V6, and improvements to the Duratec V6 to improve responsiveness.

RATINGS (SCALE OF 1-10)

Overall	Safety	Reliability	Performance	Comfort	Value
7.8	7.1	7.9	7.8	8.1	8.2

Category C

Model Description	Trade-in Value	Market Value
4 Dr GS Sdn	9935	12265
4 Dr GS Wgn	10210	12605
4 Dr LS Sdn	11040	13625
4 Dr LS Wgn	11375	14040

OPTIONS FOR SABLE

Leather Bucket Seats +675
Aluminum/Alloy Wheels[Opt on GS] +195
AM/FM Stereo Tape[Opt on GS] +110
Anti-Lock Brakes +425
Child Seat (1) +80
Chrome Wheels +405
Compact Disc Changer +355
Cruise Control +140
Keyless Entry System +130
Leather Seats[Opt on GS] +390
Power Door Locks[Opt on GS] +160
Power Moonroof +475

TRACER 1997

The Mercury Tracer is totally redesigned this year with enhancements across the board. The most noticeable improvements are in the powertrain and in the ride quality. New sheetmetal gives the Tracer a rounder, more aerodynamic appearance as well. The speedy LTS sedan is discontinued.

RATINGS (SCALE OF 1-10)

Overall	Safety	Reliability	Performance	Comfort	Value
7.2	6.6	8.6	7.2	7.3	6.2

Category E

Model Description	Trade-in Value	Market Value
4 Dr GS Sdn	6250	7815
4 Dr LS Sdn	6685	8355
4 Dr LS Wgn	6660	8320

OPTIONS FOR TRACER

Auto 4-Speed Transmission +520
Air Conditioning +550
Aluminum/Alloy Wheels +215
AM/FM Stereo Tape +210
Anti-Lock Brakes +480
Child Seat (1) +80
Compact Disc Changer +380
Cruise Control +150
Keyless Entry System +100
Power Door Locks +160
Power Windows +180

VILLAGER 1997

For 1997, the Villager offers a few more luxury items to distinguish it from the Nissan Quest. Quad captain's chairs are a nice alternative to the middle-row bench,

Don't forget to refer to the Mileage Adjustment Table at the back of this book!

 © 1999 by Edmund Publications Corporation

and the addition of rear radio controls and rear air conditioning should also make rear seat passengers happy.

RATINGS (SCALE OF 1-10)

Overall	Safety	Reliability	Performance	Comfort	Value
7.8	6.9	8.6	7.3	7.5	8.8

Category G	Trade-in Value	Market Value
2 Dr GS Cargo Van	12310	14835
2 Dr GS Pass. Van	12475	15030
2 Dr LS Pass. Van	14590	17580
2 Dr Nautica Pass. Van	16470	19840

OPTIONS FOR VILLAGER

7 Passenger Seating[Opt on GS] +370
Air Conditioning[Opt on GS Cargo Van] +550
Aluminum/Alloy Wheels[Opt on GS] +235
Anti-Lock Brakes[Opt on GS] +420
Captain Chairs (4)[Opt on LS] +430
Child Seats (2) +175
Compact Disc W/fm/tape +465
Cruise Control +145
Dual Air Conditioning +685
Dual Power Seats +430
Keyless Entry System +140
Leather Seats[Opt on LS] +520
Luggage Rack[Opt on GS] +105
Power Door Locks[Opt on GS Cargo Van] +155
Power Drivers Seat +190
Power Moonroof +600
Power Windows[Opt on GS Cargo Van] +160
Premium Sound System +245

1996 MERCURY

COUGAR 1996

New styling and powertrain improvements highlight the 1996 Cougar. Some formerly standard equipment is now optional. New options include a revamped cruise control system and a Total Anti-theft System. Four new colors debut.

RATINGS (SCALE OF 1-10)

Overall	Safety	Reliability	Performance	Comfort	Value
7.6	7.9	7.8	8	7.8	6.6

Category C	Trade-in Value	Market Value
2 Dr XR7 Cpe	8715	11320

OPTIONS FOR COUGAR

AM/FM Compact Disc Playr +215
Anti-Lock Brakes +345
Chrome Wheels +330
Cruise Control +115
Keyless Entry System +105
Leather Seats +320
Power Door Locks +135
Power Drivers Seat +160
Power Moonroof +390
Power Passenger Seat +150
Premium Sound System +220
Traction Control System +155

GRAND MARQUIS 1996

This distant descendant of the Turnpike Cruiser gets engine and transmission upgrades, a new steering wheel and a new gas cap design. Passenger power lumbar support has been deleted.

RATINGS (SCALE OF 1-10)

Overall	Safety	Reliability	Performance	Comfort	Value
8.2	8.1	8.1	7.7	8.3	8.8

Category B	Trade-in Value	Market Value
4 Dr GS Sdn	11005	13760
4 Dr LS Sdn	11650	14565

OPTIONS FOR GRAND MARQUIS

Anti-Lock Brakes +395
Cruise Control +120
Keyless Entry System +100
Leather Steering Wheel +45
Power Door Locks +140
Power Passenger Seat +170
Premium Sound System +235

MYSTIQUE 1996

More rear seat room is the big story for Mystique in 1996. Gearshift effort has been improved on manual transmissions, a new Sport Appearance Package is available, and five new colors are on the palette. Alloy wheels have been restyled on LS models.

RATINGS (SCALE OF 1-10)

Overall	Safety	Reliability	Performance	Comfort	Value
7.6	7	7.7	8.4	7.9	6.9

Category C	Trade-in Value	Market Value
4 Dr GS Sdn	6390	8295
4 Dr LS Sdn	7075	9185

OPTIONS FOR MYSTIQUE

6 cyl 2.5 L Engine +550
Auto 4-Speed Transmission +425
Air Conditioning +445
AM/FM Compact Disc Playr +215
Anti-Lock Brakes +345
Cruise Control +115
Keyless Entry System +105
Leather Seats +320
Power Antenna[Opt on GS] +45
Power Door Locks +135
Power Drivers Seat[Opt on GS] +160
Power Moonroof +390
Power Windows +170

Don't forget to refer to the Mileage Adjustment Table at the back of this book!

 © 1999 by Edmund Publications Corporation

Model Description	Trade-in Value	Market Value

SABLE 1996

Fresh off the drawing boards for 1996, and it seems the drawing boards were poorly lit. Styling is heavy-handed and homely, but definitely not dull. Otherwise, the new Sable is an excellent car, powered by new engines, suspended by new components, and innovative in nearly every way. Longer and wider sedan and wagon bodystyles are offered in GS and LS trim.

RATINGS (SCALE OF 1-10)

Overall	Safety	Reliability	Performance	Comfort	Value
7.4	7.1	7.4	7.8	8.1	6.7

Category C		
4 Dr G Sdn	8365	10860
4 Dr GS Wgn	9025	11720
4 Dr GS Sdn	8400	10910
4 Dr LS Wgn	9910	12870
4 Dr LS Sdn	9635	12515

OPTIONS FOR SABLE

AM/FM Stereo Tape[Std on LS] +90
Anti-Lock Brakes +345
Child Seat (1) +65
Chrome Wheels +330
Compact Disc Changer +290
Cruise Control +115
Keyless Entry System +105
Leather Seats +320
Power Door Locks[Opt on GS] +135
Power Drivers Seat[Opt on GS] +160
Power Moonroof +390

TRACER 1996

Automatic transmission modifications make base Tracers more responsive, and the standard 1.9-liter engine now goes 100,000 miles between tune-ups. Last year's integrated child seat continues, and Trio models are now available in all colors, including a new one called Toreador Red.

RATINGS (SCALE OF 1-10)

Overall	Safety	Reliability	Performance	Comfort	Value
7.2	6.8	8.3	7.6	7.1	6.1

Category E		
4 Dr LTS Sdn	6725	8965
4 Dr STD Sdn	5495	7325
4 Dr STD Wgn	5065	6755

OPTIONS FOR TRACER

Auto 4-Speed Transmission +425
Air Conditioning +450
AM/FM Compact Disc Playr +260
Anti-Lock Brakes +395
Child Seat (1) +65
Cruise Control[Opt on STD] +120
Luggage Rack +70
Power Door Locks +130
Power Moonroof +325
Power Windows +145

VILLAGER 1996

A passenger-side airbag is installed in a redesigned dashboard for 1996, and fresh front and rear styling updates this versatile van. Villager also gets an optional integrated child seat, automatic climate control system, and remote keyless entry system. Substantial trim and functional changes make Villager competitive once again.

RATINGS (SCALE OF 1-10)

Overall	Safety	Reliability	Performance	Comfort	Value
7.7	7	8	7.3	7.5	8.6

Category G		
2 Dr GS Pass. Van	11280	14100
2 Dr GS Cargo Van	10835	13545
2 Dr LS Pass. Van	13250	16560
2 Dr Nautica Pass. Van	13475	16845

OPTIONS FOR VILLAGER

7 Passenger Seating[Opt on GS] +300
Air Conditioning[Opt on GS Cargo Van] +450
Captain Chairs (4)[Opt on LS] +350
Child Seats (2) +145
Compact Disc W/fm/tape +380
Cruise Control +115
Dual Air Conditioning +560
Keyless Entry System +115
Leather Seats[Opt on LS] +425
Luggage Rack[Opt on GS] +85
Power Door Locks[Opt on GS Cargo Van] +125
Power Drivers Seat +155
Power Moonroof +490
Power Passenger Seat +150
Power Windows[Opt on GS Cargo Van] +130
Premium Sound System +200

1995 MERCURY

COUGAR 1995

A Sport Appearance Package is offered to spruce up the Cougar with BBS wheels and a luggage rack. Unfortunately, the trunk-mounted CD-changer is deleted from the option list. Antilock brakes and a traction-lock axle are available as separate options for the first time this year.

RATINGS (SCALE OF 1-10)

Overall	Safety	Reliability	Performance	Comfort	Value
7.9	8.7	7.9	8	7.8	7.2

Category C		
2 Dr XR7 Cpe	7095	9340

Don't forget to refer to the Mileage Adjustment Table at the back of this book!

 © 1999 by Edmund Publications Corporation

Model Description	Trade-in Value	Market Value

OPTIONS FOR COUGAR

8 cyl 4.6 L Engine +275
AM/FM Compact Disc Playr +175
Anti-Lock Brakes +285
Climate Control for AC +80
Cruise Control +95
Keyless Entry System +85
Leather Seats +260
Power Door Locks +110
Power Drivers Seat +130
Power Moonroof +320
Power Passenger Seat +120
Premium Sound System +180

GRAND MARQUIS 1995

Updated styling and an increased number of convenience features improve upon last year's model. A battery saver shuts off power to accessories or lights ten minutes after the ignition is switched off. The mast antenna has been replaced by an integrated rear window antenna. Interior updates include a 12-volt outlet in a redesigned dashboard. Enlarged stereo controls improve ease of operation and bigger gauges improve the instrument panel.

RATINGS (SCALE OF 1-10)

Overall	Safety	Reliability	Performance	Comfort	Value
8.2	8.8	7.7	7.7	8.3	8.7

Category B	Trade-in Value	Market Value
4 Dr GS Sdn	9140	11715
4 Dr LS Sdn	9690	12420

OPTIONS FOR GRAND MARQUIS

Anti-Lock Brakes +325
Climate Control for AC +80
Cruise Control +95
Keyless Entry System +80
Leather Seats +300
Power Door Locks +115
Power Passenger Seat +140
Power Sunroof +520
Premium Sound System +190

MYSTIQUE 1995

Introduced to replace the aging Topaz, the Mystique is a virtual twin to the Ford Contour. Euro-styling combined with German engineering results in a $20,000 American car that can compete with import sedans that cost nearly twice as much. You may choose between two trim levels, the base GS or the more luxurious LS. A 170-horsepower V6 engine is optional.

RATINGS (SCALE OF 1-10)

Overall	Safety	Reliability	Performance	Comfort	Value
7.6	7.5	7	8.4	7.9	7.2

Category C	Trade-in Value	Market Value
4 Dr GS Sdn	5820	7660
4 Dr LS Sdn	5930	7800

OPTIONS FOR MYSTIQUE

6 cyl 2.5 L Engine +430
Auto 4-Speed Transmission +365
Air Conditioning +360
AM/FM Compact Disc Playr +175
Anti-Lock Brakes +285
Cruise Control +95
Keyless Entry System +85
Leather Seats +260
Power Door Locks +110
Power Drivers Seat[Opt on GS] +130
Power Moonroof +320
Power Windows +140
Premium Sound System +180

SABLE 1995

Last year for the Sable in its current form. New cylinder heads and crankshafts are intended to decrease engine noise by reducing vibration. Solar control window glass makes a brief appearance on the sedan and wagon.

RATINGS (SCALE OF 1-10)

Overall	Safety	Reliability	Performance	Comfort	Value
8	7.6	7.6	8	7.8	9

Category C	Trade-in Value	Market Value
4 Dr GS Wgn	6900	9080
4 Dr GS Sdn	6665	8770
4 Dr LS Sdn	7375	9700
4 Dr LS Wgn	7885	10375

OPTIONS FOR SABLE

6 cyl 3.8 L Engine +280
AM/FM Compact Disc Playr +175
Anti-Lock Brakes[Opt on GS] +285
Chrome Wheels +270
Cruise Control +95
Dual Power Seats +265
Keyless Entry System +85
Leather Seats +260
Power Door Locks[Opt on GS] +110
Power Moonroof +320
Power Windows[Opt on GS] +140

TRACER 1995

A passenger airbag is finally available for the Tracer. Unfortunately, some engineering genius decided to retain the annoying motorized shoulder belts. An integrated child seat is introduced as an optional safety feature. The Trio package is introduced, designed to give budget shoppers the option of purchasing some of the more popular LTS features such as the spoiler, aluminum wheels and leather-wrapped steering wheel.

Don't forget to refer to the Mileage Adjustment Table at the back of this book!

 © 1999 by Edmund Publications Corporation

Model Description	Trade-in Value	Market Value

RATINGS (SCALE OF 1-10)

Overall	Safety	Reliability	Performance	Comfort	Value
7.3	7.4	8	7.6	7.1	6.6

Category E		
4 Dr LTS Sdn	5590	7655
4 Dr STD Wgn	4505	6175
4 Dr STD Sdn	4700	6435

OPTIONS FOR TRACER

Auto 4-Speed Transmission +365
Air Conditioning +370
AM/FM Compact Disc Playr +215
Anti-Lock Brakes +320
Child Seat (1) +50
Cruise Control[Opt on STD] +100
Luggage Rack +60
Power Door Locks +105
Power Moonroof +265
Power Windows +120

VILLAGER 1995

No changes for the Villager.

RATINGS (SCALE OF 1-10)

Overall	Safety	Reliability	Performance	Comfort	Value
7.7	7	7.9	7.3	7.1	9

Category G		
2 Dr GS Pass. Van	9330	11810
2 Dr GS Cargo Van	8475	10730
2 Dr LS Pass. Van	11030	13965
2 Dr Nautica Pass. Van	11770	14895

OPTIONS FOR VILLAGER

Super Sound +385
7 Passenger Seating[Opt on GS] +245
Air Conditioning[Opt on GS Cargo Van] +370
Captain Chairs (4)[Opt on LS] +285
Compact Disc W/fm/tape +310
Cruise Control[Opt on GS Cargo Van] +95
Keyless Entry System +95
Leather Seats[Opt on LS] +350
Luggage Rack[Opt on GS] +70
Power Door Locks[Opt on GS Cargo Van] +105
Power Drivers Seat +130
Power Moonroof +400
Power Passenger Seat +125
Power Windows[Opt on GS Cargo Van] +105
Premium Sound System +165

1994 MERCURY

CAPRI 1994

A passenger airbag is added. A new suspension on the XR2 improves handling. Both trim levels get a freshened exterior. Slow sales make this the final year for this car.

Category F		
2 Dr STD Conv	4740	6235

OPTIONS FOR CAPRI

Auto 4-Speed Transmission +295
Air Conditioning +310
Aluminum/Alloy Wheels +115
AM/FM Stereo Tape[Opt on STD] +75
Cruise Control +80
Leather Seats +265
Power Door Locks +75

COUGAR 1994

Dual airbags are finally available on the Cougar. The standard four-speed automatic transmission gains electronic shift controls and an overdrive lockout switch. Optional traction control joins the lineup of safety features. Updated front and rear fascias, taillamps and headlights round out the changes.

RATINGS (SCALE OF 1-10)

Overall	Safety	Reliability	Performance	Comfort	Value
8	8.7	7.7	8	7.8	7.6

Category C		
2 Dr XR7 Cpe	6220	8405

OPTIONS FOR COUGAR

8 cyl 4.6 L Engine +210
Aluminum/Alloy Wheels +105
Anti-Lock Brakes +230
Climate Control for AC +65
Compact Disc Changer +195
Cruise Control +75
Keyless Entry System +70
Leather Seats +215
Power Door Locks +90
Power Drivers Seat +105
Power Moonroof +260
Power Passenger Seat +100
Premium Sound System +145
Traction Control System +105

GRAND MARQUIS 1994

The Grand Marquis passes the stringent 1997 side-impact standards this year. Wire-spoke wheelcovers are now part of the standard equipment package.

RATINGS (SCALE OF 1-10)

Overall	Safety	Reliability	Performance	Comfort	Value
8.1	8.1	8	7.7	8.3	8.7

Category B		
4 Dr GS Sdn	7185	9580
4 Dr LS Sdn	7655	10205

OPTIONS FOR GRAND MARQUIS

Anti-Lock Brakes +265
Cruise Control +80
Keyless Entry System +65

Don't forget to refer to the Mileage Adjustment Table at the back of this book!

© 1999 by Edmund Publications Corporation

Leather Seats +245
Power Door Locks +90
Power Passenger Seat +115
Premium Sound System +155
Rear Window Defroster +60
Traction Control System +65

SABLE 1994

Rear window defroster becomes standard equipment on the sedan and wagon. The wagon gets a standard rear window wiper as well. CFC-free air conditioning is introduced to the Sable.

RATINGS (SCALE OF 1-10)

Overall	Safety	Reliability	Performance	Comfort	Value
7.9	7.6	7.4	8	7.8	8.9

Category C

Model	Trade-in Value	Market Value
4 Dr GS Sdn	5470	7390
4 Dr GS Wgn	6265	8470
4 Dr LS Sdn	6335	8560
4 Dr LS Wgn	6585	8900

OPTIONS FOR SABLE

6 cyl 3.8 L Engine +205
AM/FM Compact Disc Playr +140
Anti-Lock Brakes[Opt on GS] +230
Cruise Control +75
Keyless Entry System +70
Leather Seats +215
Power Door Locks +90
Power Drivers Seat[Opt on GS] +105
Power Moonroof +260
Power Passenger Seat +100
Power Windows[Opt on GS] +115

TOPAZ 1994

The Topaz receives CFC-free air conditioning. This will be the last year for the Topaz; Mercury is replacing it with an all-new compact called the Mystique.

RATINGS (SCALE OF 1-10)

Overall	Safety	Reliability	Performance	Comfort	Value
6.9	5.4	7.6	7.6	7.1	6.9

Category C

Model	Trade-in Value	Market Value
2 Dr GS Sdn	3635	4915
4 Dr GS Sdn	3485	4710

OPTIONS FOR TOPAZ

6 cyl 3.0 L Engine +255
Auto 3-Speed Transmission +200
Air Bag Restraint +190
Air Conditioning +295
AM/FM Stereo Tape +60
Cruise Control +75
Power Door Locks +90
Power Drivers Seat +105
Power Windows +115
Tilt Steering Wheel +55

TRACER 1994

A driver's side airbag is introduced on all models. New alloy wheels and optional antilock brakes show up on the LTS.

RATINGS (SCALE OF 1-10)

Overall	Safety	Reliability	Performance	Comfort	Value
7	6.2	7.8	7.6	7.1	6.5

Category E

Model	Trade-in Value	Market Value
4 Dr LTS Sdn	4145	5925
4 Dr STD Sdn	3725	5325
4 Dr STD Wgn	3690	5270

OPTIONS FOR TRACER

Auto 4-Speed Transmission +295
Air Conditioning +300
AM/FM Compact Disc Playr +175
Anti-Lock Brakes +265
Cruise Control[Opt on STD] +80
Luggage Rack +50
Power Door Locks +85
Power Moonroof +215
Power Windows +100
Premium Sound System +125

VILLAGER 1994

A driver airbag is installed in the Villager and a special edition luxury model debuts. Borrowing the name of an upscale men's clothier, the Nautica edition of the Villager includes such niceties as two-tone paint, alloy wheels and leather upholstery; all tastefully done in blue and white befitting a nautical theme.

RATINGS (SCALE OF 1-10)

Overall	Safety	Reliability	Performance	Comfort	Value
7.5	7.1	7.6	7.3	7.1	8.5

Category G

Model	Trade-in Value	Market Value
2 Dr GS Pass. Van	7690	9985
2 Dr GS Cargo Van	6925	8995
2 Dr LS Pass. Van	8890	11545
2 Dr Nautica Pass. Van	9505	12345

OPTIONS FOR VILLAGER

Supersound Package +335
7 Passenger Seating[Opt on GS] +200
Air Conditioning[Opt on GS Cargo Van] +300
Captain Chairs (4)[Opt on LS] +235
Compact Disc W/fm/tape +255
Cruise Control[Opt on GS Cargo Van] +80
Dual Air Conditioning +375
Keyless Entry System +75
Leather Seats[Opt on LS] +285
Luggage Rack[Opt on GS] +60
Power Door Locks[Opt on GS Cargo Van] +85
Power Drivers Seat +105

Don't forget to refer to the Mileage Adjustment Table at the back of this book!

 © 1999 by Edmund Publications Corporation

Power Moonroof +325
Power Passenger Seat +100
Power Windows[Opt on GS Cargo Van] +85
Premium Sound System +135

1993 MERCURY

CAPRI 1993

A new radio is introduced as the only change on the 1993 Capri.

Category F

Model Description	Trade-in Value	Market Value
2 Dr STD Conv	3685	4915
2 Dr XR2 Turbo Conv	4390	5850

OPTIONS FOR CAPRI

Auto 4-Speed Transmission +220
Air Conditioning[Opt on STD] +250
Aluminum/Alloy Wheels[Opt on STD] +95
AM/FM Stereo Tape[Opt on STD] +60
Cruise Control[Opt on STD] +65
Hardtop Roof +415
Leather Seats +215
Premium Sound System +125

COUGAR 1993

The LS trim level is dropped in favor of the XR-7. The XR-7 is decontented for 1993, losing the V8 engine, optional limited-slip axle and antilock brakes from the standard equipment lists. Split-fold rear seats are no longer available.

RATINGS (SCALE OF 1-10)

Overall	Safety	Reliability	Performance	Comfort	Value
6.9	5.7	7	6.8	7.8	7.5

Category C

Model Description	Trade-in Value	Market Value
2 Dr XR7 Cpe	4910	6915

OPTIONS FOR COUGAR

8 cyl 5.0 L Engine +345
Aluminum/Alloy Wheels +85
AM/FM Compact Disc Playr +115
Anti-Lock Brakes +190
Cruise Control +65
Dual Power Seats +175
Keyless Entry System +55
Leather Seats +175
Power Door Locks +70
Power Moonroof +210
Premium Sound System +120

GRAND MARQUIS 1993

A passenger airbag, an overdrive-lockout selector on the automatic gearshift, a stainless steel exhaust system, an express-down driver's window, and dual front cupholders appear on the Grand Marquis's extensive standard equipment list this year.

RATINGS (SCALE OF 1-10)

Overall	Safety	Reliability	Performance	Comfort	Value
7.9	7.2	7.8	7.5	8.3	8.6

Category B

Model Description	Trade-in Value	Market Value
4 Dr GS Sdn	6000	8220
4 Dr LS Sdn	6385	8750

OPTIONS FOR GRAND MARQUIS

Aluminum/Alloy Wheels +100
Anti-Lock Brakes +215
Cruise Control +65
Keyless Entry System +55
Leather Seats +200
Power Door Locks +75
Power Passenger Seat +95
Premium Sound System +125
Traction Control System +55

SABLE 1993

The lower body-side cladding and bumpers become body colored for 1993. Bucket seats become an option on both body styles.

RATINGS (SCALE OF 1-10)

Overall	Safety	Reliability	Performance	Comfort	Value
7.6	7.5	6.7	8	7.8	8.2

Category C

Model Description	Trade-in Value	Market Value
4 Dr GS Wgn	4465	6285
4 Dr GS Sdn	4030	5680
4 Dr LS Wgn	5020	7065
4 Dr LS Sdn	4685	6600

OPTIONS FOR SABLE

6 cyl 3.8 L Engine +170
Aluminum/Alloy Wheels +85
AM/FM Compact Disc Playr +115
Anti-Lock Brakes +190
Cruise Control +65
Keyless Entry System +55
Leather Seats +175
Power Door Locks +70
Power Drivers Seat +85
Power Passenger Seat +80
Power Sunroof +210
Power Windows[Opt on GS] +90
Premium Sound System +120

TOPAZ 1993

Mercury offers only one trim level for the Topaz this year: the lowly GS. A leather-wrapped shift-knob and console mounted cupholders are intended to make us forget the absence of the nicer trim levels.

RATINGS (SCALE OF 1-10)

Overall	Safety	Reliability	Performance	Comfort	Value
6.7	4.5	7.4	7.6	7.1	6.9

Don't forget to refer to the Mileage Adjustment Table at the back of this book!

© 1999 by Edmund Publications Corporation

Model Description	Trade-in Value	Market Value
Category C		
2 Dr GS Sdn	2890	4070
4 Dr GS Sdn	2810	3960

OPTIONS FOR TOPAZ

6 cyl 3.0 L Engine +210
Auto 3-Speed Transmission +170
Auto 4-Speed Transmission +170
Air Bag Restraint +155
Air Conditioning +240
Aluminum/Alloy Wheels +85
AM/FM Stereo Tape +50
Cruise Control +65
Power Door Locks +70
Power Drivers Seat +85
Power Windows +90
Premium Sound System +120

TRACER 1993

Beefy stabilizer arms on all trim levels improve handling. Base models receive a new fascia and the LTS receives a one-piece spoiler. All models get new interior fabrics and tail lamps.

RATINGS (SCALE OF 1-10)

Overall	Safety	Reliability	Performance	Comfort	Value
6.6	4.7	7.7	7.6	7.1	5.9

Model Description	Trade-in Value	Market Value
Category E		
4 Dr LTS Sdn	3650	5450
4 Dr STD Sdn	3040	4535
4 Dr STD Wgn	2930	4375

OPTIONS FOR TRACER

Auto 4-Speed Transmission +220
Air Conditioning +245
AM/FM Stereo Tape[Opt on STD] +95
Cruise Control[Opt on STD] +65
Luggage Rack +40
Power Door Locks +70
Power Moonroof +175
Power Steering[Std on LTS,Wgn] +75
Power Windows +80

VILLAGER 1993

Mercury joins the minivan fray by introducing a vehicle designed jointly with Nissan. Attractive styling and standard features such as antilock brakes are certainly commendable, but the absence of airbags would lead us toward another model.

RATINGS (SCALE OF 1-10)

Overall	Safety	Reliability	Performance	Comfort	Value
7	5.7	7.6	7.3	7.1	7.4

Model Description	Trade-in Value	Market Value
Category G		
2 Dr GS Cargo Van	5455	7275
2 Dr GS Pass. Van	5665	7555
2 Dr LS Pass. Van	7125	9500

OPTIONS FOR VILLAGER

Air Conditioning[Opt on GS Cargo Van] +245
Aluminum/Alloy Wheels +105
Captain Chairs (4) +190
Compact Disc W/fm/tape +205
Cruise Control[Opt on GS Cargo Van] +65
Keyless Entry System +60
Leather Seats +235
Luggage Rack[Opt on GS] +45
Power Door Locks[Opt on GS Cargo Van] +70
Power Drivers Seat +85
Power Passenger Seat +80
Power Sunroof +245
Power Windows[Opt on GS Cargo Van] +70

1992 MERCURY

CAPRI 1992

The XR2 receives 15-inch wheels, new tires and updated cabin trim. Power door locks are no longer available but cruise control is added to the options list.

Model Description	Trade-in Value	Market Value
Category F		
2 Dr STD Conv	2915	4045
2 Dr XR2 Turbo Conv	3430	4760

OPTIONS FOR CAPRI

Auto 4-Speed Transmission +180
Air Conditioning[Opt on STD] +205
Aluminum/Alloy Wheels[Opt on STD] +75
AM/FM Stereo Tape[Opt on STD] +50
Cruise Control[Opt on STD] +50
Hardtop Roof +340
Leather Seats +175
Premium Sound System +100

COUGAR 1992

The 25th anniversary edition debuts. A unique LS model becomes available this year equipped with 5.0-liter V8 engine, monochromatic colors, BBS aluminum wheels, and special trim. White sidewall tires and the anti-theft system are no longer available.

RATINGS (SCALE OF 1-10)

Overall	Safety	Reliability	Performance	Comfort	Value
6.8	5.7	6.8	6.8	7.8	6.9

Model Description	Trade-in Value	Market Value
Category C		
2 Dr LS Cpe	3835	5560
2 Dr XR7 Cpe	4270	6185

OPTIONS FOR COUGAR

8 cyl 5.0 L Engine[Opt on LS] +270
Aluminum/Alloy Wheels[Opt on LS] +70
AM/FM Compact Disc Playr +95
Anti-Lock Brakes[Opt on LS] +155
Cruise Control +50
Keyless Entry System +45
Leather Seats +145

Don't forget to refer to the Mileage Adjustment Table at the back of this book!

 © 1999 by Edmund Publications Corporation

Model Description	Trade-in Value	Market Value

Power Door Locks +60
Power Drivers Seat +70
Power Moonroof +175
Power Passenger Seat +65
Premium Sound System +100

GRAND MARQUIS 1992

New sheetmetal debuts on the Grand Marquis. Rounded styling and two additional inches in length give the car a sleeker appearance. The old V8 engine is replaced with a 4.6-liter V8 that makes between 40 and 60 more horsepower, depending on the exhaust system. A new passenger airbag is added to the options list. Antilock brakes are available in the performance and handling package. The wagon is discontinued.

RATINGS (SCALE OF 1-10)

Overall	Safety	Reliability	Performance	Comfort	Value
N/A	7.2	7.5	7.5	N/A	7.9

Category B

4 Dr GS Sdn	4590	6375
4 Dr LS Sdn	4880	6780

OPTIONS FOR GRAND MARQUIS
Aluminum/Alloy Wheels +85
AM/FM Stereo Tape +45
Anti-Lock Brakes +175
Cruise Control +55
Dual Air Bag Restraints +120
Keyless Entry System +45
Leather Seats +165
Power Door Locks +60
Power Drivers Seat +75
Power Passenger Seat +75
Premium Sound System +105

SABLE 1992

Sable gets dual airbags for front seat occupants. New sheetmetal does little to change the looks of the car. Fifteen-inch wheels replace last year's fourteen-inchers. Additional radio controls have been placed near the steering wheel and the power window buttons have been moved to the armrest. Variable-assist power steering becomes standard and the heated windshield is dropped from the options list.

RATINGS (SCALE OF 1-10)

Overall	Safety	Reliability	Performance	Comfort	Value
7.5	7	6.5	8	7.8	8.1

Category C

4 Dr GS Sdn	3135	4545
4 Dr GS Wgn	3505	5080
4 Dr LS Wgn	4130	5980
4 Dr LS Sdn	3840	5565

OPTIONS FOR SABLE
6 cyl 3.8 L Engine +135
Aluminum/Alloy Wheels +70
AM/FM Compact Disc Playr +95
Anti-Lock Brakes +155
Cruise Control +50
Keyless Entry System +45
Leather Seats +145
Power Door Locks +60
Power Drivers Seat +70
Power Moonroof +175
Power Passenger Seat +65
Power Windows[Opt on GS] +75
Premium Sound System +100

TOPAZ 1992

V6 is available for those who need a little more horsepower. Unfortunately the all-wheel drive system is dropped from the option list.

RATINGS (SCALE OF 1-10)

Overall	Safety	Reliability	Performance	Comfort	Value
6.8	4.5	7	7.6	7.1	7.6

Category C

2 Dr GS Sdn	2335	3385
4 Dr GS Sdn	2435	3525
4 Dr LS Sdn	2900	4200
4 Dr LTS Sdn	3155	4570
2 Dr XR5 Sdn	2895	4195

OPTIONS FOR TOPAZ
6 cyl 3.0 L Engine[Opt on GS,LS] +170
Auto 3-Speed Transmission +110
Air Bag Restraint +125
Air Conditioning[Opt on GS,LS] +200
Aluminum/Alloy Wheels[Opt on GS,LS] +70
AM/FM Stereo Tape[Opt on GS] +40
Cruise Control[Opt on GS,XR5] +50
Power Door Locks[Opt on GS,XR5] +60
Power Drivers Seat[Std on LTS] +70
Power Windows[Opt on GS] +75
Premium Sound System[Std on LTS] +100

TRACER 1992

No changes.

RATINGS (SCALE OF 1-10)

Overall	Safety	Reliability	Performance	Comfort	Value
6.5	4.7	7.3	7.6	7.1	5.8

Category E

4 Dr LTS Sdn	2635	4120
4 Dr STD Sdn	2175	3400
4 Dr STD Wgn	2225	3475

OPTIONS FOR TRACER
Auto 4-Speed Transmission +180
Air Conditioning +200

Don't forget to refer to the Mileage Adjustment Table at the back of this book!

 © 1999 by Edmund Publications Corporation

Model Description	Trade-in Value	Market Value

AM/FM Stereo Tape[Opt on STD] +75
Cruise Control[Opt on STD] +55
Luggage Rack +30
Power Door Locks +55
Power Moonroof +145
Power Steering[Std on LTS,Wgn] +60
Power Windows +65
Premium Sound System +85

1991 MERCURY

CAPRI 1991

This Australian-built convertible is based on the Mazda 323 platform. The 1.6-liter engine is available in turbo or regularly aspirated versions good for either 132 or 100 horsepower. An optional lift-off hardtop with a rear window defroster and interior lights is also available.

Category F		
2 Dr STD Conv	2525	3555
2 Dr XR2 Turbo Conv	2970	4185

OPTIONS FOR CAPRI

Auto 4-Speed Transmission +145
Air Conditioning[Opt on STD] +170
Aluminum/Alloy Wheels[Opt on STD] +65
AM/FM Stereo Tape[Opt on STD] +40
Hardtop Roof +280
Power Door Locks[Opt on STD] +40
Premium Sound System +85

COUGAR 1991

No significant changes to the Mercury Cougar.

RATINGS (SCALE OF 1-10)

Overall	Safety	Reliability	Performance	Comfort	Value
6.7	5.7	6.5	6.8	7.8	6.8

Category C		
2 Dr LS Cpe	2955	4515
2 Dr XR7 Cpe	3710	5705

OPTIONS FOR COUGAR

8 cyl 5.0 L Engine[Opt on LS] +220
Aluminum/Alloy Wheels[Opt on LS] +60
AM/FM Stereo Tape +35
Anti-Lock Brakes[Opt on LS] +125
Cruise Control +40
Keyless Entry System +40
Leather Seats +115
Power Door Locks +50
Power Drivers Seat +60
Power Passenger Seat +55
Power Sunroof +140
Premium Sound System +80

GRAND MARQUIS 1991

No major changes to the 1991 Grand Marquis.

Category B		
4 Dr GS Sdn	3405	4795
4 Dr LS Sdn	3580	5040

OPTIONS FOR GRAND MARQUIS

Aluminum/Alloy Wheels +65
AM/FM Stereo Tape +35
Auto Load Leveling +40
Cruise Control +45
Leather Seats +135
Power Door Locks +50
Power Drivers Seat +60
Power Passenger Seat +65
Premium Sound System +85

SABLE 1991

No significant changes to the 1991 Sable.

Category C		
4 Dr GS Sdn	2270	3495
4 Dr GS Wgn	2585	3980
4 Dr LS Sdn	2770	4260
4 Dr LS Wgn	3050	4695

OPTIONS FOR SABLE

6 cyl 3.8 L Engine +110
Aluminum/Alloy Wheels +60
AM/FM Stereo Tape +35
Anti-Lock Brakes +125
Cruise Control +40
Keyless Entry System +40
Leather Seats +115
Power Door Locks +50
Power Drivers Seat +60
Power Passenger Seat +55
Power Sunroof +140
Power Windows[Opt on GS] +60
Premium Sound System +80

TOPAZ 1991

No changes for the 1991 Topaz.

RATINGS (SCALE OF 1-10)

Overall	Safety	Reliability	Performance	Comfort	Value
6.7	4.6	7	7.2	7.1	7.4

Category C		
2 Dr GS Sdn	2085	3205
4 Dr GS Sdn	1845	2835
4 Dr LS Sdn	2145	3300
4 Dr LTS Sdn	2425	3730
2 Dr XR5 Sdn	2265	3485

OPTIONS FOR TOPAZ

Auto 3-Speed Transmission[Opt on] +110
Air Bag Restraint +100
Air Conditioning[Std on LTS] +160
Aluminum/Alloy Wheels[Opt on GS] +60
AM/FM Stereo Tape[Opt on GS] +35
Cruise Control[Opt on GS,XR5] +40

Don't forget to refer to the Mileage Adjustment Table at the back of this book!

© 1999 by Edmund Publications Corporation

Model Description	Trade-in Value	Market Value

Power Door Locks[Opt on GS,XR5] +50
Power Drivers Seat[Std on LTS] +60
Power Windows[Opt on GS] +60
Premium Sound System[Std on LTS] +80

TRACER 1991

Tracer receives a mighty makeover. Base notchback and wagon body styles share the Escort's base engine, but the up-level LTS receives a much more powerful Mazda DOHC engine that produces 127 horsepower.

RATINGS (SCALE OF 1-10)

Overall	Safety	Reliability	Performance	Comfort	Value
6.5	4.6	7.4	7.6	7.1	5.9

Category E

Model	Trade-in	Market
4 Dr LTS Sdn	2250	3815
4 Dr STD Sdn	1845	3125
4 Dr STD Wgn	1710	2895

OPTIONS FOR TRACER

Auto 4-Speed Transmission +145
Air Conditioning +165
AM/FM Stereo Tape[Opt on STD] +60
Cruise Control[Opt on STD] +45
Power Door Locks +45
Power Steering[Std on LTS,Wgn] +50
Power Sunroof +120
Power Windows +55
Premium Sound System +70

1990 MERCURY

COUGAR 1990

Contoured front headrests are introduced on the Cougar. Front and rear styling is updated.

RATINGS (SCALE OF 1-10)

Overall	Safety	Reliability	Performance	Comfort	Value
6.3	5.6	6.2	6.8	7.8	5

Category C

Model	Trade-in	Market
2 Dr LS Cpe	2370	3880
2 Dr XR7 Sprchgd Cpe	2640	4330

OPTIONS FOR COUGAR

Auto 4-Speed Transmission[Std on LS] +90
Aluminum/Alloy Wheels[Opt on LS] +50
Anti-Lock Brakes[Opt on LS] +105
Cruise Control +35
Keyless Entry System +30
Leather Seats +95
Power Door Locks +40
Power Drivers Seat +45
Power Passenger Seat +45
Power Sunroof +115
Premium Sound System +65

GRAND MARQUIS 1990

A driver airbag and tilt steering wheel are added to the standard features list.

Category B

Model	Trade-in	Market
4 Dr Colony Park GS Wgn	2400	3690
4 Dr Colony Park LS Wgn	2585	3975
4 Dr GS Sdn	2780	4275
4 Dr LS Sdn	2895	4455

OPTIONS FOR GRAND MARQUIS

Aluminum/Alloy Wheels[Opt on GS] +55
AM/FM Stereo Tape +30
Auto Load Leveling +30
Cruise Control +35
Full Vinyl Top +65
Leather Seats +110
Power Door Locks +40
Power Drivers Seat +50
Power Passenger Seat +50
Premium Sound System +70
Velour/Cloth Seats[Opt on Colony ParkGS] +35

SABLE 1990

Standard driver airbag and knee bolsters improve crash protection. Antilock brakes are optional on the sedan and a CD player is optional for both body styles. The tilt steering wheel becomes standard.

Category C

Model	Trade-in	Market
4 Dr GS Sdn	1840	3020
4 Dr GS Wgn	1815	2975
4 Dr LS Sdn	2125	3485
4 Dr LS Wgn	2200	3605

OPTIONS FOR SABLE

6 cyl 3.8 L Engine +110
Aluminum/Alloy Wheels +50
Anti-Lock Brakes +105
Cruise Control +35
Keyless Entry System +30
Leather Seats +95
Power Door Locks +40
Power Drivers Seat +45
Power Passenger Seat +45
Power Sunroof +115
Power Windows[Opt on GS] +50
Premium Sound System +65

TOPAZ 1990

No changes.

RATINGS (SCALE OF 1-10)

Overall	Safety	Reliability	Performance	Comfort	Value
6.6	4.6	6.8	7.2	7.1	7.4

Category C

Model	Trade-in	Market
2 Dr GS Sdn	1515	2480
4 Dr GS Sdn	1335	2190

Don't forget to refer to the Mileage Adjustment Table at the back of this book!

 © 1999 by Edmund Publications Corporation

Model Description	Trade-in Value	Market Value
4 Dr GS 4WD Sdn	1620	2655
4 Dr LS Sdn	1695	2780
4 Dr LS 4WD Sdn	1800	2950
4 Dr LTS Sdn	1930	3165
2 Dr XR5 Sdn	1535	2515

OPTIONS FOR TOPAZ

Auto 3-Speed Transmission[Std on 4WD] +90
Air Bag Restraint +85
Air Conditioning[Std on LTS] +130
Cruise Control[Opt on GS,XR5] +35
Power Door Locks[Opt on GS,XR5] +40
Power Drivers Seat[Std on LTS] +45
Power Windows[Opt on GS,XR5] +50

1989 MERCURY

COUGAR 1989

Redesigned to be bigger on the inside and smaller on the outside, the Cougar undergoes a complete restyle for 1989. An independent suspension and stretched wheelbase improves handling, but does not increase overall length. The LS is powered by a 3.8-liter V6. Antilock brakes are optional.

RATINGS (SCALE OF 1-10)

Overall	Safety	Reliability	Performance	Comfort	Value
6.5	5.7	6.3	6.8	7.8	5.9

Category C

Model Description	Trade-in Value	Market Value
2 Dr LS Cpe	1875	3290
2 Dr XR7 Sprchgd Cpe	2455	4310

OPTIONS FOR COUGAR

Auto 4-Speed Transmission[Std on LS] +75
Aluminum/Alloy Wheels[Opt on LS] +40
Anti-Lock Brakes[Opt on LS] +85
Cruise Control +30
Leather Seats +80
Power Door Locks +30
Power Drivers Seat +40
Power Passenger Seat +35
Power Sunroof +95
Premium Sound System +55

GRAND MARQUIS 1989

Few changes to Mercury's full-size rear-wheel drive road-warrior. A Silver Anniversary Edition is available sporting distinctive wheels, a premium sound system, six-way power front seats and a leather-wrapped steering wheel. The LS trim level requires the purchase of alloy wheels.

Category B

Model Description	Trade-in Value	Market Value
4 Dr Colony Park GS Wgn	1760	2930
4 Dr Colony Park LS Wgn	1760	2930
4 Dr GS Sdn	2245	3740
4 Dr LS Sdn	2255	3755

OPTIONS FOR GRAND MARQUIS

Aluminum/Alloy Wheels +45
Cruise Control +30
Leather Seats +90
Power Door Locks +35
Power Drivers Seat +40
Power Passenger Seat +40
Premium Sound System +55
Trip Computer +30

SABLE 1989

New headlights, turn signals, illuminated grille and parking lights appear at the front of the Sable. Engine noise is reduced by including improved dampers and isolators. The driver's side power window and power door lock controls are illuminated. New wheels are added.

Category C

Model Description	Trade-in Value	Market Value
4 Dr GS Wgn	1575	2765
4 Dr GS Sdn	1455	2550
4 Dr LS Sdn	1665	2925
4 Dr LS Wgn	1755	3080

OPTIONS FOR SABLE

6 cyl 3.8 L Engine +70
Aluminum/Alloy Wheels +40
Cruise Control +30
Leather Seats +80
Power Door Locks +30
Power Drivers Seat +40
Power Moonroof +95
Power Passenger Seat +35
Power Windows[Opt on GS] +40
Premium Sound System +55

TOPAZ 1989

The Ford Tempo's twin receives an optional driver airbag. Cargo tie-downs become standard in the luggage compartments of all Topaz models.

RATINGS (SCALE OF 1-10)

Overall	Safety	Reliability	Performance	Comfort	Value
6.3	4.6	6.6	7.2	7.1	6

Category C

Model Description	Trade-in Value	Market Value
2 Dr GS Sdn	1120	1960
4 Dr GS Sdn	1180	2075
4 Dr GS 4WD Sdn	1475	2590
4 Dr LS Sdn	1475	2590
4 Dr LTS Sdn	1585	2785

OPTIONS FOR TOPAZ

Auto 3-Speed Transmission[Std on 4WD] +70
Air Bag Restraint +70
Air Conditioning[Std on LTS] +110
Cruise Control[Opt on GS,XR5] +30
Power Door Locks[Opt on GS,XR5] +30

Don't forget to refer to the Mileage Adjustment Table at the back of this book!

 © 1999 by Edmund Publications Corporation

Model Description	Trade-in Value	Market Value
Power Drivers Seat[Std on LTS] +40		
Power Windows[Opt on GS] +40		
Premium Sound System +55		

TRACER 1989

Based on Mazda's 323, the Mercury Tracer receives only one change for 1989. The service points in the engine bay are conveniently marked with yellow paint, thus making them easier to spot for the shade-tree mechanic.

Model Description	Trade-in Value	Market Value
Category E		
2 Dr STD Hbk	785	1790
4 Dr STD Hbk	795	1810
4 Dr STD Wgn	750	1705

OPTIONS FOR TRACER

Auto 3-Speed Transmission +55
Air Conditioning +110
Aluminum/Alloy Wheels[Opt on Hbk] +45
AM/FM Stereo Tape +40
Cruise Control +30
Power Steering[Opt on STD Hbk] +35

A 15-minute phone call
could save you 15% or more
on car insurance.

1-800-555-2758

GEICO DIRECT

The Sensible Alternative

Get a great used car and
apply for financing *online*
at a price you must
see to believe!

http://www.edmunds.com

Don't forget to refer to the Mileage Adjustment Table at the back of this book!

 © 1999 by Edmund Publications Corporation

MITSUBISHI Japan

1994 Mitsubishi Diamante

1998 MITSUBISHI

3000GT 1998

SL and VR-4 models get a standard power sunroof this year.

Category F

Model Description	Trade-in Value	Market Value
2 Dr SL Cpe	23445	27580
2 Dr STD Cpe	17710	20840

OPTIONS FOR 3000GT

Auto 4-Speed Transmission[Opt on STD, SL] +750
Anti-Lock Brakes[Opt on SL] +600
Compact Disc W/fm/tape[Opt on STD] +435
Fog Lights[Opt on STD] +145
Leather Seats[Opt on STD] +590

DIAMANTE 1998

All Diamantes get standard ABS and remote keyless entry for 1998.

Category D

Model Description	Trade-in Value	Market Value
4 Dr ES Sdn	18710	22275
4 Dr LS Sdn	23595	28090

OPTIONS FOR DIAMANTE

Luxury Group +2190
Aluminum/Alloy Wheels[Opt on ES] +375
Dual Power Seats +695
Fog Lights[Opt on ES] +175
Infinity Sound System +355
Leather Seats[Opt on ES] +915
Power Drivers Seat[Opt on ES] +285
Power Moonroof[Opt on ES] +695

ECLIPSE 1998

The GSX gets a standard sunroof, power driver's seat and remote keyless entry.

Category F

Model Description	Trade-in Value	Market Value
2 Dr GS Hbk	12305	14475
2 Dr GS-T Turbo Hbk	15405	18120
2 Dr GSX Turbo 4WD Hbk	17320	20380
2 Dr RS Hbk	10820	12730
2 Dr Spyder GS Conv	15600	18350

OPTIONS FOR ECLIPSE

Auto 4-Speed Transmission +630
Air Conditioning[Opt on GS, RS] +690
Aluminum/Alloy Wheels[Opt on GS, RS] +260
AM/FM Compact Disc Playr[Opt on GS, RS] +410
Anti-Lock Brakes +600
Cruise Control[Opt on GS, RS, Spyder GS] +175
Infinity Sound System +575
Keyless Entry System[Std on GSX, Spyder GS-T] +145
Leather Seats[Std on GSX, Spyder GS-T] +590
Power Door Locks[Opt on GS, RS] +165
Power Moonroof[Std on GSX] +595
Power Windows[Opt on GS, RS] +185

GALANT 1998

Solar tinted glass makes it harder to tan in the new Galant. The ES gets a standard manual transmission, and the ES and LS have a new black grille with chrome accents. The LS also benefits from standard antilock brakes. All models have a new heavy-duty starter and battery.

Category D

Model Description	Trade-in Value	Market Value
4 Dr DE Sdn	9235	10995
4 Dr ES Sdn	11235	13375
4 Dr LS Sdn	14205	16910

OPTIONS FOR GALANT

Auto 4-Speed Transmission[Std on LS] +685
Air Conditioning[Opt on DE] +700
Aluminum/Alloy Wheels[Opt on ES] +375
AM/FM Compact Disc Playr +465
Anti-Lock Brakes[Opt on ES] +790
Fog Lights[Opt on ES] +175
Leather Seats[Opt on ES] +915
Power Moonroof[Opt on ES] +695

MIRAGE 1998

Some new colors to choose from and a new heavy duty starter and battery make the Mirage more reliable.

Category E

Model Description	Trade-in Value	Market Value
2 Dr DE Cpe	7745	9330
4 Dr DE Sdn	7835	9440
2 Dr LS Cpe	10070	12130
4 Dr LS Sdn	8750	10545

OPTIONS FOR MIRAGE

Auto 4-Speed Transmission +580
Air Conditioning[Opt on DE, Sdn] +675
AM/FM Compact Disc Playr[Opt on Sdn] +390
Anti-Lock Brakes +590

Don't forget to refer to the Mileage Adjustment Table at the back of this book!

 © 1999 by Edmund Publications Corporation

Cruise Control +185
Keyless Entry System +125
Power Door Locks +195
Power Mirrors +95
Power Moonroof +485
Power Windows +220
Tilt Steering Wheel[Opt on DE] +125

MONTERO 1998

A revised front bumper and grille, new fenders and new rear quarter panels mark the exterior changes. Inside is a new steering wheel, while the standard equipment list now includes ABS, air conditioning, third row seats and alloy wheels.

Category G	Trade-in Value	Market Value
4 Dr STD 4WD Wgn	18225	21695

OPTIONS FOR MONTERO

Premium Package +665
AM/FM Compact Disc Playr +320
Chrome Wheels +200
Compact Disc Changer +430
Heated Front Seats +210
Infinity Sound System +490
Keyless Entry System +170
Leather Seats +640
Power Drivers Seat +235
Power Moonroof +735

MONTERO SPORT 1998

Montero Sports get lots of features added to their option packages, and 4WD models now come with standard ABS.

Category G	Trade-in Value	Market Value
4 Dr ES Wgn	14625	17410
4 Dr LS Wgn	16595	19755
4 Dr LS 4WD Wgn	17625	20985
4 Dr XLS Wgn	19440	23140
4 Dr XLS 4WD Wgn	21175	25210

OPTIONS FOR MONTERO SPORT

Auto 4-Speed Transmission[Std on XLS, 2WD] +715
LS Appearance Package +990
Air Conditioning[Std on XLS] +675
Aluminum/Alloy Wheels[Opt on LS] +285
AM/FM Compact Disc Playr +320
Cruise Control[Opt on LS] +175
Keyless Entry System +170
Limited Slip Diff[Opt on LS, 2WD] +220
Power Door Locks[Opt on LS] +190
Power Mirrors +110
Power Moonroof[Opt on LS] +735
Power Windows[Opt on LS] +195
Rear Heater[Opt on LS] +170
Tutone Paint[Opt on LS] +220

1997 MITSUBISHI

3000GT 1997

A value-leader base model is introduced. It has less than stellar performance and we think that it's embarrassing that this car is in the same lineup as the earth-scorching VR-4.

RATINGS (SCALE OF 1-10)

Overall	Safety	Reliability	Performance	Comfort	Value
N/A	7.7	8.1	8.8	6.6	N/A

Category F	Trade-in Value	Market Value
2 Dr SL Cpe	19990	24085
2 Dr STD Cpe	16670	20080
2 Dr VR-4 Turbo 4WD Cpe	25215	30375

OPTIONS FOR 3000GT

Auto 4-Speed Transmission +610
Anti-Lock Brakes[Opt on SL] +490
Compact Disc W/fm/tape[Opt on STD] +355
Keyless Entry System[Std on VR-4] +120
Leather Seats[Opt on STD] +485
Power Sunroof +465

DIAMANTE 1997

After a one-year hiatus, the Diamante returns to the Mitusbishi lineup sporting clean, crisp styling, a full-load of luxury features, and a lower price. The old car barely registered on near-luxury car buyers' radar; this new one deserves consideration and a close inspection.

RATINGS (SCALE OF 1-10)

Overall	Safety	Reliability	Performance	Comfort	Value
N/A	N/A	8.8	7.4	7.5	5

Category D	Trade-in Value	Market Value
4 Dr ES Sdn	13540	16315
4 Dr LS Sdn	16620	20025

OPTIONS FOR DIAMANTE

Luxury Group +950
Aluminum/Alloy Wheels[Opt on ES] +305
Anti-Lock Brakes +645
Fog Lights[Opt on ES] +145
Infinity Sound System +290
Keyless Entry System +205
Leather Seats[Opt on ES] +750
Leather Steering Wheel[Opt on ES] +75
Power Drivers Seat[Opt on ES] +230
Power Moonroof +565

ECLIPSE 1997

Revised styling makes the attractive Eclipse drop-dead gorgeous. New interior fabrics and paint colors debut as well. Antilock brakes are now available on the GS model, and a CD player joins its standard equipment

Don't forget to refer to the Mileage Adjustment Table at the back of this book!

 © 1999 by Edmund Publications Corporation

list. Two new exterior colors, new seat fabrics and a new interior color combination round out the changes.

RATINGS (SCALE OF 1-10)

Overall	Safety	Reliability	Performance	Comfort	Value
7.2	6.8	8.7	8.4	6.6	5.3

Category F	Trade-in Value	Market Value
2 Dr GS Hbk	10970	13220
2 Dr GS-T Turbo Hbk	13660	16460
2 Dr GSX Turbo 4WD Hbk	14845	17885
2 Dr RS Hbk	9605	11575
2 Dr Spyder GS Conv	13595	16380
2 Dr Spyder GS-T Turbo Conv	16300	19635
2 Dr STD Hbk	9390	11310

OPTIONS FOR ECLIPSE

Auto 4-Speed Transmission +515
Air Conditioning[Opt on GS,RS,Spyder GS,STD] +565
Aluminum/Alloy Wheels[Opt on GS,RS] +210
Anti-Lock Brakes +490
Compact Disc W/fm/tape[Opt on GS,Spyder GS] +355
Keyless Entry System[Std on Spyder GS-T] +120
Leather Seats[Std on Spyder GS-T] +485
Power Door Locks[Opt on GS,RS] +135
Power Drivers Seat[Opt on GSX] +160
Power Moonroof +485
Power Windows[Opt on GS,RS] +150

GALANT 1997

Mitsubishi shuffles the Galant lineup, replacing the S sedan with a base model called the DE. Front and rear fascias have been redesigned, and the interiors of all models have been upgraded by the addition of more ergonomically correct center armrests, upgraded upholstery, additional sound deadening material, and a new steering wheel.

RATINGS (SCALE OF 1-10)

Overall	Safety	Reliability	Performance	Comfort	Value
7.3	6.6	8.8	8	8.3	5

Category D	Trade-in Value	Market Value
4 Dr DE Sdn	7965	9600
4 Dr ES Sdn	10235	12330
4 Dr LS Sdn	11710	14105

OPTIONS FOR GALANT

Auto 4-Speed Transmission[Opt on DE] +590
Air Conditioning[Opt on DE] +575
Aluminum/Alloy Wheels[Opt on ES] +305
AM/FM Compact Disc Playr +380
Anti-Lock Brakes +645
Fog Lights[Opt on ES] +145
Keyless Entry System[Opt on ES] +205
Leather Seats[Opt on ES] +750
Power Moonroof[Opt on ES] +565

MIRAGE 1997

The Mirage is totally redesigned for 1997, sharing little with the model it replaces. Mitsubishi claims that interior size has been increased and that NVH have been reduced.

RATINGS (SCALE OF 1-10)

Overall	Safety	Reliability	Performance	Comfort	Value
N/A	N/A	8.9	7.4	6.4	5.4

Category E	Trade-in Value	Market Value
2 Dr DE Cpe	6495	7920
4 Dr DE Sdn	6960	8485
2 Dr LS Cpe	7615	9285
4 Dr LS Sdn	7365	8985

OPTIONS FOR MIRAGE

Auto 4-Speed Transmission +465
Air Conditioning +550
Aluminum/Alloy Wheels[Opt on Sdn] +215
Anti-Lock Brakes +480
Compact Disc W/fm/tape +470
Cruise Control +150
Keyless Entry System +100
Power Door Locks +160
Power Moonroof +395
Power Steering[Opt on DE Cpe] +170
Power Windows +180

MONTERO 1997

The pricey Montero moves further up-market in anticipation of the Montero Sport's arrival to these shores. This year sees the deletion of the LS with a manual transmission, and the addition of a more powerful V6 engine. Leather seats are now available on the LS as well as the SR.

RATINGS (SCALE OF 1-10)

Overall	Safety	Reliability	Performance	Comfort	Value
N/A	N/A	8.5	7.4	7.4	3.5

Category G	Trade-in Value	Market Value
4 Dr LS 4WD Wgn	16770	19965
4 Dr SR 4WD Wgn	21035	25045

OPTIONS FOR MONTERO

Air Conditioning[Opt on LS] +550
Alarm System +240
Aluminum/Alloy Wheels[Opt on LS] +235
Anti-Lock Brakes +420
Chrome Wheels +165
Heated Front Seats +175
Keyless Entry System +140
Leather Seats[Opt on LS] +520
Luggage Rack +105
Power Drivers Seat[Opt on LS] +190
Power Moonroof[Opt on LS] +600

Don't forget to refer to the Mileage Adjustment Table at the back of this book!

 © 1999 by Edmund Publications Corporation

Model Description	Trade-in Value	Market Value

Running Boards +260
Third Seat +510
Trailer Hitch +195

MONTERO SPORT 1997

This all-new entry from Mitsubishi is poised to steal sales in the ever-growing midsized sport-utility segment. Based on the same floorpan as the full-sized Montero, the Montero Sport is shorter in length, lighter in weight, and generally more nimble than its big brother.

RATINGS (SCALE OF 1-10)

Overall	Safety	Reliability	Performance	Comfort	Value
N/A	6.6	8.4	6	7.5	N/A

Category G		
4 Dr ES Wgn	14020	16690
4 Dr LS Wgn	14300	17020
4 Dr LS 4WD Wgn	16270	19365
4 Dr XLS 4WD Wgn	19870	23655

OPTIONS FOR MONTERO SPORT

Auto 4-Speed Transmission[Std on XLS,2WD] +610
LS Appearance Package +1010
Premium Package +875
Air Conditioning[Std on XLS] +550
Aluminum/Alloy Wheels[Opt on LS] +235
Anti-Lock Brakes +420
Compact Disc W/fm/tape +465
Cruise Control[Opt on LS] +145
Infinity Sound System[Opt on LS] +400
Leather Seats[Opt on LS] +520
Limited Slip Diff +180
Luggage Rack +105
Power Door Locks[Opt on LS] +155
Power Moonroof[Opt on LS] +600
Power Windows[Opt on LS] +160
Rear Heater +140
Rear Window Wiper[Opt on ES] +105

1996 MITSUBISHI

3000GT 1996

Base model gets new cloth interior, while upper trim levels receive a choice of black or tan leather. Remote keyless entry gets panic feature, and several new colors are available.

RATINGS (SCALE OF 1-10)

Overall	Safety	Reliability	Performance	Comfort	Value
N/A	7.7	7.5	8.8	6.6	N/A

Category F		
2 Dr SL Cpe	16690	20605
2 Dr STD Cpe	14340	17700
2 Dr VR-4 Turbo 4WD Cpe	23675	29230

OPTIONS FOR 3000GT

Auto 4-Speed Transmission +480
Chrome Wheels[Opt on SL] +315
Compact Disc Changer +375
Power Sunroof +380

DIAMANTE 1996

The only Diamantes sold this year were for fleet sales. So unless you see one at a rental car auction, chances are not good that you'll find a used 1996 model.

Category D		
4 Dr ES Sdn	10615	13270

ECLIPSE 1996

Three new colors debut, audio systems are revised, and RS models can be ordered with a rear spoiler. Remote keyless entry systems get a new panic feature.

RATINGS (SCALE OF 1-10)

Overall	Safety	Reliability	Performance	Comfort	Value
6.9	6.8	8	8.4	6.6	4.5

Category F		
2 Dr GS Hbk	9550	11795
2 Dr GS-T Turbo Hbk	11980	14790
2 Dr GSX Turbo 4WD Hbk	12575	15525
2 Dr RS Hbk	8665	10695
2 Dr Spyder GS Conv	12070	14900
2 Dr STD Hbk	8625	10650
2 Dr Sypder GS-T Turbo Conv	13635	16835

OPTIONS FOR ECLIPSE

Auto 4-Speed Transmission +410
Air Conditioning[Std on GS-T,GSX] +460
Aluminum/Alloy Wheels[Std on GS-T,GSX] +170
Anti-Lock Brakes +400
Compact Disc W/fm/tape +290
Cruise Control[Std on GS-T,GSX] +115
Keyless Entry System[Opt on GS,GSX,Spyder GS] +95
Leather Seats[Std on GSX,GS-T Turbo Conv] +395
Power Drivers Seat[Std on GSX] +130
Power Sunroof +380
Rear Window Wiper[Opt on GS] +80

GALANT 1996

A Homelink transmitter is available, and a panic feature debuts on keyless entry systems. New two-tone interiors debut, and four fresh exterior colors join the palette. Other changes include new wheelcovers, expanded availability of alloy wheels, and a heavy duty defroster with timer. LS models have standard leather seating and antilock brakes are available across the line.

RATINGS (SCALE OF 1-10)

Overall	Safety	Reliability	Performance	Comfort	Value
7.3	6.6	8.3	8	8.3	5.3

Don't forget to refer to the Mileage Adjustment Table at the back of this book!

 © 1999 by Edmund Publications Corporation

Model Description	Trade-in Value	Market Value
Category D		
4 Dr ES Sdn	9730	12160
4 Dr LS Sdn	10960	13700
4 Dr S Sdn	7395	9245

OPTIONS FOR GALANT

Auto 4-Speed Transmission[Opt on S] +485
Air Conditioning[Opt on S] +470
Aluminum/Alloy Wheels[Opt on ES] +250
AM/FM Compact Disc Playr +310
AM/FM Stereo Tape[Opt on S] +200
Anti-Lock Brakes +530
Cruise Control[Opt on S] +135
Keyless Entry System +170
Power Door Locks[Opt on S] +145
Power Moonroof[Opt on ES] +465
Power Windows[Opt on S] +145

MIGHTY MAX PICKUP 1996

No changes this year, the Mighty Max's last.

Model Description	Trade-in Value	Market Value
Category G		
2 Dr STD Std Cab SB	6980	8510

OPTIONS FOR MIGHTY MAX PICKUP

Auto 4-Speed Transmission +790
Air Conditioning +450
AM/FM Stereo Tape +135
Power Steering +155
Rear Step Bumper +80

MIRAGE 1996

Four colors debut, and the Preferred Equipment Packages are revised a bit.

RATINGS (SCALE OF 1-10)

Overall	Safety	Reliability	Performance	Comfort	Value
6.5	5.5	8.1	8.2	7	3.9

Model Description	Trade-in Value	Market Value
Category E		
2 Dr LS Cpe	6595	8350
2 Dr S Cpe	4830	6115
4 Dr S Sdn	4785	6060

OPTIONS FOR MIRAGE

Auto 3-Speed Transmission[Opt on Cpe] +295
Auto 4-Speed Transmission +360
Air Conditioning +450
AM/FM Compact Disc Playr +260
AM/FM Stereo Tape[Opt on S] +170
Power Steering[Std on LS,Sdn] +140

MONTERO 1996

Refinements result in a better SUV this year. A passenger airbag has been installed, optional side steps make it easier to clamber aboard, and split-fold second row seats increase versatility. New colors, new seat fabrics and better audio systems round out the package.

RATINGS (SCALE OF 1-10)

Overall	Safety	Reliability	Performance	Comfort	Value
N/A	N/A	7.9	7.4	7.4	3.8

Model Description	Trade-in Value	Market Value
Category G		
4 Dr LS 4WD Wgn	14225	17345
4 Dr SR 4WD Wgn	18305	22320

OPTIONS FOR MONTERO

Auto 4-Speed Transmission[Opt on LS] +485
Leather/Wood Package +410
Air Conditioning[Opt on LS] +450
Aluminum/Alloy Wheels[Opt on LS] +190
Anti-Lock Brakes[Opt on LS] +345
Chrome Wheels +135
Compact Disc Changer +290
Keyless Entry System[Opt on LS] +115
Leather Seats +425
Luggage Rack +85
Power Moonroof[Opt on LS] +490
Power Sunroof +450
Running Boards +215
Trailer Hitch +160

1995 MITSUBISHI

3000GT 1995

The VR-4 gains chrome-plated alloy wheels as standard equipment.

RATINGS (SCALE OF 1-10)

Overall	Safety	Reliability	Performance	Comfort	Value
N/A	8.5	7.4	8.8	6.6	N/A

Model Description	Trade-in Value	Market Value
Category F		
2 Dr SL Cpe	13830	17290
2 Dr Spyder SL Conv	24000	30000
2 Dr STD Cpe	12190	15235
2 Dr VR-4 Turbo 4WD Cpe	20310	25390

OPTIONS FOR 3000GT

Auto 4-Speed Transmission[Opt on SL,STD] +390
Chrome Wheels[Opt on SL] +255
Compact Disc Changer[Opt on SL,STD,VR-4] +305
Power Sunroof +310

DIAMANTE 1995

The base Diamante sedan is sent out to pasture, available only to fleet purchasers such as rental car agencies. No other changes for the Mitsubishi flagship.

RATINGS (SCALE OF 1-10)

Overall	Safety	Reliability	Performance	Comfort	Value
7.3	7.1	8.3	8.4	8.4	4.3

Model Description	Trade-in Value	Market Value
Category D		
4 Dr ES Sdn	9775	12375
4 Dr LS Sdn	11745	14865
4 Dr STD Wgn	9120	11545

Don't forget to refer to the Mileage Adjustment Table at the back of this book!

 © 1999 by Edmund Publications Corporation

Model Description	Trade-in Value	Market Value

OPTIONS FOR DIAMANTE

Compact Disc Changer +300
Power Moonroof +380
Power Passenger Seat +175
Traction Control System +370

ECLIPSE 1995

Radically redesigned, the new Eclipse sports bulging shoulders and no-nonsense looks, particularly in GSX guise. Engine ratings are improved for all models, while the turbocharged GS-T and GSX produce a mighty 210 horsepower at 6,000 rpm. Antilock brakes are optional on all models. Dual airbags are finally standard on the Eclipse.

RATINGS (SCALE OF 1-10)

Overall	Safety	Reliability	Performance	Comfort	Value
6.9	7.5	7.8	8.4	6.6	4.4

Category F

Model Description	Trade-in Value	Market Value
2 Dr GS Hbk	8085	10105
2 Dr GS-T Turbo Hbk	9745	12185
2 Dr GSX Turbo 4WD Hbk	10915	13645
2 Dr RS Hbk	7365	9205

OPTIONS FOR ECLIPSE

Auto 4-Speed Transmission +340
Air Conditioning[Opt on GS,RS] +380
Aluminum/Alloy Wheels[Opt on GS,RS] +140
AM/FM Compact Disc Playr +225
Cruise Control[Opt on GS] +95
Infinity Sound System[Opt on GS] +315
Leather Seats[Std on GSX] +325
Power Door Locks[Opt on GS] +90
Power Drivers Seat[Std on GSX] +110
Power Sunroof +310
Power Windows[Opt on GS] +100

EXPO 1995

This is the last year for the Expo.

Category E

Model Description	Trade-in Value	Market Value
4 Dr STD Hbk	6890	8945

OPTIONS FOR EXPO

Air Conditioning +370
AM/FM Stereo Tape +140
Cruise Control +100
Luggage Rack +60
Power Door Locks +105
Power Windows +120

GALANT 1995

The much anticipated V6 engine never transpired in the 1995 Galant due to the increased costs and complexity involved in making the model. The 1995 Galants are available in three trim-levels, all with the 141-horsepower four-cylinder.

RATINGS (SCALE OF 1-10)

Overall	Safety	Reliability	Performance	Comfort	Value
7.2	7.2	8.3	8	8.3	4.3

Category D

Model Description	Trade-in Value	Market Value
4 Dr ES Sdn	8035	10170
4 Dr LS Sdn	8940	11315
4 Dr S Sdn	6335	8020

OPTIONS FOR GALANT

Auto 4-Speed Transmission[Opt on S] +400
Air Conditioning[Opt on S] +385
Aluminum/Alloy Wheels[Opt on ES] +205
AM/FM Compact Disc Playr +255
Anti-Lock Brakes +430
Cruise Control[Opt on S] +110
Keyless Entry System +135
Leather Seats +500
Power Door Locks[Opt on S] +120
Power Drivers Seat +155
Power Windows[Opt on S] +120

MIGHTY MAX PICKUP 1995

The Mighty Max line is drastically reduced. Remaining is a four-cylinder two-wheel drive regular-cab model.

Category G

Model Description	Trade-in Value	Market Value
2 Dr STD Std Cab SB	5060	6245

OPTIONS FOR MIGHTY MAX PICKUP

Auto 4-Speed Transmission +410
Air Conditioning +370
AM/FM Stereo Tape +110
Power Steering +130
Rear Step Bumper +65

MIRAGE 1995

The often changing Mitsubishi Mirage is once again revised, this time with dual airbags. LS versions get bigger alloy wheels.

RATINGS (SCALE OF 1-10)

Overall	Safety	Reliability	Performance	Comfort	Value
6.9	6	8	8.2	7	5.1

Category E

Model Description	Trade-in Value	Market Value
2 Dr ES Cpe	4805	6240
4 Dr ES Sdn	5590	7260
2 Dr LS Cpe	5550	7210
2 Dr S Cpe	4190	5445
4 Dr S Sdn	4375	5685

OPTIONS FOR MIRAGE

Auto 3-Speed Transmission[Opt on Cpe] +235
Auto 4-Speed Transmission +330
Air Conditioning +370
AM/FM Compact Disc Playr +215
AM/FM Stereo Tape[Opt on S] +140
Bucket Seats +50
Cruise Control[Opt on ES] +100

Don't forget to refer to the Mileage Adjustment Table at the back of this book!

© 1999 by Edmund Publications Corporation

Model Description	Trade-in Value	Market Value

Power Door Locks +105
Power Steering[Std on ES,LS,Sdn] +115
Power Windows +120
Tinted Glass[Opt on S] +45

MONTERO 1995

The Montero LS gets a more powerful V6 that offers a 26-horsepower boost over last year's marginal 151-horsepower rating. Towing capacity increases to 5,000 pounds for all models. Tricky, electronic shock absorbers return to the Montero SR's standard equipment list, letting drivers choose between soft, medium or hard setting depending on their preferences.

RATINGS (SCALE OF 1-10)

Overall	Safety	Reliability	Performance	Comfort	Value
6.8	7.3	7.9	7.4	7.4	4.3

Category G

Model	Trade-in	Market
4 Dr LS 4WD Wgn	12735	15720
4 Dr SR 4WD Wgn	15765	19460

OPTIONS FOR MONTERO

Auto 4-Speed Transmission[Opt on LS] +380
Leather/Wood Package +595
Anti-Lock Brakes[Opt on LS] +280
Chrome Wheels +110
Compact Disc W/fm/tape +310
Keyless Entry System[Opt on LS] +95
Leather Seats +350
Luggage Rack +70
Power Drivers Seat +130
Power Sunroof[Opt on LS] +365

1994 MITSUBISHI

3000GT 1994

The 3000GT gets a passenger airbag. The 3000GT VR-4 gets a totally unnecessary 20 extra horsepower. But, hey, you won't find us complaining. To harness the extra power, the VR-4 switches to a six-speed manual gearbox. Freshened styling and CFC-free air conditioning round out the changes for all models.

RATINGS (SCALE OF 1-10)

Overall	Safety	Reliability	Performance	Comfort	Value
N/A	8.5	7.7	8.8	6.6	N/A

Category F

Model	Trade-in	Market
2 Dr SL Cpe	11620	14705
2 Dr STD Cpe	9955	12605
2 Dr VR-4 Turbo 4WD Cpe	14750	18670

OPTIONS FOR 3000GT

Auto 4-Speed Transmission +325
Compact Disc Changer +250
Leather Seats[Opt on SL] +265
Sunroof +145

DIAMANTE 1994

A passenger airbag and CFC-free air conditioning make the Diamante much friendlier to its passengers and the environment. A five-door wagon model introduced late last year comes with the 175-horsepower engine that is standard in the ES sedan. New wood trim and an upgraded Infinity stereo debut on the 1994 Diamante.

RATINGS (SCALE OF 1-10)

Overall	Safety	Reliability	Performance	Comfort	Value
7.3	7.1	8.5	8.4	8.4	3.9

Category D

Model	Trade-in	Market
4 Dr ES Sdn	8135	10430
4 Dr LS Sdn	9905	12700
4 Dr STD Wgn	7490	9605

OPTIONS FOR DIAMANTE

AM/FM Compact Disc Playr +210
Anti-Lock Brakes[Std on LS] +355
Infinity Sound System[Opt on ES] +160
Keyless Entry System[Std on LS] +110
Leather Seats[Std on LS] +410
Power Drivers Seat[Std on LS] +125
Power Passenger Seat[Opt on ES] +140
Power Sunroof +270
Traction Control System +300

ECLIPSE 1994

Last year for the current edition of the Diamond Star sport coupe. Turbo engines gain a minimal boost in horsepower. Several of the models get more standard equipment in an attempt to increase sales in this edition's final year.

RATINGS (SCALE OF 1-10)

Overall	Safety	Reliability	Performance	Comfort	Value
N/A	N/A	7.8	8.4	6.8	3.9

Category F

Model	Trade-in	Market
2 Dr GS Turbo Hbk	6750	8545
2 Dr GS 1.8 Hbk	6140	7770
2 Dr GS 2.0 Hbk	6315	7995

OPTIONS FOR ECLIPSE

Auto 4-Speed Transmission +270
Air Conditioning[Opt on GS 1.8] +310
Aluminum/Alloy Wheels[Opt on GS 2.0] +115
Anti-Lock Brakes[Opt on GS] +270
Compact Disc W/fm/tape[Opt on GS 2.0] +195
Cruise Control[Opt on GS 1.8] +80
Keyless Entry System[Std on GS 2.0] +65
Leather Seats +265
Power Door Locks[Std on GS,GSX] +75
Power Windows[Std on GS,GSX] +85
Sunroof +145

Don't forget to refer to the Mileage Adjustment Table at the back of this book!

 © 1999 by Edmund Publications Corporation

Model Description	Trade-in Value	Market Value

EXPO 1994

The Expo and LRV receive a driver airbag this year. Unfortunately, the Expo loses its up-level SP model, but base models do receive better standard equipment as a result. LRVs are available only as two-wheel drive models in 1994; the AWD has been axed. This is the last year for the Expo LRV, although it will live on as the Eagle Summit wagon.

Category E

Model Description	Trade-in Value	Market Value
4 Dr STD Hbk	5470	7290

OPTIONS FOR EXPO

Auto 4-Speed Transmission +255
Air Conditioning +300
Aluminum/Alloy Wheels +120
AM/FM Stereo Tape +115
Anti-Lock Brakes +265
Cruise Control +80
Keyless Entry System +55
Luggage Rack +50
Power Door Locks +85
Power Sunroof +225
Power Windows +100

EXPO LRV 1994

Category E

Model Description	Trade-in Value	Market Value
2 Dr LRV Hbk	4965	6615
2 Dr Sport Hbk	6355	8475

OPTIONS FOR EXPO LRV

Auto 4-Speed Transmission +255
Air Conditioning[Opt on 1.8] +300
Aluminum/Alloy Wheels[Opt on 1.8] +120
AM/FM Compact Disc Playr +175
AM/FM Stereo Tape[Opt on 1.8] +115
Anti-Lock Brakes +265
Digital Clock[Opt on 1.8] +30
Luggage Rack +50
Power Door Locks[Opt on 1.8] +85
Power Sunroof +225
Rear Window Defroster +60
Rear Window Wiper[Opt on 1.8] +50

GALANT 1994

Dual airbags debut on this totally redesigned sedan. Four trim-levels are offered, ranging from the low-level S to the luxury ES and sporty GS models. An automatic transmission is standard on the ES and LS models. GS Galants come with a twin-cam engine rated at 160 horsepower.

RATINGS (SCALE OF 1-10)

Overall	Safety	Reliability	Performance	Comfort	Value
7.3	7.2	8.2	8	8.3	4.8

Category D

Model Description	Trade-in Value	Market Value
4 Dr ES Sdn	6575	8430
4 Dr GS Sdn	7415	9505
4 Dr LS Sdn	7130	9140
4 Dr S Sdn	5170	6625

OPTIONS FOR GALANT

Auto 4-Speed Transmission[Opt on GS,S] +310
Air Conditioning[Opt on S] +315
Anti-Lock Brakes +355
Compact Disc W/fm/tape[Std on GS] +360
Keyless Entry System +110

MIGHTY MAX PICKUP 1994

The Mighty Max gains a few safety features such as a high-mounted rear stop light and side-impact door guard beams. The vehicle is otherwise unchanged.

Category G

Model Description	Trade-in Value	Market Value
2 Dr STD Ext Cab SB	4775	5965
2 Dr STD Std Cab SB	4290	5360
2 Dr STD 4WD Std Cab SB	6835	8545

OPTIONS FOR MIGHTY MAX PICKUP

Auto 4-Speed Transmission +295
Air Conditioning +300
AM/FM Stereo Tape +90
Limited Slip Diff +100
Power Steering[Std on 4WD] +105
Rear Step Bumper +55
Sliding Rear Window +45
Velour/Cloth Seats[Std on 4WD] +65

MIRAGE 1994

The Mirage finally gains a standard driver airbag, but the LS loses its optional antilock brakes. The LS coupe gets the 1.8-liter engine that was formerly available only on the LS and ES sedans. S and ES coupes get power steering added to their standard equipment lists, and LS sedans get alloy wheels.

RATINGS (SCALE OF 1-10)

Overall	Safety	Reliability	Performance	Comfort	Value
N/A	N/A	8.1	8.2	7	5.7

Category E

Model Description	Trade-in Value	Market Value
2 Dr ES Cpe	3505	4675
4 Dr ES Sdn	3875	5165
2 Dr LS Cpe	4045	5395
4 Dr LS Sdn	4950	6600
2 Dr S Cpe	3090	4120
4 Dr S Sdn	3665	4885

OPTIONS FOR MIRAGE

Auto 3-Speed Transmission +180
Auto 4-Speed Transmission[Opt on ES,Cpe] +230
Air Conditioning +300
AM/FM Compact Disc Playr +175
AM/FM Stereo Tape[Std on LS] +115
Cruise Control[Opt on ES] +80
Digital Clock[Std on LS,S,Sdn] +30
Keyless Entry System[Opt on S] +55

Don't forget to refer to the Mileage Adjustment Table at the back of this book!

© 1999 by Edmund Publications Corporation

Model Description	Trade-in Value	Market Value

Power Door Locks[Std on LS] +85
Power Windows[Std on LS] +100
Tilt Steering Wheel[Opt on ES] +55

MONTERO 1994

Deciding to go the luxury sport-ute route, Mitsubishi drops its entry-level Monteros. The remaining models are the luxury-oriented LS and sporty SR. A driver airbag is standard on the 1994 Montero. Antilock brakes move from the standard equipment list to the option list of both trucks. CFC-free air conditioning, a third-row bench seat, heated outside mirrors, and a leather-wrapped steering wheel become standard equipment. SR models finally receive a gutsier engine to move this scale-tipping SUV around; a 215-horsepower V6 engine is now standard on that model.

RATINGS (SCALE OF 1-10)

Overall	Safety	Reliability	Performance	Comfort	Value
6.9	7.3	7.9	7.4	7.4	4.3

Category G

4 Dr LS 4WD Wgn	10500	13125
4 Dr SR 4WD Wgn	13510	16885

OPTIONS FOR MONTERO

Auto 4-Speed Transmission[Opt on LS] +315
Air Conditioning[Opt on LS] +300
Aluminum/Alloy Wheels +130
Anti-Lock Brakes[Opt on LS] +230
Chrome Wheels +90
Compact Disc W/fm/tape +255
Keyless Entry System[Opt on LS] +75
Leather Seats +285
Limited Slip Diff +100
Luggage Rack +60
Power Drivers Seat +105
Power Sunroof +300
Running Boards +140

PRECIS 1994

Category E

2 Dr STD Hbk	2190	2920

OPTIONS FOR PRECIS

Auto 4-Speed Transmission +240
Air Conditioning +300
AM/FM Stereo Tape +115
Power Steering +95

1993 MITSUBISHI

3000GT 1993

Leather makes its way into the top-of-the-line VR-4. Base models get bigger and better standard equipment lists that include air conditioning, power windows, power door locks, and cruise control (to name a few).

RATINGS (SCALE OF 1-10)

Overall	Safety	Reliability	Performance	Comfort	Value
N/A	6.7	7.4	8.8	6.6	N/A

Category F

2 Dr SL Cpe	9565	12420
2 Dr STD Cpe	7820	10160
2 Dr VR-4 Turbo 4WD Cpe	11810	15340

OPTIONS FOR 3000GT

Auto 4-Speed Transmission +260
Compact Disc Changer +205
Leather Seats[Opt on SL] +215
Sunroof +120

DIAMANTE 1993

Base models are now called ES and gain cruise control, a power trunk opener and steering wheel mounted stereo controls.

RATINGS (SCALE OF 1-10)

Overall	Safety	Reliability	Performance	Comfort	Value
N/A	N/A	8	8.4	8.4	3.8

Category D

4 Dr ES Sdn	6630	8725
4 Dr ES Wgn	6225	8190
4 Dr LS Sdn	7885	10375

OPTIONS FOR DIAMANTE

Diamante Euro Handling Package +505
Diamante Leather Seat Pkg +335
Aluminum/Alloy Wheels[Opt on ES] +135
AM/FM Compact Disc Playr +170
Anti-Lock Brakes[Opt on ES] +290
Keyless Entry System[Opt on ES] +90
Leather Seats[Opt on ES] +335
Power Drivers Seat[Opt on ES] +105
Power Sunroof +220
Premium Sound System[Opt on ES] +105
Traction Control System +245

ECLIPSE 1993

The GS model gets a rear spoiler. GSX Eclipses now have standard antilock brakes. Some interior changes include new seat stitching and a new manual shift knob. Exterior changes are limited to new wheels and optional graphics.

RATINGS (SCALE OF 1-10)

Overall	Safety	Reliability	Performance	Comfort	Value
N/A	N/A	7.7	8.4	6.8	4.4

Category F

2 Dr GSX Turbo 4WD Hbk	6845	8890

OPTIONS FOR ECLIPSE

Auto 4-Speed Transmission +245
Air Conditioning +250
Aluminum/Alloy Wheels +95

Don't forget to refer to the Mileage Adjustment Table at the back of this book!

 © 1999 by Edmund Publications Corporation

Model Description	Trade-in Value	Market Value

Cruise Control +65
Leather Seats +215
Power Door Locks +60
Power Windows +70
Premium Sound System +125
Rear Window Wiper +45
Sunroof +120

EXPO 1993

Mitsubishi increases the number of valves on the Expo's 2.4-liter engine, improving horsepower by twelve percent. Sport and AWD Sport Expo LRVs get the larger 2.4-liter engine found on the Expo. More equipment is now standard on the LRV Sport models.

Category E

Model Description	Trade-in Value	Market Value
4 Dr SP Hbk	5615	7690
4 Dr STD Hbk	4805	6580

OPTIONS FOR EXPO

Auto 4-Speed Transmission +210
Air Conditioning +245
AM/FM Stereo Tape[Std on SP] +95
Anti-Lock Brakes +215
Cruise Control[Std on SP] +65
Luggage Rack +40
Power Door Locks[Std on SP] +70
Power Mirrors[Std on SP] +35
Power Sunroof +185
Power Windows[Std on SP] +80
Premium Sound System +105

EXPO LRV 1993

Category E

Model Description	Trade-in Value	Market Value
2 Dr Sport Hbk	4995	6840
2 Dr STD Hbk	3980	5450

OPTIONS FOR EXPO LRV

Auto 4-Speed Transmission +205
Air Conditioning +245
AM/FM Compact Disc Playr +145
AM/FM Stereo Tape[Opt on STD] +95
Anti-Lock Brakes +215
Cruise Control[Opt on STD] +65
Luggage Rack +40
Power Door Locks[Opt on STD] +70
Power Mirrors[Opt on STD] +35
Power Sunroof +185
Power Windows[Opt on STD] +80
Premium Sound System +105
Rear Window Wiper[Opt on STD] +40

GALANT 1993

Sporty VR-4 model goes the way of the buffalo. GS and GSR models are combined into the previously named luxury LS. The former LS model is now the ES model. Base Galants are now called S models. Confused? So are we. All 1993 Galants use the SOHC 2.0-liter engine, which makes 121-horsepower this year with the addition of an extra two valves per cylinder.

RATINGS (SCALE OF 1-10)

Overall	Safety	Reliability	Performance	Comfort	Value
N/A	N/A	7.9	7.4	7.9	5.7

Category D

Model Description	Trade-in Value	Market Value
4 Dr ES Sdn	5855	7700
4 Dr LS Sdn	6445	8480
4 Dr S Sdn	4515	5940

OPTIONS FOR GALANT

Auto 4-Speed Transmission[Opt on S] +465
Air Conditioning +255
Aluminum/Alloy Wheels[Opt on ES] +135
AM/FM Compact Disc Playr +170
Cruise Control[Opt on S] +75
Power Door Locks[Opt on S] +80
Power Sunroof +220
Power Windows[Opt on S] +80
Premium Sound System +105

MIGHTY MAX PICKUP 1993

The Mighty Max is unchanged for 1993.

Category G

Model Description	Trade-in Value	Market Value
2 Dr STD Std Cab SB	3540	4535

OPTIONS FOR MIGHTY MAX PICKUP

Auto 4-Speed Transmission +275
Air Conditioning +245
AM/FM Stereo Tape +75
Bed Liner +85
Chrome Wheels +75
Power Steering[Std on 4WD] +85
Sliding Rear Window +35

MIRAGE 1993

The Mirage is totally redesigned this year, gaining size but losing weight. A coupe and sedan are offered in Base, S, ES, and LS trim-levels. A five-speed manual transmission is standard on all vehicles, although an automatic is available on all Mirages except the S coupe. Antilock brakes make their first appearance on the Mirage, becoming an available option on the LS sedan.

RATINGS (SCALE OF 1-10)

Overall	Safety	Reliability	Performance	Comfort	Value
N/A	N/A	7.9	8.2	7	6.6

Category E

Model Description	Trade-in Value	Market Value
2 Dr ES Cpe	2825	3865
4 Dr ES Sdn	3405	4665
2 Dr LS Cpe	3145	4310
4 Dr LS Sdn	4070	5575
2 Dr S Cpe	2490	3410
4 Dr S Sdn	3190	4370

Don't forget to refer to the Mileage Adjustment Table at the back of this book!

© 1999 by Edmund Publications Corporation

OPTIONS FOR MIRAGE

Auto 3-Speed Transmission +145
Auto 4-Speed Transmission +195
Air Conditioning +245
Aluminum/Alloy Wheels[Opt on Sdn] +95
Anti-Lock Brakes +215
Compact Disc W/fm/tape +210
Cruise Control[Opt on ES] +65
Power Door Locks[Opt on ES,S,LS,Cpe] +70
Power Steering[Opt on S,ES Cpe] +75
Power Windows[Opt on ES,S,LS,Cpe] +80
Tilt Steering Wheel[Opt on ES] +45
Tinted Glass[Opt on S] +30

MONTERO 1993

Shift-on-the-fly four-wheel drive is introduced to the 1993 Montero. Antilock brakes become standard equipment for the SR and optional for the RS; they were formerly standard only on the LS. Top-of-the-line Monteros may now be ordered with a leather and wood package, for those who really want to get down and dirty.

RATINGS (SCALE OF 1-10)

Overall	Safety	Reliability	Performance	Comfort	Value
6.4	5.5	7.6	7.2	7.4	4.2

Category G

Model	Trade-in Value	Market Value
4 Dr LS 4WD Wgn	10090	12935
4 Dr RS 4WD Wgn	9085	11645
4 Dr SR 4WD Wgn	10595	13585
4 Dr STD 4WD Wgn	8585	11005

OPTIONS FOR MONTERO

Auto 4-Speed Transmission[Std on LS,SR] +255
Montero Lthr & Wood Pkg +355
Air Conditioning +245
AM/FM Compact Disc Playr +115
Cruise Control[Opt on RS] +65
Fog Lights[Std on STD] +45
Leather Seats +235
Limited Slip Diff +80
Luggage Rack +45
Power Door Locks[Opt on RS] +70
Power Sunroof +245
Power Windows[Opt on RS] +70

PRECIS 1993

No changes for the last year of this little hatchback.

Category E

Model	Trade-in Value	Market Value
2 Dr STD Hbk	1960	2685

OPTIONS FOR PRECIS

Auto 4-Speed Transmission +195
Air Conditioning +245
AM/FM Stereo Tape +95
Power Steering +75
Tinted Glass +30

1992 MITSUBISHI

3000GT 1992

New paint. That's the only change for the highly touted 3000GT.

RATINGS (SCALE OF 1-10)

Overall	Safety	Reliability	Performance	Comfort	Value
N/A	6.7	7.4	8.8	6.6	N/A

Category F

Model	Trade-in Value	Market Value
2 Dr SL Cpe	7705	10270
2 Dr STD Cpe	6290	8385
2 Dr VR-4 Turbo 4WD Cpe	9840	13125

OPTIONS FOR 3000GT

Auto 4-Speed Transmission +205
Air Conditioning[Opt on STD] +205
Alarm System[Opt on STD] +60
Anti-Lock Brakes[Opt on STD] +180
Compact Disc W/fm/tape +130
Cruise Control[Opt on STD] +50
Leather Seats +175
Rear Spoiler[Opt on SL] +70
Rear Window Wiper[Opt on STD] +35
Sunroof +95

DIAMANTE 1992

As a replacement for the low-tech Sigma, the Diamante offers V6 power delivering 175-horsepower in the base model, 202-horsepower in the LS. Antilock brakes are standard on the LS and optional on the base, and a driver airbag is standard on both models. A Euro Handling Package and an electronically controlled suspension that includes traction control is an available option on the LS.

RATINGS (SCALE OF 1-10)

Overall	Safety	Reliability	Performance	Comfort	Value
N/A	N/A	8.4	8.4	8.4	4.3

Category D

Model	Trade-in Value	Market Value
4 Dr LS Sdn	5750	7770
4 Dr STD Sdn	4900	6620

OPTIONS FOR DIAMANTE

Euro Handling Pkg +405
Luxury Package +190
Aluminum/Alloy Wheels[Std on LS] +110
AM/FM Compact Disc Playr +140
Anti-Lock Brakes[Std on LS] +235
Cruise Control[Std on LS] +60
Leather Seats +275
Power Passenger Seat +95
Power Sunroof +180
Premium Sound System[Std on LS] +85

Don't forget to refer to the Mileage Adjustment Table at the back of this book!

 © 1999 by Edmund Publications Corporation

Model Description	Trade-in Value	Market Value

ECLIPSE 1992

Freshened front-end styling includes aero headlights and a new air dam. The GS-X model loses leather trim from its options list.

RATINGS (SCALE OF 1-10)

Overall	Safety	Reliability	Performance	Comfort	Value
N/A	N/A	7.5	8.4	6.8	3.3

Category F

2 Dr GS Hbk	3980	5310
2 Dr GS Turbo Hbk	4605	6140
2 Dr GSX Turbo 4WD Hbk	5430	7245
2 Dr STD Hbk	3580	4775

OPTIONS FOR ECLIPSE

4 cyl 2.0 L 16V Engine +205
Auto 4-Speed Transmission +160
Air Conditioning[Std on GSX] +205
Aluminum/Alloy Wheels[Opt on GS] +75
AM/FM Stereo Tape[Opt on STD] +50
Anti-Lock Brakes +180
Cruise Control[Opt on GS] +50
Power Door Locks[Opt on GS] +50
Power Steering[Opt on STD] +90
Power Windows[Opt on GS] +55
Rear Spoiler[Opt on GS] +70
Sunroof +95

EXPO 1992

Mitsubishi creates a van/station wagon hybrid. Designed to compete with everything from the Dodge Caravan to the Subaru Legacy wagon, the Expo seats seven while the Expo LRV seats five. Three models are available including a Sport all-wheel drive, a logical choice for residents of bad-weather states.

Category E

4 Dr SP Hbk	3865	5525
4 Dr SP 4WD Hbk	4405	6290

OPTIONS FOR EXPO

Auto 4-Speed Transmission +170
Air Conditioning +200
Aluminum/Alloy Wheels +80
Anti-Lock Brakes +175
Cruise Control +55
Luggage Rack +30
Power Door Locks +55
Power Sunroof +150
Power Windows +65
Premium Sound System +85

EXPO LRV 1992

Category E

2 Dr Sport Hbk	3655	5225
2 Dr STD Hbk	3465	4955

OPTIONS FOR EXPO LRV

Auto 4-Speed Transmission +165
Air Conditioning +200
Aluminum/Alloy Wheels +80
AM/FM Stereo Tape +75
Anti-Lock Brakes +175
Cruise Control +55
Luggage Rack +30
Power Door Locks +55
Power Sunroof +150
Power Windows +65
Premium Sound System +85
Rear Window Defroster[Opt on STD] +40
Rear Window Wiper +30
Tutone Paint[Opt on 2WD] +35

GALANT 1992

The GS-X model is discontinued in favor of ultra-high performance VR-4. A 195-horsepower engine lurks under its sedate exterior. Standard antilock brakes, four-wheel steering, and leather seating surfaces are a few of the standard equipment items found on this very competent sedan. A Euro Handling Package and an Electronically Controlled Suspension are available options on the LS model.

RATINGS (SCALE OF 1-10)

Overall	Safety	Reliability	Performance	Comfort	Value
N/A	N/A	8.2	7.4	7.9	5.3

Category D

4 Dr GS Sdn	3295	4450
4 Dr GSR Sdn	3640	4915
4 Dr LS Sdn	3395	4585
4 Dr STD Sdn	2520	3405
4 Dr VR-4 Turbo 4WD Sdn	6315	8530

OPTIONS FOR GALANT

Auto 4-Speed Transmission[Opt on GS,STD] +270
Air Conditioning[Std on VR4] +210
Aluminum/Alloy Wheels[Std on GSR,VR4] +110
AM/FM Compact Disc Playr +140
Anti-Lock Brakes[Std on VR4] +235
Cruise Control[Opt on STD] +60
Leather Seats +275
Power Door Locks[Opt on STD] +65
Power Sunroof +180
Power Windows[Opt on STD] +65
Premium Sound System[Std on VR4] +85

MIGHTY MAX PICKUP 1992

Safety-interlocks are now standard on manual transmission models, requiring the clutch to be fully depressed before the vehicle will start. The automatic transmission also gets a shift-interlock, requiring the brake to be depressed before the car can be shifted out of park. Two-wheel drive Mighty Max models lose their rear-wheel antilock brakes.

Don't forget to refer to the Mileage Adjustment Table at the back of this book!

 © 1999 by Edmund Publications Corporation

Model Description	Trade-in Value	Market Value
Category G		
2 Dr Mighty Max Std Cab SB	2955	3940

OPTIONS FOR MIGHTY MAX PICKUP
Auto 4-Speed Transmission +210
Air Conditioning +200
AM/FM Stereo Tape +60
Chrome Wheels +60
Power Steering[Std on 4WD] +70
Rear Step Bumper +35
Sliding Rear Window +30

MIRAGE 1992

Base models finally lose the sticky vinyl interior in favor of full-cloth seats. LS models receive minor exterior trim changes.

Model Description	Trade-in Value	Market Value
Category E		
4 Dr GS Sdn	2455	3510
4 Dr LS Sdn	2255	3220
2 Dr STD Hbk	2085	2980
4 Dr STD Sdn	2085	2975
2 Dr VL Hbk	1830	2615

OPTIONS FOR MIRAGE
Auto 3-Speed Transmission +125
Auto 4-Speed Transmission +160
Air Conditioning +200
Aluminum/Alloy Wheels +80
AM/FM Stereo Tape +75
Cruise Control +55
Power Steering[Std on GS] +60
Rear Window Defroster[Opt on VL,STD Sdn] +40

MONTERO 1992

An all-new Montero is introduced. The new Montero features new wheels, a new grille, more interesting sheetmetal, more curves around the edges, and a very serious looking blackout treatment on the formerly chrome accessories. Horsepower is upped but only enough to keep pace with its 125-pound weight gain. Antilock brakes are standard on the LS and optional on the SR model, working in both two- and four-wheel drive mode.

RATINGS (SCALE OF 1-10)

Overall	Safety	Reliability	Performance	Comfort	Value
6.6	5.5	7.7	7.2	7.4	5.2

Model Description	Trade-in Value	Market Value
Category G		
4 Dr LS 4WD Wgn	7950	10600
4 Dr RS 4WD Wgn	7375	9835
4 Dr SR 4WD Wgn	8290	11050
4 Dr STD 4WD Wgn	6965	9285

OPTIONS FOR MONTERO
Auto 4-Speed Transmission[Std on LS,SR] +195
Air Conditioning +200
Anti-Lock Brakes[Opt on SR] +155
Compact Disc W/fm/tape +170
Cruise Control[Opt on RS] +50
Leather Seats +190
Limited Slip Diff[Opt on SR] +65
Luggage Rack +40
Power Door Locks[Opt on RS] +55
Power Sunroof +200
Power Windows[Opt on RS] +60

PRECIS 1992

The bargain-basement Precis gets a nose job.

Model Description	Trade-in Value	Market Value
Category E		
2 Dr STD Hbk	1790	2560

OPTIONS FOR PRECIS
Auto 4-Speed Transmission +160
Air Conditioning +200
AM/FM Stereo Tape +75
Power Steering +60

1991 MITSUBISHI

3000GT 1991

Dumping the Starion in favor of the 3000GT is one of the better decisions made by Mitsubishi this decade. Gorgeous styling, exceptional handling, and available all-wheel drive characterize the improvements the 3000GT has over Mitsubishi's previous sports cars. A driver airbag is standard on all models; antilock brakes are standard on the SL and VR-4 models.

RATINGS (SCALE OF 1-10)

Overall	Safety	Reliability	Performance	Comfort	Value
N/A	6.6	7	8.8	6.6	N/A

Model Description	Trade-in Value	Market Value
Category F		
2 Dr SL Cpe	6920	9230
2 Dr STD Cpe	5575	7435
2 Dr VR-4 Turbo 4WD Cpe	8970	11960

OPTIONS FOR 3000GT
Auto 4-Speed Transmission +160
Anti-Lock Brakes[Opt on STD] +145
Compact Disc W/fm/tape +105
Cruise Control[Opt on STD] +40
Leather Seats +145
Power Windows[Opt on STD] +45
Premium Sound System[Opt on STD] +85
Rear Window Wiper[Opt on STD] +30

ECLIPSE 1991

Antilock brakes are offered on the GS-T and GSX models.

RATINGS (SCALE OF 1-10)

Overall	Safety	Reliability	Performance	Comfort	Value
N/A	N/A	7.3	8.4	6.8	4.3

Don't forget to refer to the Mileage Adjustment Table at the back of this book!

© 1999 by Edmund Publications Corporation

Model Description	Trade-in Value	Market Value
Category F		
2 Dr GS Hbk	3215	4290
2 Dr GS Turbo Hbk	3565	4755
2 Dr GSX Turbo 4WD Hbk	4245	5665
2 Dr STD Hbk	2870	3830

OPTIONS FOR ECLIPSE

4 cyl 2.0 L 16V Engine +180
Auto 3-Speed Transmission +125
Auto 4-Speed Transmission +135
Turbo Pkg +600
Air Conditioning +170
Aluminum/Alloy Wheels[Opt on GS] +65
AM/FM Stereo Tape[Std on GSX,GS] +40
Anti-Lock Brakes +145
Cruise Control[Std on GSX] +40
Power Door Locks +40
Power Steering[Opt on STD] +75
Power Windows +45
Rear Spoiler[Opt on GS] +55
Rear Window Wiper[Std on GSX] +30

GALANT 1991

A sporty GSR model is added to the lineup.

RATINGS (SCALE OF 1-10)

Overall	Safety	Reliability	Performance	Comfort	Value
N/A	N/A	8	7.4	7.9	5.2

Model Description	Trade-in Value	Market Value
Category D		
4 Dr GS Sdn	3160	4330
4 Dr GSR Sdn	3380	4630
4 Dr LS Sdn	3140	4300
4 Dr STD Sdn	2400	3285
4 Dr VR-4 Turbo 4WD Sdn	4845	6635

OPTIONS FOR GALANT

Auto 4-Speed Transmission[Opt on GS,STD] +215
Air Conditioning[Std on VR4] +170
Aluminum/Alloy Wheels[Opt on GS,LS] +90
AM/FM Compact Disc Playr +115
Anti-Lock Brakes[Opt on GS,GSX] +195
Fog Lights[Std on VR4] +45
Power Door Locks[Opt on STD] +55
Power Sunroof +150
Power Windows[Opt on STD] +55
Premium Sound System +70

MIGHTY MAX PICKUP 1991

A Special Edition Package is added to the option list, featuring wide-spoke wheels, upgraded seats, better carpet, and a tachometer for four-wheel drive models.

Model Description	Trade-in Value	Market Value
Category G		
2 Dr Mighty Max Std Cab SB	2450	3315
2 Dr Mighty Max 4WD Std Cab SB	4005	5410

OPTIONS FOR MIGHTY MAX PICKUP

Auto 3-Speed Transmission +165
Air Conditioning +165
AM/FM Stereo Tape +50
Anti-Lock Brakes +125
Chrome Wheels +50
Limited Slip Diff +55
Power Steering[Std on 4WD] +55
Rear Step Bumper +30

MIRAGE 1991

No changes for the Mirage.

Model Description	Trade-in Value	Market Value
Category E		
4 Dr GS Sdn	2775	4085
4 Dr LS Sdn	2480	3650
2 Dr STD Hbk	1930	2835
4 Dr STD Sdn	2280	3350
2 Dr VL Hbk	1485	2180

OPTIONS FOR MIRAGE

Auto 3-Speed Transmission +110
Auto 4-Speed Transmission +125
Air Conditioning +165
Aluminum/Alloy Wheels +65
AM/FM Stereo Tape +60
Cruise Control +45
Power Door Locks +45
Power Steering[Std on GS] +50
Power Windows +55
Premium Sound System +70
Rear Window Defroster[Opt on VL,STD Sdn] +30

MONTERO 1991

The slow-selling two-door Montero is dropped in favor of the popular four-door. Base models are no longer available with an automatic transmission. RS models now come standard with an automatic. The top-end LS model is available with a manual or automatic transmission.

Model Description	Trade-in Value	Market Value
Category G		
4 Dr LS 4WD Wgn	5495	7430
4 Dr RS 4WD Wgn	5290	7150
4 Dr STD 4WD Wgn	5090	6875

OPTIONS FOR MONTERO

Auto 4-Speed Transmission[Opt on LS] +140
Air Conditioning +165
Aluminum/Alloy Wheels +70
AM/FM Stereo Tape[Std on LS] +50
Power Sunroof +165
Power Windows[Opt on RS] +50
Premium Sound System +75
Rear Window Wiper[Opt on STD] +30
Theft Deterrent System +75

PRECIS 1991

No changes for the Hyundai-twin.

Model Description	Trade-in Value	Market Value
Category E		
2 Dr RS Hbk	1490	2195
2 Dr STD Hbk	1350	1980

Don't forget to refer to the Mileage Adjustment Table at the back of this book!

© 1999 by Edmund Publications Corporation

Model Description	Trade-in Value	Market Value

OPTIONS FOR PRECIS
Auto 4-Speed Transmission +120
Air Conditioning +165
AM/FM Stereo Tape +60
Power Steering +50

1990 MITSUBISHI

ECLIPSE 1990

The first car created by the Chrysler-Mitsubishi partnership, the Eclipse is available as a sporty hatchback with three available engines. Four-wheel disc brakes are standard on all models.

RATINGS (SCALE OF 1-10)

Overall	Safety	Reliability	Performance	Comfort	Value
N/A	N/A	7	8.4	6.8	3.8

Category F

Model	Trade-in Value	Market Value
2 Dr GS Hbk	2860	3810
2 Dr GS Turbo Hbk	3020	4025
2 Dr GSX Turbo 4WD Hbk	3665	4890
2 Dr STD Hbk	2590	3455

OPTIONS FOR ECLIPSE
4 cyl 2.0 L 16V Engine +140
Auto 4-Speed Transmission +105
Air Conditioning +140
Aluminum/Alloy Wheels[Std on GSX] +50
AM/FM Stereo Tape[Opt on STD] +35
Cruise Control +35
Power Door Locks +35
Power Steering[Opt on STD] +60
Power Windows +35
Sunroof +65

GALANT 1990

Mitsubishi's highly acclaimed all-wheel drive system is introduced to the American market sedan in the GS-X model. GS-X models have the same 135-horsepower engine as the GS. No other changes for the 1990 Galant.

RATINGS (SCALE OF 1-10)

Overall	Safety	Reliability	Performance	Comfort	Value
N/A	N/A	7.7	7.4	7.9	5.1

Category D

Model	Trade-in Value	Market Value
4 Dr GS Sdn	2820	3915
4 Dr GSX 4WD Sdn	3135	4355
4 Dr LS Sdn	2645	3670
4 Dr STD Sdn	2270	3150

OPTIONS FOR GALANT
Auto 4-Speed Transmission[Std on LS] +170
Air Conditioning +140
Aluminum/Alloy Wheels[Opt on LS] +75
AM/FM Stereo Tape[Opt on STD] +60
Anti-Lock Brakes +155
Power Door Locks[Opt on STD] +45
Power Sunroof +120
Power Windows[Opt on STD] +45
Premium Sound System +55

MIGHTY MAX PICKUP 1990

New four-cylinder and V6 engines are available in the 1990 Mighty Max, producing greater horsepower and torque. Models are otherwise unchanged.

Category G

Model	Trade-in Value	Market Value
2 Dr Mighty Max Std Cab SB	2280	3165
2 Dr Mighty Max 4WD Std Cab SB	2975	4130

OPTIONS FOR MIGHTY MAX PICKUP
Auto 4-Speed Transmission +140
Air Conditioning +135
AM/FM Stereo Tape +40
Power Steering[Std on 4WD] +45

MIRAGE 1990

The turbocharged model is dropped, no other changes for the Mirage.

Category E

Model	Trade-in Value	Market Value
2 Dr STD Hbk	1520	2335
2 Dr VL Hbk	1155	1775

OPTIONS FOR MIRAGE
Auto 4-Speed Transmission +75
Air Conditioning[Opt on RS,STD,VL] +135
AM/FM Stereo Tape[Opt on RS,STD,VL] +50
Power Steering[Opt on RS,STD] +40

MONTERO 1990

No major changes for the Montero.

Category G

Model	Trade-in Value	Market Value
4 Dr LS 4WD Wgn	4775	6630
4 Dr RS 4WD Wgn	4920	6835
2 Dr SP 4WD Utility	4235	5880
4 Dr STD 4WD Wgn	4585	6370

OPTIONS FOR MONTERO
Auto 4-Speed Transmission[Std on LS,Sport] +135
Air Conditioning +135
Aluminum/Alloy Wheels +55
AM/FM Stereo Tape[Opt on SP,STD] +40
Cruise Control[Std on LS] +35
Power Sunroof +135
Power Windows[Std on LS] +40
Premium Sound System +60

PRECIS 1990

New sheetmetal for Mitsubishi's econobox. This year the Precis is available as a base model or uplevel RS and LS.

Don't forget to refer to the Mileage Adjustment Table at the back of this book!

© 1999 by Edmund Publications Corporation

Model Description	Trade-in Value	Market Value
Category E		
2 Dr LS Hbk	1005	1545
2 Dr RS Hbk	945	1455
2 Dr STD Hbk	895	1375

OPTIONS FOR PRECIS

Auto 4-Speed Transmission +80
Air Conditioning +135
Aluminum/Alloy Wheels +50
AM/FM Stereo Tape[Std on LS] +50
Power Steering +40
Power Sunroof +100
Premium Sound System +55

SIGMA 1990

Mitsubishi's answer to the Accord and Camry is the updated Sigma. For 1990 it receives a 3.0-liter V6 engine as standard equipment. Antilock brakes are available as a standalone option on the Sigma for the first time. Delayed accessory power allows the driver to close windows and the sunroof for up to 30 seconds after the ignition is turned off.

Model Description	Trade-in Value	Market Value
Category D		
4 Dr Luxury Sdn	2605	3615

OPTIONS FOR SIGMA

Eurotech Pkg +340
Anti-Lock Brakes +155
Leather Seats +185
Power Sunroof +120
Premium Sound System +55

VANWAGON 1990

Model Description	Trade-in Value	Market Value
Category G		
2 Dr STD Cargo Van	1790	2485
2 Dr STD Pass. Van	2900	4030

OPTIONS FOR VANWAGON

LS Pkg +135
Air Conditioning +135
AM/FM Stereo Tape +40
Cruise Control +35
Dual Air Conditioning +165
Power Steering +45
Power Sunroof +135
Power Windows +40

1989 MITSUBISHI

GALANT 1989

The Galant is designed to replace the aging Tredia. Available only as a four-door model, the Galant has three trim levels ranging from the economical base Galant to the sporty GS model. Antilock brakes are available only on the GS, which also has Mitsubishi's Active Electronically Controlled Suspension system and a more powerful 135-horsepower engine.

RATINGS (SCALE OF 1-10)

Overall	Safety	Reliability	Performance	Comfort	Value
N/A	N/A	7.6	7.4	7.9	6.3

Model Description	Trade-in Value	Market Value
Category D		
4 Dr GS Sdn	2125	3080
4 Dr LS Sdn	2230	3230
4 Dr STD Sdn	1720	2495

OPTIONS FOR GALANT

Auto 4-Speed Transmission[Std on LS] +115
Air Conditioning +115
AM/FM Stereo Tape[Opt on STD] +50
Anti-Lock Brakes +130
Power Sunroof +100
Premium Sound System +45

MIGHTY MAX PICKUP 1989

The Mighty Max is available in two- and four-wheel drive models, offering long and short beds as well as an extended Macrocab version that has added interior space. Unfortunately, Macrocabs are available only in the two-wheel drive models. Sport models receive exterior updates for 1989 including new exterior graphics, bodyside molding, grille and bumpers.

Model Description	Trade-in Value	Market Value
Category G		
2 Dr Mighty Max Std Cab SB	1700	2465
2 Dr Mighty Max 4WD Std Cab SB	3090	4475
2 Dr Mighty Max Macro Ext Cab SB	2060	2980
2 Dr SPX Ext Cab SB	2130	3085

OPTIONS FOR MIGHTY MAX PICKUP

Auto 4-Speed Transmission +100
Sport Handling Package +130
Air Conditioning +110
AM/FM Stereo Tape +35
Cruise Control +30
Power Steering[Std on 4WD] +40
Premium Sound System +50
Sunroof +40

MIRAGE 1989

The redesigned Mirage is available as a two-door hatchback or four-door sedan. The base hatchback comes standard with a three-speed automatic transmission; the sedan is available with a manual transmission or an automatic. For sports-minded drivers, Mitsubishi offers a turbo version of the hatchback, which has a 135-horsepower engine and a standard five-speed manual transmission.

Model Description	Trade-in Value	Market Value
Category E		
4 Dr LS Sdn	1255	2055
2 Dr STD Hbk	1075	1760
2 Dr STD Turbo Hbk	1180	1930

Don't forget to refer to the Mileage Adjustment Table at the back of this book!

 © 1999 by Edmund Publications Corporation

Model Description	Trade-in Value	Market Value
4 Dr STD Sdn	1145	1880
2 Dr VL Hbk	1010	1655
4 Dr VL Sdn	1075	1765

OPTIONS FOR MIRAGE

Auto 3-Speed Transmission +65
Air Conditioning +110
Aluminum/Alloy Wheels[Opt on Sdn] +45
AM/FM Stereo Tape +40
Power Steering[Std on LS,Turbo] +35

MONTERO 1989

A new four-door body style is added and a new V6 engine is introduced. Coil springs replace leaf springs as the suspension setup on the Montero. The V6 engine is the same one found in the Dodge Caravan and is good for 143-horsepower, the four-cylinder engine is still standard on the two-door. Part-time four-wheel drive is standard on all models.

Category G

Model Description	Trade-in Value	Market Value
4 Dr LS 4WD Wgn	4165	6035
2 Dr SP 4WD Utility	3520	5100
4 Dr STD 4WD Wgn	4060	5880

OPTIONS FOR MONTERO

6 cyl 3.0 L Engine +135
Auto 4-Speed Transmission[Std on LS] +95
Montero Sport Pkg +235
Air Conditioning +110
Alarm System +50
Aluminum/Alloy Wheels +45
AM/FM Stereo Tape[Opt on SP] +35
Cruise Control[Std on LS] +30
Electric Sunroof +95
Limited Slip Diff[Std on LS] +35
Power Windows[Std on LS] +30
Premium Sound System +50

PRECIS 1989

RS and LS Precis get a new center console and armrest. A warning indicator has been added to all models allowing people to forget about the condition of their brakes until the annoying beep goes off.

Category E

Model Description	Trade-in Value	Market Value
2 Dr LS Hbk	825	1355
4 Dr LS Hbk	790	1295
2 Dr RS Hbk	755	1235
2 Dr STD Hbk	695	1135

OPTIONS FOR PRECIS

Auto 3-Speed Transmission +65
Air Conditioning +110
Aluminum/Alloy Wheels +45
AM/FM Stereo Tape[Std on LS] +40
Power Steering +35
Power Sunroof +80
Premium Sound System +45

SIGMA 1989

No changes for 1989.

Category D

Model Description	Trade-in Value	Market Value
4 Dr STD Sdn	2110	3060

OPTIONS FOR SIGMA

Eurotech Package +275
Anti-Lock Brakes +130
Leather Seats +150
Power Sunroof +100
Premium Sound System +45

VANWAGON 1989

Category G

Model Description	Trade-in Value	Market Value
2 Dr STD Cargo Van	1710	2475
2 Dr STD Pass. Van	2325	3370

OPTIONS FOR VANWAGON

LS Pkg +115
Air Conditioning +110
AM/FM Stereo Tape +35
Cruise Control +30
Dual Air Conditioning +135
Electric Sunroof +95
Power Steering +40
Power Windows +30

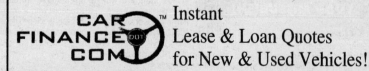

CAR FINANCE DOT COM™
Instant
Lease & Loan Quotes
for New & Used Vehicles!
www.CarFinance.com/edmunds

Don't forget to refer to the Mileage Adjustment Table at the back of this book!

 © 1999 by Edmund Publications Corporation

NISSAN Japan

1996 Nissan 300ZX

1998 NISSAN

200SX 1998

Exterior enhancements include new headlights, taillights, front and rear bumpers and revised grille. Three new colors are available for 1998.

Category F

Model	Trade-in Value	Market Value
2 Dr SE Cpe	10430	12275
2 Dr SE-R Cpe	11930	14035
2 Dr STD Cpe	8500	10000

OPTIONS FOR 200SX

Auto 4-Speed Transmission +665
Air Conditioning[Opt on STD] +690
AM/FM Compact Disc Playr[Opt on STD] +410
Anti-Lock Brakes +600
Keyless Entry System +145
Power Moonroof +595

240SX 1998

No changes to Nissan's sporty coupe.

Category F

Model	Trade-in Value	Market Value
2 Dr LE Cpe	15505	18240
2 Dr SE Cpe	13415	15785
2 Dr STD Cpe	11725	13790

OPTIONS FOR 240SX

Auto 4-Speed Transmission +665
Air Conditioning[Opt on STD] +690
Aluminum/Alloy Wheels[Opt on STD] +260
AM/FM Compact Disc Playr +410
Anti-Lock Brakes +600
Cruise Control[Opt on STD] +175
Power Door Locks[Opt on STD] +165
Power Mirrors[Opt on STD] +100
Power Moonroof[Std on LE] +595
Tilt Steering Wheel[Opt on STD] +150

ALTIMA 1998

Altima is totally, and unnecessarily, redesigned for 1998. The Altima's new look is more wedge-shaped, with a trunk that looks like it has met the working end of a band saw. Standard equipment is up, including a CD player on every model except the XE.

Category D

Model	Trade-in Value	Market Value
4 Dr GLE Sdn	12855	15300
4 Dr GXE Sdn	11555	13755
4 Dr SE Sdn	12570	14965
4 Dr XE Sdn	9620	11455

OPTIONS FOR ALTIMA

Auto 4-Speed Transmission[Std on GLE] +665
Air Conditioning[Opt on XE] +700
Aluminum/Alloy Wheels[Std on SE] +375
Anti-Lock Brakes +790
Compact Disc W/fm/tape[Opt on GXE] +800
Cruise Control[Opt on XE] +200
Keyless Entry System[Opt on GXE] +250
Leather Seats[Opt on SE] +915
Power Drivers Seat[Std on GLE] +285
Power Moonroof +695

FRONTIER 1998

Nissan introduces an all-new truck for 1998. This model, named the Frontier, is larger than the model it replaces, and has improved interior ergonomics.

Category G

Model	Trade-in Value	Market Value
2 Dr SE Ext Cab SB	12780	15215
2 Dr SE 4WD Ext Cab SB	14145	16840
2 Dr STD Std Cab SB	8930	10630
2 Dr XE Std Cab SB	9710	11555
2 Dr XE Ext Cab SB	10385	12360
2 Dr XE 4WD Std Cab SB	12215	14545
2 Dr XE 4WD Ext Cab SB	12390	14750

OPTIONS FOR FRONTIER

Auto 4-Speed Transmission[Opt on 2WD] +875
Aluminum/Alloy Wheels[Std on SE, XE 2WD Ext Cab SB] +285
Bed Liner[Opt on STD, XE, 2WD] +230
Compact Disc W/fm/tape[Opt on XE] +565
Cruise Control[Opt on XE] +175
Keyless Entry System[Opt on XE] +170
Power Door Locks[Opt on XE] +190
Power Mirrors[Opt on XE] +110
Power Windows[Opt on XE] +195
Sliding Rear Window[Opt on XE] +100
Tilt Steering Wheel[Opt on XE] +140

MAXIMA 1998

Side-impact airbags are added to the optional equipment lists of the SE and GLE models. Sterling Mist is a new color choice for this sporty sedan.

Don't forget to refer to the Mileage Adjustment Table at the back of this book!

© 1999 by Edmund Publications Corporation

Model Description	Trade-in Value	Market Value
Category D		
4 Dr GLE Sdn	17320	20620
4 Dr GXE Sdn	13635	16235
4 Dr SE Sdn	14735	17540

OPTIONS FOR MAXIMA

Auto 4-Speed Transmission[Std on GLE] +1145
Aluminum/Alloy Wheels[Opt on GXE] +375
Anti-Lock Brakes +790
Bose Sound System +605
Climate Control for AC[Opt on SE] +250
Compact Disc W/fm/tape[Opt on GXE] +800
Dual Power Seats[Opt on SE] +695
Heated Front Seats +305
Keyless Entry System[Std on GLE] +250
Leather Seats[Opt on SE] +915
Power Drivers Seat +285
Power Moonroof +695
Side Air Bag Restraint +240

PATHFINDER 1998

The only changes to the 1998 Pathfinder include chrome bumpers for the XE model, the addition of air conditioning to XE and SE standard equipment lists and additions to the XE Sport Package equipment.

Model Description	Trade-in Value	Market Value
Category G		
4 Dr LE Wgn	21225	25270
4 Dr LE 4WD Wgn	22520	26805
4 Dr SE 4WD Wgn	19430	23130
4 Dr XE Wgn	15395	18330
4 Dr XE 4WD Wgn	16870	20085

OPTIONS FOR PATHFINDER

Auto 4-Speed Transmission[Std on LE] +830
Aluminum/Alloy Wheels[Opt on XE] +285
Bose Sound System[Opt on SE] +455
Compact Disc W/fm/tape[Opt on SE] +565
Cruise Control[Opt on XE] +175
Dual Power Seats +525
Fog Lights[Opt on XE] +120
Heated Front Seats[Opt on SE] +210
Heated Power Mirrors[Opt on XE] +50
Keyless Entry System[Opt on XE] +170
Leather Seats[Opt on SE] +640
Limited Slip Diff[Std on LE] +220
Power Door Locks[Opt on XE] +190
Power Moonroof +735
Power Windows[Opt on XE] +195

QUEST 1998

No changes to the 1998 Quest.

Model Description	Trade-in Value	Market Value
Category G		
2 Dr GXE Pass. Van	15815	18830
2 Dr XE Pass. Van	15050	17920

OPTIONS FOR QUEST

Aluminum/Alloy Wheels[Opt on XE] +285
Anti-Lock Brakes[Opt on XE] +515
Captain Chairs (4)[Opt on XE] +525
Climate Control for AC +165
Compact Disc W/fm/tape[Opt on XE] +565
Dual Air Conditioning[Opt on XE] +840
Dual Power Seats +525
Leather Seats +640
Power Moonroof +735

SENTRA 1998

A new Sentra SE debuts, sporting the same 140-horespower engine and styling cues found in the 200SX SE-R coupe. Other changes include an exterior freshening that features new front and rear fascias.

Model Description	Trade-in Value	Market Value
Category E		
4 Dr GLE Sdn	10450	12590
4 Dr GXE Sdn	9225	11115
4 Dr SE Sdn	10660	12845
4 Dr STD Sdn	7130	8590
4 Dr XE Sdn	8230	9915

OPTIONS FOR SENTRA

Auto 4-Speed Transmission +665
Air Conditioning[Opt on STD] +675
Anti-Lock Brakes +590
Compact Disc W/fm/tape[Std on GLE] +575
Keyless Entry System[Opt on SE] +125
Power Moonroof +485

1997 NISSAN

200SX 1997

A spoiler is now standard on all models. An additional exterior color is the only other change for 1997.

RATINGS (SCALE OF 1-10)

Overall	Safety	Reliability	Performance	Comfort	Value
7.3	6.6	9.4	7.8	6.8	5.7

Model Description	Trade-in Value	Market Value
Category F		
2 Dr SE Cpe	8400	10120
2 Dr SE-R Cpe	9620	11590
2 Dr STD Cpe	6960	8390

OPTIONS FOR 200SX

Auto 4-Speed Transmission +545
Air Conditioning[Opt on STD] +565
AM/FM Compact Disc Playr +335
AM/FM Stereo Tape[Opt on STD] +135
Anti-Lock Brakes +490
Compact Disc Changer +455
Power Moonroof +485

240SX 1997

Extensive exterior changes update the look of the 240SX. A luxury model is introduced midyear.

Don't forget to refer to the Mileage Adjustment Table at the back of this book!

 © 1999 by Edmund Publications Corporation

Model Description	Trade-in Value	Market Value

RATINGS (SCALE OF 1-10)

Overall	Safety	Reliability	Performance	Comfort	Value
6.9	6.5	9.3	8.4	7.6	2.7

Category F		
2 Dr LE Cpe	14135	17035
2 Dr SE Cpe	12595	15175
2 Dr STD Cpe	11105	13380

OPTIONS FOR 240SX

Auto 4-Speed Transmission +555
Air Conditioning[Opt on STD] +565
Aluminum/Alloy Wheels[Opt on STD] +210
Anti-Lock Brakes +490
Cruise Control[Opt on STD] +140
Leather Seats[Opt on SE] +485
Limited Slip Diff +255
Power Door Locks[Opt on STD] +135
Power Mirrors[Opt on STD] +80
Power Moonroof[Std on LE] +485

ALTIMA 1997

1997 models are virtually identical to 1996 models, except for the addition of new emissions equipment.

RATINGS (SCALE OF 1-10)

Overall	Safety	Reliability	Performance	Comfort	Value
7.4	7	8.8	8	7.4	5.6

Category D		
4 Dr 1997.5 GLE Sdn	12965	15620
4 Dr 1997.5 GXE Sdn	10285	12390
4 Dr 1997.5 SE Sdn	11350	13675
4 Dr 1997.5 XE Sdn	8510	10255
4 Dr GLE Sdn	12395	14935
4 Dr GXE Sdn	8660	10430
4 Dr SE Sdn	11265	13570
4 Dr XE Sdn	8060	9715

OPTIONS FOR ALTIMA

Auto 4-Speed Transmission[Std on GLE] +535
Air Conditioning[Opt on GXE,XE] +575
Aluminum/Alloy Wheels[Opt on GXE] +305
Anti-Lock Brakes +645
Compact Disc W/fm/tape[Std on GLE] +655
Cruise Control[Opt on GXE,XE] +165
Keyless Entry System +205
Leather Seats[Std on GLE] +750
Leather Steering Wheel[Opt on GLE] +75
Power Moonroof[Std on GLE] +565
Rear Spoiler[Std on SE] +280

MAXIMA 1997

The Nissan Maxima gets a new grille, headlights, bumpers and taillights. New alloy wheels and fog lights on the SE, new wheel covers on the GXE, and new aluminum wheels on the GLE round out the changes.

RATINGS (SCALE OF 1-10)

Overall	Safety	Reliability	Performance	Comfort	Value
7.1	6.4	9.1	8	7.8	4.1

Category D		
4 Dr GLE Sdn	15370	18520
4 Dr GXE Sdn	12305	14825
4 Dr SE Sdn	13925	16780

OPTIONS FOR MAXIMA

Auto 4-Speed Transmission[Std on GLE] +935
Aluminum/Alloy Wheels[Opt on GXE] +305
Anti-Lock Brakes +645
Bose Sound System +495
Climate Control for AC[Opt on SE] +205
Compact Disc W/fm/tape[Opt on GXE] +655
Dual Power Seats[Opt on SE] +570
Heated Front Seats +250
Keyless Entry System[Std on GLE] +205
Leather Seats[Opt on SE] +750
Power Moonroof +565

PATHFINDER 1997

Changes to the 1997 Nissan Pathfinder include storage pockets added at all doors, a new exterior color and an available Bose sound system.

RATINGS (SCALE OF 1-10)

Overall	Safety	Reliability	Performance	Comfort	Value
7.2	7	8.9	7.4	8.3	4.6

Category G		
4 Dr LE Wgn	18685	22245
4 Dr LE 4WD Wgn	20765	24720
4 Dr SE 4WD Wgn	17695	21065
4 Dr XE Wgn	12970	15445
4 Dr XE 4WD Wgn	13490	16060

OPTIONS FOR PATHFINDER

Auto 4-Speed Transmission[Std on LE] +680
Air Conditioning[Std on LE] +550
Aluminum/Alloy Wheels[Opt on XE] +235
Bose Sound System[Opt on SE] +375
Climate Control for AC[Opt on SE] +135
Cruise Control[Opt on XE] +145
Dual Power Seats +430
Fog Lights[Opt on XE] +95
Heated Front Seats[Opt on SE] +175
Keyless Entry System[Opt on XE] +140
Leather Seats[Opt on SE] +520
Limited Slip Diff[Std on LE] +180
Luggage Rack[Opt on XE] +105
Power Door Locks[Opt on XE] +155
Power Moonroof +600
Power Windows[Opt on XE] +160
Swing Out Tire Carrier +140

Don't forget to refer to the Mileage Adjustment Table at the back of this book!

 © 1999 by Edmund Publications Corporation

Model Description	Trade-in Value	Market Value

QUEST 1997

A few new colors are the only changes to the 1997 Quest.

RATINGS (SCALE OF 1-10)

Overall	Safety	Reliability	Performance	Comfort	Value
7.8	7	8.6	7.3	7.5	8.8

Category G	Trade-in Value	Market Value
2 Dr GXE Pass. Van	16210	19295
2 Dr XE Pass. Van	12725	15150

OPTIONS FOR QUEST

Aluminum/Alloy Wheels[Opt on XE] +235
Anti-Lock Brakes[Opt on XE] +420
Captain Chairs (4)[Opt on XE] +430
Child Seat (1) +120
Compact Disc W/fm/tape +465
Cruise Control[Opt on XE] +145
Dual Air Conditioning[Opt on XE] +685
Keyless Entry System[Opt on XE] +140
Leather Seats +520
Luggage Rack[Opt on XE] +105
Power Door Locks[Opt on XE] +155
Power Moonroof +600
Power Windows[Opt on XE] +160
Steer. Whl. Radio Cntrls[Opt on XE] +125

SENTRA 1997

The base model is now simply called "Base" instead of S. Nissan works to quiet the Sentra's interior by using a bigger muffler and reducing the number of suspension-mounting points.

RATINGS (SCALE OF 1-10)

Overall	Safety	Reliability	Performance	Comfort	Value
6.9	6.6	8.5	6.4	6.9	5.9

Category E	Trade-in Value	Market Value
4 Dr GLE Sdn	9080	11075
4 Dr GXE Sdn	8020	9780
4 Dr STD Sdn	6680	8145
4 Dr XE Sdn	7240	8830

OPTIONS FOR SENTRA

Auto 4-Speed Transmission +485
Air Conditioning[Opt on STD] +550
Alarm System[Opt on GXE] +305
AM/FM Compact Disc Playr +320
Anti-Lock Brakes +480
Power Moonroof +395
Rear Spoiler +140

TRUCK 1997

No changes for 1997.

RATINGS (SCALE OF 1-10)

Overall	Safety	Reliability	Performance	Comfort	Value
N/A	5.2	8.7	6	6.1	N/A

HALF TON

Category G	Trade-in Value	Market Value
2 Dr STD Std Cab SB	6905	8220
2 Dr XE Std Cab SB	7770	9250
2 Dr XE 4WD Std Cab SB	10970	13055

KING CAB

Category G	Trade-in Value	Market Value
2 Dr SE Ext Cab SB	10945	13030
2 Dr SE 4WD Ext Cab SB	13140	15640
2 Dr XE Ext Cab SB	8920	10620
2 Dr XE 4WD Ext Cab SB	11265	13415

OPTIONS FOR TRUCK

Auto 4-Speed Transmission +680
Air Conditioning[Std on SE] +550
Aluminum/Alloy Wheels[Std on SE] +235
AM/FM Compact Disc Playr +260
Bed Liner[Std on SE] +190
Chrome Bumpers[Std on SE] +105
Cruise Control[Std on SE] +145
Power Steering[Opt on STD] +190
Privacy Glass[Opt on XE] +185
Rear Step Bumper[Opt on STD] +100
Tilt Steering Wheel[Std on SE] +115

1996 NISSAN

200SX 1996

Body color door handles and outside mirrors are newly standard on SE and SE-R models.

RATINGS (SCALE OF 1-10)

Overall	Safety	Reliability	Performance	Comfort	Value
7.3	6.6	9.2	7.8	6.8	6.1

Category F	Trade-in Value	Market Value
2 Dr SE Cpe	7680	9485
2 Dr SE-R Cpe	8840	10915
2 Dr STD Cpe	6675	8240

OPTIONS FOR 200SX

Auto 4-Speed Transmission +420
Air Conditioning[Opt on STD] +460
AM/FM Stereo Tape[Opt on STD] +110
Anti-Lock Brakes +400
Power Moonroof +395
Rear Spoiler[Opt on SE] +155

240SX 1996

Sporty new fabrics and a new grille are the only changes to the attractive 240SX.

RATINGS (SCALE OF 1-10)

Overall	Safety	Reliability	Performance	Comfort	Value
7.1	6.5	9.1	8.4	7.6	4.1

Don't forget to refer to the Mileage Adjustment Table at the back of this book!

 © 1999 by Edmund Publications Corporation

Model Description	Trade-in Value	Market Value
Category F		
2 Dr SE Cpe	10775	13300
2 Dr STD Cpe	8315	10265

OPTIONS FOR 240SX

Auto 4-Speed Transmission +435
Air Conditioning[Std on SE] +460
Aluminum/Alloy Wheels[Std on SE] +170
Anti-Lock Brakes +400
Cruise Control[Std on SE] +115
Keyless Entry System +95
Leather Seats +395
Limited Slip Diff +205
Power Door Locks[Std on SE] +110
Power Sunroof +380
Steer. Whl. Radio Cntrls +100

300ZX 1996

It's the end of the world as we know it. The final Z-car is produced for 1996.

RATINGS (SCALE OF 1-10)

Overall	Safety	Reliability	Performance	Comfort	Value
N/A	N/A	8.5	9.2	6.6	4.2

Model Description	Trade-in Value	Market Value
Category F		
2 Dr 2+2 Cpe	19505	24080
2 Dr STD Conv	22235	27450
2 Dr STD Cpe	19415	23970
2 Dr STD Turbo Cpe	22450	27715

OPTIONS FOR 300ZX

Auto 4-Speed Transmission +490
Glass Panel T-tops[Std on 2+2,Turbo] +575
Leather Seats[Std on Conv] +395
Power Drivers Seat[Std on Turbo] +130

ALTIMA 1996

New wheelcovers, power lock logic and fresh GXE upholstery update this hot-selling sedan.

RATINGS (SCALE OF 1-10)

Overall	Safety	Reliability	Performance	Comfort	Value
7.4	7	8.6	8	7.4	6

Model Description	Trade-in Value	Market Value
Category D		
4 Dr GLE Sdn	10785	13480
4 Dr GXE Sdn	7480	9350
4 Dr SE Sdn	9450	11810
4 Dr XE Sdn	6890	8615

OPTIONS FOR ALTIMA

Auto 4-Speed Transmission[Std on GLE] +455
Air Conditioning[Opt on GXE,XE] +470
AM/FM Stereo Tape[Std on SE] +200
Anti-Lock Brakes +530
Cruise Control[Opt on GXE,XE] +135
Leather Seats +610
Power Moonroof +465

MAXIMA 1996

All new for 1995, the excellent Maxima receives few changes for 1996. A four-way power passenger seat is available, a new center console cupholder will hold a Big Gulp, and two new colors grace the Maxima's decidedly dull flanks. Taillights are as ugly as ever.

RATINGS (SCALE OF 1-10)

Overall	Safety	Reliability	Performance	Comfort	Value
7.2	6.4	9	8	7.8	5.1

Model Description	Trade-in Value	Market Value
Category D		
4 Dr GLE Sdn	13600	17000
4 Dr GXE Sdn	10710	13390
4 Dr SE Sdn	11905	14880

OPTIONS FOR MAXIMA

Auto 4-Speed Transmission[Std on GLE] +695
Aluminum/Alloy Wheels[Opt on GXE] +250
Anti-Lock Brakes +530
Bose Sound System +405
Climate Control for AC[Opt on SE] +165
Compact Disc W/fm/tape[Opt on GXE] +535
Heated Front Seats +205
Keyless Entry System[Std on GLE] +170
Leather Seats[Opt on SE] +610
Power Moonroof +465

PATHFINDER 1996

Outstanding new Pathfinder debuts with dual airbags and great styling. Engine output is up, but the Pathfinder is still not going to win any drag races. The new interior is open, airy, and much more comfortable than most of its competitors.

RATINGS (SCALE OF 1-10)

Overall	Safety	Reliability	Performance	Comfort	Value
7.5	6.9	8.2	7.4	8.3	6.9

Model Description	Trade-in Value	Market Value
Category G		
4 Dr LE Wgn	16370	19960
4 Dr LE 4WD Wgn	17080	20825
4 Dr SE 4WD Wgn	15770	19235
4 Dr XE Wgn	11455	13970
4 Dr XE 4WD Wgn	12005	14640

OPTIONS FOR PATHFINDER

Auto 4-Speed Transmission[Std on LE] +545
Air Conditioning[Std on LE] +450
Climate Control for AC[Opt on SE] +110
Cruise Control[Opt on XE] +115
Dual Power Seats +350
Fog Lights[Opt on XE] +80
Heated Front Seats[Opt on SE] +140
Keyless Entry System[Opt on XE] +115
Leather Seats[Opt on SE] +425
Limited Slip Diff[Std on LE] +145
Luggage Rack[Opt on XE] +85

Don't forget to refer to the Mileage Adjustment Table at the back of this book!

 © 1999 by Edmund Publications Corporation

Power Door Locks[Opt on XE] +125
Power Moonroof +490
Power Windows[Opt on XE] +130
Swing Out Tire Carrier +115

QUEST 1996

Substantial upgrades include dual airbags, integrated child safety seats, side-impact protection meeting 1997 passenger car standards, revamped fabrics, new colors, freshened styling, and a cool in-dash six-disc CD changer. The Quest is still in the hunt.

RATINGS (SCALE OF 1-10)

Overall	Safety	Reliability	Performance	Comfort	Value
7.7	6.6	8.3	7.3	7.5	8.6

Category G

Model	Trade-in	Market
2 Dr GXE Pass. Van	13775	16795
2 Dr XE Pass. Van	10940	13345

OPTIONS FOR QUEST

Aluminum/Alloy Wheels[Opt on XE] +190
Anti-Lock Brakes[Opt on XE] +345
Child Seat (1) +95
Climate Control for AC +110
Cruise Control[Opt on XE] +115
Dual Air Conditioning[Opt on XE] +560
Keyless Entry System[Opt on XE] +115
Leather Seats +425
Luggage Rack[Opt on XE] +85
Power Door Locks[Opt on XE] +125
Power Passenger Seat +150
Power Windows[Opt on XE] +130
Privacy Glass[Opt on XE] +150

SENTRA 1996

It sure is plain Jane, huh? What we have here is a three-box sedan with Saabish rear styling. Prices have crept up, making the Sentra a hard sell against the Neon, Prizm and Cavalier. Still, you may be able to find a good deal on a former rental vehicle. We've seen tons of them at the Alamo rental lots.

RATINGS (SCALE OF 1-10)

Overall	Safety	Reliability	Performance	Comfort	Value
7	6.7	8.7	6.4	6.9	6.3

Category E

Model	Trade-in	Market
4 Dr GLE Sdn	7565	9580
4 Dr GXE Sdn	7035	8900
4 Dr STD Sdn	5565	7045
4 Dr XE Sdn	6450	8165

OPTIONS FOR SENTRA

Auto 4-Speed Transmission +435
Air Conditioning[Opt on STD] +450
AM/FM Stereo Tape[Opt on STD] +170
Anti-Lock Brakes +395

TRUCK 1996

No changes for the Truck.

RATINGS (SCALE OF 1-10)

Overall	Safety	Reliability	Performance	Comfort	Value
N/A	5.2	8.5	6	6.1	N/A

HALF TON

Category G

Model	Trade-in	Market
2 Dr STD Std Cab SB	6765	8250
2 Dr XE Std Cab SB	7460	9100
2 Dr XE 4WD Std Cab SB	9545	11640

KING CAB

Category G

Model	Trade-in	Market
2 Dr SE Ext Cab SB	9775	11920
2 Dr SE 4WD Ext Cab SB	11640	14195
2 Dr XE Ext Cab SB	8165	9960
2 Dr XE 4WD Ext Cab SB	10085	12295

OPTIONS FOR TRUCK

Auto 4-Speed Transmission +545
Air Conditioning[Std on SE] +450
Aluminum/Alloy Wheels[Std on SE] +190
AM/FM Stereo Tape +135
Center Console[Std on 2WD] +90
Chrome Bumpers[Std on SE] +90
Chrome Wheels +135
Cruise Control[Std on SE] +115
Flip-Up Sunroof[Opt on 4WD] +185
Power Steering[Opt on STD] +155
Power Windows[Opt on 4WD] +130
Privacy Glass[Std on SE] +150
Tilt Steering Wheel[Opt on Half Ton] +95

1995 NISSAN

200SX 1995

A Sentra derived 200SX is introduced to the sporting public. Basically a two-door version of the redesigned Sentra, the 200SX comes equipped with dual airbags. The 200SX has two available powerplants, a 1.6-liter four-cylinder that produces 115-horsepower or a 2.0-liter four that is good for 140 ponies.

RATINGS (SCALE OF 1-10)

Overall	Safety	Reliability	Performance	Comfort	Value
7.2	7.2	8.8	7.8	6.8	5.5

Category F

Model	Trade-in	Market
2 Dr SE Cpe	7020	8775
2 Dr SE-R Cpe	7795	9740
2 Dr STD Cpe	5815	7265

OPTIONS FOR 200SX

Auto 4-Speed Transmission +355
Air Conditioning[Opt on STD] +380

Don't forget to refer to the Mileage Adjustment Table at the back of this book!

© 1999 by Edmund Publications Corporation

AM/FM Stereo Tape[Opt on STD] +90
Anti-Lock Brakes +330
Power Moonroof +325
Rear Spoiler[Opt on SE] +130

240SX 1995

Totally redesigned, the 240SX loses its hatchback and convertible body styles. Available as a base or SE model, the 240 uses the same engine as the previous generation model. Dual airbags are standard on the new 240SX as are side door beams that help the car meet federal side-impact standards.

RATINGS (SCALE OF 1-10)

Overall	Safety	Reliability	Performance	Comfort	Value
7.1	7.1	8.9	8.4	7.6	3.5

Category F	Trade-in Value	Market Value
2 Dr SE Cpe	8580	10730
2 Dr STD Cpe	7415	9270

OPTIONS FOR 240SX

Auto 4-Speed Transmission +380
Air Conditioning[Std on SE] +380
Aluminum/Alloy Wheels[Std on SE] +140
Anti-Lock Brakes +330
Cruise Control[Std on SE] +95
Leather Seats +325
Leather Steering Wheel[Opt on SE] +55
Limited Slip Diff +170
Power Door Locks[Std on SE] +90
Power Moonroof +325

300ZX 1995

No changes for the 300ZX.

RATINGS (SCALE OF 1-10)

Overall	Safety	Reliability	Performance	Comfort	Value
N/A	N/A	8.3	9.2	6.6	4.1

Category F	Trade-in Value	Market Value
2 Dr 2+2 Cpe	16315	20390
2 Dr STD Cpe	16045	20060
2 Dr STD Conv	18780	23475
2 Dr STD Turbo Cpe	18995	23740

OPTIONS FOR 300ZX

Auto 4-Speed Transmission +400
Glass Panel T-tops[Std on 2+2,Turbo] +470
Leather Seats[Std on Conv] +325
Power Drivers Seat[Opt on STD Cpe] +110

ALTIMA 1995

Minor exterior tweaks to the grille, taillights and wheels are the only changes for this attractive compact from Tennessee.

RATINGS (SCALE OF 1-10)

Overall	Safety	Reliability	Performance	Comfort	Value
7.5	7.7	8.5	8	7.4	5.9

Category D	Trade-in Value	Market Value
4 Dr GLE Sdn	9215	11660
4 Dr GXE Sdn	6480	8200
4 Dr SE Sdn	8175	10345
4 Dr XE Sdn	6315	7995

OPTIONS FOR ALTIMA

Auto 4-Speed Transmission[Std on GLE] +370
Air Conditioning[Opt on GXE,XE] +385
Anti-Lock Brakes +430
Cruise Control[Opt on GXE,XE] +110
Power Moonroof[Opt on GXE] +380

MAXIMA 1995

Wow, what a beauty. The redesigned Maxima bows with an aerodynamic shape and a lengthened wheelbase. The new Maxima is available as a budget-minded GXE, sporty SE or luxurious GLE. All Maximas get the 190-horsepower engine previously exclusive to the SE.

RATINGS (SCALE OF 1-10)

Overall	Safety	Reliability	Performance	Comfort	Value
7.3	7	8.8	8	7.8	5

Category D	Trade-in Value	Market Value
4 Dr GLE Sdn	11815	14960
4 Dr GXE Sdn	9375	11865
4 Dr SE Sdn	10300	13040

OPTIONS FOR MAXIMA

Auto 4-Speed Transmission[Std on GLE] +580
Aluminum/Alloy Wheels[Opt on GXE] +205
Anti-Lock Brakes +430
Climate Control for AC[Opt on SE] +135
Compact Disc W/fm/tape[Std on GLE] +440
Heated Front Seats +165
Keyless Entry System[Std on GLE] +135
Leather Seats[Std on GLE] +500
Power Drivers Seat[Std on GLE] +155
Power Moonroof +380
Rear Spoiler[Std on SE] +190

PATHFINDER 1995

Whoopee. A two-wheel drive version of Nissan's ancient sport utility is now available in LE flavor.

RATINGS (SCALE OF 1-10)

Overall	Safety	Reliability	Performance	Comfort	Value
6.6	4.3	8.6	7.6	7.5	4.9

Category G	Trade-in Value	Market Value
4 Dr LE Wgn	13600	16790
4 Dr LE 4WD Wgn	14445	17835
4 Dr SE 4WD Wgn	12205	15065

Don't forget to refer to the Mileage Adjustment Table at the back of this book!

 © 1999 by Edmund Publications Corporation

Model Description	Trade-in Value	Market Value
4 Dr XE Wgn	9895	12215
4 Dr XE 4WD Wgn	10090	12455

OPTIONS FOR PATHFINDER

Auto 4-Speed Transmission[Std on LE] +545
Air Conditioning[Std on LE] +370
Camper/Towing Package +130
Compact Disc W/fm/tape[Opt on SE] +310
Cruise Control[Opt on XE] +95
Fog Lights[Opt on XE] +65
Heated Front Seats[Opt on SE] +115
Intermittent Wipers[Opt on XE] +35
Keyless Entry System[Opt on XE] +95
Leather Seats[Opt on SE] +350
Limited Slip Diff[Std on LE] +120
Power Door Locks[Opt on XE] +105
Power Windows[Opt on XE] +105
Remote Trunk Release[Opt on XE] +35
Swing Out Tire Carrier[Opt on XE] +95

QUEST 1995

GXE models get standard captain's chairs for second-row occupants. The Extra Performance Package is renamed the Handling Package. No other significant changes for the Quest.

RATINGS (SCALE OF 1-10)

Overall	Safety	Reliability	Performance	Comfort	Value
7.5	6.5	7.6	7.3	7.1	9

Model Description	Trade-in Value	Market Value
Category G		
2 Dr GXE Pass. Van	11730	14480
2 Dr XE Pass. Van	9390	11595

OPTIONS FOR QUEST

Anti-Lock Brakes[Opt on XE] +280
Cruise Control[Opt on XE] +95
Dual Air Conditioning[Opt on XE] +460
Keyless Entry System +95
Leather Seats +350
Lighted Entry System +65
Luggage Rack[Opt on XE] +70
Power Door Locks[Opt on XE] +105
Power Moonroof +400
Power Passenger Seat +125
Power Windows[Opt on XE] +105
Privacy Glass[Opt on XE] +125

SENTRA 1995

An all-new Sentra is released featuring aero styling and a stubby trunk. The 1995 Sentra is available only as a four-door sedan, the two-door model now being called the 200SX. Increased interior space is the most noticeable feature of the redesign. The engines remain unchanged from previous models.

RATINGS (SCALE OF 1-10)

Overall	Safety	Reliability	Performance	Comfort	Value
N/A	N/A	8.3	6.4	6.9	5.8

Model Description	Trade-in Value	Market Value
Category E		
4 Dr GLE Sdn	6680	8680
4 Dr GXE Sdn	5930	7705
4 Dr STD Sdn	4690	6090
4 Dr XE Sdn	5465	7100

OPTIONS FOR SENTRA

Auto 4-Speed Transmission +355
Air Conditioning[Opt on STD] +370
Anti-Lock Brakes +320

TRUCK 1995

The two-wheel drive Nissan trucks finally get rear-wheel antilock brakes.

RATINGS (SCALE OF 1-10)

Overall	Safety	Reliability	Performance	Comfort	Value
N/A	4.3	8.3	6	6.1	N/A

HALF TON

Model Description	Trade-in Value	Market Value
Category G		
2 Dr HD Std Cab LB	6805	8405
2 Dr STD Std Cab SB	5595	6905
2 Dr XE Std Cab SB	6295	7775
2 Dr XE 4WD Std Cab SB	8630	10655

KING CAB

Model Description	Trade-in Value	Market Value
Category G		
2 Dr SE V6 4WD Ext Cab SB	10590	13075
2 Dr XE Ext Cab SB	7120	8790
2 Dr XE 4WD Ext Cab SB	9170	11320
2 Dr XE V6 Ext Cab SB	7840	9675
2 Dr XE V6 4WD Ext Cab SB	9800	12100

OPTIONS FOR TRUCK

Auto 4-Speed Transmission +520
Air Conditioning[Std on SE V6] +370
AM/FM Stereo Tape[Std on SE V6] +110
Chrome Bumpers[Std on SE V6] +70
Chrome Wheels[Std on XE V6,King Cab XE 4WD Ext Cab SB] +110
Cruise Control[Opt on XE V6] +95
Flip-Up Sunroof +150
Limited Slip Diff[Opt on XE V6] +120
Power Door Locks +105
Power Steering[Std on HD,SE V6,XE V6,4WD] +130
Power Windows +105
Rear Step Bumper[Opt on STD] +65
Tilt Steering Wheel[Opt on XE V6] +80

1994 NISSAN

240SX 1994

A convertible body style is the sole offering this year as the coupe is set for a complete redesign.

Don't forget to refer to the Mileage Adjustment Table at the back of this book!

 © 1999 by Edmund Publications Corporation

Model Description	Trade-in Value	Market Value

RATINGS (SCALE OF 1-10)

Overall	Safety	Reliability	Performance	Comfort	Value
N/A	N/A	8.7	8	7.3	3.5

Category F

2 Dr SE Conv	8645	10940

OPTIONS FOR 240SX

Air Conditioning +310

300ZX 1994

A passenger airbag is a new safety feature on the 300ZX, which allows the use of manual seat belts. Remote keyless entry is another new feature for the 300ZX.

RATINGS (SCALE OF 1-10)

Overall	Safety	Reliability	Performance	Comfort	Value
N/A	N/A	8.3	9.2	6.6	3.6

Category F

2 Dr 2+2 Cpe	13855	17540
2 Dr STD Cpe	13700	17340
2 Dr STD Conv	16155	20450
2 Dr STD Turbo Cpe	15960	20200

OPTIONS FOR 300ZX

Auto 4-Speed Transmission +355
Alarm System +90
Compact Disc W/fm/tape +195
Glass Panel T-tops[Opt on STD] +385
Leather Seats[Std on Conv] +265

ALTIMA 1994

A passenger-side airbag is added to this hot-selling Tennessee-built compact. SE models gain a standard sunroof and GLEs have it as an available option.

RATINGS (SCALE OF 1-10)

Overall	Safety	Reliability	Performance	Comfort	Value
7.5	7.7	8.6	8	7.4	5.9

Category D

4 Dr GLE Sdn	7785	9985
4 Dr GXE Sdn	5585	7160
4 Dr SE Sdn	7070	9060
4 Dr XE Sdn	5200	6665

OPTIONS FOR ALTIMA

Auto 4-Speed Transmission[Std on GLE] +325
Air Conditioning[Opt on GXE,XE] +315
Aluminum/Alloy Wheels[Opt on GXE] +165
Anti-Lock Brakes +355
Compact Disc W/fm/tape +360
Cruise Control[Opt on GXE,XE] +90
Leather Seats +410
Power Antenna[Opt on GXE] +45
Power Sunroof[Opt on GXE] +270
Premium Sound System +130

MAXIMA 1994

No changes for the 1994 Maxima.

RATINGS (SCALE OF 1-10)

Overall	Safety	Reliability	Performance	Comfort	Value
N/A	N/A	8.5	8.8	7.9	4.4

Category D

4 Dr GXE Sdn	7530	9650
4 Dr SE Sdn	8120	10415

OPTIONS FOR MAXIMA

Auto 4-Speed Transmission[Opt on SE] +345
AM/FM Compact Disc Playr +210
Anti-Lock Brakes +355
Bose Sound System[Std on SE] +270
Climate Control for AC +110
Leather Seats +410
Power Drivers Seat +125
Power Passenger Seat +140
Power Sunroof +270

PATHFINDER 1994

The LE model is introduced for the country-club crowd. Standard equipment on the LE includes leather upholstery, heated seats, a CD player, and a luggage rack. All 1994 Pathfinders sport a redesigned dashboard and instrument panel. SE models get new alloy wheels and a sunroof.

RATINGS (SCALE OF 1-10)

Overall	Safety	Reliability	Performance	Comfort	Value
6.4	4.3	8.3	7.6	7.5	4.3

Category G

4 Dr LE 4WD Wgn	12720	15900
4 Dr SE 4WD Wgn	10495	13115
4 Dr XE Wgn	8230	10285
4 Dr XE 4WD Wgn	8720	10900

OPTIONS FOR PATHFINDER

Auto 4-Speed Transmission[Std on LE] +455
Air Conditioning[Std on LE] +300
Alarm System[Opt on XE] +130
Cruise Control[Opt on XE] +80
Fog Lights[Opt on XE] +55
Heated Front Seats +95
Intermittent Wipers[Opt on XE] +30
Leather Seats[Opt on SE] +285
Limited Slip Diff[Std on LE] +100
Luggage Rack[Opt on SE] +60
Power Door Locks[Opt on XE] +85
Power Windows[Opt on XE] +85
Theft Deterrent System[Opt on XE] +140

Don't forget to refer to the Mileage Adjustment Table at the back of this book!

© 1999 by Edmund Publications Corporation

Model Description	Trade-in Value	Market Value

QUEST 1994

The Quest gets a driver airbag added to its standard equipment list for 1994. GXE models can now be had with a premium audio package that includes a CD player.

RATINGS (SCALE OF 1-10)

Overall	Safety	Reliability	Performance	Comfort	Value
7.5	6.6	7.9	7.3	7.1	8.5

Category G		
2 Dr GXE Pass. Van	9975	12470
2 Dr XE Pass. Van	7845	9810

OPTIONS FOR QUEST

Aluminum/Alloy Wheels +130
Anti-Lock Brakes[Opt on XE] +230
Camper/Towing Package +105
Captain Chairs (2) +175
Compact Disc W/fm/tape +255
Cruise Control[Opt on XE] +80
Dual Air Conditioning[Opt on XE] +375
Keyless Entry System +75
Leather Seats +285
Lighted Entry System +55
Luggage Rack[Opt on XE] +60
Power Door Locks[Opt on XE] +85
Power Moonroof +325
Power Passenger Seat +100
Power Windows[Opt on XE] +85

SENTRA 1994

CFC-free coolant is now standard on vehicles equipped with air conditioning. XE models get more standard equipment that includes air conditioning, cruise control and a stereo with cassette player.

RATINGS (SCALE OF 1-10)

Overall	Safety	Reliability	Performance	Comfort	Value
N/A	N/A	8.7	7.2	7.9	5.8

Category E		
2 Dr 1994.5 Limited Sdn	4510	6010
4 Dr 1994.5 Limited Sdn	5120	6830
2 Dr E Sdn	3860	5150
4 Dr E Sdn	3730	4970
4 Dr GXE Sdn	5410	7210
2 Dr SE Sdn	4680	6240
2 Dr SE-R Sdn	5030	6705
2 Dr XE Sdn	4340	5790
4 Dr XE Sdn	4490	5985

OPTIONS FOR SENTRA

Auto 4-Speed Transmission +300
Air Bag Restraint[Std on GXE] +215
Air Conditioning[Opt on E,SE,SE-R] +300
Aluminum/Alloy Wheels[Std on GXE,SE-R] +120
AM/FM Stereo Tape[Opt on E,SE] +115
Anti-Lock Brakes +265
Cruise Control[Opt on SE,SE-R] +80
Power Steering[Opt on E] +95
Power Sunroof +225
Tilt Steering Wheel[Opt on E] +55

TRUCK 1994

The Nissan pickup gets a redesigned dashboard and a new model for 1994. The new model is called the XE.

RATINGS (SCALE OF 1-10)

Overall	Safety	Reliability	Performance	Comfort	Value
N/A	4.3	8.3	6	6.1	N/A

HALF TON

Category G		
2 Dr STD Std Cab SB	4860	6070
2 Dr V6 Std Cab LB	5680	7105
2 Dr XE Std Cab SB	5465	6830
2 Dr XE 4WD Std Cab SB	7350	9185

KING CAB

Category G		
2 Dr SE V6 Ext Cab SB	8335	10420
2 Dr SE V6 4WD Ext Cab SB	9410	11765
2 Dr XE Ext Cab SB	6135	7670
2 Dr XE 4WD Ext Cab SB	8475	10590
2 Dr XE V6 4WD Ext Cab SB	8935	11170

OPTIONS FOR TRUCK

Auto 4-Speed Transmission +420
Sport Handling Package +420
Air Conditioning +300
Aluminum/Alloy Wheels +130
AM/FM Stereo Tape[Std on SE V6,XE Std Cab SB] +90
Bed Liner +105
Chrome Bumpers[Std on SE V6] +60
Chrome Wheels[Std on SE V6] +90
Cruise Control[Opt on XE V6] +80
Flip-Up Sunroof +125
Intermittent Wipers[Opt on Half Ton,XE] +30
Limited Slip Diff +100
Power Door Locks +85
Power Steering[Std on SE V6,XE V6,4WD] +105
Power Windows +85
Rear Jump Seats[Opt on XE] +85
Sliding Rear Window[Opt on STD] +45
Tilt Steering Wheel[Opt on XE V6] +65

1993 NISSAN

240SX 1993

The luxury-oriented LE is dropped from the 240SX lineup due to poor sales. Don't worry, those with a penchant for leather can still get their kicks in a cowhide equipped SE model. Half of the 240SXs produced this year have CFC-free air conditioning.

Don't forget to refer to the Mileage Adjustment Table at the back of this book!

© 1999 by Edmund Publications Corporation

Model Description	Trade-in Value	Market Value

RATINGS (SCALE OF 1-10)

Overall	Safety	Reliability	Performance	Comfort	Value
N/A	N/A	8.8	8	7.3	4.2

Category F		
2 Dr SE Hbk	5705	7410
2 Dr SE Conv	7355	9555
2 Dr SE Cpe	5690	7390
2 Dr STD Hbk	5110	6635
2 Dr STD Cpe	4975	6465

OPTIONS FOR 240SX

Auto 4-Speed Transmission[Std on Conv] +250
Air Conditioning +250
Anti-Lock Brakes +220
Flip-Up Sunroof +120
Leather Seats +215
Limited Slip Diff +115
Power Sunroof +205
Sport Suspension +80

300ZX 1993

The first chop-top Z-car debuts this year. A basket handle behind the seats reduces body flex in the 300ZX and gives the seat belts an anchor point. No changes for the other models.

RATINGS (SCALE OF 1-10)

Overall	Safety	Reliability	Performance	Comfort	Value
N/A	N/A	8.2	9.2	6.6	3.1

Category F		
2 Dr 2+2 Cpe	11025	14320
2 Dr STD Conv	12860	16700
2 Dr STD Cpe	10840	14080
2 Dr STD Turbo Cpe	13010	16900

OPTIONS FOR 300ZX

Auto 4-Speed Transmission +290
AM/FM Stereo Tape[Opt on Cpe] +60
Glass Panel T-tops[Std on 2+2,Turbo] +315
Leather Seats +215
Premium Sound System[Std on 2+2,Turbo] +125

ALTIMA 1993

The Infiniti-inspired Altima replaces the aging Stanza. Swooping sheetmetal, a longer wheelbase, and increased cabin size distinguish the Altima from its lackluster predecessor. The Altima is powered by a twin-cam four-cylinder that produces 150 horsepower. A driver airbag is standard on the Altima, as are motorized seat belts.

RATINGS (SCALE OF 1-10)

Overall	Safety	Reliability	Performance	Comfort	Value
N/A	N/A	8.3	8	7.4	6.3

Category D		
4 Dr GLE Sdn	6760	8895
4 Dr GXE Sdn	4720	6210
4 Dr SE Sdn	5975	7860
4 Dr XE Sdn	4510	5930

OPTIONS FOR ALTIMA

Auto 4-Speed Transmission[Std on GLE] +250
Air Conditioning[Opt on GXE,XE] +255
Alarm System[Opt on SE] +170
Anti-Lock Brakes +290
Compact Disc W/fm/tape[Opt on SE] +290
Cruise Control[Opt on GXE,XE] +75
Leather Seats +335
Leather Steering Wheel[Std on SE] +35
Power Antenna[Opt on GXE] +35
Power Moonroof +255
Theft Deterrent System +130

MAXIMA 1993

The driver airbag is now standard on Nissan's front-wheel drive midsize sedan. Both cars have CFC-free air conditioning and SE models get a trick new stereo, compliments of Bose.

RATINGS (SCALE OF 1-10)

Overall	Safety	Reliability	Performance	Comfort	Value
N/A	N/A	8.2	8.8	7.9	5.6

Category D		
4 Dr GXE Sdn	6345	8350
4 Dr SE Sdn	6740	8865

OPTIONS FOR MAXIMA

Auto 4-Speed Transmission[Opt on SE] +285
Anti-Lock Brakes +290
Bose Sound System[Std on SE] +220
Climate Control for AC +90
Compact Disc W/fm/tape +290
Dual Power Seats +255
Leather Seats +335
Power Sunroof +220

NX 1993

The 2000 gets a standard T-top. New interior fabrics mark the only other changes for the NX line.

RATINGS (SCALE OF 1-10)

Overall	Safety	Reliability	Performance	Comfort	Value
N/A	N/A	7.9	8.6	6.9	4.6

Category E		
2 Dr 1600 Cpe	4005	5485
2 Dr 2000 Cpe	4880	6680

OPTIONS FOR NX

Auto 4-Speed Transmission +250
Air Conditioning +245
AM/FM Stereo Tape[Opt on 1600] +95

Don't forget to refer to the Mileage Adjustment Table at the back of this book!

 © 1999 by Edmund Publications Corporation

Model Description	Trade-in Value	Market Value

Anti-Lock Brakes +215
Cruise Control +65
Power Door Locks +70
Power Windows +80
T-Bar Roof[Opt on 1600] +275

PATHFINDER 1993

CFC-free air conditioning is standard and side-impact door beams are introduced to protect occupants. The Pathfinder's standard stereo gets its wattage increased and the SE's leather seats are now heated. How cozy.

RATINGS (SCALE OF 1-10)

Overall	Safety	Reliability	Performance	Comfort	Value
6.5	4.3	8.7	7.6	6.8	4.9

Category G

Model Description	Trade-in Value	Market Value
4 Dr SE 4WD Wgn	8905	11420
4 Dr XE Wgn	6915	8865
4 Dr XE 4WD Wgn	7490	9600

OPTIONS FOR PATHFINDER

Auto 4-Speed Transmission +380
Sport Handling Package +355
Air Conditioning[Opt on XE] +245
Aluminum/Alloy Wheels +105
Heated Front Seats +75
Leather Seats +235
Limited Slip Diff +80
Luggage Rack +45
Power Door Locks[Opt on XE] +70
Power Windows[Opt on XE] +70
Sunroof +90

QUEST 1993

After messing around with the Axxess and Nissan Van, Nissan finally gets it right on this joint project with Mercury. The Quest is a front-engine, front-wheel drive minivan that is built alongside the Villager at the Ford plant in Avon Lake, Ohio. The Quest is powered by a 3.0-liter V6 engine that produces 150-horsepower. The Quest seats seven and has standard air conditioning, a tilt steering wheel, and a stereo with cassette. Antilock brakes are optional on the Quest.

RATINGS (SCALE OF 1-10)

Overall	Safety	Reliability	Performance	Comfort	Value
6.9	5.3	7.3	7.3	7.1	7.4

Category G

Model Description	Trade-in Value	Market Value
2 Dr GXE Pass. Van	8295	10635
2 Dr STD Cargo Van	6670	8550
2 Dr XE Pass. Van	6820	8740

OPTIONS FOR QUEST

7 Passenger Seating[Opt on XE] +165
Aluminum/Alloy Wheels[Opt on XE] +105
AM/FM Stereo Tape[Std on XE] +75
Anti-Lock Brakes +185
Cruise Control[Opt on XE] +65
Dual Air Conditioning[Opt on XE] +305
Keyless Entry System +60
Leather Seats +235
Lighted Entry System +45
Luggage Rack[Opt on XE] +45
Power Door Locks[Opt on XE] +70
Power Passenger Seat +80
Power Sunroof +245
Power Windows[Opt on XE] +70
Premium Sound System[Opt on XE] +110

SENTRA 1993

A driver airbag is now standard on the GXE model. Base models ditch the Flintstone transmissions, gaining a standard five-speed manual or optional four-speed automatic in place of the archaic four-speed manual and three-speed automatic that was formerly available. All Sentras receive minor nose work that includes a redesigned grille, headlights and front fascia.

RATINGS (SCALE OF 1-10)

Overall	Safety	Reliability	Performance	Comfort	Value
N/A	N/A	8.5	7.2	7.9	4.7

Category E

Model Description	Trade-in Value	Market Value
2 Dr E Sdn	3030	4150
4 Dr E Sdn	2950	4045
4 Dr GXE Sdn	4205	5755
2 Dr SE Sdn	3425	4695
2 Dr SE-R Sdn	4030	5520
2 Dr XE Sdn	3295	4515
4 Dr XE Sdn	3320	4545

OPTIONS FOR SENTRA

Auto 4-Speed Transmission +285
Air Bag Restraint[Std on GXE] +175
Air Conditioning[Std on GXE] +245
AM/FM Stereo Tape[Std on GXE] +95
Anti-Lock Brakes +215
Cruise Control[Std on GXE] +65
Power Steering[Opt on E] +75
Power Sunroof +185

TRUCK 1993

CFC-free air conditioning debuts. No other changes to this mini-bruiser.

RATINGS (SCALE OF 1-10)

Overall	Safety	Reliability	Performance	Comfort	Value
N/A	4.3	8.4	6	6.5	N/A

HALF TON

Category G

Model Description	Trade-in Value	Market Value
2 Dr STD Std Cab SB	4150	5320
2 Dr STD Std Cab LB	4085	5235
2 Dr STD 4WD Std Cab SB	6315	8095

Don't forget to refer to the Mileage Adjustment Table at the back of this book!

 © 1999 by Edmund Publications Corporation

Model Description	Trade-in Value	Market Value

KING CAB

Category G

2 Dr SE Ext Cab SB	6420	8230
2 Dr SE 4WD Ext Cab SB	7465	9575
2 Dr STD Ext Cab SB	5235	6710
2 Dr STD 4WD Ext Cab SB	6710	8600

OPTIONS FOR TRUCK

6 cyl 3.0 L Engine[Opt on] +200
Auto 4-Speed Transmission +295
2WD Sport Pkg +265
4WD Sport Pkg +245
Air Conditioning +245
Aluminum/Alloy Wheels +105
AM/FM Stereo Tape[Std on SE,4WD] +75
Bed Liner +85
Camper/Towing Package +85
Chrome Bumpers[Std on SE] +50
Chrome Wheels[Std on King Cab,4WD] +75
Flip-Up Sunroof +100
Limited Slip Diff +80
Power Door Locks +70
Power Steering[Std on King Cab,4WD] +85
Power Windows +70

1992 NISSAN

240SX 1992

Nissan chops the top off the 240SX, adding a convertible to this versatile line of cars. Antilock brakes are made available on the LE model.

RATINGS (SCALE OF 1-10)

Overall	Safety	Reliability	Performance	Comfort	Value
N/A	N/A	8.7	8	7.3	4.1

Category F

2 Dr LE Hbk	5465	7285
2 Dr SE Conv	6615	8820
2 Dr SE Cpe	4760	6345
2 Dr SE Hbk	4820	6430
2 Dr STD Cpe	4130	5510
2 Dr STD Hbk	4225	5630

OPTIONS FOR 240SX

Auto 4-Speed Transmission[Std on Conv] +200
Air Conditioning[Std on LE] +205
Anti-Lock Brakes +180
Flip-Up Sunroof +100
Leather Seats[Opt on SE] +175
Limited Slip Diff +90
Power Sunroof +170

300ZX 1992

The driver airbag is moved to the standard equipment list this year. No other changes to this fine car.

RATINGS (SCALE OF 1-10)

Overall	Safety	Reliability	Performance	Comfort	Value
N/A	N/A	8.1	9.2	6.6	3.5

Category F

2 Dr 2+2 Cpe	9185	12245
2 Dr STD Cpe	8985	11980
2 Dr STD Turbo Cpe	11330	15110

OPTIONS FOR 300ZX

Auto 4-Speed Transmission +230
Bose Sound System[Std on 2+2,Turbo] +125
Glass Panel T-tops[Std on Turbo] +255
Leather Seats +175
Power Drivers Seat[Std on 2+2,Turbo] +60

MAXIMA 1992

The Maxima gets an available driver airbag and a bigger engine for the SE. The SE's new engine is a DOHC 190-horsepower V6. Unfortunately, the SE loses its standard sunroof. GXE and SE models receive a new grille and taillights for 1992.

RATINGS (SCALE OF 1-10)

Overall	Safety	Reliability	Performance	Comfort	Value
N/A	N/A	8	8.8	7.9	6.5

Category D

4 Dr GXE Sdn	5375	7260
4 Dr SE Sdn	5920	7995

OPTIONS FOR MAXIMA

Auto 4-Speed Transmission[Opt on SE] +230
Luxury Package +220
Air Bag Restraint +150
Anti-Lock Brakes +235
Bose Sound System[Std on SE] +180
Climate Control for AC +75
Dual Power Seats +205
Leather Seats +275
Power Sunroof +180

NX 1992

The optional T-tops are now available on the 1600. The NX 2000 is available this year with a power package that adds power windows, power door locks and cruise control.

RATINGS (SCALE OF 1-10)

Overall	Safety	Reliability	Performance	Comfort	Value
N/A	N/A	8.5	8.6	6.9	4.5

Category E

2 Dr 1600 Cpe	3180	4545
2 Dr 2000 Cpe	3810	5440

OPTIONS FOR NX

Auto 4-Speed Transmission +200
Air Conditioning +200

Don't forget to refer to the Mileage Adjustment Table at the back of this book!

© 1999 by Edmund Publications Corporation

Model Description	Trade-in Value	Market Value

AM/FM Stereo Tape[Opt on 1600] +75
Anti-Lock Brakes +175
Cruise Control +55
Power Door Locks +55
Power Windows +65
T-Tops (solid/Colored) +225

PATHFINDER 1992

Safari Green paint is a new exterior color choice for this aging veteran of the sport-ute wars. No other changes are made.

RATINGS (SCALE OF 1-10)

Overall	Safety	Reliability	Performance	Comfort	Value
6.6	4.3	8.3	7.6	6.8	6.3

Category G

Model Description	Trade-in Value	Market Value
4 Dr SE 4WD Wgn	7605	10145
4 Dr XE Wgn	6430	8570
4 Dr XE 4WD Wgn	6575	8765

OPTIONS FOR PATHFINDER

Auto 4-Speed Transmission +275
Air Conditioning[Opt on XE] +200
Aluminum/Alloy Wheels +85
AM/FM Compact Disc Playr +95
Cruise Control[Opt on XE] +50
Flip-Up Sunroof +85
Leather Seats +190
Limited Slip Diff +65
Luggage Rack +40
Power Door Locks[Opt on XE] +55
Power Windows[Opt on XE] +60
Premium Sound System +90

SENTRA 1992

A passenger's side vanity mirror and black body side moldings are now standard on the two-door Sentra. The Value Option Package (includes air conditioning, cruise control, and a stereo) is extended to the SE Sentras this year.

RATINGS (SCALE OF 1-10)

Overall	Safety	Reliability	Performance	Comfort	Value
N/A	N/A	8.3	7.2	7.9	5.1

Category E

Model Description	Trade-in Value	Market Value
2 Dr E Sdn	2520	3605
4 Dr E Sdn	2450	3500
4 Dr GXE Sdn	3530	5040
2 Dr SE Sdn	2795	3995
2 Dr SE-R Sdn	3055	4365
2 Dr XE Sdn	2675	3820
4 Dr XE Sdn	2795	3990

OPTIONS FOR SENTRA

Auto 4-Speed Transmission +200
Air Conditioning[Std on GXE] +200
AM/FM Stereo Tape[Std on GXE] +75
Anti-Lock Brakes +175
Cruise Control[Std on GXE] +55
Power Steering[Opt on E] +60
Power Sunroof +150
Rear Spoiler[Opt on XE] +50
Tilt Steering Wheel[Opt on E] +35

STANZA 1992

A sporty SE model joins the roster of available Stanzas this year. Distinguished by a blacked-out grille, fog lights, rear spoiler, and leather-wrapped steering wheel and shift knob, the SE is attempting to draw in customers who want more from their compact family sedan.

Category E

Model Description	Trade-in Value	Market Value
4 Dr GXE Sdn	3775	5395
4 Dr SE Sdn	3865	5525
4 Dr XE Sdn	2850	4070

OPTIONS FOR STANZA

Auto 4-Speed Transmission[Std on GXE] +220
Air Conditioning[Opt on XE] +200
AM/FM Stereo Tape[Opt on XE] +75
Anti-Lock Brakes +175
Cruise Control[Opt on XE] +55
Power Door Locks[Opt on XE] +55
Power Sunroof +150
Power Windows[Opt on XE] +65

TRUCK 1992

No changes for the Nissan Pickup.

RATINGS (SCALE OF 1-10)

Overall	Safety	Reliability	Performance	Comfort	Value
N/A	4	8.1	6	6.5	N/A

HALF TON

Category G

Model Description	Trade-in Value	Market Value
2 Dr STD Std Cab SB	3230	4310
2 Dr STD Std Cab LB	3645	4860
2 Dr STD 4WD Std Cab SB	5380	7170

KING CAB

Category G

Model Description	Trade-in Value	Market Value
2 Dr SE Ext Cab SB	5010	6680
2 Dr SE 4WD Ext Cab SB	6195	8255
2 Dr STD Ext Cab SB	4225	5630
2 Dr STD 4WD Ext Cab SB	5530	7370

OPTIONS FOR TRUCK

6 cyl 3.0 L Engine +185
Auto 4-Speed Transmission +225
Air Conditioning +200
Aluminum/Alloy Wheels +85
AM/FM Stereo Tape +60
Bed Liner[Std on SE] +70
Chrome Bumpers +40
Chrome Wheels[Opt on 2WD] +60
Flip-Up Sunroof +85

Don't forget to refer to the Mileage Adjustment Table at the back of this book!

 © 1999 by Edmund Publications Corporation

Limited Slip Diff +65
Power Door Locks +55
Power Steering[Std on SE,4WD] +70
Power Windows +60
Rear Step Bumper +35

1991 NISSAN

240SX 1991

More gadgets for the Nissan sport coupe. Four-wheel steering and antilock brakes are the latest additions to Nissan's spry pocket-rocket. The 2.4-liter DOHC inline-four produces fifteen more horsepower than last year.

RATINGS (SCALE OF 1-10)

Overall	Safety	Reliability	Performance	Comfort	Value
N/A	N/A	8.4	8	7.3	4.5

Category F

Model	Trade-in	Market
2 Dr LE Hbk	4565	6085
2 Dr Limited Hbk	4625	6165
2 Dr SE Cpe	3950	5270
2 Dr SE Hbk	4055	5410
2 Dr STD Cpe	3535	4715
2 Dr STD Hbk	3605	4810

OPTIONS FOR 240SX

Auto 4-Speed Transmission +165
Air Conditioning[Opt on SE,STD] +170
Anti-Lock Brakes +145
Flip-Up Sunroof +80
Leather Seats[Opt on SE] +145
Power Sunroof +140
Theft Deterrent System +35

300ZX 1991

The 300ZX is available with the four-wheel steering and antilock brakes. A driver airbag joins the options list this year.

RATINGS (SCALE OF 1-10)

Overall	Safety	Reliability	Performance	Comfort	Value
N/A	N/A	7.8	9.2	6.6	3.9

Category F

Model	Trade-in	Market
2 Dr 2+2 Cpe	8005	10675
2 Dr STD Cpe	7730	10310
2 Dr STD Turbo Cpe	9570	12765

OPTIONS FOR 300ZX

Auto 4-Speed Transmission +160
Air Bag Restraint +100
Bose Sound System +100
Glass Panel T-tops +210
Leather Seats +145
Power Drivers Seat +50

MAXIMA 1991

Antilock brakes are added to the options list of the capable Maxima.

RATINGS (SCALE OF 1-10)

Overall	Safety	Reliability	Performance	Comfort	Value
N/A	N/A	7.8	8.8	7.9	6.9

Category D

Model	Trade-in	Market
4 Dr GXE Sdn	4505	6170
4 Dr SE Sdn	5060	6930

OPTIONS FOR MAXIMA

Auto 4-Speed Transmission[Opt on SE] +185
Anti-Lock Brakes +195
Bose Sound System[Std on SE] +145
Compact Disc W/fm/tape +195
Leather Seats +225
Power Drivers Seat +70
Power Sunroof[Std on SE] +150

NX 1991

The replacement for the Nissan Pulsar appears in the guise of the NX twins. Available with the same engines found in the Nissan Sentra, the NX duo are designed to be a sportier alternative to their pedestrian cousins. Both models feature a driver airbag, a two-door body style and front-wheel drive. Antilock brakes are available on the NX 2000 equipped with a manual transmission.

RATINGS (SCALE OF 1-10)

Overall	Safety	Reliability	Performance	Comfort	Value
N/A	N/A	8	8.6	6.9	4.9

Category E

Model	Trade-in	Market
2 Dr 1600 Cpe	2590	3810
2 Dr 2000 Cpe	3180	4675

OPTIONS FOR NX

Auto 4-Speed Transmission +165
Air Conditioning +165
AM/FM Stereo Tape[Opt on 1600] +60
Anti-Lock Brakes +145
T-Tops (solid/Colored) +180

PATHFINDER 1991

The two-door version of Nissan's sport-utility wagon is dropped in favor of the much better selling four-door. Reaching a new level of refinement, Nissan makes leather seating surfaces available on the top-end SE model. All '91 Pathfinders get rear-wheel antilock brakes.

RATINGS (SCALE OF 1-10)

Overall	Safety	Reliability	Performance	Comfort	Value
6.6	4.3	7.9	7.6	6.8	6.6

Don't forget to refer to the Mileage Adjustment Table at the back of this book!

 © 1999 by Edmund Publications Corporation

Model Description	Trade-in Value	Market Value
Category G		
4 Dr SE 4WD Wgn	6755	9125
4 Dr XE Wgn	6080	8220
4 Dr XE 4WD Wgn	6150	8310

OPTIONS FOR PATHFINDER

Auto 4-Speed Transmission +215
Air Conditioning[Opt on XE] +165
Aluminum/Alloy Wheels +70
AM/FM Compact Disc Playr +80
Cruise Control[Std on SE,2WD] +45
Leather Seats +155
Limited Slip Diff +55
Luggage Rack +30
Power Door Locks[Opt on XE] +45
Power Windows[Opt on XE] +50
Sunroof +60
Swing Out Tire Carrier +40

SENTRA 1991

The Nissan Sentra is totally redesigned for 1991. Edges are smoothed out and corners are rounded, giving the '91 Sentra a more substantial feel. A racy SE-R is introduced with an outstanding little 140-horsepower engine. All other Sentras get a 110-horsepower engine that is about average for this class. A four-speed automatic transmission is available on all Sentras but the SE-R.

RATINGS (SCALE OF 1-10)

Overall	Safety	Reliability	Performance	Comfort	Value
N/A	N/A	8	7.2	7.9	6

Model Description	Trade-in Value	Market Value
Category E		
2 Dr E Sdn	2085	3070
4 Dr E Sdn	2090	3075
4 Dr GXE Sdn	2930	4310
2 Dr SE Sdn	2425	3565
2 Dr SE-R Sdn	2515	3700
2 Dr XE Sdn	2300	3380
4 Dr XE Sdn	2315	3405

OPTIONS FOR SENTRA

Auto 3-Speed Transmission +140
Auto 4-Speed Transmission +180
Air Conditioning[Std on GXE] +165
AM/FM Stereo Tape[Std on GXE] +60
Anti-Lock Brakes +145
Cruise Control[Std on GXE] +45
Power Steering[Opt on E] +50
Power Sunroof +120
Tilt Steering Wheel[Opt on E Sdn] +30

STANZA 1991

Four-wheel antilock brakes are a new option on the Stanza GXE. No other changes for the recently redesigned sedan from Nissan.

Model Description	Trade-in Value	Market Value
Category E		
4 Dr GXE Sdn	3115	4580
4 Dr XE Sdn	2565	3770

OPTIONS FOR STANZA

Auto 4-Speed Transmission +150
Air Conditioning[Opt on XE] +165
AM/FM Stereo Tape[Opt on XE] +60
Anti-Lock Brakes +145
Cruise Control[Opt on XE] +45
Power Door Locks[Opt on XE] +45
Power Sunroof +120
Power Windows[Opt on XE] +55

TRUCK 1991

The regular cab six-cylinder four-wheel drive model is dropped. The remaining Nissan four-wheel drives are equipped with rear-wheel antilock brakes.

RATINGS (SCALE OF 1-10)

Overall	Safety	Reliability	Performance	Comfort	Value
N/A	3.9	7.4	6	6.5	N/A

HALF TON

Model Description	Trade-in Value	Market Value
Category G		
2 Dr STD Std Cab SB	2850	3850
2 Dr STD Std Cab LB	3220	4350
2 Dr STD 4WD Std Cab SB	4635	6265

KING CAB

Model Description	Trade-in Value	Market Value
Category G		
2 Dr SE Ext Cab SB	4460	6030
2 Dr SE 4WD Ext Cab SB	5655	7640
2 Dr STD Ext Cab SB	3820	5160
2 Dr STD 4WD Ext Cab SB	4990	6740

OPTIONS FOR TRUCK

6 cyl 3.0 L Engine[Std on King Cab,LB] +145
Auto 4-Speed Transmission +175
Chrome Pkg +165
Air Conditioning +165
Aluminum/Alloy Wheels +70
AM/FM Stereo Tape[Std on SE] +50
Bed Liner +55
Chrome Bumpers +30
Chrome Wheels[Std on SE,4WD] +50
Limited Slip Diff +55
Power Door Locks +45
Power Steering[Std on King Cab,4WD] +55
Power Windows +50
Sunroof +60

1990 NISSAN

240SX 1990

After last year's amazing innovations the designers at Nissan decided not to mess with the 240SX, offering a

Don't forget to refer to the Mileage Adjustment Table at the back of this book!

 © 1999 by Edmund Publications Corporation

Model Description	Trade-in Value	Market Value

standard power antenna and an upgraded stereo as the only modifications.

RATINGS (SCALE OF 1-10)

Overall	Safety	Reliability	Performance	Comfort	Value
N/A	N/A	7.9	8	7.3	3.8

Category F	Trade-in Value	Market Value
2 Dr SE Hbk	3350	4470
2 Dr XE Cpe	3290	4385

OPTIONS FOR 240SX

Auto 4-Speed Transmission +135
Air Conditioning +140
Aluminum/Alloy Wheels +50
AM/FM Stereo Tape +35
Anti-Lock Brakes +120
Cruise Control +35
Power Door Locks +35
Power Sunroof +115
Power Windows +35
Premium Sound System +70
Sport Suspension +45

300ZX 1990

Cutting-edge styling and exceptional performance launch the new 300ZX onto our top-ten list of all-time favorite sports cars. Available as a two-seater or a two-plus-two, the 300ZX can move its occupants hither and yon with alacrity. An available turbo engine in the two-seater makes the 300ZX even more fun.

RATINGS (SCALE OF 1-10)

Overall	Safety	Reliability	Performance	Comfort	Value
N/A	N/A	7.6	9.2	6.6	3.3

Category F	Trade-in Value	Market Value
2 Dr GS Cpe	7070	9425
2 Dr GS 2+2 Cpe	7160	9550
2 Dr STD Turbo Cpe	8660	11550

OPTIONS FOR 300ZX

Auto 4-Speed Transmission +130
Electronics Pkg +150
Bose Sound System[Std on STD] +85
Climate Control for AC +30
Digital Instrument Panel +120
Leather Seats +120
Power Drivers Seat +40
Premium Sound System +70

AXXESS 1990

What's that? This is the most frequently asked question regarding the Axxess. The Axxess replaces the now defunct Stanza wagon and is sandwiched between minivans and compact station wagons in size and utility. The Axxess offers interesting features such as available four-wheel drive and dual sliding passenger doors that allow the middle row passengers an entrance or exit from either side of the vehicle.

Category G	Trade-in Value	Market Value
2 Dr SE Pass. Van	3400	4720
2 Dr SE 4WD Pass. Van	3465	4810
2 Dr XE Pass. Van	2740	3805
2 Dr XE 4WD Pass. Van	3235	4495

OPTIONS FOR AXXESS

Auto 4-Speed Transmission[Opt on XE] +125
Air Conditioning[Opt on XE] +135
Cruise Control[Opt on XE] +35
Power Sunroof[Opt on XE] +135
Power Windows[Opt on XE] +40

MAXIMA 1990

The radio is upgraded and there are a few more colors available for the 1990 Maxima.

RATINGS (SCALE OF 1-10)

Overall	Safety	Reliability	Performance	Comfort	Value
N/A	N/A	7.6	8.8	7.9	5.1

Category D	Trade-in Value	Market Value
4 Dr GXE Sdn	4120	5725
4 Dr SE Sdn	4420	6140

OPTIONS FOR MAXIMA

Auto 4-Speed Transmission[Opt on SE] +155
Electronics Pkg +170
AM/FM Compact Disc Playr +95
Anti-Lock Brakes +155
Bose Sound System[Std on SE] +120
Climate Control for AC +50
Digital Instrument Panel +90
Leather Seats +185
Power Drivers Seat +55
Power Passenger Seat +65
Power Sunroof[Std on SE] +120
Rear Spoiler[Std on SE] +70

PATHFINDER 1990

Nissan joins the four-door sport-ute frenzy by adding two doors to the popular Pathfinder. No other changes are made this year.

RATINGS (SCALE OF 1-10)

Overall	Safety	Reliability	Performance	Comfort	Value
6.5	4	7.9	7.6	6.8	6.1

Category G	Trade-in Value	Market Value
2 Dr SE 4WD Utility	5980	8305
4 Dr SE 4WD Wgn	5665	7870
4 Dr XE Wgn	3865	5370
4 Dr XE 4WD Wgn	5580	7750

OPTIONS FOR PATHFINDER

Auto 4-Speed Transmission +170
Power Plus Pkg +250

Don't forget to refer to the Mileage Adjustment Table at the back of this book!

© 1999 by Edmund Publications Corporation

Model Description	Trade-in Value	Market Value

Sport Handling Package +135
Air Conditioning[Opt on XE] +135
Aluminum/Alloy Wheels[Opt on Wgn] +55
Chrome Wheels +40
Cruise Control[Opt on XE] +35
Limited Slip Diff[Opt on Wgn] +45
Power Door Locks[Opt on XE] +40
Power Windows[Opt on XE] +40
Sunroof[Opt on Wgn] +50

PULSAR 1990

No changes for 1990.

Category E

2 Dr NX XE Cpe	1845	2835

OPTIONS FOR PULSAR

Auto 3-Speed Transmission +90
Air Conditioning +135
AM/FM Stereo Tape +50
Theft Deterrent System +30

SENTRA 1990

The bargain-basement Sentra E has been dropped from the model list. No other changes are made.

Category E

2 Dr SE Cpe	1980	3045
2 Dr STD Sdn	1400	2155
2 Dr XE Cpe	1925	2965
2 Dr XE Sdn	1655	2550
4 Dr XE Sdn	1710	2630
4 Dr XE Wgn	1895	2915

OPTIONS FOR SENTRA

Auto 3-Speed Transmission +110
Air Conditioning +135
AM/FM Stereo Tape +50
Power Steering +40
Sunroof[Opt on XE] +55

STANZA 1990

An all new Stanza debuts in 1990. The new Stanza has the same engine as the sporty 240SX but continues with a tired suspension and uninteresting styling. Better luck next time.

Category E

4 Dr GXE Sdn	2630	4045
4 Dr XE Sdn	2235	3440

OPTIONS FOR STANZA

Auto 4-Speed Transmission +130
Air Conditioning[Opt on XE] +135
Aluminum/Alloy Wheels[Opt on XE] +50
AM/FM Stereo Tape[Opt on XE] +50
Anti-Lock Brakes +120
Cruise Control[Opt on XE] +35
Power Door Locks[Opt on XE] +40
Power Sunroof +100
Power Windows[Opt on XE] +45

TRUCK 1990

No significant changes for the Nissan pickup.

RATINGS (SCALE OF 1-10)

Overall	Safety	Reliability	Performance	Comfort	Value
N/A	3.9	7.4	6	6.5	N/A

HALF TON

Category G

2 Dr STD Std Cab SB	2460	3415
2 Dr STD Std Cab LB	2625	3645
2 Dr STD 4WD Std Cab SB	3730	5180

KING CAB

Category G

2 Dr SE Ext Cab SB	4000	5555
2 Dr SE 4WD Ext Cab SB	5055	7020
2 Dr STD Ext Cab SB	3270	4540
2 Dr STD 4WD Ext Cab SB	4340	6030

OPTIONS FOR TRUCK

6 cyl 3.0 L Engine[Std on King Cab] +145
Auto 4-Speed Transmission +155
Black Value Pkg +145
Chrome Value Pkg +160
Air Conditioning +135
Aluminum/Alloy Wheels +55
AM/FM Stereo Tape[Std on SE] +40
Bed Liner +45
Chrome Wheels[Opt on Half Ton] +40
Flip-Up Sunroof +55
Limited Slip Diff +45
Power Door Locks +40
Power Steering[Std on King Cab,4WD,LB] +45
Power Windows +40
Sunroof +50

1989 NISSAN

240SX 1989

A new nickel-missile replaces the lethargic 200SX. A 140-horsepower engine drives the rear-wheels of this sporty little car. The 240SX can be had as a two-door coupe or hatchback. New from the Department of Interior Gadgetry is the Nissan heads-up display. The HUD projects the driver's speed onto the lower left-hand corner of the windshield, making it easier to keep track of one's forward progress.

RATINGS (SCALE OF 1-10)

Overall	Safety	Reliability	Performance	Comfort	Value
N/A	N/A	7.8	8	7.3	3.2

Category F

2 Dr SE Hbk	2705	3760
2 Dr XE Cpe	2695	3745

Don't forget to refer to the Mileage Adjustment Table at the back of this book!

© 1999 by Edmund Publications Corporation

Model Description	Trade-in Value	Market Value

OPTIONS FOR 240SX

Auto 4-Speed Transmission +105
Air Conditioning +115
Aluminum/Alloy Wheels +40
Anti-Lock Brakes +100
Cruise Control +30
Power Sunroof +90
Power Windows +30

300ZX 1989

The 300ZX receives no changes.

Category F		
2 Dr GS Cpe	3750	5205
2 Dr GS 2+2 Cpe	3890	5400
2 Dr STD Turbo Cpe	4105	5705

OPTIONS FOR 300ZX

Auto 4-Speed Transmission +100
Digital Instrument Panel +95
Leather Seats +95
Power Drivers Seat +30
Premium Sound System +55

MAXIMA 1989

The Nissan Maxima is completely redesigned for 1989, gaining soft edges and round corners. The four-door wagon is dropped, leaving the sedan as the only Maxima offering. The wheelbase is stretched on the new Maxima, increasing the car's interior space enough to move it from the EPA's compact to midsize class. Luxury GXE or sporty SE trim-levels allow the buyers to choose the type of Maxima best suited to their personalities.

RATINGS (SCALE OF 1-10)

Overall	Safety	Reliability	Performance	Comfort	Value
N/A	N/A	7.4	8.8	7.9	5

Category D		
4 Dr GXE Sdn	3385	4905
4 Dr SE Sdn	3525	5110

OPTIONS FOR MAXIMA

Auto 4-Speed Transmission[Opt on SE] +120
Electronics Pkg +145
Anti-Lock Brakes +130
Climate Control for AC +40
Digital Instrument Panel +70
Leather Seats +150
Power Drivers Seat +45
Power Passenger Seat +50
Power Sunroof[Std on SE] +100

PATHFINDER 1989

One of the original compact SUVs, the Pathfinder moves into 1989 with on-demand four-wheel drive that allows drivers to shift into four-wheel drive at speeds under 25 mph without stopping to lock the hubs.

RATINGS (SCALE OF 1-10)

Overall	Safety	Reliability	Performance	Comfort	Value
6.4	3.8	7.7	7.6	6.8	5.9

Category G		
2 Dr SE 4WD Utility	4825	6995
2 Dr SE Sport 4WD Utility	4900	7100
2 Dr XE Utility	4280	6205
2 Dr XE 4WD Utility	4625	6700

OPTIONS FOR PATHFINDER

Auto 4-Speed Transmission +140
Power Plus Pkg +250
Air Conditioning[Opt on XE] +110
Chrome Wheels[Opt on XE] +30
Cruise Control[Opt on XE] +30
Limited Slip Diff[Opt on XE] +35
Power Door Locks[Opt on XE] +30
Power Windows[Opt on XE] +30

PULSAR 1989

A new cylinder head for the 1.6-liter engine boosts the Pulsar's horsepower from 69 to 90. The ill-conceived Sportback has been dropped from the list of the Pulsar's available options.

Category E		
2 Dr NX SE Cpe	1635	2680
2 Dr NX XE Cpe	1515	2485

OPTIONS FOR PULSAR

Auto 3-Speed Transmission +70
Auto 4-Speed Transmission +100
Air Conditioning +110
Alarm System +60
AM/FM Stereo Tape +40

SENTRA 1989

A new cylinder head gives the '89 Sentra 21 more horsepower than last year.

Category E		
2 Dr E Sdn	1115	1830
4 Dr E Sdn	1175	1930
4 Dr E Wgn	1685	2765
2 Dr SE Cpe	1575	2580
2 Dr STD Sdn	1100	1800
2 Dr XE Sdn	1285	2110
2 Dr XE Cpe	1475	2420
4 Dr XE Sdn	1415	2320
4 Dr XE Wgn	1840	3015

OPTIONS FOR SENTRA

Auto 3-Speed Transmission +115
Air Conditioning +110
AM/FM Stereo Tape +40
Flip-Up Sunroof[Opt on XE] +50
Power Steering[Opt on E] +35

Don't forget to refer to the Mileage Adjustment Table at the back of this book!

 © 1999 by Edmund Publications Corporation

Model Description	Trade-in Value	Market Value

STANZA 1989

The Stanza wagon has been dropped from the lineup. Sedans are still available as E or GXE models, depending on your budget, with only minor changes to the exterior.

Category E

Model Description	Trade-in Value	Market Value
4 Dr E Sdn	1640	2690
4 Dr GXE Sdn	1745	2865

OPTIONS FOR STANZA

Auto 4-Speed Transmission +100
Air Conditioning +110
Alarm System +60
Aluminum/Alloy Wheels +45
AM/FM Stereo Tape[Opt on E] +40
Power Sunroof +80

TRUCK 1989

Nissan pickups are available as regular or King cabs, with two bed lengths to choose from. Three trim-levels and two engine choices are designed to fit the needs of most compact pickup truck buyers.

RATINGS (SCALE OF 1-10)

Overall	Safety	Reliability	Performance	Comfort	Value
N/A	3.9	7.2	6	6.5	N/A

For a guaranteed low price on a new car in your area, call 1-800-CAR-CLUB

HALF TON

Category G

Model Description	Trade-in Value	Market Value
2 Dr E Std Cab SB	2225	3225
2 Dr E Std Cab LB	2225	3225
2 Dr E 4WD Std Cab SB	3470	5030
2 Dr Special Std Cab SB	2425	3515
2 Dr Special Std Cab LB	2425	3515
2 Dr Special 4WD Std Cab SB	3620	5245

KING CAB

Category G

Model Description	Trade-in Value	Market Value
2 Dr E Ext Cab SB	2615	3790
2 Dr E 4WD Ext Cab SB	3605	5230
2 Dr SE Ext Cab SB	2910	4220
2 Dr SE 4WD Ext Cab SB	4260	6175
2 Dr Special Ext Cab SB	2775	4020
2 Dr Special 4WD Ext Cab SB	3690	5345

OPTIONS FOR TRUCK

6 cyl 3.0 L Engine +135
Auto 4-Speed Transmission +115
Power Pkg +110
Air Conditioning +110
Aluminum/Alloy Wheels +45
AM/FM Stereo Tape +35
Bed Liner +40
Chrome Wheels[Opt on E] +30
Limited Slip Diff +35
Power Door Locks +30
Power Steering[Opt on Half Ton] +40
Power Windows +30
Rear Jump Seats[Opt on E] +30
Sunroof +40

Major Savings On An Extended Warranty

"YOU DESERVE THE BEST"

Call today for your free quote.

Pay up to 50% less than dealership prices!

http://www.edmunds.com/warranty 1-800-580-9889

Don't forget to refer to the Mileage Adjustment Table at the back of this book!

 © 1999 by Edmund Publications Corporation

Model Description	Trade-in Value	Market Value

OLDSMOBILE USA

1996 Oldsmobile Achieva

1998 OLDSMOBILE

ACHIEVA 1998

Oldsmobile limited sales of the Achieva to fleets for 1998, so if you're considering one, it's probably a former rental car.

Category C

4 Dr SL Sdn	9195	11080

AURORA 1998

Status quo in Auroraville, but second-generation airbags have been added.

Category A

4 Dr STD Sdn	22550	26530

OPTIONS FOR AURORA

Bose Sound System +570
Chrome Wheels +930
Heated Front Seats +165
Power Moonroof +1190

BRAVADA 1998

Front styling is revised, and new body-side cladding alters the Bravada's profile. Inside, dual second generation airbags are housed in a new dashboard. A heated driver's side exterior mirror is newly standard, while heated front seats have been added to the options roster. Battery rundown protection and a theft deterrent system are new standard features.

Category G

4 Dr STD 4WD Wgn	19785	23555

OPTIONS FOR BRAVADA

Compact Disc W/fm/tape +565
Heated Front Seats +210
Power Moonroof +735

CUTLASS 1998

No changes to Oldsmobile's fresh bread-and butter sedan, except for the addition of second-generation airbags.

Category C

4 Dr GL Sdn	12460	15010
4 Dr GLS Sdn	13830	16665

OPTIONS FOR CUTLASS

Aluminum/Alloy Wheels[Opt on GL] +240
Compact Disc W/fm/tape +310
Keyless Entry System[Opt on GL] +155
Power Drivers Seat[Opt on GL] +235
Power Mirrors[Opt on GL] +90
Power Moonroof +580
Power Windows[Opt on GL] +255

EIGHTY-EIGHT 1998

Virtually nothing, unless you find a new fuel cap, better access to rear seat belts, new ABS wheel speed sensors, deletion of the "unleaded fuel only" label from the inside of the fuel door and a couple of new colors intriguing. Second-generation airbags are standard.

Category B

4 Dr LS Sdn	15315	18450
4 Dr STD Sdn	13790	16615

OPTIONS FOR EIGHTY-EIGHT

Aluminum/Alloy Wheels[Std on LS] +275
Compact Disc W/fm/tape +325
Dual Power Seats +300
Keyless Entry System[Std on LS] +145
Leather Seats +550

INTRIGUE 1998

Oldsmobile dumps the stodgy Cutlass Supreme for the Intrigue: a suave, sophisticated, sporty sedan designed to take on the best of the imports. Too bad they forgot the "reliability" portion of the recipe. Second-generation airbags are standard equipment.

Category B

4 Dr GL Sdn	15450	18610
4 Dr GLS Sdn	17470	21050
4 Dr STD Sdn	14985	18050

OPTIONS FOR INTRIGUE

Bose Sound System +640
Chrome Wheels +610
Compact Disc W/fm/tape[Std on GLS] +325
Keyless Entry System[Opt on STD] +145
Leather Seats[Opt on GL] +550
Power Drivers Seat[Std on GL] +250
Power Moonroof +825

Don't forget to refer to the Mileage Adjustment Table at the back of this book!

 © 1999 by Edmund Publications Corporation

LSS 1998

New colors, improved ABS, a revised electrochromic rearview mirror, second-generation airbags and a redesigned fuel cap are the major changes for 1998.

Category C

Model Description	Trade-in Value	Market Value
4 Dr STD Sdn	17475	21055

OPTIONS FOR LSS

Chrome Wheels +495
Power Moonroof +580

REGENCY 1998

Minor changes to this retirement village special for '98. The ABS is upgraded, it's easier to get at the rear seat belts, colors are revised and the "unleaded fuel only" label is removed from the inside of the fuel door.

Category A

Model Description	Trade-in Value	Market Value
4 Dr STD Sdn	16975	19970

OPTIONS FOR REGENCY

Power Moonroof +1190

SILHOUETTE 1998

Side-impact airbags are standard for front seat passengers, and Oldsmobile is building more short-wheelbase vans with dual sliding doors. Front airbags get second generation technology, which results in slower deployment speeds. Midyear, a Premiere Edition debuted, loaded with standard features including a TV/VCP setup in back.

Category G

Model Description	Trade-in Value	Market Value
2 Dr GL Pass. Van Ext	16090	19155
2 Dr GLS Pass. Van Ext	18345	21840
2 Dr GS Pass. Van	16970	20205
2 Dr Premiere Pass. Van Ext	21895	26065

OPTIONS FOR SILHOUETTE

Aluminum/Alloy Wheels[Opt on GL, GS] +285
Auto Load Leveling[Opt on GL, GS] +190
Captain Chairs (2) +395
Compact Disc W/fm/tape[Std on Premiere] +565
Dual Air Conditioning[Opt on GL, GLS] +840
Dual Power Seats[Opt on GL] +525
Keyless Entry System[Opt on GL] +170
Leather Seats +640
Privacy Glass[Opt on GL] +225
Traction Control System[Std on Premiere] +245

1997 OLDSMOBILE

ACHIEVA 1997

Side-impact standards are met, and standard equipment lists are enhanced. Series II Coupe gets new alloy wheels, and the lineup has been simplified.

RATINGS (SCALE OF 1-10)

Overall	Safety	Reliability	Performance	Comfort	Value
7.7	7.5	8.1	8.4	7.6	6.8

Category C

Model Description	Trade-in Value	Market Value
2 Dr SC Series I Cpe	8235	10165
2 Dr SC Series II Cpe	8775	10830
4 Dr SL Series I Sdn	8020	9900
4 Dr SL Series II Sdn	8595	10615

OPTIONS FOR ACHIEVA

6 cyl 3.1 L Engine +295
Compact Disc W/fm/tape +250
Cruise Control[Opt on SL Series I] +140
Fog Lights[Opt on SL Series II] +65
Keyless Entry System +130
Leather Steering Wheel[Opt on SL Series II] +65
Power Drivers Seat +195
Power Moonroof +475
Power Windows[Opt on SC Series I,SL Series I] +205
Rear Spoiler[Opt on SL Series II] +110

AURORA 1997

Larger front brakes, an in-dash CD player for the Bose sound system, a tilt-down right-hand exterior mirror for backing assistance, an integrated rearview mirror compass, and a three-channel garage door opener are added this year.

RATINGS (SCALE OF 1-10)

Overall	Safety	Reliability	Performance	Comfort	Value
8.4	7.1	8.5	8.8	9	8.7

Category A

Model Description	Trade-in Value	Market Value
4 Dr STD Sdn	19870	23375

OPTIONS FOR AURORA

Bose Sound System +465
Chrome Wheels +760
Compact Disc Changer +590
Heated Front Seats +135
Power Moonroof +970

BRAVADA 1997

Bravada drops the split-tailgate arrangement at the rear in favor of a top-hinged liftgate with separately lifting glass. So, tailgate parties aren't as convenient, but loading cargo sure is easier. Also new to the options list is a power tilt and slide sunroof. Included with the hole in the roof are a mini-overhead console, a pop-up wind deflector, and a sun shade. Rear disc brakes replace the former drums, combining with the front discs to provide better stopping ability.

RATINGS (SCALE OF 1-10)

Overall	Safety	Reliability	Performance	Comfort	Value
7.3	5.3	8.4	8	8	6.6

Don't forget to refer to the Mileage Adjustment Table at the back of this book!

 © 1999 by Edmund Publications Corporation

Category G

4 Dr STD 4WD Wgn	17365	20925

OPTIONS FOR BRAVADA

AM/FM Compact Disc Playr +260
Camper/Towing Package +195
Gold Package +320
Power Moonroof +600

CUTLASS 1997

Oldsmobile retires the Ciera and introduces the Cutlass, based on the same platform as Chevy's new Malibu. Cutlass is more upscale that its Chevrolet counterpart, offering a slightly more powerful V-6 engine on all models, and a sunroof option, standard leather interior, and larger wheels on the GLS.

RATINGS (SCALE OF 1-10)

Overall	Safety	Reliability	Performance	Comfort	Value
7.8	7.5	8.8	8.4	8.3	6

Category C

4 Dr GLS Sdn	11920	14715
4 Dr STD Sdn	10675	13180

OPTIONS FOR CUTLASS

Aluminum/Alloy Wheels[Opt on STD] +195
Compact Disc W/fm/tape +250
Keyless Entry System[Opt on STD] +130
Power Drivers Seat[Opt on STD] +195
Power Moonroof +475
Power Windows[Opt on STD] +205

CUTLASS SUPREME 1997

Alloy wheels and a power trunk release are added to the standard equipment list, while coupes gain side-impact protection that meets federal safety standards. The 3.4-liter DOHC V-6 engine is dropped from the options list.

RATINGS (SCALE OF 1-10)

Overall	Safety	Reliability	Performance	Comfort	Value
8	7.6	8.3	8.2	8.3	7.7

Category C

2 Dr SL Series I Cpe	10595	13080
4 Dr SL Series I Sdn	10605	13090
2 Dr SL Series II Cpe	10760	13285
4 Dr SL Series II Sdn	10735	13255
2 Dr SL Series III Cpe	11040	13625
4 Dr SL Series III Sdn	10990	13565

OPTIONS FOR CUTLASS SUPREME

Compact Disc W/fm/tape +250
Keyless Entry System[Opt on SL Series I] +130
Power Drivers Seat[Opt on SL Series I] +195
Power Moonroof +475

EIGHTY-EIGHT 1997

Side-impact protection is upgraded to federal safety standards, interiors are improved, and new Oldsmobile logos adorn the body.

RATINGS (SCALE OF 1-10)

Overall	Safety	Reliability	Performance	Comfort	Value
8.3	7.6	8.5	8.5	8.4	8.4

Category B

4 Dr LS Sdn	12750	15550
4 Dr STD Sdn	11745	14320

OPTIONS FOR EIGHTY-EIGHT

Aluminum/Alloy Wheels[Std on LS] +225
Compact Disc W/fm/tape +265
Dual Power Seats +245
Leather Seats +450

LSS 1997

Minor changes accompany Oldsmobile's euro-flavored sedan into 1997. The center console and shifter are new, and other interior upgrades have been made. New, more prominent badging has been added to the exterior. Finally, the final-drive ratio has been changed to 2.93:1 from 2.97:1.

RATINGS (SCALE OF 1-10)

Overall	Safety	Reliability	Performance	Comfort	Value
8.3	7.6	8.5	8.4	8.6	8.4

Category C

4 Dr STD Sdn	14990	18505

OPTIONS FOR LSS

Chrome Wheels +405
Power Moonroof +475

REGENCY 1997

New name for an old concept. Look closely...see the old Eighty Eight before 1996's restyle? Regency takes over where the Ninety Eight left off, satisfying traditional Oldsmobile buyers.

RATINGS (SCALE OF 1-10)

Overall	Safety	Reliability	Performance	Comfort	Value
N/A	N/A	N/A	8.5	N/A	N/A

Category A

4 Dr STD Sdn	15975	18790

OPTIONS FOR REGENCY

Power Moonroof +970

SILHOUETTE 1997

Completely redesigned, the new Silhouette comes in several trim levels and two sizes, each with a healthy load of standard equipment.

Don't forget to refer to the Mileage Adjustment Table at the back of this book!

 © 1999 by Edmund Publications Corporation

Model Description	Trade-in Value	Market Value

RATINGS (SCALE OF 1-10)

Overall	Safety	Reliability	Performance	Comfort	Value
7.6	7.2	8.2	7.8	7.9	6.8

Category G

Model Description	Trade-in Value	Market Value
2 Dr GL Pass. Van Ext	15230	18350
2 Dr GLS Pass. Van Ext	15840	19085
2 Dr STD Pass. Van Ext	15300	18435
2 Dr STD Pass. Van	13790	16615

OPTIONS FOR SILHOUETTE

Aluminum/Alloy Wheels[Opt on GL] +235
Auto Load Leveling[Opt on GL] +155
Child Seats (2) +175
Compact Disc W/fm/tape +465
Dual Air Conditioning[Opt on GL] +685
Leather Seats +520
Power Moonroof +600
Privacy Glass[Opt on STD] +185
Sliding Driver Side Door +365
Traction Control System[Opt on GL] +200

1996 OLDSMOBILE

ACHIEVA 1996

Substantial upgrades make the Achieva palatable for 1996. A new interior with dual airbags, standard air conditioning, a new base engine, daytime running lights, a theft-deterrent system and optional traction control make this Oldsmobile an excellent value in the compact class.

RATINGS (SCALE OF 1-10)

Overall	Safety	Reliability	Performance	Comfort	Value
7.8	7.5	8.1	8.4	7.6	7.3

Category C

Model Description	Trade-in Value	Market Value
2 Dr SC Series I Cpe	5945	7720
2 Dr SC Series II Cpe	6515	8465
2 Dr SC Series III Cpe	6785	8815
4 Dr SL Series II Sdn	6480	8415
4 Dr SL Series III Sdn	6900	8960

OPTIONS FOR ACHIEVA

6 cyl 3.1 L Engine +250
Auto 4-Speed Transmission[Opt on SC Series II,SL Series II] +435
Compact Disc W/fm/tape +205
Cruise Control[Opt on SC Series II,SL Series II] +115
Fog Lights +55
Keyless Entry System +105
Power Drivers Seat +160
Power Sunroof +385

AURORA 1996

Daytime running lights are added, and looking through the backlight won't make your eyes water from distortions anymore. We knew it was only a matter of time before some goofball decided chrome wheels and a gold package would look great on the otherwise classy Aurora. The new Oldsmobile? What's that? When do we get the fake convertible roof, guys?

RATINGS (SCALE OF 1-10)

Overall	Safety	Reliability	Performance	Comfort	Value
8.1	7.1	8.3	8.8	9	7.4

Category A

Model Description	Trade-in Value	Market Value
4 Dr STD Sdn	15830	19545

OPTIONS FOR AURORA

Bose Sound System +380
Chrome Wheels +620
Compact Disc Changer +485
Heated Front Seats +110
Power Moonroof +795

BRAVADA 1996

Nice truck, but how many luxury SUV's do we really need? The only thing different about the Bravada to differentiate it from the Chevy Blazer and GMC Jimmy are the seats, front styling, trim — and the price tag.

RATINGS (SCALE OF 1-10)

Overall	Safety	Reliability	Performance	Comfort	Value
7.3	5.3	8.1	8	8	7.1

Category G

Model Description	Trade-in Value	Market Value
4 Dr STD 4WD Wgn	14945	18680

OPTIONS FOR BRAVADA

AM/FM Compact Disc Playr +215
Camper/Towing Package +160
Gold Package +265

CIERA 1996

Bestseller prepares for retirement at the end of the year, receiving badge revisions, some additional standard equipment and an improved, optional V6 engine.

RATINGS (SCALE OF 1-10)

Overall	Safety	Reliability	Performance	Comfort	Value
7.6	6.5	7.8	7.4	7.6	8.5

Category C

Model Description	Trade-in Value	Market Value
4 Dr SL Wgn	7560	9815
4 Dr SL Series I Sdn	6920	8990
4 Dr SL Series II Sdn	7380	9585

OPTIONS FOR CIERA

6 cyl 3.1 L Engine[Opt on SL Series I] +250
AM/FM Compact Disc Playr +215
Cruise Control[Std on SL Series II] +115
Keyless Entry System +105
Luggage Rack +65
Power Drivers Seat +160
Power Windows[Std on SL Series II] +170
Third Seat +95

Don't forget to refer to the Mileage Adjustment Table at the back of this book!

 © 1999 by Edmund Publications Corporation

Model Description	Trade-in Value	Market Value

CUTLASS SUPREME 1996

The convertible has been retired. The sedan and coupe enjoy their last year in production, receiving engine upgrades for 1996.

RATINGS (SCALE OF 1-10)

Overall	Safety	Reliability	Performance	Comfort	Value
7.9	7.6	8	8.2	8.3	7.6

Category C

2 Dr SL Series I Cpe	8380	10885
4 Dr SL Series I Sdn	8855	11500
2 Dr SL Series II Cpe	8515	11060
4 Dr SL Series II Sdn	9045	11750
2 Dr SL Series III Cpe	8770	11390
4 Dr SL Series III Sdn	9195	11945
2 Dr SL Series IV Cpe	9140	11865
4 Dr SL Series IV Sdn	9705	12605

OPTIONS FOR CUTLASS SUPREME

6 cyl 3.4 L Engine +670
Compact Disc W/fm/tape[Std on SL Series IV] +205
Keyless Entry System[Opt on SL Series II,SL Series I Sdn] +105
Leather Seats[Opt on SL Series I] +320
Power Drivers Seat[Std on SL Series IV] +160
Power Moonroof +390
Rear Spoiler +90

EIGHTY-EIGHT 1996

Royale designation dropped, and the Eighty Eight gets fresh Aurora-inspired styling front and rear. Standard equipment levels go up, and daytime running lights are added.

RATINGS (SCALE OF 1-10)

Overall	Safety	Reliability	Performance	Comfort	Value
8.2	7.5	8.2	8.5	8.4	8.3

Category B

4 Dr LS Sdn	10630	13290
4 Dr LSS Sdn	11480	14350
4 Dr STD Sdn	9485	11860

OPTIONS FOR EIGHTY-EIGHT

Chrome Wheels +405
Compact Disc W/fm/tape +220
Cruise Control[Opt on STD] +120
Leather Seats[Std on LSS] +370
Power Drivers Seat[Opt on STD] +165
Power Moonroof +550
Traction Control System[Opt on LS] +100

NINETY-EIGHT 1996

Supercharged engine dropped from this model, and daytime running lamps have been added. Don't expect a 1997 Ninety Eight.

RATINGS (SCALE OF 1-10)

Overall	Safety	Reliability	Performance	Comfort	Value
8	7.5	8.1	7.9	8.1	8.3

Category A

4 Dr Series I Sdn	13110	16185
4 Dr Series II Sdn	13360	16490

OPTIONS FOR NINETY-EIGHT

Compact Disc W/fm/tape +390
Power Sunroof +760
Traction Control System[Opt on Series I] +120

SILHOUETTE 1996

New 180-horsepower 3.4-liter V6 makes the Silhouette better resemble Japan's bullet train.

RATINGS (SCALE OF 1-10)

Overall	Safety	Reliability	Performance	Comfort	Value
7.6	6.4	8.1	7.5	7.4	8.6

Category G

2 Dr Series I Pass. Van	11030	13785
2 Dr Series II Pass. Van	11670	14585

OPTIONS FOR SILHOUETTE

AM/FM Compact Disc Playr +215
Auto Load Leveling +125
Child Seats (2) +145
Dual Air Conditioning +560
Power Sliding Door[Opt on Series I] +195

1995 OLDSMOBILE

ACHIEVA 1995

Fewer options and powertrains are available; SOHC and high-output Quad 4 engines are gone. Standard engine makes 150 horsepower this year, up from 115 in 1994. A V6 is optional. Air conditioning is standard.

RATINGS (SCALE OF 1-10)

Overall	Safety	Reliability	Performance	Comfort	Value
7.7	6.6	8.2	8.4	7.9	7.2

Category C

4 Dr S Sdn	4985	6560
2 Dr S Series I Cpe	5065	6665
2 Dr S Series II Cpe	5695	7495

OPTIONS FOR ACHIEVA

6 cyl 3.1 L Engine +215
Auto 3-Speed Transmission +165
Auto 4-Speed Transmission[Std on S Series II] +335
Air Conditioning[Std on S Series II] +360
AM/FM Stereo Tape[Std on S Series II] +75
Cruise Control[Std on S Series II] +95
Keyless Entry System +85
Power Windows[Std on S Series II] +140
Rear Spoiler +75

Don't forget to refer to the Mileage Adjustment Table at the back of this book!

 © 1999 by Edmund Publications Corporation

AURORA 1995

World-class V8 front-drive luxury sedan features cutting-edge styling, dual airbags, ABS and traction control.

RATINGS (SCALE OF 1-10)

Overall	Safety	Reliability	Performance	Comfort	Value
8.2	7.8	8	8.8	9	7.3

Category A

Model Description	Trade-in Value	Market Value
4 Dr STD Sdn	12735	15920

OPTIONS FOR AURORA

Bose Sound System +310
Heated Front Seats +90
Power Moonroof +650

CIERA 1995

Offered in a single trim level this year. Rear defroster and cassette player are standard. Brake/transmission shift interlock is new.

RATINGS (SCALE OF 1-10)

Overall	Safety	Reliability	Performance	Comfort	Value
7.8	7.1	7.7	7.4	7.6	9

Category C

Model Description	Trade-in Value	Market Value
4 Dr SL Wgn	6810	8960
4 Dr SL Sdn	6195	8155

OPTIONS FOR CIERA

6 cyl 3.1 L Engine[Opt on Sdn] +215
Aluminum/Alloy Wheels +130
AM/FM Stereo Tape[Opt on Wgn] +75
Cruise Control[Opt on Wgn] +95
Keyless Entry System +85
Luggage Rack +55
Power Drivers Seat +130
Power Windows +140
Third Seat +75
Woodgrain Applique +140

CUTLASS SUPREME 1995

Redesigned dashboard equipped with dual airbags debuts. Single trim level offered this year. Front bench seat is no longer available. Front seatbelts are mounted to door pillars instead of doors. Air conditioning, power windows, power locks, tilt steering, and cassette player are standard on all models.

RATINGS (SCALE OF 1-10)

Overall	Safety	Reliability	Performance	Comfort	Value
8	8.2	7.3	8.2	8.3	8

Category C

Model Description	Trade-in Value	Market Value
2 Dr S Cpe	7855	10335
4 Dr S Sdn	7580	9970
2 Dr STD Conv	9625	12665

OPTIONS FOR CUTLASS SUPREME

6 cyl 3.4 L Engine +550
Compact Disc W/fm/tape +170
Cruise Control[Opt on Sdn] +95
Fog Lights[Opt on Sdn] +45
Keyless Entry System[Opt on Sdn] +85
Leather Seats[Opt on S] +260
Power Drivers Seat[Opt on S] +130
Power Moonroof +320

EIGHTY-EIGHT ROYALE 1995

Engine upgraded to 3800 Series II status, and supercharged 3.8-liter V6 is a new option on LSS models. New on-board navigation system called Guidestar was a $1,995 option, originally available only in California.

RATINGS (SCALE OF 1-10)

Overall	Safety	Reliability	Performance	Comfort	Value
N/A	8.4	8	8.5	N/A	N/A

Category B

Model Description	Trade-in Value	Market Value
4 Dr LS Sdn	9495	12175
4 Dr LSS Sdn	9950	12755
4 Dr LSS Sprchgd Sdn	10485	13445
4 Dr STD Sdn	8380	10745

OPTIONS FOR EIGHTY-EIGHT ROYALE

Compact Disc W/fm/tape +180
Cruise Control[Opt on STD] +95
Leather Seats[Std on LSS] +300
Power Drivers Seat[Opt on STD] +135
Traction Control System[Std on LSS] +80

NINETY-EIGHT 1995

Engine upgraded to 3800 Series II status. Alloy wheels are standard. Flash-to-pass is new standard feature.

RATINGS (SCALE OF 1-10)

Overall	Safety	Reliability	Performance	Comfort	Value
8	8.4	8	7.9	8.1	7.6

Category A

Model Description	Trade-in Value	Market Value
4 Dr STD Sdn	10980	13730

OPTIONS FOR NINETY-EIGHT

Compact Disc W/fm/tape +320
Keyless Entry System +115
Power Moonroof +650
Steer. Whl. Radio Cntrls +90
Traction Control System +95

SILHOUETTE 1995

3.1-liter V6 engine dropped in favor of more powerful 3.8-liter V6.

RATINGS (SCALE OF 1-10)

Overall	Safety	Reliability	Performance	Comfort	Value
7.5	6.9	7.7	7.5	7.4	8

Don't forget to refer to the Mileage Adjustment Table at the back of this book!

© 1999 by Edmund Publications Corporation

Model Description	Trade-in Value	Market Value
Category G		
2 Dr STD Pass. Van	9700	12280

OPTIONS FOR SILHOUETTE

AM/FM Compact Disc Playr +175
Child Seats (2) +115
Dual Air Conditioning +460
Keyless Entry System +95
Leather Seats +350
Power Drivers Seat +130
Traction Control System +135

1994 OLDSMOBILE

ACHIEVA 1994

Driver airbag debuts. 3.1-liter V6 replaces 3.3-liter V6 on options sheet. Hot-rod SCX gone from lineup.

RATINGS (SCALE OF 1-10)

Overall	Safety	Reliability	Performance	Comfort	Value
7.6	6.6	8.1	8.4	7.9	7.1

Model Description	Trade-in Value	Market Value
Category C		
2 Dr S Cpe	4445	6005
4 Dr S Sdn	4500	6080
2 Dr SC Cpe	5810	7850
4 Dr SL Sdn	5815	7855

OPTIONS FOR ACHIEVA

6 cyl 3.1 L Engine +195
Auto 3-Speed Transmission +205
Auto 4-Speed Transmission +280
Air Conditioning[Opt on S] +295
AM/FM Stereo Tape[Opt on S] +60
Astro Roof +265
Cruise Control[Opt on S] +75
Leather Seats +215
Power Drivers Seat +105
Power Mirrors[Opt on S] +40
Power Windows +115

BRAVADA 1994

New Special Edition model has gold trim. Doors get guard beams. Shock absorbers are softened for a better ride.

RATINGS (SCALE OF 1-10)

Overall	Safety	Reliability	Performance	Comfort	Value
6.2	5.1	7.2	6.8	7.1	4.7

Model Description	Trade-in Value	Market Value
Category G		
4 Dr Special Edition 4WD Wgn	9915	12880
4 Dr STD 4WD Wgn	9590	12455

OPTIONS FOR BRAVADA

AM/FM Compact Disc Playr +145
Camper/Towing Package[Opt on STD] +105
Electronic Gauges[Opt on STD] +100
Gold Package[Opt on STD] +175
Leather Seats[Opt on STD] +285
Swing Out Tire Carrier[Opt on STD] +75

CUTLASS CIERA 1994

Driver airbag and ABS standard for all models. Four-cylinder engine back in base models, producing 120 horsepower. A 3.1-liter V6 replaces last year's 3.3-liter V6. Variable-assist steering is a new option on sedans. SL replaced by Special Edition models.

RATINGS (SCALE OF 1-10)

Overall	Safety	Reliability	Performance	Comfort	Value
7.6	7.1	7.3	7.4	7.6	8.3

Model Description	Trade-in Value	Market Value
Category C		
4 Dr S Wgn	5085	6870
4 Dr S Sdn	5235	7075
4 Dr Special Edition Sdn	5670	7665
4 Dr Special Edition Wgn	5430	7340

OPTIONS FOR CUTLASS CIERA

6 cyl 3.1 L Engine[Opt on S Sdn] +195
AM/FM Stereo Tape[Opt on S] +60
Cruise Control[Opt on S] +75
Keyless Entry System +70
Leather Seats +215
Power Drivers Seat[Opt on S] +105
Power Windows[Opt on S] +115
Premium Sound System +145
Third Seat[Opt on S] +60
Woodgrain Applique +115

CUTLASS SUPREME 1994

Driver airbag added and ABS is made standard on all models. International Series dropped. Special Editions are on sale, carrying one-price stickers and a healthy load of standard equipment. 3.1-liter V6 makes 20 more horsepower. 3.4-liter V6 makes 15 more horsepower. New standard features include tilt steering, intermittent wipers, Pass-Key theft deterrent system, and rear defogger.

RATINGS (SCALE OF 1-10)

Overall	Safety	Reliability	Performance	Comfort	Value
7.8	7.5	6.7	8.2	8	8.4

Model Description	Trade-in Value	Market Value
Category C		
2 Dr S Cpe	6290	8500
4 Dr S Sdn	6180	8350
2 Dr Special Edition Cpe	6545	8845
4 Dr Special Edition Sdn	6470	8745
2 Dr STD Conv	8790	11880

OPTIONS FOR CUTLASS SUPREME

6 cyl 3.4 L Engine +485
Climate Control for AC[Opt on S Cpe] +65
Cruise Control[Opt on S] +75

Don't forget to refer to the Mileage Adjustment Table at the back of this book!

© 1999 by Edmund Publications Corporation

Keyless Entry System +70
Leather Seats[Std on STD] +215
Lighted Entry System[Opt on STD] +60
Power Drivers Seat[Std on STD] +105
Power Moonroof +260
Power Passenger Seat +100
Power Windows[Opt on S] +115
Premium Sound System +145
Remote Trunk Release[Std on STD] +30

EIGHTY-EIGHT ROYALE 1994

Passenger airbag is housed in a new dashboard featuring more compact layout and new four-spoke steering wheel. Grille is body-color. Headlamps and turn signals are restyled. Traction control system can now reduce engine power as well as apply brakes to slipping wheel. New Special Edition model is available.

RATINGS (SCALE OF 1-10)

Overall	Safety	Reliability	Performance	Comfort	Value
N/A	8.4	7.9	8.3	N/A	N/A

Category B

Model	Trade-in Value	Market Value
4 Dr LS Sdn	7185	9580
4 Dr LSS Sdn	7480	9970
4 Dr Special Edition Sdn	7000	9335
4 Dr STD Sdn	6665	8890

OPTIONS FOR EIGHTY-EIGHT ROYALE

Compact Disc W/fm/tape +145
Cruise Control[Opt on STD] +80
Keyless Entry System +65
Leather Seats[Std on LS Special Edit.] +245
Power Drivers Seat[Opt on LS,STD] +110
Traction Control System +65

NINETY-EIGHT 1994

Passenger airbag is housed in a new dashboard featuring more compact layout. Touring Sedan is dropped, and a Special Edition is added. Supercharged engine is now available on the Elite, and it gains horsepower and torque. Traction control system can now reduce engine power as well as apply brakes to slipping wheel. There is an additional inch of seat travel. The grille and headlamps are restyled.

RATINGS (SCALE OF 1-10)

Overall	Safety	Reliability	Performance	Comfort	Value
8.1	8.4	7.9	7.7	8.1	8.6

Category A

Model	Trade-in Value	Market Value
4 Dr Elite Sdn	8675	11125
4 Dr Special Edition Sdn	8105	10390
4 Dr STD Sdn	7805	10005

OPTIONS FOR NINETY-EIGHT

Astro Roof +510
Compact Disc W/fm/tape +260
Keyless Entry System[Opt on STD] +90
Leather Seats[Opt on Elite,STD] +255
Power Passenger Seat[Opt on STD] +115
Traction Control System +80

SILHOUETTE 1994

Driver airbag added to standard equipment list. Traction control and integrated child seats are new options. Power sliding side door debuts. New Special Edition model is available.

RATINGS (SCALE OF 1-10)

Overall	Safety	Reliability	Performance	Comfort	Value
7.6	6.9	7.6	7.5	7.4	8.5

Category G

Model	Trade-in Value	Market Value
2 Dr Special Edition Pass. Van	7560	9815
2 Dr STD Pass. Van	7310	9490

OPTIONS FOR SILHOUETTE

6 cyl 3.8 L Engine[Opt on STD] +160
AM/FM Compact Disc Playr +145
AM/FM Stereo Tape[Opt on STD] +90
Child Seats (2) +95
Cruise Control[Opt on STD] +80
Keyless Entry System +75
Leather Seats +285
Luggage Rack[Opt on STD] +60
Power Door Locks[Opt on STD] +85
Power Drivers Seat +105
Power Windows[Opt on STD] +85
Traction Control System +110

1993 OLDSMOBILE

ACHIEVA 1993

All four-cylinder engines lose five horsepower, thanks to emissions regulations. They also get new engine mounts and other revisions aimed at making them smoother and quieter. Battery rundown protection is new standard feature.

RATINGS (SCALE OF 1-10)

Overall	Safety	Reliability	Performance	Comfort	Value
7	4.3	7.4	8.4	7.9	6.9

Category C

Model	Trade-in Value	Market Value
2 Dr S Cpe	3455	4865
4 Dr S Sdn	3495	4925
2 Dr SL Cpe	4340	6115
4 Dr SL Sdn	4345	6120

OPTIONS FOR ACHIEVA

4 cyl 2.3 L Quad 4 Engine +125
6 cyl 3.3 L Engine[Opt on S,Sdn] +165
Auto 3-Speed Transmission[Opt on S] +170
Achieva SC Performance Pkg +425
Achieva SCX Performance Pkg +655
Air Conditioning +240
Aluminum/Alloy Wheels +85

Don't forget to refer to the Mileage Adjustment Table at the back of this book!

 © 1999 by Edmund Publications Corporation

Model Description	Trade-in Value	Market Value

AM/FM Stereo Tape[Opt on S] +50
Cruise Control +65
Keyless Entry System +55
Power Drivers Seat +85
Power Windows +90

BRAVADA 1993

Electronic shift controls added to transmission. Gold Package is new option. Driver's seat gets six-way power adjustment. Both front seats gain power lumbar adjusters. Sun visors get extender panels, and a new overhead console with compass is added.

RATINGS (SCALE OF 1-10)

Overall	Safety	Reliability	Performance	Comfort	Value
6.4	5.2	7.3	6.8	7.1	5.6

Category G

4 Dr STD 4WD Wgn	7860	10480

OPTIONS FOR BRAVADA

AM/FM Compact Disc Playr +115
Camper/Towing Package +85
Electronic Gauges +80
Leather Seats +235
Swing Out Tire Carrier +60

CUTLASS CIERA 1993

Driver airbag is standard on SL; optional on S. Four-cylinder engine dropped in favor of standard V6 power. Air conditioning also makes the standard equipment list. SL sedans get a trunk cargo net; SL wagons get a cargo cover. Leather is new option on base model.

RATINGS (SCALE OF 1-10)

Overall	Safety	Reliability	Performance	Comfort	Value
7.4	6.1	7.2	7.4	7.6	8.8

Category C

4 Dr S Sdn	3890	5480
4 Dr S Cruiser Wgn	4375	6160
4 Dr SL Sdn	4485	6315
4 Dr SL Cruiser Wgn	5170	7285

OPTIONS FOR CUTLASS CIERA

6 cyl 3.3 L Engine[Opt on S,S Cruiser] +165
Auto 4-Speed Transmission[Std on SL Cruiser] +60
Air Bag Restraint[Opt on S,S Cruiser] +155
Aluminum/Alloy Wheels +85
AM/FM Stereo Tape[Opt on S,S Cruiser] +50
Cruise Control +65
Keyless Entry System +55
Leather Seats +175
Power Drivers Seat +85
Power Windows +90
Premium Sound System +120
Third Seat[Opt on S Cruiser] +50
Woodgrain Applique +95

CUTLASS SUPREME 1993

3.4-liter twin-cam engine now available in convertible, but can't be ordered with five-speed transmission anymore. International Series gets new alloys, and all models are equipped with automatic power door locks.

RATINGS (SCALE OF 1-10)

Overall	Safety	Reliability	Performance	Comfort	Value
7.3	5.3	7	8.2	8	7.9

Category C

2 Dr International Cpe	6475	9120
4 Dr International Sdn	6445	9075
2 Dr S Cpe	4745	6680
4 Dr S Sdn	4520	6365
2 Dr Special Cpe	5080	7150
4 Dr Special Sdn	4830	6805
2 Dr STD Conv	6980	9830

OPTIONS FOR CUTLASS SUPREME

6 cyl 3.4 L Engine[Opt on S,STD] +405
Auto 4-Speed Transmission[Opt on S] +55
Aluminum/Alloy Wheels[Opt on S] +85
AM/FM Stereo Tape[Opt on S] +50
Anti-Lock Brakes[Opt on S,STD] +190
Climate Control for AC[Opt on S,STD] +55
Cruise Control[Opt on S,STD] +65
Leather Seats +175
Power Drivers Seat[Opt on S,STD] +85
Power Sunroof +210
Power Windows[Std on Special,STD] +90
Premium Sound System +120
Steer. Whl. Radio Cntrls[Opt on S,STD] +50

EIGHTY-EIGHT ROYALE 1993

ABS is standard on all models. Engine makes more torque. LSS gets new alloy wheels and variable-assist power steering.

RATINGS (SCALE OF 1-10)

Overall	Safety	Reliability	Performance	Comfort	Value
N/A	7	7.7	8.3	N/A	N/A

Category B

4 Dr LS Sdn	6315	8650
4 Dr STD Sdn	5620	7700

OPTIONS FOR EIGHTY-EIGHT ROYALE

LSS Package +370
Aluminum/Alloy Wheels +100
AM/FM Stereo Tape[Std on LS] +55
Auto Load Leveling +55
Cruise Control[Std on LS] +65
Leather Seats +200
Power Door Locks[Std on LS] +75
Power Drivers Seat +90
Premium Sound System +125
Traction Control System +55

Don't forget to refer to the Mileage Adjustment Table at the back of this book!

 © 1999 by Edmund Publications Corporation

Model Description	Trade-in Value	Market Value

NINETY-EIGHT 1993

Base V6 makes more torque. Touring Sedan gets body-color grille and headlight trim. Base model loses standard cassette player.

RATINGS (SCALE OF 1-10)

Overall	Safety	Reliability	Performance	Comfort	Value
N/A	N/A	7.8	7.7	7.7	8.6

Category A	Trade-in Value	Market Value
4 Dr Regency Sdn	6580	8775
4 Dr Regency Elite Sdn	7370	9830
4 Dr Regency Touring Sdn	8300	11065
4 Dr Special Sdn	6865	9155

OPTIONS FOR NINETY-EIGHT

Aluminum/Alloy Wheels[Opt on Regency] +125
AM/FM Stereo Tape[Opt on Regency] +45
Keyless Entry System[Opt on Regency] +75
Leather Seats[Opt on Regency,Regency Elite] +210
Power Passenger Seat +90
Power Sunroof +415
Premium Sound System[Std on Regency Touring] +135
Steer. Whl. Radio Cntrls[Opt on Regency] +60

SILHOUETTE 1993

Subtle restyle includes front and rear fascias, as well as alloy wheels. Optional V6 makes more power.

RATINGS (SCALE OF 1-10)

Overall	Safety	Reliability	Performance	Comfort	Value
7.2	5.8	6.9	7.5	7.4	8.3

Category G	Trade-in Value	Market Value
2 Dr STD Pass. Van	5615	7485

OPTIONS FOR SILHOUETTE

6 cyl 3.8 L Engine +185
Auto 4-Speed Transmission +120
AM/FM Compact Disc Playr +115
Auto Load Leveling +70
Cruise Control +65
Dual Air Conditioning +305
Leather Seats +235
Luggage Rack +45
Power Door Locks +70
Power Drivers Seat +85
Power Windows +70
Sunroof +90

For expert advice in selecting/buying/leasing a car, call

1-900-AUTOPRO

($2.00 per minute)

1992 OLDSMOBILE

ACHIEVA 1992

Cutlass Calais replacement. SCX coupe is hot-rod of the bunch, featuring a 190-horsepower Quad 4 engine. ABS is standard. Computer Command Ride is optional on SL and SC, and allows driver to select one of three suspension settings.

RATINGS (SCALE OF 1-10)

Overall	Safety	Reliability	Performance	Comfort	Value
7.1	4.4	7.7	8.4	7.9	6.9

Category C	Trade-in Value	Market Value
2 Dr S Cpe	3020	4380
4 Dr S Sdn	2995	4345
2 Dr SCX Cpe	3655	5295
2 Dr SL Cpe	3415	4950
4 Dr SL Sdn	3550	5145

OPTIONS FOR ACHIEVA

4 cyl 2.3 L Quad 4 Engine[Opt on S] +100
6 cyl 3.3 L Engine +125
Auto 3-Speed Transmission[Opt on S] +135
Sport Performance Pkg +320
Air Conditioning +200
AM/FM Stereo Tape[Std on SL] +40
Cruise Control +50
Keyless Entry System +45
Power Drivers Seat +70
Power Windows +75
Rear Spoiler[Std on SCX] +40
Rear Window Defroster[Std on SCX] +40
Tilt Steering Wheel +35

BRAVADA 1992

CD player and outside spare tire carrier are new options. New speedometer placed in dashboard. Midyear, a 200-horsepower V6 is added.

RATINGS (SCALE OF 1-10)

Overall	Safety	Reliability	Performance	Comfort	Value
5.9	3.9	7.1	6.4	7.1	5.1

Category G	Trade-in Value	Market Value
4 Dr STD 4WD Wgn	6505	8915

OPTIONS FOR BRAVADA

AM/FM Compact Disc Playr +95
Camper/Towing Package +70
Electronic Gauges +65
Leather Seats +190
Swing Out Tire Carrier +50

CUSTOM CRUISER 1992

A more powerful 5.7-liter V8 is newly optional.

Don't forget to refer to the Mileage Adjustment Table at the back of this book!

 © 1999 by Edmund Publications Corporation

Model Description	Trade-in Value	Market Value
Category C		
4 Dr STD Wgn	5155	7470

OPTIONS FOR CUSTOM CRUISER

8 cyl 5.7 L Engine +60
Aluminum/Alloy Wheels +70
Cruise Control +50
Power Door Locks +60
Power Drivers Seat +70
Power Windows +75
Premium Sound System +100
Rear Window Defroster +40

CUTLASS CIERA 1992

Coupe is given the ax, and base sedan disappears. Automatic door locks made standard.

RATINGS (SCALE OF 1-10)

Overall	Safety	Reliability	Performance	Comfort	Value
7.1	4.7	7.1	7.4	7.6	8.7

Model Description	Trade-in Value	Market Value
Category C		
4 Dr S Sdn	3110	4510
4 Dr S Cruiser Wgn	3435	4980
4 Dr SL Sdn	3750	5435
4 Dr SL Cruiser Wgn	4155	6025

OPTIONS FOR CUTLASS CIERA

6 cyl 3.3 L Engine[Opt on S,S Cruiser] +125
Auto 4-Speed Transmission[Std on SL Cruiser] +50
Air Conditioning[Opt on S,S Cruiser] +200
Aluminum/Alloy Wheels +70
AM/FM Stereo Tape[Opt on S,S Cruiser] +40
Cruise Control +50
Leather Seats +145
Power Drivers Seat[Opt on S] +70
Power Windows +75
Premium Sound System +100
Third Seat[Opt on S Cruiser] +40
Woodgrain Applique +75

CUTLASS SUPREME 1992

Styling is updated front and rear. Four-cylinder engine dropped. International Series models get 3.4-liter twin-cam engine, heads-up instrument display and ABS standard. Sedans get folding rear seatback. Alloys are standard on SL models.

RATINGS (SCALE OF 1-10)

Overall	Safety	Reliability	Performance	Comfort	Value
7.4	5.4	7.1	8.2	8	8.3

Model Description	Trade-in Value	Market Value
Category C		
2 Dr International Cpe	4895	7095
4 Dr International Sdn	5230	7580
2 Dr S Cpe	3630	5260
4 Dr S Sdn	3850	5580
2 Dr STD Conv	6050	8765

OPTIONS FOR CUTLASS SUPREME

6 cyl 3.4 L Engine +295
Auto 4-Speed Transmission[Std on STD] +45
Aluminum/Alloy Wheels[Opt on S] +70
AM/FM Stereo Tape[Opt on S] +40
Anti-Lock Brakes[Opt on S,STD] +155
Astro Roof +180
Auto Load Leveling +55
Climate Control for AC[Opt on S,STD] +45
Cruise Control[Opt on S,STD] +50
Keyless Entry System[Opt on S,STD] +45
Leather Seats +145
Power Door Locks[Opt on S,STD] +60
Power Windows[Std on STD] +75

EIGHTY-EIGHT ROYALE 1992

Redesigned and based on Ninety-Eight platform. Available only as a sedan; coupe dropped from lineup. Driver airbag is standard. LS models have standard ABS; this feature is optional on base models. 3.8-liter V6 makes 170 horsepower. Passenger and cargo volume are both up. Traction control is optional on LS models. Midyear, an LSS model debuted with FE3 suspension, alloy wheels and bucket seats.

RATINGS (SCALE OF 1-10)

Overall	Safety	Reliability	Performance	Comfort	Value
N/A	7	7.6	8.3	N/A	N/A

Model Description	Trade-in Value	Market Value
Category B		
4 Dr LS Sdn	5090	7070
4 Dr STD Sdn	4505	6260

OPTIONS FOR EIGHTY-EIGHT ROYALE

LSS Package +340
Aluminum/Alloy Wheels +85
AM/FM Stereo Tape[Std on LS] +45
Anti-Lock Brakes[Std on LS] +175
Auto Load Leveling +45
Climate Control for AC +45
Cruise Control[Std on LS] +55
Keyless Entry System +45
Leather Seats +165
Power Door Locks[Std on LS] +60
Power Drivers Seat +75
Power Passenger Seat +75
Premium Sound System +105
Traction Control System +45

NINETY-EIGHT 1992

Supercharged engine is optional on Touring Sedan. Traction control is optional on any model.

RATINGS (SCALE OF 1-10)

Overall	Safety	Reliability	Performance	Comfort	Value
N/A	N/A	7.3	7.7	7.7	7.9

Don't forget to refer to the Mileage Adjustment Table at the back of this book!

© 1999 by Edmund Publications Corporation

Model Description	Trade-in Value	Market Value
Category A		
4 Dr Regency Sdn	5290	7350
4 Dr Regency Elite Sdn	5785	8030
4 Dr Regency Touring Sdn	6560	9110

OPTIONS FOR NINETY-EIGHT

Aluminum/Alloy Wheels[Opt on Regency] +105
AM/FM Compact Disc Playr +130
Astro Roof +340
Digital Instrument Panel +65
Dual Power Seats +95
Keyless Entry System +60
Leather Seats[Std on Regency Touring] +170
Premium Sound System +110
Traction Control System +55

SILHOUETTE 1992

Newly optional 165-horsepower 3.8-liter V6 is highly recommended. ABS is made standard. Larger wheels and tires are standard. New options include sunroof, remote keyless entry and rear climate controls.

RATINGS (SCALE OF 1-10)

Overall	Safety	Reliability	Performance	Comfort	Value
7.3	5.9	7.2	7.5	7.4	8.3

Model Description	Trade-in Value	Market Value
Category G		
2 Dr STD Pass. Van	4710	6455

OPTIONS FOR SILHOUETTE

6 cyl 3.8 L Engine +160
Auto 4-Speed Transmission +50
AM/FM Compact Disc Playr +95
Auto Load Leveling +55
Cruise Control +50
Dual Air Conditioning +250
Keyless Entry System +50
Leather Seats +190
Luggage Rack +40
Power Door Locks +55
Power Windows +60

TORONADO 1992

Trofeo gets firmer suspension and bigger wheels and tires.

Model Description	Trade-in Value	Market Value
Category B		
2 Dr STD Cpe	5550	7710
2 Dr Trofeo Cpe	6410	8905

OPTIONS FOR TORONADO

Visual Info System +315
AM/FM Compact Disc Playr +75
Astro Roof +310
Leather Seats[Opt on STD] +165
Power Passenger Seat[Opt on STD] +75
Premium Sound System +105

1991 OLDSMOBILE

BRAVADA 1991

Olds markets a gussied-up S10 Blazer. Features all-wheel drive and four-wheel ABS. Remote keyless entry is standard.

RATINGS (SCALE OF 1-10)

Overall	Safety	Reliability	Performance	Comfort	Value
5.7	3.8	6.7	6.4	7.1	4.5

Model Description	Trade-in Value	Market Value
Category G		
4 Dr STD 4WD Wgn	5630	8045

OPTIONS FOR BRAVADA

Camper/Towing Package +60
Leather Seats +155

CUSTOM CRUISER 1991

Behemoth wagon based on same chassis and bodywork as Caprice and Roadmaster joins lineup. Features eight-passenger seating, glass Vista Roof treatment, ABS and driver airbag. Leather is optional.

Model Description	Trade-in Value	Market Value
Category C		
4 Dr STD Wgn	4195	6450

OPTIONS FOR CUSTOM CRUISER

Aluminum/Alloy Wheels +60
AM/FM Stereo Tape +35
Cruise Control +40
Leather Seats +115
Power Door Locks +50
Power Drivers Seat +60
Power Passenger Seat +55
Power Windows +60
Premium Sound System +80

CUTLASS CALAIS 1991

Quad 442 gets performance tires. International Series has standard ABS.

Model Description	Trade-in Value	Market Value
Category C		
2 Dr International Cpe	3115	4790
4 Dr International Sdn	3150	4845
2 Dr S Cpe	2325	3580
4 Dr S Sdn	2420	3720
2 Dr SL Cpe	2775	4265
4 Dr SL Sdn	2850	4380
2 Dr STD Cpe	2150	3305
4 Dr STD Sdn	2185	3365

OPTIONS FOR CUTLASS CALAIS

4 cyl 2.3 L Quad 4 Engine[Opt on S,STD] +130
6 cyl 3.3 L Engine +125
Auto 3-Speed Transmission[Std on SL] +70
Quad 442 Performance Pkg +345
Air Conditioning[Opt on S,STD] +160

Don't forget to refer to the Mileage Adjustment Table at the back of this book!

 © 1999 by Edmund Publications Corporation

Model Description	Trade-in Value	Market Value

Aluminum/Alloy Wheels[Opt on S] +60
AM/FM Stereo Tape[Opt on S,STD] +35
Cruise Control +40
Leather Seats +115
Power Door Locks +50
Power Drivers Seat +60
Power Windows +60
Premium Sound System +80

CUTLASS CIERA 1991

No changes.

RATINGS (SCALE OF 1-10)

Overall	Safety	Reliability	Performance	Comfort	Value
6.9	4.6	6.5	7.4	7.6	8.3

Category C

Model Description	Trade-in Value	Market Value
2 Dr S Cpe	2395	3685
4 Dr S Sdn	2450	3770
4 Dr S Cruiser Wgn	2580	3970
4 Dr SL Sdn	2905	4470
4 Dr SL Cruiser Wgn	3095	4760
4 Dr STD Sdn	2255	3470

OPTIONS FOR CUTLASS CIERA

6 cyl 3.3 L Engine[Std on SL,SL Cruiser] +125
Auto 4-Speed Transmission[Opt on S,SL] +40
Sport Appearance Package +165
Air Conditioning[Std on SL,SL Cruiser] +160
Aluminum/Alloy Wheels +60
AM/FM Stereo Tape[Std on SL,SL Cruiser] +35
Cruise Control +40
Leather Seats +115
Power Door Locks +50
Power Drivers Seat +60
Power Windows +60
Premium Sound System +80
Third Seat[Opt on S Cruiser] +35
Woodgrain Applique +65

CUTLASS SUPREME 1991

3.4-liter twin-cam V6 debuts on options list, equipped with a five-speed in coupes and an automatic in sedans.

RATINGS (SCALE OF 1-10)

Overall	Safety	Reliability	Performance	Comfort	Value
7.2	5.3	6.5	8.2	8	8.2

Category C

Model Description	Trade-in Value	Market Value
2 Dr International Cpe	3650	5615
4 Dr International Sdn	3580	5505
2 Dr SL Cpe	3240	4980
4 Dr SL Sdn	3175	4885
2 Dr STD Conv	4945	7605
2 Dr STD Cpe	2725	4190
4 Dr STD Sdn	2705	4165

OPTIONS FOR CUTLASS SUPREME

6 cyl 3.1 L Engine[Std on International,SL,Conv] +75
6 cyl 3.4 L Engine +105
Aluminum/Alloy Wheels[Std on International,SL, Conv] +60
AM/FM Stereo Tape[Std on International,SL,Conv] +35
Anti-Lock Brakes +125
Climate Control for AC[Opt on SL,STD] +35
Cruise Control[Opt on SL,STD] +40
Leather Seats +115
Power Door Locks[Opt on SL,STD] +50
Power Drivers Seat +60
Power Sunroof +140
Power Windows[Std on Conv] +60
Premium Sound System +80
Steer. Whl. Radio Cntrls[Opt on SL,STD] +30

EIGHTY-EIGHT ROYALE 1991

No changes.

Category B

Model Description	Trade-in Value	Market Value
2 Dr Brougham Cpe	3600	5075
4 Dr Brougham Sdn	3855	5430
2 Dr STD Cpe	3190	4495
4 Dr STD Sdn	3355	4725

OPTIONS FOR EIGHTY-EIGHT ROYALE

Touring Suspension +155
Air Bag Restraint +130
Aluminum/Alloy Wheels +65
AM/FM Stereo Tape[Opt on STD] +35
Anti-Lock Brakes +145
Cruise Control +45
Keyless Entry System +35
Leather Seats +135
Power Door Locks +50
Power Drivers Seat[Opt on STD] +60
Power Passenger Seat +65
Power Windows +60
Premium Sound System +85

NINETY-EIGHT 1991

Total redesign gives Ninety-Eight nine inches of additional length. Automatic load leveling, ABS, child-proof rear door locks, driver airbag, and automatic climate controls are standard. Touring Sedan again available.

RATINGS (SCALE OF 1-10)

Overall	Safety	Reliability	Performance	Comfort	Value
N/A	N/A	7.3	7.7	7.7	8

Category A

Model Description	Trade-in Value	Market Value
4 Dr Regency Elite Sdn	4465	6380
4 Dr Touring Sdn	5160	7375

OPTIONS FOR NINETY-EIGHT

Aluminum/Alloy Wheels[Std on Touring] +85
AM/FM Compact Disc Playr +105
Astro Roof +275

Don't forget to refer to the Mileage Adjustment Table at the back of this book!

© 1999 by Edmund Publications Corporation

Model Description	Trade-in Value	Market Value

Leather Seats[Std on Touring] +140
Power Passenger Seat[Std on Touring] +60
Premium Sound System[Std on Touring] +90

SILHOUETTE 1991

No changes.

RATINGS (SCALE OF 1-10)

Overall	Safety	Reliability	Performance	Comfort	Value
6.8	4.9	7.1	7	7.4	7.7

Category G

2 Dr STD Pass. Van	3750	5360

OPTIONS FOR SILHOUETTE

AM/FM Compact Disc Playr +80
Auto Load Leveling +45
Cruise Control +45
Leather Seats +155
Luggage Rack +30
Power Door Locks +45
Power Drivers Seat +55
Power Windows +50
Premium Sound System +75

TORONADO 1991

Remote keyless entry standard. Hands-free mobile phone is optional.

Category B

2 Dr STD Cpe	4725	6655
2 Dr Trofeo Cpe	5415	7630

OPTIONS FOR TORONADO

Visual Info System +260
AM/FM Compact Disc Playr +65
Leather Seats[Opt on STD] +135
Power Sunroof +235
Premium Sound System +85

1990 OLDSMOBILE

CUSTOM CRUISER 1990

No changes for 1990.

Category B

4 Dr STD Wgn	2445	3760

OPTIONS FOR CUSTOM CRUISER

Aluminum/Alloy Wheels +55
AM/FM Stereo Tape +30
Auto Load Leveling +30
Cruise Control +35
Power Door Locks +40
Power Drivers Seat +50
Power Passenger Seat +50
Power Windows +50
Woodgrain Applique +65

CUTLASS CALAIS 1990

New Quad 442 option includes high-output Quad 4 engine, sport suspension, and manual transmission. Remote keyless entry and a CD player are new options.

Category C

2 Dr International Cpe	2190	3595
4 Dr International Sdn	2195	3600
2 Dr S Cpe	1680	2755
4 Dr S Sdn	1715	2810
2 Dr SL Cpe	1855	3035
4 Dr SL Sdn	1980	3245
2 Dr STD Cpe	1670	2735
4 Dr STD Sdn	1615	2650

OPTIONS FOR CUTLASS CALAIS

4 cyl 2.3 L Quad 4 Engine[Std on SL] +100
6 cyl 3.3 L Engine +100
Auto 3-Speed Transmission[Std on SL] +60
Quad 442 Pkg +275
Air Conditioning[Opt on S,SL,STD] +130
Aluminum/Alloy Wheels[Opt on S] +50
Cruise Control +35
Keyless Entry System +30
Leather Seats +95
Power Door Locks +40
Power Drivers Seat +45
Power Windows +50
Premium Sound System +65
Sunroof +60

CUTLASS CIERA 1990

2.8-liter V6 option disappears. Manual transmission dropped. Door-mounted passive seatbelts are added for front seat passengers. Seats have been upgraded.

RATINGS (SCALE OF 1-10)

Overall	Safety	Reliability	Performance	Comfort	Value
6.7	4.4	6.5	7.4	7.6	7.6

Category C

2 Dr International Cpe	2095	3435
4 Dr International Sdn	2295	3760
2 Dr S Cpe	1785	2930
4 Dr S Sdn	1735	2845
4 Dr S Cruiser Wgn	1855	3040
4 Dr SL Sdn	2165	3550
4 Dr SL Cruiser Wgn	2210	3625
4 Dr STD Sdn	1705	2795

OPTIONS FOR CUTLASS CIERA

6 cyl 3.3 L Engine[Opt on S,S Cruiser,STD] +100
Auto 4-Speed Transmission[Opt on S,S Cruiser,SL] +35
Air Conditioning[Opt on S,S Cruiser,STD] +130
Aluminum/Alloy Wheels[Std on International] +50
Cruise Control +35
Dual Power Seats +95
Leather Seats +95

Don't forget to refer to the Mileage Adjustment Table at the back of this book!

 © 1999 by Edmund Publications Corporation

Power Door Locks +40
Power Sunroof +115
Power Windows +50
Premium Sound System +65
Third Seat[Opt on S Cruiser] +30
Woodgrain Applique +50

CUTLASS SUPREME 1990

A sedan joins the lineup. International Series gets high-output Quad 4 engine, teamed with five-speed manual transmission.

RATINGS (SCALE OF 1-10)

Overall	Safety	Reliability	Performance	Comfort	Value
7.1	5.2	6.1	8.2	8	8.1

Category C

Model	Trade-in	Market
2 Dr International Cpe	2545	4175
4 Dr International Sdn	2550	4185
2 Dr SL Cpe	2345	3845
4 Dr SL Sdn	2420	3965
2 Dr STD Cpe	2025	3315
4 Dr STD Sdn	2110	3460

OPTIONS FOR CUTLASS SUPREME

6 cyl 3.1 L Engine[Std on SL,Conv] +100
Aluminum/Alloy Wheels[Opt on STD] +50
Anti-Lock Brakes +105
Astro Roof +120
Climate Control for AC +30
Cruise Control +35
Leather Seats +95
Power Door Locks[Opt on SL,STD] +40
Power Drivers Seat[Opt on SL,STD] +45
Power Windows[Std on Conv] +50
Premium Sound System +65

EIGHTY-EIGHT ROYALE 1990

Minor styling updates front and rear. A power auto-down driver's window, and remote keyless entry are new options.

Category B

Model	Trade-in	Market
2 Dr Brougham Cpe	2730	4200
4 Dr Brougham Sdn	3105	4775
2 Dr STD Cpe	2640	4065
4 Dr STD Sdn	2865	4405

OPTIONS FOR EIGHTY-EIGHT ROYALE

Touring Ride & Handling Package +130
Air Bag Restraint +105
Aluminum/Alloy Wheels +55
AM/FM Stereo Tape[Opt on STD] +30
Anti-Lock Brakes +120
Auto Load Leveling +30
Cruise Control +35
Keyless Entry System +30
Leather Seats +110
Power Door Locks +40
Power Drivers Seat +50
Power Passenger Seat +50
Power Windows +50
Premium Sound System +70

NINETY-EIGHT 1990

Minor styling updates front and rear. Express-down feature for the power driver's window is standard this year. Optional astroroof has an express-open feature. Remote keyless entry is a new option. Center armrest is redesigned to accommodate optional CD player.

Category A

Model	Trade-in	Market
4 Dr Touring Sdn	3960	5915
4 Dr Regency Sdn	2810	4195
4 Dr Regency Brougham Sdn	2955	4410

OPTIONS FOR NINETY-EIGHT

Air Bag Restraint +140
Aluminum/Alloy Wheels[Opt on Regency] +70
AM/FM Compact Disc Playr +85
Anti-Lock Brakes[Std on Touring] +155
Astro Roof +225
Cruise Control[Opt on Regency] +30
Keyless Entry System +40
Leather Seats[Std on Touring] +115
Power Passenger Seat[Std on Touring] +50
Premium Sound System[Std on Touring] +75
Steer. Whl. Radio Cntrls[Std on Touring] +30

SILHOUETTE 1990

Underpowered minivan with lots of standard equipment. 3.1-liter V6 offers a measly 120 horsepower.

RATINGS (SCALE OF 1-10)

Overall	Safety	Reliability	Performance	Comfort	Value
6.7	4.9	7	7	7.4	7.2

Category G

Model	Trade-in	Market
2 Dr STD Pass. Van	3020	4570

OPTIONS FOR SILHOUETTE

AM/FM Stereo Tape +40
Cruise Control +35
Leather Seats +125
Power Door Locks +40
Power Drivers Seat +45
Power Windows +40
Premium Sound System +60

TORONADO 1990

Redesigned inside and out. Car is more than a foot longer than last year. Trunk is 2.5 cubic feet larger. Driver airbag is a new option on base models; standard on Trofeo. Dash features full analog gauges. Suspension is revamped and features automatic load leveling.

Don't forget to refer to the Mileage Adjustment Table at the back of this book!

 © 1999 by Edmund Publications Corporation

Model Description	Trade-in Value	Market Value
Category B		
2 Dr STD Cpe	3265	5020
2 Dr Trofeo Cpe	3685	5670

OPTIONS FOR TORONADO

Visual Information Center +190
AM/FM Compact Disc Playr +50
Anti-Lock Brakes[Opt on STD] +120
Astro Roof +205
Bose Sound System +125
Leather Seats[Opt on STD] +110

1989 OLDSMOBILE

CUSTOM CRUISER 1989

Three-point rear shoulder belts are added.

Model Description	Trade-in Value	Market Value
Category B		
4 Dr STD Wgn	1700	2830

OPTIONS FOR CUSTOM CRUISER

Cruise Control +30
Power Door Locks +35
Power Drivers Seat +40
Power Passenger Seat +40
Power Windows +40
Woodgrain Applique +50

CUTLASS CALAIS 1989

New 3.3-liter V6 is optional on S and SL models. Midyear, a high-output Quad 4 engine went into International Series model, good for 185 horsepower. Base engine gets 12 horsepower bump to 110. New grilles, taillights and fascias debut. Power sunroof is new option.

Model Description	Trade-in Value	Market Value
Category C		
2 Dr International Cpe	1630	2860
4 Dr International Sdn	1720	3015
2 Dr S Cpe	1485	2605
4 Dr S Sdn	1585	2780
2 Dr SL Cpe	1575	2765
4 Dr SL Sdn	1635	2870
2 Dr STD Cpe	1450	2545
4 Dr STD Sdn	1520	2665

OPTIONS FOR CUTLASS CALAIS

4 cyl 2.3 L Quad 4 Engine[Opt on S,SL] +90
6 cyl 3.3 L Engine +95
Auto 3-Speed Transmission +60
Quad 4 Pkg +155
Air Conditioning[Opt on S,SL,STD] +110
Aluminum/Alloy Wheels[Opt on S,SL,STD] +40
Cruise Control +30
Leather Seats +80
Power Door Locks +30
Power Drivers Seat +40
Power Windows +40
Premium Sound System +55
Sunroof +50

CUTLASS CIERA 1989

Styling is freshened with revised sheetmetal, grilles and moldings. New 3.3-liter V6 replaces old 3.8-liter unit. Base four-cylinder gets more horsepower, and midlevel 2.8-liter V6 returns with no change. Power sunroof is new option.

RATINGS (SCALE OF 1-10)

Overall	Safety	Reliability	Performance	Comfort	Value
6.8	4.5	6.6	7.4	7.6	8

Model Description	Trade-in Value	Market Value
Category C		
4 Dr Cruiser Wgn	1270	2225
2 Dr International Cpe	1885	3305
4 Dr International Sdn	1865	3270
2 Dr SL Cpe	1520	2665
4 Dr SL Sdn	1445	2535
4 Dr SL Cruiser Wgn	1520	2665
2 Dr STD Cpe	1215	2130
4 Dr STD Sdn	1335	2340

OPTIONS FOR CUTLASS CIERA

6 cyl 2.8 L Engine +85
6 cyl 3.3 L Engine[Std on International] +95
Air Conditioning[Std on International] +110
Aluminum/Alloy Wheels[Std on International] +40
Cruise Control +30
Leather Seats +80
Power Door Locks +30
Power Drivers Seat +40
Power Sunroof +95
Power Windows +40
Premium Sound System +55
Woodgrain Applique +40

CUTLASS SUPREME 1989

Air conditioning is made standard, ABS is optional, and a 3.1-liter V6 arrives midyear to replace 2.8-liter V6 as the standard engine. Cars with manual transmissions will continue to use 2.8-liter unit. Three-point rear seatbelts are added, and a power sunroof, remote keyless entry, CD player, and trip computer join the options list. International Series can be equipped with heads-up instrument display.

RATINGS (SCALE OF 1-10)

Overall	Safety	Reliability	Performance	Comfort	Value
6.9	5	5.9	7.8	8	7.7

Model Description	Trade-in Value	Market Value
Category C		
2 Dr International Cpe	1935	3395
2 Dr SL Cpe	1785	3130
2 Dr STD Cpe	1735	3040

Don't forget to refer to the Mileage Adjustment Table at the back of this book!

 © 1999 by Edmund Publications Corporation

Model Description	Trade-in Value	Market Value

OPTIONS FOR CUTLASS SUPREME

6 cyl 2.8 L Engine[Opt on SL,STD] +85
Auto 4-Speed Transmission +85
Aluminum/Alloy Wheels[Opt on STD] +40
Anti-Lock Brakes +85
Cruise Control +30
Leather Seats +80
Power Door Locks[Opt on SL,STD] +30
Power Drivers Seat[Opt on SL,STD] +40
Power Sunroof +95
Power Windows +40
Premium Sound System +55

EIGHTY-EIGHT ROYALE 1989

"Delta" moniker disappears for no good reason. A fully automatic climate control system is now standard. A CD player joined the options list midyear. Power sunroof option dropped. Driver airbag is optional on sedan. ABS is optional on all models.

Category B

Model Description	Trade-in Value	Market Value
2 Dr Brougham Cpe	1980	3305
4 Dr Brougham Sdn	2170	3615
2 Dr STD Cpe	1790	2985
4 Dr STD Sdn	2100	3500

OPTIONS FOR EIGHTY-EIGHT ROYALE

Air Bag Restraint +90
Aluminum/Alloy Wheels +45
Anti-Lock Brakes +95
Cruise Control +30
Dual Power Seats +50
Leather Seats +90
Power Door Locks +35
Power Windows +40
Premium Sound System +55

NINETY-EIGHT 1989

A driver airbag is optional this year on base Ninety-Eight. To meet passive restraint laws, automatic seatbelts are standard for front passengers. Rear passengers get three-point harnesses. Steering wheel controls for climate and audio are standard on Touring Sedan, optional on base Ninety-Eight. A CD player hit the options list midyear. Touring Sedans get trip computer, automatic door locks, cassette player and high-performance tires. ABS is standard on Touring Sedan, optional on base Ninety-Eight.

Category A

Model Description	Trade-in Value	Market Value
4 Dr Touring Sdn	3070	4875
4 Dr Regency Sdn	2200	3495
4 Dr Regency Brougham Sdn	2370	3765

OPTIONS FOR NINETY-EIGHT

Air Bag Restraint +115
Aluminum/Alloy Wheels[Opt on Regency] +55
AM/FM Compact Disc Playr +70
Anti-Lock Brakes[Std on Touring] +125
Astro Roof +185
Leather Seats[Std on Touring] +95
Power Passenger Seat[Std on Touring] +40
Premium Sound System +60

TORONADO 1989

A color CRT, called the Visual Information Center, is optional. It controls climate and audio functions. As if this isn't confusing enough, you can control the same functions using steering wheel controls, which are standard on Trofeo and optional on base models. Trofeo also gets ABS and automatic door locks. Base models gain bucket seats, console and alloy wheels. A bench seat and ABS are optional on base Toronados.

Category B

Model Description	Trade-in Value	Market Value
2 Dr STD Cpe	2385	3975
2 Dr Trofeo Cpe	2440	4065

OPTIONS FOR TORONADO

Visual Information Center +175
Anti-Lock Brakes[Opt on STD] +95
Astro Roof +170
Leather Seats[Opt on STD] +90
Premium Sound System +55

Instant
Lease & Loan Quotes
for New & Used Vehicles!

www.CarFinance.com/edmunds

Don't forget to refer to the Mileage Adjustment Table at the back of this book!

 © 1999 by Edmund Publications Corporation

PLYMOUTH USA

1995 Plymouth Neon

1998 PLYMOUTH

BREEZE 1998

Availability of a 2.4-liter engine brings150 horsepower and 167 foot-pounds of torque, and that's just what the Breeze needs to live up to its name. Both engines can meet California emissions regulations, and new engine mounts helps make them quieter. An Expresso package adds some aesthetic changes: a power sunroof is now optional, the interior becomes Agate and outside, there are six new colors to choose from.

Model Description	Trade-in Value	Market Value
Category C		
4 Dr Expresso Sdn	9660	11640
4 Dr STD Sdn	9405	11330

OPTIONS FOR BREEZE

4 cyl 2.4 L Engine +375
Auto 4-Speed Transmission +875
Aluminum/Alloy Wheels +240
AM/FM Compact Disc Playr +320
Anti-Lock Brakes +520
Cruise Control +170
Keyless Entry System +155
Power Door Locks +200
Power Sunroof +580
Power Windows +255

NEON 1998

Model year 1998 Neons are made quieter by the addition of a structural oil pan. California and other emission-regulating states get an LEV (Low Emission Vehicle) engine calibration. Also changed this year are ABS, a new ignition key lock and the addition of four new colors.

Model Description	Trade-in Value	Market Value
Category E		
2 Dr Competition Cpe	8640	10535
4 Dr Competition Sdn	8810	10745
2 Dr Expresso Cpe	8425	10275
4 Dr Expresso Sdn	8185	9980
2 Dr Highline Cpe	7875	9605
4 Dr Highline Sdn	7875	9605
4 Dr Style Sdn	10125	12345

OPTIONS FOR NEON

Auto 3-Speed Transmission +500
Competition Package +1310
Air Conditioning[Std on Expresso, Style] +675
Aluminum/Alloy Wheels[Std on Style] +265
AM/FM Compact Disc Playr +390
Anti-Lock Brakes +590
Cruise Control +185
Keyless Entry System +125
Power Door Locks +195
Power Mirrors +95
Power Moonroof +485
Power Windows +220
Rear Window Defroster[Opt on Competition] +135
Tilt Steering Wheel +125

VOYAGER 1998

Expresso Decor Package, four new exterior colors, and "next generation" depowered airbags sum up the changes this year.

Model Description	Trade-in Value	Market Value
Category G		
2 Dr Expresso Pass. Van	15075	17945
2 Dr Grand Pass. Van	14215	16920
2 Dr Grand Expresso Pass. Van	16735	19920
2 Dr Grand SE Pass. Van	15550	18510
2 Dr SE Pass. Van	13895	16545
2 Dr STD Pass. Van	12575	14970

OPTIONS FOR VOYAGER

6 cyl 3.0 L Engine[Opt on STD] +360
6 cyl 3.3 L Engine +430
6 cyl 3.3 L FLEX Engine +165
Auto 4-Speed Transmission[Opt on Grand,STD] +210
Air Conditioning[Opt on Grand, Grand SE, SE, STD] +675
Aluminum/Alloy Wheels +285
Anti-Lock Brakes[Opt on Grand, STD] +515
Compact Disc W/fm/tape[Opt on Grand SE,SE] +565
Cruise Control[Opt on Grand, STD] +175
Keyless Entry System +170
Power Door Locks +190
Power Mirrors[Opt on Grand, STD] +110
Power Windows +195
Rear Window Defroster[Opt on Grand, Grand SE, SE, STD] +140
Sliding Driver Side Door[Opt on STD] +445
Sunscreen Glass[Opt on Grand, Grand SE, SE, STD] +295
Tilt Steering Wheel[Opt on Grand, STD] +140

Don't forget to refer to the Mileage Adjustment Table at the back of this book!

 © 1999 by Edmund Publications Corporation

1997 PLYMOUTH

BREEZE 1997

Plymouth is inching the Breeze up-market in both price and content. This year sees a fairly sizable price hike and the addition of luxury options such as an in-dash CD changer. Changes to the standard equipment list brings a nicer center console, improved basic stereos, and increased flow rear seat heater ducts.

RATINGS (SCALE OF 1-10)

Overall	Safety	Reliability	Performance	Comfort	Value
N/A	N/A	7.2	6.6	7.1	7

Category C

Model Description	Trade-in Value	Market Value
4 Dr STD Sdn	7750	9565

OPTIONS FOR BREEZE

Auto 4-Speed Transmission +690
Aluminum/Alloy Wheels +195
AM/FM Compact Disc Playr +260
Anti-Lock Brakes +425
Child Seat (1) +80
Cruise Control +140
Keyless Entry System +130
Power Door Locks +160
Power Windows +205

NEON 1997

1997 Neons are made quieter with the addition of a structural oil pan. Other changes include new optional radios, a new seat fabric, new wheels and wheel covers, and a few new paint colors.

RATINGS (SCALE OF 1-10)

Overall	Safety	Reliability	Performance	Comfort	Value
7.4	6.4	8.2	7.4	7.6	7.4

Category E

Model Description	Trade-in Value	Market Value
2 Dr Expresso Cpe	8185	10230
4 Dr Expresso Sdn	8210	10260
2 Dr Highline Cpe	6920	8655
4 Dr Highline Sdn	7060	8820
2 Dr STD Cpe	6055	7570
4 Dr STD Sdn	5940	7425

OPTIONS FOR NEON

4 cyl 2.0 L DOHC Engine +100
Auto 3-Speed Transmission +395
Competition Package +850
Air Conditioning[Opt on STD] +550
Aluminum/Alloy Wheels +215
AM/FM Compact Disc Playr +320
Anti-Lock Brakes +480
Child Seat (1) +80
Keyless Entry System +100
Power Door Locks +160
Power Moonroof +395
Power Windows +180

PROWLER 1997

Category K

Model Description	Trade-in Value	Market Value
2 Dr STD Conv	41195	49045

VOYAGER 1997

For 1997, the Plymouth minivans receive a cornucopia of changes. This year brings new wheel covers, improved antilock braking systems, an accident response system that unlocks the doors and turns on the interior lights if the air bags deploy, better radios, a quieter interior, and more optional equipment for Base and SE models.

RATINGS (SCALE OF 1-10)

Overall	Safety	Reliability	Performance	Comfort	Value
7.6	7.5	8	6.6	7.4	8.3

Category G

Model Description	Trade-in Value	Market Value
2 Dr Grand Pass. Van	11840	14265
2 Dr Grand SE Pass. Van	13225	15935
2 Dr SE Pass. Van	12055	14525
2 Dr STD Pass. Van	10825	13040

OPTIONS FOR VOYAGER

6 cyl 3.0 L Engine +470
6 cyl 3.3 L Engine +620
Auto 4-Speed Transmission[Opt on Grand,STD] +165
7 Passenger Seating[Opt on STD] +370
Air Conditioning +550
Aluminum/Alloy Wheels +235
Anti-Lock Brakes[Opt on Grand,STD] +420
Auto Load Leveling +155
Captain Chairs (4) +430
Child Seats (2) +175
Compact Disc W/fm/tape +465
Cruise Control[Opt on Grand,STD] +145
Dual Air Conditioning +685
Keyless Entry System +140
Luggage Rack +105
Power Door Locks +155
Power Drivers Seat +190
Power Windows +160
Sliding Driver Side Door +365

1996 PLYMOUTH

BREEZE 1996

The Breeze is introduced this year as Chrysler Corporation's bargain-basement midsize sedan. Nicely equipped with air conditioning and a decent stereo, the Breeze has a surprising amount of interior room.

RATINGS (SCALE OF 1-10)

Overall	Safety	Reliability	Performance	Comfort	Value
N/A	N/A	6.6	6.6	7.1	6.4

Don't forget to refer to the Mileage Adjustment Table at the back of this book!

© 1999 by Edmund Publications Corporation

Model Description	Trade-in Value	Market Value
Category C		
4 Dr STD Sdn	6540	8490

OPTIONS FOR BREEZE

Auto 4-Speed Transmission +575
Air Conditioning +445
Anti-Lock Brakes +345
Child Seat (1) +65
Compact Disc W/fm/tape +205
Keyless Entry System +105
Power Door Locks +135
Power Sunroof +385
Power Windows +170

NEON 1996

Antilock brakes are optional across the line, and base models get more standard equipment for 1996. A value-packed Expresso package is aimed at twenty-something first-time buyers. A base coupe is newly available, and all Neons are supposedly quieter than last year. A power sunroof joins the options list, and a remote keyless entry system with panic alarm is available.

RATINGS (SCALE OF 1-10)

Overall	Safety	Reliability	Performance	Comfort	Value
7.2	6.3	7.3	7.4	7.6	7.2

Model Description	Trade-in Value	Market Value
Category E		
2 Dr Highline Cpe	5775	7700
4 Dr Highline Sdn	5890	7850
2 Dr Sport Cpe	6255	8335
4 Dr Sport Sdn	5995	7990
2 Dr STD Cpe	5255	7005
4 Dr STD Sdn	5205	6940

OPTIONS FOR NEON

4 cyl 2.0 L DOHC Engine +80
Auto 3-Speed Transmission +325
Competition Package +560
Air Conditioning +450
Aluminum/Alloy Wheels +175
AM/FM Compact Disc Playr +260
Anti-Lock Brakes +395
Child Seat (1) +65
Cruise Control +120
Keyless Entry System +80
Power Door Locks[Std on Sport] +130
Power Moonroof +325
Power Windows +145
Rear Spoiler +115
Tilt Steering Wheel[Std on Sport] +85

VOYAGER 1996

Chrysler's stylists and engineers have achieved what many thought was impossible: they substantially improved upon their original formula in every way. Interior comfort is top-notch, and the left-hand passenger door is an industry first.

RATINGS (SCALE OF 1-10)

Overall	Safety	Reliability	Performance	Comfort	Value
7.3	7.3	7	6.6	7.4	8.1

Model Description	Trade-in Value	Market Value
Category G		
2 Dr Grand Pass. Van	10175	12720
2 Dr Grand SE Pass. Van	11000	13750
2 Dr SE Pass. Van	10115	12645
2 Dr STD Pass. Van	9080	11350

OPTIONS FOR VOYAGER

6 cyl 3.0 L Engine[Std on Grand] +390
6 cyl 3.3 L Engine +470
7 Passenger Seating[Opt on STD] +300
Air Conditioning +450
Aluminum/Alloy Wheels +190
Anti-Lock Brakes[Opt on Grand,STD] +345
Captain Chairs (4) +350
Child Seats (2) +145
Compact Disc W/fm/tape +380
Cruise Control[Opt on Grand,STD] +115
Dual Air Conditioning +560
Keyless Entry System +115
Luggage Rack +85
Power Door Locks +125
Power Windows +130
Premium Sound System +200
Sliding Driver Side Door +295

1995 PLYMOUTH

ACCLAIM 1995

The Acclaim is into the home stretch of its career.

RATINGS (SCALE OF 1-10)

Overall	Safety	Reliability	Performance	Comfort	Value
7.1	6.7	8	6.8	7.4	6.8

Model Description	Trade-in Value	Market Value
Category C		
4 Dr STD Sdn	5340	7030

OPTIONS FOR ACCLAIM

6 cyl 3.0 L Engine +355
Aluminum/Alloy Wheels +130
Power Door Locks +110
Power Drivers Seat +130
Power Windows +140

NEON 1995

The all-new Neon is introduced as Plymouth's entry in the compact car class. Roomy, cute and quick are three of the best adjectives we can find for this car. Unfortunately, Chrysler Corporation is still grappling with reliability and noise issues. The Neon is available in coupe and sedan bodystyles in three trim-levels. Safety equipment includes standard dual airbags, optional antilock brakes and an optional integrated child seat.

Don't forget to refer to the Mileage Adjustment Table at the back of this book!

 © 1999 by Edmund Publications Corporation

Model Description	Trade-in Value	Market Value

RATINGS (SCALE OF 1-10)

Overall	Safety	Reliability	Performance	Comfort	Value
7	6.1	6.7	7.4	7.6	7.1

Category E

Model Description	Trade-in Value	Market Value
2 Dr Highline Cpe	4830	6620
4 Dr Highline Sdn	4725	6470
2 Dr Sport Cpe	5275	7230
4 Dr Sport Sdn	5220	7150
4 Dr STD Sdn	4285	5870

OPTIONS FOR NEON

4 cyl 2.0 L DOHC Engine[Std on Sport] +65
Auto 3-Speed Transmission +225
Air Conditioning +370
AM/FM Compact Disc Playr +215
Anti-Lock Brakes[Std on Sport] +320
Child Seat (1) +50
Cruise Control +100
Leather Seats +405
Power Door Locks[Std on Sport] +105
Power Windows +120
Tilt Steering Wheel[Std on Sport] +70

VOYAGER 1995

A 3.3-liter V6 natural gas engine is available this year. Plymouth introduces a snazzy Rallye package for those trying to disguise the fact that they are driving a minivan.

RATINGS (SCALE OF 1-10)

Overall	Safety	Reliability	Performance	Comfort	Value
7.9	8.3	7.1	7.4	8.3	8.6

Category G

Model Description	Trade-in Value	Market Value
2 Dr Grand Pass. Van	7655	9690
2 Dr Grand LE Pass. Van	10255	12985
2 Dr Grand LE 4WD Pass. Van	10905	13805
2 Dr Grand SE Pass. Van	8515	10775
2 Dr Grand SE 4WD Pass. Van	8935	11310
2 Dr LE Pass. Van	9080	11490
2 Dr SE Pass. Van	7575	9590
2 Dr STD Pass. Van	6465	8185

OPTIONS FOR VOYAGER

6 cyl 3.0 L Engine[Opt on STD] +105
6 cyl 3.3 L Engine[Opt on LE,SE,STD] +325
6 cyl 3.8 L Engine +185
Auto 4-Speed Transmission[Opt on SE,STD] +90
7 Passenger Seating[Opt on STD] +245
Air Conditioning[Std on Grand LE,LE] +370
Anti-Lock Brakes[Std on Grand LE,LE,4WD] +280
Captain Chairs (4) +285
Child Seats (2) +115
Compact Disc W/fm/tape +310
Cruise Control[Opt on Grand,STD] +95
Dual Air Conditioning +460
Keyless Entry System[Opt on Grand SE,SE] +95
Leather Seats +350
Luggage Rack +70
Power Door Locks[Std on Grand LE,LE] +105
Power Drivers Seat +130
Power Windows +105

1994 PLYMOUTH

ACCLAIM 1994

The Acclaim gains a motorized passenger seatbelt. The flexible-fuel model is now available to retail customers.

RATINGS (SCALE OF 1-10)

Overall	Safety	Reliability	Performance	Comfort	Value
7.2	6.6	7.7	6.8	7.4	7.5

Category C

Model Description	Trade-in Value	Market Value
4 Dr STD Sdn	4105	5545

OPTIONS FOR ACCLAIM

6 cyl 3.0 L Engine +255
Auto 4-Speed Transmission +65
Air Conditioning +295
AM/FM Stereo Tape +60
Anti-Lock Brakes +230
Cruise Control +75
Power Door Locks +90
Power Drivers Seat +105
Power Windows +115
Rear Window Defroster +60
Tilt Steering Wheel +55

COLT 1994

A driver's airbag is now standard on the Colt. CFC-free air conditioning optional.

RATINGS (SCALE OF 1-10)

Overall	Safety	Reliability	Performance	Comfort	Value
6.6	5.5	7.4	8	7.4	4.7

Category E

Model Description	Trade-in Value	Market Value
2 Dr GL Sdn	3775	5395
4 Dr GL Sdn	4355	6225
4 Dr SE Wgn	3775	5395
2 Dr STD Sdn	3325	4750
4 Dr STD Wgn	3545	5060
4 Dr STD Sdn	4180	5975

OPTIONS FOR COLT

4 cyl 1.8 L Engine[Opt on GL Sdn] +165
4 cyl 2.4 L Engine[Opt on STD Wgn] +65
Auto 3-Speed Transmission +190
Auto 4-Speed Transmission +255
Air Conditioning +300
Aluminum/Alloy Wheels +120
AM/FM Stereo Tape +115
Anti-Lock Brakes +265
Cruise Control +80
Keyless Entry System +55
Power Door Locks[Std on SE] +85

Don't forget to refer to the Mileage Adjustment Table at the back of this book!

© 1999 by Edmund Publications Corporation

Model Description	Trade-in Value	Market Value

Power Windows +100
Rear Window Wiper[Std on SE,4WD] +50

LASER 1994

The final year for the Laser brings automatic-locking retractors for rear seats, making them more compatible for child seats.

RATINGS (SCALE OF 1-10)

Overall	Safety	Reliability	Performance	Comfort	Value
N/A	N/A	7.8	8.4	6.8	3.9

Category C	Trade-in Value	Market Value
2 Dr RS Hbk	4780	6460
2 Dr STD Hbk	4240	5730

OPTIONS FOR LASER

Auto 4-Speed Transmission +265
Air Conditioning +295
Aluminum/Alloy Wheels[Opt on 2WD] +105
AM/FM Compact Disc Playr +140
Anti-Lock Brakes +230
Cruise Control +75
Power Door Locks +90
Power Windows +115
Premium Sound System +145
Rear Spoiler[Std on RS] +60
Rear Window Wiper +55
Sunroof +135

SUNDANCE 1994

The Sundance gets a motorized passenger shoulder belt and CFC-free air conditioning.

RATINGS (SCALE OF 1-10)

Overall	Safety	Reliability	Performance	Comfort	Value
6.5	6.5	7.1	7.2	6.8	5.2

Category E	Trade-in Value	Market Value
2 Dr Duster Hbk	3640	5200
4 Dr Duster Hbk	3655	5220
2 Dr STD Hbk	3375	4820
4 Dr STD Hbk	3450	4930

OPTIONS FOR SUNDANCE

4 cyl 2.5 L Engine[Opt on STD] +105
6 cyl 3.0 L Engine +295
Auto 3-Speed Transmission +205
Auto 4-Speed Transmission +270
Air Conditioning +300
Aluminum/Alloy Wheels +120
AM/FM Compact Disc Playr +175
Anti-Lock Brakes +265
Cruise Control +80
Power Door Locks +85
Power Drivers Seat +110
Power Windows +100
Premium Sound System +125

VOYAGER 1994

New safety features include a passenger airbag and side-impact door beams that meet federal 1997 passenger car standards. Other changes include a new dashboard, optional integrated child seats and new body moldings.

RATINGS (SCALE OF 1-10)

Overall	Safety	Reliability	Performance	Comfort	Value
7.7	8.3	6.8	7.4	8.3	7.9

Category G	Trade-in Value	Market Value
2 Dr Grand Pass. Van	6315	8200
2 Dr Grand LE Pass. Van	8180	10625
2 Dr Grand LE 4WD Pass. Van	8445	10970
2 Dr Grand SE Pass. Van	6775	8795
2 Dr Grand SE 4WD Pass. Van	7175	9320
2 Dr LE Pass. Van	7395	9605
2 Dr SE Pass. Van	6190	8035
2 Dr STD Pass. Van	5195	6745

OPTIONS FOR VOYAGER

6 cyl 3.0 L Engine[Opt on STD] +40
6 cyl 3.3 L Engine +225
6 cyl 3.8 L Engine +160
Auto 3-Speed Transmission[Opt on STD] +130
Auto 4-Speed Transmission[Opt on Grand,LE, SE,STD] +225
7 Passenger Seating[Std on Grand SE,SE] +200
Air Conditioning[Std on Grand LE,LE] +300
Aluminum/Alloy Wheels +130
AM/FM Compact Disc Playr +145
AM/FM Stereo Tape[Opt on Grand,STD] +90
Anti-Lock Brakes[Std on 4WD] +230
Captain Chairs (4) +235
Child Seats (2) +95
Cruise Control[Opt on Grand,STD] +80
Dual Air Conditioning +375
Infinity Sound System +220
Keyless Entry System[Opt on Grand SE,SE] +75
Leather Seats +285
Luggage Rack +60
Power Door Locks[Std on Grand LE,LE] +85
Power Drivers Seat +105
Power Windows[Std on LE] +85

1993 PLYMOUTH

ACCLAIM 1993

The Acclaim is now available to fleet purchasers as a flexible-fuel vehicle, able to run on a fuel mix that is 85 percent methanol.

RATINGS (SCALE OF 1-10)

Overall	Safety	Reliability	Performance	Comfort	Value
7.1	6.1	7.8	6.8	7.4	7.4

Don't forget to refer to the Mileage Adjustment Table at the back of this book!

© 1999 by Edmund Publications Corporation

Model Description	Trade-in Value	Market Value
Category C		
4 Dr STD Sdn	2950	4155

OPTIONS FOR ACCLAIM

6 cyl 3.0 L Engine +210
Auto 3-Speed Transmission +170
Auto 4-Speed Transmission +210
Air Conditioning +240
Aluminum/Alloy Wheels +85
AM/FM Stereo Tape +50
Anti-Lock Brakes +190
Cruise Control +65
Power Door Locks +70
Power Drivers Seat +85
Power Windows +90

COLT 1993

The Colt is redesigned for 1993. The hatchback is dropped in favor of two- and four-door notchback styles and the GL model is equipped with a 113-horsepower engine that is optional on the base.

RATINGS (SCALE OF 1-10)

Overall	Safety	Reliability	Performance	Comfort	Value
N/A	N/A	7.3	8	7.4	6.6

Model Description	Trade-in Value	Market Value
Category E		
2 Dr GL Sdn	2585	3860
4 Dr GL Sdn	3050	4550
4 Dr SE Wgn	4245	6340
2 Dr STD Sdn	2410	3595
4 Dr STD Wgn	3945	5885
4 Dr STD Sdn	2865	4275

OPTIONS FOR COLT

4 cyl 1.8 L Engine[Std on GL,Wgn] +115
4 cyl 2.4 L Engine[Std on SE] +55
Auto 3-Speed Transmission +155
Auto 4-Speed Transmission +210
Air Conditioning +245
Aluminum/Alloy Wheels +95
AM/FM Stereo Tape +95
Anti-Lock Brakes +215
Cruise Control +65
Keyless Entry System +45
Power Door Locks +70
Power Steering[Opt on GL,Sdn] +75
Power Windows +80
Rear Window Wiper[Std on] +40

LASER 1993

The all-wheel drive Laser is now available with an automatic transmission. New alloy wheels are introduced to all but the base Laser. A gold package is available for those of you wanting the ever-popular midlife crisis look.

RATINGS (SCALE OF 1-10)

Overall	Safety	Reliability	Performance	Comfort	Value
N/A	N/A	8	8.4	6.8	4.4

Model Description	Trade-in Value	Market Value
Category C		
2 Dr RS Hbk	3885	5475
2 Dr STD Hbk	3450	4855

OPTIONS FOR LASER

Auto 4-Speed Transmission +215
Air Conditioning +240
Aluminum/Alloy Wheels[Opt on 2WD] +85
Anti-Lock Brakes +190
Cruise Control +65
Power Door Locks +70
Power Windows +90
Premium Sound System +120
Sunroof +110

SUNDANCE 1993

The Sundance is available with antilock brakes in 1993.

RATINGS (SCALE OF 1-10)

Overall	Safety	Reliability	Performance	Comfort	Value
6.7	6.5	7.9	7.2	6.8	5.1

Model Description	Trade-in Value	Market Value
Category E		
2 Dr Duster Hbk	2745	4095
4 Dr Duster Hbk	2765	4130
2 Dr STD Hbk	2510	3750
4 Dr STD Hbk	2550	3805

OPTIONS FOR SUNDANCE

4 cyl 2.5 L Engine[Opt on STD] +85
6 cyl 3.0 L Engine +210
Auto 3-Speed Transmission +170
Auto 4-Speed Transmission +210
Air Conditioning +245
Aluminum/Alloy Wheels +95
AM/FM Compact Disc Playr +145
Anti-Lock Brakes +215
Cruise Control +65
Power Door Locks +70
Power Drivers Seat +90
Power Windows +80
Premium Sound System +105

VOYAGER 1993

Front shoulder belts are now height adjustable on the Voyager. All-wheel drive models gain new exterior and interior options.

RATINGS (SCALE OF 1-10)

Overall	Safety	Reliability	Performance	Comfort	Value
7.4	6.5	6.6	7.4	8.3	8.3

Model Description	Trade-in Value	Market Value
Category G		
2 Dr Grand Pass. Van	5050	6735
2 Dr Grand LE Pass. Van	6645	8860

Don't forget to refer to the Mileage Adjustment Table at the back of this book!

© 1999 by Edmund Publications Corporation

Model Description	Trade-in Value	Market Value
2 Dr Grand LE 4WD Pass. Van	6840	9120
2 Dr Grand SE Pass. Van	5540	7390
2 Dr Grand SE 4WD Pass. Van	5695	7595
2 Dr LE Pass. Van	6290	8390
2 Dr LE 4WD Pass. Van	6845	9130
2 Dr SE Pass. Van	4665	6220
2 Dr SE 4WD Pass. Van	5720	7630
2 Dr STD Pass. Van	4000	5335

OPTIONS FOR VOYAGER

6 cyl 3.0 L Engine[Opt on SE,STD] +115
6 cyl 3.3 L Engine[Std on Grand LE,Grand SE, 4WD] +200
Auto 3-Speed Transmission +70
Auto 4-Speed Transmission +180
7 Passenger Seating +165
Air Conditioning[Std on Grand LE,LE] +245
Aluminum/Alloy Wheels +105
AM/FM Compact Disc Playr +115
Anti-Lock Brakes +185
Captain Chairs (4) +190
Child Seats (2) +80
Cruise Control[Std on Grand LE,LE] +65
Dual Air Conditioning +305
Luggage Rack +45
Power Door Locks[Std on Grand LE] +70
Power Drivers Seat +85
Power Windows[Std on LE] +70
Premium Sound System +110
Velour/Cloth Seats[Opt on STD] +55
Woodgrain Applique +100

1992 PLYMOUTH

ACCLAIM 1992

Plymouth trims the fat, offering the Acclaim in only one trim level for 1992. The remaining Acclaim can be had with four-cylinder or V6 power.

RATINGS (SCALE OF 1-10)

Overall	Safety	Reliability	Performance	Comfort	Value
7.1	6.1	7.5	6.8	7.4	7.8

Category C

Model Description	Trade-in Value	Market Value
4 Dr STD Sdn	2385	3460

OPTIONS FOR ACCLAIM

6 cyl 3.0 L Engine +170
Auto 3-Speed Transmission +135
Auto 4-Speed Transmission +155
Air Conditioning +200
Aluminum/Alloy Wheels +70
AM/FM Stereo Tape +40
Anti-Lock Brakes +155
Cruise Control +50
Power Door Locks +60
Power Drivers Seat +70
Power Windows +75
Premium Sound System +100

COLT 1992

Factory options list is pared in a cost-savings measure. A 113-horsepower engine is standard and a 118-horsepower engine is optional.

Category E

Model Description	Trade-in Value	Market Value
2 Dr GL Hbk	2210	3455
4 Dr SE Wgn	3090	4825
2 Dr STD Hbk	1945	3035
4 Dr STD Wgn	2845	4450

OPTIONS FOR COLT

4 cyl 2.4 L Engine +45
Auto 3-Speed Transmission +135
Auto 4-Speed Transmission +175
Air Conditioning +200
AM/FM Stereo Tape +75
Anti-Lock Brakes +175
Cruise Control +55
Power Door Locks +55
Power Windows +65
Rear Window Wiper[Opt on GL] +30

LASER 1992

The Laser gains all-wheel drive as an option that greatly improves handling. Front and rear styling changes include headlights, taillamps, and a new rear spoiler on turbo models.

RATINGS (SCALE OF 1-10)

Overall	Safety	Reliability	Performance	Comfort	Value
N/A	N/A	7.8	8.4	6.8	3.3

Category C

Model Description	Trade-in Value	Market Value
2 Dr RS Hbk	3445	4995
2 Dr RS Turbo Hbk	3495	5070
2 Dr RS Turbo 4WD Hbk	4090	5930
2 Dr STD Hbk	3085	4470

OPTIONS FOR LASER

Auto 4-Speed Transmission +180
Air Conditioning +200
Aluminum/Alloy Wheels[Opt on 2WD] +70
AM/FM Stereo Tape[Std on RS] +40
Anti-Lock Brakes +155
Cruise Control +50
Power Door Locks +60
Power Windows +75
Premium Sound System +100
Sunroof +90

SUNDANCE 1992

The RS trim level is dropped due to poor sales. No other changes to the Sundance.

RATINGS (SCALE OF 1-10)

Overall	Safety	Reliability	Performance	Comfort	Value
6.5	5.9	7.1	7.2	6.8	5.4

Don't forget to refer to the Mileage Adjustment Table at the back of this book!

 © 1999 by Edmund Publications Corporation

Model Description	Trade-in Value	Market Value
Category E		
2 Dr America Hbk	1895	2965
4 Dr America Hbk	1960	3065
2 Dr Duster Hbk	2300	3590
4 Dr Duster Hbk	2380	3720
2 Dr Highline Hbk	2125	3320
4 Dr Highline Hbk	2190	3425

OPTIONS FOR SUNDANCE

4 cyl 2.5 L Engine[Std on Duster] +70
6 cyl 3.0 L Engine +180
Auto 3-Speed Transmission +135
Auto 4-Speed Transmission +170
Air Conditioning +200
Aluminum/Alloy Wheels +80
AM/FM Compact Disc Playr +115
Cruise Control +55
Power Door Locks +55
Power Drivers Seat +75
Power Windows +65
Premium Sound System +85
Sunroof +85

VOYAGER 1992

The driver airbag first seen on the 1991 model becomes standard in 1992. An integrated child seat is available for those with toddlers.

RATINGS (SCALE OF 1-10)

Overall	Safety	Reliability	Performance	Comfort	Value
7.1	5.8	5.8	7.4	8.3	8.2

Model Description	Trade-in Value	Market Value
Category G		
2 Dr Grand Pass. Van	4115	5635
2 Dr Grand LE Pass. Van	5550	7600
2 Dr Grand LE 4WD Pass. Van	5715	7830
2 Dr Grand SE Pass. Van	4470	6125
2 Dr Grand SE 4WD Pass. Van	4790	6560
2 Dr LE Pass. Van	4950	6780
2 Dr LE 4WD Pass. Van	5575	7635
2 Dr LX Pass. Van	4870	6670
2 Dr LX 4WD Pass. Van	5535	7580
2 Dr SE Pass. Van	3785	5185
2 Dr SE 4WD Pass. Van	4450	6095
2 Dr STD Pass. Van	3240	4440

OPTIONS FOR VOYAGER

6 cyl 3.0 L Engine[Opt on SE,STD] +95
6 cyl 3.3 L Engine[Std on Grand LE,Grand SE, 4WD] +185
Auto 3-Speed Transmission +40
Auto 4-Speed Transmission +140
7 Passenger Seating[Opt on STD] +135
Air Conditioning[Std on Grand LE,LE,LX] +200
Aluminum/Alloy Wheels[Std on LX] +85
AM/FM Stereo Tape +60
Cruise Control[Std on Grand LE,LE,LX] +50
Lighted Entry System +35
Luggage Rack +40
Overhead Console[Std on Grand LE,LE,LX] +45
Power Door Locks[Std on Grand LE,LE,LX] +55
Power Windows +60
Rear Window Defroster[Std on Grand LE,LE,LX] +40
Tilt Steering Wheel[Std on Grand LE,LE,LX] +40
Woodgrain Applique[Std on LE] +85

1991 PLYMOUTH

ACCLAIM 1991

Four-wheel antilock brakes are introduced as an option on the 1991 Acclaim.

RATINGS (SCALE OF 1-10)

Overall	Safety	Reliability	Performance	Comfort	Value
7.1	6	7.2	6.8	7.4	8.3

Model Description	Trade-in Value	Market Value
Category C		
4 Dr LE Sdn	2365	3640
4 Dr LX Sdn	2625	4035
4 Dr STD Sdn	2005	3080

OPTIONS FOR ACCLAIM

6 cyl 3.0 L Engine[Std on LX] +135
Auto 3-Speed Transmission[Opt on STD] +75
Auto 4-Speed Transmission[Opt on LE] +110
Air Conditioning +160
Aluminum/Alloy Wheels[Std on LX] +60
AM/FM Stereo Tape[Std on LX] +35
Anti-Lock Brakes +125
Cruise Control[Opt on STD] +40
Power Door Locks +50
Power Drivers Seat +60
Power Windows +60
Premium Sound System +80

COLT 1991

No changes to the Colt.

Model Description	Trade-in Value	Market Value
Category E		
2 Dr GL Hbk	1445	2450
2 Dr STD Hbk	1365	2310
4 Dr Vista Wgn	2010	3410
4 Dr Vista 4WD Wgn	2245	3810

OPTIONS FOR COLT

Auto 3-Speed Transmission +105
Air Conditioning +165
Aluminum/Alloy Wheels +65
AM/FM Stereo Tape +60
Cruise Control +45
Power Door Locks +45
Power Steering[Std on 4WD] +50
Power Windows +55

LASER 1991

No major changes for the '91 Laser.

Don't forget to refer to the Mileage Adjustment Table at the back of this book!

 © 1999 by Edmund Publications Corporation

Model Description	Trade-in Value	Market Value

RATINGS (SCALE OF 1-10)

Overall	Safety	Reliability	Performance	Comfort	Value
N/A	N/A	7.5	8.4	6.8	3.3

Category C		
2 Dr RS Hbk	2545	3915
2 Dr RS Turbo Hbk	2735	4210
2 Dr STD Hbk	2275	3500

OPTIONS FOR LASER

Auto 4-Speed Transmission +135
Air Conditioning +160
Aluminum/Alloy Wheels +60
AM/FM Stereo Tape[Std on RS] +35
Anti-Lock Brakes +125
Cruise Control +40
Power Door Locks +50
Power Windows +60
Premium Sound System +80
Sunroof +75

SUNDANCE 1991

No major changes to the bargain-basement Sundance.

RATINGS (SCALE OF 1-10)

Overall	Safety	Reliability	Performance	Comfort	Value
6.4	5.8	6.3	7.4	6.8	5.8

Category E		
2 Dr America Hbk	1505	2550
4 Dr America Hbk	1760	2985
2 Dr Highline Hbk	1635	2770
4 Dr Highline Hbk	1910	3240
2 Dr RS Hbk	1650	2800
4 Dr RS Hbk	1925	3265

OPTIONS FOR SUNDANCE

4 cyl 2.5 L Engine[Std on RS] +55
Auto 3-Speed Transmission +110
Air Conditioning +165
Aluminum/Alloy Wheels +65
AM/FM Stereo Tape[Std on RS] +60
Cruise Control +45
Power Door Locks +45
Power Drivers Seat +60
Power Windows +55
Premium Sound System +70
Sunroof +70

VOYAGER 1991

Big changes for the all-new Plymouth Voyager. New sheetmetal, available antilock brakes and optional all-wheel drive are new features for the Voyager. A driver airbag also debuts on the Voyager. An LX model joins the Voyager lineup sporting a front air dam, fog lights and alloy wheels.

RATINGS (SCALE OF 1-10)

Overall	Safety	Reliability	Performance	Comfort	Value
7	5.3	5.6	7.4	8.3	8.6

Category G		
2 Dr Grand LE Pass. Van	3950	5645
2 Dr Grand LE 4WD Pass. Van	4465	6380
2 Dr Grand SE Pass. Van	3160	4510
2 Dr Grand SE 4WD Pass. Van	3830	5470
2 Dr LE Pass. Van	3950	5645
2 Dr LE 4WD Pass. Van	4655	6650
2 Dr LX Pass. Van	3825	5465
2 Dr LX 4WD Pass. Van	4510	6440
2 Dr SE Pass. Van	2985	4260
2 Dr SE 4WD Pass. Van	3820	5455
2 Dr STD Pass. Van	2555	3650

OPTIONS FOR VOYAGER

6 cyl 3.0 L Engine[Std on LX] +115
6 cyl 3.3 L Engine[Std on Grand LE,Grand SE, 4WD] +145
Auto 4-Speed Transmission[Std on Grand LE, Grand SE,LX,4WD] +35
Luxury Package +225
7 Passenger Seating[Opt on STD] +110
Air Bag Restraint[Std on STD] +100
Air Conditioning[Std on Grand LE,LE,LX] +165
Aluminum/Alloy Wheels[Std on LX] +70
AM/FM Stereo Tape +50
Anti-Lock Brakes +125
Captain Chairs (4) +130
Cruise Control[Std on Grand LE,LE,LX] +45
Dual Air Conditioning +205
Leather Seats +155
Luggage Rack +30
Power Door Locks[Std on Grand LE,LE,LX] +45
Power Drivers Seat +55
Power Windows +50
Premium Sound System +75

1990 PLYMOUTH

ACCLAIM 1990

The 1990 Acclaim gains a driver's side airbag and available V6 power in all of its models.

RATINGS (SCALE OF 1-10)

Overall	Safety	Reliability	Performance	Comfort	Value
7	5.6	7.2	6.8	7.4	8.2

Category C		
4 Dr LE Sdn	1615	2645
4 Dr LE Turbo Sdn	1805	2965
4 Dr LX Sdn	2040	3345
4 Dr STD Sdn	1450	2380
4 Dr STD Turbo Sdn	1565	2565

Don't forget to refer to the Mileage Adjustment Table at the back of this book!

 © 1999 by Edmund Publications Corporation

Model Description	Trade-in Value	Market Value

OPTIONS FOR ACCLAIM

6 cyl 3.0 L Engine[Std on LX] +110
Auto 3-Speed Transmission[Std on LX] +95
Auto 4-Speed Transmission[Std on LX] +105
Air Conditioning +130
Aluminum/Alloy Wheels[Std on LX] +50
Cruise Control[Opt on STD] +35
Power Door Locks +40
Power Drivers Seat +45
Power Windows +50
Premium Sound System +65
Sunroof +60

COLT 1990

No changes for 1990.

Category E		
4 Dr DL 4WD Wgn	1940	3730
2 Dr GL Hbk	1020	1960
2 Dr GT Hbk	1355	2605
2 Dr STD Hbk	930	1790
4 Dr STD Wgn	1725	3315
4 Dr STD 4WD Wgn	1900	3650

OPTIONS FOR COLT

Auto 3-Speed Transmission +85
Auto 4-Speed Transmission +110
Performance Pkg +250
Sport Appearance Package +135
Air Conditioning +135
Aluminum/Alloy Wheels +50
AM/FM Stereo Tape +50
Cruise Control +35
Power Door Locks +40
Power Windows +45

HORIZON 1990

No changes for 1990.

Category E		
4 Dr America Hbk	725	1400

OPTIONS FOR HORIZON

Auto 3-Speed Transmission +80
Air Conditioning +135
Aluminum/Alloy Wheels +50
AM/FM Stereo Tape +50
Power Steering +40

LASER 1990

Based on the Mitsubishi Eclipse, the Laser is designed to compete with the Probe, MX-6 and Daytona. A 92-horsepower powerplant is standard on Base and RS models, but the RS can be had with DOHC 2.0-liter four-cylinder engine that makes 135 horsepower.

RATINGS (SCALE OF 1-10)

Overall	Safety	Reliability	Performance	Comfort	Value
N/A	N/A	6.7	8.4	6.8	2.8

Category C		
2 Dr RS Hbk	1915	3135
2 Dr RS Turbo Hbk	2220	3640
2 Dr STD Hbk	1855	3040

OPTIONS FOR LASER

4 cyl 2.0 L Engine +145
Auto 4-Speed Transmission +115
Air Conditioning +130
Aluminum/Alloy Wheels +50
Cruise Control +35
Power Door Locks +40
Power Windows +50
Premium Sound System +65
Sunroof +60

SUNDANCE 1990

A driver airbag becomes standard on all Sundances. The dashboard is slightly changed and it includes a better stereo.

RATINGS (SCALE OF 1-10)

Overall	Safety	Reliability	Performance	Comfort	Value
6.7	5.6	6.9	7.4	6.8	6.8

Category E		
2 Dr RS Hbk	1295	2495
2 Dr RS Turbo Hbk	1470	2830
4 Dr RS Hbk	1355	2610
4 Dr RS Turbo Hbk	1545	2970
2 Dr STD Hbk	1235	2380
2 Dr STD Turbo Hbk	1390	2670
4 Dr STD Hbk	1335	2570
4 Dr STD Turbo Hbk	1490	2860

OPTIONS FOR SUNDANCE

4 cyl 2.5 L Engine[Std on RS Hbk] +45
Auto 3-Speed Transmission +90
Air Conditioning +135
Aluminum/Alloy Wheels[Std on RS] +50
AM/FM Stereo Tape[Std on RS] +50
Cruise Control +35
Power Door Locks +40
Power Drivers Seat +50
Power Windows +45
Sunroof +55

VOYAGER 1990

The Voyager and Grand Voyager get a 20-gallon fuel tank and the Grand Voyager gets a larger V6 engine.

Category G		
2 Dr Grand LE Pass. Van	2915	4415
2 Dr Grand SE Pass. Van	2530	3830
2 Dr LE Pass. Van	2580	3910
2 Dr LE Turbo Pass. Van	2625	3980
2 Dr LX Pass. Van	2625	3975
2 Dr LX Turbo Pass. Van	2640	3995

Don't forget to refer to the Mileage Adjustment Table at the back of this book!

© 1999 by Edmund Publications Corporation

Model Description	Trade-in Value	Market Value
2 Dr SE Pass. Van	2170	3285
2 Dr SE Turbo Pass. Van	2240	3395
2 Dr STD Pass. Van	1955	2960
2 Dr STD Turbo Pass. Van	2180	3305

OPTIONS FOR VOYAGER

6 cyl 3.0 L Engine[Std on LX] +145
Auto 3-Speed Transmission +95
Auto 4-Speed Transmission[Opt on LE,SE] +120
Sun Roof Pkg +135
7 Passenger Seating[Opt on SE,STD] +90
Air Conditioning[Std on Grand LE,LE,LX] +135
Aluminum/Alloy Wheels[Std on LX] +55
AM/FM Stereo Tape +40
Cruise Control[Std on Grand LE,LE,LX] +35
Dual Air Conditioning +165
Leather Seats +125
Power Door Locks[Std on Grand LE,LE,LX] +40
Power Drivers Seat +45
Power Sunroof +135
Power Windows[Std on Grand LE,LE,LX] +40
Premium Sound System +60
Woodgrain Applique +55

1989 PLYMOUTH

ACCLAIM 1989

The Plymouth Acclaim is based on Chrysler's A-car platform. A longer wheelbase provides a more supple ride than the K-car and improved rear passenger legroom. Base and LE models are equipped with a 100-horsepower four-cylinder engines. They can, however, be equipped with a 150-horsepower turbocharged four-cylinder. LX models have a V6 that offers a smooth 141 horsepower.

RATINGS (SCALE OF 1-10)

Overall	Safety	Reliability	Performance	Comfort	Value
N/A	N/A	7.1	6.8	7.4	7.6

Category C

Model Description	Trade-in Value	Market Value
4 Dr LE Sdn	1240	2180
4 Dr LE Turbo Sdn	1350	2365
4 Dr LX Sdn	1675	2940
4 Dr STD Sdn	1175	2065
4 Dr STD Turbo Sdn	1220	2140

OPTIONS FOR ACCLAIM

Auto 3-Speed Transmission +75
Air Conditioning +110
Cruise Control[Opt on STD] +30
Power Door Locks +30
Power Drivers Seat +40
Power Windows +40
Premium Sound System +55
Sunroof +50

COLT 1989

The hatchback is redesigned and the wagon is now available with four-wheel drive. Base models have an 81-horsepower engine; four-wheel drive models have an 87-horsepower engine. On the Colt Vista, shoulder safety belts are now standard for rear outboard passengers. Power windows get an express-down feature.

Category E

Model Description	Trade-in Value	Market Value
4 Dr DL Wgn	1020	2320
4 Dr DL 4WD Wgn	1290	2930
2 Dr E Hbk	705	1605
2 Dr GT Hbk	815	1855
2 Dr GT Turbo Hbk	1120	2540
2 Dr STD Hbk	650	1475
4 Dr STD Wgn	980	2230
4 Dr STD 4WD Wgn	1270	2890
4 Dr Vista Wgn	940	2140
4 Dr Vista 4WD Wgn	1105	2515

OPTIONS FOR COLT

Auto 3-Speed Transmission +65
Air Conditioning +110
Aluminum/Alloy Wheels +45
AM/FM Stereo Tape +40
Cruise Control +30
Power Door Locks +30
Power Steering[Std on Turbo,Vista 4WD Wgn] +35
Power Windows +35
Premium Sound System +45

GRAN FURY 1989

The Gran Fury is retired this year with no changes.

Category C

Model Description	Trade-in Value	Market Value
4 Dr Salon Sdn	895	1575

OPTIONS FOR GRAN FURY

Air Conditioning +110
Aluminum/Alloy Wheels +40
Cruise Control +30
Power Door Locks +30
Power Windows +40

HORIZON 1989

Service points in the engine compartment have been brightly marked for the Horizon. Good thing, you'll need it.

Category E

Model Description	Trade-in Value	Market Value
4 Dr America Hbk	540	1230

OPTIONS FOR HORIZON

Auto 3-Speed Transmission +70
Air Conditioning +110
AM/FM Stereo Tape +40
Power Steering +35

Don't forget to refer to the Mileage Adjustment Table at the back of this book!

 © 1999 by Edmund Publications Corporation

Model Description	Trade-in Value	Market Value

RELIANT 1989

Service points in the engine compartment are marked with bright paint; good thing because this car will need plenty of service. The suspension has been improved to decrease ride-harshness and the engine noises are supposed to be dampened. A four-speaker stereo is a new option on the '89 Reliant America.

Category C

Model Description	Trade-in Value	Market Value
2 Dr America Sdn	815	1430
4 Dr America Sdn	885	1550

OPTIONS FOR RELIANT

4 cyl 2.5 L Engine +40
Auto 3-Speed Transmission +75
Air Conditioning +110
Cruise Control +30
Power Door Locks +30
Power Steering +35

SUNDANCE 1989

A new grille and headlights change the front-end appearance of the Sundance. A 2.5-liter turbo engine replaces last year's 2.2-liter in the high-performance RS model.

RATINGS (SCALE OF 1-10)

Overall	Safety	Reliability	Performance	Comfort	Value
6.4	4.5	6.4	7.4	6.8	6.7

Category E

Model Description	Trade-in Value	Market Value
2 Dr STD Hbk	810	1845
2 Dr STD Turbo Hbk	930	2115
4 Dr STD Hbk	835	1895
4 Dr STD Turbo Hbk	885	2015

OPTIONS FOR SUNDANCE

4 cyl 2.5 L Engine +40
Auto 3-Speed Transmission +75
Air Conditioning +110
Aluminum/Alloy Wheels +45
AM/FM Stereo Tape +40
Cruise Control +30
Flip-Up Sunroof +50
Power Door Locks +30
Power Drivers Seat +40
Power Windows +35
Premium Sound System +45

VOYAGER 1989

A turbo engine is available on short-wheelbase SE and LE Voyagers. A new four-speed automatic transmission is standard on the Grand Voyager LE.

Category G

Model Description	Trade-in Value	Market Value
2 Dr Grand LE Pass. Van	2110	3460
2 Dr Grand LE Turbo Pass. Van	2090	3430
2 Dr Grand SE Pass. Van	1840	3015
2 Dr Grand SE Turbo Pass. Van	1720	2820
2 Dr LE Pass. Van	1840	3020
2 Dr LE Turbo Pass. Van	1825	2990
2 Dr SE Pass. Van	1760	2885
2 Dr SE Turbo Pass. Van	1705	2795
2 Dr STD Pass. Van	1520	2490
2 Dr STD Turbo Pass. Van	1415	2320

OPTIONS FOR VOYAGER

6 cyl 3.0 L Engine[Std on Grand LE] +135
Auto 3-Speed Transmission +60
Auto 4-Speed Transmission[Std on Grand LE] +100
7 Passenger Seating[Opt on LE,SE,STD] +75
Air Conditioning[Std on Grand LE,LE] +110
Aluminum/Alloy Wheels +45
AM/FM Stereo Tape +35
Cruise Control +30
Dual Air Conditioning +135
Leather Seats +105
Power Door Locks +30
Power Drivers Seat +40
Power Sunroof +110
Power Windows +30
Premium Sound System +50

Instant
Lease & Loan Quotes
for New & Used Vehicles!
www.CarFinance.com/edmunds

Don't forget to refer to the Mileage Adjustment Table at the back of this book!

 © 1999 by Edmund Publications Corporation

Model Description	Trade-in Value	Market Value

PONTIAC USA

1996 Pontiac Firebird Coupe

1998 PONTIAC

BONNEVILLE 1998

Second-generation airbags are standard, the SE comes with a standard decklid spoiler, and the SSE gets more standard equipment. New colors freshen the rapidly aging Bonneville.

Category B

Model Description	Trade-in Value	Market Value
4 Dr SE Sdn	14830	17865
4 Dr SLE Sdn	15090	18185
4 Dr SSE Sdn	17990	21675
4 Dr SSEi Sprchgd Sdn	18470	22250

OPTIONS FOR BONNEVILLE

Aluminum/Alloy Wheels[Opt on SE] +275
AM/FM Compact Disc Playr[Opt on SE, SLE] +260
Chrome Wheels +610
Dual Power Seats[Opt on SE, SLE] +300
Keyless Entry System[Opt on SE] +145
Power Drivers Seat[Opt on SE] +250
Power Mirrors[Opt on SE] +80
Power Moonroof +825
Premium Sound System[Opt on SE] +350
Traction Control System[Opt on SE, SLE] +150

FIREBIRD 1998

Firebirds get a minor restyle that is most evident from the front end. Also on tap for Formula and Trans Am models is a de-tuned Corvette engine making 305 horsepower without Ram Air induction. Base models can be equipped with a new Sport Appearance Package, and two new exterior colors debut. Second-generation airbags are standard.

Category F

Model Description	Trade-in Value	Market Value
2 Dr Formula Cpe	17430	21255
2 Dr STD Conv	16720	20390
2 Dr STD Cpe	12840	15655
2 Dr Trans Am Conv	20365	24840
2 Dr Trans Am Cpe	18665	22760

OPTIONS FOR FIREBIRD

Auto 4-Speed Transmission[Opt on STD] +675
AutoCross Performance Pkg +975
Performance Handling Package +2575
Sport Appearance Package +825
Chrome Wheels +470
Glass Panel T-tops[Std on Trans Am Cpe] +860
Keyless Entry System[Std on Trans Am, Conv] +145
Leather Seats[Std on Trans Am] +590
Power Door Locks[Opt on STD Cpe] +165
Power Drivers Seat[Std on Trans Am] +195
Power Mirrors[Opt on STD Cpe] +100
Power Windows[Opt on STD Cpe] +185
Traction Control System +585

GRAND AM 1998

Second generation airbags are newly standard, and option groups are simplified.

Category C

Model Description	Trade-in Value	Market Value
2 Dr GT Cpe	10220	12310
4 Dr GT Sdn	10325	12435
2 Dr SE Cpe	9305	11210
4 Dr SE Sdn	9600	11565

OPTIONS FOR GRAND AM

6 cyl 3.1 L Engine +370
Auto 4-Speed Transmission +675
Aluminum/Alloy Wheels[Opt on SE] +240
AM/FM Compact Disc Playr +320
Cruise Control +170
Keyless Entry System +155
Leather Seats +480
Power Drivers Seat +235
Power Mirrors +90
Power Moonroof +580
Power Windows +255
Premium Sound System +330
Rear Window Defroster +135
Tilt Steering Wheel[Opt on SE] +125
Traction Control System +235

GRAND PRIX 1998

Supercharged GTP models get traction control, and new colors are available inside and out. Second-generation airbags debut as standard equipment.

Category C

Model Description	Trade-in Value	Market Value
2 Dr GT Cpe	15325	18460
4 Dr GT Sdn	14960	18025
2 Dr GTP Sprchgd Cpe	15620	18815
4 Dr GTP Sprchgd Sdn	15510	18685
4 Dr SE Sdn	14040	16915

Don't forget to refer to the Mileage Adjustment Table at the back of this book!

 © 1999 by Edmund Publications Corporation

Model Description	Trade-in Value	Market Value

OPTIONS FOR GRAND PRIX

6 cyl 3.8 L Engine[Opt on SE] +360
Aluminum/Alloy Wheels[Opt on SE] +240
AM/FM Compact Disc Playr +320
Climate Control for AC +150
Cruise Control[Opt on SE] +170
Heads-up Display +210
Keyless Entry System +155
Leather Seats +480
Power Drivers Seat +235
Power Moonroof +580
Premium Sound System[Opt on SE] +330
Trip Computer[Std on GTP] +155

SUNFIRE 1998

All coupes have a rear spoiler, a new six-speaker sound system is available, the base four-cylinder gets some additional low-end punch, and Topaz Gold Metallic is added to the paint color chart. Second-generation airbags are added as standard equipment.

Category E

Model Description	Trade-in Value	Market Value
2 Dr GT Cpe	10535	12845
2 Dr SE Conv	11545	14075
2 Dr SE Cpe	9225	11250
4 Dr SE Sdn	9010	10990

OPTIONS FOR SUNFIRE

4 cyl 2.4 L Engine[Opt on SE] +375
Auto 3-Speed Transmission +500
Auto 4-Speed Transmission[Std on Conv] +675
Air Conditioning[Std on GT, Conv] +675
Aluminum/Alloy Wheels[Opt on SE] +265
AM/FM Compact Disc Playr[Std on GT, Conv] +390
Cruise Control[Std on Conv] +185
Keyless Entry System +125
Power Door Locks +195
Power Mirrors +95
Power Moonroof +485
Power Windows +220
Premium Sound System +285
Rear Window Defroster[Std on GT, Conv] +135
Tilt Steering Wheel[Std on GT, Conv] +125

TRANS SPORT 1998

Short-wheelbase models get the dual sliding doors and power sliding door options. Side-impact airbags are standard, and a white two-tone paint job is new. Second generation airbags are standard for front seat occupants.

Category G

Model Description	Trade-in Value	Market Value
2 Dr Montana Pass. Van Ext	17165	20435
2 Dr Montana Pass. Van	16675	19855
2 Dr STD Pass. Van Ext	16440	19570
2 Dr STD Pass. Van	14575	17350

OPTIONS FOR TRANS SPORT

Aluminum/Alloy Wheels[Opt on STD] +285
Auto Load Leveling[Opt on STD] +190
Captain Chairs (4) +525
Compact Disc W/fm/tape +565
Cruise Control[Std on Pass. Van Ext] +175
Dual Air Conditioning +840
Dual Power Seats +525
Keyless Entry System +170
Leather Seats +640
Power Drivers Seat +235
Power Windows +195
Premium Sound System +300
Privacy Glass +225
Rear Window Defroster +140
Sliding Driver Side Door[Std on Montana, Pass. Van Ext] +445
Traction Control System[Opt on STD] +245

1997 PONTIAC

BONNEVILLE 1997

Changes for 1997 are few. Supercharged Bonnevilles get a new transmission, a new Delco/Bose premium sound system is optional on the SSE, and the EYE CUE head-up display has a new motorized adjustment feature. Two new exterior colors, a new interior color and a new interior fabric liven the aging Bonneville visually.

RATINGS (SCALE OF 1-10)

Overall	Safety	Reliability	Performance	Comfort	Value
8.1	7.6	8.5	8.3	7.8	8.4

Category B

Model Description	Trade-in Value	Market Value
4 Dr SE Sdn	12175	14850
4 Dr SE Sprchgd Sdn	12485	15225
4 Dr SSE Sdn	16480	20100

OPTIONS FOR BONNEVILLE

Computer Command Ride Pkg +565
Aluminum/Alloy Wheels[Opt on SE] +225
Chrome Wheels +495
Compact Disc W/fm/tape +265
Dual Power Seats +245
Keyless Entry System[Opt on SE] +120
Leather Seats +450
Power Moonroof +675
Premium Sound System[Opt on SE] +285
Steer. Whl. Radio Cntrls[Opt on SE] +95
Traction Control System +120

FIREBIRD 1997

Pontiac upgrades the Firebird in several ways for 1997. Performance freaks will appreciate the addition of Ram Air induction to the options list of the Formula and Trans Am convertibles. Audiophiles will be blown away by the newly optional 500-watt Monsoon sound system. Luxury intenders can get power seats swathed in leather this year. Safety-conscious buyers will find daytime running

Don't forget to refer to the Mileage Adjustment Table at the back of this book!

 © 1999 by Edmund Publications Corporation

lights. Additional cosmetic and comfort items keep the fourth-generation Firebird fresh for its fifth year.

RATINGS (SCALE OF 1-10)

Overall	Safety	Reliability	Performance	Comfort	Value
7.4	8.3	8	9.1	7.4	4.2

Category F

Model Description	Trade-in Value	Market Value
2 Dr Formula Conv	16170	19720
2 Dr Formula Cpe	13580	16560
2 Dr STD Conv	13710	16720
2 Dr STD Cpe	10660	13000
2 Dr Trans Am Conv	16615	20265
2 Dr Trans Am Cpe	13695	16700

OPTIONS FOR FIREBIRD

Auto 4-Speed Transmission[Opt on STD] +555
Performance Handling Package +1770
Performance Package +800
Sport Appearance Package +915
AM/FM Compact Disc Playr +335
Chrome Wheels +385
Cruise Control[Std on Trans Am,Conv] +140
Glass Panel T-tops +700
Keyless Entry System[Opt on Formula,STD] +120
Leather Seats +485
Power Door Locks[Std on Trans Am,Conv] +135
Power Drivers Seat +160
Power Windows[Std on Trans Am,Conv] +150
Steer. Whl. Radio Cntrls[Opt on Formula,STD] +120
Traction Control System +480

GRAND AM 1997

Very minimal changes this year as Pontiac concentrates on Grand Prix and Trans Sport launches. Air conditioning is now standard (though press kit does contradict itself, claiming it is standard on SE in one place, and saying it's optional in another). Also, we think three new colors are added, even though the press kit lists only two. Guess Pontiac P.R. was a bit busy during the summer of 1996.

RATINGS (SCALE OF 1-10)

Overall	Safety	Reliability	Performance	Comfort	Value
7.5	7.4	7.8	8.2	7.4	6.9

Category C

Model Description	Trade-in Value	Market Value
2 Dr GT Cpe	9695	11970
4 Dr GT Sdn	9450	11665
2 Dr SE Cpe	8185	10105
4 Dr SE Sdn	8210	10135

OPTIONS FOR GRAND AM

6 cyl 3.1 L Engine +295
Auto 4-Speed Transmission +550
Aluminum/Alloy Wheels[Opt on SE] +195
Compact Disc W/fm/tape +250
Cruise Control +140
Keyless Entry System +130
Leather Seats +390
Power Drivers Seat +195
Power Moonroof +475
Power Windows +205
Premium Sound System +270

GRAND PRIX 1997

Pontiac redesigns the Grand Prix for 1997, giving buyers slick new styling, a longer and wider wheelbase, and available supercharged V6 power on GT models. Traction control, antilock brakes, dual airbags and side-impact protection are standard. Optional is a built-in child safety seat.

RATINGS (SCALE OF 1-10)

Overall	Safety	Reliability	Performance	Comfort	Value
7.7	7.7	8.7	8.8	7.9	5.6

Category C

Model Description	Trade-in Value	Market Value
2 Dr GT Cpe	13205	16300
4 Dr GT Sdn	13475	16635
2 Dr GTP Sprchgd Cpe	14345	17710
4 Dr GTP Sprchgd Sdn	14285	17635
4 Dr SE Sdn	11960	14765

OPTIONS FOR GRAND PRIX

6 cyl 3.8 L Engine[Opt on SE] +280
Aluminum/Alloy Wheels[Opt on SE] +195
Child Seat (1) +80
Climate Control for AC +120
Compact Disc W/fm/tape +250
Cruise Control[Opt on SE,Cpe] +140
Keyless Entry System +130
Leather Seats +390
Power Drivers Seat +195
Power Moonroof +475
Premium Sound System +270
Trip Computer[Std on GTP] +125

SUNFIRE 1997

SE Convertible gets a higher level of standard equipment, including an automatic transmission. All models meet 1997 side-impact standards, coupes get a new front seatbelt guide loop, and a new Sports Interior trim debuts called Patina/Redondo cloth.

RATINGS (SCALE OF 1-10)

Overall	Safety	Reliability	Performance	Comfort	Value
7	6.3	8.4	6.8	7.1	6.4

Category E

Model Description	Trade-in Value	Market Value
2 Dr GT Cpe	8805	11010
2 Dr SE Conv	9185	11485
2 Dr SE Cpe	7635	9540
4 Dr SE Sdn	7600	9500

OPTIONS FOR SUNFIRE

4 cyl 2.4 L Engine[Opt on SE] +290
Auto 3-Speed Transmission +375

Don't forget to refer to the Mileage Adjustment Table at the back of this book!

 © 1999 by Edmund Publications Corporation

Model Description	Trade-in Value	Market Value

Auto 4-Speed Transmission[Std on Conv] +550
Air Conditioning[Std on Conv] +550
Aluminum/Alloy Wheels[Opt on SE] +215
AM/FM Compact Disc Playr +320
Cruise Control[Std on Conv] +150
Keyless Entry System +100
Overhead Console[Std on Conv] +75
Power Door Locks +160
Power Moonroof +395
Power Windows +180
Premium Sound System +230
Rear Spoiler[Std on GT,Conv] +140
Tilt Steering Wheel[Std on GT,Conv] +100

TRANS SPORT 1997

After years of taking it on the chin, Pontiac redesigns the Trans Sport and lands one squarely in Chrysler's face. This van is good-looking, loaded with features and fun to drive. Wait. Did we say fun to drive?

RATINGS (SCALE OF 1-10)

Overall	Safety	Reliability	Performance	Comfort	Value
7.5	7.2	7.9	7.8	7.9	6.8

Category G

Model	Trade-in	Market
2 Dr SE Pass. Van	13525	16300
2 Dr SE Pass. Van Ext	13690	16495

OPTIONS FOR TRANS SPORT

7 Passenger Seating[Opt on Pass. Van] +370
Aluminum/Alloy Wheels +235
Auto Load Leveling +155
Captain Chairs (4) +430
Child Seats (2) +175
Compact Disc W/fm/tape +465
Cruise Control +145
Dual Power Seats +430
Keyless Entry System +140
Leather Seats +520
Luggage Rack +105
Power Windows +160
Premium Sound System +245
Rear Heater +140
Sliding Driver Side Door +365

1996 PONTIAC

BONNEVILLE 1996

The Series II V6 has been supercharged for 1996, pumping out 240 horsepower. Styling front and rear has been tweaked, and daytime running lights debut.

RATINGS (SCALE OF 1-10)

Overall	Safety	Reliability	Performance	Comfort	Value
8	7.5	8	8.3	7.8	8.3

Category B

Model	Trade-in	Market
4 Dr SE Sdn	10245	12805
4 Dr SE Sprchgd Sdn	10530	13165
4 Dr SSE Sdn	13480	16850
4 Dr SSE Sprchgd Sdn	13630	17040

OPTIONS FOR BONNEVILLE

Computer Command Ride Pkg +525
SSEi Supercharger Package +605
Chrome Wheels +405
Climate Control for AC[Opt on SE] +100
Compact Disc W/fm/tape +220
Keyless Entry System[Opt on SE] +100
Leather Seats +370
Power Drivers Seat[Opt on SE] +165
Power Moonroof +550
Power Passenger Seat +170
Premium Sound System[Opt on SE] +235
Traction Control System +100

FIREBIRD 1996

A new standard V6 makes 40 more horsepower than the old one. The LT1 V8 also makes more power, particularly when equipped with Ram Air induction. A new color livens up the exterior, as if it needed it.

RATINGS (SCALE OF 1-10)

Overall	Safety	Reliability	Performance	Comfort	Value
7.4	8.4	7.8	9.1	7.4	4.6

Category F

Model	Trade-in	Market
2 Dr Formula Cpe	11150	13935
2 Dr Formula Conv	13745	17185
2 Dr STD Cpe	8665	10835
2 Dr STD Conv	11225	14030
2 Dr Trans Am Conv	13910	17390
2 Dr Trans Am Cpe	11685	14605

OPTIONS FOR FIREBIRD

Auto 4-Speed Transmission +415
Performance Handling Package +1415
Air Conditioning[Opt on STD Cpe] +460
AM/FM Compact Disc Playr +275
Chrome Wheels +315
Cruise Control[Std on Trans Am,Conv] +115
Glass Panel T-tops +575
Keyless Entry System[Opt on Formula,STD,Cpe] +95
Leather Seats +395
Power Door Locks[Std on Trans Am,Conv] +110
Power Drivers Seat +130
Power Windows[Std on Trans Am,Conv] +125
Premium Sound System[Std on Trans Am,Conv] +225
Steer. Whl. Radio Cntrls[Opt on Formula,STD,Cpe] +100

Don't forget to refer to the Mileage Adjustment Table at the back of this book!

 © 1999 by Edmund Publications Corporation

GRAND AM 1996

New styling, a new base engine, and ... what's this? Dual airbags and body-mounted seatbelts? Will wonders never cease?

RATINGS (SCALE OF 1-10)

Overall	Safety	Reliability	Performance	Comfort	Value
7.5	7.4	7.3	8.2	7.4	7.2

Category C		
2 Dr GT Cpe	8200	10650
4 Dr GT Sdn	8065	10475
2 Dr SE Cpe	6580	8545
4 Dr SE Sdn	6490	8425

OPTIONS FOR GRAND AM

6 cyl 3.1 L Engine +250
Auto 4-Speed Transmission +415
Air Conditioning[Opt on SE] +445
Compact Disc W/fm/tape +205
Cruise Control +115
Keyless Entry System +105
Leather Seats +320
Power Drivers Seat +160
Power Moonroof +390
Power Windows +170
Premium Sound System +220

GRAND PRIX 1996

Minor trim and powertrain improvements to the only car in GM's stable that still has those stupid door-mounted seatbelts. Do yourself a favor. Buy the 1997 GP.

RATINGS (SCALE OF 1-10)

Overall	Safety	Reliability	Performance	Comfort	Value
7.4	7.2	8	8	7.3	6.5

Category C		
4 Dr GT Sdn	9025	11725
2 Dr GTP Cpe	10170	13210
2 Dr SE Cpe	9370	12170
4 Dr SE Sdn	8330	10815

OPTIONS FOR GRAND PRIX

GT Performance Pkg +500
Aluminum/Alloy Wheels[Opt on SE] +160
AM/FM Compact Disc Playr +215
Anti-Lock Brakes[Opt on SE] +345
Cruise Control[Opt on GT,Sdn] +115
Keyless Entry System +105
Leather Seats +320
Power Drivers Seat +160
Power Moonroof +390
Premium Sound System +220
Sport Suspension[Opt on SE] +95
Trip Computer +105

SUNFIRE 1996

Traction control, remote keyless entry and steering wheel radio controls are newly available. Old Quad 4 engine dumped in favor of new 2.4-liter twin-cam engine. Two new paint choices spiff up the exterior.

RATINGS (SCALE OF 1-10)

Overall	Safety	Reliability	Performance	Comfort	Value
6.9	6.2	7.7	6.8	7.1	6.7

Category E		
2 Dr GT Cpe	7245	9660
2 Dr SE Conv	8560	11410
2 Dr SE Cpe	6310	8410
4 Dr SE Sdn	6445	8590

OPTIONS FOR SUNFIRE

4 cyl 2.4 L Engine[Opt on SE] +185
Auto 3-Speed Transmission[Std on Conv] +285
Auto 4-Speed Transmission +340
Air Conditioning[Std on Conv] +450
AM/FM Compact Disc Playr +260
Cruise Control +120
Keyless Entry System +80
Power Door Locks +130
Power Sunroof +335
Power Windows +145
Premium Sound System +190
Traction Control System +30

TRANS SPORT 1996

A 180-horsepower 3.4-liter V6 replaces last year's pathetic base engine as well as the optional 3.8-liter V6. Front air conditioning is standard equipment for 1996.

RATINGS (SCALE OF 1-10)

Overall	Safety	Reliability	Performance	Comfort	Value
7.4	6.4	7.6	7.2	7.1	8.6

Category G		
2 Dr SE Pass. Van	10045	12555

OPTIONS FOR TRANS SPORT

7 Passenger Seating +300
Air Conditioning +450
Auto Load Leveling +125
Child Seats (2) +145
Cruise Control +115
Dual Air Conditioning +560
Keyless Entry System +115
Leather Seats +425
Power Door Locks +125
Power Drivers Seat +155
Power Sliding Door +195
Power Windows +130
Premium Sound System +200
Traction Control System +165

Don't forget to refer to the Mileage Adjustment Table at the back of this book!

 © 1999 by Edmund Publications Corporation

1995 PONTIAC

BONNEVILLE 1995

Base engine is upgraded to 3800 Series II status, gaining 35 horsepower in the process. SE models with the SLE package can be ordered with the supercharged 3.8-liter V6. Computer Command Ride is made available on SE models.

RATINGS (SCALE OF 1-10)

Overall	Safety	Reliability	Performance	Comfort	Value
8.1	8.4	8	8.3	7.8	8.2

Category B

Model	Trade-in Value	Market Value
4 Dr SE Sdn	8540	10950
4 Dr SE Sprchgd Sdn	9175	11760
4 Dr SSE Sdn	11220	14385
4 Dr SSEi Sprchgd Sdn	11625	14905

OPTIONS FOR BONNEVILLE

Articulating Lthr Seats +490
Climate Control for AC +80
Dual Power Seats +160
Keyless Entry System +80
Leather Seats +300
Power Moonroof +450
Premium Sound System[Opt on SE] +190
Steer. Whl. Radio Cntrls +65

FIREBIRD 1995

Traction control is added as an option on Formula and Trans Am. Trans Am GT is dropped from lineup. Californians get a 3.8-liter V6 equipped with an automatic transmission on base models instead of the 3.4-liter V6. The new engine meets strict emissions standards in that state, and makes 40 additional horsepower.

RATINGS (SCALE OF 1-10)

Overall	Safety	Reliability	Performance	Comfort	Value
7.4	9.1	7.3	8.9	7.4	4.4

Category F

Model	Trade-in Value	Market Value
2 Dr Formula Conv	12020	15410
2 Dr Formula Cpe	9140	11720
2 Dr STD Conv	9720	12460
2 Dr STD Cpe	7555	9685
2 Dr Trans Am Conv	12185	15625
2 Dr Trans Am Cpe	10220	13105

OPTIONS FOR FIREBIRD

Auto 4-Speed Transmission +345
Air Conditioning[Std on Trans Am,Conv] +380
AM/FM Compact Disc Playr +225
Cruise Control[Std on Trans Am,Conv] +95
Glass Panel T-tops +470
Keyless Entry System[Opt on Formula,STD] +80
Leather Seats[Opt on Formula,STD] +325
Power Door Locks[Std on Trans Am,Conv] +90
Power Windows[Std on Trans Am,Conv] +100
Premium Sound System[Opt on Formula,STD] +185
Steer. Whl. Radio Cntrls +80
Traction Control System +320

GRAND AM 1995

Base engine upgraded to a 150-horsepower version of the Quad 4. High-output Quad 4 motor is dropped from the GT, which now uses the same standard and optional powerplants as the SE. Variable-effort power steering is a new option on GT models, rear suspensions are redesigned, and SE models get restyled wheelcovers and alloy wheels.

RATINGS (SCALE OF 1-10)

Overall	Safety	Reliability	Performance	Comfort	Value
7.2	6.8	7.7	8.2	7.3	6.1

Category C

Model	Trade-in Value	Market Value
2 Dr GT Cpe	6965	9165
4 Dr GT Sdn	6805	8955
2 Dr SE Cpe	6000	7890
4 Dr SE Sdn	5695	7495

OPTIONS FOR GRAND AM

6 cyl 3.1 L Engine +215
Auto 3-Speed Transmission +250
Auto 4-Speed Transmission +335
Air Conditioning[Opt on SE] +360
AM/FM Compact Disc Playr +175
Cruise Control +95
Intermittent Wipers[Std on GT] +30
Keyless Entry System +85
Leather Seats +260
Power Drivers Seat +130
Power Moonroof +320
Power Windows +140
Premium Sound System +180

GRAND PRIX 1995

Brake/transmission shift interlock is added. GT coupe dropped in favor of GTP Package. GT sedan continues. Variable-effort steering is added to GTP and GT. New alloys debut on GT and GTP. Coupes can be equipped with a White Appearance Package, which includes color-keyed alloys and special pinstriping. Floor consoles are redesigned on models with bucket seats.

RATINGS (SCALE OF 1-10)

Overall	Safety	Reliability	Performance	Comfort	Value
7.7	7.7	7.4	8	7.3	8

Category C

Model	Trade-in Value	Market Value
4 Dr GT Sdn	8070	10620
2 Dr GTP Cpe	8720	11475
2 Dr SE Cpe	7900	10400
4 Dr SE Sdn	7290	9590

Don't forget to refer to the Mileage Adjustment Table at the back of this book!

© 1999 by Edmund Publications Corporation

Model Description	Trade-in Value	Market Value

OPTIONS FOR GRAND PRIX

AM/FM Compact Disc Playr +175
Anti-Lock Brakes[Opt on SE] +285
Cruise Control +95
Keyless Entry System +85
Leather Seats +260
Power Drivers Seat +130
Power Moonroof +320
Premium Sound System +180
Sport Suspension[Opt on SE] +80
Trip Computer +85

SUNFIRE 1995

All-new replacement for aged Sunbird comes in SE coupe or sedan, and GT coupe trim levels. An SE convertible debuted midyear. Dual airbags, ABS, tilt steering and tachometer are standard. Base engine is a 2.2-liter four cylinder good for 120 horsepower. GT models get a 150-horsepower Quad 4 engine, which is optional on SE. Order the four-speed automatic transmission, and you'll get traction control.

RATINGS (SCALE OF 1-10)

Overall	Safety	Reliability	Performance	Comfort	Value
7.1	6.7	7.6	6.8	7.1	7.1

Category E

2 Dr GT Cpe	6215	8515
2 Dr SE Conv	6480	8875
2 Dr SE Cpe	5725	7845
4 Dr SE Sdn	5690	7795

OPTIONS FOR SUNFIRE

4 cyl 2.3 L Quad 4 Engine[Opt on SE] +175
Auto 3-Speed Transmission[Std on Conv] +210
Auto 4-Speed Transmission +220
Air Conditioning +370
AM/FM Compact Disc Playr +215
Cruise Control +100
Power Door Locks +105
Power Sunroof +275
Power Windows +120
Premium Sound System +155
Tilt Steering Wheel[Std on GT,Conv] +70

TRANS SPORT 1995

A brake/transmission shift interlock is added. New overhead console includes outside temperature gauge, compass and storage bin.

RATINGS (SCALE OF 1-10)

Overall	Safety	Reliability	Performance	Comfort	Value
7.3	6.9	7.2	7.2	7.1	8

Category G

2 Dr SE Pass. Van	8365	10590

OPTIONS FOR TRANS SPORT

6 cyl 3.8 L Engine +185
Auto 4-Speed Transmission +90
7 Passenger Seating +245
Air Conditioning +370
AM/FM Compact Disc Playr +175
Auto Load Leveling +105
Child Seats (2) +115
Cruise Control +95
Dual Air Conditioning +460
Keyless Entry System +95
Leather Seats +350
Luggage Rack +70
Power Door Locks +105
Power Windows +105
Premium Sound System +165
Traction Control System +135

1994 PONTIAC

BONNEVILLE 1994

Dual airbags are standard. SE and SSE trim levels are available. Californians get SLE model. SSEi is an option package on SSE. Supercharged engine in SSEi package gets 20 more horsepower. Automatic transmission gains "Normal" and "Performance" shift modes when hooked to supercharged engine. Traction control gains ability to retard engine power as well as apply brakes to slow spinning wheel(s). Get traction control on the SSE, and you can opt for Computer Command Ride, a suspension package that automatically adjusts the suspension to meet the demands of the driver.

RATINGS (SCALE OF 1-10)

Overall	Safety	Reliability	Performance	Comfort	Value
8.1	8.4	7.8	8.1	7.8	8.6

Category B

4 Dr SE Sdn	6680	8910
4 Dr SSE Sdn	9355	12470
4 Dr SSEi Sprchgd Sdn	9625	12835

OPTIONS FOR BONNEVILLE

Sport Luxury Edition Pkg +280
Climate Control for AC +65
Compact Disc W/fm/tape +145
Cruise Control[Opt on SE] +80
Keyless Entry System +65
Leather Seats +245
Power Drivers Seat[Opt on SE] +110
Power Moonroof +370
Power Passenger Seat +115
Premium Sound System[Opt on SE] +155
Sport Suspension +145
Traction Control System +65

Don't forget to refer to the Mileage Adjustment Table at the back of this book!

 © 1999 by Edmund Publications Corporation

Model Description	Trade-in Value	Market Value

FIREBIRD 1994

Trans Am GT debuts. Six-speed transmission is saddled with a first-to-fourth skip shift feature designed to improve fuel economy. Automatic is new electronically controlled unit with the V8 engine, and it features "Normal" and "Performance" modes. Remote keyless entry, cassette player, and leather-wrapped steering wheel move from the Trans Am standard equipment list to the options sheet. T/A also loses Batwing rear spoiler to GT, taking Formula's more subdued rear treatment. Convertible debuts at midyear.

RATINGS (SCALE OF 1-10)

Overall	Safety	Reliability	Performance	Comfort	Value
7.6	9.2	7.5	8.9	7.4	4.9

Category F

Model	Trade-in Value	Market Value
2 Dr Formula Conv	12170	16010
2 Dr Formula Cpe	7845	10325
2 Dr STD Conv	9690	12750
2 Dr STD Cpe	6080	8000
2 Dr Trans Am Cpe	8990	11830
2 Dr Trans Am GT Conv	13135	17285
2 Dr Trans Am GT Cpe	9550	12565

OPTIONS FOR FIREBIRD

Auto 4-Speed Transmission +265
Air Conditioning[Opt on STD Cpe] +310
Compact Disc W/fm/tape +195
Cruise Control[Opt on Formula Cpe,STD Cpe] +80
Glass Panel T-tops +385
Keyless Entry System[Opt on Formula,STD, Trans Am] +65
Leather Seats[Std on Trans Am GT Conv] +265
Power Door Locks[Opt on Formula Cpe,STD Cpe] +75
Power Drivers Seat +90
Power Windows[Opt on STD Cpe,Formula Cpe] +85
Premium Sound System[Opt on Formula,STD, Trans Am] +150
Steer. Whl. Radio Cntrls +65

GRAND AM 1994

Driver airbag added. A 3.1-liter V6 replaces last year's optional 3.3-liter V6. Four-speed automatic debuts; standard with V6 and optional on four-cylinder models.

RATINGS (SCALE OF 1-10)

Overall	Safety	Reliability	Performance	Comfort	Value
7.2	6.6	7.6	8.2	7.3	6.1

Category C

Model	Trade-in Value	Market Value
2 Dr GT Cpe	6130	8280
4 Dr GT Sdn	6070	8200
2 Dr SE Cpe	4900	6625
4 Dr SE Sdn	4675	6315

OPTIONS FOR GRAND AM

6 cyl 3.1 L Engine +195
Auto 3-Speed Transmission +205
Auto 4-Speed Transmission +280
Air Conditioning[Opt on SE] +295
AM/FM Compact Disc Playr +140
Cruise Control +75
Keyless Entry System +70
Leather Seats +215
Power Drivers Seat +105
Power Windows +115
Premium Sound System +145

GRAND PRIX 1994

Interior is redesigned to accommodate dual airbags. LE and STE sedans are dropped; GT and GTP become option packages on SE coupe. A GT package is available on SE sedan, and includes 3.4-liter V6, alloys, low-profile tires, ABS, and sport suspension. Front seatbelts are anchored to pillars instead of doors on sedan; coupe retains door-mounted belts. 3.1-liter V6 is up 20 horsepower. Twin-cam 3.4-liter V6 is up ten horsepower. Five-speed manual and three-speed automatic transmissions are dropped in favor of four-speed automatic. Coupes gain standard equipment, including 16-inch alloys, cruise, and leather-wrapped steering wheel with integral radio controls.

RATINGS (SCALE OF 1-10)

Overall	Safety	Reliability	Performance	Comfort	Value
7.8	7.8	7.5	8	7.3	8.4

Category C

Model	Trade-in Value	Market Value
2 Dr SE Cpe	6625	8955
4 Dr SE Sdn	6105	8250

OPTIONS FOR GRAND PRIX

6 cyl 3.4 L Engine +415
GT Performance Package +600
AM/FM Compact Disc Playr +140
AM/FM Stereo Tape[Opt on Sdn] +60
Anti-Lock Brakes +230
Cruise Control[Opt on Sdn] +75
Keyless Entry System +70
Leather Seats +215
Power Drivers Seat +105
Power Sunroof +260
Premium Sound System +145
Sport Suspension +65
Trip Computer +70

SUNBIRD 1994

GT coupe, SE convertible and SE sedan vanish. Surviving are LE models and an SE coupe that comes standard with the GT's old body work. Convertibles get alloys and rear spoiler standard. SE comes with a 3.1-liter V6 standard.

Don't forget to refer to the Mileage Adjustment Table at the back of this book!

 © 1999 by Edmund Publications Corporation

RATINGS (SCALE OF 1-10)

Overall	Safety	Reliability	Performance	Comfort	Value
6.5	5.6	7.7	6.6	6.8	5.9

Category E

Model Description	Trade-in Value	Market Value
2 Dr LE Conv	5010	7155
2 Dr LE Cpe	3970	5670
4 Dr LE Sdn	3995	5710
2 Dr SE Cpe	4700	6715

OPTIONS FOR SUNBIRD

6 cyl 3.1 L Engine[Opt on LE] +275
Auto 3-Speed Transmission +185
Air Conditioning +300
Aluminum/Alloy Wheels +120
AM/FM Compact Disc Playr +175
Cruise Control +80
Power Windows[Std on Conv] +100
Rear Spoiler[Std on SE,Conv] +75
Sunroof +130

TRANS SPORT 1994

Driver airbag debuts and new front styling improves doorstop looks. Dashboard gets styling tweak to shorten visual acreage on top. A power sliding side door and integrated child seats are newly optional. Automatic power door locks are added, and rear seats gain a fold-and-stow feature. Traction control is made available at midyear; requires 3.8-liter engine.

RATINGS (SCALE OF 1-10)

Overall	Safety	Reliability	Performance	Comfort	Value
7.4	6.9	7.1	7.2	7.1	8.5

Category G

Model Description	Trade-in Value	Market Value
2 Dr SE Pass. Van	6535	8490

OPTIONS FOR TRANS SPORT

6 cyl 3.8 L Engine +160
7 Passenger Seating +200
Air Conditioning +300
AM/FM Compact Disc Playr +145
Auto Load Leveling +85
Child Seats (2) +95
Cruise Control +80
Dual Air Conditioning +375
Keyless Entry System +75
Leather Seats +285
Luggage Rack +60
Power Door Locks +85
Power Drivers Seat +105
Power Windows +85
Premium Sound System +135
Traction Control System +110

1993 PONTIAC

BONNEVILLE 1993

SSE gets supercharged engine option. ABS is standard on all models. Sport Luxury Edition (SLE) for SE includes chrome grille, decklid spoiler, cross-lace alloy wheels, bigger tires, leather seats, and performance-oriented transaxle ratio.

RATINGS (SCALE OF 1-10)

Overall	Safety	Reliability	Performance	Comfort	Value
7.8	7.5	7.6	8.1	7.8	8

Category B

Model Description	Trade-in Value	Market Value
4 Dr SE Sdn	5505	7540
4 Dr SSE Sdn	7095	9720
4 Dr SSE Sprchgd Sdn	7295	9990
4 Dr SSEi Sprchgd Sdn	7555	10350

OPTIONS FOR BONNEVILLE

Aluminum/Alloy Wheels[Opt on SE] +100
Climate Control for AC[Opt on SSE] +55
Cruise Control[Opt on SE] +65
Keyless Entry System[Std on SSEi] +55
Leather Seats[Std on SSEi] +200
Power Drivers Seat[Opt on SE] +90
Power Passenger Seat +95
Power Sunroof +350
Premium Sound System[Opt on SE] +125
Traction Control System[Std on SSEi] +55

FIREBIRD 1993

Brand new car debuts, marking first redesign since 1982. Base, Formula and Trans Am trim levels are available. Base car powered by 160-horsepower 3.4-liter V6. Formula and T/A get 5.7-liter V8 worth 275 horsepower. Formula and T/A get a standard six-speed manual transmission. Dual airbags and ABS are standard.

RATINGS (SCALE OF 1-10)

Overall	Safety	Reliability	Performance	Comfort	Value
7.2	9.1	7	8.9	7.4	3.8

Category F

Model Description	Trade-in Value	Market Value
2 Dr Formula Cpe	7025	9365
2 Dr STD Cpe	5885	7850
2 Dr Trans Am Cpe	7790	10385

OPTIONS FOR FIREBIRD

Auto 4-Speed Transmission +180
Air Conditioning[Opt on STD] +250
AM/FM Compact Disc Playr +150
Cruise Control[Std on Trans Am] +65
Keyless Entry System[Opt on STD] +50

Don't forget to refer to the Mileage Adjustment Table at the back of this book!

© 1999 by Edmund Publications Corporation

Model Description	Trade-in Value	Market Value

Leather Seats[Std on Trans Am] +215
Power Door Locks[Std on Trans Am] +60
Power Drivers Seat +70
Power Windows[Std on Trans Am] +70
Premium Sound System[Opt on STD] +125

GRAND AM 1993

Four-cylinder engines lose five horsepower, but gain modifications designed to reduce engine noise. Climate controls are revised, instrument panel graphics are revised on the SE, and battery-saver protection is added.

RATINGS (SCALE OF 1-10)

Overall	Safety	Reliability	Performance	Comfort	Value
6.8	4.4	7.2	8.2	7.3	6.9

Category C

Model Description	Trade-in Value	Market Value
2 Dr GT Cpe	4870	6860
4 Dr GT Sdn	4745	6685
2 Dr SE Cpe	3930	5535
4 Dr SE Sdn	3770	5310

OPTIONS FOR GRAND AM

4 cyl 2.3 L Quad 4 Engine[Opt on SE] +125
6 cyl 3.3 L Engine +165
Auto 3-Speed Transmission +170
Air Conditioning +240
Aluminum/Alloy Wheels[Opt on SE] +85
AM/FM Compact Disc Playr +115
Cruise Control +65
Power Drivers Seat +85
Power Windows +90
Premium Sound System +120

GRAND PRIX 1993

An electronically-controlled four-speed automatic is optional on LE sedan and SE coupe. A Sport Appearance Package for the LE sedan includes aero body panels, heads-up display, and bucket seats with console. Automatic door locks are standard. Chime added to warn driver if turn signal has been on for more than half a mile.

RATINGS (SCALE OF 1-10)

Overall	Safety	Reliability	Performance	Comfort	Value
7.2	5.4	7.2	8	7	8.3

Category C

Model Description	Trade-in Value	Market Value
2 Dr GT Cpe	6955	9795
4 Dr LE Sdn	4510	6350
2 Dr SE Cpe	5110	7195
4 Dr SE Sdn	5110	7200
4 Dr STE Sdn	7065	9950

OPTIONS FOR GRAND PRIX

6 cyl 3.4 L Engine +300
Auto 4-Speed Transmission[Opt on LE,SE] +70
Aero Performance Pkg +645
Aluminum/Alloy Wheels[Opt on LE,SE Cpe] +85
AM/FM Compact Disc Playr +115
Anti-Lock Brakes[Opt on LE,SE] +190
Cruise Control[Opt on LE,SE] +65
Keyless Entry System[Std on STE] +55
Leather Seats +175
Power Sunroof +210
Power Windows[Opt on LE,SE] +90
Premium Sound System[Opt on LE,SE] +120
Trip Computer[Opt on SE] +55

LE MANS 1993

New front styling and revised taillights debut. New moldings and wheelcovers complete the minor makeover.

Category E

Model Description	Trade-in Value	Market Value
2 Dr SE Cpe	2360	3520
4 Dr SE Sdn	2110	3150
2 Dr Value Leader Cpe	1750	2610

OPTIONS FOR LE MANS

Auto 3-Speed Transmission +145
Air Conditioning +245
AM/FM Stereo Tape +95
Power Steering +75
Sunroof +105

SUNBIRD 1993

Base models can be equipped with a V6, and midline coupe gets Sport Appearance Package, which includes GT styling.

RATINGS (SCALE OF 1-10)

Overall	Safety	Reliability	Performance	Comfort	Value
6.7	5.6	7.7	6.6	6.8	6.9

Category E

Model Description	Trade-in Value	Market Value
2 Dr GT Cpe	4455	6650
2 Dr LE Cpe	3135	4680
4 Dr LE Sdn	3140	4685
2 Dr SE Conv	4175	6230
2 Dr SE Cpe	3325	4960
4 Dr SE Sdn	3450	5150

OPTIONS FOR SUNBIRD

6 cyl 3.1 L Engine[Std on GT] +180
Auto 3-Speed Transmission +150
Air Conditioning +245
Aluminum/Alloy Wheels[Std on GT] +95
AM/FM Compact Disc Playr +145
Cruise Control +65
Power Windows[Std on Conv] +80
Rear Spoiler[Std on GT] +60
Sunroof +105
Tilt Steering Wheel +45

Don't forget to refer to the Mileage Adjustment Table at the back of this book!

 © 1999 by Edmund Publications Corporation

Model Description	Trade-in Value	Market Value

TRANS SPORT 1993

GT model canceled. SE is only trim level. Leather seats and steering wheel controls for the radio have been added to the options sheet. Climate controls are bigger. Sunroof becomes optional midyear.

RATINGS (SCALE OF 1-10)

Overall	Safety	Reliability	Performance	Comfort	Value
7	5.8	6.4	7.2	7.1	8.3

Category G

2 Dr SE Pass. Van	5200	6930

OPTIONS FOR TRANS SPORT

6 cyl 3.8 L Engine +185
Air Conditioning +245
Aluminum/Alloy Wheels +105
AM/FM Compact Disc Playr +115
Cruise Control +65
Dual Air Conditioning +305
Keyless Entry System +60
Leather Seats +235
Luggage Rack +45
Power Door Locks +70
Power Drivers Seat +85
Power Windows +70
Premium Sound System +110

1992 PONTIAC

BONNEVILLE 1992

Earns restyle that swaps stodgy, three-box design theme for flowing lines reminiscent of the Jaguar XJ6. LE trim level dies. 3.8-liter V6 gets five additional horsepower. SSEi has a supercharged V6 worth 205 horsepower and standard traction control. Traction control is optional on other Bonnevilles. ABS is standard on SSE and SSEi; optional on SE with Sport Appearance Package. A passenger airbag is standard on SSEi, optional on SSE. A heads-up display is standard on SSEi and optional on SSE.

RATINGS (SCALE OF 1-10)

Overall	Safety	Reliability	Performance	Comfort	Value
7.6	6.9	7.2	8.1	7.8	7.9

Category B

4 Dr SE Sdn	4330	6010
4 Dr SSE Sdn	5845	8120
4 Dr SSE Sprchgd Sdn	6195	8605
4 Dr SSEi Sprchgd Sdn	6295	8745

OPTIONS FOR BONNEVILLE

Aluminum/Alloy Wheels[Opt on SE] +85
AM/FM Stereo Tape +45
Anti-Lock Brakes[Opt on SE] +175
Climate Control for AC +45
Cruise Control[Opt on SE] +55
Keyless Entry System +45
Leather Seats +165
Power Drivers Seat[Opt on SE] +75
Power Moonroof +245
Power Passenger Seat[Opt on SSE] +75
Power Sunroof +285
Premium Sound System[Opt on SE] +105
Traction Control System[Std on SSEi] +45

FIREBIRD 1992

Pontiac takes great pains to reduce the number of squeaks and rattles in the Firebird. Body has been stiffened for a tighter feel. Performance Equipment Group is available on Formula and Trans Am coupes, and boosts tuned-port 5.0-liter to 230 horsepower.

Category F

2 Dr Formula Cpe	5110	7100
2 Dr STD Conv	4465	6200
2 Dr STD Cpe	4195	5830
2 Dr Trans Am Cpe	5800	8060
2 Dr Trans Am Conv	7165	9950

OPTIONS FOR FIREBIRD

8 cyl 5.0 L Engine[Opt on STD] +90
8 cyl 5.0 L TPI Engine[Opt on Formula] +110
8 cyl 5.7 L Engine[Std on Trans Am GTA] +180
Auto 4-Speed Transmission +130
Air Conditioning[Opt on STD] +205
AM/FM Compact Disc Playr +120
Cruise Control[Std on Trans Am GTA] +50
Glass Panel T-tops +255
Leather Seats +175
Limited Slip Diff[Opt on Formula,STD] +90
Power Door Locks[Std on Trans Am GTA] +50
Power Windows[Std on Trans Am GTA] +55
Premium Sound System[Std on Trans Am GTA] +100

GRAND AM 1992

Redesign nets Grand Am swoopy look, standard ABS and optional V6 power. Car is now based on same platform as Chevy Corsica/Beretta. SE and GT models are available. Standard engine is a 120-horsepower SOHC engine. GT gets 180-horsepower Quad 4. Optional on both is a 3.3-liter V6. Hook an automatic to the Quad 4 engine and horsepower drops to 160 horsepower.

RATINGS (SCALE OF 1-10)

Overall	Safety	Reliability	Performance	Comfort	Value
6.5	4.3	6.7	8.2	7.3	5.8

Category C

2 Dr GT Cpe	3880	5620
4 Dr GT Sdn	3875	5620
2 Dr SE Cpe	3050	4420
4 Dr SE Sdn	3015	4375

Don't forget to refer to the Mileage Adjustment Table at the back of this book!

 © 1999 by Edmund Publications Corporation

OPTIONS FOR GRAND AM

4 cyl 2.3 L Engine +100
6 cyl 3.3 L Engine +125
Auto 3-Speed Transmission +135
Air Conditioning +200
Aluminum/Alloy Wheels[Opt on SE] +70
AM/FM Compact Disc Playr +95
Cruise Control +50
Power Drivers Seat +70
Power Windows +75

GRAND PRIX 1992

All sedans get STE light-bar front styling treatment. Base 160-horsepower Quad 4 motor replaced by 140-horsepower 3.1-liter V6. GTP coupe still has 210-horsepower twin-cam V6 standard. ABS is standard on GT, GTP, and STE; optional on LE and SE. Base SE coupes can be dressed in GT lower-body extensions.

RATINGS (SCALE OF 1-10)

Overall	Safety	Reliability	Performance	Comfort	Value
7.1	5.4	7.1	8	7	8

Category C	Trade-in Value	Market Value
2 Dr GT Cpe	5580	8085
4 Dr LE Sdn	3635	5270
2 Dr SE Cpe	4115	5965
4 Dr SE Sdn	4090	5925
4 Dr STE Sdn	5860	8495

OPTIONS FOR GRAND PRIX

6 cyl 3.4 L Engine +240
Auto 4-Speed Transmission[Opt on LE,SE] +50
Aero Performance Pkg +600
Aluminum/Alloy Wheels[Opt on LE,SE Cpe] +70
AM/FM Stereo Tape +40
Anti-Lock Brakes[Opt on LE,SE] +155
Cruise Control[Opt on LE,SE] +50
Keyless Entry System[Std on STE] +45
Leather Seats +145
Power Door Locks[Opt on LE,SE] +60
Power Drivers Seat[Std on STE] +70
Power Sunroof +170
Power Windows[Opt on LE,SE] +75
Premium Sound System[Opt on LE,SE] +100
Trip Computer[Std on STE] +45

LE MANS 1992

LE designation swapped for SE nomenclature. Coupe gets amber turn signals.

Category E	Trade-in Value	Market Value
2 Dr SE Cpe	1660	2595
4 Dr SE Sdn	1620	2535
2 Dr Value Leader Cpe	1205	1880

OPTIONS FOR LE MANS

Auto 3-Speed Transmission +115
Air Conditioning +200
AM/FM Stereo Tape +75
Power Steering +60
Sunroof +85

SUNBIRD 1992

ABS is standard. LE designation extended to base coupe and sedan. 2.0-liter four-cylinder engine gets 15 more horsepower. Brake/transmission shift interlock is added. Fuel capacity jumps to 15.2 gallons. Automatic door locks lock doors when automatic is shifted from "Park" or manually shifted car begins moving forward. Convertible gets glass rear window at midyear.

RATINGS (SCALE OF 1-10)

Overall	Safety	Reliability	Performance	Comfort	Value
6.3	5.5	7.3	6.6	6.8	5.4

Category E	Trade-in Value	Market Value
2 Dr GT Cpe	3590	5610
2 Dr LE Cpe	2505	3915
4 Dr LE Sdn	2585	4040
2 Dr SE Conv	3450	5390
2 Dr SE Cpe	2805	4385
4 Dr SE Sdn	2850	4450

OPTIONS FOR SUNBIRD

6 cyl 3.1 L Engine[Opt on SE] +145
Auto 3-Speed Transmission +120
Air Conditioning +200
Aluminum/Alloy Wheels[Std on GT] +80
AM/FM Compact Disc Playr +115
Cruise Control +55
Power Windows[Std on Conv] +65
Rear Spoiler[Std on GT] +50
Sunroof +85
Tilt Steering Wheel +35

TRANS SPORT 1992

ABS is standard. SE becomes base model; new top-of-the-line is the GT. GT gets a standard 3.8-liter V6 good for 165 horsepower. SE retains old 3.1-liter, but offers the bigger motor as an option. 15-inch wheels replace 14-inch wheels on both models. Remote keyless entry and rear climate controls are added to the options list.

RATINGS (SCALE OF 1-10)

Overall	Safety	Reliability	Performance	Comfort	Value
7	5.9	6.7	7.2	7.1	8.3

Category G	Trade-in Value	Market Value
2 Dr GT Pass. Van	5420	7430
2 Dr SE Pass. Van	4300	5890

OPTIONS FOR TRANS SPORT

6 cyl 3.8 L Engine[Opt on SE] +160
7 Passenger Seating +135
Air Conditioning[Opt on SE] +200

Don't forget to refer to the Mileage Adjustment Table at the back of this book!

 © 1999 by Edmund Publications Corporation

Model Description	Trade-in Value	Market Value

Aluminum/Alloy Wheels[Opt on SE] +85
AM/FM Compact Disc Playr +95
Auto Load Leveling[Opt on SE] +55
Cruise Control[Opt on SE] +50
Dual Air Conditioning +250
Keyless Entry System +50
Luggage Rack +40
Power Door Locks +55
Power Drivers Seat +70
Power Windows +60
Tilt Steering Wheel[Opt on SE] +40

1991 PONTIAC

6000 — 1991

No changes.

Category C

Model Description	Trade-in Value	Market Value
4 Dr LE Sdn	2185	3360
4 Dr LE Wgn	3115	4795
4 Dr SE Sdn	2955	4545

OPTIONS FOR 6000

6 cyl 3.1 L Engine[Std on SE,Wgn] +105
Auto 4-Speed Transmission[Std on SE,Wgn] +40
Air Conditioning[Std on SE,Wgn] +160
AM/FM Stereo Tape[Opt on LE] +35
Cruise Control[Opt on LE] +40
Power Door Locks[Opt on LE] +50
Power Drivers Seat +60
Power Windows[Opt on LE] +60
Premium Sound System +80
Woodgrain Applique +65

BONNEVILLE — 1991

Brake/transmission shift interlock is added.

Category B

Model Description	Trade-in Value	Market Value
4 Dr LE Sdn	3085	4345
4 Dr SE Sdn	3935	5545
4 Dr SSE Sdn	4890	6885

OPTIONS FOR BONNEVILLE

AM/FM Stereo Tape[Opt on LE] +35
Anti-Lock Brakes[Std on SSE] +145
Climate Control for AC +35
Cruise Control[Opt on LE] +45
Keyless Entry System[Std on SSE] +35
Leather Seats +135
Power Door Locks[Opt on LE] +50
Power Drivers Seat[Opt on LE] +60
Power Moonroof +200
Power Windows[Opt on LE] +60
Premium Sound System[Std on SSE] +85
Steer. Whl. Radio Cntrls[Std on SSE] +30

FIREBIRD — 1991

Top level V8 engines get more horsepower. Front and rear styling is freshened. Rocker panel extensions are restyled. Base coupes get new Sport Appearance Package. Formula can be ordered with 5.7-liter engine option.

Category F

Model Description	Trade-in Value	Market Value
2 Dr Formula Cpe	4280	6030
2 Dr STD Cpe	3440	4845
2 Dr Trans Am Conv	6480	9125
2 Dr Trans Am Cpe	5155	7260
2 Dr Trans Am GTA Cpe	5630	7930

OPTIONS FOR FIREBIRD

8 cyl 5.0 L Engine[Opt on STD] +70
8 cyl 5.7 L Engine[Std on Trans Am GTA] +95
Auto 4-Speed Transmission[Std on STD Conv] +105
Air Conditioning[Opt on STD] +170
AM/FM Compact Disc Playr +100
Cruise Control[Std on Trans Am GTA] +40
Leather Seats +145
Limited Slip Diff[Opt on Formula,STD] +75
Power Door Locks[Std on Trans Am GTA] +40
Power Windows[Std on Trans Am GTA] +45
Premium Sound System[Std on Trans Am GTA] +85
T-Tops (solid/Colored) +190

GRAND AM — 1991

ABS is standard on SE. Larger, vented front rotors increase stopping ability on SE. LE with Sport Performance Package adds several SE goodies, like high-output Quad 4 engine, alloy wheels, exterior trim, and a revised suspension.

Category C

Model Description	Trade-in Value	Market Value
2 Dr LE Cpe	2335	3590
4 Dr LE Sdn	2225	3420
2 Dr SE Cpe	3205	4930
4 Dr SE Sdn	2985	4590
2 Dr STD Cpe	2270	3490
4 Dr STD Sdn	2120	3260

OPTIONS FOR GRAND AM

4 cyl 2.3 L Quad 4 Engine[Opt on LE] +130
Auto 3-Speed Transmission +110
Sport Performance Pkg +195
Air Conditioning[Std on SE] +160
AM/FM Compact Disc Playr +80
Cruise Control[Std on SE] +40
Power Door Locks[Opt on LE] +50
Power Drivers Seat +60
Power Windows[Opt on LE] +60
Rear Window Defroster +35
Sunroof +75
Tilt Steering Wheel[Std on SE] +30

GRAND PRIX — 1991

LE and Turbo coupes dropped; GT coupe added. A twin-cam V6 with five-speed transmission is optional.

Don't forget to refer to the Mileage Adjustment Table at the back of this book!

 © 1999 by Edmund Publications Corporation

Model Description	Trade-in Value	Market Value

RATINGS (SCALE OF 1-10)

Overall	Safety	Reliability	Performance	Comfort	Value
7	5.3	6.4	8	7	8.1

Category C		
2 Dr GT Cpe	4305	6625
4 Dr LE Sdn	2705	4165
2 Dr SE Cpe	3205	4930
4 Dr SE Sdn	3000	4615
4 Dr STE Sdn	4285	6595

OPTIONS FOR GRAND PRIX

6 cyl 3.1 L Engine[Opt on LE,SE] +105
6 cyl 3.4 L Engine +190
Auto 4-Speed Transmission[Opt on LE,SE] +40
Aero Performance Pkg +465
AM/FM Stereo Tape +35
Anti-Lock Brakes +125
Cruise Control[Opt on LE,SE] +40
Keyless Entry System[Std on STE] +40
Leather Seats +115
Power Door Locks[Opt on LE,SE] +50
Power Drivers Seat[Opt on LE,SE] +60
Power Sunroof +140
Power Windows[Opt on LE,SE] +60
Premium Sound System[Opt on SE] +80
Steer. Whl. Radio Cntrls[Opt on SE] +30

LE MANS 1991

Sporty GSE dropped.

Category E		
2 Dr LE Cpe	1170	1985
4 Dr LE Sdn	1285	2180
2 Dr Value Leader Cpe	1000	1695

OPTIONS FOR LE MANS

Auto 3-Speed Transmission +90
Air Conditioning +165
AM/FM Stereo Tape +60
Power Steering +50
Sunroof +70

SUNBIRD 1991

Turbo engine dropped in favor of 3.1-liter V6. Six-cylinder makes 25 fewer horsepower than previous turbo. GT gets new alloys.

RATINGS (SCALE OF 1-10)

Overall	Safety	Reliability	Performance	Comfort	Value
6.1	4.5	7.1	6.6	6.8	5.3

Category E		
2 Dr GT Cpe	3110	5270
2 Dr LE Conv	2595	4400
2 Dr LE Cpe	1920	3260
4 Dr LE Sdn	2050	3480
2 Dr SE Cpe	2250	3810
2 Dr STD Cpe	1665	2820
4 Dr STD Sdn	1780	3020

OPTIONS FOR SUNBIRD

6 cyl 3.1 L Engine[Std on GT] +135
Auto 3-Speed Transmission +95
Air Conditioning +165
AM/FM Compact Disc Playr +95
Cruise Control +45
Power Door Locks[Std on Conv] +45
Power Windows[Std on Conv] +55
Sunroof +70
Tilt Steering Wheel +30

TRANS SPORT 1991

No changes.

RATINGS (SCALE OF 1-10)

Overall	Safety	Reliability	Performance	Comfort	Value
6.6	4.9	6.5	6.8	7.1	7.7

Category G		
2 Dr SE Pass. Van	3580	5110
2 Dr STD Pass. Van	3050	4355

OPTIONS FOR TRANS SPORT

7 Passenger Seating +110
Air Conditioning[Std on SE] +165
Aluminum/Alloy Wheels[Std on SE] +70
AM/FM Stereo Tape[Std on SE] +50
Cruise Control[Std on SE] +45
Luggage Rack +30
Power Door Locks +45
Power Drivers Seat +55
Power Windows +50
Premium Sound System +75

1990 PONTIAC

6000 1990

STE dropped. S/E gains all-wheel drive option. 3.1-liter V6 replaces 2.8-liter V6, and makes more power. Air conditioning standard on all except LE sedan.

Category C		
4 Dr LE Sdn	1765	2890
4 Dr LE Wgn	2210	3625
4 Dr SE Sdn	2330	3820
4 Dr SE Wgn	2605	4270
4 Dr SE 4WD Sdn	2675	4385

OPTIONS FOR 6000

6 cyl 3.1 L Engine[Std on SE,Wgn] +100
Auto 4-Speed Transmission[Std on SE,Wgn] +35
Air Conditioning[Std on SE,Wgn] +130
Aluminum/Alloy Wheels[Opt on LE] +50
Cruise Control[Opt on LE] +35
Power Door Locks[Opt on LE] +40

Don't forget to refer to the Mileage Adjustment Table at the back of this book!

 © 1999 by Edmund Publications Corporation

Model Description	Trade-in Value	Market Value

Power Drivers Seat +45
Power Windows[Opt on LE] +50
Premium Sound System +65
Woodgrain Applique +50

BONNEVILLE 1990

Front body/frame structure is redesigned. SSE gets new grille. LE and SE get new taillights. Remote keyless entry is new option. Power windows come with driver's express-down window. SE gets rear spoiler, fog lights and power trunk release standard. Alloy wheels are new. Bench seat is replaced by a 55/45 split bench.

Category B

4 Dr LE Sdn	2725	4190
4 Dr SE Sdn	2825	4345
4 Dr SSE Sdn	3480	5350

OPTIONS FOR BONNEVILLE

Aluminum/Alloy Wheels[Opt on LE] +55
AM/FM Stereo Tape[Opt on LE] +30
Anti-Lock Brakes[Std on SSE] +120
Climate Control for AC +30
Cruise Control[Std on SSE] +35
Keyless Entry System[Opt on SE] +30
Leather Seats +110
Power Door Locks[Opt on LE] +40
Power Drivers Seat[Std on SSE] +50
Power Passenger Seat[Std on SSE] +50
Power Sunroof +190
Power Windows[Opt on LE] +50
Premium Sound System[Opt on SE] +70

FIREBIRD 1990

Driver airbag is added. A 3.1-liter V6 replaces the 2.8-liter V6. 5.0-liter V8 drops throttle body fuel injection in favor of tuned-port fuel injection (except on base model and Formula). All models get dual body-color mirrors. Base cars get new interior trim. Some dashboard switchgear has been modified.

Category F

2 Dr Formula Cpe	3410	4940
2 Dr STD Cpe	2535	3675
2 Dr Trans Am Cpe	3920	5680
2 Dr Trans Am GTA Cpe	5425	7860

OPTIONS FOR FIREBIRD

8 cyl 5.0 L Engine[Std on Trans Am] +80
8 cyl 5.7 L Engine[Std on Trans Am GTA] +90
Auto 4-Speed Transmission +85
Air Conditioning[Opt on STD] +140
AM/FM Compact Disc Playr +80
Cruise Control +35
Leather Seats +120
Limited Slip Diff[Opt on Formula] +60
Power Door Locks +35
Power Windows[Std on Trans Am GTA] +35
T-Tops (solid/Colored) +155

GRAND AM 1990

Turbocharged engine dumped in favor of high-output Quad 4 motor. It is standard on SE model. Base Quad 4 engine is up ten horsepower this year. Express-down power windows are optional. SE gets 16-inch alloys.

Category C

2 Dr LE Cpe	1710	2800
4 Dr LE Sdn	1790	2930
2 Dr SE Cpe	2175	3565
4 Dr SE Sdn	2220	3635

OPTIONS FOR GRAND AM

4 cyl 2.3 L Quad 4 Engine[Opt on LE] +100
Auto 3-Speed Transmission +90
Air Conditioning[Opt on LE] +130
Aluminum/Alloy Wheels[Opt on LE] +50
Cruise Control[Opt on LE] +35
Power Door Locks[Opt on LE] +40
Power Drivers Seat +45
Power Windows[Opt on LE] +50
Premium Sound System +65
Sunroof +60

GRAND PRIX 1990

Sedan debuts, in LE and STE trim. STE includes remote keyless entry. Turbo coupe becomes regular production model. 2.8-liter V6 dumped in favor of 3.1-liter V6. A Quad 4 engine is available for the first time, and is standard on LE. STE sedan and SE coupe get smoother V6 power.

RATINGS (SCALE OF 1-10)

Overall	Safety	Reliability	Performance	Comfort	Value
6.9	5.2	6.1	8	7	8.1

Category C

2 Dr LE Cpe	2160	3540
4 Dr LE Sdn	2270	3725
2 Dr SE Cpe	2855	4685
2 Dr SE Turbo Cpe	3260	5340
4 Dr STE Sdn	3125	5125
4 Dr STE Turbo Sdn	3180	5215

OPTIONS FOR GRAND PRIX

6 cyl 3.1 L Engine[Opt on LE] +100
Auto 4-Speed Transmission +80
Aluminum/Alloy Wheels[Opt on LE] +50
Anti-Lock Brakes +105
Cruise Control[Opt on LE] +35
Keyless Entry System[Std on STE] +30
Leather Seats +95
Power Door Locks[Opt on LE] +40
Power Drivers Seat[Opt on LE] +45
Power Passenger Seat +45
Power Sunroof +115
Power Windows[Opt on LE] +50
Premium Sound System[Opt on LE] +65

Don't forget to refer to the Mileage Adjustment Table at the back of this book!

 © 1999 by Edmund Publications Corporation

Model Description	Trade-in Value	Market Value

LE MANS 1990

SE sedan dropped from lineup. Motorized seatbelts appear. GSE gets quicker steering. Cars with 1.6-liter engine get better brakes. Suspensions retuned for better performance and quieter ride.

Category E

Model Description	Trade-in Value	Market Value
2 Dr GSE Cpe	1200	2305
2 Dr LE Cpe	895	1725
4 Dr LE Sdn	1005	1935
2 Dr Value Leader Cpe	730	1405

OPTIONS FOR LE MANS

Auto 3-Speed Transmission +75
Air Conditioning[Std on GSE] +135
AM/FM Stereo Tape +50
Power Steering[Opt on LE] +40
Sunroof +55

SUNBIRD 1990

GT convertible switches to LE trim in cost-cutting move. SE and GT get new front styling. Passive restraint seatbelts are added. Turbo option dropped for SE model; is included in a sports package for LE convertible, along with GT suspension and steering.

RATINGS (SCALE OF 1-10)

Overall	Safety	Reliability	Performance	Comfort	Value
6.2	4.6	7.1	6.6	6.8	6.2

Category E

Model Description	Trade-in Value	Market Value
2 Dr GT Cpe	1865	3590
2 Dr GT Turbo Cpe	1900	3650
2 Dr LE Cpe	1285	2475
2 Dr LE Conv	1735	3340
2 Dr LE Turbo Conv	1800	3465
4 Dr LE Sdn	1180	2270
2 Dr SE Cpe	1400	2690

OPTIONS FOR SUNBIRD

Auto 3-Speed Transmission +75
Air Conditioning +135
Aluminum/Alloy Wheels[Std on GT] +50
AM/FM Stereo Tape +50
Cruise Control +35
Power Door Locks +40
Power Steering[Std on GT,SE,Conv] +40
Power Windows +45
Premium Sound System +55
Rear Spoiler[Opt on LE] +35
Sunroof +55

TRANS SPORT 1990

Weak-kneed minivan debuts with pathetic 120-horsepower V6 and plastic composite body panels. Load-leveling suspension is standard. Seating is modular in style, providing space for up to seven occupants.

RATINGS (SCALE OF 1-10)

Overall	Safety	Reliability	Performance	Comfort	Value
6.5	4.9	6.4	6.8	7.1	7.2

Category G

Model Description	Trade-in Value	Market Value
2 Dr SE Pass. Van	3270	4950
2 Dr STD Pass. Van	2910	4410

OPTIONS FOR TRANS SPORT

7 Passenger Seating +90
Air Conditioning[Std on SE] +135
Aluminum/Alloy Wheels[Std on SE] +55
AM/FM Stereo Tape[Std on SE] +40
Cruise Control[Std on SE] +35
Power Door Locks +40
Power Drivers Seat +45
Power Windows +40
Premium Sound System +60
Privacy Glass[Std on SE] +45

1989 PONTIAC

6000 1989

STE is available only with all-wheel drive. Sedans get new rounded rear styling, featuring STE-style taillights and trunk lid. LE and S/E get integrated fog lamps just like STE. S/E gets body-color grille and moldings. STE is only 6000 to get 3.1-liter V-6 and ABS, and is available only in red or blue. Standard four-cylinder engine makes more horsepower. CD player added to options list. Manual transmission option is dropped.

Category C

Model Description	Trade-in Value	Market Value
4 Dr LE Wgn	1375	2410
4 Dr LE Sdn	1415	2485
4 Dr SE Sdn	1500	2630
4 Dr SE Wgn	1700	2980

OPTIONS FOR 6000

6 cyl 2.8 L Engine[Std on SE,STE,Wgn] +85
Air Conditioning[Std on STE] +110
Aluminum/Alloy Wheels[Opt on LE] +40
Cruise Control[Opt on LE] +30
Power Door Locks[Opt on LE] +30
Power Drivers Seat[Std on STE] +40
Power Windows[Opt on LE] +40
Premium Sound System +55
Woodgrain Applique +40

BONNEVILLE 1989

SSE's optional ABS trickles down to LE and SE trim levels, while SSE gets new seats and new center console. Steering wheel controls for the stereo are

Don't forget to refer to the Mileage Adjustment Table at the back of this book!

 © 1999 by Edmund Publications Corporation

Model Description	Trade-in Value	Market Value

simplified. SSE sound system gets larger speakers and a subwoofer.

Category B

4 Dr LE Sdn	1920	3200
4 Dr SE Sdn	2140	3565
4 Dr SSE Sdn	2500	4165

OPTIONS FOR BONNEVILLE

Aluminum/Alloy Wheels[Opt on LE] +45
Anti-Lock Brakes[Std on SSE] +95
Cruise Control[Opt on LE] +30
Leather Seats +90
Power Door Locks[Std on SSE] +35
Power Drivers Seat +40
Power Passenger Seat +40
Power Sunroof +155
Power Windows[Opt on LE] +40
Premium Sound System[Std on SSE] +55

FIREBIRD 1989

Twentieth-Anniversary Edition debuts midyear sporting turbocharged 3.8-liter V6. 1,500 are built. All Firebirds get rear disc brakes and a theft-deterrent system. A CD player is a new option. Air conditioning is made standard on Formula and Trans Am.

Category F

2 Dr Formula Cpe	2980	4445
2 Dr STD Cpe	2435	3635
2 Dr Trans Am Cpe	3565	5325
2 Dr Trans Am GTA Cpe	4240	6330
2 Dr Trans Am 20th Anniv. Turbo Cpe	6325	9440

OPTIONS FOR FIREBIRD

8 cyl 5.0 L Engine[Opt on STD,Trans Am GTA] +55
8 cyl 5.0 L Engine +100
8 cyl 5.7 L Engine[Std on Trans Am GTA] +140
Auto 4-Speed Transmission[Opt on Formula,STD,Trans Am] +70
Air Conditioning[Opt on STD] +115
Cruise Control[Opt on Formula,STD,Trans Am] +30
Leather Seats +95
Limited Slip Diff +50
Power Windows[Opt on Formula,STD,Trans Am] +30
Premium Sound System[Opt on Trans Am] +55
T-Tops (solid/Colored) +125

GRAND AM 1989

Styling is updated front and rear. Base engine makes more power. SE gets turbocharged 2.0-liter engine. A Quad 4 motor is optional on both trim levels.

Category C

2 Dr LE Cpe	1380	2425
4 Dr LE Sdn	1410	2475
2 Dr SE Cpe	1650	2895
2 Dr SE Turbo Cpe	1745	3065
4 Dr SE Sdn	1445	2535
4 Dr SE Turbo Sdn	1520	2670

OPTIONS FOR GRAND AM

4 cyl 2.3 L Quad 4 Engine[Opt on LE] +90
Auto 3-Speed Transmission +65
Air Conditioning +110
Aluminum/Alloy Wheels[Opt on LE] +40
Cruise Control[Opt on LE] +30
Power Door Locks[Opt on LE] +30
Power Drivers Seat +40
Power Windows +40
Premium Sound System +55
Sunroof +50

GRAND PRIX 1989

ABS is newly optional. A 3.1-liter V6 replaces the 2.8-liter V6 as the standard engine in models with an automatic. Manually shifted cars will continue to use the smaller engine. Air conditioning is standard on all models. Power sunroof, steering wheel radio controls and remote keyless entry are new options. Midyear, a McLaren Turbo Grand Prix is introduced, painted red or black. All 2,000 examples feature ABS, a power sunroof and leather seats.

RATINGS (SCALE OF 1-10)

Overall	Safety	Reliability	Performance	Comfort	Value
6.2	5	5.9	7.8	7	5.4

Category C

2 Dr LE Cpe	1740	3055
2 Dr SE Cpe	1975	3470
2 Dr SE Turbo Cpe	3285	5760
2 Dr STD Cpe	1590	2790

OPTIONS FOR GRAND PRIX

6 cyl 2.8 L Engine[Std on SE] +85
Auto 4-Speed Transmission +85
Aluminum/Alloy Wheels[Std on SE] +40
Anti-Lock Brakes +85
Cruise Control[Std on SE] +30
Leather Seats +80
Power Door Locks[Std on Turbo] +30
Power Drivers Seat[Std on SE] +40
Power Passenger Seat[Opt on] +35
Power Sunroof +95
Power Windows[Opt on STD] +40
Premium Sound System[Std on Turbo] +55

LE MANS 1989

Sunroof is added to options list.

Category E

2 Dr GSE Cpe	795	1805
2 Dr LE Cpe	640	1460
4 Dr LE Sdn	650	1475
4 Dr SE Sdn	650	1480
2 Dr STD Cpe	600	1370

Don't forget to refer to the Mileage Adjustment Table at the back of this book!

© 1999 by Edmund Publications Corporation

Model Description	Trade-in Value	Market Value

OPTIONS FOR LE MANS
Auto 3-Speed Transmission +55
Air Conditioning +110
AM/FM Stereo Tape +40
Cruise Control +30
Power Steering[Std on GSE] +35
Sunroof +45

SAFARI 1989

Full-size wagon gets rear shoulder belts.

Category B		
4 Dr STD Wgn	1690	2815

OPTIONS FOR SAFARI
Cruise Control +30
Power Door Locks +35
Power Drivers Seat +40
Power Windows +40
Premium Sound System +55
Woodgrain Applique +50

SUNBIRD 1989

Revised instrument panel debuts. Wagon model disappears. LE models get new front styling. CD player added to options list.

RATINGS (SCALE OF 1-10)

Overall	Safety	Reliability	Performance	Comfort	Value
6.6	5.7	6.7	6.6	6.8	7.3

Category E		
2 Dr GT Cpe	1035	2350
2 Dr GT Conv	1790	4070
2 Dr GT Turbo Cpe	1095	2490
2 Dr GT Turbo Conv	1880	4270
2 Dr LE Cpe	780	1775
4 Dr LE Sdn	890	2030
2 Dr SE Cpe	980	2230

OPTIONS FOR SUNBIRD
Auto 3-Speed Transmission +55
Air Conditioning +110
Aluminum/Alloy Wheels[Std on GT] +45
AM/FM Stereo Tape +40
Cruise Control +30
Power Door Locks[Std on Conv] +30
Power Drivers Seat +40
Power Steering[Std on GT] +35
Power Windows[Std on Conv] +35
Sunroof +45

Get a great used car and apply for financing *online* at a price you must see to believe!

http://www.edmunds.com

Don't forget to refer to the Mileage Adjustment Table at the back of this book!

 © 1999 by Edmund Publications Corporation

PORSCHE Germany

1997 Porsche 911

1998 PORSCHE

911 1998

The current-generation 911 goes the way of the dodo at year's end, when it will be replaced by the next evolutionary step toward the perfect driving machine.

Category J

Model	Trade-in Value	Market Value
2 Dr Carrera Conv	60385	70215
2 Dr Carrera S Cpe	53035	61670
2 Dr Targa Cpe	58765	68330

OPTIONS FOR 911

Auto 4-Speed Transmission +2715
5-Spoke Cast Alloy Wheels +1200
Aero Kit +5860
Digital Sound Radio Equip +1725
F&R Aero Spoilers Kit +5120
Hi-Fi Sound Radio Equip. +775
Leather Door Panels +1570
Leather Interior Trim +3320
Leather/Vinyl Inter. Trim +1285
Litronic Headlamps +1275
Rootwood Steering Wheel +1545
Special Chassis +1330
Special Leather Int. Trim +3900
Sport Chassis W/18" Whls +2040
Sport Classic Wheels +1535
Targa Wheels +1375
Technology Alloy Wheels +2685
Technology Pressure Whls. +1485
Wood Dash +5410
AM/FM Compact Disc Playr +450
Compact Disc Changer +815
Dual Power Seats +610
Heated Front Seats +345
Leather Seats +855
Limited Slip Diff[Std on Carrera 4S, 4WD] +820
Onboard Computer +360
Special Factory Paint +1460
Traction Control System[Opt on 2WD] +1095

BOXSTER 1998

Side air bags are standard for 1998.

Category J

Model	Trade-in Value	Market Value
2 Dr STD Conv	40205	46750

OPTIONS FOR BOXSTER

Auto 5-Speed Transmission +2670
Boxster Design Wheels +1230
Leather Seat/Interior Trm +1655
Special Leather Seat Trim +1970
Sport Classic Wheels +2070
Sport Handling Package +1670
Technic Sport Package +1000
AM/FM Compact Disc Playr +450
Compact Disc Changer +815
Cruise Control +390
Heated Front Seats +345
Onboard Computer +360

1997 PORSCHE

911 1997

The only change to this year's Porsche 911 is the availability of a Porsche-engineered child seat that will deactivate the passenger airbag when it is in place.

Category J

Model	Trade-in Value	Market Value
2 Dr Carrera Cpe	47230	54920
2 Dr Carrera Conv	56890	66150
2 Dr Targa Cpe	56960	66230
2 Dr Turbo 4WD Cpe	81715	95015
2 Dr Turbo S 4WD Cpe	88135	102485

OPTIONS FOR 911

Auto 4-Speed Transmission +2220
5 Spoke Light Alloy Whls +935
Aluminum/Chrome Package +1410
Carbon/Alloy Brake and Shifter +565
Carbon/Lth Steering Wheel +1070
Digital Sound Radio +780
Leather Door Panels +1285
Leather Sun Visors +575
Pearlescent White Paint +8320
Wood Dash +2960
AM/FM Compact Disc Playr +370
Compact Disc Changer +665
Dual Power Seats[Std on Turbo,Turbo S] +500
Hardtop Roof +1915
Heated Front Seats[Std on Turbo S] +280
Leather Seats[Std on Turbo,Turbo S] +700
Limited Slip Diff[Opt on Targa,2WD] +670
Onboard Computer[Std on Turbo,Turbo S] +295

Don't forget to refer to the Mileage Adjustment Table at the back of this book!

 © 1999 by Edmund Publications Corporation

Model Description	Trade-in Value	Market Value

BOXSTER 1997

This all-new roadster is introduced to compete in the revitalized midpriced sports car category. The Boxster features a 2.5-liter six-cylinder engine, a five-speed manual or five-speed Tiptronic transmission, and a power top that closes in an impressive 12 seconds.

Category J

Model Description	Trade-in Value	Market Value
2 Dr Sport Touring Conv	37155	43205
2 Dr STD Conv	36440	42370

OPTIONS FOR BOXSTER

Auto 5-Speed Transmission +1185
Aerokit +3865
Boxster-design Wheels +900
Color Keyed Rear Spoiler +1060
Leather Seat Trim +1465
Rain Sensing Windshield +1015
Special Leather Seat Trim +1745
Sport Classic Wheels +1830
Sport Handling Package +2215
Compact Disc Changer[Opt on STD] +665
Compact Disc W/fm/tape +485
Cruise Control +320
Hardtop Roof +1915
Heated Front Seats +280
Onboard Computer[Opt on STD] +295
Traction Control System +895

1996 PORSCHE

911 1996

Trick Targa model joins the lineup, and power is up in midrange revs. New Carrera 4S model provides Turbo looks without Turbo price or performance. Bigger wheels are standard across the line, as well as Litronic headlights. New stereos and exterior colors compliment one new interior color this year. Remote keyless entry system gets an immobilizer feature.

Category J

Model Description	Trade-in Value	Market Value
2 Dr Carrera Cpe	41020	48835
2 Dr Carrera Conv	48520	57760
2 Dr STD Turbo 4WD Cpe	75335	89685
2 Dr Targa Cpe	46905	55835

OPTIONS FOR 911

Auto 4-Speed Transmission +1720
5 Spoke Light Alloy Whls +750
Door Panel Pkg +1035
Leather Door Panels +1035
Pearlescent White Paint +6690
Seat Pkg +955
Steering Wheel Pkg +660
Wood Dash +2380
AM/FM Compact Disc Playr +300
Compact Disc Changer +545
Dual Power Seats[Std on STD] +410
Heated Front Seats +230
Leather Seats[Std on STD] +570
Limited Slip Diff[Opt on 2WD] +550
Onboard Computer +240

1995 PORSCHE

911 1995

Category J

Model Description	Trade-in Value	Market Value
2 Dr Carrera Cpe	34270	41290
2 Dr Carrera Conv	39960	48145

OPTIONS FOR 911

Auto 4-Speed Transmission +1405
5 Spoke Light Alloy Whls +615
Active Brake Differential +405
Color To Sample Paint +1115
Door Panel Pkg +845
Hi-fi Sound W/amplifier +415
Leather Door Panels +845
Pearlescent White Paint +5465
Pressure Cast Alloy Whls +615
Seat Pkg +780
Steering Wheel Pkg +540
Telephone Handset Kit +425
Wood Dash +1945
AM/FM Compact Disc Playr +245
Compact Disc Changer +445
Dual Power Seats +335
Heated Front Seats +185
Leather Seats +465
Limited Slip Diff[Opt on 2WD] +450
Onboard Computer +195
Rear Window Wiper +155

968 1995

Category J

Model Description	Trade-in Value	Market Value
2 Dr STD Cpe	19570	23580

OPTIONS FOR 968

Auto 4-Speed Transmission +1405
Compact Disc Changer +445
Compact Disc W/fm/tape +325
Heated Front Seats +185
Leather Seats +465
Limited Slip Diff +450
Power Drivers Seat +150
Power Passenger Seat +150

1994 PORSCHE

911 1994

Category J

Model Description	Trade-in Value	Market Value
2 Dr America Roadster Conv	30630	37355
2 Dr Cabriolet Conv	35765	43615
2 Dr Carrera Cpe	28875	35215
2 Dr Carrera Turbo Cpe	49865	60810
2 Dr RS America Cpe	23050	28110

Don't forget to refer to the Mileage Adjustment Table at the back of this book!

 © 1999 by Edmund Publications Corporation

Model Description	Trade-in Value	Market Value
2 Dr Speedster Conv	29710	36230
2 Dr Targa Cpe	29510	35985
2 Dr Wide Body Cpe	29910	36475

OPTIONS FOR 911
Auto 4-Speed Transmission +1170
5-Spoke 17-Inch Wheels +510
Boot Cover +960
Leather Headliner +505
Rootwood Dashboard +1615
Special Leather Console +715
Air Conditioning[Std on Cabriolet,Carrera,Targa,Wide Body] +1035
AM/FM Compact Disc Playr +200
Climate Control for AC[Opt on RS America, Speedster] +80
Compact Disc Changer +365
Cruise Control[Opt on Speedster] +175
Hardtop Roof +1045
Headlight Washers[Opt on Targa] +90
Heated Front Seats +155
Limited Slip Diff[Std on Turbo] +365
Onboard Computer[Std on Turbo] +160
Power Drivers Seat +120
Power Passenger Seat +120
Power Sunroof[Opt on RS America] +455
Rear Window Wiper[Std on Turbo] +125

968 — 1994

Category J

Model Description	Trade-in Value	Market Value
2 Dr Cabriolet Conv	19845	24200
2 Dr STD Cpe	16815	20505

OPTIONS FOR 968
Auto 4-Speed Transmission +1170
5-Spoke 17-Inch Wheels +510
Leather Boot Cover +960
Rootwood Package +895
Sport Chassis +750
AM/FM Compact Disc Playr +200
Compact Disc Changer +365
Heated Front Seats +155
Leather Seats +380
Limited Slip Diff +365
Power Drivers Seat +120
Power Passenger Seat +120
Premium Sound System +340

1993 PORSCHE

911 — 1993

Category J

Model Description	Trade-in Value	Market Value
2 Dr Cabriolet Conv	31100	38395
2 Dr Carrera Cpe	26620	32865
2 Dr RS America Cpe	24320	30025
2 Dr Targa Cpe	27935	34485

OPTIONS FOR 911
Auto 4-Speed Transmission +955
Air Conditioning[Std on Cabriolet Conv,Carrera 4WD Cpe] +845
AM/FM Compact Disc Playr +165
Climate Control for AC[Opt on RS America] +65
Compact Disc Changer +295
Dual Power Seats +225
Leather Seats[Opt on Cabriolet] +310
Limited Slip Diff +300
Power Sunroof[Std on Carrera] +370

968 — 1993

Category J

Model Description	Trade-in Value	Market Value
2 Dr STD Cpe	12350	15250

OPTIONS FOR 968
Auto 4-Speed Transmission +955
5-Spoke 17-Inch Wheels +420
968 Special Chassis +610
Leather Piping All Seats +440
Lthr Interior W/Blck Belt +1665
Lthr Interior W/Lthr Belt +1050
MetallicPaint To Sample +515
Painted Rims +325
Special Leather Upholstry +1180
Compact Disc Changer +295
Heated Front Seats +125
Leather Seats +310
Limited Slip Diff +300
Sport Seats +240

1992 PORSCHE

911 — 1992

Category J

Model Description	Trade-in Value	Market Value
2 Dr Cabriolet Conv	28540	36125
2 Dr Carrera Cpe	22245	28160
2 Dr STD Turbo Cpe	33470	42370
2 Dr Targa Cpe	23940	30305

OPTIONS FOR 911
Auto 4-Speed Transmission +770
Rear Window Washing Systm +190
Climate Control for AC[Opt on America Roadster] +55
Dual Power Seats[Std on STD] +180
Heated Front Seats +100
Leather Seats[Opt on America Roadster] +255
Onboard Computer[Std on STD] +105
Rear Window Wiper[Opt on Carrera] +85

968 — 1992

Category J

Model Description	Trade-in Value	Market Value
2 Dr Cabriolet Conv	15000	18990
2 Dr STD Cpe	11530	14595

OPTIONS FOR 968
Auto 4-Speed Transmission +770
AM/FM Compact Disc Playr +135

Don't forget to refer to the Mileage Adjustment Table at the back of this book!

 © 1999 by Edmund Publications Corporation

Model Description	Trade-in Value	Market Value

Compact Disc Changer +245
Heated Front Seats +100
Leather Seats +255
Limited Slip Diff +245
Power Drivers Seat +80
Power Passenger Seat +80

1991 PORSCHE

911 — 1991

Category J

Model Description	Trade-in Value	Market Value
2 Dr Carrera Cpe	20720	26910
2 Dr Carrera 4 4WD Cpe	21865	28395
2 Dr Carrera 4 Targa 4WD Cpe	22085	28680
2 Dr Carrera Cabrio Conv	23415	30410
2 Dr Carrera Targa Cpe	21725	28215
2 Dr STD Turbo Cpe	31160	40465

OPTIONS FOR 911

Auto 4-Speed Transmission +565
All Leather Interior +1925
Car Color Rims +195
Forged Alloy Wheels +320
Leather Boot Cover +450
Leather Headliner +205
Leather Instr Panel +270
AM/FM Compact Disc Playr +110
Leather Seats[Std on STD] +210
Limited Slip Diff +200
Onboard Computer +85
Power Drivers Seat[Std on STD] +65
Power Passenger Seat[Std on STD] +65

944 S2 — 1991

Category F

Model Description	Trade-in Value	Market Value
2 Dr Cabriolet Conv	13600	18130
2 Dr STD Cpe	10590	14120

OPTIONS FOR 944 S2

16-Inch Disc Wheels +400
Sport Chassis +395
AM/FM Compact Disc Playr +100
Dual Power Seats +170
Leather Seats +145
Limited Slip Diff +75
Premium Sound System +85

1990 PORSCHE

911 — 1990

Category J

Model Description	Trade-in Value	Market Value
2 Dr Carrera Cpe	19380	25835
2 Dr Carrera 4 4WD Cpe	20825	27765
2 Dr Carrera Cabrio Conv	22130	29510
2 Dr Carrera Targa Conv	19180	25575

OPTIONS FOR 911

Auto 4-Speed Transmission +460
Forged Alloy Wheels +255
Leather Boot Cover +365
Leather Headliner +170
Leather Instrument Panel +220
Supple Leather Seat Trim +480
AM/FM Compact Disc Playr +90
Heated Drivers Seat +45
Leather Seats +170
Limited Slip Diff +165
Power Drivers Seat +55
Power Passenger Seat +55

928 — 1990

Category J

Model Description	Trade-in Value	Market Value
2 Dr STD Cpe	15450	20600

OPTIONS FOR 928

All Leather Interior +905
Passenger Positrol Seats +160
AM/FM Compact Disc Playr +90

944 S2 — 1990

Category F

Model Description	Trade-in Value	Market Value
2 Dr Cabriolet Conv	12275	16370
2 Dr STD Cpe	9515	12685

OPTIONS FOR 944 S2

16-Inch Disc Wheels +315
Sport Chassis +325
AM/FM Compact Disc Playr +80
Heated Drivers Seat +40
Leather Seats +120
Limited Slip Diff +60
Power Drivers Seat +40
Power Passenger Seat +50
Premium Sound System +70

1989 PORSCHE

911 — 1989

Category J

Model Description	Trade-in Value	Market Value
2 Dr Cabriolet Conv	20365	27900
2 Dr Carrera 4WD Cpe	18650	25545
2 Dr STD Cpe	17320	23725
2 Dr Targa Cpe	17460	23920

OPTIONS FOR 911

Rootwood Instrument Panel +540
Special Edition Pkg +650
Air Conditioning[Opt on Speedster] +380
AM/FM Compact Disc Playr +75
Limited Slip Diff[Std on Turbo] +135

Don't forget to refer to the Mileage Adjustment Table at the back of this book!

 © 1999 by Edmund Publications Corporation

928S4 — 1989

Category J

Model Description	Trade-in Value	Market Value
2 Dr STD Cpe	12910	17685

OPTIONS FOR 928S4

Leather Headliner +215
Leather Instrument Panel +215
Paint Option +225
Rootwood Instrument Panel +705
AM/FM Compact Disc Playr +75
Heated Drivers Seat +35
Limited Slip Diff +135

944 — 1989

Category F

Model Description	Trade-in Value	Market Value
2 Dr S Cpe	6620	9195
2 Dr STD Cpe	6075	8435
2 Dr STD Turbo Cpe	9850	13680

OPTIONS FOR 944

Auto 3-Speed Transmission +145
16-Inch Cast Alloy Wheels +120
16-Inch Disc Wheels +325
Rear Turbo Spoiler +115
Sport Chassis +145
AM/FM Compact Disc Playr +65
Heated Front Seats +45
Leather Seats +95
Limited Slip Diff[Std on Turbo] +50
Power Drivers Seat +30
Power Passenger Seat +40
Premium Sound System[Std on Turbo] +55

A 15-minute phone call could save you 15% or more on car insurance.

1-800-555-2758

The Sensible Alternative

Get a great used car and apply for financing *online* at a price you must see to believe!

http://www.edmunds.com

Don't forget to refer to the Mileage Adjustment Table at the back of this book!

 © 1999 by Edmund Publications Corporation

Model Description	Trade-in Value	Market Value

SAAB Sweden

1997 Saab 900 Convertible

1998 SAAB

900 1998

The Saab 900 three-door hatchback gets the same turbocharged engine as the SE models this year. Other changes include the addition of body-color front and rear bumpers.

Category J

Model Description	Trade-in Value	Market Value
2 Dr S Conv	24585	28585
2 Dr S Turbo Hbk	19485	22655
4 Dr S Hbk	19790	23010
2 Dr SE Turbo Hbk	22095	25695
4 Dr SE Turbo Hbk	22775	26485

OPTIONS FOR 900

Auto 4-Speed Transmission +850
Leather Seats[Std on SE, Conv] +855
Power Moonroof[Opt on S] +760

9000 1998

No changes to the aging 9000.

Category J

Model Description	Trade-in Value	Market Value
4 Dr CSE Turbo Hbk	22850	26570

OPTIONS FOR 9000

Auto 4-Speed Transmission +870

1997 SAAB

900 1997

No significant changes for the 1997 Saab 900.

RATINGS (SCALE OF 1-10)

Overall	Safety	Reliability	Performance	Comfort	Value
7.5	7.1	8	8.6	7.9	5.7

Category J

Model Description	Trade-in Value	Market Value
2 Dr S Conv	21575	25085
2 Dr S Hbk	16885	19635
4 Dr S Hbk	16520	19210
2 Dr SE Turbo Conv	23170	26940
2 Dr SE Turbo Hbk	19890	23125
4 Dr SE Turbo Hbk	20065	23335
2 Dr SE Talladega Turbo Conv	23380	27185
2 Dr SE Talladega Turbo Hbk	20140	23420
4 Dr SE Talladega Turbo Hbk	20265	23565
2 Dr SE V6 Conv	24555	28555
4 Dr SE V6 Hbk	20750	24125

OPTIONS FOR 900

Auto 4-Speed Transmission[Std on SE V6] +685
Child Seats (2) +170
Leather Seats[Opt on S Hbk] +700
Power Moonroof[Opt on S] +620

9000 1997

No changes to this aging model.

RATINGS (SCALE OF 1-10)

Overall	Safety	Reliability	Performance	Comfort	Value
7.6	7.4	8.3	8.8	8.4	5.3

Category J

Model Description	Trade-in Value	Market Value
4 Dr Aero Turbo Hbk	24680	28700
4 Dr CS Turbo Hbk	18305	21285
4 Dr CSE Turbo Hbk	21535	25040
4 Dr CSE Anniversary Turbo Hbk	21900	25465

OPTIONS FOR 9000

Auto 4-Speed Transmission[Std on CSE V6] +710
Dual Power Seats[Opt on CS] +500
Leather Seats[Opt on CS] +700
Power Moonroof[Opt on CS] +620

1996 SAAB

900 1996

The popular Saab 900 SE five-door is available this year with the amazing turbocharged four-cylinder engine. All turbo models have an optional automatic transmission, and V6 models will be available only with an automatic. Adjustable driver lumbar support is now standard on all 900 models.

RATINGS (SCALE OF 1-10)

Overall	Safety	Reliability	Performance	Comfort	Value
7.3	7	7.5	8.6	7.9	5.4

Category J

Model Description	Trade-in Value	Market Value
2 Dr S Hbk	13355	15900
2 Dr S Conv	18420	21925
4 Dr S Hbk	13860	16500
2 Dr SE Turbo Hbk	16610	19770

Don't forget to refer to the Mileage Adjustment Table at the back of this book!

© 1999 by Edmund Publications Corporation

Model Description	Trade-in Value	Market Value
2 Dr SE Turbo Conv	20395	24275
4 Dr SE Turbo Hbk	16260	19360
2 Dr SE V6 Conv	21015	25020
4 Dr SE V6 Hbk	16525	19670

OPTIONS FOR 900

Auto 4-Speed Transmission[Opt on S,SE] +545
Child Seats (2) +140
Leather Seats[Std on SE,SE V6,Conv] +570
Power Moonroof[Opt on S] +510

9000 1996

The 9000 sedans are dropped, leaving only the hatchback bodystyle. Cupholders for rear seat passengers, new upholstery for the CS, and new three-spoke alloy wheels for the CS and CSE round out the major developments for this year's model.

RATINGS (SCALE OF 1-10)

Overall	Safety	Reliability	Performance	Comfort	Value
7.9	7.4	8	8.8	8.4	6.9

Category J

4 Dr Aero Turbo Hbk	19535	23255
4 Dr CS Turbo Hbk	14755	17565
4 Dr CSE Turbo Hbk	17235	20520

OPTIONS FOR 9000

Auto 4-Speed Transmission[Opt on CS,CSE] +570
Dual Power Seats[Opt on CS] +410
Leather Seats[Opt on CS] +570
Power Moonroof[Opt on CS] +510

1995 SAAB

900 1995

Daytime Running Lights (DRLs) are now standard on the 900.

RATINGS (SCALE OF 1-10)

Overall	Safety	Reliability	Performance	Comfort	Value
7.1	7.6	7	8.6	7.9	4.2

Category J

2 Dr S Conv	15160	18270
2 Dr S Hbk	11710	14105
4 Dr S Hbk	11450	13795
2 Dr SE Conv	16765	20200
2 Dr SE Turbo Conv	18095	21805
2 Dr SE Turbo Hbk	15390	18540
4 Dr SE Hbk	13785	16610

OPTIONS FOR 900

Auto 4-Speed Transmission +445
Aluminum/Alloy Wheels[Std on SE,Conv] +170
AM/FM Compact Disc Playr +245
Compact Disc Changer[Opt on Hbk] +445
Leather Seats[Std on SE,Conv] +465
Power Moonroof[Opt on S] +415

9000 1995

Saab adds a light-pressure turbo and a V6 to their large-car engine roster. V6 cars come only with an automatic transmission. Daytime running lights (DRLs) become standard on all 9000s this year.

RATINGS (SCALE OF 1-10)

Overall	Safety	Reliability	Performance	Comfort	Value
8	8.1	7.8	8.8	8.4	6.8

Category J

4 Dr Aero Turbo Hbk	17480	21060
4 Dr CDE Sdn	14655	17655
4 Dr CS Turbo Hbk	12795	15415
4 Dr CSE Hbk	14500	17465
4 Dr CSE Turbo Hbk	14860	17905

OPTIONS FOR 9000

Auto 4-Speed Transmission[Opt on Aero,CS,Turbo] +310
Leather Seats[Opt on CS] +465
Power Moonroof[Opt on CS] +415

1994 SAAB

900 1994

A totally new Saab is introduced with a little help from GM. The new 900 is available as two-door and four-door hatchbacks or a two-door convertible. The 900SE four-door features a V6 engine that was developed by GM for use in its Opels. Saab gets a new optional automatic transmission as well that offers three types of driving modes: sport, winter and economy. Saab's very cool black panel instrument cluster and dual airbags debut on this vehicle as well.

RATINGS (SCALE OF 1-10)

Overall	Safety	Reliability	Performance	Comfort	Value
6.9	7.6	6.9	8.6	7.9	3.6

Category J

2 Dr Commemorative Turbo Conv	15320	18680
2 Dr S Conv	12540	15290
2 Dr S Hbk	10050	12255
4 Dr S Hbk	9670	11795
2 Dr SE Turbo Hbk	13235	16140
4 Dr SE Hbk	11680	14245
2 Dr STD Turbo Conv	14965	18250

OPTIONS FOR 900

6 cyl 2.5 L Engine[Opt on S] +850
Auto 3-Speed Transmission +250
Auto 4-Speed Transmission +260
Aluminum/Alloy Wheels[Opt on S Hbk] +140
Child Seats (2) +95

Don't forget to refer to the Mileage Adjustment Table at the back of this book!

© 1999 by Edmund Publications Corporation

Model Description	Trade-in Value	Market Value

Compact Disc W/fm/tape[Opt on S] +265
Leather Seats[Opt on S] +380
Power Drivers Seat[Opt on S Hbk,SE Hbk] +120
Power Moonroof[Opt on S] +340
Power Passenger Seat[Opt on SE Hbk,S Hbk] +120
Power Sunroof +455
Traction Control System[Opt on S] +490

9000 — 1994

Dual airbags for the 9000! CS models get front and rear fog lights. Unfortunately, traction control is dropped for all models.

RATINGS (SCALE OF 1-10)

Overall	Safety	Reliability	Performance	Comfort	Value
7.7	8	7.2	8.8	8.4	6.2

Category J

Model Description	Trade-in Value	Market Value
4 Dr Aero Turbo Hbk	13495	16460
4 Dr CD Turbo Sdn	11920	14540
4 Dr CDE Sdn	12585	15350
4 Dr CDE Turbo Sdn	11920	14535
4 Dr CS Hbk	10430	12720
4 Dr CS Turbo Hbk	10995	13410
4 Dr CSE Hbk	11285	13765
4 Dr CSE Turbo Hbk	12060	14705

OPTIONS FOR 9000

Auto 4-Speed Transmission +305
Compact Disc W/fm/tape +265
Leather Seats[Opt on CD,CS] +380
Power Moonroof[Opt on CD] +340
Rear Spoiler[Opt on CSE] +140
Traction Control System +490

1993 SAAB

900 — 1993

Base 900 models replace the 900S. The equipment that was standard on the 900S is now part of a preferred equipment package. The convertible can now get a blue or tan top.

RATINGS (SCALE OF 1-10)

Overall	Safety	Reliability	Performance	Comfort	Value
N/A	N/A	7.3	8.4	7.5	4.2

Category D

Model Description	Trade-in Value	Market Value
2 Dr Commemorative Turbo Hbk	11040	14920
2 Dr S Hbk	6795	9185
2 Dr S Conv	10155	13720
4 Dr S Sdn	6735	9105
2 Dr S Luxury Hbk	7210	9745
4 Dr S Luxury Sdn	7180	9705
2 Dr STD Turbo Conv	10695	14455
2 Dr STD Turbo Hbk	10300	13920

OPTIONS FOR 900

Auto 3-Speed Transmission +210

9000 — 1993

New nomenclature reflects Saab's current identity crisis. Base models are now called the CS and CD; luxury models are called CSE and CDE. Hatchbacks get more sedan-like styling that increases their length by four inches. A new Aero hatchback enters the lineup. The Aero is the fastest vehicle in the large-car class. It is powered by a 225-horsepower version of the inline-four found in the other turbo models, and it offers exceptional handling.

RATINGS (SCALE OF 1-10)

Overall	Safety	Reliability	Performance	Comfort	Value
7.7	6.5	6.7	8.8	8.4	8.1

Category J

Model Description	Trade-in Value	Market Value
4 Dr Aero Turbo Hbk	10890	13445
4 Dr CD Sdn	8915	11010
4 Dr CD Turbo Sdn	7780	9600
4 Dr CDE Sdn	10055	12415
4 Dr CDE Turbo Sdn	9315	11500
4 Dr CS Hbk	8880	10960
4 Dr CS Turbo Hbk	9440	11655
4 Dr CSE Hbk	9605	11860
4 Dr CSE Turbo Hbk	10120	12495

OPTIONS FOR 9000

Auto 4-Speed Transmission[Std on CD Sdn] +245
Leather Seats[Opt on CD,CS] +310
Power Sunroof[Opt on CD,CS] +370

1992 SAAB

900 — 1992

Saab Turbo SPG is dropped from the 900 lineup. Base models gain power windows and power/heated outside mirrors. 900S models get new alloy wheels and convertibles get freshened exterior and interior styling. Turbo models get new wheels, tires and a compact disc player.

RATINGS (SCALE OF 1-10)

Overall	Safety	Reliability	Performance	Comfort	Value
N/A	N/A	7.1	8.4	7.5	3.6

Category D

Model Description	Trade-in Value	Market Value
2 Dr S Conv	8275	11335
2 Dr S Hbk	6015	8240
4 Dr S Sdn	6250	8560
2 Dr STD Hbk	5285	7240
2 Dr STD Turbo Hbk	8370	11470
2 Dr STD Turbo Conv	9520	13040
4 Dr STD Sdn	5565	7620

Don't forget to refer to the Mileage Adjustment Table at the back of this book!

 © 1999 by Edmund Publications Corporation

Model Description	Trade-in Value	Market Value

OPTIONS FOR 900

Auto 3-Speed Transmission +165
Auto 4-Speed Transmission +165

9000 1992

A limited-edition Griffin Edition is introduced as the *crème de la crème* 9000 for 1992. It is available only as a four-door turbo sedan. All turbo models get traction control for 1992. All Saab 9000s get a sunroof as well.

RATINGS (SCALE OF 1-10)

Overall	Safety	Reliability	Performance	Comfort	Value
7.4	6.6	6.9	8.8	8.4	6.6

Model Description	Trade-in Value	Market Value
Category D		
4 Dr CD Sdn	7000	9590
4 Dr CD Turbo Sdn	7425	10170
4 Dr S Hbk	6695	9175
4 Dr STD Hbk	6190	8480
4 Dr STD Turbo Hbk	7225	9900
Category J		
4 Dr CD Griffin Turbo Sdn	8235	10425

OPTIONS FOR 9000

Auto 4-Speed Transmission[Std on CD] +215
Rear Window Wiper +35

1991 SAAB

900 1991

The Turbo sedan is dropped from the 900 lineup.

RATINGS (SCALE OF 1-10)

Overall	Safety	Reliability	Performance	Comfort	Value
N/A	N/A	6.9	8.4	7.5	3.5

Model Description	Trade-in Value	Market Value
Category D		
2 Dr S Hbk	4815	6595
2 Dr S Conv	7355	10080
4 Dr S Sdn	4640	6355
2 Dr SE Turbo Conv	8630	11825
2 Dr SPG Turbo Hbk	6865	9405
2 Dr STD Hbk	4175	5715
2 Dr STD Turbo Hbk	6720	9205
2 Dr STD Turbo Conv	8425	11540
4 Dr STD Sdn	3960	5425

OPTIONS FOR 900

Auto 3-Speed Transmission +115

9000 1991

Turbo CD Sedan is introduced.

RATINGS (SCALE OF 1-10)

Overall	Safety	Reliability	Performance	Comfort	Value
7.5	6.7	6.9	8.8	8.4	6.9

Model Description	Trade-in Value	Market Value
Category D		
4 Dr CD Sdn	5355	7340
4 Dr CD Turbo Sdn	5850	8015
4 Dr S Hbk	5240	7175
4 Dr STD Hbk	4650	6365
4 Dr STD Turbo Hbk	5930	8120

OPTIONS FOR 9000

Auto 4-Speed Transmission[Std on CD] +150

1990 SAAB

900 1990

A driver airbag is added to the standard equipment list.

RATINGS (SCALE OF 1-10)

Overall	Safety	Reliability	Performance	Comfort	Value
N/A	N/A	6.9	8.4	7.5	3.4

Model Description	Trade-in Value	Market Value
Category D		
2 Dr S Hbk	3935	5395
4 Dr S Sdn	3860	5290
2 Dr SPG Turbo Hbk	5545	7595
2 Dr STD Hbk	3290	4510
2 Dr STD Turbo Conv	6830	9355
2 Dr STD Turbo Hbk	5185	7100
4 Dr STD Sdn	3195	4375
4 Dr STD Turbo Sdn	5380	7375

OPTIONS FOR 900

Auto 3-Speed Transmission +95

9000 1990

A new turbocharger is added to Turbo models, as is a direct injection fuel system.

RATINGS (SCALE OF 1-10)

Overall	Safety	Reliability	Performance	Comfort	Value
7.4	6.7	6.7	8.4	8.4	6.8

Model Description	Trade-in Value	Market Value
Category D		
4 Dr CD Turbo Sdn	4840	6630
4 Dr S Hbk	4050	5550
4 Dr S Sdn	4365	5980
4 Dr STD Turbo Hbk	4820	6600

OPTIONS FOR 9000

Auto 4-Speed Transmission +125
Leather Seats[Opt on S] +185
Power Sunroof[Opt on S Hbk] +120

For a guaranteed low price on a new car in your area, call

1-800-CAR-CLUB

Don't forget to refer to the Mileage Adjustment Table at the back of this book!

 © 1999 by Edmund Publications Corporation

Model Description	Trade-in Value	Market Value

1989 SAAB

900 — 1989

Saab Turbo four-door is resurrected. An SPG Package adds high performance options to the two-door Saab 900 Turbo. The 900's naturally aspirated engine gets a boost in horsepower.

RATINGS (SCALE OF 1-10)

Overall	Safety	Reliability	Performance	Comfort	Value
N/A	N/A	6.4	8.4	7.5	3.8

Category D

Model Description	Trade-in Value	Market Value
2 Dr S Hbk	2765	4010
4 Dr S Sdn	2795	4050
2 Dr STD Hbk	2690	3900
2 Dr STD Turbo Conv	5660	8205
2 Dr STD Turbo Hbk	3820	5535
4 Dr STD Sdn	2755	3990
4 Dr STD Turbo Sdn	3575	5185

OPTIONS FOR 900

Auto 3-Speed Transmission +70
Cruise Control[Std on S,SPG,Conv,Turbo] +35
Leather Seats[Std on Conv] +150
Power Drivers Seat +45

9000 — 1989

A traditional sedan is introduced as the new flagship for the 9000-Series. A giant trunk and slightly longer body distinguish it from the previous hatchbacks. Features unique to the CD sedan include standard fog lights, front spoiler and a slightly freshened front end. Base models get leather upholstery as an available option.

RATINGS (SCALE OF 1-10)

Overall	Safety	Reliability	Performance	Comfort	Value
7	6.1	6.1	8.4	8.4	6

Category D

Model Description	Trade-in Value	Market Value
4 Dr CD Turbo Sdn	3290	4765
4 Dr S Sdn	2990	4335
4 Dr S Hbk	2880	4175
4 Dr STD Turbo Hbk	3435	4975

OPTIONS FOR 9000

Auto 4-Speed Transmission +95
Air Bag Restraint +80
Leather Seats[Std on STD] +150

Edmund's

Get answers from our editors, scope out smart shopping strategies and share your experiences in our new talk area. Just enter the following address in your web browser:

http://townhall.edmunds.com

Don't forget to refer to the Mileage Adjustment Table at the back of this book!

© 1999 by Edmund Publications Corporation

SATURN USA

1997 Saturn SL2

1998 SATURN

SC 1998

Refinement is the name of the game for 1998. Improvements to the suspension, transmission and engine blocks are designed to smooth the ride, reduce noise, increase durability and provide slick shifts. Second-generation airbags deploy with less force than the old ones. A child seatbelt comfort guide has been added in the back seat, and SC1 models have a new wheel design. Dark Blue is the single new color.

Category E

Model Description	Trade-in Value	Market Value
2 Dr SC1 Cpe	9155	11165
2 Dr SC2 Cpe	9950	12135

OPTIONS FOR SC

Auto 4-Speed Transmission +715
Air Conditioning[Opt on SC1] +675
Aluminum/Alloy Wheels +265
AM/FM Compact Disc Playr +390
Anti-Lock Brakes +590
Cruise Control +185
Keyless Entry System +125
Leather Seats +740
Power Door Locks +195
Power Mirrors +95
Power Sunroof +500
Power Windows +220
Premium Sound System +285
Traction Control System +40

SL 1998

Minor trim modifications, reduced force airbags, and hardware improvements to stifle unwanted noise, vibration and harshness are on tap for 1998.

Category E

Model Description	Trade-in Value	Market Value
4 Dr SL1 Sdn	8475	10335
4 Dr SL2 Sdn	9270	11300
4 Dr STD Sdn	8280	10095

OPTIONS FOR SL

Auto 4-Speed Transmission +715
Air Conditioning[Std on SL2] +675
Aluminum/Alloy Wheels +265
AM/FM Compact Disc Playr +390
Anti-Lock Brakes +590
Cruise Control +185
Keyless Entry System +125
Leather Seats +740
Power Door Locks +195
Power Mirrors +95
Power Sunroof +500
Power Windows +220
Premium Sound System +285
Traction Control System +40

SW 1998

Fresh colors, revised fabrics, redesigned wheels, reduced force airbags and more attempts at turning the SW into a conveyance in which a conversation can be conducted at normal voice levels are new for 1998.

Category E

Model Description	Trade-in Value	Market Value
4 Dr SW2 Wgn	10240	12490

OPTIONS FOR SW

Auto 4-Speed Transmission +715
Air Conditioning[Opt on SW1] +675
Aluminum/Alloy Wheels +265
AM/FM Compact Disc Playr +390
Anti-Lock Brakes +590
Cruise Control +185
Keyless Entry System +125
Leather Seats +740
Power Door Locks +195
Power Mirrors +95
Power Windows +220
Premium Sound System +285
Traction Control System +40

1997 SATURN

SC 1997

Saturn restyles its sport coupe, moving it to the SL/SW platform in the process. The result is a larger, roomier and heavier car. Dashboard is carried over, but interior trim is new. Newly optional is an in-dash CD player. More steps are taken to reduce noise, vibration and harshness.

RATINGS (SCALE OF 1-10)

Overall	Safety	Reliability	Performance	Comfort	Value
N/A	N/A	8.7	7.8	7	7.9

Don't forget to refer to the Mileage Adjustment Table at the back of this book!

 © 1999 by Edmund Publications Corporation

Model Description	Trade-in Value	Market Value
Category E		
2 Dr SC1 Cpe	8400	10500
2 Dr SC2 Cpe	8720	10900

OPTIONS FOR SC

Auto 4-Speed Transmission +535
Air Conditioning +550
Aluminum/Alloy Wheels +215
AM/FM Compact Disc Playr +320
Anti-Lock Brakes +480
Cruise Control +150
Leather Seats +605
Power Door Locks +160
Power Sunroof +410
Power Windows +180
Premium Sound System +230
Rear Spoiler[Opt on SC1] +140

SL 1997

Once again, Saturn attempts to quell noise, vibration, and harshness (NVH) with improved engine mounts, revised torque struts, thicker dash mat, and non-asbestos organic front brake pads. Other changes are limited to new colors, an optional in-dash CD player, a panic mode for the security system, and a low-fuel indicator.

RATINGS (SCALE OF 1-10)

Overall	Safety	Reliability	Performance	Comfort	Value
7.9	6.8	8.7	8.3	7.4	8.2

Model Description	Trade-in Value	Market Value
Category E		
4 Dr SL1 Sdn	7570	9465
4 Dr SL2 Sdn	8010	10010
4 Dr STD Sdn	7410	9260

OPTIONS FOR SL

Auto 4-Speed Transmission +560
Air Conditioning +550
Aluminum/Alloy Wheels +215
AM/FM Compact Disc Playr +320
Anti-Lock Brakes +480
Cruise Control +150
Keyless Entry System +100
Leather Seats +605
Power Door Locks +160
Power Sunroof +410
Power Windows +180
Premium Sound System +230
Traction Control System +35

SW 1997

Once again, Saturn attempts to quell noise, vibration, and harshness (NVH) with improved engine mounts, revised torque struts, thicker dash mat, and non-asbestos organic front brake pads. Other changes are limited to a new color, an optional in-dash CD player, a panic mode for the security system, and a low-fuel indicator.

RATINGS (SCALE OF 1-10)

Overall	Safety	Reliability	Performance	Comfort	Value
7.9	6.6	8.7	8.2	7.5	8.4

Model Description	Trade-in Value	Market Value
Category E		
4 Dr SW1 Wgn	8380	10475
4 Dr SW2 Wgn	8480	10600

OPTIONS FOR SW

Auto 4-Speed Transmission +560
Air Conditioning +550
Aluminum/Alloy Wheels +215
AM/FM Compact Disc Playr +320
Anti-Lock Brakes +480
Cruise Control +150
Keyless Entry System +100
Leather Seats +605
Power Door Locks +160
Power Windows +180
Premium Sound System +230

1996 SATURN

SC 1996

Coupe carries over in anticipation of all-new styling to arrive for 1997. Traction control can now be ordered with the manual transmission and antilock brake system.

RATINGS (SCALE OF 1-10)

Overall	Safety	Reliability	Performance	Comfort	Value
7.7	6.6	8.5	8.5	7.1	7.6

Model Description	Trade-in Value	Market Value
Category E		
2 Dr SC1 Cpe	6595	8795
2 Dr SC2 Cpe	7060	9415

OPTIONS FOR SC

Auto 4-Speed Transmission +430
Air Conditioning +450
Aluminum/Alloy Wheels +175
AM/FM Stereo Tape +170
Anti-Lock Brakes +395
Compact Disc Changer +310
Cruise Control +120
Keyless Entry System +80
Leather Seats +495
Power Door Locks +130
Power Sunroof +335
Power Windows +145
Premium Sound System +190
Traction Control System +30

SL 1996

New bodywork and interior improvements make the SL an excellent value in the compact sedan class. SL's meet 1997 side-impact standards for the first time. A five-speed and traction control are no longer mutually exclusive items. The back seat is actually livable this

Don't forget to refer to the Mileage Adjustment Table at the back of this book!

 © 1999 by Edmund Publications Corporation

year. Daytime running lights are standard, and rain water won't leak all over your stuff anymore when you open the trunk.

RATINGS (SCALE OF 1-10)

Overall	Safety	Reliability	Performance	Comfort	Value
7.8	6.8	8.5	8.3	7.4	7.8

Category E

Model	Trade-in Value	Market Value
4 Dr SL1 Sdn	6280	8375
4 Dr SL2 Sdn	6650	8865
4 Dr STD Sdn	6105	8140

OPTIONS FOR SL

Auto 4-Speed Transmission +430
Air Conditioning +450
Aluminum/Alloy Wheels +175
AM/FM Compact Disc Playr +260
Anti-Lock Brakes +395
Cruise Control +120
Keyless Entry System +80
Leather Seats +495
Power Door Locks +130
Power Sunroof +335
Power Windows +145
Premium Sound System +190
Traction Control System +30

SW 1996

Sporty wagon gets more conventional, but more attractive, plastic panels for 1996. Wagon meets 1997 side-impact standards this year, and five-speed models can be equipped with traction control. The rear seat is more comfortable, and head room is improved. Daytime running lights debut. Avoid new purple color, unless you want the kids calling your car the Barneymobile in front of friends and relatives.

RATINGS (SCALE OF 1-10)

Overall	Safety	Reliability	Performance	Comfort	Value
7.8	6.6	8.5	8.2	7.5	8.1

Category E

Model	Trade-in Value	Market Value
4 Dr SW1 Wgn	7135	9515
4 Dr SW2 Wgn	7410	9880

OPTIONS FOR SW

Auto 4-Speed Transmission +430
Air Conditioning +450
Aluminum/Alloy Wheels +175
AM/FM Stereo Tape +170
Anti-Lock Brakes +395
Cruise Control +120
Keyless Entry System +80
Leather Seats +495
Power Door Locks +130
Power Windows +145
Premium Sound System +190
Traction Control System +30

1995 SATURN

SC 1995

Dashboard is redesigned and now contains two airbags. Base engine is rated at 100 horsepower, up 15 from last year. With the automatic transmission, traction control is included with optional ABS. Styling is cleaned up front and rear. Manual three-point front seatbelts replace automatic type. SC1 gets new bucket seats.

RATINGS (SCALE OF 1-10)

Overall	Safety	Reliability	Performance	Comfort	Value
7.6	7.2	7.9	8.5	7.1	7.5

Category E

Model	Trade-in Value	Market Value
2 Dr SC1 Cpe	5965	8170
2 Dr SC2 Cpe	6140	8410

OPTIONS FOR SC

Auto 4-Speed Transmission +365
Air Conditioning +370
Aluminum/Alloy Wheels +145
AM/FM Stereo Tape +140
Anti-Lock Brakes +320
Cruise Control +100
Keyless Entry System +65
Leather Seats +405
Power Door Locks +105
Power Sunroof +275
Power Windows +120
Premium Sound System +155

SL 1995

Dashboard is redesigned and now contains two airbags. Base engine is rated at 100 horsepower, up 15 from last year. With the automatic transmission, traction control is included with optional ABS. Styling is cleaned up front and rear. Manual three-point front seatbelts replace automatic type.

RATINGS (SCALE OF 1-10)

Overall	Safety	Reliability	Performance	Comfort	Value
7.8	7.3	8.2	8.3	7.5	7.8

Category E

Model	Trade-in Value	Market Value
4 Dr SL1 Sdn	5320	7285
4 Dr SL2 Sdn	5815	7965
4 Dr STD Sdn	5145	7050

OPTIONS FOR SL

Auto 4-Speed Transmission +365
Air Conditioning +370
Aluminum/Alloy Wheels +145
AM/FM Stereo Tape +140
Anti-Lock Brakes +320
Compact Disc Changer +255
Cruise Control +100
Leather Seats +405

Don't forget to refer to the Mileage Adjustment Table at the back of this book!

 © 1999 by Edmund Publications Corporation

Model Description	Trade-in Value	Market Value

Power Door Locks +105
Power Mirrors +50
Power Sunroof +275
Power Windows +120
Premium Sound System +155

SW 1995

Dashboard is redesigned and now contains two airbags. Base engine is rated at 100 horsepower, up 15 from last year. With the automatic transmission, traction control is included with optional ABS. Styling is cleaned up front and rear. Manual three-point front seatbelts replace automatic type.

RATINGS (SCALE OF 1-10)

Overall	Safety	Reliability	Performance	Comfort	Value
7.9	7.3	8.2	8.2	7.5	8

Category E

	Trade-in Value	Market Value
4 Dr SW1 Wgn	5985	8200
4 Dr SW2 Wgn	6120	8385

OPTIONS FOR SW

Auto 4-Speed Transmission +365
Air Conditioning +370
Aluminum/Alloy Wheels +145
AM/FM Stereo Tape +140
Anti-Lock Brakes +320
Cruise Control +100
Leather Seats +405
Power Door Locks +105
Power Windows +120
Premium Sound System +155

1994 SATURN

SC 1994

CFC-free refrigerant is added to air conditioning system. Automatic transmission's "Performance" mode is recalibrated to give smoother shifts. New central unlocking feature on power door locks allows all doors to be unlocked with a twist of the key. New alloy wheels are optional on SC1.

RATINGS (SCALE OF 1-10)

Overall	Safety	Reliability	Performance	Comfort	Value
7.2	5.5	7.9	8.3	7.3	6.9

Category E

	Trade-in Value	Market Value
2 Dr SC1 Cpe	4840	6910
2 Dr SC2 Cpe	5140	7345

OPTIONS FOR SC

Auto 4-Speed Transmission +295
Air Conditioning +300
Aluminum/Alloy Wheels +120
AM/FM Compact Disc Playr +175
Anti-Lock Brakes +265
Cruise Control +80
Leather Seats +330
Power Door Locks +85
Power Sunroof +225
Power Windows +100
Premium Sound System +125

SL 1994

CFC-free refrigerant is added to air conditioning system. Automatic transmission's "Performance" mode is recalibrated to give smoother shifts. New central unlocking feature on power door locks allows all doors to be unlocked with a twist of the key. New alloy wheels are optional on SL2.

RATINGS (SCALE OF 1-10)

Overall	Safety	Reliability	Performance	Comfort	Value
7.3	5.5	8.1	8.1	7.6	7.3

Category E

	Trade-in Value	Market Value
4 Dr SL1 Sdn	4325	6180
4 Dr SL2 Sdn	4735	6765
4 Dr STD Sdn	4320	6170

OPTIONS FOR SL

Auto 4-Speed Transmission +295
Air Conditioning +300
Aluminum/Alloy Wheels +120
AM/FM Compact Disc Playr +175
Anti-Lock Brakes +265
Cruise Control +80
Leather Seats +330
Power Door Locks +85
Power Steering[Opt on STD] +95
Power Sunroof +225
Power Windows +100
Premium Sound System +125

SW 1994

CFC-free refrigerant is added to air conditioning system. Automatic transmission's "Performance" mode is recalibrated to give smoother shifts. New central unlocking feature on power door locks allows all doors to be unlocked with a twist of the key. New alloy wheels are optional on SW2.

RATINGS (SCALE OF 1-10)

Overall	Safety	Reliability	Performance	Comfort	Value
7.3	5.5	8.1	7.9	7.6	7.5

Category E

	Trade-in Value	Market Value
4 Dr SW1 Wgn	4985	7120
4 Dr SW2 Wgn	5095	7280

OPTIONS FOR SW

Auto 4-Speed Transmission +295
Air Conditioning +300
Aluminum/Alloy Wheels +120
AM/FM Compact Disc Playr +175
AM/FM Stereo Tape +115

Don't forget to refer to the Mileage Adjustment Table at the back of this book!

 © 1999 by Edmund Publications Corporation

Anti-Lock Brakes +265
Cruise Control +80
Leather Seats +330
Power Door Locks +85
Power Windows +100
Premium Sound System +125

1993 SATURN

SC 1993

Driver airbag added. Cars with ABS and automatic transmission can be ordered with traction control. SC coupe equipped with same 85-horsepower 1.9-liter engine as in SL.

RATINGS (SCALE OF 1-10)

Overall	Safety	Reliability	Performance	Comfort	Value
7.1	5.3	7.7	8.3	7.3	6.8

Category E

Model	Trade-in	Market
2 Dr SC1 Cpe	4045	6040
2 Dr SC2 Cpe	4250	6345

OPTIONS FOR SC

Auto 4-Speed Transmission +225
Air Conditioning +245
Aluminum/Alloy Wheels[Opt on SC1] +95
AM/FM Compact Disc Playr +145
AM/FM Stereo Tape +95
Anti-Lock Brakes +215
Cruise Control +65
Leather Seats +270
Power Door Locks +70
Power Sunroof +185
Power Windows +80
Premium Sound System +105

SL 1993

Driver airbag added. SL2 gets new front fascia and optional fog lights. Cars with ABS and automatic transmission can be ordered with traction control. SL2 suspension provides softer ride.

RATINGS (SCALE OF 1-10)

Overall	Safety	Reliability	Performance	Comfort	Value
7.2	5.3	7.7	8.1	7.6	7.2

Category E

Model	Trade-in	Market
4 Dr SL1 Sdn	3690	5505
4 Dr SL2 Sdn	3900	5820
4 Dr STD Sdn	3440	5135

OPTIONS FOR SL

Auto 4-Speed Transmission +225
Air Conditioning +245
Aluminum/Alloy Wheels[Opt on SL1] +95
AM/FM Compact Disc Playr +145
Anti-Lock Brakes +215
Cruise Control +65
Leather Seats +270
Power Door Locks +70
Power Moonroof +175
Power Sunroof +185
Power Windows +80
Premium Sound System +105

SW 1993

Driver airbag added, and is standard on SW. Cars with ABS and automatic transmission can be ordered with traction control. New station wagon model comes in SW1 and SW2 trim, and rear wiper/washer and defogger are standard. SW1 equipped with same 85-horsepower 1.9-liter engine as in SL. SW2 gets twin-cam 124-horsepower engine and SL2's sport suspension.

RATINGS (SCALE OF 1-10)

Overall	Safety	Reliability	Performance	Comfort	Value
7.2	5.3	7.7	7.9	7.6	7.4

Category E

Model	Trade-in	Market
4 Dr SW1 Wgn	4030	6015
4 Dr SW2 Wgn	4315	6440

OPTIONS FOR SW

Auto 4-Speed Transmission +225
Air Conditioning +245
Aluminum/Alloy Wheels +95
AM/FM Compact Disc Playr +145
Anti-Lock Brakes +215
Cruise Control +65
Power Door Locks +70
Power Windows +80
Premium Sound System +105

1992 SATURN

SC 1992

New engine and transmission mounting system supposedly cuts down on noise and vibration. Passenger compartment gets added acoustic insulation. Alloy wheels are redesigned.

RATINGS (SCALE OF 1-10)

Overall	Safety	Reliability	Performance	Comfort	Value
6.6	4.4	7.6	8.6	7.3	5.3

Category E

Model	Trade-in	Market
2 Dr SC2 Cpe	3325	5190

OPTIONS FOR SC

Auto 4-Speed Transmission +215
Air Bag Restraint +145
Air Conditioning +200
AM/FM Compact Disc Playr +115
Anti-Lock Brakes +175
Cruise Control +55
Leather Seats +220
Power Door Locks +55

Don't forget to refer to the Mileage Adjustment Table at the back of this book!

 © 1999 by Edmund Publications Corporation

Model Description	Trade-in Value	Market Value

Power Sunroof +150
Power Windows +65
Premium Sound System +85

SL 1992

New engine and transmission mounting system supposedly cuts down on noise and vibration. Passenger compartment gets added acoustic insulation. Leather and a rear deck spoiler are new for SL2 models. Alloy wheels are redesigned.

RATINGS (SCALE OF 1-10)

Overall	Safety	Reliability	Performance	Comfort	Value
6.8	4.5	8.1	8.1	7.6	5.6

Category E

Model Description	Trade-in Value	Market Value
4 Dr SL1 Sdn	2935	4585
4 Dr SL2 Sdn	2945	4605
4 Dr STD Sdn	2710	4235

OPTIONS FOR SL

Auto 4-Speed Transmission +175
Air Bag Restraint +145
Air Conditioning +200
AM/FM Compact Disc Playr +115
Anti-Lock Brakes +175
Cruise Control +55
Leather Seats +220
Power Door Locks +55
Power Sunroof +150
Power Windows +65
Premium Sound System +85

1991 SATURN

SC 1991

Saturn coupe comes with a dual overhead cam engine, sport-tuned suspension, alloy wheels, and speed rated tires. All body panels except hood, roof and trunk lid are made of plastic composite materials on all models, and ABS is optional.

RATINGS (SCALE OF 1-10)

Overall	Safety	Reliability	Performance	Comfort	Value
6.5	3.5	8	8.6	7.3	5.2

A 15-minute phone call could save you 15% or more on car insurance.
1-800-555-2758
GEICO DIRECT

Category E

Model Description	Trade-in Value	Market Value
2 Dr SC2 Cpe	2690	4560

OPTIONS FOR SC

Auto 4-Speed Transmission +140
Air Conditioning +165
AM/FM Compact Disc Playr +95
Anti-Lock Brakes +145
Cruise Control +45
Power Door Locks +45
Power Sunroof +120
Power Windows +55
Premium Sound System +70

SL 1991

Featuring an underpowered 1.9-liter engine and uninspired ergonomics, first Saturn sedan isn't all it's cracked up to be. The SL is very basic, with manual steering and transmission. Variable-effort steering, adjustable steering column, tachometer, and remote fuel door and trunk lid releases are standard on SL1. SL2 adds more powerful engine, sport-tuned suspension, alloy wheels, body-color bumpers, and speed-rated tires. All body panels except hood, roof and trunk lid are made of plastic composite materials on all models, and ABS is optional.

RATINGS (SCALE OF 1-10)

Overall	Safety	Reliability	Performance	Comfort	Value
6.6	3.6	8.4	8.1	7.6	5.5

Category E

Model Description	Trade-in Value	Market Value
4 Dr SL1 Sdn	2450	4155
4 Dr SL2 Sdn	2515	4265
4 Dr STD Sdn	2025	3430

OPTIONS FOR SL

Auto 4-Speed Transmission +140
Air Conditioning +165
AM/FM Compact Disc Playr +95
AM/FM Stereo Tape +60
Anti-Lock Brakes +145
Cruise Control +45
Power Door Locks +45
Power Sunroof +120
Power Windows +55
Premium Sound System +70

Get a great used car and apply for financing *online* at a price you must see to believe !
http://edmunds.com

Don't forget to refer to the Mileage Adjustment Table at the back of this book!

 © 1999 by Edmund Publications Corporation

SUBARU — Japan

1994 Subaru Justy

1998 SUBARU

FORESTER — 1998

Subaru attacks the mini-SUV market head-on with the Forester, which actually constitutes an SUV body on an Impreza platform with a Legacy engine under the hood. The most car-like of the mini-utes, Forester is also the most powerful. Airbags remain the full power variety, despite new rules allowing lower deployment speeds.

Category G

Model Description	Trade-in Value	Market Value
4 Dr L 4WD Wgn	14890	17725
4 Dr S 4WD Wgn	16800	20000
4 Dr STD 4WD Wgn	14320	17050

OPTIONS FOR FORESTER

Auto 4-Speed Transmission +655
Aluminum/Alloy Wheels[Std on S] +285
AM/FM Compact Disc Playr +320
Cruise Control[Std on S] +175
Heated Front Seats +210
Heated Power Mirrors +50
Keyless Entry System +170
Leather Seats +640

IMPREZA — 1998

Impreza gets a new dashboard and revised door panels. The entry-level Brighton coupe is dropped, and the high-end 2.5RS coupe is added. No depowered airbags here.

Category E

Model Description	Trade-in Value	Market Value
2 Dr L 4WD Cpe	12345	14875
4 Dr L 4WD Sdn	11420	13760
4 Dr L 4WD Wgn	11095	13365
4 Dr Outback Sport 4WD Wgn	12555	15130
2 Dr RS 4WD Cpe	14830	17865

OPTIONS FOR IMPREZA

Auto 4-Speed Transmission +665
Aluminum/Alloy Wheels[Std on RS] +265
AM/FM Compact Disc Playr +390
Cruise Control +185
Fog Lights[Std on RS] +125
Keyless Entry System +125

LEGACY — 1998

Prices remain stable while equipment is shuffled and the LSi model is dropped. All Legacy sedans and wagons except the Outback sport the grille and multi-reflector halogen lights found on the 2.5GT. A new Limited model joins the 2.5GT lineup, and a dual power moonroof package is available for the Outback Limited wagon. Outbacks get new alloy wheels, an overhead console and longer splash guards, while mid-year Outback Limiteds with revised trim and added content were dubbed 30th Anniversary models. The cold weather package has heated windshield wiper nozzles this year instead of an engine block heater. The Brighton wagon's stereo loses half its wattage, Limited models have a standard CD player and the base Outback comes with a Weatherband radio. Full power airbags continue, despite new government rules allowing automakers to install reduced force bags to better protect small adults.

Category D

Model Description	Trade-in Value	Market Value
4 Dr Brighton 4WD Wgn	11635	13850
4 Dr GT 4WD Sdn	16035	19090
4 Dr GT 4WD Wgn	15630	18610
4 Dr GT Limited 4WD Sdn	17180	20450
4 Dr L 4WD Wgn	14200	16905
4 Dr L 4WD Sdn	13000	15480
4 Dr Outback 4WD Wgn	15990	19035
4 Dr Outback Limited 4WD Wgn	16520	19665

OPTIONS FOR LEGACY

Auto 4-Speed Transmission[Std on GT Limited] +665
Aluminum/Alloy Wheels[Opt on Brighton, L] +375
AM/FM Compact Disc Playr[Std on Limited] +465
Cruise Control[Opt on Brighton] +200
Dual Sunroof[Opt on Outback Limited] +995
Fog Lights[Opt on Brighton, L] +175
Heated Front Seats[Opt on Outback] +305
Heated Power Mirrors[Opt on Outback] +75
Keyless Entry System +250
Leather Seats[Opt on GT, Outback] +915

1997 SUBARU

IMPREZA — 1997

Imprezas receive a facelifted front end that includes a Hemi-sized hood scoop. A new Outback Sport Wagon debuts, with nearly six-inches of additional ground clearance, fog lights, and a slightly raised roof. LX model

Don't forget to refer to the Mileage Adjustment Table at the back of this book!

 © 1999 by Edmund Publications Corporation

Model Description	Trade-in Value	Market Value

disappears, which means only the Outback is equipped with ABS. Power and torque for both Impreza engines is up for 1997, and some new colors are available. HVAC controls are revised.

RATINGS (SCALE OF 1-10)

Overall	Safety	Reliability	Performance	Comfort	Value
7.6	6.8	9.1	7.8	7.4	6.8

Category E		
2 Dr Brighton 4WD Cpe	8965	10930
2 Dr L 4WD Cpe	10175	12410
4 Dr L 4WD Wgn	9835	11990
4 Dr L 4WD Sdn	9920	12100
4 Dr Outback Sport 4WD Wgn	11240	13710

OPTIONS FOR IMPREZA

4 cyl 2.2 L Engine[Opt on Brighton] +135
Auto 4-Speed Transmission +545
Aluminum/Alloy Wheels +215
AM/FM Compact Disc Playr +320
Compact Disc Changer +380
Cruise Control +150
Fog Lights[Std on L 4WD Cpe] +105
Keyless Entry System +100
Luggage Rack[Opt on L] +90
Rear Spoiler[Opt on Brighton,Sdn] +140

LEGACY 1997

Front-wheel drive models are given the ax as Subaru returns to its all-wheel drive roots. Power and torque are up marginally with the base 2.2-liter engine. All Outback models are now powered by a similarly stronger 2.5-liter motor, which is newly available with a manual transmission. L models gain cruise control, anti-lock brakes, and power door locks as standard equipment. GT's get a manual transmission, larger tires, and revised styling. The Outback lineup is expanded with the introduction of a Limited model, which includes a leather interior, new alloy wheels, fresh exterior colors, and woodgrain interior trim.

RATINGS (SCALE OF 1-10)

Overall	Safety	Reliability	Performance	Comfort	Value
7.8	7.5	8.8	7.6	7.5	7.5

Category D		
4 Dr Brighton 4WD Wgn	10080	12145
4 Dr GT 4WD Wgn	13725	16540
4 Dr GT 4WD Sdn	13885	16725
4 Dr L 4WD Wgn	12445	14995
4 Dr L 4WD Sdn	11405	13740
4 Dr LSi 4WD Wgn	14705	17715
4 Dr LSi 4WD Sdn	14925	17985
4 Dr Outback 4WD Wgn	14045	16920
4 Dr Outback Limited 4WD Wgn	14310	17240

OPTIONS FOR LEGACY

Auto 4-Speed Transmission[Std on LSi] +540
Alarm System[Std on LSi] +380
Aluminum/Alloy Wheels[Opt on Brighton,L] +305
AM/FM Compact Disc Playr +380
Compact Disc Changer[Std on LSi] +655
Compact Disc W/fm/tape +450
Cruise Control[Opt on Brighton] +165
Heated Front Seats[Opt on Outback] +250
Keyless Entry System +205
Leather Seats[Opt on GT,Outback] +750
Luggage Rack[Opt on Brighton,L,LSi] +185

1996 SUBARU

IMPREZA 1996

The formerly optional 2.2-liter engine is standard across the board, except in the new budget-minded Brighton AWD Coupe. A new grille accompanies the bigger engine, and a five-speed is available as well.

RATINGS (SCALE OF 1-10)

Overall	Safety	Reliability	Performance	Comfort	Value
7.6	6.6	9.1	7.8	7.4	7.2

Category E		
2 Dr Brighton 4WD Cpe	7290	9225
2 Dr L 4WD Cpe	8275	10475
4 Dr L 4WD Sdn	8165	10335
4 Dr L 4WD Wgn	8540	10810
2 Dr LX 4WD Cpe	9290	11760
4 Dr LX 4WD Wgn	9780	12380
4 Dr LX 4WD Sdn	9355	11845
4 Dr Outback 4WD Wgn	9945	12590

OPTIONS FOR IMPREZA

Auto 4-Speed Transmission[Opt on L,Outback,Cpe] +435
Aluminum/Alloy Wheels[Std on LX 4WD Cpe] +175
AM/FM Compact Disc Playr +260
Anti-Lock Brakes[Opt on L] +395
Compact Disc Changer +310
Cruise Control +120
Luggage Rack[Opt on L,LX] +70

LEGACY 1996

A new sport model debuts, with a larger, more powerful engine. The 2.5GT is available in sedan or wagon format. The luxury-oriented LSi model also gets the new motor. A knobby-tired, raised-roof Outback wagon appears, offering 7.3 inches of ground clearance and an optional 2.5-liter engine. Designed specifically for American consumers, the Outback provides a car-like ride with light-duty off-road ability.

RATINGS (SCALE OF 1-10)

Overall	Safety	Reliability	Performance	Comfort	Value
7.7	7.5	8.6	7.4	7.5	7.4

Don't forget to refer to the Mileage Adjustment Table at the back of this book!

 © 1999 by Edmund Publications Corporation

SUBARU 96-95

Model Description	Trade-in Value	Market Value
Category D		
4 Dr Brighton 4WD Wgn	8500	10620
4 Dr GT 4WD Wgn	12340	15420
4 Dr GT 4WD Sdn	12295	15370
4 Dr L 4WD Sdn	9370	11710
4 Dr L 4WD Wgn	9405	11760
4 Dr LS 4WD Wgn	11760	14705
4 Dr LS 4WD Sdn	11680	14605
4 Dr LSi 4WD Sdn	13080	16350
4 Dr LSi 4WD Wgn	13090	16365
4 Dr Outback 4WD Wgn	12370	15465

OPTIONS FOR LEGACY

4 cyl 2.5 L DOHC Engine[Std on GT,LSi] +105
Auto 4-Speed Transmission[Std on GT,LS,LSi] +415
Aluminum/Alloy Wheels[Opt on L] +250
Anti-Lock Brakes[Opt on L] +530
Compact Disc W/fm/tape +535
Cruise Control[Opt on Brighton,L] +135
Heated Front Seats +205
Keyless Entry System +170
Luggage Rack[Opt on Brighton] +150

SVX 1996

Umm ... the L model gets standard solar-reduction glass this year. Whoopee.

Model Description	Trade-in Value	Market Value
Category F		
2 Dr L 4WD Cpe	12265	15140
2 Dr LSi 4WD Cpe	15025	18550

OPTIONS FOR SVX

AM/FM Compact Disc Playr +275

1995 SUBARU

IMPREZA 1995

An Impreza coupe and an Outback Wagon are added to Subaru's subcompact line of cars in an attempt to broaden their appeal with sporting and outdoor enthusiasts. Top-of-the-line LX model is introduced, replacing the LS trim-level, with an available 2.2-liter engine taken from the Legacy. Unfortunately it is available only with an automatic transmission.

RATINGS (SCALE OF 1-10)

Overall	Safety	Reliability	Performance	Comfort	Value
7.7	7.3	9	7.8	7.4	7.1

Model Description	Trade-in Value	Market Value
Category E		
2 Dr L 4WD Cpe	6320	8205
4 Dr L 4WD Wgn	7225	9380
4 Dr L 4WD Sdn	7050	9155
4 Dr L Special Edit. 4WD Sdn	7095	9215
4 Dr L Special Edit. 4WD Wgn	7270	9440
2 Dr LX 4WD Cpe	7610	9885
4 Dr LX 4WD Wgn	8015	10410
4 Dr LX 4WD Sdn	8050	10455
4 Dr Outback 4WD Wgn	8165	10605
4 Dr Outback Spec. Ed. 4WD Wgn	8275	10745

OPTIONS FOR IMPREZA

4 cyl 2.2 L Engine[Std on LX] +430
Auto 4-Speed Transmission[Std on L Spec. Edition,LX,L Special Edit. 4WD Sdn] +355
4-WD Active Safety Group +805
Air Conditioning[Opt on STD,L 4WD Cpe] +370
Aluminum/Alloy Wheels[Std on LX 4WD Sdn] +145
AM/FM Compact Disc Playr +215
Anti-Lock Brakes[Opt on L] +320
Cruise Control +100
Luggage Rack[Opt on L,L Special Edit.,LX] +60

LEGACY 1995

New sheetmetal freshens the flanks of one of our favorite compact sedans and wagons. Unfortunately the turbocharged engine has been dropped, leaving the Legacy with a rather anemic 2.2-liter four-cylinder that produces a meager 135 horsepower. The "value leader" Brighton wagon is introduced for budding naturalists. It includes all-wheel drive, air conditioning and a stereo with cassette. The Outback Wagon is also introduced as an alternative to the burgeoning SUV market.

RATINGS (SCALE OF 1-10)

Overall	Safety	Reliability	Performance	Comfort	Value
7.6	7.7	8.5	7.4	7.5	6.9

Model Description	Trade-in Value	Market Value
Category D		
4 Dr Brighton 4WD Wgn	7820	9895
4 Dr L Sdn	7775	9840
4 Dr L 4WD Sdn	8570	10850
4 Dr L 4WD Wgn	8395	10630
4 Dr LS 4WD Sdn	10165	12870
4 Dr LS 4WD Wgn	10305	13040
4 Dr LSi 4WD Wgn	10505	13300
4 Dr LSi 4WD Sdn	10280	13015
4 Dr Outback 4WD Wgn	10160	12860
4 Dr STD Sdn	7775	9840

OPTIONS FOR LEGACY

Auto 4-Speed Transmission[Std on LS,LSi] +355
Air Conditioning[Opt on STD] +385
Aluminum/Alloy Wheels[Opt on Brighton,L,STD] +205
AM/FM Compact Disc Playr[Std on LSi] +255
Anti-Lock Brakes[Opt on L] +430
Compact Disc Changer +300
Cruise Control[Opt on Brighton,L,STD] +110
Luggage Rack[Std on LSi,Outback] +125
Power Antenna[Opt on L] +55
Power Moonroof[Opt on L] +380

Don't forget to refer to the Mileage Adjustment Table at the back of this book!

 © 1999 by Edmund Publications Corporation

Model Description	Trade-in Value	Market Value

SVX 1995

Dual airbags are extended to the base model.

Category F

2 Dr L Cpe	9600	12005
2 Dr L 4WD Cpe	10410	13015
2 Dr LS Cpe	11250	14060
2 Dr LSi 4WD Cpe	12590	15735

1994 SUBARU

IMPREZA 1994

A passenger airbag joins the driver's airbag on all models. LS Imprezas have standard antilock brakes, automatic transmission and sunroof.

RATINGS (SCALE OF 1-10)

Overall	Safety	Reliability	Performance	Comfort	Value
7.6	6.8	9	7.6	7.4	7.1

Category E

4 Dr L 4WD Wgn	5760	7675
4 Dr L 4WD Sdn	5200	6935
4 Dr LS 4WD Wgn	6910	9215
4 Dr LS 4WD Sdn	6385	8515

OPTIONS FOR IMPREZA

Auto 4-Speed Transmission[Std on LS] +295
Air Conditioning[Std on LS] +300
AM/FM Stereo Tape[Std on LS] +115
Anti-Lock Brakes[Std on LS] +265
Dual Air Bag Restraints[Std on LS] +230
Power Door Locks[Std on LS] +85
Power Sunroof[Std on LS] +225
Power Windows[Std on LS] +100

JUSTY 1994

Continuously variable transmission is no longer available. Base models gain a standard rear-wheel defroster. Last year for the Justy runabout.

Category E

2 Dr DL Hbk	3000	4000

OPTIONS FOR JUSTY

Air Conditioning +300

LEGACY 1994

Antilock brakes become optional on the L sedan.

RATINGS (SCALE OF 1-10)

Overall	Safety	Reliability	Performance	Comfort	Value
N/A	N/A	8.1	8.3	7.8	6.8

Category D

4 Dr L Sdn	5435	6970
4 Dr L 4WD Wgn	6600	8460
4 Dr L 4WD Sdn	6150	7885
4 Dr LS Sdn	8010	10270
4 Dr LS 4WD Wgn	8485	10875
4 Dr LS 4WD Sdn	8485	10880
4 Dr LSi 4WD Wgn	8870	11375
4 Dr LSi 4WD Sdn	8725	11190

OPTIONS FOR LEGACY

Auto 4-Speed Transmission[Opt on L] +295
Air Conditioning[Opt on L] +315
Aluminum/Alloy Wheels[Opt on L] +165
AM/FM Compact Disc Playr +210
Anti-Lock Brakes[Opt on L] +355
Cruise Control[Opt on L] +90
Graphic Equalizer[Opt on L] +70
Keyless Entry System +110
Luggage Rack +100
Power Door Locks[Opt on L] +100
Power Moonroof[Opt on L,LS 4WD Sdn] +310
Power Windows[Opt on L] +100
Premium Sound System +130

LOYALE 1994

The Loyale is available only in the wagon bodystyle and is seeing its last year as the Impreza is set to take over the duties of all-wheel drive subcompact in Subaru's lineup.

Category D

4 Dr STD 4WD Wgn	5830	7475

OPTIONS FOR LOYALE

Auto 3-Speed Transmission +205
AM/FM Stereo Tape +135
Cruise Control +90
Luggage Rack +100

SVX 1994

Subaru introduces two-wheel drive "value leaders" to the SVX lineup called the L and LS. These new SVXs offer the same 3.3-liter V6 found in the LSi, and antilock brakes are standard on the LS . A passenger airbag becomes standard on the uplevel LS and LSi models.

Category F

2 Dr L Cpe	8675	10980
2 Dr LS Cpe	9960	12610
2 Dr LSi 4WD Cpe	11315	14320

OPTIONS FOR SVX

Dual Air Bag Restraints[Opt on L] +185

1993 SUBARU

IMPREZA 1993

Designed as a replacement for the aging Loyale, the Impreza is a subcompact available as a sedan or wagon. A driver airbag and available antilock brakes are important safety features included on the Impreza that

Don't forget to refer to the Mileage Adjustment Table at the back of this book!

 © 1999 by Edmund Publications Corporation

Model Description	Trade-in Value	Market Value

never found their way to the Loyale. The Impreza is powered by a 1.8-liter 118-horsepower engine. Front-wheel drive and full-time all-wheel drive models are offered.

RATINGS (SCALE OF 1-10)

Overall	Safety	Reliability	Performance	Comfort	Value
N/A	N/A	8.7	7.6	7.4	7.1

Category E		
4 Dr L Sdn	4310	5905
4 Dr L 4WD Sdn	5070	6945
4 Dr L 4WD Wgn	4500	6165
4 Dr LS Sdn	5115	7005
4 Dr LS 4WD Wgn	5195	7115
4 Dr LS 4WD Sdn	5700	7805
4 Dr STD Sdn	3380	4630

OPTIONS FOR IMPREZA

Auto 4-Speed Transmission[Opt on L] +245
Air Conditioning[Opt on STD] +245
Aluminum/Alloy Wheels +95
AM/FM Stereo Tape +95

JUSTY 1993

The base Justy gets a larger engine that increases horsepower to GL standards.

Category E		
2 Dr GL Hbk	2470	3380
4 Dr GL Hbk	2665	3655
2 Dr STD Hbk	2100	2880

OPTIONS FOR JUSTY

Air Conditioning +245
AM/FM Stereo Tape +95

LEGACY 1993

A driver airbag is now standard on all Legacys. Touring wagons and LSi wagons were introduced in 1992 as upscale versions of the Legacy. Commendably, antilock brakes are now standard on all Legacys except the L models. Several new trim-levels of the Legacy are available for 1993. Based on the L wagon, these models are geared to appeal to different groups of outdoor enthusiasts such as skiers, beach combers and campers. The standard equipment lists of these models reflects the differences in their target market, such as heated seats and a ski rack on the Alpine model.

RATINGS (SCALE OF 1-10)

Overall	Safety	Reliability	Performance	Comfort	Value
N/A	N/A	8.1	8.3	7.8	6.8

Category D		
4 Dr L Sdn	4570	6010
4 Dr L 4WD Sdn	5175	6810
4 Dr L 4WD Wgn	6285	8270
4 Dr LS Sdn	5445	7165
4 Dr LS 4WD Sdn	6050	7960
4 Dr LS 4WD Wgn	6955	9150
4 Dr LSi 4WD Wgn	6585	8665
4 Dr LSi 4WD Sdn	6360	8370

OPTIONS FOR LEGACY

Auto 4-Speed Transmission[Opt on L,Sport] +245
Anti-Lock Brakes[Opt on L Wgn] +290
Compact Disc W/fm/tape[Opt on LS] +290
Luggage Rack[Std on L] +80

LOYALE 1993

New colors are the only changes to the Loyale.

Category D		
4 Dr FWD Wgn	4345	5715
4 Dr FWD Sdn	3700	4870
4 Dr STD 4WD Sdn	3980	5235
4 Dr STD 4WD Wgn	4555	5995

OPTIONS FOR LOYALE

Auto 3-Speed Transmission +165
AM/FM Stereo Tape +110
Luggage Rack +80

1992 SUBARU

LEGACY 1992

A driver airbag is now standard on the Legacy LS and LSi; it is optional on L model. A trunk pass-through opening in the rear seats, rear heater ducts, and cupholders integrated into the dashboard give more utility to the passengers.

RATINGS (SCALE OF 1-10)

Overall	Safety	Reliability	Performance	Comfort	Value
N/A	N/A	7.6	8.3	7.8	6.2

Category D		
4 Dr L Sdn	3925	5305
4 Dr L 4WD Sdn	4450	6010
4 Dr L 4WD Wgn	4730	6390
4 Dr LS Sdn	4285	5790
4 Dr LS 4WD Sdn	4765	6440
4 Dr LS 4WD Wgn	5810	7850
4 Dr LSi Sdn	5050	6825
4 Dr LSi 4WD Sdn	5570	7530
4 Dr Sport Turbo 4WD Sdn	6325	8545

OPTIONS FOR LEGACY

Auto 4-Speed Transmission[Opt on L,Sport] +190
Air Bag Restraint[Std on Sport,LS Sdn] +150
Air Conditioning[Opt on L] +210
Anti-Lock Brakes[Opt on L] +235
Compact Disc W/fm/tape[Opt on L] +240
Luggage Rack +65
Power Door Locks[Opt on L] +65

Don't forget to refer to the Mileage Adjustment Table at the back of this book!

© 1999 by Edmund Publications Corporation

Model Description	Trade-in Value	Market Value

Power Windows[Opt on L] +65
Premium Sound System[Opt on L] +85

LOYALE 1992

Still no changes for the Loyale.

Category D

Model Description	Trade-in Value	Market Value
4 Dr STD Sdn	2850	3850
4 Dr STD Wgn	3245	4385
4 Dr STD 4WD Sdn	3305	4465
4 Dr STD 4WD Wgn	3865	5225

OPTIONS FOR LOYALE

Auto 3-Speed Transmission +135
AM/FM Stereo Tape +90

SVX 1992

Subaru replaces the odd XT6 with the equally unusual SVX. Performance numbers are quite good with the standard 3.3-liter V6 engine and standard all-wheel drive. The strange two-piece side windows, designed to decrease interior turbulence when the window is opened, leave something to be desired. Antilock brakes and a driver airbag are standard.

Category F

Model Description	Trade-in Value	Market Value
2 Dr STD 4WD Cpe	6750	9005

OPTIONS FOR SVX

Compact Disc W/fm/tape +130
Leather Seats +175
Power Drivers Seat +60
Power Sunroof +170

1991 SUBARU

JUSTY 1991

The Subaru Justy is unchanged.

Category E

Model Description	Trade-in Value	Market Value
2 Dr GL Hbk	1490	2190
2 Dr GL 4WD Hbk	1785	2625
4 Dr GL 4WD Hbk	1680	2470
2 Dr STD Hbk	1295	1905

OPTIONS FOR JUSTY

Auto 3-Speed Transmission +105
Air Conditioning +165
AM/FM Stereo[Std on GL] +60
AM/FM Stereo Tape +60

LEGACY 1991

Turbo power is now available on the Legacy Sport sedan. The boosted engine produces 160-horsepower and 180-lbs./ft. of torque; not too shabby for a family hauler.

RATINGS (SCALE OF 1-10)

Overall	Safety	Reliability	Performance	Comfort	Value
N/A	N/A	7.2	8.3	7.8	6.5

Category D

Model Description	Trade-in Value	Market Value
4 Dr L Sdn	2835	3885
4 Dr L 4WD Wgn	3565	4880
4 Dr L 4WD Sdn	3395	4650
4 Dr L Plus Sdn	3240	4440
4 Dr L Plus 4WD Sdn	3575	4895
4 Dr L Plus 4WD Wgn	3675	5035
4 Dr LS Sdn	3660	5015
4 Dr LS 4WD Wgn	4275	5860
4 Dr LS 4WD Sdn	4110	5625
4 Dr LSi Sdn	3775	5170
4 Dr LSi 4WD Sdn	4220	5780
4 Dr Sport Turbo 4WD Sdn	4770	6535

OPTIONS FOR LEGACY

Auto 4-Speed Transmission[Std on LSi] +155
Air Conditioning[Opt on L] +170
AM/FM Stereo Tape +75
Anti-Lock Brakes[Opt on L,L Plus] +195
Climate Control for AC +60
Cruise Control[Opt on L] +50
Luggage Rack +55
Power Door Locks[Opt on L] +55
Power Windows[Std on L Plus,LS,LSi,Sport,L 4WD Wgn] +55
Premium Sound System[Opt on L] +70

LOYALE 1991

No changes to the ever-popular Loyale.

Category D

Model Description	Trade-in Value	Market Value
4 Dr STD Wgn	2850	3900
4 Dr STD Sdn	2300	3155
4 Dr STD 4WD Wgn	3295	4515
4 Dr STD 4WD Sdn	2830	3875

OPTIONS FOR LOYALE

Auto 3-Speed Transmission +110
AM/FM Stereo Tape +75
Luggage Rack +55
Sunroof +85

XT 1991

The car with the weirdest steering wheel in the world enters its final year of production with no changes.

Category F

Model Description	Trade-in Value	Market Value
2 Dr GL Cpe	3120	4155
2 Dr XT6 Cpe	3880	5170

OPTIONS FOR XT

Auto 4-Speed Transmission[Opt on GL,4WD] +155
Air Conditioning[Opt on GL] +170
AM/FM Stereo Tape +40

Don't forget to refer to the Mileage Adjustment Table at the back of this book!

 © 1999 by Edmund Publications Corporation

Model Description	Trade-in Value	Market Value

1990 SUBARU

JUSTY 1990

Goodness, gracious, great gobs of gimmickry: the Subaru's ECVT (gearless automatic transmission) is available with the four-wheel drive Justy. We can't imagine where you would take this car for repairs, but we are certain that the one mechanic in the world who can fix it lives in a very expensive house. Fuel-injection technology trickles down to the Justy, increasing horsepower by a whopping 15 percent. That brings the Justy up to a tire-smokin' 70-horsepower for those of you keeping track.

Category E

Model Description	Trade-in Value	Market Value
2 Dr DL Hbk	1035	1595
2 Dr GL Hbk	1230	1890
2 Dr GL 4WD Hbk	1495	2295
4 Dr GL 4WD Hbk	1515	2330

OPTIONS FOR JUSTY

Auto 3-Speed Transmission +90
Air Conditioning +135
AM/FM Stereo Tape +50

LEGACY 1990

The Legacy is an entirely new line that is geared toward a more traditional audience than the Coupe/Sedan/Wagon. The Legacy is the largest vehicle produced by Subaru and is available as a sedan or wagon. A multi-valve engine is offered for the first time on a Subaru, as are the optional antilock brakes.

RATINGS (SCALE OF 1-10)

Overall	Safety	Reliability	Performance	Comfort	Value
N/A	N/A	6.7	8.3	7.8	5.9

Category D

Model Description	Trade-in Value	Market Value
4 Dr L Wgn	2590	3595
4 Dr L Sdn	2545	3535
4 Dr L 4WD Wgn	2960	4110
4 Dr L 4WD Sdn	2960	4110
4 Dr LS Sdn	2895	4020
4 Dr LS 4WD Wgn	3425	4755
4 Dr LS 4WD Sdn	3310	4600
4 Dr STD Sdn	2335	3240

OPTIONS FOR LEGACY

Auto 4-Speed Transmission +125
Air Conditioning[Std on LS] +140
AM/FM Stereo Tape +60
Anti-Lock Brakes[Opt on L,Wgn,4WD] +155
Cruise Control[Opt on L] +40
Premium Sound System[Std on LS,L 4WD Sdn] +55

LOYALE 1990

Subaru's popular Sedan/Wagon/Coupe line is renamed in a move toward traditional vehicle marketing. No other changes for this line of cars.

Category D

Model Description	Trade-in Value	Market Value
2 Dr STD Hbk	1960	2725
2 Dr STD 4WD Hbk	2450	3400
4 Dr STD Wgn	1855	2575
4 Dr STD Sdn	2010	2790
4 Dr STD 4WD Wgn	2230	3095
4 Dr STD 4WD Sdn	2605	3615
4 Dr STD Turbo 4WD Wgn	2480	3440

OPTIONS FOR LOYALE

Auto 3-Speed Transmission +90
Auto 4-Speed Transmission[Opt on Wgn] +110
Air Conditioning[Opt on Hbk,2WD,Non-turbo models] +140
AM/FM Stereo Tape +60
Auto Locking Hubs (4WD) +170
Luggage Rack +45
Power Door Locks[Opt on 2WD,STD 4WD Wgn] +45
Power Windows[Opt on 2WD,STD 4WD Wgn] +45

1989 SUBARU

DL 1989

The Coupe gains Subaru's Active four-wheel drive system as an available option. This line of vehicles is replaced with the all-new Subaru Legacy in 1990.

Category E

Model Description	Trade-in Value	Market Value
2 Dr STD Cpe	1345	2205
4 Dr STD Sdn	1255	2055
4 Dr STD Wgn	1145	1875
4 Dr STD 4WD Wgn	1450	2380

OPTIONS FOR DL

Auto 3-Speed Transmission +75
Air Conditioning +110
AM/FM Stereo Tape +40

GL 1989

The Coupe gains Subaru's Active four-wheel drive system as an available option. The Touring Wagon is a new model which offers added headroom and legroom, and it can be had with a normally aspirated or turbo engine. Front-wheel and four-wheel drive Touring Wagons are both available. The venerable Hatchback is now available only in the GL trim-level; part-time four-wheel drive is still available.

Category E

Model Description	Trade-in Value	Market Value
2 Dr STD Cpe	1640	2690
2 Dr STD 4WD Hbk	1475	2420

Don't forget to refer to the Mileage Adjustment Table at the back of this book!

 © 1999 by Edmund Publications Corporation

Model Description	Trade-in Value	Market Value
2 Dr STD 4WD Cpe	1905	3125
4 Dr STD Sdn	1675	2745
4 Dr STD Wgn	1390	2275
4 Dr STD 4WD Sdn	1935	3175
4 Dr STD 4WD Wgn	1720	2820
4 Dr STD Turbo 4WD Wgn	1705	2795

OPTIONS FOR GL

Auto 3-Speed Transmission[Std on STD Turbo Sdn] +75
Auto 4-Speed Transmission +75
Air Conditioning +110
AM/FM Stereo Tape +40
Cruise Control +30

JUSTY 1989

Innovative continuous variable transmission is optional on the Justy in 1989. This gearless transmission is supposed to offer more spirited acceleration than traditional automatics. GL and RS Justys get larger wheels and beefier stabilizer bars.

Category E

Model Description	Trade-in Value	Market Value
2 Dr DL Hbk	890	1460
2 Dr GL Hbk	910	1490
2 Dr GL 4WD Hbk	1235	2025

OPTIONS FOR JUSTY

Auto 3-Speed Transmission +75
Air Conditioning +110
AM/FM Stereo Tape +40

XT 1989

New high-performance tires for top-end XT is the only change for this funky sports car from Subaru.

Category F

Model Description	Trade-in Value	Market Value
2 Dr GL Cpe	1590	2210
2 Dr XT6 Cpe	2145	2980
2 Dr XT6 4WD Cpe	2410	3350

OPTIONS FOR XT

Auto 3-Speed Transmission +105
Auto 4-Speed Transmission[Opt on 4WD] +105
Air Conditioning[Opt on GL] +115
Cruise Control[Std on XT6,2WD] +30

Instant Lease & Loan Quotes for New & Used Vehicles!

www.CarFinance.com/edmunds

A 15-minute phone call could save you 15% or more on car insurance.

1-800-555-2758

The Sensible Alternative

Don't forget to refer to the Mileage Adjustment Table at the back of this book!

© 1999 by Edmund Publications Corporation

Model Description	Trade-in Value	Market Value

SUZUKI Japan

1998 Suzuki Esteem

1998 SUZUKI

ESTEEM 1998

A wagon adds diversity to the Esteem lineup.

Category E

Model Description	Trade-in Value	Market Value
4 Dr GL Sdn	7870	9480
4 Dr GL Wgn	7900	9520
4 Dr GL SE Wgn	9655	11635
4 Dr GLX Sdn	9320	11225
4 Dr GLX Wgn	9320	11230
4 Dr GLX SE Wgn	10385	12515

OPTIONS FOR ESTEEM

Auto 4-Speed Transmission[Opt on GL, GLX] +830
Anti-Lock Brakes +590
Cruise Control +185

SIDEKICK 1998

A couple of new colors debut.

Category G

Model Description	Trade-in Value	Market Value
4 Dr JX 4WD Wgn	8825	10505
4 Dr Sport JLX 4WD Wgn	12135	14450
4 Dr Sport JX 4WD Wgn	11135	13255
4 Dr Sport JX SE 4WD Wgn	11220	13360

OPTIONS FOR SIDEKICK

Auto 4-Speed Transmission +820
Air Conditioning[Opt on JS, JX] +675
Anti-Lock Brakes[Std on Sport JLX] +515

SWIFT 1998

Swift's engine makes nine more horsepower this year, and one more pound of torque.

Category E

Model Description	Trade-in Value	Market Value
2 Dr STD Hbk	5805	6995

OPTIONS FOR SWIFT

Auto 3-Speed Transmission +540
Air Conditioning +675
Anti-Lock Brakes +590

1997 SUZUKI

ESTEEM 1997

No changes to the economical Esteem.

Category E

Model Description	Trade-in Value	Market Value
4 Dr GL Sdn	7000	8535
4 Dr GLX Sdn	8030	9795

OPTIONS FOR ESTEEM

Auto 4-Speed Transmission +680
Anti-Lock Brakes +480
Cruise Control +150

SIDEKICK 1997

A JS Sport 2WD model is added to the Sidekick lineup. It has a DOHC engine that makes 120 horsepower at 6500 rpm. There are no changes to the rest of the Sidekick line.

RATINGS (SCALE OF 1-10)

Overall	Safety	Reliability	Performance	Comfort	Value
6.3	5.5	8.5	7	6.9	3.4

Category G

Model Description	Trade-in Value	Market Value
2 Dr JX 4WD Conv	9345	11125
4 Dr JX 4WD Wgn	10290	12250
4 Dr Sport JLX 4WD Wgn	12135	14445
4 Dr Sport JX 4WD Wgn	10965	13050

OPTIONS FOR SIDEKICK

Auto 3-Speed Transmission +410
Auto 4-Speed Transmission +670
Air Conditioning[Opt on JS,JX] +550
AM/FM Stereo Tape[Opt on Conv] +165
Anti-Lock Brakes[Std on Sport JLX] +420

SWIFT 1997

New paint colors (Victory Red and Bright Teal Metallic) and new seat coverings are the only changes to the 1996 Swift.

RATINGS (SCALE OF 1-10)

Overall	Safety	Reliability	Performance	Comfort	Value
6.4	6.5	8.3	6.6	6.4	4.4

Category E

Model Description	Trade-in Value	Market Value
2 Dr STD Hbk	5035	6140

OPTIONS FOR SWIFT

Auto 3-Speed Transmission +440
Air Conditioning +550
AM/FM Stereo Tape +210
Anti-Lock Brakes +480

Don't forget to refer to the Mileage Adjustment Table at the back of this book!

© 1999 by Edmund Publications Corporation

Model Description	Trade-in Value	Market Value

X-90 1997

No changes to Suzuki's interesting alternative to AWD vehicles.

RATINGS (SCALE OF 1-10)

Overall	Safety	Reliability	Performance	Comfort	Value
N/A	5.5	N/A	6.2	6.6	N/A

Category G

2 Dr STD 4WD Utility	8100	9645

OPTIONS FOR X-90

Auto 4-Speed Transmission +645
Air Conditioning +550
AM/FM Stereo Tape[Opt on 2WD] +165
Anti-Lock Brakes +420
Cruise Control +145

1996 SUZUKI

ESTEEM 1996

New for 1996 are daytime running lights, standard air conditioning and body-color bumpers on the GL.

Category E

4 Dr GL Sdn	5790	7330
4 Dr GLX Sdn	6550	8290

OPTIONS FOR ESTEEM

Auto 4-Speed Transmission +545
AM/FM Stereo Tape[Opt on GL] +170
Anti-Lock Brakes +395
Cruise Control +120

SIDEKICK 1996

Lots of changes to this mini SUV: the 16-valve, 95-horsepower engine is available across the board (except in the Sport), and dual airbags are housed in a revised instrument panel. New fabrics, colors and styling revisions update the Sidekick nicely. All-new for 1996 is a Sport variant, equipped with lots of exclusive standard equipment, a 120-horsepower twin-cam motor, a wider track, two-tone paint and a dorky chrome grille.

RATINGS (SCALE OF 1-10)

Overall	Safety	Reliability	Performance	Comfort	Value
6.2	5.5	8	7	6.9	3.8

Category G

2 Dr JS Conv	6135	7480
2 Dr JX 4WD Conv	7125	8690
4 Dr JX 4WD Wgn	8760	10685
4 Dr Sport JLX 4WD Wgn	10210	12450
4 Dr Sport JX 4WD Wgn	9110	11110

OPTIONS FOR SIDEKICK

Auto 3-Speed Transmission +330
Auto 4-Speed Transmission +535
Air Conditioning[Opt on JS,JX] +450
Anti-Lock Brakes[Opt on JS,JX] +345

SWIFT 1996

Oh boy. Two new colors and new seat fabrics. Whoopee.

RATINGS (SCALE OF 1-10)

Overall	Safety	Reliability	Performance	Comfort	Value
6.4	6.5	8.2	6.6	6.4	4.3

Category E

2 Dr STD Hbk	4560	5775

OPTIONS FOR SWIFT

Auto 3-Speed Transmission +355
Air Conditioning +450
AM/FM Stereo Tape +170
Anti-Lock Brakes +395

X-90 1996

Based on Sidekick platform, this new concept features a two-seat cockpit, T-top roof, conventional trunk, and available four-wheel drive. Loaded with standard equipment, the X-90 is an interesting vehicle indeed.

RATINGS (SCALE OF 1-10)

Overall	Safety	Reliability	Performance	Comfort	Value
N/A	5.5	N/A	6.2	6.6	N/A

Category G

2 Dr STD Utility	6755	8235
2 Dr STD 4WD Utility	6945	8470

OPTIONS FOR X-90

Auto 4-Speed Transmission +520
Air Conditioning +450

1995 SUZUKI

ESTEEM 1995

The 1995 Esteem is Suzuki's latest entry in the hotly contested subcompact car market. The Esteem has standard antilock brakes and dual airbags but is saddled with a 1.6-liter engine. Competition from Toyota, Geo and Honda is stiff, but low resale values may make this car worthwhile.

Category E

4 Dr GL Sdn	5015	6510
4 Dr GLX Sdn	5445	7075

OPTIONS FOR ESTEEM

Auto 4-Speed Transmission +445
Air Conditioning +370
Anti-Lock Brakes +320
Cruise Control +100

Don't forget to refer to the Mileage Adjustment Table at the back of this book!

 © 1999 by Edmund Publications Corporation

Model Description	Trade-in Value	Market Value

SIDEKICK 1995

The convertible model gets a new top.

RATINGS (SCALE OF 1-10)

Overall	Safety	Reliability	Performance	Comfort	Value
5.8	2.7	8.1	6.8	6.9	4.7

Category G

Model Description	Trade-in Value	Market Value
4 Dr JLX 4WD Wgn	6825	8430
2 Dr JS Conv	5480	6770
4 Dr JS Wgn	5505	6795
2 Dr JX 4WD Conv	6250	7715
4 Dr JX 4WD Wgn	6635	8190

OPTIONS FOR SIDEKICK

Auto 3-Speed Transmission +270
Auto 4-Speed Transmission +405
Air Conditioning +370
Luggage Rack +70

SWIFT 1995

The sedan is dropped and dual airbags are added. Antilock brakes become a much appreciated option. The two-door GT hatchback has also been dropped.

RATINGS (SCALE OF 1-10)

Overall	Safety	Reliability	Performance	Comfort	Value
6.6	7.1	8	6.6	6.4	4.7

Category E

Model Description	Trade-in Value	Market Value
2 Dr STD Hbk	3420	4440

OPTIONS FOR SWIFT

Auto 3-Speed Transmission +515
Air Conditioning +370
AM/FM Stereo Tape +140
Anti-Lock Brakes +320

1994 SUZUKI

SAMURAI 1994

Another Samurai commits Hari-Kari; the two-wheel drive model is no longer available. Other changes are limited to the addition of a high-mounted rear brake light.

Category G

Model Description	Trade-in Value	Market Value
2 Dr JL 4WD Conv	4290	5365

OPTIONS FOR SAMURAI

Air Conditioning +300

SIDEKICK 1994

All Sidekicks get an alarm and a tilt steering wheel as standard equipment this year. A high-mounted rear brake light is a new safety item found on all Sidekicks.

RATINGS (SCALE OF 1-10)

Overall	Safety	Reliability	Performance	Comfort	Value
5.6	2.7	8	6.8	6.9	3.7

Category G

Model Description	Trade-in Value	Market Value
4 Dr JLX 4WD Wgn	6295	7870
2 Dr JX 4WD Conv	5730	7160
4 Dr JX 4WD Wgn	5750	7185

OPTIONS FOR SIDEKICK

Auto 3-Speed Transmission +225
Auto 4-Speed Transmission +350
Air Conditioning +300
Flip-Up Sunroof +125

SWIFT 1994

The GA hatchback gets a cargo cover and both GA models get a right sideview mirror. Will wonders never cease?

Category E

Model Description	Trade-in Value	Market Value
2 Dr GA Hbk	2905	3870
4 Dr GA Sdn	3070	4090
4 Dr GS Sdn	3660	4875
2 Dr GT Hbk	3885	5180

OPTIONS FOR SWIFT

Auto 3-Speed Transmission +235
Air Conditioning +300
AM/FM Stereo Tape[Opt on GA] +115

1993 SUZUKI

SAMURAI 1993

When are they going to retire this thing? The Samurai continues unchanged.

Category G

Model Description	Trade-in Value	Market Value
2 Dr JL 4WD Conv	2940	3770

OPTIONS FOR SAMURAI

Air Conditioning +245
AM/FM Stereo Tape +75

SIDEKICK 1993

No changes for the Sidekick.

RATINGS (SCALE OF 1-10)

Overall	Safety	Reliability	Performance	Comfort	Value
5.6	2.7	7.9	6.8	6.9	3.6

Category G

Model Description	Trade-in Value	Market Value
4 Dr JLX 4WD Wgn	5570	7140
2 Dr JX 4WD Conv	4300	5510
4 Dr JX 4WD Wgn	5205	6670

Don't forget to refer to the Mileage Adjustment Table at the back of this book!

© 1999 by Edmund Publications Corporation

Model Description	Trade-in Value	Market Value

OPTIONS FOR SIDEKICK
Auto 3-Speed Transmission +200
Auto 4-Speed Transmission +275
Air Conditioning +245
AM/FM Stereo Tape[Opt on Conv] +75
Hardtop Roof +235

SWIFT 1993

The doors lock when the Swift reaches speeds of 8 mph or more; apparently Suzuki thinks that anyone crazy enough to buy this car won't be able to figure out how to do this on their own.

Category E

Model Description	Trade-in Value	Market Value
2 Dr GA Hbk	2230	3060
4 Dr GA Sdn	2170	2975
4 Dr GS Sdn	2535	3475
2 Dr GT Hbk	2730	3740

OPTIONS FOR SWIFT
Auto 3-Speed Transmission +180
Air Conditioning +245
AM/FM Stereo Tape[Opt on GA] +95

1992 SUZUKI

SAMURAI 1992

The Samurai loses a trim-level, making it available only as a two-wheel drive JA or four-wheel drive JL. The JL model loses its back seat.

Category G

Model Description	Trade-in Value	Market Value
2 Dr JL 4WD Conv	2770	3690

OPTIONS FOR SAMURAI
Air Conditioning +200
AM/FM Stereo Tape +60

SIDEKICK 1992

Four-door models receive an increase of 15 horsepower and a four-speed automatic transmission. All Sidekicks get a redesigned instrument panel.

RATINGS (SCALE OF 1-10)

Overall	Safety	Reliability	Performance	Comfort	Value
5.5	2.4	7.5	6.8	6.9	4

Category G

Model Description	Trade-in Value	Market Value
4 Dr JLX 4WD Wgn	4235	5645
2 Dr JX 4WD Conv	3570	4760
4 Dr JX 4WD Wgn	4060	5415

OPTIONS FOR SIDEKICK
Auto 3-Speed Transmission +205
Air Conditioning +200
AM/FM Stereo Tape[Std on JX,JS Wgn] +60
Chrome Wheels[Opt on JX] +60
Hardtop Roof +190
Leather Seats +190

SWIFT 1992

All Swifts get a redesigned front and rear fascia as well as a new dashboard. GS sedans receive power steering and new hub caps.

Category E

Model Description	Trade-in Value	Market Value
2 Dr GA Hbk	2025	2890
4 Dr GA Sdn	2010	2870
4 Dr GS Sdn	2290	3270
2 Dr GT Hbk	2315	3310

OPTIONS FOR SWIFT
Auto 3-Speed Transmission +145
Air Conditioning +200
AM/FM Stereo Tape[Std on GT] +75

1991 SUZUKI

SAMURAI 1991

The Samurai receives a freshened front-end that includes a new grille.

Category G

Model Description	Trade-in Value	Market Value
2 Dr JL 4WD Conv	2295	3105

OPTIONS FOR SAMURAI
Air Conditioning +165
AM/FM Stereo Tape +50

SIDEKICK 1991

A four-door Sidekick is introduced, offering more passenger and cargo room.

RATINGS (SCALE OF 1-10)

Overall	Safety	Reliability	Performance	Comfort	Value
5.6	2.4	7.6	6.8	6.9	4.5

Category G

Model Description	Trade-in Value	Market Value
2 Dr JL 4WD Conv	2860	3870
4 Dr JLX 4WD Wgn	3845	5195
2 Dr JX 4WD Conv	3175	4290
4 Dr JX 4WD Wgn	3710	5010

OPTIONS FOR SIDEKICK
Auto 3-Speed Transmission +120
Air Conditioning +165
AM/FM Stereo Tape[Opt on JL,JS] +50

SWIFT 1991

A GS sedan is introduced to the Swift lineup, offering first-time buyers a touch more luxury than is found in the base model.

Category E

Model Description	Trade-in Value	Market Value
2 Dr GA Hbk	1500	2210
4 Dr GA Sdn	1670	2460
4 Dr GS Sdn	1920	2820
2 Dr GT Hbk	1825	2680

Don't forget to refer to the Mileage Adjustment Table at the back of this book!

© 1999 by Edmund Publications Corporation

Model Description	Trade-in Value	Market Value

OPTIONS FOR SWIFT

Auto 3-Speed Transmission +120
Air Conditioning +165
AM/FM Stereo Tape[Opt on GA] +60

1990 SUZUKI

SAMURAI 1990

No changes to the Samurai.

Category G		
2 Dr JL 4WD Conv	2065	2870

OPTIONS FOR SAMURAI

Air Conditioning +135
AM/FM Stereo Tape +40

SIDEKICK 1990

No changes for the mini sport-ute from Suzuki.

RATINGS (SCALE OF 1-10)

Overall	Safety	Reliability	Performance	Comfort	Value
5.5	2.4	7.2	6.8	6.9	4.3

Category G		
2 Dr JLX 4WD Conv	3230	4485
2 Dr JS Conv	2265	3145
2 Dr JX 4WD Conv	2635	3660

OPTIONS FOR SIDEKICK

Auto 3-Speed Transmission +100
Air Conditioning +135
AM/FM Stereo Tape[Std on JLX] +40

SWIFT 1990

A base hatchback, called the GA, and a sedan are introduced for 1990. The GTi is renamed the GT after a run-in with the people at Volkswagen.

Category E		
2 Dr GA Hbk	1120	1725
4 Dr GA Sdn	1405	2160
2 Dr GL Hbk	1210	1865
4 Dr GL Sdn	1435	2210
2 Dr GLX Hbk	1345	2070
4 Dr GS Sdn	1485	2280
2 Dr GT Hbk	1505	2315

Get a great used car and apply for financing *online* at a price you must see to believe !

http://edmunds.com

OPTIONS FOR SWIFT

Auto 3-Speed Transmission +100
Air Conditioning +135
AM/FM Stereo Tape[Std on GS,GT] +50

1989 SUZUKI

SIDEKICK 1989

A bigger, more stable off-road vehicle is introduced to bolster the sales of the ailing Samurai. A larger available engine, wider track, and longer wheelbase increase passenger comfort and safety.

RATINGS (SCALE OF 1-10)

Overall	Safety	Reliability	Performance	Comfort	Value
5.7	2.4	7	6.8	6.9	5.3

Category G		
2 Dr JA 4WD Conv	2300	3330
2 Dr JLX 4WD Conv	2590	3750
2 Dr JLX 4WD Utility	2575	3735
2 Dr JX 4WD Conv	2475	3585
2 Dr JX 4WD Utility	2430	3520

OPTIONS FOR SIDEKICK

Auto 3-Speed Transmission[Opt on JX] +70
Air Conditioning +110
Aluminum/Alloy Wheels +45
AM/FM Stereo Tape[Opt on JA] +35
Auto Locking Hubs (4WD) +35
Cruise Control +30
Power Door Locks +30
Power Steering +40
Power Windows +30

SWIFT 1989

The anything-but-Swift is brought to these shores as Suzuki's first passenger car. The Swift is available as a budget-minded four door or racy two-door hatchback.

Category E		
4 Dr GLX Hbk	1135	1860
2 Dr GTi Hbk	1010	1655

OPTIONS FOR SWIFT

Auto 3-Speed Transmission[Opt on GTi] +135
Air Conditioning +110
AM/FM Stereo Tape[Opt on GLX] +40
Sunroof +45

For expert advice in selecting/buying/leasing a car, call

1-900-AUTOPRO

($2.00 per minute)

Don't forget to refer to the Mileage Adjustment Table at the back of this book!

 © 1999 by Edmund Publications Corporation

TOYOTA Japan

1994 Toyota Corolla

1998 TOYOTA

4RUNNER 1998

For 1998, the Toyota 4Runner gets rotary HVAC controls, a new four-spoke steering wheel and revised audio control head units.

Category G

Model	Trade-in Value	Market Value
4 Dr Limited Wgn	25530	30395
4 Dr Limited 4WD Wgn	26360	31385
4 Dr SR5 Wgn	18215	21685
4 Dr SR5 4WD Wgn	19170	22820
4 Dr STD Wgn	15135	18020
4 Dr STD 4WD Wgn	16850	20060

OPTIONS FOR 4RUNNER

Auto 4-Speed Transmission[Std on Limited, SR5 2WD] +750
Black Elite Package +760
Elite Package +760
Sports Package +650
Air Conditioning[Std on Limited] +675
Aluminum/Alloy Wheels[Std on Limited] +285
Anti-Lock Brakes[Opt on STD] +515
Compact Disc Changer +565
Compact Disc W/fm/tape +430
Cruise Control[Std on Limited] +175
Fog Lights +120
Keyless Entry System +170
Leather Seats[Opt on SR5] +640
Power Door Locks[Opt on STD] +190
Power Mirrors[Opt on STD] +110
Power Moonroof +735
Power Windows[Std on Limited] +195
Privacy Glass[Opt on STD] +225
Rear Window Defroster[Opt on STD] +140
Rear Window Wiper[Opt on STD] +125
Running Boards[Opt on SR5,STD] +320
Tilt Steering Wheel[Opt on STD] +140

AVALON 1998

The Avalon gets side-impact airbags, new headlights and taillamps, a new grille, a new trunk lid and pretensioner seatbelts with force limiters.

Category D

Model	Trade-in Value	Market Value
4 Dr XL Sdn	16855	20065
4 Dr XLS Sdn	19625	23360

OPTIONS FOR AVALON

Leather Bucket Seat Pkg. +645
Aluminum/Alloy Wheels[Opt on XL] +375
AM/FM Compact Disc Playr[Opt on XL] +465
Dual Power Seats[Opt on XL] +695
Heated Front Seats +305
Heated Power Mirrors[Opt on XL] +75
Leather Seats +915
Power Moonroof +695
Traction Control System +675

CAMRY 1998

Side-impact airbags debut on the recently redesigned Camry. Depowered front airbags further enhance this car's ability to protect its occupant in a crash. An engine immobilizer feature is now part of the theft-deterrent package.

Category D

Model	Trade-in Value	Market Value
4 Dr CE Sdn	10905	12980
4 Dr CE V6 Sdn	12460	14835
4 Dr LE Sdn	13875	16515
4 Dr LE V6 Sdn	15355	18280
4 Dr XLE Sdn	15600	18570
4 Dr XLE V6 Sdn	16395	19515

OPTIONS FOR CAMRY

Auto 4-Speed Transmission[Opt on CE] +665
Black Elite Package +680
Air Conditioning[Opt on CE, CE V6] +700
Aluminum/Alloy Wheels[Std on XLE, XLE V6] +375
AM/FM Compact Disc Playr[Std on XLE, XLE V6] +465
Anti-Lock Brakes[Opt on CE 4 cyl.] +790
Cruise Control[Opt on CE, CE V6] +200
Keyless Entry System[Std on XLE, XLE V6] +250
Leather Seats +915
Power Door Locks[Opt on CE, CE V6] +220
Power Drivers Seat +285
Power Mirrors[Opt on CE, CE V6] +135
Power Moonroof +695
Power Windows[Opt on CE, CE V6] +220
Side Air Bag Restraint +240
Traction Control System +675

Don't forget to refer to the Mileage Adjustment Table at the back of this book!

 © 1999 by Edmund Publications Corporation

Model Description	Trade-in Value	Market Value

COROLLA 1998

The Toyota Corolla is completely redesigned this year with a new engine, new sheetmetal and a new standard for safety in compact cars: optional front passenger side-impact airbags.

Category E

Model Description	Trade-in Value	Market Value
4 Dr CE Sdn	9735	11725
4 Dr LE Sdn	10740	12940
4 Dr VE Sdn	8355	10065

OPTIONS FOR COROLLA

Auto 3-Speed Transmission +415
Auto 4-Speed Transmission +665
Air Conditioning[Opt on VE] +675
Aluminum/Alloy Wheels +265
AM/FM Compact Disc Playr +390
Anti-Lock Brakes +590
Cruise Control +185
Keyless Entry System +125
Power Door Locks[Opt on CE] +195
Power Moonroof +485
Power Windows[Opt on CE] +220
Rear Window Defroster[Opt on VE] +135
Side Air Bag Restraint +220
Tachometer[Opt on CE] +65

LAND CRUISER 1998

For 1998, Land Cruiser gets a more powerful V8 engine, standard ABS, an increase in structural rigidity, an improved suspension system, increased passenger and cargo room and a slew of new colors.

Category G

Model Description	Trade-in Value	Market Value
4 Dr STD 4WD Wgn	30910	36795

OPTIONS FOR LAND CRUISER

Convenience Package +635
Third Seat Package +915
Leather Seats +640
Locking Differential +250
Power Moonroof +735
Running Boards +320
Third Seat +625

RAV4 1998

Toyota's jellybean enters its third year of production with minor changes to the grille, headlights, taillamps and interior. Four-door RAV4s get new seat fabric. A late-year introduction of the new RAV4 convertible makes this sport-ute more appealing for those who live in the sunbelt.

Category G

Model Description	Trade-in Value	Market Value
2 Dr STD Utility	12900	15360
2 Dr STD 4WD Conv	14105	16795
2 Dr STD 4WD Utility	13985	16650
4 Dr STD Wgn	13355	15900
4 Dr STD 4WD Wgn	15920	18950

OPTIONS FOR RAV4

Auto 4-Speed Transmission +875
Air Conditioning +675
Aluminum/Alloy Wheels +285
AM/FM Compact Disc Playr +320
Anti-Lock Brakes +515
Cruise Control +175
Keyless Entry System +170
Power Door Locks +190
Power Mirrors +110
Power Windows +195
Tilt Steering Wheel[Std on Wgn] +140

SIENNA 1998

A new minivan from Toyota brings some innovation to the family truckster market. A powerful 194-horsepower V6 engine rests under the hood of all models. Safety equipment includes standard anti-lock brakes, low tire pressure warning systems and five mph front and rear bumpers. Sienna boasts outstanding crash test scores.

Category G

Model Description	Trade-in Value	Market Value
2 Dr CE Pass. Van	16335	19445
2 Dr LE Pass. Van	18400	21905
2 Dr XLE Pass. Van	21705	25840

OPTIONS FOR SIENNA

Aluminum/Alloy Wheels[Opt on LE] +285
AM/FM Compact Disc Playr[Std on XLE] +320
Captain Chairs (4)[Opt on LE] +525
Cruise Control[Opt on CE] +175
Dual Air Conditioning[Opt on CE] +840
Heated Power Mirrors[Std on XLE] +50
Keyless Entry System[Std on XLE] +170
Leather Seats +640
Power Door Locks[Opt on CE] +190
Power Drivers Seat +235
Power Mirrors[Opt on CE] +110
Power Moonroof +735
Power Windows[Opt on CE] +195
Privacy Glass[Opt on CE] +225
Rear Window Defroster[Opt on CE] +140
Sliding Driver Side Door +445

T100 1998

No changes to Toyota's full-size truck.

Category H

Model Description	Trade-in Value	Market Value
2 Dr DX 4WD Ext Cab SB	17535	20625
2 Dr SR5 4WD Ext Cab SB	18515	21780

OPTIONS FOR T100

Auto 4-Speed Transmission +750
Air Conditioning +670
Aluminum/Alloy Wheels +260
AM/FM Compact Disc Playr +245
Anti-Lock Brakes +420
Bed Liner +185
Cruise Control +160
Keyless Entry System +125

Don't forget to refer to the Mileage Adjustment Table at the back of this book!

 © 1999 by Edmund Publications Corporation

Model Description	Trade-in Value	Market Value

Power Door Locks +155
Power Mirrors +85
Power Windows +160
Privacy Glass[Opt on DX] +140
Sliding Rear Window[Std on SR5] +95
Tilt Steering Wheel[Std on SR5] +150
Velour/Cloth Seats[Opt on STD] +110

TACOMA 1998

The 1998 four-wheel drive Tacomas receive fresh front-end styling that makes them more closely resemble their two-wheel drive brothers. A new option package appears for 1998 as well; the TRD (no, not short for "turd") Off-Road Package for extended cab models is designed to make the Tacoma appeal to would-be Baja 1000 racers. On the safety front, Toyota introduces a passenger's side airbag that can be deactivated with a cut-off switch, making the Tacoma somewhat safer for children and short adults. Toyota also offers a new Tacoma PreRunner for 1998, billing it as a two-wheel drive truck with four-wheel drive performance.

Category G

Model Description	Trade-in Value	Market Value
2 Dr Limited 4WD Ext Cab SB	18115	21570
2 Dr Prerunner Ext Cab SB	14055	16735
2 Dr Prerunner V6 Ext Cab SB	14800	17615
2 Dr SR5 Ext Cab SB	12500	14880
2 Dr SR5 4WD Ext Cab SB	14665	17460
2 Dr SR5 V6 Ext Cab SB	12895	15355
2 Dr SR5 V6 4WD Ext Cab SB	15155	18045
2 Dr STD Ext Cab SB	11025	13125
2 Dr STD Std Cab SB	8990	10705
2 Dr STD 4WD Ext Cab SB	13725	16335
2 Dr STD 4WD Std Cab SB	12130	14440
2 Dr V6 Ext Cab SB	11395	13565
2 Dr V6 4WD Ext Cab SB	14585	17360

OPTIONS FOR TACOMA

Auto 4-Speed Transmission[Std on Prerunner, Prerunner V6] +690
Off-Road Package +865
Air Conditioning[Opt on Limited, STD, V6] +675
Aluminum/Alloy Wheels[Std on Limited] +285
AM/FM Compact Disc Playr +320
Anti-Lock Brakes +515
Auto Locking Hubs (4WD)[Std on Limited] +220
Bed Liner +230
Cruise Control[Std on Limited] +175
Flip-Up Sunroof +280
Keyless Entry System +170
Power Door Locks[Std on Limited] +190
Power Steering[Opt on STD 4 cyl.] +235
Power Windows[Std on Limited] +195
Sliding Rear Window[Opt on STD, V6] +100
Tilt Steering Wheel[Std on Limited] +140

TERCEL 1998

For 1998, the Tercel is available exclusively as a two-door CE model with additional standard features like color-keyed grille and bumpers, rear seat headrests, AM/FM stereo with cassette, air conditioning, digital clock and power steering.

Category E

Model Description	Trade-in Value	Market Value
2 Dr CE Sdn	8060	9710

OPTIONS FOR TERCEL

Auto 3-Speed Transmission +415
AM/FM Compact Disc Playr +390
Anti-Lock Brakes +590
Keyless Entry System +125
Power Door Locks +195
Power Windows +220
Rear Window Defroster +135

1997 TOYOTA

4RUNNER 1997

Toyota's hot-selling redesign receives minor changes. The most noticeable is the addition of the 2WD Limited to the model lineup. SR5 models receive new interior fabrics.

RATINGS (SCALE OF 1-10)

Overall	Safety	Reliability	Performance	Comfort	Value
6.6	6.6	9.1	6.6	6.9	4.1

Category G

Model Description	Trade-in Value	Market Value
4 Dr Limited Wgn	23455	27920
4 Dr Limited 4WD Wgn	24155	28755
4 Dr SR5 Wgn	17800	21195
4 Dr SR5 4WD Wgn	18035	21470
4 Dr STD Wgn	13615	16210
4 Dr STD 4WD Wgn	14550	17320

OPTIONS FOR 4RUNNER

Auto 4-Speed Transmission[Opt on STD,SR5 4WD Wgn] +610
Elite Package +745
Walnut Wood Dash +540
Air Conditioning[Opt on SR5,STD] +550
Aluminum/Alloy Wheels[Opt on SR5,STD] +235
Anti-Lock Brakes[Opt on STD] +420
Compact Disc W/fm/tape +465
Cruise Control[Opt on SR5,STD] +145
Keyless Entry System +140
Leather Seats[Opt on SR5,STD] +520
Locking Differential +205
Luggage Rack +105
Power Door Locks[Opt on STD] +155
Power Moonroof +600
Power Windows[Opt on SR5,STD] +160
Rear Heater +140
Running Boards[Opt on SR5,STD] +260

Don't forget to refer to the Mileage Adjustment Table at the back of this book!

 © 1999 by Edmund Publications Corporation

AVALON 1997

More power, more torque, and added standard features make the Avalon one of the most appealing full-sized sedans

RATINGS (SCALE OF 1-10)

Overall	Safety	Reliability	Performance	Comfort	Value
8.1	8	9.2	8	8.4	6.7

Model Description	Trade-in Value	Market Value
Category D		
4 Dr XL Sdn	15360	18510
4 Dr XLS Sdn	17615	21220

OPTIONS FOR AVALON

Power Bench Seat +555
Aluminum/Alloy Wheels[Opt on XL] +305
Compact Disc W/fm/tape +655
Dual Power Seats[Opt on XL] +570
Leather Seats +750
Power Moonroof +565
Traction Control System +550

CAMRY 1997

Toyota plays the market conservatively with the all-new Camry, giving consumers exactly what they want; a roomy, attractive, feature-laden car with available V6 performance and the promise of excellent reliability as well as resale value. The Camry is the new standard for midsized sedans.

RATINGS (SCALE OF 1-10)

Overall	Safety	Reliability	Performance	Comfort	Value
7.6	7.3	8.9	8.6	8.1	5.1

Model Description	Trade-in Value	Market Value
Category D		
4 Dr CE Sdn	10095	12165
4 Dr CE V6 Sdn	11360	13685
4 Dr LE Sdn	12680	15280
4 Dr LE V6 Sdn	14000	16865
4 Dr XLE Sdn	14010	16880
4 Dr XLE V6 Sdn	15215	18330

OPTIONS FOR CAMRY

Auto 4-Speed Transmission[Opt on CE] +545
6-disc CD Autochanger +545
Elite Package +970
Air Conditioning[Opt on CE,CE V6] +575
Aluminum/Alloy Wheels[Std on XLE,XLE V6] +305
Anti-Lock Brakes[Opt on CE] +645
Child Seat (1) +90
Compact Disc W/fm/tape +655
Cruise Control[Opt on CE,CE V6] +165
Keyless Entry System[Std on XLE,XLE V6] +205
Leather Seats +750
Power Door Locks[Opt on CE,CE V6] +180
Power Moonroof +565
Power Windows[Opt on CE,CE V6] +180
Traction Control System +550

CELICA 1997

GT Coupe is gone, and Fiesta Blue Metallic can be specified for cars equipped with black sport cloth interior.

RATINGS (SCALE OF 1-10)

Overall	Safety	Reliability	Performance	Comfort	Value
N/A	N/A	9.6	8.2	7.6	4.3

Model Description	Trade-in Value	Market Value
Category F		
2 Dr GT Conv	15380	18530
2 Dr GT Hbk	14485	17450
2 Dr GT Limited Edit. Conv	16640	20045
2 Dr ST Cpe	11875	14310
2 Dr ST Hbk	12120	14600
2 Dr ST Limited Edit. Hbk	13405	16150

OPTIONS FOR CELICA

Auto 4-Speed Transmission +545
Air Conditioning[Opt on GT,ST] +565
Aluminum/Alloy Wheels[Opt on GT,ST] +210
Anti-Lock Brakes +490
Compact Disc W/fm/tape[Opt on GT] +355
Cruise Control[Opt on GT,ST] +140
Leather Seats +485
Power Door Locks[Opt on ST] +135
Power Moonroof +485
Power Windows[Opt on ST] +150
Premium Sound System +280
Sport Suspension +175

COROLLA 1997

The Classic Edition (CE) debuts and the slow-selling DX Wagon gets the ax.

RATINGS (SCALE OF 1-10)

Overall	Safety	Reliability	Performance	Comfort	Value
7.3	6.6	9.3	7.8	8.1	4.4

Model Description	Trade-in Value	Market Value
Category E		
4 Dr CE Sdn	8870	10820
4 Dr DX Sdn	8210	10015
4 Dr STD Sdn	7635	9310

OPTIONS FOR COROLLA

Auto 3-Speed Transmission +340
Auto 4-Speed Transmission +440
Air Conditioning[Std on CE] +550
Aluminum/Alloy Wheels +215
Anti-Lock Brakes +480
Child Seat (1) +80
Compact Disc W/fm/tape +470
Cruise Control +150
Gold Package +265
Power Door Locks[Opt on DX] +160
Power Sunroof +410
Power Windows[Opt on DX] +180

Don't forget to refer to the Mileage Adjustment Table at the back of this book!

 © 1999 by Edmund Publications Corporation

Model Description	Trade-in Value	Market Value

LAND CRUISER 1997

The Black Package is discontinued, but black paint becomes an available color choice. A 40th-Anniversary Package lets buyers slather their Cruiser in leather and choose one of two unique paint schemes.

RATINGS (SCALE OF 1-10)

Overall	Safety	Reliability	Performance	Comfort	Value
N/A	N/A	9.1	7.8	8	N/A

Category G		
4 Dr 40th Anniv. Ltd. 4WD Wgn	31040	36950
4 Dr STD 4WD Wgn	26990	32130

OPTIONS FOR LAND CRUISER

Burlwood Dash +540
Convenience Package +545
Leather Trim Package +1900
Third Seat Package +810
Aluminum/Alloy Wheels +235
Compact Disc Changer +350
Compact Disc W/fm/tape +465
Dual Power Seats[Opt on STD] +430
Keyless Entry System +140
Leather Seats[Opt on STD] +520
Locking Differential +205
Luggage Rack +105
Power Moonroof +600
Running Boards +260
Third Seat[Opt on STD] +510

PASEO 1997

For some reason, Toyota product planners took a look at the cheap convertible market and thought, "Hmmm...a convertible Tercel with fancy styling will just kill the Sunfire SE Convertible's sales and make us rich." Coupes get dual-visor vanity mirrors, fresh door trim and rotary-heater controls.

RATINGS (SCALE OF 1-10)

Overall	Safety	Reliability	Performance	Comfort	Value
N/A	6.6	N/A	7	6.9	N/A

Category E		
2 Dr STD Cpe	8740	10660
2 Dr STD Conv	9625	11740

OPTIONS FOR PASEO

Auto 4-Speed Transmission +545
Air Conditioning +550
Aluminum/Alloy Wheels +215
AM/FM Compact Disc Playr +320
Anti-Lock Brakes +480
Cruise Control +150
Flip-Up Sunroof +240
Power Door Locks +160
Power Windows +180

PREVIA 1997

RATINGS (SCALE OF 1-10)

Overall	Safety	Reliability	Performance	Comfort	Value
7.5	6.7	8.8	7.7	7.3	6.8

Category G		
2 Dr DX Sprchgd Pass. Van	14475	17230
2 Dr LE Sprchgd Pass. Van	18360	21855

OPTIONS FOR PREVIA

Aluminum/Alloy Wheels +235
Anti-Lock Brakes +420
Captain Chairs (4) +430
Compact Disc W/fm/tape +465
Cruise Control[Opt on DX] +145
Dual Air Conditioning[Opt on DX] +685
Keyless Entry System +140
Leather Seats +520
Luggage Rack +105
Power Door Locks[Opt on DX] +155
Power Moonroof +600
Power Windows[Opt on DX] +160
Premium Sound System +245
Running Boards +260

RAV4 1997

New fabric debuts on the two-door RAV, and a sunroof is finally available on the four-door. Improvements have also been made by using sound deadening material in the dash area, reducing engine noise in the passenger compartment.

RATINGS (SCALE OF 1-10)

Overall	Safety	Reliability	Performance	Comfort	Value
N/A	N/A	9.1	7	6.4	N/A

Category G		
2 Dr STD Utility	11870	14130
2 Dr STD 4WD Utility	12470	14845
4 Dr STD Wgn	12500	14880
4 Dr STD 4WD Wgn	13170	15680

OPTIONS FOR RAV4

Auto 4-Speed Transmission +715
Air Conditioning +550
Aluminum/Alloy Wheels +235
AM/FM Compact Disc Playr +260
Anti-Lock Brakes +420
Cruise Control +145
Keyless Entry System +140
Leather Seats +520
Power Door Locks +155
Power Moonroof +600
Power Windows +160
Tilt Steering Wheel +115

Don't forget to refer to the Mileage Adjustment Table at the back of this book!

 © 1999 by Edmund Publications Corporation

Model Description	Trade-in Value	Market Value

SUPRA 1997

Turbo models get the six-speed manual transmission back, but the bigger news details massive price cuts. Turbos with automatics are $12,000 dollars less expensive than last year! All Supras commemorate the nameplate's 15th anniversary with a rear spoiler, premium sound and special badging. Despite price cuts, equipment levels are enhanced across the board.

Category F		
2 Dr STD Hbk	23240	28005
2 Dr STD Turbo Hbk	26600	32050

OPTIONS FOR SUPRA

6-Speed Transmission +1155
Auto 4-Speed Transmission[Std on Turbo] +610
Sport Roof +2510
Compact Disc Changer +455
Compact Disc W/fm/tape[Std on Turbo] +355
Keyless Entry System +120
Leather Seats[Std on Turbo] +485
Power Drivers Seat[Std on Turbo] +160

T100 1997

Two new colors debut and the optional wheel and tire packages are larger this year. Standard models get radio pre-wiring, midlevel models get fabric door trim panels, and SR5 models get chrome wheel arches.

RATINGS (SCALE OF 1-10)

Overall	Safety	Reliability	Performance	Comfort	Value
N/A	6.3	9.3	7.1	7.7	N/A

Category H		
2 Dr SR5 Ext Cab SB	14030	16705
2 Dr SR5 4WD Ext Cab SB	15990	19035
2 Dr STD Ext Cab SB	13725	16340
2 Dr STD Std Cab LB	11530	13730
2 Dr STD 4WD Ext Cab SB	14800	17620

OPTIONS FOR T100

Auto 4-Speed Transmission +610
Air Conditioning +550
Aluminum/Alloy Wheels +210
AM/FM Compact Disc Playr +200
Anti-Lock Brakes +345
Bed Liner +155
Chrome Wheels +200
Cruise Control +130
Keyless Entry System +110
Power Door Locks +125
Power Windows +130
Premium Sound System +275
Rear Step Bumper +105
Running Boards +200
Velour/Cloth Seats[Opt on Std Cab] +90

TACOMA 1997

The 1997 Tacoma receives several new value packages that make optioning the truck easier. A locking rear-wheel differential is now available on all 4WD models. Bucket seats can be had on all Xtracab Tacomas this year; not just the SR5. Two-wheel drive models have new headlamps and a new grille that make the vehicle look more like the T100.

RATINGS (SCALE OF 1-10)

Overall	Safety	Reliability	Performance	Comfort	Value
N/A	4.8	9.6	7.2	7	N/A

Category G		
2 Dr SR5 4WD Ext Cab SB	14985	17840
2 Dr STD Ext Cab SB	10585	12600
2 Dr STD Std Cab SB	10025	11935
2 Dr STD 4WD Std Cab SB	12105	14410
2 Dr STD 4WD Ext Cab SB	12830	15275
2 Dr V6 Ext Cab SB	11285	13435
2 Dr V6 4WD Ext Cab SB	13275	15805
2 Dr V6 4WD Std Cab SB	12455	14825

OPTIONS FOR TACOMA

Auto 4-Speed Transmission +575
Air Conditioning +550
Aluminum/Alloy Wheels[Std on SR5] +235
Anti-Lock Brakes +420
Auto Locking Hubs (4WD)[Std on SR5] +180
Bed Liner +190
Compact Disc W/fm/tape +465
Cruise Control +145
Power Door Locks +155
Power Steering[Std on SR5,V6,4WD] +190
Power Windows +160
Rear Step Bumper[Std on V6,Ext Cab,4WD] +100
Running Boards +260

TERCEL 1997

Standard and DX trim levels are shelved in favor of CE trim for all Tercels. All models have upgraded cloth trim, new rotary heater controls, a trip odometer, and a storage console. New wheelcovers adorn standard 14-inch wheels.

RATINGS (SCALE OF 1-10)

Overall	Safety	Reliability	Performance	Comfort	Value
6.9	6.3	9.2	6.6	7	5.5

Category E		
2 Dr CE Sdn	6595	8040
4 Dr CE Sdn	7150	8715
2 Dr Limited Edition Sdn	6785	8275

Don't forget to refer to the Mileage Adjustment Table at the back of this book!

 © 1999 by Edmund Publications Corporation

Model Description	Trade-in Value	Market Value

OPTIONS FOR TERCEL

Auto 3-Speed Transmission +345
Auto 4-Speed Transmission +475
Air Conditioning +550
AM/FM Compact Disc Playr +320
Anti-Lock Brakes +480
Keyless Entry System +100
Power Door Locks +160
Power Steering +170
Power Windows +180

1996 TOYOTA

4RUNNER 1996

A cool new 4Runner with a potent V6, big bruiser styling, and lots more interior room debuts. This thing annihilates most compact off-road vehicles.

RATINGS (SCALE OF 1-10)

Overall	Safety	Reliability	Performance	Comfort	Value
6.7	6.6	8.9	6.6	6.9	4.5

Category G

Model Description	Trade-in Value	Market Value
4 Dr Limited 4WD Wgn	21865	26660
4 Dr SR5 Wgn	16370	19965
4 Dr SR5 4WD Wgn	16485	20105
4 Dr STD Wgn	13010	15865
4 Dr STD 4WD Wgn	13360	16295

OPTIONS FOR 4RUNNER

Auto 4-Speed Transmission[Opt on STD,SR5 4WD Wgn] +490
Walnut Wood Dash +435
Air Conditioning[Opt on SR5,STD] +450
Aluminum/Alloy Wheels[Opt on SR5,STD] +190
Anti-Lock Brakes[Opt on STD] +345
Compact Disc W/fm/tape +380
Cruise Control[Opt on SR5,STD] +115
Keyless Entry System +115
Leather Seats[Opt on SR5] +425
Locking Differential +165
Luggage Rack +85
Power Door Locks[Opt on STD] +125
Power Moonroof +490
Power Windows[Opt on 2WD] +130
Rear Heater +115
Running Boards +215
Trailer Hitch +160

AVALON 1996

No changes as cloud car floats into its second year.

RATINGS (SCALE OF 1-10)

Overall	Safety	Reliability	Performance	Comfort	Value
7.9	7.6	8.9	8	8.4	6.6

Category D

Model Description	Trade-in Value	Market Value
4 Dr XL Sdn	12750	15940
4 Dr XLS Sdn	14685	18360

OPTIONS FOR AVALON

Power Bench Seat +440
Aluminum/Alloy Wheels[Opt on XL] +250
Anti-Lock Brakes[Opt on XL] +530
Compact Disc W/fm/tape +535
Dual Power Seats[Opt on XL] +465
Leather Seats +610
Power Moonroof +465
Premium Sound System[Opt on XL] +195

CAMRY 1996

The 1996 Camry remains virtually unchanged from last year's model. Minor engine adjustments mean that the four-cylinder is fully compliant with all On-Board Diagnostic standards, and is now certified as a Transitional Low Emission Vehicle powerplant. Additionally, the interior of the DX line gets a new seat fabric, the LE Sedan is available with a leather package, and the Wagon can now be ordered with power-operated driver and passenger seats.

RATINGS (SCALE OF 1-10)

Overall	Safety	Reliability	Performance	Comfort	Value
7.7	6.7	8.7	8.6	8.4	5.9

Category D

Model Description	Trade-in Value	Market Value
4 Dr Collector Sdn	13600	17000
2 Dr DX Cpe	8585	10730
4 Dr DX Sdn	8935	11165
2 Dr LE Cpe	10915	13640
4 Dr LE Wgn	11095	13865
4 Dr LE Sdn	11005	13755
2 Dr LE V6 Cpe	11370	14210
4 Dr LE V6 Sdn	12120	15145
4 Dr LE V6 Wgn	12225	15280
2 Dr SE Cpe	12675	15840
4 Dr SE Sdn	13115	16395
4 Dr XLE Sdn	12435	15545
4 Dr XLE V6 Sdn	13420	16770

OPTIONS FOR CAMRY

Auto 4-Speed Transmission[Opt on DX] +435
Elite Package +680
Air Conditioning[Opt on DX] +470
Anti-Lock Brakes[Std on XLE,XLE V6] +530
Compact Disc W/fm/tape[Std on Collector] +535
Cruise Control[Opt on DX] +135
Keyless Entry System +170
Leather Seats[Std on Collector] +610
Power Door Locks[Opt on DX] +145
Power Drivers Seat[Opt on LE,LE V6] +190
Power Moonroof +465
Power Passenger Seat +210
Power Windows[Opt on DX] +145
Premium Sound System +195

Don't forget to refer to the Mileage Adjustment Table at the back of this book!

 © 1999 by Edmund Publications Corporation

Model Description	Trade-in Value	Market Value

CELICA 1996

Minor front end freshening doesn't help much. A new spoiler, new wheelcovers, two new colors, and revised fabrics debut this year.

RATINGS (SCALE OF 1-10)

Overall	Safety	Reliability	Performance	Comfort	Value
N/A	N/A	9.3	8.2	7.6	4.3

Model Description	Trade-in Value	Market Value
Category F		
2 Dr GT Conv	14420	17805
2 Dr GT Cpe	12210	15070
2 Dr GT Hbk	12540	15485
2 Dr GT 25th Anniv. Conv	14015	17300
2 Dr ST Cpe	10635	13130
2 Dr ST Hbk	10765	13295
2 Dr ST 25th Anniv. Hbk	12200	15060

OPTIONS FOR CELICA

Auto 4-Speed Transmission +435
Leather Sport Package +580
Air Conditioning[Opt on GT,ST] +460
Anti-Lock Brakes +400
Compact Disc W/fm/tape[Opt on GT] +290
Cruise Control[Opt on GT,ST] +115
Keyless Entry System +95
Leather Seats +395
Power Door Locks[Opt on ST] +110
Power Moonroof[Opt on GT,ST] +395
Power Windows[Opt on ST] +125
Premium Sound System +225
Sport Suspension +145

COROLLA 1996

The Toyota Corolla heads into 1996 with a redesigned front and rear fascia, three new colors, new wheel covers, an optional integrated child seat, and a revised interior. Additionally, the five-speed manual transmission has been revised for a better feel and more positive gear engagement.

RATINGS (SCALE OF 1-10)

Overall	Safety	Reliability	Performance	Comfort	Value
7.3	6.5	9	7.8	8.1	5.2

Model Description	Trade-in Value	Market Value
Category E		
4 Dr DX Wgn	7695	9740
4 Dr DX Sdn	7365	9320
4 Dr STD Sdn	6985	8840

OPTIONS FOR COROLLA

Auto 3-Speed Transmission +265
Auto 4-Speed Transmission +435
Air Conditioning +450
Anti-Lock Brakes +395
Child Seat (1) +65
Cruise Control +120
Keyless Entry System +80
Power Door Locks +130
Power Sunroof +335
Power Windows +145

LAND CRUISER 1996

The Black Paint Package debuts, for those who enjoy spending long hours maintaining the finish on their truck.

RATINGS (SCALE OF 1-10)

Overall	Safety	Reliability	Performance	Comfort	Value
N/A	N/A	8.9	7.8	8	N/A

Model Description	Trade-in Value	Market Value
Category G		
4 Dr STD 4WD Wgn	24715	30140

OPTIONS FOR LAND CRUISER

Burlwood Dash +435
Leather Trim Package +1675
Third Seat Package +825
Compact Disc Changer +380
Compact Disc W/fm/tape +290
Dual Power Seats +350
Keyless Entry System +115
Leather Seats +425
Power Moonroof +490
Running Boards +215
Third Seat +420

PASEO 1996

All new Paseo looks like last year's car, but is much improved. It now meets 1997 passenger car safety standards, and has a split-fold rear seat.

RATINGS (SCALE OF 1-10)

Overall	Safety	Reliability	Performance	Comfort	Value
N/A	6.6	N/A	7	6.9	N/A

Model Description	Trade-in Value	Market Value
Category E		
2 Dr STD Cpe	7535	9540

OPTIONS FOR PASEO

Auto 4-Speed Transmission +435
Air Conditioning +450
AM/FM Stereo Tape +170
Rear Spoiler +115
Rear Window Defroster +90

PREVIA 1996

Supercharged engines for everyone!

RATINGS (SCALE OF 1-10)

Overall	Safety	Reliability	Performance	Comfort	Value
7.6	6.8	9	7.7	7.3	7.3

Model Description	Trade-in Value	Market Value
Category G		
2 Dr DX Sprchgd Pass. Van	12540	15290
2 Dr LE Sprchgd Pass. Van	16295	19870

Don't forget to refer to the Mileage Adjustment Table at the back of this book!

 © 1999 by Edmund Publications Corporation

Model Description	Trade-in Value	Market Value

OPTIONS FOR PREVIA

Aluminum/Alloy Wheels +190
Anti-Lock Brakes +345
Captain Chairs (4) +350
Compact Disc W/fm/tape +380
Cruise Control[Opt on DX] +115
Dual Air Conditioning[Opt on DX] +560
Keyless Entry System +115
Leather Seats +425
Luggage Rack +85
Power Door Locks[Opt on DX] +125
Power Moonroof +490
Power Windows[Opt on DX] +130
Premium Sound System +200
Running Boards +215

RAV4 1996

A cool new mini-ute based on passenger car mechanicals debuts this year. Available as a two-door or four-door, the RAV4 has a gutsy powerplant and cute-as-can-be styling. We like the RAV, but think that the Jeep Cherokee offers more bang-for-the-buck.

RATINGS (SCALE OF 1-10)

Overall	Safety	Reliability	Performance	Comfort	Value
N/A	N/A	9	7	6.4	N/A

Category G		
2 Dr STD Utility	10520	12830
2 Dr STD 4WD Utility	11685	14250
4 Dr STD Wgn	10790	13160
4 Dr STD 4WD Wgn	12045	14690

OPTIONS FOR RAV4

Auto 4-Speed Transmission +575
Air Conditioning +450
Aluminum/Alloy Wheels +190
AM/FM Compact Disc Playr +215
Anti-Lock Brakes +345
Cruise Control +115
Keyless Entry System +115
Luggage Rack +85
Power Door Locks +125
Power Windows +130

SUPRA 1996

Manual transmission Turbo models are history, thanks to stringent emission regulations. Don't worry, they're back for 1997.

Category F		
2 Dr STD Hbk	20030	24730

OPTIONS FOR SUPRA

Auto 4-Speed Transmission[Std on Turbo] +490
Sport Roof +1365
Compact Disc Changer +375
Compact Disc W/fm/tape +290
Dual Power Seats +470
Keyless Entry System +95
Leather Seats +395
Limited Slip Diff[Std on Turbo] +205

T100 1996

Essentially a carryover, but DX models are scrapped. Strangely, regular cabs can't be equipped with cruise control anymore. A new shade of red is offered, and tan interiors are offered in a wider variety of trucks.

RATINGS (SCALE OF 1-10)

Overall	Safety	Reliability	Performance	Comfort	Value
N/A	6.2	8.7	7.1	7.7	N/A

Category H		
2 Dr SR5 Ext Cab SB	13300	16025
2 Dr SR5 4WD Ext Cab SB	14085	16970
2 Dr STD Ext Cab SB	11260	13570
2 Dr STD Std Cab LB	8565	10320
2 Dr STD 4WD Ext Cab SB	12385	14925

OPTIONS FOR T100

Auto 4-Speed Transmission +490
Air Conditioning +450
Aluminum/Alloy Wheels +175
AM/FM Compact Disc Playr +165
Anti-Lock Brakes +280
Bed Liner +125
Chrome Wheels +165
Cruise Control +105
Keyless Entry System +90
Power Door Locks +105
Power Windows +105
Premium Sound System +225
Rear Step Bumper +85
Running Boards +165
Velour/Cloth Seats[Opt on Std Cab] +75

TACOMA 1996

Regular Cab 4WD models can be equipped with a new Off-Road Package.

RATINGS (SCALE OF 1-10)

Overall	Safety	Reliability	Performance	Comfort	Value
N/A	4.6	8.9	7.2	7	N/A

Category G		
2 Dr SR5 4WD Ext Cab SB	13390	16330
2 Dr STD Ext Cab SB	9290	11330
2 Dr STD Std Cab SB	9205	11225
2 Dr STD 4WD Std Cab SB	11335	13825
2 Dr STD 4WD Ext Cab SB	11380	13875
2 Dr V6 Ext Cab SB	9790	11940
2 Dr V6 4WD Ext Cab SB	11865	14470
2 Dr V6 4WD Std Cab SB	11655	14210

Don't forget to refer to the Mileage Adjustment Table at the back of this book!

 © 1999 by Edmund Publications Corporation

Model Description	Trade-in Value	Market Value

OPTIONS FOR TACOMA

Auto 4-Speed Transmission +465
Off Road Package +565
Wheel Pkg +540
Air Conditioning +450
Aluminum/Alloy Wheels +190
AM/FM Compact Disc Playr +215
Anti-Lock Brakes +345
Auto Locking Hubs (4WD)[Std on SR5] +145
Bed Liner +155
Cruise Control +115
Keyless Entry System +115
Power Door Locks +125
Power Steering[Std on SR5,V6,4WD] +155
Power Windows +130
Rear Step Bumper +80
Running Boards +215

TERCEL 1996

Base cars can be equipped with fabric seats, and a ... ha,ha,ha ... "Sports" package is available.

RATINGS (SCALE OF 1-10)

Overall	Safety	Reliability	Performance	Comfort	Value
6.9	6.3	9.1	6.6	7	5.4

Category E

Model Description	Trade-in Value	Market Value
2 Dr DX Sdn	6420	8125
4 Dr DX Sdn	6370	8065
2 Dr STD Sdn	5630	7125

OPTIONS FOR TERCEL

Auto 3-Speed Transmission +380
Auto 4-Speed Transmission +380
Air Conditioning +450
AM/FM Compact Disc Playr +260
Anti-Lock Brakes +395
Electric Sunroof +230
Keyless Entry System +80
Power Door Locks +130
Power Steering +140
Power Windows +145
Rear Window Defroster +90

1995 TOYOTA

4RUNNER 1995

V6 models get new tape stripes. Whoo-hoo!

RATINGS (SCALE OF 1-10)

Overall	Safety	Reliability	Performance	Comfort	Value
6.3	3.9	9.1	7	7	4.5

Category G

Model Description	Trade-in Value	Market Value
4 Dr Limited 4WD Wgn	14910	18405
4 Dr SR5 Wgn	13020	16070
4 Dr SR5 4WD Wgn	13315	16435
4 Dr SR5 V6 4WD Wgn	13840	17085

OPTIONS FOR 4RUNNER

Auto 4-Speed Transmission[Std on 2WD] +470
Value Package +430
Air Conditioning[Std on Limited] +370
Anti-Lock Brakes +280
Compact Disc W/fm/tape +310
Cruise Control[Std on Limited] +95
Gold Package +215
Leather Seats[Opt on SR5 V6] +350
Luggage Rack[Std on Limited] +70
Power Door Locks[Std on Limited] +105
Power Moonroof +400
Power Windows[Opt on SR5 V6,2WD] +105
Premium Sound System +165
Rear Heater +95
Running Boards +175

AVALON 1995

Marginally larger than the Camry, the Avalon is a true six-passenger sedan set to conquer Buick LeSabre and Ford Crown Victoria. Dual airbags, power windows, power mirrors, and power locks are standard. ABS is optional. Mechanicals are mostly Camry-based.

RATINGS (SCALE OF 1-10)

Overall	Safety	Reliability	Performance	Comfort	Value
8	8.3	8.6	8	8.4	6.6

Category D

Model Description	Trade-in Value	Market Value
4 Dr XL Sdn	11690	14795
4 Dr XLS Sdn	13300	16835

OPTIONS FOR AVALON

Power Bench Seat +355
Aluminum/Alloy Wheels[Opt on XL] +205
Anti-Lock Brakes[Opt on XL] +430
Compact Disc W/fm/tape +440
Dual Power Seats +380
Leather Seats +500
Power Moonroof +380
Premium Sound System[Opt on XL] +155

CAMRY 1995

Front and rear styling is updated, ABS is standard on XLE model, and Camry now meets 1997 side-impact protection standards. DX wagon dumped from lineup.

RATINGS (SCALE OF 1-10)

Overall	Safety	Reliability	Performance	Comfort	Value
7.9	7.4	9	8.6	8.4	6.2

Category D

Model Description	Trade-in Value	Market Value
2 Dr DX Cpe	7885	9985
4 Dr DX Sdn	8075	10220
2 Dr LE Cpe	9510	12035
4 Dr LE Sdn	9810	12415
4 Dr LE Wgn	10260	12990
2 Dr LE V6 Cpe	10365	13120

Don't forget to refer to the Mileage Adjustment Table at the back of this book!

 © 1999 by Edmund Publications Corporation

Model Description	Trade-in Value	Market Value
4 Dr LE V6 Wgn	11100	14050
4 Dr LE V6 Sdn	10650	13480
2 Dr SE Cpe	11240	14230
4 Dr SE Sdn	11570	14645
4 Dr XLE Sdn	11035	13970
4 Dr XLE V6 Sdn	11700	14815

OPTIONS FOR CAMRY

Auto 4-Speed Transmission[Opt on DX] +355
Elite Package +565
Leather Trim Pkg +405
Air Conditioning[Opt on DX] +385
Anti-Lock Brakes[Std on XLE,XLE V6] +430
Compact Disc W/fm/tape +440
Cruise Control[Opt on DX] +110
Leather Seats +500
Power Door Locks[Opt on DX] +120
Power Drivers Seat[Std on XLE,XLE V6] +155
Power Moonroof +380
Power Passenger Seat +175
Power Windows[Opt on DX] +120
Premium Sound System +155

CELICA 1995

GT convertible returns to lineup, available in red, white, blue or black.

RATINGS (SCALE OF 1-10)

Overall	Safety	Reliability	Performance	Comfort	Value
N/A	N/A	8.7	8.2	7.6	4.2

Category F

Model Description	Trade-in Value	Market Value
2 Dr GT Cpe	10475	13095
2 Dr GT Hbk	10695	13370
2 Dr GT Conv	12220	15275
2 Dr ST Hbk	9190	11485
2 Dr ST Cpe	9005	11255

OPTIONS FOR CELICA

Auto 4-Speed Transmission +355
Air Conditioning +380
Anti-Lock Brakes +330
Compact Disc W/fm/tape +240
Cruise Control +95
Leather Seats +325
Power Door Locks[Opt on ST] +90
Power Moonroof +325
Power Windows[Opt on ST] +100
Premium Sound System +185
Sport Suspension +120

COROLLA 1995

1.8-liter engine loses ten horsepower to meet stricter emissions regulations. Torque is up, though. DX models get new interior fabric.

RATINGS (SCALE OF 1-10)

Overall	Safety	Reliability	Performance	Comfort	Value
7.5	7.2	8.9	7.8	8.1	5.6

Category E

Model Description	Trade-in Value	Market Value
4 Dr DX Wgn	6700	8700
4 Dr DX Sdn	6585	8555
4 Dr LE Sdn	8080	10490
4 Dr STD Sdn	6260	8130

OPTIONS FOR COROLLA

Auto 3-Speed Transmission +225
Auto 4-Speed Transmission[Opt on DX] +290
Air Conditioning[Std on LE] +370
Aluminum/Alloy Wheels +145
AM/FM Compact Disc Playr +215
Anti-Lock Brakes +320
Cruise Control[Opt on DX] +100
Gold Package +175
Power Door Locks[Opt on DX] +105
Power Sunroof +275
Power Windows[Opt on DX] +120
Premium Sound System +155

LAND CRUISER 1995

Redesigned dashboard carries dual airbags, and ABS is now standard. Revised grille carries Toyota logo rather than nameplate.

RATINGS (SCALE OF 1-10)

Overall	Safety	Reliability	Performance	Comfort	Value
N/A	N/A	8.8	7.8	8	N/A

Category G

Model Description	Trade-in Value	Market Value
4 Dr STD 4WD Wgn	22630	27935

OPTIONS FOR LAND CRUISER

Leather Trim Pkg +1050
Third Seat Pkg +495
Compact Disc Changer +310
Compact Disc W/fm/tape +235
Dual Power Seats +285
Leather Seats +350
Locking Differential +135
Luggage Rack +70
Power Moonroof +400
Running Boards +175
Third Seat +340

MR2 1995

Final year for Mister Two. Several states lose Turbo model, which wouldn't pass emissions regulations. Base models with T-bar roof get power windows and locks standard.

Category F

Model Description	Trade-in Value	Market Value
2 Dr STD Cpe	12790	15990

Don't forget to refer to the Mileage Adjustment Table at the back of this book!

 © 1999 by Edmund Publications Corporation

Model Description	Trade-in Value	Market Value

OPTIONS FOR MR2

Auto 4-Speed Transmission +355
T-Bar Roof Pkg +475
Air Conditioning +380
Anti-Lock Brakes +330
Compact Disc W/fm/tape +240
Cruise Control[Std on Turbo] +95
Flip-Up Sunroof +180
Leather Seats +325
Power Door Locks[Std on Turbo] +90
Power Drivers Seat +110
Power Windows[Std on Turbo] +100

PASEO 1995

Several states with strict emissions laws get detuned Paseo for 1995.

RATINGS (SCALE OF 1-10)

Overall	Safety	Reliability	Performance	Comfort	Value
N/A	5.9	N/A	7.8	7.1	N/A

Model Description	Trade-in Value	Market Value
Category E		
2 Dr STD Cpe	6360	8255

OPTIONS FOR PASEO

Auto 4-Speed Transmission +355
Air Conditioning +370
AM/FM Stereo Tape +140

PICKUP 1995

No changes.

HALF TON

Model Description	Trade-in Value	Market Value
Category G		
2 Dr DX Ext Cab SB	8835	10905
2 Dr DX Std Cab SB	7700	9505
2 Dr DX 4WD Ext Cab SB	10195	12585
2 Dr DX 4WD Std Cab SB	8575	10585
2 Dr DX V6 Ext Cab SB	9330	11515
2 Dr DX V6 4WD Ext Cab SB	10740	13255
2 Dr DX V6 4WD Std Cab SB	9125	11265
2 Dr SR5 Ext Cab SB	10290	12705
2 Dr SR5 4WD Ext Cab SB	11390	14060
2 Dr STD Std Cab SB	7070	8725

OPTIONS FOR PICKUP

Auto 4-Speed Transmission +430
Air Conditioning +370
Aluminum/Alloy Wheels +155
AM/FM Stereo Tape +110
Anti-Lock Brakes +280
Auto Locking Hubs (4WD) +120
Bed Liner +125
Chrome Wheels +110
Cruise Control +95
Intermittent Wipers[Opt on DX] +35
Power Door Locks +105
Power Steering[Opt on DX,STD] +130
Power Windows +105
Premium Sound System +165
Rear Step Bumper +65
Running Boards +175

PREVIA 1995

Seatback map pockets and an illuminated driver's visor vanity mirror are standard on all models.

RATINGS (SCALE OF 1-10)

Overall	Safety	Reliability	Performance	Comfort	Value
7.8	7.4	8.8	7.7	7.3	7.7

Model Description	Trade-in Value	Market Value
Category G		
2 Dr DX Pass. Van	10805	13340
2 Dr DX Sprchgd Pass. Van	11000	13580
2 Dr DX 4WD Pass. Van	11460	14145
2 Dr LE Pass. Van	13945	17215
2 Dr LE Sprchgd Pass. Van	14050	17345
2 Dr LE 4WD Pass. Van	14380	17750

OPTIONS FOR PREVIA

Dual Moonroofs +635
Aluminum/Alloy Wheels +155
Anti-Lock Brakes +280
Captain Chairs (2) +215
Compact Disc W/fm/tape +310
Cruise Control[Opt on DX] +95
Dual Air Conditioning[Opt on DX] +460
Leather Seats +350
Luggage Rack +70
Power Door Locks[Opt on DX] +105
Power Moonroof +400
Power Windows[Opt on DX] +105
Premium Sound System +165
Running Boards +175

SUPRA 1995

No changes.

Model Description	Trade-in Value	Market Value
Category F		
2 Dr STD Hbk	17255	21570
2 Dr STD Turbo Hbk	19870	24840

OPTIONS FOR SUPRA

Auto 4-Speed Transmission +470
Sport Roof +515
Compact Disc W/fm/tape +240
Leather Seats +325
Limited Slip Diff[Std on Turbo] +170
Power Drivers Seat[Std on Turbo] +110

T100 1995

The 1995 T100 adds an extended-cab body style to fill out this midsized truck's lineup. A much more powerful DOHC V6 engine is introduced this year as are four-wheel antilock brakes. The antilock brakes are available only on DX and Xtracab models equipped V6 engine.

Don't forget to refer to the Mileage Adjustment Table at the back of this book!

 © 1999 by Edmund Publications Corporation

Model Description	Trade-in Value	Market Value

RATINGS (SCALE OF 1-10)

Overall	Safety	Reliability	Performance	Comfort	Value
N/A	6.9	9.1	7.1	7.7	N/A

Category H		
2 Dr DX Ext Cab SB	9505	11735
2 Dr DX Std Cab LB	9305	11490
2 Dr DX 4WD Ext Cab SB	11020	13605
2 Dr DX 4WD Std Cab LB	10370	12800
2 Dr DX 1 Ton Std Cab LB	9925	12255
2 Dr SR5 Ext Cab SB	10785	13310
2 Dr SR5 4WD Ext Cab SB	12165	15015
2 Dr STD Std Cab LB	8020	9905
2 Dr V6 Std Cab LB	8685	10720

OPTIONS FOR T100

Auto 4-Speed Transmission +400
Air Conditioning +365
Aluminum/Alloy Wheels +140
AM/FM Compact Disc Playr +135
Anti-Lock Brakes +230
Bed Liner +100
Chrome Wheels +135
Cruise Control +90
Power Door Locks +85
Power Windows +85
Premium Sound System +185
Rear Step Bumper +70
Running Boards +135
Velour/Cloth Seats[Opt on STD] +60

TACOMA 1995

Toyota puts a city on wheels. No. New compact pickup with a real name debuted in March, 1995. Optional four-wheel ABS, a driver airbag, and potent new engines are highlights of the new design. Rack and pinion steering replaces the old recirculating ball-type on the old truck. Front seatbelts are height adjustable.

RATINGS (SCALE OF 1-10)

Overall	Safety	Reliability	Performance	Comfort	Value
N/A	5.1	8.7	7.2	7	N/A

Category G		
2 Dr SR5 4WD Ext Cab SB	12095	14935
2 Dr STD Std Cab SB	8515	10510
2 Dr STD Ext Cab SB	8750	10805
2 Dr STD 4WD Ext Cab SB	10385	12820
2 Dr STD 4WD Std Cab SB	10035	12390
2 Dr V6 Ext Cab SB	8930	11025
2 Dr V6 4WD Ext Cab SB	10845	13385
2 Dr V6 4WD Std Cab SB	10470	12925

OPTIONS FOR TACOMA

Auto 4-Speed Transmission +380
Wheel Pkg +440
Air Conditioning +370
AM/FM Stereo Tape +110
Anti-Lock Brakes +280
Auto Locking Hubs (4WD) +120
Bed Liner +125
Chrome Bumpers[Std on SR5] +70
Cruise Control +95
Power Door Locks +105
Power Windows +105
Tachometer[Std on SR5] +30

TERCEL 1995

Redesigned, but based on 1991-1994 generation. Coupe and sedan body styles. Coupe available in Standard and DX trim; sedan comes in DX flavor only. Dual airbags are standard. Height-adjustable seat belts are new. Car now meets 1997 side-impact standards. Engine is more powerful than before.

RATINGS (SCALE OF 1-10)

Overall	Safety	Reliability	Performance	Comfort	Value
6.9	6.9	8.9	6.6	7	5.3

Category E		
2 Dr DX Sdn	5570	7230
4 Dr DX Sdn	5595	7265
2 Dr STD Sdn	5110	6635

OPTIONS FOR TERCEL

Auto 3-Speed Transmission +310
Auto 4-Speed Transmission +315
Air Conditioning +370
AM/FM Compact Disc Playr +215
Anti-Lock Brakes +320
Power Door Locks +105
Power Steering +115
Power Windows +120

1994 TOYOTA

4RUNNER 1994

Four-wheel ABS available on models with V6 engine. Side-door guard beams added. Air conditioners get CFC-free refrigerant. Optional leather can be had in new Oak color.

RATINGS (SCALE OF 1-10)

Overall	Safety	Reliability	Performance	Comfort	Value
6.3	3.9	9	7	7	4.4

Category G		
4 Dr SR5 4WD Wgn	11385	14230
4 Dr SR5 V6 Wgn	11195	13990
4 Dr SR5 V6 4WD Wgn	11910	14885

OPTIONS FOR 4RUNNER

Auto 4-Speed Transmission[Std on 2WD] +390
Air Conditioning +300
Anti-Lock Brakes +230

Don't forget to refer to the Mileage Adjustment Table at the back of this book!

 © 1999 by Edmund Publications Corporation

Compact Disc W/fm/tape +255
Cruise Control +80
Leather Seats +285
Luggage Rack +60
Power Door Locks +85
Power Moonroof +325
Power Windows +85
Premium Sound System +135
Rear Heater +75
Running Boards +140

CAMRY 1994

Coupe body style debuts in DX, LE and SE form. All Camrys get passenger airbag. V6 engine is tweaked for more power. New fuzzy logic controls govern automatic transmission. SE models get standard power windows, locks, mirrors and cruise control.

RATINGS (SCALE OF 1-10)

Overall	Safety	Reliability	Performance	Comfort	Value
8	7.4	8.9	8.6	8.4	6.7

Category D

Model	Trade-in Value	Market Value
2 Dr DX Cpe	6735	8635
4 Dr DX Sdn	6920	8870
4 Dr DX Wgn	7905	10135
2 Dr LE Cpe	7910	10145
4 Dr LE Sdn	8040	10305
4 Dr LE Wgn	8940	11460
2 Dr LE V6 Cpe	8670	11115
4 Dr LE V6 Sdn	8850	11345
4 Dr LE V6 Wgn	9640	12355
2 Dr SE Cpe	9365	12005
4 Dr SE Sdn	9655	12380
4 Dr XLE Sdn	9410	12060
4 Dr XLE V6 Sdn	9980	12795

OPTIONS FOR CAMRY

Auto 4-Speed Transmission[Opt on DX Sdn, DX Cpe] +295
Elite Package +425
Air Conditioning[Opt on DX] +315
Anti-Lock Brakes +355
Compact Disc W/fm/tape +360
Cruise Control[Opt on DX] +90
Leather Seats +410
Power Door Locks[Opt on DX] +100
Power Drivers Seat[Opt on LE,LE V6] +125
Power Moonroof[Std on XLE,XLE V6] +310
Premium Sound System +130

CELICA 1994

Redesigned coupe and liftback debut. Turbocharged All-Trac is gone. ST and GT are only trim levels. Dual airbags are standard; ABS is optional. Power mirrors and driver's seat height adjuster are standard.

RATINGS (SCALE OF 1-10)

Overall	Safety	Reliability	Performance	Comfort	Value
N/A	N/A	9.6	8.2	7.6	5.3

Category F

Model	Trade-in Value	Market Value
2 Dr GT Hbk	8265	10460
2 Dr GT Cpe	8260	10455
2 Dr ST Hbk	7305	9245
2 Dr ST Cpe	6965	8815

OPTIONS FOR CELICA

Auto 4-Speed Transmission +295
Air Conditioning +310
Anti-Lock Brakes +270
Compact Disc W/fm/tape +195
Cruise Control +80
Leather Seats +265
Power Door Locks[Opt on ST] +75
Power Drivers Seat +90
Power Sunroof +255
Power Windows[Opt on ST] +85
Premium Sound System +150
Sport Suspension +95

COROLLA 1994

Passenger airbag added. Passenger seatbelts have automatic locking retractors. CFC-free refrigerant is added to air conditioning system.

RATINGS (SCALE OF 1-10)

Overall	Safety	Reliability	Performance	Comfort	Value
7.5	7.2	8.8	7.8	8.1	5.6

Category E

Model	Trade-in Value	Market Value
4 Dr DX Wgn	5935	7915
4 Dr DX Sdn	5380	7175
4 Dr LE Sdn	7000	9330
4 Dr STD Sdn	4845	6460

OPTIONS FOR COROLLA

Auto 3-Speed Transmission +150
Auto 4-Speed Transmission[Opt on DX] +185
Air Conditioning[Std on LE] +300
Aluminum/Alloy Wheels +120
AM/FM Compact Disc Playr +175
Anti-Lock Brakes +265
Cruise Control[Opt on DX] +80
Power Door Locks[Opt on DX] +85
Power Sunroof +225
Power Windows[Opt on DX] +100
Premium Sound System +125

LAND CRUISER 1994

Standard sound system has nine speakers instead of five. Passenger seatbelts have automatic locking retractors.

Don't forget to refer to the Mileage Adjustment Table at the back of this book!

 © 1999 by Edmund Publications Corporation

RATINGS (SCALE OF 1-10)

Overall	Safety	Reliability	Performance	Comfort	Value
N/A	N/A	8.8	7.8	7.9	N/A

Category G

Model	Trade-in	Market
4 Dr STD 4WD Wgn	20170	25210

OPTIONS FOR LAND CRUISER

Leather Trim Package +775
Third Rear Seat Package +520
Anti-Lock Brakes +230
Compact Disc W/fm/tape +255
Leather Seats +285
Limited Slip Diff +100
Luggage Rack +60
Power Drivers Seat +105
Power Moonroof +325
Power Passenger Seat +100
Running Boards +140
Third Seat +280

MR2 1994

Passenger airbag debuts. ABS made standard. Taillights are revised, and the suspension gets further fine-tuning. Base models get standard air conditioning, which is CFC-free on both models.

Category F

Model	Trade-in	Market
2 Dr STD Cpe	10755	13615

OPTIONS FOR MR2

Auto 4-Speed Transmission +295
Anti-Lock Brakes +270
Compact Disc W/fm/tape +195
Cruise Control[Std on Turbo] +80
Flip-Up Sunroof +145
Leather Seats +265
Power Door Locks[Std on Turbo] +75
Power Windows[Std on Turbo] +85
Premium Sound System[Std on Turbo] +150
T-Bar Roof[Std on Turbo] +315

PASEO 1994

CFC-free A/C added. Passenger seatbelts get automatic locking retractors.

RATINGS (SCALE OF 1-10)

Overall	Safety	Reliability	Performance	Comfort	Value
N/A	5.9	N/A	7.8	7.1	N/A

Category E

Model	Trade-in	Market
2 Dr STD Cpe	5170	6890

OPTIONS FOR PASEO

Auto 4-Speed Transmission +295
Air Conditioning +300
AM/FM Stereo Tape +115
Anti-Lock Brakes +265
Cruise Control +80
Pop-Up Moonroof +150

PICKUP 1994

Longbed models dropped. Side-door guard beams have been added.

RATINGS (SCALE OF 1-10)

Overall	Safety	Reliability	Performance	Comfort	Value
N/A	4.5	9.2	7.1	7.1	N/A

HALF TON

Category G

Model	Trade-in	Market
2 Dr DX Ext Cab SB	6890	8615
2 Dr DX Std Cab SB	6620	8270
2 Dr DX 4WD Std Cab SB	7785	9730
2 Dr DX 4WD Ext Cab SB	8535	10665
2 Dr DX V6 Ext Cab SB	7320	9150
2 Dr DX V6 4WD Std Cab SB	8265	10330
2 Dr DX V6 4WD Ext Cab SB	9045	11305
2 Dr SR5 V6 Ext Cab SB	8025	10035
2 Dr SR5 V6 4WD Ext Cab SB	9710	12140
2 Dr STD Std Cab SB	6055	7570

OPTIONS FOR PICKUP

Auto 4-Speed Transmission +355
Air Conditioning +300
AM/FM Stereo Tape +90
Anti-Lock Rear Brakes[Std on SR5 V6] +105
Auto Locking Hubs (4WD)[Opt on DX V6] +100
Bed Liner +105
Cruise Control +80
Power Door Locks +85
Power Steering[Opt on DX,STD] +105
Power Windows +85
Premium Sound System +135
Rear Jump Seats +85
Rear Step Bumper +55
Running Boards +140
Tilt Steering Wheel[Std on SR5 V6] +65

PREVIA 1994

Passenger airbag added. Supercharged engine included on S/C models. Manual transmission is dropped. CFC-free air conditioning is new. Leather is available on LE models. New front bucket seats are installed.

RATINGS (SCALE OF 1-10)

Overall	Safety	Reliability	Performance	Comfort	Value
7.7	7.4	8.9	7.7	7.3	7.2

Category G

Model	Trade-in	Market
2 Dr DX Pass. Van	8895	11115
2 Dr DX 4WD Pass. Van	9665	12080
2 Dr LE Pass. Van	11090	13860
2 Dr LE 4WD Pass. Van	11760	14705

Don't forget to refer to the Mileage Adjustment Table at the back of this book!

 © 1999 by Edmund Publications Corporation

OPTIONS FOR PREVIA

Dual Moonroofs +575
Anti-Lock Brakes +230
Captain Chairs (2) +175
Compact Disc W/fm/tape +255
Cruise Control[Opt on DX] +80
Dual Air Conditioning[Opt on DX] +375
Luggage Rack +60
Power Door Locks[Opt on DX] +85
Power Moonroof +325
Power Windows[Opt on DX] +85
Premium Sound System +135
Running Boards +140

SUPRA 1994

Base model gets revised final-drive ratio for improved launch.

Category F

Model	Trade-in Value	Market Value
2 Dr STD Hbk	16255	20575
2 Dr STD Turbo Hbk	17235	21815

OPTIONS FOR SUPRA

Auto 4-Speed Transmission +335
Sport Roof +410
Compact Disc W/fm/tape +195
Leather Seats +265
Limited Slip Diff[Std on Turbo] +140

T100 1994

Driver airbag is added, and base models get four-cylinder engine. Side-door guard beams are installed, and beds get cargo tie-down hooks. Formerly standard rear ABS is now optional on base and DX trucks.

RATINGS (SCALE OF 1-10)

Overall	Safety	Reliability	Performance	Comfort	Value
N/A	6.7	9	6.9	7.7	N/A

Category H

Model	Trade-in Value	Market Value
2 Dr DX Std Cab LB	8470	10460
2 Dr DX 4WD Std Cab LB	8860	10940
2 Dr DX 1 Ton Std Cab LB	8965	11065
2 Dr SR5 Std Cab LB	9315	11500
2 Dr SR5 4WD Std Cab LB	9740	12025
2 Dr STD Std Cab LB	7470	9220

OPTIONS FOR T100

Auto 4-Speed Transmission +335
Air Conditioning +300
AM/FM Compact Disc Playr +110
Anti-Lock Rear Brakes[Std on SR5] +85
Bed Liner +85
Cruise Control +70
Power Door Locks +70
Power Windows +70
Premium Sound System +150
Rear Step Bumper +60

TERCEL 1994

CFC-free refrigerant added to optional A/C. Passenger seatbelts get automatic locking retractors. LE sedan is dropped.

RATINGS (SCALE OF 1-10)

Overall	Safety	Reliability	Performance	Comfort	Value
N/A	N/A	8.9	7.2	7.1	5.4

Category E

Model	Trade-in Value	Market Value
2 Dr DX Sdn	4190	5585
4 Dr DX Sdn	4285	5715
2 Dr STD Sdn	3665	4890

OPTIONS FOR TERCEL

Auto 3-Speed Transmission +185
Air Conditioning +300
AM/FM Stereo Tape +115
Anti-Lock Brakes +265
Power Steering +95

1993 TOYOTA

4RUNNER 1993

Two-door model is dropped from lineup, a victim of import tariffs. Four-wheel drive models come standard with 4WDemand system. Alloy wheels available only on V6 models, and now include chrome package.

RATINGS (SCALE OF 1-10)

Overall	Safety	Reliability	Performance	Comfort	Value
6.3	3.9	8.8	7	7	4.9

Category G

Model	Trade-in Value	Market Value
4 Dr SR5 4WD Wgn	9640	12360
4 Dr SR5 V6 Wgn	9620	12335
4 Dr SR5 V6 4WD Wgn	10165	13030

OPTIONS FOR 4RUNNER

Auto 4-Speed Transmission[Opt on 4WD] +320
Air Conditioning +245
Aluminum/Alloy Wheels +105
Anti-Lock Rear Brakes[Opt on SR5] +85
Compact Disc W/fm/tape +205
Cruise Control +65
Leather Seats +235
Luggage Rack +45
Power Door Locks +70
Power Moonroof +265
Power Windows +70
Premium Sound System +110
Rear Heater +65
Running Boards +115

CAMRY 1993

DX models get color-keyed bodyside moldings. Oak is a new interior color.

Don't forget to refer to the Mileage Adjustment Table at the back of this book!

 © 1999 by Edmund Publications Corporation

RATINGS (SCALE OF 1-10)

Overall	Safety	Reliability	Performance	Comfort	Value
N/A	N/A	8.9	8.6	8.4	6.6

Model Description	Trade-in Value	Market Value
Category D		
4 Dr DX Wgn	6705	8820
4 Dr DX Sdn	5770	7595
4 Dr DX V6 Sdn	6595	8675
4 Dr LE Sdn	6830	8985
4 Dr LE Wgn	7195	9465
4 Dr LE V6 Wgn	7825	10300
4 Dr LE V6 Sdn	7205	9480
4 Dr SE Sdn	7630	10040
4 Dr XLE Sdn	7545	9925
4 Dr XLE V6 Sdn	8025	10560

OPTIONS FOR CAMRY

Auto 4-Speed Transmission[Opt on SE,DX Sdn] +245
Air Conditioning[Opt on DX,DX V6] +255
AM/FM Compact Disc Playr +170
Anti-Lock Brakes +290
Cruise Control[Opt on DX,DX V6,SE] +75
Leather Seats +335
Power Door Locks[Opt on SE] +80
Power Moonroof[Std on XLE,XLE V6] +255
Power Windows[Opt on SE] +80
Premium Sound System +105

CELICA 1993

ABS is standard on All-Trac model; optional for first time on GT convertible.

Model Description	Trade-in Value	Market Value
Category F		
2 Dr GT Conv	8205	10655
2 Dr GT Cpe	6650	8635
2 Dr GT Hbk	6535	8485
2 Dr GT-S Hbk	7370	9570
2 Dr ST Cpe	5880	7640

OPTIONS FOR CELICA

Auto 4-Speed Transmission +235
Air Conditioning[Std on STD] +250
Aluminum/Alloy Wheels[Opt on GT] +95
Anti-Lock Brakes[Std on STD] +220
Cruise Control[Std on STD] +65
Leather Seats[Std on STD] +215
Power Door Locks[Std on STD] +60
Power Drivers Seat[Std on STD] +70
Power Sunroof[Std on STD,Conv] +205
Power Windows[Std on STD] +70

COROLLA 1993

All-new Corolla arrives with driver airbag. Sedan and wagon body styles available. All-Trac wagon dies. Interior volume increases enough to move Corolla out of subcompact classification. Height-adjustable seat belts are standard. ABS optional on all models.

RATINGS (SCALE OF 1-10)

Overall	Safety	Reliability	Performance	Comfort	Value
7.3	5.8	8.7	7.8	8.1	6.1

Model Description	Trade-in Value	Market Value
Category E		
4 Dr DX Wgn	4725	6470
4 Dr DX Sdn	4495	6160
4 Dr LE Sdn	5470	7490
4 Dr STD Sdn	4010	5490

OPTIONS FOR COROLLA

Auto 3-Speed Transmission +150
Auto 4-Speed Transmission[Opt on DX] +245
Air Conditioning[Std on LE] +245
Aluminum/Alloy Wheels +95
AM/FM Stereo Tape +95
Anti-Lock Brakes +215
Cruise Control[Opt on DX] +65
Power Door Locks[Opt on DX] +70
Power Sunroof +185
Power Windows[Opt on DX] +80

LAND CRUISER 1993

New 4.5-liter inline six pumps out 57 more horsepower than last year's engine; output is up to 212. Air conditioning and cruise control are added to the standard equipment list. Front and rear differential locks are newly optional. New leather package is available. Side-door guard beams added.

RATINGS (SCALE OF 1-10)

Overall	Safety	Reliability	Performance	Comfort	Value
N/A	N/A	8.7	7.8	7.9	N/A

Model Description	Trade-in Value	Market Value
Category G		
4 Dr STD 4WD Wgn	16050	20575

OPTIONS FOR LAND CRUISER

Leather Trim Package +755
Alarm System +105
Aluminum/Alloy Wheels +105
Anti-Lock Brakes +185
Compact Disc Changer +205
Compact Disc W/fm/tape +155
Dual Power Seats +190
Leather Seats +235
Locking Differential +90
Luggage Rack +45
Power Moonroof +265
Running Boards +115
Third Seat +230

MR2 1993

Suspension revisions aim to cure quirky cornering characteristics. All Turbos come with a standard T-bar roof. Base MR2s get V-rated tires, and alloy wheels have been redesigned. An eight-speaker stereo, air conditioning, cruise, power windows, and power door locks are all newly standard on Turbo.

Don't forget to refer to the Mileage Adjustment Table at the back of this book!

 © 1999 by Edmund Publications Corporation

Model Description	Trade-in Value	Market Value
Category F		
2 Dr STD Cpe	7300	9480
2 Dr STD Turbo Cpe	8775	11395

OPTIONS FOR MR2

Auto 4-Speed Transmission +245
Air Conditioning +250
Anti-Lock Brakes +220
Compact Disc W/fm/tape +160
Cruise Control[Std on Turbo] +65
Leather Seats +215
Limited Slip Diff +115
Power Door Locks[Std on Turbo] +60
Power Windows[Std on Turbo] +70
Premium Sound System +125
T-Tops (solid/Colored)[Std on Turbo] +280

PASEO 1993

Driver airbag added, and ABS is now optional. Interior fabrics are revised. Two new colors.

RATINGS (SCALE OF 1-10)

Overall	Safety	Reliability	Performance	Comfort	Value
N/A	5.9	N/A	7.8	7.1	N/A

Model Description	Trade-in Value	Market Value
Category E		
2 Dr STD Cpe	4300	5890

OPTIONS FOR PASEO

Auto 4-Speed Transmission +245
Air Conditioning +245
Aluminum/Alloy Wheels +95
AM/FM Stereo Tape +95
Anti-Lock Brakes +215
Cruise Control +65
Moonroof +115

PICKUP 1993

One-ton and 4WD longbed dropped.

RATINGS (SCALE OF 1-10)

Overall	Safety	Reliability	Performance	Comfort	Value
N/A	4.4	8.8	7.1	7.1	N/A

HALF TON

Model Description	Trade-in Value	Market Value
Category G		
2 Dr Deluxe Std Cab SB	5685	7290
2 Dr Deluxe Ext Cab SB	6565	8420
2 Dr Deluxe Std Cab LB	5735	7350
2 Dr Deluxe 4WD Std Cab SB	6760	8670
2 Dr Deluxe 4WD Ext Cab SB	7415	9505
2 Dr Deluxe V6 Ext Cab SB	6660	8535
2 Dr Deluxe V6 4WD Ext Cab SB	7765	9960
2 Dr SR5 V6 Ext Cab SB	7305	9365
2 Dr SR5 V6 4WD Ext Cab SB	8310	10655
2 Dr STD Std Cab SB	5355	6865

OPTIONS FOR PICKUP

6 cyl 3.0 L Engine[Opt on Deluxe] +200
Auto 4-Speed Transmission +280
Air Conditioning +245
Aluminum/Alloy Wheels +105
AM/FM Stereo Tape +75
Anti-Lock Rear Brakes[Std on SR5 V6] +85
Auto Locking Hubs (4WD) +80
Bed Liner +85
Cruise Control +65
Power Door Locks +70
Power Steering[Opt on Deluxe,STD] +85
Power Windows +70
Premium Sound System +110
Rear Step Bumper +45
Velour/Cloth Seats[Opt on STD] +55

PREVIA 1993

All Previas seat seven instead of five. Only 2WD DX can be equipped with manual transmission. All-Tracs and 2WD LE get rear disc brakes.

RATINGS (SCALE OF 1-10)

Overall	Safety	Reliability	Performance	Comfort	Value
7	5.4	8.8	7.5	7.3	5.9

Model Description	Trade-in Value	Market Value
Category G		
2 Dr Deluxe Pass. Van	6685	8570
2 Dr Deluxe 4WD Pass. Van	7515	9635
2 Dr LE Pass. Van	8715	11170
2 Dr LE 4WD Pass. Van	8895	11400

OPTIONS FOR PREVIA

Auto 4-Speed Transmission[Std on LE,4WD] +245
Aluminum/Alloy Wheels +105
Anti-Lock Brakes +185
Captain Chairs (2) +145
Compact Disc W/fm/tape +205
Cruise Control[Std on LE] +65
Dual Air Conditioning[Std on LE] +305
Luggage Rack +45
Power Door Locks[Std on LE] +70
Power Sunroof +245
Power Windows[Std on LE] +70

SUPRA 1993

Debuted in summer 1993. All-new car features dual airbags and ABS. Twin Turbo model has 320 horsepower and traction control.

Model Description	Trade-in Value	Market Value
Category F		
2 Dr STD Hbk	13070	16970
2 Dr STD Turbo Hbk	15495	20120

OPTIONS FOR SUPRA

Auto 4-Speed Transmission +135
AM/FM Compact Disc Playr +150
Leather Seats +215

Don't forget to refer to the Mileage Adjustment Table at the back of this book!

© 1999 by Edmund Publications Corporation

Model Description	Trade-in Value	Market Value	Model Description	Trade-in Value	Market Value

Limited Slip Diff[Std on Turbo] +115
Power Sunroof +205
T-Tops (solid/Colored) +280

T100 1993

New full-size Toyota pickup designed to battle Chevy C/K, Ford F-Series and Dodge Ram. 150-horsepower V6 is only powerplant. One-ton model handles 2,570 lbs.

RATINGS (SCALE OF 1-10)

Overall	Safety	Reliability	Performance	Comfort	Value
N/A	N/A	8.9	6.9	7.7	N/A

Category H	Trade-in Value	Market Value
2 Dr 1 Ton Std Cab LB	6745	8225
2 Dr SR5 Std Cab LB	7110	8670
2 Dr SR5 4WD Std Cab LB	8210	10015
2 Dr STD Std Cab LB	6295	7675
2 Dr STD 4WD Std Cab LB	7275	8870

OPTIONS FOR T100

Auto 4-Speed Transmission +275
Air Conditioning +245
Aluminum/Alloy Wheels +95
AM/FM Compact Disc Playr +90
Bed Liner +70
Cruise Control +60
Power Door Locks +55
Power Windows +60
Premium Sound System +125
Rear Step Bumper +45

TERCEL 1993

Driver airbag added, and ABS is optional for first time. Sedans get height-adjustable seatbelts. Exteriors get a new grille. DX models get body-color bumpers and moldings. Airbag is housed in new steering wheel. LE gets standard power steering.

RATINGS (SCALE OF 1-10)

Overall	Safety	Reliability	Performance	Comfort	Value
N/A	N/A	8.7	7.2	7.1	5.3

Category E	Trade-in Value	Market Value
2 Dr DX Sdn	3430	4695
4 Dr DX Sdn	3415	4680
4 Dr LE Sdn	3770	5165
2 Dr STD Sdn	2900	3975

OPTIONS FOR TERCEL

Auto 3-Speed Transmission +150
Air Conditioning +245
AM/FM Stereo Tape +95
Anti-Lock Brakes +215
Power Steering +75

1992 TOYOTA

4RUNNER 1992

New grille, front bumper and aero headlights debut. Power steering and a rear wiper/washer are standard on all models. Spare tire is moved underneath body of truck. Leather seats are newly optional on four-door models with a V6 engine.

RATINGS (SCALE OF 1-10)

Overall	Safety	Reliability	Performance	Comfort	Value
6.3	3.9	8.5	7	7	5.2

Category G	Trade-in Value	Market Value
2 Dr SR5 4WD Utility	8840	11790
4 Dr SR5 Wgn	8100	10800
4 Dr SR5 4WD Wgn	8855	11805

OPTIONS FOR 4RUNNER

6 cyl 3.0 L Engine[Std on Utility,2WD] +185
Auto 4-Speed Transmission[Opt on 4WD] +270
Air Conditioning +200
Aluminum/Alloy Wheels +85
Anti-Lock Rear Brakes +70
Auto Locking Hubs (4WD) +65
Compact Disc W/fm/tape +170
Cruise Control +50
Leather Seats +190
Luggage Rack +40
Power Door Locks +55
Power Sunroof +200
Power Windows +60
Premium Sound System +90
Rear Heater +50
Running Boards +95

CAMRY 1992

Redesign nets a driver airbag, larger engines, more interior volume and a sporty SE model. All-Trac has been dropped. ABS is optional across all trim levels and body styles.

RATINGS (SCALE OF 1-10)

Overall	Safety	Reliability	Performance	Comfort	Value
N/A	N/A	8.6	8.6	8.4	6.9

Category D	Trade-in Value	Market Value
4 Dr Deluxe Sdn	5100	6890
4 Dr Deluxe Wgn	5835	7885
4 Dr LE Sdn	5840	7890
4 Dr LE Wgn	6445	8710
4 Dr SE Sdn	6565	8875
4 Dr XLE Sdn	6640	8975

OPTIONS FOR CAMRY

6 cyl 3.0 L Engine[Std on SE] +335
Auto 4-Speed Transmission[Std on LE,XLE,Wgn] +195
Air Conditioning[Opt on Deluxe] +210

Don't forget to refer to the Mileage Adjustment Table at the back of this book!

 © 1999 by Edmund Publications Corporation

Model Description	Trade-in Value	Market Value

Aluminum/Alloy Wheels[Std on XLE] +110
Anti-Lock Brakes +235
Compact Disc W/fm/tape +240
Cruise Control[Std on LE,XLE] +60
Leather Seats +275
Power Door Locks[Opt on SE] +65
Power Moonroof[Std on XLE] +205
Power Windows[Opt on SE] +65
Premium Sound System +85

CELICA 1992

Subtle restyling, larger wheels and tires, and wider availability of ABS.

Category F

Model Description	Trade-in Value	Market Value
2 Dr GT Cpe	5355	7140
2 Dr GT Conv	7095	9465
2 Dr GT Hbk	5530	7370
2 Dr GT-S Hbk	6145	8190
2 Dr ST Cpe	4670	6225
2 Dr STD Turbo 4WD Hbk	7290	9715

OPTIONS FOR CELICA

Auto 4-Speed Transmission +175
Air Conditioning +205
Aluminum/Alloy Wheels[Opt on GT] +75
Anti-Lock Brakes +180
Compact Disc W/fm/tape +130
Cruise Control +50
Leather Seats +175
Power Door Locks[Std on STD] +50
Power Drivers Seat +60
Power Sunroof +170
Power Windows[Std on STD] +55
Premium Sound System +100

COROLLA 1992

LE sedan comes with an automatic only. Coupe body style is dropped.

Category E

Model Description	Trade-in Value	Market Value
4 Dr Deluxe Wgn	3340	4770
4 Dr Deluxe Sdn	3330	4755
4 Dr Deluxe 4WD Wgn	4585	6550
4 Dr LE Sdn	3800	5430
4 Dr STD Sdn	2955	4220

OPTIONS FOR COROLLA

Auto 3-Speed Transmission +120
Auto 4-Speed Transmission[Std on LE] +195
Air Conditioning +200
Aluminum/Alloy Wheels +80
AM/FM Stereo Tape +75
Cruise Control +55
Power Door Locks +55
Power Steering[Std on LE] +60
Power Sunroof +150
Power Windows +65

CRESSIDA 1992

No changes.

Category D

Model Description	Trade-in Value	Market Value
4 Dr STD Sdn	6725	9090

OPTIONS FOR CRESSIDA

Anti-Lock Brakes +235
Dual Power Seats +205
Leather Seats +275
Power Moonroof +205

LAND CRUISER 1992

Power windows, locks and outside mirrors are standard this year.

RATINGS (SCALE OF 1-10)

Overall	Safety	Reliability	Performance	Comfort	Value
N/A	N/A	8.5	7.4	7.9	N/A

Category G

Model Description	Trade-in Value	Market Value
4 Dr STD 4WD Wgn	12640	16855

OPTIONS FOR LAND CRUISER

Air Conditioning +200
Aluminum/Alloy Wheels +85
Compact Disc W/fm/tape +170
Cruise Control +50
Leather Seats +190
Luggage Rack +40
Power Sunroof +200
Premium Sound System +90
Third Seat +185

MR2 1992

ABS is optional.

Category F

Model Description	Trade-in Value	Market Value
2 Dr STD Cpe	6040	8050
2 Dr STD Turbo Cpe	6530	8710

OPTIONS FOR MR2

Auto 4-Speed Transmission +195
Air Conditioning +205
Anti-Lock Brakes +180
Compact Disc W/fm/tape +130
Cruise Control +50
Leather Seats +175
Power Door Locks +50
Power Windows +55
Premium Sound System +100
T-Tops (solid/Colored) +230

PASEO 1992

Sporty version of the Tercel offers more horsepower, stiffer suspension, and racier bodywork than its more pedestrian counterpart.

Don't forget to refer to the Mileage Adjustment Table at the back of this book!

 © 1999 by Edmund Publications Corporation

Model Description	Trade-in Value	Market Value

RATINGS (SCALE OF 1-10)

Overall	Safety	Reliability	Performance	Comfort	Value
N/A	3.6	N/A	7.8	7.1	N/A

Category E

Model	Trade-in	Market
2 Dr STD Cpe	3525	5040

OPTIONS FOR PASEO

Auto 4-Speed Transmission +195
Air Conditioning +200
Aluminum/Alloy Wheels +80
AM/FM Stereo Tape +75
Cruise Control +55
Moonroof +95

PICKUP 1992

New front grille debuts. Storage compartment is added to dashboard. Two-wheel drive models get full wheelcovers. Four-wheel drive models get new steel wheels and passenger assist grip.

RATINGS (SCALE OF 1-10)

Overall	Safety	Reliability	Performance	Comfort	Value
N/A	3.7	9.1	7.1	7.1	N/A

HALFTON

Category G

Model	Trade-in	Market
2 Dr Deluxe Std Cab SB	4640	6190
2 Dr Deluxe Ext Cab SB	5735	7645
2 Dr Deluxe Std Cab LB	4700	6265
2 Dr Deluxe 4WD Std Cab SB	5850	7800
2 Dr Deluxe 4WD Ext Cab SB	6715	8950
2 Dr Deluxe 4WD Std Cab LB	5920	7895
2 Dr SR5 Ext Cab SB	6425	8565
2 Dr SR5 4WD Ext Cab SB	7300	9730
2 Dr STD Std Cab SB	4390	5850

OPTIONS FOR PICKUP

6 cyl 3.0 L Engine[Opt on Deluxe] +185
Auto 4-Speed Transmission +215
Air Conditioning +200
Aluminum/Alloy Wheels +85
AM/FM Stereo Tape +60
Anti-Lock Brakes[Std on SR5] +155
Auto Locking Hubs (4WD)[Std on SR5] +65
Cruise Control +50
Power Door Locks +55
Power Steering[Std on One Ton,SR5] +70
Power Windows +60
Rear Jump Seats[Opt on One Ton,Deluxe,4WD] +55
Rear Step Bumper +35
Velour/Cloth Seats[Opt on SR5,STD,Std Cab] +45

PREVIA 1992

Driver airbag is added, and with new knee bolsters under the dash and a third brake light, the 1992 Previa becomes the first minivan to meet passenger car safety requirements, including standards for roof crush and side-impact protection. ABS is newly optional on DX models. LE models get standard power windows, locks and mirrors.

RATINGS (SCALE OF 1-10)

Overall	Safety	Reliability	Performance	Comfort	Value
7	5.2	8.6	7.5	7.3	6.3

Category G

Model	Trade-in	Market
2 Dr Deluxe Pass. Van	6070	8095
2 Dr Deluxe 4WD Pass. Van	6530	8710
2 Dr LE Pass. Van	7185	9580
2 Dr LE 4WD Pass. Van	7895	10525

OPTIONS FOR PREVIA

Auto 4-Speed Transmission[Std on LE] +205
Aluminum/Alloy Wheels +85
AM/FM Stereo Tape +60
Anti-Lock Brakes +155
Captain Chairs (2) +120
Cruise Control[Std on LE] +50
Dual Air Conditioning[Std on LE] +250
Luggage Rack +40
Power Door Locks[Std on LE] +55
Power Windows[Std on LE] +60
Premium Sound System +90

SUPRA 1992

Automatic transmission gets revised shift points.

Category F

Model	Trade-in	Market
2 Dr STD Hbk	6835	9115
2 Dr STD Turbo Hbk	8160	10875

OPTIONS FOR SUPRA

Auto 4-Speed Transmission +185
AM/FM Compact Disc Playr +120
Anti-Lock Brakes[Std on Turbo] +180
Leather Seats +175
Limited Slip Diff[Std on Turbo] +90
Solid Targa Top +245

TERCEL 1992

No changes.

RATINGS (SCALE OF 1-10)

Overall	Safety	Reliability	Performance	Comfort	Value
N/A	N/A	8.5	7.2	7.1	5.2

Category E

Model	Trade-in	Market
2 Dr DX Sdn	2850	4075
4 Dr DX Sdn	3020	4315
4 Dr LE Sdn	3280	4685
2 Dr STD Sdn	2560	3655

OPTIONS FOR TERCEL

Auto 3-Speed Transmission +120
Air Conditioning +200
AM/FM Stereo Tape +75
Power Steering +60

Don't forget to refer to the Mileage Adjustment Table at the back of this book!

© 1999 by Edmund Publications Corporation

Model Description	Trade-in Value	Market Value

1991 TOYOTA

4RUNNER 1991

No changes.

RATINGS (SCALE OF 1-10)

Overall	Safety	Reliability	Performance	Comfort	Value
6.2	3.9	8.3	7	7	4.6

Category G

Model Description	Trade-in Value	Market Value
2 Dr SR5 4WD Utility	7695	10395
4 Dr SR5 Wgn	6615	8940
4 Dr SR5 4WD Wgn	7735	10450
4 Dr SR5 V6 4WD Wgn	7885	10655

OPTIONS FOR 4RUNNER

6 cyl 3.0 L Engine[Opt on SR5] +145
Auto 4-Speed Transmission[Std on 2WD] +190
Air Conditioning +165
Aluminum/Alloy Wheels +70
Anti-Lock Brakes[Opt on SR5] +125
Compact Disc W/fm/tape +140
Cruise Control +45
Luggage Rack +30
Power Door Locks +45
Power Moonroof +180
Power Windows +50
Premium Sound System +75
Rear Heater +40
Running Boards +80

CAMRY 1991

No changes.

Category D

Model Description	Trade-in Value	Market Value
4 Dr Deluxe Sdn	3605	4940
4 Dr Deluxe Wgn	3590	4915
4 Dr Deluxe 4WD Sdn	4140	5670
4 Dr LE Wgn	4610	6315
4 Dr LE Sdn	4190	5740
4 Dr LE 4WD Sdn	4600	6300
4 Dr LE V6 Sdn	4820	6605
4 Dr STD Sdn	3420	4685

OPTIONS FOR CAMRY

6 cyl 2.5 L Engine[Opt on Deluxe] +255
Auto 4-Speed Transmission[Std on LE,LE V6,Wgn, 4WD] +135
Air Conditioning[Std on LE V6,LE Wgn] +170
Anti-Lock Brakes +195
Cruise Control[Std on LE V6,LE Wgn] +50
Leather Seats +225
Power Door Locks[Std on LE V6,LE Wgn] +55
Power Drivers Seat +70
Power Sunroof +150
Power Windows[Std on LE V6,LE Wgn] +55

CELICA 1991

Driver airbag added.

Category F

Model Description	Trade-in Value	Market Value
2 Dr GT Conv	6205	8275
2 Dr GT Cpe	4485	5975
2 Dr GT Hbk	4600	6130
2 Dr GT-S Hbk	5225	6965
2 Dr ST Cpe	4045	5395
2 Dr STD Turbo 4WD Hbk	6385	8515

OPTIONS FOR CELICA

Auto 4-Speed Transmission +135
Air Conditioning +170
Aluminum/Alloy Wheels[Opt on GT,ST] +65
Anti-Lock Brakes +145
Compact Disc W/fm/tape +105
Cruise Control[Std on STD] +40
Leather Seats +145
Power Door Locks[Std on STD] +40
Power Sunroof +140
Power Windows[Std on STD] +45
Premium Sound System +85

COROLLA 1991

All-Trac sedan dropped.

Category E

Model Description	Trade-in Value	Market Value
4 Dr Deluxe Sdn	2800	4120
4 Dr Deluxe Wgn	2975	4375
4 Dr Deluxe 4WD Wgn	3860	5675
2 Dr GT-S Cpe	3600	5295
4 Dr LE Sdn	3125	4600
2 Dr SR5 Cpe	3415	5025
4 Dr STD Sdn	2555	3755

OPTIONS FOR COROLLA

Auto 3-Speed Transmission +95
Auto 4-Speed Transmission +140
Air Conditioning +165
Aluminum/Alloy Wheels +65
AM/FM Stereo Tape +60
Cruise Control +45
Power Door Locks +45
Power Steering[Std on GT-S,LE] +50
Power Sunroof +120
Power Windows +55

CRESSIDA 1991

No changes.

Category D

Model Description	Trade-in Value	Market Value
4 Dr Luxury Sdn	5785	7930

OPTIONS FOR CRESSIDA

Anti-Lock Brakes +195
Leather Seats +225
Power Drivers Seat +70
Power Passenger Seat +75
Power Sunroof +150

Don't forget to refer to the Mileage Adjustment Table at the back of this book!

 © 1999 by Edmund Publications Corporation

Model Description	Trade-in Value	Market Value

LAND CRUISER 1991

All-new design debuted in March, 1990. Features permanent 4WD. Coil springs replace leaf springs. 4.0-liter inline six makes 155 horsepower. Optional third seat allows truck to carry seven passengers.

RATINGS (SCALE OF 1-10)

Overall	Safety	Reliability	Performance	Comfort	Value
N/A	N/A	8.2	7.4	7.9	N/A

Category G

Model Description	Trade-in Value	Market Value
4 Dr STD 4WD Wgn	11045	14925

OPTIONS FOR LAND CRUISER

Air Conditioning +165
Aluminum/Alloy Wheels +70
Compact Disc W/fm/tape +140
Cruise Control +45
Power Door Locks +45
Power Sunroof +165
Power Windows +50
Premium Sound System +75
Third Seat +150

MR2 1991

Back after one-year hiatus. Ferrari styling themes, driver airbag and optional turbocharged power make this one a winner.

Category F

Model Description	Trade-in Value	Market Value
2 Dr STD Cpe	5745	7660
2 Dr STD Turbo Cpe	6210	8275

OPTIONS FOR MR2

Auto 4-Speed Transmission +150
Air Conditioning +170
Anti-Lock Brakes +145
Compact Disc W/fm/tape +105
Cruise Control +40
Leather Seats +145
Power Door Locks +40
Power Windows +45
Premium Sound System +85

PICKUP 1991

Wider availability of shift-on-the-fly 4WD and rear ABS. All engines have fuel injection. Four-speed manual transmission dropped. SR5 trim available only with V6 engine, and SR5s get new graphics and seat fabric.

RATINGS (SCALE OF 1-10)

Overall	Safety	Reliability	Performance	Comfort	Value
N/A	3.7	9	7.1	7.1	N/A

HALF TON

Category G

Model Description	Trade-in Value	Market Value
2 Dr Deluxe Std Cab SB	4155	5615
2 Dr Deluxe Ext Cab SB	5080	6865
2 Dr Deluxe Std Cab LB	4215	5700
2 Dr Deluxe 4WD Std Cab SB	5140	6950
2 Dr Deluxe 4WD Ext Cab SB	6080	8220
2 Dr Deluxe 4WD Std Cab LB	5205	7035
2 Dr SR5 Ext Cab SB	5710	7715
2 Dr SR5 4WD Ext Cab SB	6430	8685
2 Dr STD Std Cab SB	4125	5570

OPTIONS FOR PICKUP

6 cyl 3.0 L Engine[Opt on Deluxe] +145
Auto 3-Speed Transmission +135
Auto 4-Speed Transmission +175
Air Conditioning +165
Aluminum/Alloy Wheels +70
AM/FM Stereo Tape +50
Anti-Lock Brakes +125
Auto Locking Hubs (4WD)[Std on SR5] +55
Bed Liner +55
Bucket Seats[Std on SR5,Ext Cab] +60
Cruise Control +45
Power Door Locks +45
Power Steering[Std on One Ton,SR5] +55
Power Windows +50
Rear Jump Seats[Std on SR5] +45
Rear Step Bumper +30

PREVIA 1991

Replaced Van in March, 1990. Employs midengine design driving the rear or all four wheels. ABS is optional on LE models.

RATINGS (SCALE OF 1-10)

Overall	Safety	Reliability	Performance	Comfort	Value
7.1	4.3	8.2	7.5	7.3	7.9

Category G

Model Description	Trade-in Value	Market Value
2 Dr Deluxe Pass. Van	4815	6505
2 Dr Deluxe 4WD Pass. Van	5250	7095
2 Dr LE Pass. Van	6130	8285
2 Dr LE 4WD Pass. Van	6500	8785

OPTIONS FOR PREVIA

Auto 4-Speed Transmission[Std on LE] +160
7 Passenger Seating[Std on LE] +110
Air Conditioning +165
Aluminum/Alloy Wheels +70
AM/FM Stereo Tape +50
Anti-Lock Brakes +125
Captain Chairs (4) +130
Cruise Control[Std on LE] +45
Dual Air Conditioning[Std on LE] +205
Power Door Locks[Std on LE] +45
Power Windows +50
Premium Sound System +75

Don't forget to refer to the Mileage Adjustment Table at the back of this book!

 © 1999 by Edmund Publications Corporation

Model Description	Trade-in Value	Market Value

SUPRA 1991

ABS made standard on Turbo.

Category F

2 Dr STD Hbk	5845	7795
2 Dr STD Turbo Hbk	6710	8945

OPTIONS FOR SUPRA

Auto 4-Speed Transmission +150
Sport Handling Package +160
AM/FM Compact Disc Playr +100
Anti-Lock Brakes[Std on Turbo] +145
Leather Seats +145
Power Drivers Seat +50
Power Sunroof +140
Solid Targa Top +200

TERCEL 1991

Redesigned Tercel available in coupe and sedan versions only.

RATINGS (SCALE OF 1-10)

Overall	Safety	Reliability	Performance	Comfort	Value
N/A	N/A	8.4	7.2	7.1	4.7

Category E

2 Dr DX Sdn	2435	3580
4 Dr DX Sdn	2560	3765
4 Dr LE Sdn	2785	4095
2 Dr STD Sdn	2210	3250

OPTIONS FOR TERCEL

Auto 3-Speed Transmission +95
Air Conditioning +165
AM/FM Stereo Tape +60
Power Steering[Opt on DX] +50

1990 TOYOTA

4RUNNER 1990

Introduced in mid-1989, the 1990 4Runner is based on the 1989 Pickup. Rear ABS is standard, but works only in 2WD. Removable rear roof section disappears. Shift-on-the-fly 4WD is now optional. Two- and four-door models are available.

RATINGS (SCALE OF 1-10)

Overall	Safety	Reliability	Performance	Comfort	Value
6.1	3.9	8.2	7	7	4.6

Category G

2 Dr SR5 4WD Utility	6295	8745
4 Dr SR5 Wgn	5955	8270
4 Dr SR5 4WD Wgn	6470	8985
2 Dr SR5 V6 4WD Utility	6555	9105
4 Dr SR5 V6 Wgn	6140	8525
4 Dr SR5 V6 4WD Wgn	6795	9435

OPTIONS FOR 4RUNNER

Auto 4-Speed Transmission[Std on 2WD] +185
Compact Disc/Power Pkg +215
Air Conditioning +135
Aluminum/Alloy Wheels +55
Anti-Lock Brakes[Std on SR5 V6,2WD] +100
Auto Locking Hubs (4WD) +45
Compact Disc W/fm/tape +115
Cruise Control +35
Power Door Locks +40
Power Moonroof +145
Power Windows[Opt on SR5,Wgn] +40
Premium Sound System +60
Rear Heater +35
Running Boards +65

CAMRY 1990

Base models get new seat fabric and dual cupholders. V6 models get more power. Optional split-folding rear seats are available on Deluxe.

Category D

4 Dr Deluxe Wgn	3430	4765
4 Dr Deluxe Sdn	3065	4255
4 Dr LE Sdn	3330	4625
4 Dr LE Wgn	4165	5785
4 Dr STD Sdn	2900	4025

OPTIONS FOR CAMRY

6 cyl 2.5 L Engine[Opt on Deluxe,Sdn] +180
Auto 4-Speed Transmission[Std on LE,Wgn] +110
Air Conditioning[Std on LE Wgn] +140
Aluminum/Alloy Wheels +75
AM/FM Stereo Tape[Std on LE Wgn] +60
Anti-Lock Brakes +155
Cruise Control[Std on LE Wgn] +40
Leather Seats +185
Power Door Locks[Opt on Deluxe,Sdn] +45
Power Drivers Seat +55
Power Sunroof +120
Power Windows[Opt on Deluxe,Sdn] +45
Premium Sound System +55

CELICA 1990

Completely redesigned for 1990. GT-S engine is larger. All-Trac Turbo still for sale. Audio systems are substantially upgraded.

Category F

2 Dr GT Cpe	3620	4830
2 Dr GT Hbk	3785	5045
2 Dr GT-S Hbk	4220	5625
2 Dr ST Cpe	3385	4515
2 Dr STD Turbo 4WD Hbk	4660	6215

OPTIONS FOR CELICA

Auto 4-Speed Transmission +115
Air Conditioning +140
Aluminum/Alloy Wheels[Opt on GT] +50

Don't forget to refer to the Mileage Adjustment Table at the back of this book!

© 1999 by Edmund Publications Corporation

Model Description	Trade-in Value	Market Value

Compact Disc W/fm/tape +85
Cruise Control[Std on STD] +35
Leather Seats +120
Power Door Locks[Std on STD] +35
Power Drivers Seat +40
Power Sunroof +115
Power Windows[Std on STD] +35
Premium Sound System +70

COROLLA 1990

Fuel injection standard on all Corollas. GT-S model gets more horsepower. All other Corollas get 100-horsepower engine.

Category E

Model Description	Trade-in Value	Market Value
4 Dr Deluxe Wgn	2470	3795
4 Dr Deluxe Sdn	2310	3555
2 Dr GT-S Cpe	2875	4425
4 Dr LE Sdn	2490	3835
2 Dr SR5 Cpe	2740	4215
4 Dr STD Sdn	2125	3270

OPTIONS FOR COROLLA

Auto 3-Speed Transmission +80
Auto 4-Speed Transmission +110
Air Conditioning +135
Aluminum/Alloy Wheels +50
AM/FM Stereo Tape +50
Cruise Control +35
Power Door Locks +40
Power Sunroof +100
Power Windows +45
Premium Sound System +55

CRESSIDA 1990

No changes.

Category D

Model Description	Trade-in Value	Market Value
4 Dr Luxury Sdn	4695	6525

OPTIONS FOR CRESSIDA

Anti-Lock Brakes +155
Leather Seats +185
Power Drivers Seat +55
Power Sunroof +120

LAND CRUISER 1990

No changes.

Category G

Model Description	Trade-in Value	Market Value
4 Dr STD 4WD Wgn	7855	10910

OPTIONS FOR LAND CRUISER

Air Conditioning +135
AM/FM Stereo Tape +40
Power Door Locks +40
Power Windows +40

PICKUP 1990

SR5 V6 models get rear wheel ABS standard. This feature is optional on SR5 four-cylinder trucks.

RATINGS (SCALE OF 1-10)

Overall	Safety	Reliability	Performance	Comfort	Value
N/A	3.7	8.7	7.1	7.1	N/A

HALF TON

Category G

Model Description	Trade-in Value	Market Value
2 Dr Deluxe Std Cab SB	3555	4935
2 Dr Deluxe Ext Cab SB	4585	6365
2 Dr Deluxe Std Cab LB	3770	5240
2 Dr Deluxe 4WD Ext Cab SB	5475	7600
2 Dr Deluxe 4WD Std Cab SB	4635	6440
2 Dr Deluxe 4WD Std Cab LB	4355	6050
2 Dr SR5 Ext Cab SB	5170	7180
2 Dr SR5 Std Cab LB	4190	5815
2 Dr SR5 4WD Std Cab SB	4925	6840
2 Dr SR5 4WD Ext Cab SB	5780	8030
2 Dr STD Std Cab SB	3420	4750

OPTIONS FOR PICKUP

6 cyl 3.0 L Engine[Std on One Ton] +145
Auto 4-Speed Transmission +135
Air Conditioning +135
Aluminum/Alloy Wheels +55
AM/FM Stereo Tape +40
Anti-Lock Brakes +100
Auto Locking Hubs (4WD) +45
Bucket Seats[Std on Ext Cab] +50
Chrome Wheels +40
Cruise Control +35
Power Door Locks +40
Power Steering[Std on One Ton] +45
Power Windows +40
Premium Sound System +60
Rear Jump Seats[Std on SR5] +40

SUPRA 1990

Driver airbag added. ABS is optional.

Category F

Model Description	Trade-in Value	Market Value
2 Dr STD Hbk	5140	6850
2 Dr STD Turbo Hbk	5875	7830

OPTIONS FOR SUPRA

Auto 4-Speed Transmission +125
Sport Handling Package +130
AM/FM Compact Disc Playr +80
Anti-Lock Brakes +120
Leather Seats +120
Power Drivers Seat +40
Solid Targa Top +165

TERCEL 1990

Four-door hatchback model dropped, and two-door Deluxe hatchback axed. Passive restraints added, and automatic transmissions get shift interlock.

Don't forget to refer to the Mileage Adjustment Table at the back of this book!

 © 1999 by Edmund Publications Corporation

Model Description	Trade-in Value	Market Value
Category E		
2 Dr Base Hbk	1885	2900
2 Dr Deluxe Cpe	1785	2745
2 Dr EZ Hbk	1530	2355
2 Dr STD Cpe	1690	2605
2 Dr STD Hbk	1790	2755

OPTIONS FOR TERCEL

Auto 3-Speed Transmission +75
Air Conditioning +135
AM/FM Stereo Tape +50
Power Steering[Opt on STD] +40

1989 TOYOTA

4RUNNER 1989

No changes in 1989.

Model Description	Trade-in Value	Market Value
Category G		
2 Dr Deluxe 4WD Utility	4875	7060
2 Dr SR5 4WD Utility	5250	7610

OPTIONS FOR 4RUNNER

6 cyl 3.0 L Engine +135
Auto 4-Speed Transmission +155
Air Conditioning +110
Aluminum/Alloy Wheels +45
AM/FM Stereo Tape +35
Cruise Control +30
Moonroof +50
Power Door Locks +30
Power Windows +30
Premium Sound System +50
Rear Heater +30

CAMRY 1989

All-Trac 4WD sedan gets optional automatic transmission. Five-speed LE All-Trac dropped. Camrys with four-cylinder engine get redesigned engine mounts. ABS is optional on LE V6 models, and on All-Trac. All-Trac models available only with four-cylinder engine.

Model Description	Trade-in Value	Market Value
Category D		
4 Dr Deluxe Sdn	2695	3905
4 Dr Deluxe Wgn	2760	4000
4 Dr LE Wgn	3050	4415
4 Dr LE Sdn	2910	4220
4 Dr LE 4WD Sdn	3380	4900
4 Dr STD Sdn	2350	3405

OPTIONS FOR CAMRY

6 cyl 2.5 L Engine +155
Auto 4-Speed Transmission[Std on LE] +100
Air Conditioning +115
AM/FM Stereo Tape +50
Anti-Lock Brakes +130
Cruise Control +35
Power Door Locks +35
Power Drivers Seat +45
Power Moonroof +115
Power Windows +35
Premium Sound System +45

CELICA 1989

ST and GT models get full wheelcovers. GT can be ordered with rear spoiler. ABS is optional on GT-S and All-Trac Turbo. Rare All-Trac Turbo boasts 190 horsepower, 55 more than GT-S model.

Model Description	Trade-in Value	Market Value
Category F		
2 Dr GT Hbk	2520	3500
2 Dr GT Conv	3545	4925
2 Dr GT Cpe	2520	3500
2 Dr GT-S Cpe	2720	3780
2 Dr GT-S Hbk	2595	3600
2 Dr ST Cpe	2195	3050

OPTIONS FOR CELICA

Auto 4-Speed Transmission +90
Air Conditioning +115
Aluminum/Alloy Wheels[Opt on GT] +40
Anti-Lock Brakes +100
Cruise Control +30
Leather Seats +95
Power Sunroof +90
Power Windows[Std on STD] +30
Premium Sound System +55

COROLLA 1989

All-Trac Deluxe sedan added to lineup.

Model Description	Trade-in Value	Market Value
Category E		
4 Dr Deluxe Sdn	1735	2845
4 Dr Deluxe Wgn	1800	2950
4 Dr Deluxe 4WD Wgn	2395	3925
2 Dr GT-S Cpe	2010	3295
4 Dr LE Sdn	1765	2895
2 Dr SR5 Cpe	1830	3000
4 Dr SR5 4WD Wgn	2410	3950

OPTIONS FOR COROLLA

Auto 3-Speed Transmission +65
Auto 4-Speed Transmission +95
Air Conditioning +110
Aluminum/Alloy Wheels +45
AM/FM Stereo Tape +40
Cruise Control +30
Power Door Locks +30
Power Sunroof +80
Power Windows +35
Premium Sound System +45

CRESSIDA 1989

All-new design debuts with detuned version of Supra's 3.0-liter V6. ABS is optional.

Model Description	Trade-in Value	Market Value
Category D		
4 Dr Luxury Sdn	3790	5490

Don't forget to refer to the Mileage Adjustment Table at the back of this book!

 © 1999 by Edmund Publications Corporation

Model Description	Trade-in Value	Market Value

OPTIONS FOR CRESSIDA

Anti-Lock Brakes +130
Leather Seats +150
Power Drivers Seat +45
Power Sunroof +100

LAND CRUISER 1989

No changes.

Category G

Model Description	Trade-in Value	Market Value
4 Dr STD 4WD Wgn	6570	9520

OPTIONS FOR LAND CRUISER

Air Conditioning +110
AM/FM Stereo Tape +35
Power Door Locks +30
Power Windows +30

MR2 1989

Supercharged models get a standard rear stabilizer bar.

Category F

Model Description	Trade-in Value	Market Value
2 Dr STD Cpe	2610	3625
2 Dr STD Sprchgd Cpe	2945	4085

OPTIONS FOR MR2

Auto 4-Speed Transmission +100
Air Conditioning +115
Aluminum/Alloy Wheels[Std on Sprchgd] +40
Cruise Control +30
Leather Seats +95
Power Windows +30
Premium Sound System +55
Rear Spoiler[Std on Sprchgd] +40
T-Tops (solid/Colored)[Std on Sprchgd] +125

PICKUP 1989

All-new design debuts, featuring optional V6 power. Extended-cab models include forward facing bench seat with three-point seatbelts. One-ton 2WD model available with 5,000-lb. towing capacity.

RATINGS (SCALE OF 1-10)

Overall	Safety	Reliability	Performance	Comfort	Value
N/A	3.4	8.7	7.1	7.1	N/A

HALF TON

Category G

Model Description	Trade-in Value	Market Value
2 Dr Deluxe Std Cab SB	3055	4425
2 Dr Deluxe Ext Cab SB	3665	5310
2 Dr Deluxe Std Cab LB	3075	4460
2 Dr Deluxe 4WD Std Cab SB	3730	5410
2 Dr Deluxe 4WD Ext Cab SB	4600	6670
2 Dr Deluxe 4WD Std Cab LB	3985	5775
2 Dr SR5 Ext Cab SB	4505	6530
2 Dr SR5 Std Cab LB	3210	4650
2 Dr SR5 4WD Ext Cab SB	4810	6970
2 Dr SR5 4WD Std Cab SB	4450	6450
2 Dr STD Std Cab SB	2710	3930

ONE TON

Category G

Model Description	Trade-in Value	Market Value
2 Dr STD Std Cab LB	3635	5270

OPTIONS FOR PICKUP

6 cyl 3.0 L Engine[Std on One Ton] +135
Auto 4-Speed Transmission +120
Air Conditioning +110
Aluminum/Alloy Wheels +45
AM/FM Stereo Tape +35
Auto Locking Hubs (4WD) +35
Chrome Wheels +30
Cruise Control +30
Power Door Locks +30
Power Steering[Std on One Ton,Half Ton SR5 4WD Ext Cab SB,Half Ton SR5 4WD Std Cab SB] +40
Power Windows +30
Premium Sound System +50

SUPRA 1989

Automatic transmission gets a shift lock, suspensions are retuned, and Turbos get more power. Speed-sensitive steering is optional on base models and standard on Turbos. Minor styling changes inside and out.

Category F

Model Description	Trade-in Value	Market Value
2 Dr STD Hbk	4085	5675
2 Dr STD Turbo Hbk	4480	6220

OPTIONS FOR SUPRA

Auto 4-Speed Transmission +100
AM/FM Compact Disc Playr +65
Anti-Lock Brakes +100
Leather Seats +95
Limited Slip Diff[Std on Turbo] +50
Power Drivers Seat +30
Rear Spoiler[Std on Turbo] +40
Solid Targa Top +135
Sport Suspension +35

TERCEL 1989

Upgraded seat fabrics, dual outside mirrors, and optional full wheelcovers on Deluxe models.

Category E

Model Description	Trade-in Value	Market Value
2 Dr Deluxe Cpe	1460	2395
2 Dr Deluxe Hbk	1285	2105
4 Dr Deluxe Hbk	1255	2055
2 Dr EZ Hbk	1250	2050
2 Dr STD Cpe	1245	2040
2 Dr STD Hbk	1215	1990

OPTIONS FOR TERCEL

5-Speed Transmission[Std on Deluxe,Cpe] +115
Auto 3-Speed Transmission +85
Air Conditioning +110

Don't forget to refer to the Mileage Adjustment Table at the back of this book!

 © 1999 by Edmund Publications Corporation

Model Description	Trade-in Value	Market Value

AM/FM Stereo Tape +40
Cruise Control +30
Power Steering +35

VANWAGON 1989

New colors and three-point seatbelts debut. Four-wheel drive Deluxe model added; five-speed 4WD LE is dropped. Final year for Igloo cooler on wheels.

Category G		
2 Dr Deluxe Pass. Van	2480	3590
2 Dr LE Pass. Van	2610	3785
2 Dr LE 4WD Pass. Van	3270	4740
2 Dr Panel Cargo Van	1630	2365
2 Dr Window Cargo Van	1980	2870

OPTIONS FOR VANWAGON
Auto 4-Speed Transmission[Opt onDeluxe, Window,2WD] +90
Dual Sunroof Package +100
Air Conditioning +110
Aluminum/Alloy Wheels +45
AM/FM Stereo Tape +35
Captain Chairs (2) +65
Chrome Wheels +30
Cruise Control +30
Dual Air Conditioning +135
Power Door Locks[Std on LE] +30
Power Windows +30
Premium Sound System +50
Rear Heater[Std on Deluxe,LE] +30

Instant
Lease & Loan Quotes
for New & Used Vehicles!
www.CarFinance.com/edmunds

Major Savings
On An
Extended Warranty
"YOU DESERVE THE BEST"
Call today for your free quote.
Pay up to 50% less than dealership prices!
http://www.edmunds.com/warranty 1-800-580-9889

Don't forget to refer to the Mileage Adjustment Table at the back of this book!

 © 1999 by Edmund Publications Corporation

VOLKSWAGEN Germany

1996 Volkswagen Cabrio

1998 VOLKSWAGEN

CABRIO 1998

The Highline trim designation is replaced by more sensible GLS nomenclature, though we'd prefer to see something like GTI grace the rear flanks of this drop-top. New GLS models gets a power top, making the Cabrio easier to live with. Optional are side impact airbags mounted inside the seats. Newly standard on both base and GLS are door pocket liners, a trunk cargo net and sport seats with height adjustment. Still no much-needed power boost.

Model Description	Trade-in Value	Market Value
Category F		
2 Dr GL Conv	14420	16965
2 Dr GLS Conv	16180	19035

OPTIONS FOR CABRIO

Auto 4-Speed Transmission +725
Air Conditioning[Opt on GL] +690
Aluminum/Alloy Wheels[Opt on GL] +260
Compact Disc Changer +560
Cruise Control[Opt on GL] +175
Heated Front Seats +280
Heated Power Mirrors[Opt on GL] +235
Keyless Entry System +145
Power Windows[Opt on GL] +185
Side Air Bag Restraint +325

GOLF 1998

All Golfs get standard remote keyless entry. GL has revised wheel covers.

Model Description	Trade-in Value	Market Value
Category E		
4 Dr GL Hbk	10245	12490
4 Dr K2 Hbk	11990	14620
4 Dr Wolfsburg Hbk	12850	15670

OPTIONS FOR GOLF

Auto 4-Speed Transmission +725
Air Conditioning[Std on Wolfsburg] +675
Anti-Lock Brakes +590
Compact Disc Changer +465
Cruise Control +185
Power Moonroof[Std on Wolfsburg] +485
Power Windows[Std on K2] +220
Side Air Bag Restraint +220

GTI 1998

GTI VR6 receives several cosmetic upgrades taken from the 1997 Driver's Edition. Among them are a chrome-tipped exhaust pipe, silver/white-faced instruments, embossed sill covers, leather-wrapped steering wheel, shift boot and handbrake lever (with stitching designed to coordinate with new Sport-Jacquard seat fabric) and the aluminum ball shift knob. Exclusive to the VR6 for 1998 are the Speedline 15-inch alloys from the Driver's Edition and one-touch up power windows with pinch protection. All GTIs get standard remote keyless entry.

Model Description	Trade-in Value	Market Value
Category E		
2 Dr STD Hbk	11975	14600
Category F		
2 Dr VR6 Hbk	14460	17635

OPTIONS FOR GTI

Auto 4-Speed Transmission +725
AM/FM Compact Disc Playr +390
Compact Disc Changer +465
Leather Seats +740
Side Air Bag Restraint +220

JETTA 1998

The TDI has finally arrived. New wheel covers and colors spruce up the exterior for another year, while remote keyless entry makes it easier to lock and unlock the Jetta. GLX models have new one-touch up power windows with pinch protection.

Model Description	Trade-in Value	Market Value
Category D		
4 Dr GL Sdn	10210	12010
4 Dr GLS Sdn	12490	14695
4 Dr GLX Sdn	16065	18900
4 Dr GT Sdn	10550	12410
4 Dr K2 Sdn	12105	14240
4 Dr TDI Turbodsl Sdn	11550	13590
4 Dr Wolfsburg Sdn	12500	14710

OPTIONS FOR JETTA

Auto 4-Speed Transmission +740
Air Conditioning[Opt on GL, GT, TDI] +700
Aluminum/Alloy Wheels[Opt on GL, TDI] +375
Anti-Lock Brakes[Std on GLX] +790
Bose Sound System[Opt on GLS] +605
Compact Disc Changer[Std on Wolfsburg] +550
Cruise Control[Std on GLS, GLX, TDI] +200
Heated Front Seats +305

Don't forget to refer to the Mileage Adjustment Table at the back of this book!

© 1999 by Edmund Publications Corporation

Heated Power Mirrors[Std on GLS, GLX] +75
Leather Seats +915
Power Moonroof[Std on GLX, Wolfsburg] +695
Power Windows[Std on GLS, GLX] +220
Side Air Bag Restraint +240

NEW BEETLE 1998

Volkswagen attempts to revive a legend using retro styling touches wrapped around Golf underpinnings.

Category E

Model Description	Trade-in Value	Market Value
2 Dr STD Sdn	15015	18310
2 Dr TDI Turbodsl Sdn	15885	19370

OPTIONS FOR NEW BEETLE

Auto 4-Speed Transmission +765
Aluminum/Alloy Wheels +265
Anti-Lock Brakes +590
Compact Disc Changer +465
Cruise Control[Std on TDI] +185
Fog Lights +125
Heated Front Seats +125
Power Windows +220

PASSAT 1998

An all-new Passat arrives wearing stylish sheetmetal over a stretched Audi A4 platform. Engine choices include a spunky turbocharged four or a silky V6.

Category D

Model Description	Trade-in Value	Market Value
4 Dr GLS Turbo Wgn	16740	19695
4 Dr GLS Turbo Sdn	16495	19405
4 Dr GLS V6 Sdn	16915	19900

OPTIONS FOR PASSAT

Auto 5-Speed Transmission +895
Heated Front Seats[Std on GLX] +305
Leather Seats[Std on GLX] +915
Power Moonroof[Std on GLX] +695

1997 VOLKSWAGEN

CABRIO 1997

Cabrio comes in two trim levels for 1997: Base and Highline. Base models are decontented versions of last year's car, priced a couple thousand dollars lower to entice young drivers. Highline models have standard alloy wheels, fog lights and leather seats. Engines have a redesigned cylinder head resulting in quieter operation.

RATINGS (SCALE OF 1-10)

Overall	Safety	Reliability	Performance	Comfort	Value
7	6.1	8.9	7.8	6.4	5.7

Category F

Model Description	Trade-in Value	Market Value
2 Dr Highline Conv	13715	16135
2 Dr STD Conv	12665	14900

OPTIONS FOR CABRIO

Auto 4-Speed Transmission +595
Air Conditioning[Opt on STD] +565
Aluminum/Alloy Wheels[Opt on STD] +210
AM/FM Stereo Tape +135
Compact Disc Changer +455
Cruise Control[Opt on STD] +140
Heated Front Seats +230
Power Windows[Opt on STD] +150

GOLF 1997

GTI VR6 gets a lowered suspension for improved handling, and a redesigned cylinder head quiets GL and GTI models. A K2 edition debuted in December, 1996, sporting heated front seats, premium sound, and a rack with either skis or a snowboard attached. Spring, 1997 brought a slick Trek model with alloys and a bike up top.

RATINGS (SCALE OF 1-10)

Overall	Safety	Reliability	Performance	Comfort	Value
7.3	5.9	8.4	8.6	7.6	6

Category E

Model Description	Trade-in Value	Market Value
2 Dr GL Hbk	9770	12215
4 Dr GL Hbk	8865	11085
4 Dr K2 Hbk	9020	11275
4 Dr Trek Hbk	9225	11530

OPTIONS FOR GOLF

Auto 4-Speed Transmission +445
Air Conditioning +550
AM/FM Stereo Tape[Std on K2] +210
Anti-Lock Brakes +480
Compact Disc Changer +380
Power Moonroof +395

GTI 1997

Category E

Model Description	Trade-in Value	Market Value
2 Dr STD Hbk	10370	12960

Category F

Model Description	Trade-in Value	Market Value
2 Dr VR6 Hbk	13055	15360

OPTIONS FOR GTI

Auto 4-Speed Transmission +595
Compact Disc Changer +380
Leather Seats +485

JETTA 1997

Wolfsburg models are gone, and the Jetta GT arrives sporting the look of the GLX without that darn expensive VR6 engine. Trek gets alloy wheels. GL, GLS, Trek and GT run more quietly, thanks to a new cylinder head design.

RATINGS (SCALE OF 1-10)

Overall	Safety	Reliability	Performance	Comfort	Value
7.2	5.9	8.1	8.6	7.6	5.9

Don't forget to refer to the Mileage Adjustment Table at the back of this book!

 © 1999 by Edmund Publications Corporation

Model Description	Trade-in Value	Market Value
Category D		
4 Dr GL Sdn	9415	11345
4 Dr GLS Sdn	11425	13765
4 Dr GLX Sdn	13500	16265
4 Dr GT Sdn	9655	11630
4 Dr Trek Sdn	9530	11485

OPTIONS FOR JETTA

Auto 4-Speed Transmission +600
Air Conditioning[Std on GLS,GLX] +575
Aluminum/Alloy Wheels[Opt on GL] +305
AM/FM Compact Disc Playr +380
Anti-Lock Brakes[Std on GLX] +645
Bose Sound System[Opt on GLS] +495
Cruise Control[Opt on GL,GT,Trek] +165
Heated Front Seats +250
Heated Power Mirrors[Opt on Trek] +60
Leather Seats +750
Power Moonroof[Std on GLX] +565
Power Windows[Opt on Trek] +180

PASSAT 1997

GLS model vanishes from radar as Volkswagen prepares for launch of all-new Passat in mid-1997.

RATINGS (SCALE OF 1-10)

Overall	Safety	Reliability	Performance	Comfort	Value
7.1	7.2	8.4	8	8	3.8

Model Description	Trade-in Value	Market Value
Category D		
4 Dr GLX Wgn	13400	16145
4 Dr GLX Sdn	13100	15780
4 Dr TDI Turbodsl Sdn	13345	16080

OPTIONS FOR PASSAT

Auto 4-Speed Transmission +600
Anti-Lock Brakes[Opt on TDI] +645
Compact Disc Changer +450
Heated Front Seats +250
Leather Seats +750
Power Moonroof +565

1996 VOLKSWAGEN

CABRIO 1996

Daytime running lights and new body-color side moldings alter the exterior appearance of the 1996 Cabrio. A new color scheme also livens things up. Central locking and unlocking switch is dash mounted.

RATINGS (SCALE OF 1-10)

Overall	Safety	Reliability	Performance	Comfort	Value
7	6.1	8.7	7.8	6.4	6

Model Description	Trade-in Value	Market Value
Category F		
2 Dr STD Conv	11835	14260

OPTIONS FOR CABRIO

Auto 4-Speed Transmission +460
Air Conditioning +460
Aluminum/Alloy Wheels +170
Leather Seats +395

GOLF 1996

The Golf Sport becomes the GTI, powered by a 2.0-liter four-cylinder with alloys, sport seats, and smoke-tinted taillights. GTI VR6 continues, with firmer front suspension, three new colors, and new "Pininfarina" style alloy wheels. Black leather seats are newly optional on GTI VR6. Automatic transmissions are smoother this year.

RATINGS (SCALE OF 1-10)

Overall	Safety	Reliability	Performance	Comfort	Value
7.3	5.9	8.1	8.6	7.6	6.4

Model Description	Trade-in Value	Market Value
Category E		
4 Dr GL Hbk	8050	10190

OPTIONS FOR GOLF

Auto 4-Speed Transmission +480
Air Conditioning +450
AM/FM Stereo Tape +170
Anti-Lock Brakes +395
Compact Disc Changer +310
Power Moonroof +325

GTI 1996

Model Description	Trade-in Value	Market Value
Category E		
2 Dr STD Hbk	9640	12205
Category F		
2 Dr VR6 Hbk	11585	13955

OPTIONS FOR GTI

Auto 4-Speed Transmission +480
Compact Disc Changer +310
Leather Seats +395

JETTA 1996

A new grille is added up front. GLX models get a firmer front suspension and new "Bugatti" style wheels. New colors sum up the changes.

RATINGS (SCALE OF 1-10)

Overall	Safety	Reliability	Performance	Comfort	Value
7.2	5.9	7.8	8.6	7.6	6.3

Model Description	Trade-in Value	Market Value
Category D		
4 Dr City Sdn	8105	10130
4 Dr GL Sdn	8210	10265
4 Dr GLS Sdn	9695	12120
4 Dr GLX Sdn	11625	14530
4 Dr Trek Limited Ed. Sdn	8370	10460
4 Dr Wolfsburg Sdn	8840	11055

Don't forget to refer to the Mileage Adjustment Table at the back of this book!

 © 1999 by Edmund Publications Corporation

Model Description	Trade-in Value	Market Value

OPTIONS FOR JETTA

Auto 4-Speed Transmission +500
Air Conditioning[Std on GLS,GLX] +470
Aluminum/Alloy Wheels[Opt on GL] +250
AM/FM Compact Disc Playr[Std on TDI] +310
Anti-Lock Brakes[Std on GLX] +530
Bose Sound System[Opt on GLS] +405
Cruise Control[Std on GLS,GLX] +135
Heated Front Seats +205
Leather Seats +610
Power Moonroof[Std on GLX,Wolfsburg] +465

PASSAT 1996

Daytime running lights debut, two new colors are added to the palette, and a new price-leader GLS model powered by a 2.0-liter, 115-horsepower, four-cylinder engine is introduced. Midyear, a Turbo Direct Injection (TDI) diesel model appears in sedan and wagon form.

RATINGS (SCALE OF 1-10)

Overall	Safety	Reliability	Performance	Comfort	Value
7.1	7.2	8.3	8	8	4.3

Category D

Model	Trade-in	Market
4 Dr GLS Sdn	9565	11955
4 Dr GLX Sdn	11225	14035
4 Dr GLX Wgn	11155	13945
4 Dr TDI Turbodsl Sdn	11320	14145
4 Dr TDI Turbodsl Wgn	11640	14550

OPTIONS FOR PASSAT

Auto 4-Speed Transmission +435
Anti-Lock Brakes[Std on GLX] +530
Compact Disc Changer +365
Heated Front Seats +205
Leather Seats +610
Power Moonroof +465

1995 VOLKSWAGEN

CABRIO 1995

Dual airbags, ABS, and 115-horsepower engine are standard on this Golf derivative. Manual top only.

RATINGS (SCALE OF 1-10)

Overall	Safety	Reliability	Performance	Comfort	Value
6.8	6.7	8.4	7.8	6.4	4.9

Category F

Model	Trade-in	Market
2 Dr STD Conv	10445	12735

OPTIONS FOR CABRIO

Auto 4-Speed Transmission +390
Air Conditioning +380
Aluminum/Alloy Wheels +140
Compact Disc Changer +305
Leather Seats +325

EUROVAN 1995

Category G

Model	Trade-in	Market
2 Dr Camp Mobile Pass. Van	14085	19035

OPTIONS FOR EUROVAN

Auto 4-Speed Transmission +445

GOLF 1995

GTI VR6 debuts, with 2.8-liter V6, ABS, and traction control. Entry-level City trim level introduced for four-door models. Two-door Golf switches from GL to Sport designation, and includes spoked alloy wheels and blacked out taillights. Golf meets 1997 side-impact standards. Front seatbelts have height adjusters and emergency tensioners. Daytime running lights are standard on all Golf models.

RATINGS (SCALE OF 1-10)

Overall	Safety	Reliability	Performance	Comfort	Value
7.1	6.4	7.5	8.6	7.6	5.3

Model	Trade-in	Market
Category E		
4 Dr Celebration Hbk	6785	8700
4 Dr City Hbk	6620	8485
2 Dr GL Hbk	7255	9300
4 Dr GL Hbk	7105	9105
2 Dr Sport Hbk	7610	9760
4 Dr STD Hbk	6675	8560
Category F		
2 Dr GTI VR6 Hbk	10030	12230

OPTIONS FOR GOLF

Auto 4-Speed Transmission +390
Air Conditioning[Std on GTIVR6,GL,Sport] +370
Aluminum/Alloy Wheels[Opt on GL] +140
AM/FM Stereo Tape[Opt on City,STD] +90
Anti-Lock Brakes[Std on GTIVR6] +320
Compact Disc Changer +255
Power Moonroof[Std on GTIVR6,Sport] +265
Premium Sound System +155

JETTA 1995

Entry-level City trim level introduced. Jetta meets 1997 side-impact standards. Front seatbelts have height adjusters and emergency tensioners. Daytime running lights are standard on all Jetta models.

RATINGS (SCALE OF 1-10)

Overall	Safety	Reliability	Performance	Comfort	Value
7	6.4	7.2	8.6	7.6	5.2

Category D

Model	Trade-in	Market
4 Dr Celebration Sdn	6745	8540
4 Dr City Sdn	6635	8400
4 Dr GL Sdn	7595	9615

Don't forget to refer to the Mileage Adjustment Table at the back of this book!

 © 1999 by Edmund Publications Corporation

Model Description	Trade-in Value	Market Value
4 Dr GLS Sdn	8505	10765
4 Dr GLX Sdn	10420	13190
4 Dr STD Sdn	7050	8925

OPTIONS FOR JETTA

Auto 4-Speed Transmission +390
Air Conditioning[Std on GL,GLS,GLX,STD] +385
Alarm System[Opt on Celebration] +255
AM/FM Stereo Tape[Std on GL,GLS,GLX] +165
Anti-Lock Brakes[Std on GLX] +430
Compact Disc Changer +300
Leather Seats +500
Power Moonroof[Std on GLS,GLX] +380

PASSAT 1995

Reskinned for 1995, VW adds dual airbags, three-point seatbelts, and side-impact protection that meets 1997 safety standards. Climate control system gains dust and pollen filter. GLX is only trim level.

RATINGS (SCALE OF 1-10)

Overall	Safety	Reliability	Performance	Comfort	Value
7.1	7.7	7.8	8	8	4.2

Category D

Model Description	Trade-in Value	Market Value
4 Dr GLS Sdn	8085	10230
4 Dr GLX Sdn	10095	12780
4 Dr GLX Wgn	9135	11560

OPTIONS FOR PASSAT

Auto 4-Speed Transmission +355
Anti-Lock Brakes[Opt on GLS] +430
Compact Disc Changer +300
Heated Front Seats +165
Leather Seats +500
Power Moonroof +380

1994 VOLKSWAGEN

GOLF 1994

Two-door GL debuts. ABS is optional. Dual airbags are phased in shortly after 1994 production begins.

RATINGS (SCALE OF 1-10)

Overall	Safety	Reliability	Performance	Comfort	Value
7.2	6.4	7.3	8.6	7.6	6.2

Category E

Model Description	Trade-in Value	Market Value
2 Dr GL Hbk	5635	7515
4 Dr GL Hbk	5910	7880

OPTIONS FOR GOLF

Auto 4-Speed Transmission +325
Air Conditioning +300
Aluminum/Alloy Wheels +120
AM/FM Stereo Tape +115
Anti-Lock Brakes +265
Dual Air Bag Restraints +230
Power Moonroof +215

JETTA 1994

GLS and GLX models arrive this year. ABS is optional on GL and GLS; standard on GLX. Dual airbags are phased in shortly after 1994 production begins. GLX features 2.8-liter V6 and traction control.

RATINGS (SCALE OF 1-10)

Overall	Safety	Reliability	Performance	Comfort	Value
7.1	6.3	6.7	8.6	7.6	6.1

Category D

Model Description	Trade-in Value	Market Value
4 Dr GL Sdn	6000	7795
4 Dr GLS Sdn	7060	9170
4 Dr GLX Sdn	9010	11705
4 Dr Limited Edition Sdn	6330	8220

OPTIONS FOR JETTA

Auto 4-Speed Transmission +345
Air Conditioning[Std on GLS,GLX] +315
Aluminum/Alloy Wheels[Std on GLX] +165
AM/FM Stereo Tape[Opt on GL] +135
Anti-Lock Brakes[Std on GLX] +355
Compact Disc Changer +245
Cruise Control[Std on GLS,GLX] +90
Dual Air Bag Restraints +230
Leather Seats +410
Power Moonroof +310
Premium Sound System +130

PASSAT 1994

GL dropped, leaving only the V6 GLX. ABS and traction control are standard. Adaptive dual-mode transmission debuts.

RATINGS (SCALE OF 1-10)

Overall	Safety	Reliability	Performance	Comfort	Value
6.7	4.9	7.9	8	8	4.6

Category D

Model Description	Trade-in Value	Market Value
4 Dr GLX Sdn	8445	10970
4 Dr GLX Wgn	8955	11630

OPTIONS FOR PASSAT

Auto 4-Speed Transmission +325
Compact Disc Changer +245
Heated Front Seats +135
Leather Seats +410

1993 VOLKSWAGEN

CABRIOLET 1993

Carat replaced by Classic. Base models get leatherette upholstery option. Audio systems are upgraded, and CD player joins options list.

Category F

Model Description	Trade-in Value	Market Value
2 Dr Classic Conv	7385	9590
2 Dr STD Conv	7070	9185

Don't forget to refer to the Mileage Adjustment Table at the back of this book!

 © 1999 by Edmund Publications Corporation

Model Description	Trade-in Value	Market Value

OPTIONS FOR CABRIOLET

Auto 3-Speed Transmission +180
Air Conditioning[Opt on STD] +250
Compact Disc Changer +205

CORRADO 1993

In mid-1992, supercharged four-cylinder engine was replaced by 2.8-liter V6. V6 model designated SLC. ABS and traction control are standard. BBS wheels dumped in favor of five-spoke VW design. Fuel capacity up four gallons, and front styling is tweaked. A/C is CFC-free. Radio turns off with ignition switch.

Category F		
2 Dr SLC Cpe	8725	11330

OPTIONS FOR CORRADO

Auto 4-Speed Transmission +265
Heated Front Seats +100
Leather Seats +215
Power Sunroof +205

EUROVAN 1993

The EuroVan is introduced as a replacement for the aging Vanagon. Major differences over the previous generation Volkswagen van are the switch to a front-engine/front-wheel drive platform. Antilock brakes are available on the EuroVan, and it has a 2.5-liter four-cylinder engine that produces 109-horsepower. A five-speed manual transmission is standard, a four-speed automatic is optional.

Category G		
2 Dr CL Pass. Van	5575	7965
2 Dr GL Pass. Van	6910	9875
2 Dr MV Pass. Van	7700	11000

OPTIONS FOR EUROVAN

Auto 4-Speed Transmission +270
Weekender Pkg +765
AM/FM Stereo Tape[Opt on CL] +75
Anti-Lock Brakes +185
Cruise Control +65
Dual Air Conditioning[Opt on CL] +305
Power Door Locks +70
Power Windows +70

FOX 1993

Air conditioning is standard. Five-speed transmission replaces four-speed unit on Base coupe. Base model gets wheelcovers, dual outside mirrors, body-color bumpers and bigger tires. GL model gets upgraded interior trim.

Category E		
2 Dr Wolfsburg Sdn	2515	3445
4 Dr Wolfsburg GL Sdn	2745	3760

OPTIONS FOR FOX

AM/FM Stereo Tape +95

GOLF 1993

All new Golf debuts, but a strike at the assembly plant in Mexico restricts sales to Southern California and parts of New England.

Category E		
4 Dr GL Hbk	4860	6660

OPTIONS FOR GOLF

Auto 4-Speed Transmission +265
Air Conditioning +245
AM/FM Stereo Tape +95
Power Sunroof +185

JETTA 1993

All new Jetta debuts, but a strike at the assembly plant in Mexico restricts sales to Southern California and parts of New England.

Category D		
4 Dr GL Sdn	5430	7340

OPTIONS FOR JETTA

Auto 4-Speed Transmission +265
Air Conditioning +255
AM/FM Stereo Tape +110
Power Sunroof +220

PASSAT 1993

GLX trim level introduced, with 2.8-liter V6, ABS and traction control. Fog lamps and six-spoke alloys indicate GLX model. CL trim dropped. GL gets suspension modifications. All models get trip computer and CFC-free air conditioning.

RATINGS (SCALE OF 1-10)

Overall	Safety	Reliability	Performance	Comfort	Value
6.3	4.8	7.3	8	8	3.5

Category D		
4 Dr GL Sdn	5940	8025
4 Dr GLX Sdn	6965	9415
4 Dr GLX Wgn	6815	9210

OPTIONS FOR PASSAT

Auto 4-Speed Transmission +265
Leather Seats +335
Power Sunroof[Opt on GL] +220

1992 VOLKSWAGEN

CABRIOLET 1992

Etienne Aigner edition dropped. Three-point seatbelts are added to the back seat. Base model gets full wheelcovers. Radio turns off with ignition switch.

Category F		
2 Dr Carat Conv	5985	7980
2 Dr STD Conv	5945	7930
2 Dr Wolfsburg Class. Conv	6100	8135

Don't forget to refer to the Mileage Adjustment Table at the back of this book!

 © 1999 by Edmund Publications Corporation

Model Description	Trade-in Value	Market Value

OPTIONS FOR CABRIOLET
Auto 3-Speed Transmission +135
Auto 4-Speed Transmission +135
Power Converible Top +205
Air Conditioning[Opt on Carat,STD] +205

CORRADO 1992

No changes.

Model Description	Trade-in Value	Market Value
Category F		
2 Dr SLC Cpe	7135	9510
2 Dr STD Sprchgd Cpe	6915	9220

OPTIONS FOR CORRADO
Auto 4-Speed Transmission +195
AM/FM Stereo Tape[Opt on STD] +50
Anti-Lock Brakes[Opt on STD] +180
Heated Front Seats +85
Leather Seats +175
Power Sunroof +170

FOX 1992

Radio turns off with ignition switch.

Model Description	Trade-in Value	Market Value
Category E		
4 Dr GL Sdn	2745	3920
2 Dr STD Sdn	1820	2600

OPTIONS FOR FOX
Air Conditioning[Std on GL] +200
AM/FM Stereo Tape +75

GOLF 1992

Radio turns off with ignition switch.

Model Description	Trade-in Value	Market Value
Category E		
2 Dr GL Hbk	3245	4635
4 Dr GL Hbk	3305	4720
Category F		
2 Dr GTI Hbk	4210	5610
2 Dr GTI 16V Hbk	4795	6395

OPTIONS FOR GOLF
Auto 3-Speed Transmission +135
Air Conditioning +200
Aluminum/Alloy Wheels[Opt on GL] +75
AM/FM Stereo Tape +50
Sunroof +85

JETTA 1992

ECOdiesel debuts, featuring turbocharging and fewer pollutants. Two-door model dropped. GL models get new wheelcovers. Radio turns off with ignition switch.

Model Description	Trade-in Value	Market Value
Category D		
4 Dr Carat Sdn	3905	5350
4 Dr GL Sdn	3515	4815
4 Dr GLI Sdn	4695	6430

OPTIONS FOR JETTA
Auto 3-Speed Transmission +135
Air Conditioning +210
Aluminum/Alloy Wheels[Opt on GL] +110
AM/FM Stereo Tape[Std on GLI] +90
Anti-Lock Brakes +235
Cruise Control[Std on Carat] +60
Power Windows[Opt on GLI] +65
Rear Spoiler[Opt on GL] +105
Sunroof +105

PASSAT 1992

New entry-level CL trim level introduced.

RATINGS (SCALE OF 1-10)

Overall	Safety	Reliability	Performance	Comfort	Value
6.4	4.4	7.4	7.6	8	4.4

Model Description	Trade-in Value	Market Value
Category D		
4 Dr CL Sdn	3615	4950
4 Dr GL Sdn	4415	6050
4 Dr GL Wgn	4380	6000

OPTIONS FOR PASSAT
Auto 4-Speed Transmission +195
Air Conditioning[Opt on CL] +210
Aluminum/Alloy Wheels +110
AM/FM Stereo Tape[Opt on CL] +90
Anti-Lock Brakes +235
Compact Disc Changer +165
Heated Front Seats +90
Leather Seats +275
Power Sunroof +180

1991 VOLKSWAGEN

CABRIOLET 1991

Airbag added to steering wheel. Etienne Aigner edition debuts.

Model Description	Trade-in Value	Market Value
Category F		
2 Dr STD Conv	4575	6095

OPTIONS FOR CABRIOLET
Auto 3-Speed Transmission +105
Air Conditioning +170
Aluminum/Alloy Wheels +65
Cruise Control +40
Leather Seats +145

CORRADO 1991

BBS alloy wheels are added as standard equipment.

Model Description	Trade-in Value	Market Value
Category F		
2 Dr STD Sprchgd Cpe	4870	6495

OPTIONS FOR CORRADO
Auto 4-Speed Transmission +160
Anti-Lock Brakes +145
Heated Front Seats +70
Leather Seats +145
Power Sunroof +140

Don't forget to refer to the Mileage Adjustment Table at the back of this book!

 © 1999 by Edmund Publications Corporation

Model Description	Trade-in Value	Market Value

FOX 1991

Restyled front end features flush headlamps. Wagon dropped. Lineup trimmed to Base coupe and GL sedan.

Model Description	Trade-in Value	Market Value
Category E		
4 Dr GL Sdn	1650	2425
2 Dr STD Sdn	1430	2100

OPTIONS FOR FOX

Air Conditioning +165
AM/FM Stereo Tape +60

GOLF 1991

BBS wheels added to GTI 16V as standard equipment.

Model Description	Trade-in Value	Market Value
Category E		
2 Dr GL Hbk	2440	3590
4 Dr GL Hbk	2535	3730
Category F		
2 Dr GTI Hbk	3620	4825
2 Dr GTI 16V Hbk	4150	5530

OPTIONS FOR GOLF

Auto 3-Speed Transmission +105
Air Conditioning +165
Aluminum/Alloy Wheels[Opt on GL] +65
AM/FM Stereo Tape +40
Sunroof +70

JETTA 1991

GLI 16V gets standard BBS alloys.

Model Description	Trade-in Value	Market Value
Category D		
4 Dr Carat Sdn	3290	4505
2 Dr GL Sdn	2895	3970
4 Dr GL Sdn	3000	4110
4 Dr GL Dsl Sdn	2950	4040
4 Dr GLI 16V Sdn	3920	5370

OPTIONS FOR JETTA

Auto 3-Speed Transmission +105
Air Conditioning +170
Aluminum/Alloy Wheels[Opt on GL] +90
AM/FM Stereo Tape[Std on GLI 16V] +75
Anti-Lock Brakes +195
Cruise Control[Std on Carat] +50
Power Windows[Std on Carat] +55
Sunroof +85

PASSAT 1991

No changes.

RATINGS (SCALE OF 1-10)

Overall	Safety	Reliability	Performance	Comfort	Value
6.5	4.4	7.2	7.6	8	5.3

Model Description	Trade-in Value	Market Value
Category D		
4 Dr GL Sdn	3395	4655
4 Dr GL Wgn	3730	5105

OPTIONS FOR PASSAT

Auto 4-Speed Transmission +160
Aluminum/Alloy Wheels +90
AM/FM Stereo Tape +75
Anti-Lock Brakes +195
Cruise Control +50
Leather Seats +225
Power Door Locks +55
Power Sunroof +150
Power Windows +55

VANAGON 1991

No changes. Final year for Vanagon.

Model Description	Trade-in Value	Market Value
Category G		
2 Dr Carat Pass. Van	6520	10030
2 Dr GL Pass. Van	5940	9140
2 Dr GL Camper Pass. Van	7875	12115
2 Dr Multi Pass. Van	4520	6955
2 Dr STD Pass. Van	4165	6405

OPTIONS FOR VANAGON

Auto 3-Speed Transmission +80
Auto 4-Speed Transmission +105
Air Conditioning[Opt on STD,Syncro] +165
Aluminum/Alloy Wheels[Opt on GL,GL Camper] +70
AM/FM Stereo Tape +50
Cruise Control[Std on Carat,GL Syncro,Multi] +45
Power Door Locks[Std on Carat,GL Syncro,Multi] +45
Power Windows[Std on Carat,GL Syncro,Multi] +50

1990 VOLKSWAGEN

CABRIOLET 1990

No changes.

Model Description	Trade-in Value	Market Value
Category F		
2 Dr Best Seller Conv	4565	6085
2 Dr Boutique Conv	4540	6050
2 Dr STD Conv	4070	5425

OPTIONS FOR CABRIOLET

Auto 3-Speed Transmission +85
Air Conditioning +140
Cruise Control +35

CORRADO 1990

Scirroco replacement moves slightly upscale, featuring supercharged Golf engine, optional ABS, and motorized seatbelts.

Model Description	Trade-in Value	Market Value
Category F		
2 Dr STD Sprchgd Cpe	4410	5880

OPTIONS FOR CORRADO

Anti-Lock Brakes +120
Leather Seats +120
Power Sunroof +115

Don't forget to refer to the Mileage Adjustment Table at the back of this book!

 © 1999 by Edmund Publications Corporation

Model Description	Trade-in Value	Market Value

FOX 1990

No changes.

Category E

2 Dr GL Wgn	1365	2070
4 Dr GL Sdn	1385	2100
2 Dr GL Sport Sdn	1460	2210
2 Dr STD Sdn	1220	1845

OPTIONS FOR FOX

Air Conditioning +135
AM/FM Stereo Tape +50
Sunroof +55

GOLF 1990

Lineup trimmed to Base and GL models. GTI drops Golf designation. Lower cost GTI debuts with 105-horsepower eight-valve engine and rear drum brakes.

Category E		
2 Dr GL Hbk	1985	3005
4 Dr GL Hbk	2035	3085
Category F		
2 Dr GTI Hbk	2670	3565

OPTIONS FOR GOLF

Auto 3-Speed Transmission +85
Air Conditioning +135
Aluminum/Alloy Wheels[Opt on GL] +50
AM/FM Stereo Tape +35
Cruise Control +35
Power Steering[Opt on GL] +40
Premium Sound System +55
Sunroof +55

JETTA 1990

No changes.

Category D

4 Dr Carat Sdn	2720	3730
2 Dr GL Sdn	2540	3480
4 Dr GL Sdn	2665	3650
4 Dr GLI 16V Sdn	3510	4805
4 Dr STD Dsl Sdn	2055	2810

OPTIONS FOR JETTA

Auto 3-Speed Transmission +85
Air Conditioning +140
Aluminum/Alloy Wheels[Opt on Carat] +75
AM/FM Stereo Tape +60
Anti-Lock Brakes +155
Cruise Control +40
Power Windows +45
Premium Sound System +55
Sunroof +70

PASSAT 1990

Delayed Quantum replacement debuts. Sedan and wagon are available in GL trim, with 134-horsepower engine. ABS is optional.

RATINGS (SCALE OF 1-10)

Overall	Safety	Reliability	Performance	Comfort	Value
6.2	4.4	6.9	7.6	8	4.2

Category D

4 Dr GL Sdn	3115	4265
4 Dr GL Wgn	3225	4420

OPTIONS FOR PASSAT

Auto 4-Speed Transmission[Opt on Sdn] +130
Aluminum/Alloy Wheels +75
AM/FM Stereo Tape +60
Anti-Lock Brakes +155
Cruise Control +40
Leather Seats +185
Power Door Locks +45
Power Sunroof +120
Power Windows +45
Premium Sound System +55

VANAGON 1990

No changes.

Category G

2 Dr Carat Pass. Van	5295	8545
2 Dr GL Pass. Van	4810	7760
2 Dr GL Camper Pass. Van	6030	9725
2 Dr Multi Van Pass. Van	4255	6860
2 Dr STD Pass. Van	3535	5705

OPTIONS FOR VANAGON

Auto 3-Speed Transmission[Std on Carat,Multi Van] +85
Air Conditioning[Opt on Multi Van,STD] +135
Aluminum/Alloy Wheels[Opt on GL,GL Camper] +55
AM/FM Stereo Tape +40
Cruise Control[Opt on GL,GL Camper,STD] +35
Power Door Locks[Opt on GL,GL Camper,STD] +40
Power Windows[Opt on GL,GL Camper,STD] +40

1989 VOLKSWAGEN

CABRIOLET 1989

No changes.

Category F

2 Dr Best Seller Conv	3200	4440
2 Dr Boutique Conv.	3235	4495
2 Dr STD Conv	3125	4345
2 Dr Wolfsburg LTD Conv	3270	4540

OPTIONS FOR CABRIOLET

Auto 3-Speed Transmission +70
Air Conditioning +115
Cruise Control +30

FOX 1989

Two-door model gets GL and GL Sport trim levels, as well as an optional removable sunroof. Wagons lose their five-speed manual transmission.

Don't forget to refer to the Mileage Adjustment Table at the back of this book!

 © 1999 by Edmund Publications Corporation

Model Description	Trade-in Value	Market Value
Category E		
2 Dr GL Wgn	1005	1705
2 Dr GL Sdn	1045	1775
4 Dr GL Sdn	1055	1790
2 Dr GL Sport Sdn	1075	1820
4 Dr GL Sport Sdn	1115	1895
2 Dr STD Sdn	995	1690

OPTIONS FOR FOX

Air Conditioning +110
AM/FM Stereo Tape[Std on Wolfsburg GL] +40
Sunroof +45

GOLF 1989

GT models disappear.

Model Description	Trade-in Value	Market Value
Category E		
2 Dr GL Hbk	1510	2560
4 Dr GL Hbk	1555	2640
2 Dr STD Hbk	1395	2360
4 Dr Wolfsburg GL Hbk	1575	2670
Category F		
2 Dr GTI 16V Hbk	2350	3265

OPTIONS FOR GOLF

Auto 3-Speed Transmission +70
Air Conditioning +110
Cruise Control +30
Power Windows +30
Sunroof +45

JETTA 1989

Carat and GLI 16V get optional ABS. Diesel model debuts.

Model Description	Trade-in Value	Market Value
Category D		
4 Dr Carat Sdn	2150	3120
4 Dr GL Sdn	2015	2920
4 Dr GLI 16V Sdn	2435	3530
2 Dr STD Sdn	1795	2600
4 Dr STD Sdn	1920	2785
4 Dr STD Dsl Sdn	1875	2720
4 Dr Wolfsburg GL Sdn	2140	3105
4 Dr Wolfsburg GLI Sdn	2565	3720

OPTIONS FOR JETTA

Auto 3-Speed Transmission +70
Air Conditioning[Std on Carat,Wolfsburg GLI] +115
AM/FM Stereo Tape[Opt on GL,GLI 16V,STD] +50
Anti-Lock Brakes +130
Cruise Control[Std on Carat] +35
Power Door Locks[Std on Carat,Wolfsburg GLI] +35
Power Windows[Std on Carat,Wolfsburg GLI] +35
Sunroof[Std on Wolfsburg GLI] +60

VANAGON 1989

Carat model added, and all Vanagons get new bumpers.

Model Description	Trade-in Value	Market Value
Category G		
2 Dr GL Pass. Van	4015	6925
2 Dr GL Camper Pass. Van	5170	8915
2 Dr GL Carat Pass. Van	4615	7955

OPTIONS FOR VANAGON

Auto 3-Speed Transmission +70
Air Conditioning +110
Aluminum/Alloy Wheels[Std on GL Carat] +45
AM/FM Stereo Tape +35
Cruise Control +30
Power Door Locks[Std on GL Carat] +30
Power Windows +30

For a guaranteed low price on a new car in your area, call
1-800-CAR-CLUB

Get a great used car and apply for financing online at a price you must see to believe !
http://edmunds.com

A 15-minute phone call could save you 15% or more on car insurance.
1-800-555-2758
GEICO DIRECT

 © 1999 by Edmund Publications Corporation

VOLVO Sweden

1997 Volvo 960

1998 VOLVO

C70 1998

Volvo performs a slam-dunk with its first new coupe in years; the convertible is somewhat less thrilling. Modeled on the S70 chassis, the C70 shares sheetmetal with the S70 from the windshield forward, and is powered by the same set of turbocharged powerplants.

Category L

Model Description	Trade-in Value	Market Value
2 Dr STD Turbo Cpe	27740	32635

OPTIONS FOR C70

Auto 4-Speed Transmission +810
Heated Front Seats +385
Traction Control System +1330

S70 1998

Volvo's 850 sedan gets a new name, new nose, body-color trim, stronger side-impact protection, more powerful turbo engines, redesigned interior, and revised suspension. A great car has been made better.

Category L

Model Description	Trade-in Value	Market Value
4 Dr GLT Turbo Sdn	20700	24355
4 Dr GT Sdn	18940	22280
4 Dr STD Sdn	17355	20420
4 Dr T-5 Turbo Sdn	23505	27650

OPTIONS FOR S70

Auto 4-Speed Transmission[Std on GLT] +810
Aluminum/Alloy Wheels[Opt on STD] +345
Compact Disc W/fm/tape[Std on T-5] +605
Dual Power Seats[Std on T-5] +725
Heated Front Seats +385
Leather Seats +1015
Sport Suspension +135
Traction Control System +1330
Trip Computer[Std on T-5] +230

S90 1998

Absolutely nothing changes on this aged warhorse.

Category L

Model Description	Trade-in Value	Market Value
4 Dr STD Sdn	23055	27120

OPTIONS FOR S90

Compact Disc W/fm/tape +605
Heated Front Seats +385

V70 1998

Volvo's 850 wagon gets a new name, new nose, body-color trim, stronger side-impact protection, more powerful turbo engines, redesigned interior and revised suspension. A great car has been made better. All-wheel drive versions arrive to battle luxury SUVs and the hot-selling Subaru Legacy.

Category L

Model Description	Trade-in Value	Market Value
4 Dr GLT Turbo Wgn	23085	27160
4 Dr GT Wgn	22560	26540
4 Dr R Turbo 4WD Wgn	28735	33810
4 Dr STD Wgn	21550	25355
4 Dr STD Turbo 4WD Wgn	24205	28475
4 Dr T-5 Turbo Wgn	25075	29500
4 Dr XC Turbo 4WD Wgn	25310	29775

OPTIONS FOR V70

Auto 4-Speed Transmission[Std on GLT, R, XC, 4WD] +810
Aluminum/Alloy Wheels[Opt on STD] +345
Auto Load Leveling[Std on R, XC, 4WD] +895
Compact Disc W/fm/tape[Std on T-5] +605
Dual Power Seats[Std on R, T-5, XC] +725
Heated Front Seats[Std on R, XC, 4WD] +385
Leather Seats[Std on R, XC] +1015
Power Drivers Seat[Std on GLT, GT, 4WD] +355
Power Moonroof[Opt on STD, XC] +745
Sport Suspension +135
Traction Control System[Std on R, XC, 4WD] +1330
Trip Computer[Std on R, T-5, XC] +230

V90 1998

Absolutely nothing changes on this aged warhorse.

Category L

Model Description	Trade-in Value	Market Value
4 Dr STD Wgn	25225	29675

OPTIONS FOR V90

Auto Load Leveling +895
Compact Disc W/fm/tape +605
Heated Front Seats +385

Don't forget to refer to the Mileage Adjustment Table at the back of this book!

 © 1999 by Edmund Publications Corporation

Model Description	Trade-in Value	Market Value

1997 VOLVO

850 1997

Looking for the Turbo? Inexplicably, Volvo tossed two decades of tradition and the Turbo nameplate out the door. The Turbo is now known as the T-5. GLT models get a new engine that makes 22 more horsepower than last year, and peak torque at a low 1,800 rpm. Base and GLT models meet Transitional Low Emission Vehicle (TLEV) regulations this year.

RATINGS (SCALE OF 1-10)

Overall	Safety	Reliability	Performance	Comfort	Value
8.5	8.6	8.8	8.8	8.3	8.2

Category L

Model Description	Trade-in Value	Market Value
4 Dr GLT Turbo Wgn	20035	23850
4 Dr GLT Turbo Sdn	18800	22380
4 Dr R Turbo Wgn	23930	28490
4 Dr R Turbo Sdn	23055	27445
4 Dr STD Wgn	19455	23160
4 Dr STD Sdn	16755	19945
4 Dr T-5 Turbo Wgn	22355	26615
4 Dr T-5 Turbo Sdn	21485	25580

OPTIONS FOR 850

Auto 4-Speed Transmission[Opt on STD] +660
Grand Touring Package +680
Wood Trim Package +550
Aluminum/Alloy Wheels[Opt on STD] +280
Auto Load Leveling[Std on R] +730
Compact Disc W/fm/tape[Std on R,T-5] +495
Dual Power Seats[Std on R,T-5] +590
Keyless Entry System[Opt on STD] +170
Leather Seats[Std on R] +830
Power Moonroof[Opt on STD] +610
Sport Suspension[Std on R] +110
Traction Control System[Std on R] +1085
Trip Computer[Std on R,T-5] +190

960 1997

Automatic load leveling joins the options list for the wagon, while tailored leather seating is no longer available on the wagon.

RATINGS (SCALE OF 1-10)

Overall	Safety	Reliability	Performance	Comfort	Value
8.3	8.5	9	8.8	8	7.2

Category L

Model Description	Trade-in Value	Market Value
4 Dr STD Sdn	19980	23785
4 Dr STD Wgn	21555	25660

OPTIONS FOR 960

Auto Load Leveling +730
Compact Disc W/fm/tape +495

S90 1997

Midyear, Volvo went and switched names for the 960. The sedan is now known as S90, while the wagon is now the V90.

RATINGS (SCALE OF 1-10)

Overall	Safety	Reliability	Performance	Comfort	Value
8.3	8.5	9	8.8	8	7.2

Category L

Model Description	Trade-in Value	Market Value
4 Dr STD Sdn	20015	23825

V90 1997

Midyear, Volvo went and switched names for the 960. The sedan is now known as S90, while the wagon is now the V90.

RATINGS (SCALE OF 1-10)

Overall	Safety	Reliability	Performance	Comfort	Value
8.3	8.5	9	8.8	8	7.2

Category L

Model Description	Trade-in Value	Market Value
4 Dr STD Wgn	21595	25710

1996 VOLVO

850 1996

This year all Volvo 850s are equipped with front seat side-impact airbags, optional traction control (TRACS), and a life insurance policy that pays $250,000 to the estate of any occupant who loses their life in the 850 as the result of an accident.

RATINGS (SCALE OF 1-10)

Overall	Safety	Reliability	Performance	Comfort	Value
8.6	8.6	8.7	8.6	8.3	8.7

Category L

Model Description	Trade-in Value	Market Value
4 Dr GLT Sdn	16025	19075
4 Dr GLT Wgn	17225	20510
4 Dr Platinum Ltd. Ed. Turbo Wgn	21445	25530
4 Dr Platinum Ltd. Ed. Turbo Sdn	19600	23330
4 Dr R Turbo Wgn	22160	26380
4 Dr R Turbo Sdn	20370	24250
4 Dr STD Wgn	16310	19415
4 Dr STD Sdn	15110	17990
4 Dr STD Turbo Wgn	19415	23110
4 Dr STD Turbo Sdn	17520	20860

OPTIONS FOR 850

Auto 4-Speed Transmission[Opt on GLT,Non-turbo models] +530
Grand Touring Package +615
Aluminum/Alloy Wheels[Opt on STD Sdn,STD Wgn] +230
Auto Load Leveling[Opt on GLT,STD] +595
Dual Power Seats[Std on R] +485

Don't forget to refer to the Mileage Adjustment Table at the back of this book!

 © 1999 by Edmund Publications Corporation

Model Description	Trade-in Value	Market Value

Keyless Entry System[Opt on STD Wgn,STD Sdn] +140
Leather Seats[Opt on GLT,STD] +680
Sport Suspension[Std on R] +90
Traction Control System[Opt on GLT,STD] +890
Trip Computer[Opt on Non-turbo models] +155

960 1996

This year all Volvo 960s are equipped with front seat side-impact airbags, a multi-step power door locking system that increases driver safety when entering the vehicle in parking lots, and a life insurance policy that pays $250,000 to the estate of any occupant who loses their life in the 960 as a result of a car accident.

RATINGS (SCALE OF 1-10)

Overall	Safety	Reliability	Performance	Comfort	Value
8.3	8.5	8.7	8.8	8	7.5

Category L

4 Dr STD Wgn	18540	22070
4 Dr STD Sdn	17745	21125

OPTIONS FOR 960

AM/FM Compact Disc Playr +430

1995 VOLVO

850 1995

Side airbags are standard on all 850 Turbos this year; optional on other 850s. All models get Turbo's rounded front styling.

RATINGS (SCALE OF 1-10)

Overall	Safety	Reliability	Performance	Comfort	Value
8.4	8.6	8.1	8.6	8.3	8.6

Category L

4 Dr GLT Wgn	14930	18205
4 Dr GLT Sdn	13720	16730
4 Dr STD Wgn	13910	16960
4 Dr STD Sdn	12970	15815
4 Dr STD Turbo Sdn	16560	20195
4 Dr STD Turbo Wgn	15775	19240
4 Dr T-5R Turbo Wgn	17220	21000
4 Dr T-5R Turbo Sdn	17635	21510

OPTIONS FOR 850

Auto 4-Speed Transmission[Std on T-5R,Turbo] +400
Grand Lux Package +510
Grand Touring Package +375
Aluminum/Alloy Wheels[Std on GLT,T-5R,Turbo] +190
Climate Control for AC[Std on T-5R,Turbo] +160
Compact Disc W/fm/tape +330
Keyless Entry System[Std on GLT,T-5R,Turbo] +115
Leather Seats[Std on T-5R,STD Turbo Sdn] +555
Power Drivers Seat[Std on GLT,T-5R,Turbo] +195
Power Passenger Seat[Opt on STD,GLT Wgn] +180
Side Air Bag Restraint[Std on T-5R,Turbo,GLT Sdn] +225
Traction Control System[Std on T-5R] +725
Trip Computer[Opt on GLT] +125

940 1995

Daytime running lights debut. Level I and Level II trim is dropped in favor of less confusing base and Turbo designations.

RATINGS (SCALE OF 1-10)

Overall	Safety	Reliability	Performance	Comfort	Value
8	8.2	8.5	8	7.9	7.5

Category L

4 Dr STD Sdn	12750	15545
4 Dr STD Wgn	13225	16130
4 Dr STD Turbo Sdn	13360	16290
4 Dr STD Turbo Wgn	13975	17045

OPTIONS FOR 940

Aluminum/Alloy Wheels +190
Leather Seats +555
Power Drivers Seat +195
Power Moonroof +405

960 1995

Substantially revised with new sheetmetal and detuned powertrain. Horsepower is down to 181 from 201, thanks to emissions standards. Daytime running lights are added. The dashboard is softened with more curves and contours. Suspensions are revised, and larger tires are standard. Other new standard equipment includes remote locking, an alarm system, headlight wipers and washers, and wood interior trim.

RATINGS (SCALE OF 1-10)

Overall	Safety	Reliability	Performance	Comfort	Value
8	8.3	7.8	8.8	8	7.3

Category L

4 Dr STD Wgn	15060	18365
4 Dr STD Sdn	14695	17925

OPTIONS FOR 960

Compact Disc Changer +530
Leather Seats +555
Rear Window Wiper +135

1994 VOLVO

850 1994

Turbo model debuts with 222-horsepower 2.3-liter five-cylinder engine, and a wagon body style is introduced with standard integrated child seat. Turbo is available in either sedan or wagon format. Warranty is upped to 4 years/50,000 miles.

Don't forget to refer to the Mileage Adjustment Table at the back of this book!

© 1999 by Edmund Publications Corporation

Model Description	Trade-in Value	Market Value

RATINGS (SCALE OF 1-10)

Overall	Safety	Reliability	Performance	Comfort	Value
8.4	8.7	8	8.6	8.3	8.4

Category L

Model Description	Trade-in Value	Market Value
4 Dr GLT Sdn	11820	14770
4 Dr GLTS Wgn	13000	16255
4 Dr GLTS Sdn	12360	15450
4 Dr STD Turbo Sdn	12780	15975
4 Dr STD Turbo Wgn	14600	18245

OPTIONS FOR 850

Auto 4-Speed Transmission[Opt on GLT,GLTS,Sdn] +250
Aluminum/Alloy Wheels[Std on GLTS,Wgn] +155
Auto Load Leveling +400
Climate Control for AC[Std on STD] +130
Leather Seats[Opt on GLT,GLTS,Sdn] +455
Power Drivers Seat[Std on GLTS,Wgn] +160
Power Passenger Seat +150
Sport Suspension +60
Traction Control System +595
Trip Computer[Std on STD] +105

940 1994

940 gets passenger airbag. Level I 940s have 114-horsepower 2.3-liter engine; equip a 940 with Level II trim and you get a turbocharged version of this engine.

RATINGS (SCALE OF 1-10)

Overall	Safety	Reliability	Performance	Comfort	Value
8	8.2	8.3	8	8	7.4

Category L

Model Description	Trade-in Value	Market Value
4 Dr STD Sdn	10535	13170
4 Dr STD Wgn	11010	13760
4 Dr STD Turbo Sdn	11440	14300
4 Dr STD Turbo Wgn	12420	15525

OPTIONS FOR 940

Aluminum/Alloy Wheels[Std on Turbo] +155
Leather Seats[Std on Turbo] +455
Power Drivers Seat[Std on Turbo] +160
Power Passenger Seat +150
Power Sunroof[Std on Turbo] +340

960 1994

Base 960 is heavily decontented, and is available only in sedan format. Level II 960 adds leather, moonroof and other nice stuff.

RATINGS (SCALE OF 1-10)

Overall	Safety	Reliability	Performance	Comfort	Value
8.1	8.4	8	8.8	8.1	7.4

Category L

Model Description	Trade-in Value	Market Value
4 Dr Level II Sdn	12100	15125
4 Dr Level II Wgn	13620	17025
4 Dr STD Sdn	11340	14180

OPTIONS FOR 960

Aluminum/Alloy Wheels[Opt on STD] +155
Compact Disc Changer +435
Compact Disc W/fm/tape +270
Leather Seats[Opt on STD] +455
Power Moonroof +335
Power Passenger Seat[Std on Wgn] +150
Premium Sound System +290

1993 VOLVO

240 1993

GL model dropped, again. Metallic paint doesn't cost extra this year, air conditioning gets CFC-free refrigerant, and plush floormats are standard.

Category L

Model Description	Trade-in Value	Market Value
4 Dr STD Sdn	8110	10265
4 Dr STD Wgn	8825	11170

OPTIONS FOR 240

Auto 4-Speed Transmission +205
Aluminum/Alloy Wheels +125
Heated Front Seats +140
Leather Seats +370
Limited Slip Diff +395

850 1993

740 replacement arrives with 168-horsepower inline five-cylinder engine. Dual airbags and ABS are standard. Automatic transmission has "Economy" and "Sport" shift modes, as well as a winter second-gear start feature. Car meets 1997 side-impact standards, traction control is optional, and sedans have standard integrated child safety seats. Wagon not available.

RATINGS (SCALE OF 1-10)

Overall	Safety	Reliability	Performance	Comfort	Value
8.3	8.7	8.3	8.6	8.3	7.4

Category L

Model Description	Trade-in Value	Market Value
4 Dr GLT Sdn	9730	12315
4 Dr GLTS Sdn	10265	12995

OPTIONS FOR 850

Auto 4-Speed Transmission +225
Keyless Entry System[Opt on GLT] +75
Leather Seats[Opt on GLT] +370
Traction Control System +485
Trip Computer +85

940 1993

Wagons have integrated child seats. All stereos have anti-theft feature, and air conditioning is free of CFCs. Wagons have an extra four gallons of fuel capacity and a revised rear seat. 940 GL dropped, but a base sedan and wagon continue.

Don't forget to refer to the Mileage Adjustment Table at the back of this book!

 © 1999 by Edmund Publications Corporation

Model Description	Trade-in Value	Market Value

RATINGS (SCALE OF 1-10)

Overall	Safety	Reliability	Performance	Comfort	Value
7.7	7.6	7.9	8	8	6.8

Category L

4 Dr S Wgn	10370	13125
4 Dr S Sdn	10040	12710
4 Dr STD Sdn	9645	12205
4 Dr STD Wgn	10080	12760
4 Dr STD Turbo Sdn	10420	13190
4 Dr STD Turbo Wgn	10660	13495

OPTIONS FOR 940

Aluminum/Alloy Wheels[Std on S,Sdn,Turbo] +125
Power Passenger Seat +120

960 — 1993

960 gets passenger airbag. Wagons have integrated child seats. All stereos have anti-theft feature, and air conditioning is free of CFCs. Wagons have an extra four gallons of fuel capacity and a revised rear seat.

RATINGS (SCALE OF 1-10)

Overall	Safety	Reliability	Performance	Comfort	Value
7.9	7.7	7.9	8.8	8.1	6.8

Category L

4 Dr STD Sdn	10270	13000
4 Dr STD Wgn	11170	14140

1992 VOLVO

240 — 1992

ABS is newly standard. GL model returns as top-of-the-line, and adds a sunroof and heated mirrors, among other items, over the base car. GL grille is chrome rather than matte black.

Category L

4 Dr GL Sdn	7280	9455
4 Dr STD Wgn	7090	9210
4 Dr STD Sdn	6840	8885

OPTIONS FOR 240

Auto 4-Speed Transmission +165
Aluminum/Alloy Wheels +105
Anti-Lock Brakes[Std on Wgn] +270
Heated Front Seats[Std on GL] +115
Leather Seats +305
Limited Slip Diff[Std on GL] +320

740 — 1992

ABS is standard across the board. A locking differential is newly standard. Turbo sedan and 780 coupe have been dropped. Turbo wagon continues.

Category L

4 Dr GL Wgn	8425	10945
4 Dr STD Wgn	7765	10085
4 Dr STD Sdn	8025	10425
4 Dr STD Turbo Wgn	8995	11685

OPTIONS FOR 740

Aluminum/Alloy Wheels[Std on Turbo] +105
Leather Seats +305

940 — 1992

940 GLE, and its twin-cam engine, is discontinued for 1992.

RATINGS (SCALE OF 1-10)

Overall	Safety	Reliability	Performance	Comfort	Value
N/A	N/A	8.2	8	8	7.3

Category L

4 Dr GL Sdn	7355	9550
4 Dr STD Turbo Sdn	8185	10630

OPTIONS FOR 940

Aluminum/Alloy Wheels[Opt on GL] +105
Leather Seats[Opt on GL] +305
Power Drivers Seat[Opt on GL] +105
Power Passenger Seat +100

960 — 1992

960 model replaces 940 SE in lineup; is powered by 2.9-liter twin-cam inline-six good for 201 horsepower.

RATINGS (SCALE OF 1-10)

Overall	Safety	Reliability	Performance	Comfort	Value
N/A	N/A	7.8	8.8	8.1	7.3

Category L

4 Dr STD Wgn	9365	12165
4 Dr STD Sdn	7720	10025

1991 VOLVO

240 — 1991

SE wagon added to lineup. DL trim dropped, leaving base trim.

Category L

4 Dr SE Wgn	6660	8765
4 Dr STD Sdn	5420	7130
4 Dr STD Wgn	6070	7990

OPTIONS FOR 240

Auto 4-Speed Transmission[Std on SE] +135
Anti-Lock Brakes[Std on SE] +220
Leather Seats[Std on SE] +250
Sunroof +115

740 — 1991

DOHC motor dropped from lineup.

Don't forget to refer to the Mileage Adjustment Table at the back of this book!

 © 1999 by Edmund Publications Corporation

Model Description	Trade-in Value	Market Value
Category L		
4 Dr SE Turbo Wgn	7845	10325
4 Dr SE Turbo Sdn	6495	8545
4 Dr STD Wgn	6295	8280
4 Dr STD Sdn	5850	7700
4 Dr STD Turbo Sdn	5950	7830
4 Dr STD Turbo Wgn	7055	9285

OPTIONS FOR 740

Auto 4-Speed Transmission[Std on SE,Non-turbo models] +135
Anti-Lock Brakes[Std on SE,Turbo] +220
Leather Seats +250
Limited Slip Diff[Std on SE,Turbo] +265
Sunroof +115

940 — 1991

New series of cars is basically renamed 760 series from last year. Base GLEs have twin-cam engine. Turbos and SE Turbos have slightly more powerful 162-horsepower engine.

RATINGS (SCALE OF 1-10)

Overall	Safety	Reliability	Performance	Comfort	Value
N/A	N/A	7.9	8	8	7.8

Model Description	Trade-in Value	Market Value
Category L		
4 Dr GLE Sdn	6565	8635
4 Dr GLE Wgn	6695	8810
4 Dr SE Turbo Sdn	7610	10010
4 Dr SE Turbo Wgn	7770	10225
4 Dr STD Turbo Wgn	7115	9365
4 Dr STD Turbo Sdn	7040	9260

OPTIONS FOR 940

Leather Seats[Opt on GLE] +250

1990 VOLVO

240 — 1990

A driver airbag and knee bolsters are standard this year on all models. 240GL dropped, and a base 240 is added below the 240DL. Wagons get a new tailgate with flush-mounted glass.

Model Description	Trade-in Value	Market Value
Category L		
4 Dr DL Wgn	4985	6735
4 Dr DL Sdn	5090	6875
4 Dr STD Wgn	4365	5900
4 Dr STD Sdn	4565	6170

OPTIONS FOR 240

Auto 4-Speed Transmission +105
Sunroof +95

740 — 1990

740 GL gets driver airbag, and all 740s have new sheetmetal that closely resembles 760. New Generation III turbo engine is introduced.

Model Description	Trade-in Value	Market Value
Category L		
4 Dr GL Wgn	5050	6825
4 Dr GL Sdn	4515	6105
4 Dr GLE Sdn	5125	6930
4 Dr GLE Wgn	5255	7100
4 Dr STD Sdn	4400	5950
4 Dr STD Wgn	4945	6685
4 Dr STD Turbo Sdn	5350	7230
4 Dr STD Turbo Wgn	5840	7895

OPTIONS FOR 740

Auto 4-Speed Transmission +100
Aluminum/Alloy Wheels[Opt on GL] +70
Anti-Lock Brakes[Std on GLE,Turbo] +180
Leather Seats +200

760 — 1990

New Generation III turbo engine is introduced.

Model Description	Trade-in Value	Market Value
Category L		
4 Dr GLE Sdn	4995	6745
4 Dr GLE Turbo Sdn	5505	7435
4 Dr GLE Turbo Wgn	6160	8325

OPTIONS FOR 760

Leather Seats[Opt on Sdn] +200

1989 VOLVO

240 — 1989

All models get rear headrests. DL trim level gets new wheel covers and optional factory-installed power windows, and DL wagons can be equipped with cloth rather than vinyl at no extra cost.

Model Description	Trade-in Value	Market Value
Category L		
4 Dr DL Sdn	3655	5010
4 Dr DL Wgn	4040	5535
4 Dr GL Sdn	3845	5270

OPTIONS FOR 240

Auto 4-Speed Transmission[Opt on DL] +75
Leather Seats[Opt on Sdn] +165
Power Windows[Opt on DL] +35

740 — 1989

740 GLE models built after January get a new twin-cam engine, which boosts power 25 percent. GLEs also have a driver airbag as standard equipment and larger tires. Entry-level model is now 740 GL, and is only model in series that doesn't have airbag. ABS is standard on all models except 740 GL.

Don't forget to refer to the Mileage Adjustment Table at the back of this book!

 © 1999 by Edmund Publications Corporation

Model Description	Trade-in Value	Market Value
Category L		
4 Dr GL Wgn	4365	5980
4 Dr GL Sdn	3755	5145
4 Dr GLE Wgn	4650	6370
4 Dr GLE Sdn	3940	5400
4 Dr STD Turbo Wgn	4835	6625
4 Dr STD Turbo Sdn	4290	5875

OPTIONS FOR 740

Auto 4-Speed Transmission +70
Air Bag Restraint[Opt on GL] +90
Aluminum/Alloy Wheels[Opt on GL] +55
Anti-Lock Brakes[Opt on GL] +145
Leather Seats[Opt on GL,STD,Sdn] +165

760 1989

GLEs have a driver airbag as standard equipment and larger tires. ABS is standard on all models.

Model Description	Trade-in Value	Market Value
Category L		
4 Dr GLE Sdn	4090	5605
4 Dr STD Turbo Sdn	4415	6050
4 Dr STD Turbo Wgn	5190	7110

780 1989

GLEs have a driver airbag as standard equipment and larger tires. ABS is standard on all models. 780 coupe gets more powerful turbocharged engine and new alloy wheels.

Model Description	Trade-in Value	Market Value
Category L		
2 Dr GLE Cpe	5170	7085
2 Dr GLE Turbo Cpe	5570	7635

Major Savings On An Extended Warranty
"YOU DESERVE THE BEST"
Call today for your free quote.
Pay up to 50% less than dealership prices!
http://www.edmunds.com/warranty 1-800-580-9889

A 15-minute phone call could save you 15% or more on car insurance.
1-800-555-2758

The Sensible Alternative

Don't forget to refer to the Mileage Adjustment Table at the back of this book!

© 1999 by Edmund Publications Corporation

Unbiased information is not toll-free.

With 1-900-AUTOPRO℠, you know what you want and what it should cost BEFORE you walk into the showroom. **1-900-AUTOPRO is not affiliated with any manufacturer. We give you unbiased information.**

Knowledge is power. 1-900-AUTOPRO gives you the inside story on any new car on the market. With a single phone call, you can learn DEALER INVOICE and retail prices, standard and optional equipment, manufacturers' rebates, financing options...everything! Learn exactly what you should expect to pay for the vehicle of your choice, and get valuable advice on how to negotiate the best possible deal.

When you call a 1-900-AUTOPRO advisor, you'll immediately get any information you request and, if you like, we will fax or mail you a FREE printout of your price summary.

"The experts at 1-900-AUTOPRO will provide you with
complete up-to-date automobile information
and money-saving purchasing advice that goes
well beyond the contents of our books.
Your call will be well worth its cost."
Publisher, Edmunds Publications
ONLY $2.00 per minute
for Edmund's Readers – must be 18 yrs. or older
1-900-AUTOPRO
A SERVICE OF 1-900-AUTOFAX INCORPORATED (1-900-288-6776) BUFFALO, NY
AWARD WINNING SERVICE SINCE 1990

ABBREVIATIONS

16V	16-valve
24V	24-valve
32V	32-valve
2WD	Two-wheel Drive
3A/4A/5A	3-speed/4-speed/ 5-speed Automatic Transmission
4M/5M/6M	4-speed/5-speed/ 6-speed Manual Transmission
4Sp/5Sp/6Sp	4-speed/5-speed/ 6-speed Manual Transmission
4WD	Four-wheel Drive
4WS	Four-wheel Steering
A/S	All-season Tires
A/T	All-terrain Tires
A/C	Air Conditioning
A/M	Auto-manual Transmission
ABS	Anti-lock Braking System
AC	Air Conditioning
ALR	Automatic Locking Retractor Seat Belt
Amp	Ampere(s)
AS	All-season Tires
AT	Automatic Transmission
AT-3	3-speed Automatic Transmission
AT-4	4-speed Automatic Transmission
Auto	Automatic
Aux	Auxiliary
Auxl	Auxiliary
Avail	Available
AWD	All-wheel Drive
Blk	Black
BSW	Black Sidewall Tires
BW	Blackwall Tires
Cptn	Captain
Cass	Cassette
CD	Compact Disc
CFC	Chloroflorocarbon
CID	Cubic Inch Displacement
Cntry	Country
Conv	Convertible
Cpe	Coupe
Ctrl	Control
Cu Ft	Cubic Foot (Feet)
Cu In	Cubic Inch(es)
Cust	Custom
CVT	Continuously Variable Transmission
Cvrs	Covers
Cyl	Cylinder
DC	Direct Current
DFRS	Dual Facing Rear Seats
DME	Digital Motor Electronics
DOHC	Dual Overhead Cam Engine
Dr	Door
DRLs	Daytime Running Lights
Drv	Drive
DRW	Dual Rear Wheels
Dsl	Diesel Engine
ECT	Electronically Controlled Transmission
EEC	Electronic Engine Control
EFI	Electronic Fuel Injection
ELR	Emergency Locking Retractor Seat Belt
Eng	Engine
Equip	Equipment
ETR	Electronically Tuned Radio
ETS	Electronically Tuned Stereo
Ext	Extended
FI	Fuel Injection
Ft	Foot (Feet)
FWD	Front-wheel Drive
Gal	Gallon
Grp	Group
GVW	Gross Vehicle Weight
GVWR	Gross Vehicle Weight Rating
H4	Horizontally-opposed, Four-cylinder Engine

 © 1999 by Edmund Publications Corporation

ABBREVIATIONS 2

H6	Horizontally-opposed, Six-cylinder Engine
Hbk	Hatchback
HD	Heavy Duty
HO	High Output
HP	Horsepower
HUD	Heads Up Display
HVAC	Heating/Ventilation/ Air Conditioning
I4	Inline Type, Four-cylinder Engine
I5	Inline Type, Five-cylinder Engine
I6	Inline Type, Six-cylinder Engine
Illum	Illuminated
Incls	Includes
Incld	Included
Kw	Kilowatt
L	Liter
L4	Inline Type, Four-cylinder Engine
L5	Inline Type, Five-cylinder Engine
L6	Inline Type, Six-cylinder Engine
L/R	Left and Right
LB	Longbed
Lbk	Liftback
Lb/ft	Pounds/Feet (measurement of engine torque)
Lb(s)	Pound(s)
LCD	Liquid Crystal Display
LD	Light Duty
LED	Light Emitting Diode
LH	Left Hand
Ltd	Limited
Lthr	Leather
Lugg	Luggage
LWB	Long Wheelbase
M+S	Mud and Snow Tires
Man	Manual
Max	Maximum
Med	Medium
Min	Minimum
Mm	Millimeter
MPFI	Multi-point Fuel Injection
Mpg	Miles Per Gallon
Mph	Miles Per Hour
MPI	Multi-point Fuel Injection
MT	Manual Transmission
Mus	Music
N/A	Not Available or Not Applicable
NA	Not Available or Not Applicable
Nbk	Notchback
N/C	No Charge
NC	No Charge
OBD II	On-board Diagnostic System
OD	Overdrive
OHC	Overhead Camshaft Engine
OHV	Overhead Valve Engine
Opt	Optional
OS	Outside
OWL	Outline White-letter Tires
P/U	Pickup Truck
Pass	Passenger
PDL	Power Door Locks
PEG	Preferred Equipment Group
PEP	Preferred Equipment Package
PGM-FI	Programmed Fuel Injection
Pkg	Package
Pkup	Pickup Truck
Prem	Premium
PS	Power Steering
Psngr	Passenger
PW	Power Windows
Pwr	Power
Reg	Regular
Req'd	Required
Req's	Requires
RH	Right Hand
Rpm	Revolutions Per Minute

 © 1999 by Edmund Publications Corporation

RWD	Rear-wheel Drive
RWL	Raised White-letter Tires
SB	Shortbed
SBR	Steel-belted Radial Tires
Sdn	Sedan
SEFI	Sequential Fuel Injection
SFI	Sequential Fuel Injection
SLA	Short/Long Arm Suspension
Snrf	Sunroof
SOHC	Single Overhead Camshaft Engine
Spd	Speed
SPFI	Sequential Port Fuel Injection
Spt	Sport
SRS	Supplemental Restraint System (Airbag)
SRW	Single Rear Wheels
Std	Standard
Sts	Seats
Sunscrn	Sunscreen
SUV	Sport/Utility Vehicle
S/W	Station Wagon
SWB	Short Wheelbase
Sys	System
Tach	Tachometer
TBI	Throttle Body Fuel Injection
TCS	Traction Control System
TD	Turbo-diesel Engine
Temp	Temperature
TPI	Tuned Port Fuel Injection
Trans	Transmission
TrbDsl	Turbo-diesel Engine
Trbo	Turbocharged Engine
V6	V-type, Six-cylinder Engine
V8	V-type, Eight-cylinder Engine
V10	V-type, Ten-cylinder Engine
V12	V-type, Twelve-cylinder Engine
VTEC	Variable Valve Timing and Lift Electronic Control
W/	With
W/O	Without
W/T	Work Truck
WB	Wheelbase
Wgn	Wagon
Whl(s)	Wheel(s)
Wndw	Window(s)
WS	Wideside
WSW	White Sidewall Tires
X-Cab	Extended Cab Pickup

 © 1999 by Edmund Publications Corporation

FREQUENTLY ASKED QUESTIONS

1. Why does Edmund's® used car pricing differ from other price guides?

Each guide uses different sources to determine pricing. You must keep in mind that these publications, and Edmund's®, are to be considered guides. The values contained within are not absolute; they are intended to give the user a range of values to consider when determining a fair price. Used car values depend on mileage, vehicle condition, geographic location, model popularity, seasonal demand, and even color.

Keep in mind that the dealer will use whatever pricing guide works to their advantage in the deal. By providing pricing that favors the dealer, other guides make big bucks on subscriptions to industry personnel. Some even publish two different pricing guides; one for consumers, and one for dealers. Rarely do dealers use Edmund's. We believe that speaks volumes about the fairness of our published pricing to the consumer.

The most important thing to remember about buying, selling, or trading a used car is this: a used car is only worth as much as somebody is willing to pay for it.

2. When is a car considered used?

Technically, a vehicle is considered used if it has been titled. However, some dealers can rack up hundreds or thousands of miles on a new car without titling it. In these cases, the ethical definition of a used car should include any car used for extensive demonstration or personal use by dealership staff members. The only miles a new car should have on the odometer when purchased are those put on during previous test drives by prospective buyers (at dealerships where demonstrators are not used), and any miles driven during a dealer trade, within a reasonable limit. If the new car you're considering has more than 300 miles on the odometer, you should question how the car accumulated so many miles, and request a discount for the excessive mileage. We think a discount amounting to a dime a mile is a fair charge for wear and tear inflicted by the dealership.

A car should not be considered used if it is a brand-new leftover from a previous model year. However, it should be discounted, because many manufacturers offer dealers incentives designed to help the dealer lower prices and clear out old stock.

3. How often is Edmund's® used car pricing updated?

We update our used car pricing quarterly.

© 1999 by Edmund Publications Corporation

4. Why did the used car I'm considering take a nasty drop in the ratings recently?

Edmund's® updates used car ratings annually, usually early in the summer. We also tend to fiddle with the formulas that create the ratings, in an effort to make the ratings more accurate. If you find that the rating has changed recently, it's only because fresh data is available and we've finished our annual update.

Keep in mind that pricing is different from ratings. Pricing is updated quarterly throughout the year; ratings are updated once per year.

5. Why don't you have a listing for the late-model used car I want to buy or sell?

To generate an accurate value for any given used car, there must be enough used examples on the market to include in the sample. Most often, the reason we don't provide a listing is because there aren't enough examples to generate an accurate value. For special interest models, such as the Volkswagen Corrado or Merkur XR4ti, try consulting a specialty car value guide at your local bookstore, or contact a dealer who specializes in these types of cars for information.

6. Do you have pricing for used cars older than 1989?

No, we do not. After a decade on the road, most cars have depreciated to the point where fluctuations in values are slight and do not have much impact on the transaction price. Older models will sell easily and for top-dollar if they are in excellent condition. Specialty models are covered by a variety of guides that you can buy in your local bookstore, or you can consult the classifieds in such publications as *AutoWeek*, *Hemmings Motor News*, and *The DuPont Registry*.

7. How do I determine a fair price for a used car?

Edmund's® publishes a Market Value, which is based on average asking and transaction prices by dealers and private owners nationwide. As a buyer or seller, you'll want to get as close to Market Value as possible.

8. Why won't the dealer give me wholesale value for my trade-in?

When a dealership takes a car in on trade, it is responsible for the car. Before the trade-in can be sold, it must be inspected and often repaired. Sometimes, emissions work is necessary. All this inspection and repair work costs the dealership money. If the trade is in good condition and has low miles, the dealer will put the car on the used car lot for retail price. When the car sells, it is rarely for retail price, so the profit margin is shaved. The less you accept for the trade-in, the more room the

 © 1999 by Edmund Publications Corporation

dealer has to make a deal with a prospective buyer, and the more money the dealer will make thanks to increased profit margins.

If the car doesn't sell, if it has high miles, or it is in poor condition, the dealer will have to wholesale it. The dealer will likely sell the car for below wholesale value at the auction, and expects to recoup some of the money spent reconditioning and inspecting the car. If the dealer offered you wholesale price when you traded the car in, he wouldn't make the money back in the event that the trade-in went to auction.

It is this practice that convinced us to change our used car format to include Trade-in Value rather than Wholesale value. Edmund's® Trade-in Value is almost always lower than the Wholesale value published by other guides (after optional equipment and mileage adjustments), and we think this price more accurately reflects the real value of a trade-in to a dealer.

Regardless of the condition of your car, the dealer will anticipate taking the car to auction, and will leave room to make money in that event. Your best bet is to sell your car on your own to a private party, and forget about trading in.

9. How much does an extended warranty cost the warranty company?

The cost of an extended warranty is based upon the degree of probability that any given vehicle will require repairs during the extended warranty period. Reliability records and repair cost information for a vehicle are evaluated to forecast potential future repair costs, and the extended warranty company will then charge a premium adequate enough to cover the potential cost of repairing the vehicle during the warranty period, while still making a profit. It is important to note that the cost of an extended warranty includes administrative costs for handling paperwork and claims, and insurance to guarantee that claims will be paid.

Extended warranty costs are based on averages, so the cost of applying an extended warranty to any given make and model of car can vary from consumer to consumer. Let's say you bought a $1,000 extended warranty for two identical Brand X vehicles: Car A and Car B. During the extended warranty period, Car A never breaks, so the extended warranty is never used. At the same time, Car B suffers bills amounting to $1,200 for transmission and valve problems. Profit on the warranty sold for Car A will counterbalance the loss suffered on Car B. Extended warranty companies sell thousands of warranties annually, and are able to make a profit when the actual loss experience is lower than the forecast potential for future repair. In other words, when sales exceed overhead the company makes money.

You can purchase an extended warranty several ways, and we recommend shopping around for the best price. Start with the warranty providers, such as Warranty

 © 1999 by Edmund Publications Corporation

Gold, and then compare to what the dealer can offer. The majority of the time, the dealer cannot beat your best price from a warranty provider because of the markup a dealer must charge to make a profit on the extended warranty offered. Also, when shopping extended warranties, be sure the policies are comparable in terms of deductible costs, covered parts and the amount of labor that will be paid for.

10. Can I negotiate price at a Saturn dealer?

No, you cannot. All Saturn dealers operate under a strict no-haggle policy, even for used cars. You can, however, demand top dollar for your trade and/or a lower interest rate to lower the overall cost of the deal.

11. Who sets the residual value for a lease?

The financing institution that is handling the lease for the dealership sets the residual value, which can be affected by market forces and vehicle popularity. When shopping leases, it is important to shop different financing institutions for the highest residual value and the lowest interest rate.

12. I want to pay cash for my car. Do I have an advantage?

Not necessarily. You must remember that no matter how you pay for your car, it's all cash to the dealer. In the old days when dealers carried your note, you could save money by paying cash because there was no risk to the dealer. Today, dealerships finance through one of several lending institutions (banks, credit unions, or the automaker's captive financing division) who pay them cash when the contract is presented. In fact, if dealerships do the financing on your behalf, they tend to make more money on your contract in the form of a reserve; anywhere from ½ to 1 point spread on the interest. For example, if the published rate is 8.75%, the lender to dealer rate may be discounted to 8%; the .75% is the reserve held by the dealer as additional profit. This may not sound like much, but it adds up to hundreds of thousands of dollars a year at larger dealerships. This is the reason you should always arrange financing before going to the dealership, and then ask the dealer if they can beat your pre-approved rate. In most cases, they cannot, because of the reserve.

Paying cash is an advantage if you suffer from poor credit or bankruptcy, because it allows you to avoid the higher interest rates charged on loans to people with past credit problems. The bottom line is that if you think you can invest your money at a higher return than the interest rate of the car, you could actually save money by not paying cash.

 © 1999 by Edmund Publications Corporation

13. When is the best time to purchase a car from a dealer?

There's as much advice about when is the best time to visit a dealer as there are days in a year. Some say that Mondays are good because business is slower on Monday than on the weekend. Some say holidays like Thanksgiving are good for the same reason: nobody else will be there, and the sales team will be hungry for a sale. Others advise to go when it's raining or snowing; after all, who wants to look at a car and get wet? Then there's the advice that the end of the month is the best time because the dealership needs to make its "quota" of car sales and will be more willing to cut a deal. Still others advise not to buy a car until the end of the model year, or in slow months like August or December when people are busy thinking about going back to school or shopping for Christmas gifts rather than buying a new car.

Our advice is don't buy a car until you need one. That's usually the best time. By then you have saved enough for a substantial down payment, and you've had plenty of time to do your research for the lowest interest rate, and you know all the current incentives and rebates. There is no way to tell when is the best time to buy other than personal need.

If a dealer has already made his target sales for the month, you're not going to have any advantage by showing up on the 31st of the month. While there may be something to say for going to a dealership on a weekday near the end of the month on Thanksgiving at five o'clock during a raging blizzard, your best bet is to track incentives and rebates, don't buy hot new models, and do your research first.

14. What's the difference between a demo car and a program car?

A demo car is one used by the dealership as a demonstrator to potential buyers. Often, dealership personnel will use the car as personal transportation. A program car is a former rental car, purchased at auction by the dealership. Either type of car is more likely to have been abused than a brand-new car or a used car offered for sale by a private owner.

15. How can I determine what a dealer paid for a used car at auction or in trade?

Unless the dealer honestly discloses this amount, you can't determine an exact "invoice" price. However, by pushing for the best deal you will find the point where the dealer firms up on price. When this happens, you've gotten about as low as you can go; any lower and the dealer figures it would be better to just hang on to the car.

 © 1999 by Edmund Publications Corporation

16. Is it fair for a dealer to ask if my trade has ever been wrecked, or damaged in any way?

Certainly. If you were buying a car from a used car dealer, you'd want to know the same thing, wouldn't you?

17. What is a trim level?

Most cars and trucks on the market today are available in various levels of trim with various levels of standard equipment. To distinguish between base models and better appointed or sporty models, manufacturers will add a numeric or alphabetic designation after the model name. For example, the Ford Taurus is sold in LX, SE, and SHO trim levels. Similarly, the Nissan Maxima is sold in GXE, SE, and GLE trim levels. Not all trim level designations appear after the model name. Acura sells a 3.2TL and a 3.5RL. BMW's 3-Series model comes in several alphanumeric trim levels: 318ti, 323i, 323is, 323iC, 328i, 328is, 328iC, and M3.

18. What is a secret warranty, and how can I find out if any exist for my car?

A secret warranty, actually called a technical service bulletin (TSB), is a notice that dealer service departments receive from manufacturers regarding suggested repairs to solve common complaints. The dealer is instructed to replace or repair these parts free of charge while the vehicle is under warranty or if the customer complains about a problem while the car is under warranty, but the TSB repair is not available at the time of the complaint. By law, TSB repairs covering emissions equipment are free of charge to the customer for up to 100,000 miles. If a TSB has been issued for your vehicle, but your situation does not meet any of the three listed criteria, then you are responsible for the cost of the repairs. You can get a list of TSBs for your car by contacting the National Highway and Traffic Safety Administration (NHTSA) at http://www.nhtsa.dot.gov and conducting a search for the information.

19. The new model year rollout is occurring. How will this affect used car values?

When you buy a new car, and it doesn't matter if it's an Acura or a Chevy, it depreciates the second it is titled in your name. Why? It has become a used car. Used cars age and accumulate mileage, and as they age and accumulate mileage they lose value. This is a constant process. Almost all used cars lose their value at a relatively steady rate, it's just that some makes like Acura lose value at a slower rate then other makes like Chevy.

 © 1999 by Edmund Publications Corporation

Just because our value guides are published quarterly doesn't mean that a car isn't losing value during that quarter. Used car prices are never static. That's why we tell people that used car values supplied by ANY publication are to be used simply as a guide to help you determine a fair price.

Because used car prices are not static the introduction of a new model year doesn't alter them much, if at all. One exception this year might affect the 1997/1998 Acura 3.2TL. The 1999 model is completely redesigned, content and size have been boosted, and the price has been dropped by several thousand dollars. This will likely affect used 1997 and 1998 TL prices in an adverse fashion.

Let's continue with our Acura example. Since the 1999 Integra is essentially a carbon copy of the 1998 Integra, and pricing is going up slightly, used Integra pricing will remain stable, depreciating at a steady rate. However, a 1998 Integra has already depreciated quite a bit from the price when it was new, and just because a 1999 model is in the showrooms, that doesn't mean the 1998 will suffer a burp in depreciation and be devalued at twice the rate for a month.

Depreciation of used cars is almost always a steady, predictable process. Factor in climate, geographic region, supply & demand, etc., and that's where you get most of the fluctuations. Other factors, such as the scenario described above regarding the TL and the whole Acura SLX/Isuzu Trooper rollover scare from a few years ago, can further alter valuations. And what would happen to Expedition/Suburban values if gas prices ever doubled? They'd drop in the toilet.

The bottom line is that the introduction of new model year vehicles generally doesn't alter used vehicle pricing much, if at all.

20. How do manufacturer certified used car programs affect used car values?

Remember that our data samples include several sources, including advertised and selling prices from dealers who sell manufacturer certified used cars. However, our data is also representative of a given vehicle in average condition, and most manufacturer certified used cars are in good to excellent condition. Furthermore, the dealership spends anywhere from $500 to $1,000 to certify a used car to manufacturer specification. If you are shopping for a manufacturer certified used car, you will need to take vehicle condition and the costs associated with the certification process into account when trying to determine a fair price.

 © 1999 by Edmund Publications Corporation

REVIEW: 1997 GMC JIMMY

When Beauty Is Only Skin Deep

By Christian J. Wardlaw
photography courtesy of General Motors

Peering out the kitchen window at the crimson GMC Jimmy SLE sitting in front of the house, I thought to myself, "Now that's a good-looking truck." The paint matched the red GMC lettering on the wheel caps, the grille, and the liftgate, and contrasted deeply with the chrome grille accents, gray cloth interior, and bright bodyside moldings. Very nice to look at, our test Jimmy.

The keys hung on a hook nearby. Snatching them from their perch, I headed out to the Jimmy for a quick drive. We'd enjoyed previous GM sport-utes from Chevrolet and Oldsmobile (the Blazer and Bravada are essentially the same truck as the Jimmy but with minor styling and content modifications), so I wasn't expecting anything different from the Jimmy. As I walked up to the driver's door, I glanced down to find the remote keyless entry button on the fob. There wasn't one, because there wasn't a fob, which makes sense, because our Jimmy didn't have a remote keyless entry system. So, I unlocked the door manually, thinking it odd that our test truck wasn't equipped with this ubiquitous convenience feature.

The Jimmy has a low step-in height, so getting behind the wheel was easy. Once seated, I reached to the lower left side of the seat for the power adjustments that have made previous test Blazers and Bravadas so darn comfortable. Hmmm. Nothing there, but a lever was sticking out from under the front of the seat that allowed fore and aft travel, and a knob on the side

pushed a flimsy-feeling lumbar support into my back. I tried to move the seat for more leg room, but to no avail. After wrestling with the lever for a moment, I realized that the seat already was positioned at its maximum rearward travel position.

Despite the presence of a power sunroof and a CD player, I'm thinking at this point that our 4WD Jimmy must be lightly equipped to lack remote keyless entry and a power driver's seat, and if it's lightly equipped, then it must be a screaming bargain in comparison to $31,000 all-wheel drive models like the leather-lined Oldsmobile Bravada and larger V8-powered Mercury Mountaineer.

With a twist of the key, a Vortec 4300 V6 fires to life under the Jimmy's broad-shouldered hood. Making 190 horsepower and 250 lb.-ft. of torque, this 4.3-liter engine provides pretty good oomph for a heavy sport-ute. Even a light foot on the throttle gets the Jimmy moving quickly, and so I more or less idled the truck to the mailboxes on the left side of my street. Then I applied the brakes, lightly of course, because I wasn't going very fast. At first, nothing happened, and I thought for a moment that I might bump the Chevy Astro Van parked on the street in front of me. Then, firmer pressure on the brake finally engaged the front discs and rear drums, and the Jimmy lurched to a halt. Ah yes, I'd forgotten to reacquaint myself with GM's 'dead pedal' brake system, deemed squishy later in the week by my wife.

After checking the mailbox, I head for the FedEx office a few miles from home. To get there, I must traverse a deep dip through a dry wash, which can usually be taken at 55 mph with any competent vehicle. The Jimmy's suspension fully compressed at that speed, and lifted a wheel coming up the other side, the first time any car I've driven through the wash has behaved in such a manner. Later, as I approach the FedEx office, another series of smaller pavement undulations sent the Jimmy into spastic suspension convulsions. Is it possible that, after a 9 month hiatus from GM's compact SUV models, I've somehow forgotten all about this handling trait, or is the Jimmy in particular the lousy driver of the trio?

Turning into the FedEx office, I notice that the steering wheel is about two sizes too big for the Jimmy's interior. Culled from the Sierra full-size pickup, where it actually fits in with the topography reasonably well, the steering wheel is far too large for Jimmy's compact interior dimensions. After parking, I retrieve the computer monitor that a colleague in New York needs for a new system. Our Jimmy is equipped with a liftgate, new for 1997. All previous models had a clamshell arrangement that made tailgate parties fun but were a hassle during the 364 days a year you weren't barbecuing from the rear of your truck. The monitor has been set upon the cargo net, because the net is very difficult to remove, and I didn't feel much like taking the time to uninstall it. Later, I do uninstall it to help friends move their belongings to a new apartment. Upon re-installation, I find that the cargo hooks to which the bottom of the net attaches are nearly impossible to pry up from the cargo floor without the help of a flathead screwdriver.

On the way back home from FedEx, I'm stopped at the bottom of a hill by a traffic signal. Next to me is a first-generation 4WD Ford Explorer with a manual transmission. To my surprise, the Explorer keeps up with the Jimmy through 1st gear, gains a bit of ground in 2nd gear, and stays with me through 3rd gear. Granted, I had the air conditioner running, but the Vortec 4300 V6 has been raved about by our staff, and other auto journalists, for its power and accelerative abilities. How could that wheezy old Ford keep up?

Less than an hour later, I'm gazing at the window sticker GMC supplied with the Jimmy. To my surprise, our test Jimmy runs a hair over $29,000. The V6 is rated 21 mpg highway and a truly disappointing 16 mpg in the city, and that's with a light foot. Why bother with a V6 if the gas mileage is going to be so low? Ah ha, our truck is equipped with the optional Luxury Ride Suspension. That explains its dead-on impression of a Buick Roadmaster Estate wagon through dips and over bumps. The power driver's seat and remote keyless entry would only run another $375, and cost cutters could excise the power sunroof, the trailering equipment, and the HomeLink system to drop the sticker another grand. But even so, the Jimmy doesn't seem like a good deal.

Why not? There are two reasons. First is the existence of the Oldsmobile Bravada. With standard leather, special seats that are twice as good as those in our test Jimmy, standard all-wheel drive, a superb sound system, adjustable headrests, power lumbar support, and standard remote keyless entry, the

Bravada seems worth the extra $2,500 over the Jimmy, or the Chevy Blazer for that matter. Second is the existence of the Jeep Cherokee. Sized about the same as the compact sport-utilities from General Motors, a loaded Cherokee Sport comes in thousands less than our test Jimmy, and is more comfortable, more fun to drive, and slightly speedier since it boasts a lower curb weight. The Jimmy offers better ergonomics than the Jeep, and a split folding rear seat (which doesn't come on the Jeep unless you get creative with your Stihl saw), but money is money, am I right?

After a week and 400 miles with the Jimmy, I asked my wife to drive it and give me some opinions. She didn't find it very powerful, and complained about the acceleration. She thought it was ridiculous that a $29,000 vehicle didn't have a power driver's seat or remote keyless entry. She called the brakes squishy. She said that this particular Jimmy's ride reminded her of the Buick Park Avenue and the Cadillac DeVille, the only two test vehicles that have ever made her ill (she suffers from motion sickness). Otherwise, she liked it, particularly the low step-in height.

I like it too, but not as well as other models in this same price range. It's adequate in all respects, with no stand out attributes except for the small amount of space it occupies in my garage and the large radio station pre-set buttons. Over time, you familiarize yourself with the transmission's shift pattern and learn to make the most of the Vortec V6's powerband. You learn to stomp on the brakes at the outset, or risk coasting into an intersection after your foot tells you the brake has been applied but the truck tells you they have not. You find a reasonably comfortable driving position, despite the huge steering wheel and the fact that your legs are shunted slightly to the left because the large transmission tunnel intrudes on passenger foot space. You get used to mediocre fuel economy, because all your pals have SUVs that guzzle gas too. The problem with the GMC Jimmy is the Ford Explorer-sized price tag on a Jeep Cherokee-sized vehicle.

CAR
FINANCE
DOT
COM
TM
Instant
Lease & Loan Quotes
for New & Used Vehicles!
www.CarFinance.com/edmunds

REVIEW: 1996 CHEVROLET BLAZER

Good Things Come In Small Packages

By Christian J. Wardlaw
photography courtesy of General Motors

When Chevrolet issued a pint-sized edition of the full-size Blazer in 1983, it pioneered a market segment that experienced explosive growth during the following decade. Sadly, Chevrolet missed the boat, failing to capitalize on the popularity of four-door compact SUVs until 1990. Based on S-10 pickup parts and featuring squared-off, rugged good looks, the S-10 Blazer was initially available in a two-door bodystyle only. In 1984, Jeep brought the Cherokee to the party in two- and four-door configurations, and soon eclipsed the S-10 Blazer in sales and panache. Cherokees became the hot family vehicle to own in snooty social circles, while the S-10 Blazer plodded along for seven sales seasons without the benefit of two additional portals or luxury trimmings. By then, Ford had dumped the dopey Bronco II and was poised to reap huge sales with the all-new Explorer. Soon thereafter, Jeep unleashed the Grand Cherokee, and the S-10 Blazer was relegated to die-hard GM fans and bargain basement buyers who didn't want the equally ancient Cherokee.

Chevrolet fixed this situation with a 1995 redesign of the compact Blazer. Again based on S-10 mechanicals, the new Blazer dropped the S-10 nomenclature, adopting the name of its full-size counterpart, which Chevy renamed Tahoe. Chevy's new Blazer represented a quantum leap in terms of performance, styling, and space, and it still offered real value in comparison to many competitors. Still ruggedly attractive, the new Blazer fell short in just one critical area. More on that later.

REVIEW: 1996 CHEVROLET BLAZER

We sampled a 1996 Blazer LS four-door equipped with shift-on-the-fly four-wheel drive. Painted bright red and sporting attractive alloy wheels shod with white-letter tires, our test Blazer looked very sporty. It drove that way too, thanks to the Vortec 4.3-liter V-6 engine under the short, sloping hood. Making 190 horsepower at 4400 rpm, and 250 lb./ft. of torque at 2800 rpm, the Blazer we drove pulled well at low speeds, but had trouble with highway passing when cruising at 70 mph. The Blazer's abundant low speed torque, small size, and good visibility make for a fun vehicle to drive around town. Ours was equipped with a comfortable and multi-adjustable 6-way power driver's seat, and we certainly recommend it. Driver comfort with this optional seat is outstanding. Passengers, however, must sit on significantly less comfortable chairs. The front and rear passenger seats are mounted too low to provide adequate leg support.

On tough off-road trails, the nimble Blazer acquitted itself well, handling the most difficult terrain we could find in the mountains west of Boulder, Colorado. The all-season tires didn't bite as deeply as all-terrain tires would have, and we had to make several second or third attempts through more difficult passages, but never were we fearful that we'd get the Blazer stuck and have to hoof it back into town. The only disconcerting thing about the Blazer's off-road characteristics was the tendency for the doors to shudder forcefully in their jambs, and the agonizing clatter of various plastic interior bits as they shook in their settings. Simply put, the interior of the Blazer felt like it would fall apart quickly if used extensively for off-road travel.

At $28,000, our test Blazer was well trimmed. Power convenience items, heavy-duty off-road hardware, an upgraded exterior appearance package, and a cool overhead console with compass, temperature display, reading lights, and storage were all part of the final tally. Want more luxurious surroundings? Step up to LT Decor, which adds leather seats, a premium sound system, and unique aluminum wheels, among other goodies. Toss on all-wheel drive for another $200, and you've just saved yourself a couple hundred bucks off the price of an Oldsmobile Bravada. Still, loaded like this, the Blazer is rapidly approaching the $30,000 price point. You might as well get into a Tahoe for a few extra bucks a month. We feel the Blazer is a better buy when trimmed to lesser specifications. Paying thirty large for a compact sport/ute falling on the small side of the spectrum seems foolish to us.

Small the Blazer may be, but Chevrolet's claim that the cargo hold is designed to accommodate a full-size washer or dryer is true. We moved a medium-sized washer in the Blazer one weekend, and it fit with plenty of room to spare. The rear seat is ridiculously simple to fold, resulting in a nice, flat load floor. Chevrolet claims that the Blazer will hold 37.3 cubic feet of stuff with the rear seat upright, but that measurement is from floor to ceiling. Halve that figure for a real world volume. Loading cargo can be difficult since Chevrolet opted to use a split-tailgate arrangement to the rear rather than a more sensible hatch, but engineers make up for this deficiency somewhat by making the optional pull-out cargo shade accessible from the side of the cargo bay where it never has to be removed. Additionally, our LS test vehicle came with durable, commodious netting that stretched across the cargo area just forward of the tailgate; handy when loading items through the flip-up rear window.

Yep, the Blazer certainly does grow on you. Fun to drive and easy to wheel about town, it can also handle most off-road demands its owners will ever make. Sparsely equipped, it represents real value and handily fits into the market gap between mini- and mid-sized SUVs. Still, we cannot recommend this vehicle. See, it only has one airbag, installed inside the steering wheel hub to protect the driver. No big deal, right? Well, not if the Blazer scored well in crash tests conducted by the National Highway and Traffic Safety Administration as part of the New Car Assessment Program. Unfortunately, it doesn't. The front passenger of a Chevy Blazer currently stands a 45% chance of suffering a life threatening injury in a 35 mph head-on collision with an object equivalent in size and weight to the Blazer. This score is the worst of all SUVs tested since 1994, and is simply unacceptable. Chevrolet expects to install a passenger airbag for the 1998 model year. We suggest waiting until then before considering the Blazer for duty as a family hauler.

It's too bad about those crash test scores. We genuinely enjoyed our time with the Blazer, and it impressed us as a capable urban and off-road runner. Basically, the Chevrolet Blazer proves the old maxim true; good things do come in small packages.

REVIEW: 1996 OLDSMOBILE BRAVADA

Rugged Luxury on a Budget

By Christian J. Wardlaw
photography courtesy of General Motors

Luxury sport/utilities can sometimes be hard to take seriously. Softer suspension settings, leather seats, and a nice stereo can't really conceal the hard-working truck origins of most upper-end SUVs. Furthermore, most luxury SUV buyers simply want to promote an image or lifestyle that says, "I'm a unique, prosperous, adventurous, physically active individual that doesn't fit a corporate mold." Land Rovers, the most serious and able of the breed, are more likely to be found parked in front of a two-story colonial 40 minutes from downtown than on top of a mountain in Utah. In direct contrast to the message they send, they're likely to be owned by middle-aged and overweight folk suffering the stress of rampant downsizing and impending mergers. Yes, it's tough to take a luxury sport/ute seriously, when their most demanding task is to impress the valet or track through six-inches of snow.

Auto manufacturers are riding the luxury SUV trend all the way to the bank. Production costs on these trucks are low, and profit margins are high. Dealers like selling them too; often, their popularity means added profit. Most models in this class are lousy values, and are tastelessly decorated with garish two-tone paint, bulging wheel flares, overblown gold packages, massive bodyside cladding, and the like. As if this ornamentation wasn't enough, owners tack on aftermarket items like brush guards and running boards. Looking at the darn things, you'd think the owners were ready to travel the Serengeti, when they're really headed for the Safeway.

REVIEW: 1996 OLDSMOBILE BRAVADA

The Oldsmobile Bravada, at $29,995, may be the best value on the luxury SUV market, and can be taken seriously, thanks to its restrained styling and excellent off-road prowess. All things considered, the only sport/utes on the market that come close to offering what the Bravada can at this price point are corporate cousins of Oldsmobile's SUV, the Chevrolet Blazer LT and GMC Jimmy SLT. Of course, you could always step down a rung and get into less refined vehicles like the Honda Passport EX, Jeep Cherokee Country, or Isuzu Rodeo, but then you'd be missing out on the Bravada's super-comfortable driver's seat, outstanding sound system, solid chassis, modern engineering, and all-wheel drive.

Let's examine the standard equipment list for the Oldsmobile Bravada. Hardware includes a 4.3-liter, 190-horsepower V-6 engine sending power to all four wheels, with 65% of available torque headed to the rear axle. A locking rear differential splits torque evenly if wheel slippage is detected under 20 mph. Ground clearance is a generous 7.7 inches, and the Bravada can tow 5,000 pounds right out of the box. Four-wheel anti-lock brakes are standard. Luxury touches include remote keyless entry, aluminum wheels, leather seats, 6-way power driver's seat, overhead storage console with trip computer and digital compass, a top-notch audio system, privacy glass, requisite power accessories, and unconvincing wood trim. Only 8 options are available, including a CD player, a gold package, a towing package, no-charge cloth seats, and different tires. Fully loaded, a Bravada undercuts a base Ford Explorer Eddie Bauer V-6 with part-time 4WD and no optional equipment. If that's not value, what is?

Value isn't the only game in town. Any respectable SUV should be able to clamber up trails that barely hint at two-track travel. We drove the Bravada up one such trail, and were pleasantly surprised at its ability to traverse washes and squeeze between trees. Certainly, the locking rear differential and excellent low-end torque provided by the 4.3-liter V-6 had a hand in lending the Bravada trailblazing ability, but the vehicle's structure didn't release any signs of stress or flex while driving through gullies. The suspension soaked up bounces and bumps with ease. On graded dirt road, however, washboard surfaces caused passenger doors to rattle in their frames violently, and a resonant thrum echoed throughout the cabin, assaulting our eardrums more than Fran Drescher's scratchy, whiny voice. At least the Bravada was stable in rough turns. The only time the truck lost its composure was during throttle lift-off or slight braking while traveling around bends that had suffered severe water run-off. A goose of the gas pedal easily straightened the Bravada out in these situations. Off-road, the anti-lock brakes seemed quick to engage, and offered more activation noise than pulsation through the brake pedal to let you know the ABS was doing its job. Overall, it was quite an agreeable off-road companion.

Unfortunately, most luxury sport/utility buyers don't venture any further off-road than the corn stand 50 yards to the right of Highway 287. That's OK in the Bravada. Highway cruising is comfortable, thanks to a somewhat softly tuned suspension and an excellent driver's seat. Wind noise created by the fixed-mast antenna, roof rack, and large side mirrors is deafening at speeds above 70 mph, but a twist of the volume knob takes care of that problem right quick. The sound system might not look like much, but it sounds great. Visibility is very good, and most controls are easy to find, see, and use. Around town, the V-6 pulls nicely, but trying to pass or travel up a slight grade at freeway speeds leaves the motor gasping for breath. We managed to get the Bravada up to 95 mph, but it certainly wasn't happy anywhere above 80 mph. Braking from lofty speeds is acceptable, but our test Bravada suffered brake fade quickly. Lower speed errand running is fun in the Bravada. It's small and strong enough to zip through stagnant traffic, and features a command-of-the-road seating position along with evident heft, which contributes to a feeling of safety. However, parking the Bravada can be cumbersome, due to a large turning circle. The verdict? Urban driving is fun in the Bravada, thanks to its compact size and eager engine. Highway driving is a chore, thanks to excessive wind noise and its winded engine. Despite the comfortable driver's seat, nearly perfect driving position and compliant on-road ride, we wouldn't want to take the Bravada on a cross-country trip.

Long distance travel in the Bravada is less than enticing for a couple of other reasons. Adult passengers will not be nearly as comfortable as the driver. Passenger seating positions are low, and the seats offer little in the way of leg and thigh support. Additionally, rear passengers don't have anyplace to put their feet, because they won't fit under the front seats. The result is an eat-your-knees-for-breakfast seating position for rear passengers. Finding room for passengers' cargo might be difficult as well. The Bravada's cargo area is noticeably smaller than class-leader Ford Explorer. And, loading the cargo bay with a week's worth of supplies isn't very convenient because of the Bravada's tailgate design. To load or unload rearmost cargo, you must stretch over the lowered tailgate, which can easily dirty clothes. Oldsmobile ought to consider installing a hatch-style or swing-out cargo door sometime before the Bravada's next redesign.

Aesthetically, the Bravada's interior suffers the same malady that plagues most other GM products; cheap plastic trim. Admittedly, Bravada stylists have done an admirable job of disguising the chintzy look that other vehicles sharing this basic interior design possess, but the glovebox door is one glaring example of the brittle, cheesy plastic found across the line at GM. Why not cover this door in the soft vinyl that dresses the top of the dash? At least the large knobs and buttons of most controls are easy to spot and use, though we wish their glossy gray plastic finish had better texture. Another nit pick is the turn signal stalk controls. Must 11 separate functions controlling wipers, hi-beams, cruise control, and turn signals be lumped onto a single stalk? With the gearshift located on the floor in the Bravada, there's room on the right hand side of the steering column for another stalk, and we don't see anything but an airbag and a horn pad located on the steering wheel. Fake wood covers the forward part of the console and the power window surrounds on the door panels. It looks OK, and serves to break up the gray monotony of the interior, but the wood on the door panels seems misplaced.

Outside, stylists have done a commendable job of distancing the Bravada from clones at Chevrolet and GMC showrooms without resorting to tacky decoration. Slightly overdone ribbed body cladding and busy grillwork around the fog lights are our only complaints. Our test Bravada was dark green with a gray leather interior. No two-tone paint, no chrome, no gold package, no added fender blisters, no pinstriping, no running boards, and no oversize driving lights. Our Bravada looked purposeful and luxurious simultaneously. Think all that add-on stuff will make your SUV more exclusive? During our two-hour test drive, we passed three white-over-gold Explorer Eddie Bauers in all their bloated, fat-fendered, chrome-wheeled glory. Didn't see a single Bravada on the road. How's that for exclusivity?

By now, you're getting the idea that we liked the Bravada. You're right. We think it's an excellent package at an excellent price. Sure, we quibble with certain aspects of this luxury SUV, but nobody builds a perfect vehicle; not even Lexus. Still, we cannot recommend the Bravada. Why, you ask? It's simple. The Bravada is currently equipped with a single airbag for the driver, which is no big deal to many people who prefer not to have a bag of explosive materials pointed at their face. The problem is that the Bravada posts very poor crash test scores for front seat passengers, according to results gathered by the National Highway and Traffic Safety Administration for the structurally identical Chevrolet Blazer. Drivers fare OK (3 stars out of 5), thanks to the airbag in the steering wheel. The front passenger, who doesn't benefit from an airbag, risks a 45% chance or better of sustaining a life-threatening injury riding in a Bravada that collides head-on into an object as heavy as the Bravada, at a speed of 35 mph. Compare this figure (1 star out of 5) with scores garnered by the Ford Explorer (4 stars out of 5), the Jeep Grand Cherokee (4 stars out of 5), and the Honda Passport/Isuzu Rodeo twins (3 stars out of 5).

The Bravada is slated to get a redesigned dashboard and passenger airbag in 1998. We think we'll wait to see how well that model performs in government crash testing before recommending this very attractive, very capable, and relatively inexpensive luxury SUV.

Notes

 © 1999 by Edmund Publications Corporation

Notes

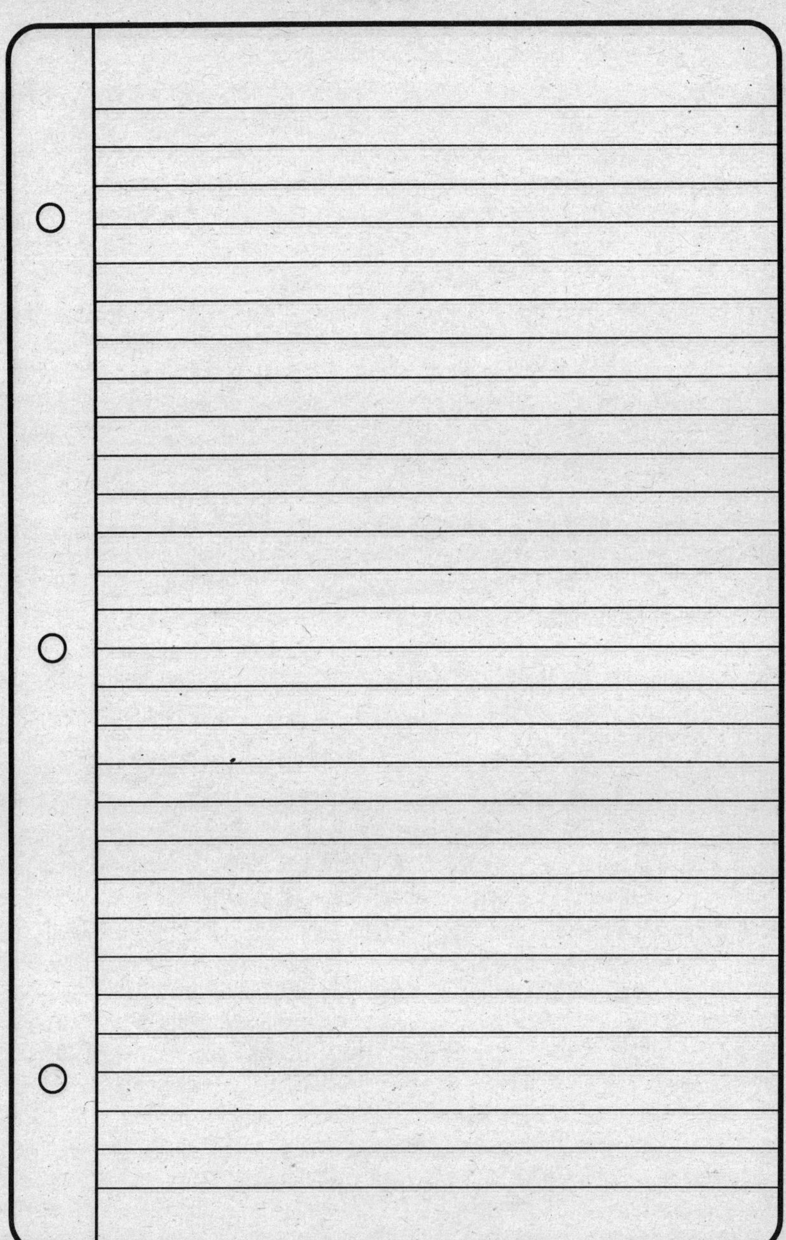

 © 1999 by Edmund Publications Corporation

Notes

 © 1999 by Edmund Publications Corporation

Edmund's®

BUYER'S DECISION GUIDES SCHEDULED RELEASE DATES FOR 1999/2000*

VOL. 33/34		RELEASE DATE	COVER DATE
N3301	NEW CARS:Prices & Reviews[American & Import]	MAR 99	SPRING 99
S3301	NEW TRUCKS:Prices & Reviews[American & Import]	MAR 99	SPRING 99
U3302	USED CARS:Prices & Ratings	APR 99	SUMMER 99
N3302	NEW CARS:Prices & Reviews[American & Import]	JUN 99	SUMMER 99
S3302	NEW TRUCKS:Prices & Reviews[American & Import]	JUN 99	SUMMER 99
U3303	USED CARS:Prices & Ratings	JUL 99	FALL 99
N3303	NEW CARS:Prices & Reviews[American & Import]	SEPT 99	FALL 99
S3303	NEW TRUCKS:Prices & Reviews[American & Import]	SEPT 99	FALL 99
U3304	USED CARS:Prices & Ratings	OCT 99	WINTER 99
N3304	NEW CARS:Prices & Reviews[American & Import]	DEC 99	WINTER 00
S3304	NEW TRUCKS:Prices & Reviews[American & Import]	DEC 99	WINTER 00
U3401	USED CARS:Prices & Ratings	JAN 00	SPRING 00

**Subject to Change*

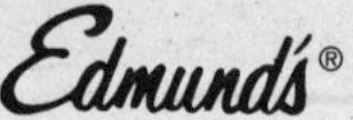

SINGLE COPIES / ORDER FORM

Please send me:

☐ **USED CARS: PRICES & RATINGS** *(includes S&H)* **$13.99**

☐ **NEW CARS**
—American & Import *(includes S&H)* **$13.99**

☐ **NEW TRUCKS [PICKUPS, VANS & SPORT UTILITIES]**
—American & Import *(includes S&H)* **$13.99**

Name ____________________

Address ____________________

City, State, Zip ____________________

Phone ____________________

PAYMENT: __ MASTERCARD __ VISA __ CHECK or MONEY ORDER $__________

Make check or money order payable to:

Edmund Publications Corporation *P.O.Box 338, Shrub Oaks, NY 10588*

For more information or to order by phone, call ***(914) 962-6297***

Credit Card # ____________________ Exp. Date: __________

Cardholder Name: ____________________

Signature ____________________

Prices above include shipping within the U.S. and Canada only. Other countries, please add $7.00 to the price ($13.99+$7.00) per book (via air mail) and $2.00 to the price ($13.99+$2.00) per book (surface mail). Please pay through an American Bank or with American Currency. Rates subject to change without notice.

On The Internet

http://www.PriceAutoOutlet.com/edmunds

Price Auto Outlet is a revolutionary used car buying and financing system that offers you a truly exceptional value on the finest quality used cars. We're able to do this because we use the Internet to cut overhead and marketing costs and bring used cars- that were previously made available primarily to wholesale buyers- directly to you.

- Huge Selection of Premium Used Cars
- Extraordinary Low Prices
- 6 Month/6,000-mile Warranty
- 80 Point Full Inspection
- Special Loan Rates
- Affordable Lease Plans
- Instant Anonymous Pre-Qualification
- On-Line Credit Decisions

No Haggling! No Salespeople!
No Sales Pressure!
Purchase at your own pace!

www.PriceAutoOutlet.com/edmunds

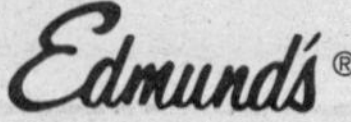

SUBSCRIPTIONS / ORDER FORM

BUYER'S PRICE GUIDES

Please send me a one year subscription for:

☐ **USED CAR PRICES & RATINGS**
AMERICAN & IMPORT (package price includes $10.00 S&H) **$34.00**
Canada $40.00/Foreign Countries $48.00 (includes air mail S&H)
4 issues/yr

☐ **NEW CARS**
AMERICAN & IMPORT (package price includes $10.00 S&H) **$34.00**
Canada $40.00/Foreign Countries $48.00 (includes air mail S&H)
4 issues/yr

☐ **NEW TRUCKS [PICKUPS, VANS & SPORT UTILITIES]**
AMERICAN & IMPORT (package price includes $10.00 S&H) **$34.00**
Canada $40.00/Foreign Countries $48.00 (includes air mail S&H)
4 issues/yr

Name ______________________________

Address ______________________________

City, State, Zip ______________________________

PAYMENT:__ MC __ VISA __ Check or Money Order-Amount $______ **Rates subject to change without notice**

Make check or money order payable to:
Edmund Publications Corporation *P.O.Box 338, Shrub Oaks, NY 10588*
*For more information or to order by phone, call **(914) 962-6297***

Credit Card # ______________________ Exp. Date: __________

Cardholder Name: ______________________________

Signature ______________________________

Protect and Enhance YOUR Investment with the Best Extended Warranty available

Savings to 50% off Dealer's Extended Warranty Prices!

Edmunds Teams up with Warranty Gold to offer You the Best Deal on Peace of Mind when Owning, Buying, or Selling Your Vehicle!

FREE QUOTE

http://www.edmunds.com/warranty
1-800-580-9889

MILEAGE TABLE

Top Row: Average Mileage Range
Bottom Row: Cents per mile to add/subtract if mileage is outside of range

Category	98	97	96	95	94	93	92	91	90	89
A	12,200-16,200 +/- 11 cents	25,100-29,100 +/- 11 cents	35,100-39,100 +/- 10 cents	47,600-51,600 +/- 10 cents	60,300-64,300 +/- 9 cents	70,600-74,600 +/- 9 cents	83,700-87,700 +/- 8 cents	95,400-99,400 +/- 8 cents	101,900-105,900 +/- 7 cents	109,800-113,800 +/- 7 cents
B	13,200-17,200 +/- 10 cents	26,700-30,700 +/- 10 cents	39,000-43,000 +/- 9 cents	53,700-57,700 +/- 9 cents	66,000-70,000 +/- 8 cents	78,300-82,300 +/- 8 cents	87,500-91,500 +/- 7 cents	96,400-100,400 +/- 7 cents	102,400-106,400 +/- 6 cents	104,400-108,400 +/- 6 cents
C	11,800-15,800 +/- 9 cents	26,800-30,800 +/- 9 cents	39,000-43,000 +/- 8 cents	53,400-57,400 +/- 8 cents	66,400-70,400 +/- 7 cents	78,100-82,100 +/- 7 cents	87,300-91,300 +/- 6 cents	94,800-98,800 +/- 6 cents	100,300-104,300 +/- 5 cents	104,000-108,000 +/- 5 cents
D	10,200-14,200 +/- 9 cents	23,600-27,600 +/- 9 cents	36,100-40,100 +/- 8 cents	50,100-54,100 +/- 8 cents	63,500-67,500 +/- 7 cents	77,100-81,100 +/- 7 cents	89,000-93,000 +/- 6 cents	98,600-102,600 +/- 6 cents	108,900-112,900 +/- 5 cents	116,800-120,800 +/- 5 cents
E	9,600-13,600 +/- 8 cents	22,200-26,200 +/- 8 cents	36,100-40,100 +/- 7.5 cents	51,600-55,600 +/- 7.5 cents	65,400-69,400 +/- 7 cents	78,300-82,300 +/- 7 cents	88,800-92,800 +/-6 cents	98,600-102,600 +/- 6 cents	106,800-110,800 +/- 5 cents	112,500-116,500 +/- 5 cents
F	8,200-12,200 +/- 9 cents	19,400-23,400 +/- 9 cents	30,900-34,900 +/- 8 cents	44,100-48,100 +/- 8 cents	57,900-61,900 +/- 7 cents	69,600-73,600 +/- 7 cents	81,100-85,100 +/- 6 cents	90,400-94,400 +/- 6 cents	97,300-101,300 +/- 5 cents	103,800-107,800 +/- 5 cents
G	9,900-13,900 +/- 9 cents	22,900-26,900 +/- 9 cents	37,500-41,500 +/- 8 cents	53,300-57,300 +/- 8 cents	68,100-72,100 +/- 7 cents	80,900-84,900 +/- 7 cents	93,400-97,400 +/- 6 cents	102,400-106,400 +/- 6 cents	111,600-115,600 +/- 5 cents	118,200-122,200 +/- 5 cents
H	10,200-14,200 +/- 9 cents	23,500-27,500 +/- 9 cents	38,900-42,900 +/- 8 cents	54,800-58,800 +/- 8 cents	68,000-72,000 +/- 7 cents	79,500-83,500 +/- 7 cents	89,600-93,600 +/- 6 cents	98,000-102,000 +/- 6 cents	101,700-105,700 +/- 5 cents	107,200-111,200 +/- 5 cents
I	7,800-11,800 +/- 12 cents	18,600-22,600 +/- 12 cents	30,300-34,300 +/- 11 cents	42,900-46,900 +/- 11 cents	56,500-60,500 +/- 11 cents	65,400-69,400 +/- 11 cents	73,400-77,400 +/- 11 cents	80,500-84,500 +/- 11 cents	87,200-91,200 +/- 10 cents	91,400-95,400 +/- 10 cents
J	6,900-10,900 +/- 11 cents	16,600-20,600 +/- 11 cents	28,300-32,300 +/- 10 cents	41,200-45,200 +/- 10 cents	48,900-52,900 +/- 9 cents	60,400-64,400 +/- 9 cents	62,100-66,100 +/- 8 cents	69,900-73,900 +/- 8 cents	73,400-77,400 +/- 7 cents	78,000-82,000 +/- 7 cents
K	3,600-5,600 +/- 14 cents	8,600-10,600 +/- 14 cents	14,000-16,000 +/- 14 cents	19,800-21,800 +/- 14 cents	26,000-28,000 +/- 13 cents	30,200-32,200 +/- 13 cents	34,100-36,100 +/- 13 cents	37,600-39,600 +/- 13 cents	40,700-42,700 +/- 12 cents	43,400-45,400 +/- 12 cents
L	8,500-12,500 +/- 14 cents	19,300-23,300 +/- 14 cents	32,800-36,800 +/- 14 cents	44,800-48,800 +/- 14 cents	57,400-61,400 +/- 13 cents	69,900-73,900 +/- 13 cents	83,600-87,600 +/- 13 cents	94,500-98,500 +/- 13 cents	106,900-110,900 +/- 12 cents	114,400-118,400 +/- 12 cents

* Mileage adjustment is not to exceed 50% of vehicle's adjusted trade-in value!

© 1999 by Edmund Publications Corporation